VISUAL ENCYCLOPEDIA

EXTERNAL FEATURES OF A BUTTERFLY

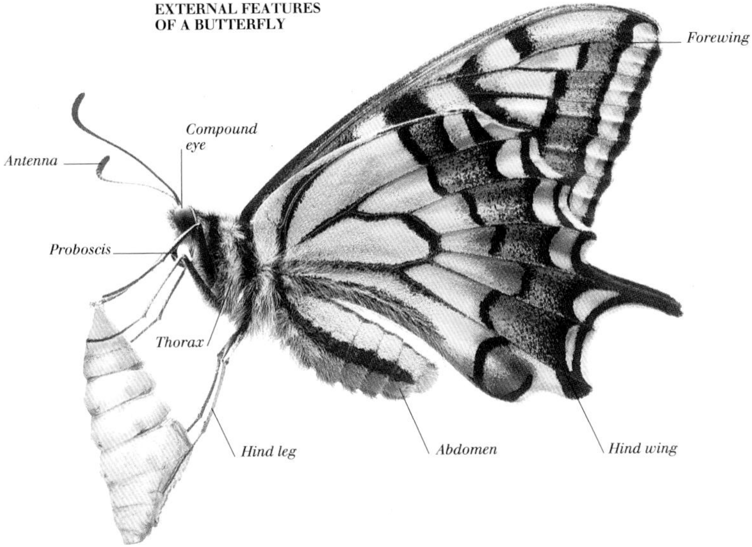

INTERNAL FEATURES OF BRACHIOSAURUS

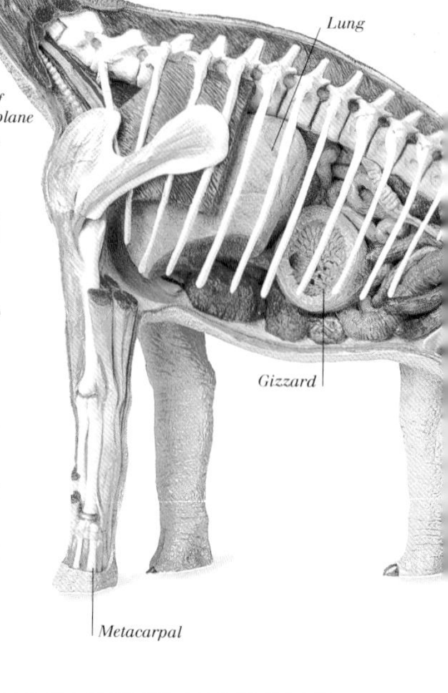

Cervical musculature
Lung
Gizzard
Metacarpal

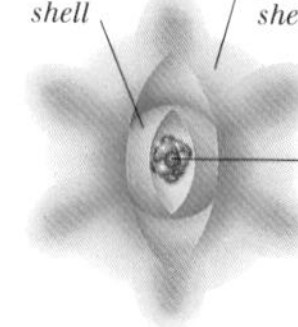

First electron shell
Second electron shell
Nucleus

ANATOMY OF A FLUORINE–19 ATOM

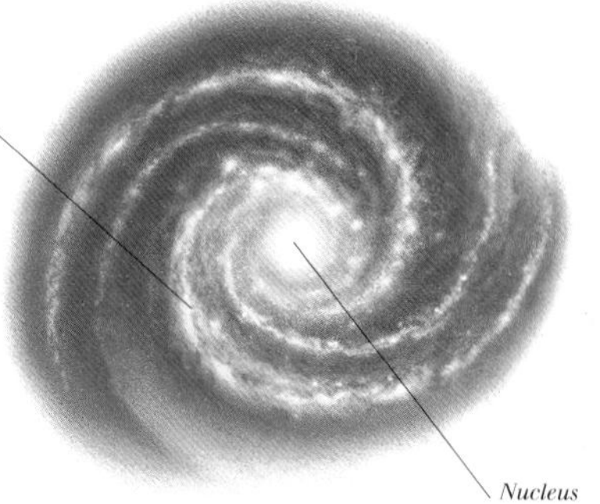

Location of Solar System
Nucleus

OVERHEAD VIEW OF OUR GALAXY

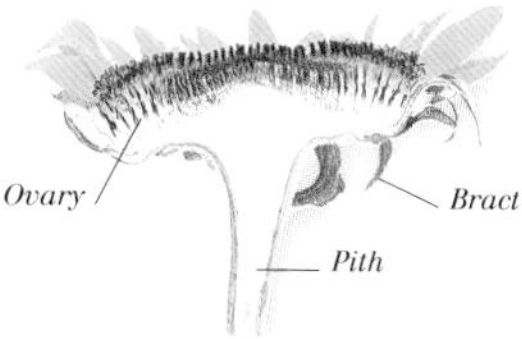

Ovary
Bract
Pith

LONGITUDINAL SECTION THROUGH SUNFLOWER INFLORESCENCE

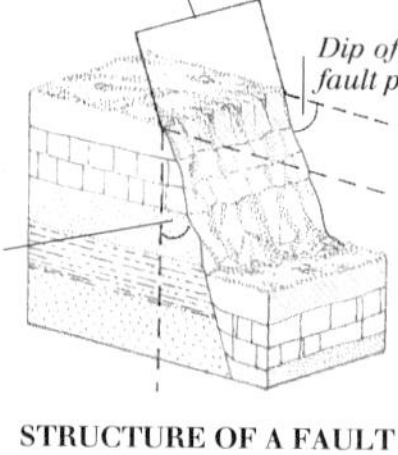

Fault plane
Dip of fault plane
Hade of fault plane

STRUCTURE OF A FAULT

Exhaust port

VELOCETTE OHV ENGINE

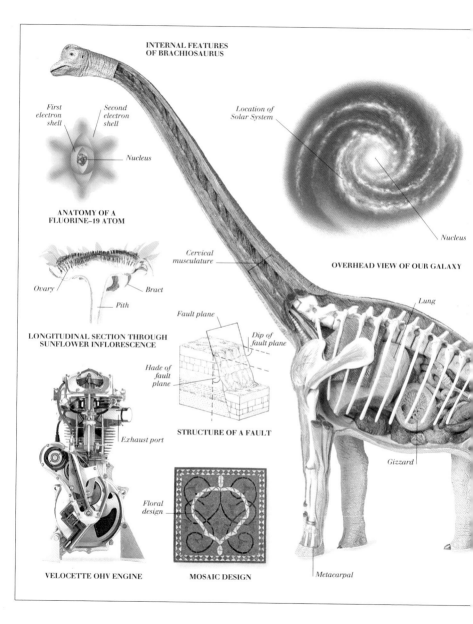

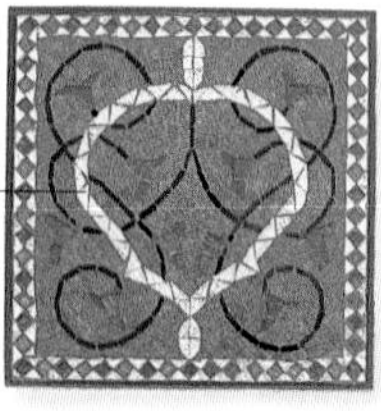

Floral design

MOSAIC DESIGN

VISUAL ENCYCLOPEDIA

BOW OF A 74–GUN SHIP

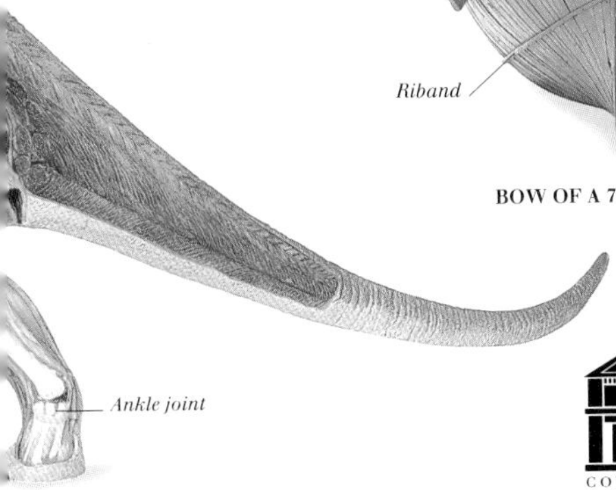

COVENT GARDEN BOOKS

A DORLING KINDERSLEY BOOK

www.dk.com

PROJECT ART EDITORS HEATHER MCCARRY, JOHNNY PAU, CHRIS WALKER, KEVIN WILLIAMS
DESIGNER SIMON MURRELL

PROJECT EDITORS LUISA CARUSO, PETER JONES, JANE MASON, GEOFFREY STALKER
EDITOR JO EVANS

DTP DESIGNER ZIRRINIA AUSTIN
PICTURE RESEARCHER CHARLOTTE BUSH

MANAGING ART EDITOR TONI KAY
SENIOR EDITOR ROGER TRITTON
MANAGING EDITOR SEAN MOORE

PRODUCTION MANAGER HILARY STEPHENS

ANATOMICAL AND BOTANICAL MODELS SUPPLIED BY SOMSO MODELLE, COBURG, GERMANY

Sound-hole
Hollow body
Bridge
Headstock

ACOUSTIC GUITAR

THIS 2000 EDITION PUBLISHED BY COVENT GARDEN BOOKS

FIRST PUBLISHED IN GREAT BRITAIN IN 1998
PREVIOUSLY PUBLISHED AS 'ULTIMATE VISUAL DICTIONARY' IN 1994
BY DORLING KINDERSLEY LIMITED,
9 HENRIETTA STREET, LONDON WC2E 8PS

2 4 6 8 10 9 7 5 3 1

A CIP CATALOGUE RECORD FOR THIS BOOK IS AVAILABLE FROM THE BRITISH LIBRARY

ISBN 1 8718 5487 3

REPRODUCED BY COLOURSCAN, SINGAPORE

Printed in Singapore

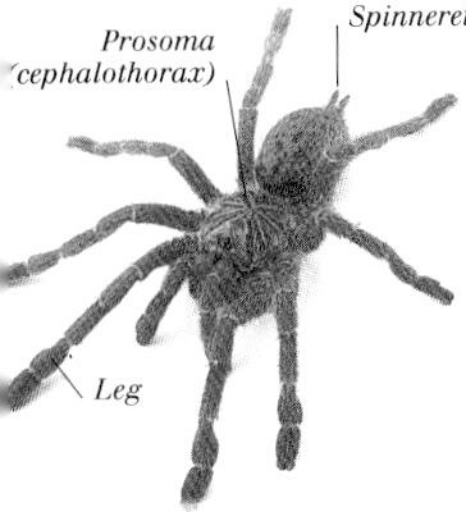
Prosoma
(cephalothorax)
Spinneret
Leg

EXTERNAL FEATURES OF A SPIDER

Canopy
Fin
G-BNHB
Main landing gear

SIDE VIEW OF ARV SUPER 2 AEROPLANE

CONTENTS

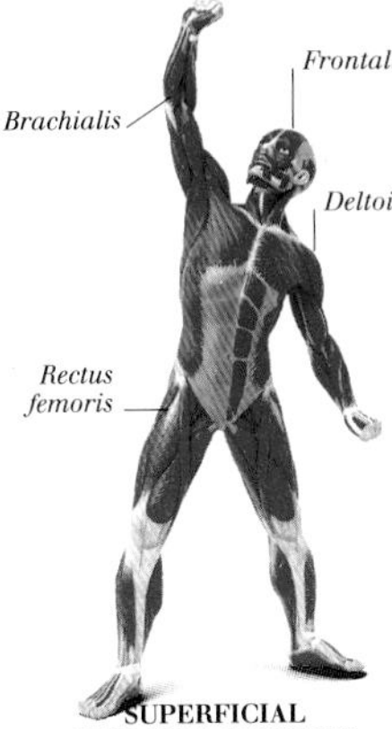
Brachialis
Frontalis
Deltoid
Rectus femoris

SUPERFICIAL SKELETAL MUSCLES

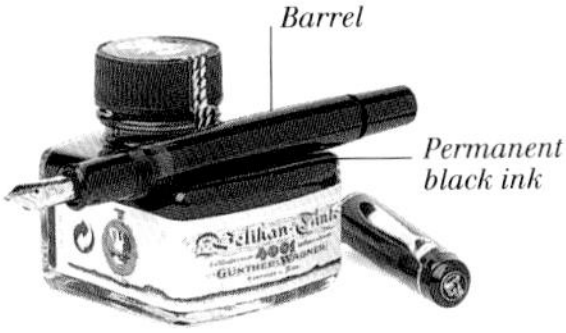
Barrel
Permanent black ink

FOUNTAIN PEN AND INK

Architrave
Podium

TEMPLE OF VESTA, TIVOLI, ITALY, c. 80 BC

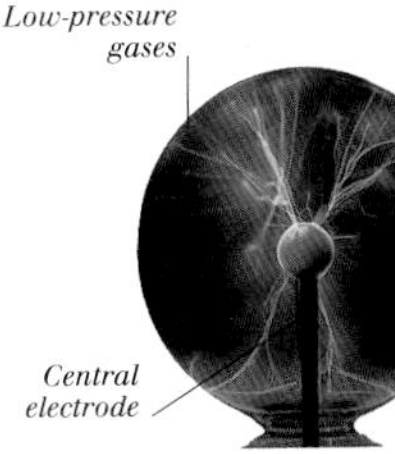
Low-pressure gases
Central electrode

BALL CONTAINING HIGH-TEMPERATURE GAS (PLASMA)

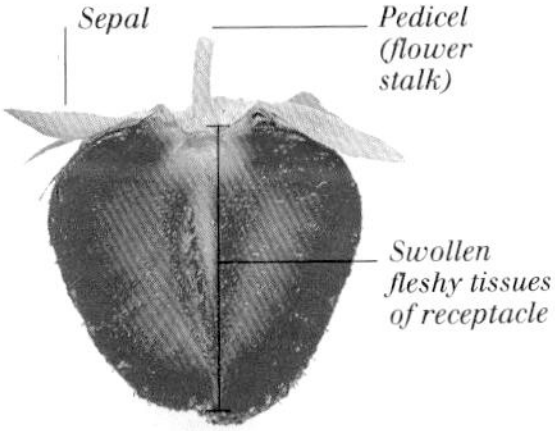
Sepal
Pedicel (flower stalk)
Swollen fleshy tissues of receptacle

LONGITUDINAL SECTION THROUGH A STRAWBERRY

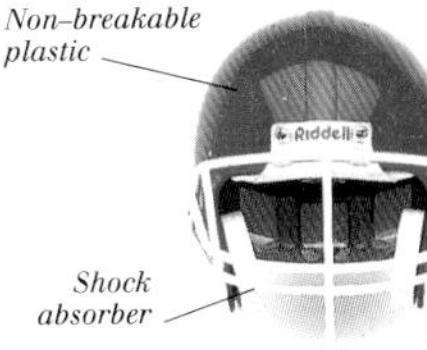
Non-breakable plastic
Riddell
Shock absorber

AMERICAN FOOTBALL HELMET

Introduction

THE VISUAL ENCYCLOPEDIA provides a link between pictures and words in a way that no ordinary encyclopedia ever has. Most encyclopedias simply tell you what a word means, but the *VISUAL ENCYCLOPEDIA* shows you, through a combination of a concise introductions, informative captions, detailed annotations, and explicit photographs and illustrations. In the *VISUAL ENCYCLOPEDIA*, pictures define the annotations around them. You do not read definitions of the annotated words, you see them. The highly accessible format of the *VISUAL ENCYCLOPEDIA*, the thoroughness of its annotations, and the range of its subject matter make it a unique and helpful reference tool.

How to use the VISUAL ENCYCLOPEDIA

You will find the *VISUAL ENCYCLOPEDIA* simple to use. Instead of being organized alphabetically, it is divided by subject into 14 sections – THE UNIVERSE, PREHISTORIC EARTH, PLANTS, ANIMALS, THE HUMAN BODY, etc. Each section begins with a table of contents listing the major entries within that section. For example, THE VISUAL ARTS section has entries on *Drawing*, *Tempera*, *Fresco*, *Oils*, *Watercolour*, *Pastels*, *Acrylics*, *Calligraphy*, *Printmaking*, *Mosaic*, and *Sculpture*. Every entry has a short introduction explaining the purpose of the photographs and illustrations, and the significance of the annotations.

If you know what something looks like, but don't know its name, turn to the annotations surrounding the pictures; if you know a word, but don't know what it refers to, use the comprehensive index to direct you to the appropriate page.

Suppose that you want to know what the bone at the end of your little finger is called. With a standard encyclopedia, you wouldn't know where to begin. But with the *VISUAL ENCYCLOPEDIA* you simply turn to the entry called *Hands* – within THE HUMAN BODY section – where you will find four fully annotated, colour photographs showing the skin, muscles, and bones of the human hand. In this entry you will quickly find that the bone you are searching for is called the distal phalanx, and for good measure you will discover that it is attached to the middle phalanx by the distal interphalangeal joint.

Perhaps you want to know what a catalytic converter looks like. If you look up "catalytic converter" in an ordinary encyclopedia, you will be told what it is and possibly what it does – but you will not be able to tell what shape it is or what it is made of. However, if you look up "catalytic converter" in the index of the *VISUAL ENCYCLOPEDIA*, you will be directed to the *Modern engines* entry on page 344 – where the introduction gives you basic information about what a catalytic converter is – and to page 350 – where there is a spectacular exploded-view photograph of the mechanics of a Renault Clio. From these pages you will find out not only what a catalytic converter looks like, but also that it is attached at one end to an exhaust downpipe and at the other to a silencer.

Whatever it is that you want to find a name for, or whatever name you want to find a picture for, you will find it quickly and easily in the *VISUAL ENCYCLOPEDIA*. Perhaps you need to know where the vamp on a shoe is; or how to tell obovate and lanceolate leaves apart; or what a spiral galaxy looks like; or whether birds have nostrils. With the *VISUAL ENCYCLOPEDIA* at hand, the answers to each of these questions, and thousands more, are readily available.

The *VISUAL ENCYCLOPEDIA* does not just tell you what the names of the different parts of an object are. The photographs, illustrations, and annotations are all specially arranged to help you understand which parts relate to one another and how objects function.

With the *VISUAL ENCYCLOPEDIA* you can find in seconds the words or pictures that you are looking for; or you can simply browse through the pages of the book for your own pleasure. The *VISUAL ENCYCLOPEDIA* is not intended to replace a standard dictionary or encyclopedia, but is instead a stimulating and valuable companion to ordinary reference volumes. Giving you access to the language that is used by astronomers and architects, musicians and mechanics, scientists and sportspeople, it is the ideal reference book for specialists and generalists of all ages.

Sections of the Visual Encyclopedia

The 14 sections of the *Visual Encyclopedia* contain a total of more than 30,000 terms, encompassing a wide range of topics:

- In the first section, The Universe, spectacular photographs and illustrations are used to show the names of the stars and planets and to explain the structure of solar systems, galaxies, nebulae, comets, and black holes.

- Prehistoric Earth tells the story in annotations of how our own planet has evolved since its formation. It includes examples of prehistoric flora and fauna, and fascinating dinosaur models – some with parts of the body stripped away to show anatomical sections.

- Plants covers a huge range of species – from the familiar to the exotic. In addition to the colour photographs of plants included in this section, there is a series of micrographic photographs illustrating plant details – such as pollen grains, spores, and cross-sections of stems and roots – in close-up.

- In the Animals section, skeletons, anatomical diagrams, and different parts of animals' bodies have been meticulously annotated. This section provides a comprehensive guide to the vocabulary of zoological classification and animal physiology.

- The structure of the human body, its parts, and its systems are presented in The Human Body. The section includes lifelike, three-dimensional models and the latest false-colour images. Clear and authoritative annotations indicate the correct anatomical terms.

- Geology, Geography, and Meteorology describes the structure of the Earth – from the inner core to the exosphere – and the physical phenomena – such as volcanoes, rivers, glaciers, and climate – that shape its surface.

- Physics and Chemistry is a visual journey through the fundamental principles underlying the physical universe and provides the essential vocabulary of these sciences.

- In Rail and Road, a wide range of trains, trams and buses, cars, bicycles, and motorcycles are described. Exploded-view photographs show mechanical details with striking clarity.

- Sea and Air gives the names for hundreds of parts of ships and aeroplanes. The section includes civil and fighting craft, both historical and modern.

- The Visual Arts shows the equipment and materials used by painters, sculptors, printers, and other artists. Well-known compositions have been chosen to illustrate specific artistic techniques and effects.

- Architecture includes photographs of exemplary architectural models and illustrates dozens of additional features such as columns, domes, and arches.

- Music provides a visual introduction to the special language of music and musical instruments. It includes clearly annotated photographs of each of the major groups of traditional instruments – brass, woodwind, strings, and percussion – together with modern electronic instruments.

- The Sports section is a guide to the playing areas, formations, equipment, and techniques needed for many of today's most popular sports.

- In Everyday Things, familiar objects, such as shoes, clocks, and toasters, are taken apart – down to the very last screw or length of thread – to show their inner workings and to give a special insight into the language that is used by their manufacturers.

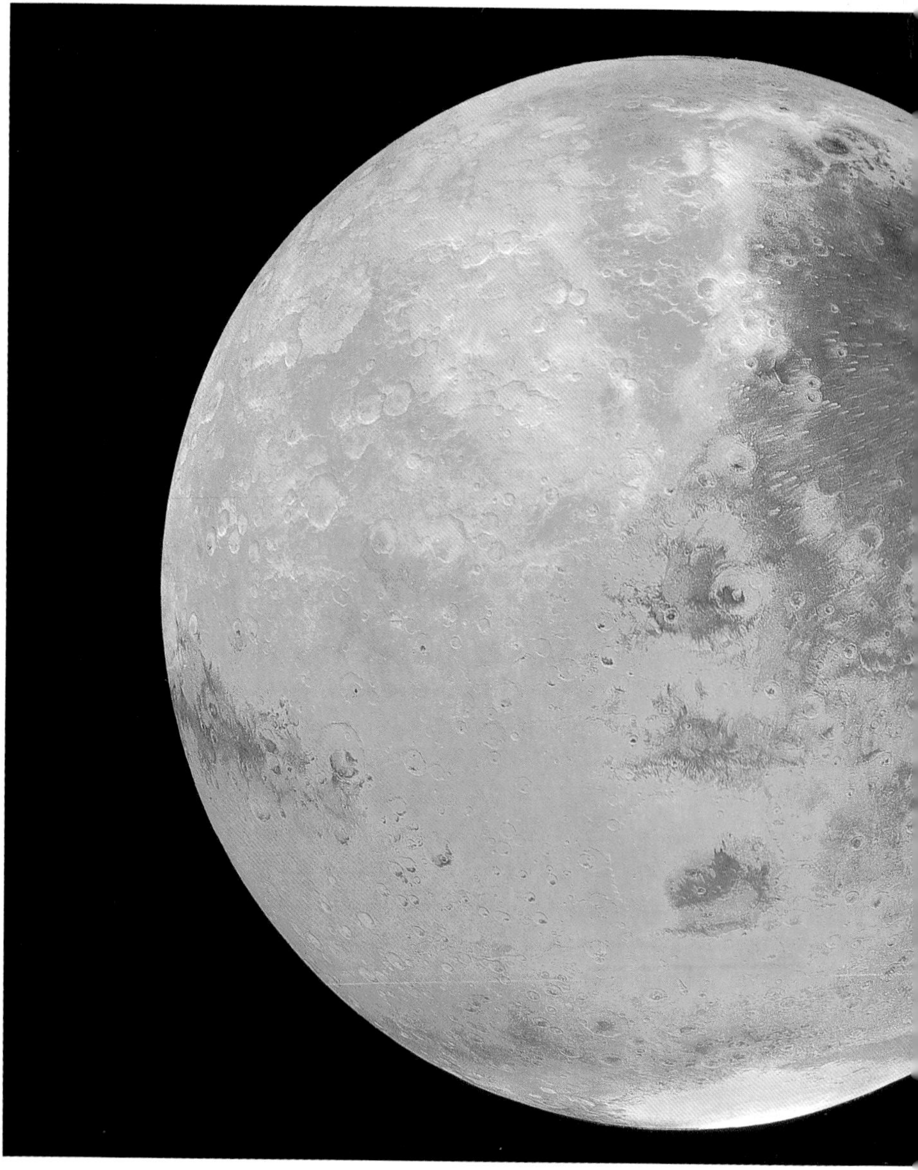

THE UNIVERSE

Anatomy of the Universe

THE UNIVERSE CONTAINS EVERYTHING that exists, from the tiniest subatomic particles to galactic superclusters (the largest structures known). Nobody knows how big the Universe is, but astronomers estimate that it contains about 100 billion galaxies, each comprising an average of 100 billion stars. The most widely accepted theory about the origin of the Universe is the Big Bang theory, which states that the Universe came into being in a huge explosion – the Big Bang – that took place between 10 and 20 billion years ago. The Universe initially consisted of a very hot, dense fireball of expanding, cooling gas. After about one million years, the gas probably began to condense into localized clumps called protogalaxies. During the next five billion years, the protogalaxies continued condensing, forming galaxies in which stars were being born. Today, billions of years later, the Universe as a whole is still expanding, although there are localized areas in which objects are held together by gravity; for example, many galaxies are found in clusters. The Big Bang theory is supported by the discovery of faint, cool background radiation coming evenly from all directions. This radiation is believed to be the remnant of the radiation produced by the Big Bang. Small "ripples" in the temperature of the cosmic background radiation are thought to be evidence of slight fluctuations in the density of the early Universe, which resulted in the formation of galaxies. Astronomers do not yet know if the Universe is "closed", which means it will eventually stop expanding and begin to contract, or if it is "open", which means it will continue expanding forever.

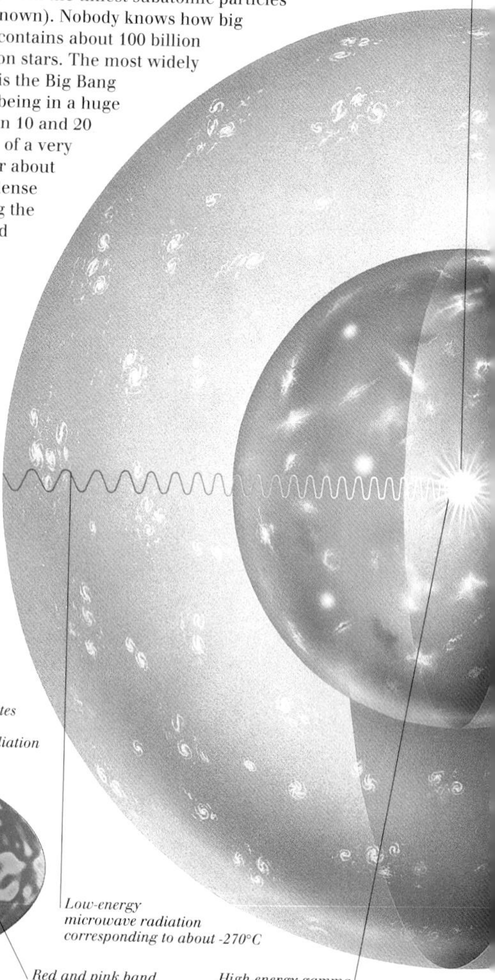
Fireball of rapidly expanding, extreme[ly] hot gas lasting abou[t] one million years
Low-energy microwave radiation corresponding to about -270°C
High-energy gamma radiation corresponding to about 3,000°C

FALSE-COLOUR MICROWAVE MAP OF COSMIC BACKGROUND RADIATION

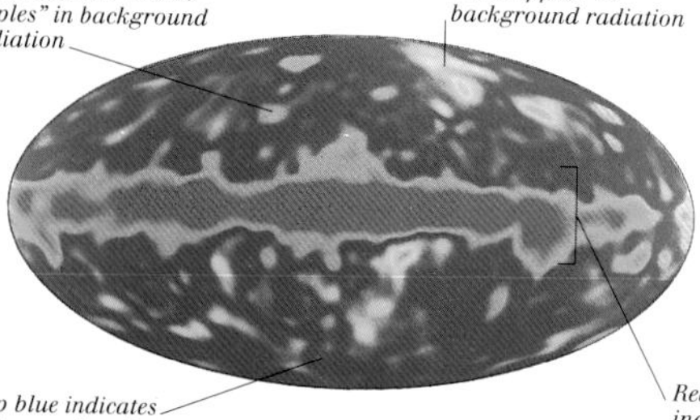
Pink indicates "warm ripples" in background radiation
Pale blue indicates "cool ripples" in background radiation
Deep blue indicates background radiation corresponding to -270.3°C (remnant of the Big Bang)
Red and pink band indicates radiation from our galaxy

ORIGIN AND EXPANSION OF THE UNIVERSE

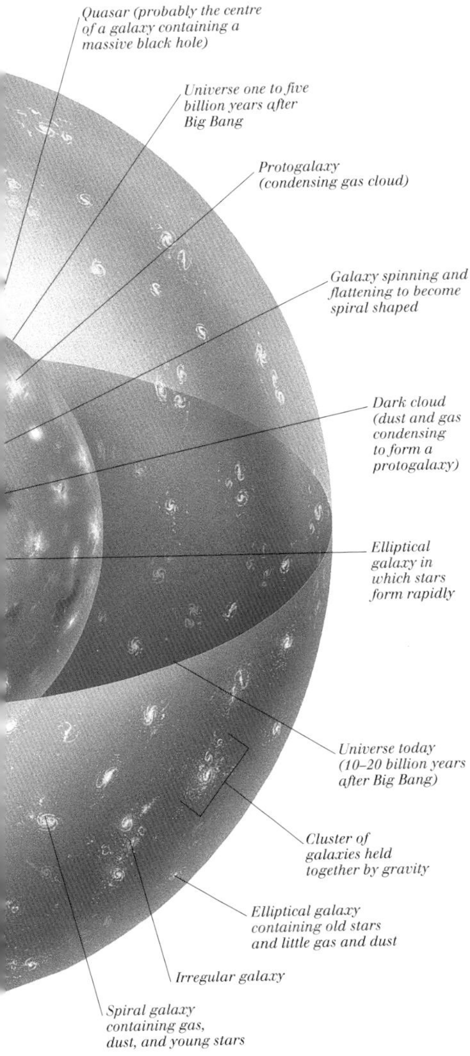
Quasar (probably the centre of a galaxy containing a massive black hole)
Universe one to five billion years after Big Bang
Protogalaxy (condensing gas cloud)
Galaxy spinning and flattening to become spiral shaped
Dark cloud (dust and gas condensing to form a protogalaxy)
Elliptical galaxy in which stars form rapidly
Universe today (10–20 billion years after Big Bang)
Cluster of galaxies held together by gravity
Elliptical galaxy containing old stars and little gas and dust
Irregular galaxy
Spiral galaxy containing gas, dust, and young stars

OBJECTS IN THE UNIVERSE

CLUSTER OF GALAXIES IN VIRGO

FALSE-COLOUR IMAGE OF 3C273 (QUASAR)

NGC 4406 (ELLIPTICAL GALAXY)

NGC 5236 (SPIRAL GALAXY)

NGC 6822 (IRREGULAR GALAXY)

THE ROSETTE NEBULA (EMISSION NEBULA)

THE JEWEL BOX (STAR CLUSTER)

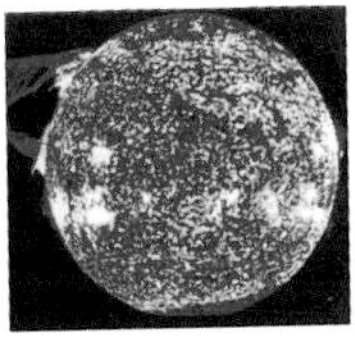

THE SUN (MAIN SEQUENCE STAR)

EARTH

THE MOON

Galaxies

SOMBRERO,
A SPIRAL GALAXY

A GALAXY IS A HUGE MASS OF STARS, nebulae, and interstellar material. The smallest galaxies contain about 100,000 stars, while the largest contain up to 3,000 billion stars. There are three main types of galaxy, classified according to their shape: elliptical, which are oval shaped; spiral, which have arms spiralling outwards from a central bulge; and irregular, which have no obvious shape. Sometimes, the shape of a galaxy is distorted by a collision with another galaxy. Quasars (quasi-stellar objects) are thought to be galactic nuclei but are so far away that their exact nature is still uncertain. They are compact, highly luminous objects in the outer reaches of the known Universe: while the furthest known "ordinary" galaxies are about 10 billion light years away, the furthest known quasar is about 15 billion light years away. Active galaxies, such as Seyfert galaxies and radio galaxies, emit intense radiation. In a Seyfert galaxy, this radiation comes from the galactic nucleus; in a radio galaxy, it also comes from huge lobes on either side of the galaxy. The radiation from active galaxies and quasars is thought to be caused by black holes (see pp. 28-29).

OPTICAL IMAGE OF NGC 4486 (ELLIPTICAL GALAXY)

Globular cluster containing very old red giants
Central region containing old red giants
Less densely populated region
Neighbouring galaxy

OPTICAL IMAGE OF LARGE MAGELLANIC CLOUD (IRREGULAR GALAXY)

Tarantula Nebula
Dust cloud obscuring light from stars
Emission nebula
Light from stars

OPTICAL IMAGE OF NGC 2997 (SPIRAL GALAXY)

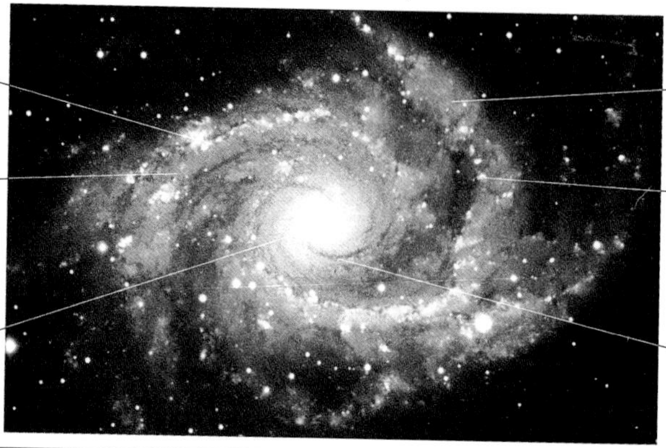
Glowing nebula in spiral arm
Spiral arm containing young stars
Galactic nucleus containing old stars
Dust in spiral arm reflecting blue light from hot young stars
Hot, ionized hydrogen gas emitting red light
Dust lane

OPTICAL IMAGE OF CENTAURUS A (RADIO GALAXY)

Dust lane crossing elliptical galaxy
Galactic nucleus containing powerful source of radiation
Light from old stars

FALSE-COLOUR RADIO IMAGE OF CENTAURUS A

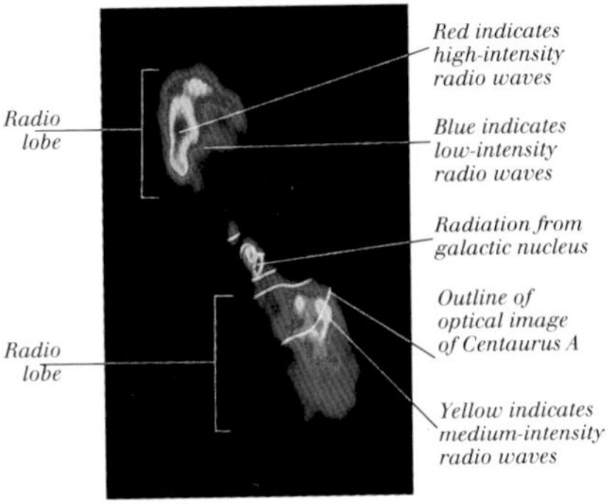
Radio lobe
Red indicates high-intensity radio waves
Blue indicates low-intensity radio waves
Radiation from galactic nucleus
Outline of optical image of Centaurus A
Radio lobe
Yellow indicates medium-intensity radio waves

FALSE-COLOUR RADIO IMAGE OF 3C273 (QUASAR)

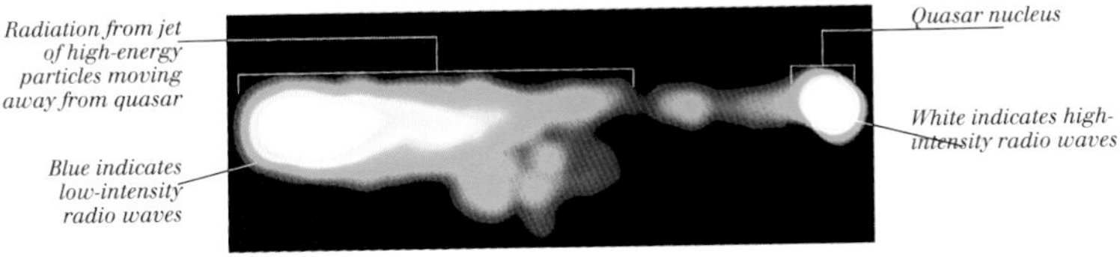
Radiation from jet of high-energy particles moving away from quasar
Blue indicates low-intensity radio waves
Quasar nucleus
White indicates high-intensity radio waves

OPTICAL IMAGE OF NGC 1566 (SEYFERT GALAXY)

Nebula in spiral arm
Compact nucleus emitting intense radiation
Spiral arm

FALSE-COLOUR OPTICAL IMAGE OF NGC 5754 (TWO COLLIDING GALAXIES)

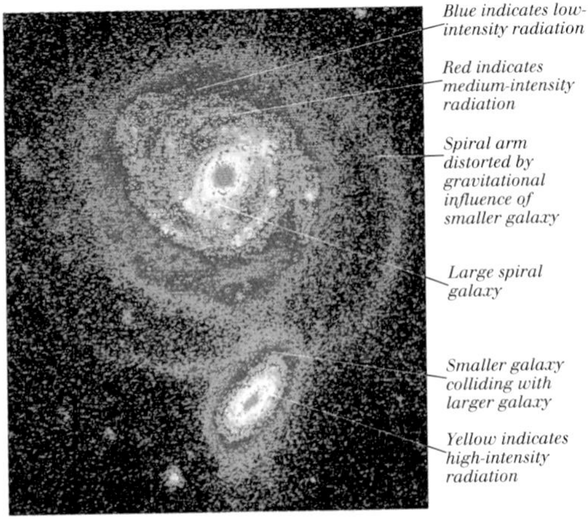
Blue indicates low-intensity radiation
Red indicates medium-intensity radiation
Spiral arm distorted by gravitational influence of smaller galaxy
Large spiral galaxy
Smaller galaxy colliding with larger galaxy
Yellow indicates high-intensity radiation

The Milky Way

VIEW TOWARDS GALACTIC CENTRE

THE MILKY WAY IS THE NAME GIVEN TO THE FAINT BAND OF LIGHT that stretches across the night sky. This light comes from stars and nebulae in our galaxy, known as the Milky Way Galaxy or simply as "the Galaxy". The Galaxy is shaped like a spiral, with a dense central bulge that is encircled by four arms spiralling outwards and surrounded by a less dense halo. We cannot see the spiral shape because the Solar System is in one of the spiral arms, the Orion Arm (also called the Local Arm). From our position, the centre of the Galaxy is completely obscured by dust clouds; as a result, optical maps give only a limited view of the Galaxy. However, a more complete picture can be obtained by studying radio, infra-red, and other radiation. The central bulge of the Galaxy is a relatively small, dense sphere that contains mainly older red and yellow stars. The halo is a less dense region in which the oldest stars are situated; some of these stars may be as old as the Galaxy itself (possibly 15 billion years). The spiral arms contain mainly hot, young, blue stars, as well as nebulae (clouds of dust and gas inside which stars are born). The Galaxy is vast, about 100,000 light years across (a light year is about 9,460 billion kilometres); in comparison, the Solar System seems small, at about 12 light hours across (about 13 billion kilometres). The entire Galaxy is rotating in space, although the inner stars travel faster than those further out. The Sun, which is about two-thirds out from the centre, completes one lap of the Galaxy about every 220 million years.

SIDE VIEW OF OUR GALAXY

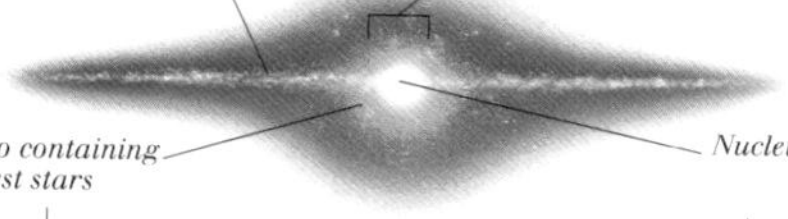

OVERHEAD VIEW OF OUR GALAXY

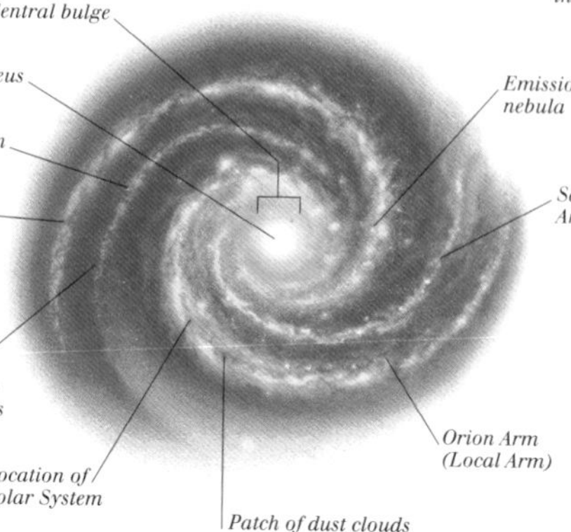

PANORAMIC OPTICAL MAP OF OUR GALAXY AND NEARBY GALAXIES

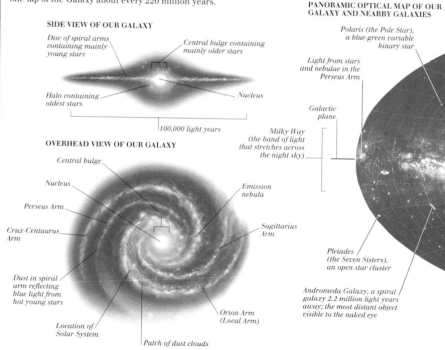

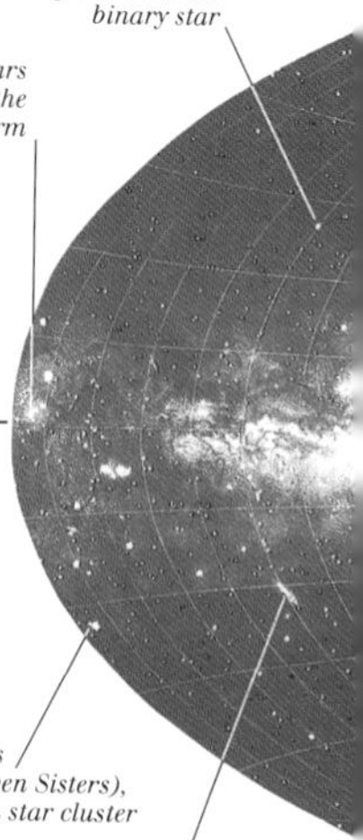

PANORAMIC RADIO MAP OF OUR GALAXY

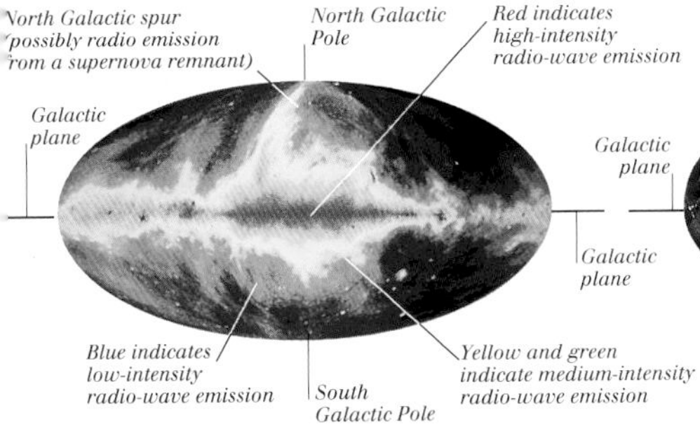
Vorth Galactic spur
'possibly radio emission
'rom a supernova remnant)
North Galactic
Pole
Red indicates
high-intensity
radio-wave emission
Galactic
plane
Galactic
plane
Blue indicates
low-intensity
radio-wave emission
South
Galactic Pole
Yellow and green
indicate medium-intensity
radio-wave emission

PANORAMIC INFRA-RED MAP OF OUR GALAXY

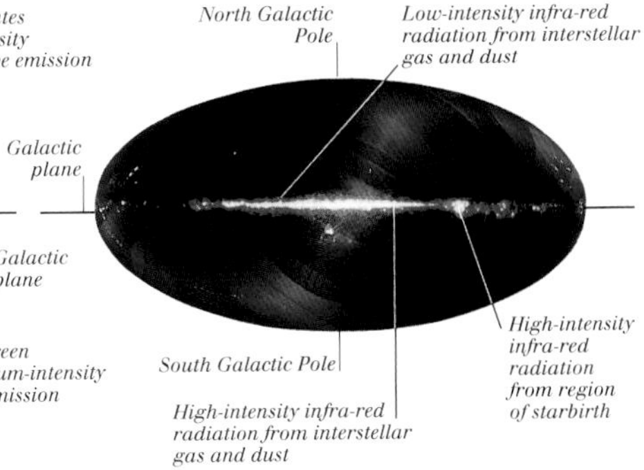
North Galactic
Pole
Low-intensity infra-red
radiation from interstellar
gas and dust
Galactic
plane
South Galactic Pole
High-intensity infra-red
radiation from interstellar
gas and dust
High-intensity
infra-red
radiation
from region
of starbirth

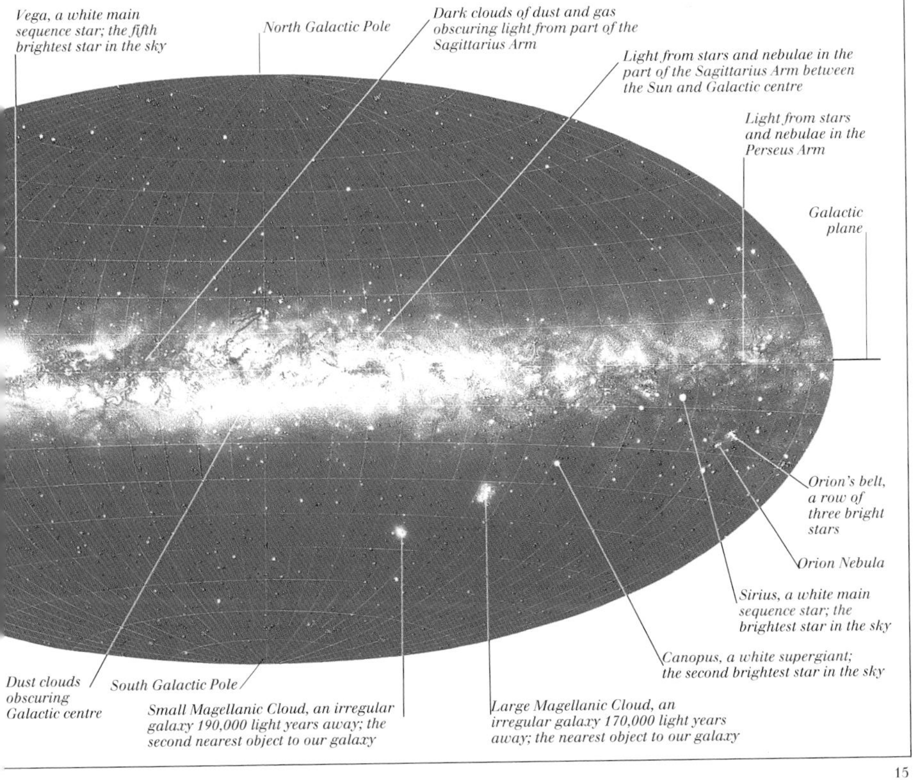
Vega, a white main
sequence star; the fifth
brightest star in the sky
North Galactic Pole
Dark clouds of dust and gas
obscuring light from part of the
Sagittarius Arm
Light from stars and nebulae in the
part of the Sagittarius Arm between
the Sun and Galactic centre
Light from stars
and nebulae in the
Perseus Arm
Galactic
plane
Orion's belt,
a row of
three bright
stars
Orion Nebula
Sirius, a white main
sequence star; the
brightest star in the sky
Canopus, a white supergiant;
the second brightest star in the sky
Dust clouds
obscuring
Galactic centre
South Galactic Pole
Small Magellanic Cloud, an irregular
galaxy 190,000 light years away; the
second nearest object to our galaxy
Large Magellanic Cloud, an
irregular galaxy 170,000 light years
away; the nearest object to our galaxy

Nebulae and star clusters

HODGE 11, A GLOBULAR CLUSTER

A NEBULA IS A CLOUD OF DUST AND GAS inside a galaxy. Nebulae become visible if the gas glows, or if the cloud reflects starlight or obscures light from more distant objects. Emission nebulae shine because their gas emits light when it is stimulated by radiation from hot young stars. Reflection nebulae shine because their dust reflects light from stars in or around the nebula. Dark nebulae appear as silhouettes because they block out light from shining nebulae or stars behind them. Two types of nebula are associated with dying stars: planetary nebulae and supernova remnants. Both consist of expanding shells of gas that were once the outer layers of a star. A planetary nebula is a gas shell drifting away from a dying stellar core. A supernova remnant is a gas shell moving away from a stellar core at great speed following a violent explosion called a supernova (see pp. 26-27). Stars are often found in groups known as clusters. Open clusters are loose groups of a few thousand young stars that were born in the same cloud and are drifting apart. Globular clusters are densely packed, roughly spherical groups of hundreds of thousands of older stars.

TRIFID NEBULA (EMISSION NEBULA)

Reflection nebula

Emission nebula

Dust lane

Starbirth region (area in which dust and gas clump together to form stars)

PLEIADES (OPEN STAR CLUSTER) WITH A REFLECTION NEBULA

Wisps of dust and hydrogen gas remaining from cloud in which stars formed

Young star in an open cluster of 300–500 stars

Reflection nebula

HORSEHEAD NEBULA (DARK NEBULA)

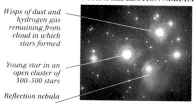

Glowing filament of hot, ionized hydrogen gas

Alnitak (star in Orion's belt)

Dust lane

Emission nebula

Star near southern end of Orion's belt

Emission nebula

Horsehead Nebula

Reflection nebula

Dark nebula obscuring light from distant stars

ORION NEBULA (DIFFUSE EMISSION NEBULA)

Glowing cloud of dust nd hydrogen gas forming part of Orion Nebula
Dust cloud
Trapezium group of four young stars)
Red light from hot, ionized ydrogen gas
Gas cloud emitting light due to ultraviolet radiation from the four young Trapezium stars
Green light from hot, ionized oxygen gas
Glowing filament of hot, ionized hydrogen gas

VELA SUPERNOVA REMNANT

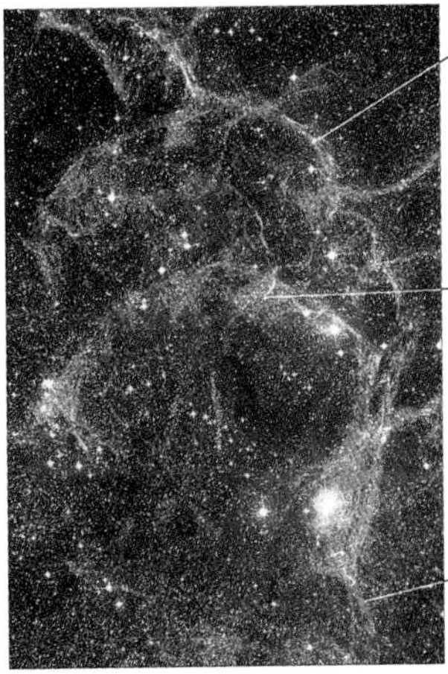
Supernova remnant (gas shell consisting of outer layers of star thrown off in supernova explosion)
Hydrogen gas emitting red light due to being heated by supernova explosion
Glowing filament of hot, ionized hydrogen gas

HELIX NEBULA (PLANETARY NEBULA)

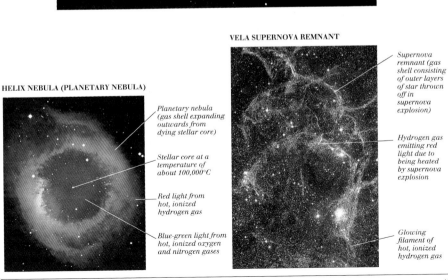

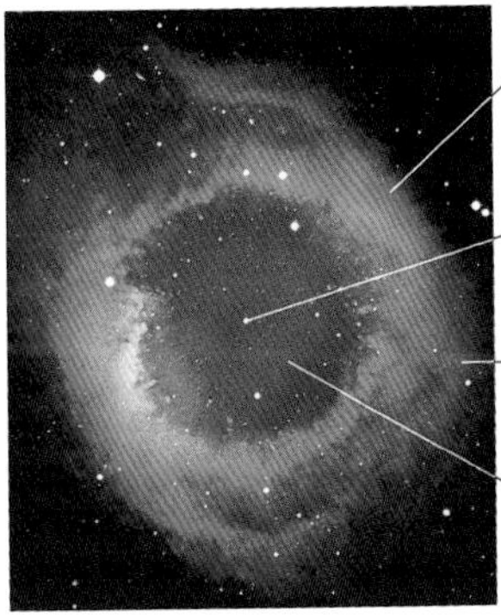
Planetary nebula (gas shell expanding outwards from dying stellar core)
Stellar core at a temperature of about 100,000°C
Red light from hot, ionized hydrogen gas
Blue-green light from hot, ionized oxygen and nitrogen gases

Stars of northern skies

WHEN YOU LOOK AT THE NORTHERN SKY, you look away from the densely populated Galactic centre, so the northern sky generally appears less bright than the southern sky (see pp. 20-21). Among the best-known sights in the northern sky are the constellations Ursa Major (the Great Bear) and Orion. Some ancient civilizations believed that the stars were fixed to a celestial sphere surrounding the Earth, and modern maps of the sky are based on a similar idea. The North and South Poles of this imaginary celestial sphere are directly above the North and South Poles of the Earth, at the points where the Earth's axis of rotation intersects the sphere. The celestial North Pole is at the centre of the map shown here, and Polaris (the Pole Star) lies very close to it. The celestial equator marks a projection of the Earth's equator on the sphere. The ecliptic marks the path of the Sun across the sky as the Earth orbits the Sun. The Moon and planets move against the background of the stars because the stars are much more distant; the nearest star outside the Solar System (Proxima Centauri) is more than 50,000 times further away than the planet Jupiter.

ORION

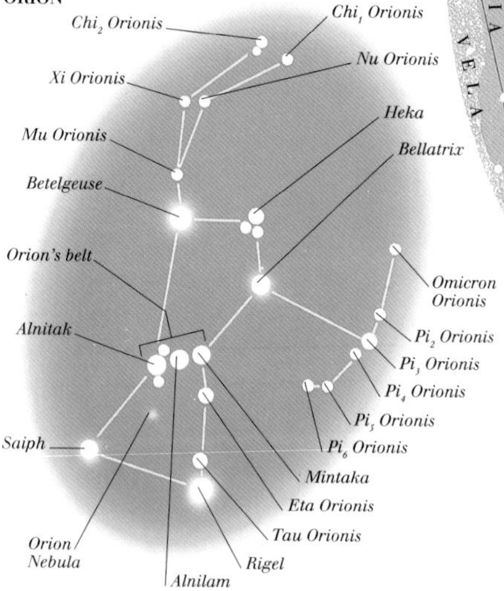

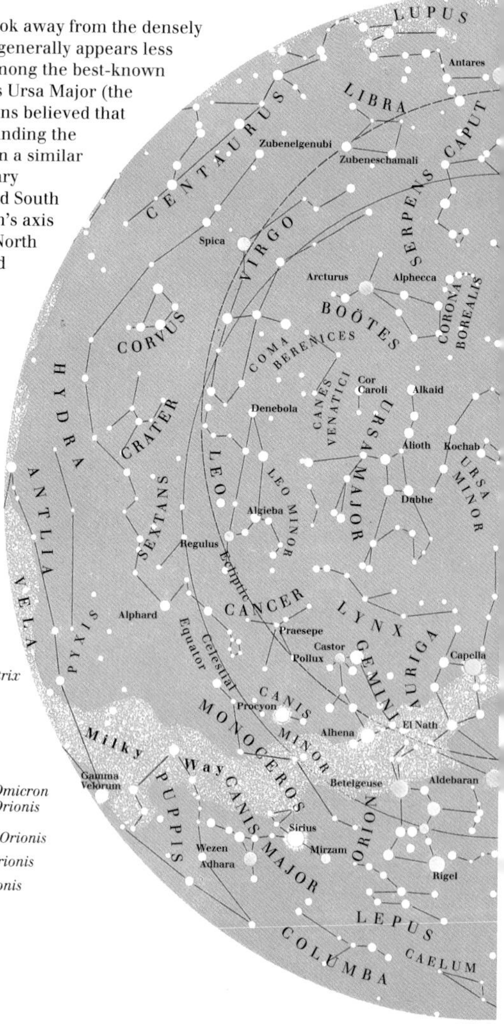

VISIBLE STARS IN THE NORTHERN SKY

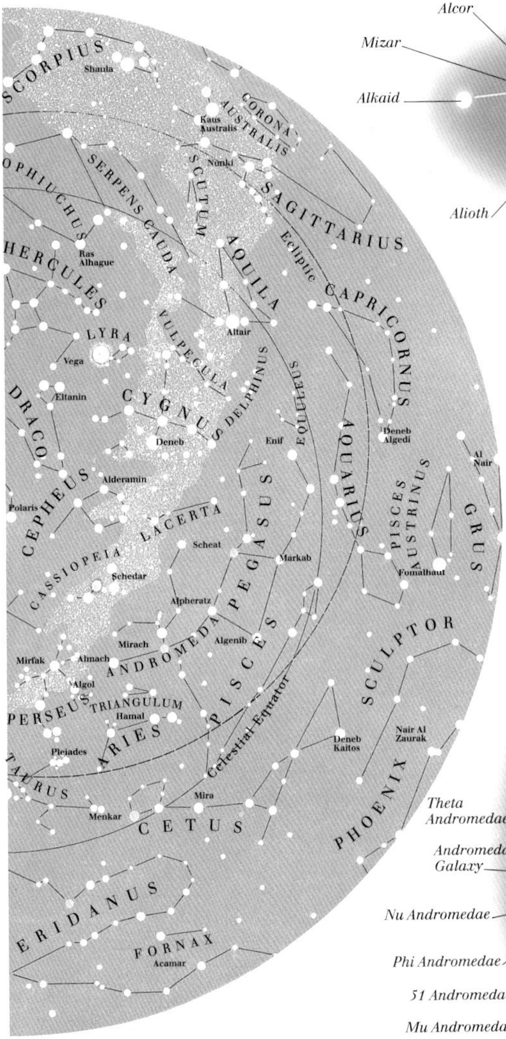
SCORPIUS
Shaula
CORONA AUSTRALIS
Kaus Australis
Nunki
OPHIUCHUS
SERPENS CAUDA
SCUTUM
SAGITTARIUS
HERCULES
Ras Alhague
AQUILA
Ecliptic
CAPRICORNUS
LYRA
Vega
Altair
VULPECULA
DELPHINUS
EQUULEUS
DRACO
Eltanin
CYGNUS
Deneb
Enif
AQUARIUS
Deneb Algedi
Al Nair
CEPHEUS
Alderamin
PISCES AUSTRINUS
GRUS
Polaris
LACERTA
PEGASUS
Scheat
Markab
CASSIOPEIA
Schedar
Fomalhaut
Alpheratz
SCULPTOR
ANDROMEDA
Mirach
Algenib
Mirfak
Almach
Algol
PISCES
PERSEUS
TRIANGULUM
Hamal
Celestial Equator
ARIES
Deneb Kaitos
Nair Al Zaurak
Pleiades
TAURUS
Mira
PHOENIX
Menkar
CETUS
ERIDANUS
FORNAX
Acamar

THE PLOUGH, PART OF URSA MAJOR (THE GREAT BEAR)

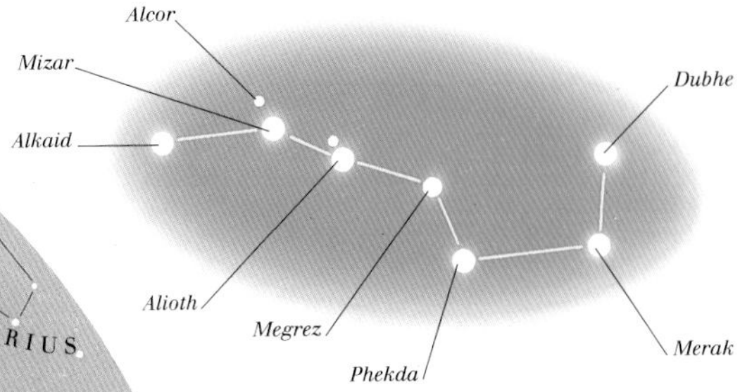
Alcor
Mizar
Dubhe
Alkaid
Alioth
Megrez
Phekda
Merak

PEGASUS AND ANDROMEDA

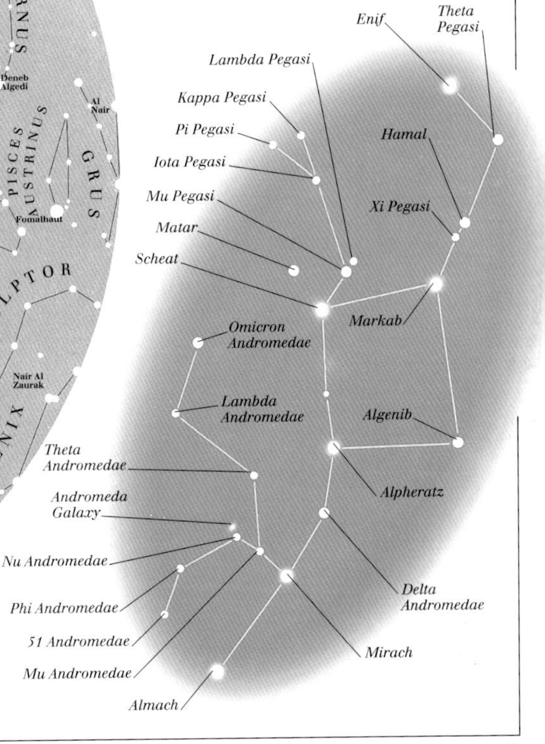
Enif
Theta Pegasi
Lambda Pegasi
Kappa Pegasi
Pi Pegasi
Hamal
Iota Pegasi
Mu Pegasi
Xi Pegasi
Matar
Scheat
Omicron Andromedae
Markab
Lambda Andromedae
Algenib
Theta Andromedae
Alpheratz
Andromeda Galaxy
Nu Andromedae
Delta Andromedae
Phi Andromedae
51 Andromedae
Mirach
Mu Andromedae
Almach

Stars of southern skies

WHEN YOU LOOK AT THE SOUTHERN SKY, you look towards the Galactic centre, which has a huge population of stars. As a result, the Milky Way appears brighter in the southern sky than in the northern sky (see pp. 18-19). The southern sky is rich in nebulae and star clusters. It contains the Large and Small Magellanic Clouds, which are the two nearest galaxies to our own. Stars make fixed patterns in the sky called constellations. However, the constellations are only apparent groupings of stars, since the distances to the stars in a constellation may vary enormously. The shapes of constellations may change over many thousands of years due to the relative motions of stars. The movement of the constellations across the sky is due to the Earth's motion in space. The daily rotation of the Earth causes the constellations to move across the sky from east to west, and the orbit of the Earth around the Sun causes different areas of sky to be visible in different seasons. The visibility of areas of sky also depends on the location of the observer. For instance, stars near the celestial equator may be seen from either hemisphere at some time during the year, whereas stars close to the celestial poles (the celestial South Pole is at the centre of the map shown here) can never be seen from the opposite hemisphere.

HYDRUS (THE WATER SNAKE) AND MENSA (THE TABLE)

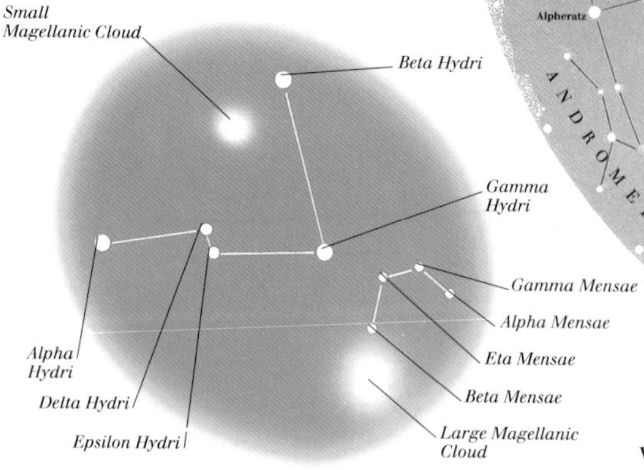
Small Magellanic Cloud
Beta Hydri
Gamma Hydri
Gamma Mensae
Alpha Mensae
Eta Mensae
Beta Mensae
Large Magellanic Cloud
Alpha Hydri
Delta Hydri
Epsilon Hydri

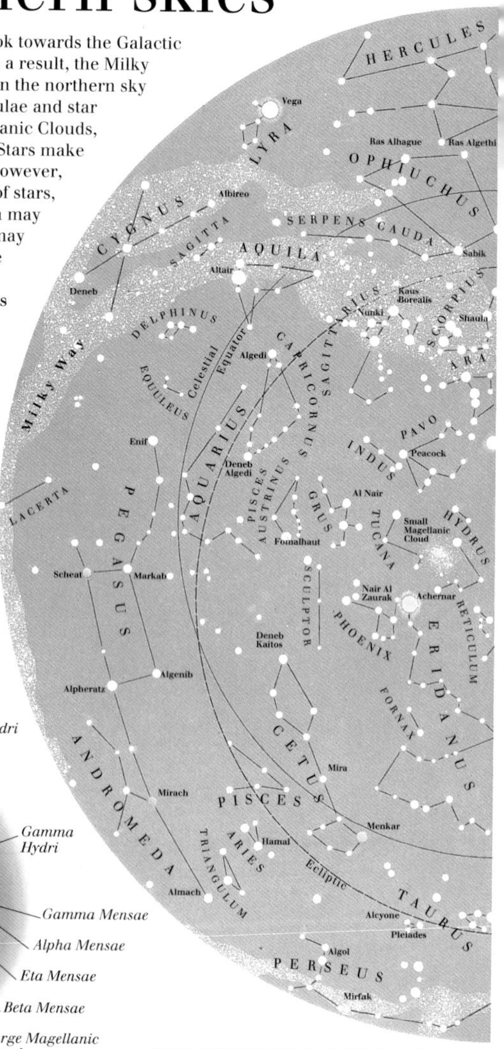
HERCULES
Vega
LYRA
Ras Alhague
Ras Algethi
OPHIUCHUS
Albireo
CYGNUS
SERPENS CAUDA
SAGITTA
AQUILA
Sabik
Altair
Deneb
Kaus Borealis
SCORPIUS
Nunki
Shaula
DELPHINUS
SAGITTARIUS
Milky Way
Celestial Equator
Algedi
CAPRICORNUS
ARA
EQUULEUS
PAVO
Enif
INDUS
Peacock
AQUARIUS
Deneb Algedi
PISCES AUSTRINUS
Al Nair
LACERTA
PEGASUS
GRUS
TUCANA
Small Magellanic Cloud
HYDRUS
Fomalhaut
Scheat
Markab
SCULPTOR
Nair Al Zaurak
Achernar
RETICULUM
PHOENIX
Deneb Kaitos
ERIDANUS
Algenib
Alpheratz
FORNAX
CETUS
ANDROMEDA
Mira
Mirach
PISCES
Menkar
TRIANGULUM
ARIES
Hamal
Ecliptic
Almach
TAURUS
Alcyone
Pleiades
Algol
PERSEUS
Mirfak

VISIBLE STARS IN THE SOUTHERN SKY

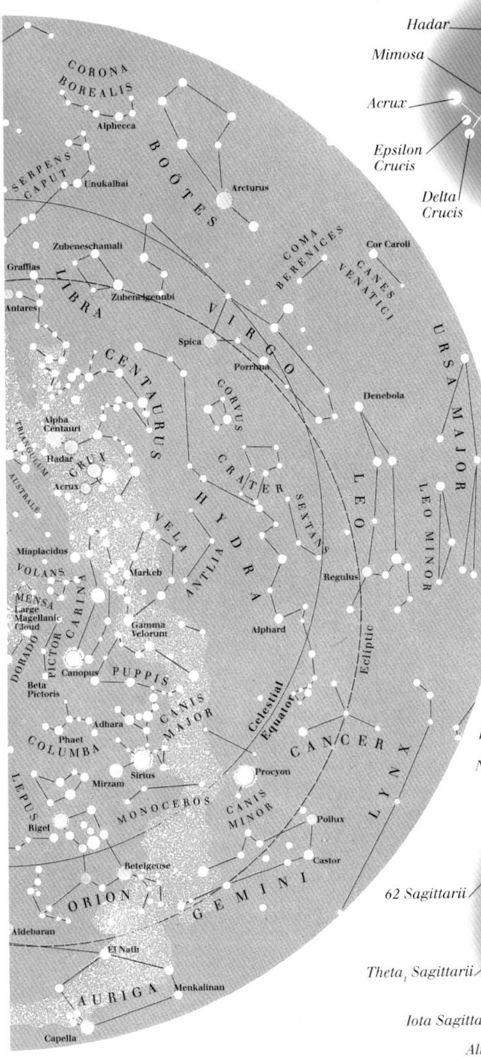

CENTAURUS (THE CENTAUR) AND CRUX (THE SOUTHERN CROSS)

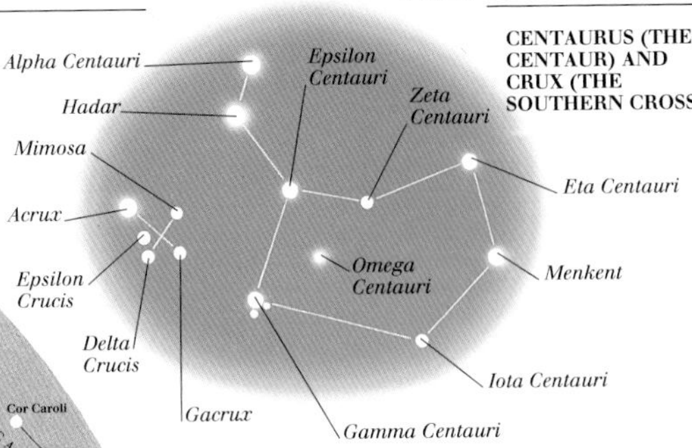
Alpha Centauri
Epsilon Centauri
Hadar
Zeta Centauri
Mimosa
Eta Centauri
Acrux
Omega Centauri
Menkent
Epsilon Crucis
Delta Crucis
Iota Centauri
Gacrux
Gamma Centauri

CANIS MAJOR (THE GREAT DOG)

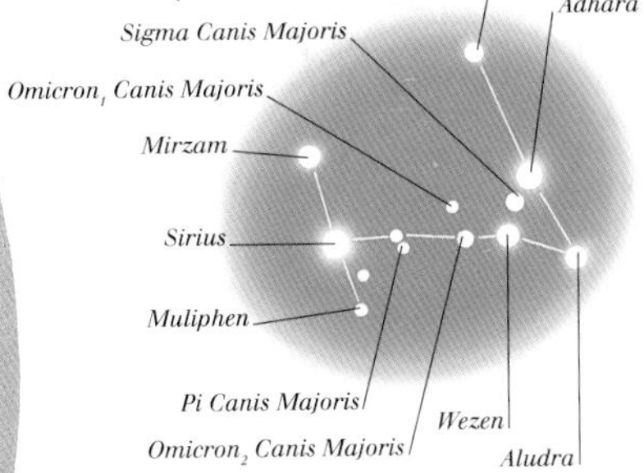
Furud
Adhara
Sigma Canis Majoris
Omicron$_1$ Canis Majoris
Mirzam
Sirius
Muliphen
Pi Canis Majoris
Wezen
Omicron$_2$ Canis Majoris
Aludra

SAGITTARIUS (THE ARCHER)

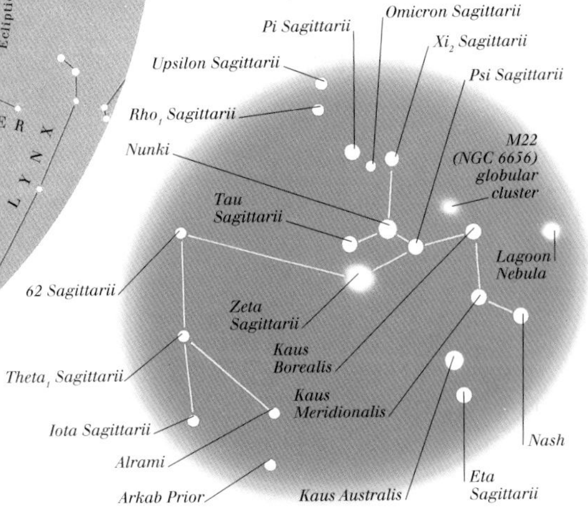
Omicron Sagittarii
Pi Sagittarii
Xi$_2$ Sagittarii
Upsilon Sagittarii
Psi Sagittarii
Rho$_1$ Sagittarii
M22 (NGC 6656) globular cluster
Nunki
Tau Sagittarii
Lagoon Nebula
62 Sagittarii
Zeta Sagittarii
Kaus Borealis
Theta$_1$ Sagittarii
Kaus Meridionalis
Iota Sagittarii
Nash
Alrami
Eta Sagittarii
Arkab Prior
Kaus Australis

Stars

OPEN STAR CLUSTER AND DUST CLOUD

STARS ARE BODIES of hot, glowing gas that are born in nebulae (see pp. 24-27). They vary enormously in size, mass, and temperature: diameters range from about 450 times smaller to over 1,000 times bigger than that of the Sun; masses range from about a twentieth to over 50 solar masses; and surface temperatures range from about 3,000°C to over 50,000°C. The colour of a star is determined by its temperature: the hottest stars are blue and the coolest are red. The Sun, with a surface temperature of 5,500°C, is between these extremes and appears yellow. The energy emitted by a shining star is produced by nuclear fusion in the star's core. The brightness of a star is measured in magnitudes – the brighter the star, the lower its magnitude. There are two types of magnitude: apparent magnitude, which is the brightness seen from Earth, and absolute magnitude, which is the brightness that would be seen from a standard distance of 10 parsecs (32.6 light years). The light emitted by a star may be split to form a spectrum containing a series of dark lines (absorption lines). The patterns of lines indicate the presence of particular chemical elements, enabling astronomers to deduce the composition of the star's atmosphere. The magnitude and spectral type (colour) of stars may be plotted on a graph called a Hertzsprung-Russell diagram, which shows that stars tend to fall into several well-defined groups. The principal groups are main sequence stars (those which are fusing hydrogen to form helium), giants, supergiants, and white dwarfs.

STAR SIZES

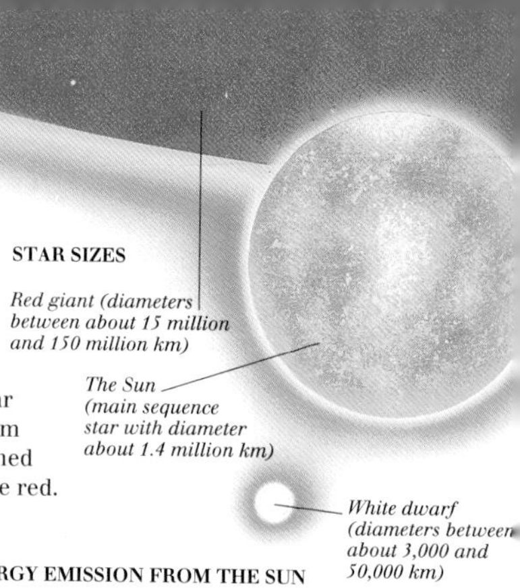

Red giant (diameters between about 15 million and 150 million km)
The Sun (main sequence star with diameter about 1.4 million km)
White dwarf (diameters between about 3,000 and 50,000 km)

ENERGY EMISSION FROM THE SUN

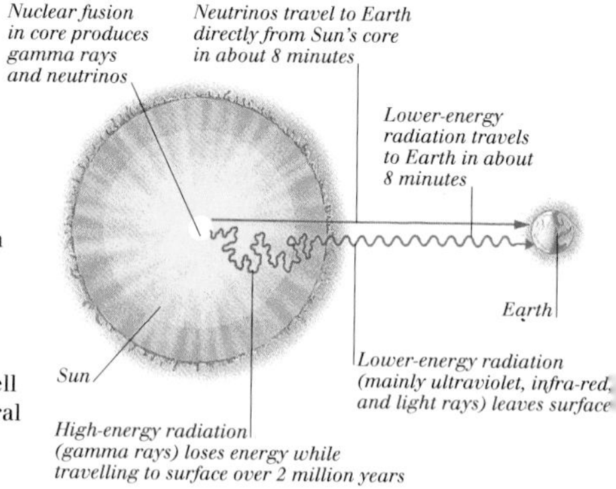

Nuclear fusion in core produces gamma rays and neutrinos
Neutrinos travel to Earth directly from Sun's core in about 8 minutes
Lower-energy radiation travels to Earth in about 8 minutes
Earth
Sun
Lower-energy radiation (mainly ultraviolet, infra-red, and light rays) leaves surface
High-energy radiation (gamma rays) loses energy while travelling to surface over 2 million years

STAR MAGNITUDES

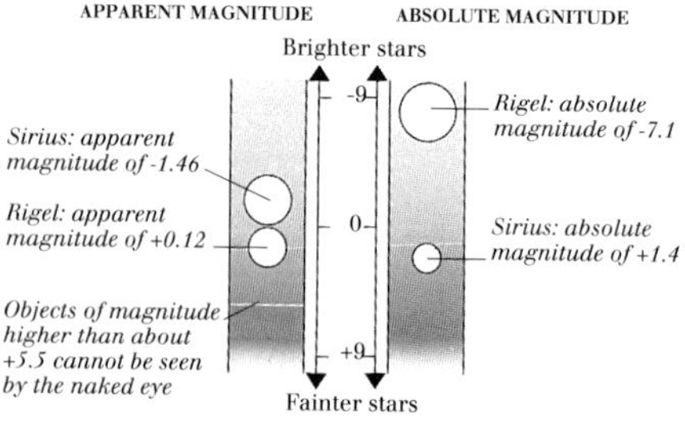

APPARENT MAGNITUDE
ABSOLUTE MAGNITUDE
Brighter stars
-9
0
+9
Fainter stars
Sirius: apparent magnitude of -1.46
Rigel: apparent magnitude of +0.12
Objects of magnitude higher than about +5.5 cannot be seen by the naked eye
Rigel: absolute magnitude of -7.1
Sirius: absolute magnitude of +1.4

NUCLEAR FUSION IN MAIN SEQUENCE STARS LIKE THE SUN

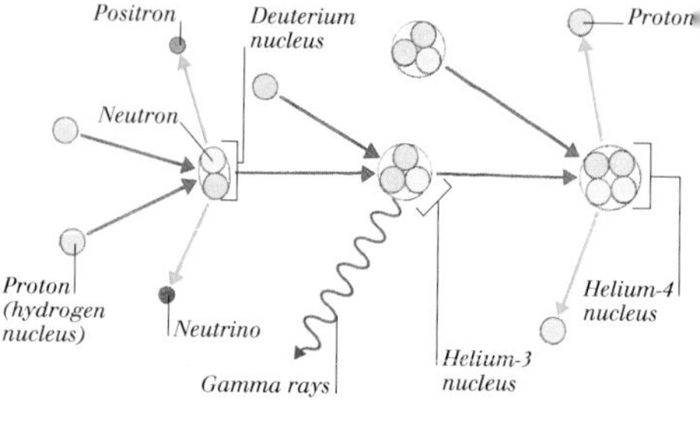

Positron
Deuterium nucleus
Proton
Neutron
Proton (hydrogen nucleus)
Neutrino
Gamma rays
Helium-3 nucleus
Helium-4 nucleus

HERTZSPRUNG-RUSSELL DIAGRAM

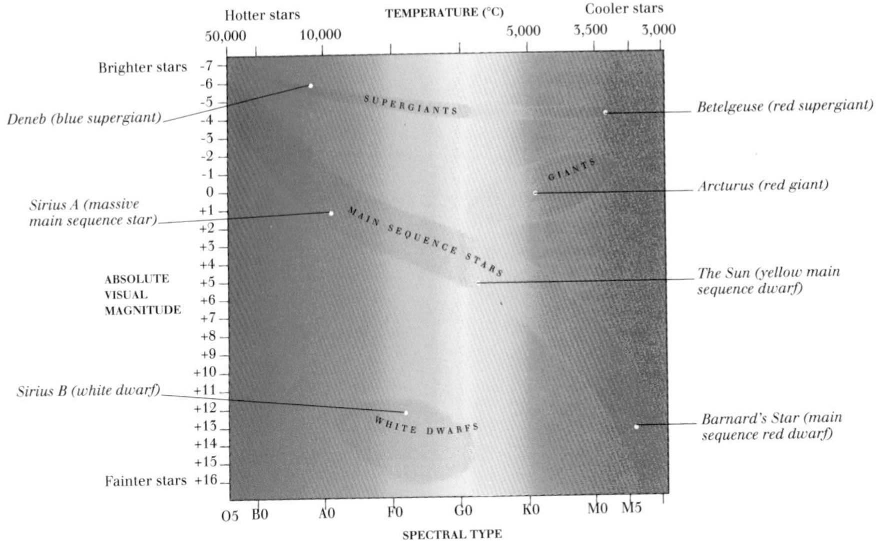
Hotter stars
TEMPERATURE (°C)
Cooler stars
50,000
10,000
5,000
3,500
3,000
Brighter stars
-7
-6
-5
-4
-3
-2
-1
0
+1
+2
+3
+4
+5
+6
+7
+8
+9
+10
+11
+12
+13
+14
+15
+16
Fainter stars
ABSOLUTE VISUAL MAGNITUDE
Deneb (blue supergiant)
SUPERGIANTS
Betelgeuse (red supergiant)
GIANTS
Arcturus (red giant)
Sirius A (massive main sequence star)
MAIN SEQUENCE STARS
The Sun (yellow main sequence dwarf)
Sirius B (white dwarf)
WHITE DWARFS
Barnard's Star (main sequence red dwarf)
O5
B0
A0
F0
G0
K0
M0
M5
SPECTRAL TYPE

STELLAR SPECTRAL ABSORPTION LINES

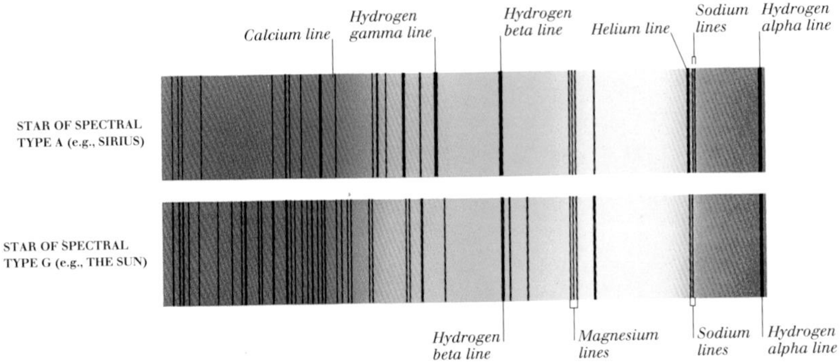
Calcium line
Hydrogen gamma line
Hydrogen beta line
Helium line
Sodium lines
Hydrogen alpha line
STAR OF SPECTRAL TYPE A (e.g., SIRIUS)
STAR OF SPECTRAL TYPE G (e.g., THE SUN)
Hydrogen beta line
Magnesium lines
Sodium lines
Hydrogen alpha line

Small stars

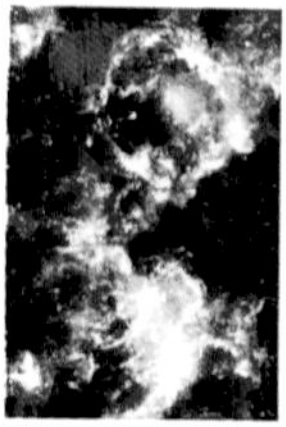

REGION OF STAR FORMATION IN ORION

SMALL STARS HAVE A MASS of up to about one and a half times that of the Sun. They begin to form when a region of higher density in a nebula condenses into a huge globule of gas and dust that contracts under its own gravity. Within a globule, regions of condensing matter heat up and begin to glow, forming protostars. If a protostar contains enough matter, the central temperature reaches about 15 million °C. At this temperature, nuclear reactions in which hydrogen fuses to form helium can start. This process releases energy, which prevents the star from contracting further and also causes it to shine; it is now a main sequence star. A star of about one solar mass remains in the main sequence for about 10 billion years, until the hydrogen in the star's core has been converted into helium. The helium core then contracts again, and nuclear reactions continue in a shell around the core. The core becomes hot enough for helium to fuse to form carbon, while the outer layers of the star expand, cool, and shine less brightly. The expanding star is known as a red giant. When the helium in the core runs out, the outer layers of the star may drift off as an expanding gas shell called a planetary nebula. The remaining core (about 80 per cent of the original star) is now in its final stages. It becomes a white dwarf star that gradually cools and dims. When it finally stops shining altogether, the dead star will become a black dwarf.

STRUCTURE OF A MAIN SEQUENCE STAR

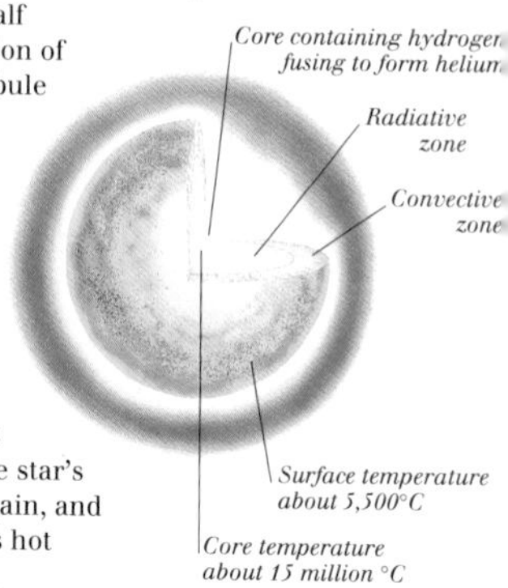

Core containing hydrogen fusing to form helium
Radiative zone
Convective zone
Surface temperature about 5,500°C
Core temperature about 15 million °C

STRUCTURE OF A NEBULA

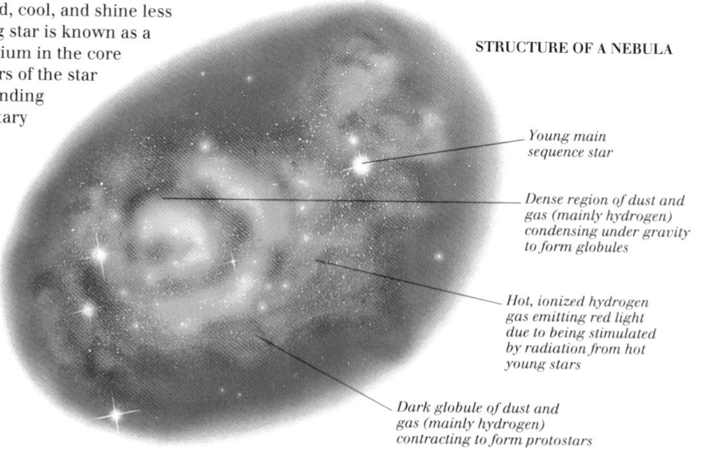

Young main sequence star
Dense region of dust and gas (mainly hydrogen) condensing under gravity to form globules
Hot, ionized hydrogen gas emitting red light due to being stimulated by radiation from hot young stars
Dark globule of dust and gas (mainly hydrogen) contracting to form protostars

LIFE OF A SMALL STAR OF ABOUT ONE SOLAR MASS

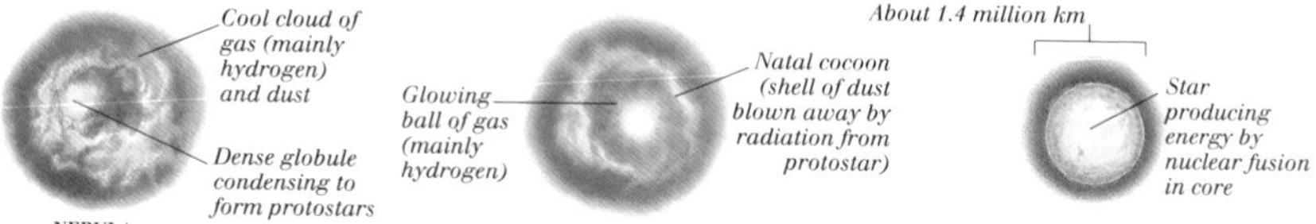

Cool cloud of gas (mainly hydrogen) and dust
Dense globule condensing to form protostars
Glowing ball of gas (mainly hydrogen)
Natal cocoon (shell of dust blown away by radiation from protostar)
About 1.4 million km
Star producing energy by nuclear fusion in core

NEBULA

PROTOSTAR
Duration: 50 million years

MAIN SEQUENCE STAR
Duration: 10 billion years

STRUCTURE OF A RED GIANT

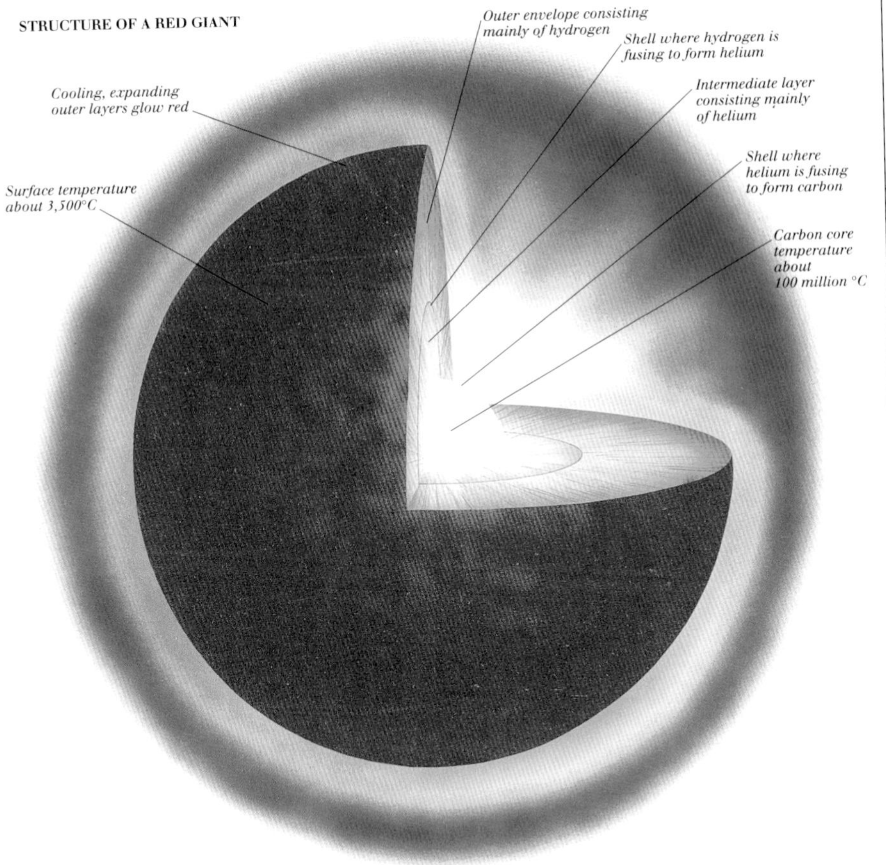
Outer envelope consisting mainly of hydrogen
Shell where hydrogen is fusing to form helium
Intermediate layer consisting mainly of helium
Shell where helium is fusing to form carbon
Carbon core temperature about 100 million °C
Cooling, expanding outer layers glow red
Surface temperature about 3,500°C

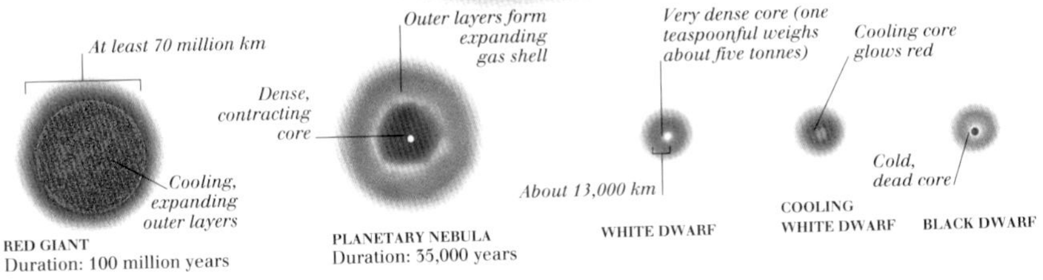
At least 70 million km
Cooling, expanding outer layers
RED GIANT
Duration: 100 million years
Outer layers form expanding gas shell
Dense, contracting core
PLANETARY NEBULA
Duration: 35,000 years
Very dense core (one teaspoonful weighs about five tonnes)
About 13,000 km
WHITE DWARF
Cooling core glows red
COOLING WHITE DWARF
Cold, dead core
BLACK DWARF

Massive stars

MASSIVE STARS HAVE A MASS AT LEAST THREE TIMES that of the Sun, and some stars are as massive as about 50 Suns. A massive star evolves in a similar way to a small star until it reaches the main sequence stage (see pp. 24-25). During the main sequence, a star shines steadily until the hydrogen in its core has fused to form helium. This process takes billions of years in a small star, but only millions of years in a massive star. A massive star then becomes a red supergiant, which initially consists of a helium core surrounded by outer layers of cooling, expanding gas. Over the next few million years, a series of nuclear reactions form different elements in shells around an iron core. The core eventually collapses in less than a second, causing a massive explosion called a supernova, in which a shock wave blows away the outer layers of the star. Supernovae shine brighter than an entire galaxy for a short time. Sometimes, the core survives the supernova explosion. If the surviving core is between about one and a half and three solar masses, it contracts to become a tiny, dense neutron star. If the core is considerably greater than three solar masses, it contracts to become a black hole (see pp. 28-29).

SUPERNOVA

TARANTULA NEBULA BEFORE SUPERNOVA

STRUCTURE OF A RED SUPERGIANT

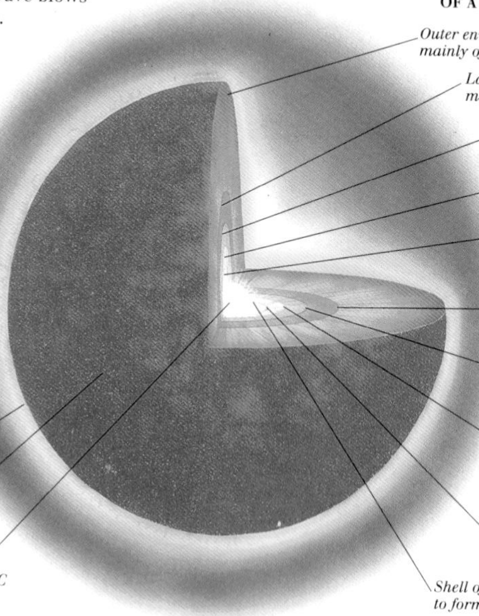
Outer envelope consisting mainly of hydrogen
Layer consisting mainly of helium
Layer consisting mainly of carbon
Layer consisting mainly of oxygen
Layer consisting mainly of silicon
Shell of hydrogen fusing to form helium
Shell of helium fusing to form carbon
Shell of carbon fusing to form oxygen
Shell of oxygen fusing to form silicon
Shell of silicon fusing to form iron core
Surface temperature about 3,000°C
Cooling, expanding outer layers glow red
Core of mainly iron at a temperature of 3–5 billion °C

LIFE OF A MASSIVE STAR OF ABOUT 10 SOLAR MASSES

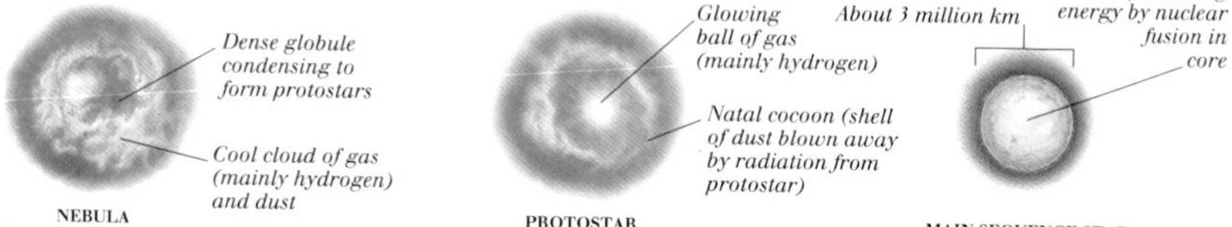
Dense globule condensing to form protostars
Cool cloud of gas (mainly hydrogen) and dust
Glowing ball of gas (mainly hydrogen)
Natal cocoon (shell of dust blown away by radiation from protostar)
About 3 million km
Star producing energy by nuclear fusion in core

NEBULA

PROTOSTAR
Duration: a few hundred thousand years

MAIN SEQUENCE STAR
Duration: 10 million years

FEATURES OF A SUPERNOVA

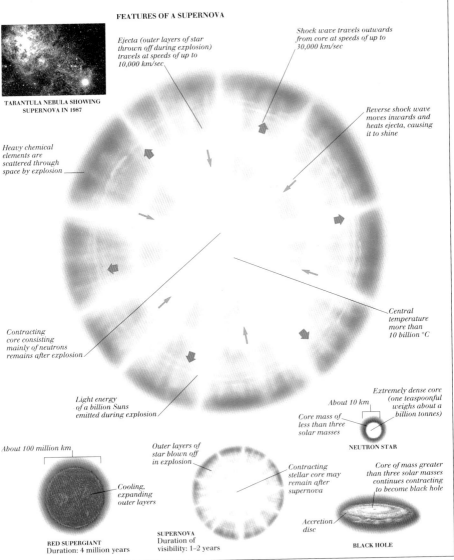

TARANTULA NEBULA SHOWING SUPERNOVA IN 1987

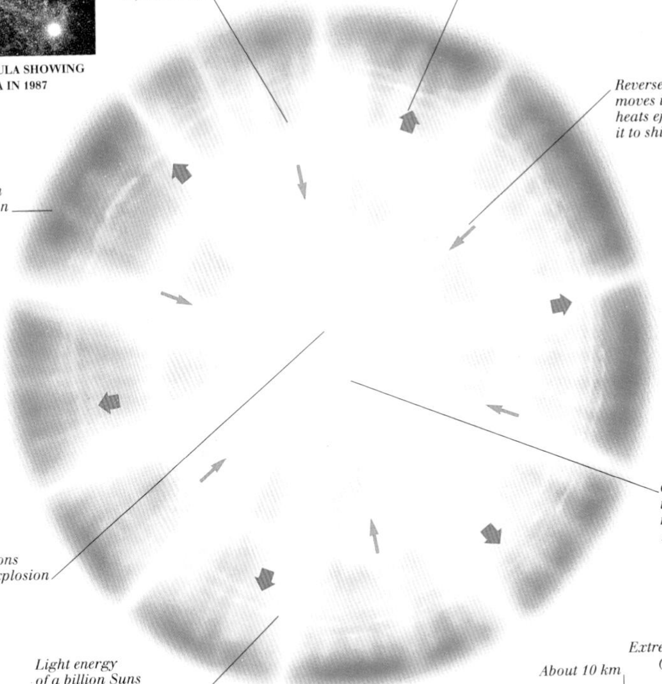
Ejecta (outer layers of star thrown off during explosion) travels at speeds of up to 10,000 km/sec
Shock wave travels outwards from core at speeds of up to 30,000 km/sec
Reverse shock wave moves inwards and heats ejecta, causing it to shine
Heavy chemical elements are scattered through space by explosion
Central temperature more than 10 billion °C
Contracting core consisting mainly of neutrons remains after explosion
Light energy of a billion Suns emitted during explosion

About 10 km
Extremely dense core (one teaspoonful weighs about a billion tonnes)
Core mass of less than three solar masses

NEUTRON STAR

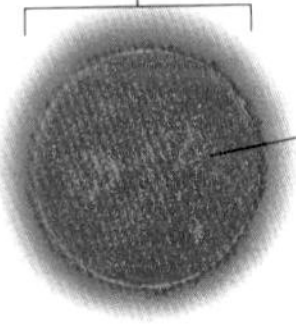
About 100 million km
Cooling, expanding outer layers

RED SUPERGIANT
Duration: 4 million years

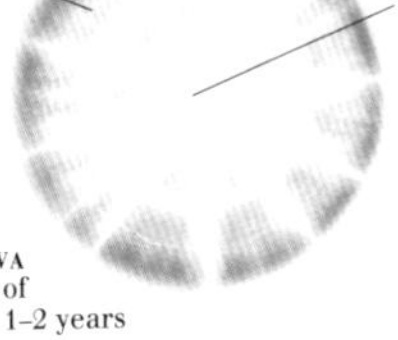
Outer layers of star blown off in explosion
Contracting stellar core may remain after supernova

SUPERNOVA
Duration of visibility: 1–2 years

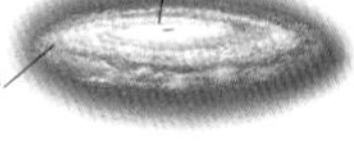
Core of mass greater than three solar masses continues contracting to become black hole
Accretion disc

BLACK HOLE

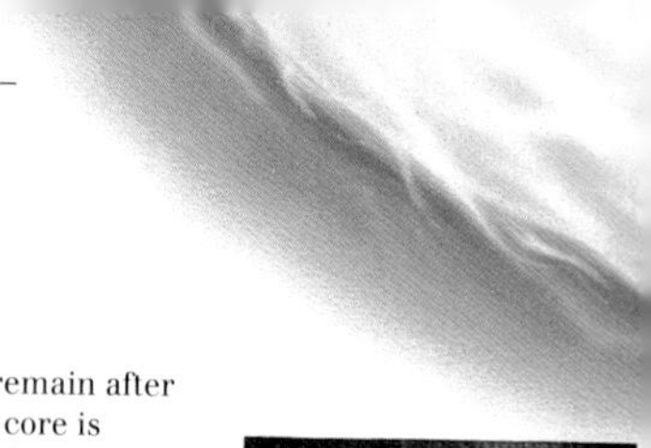

Neutron stars and black holes

NEUTRON STARS AND BLACK HOLES form from the stellar cores that remain after stars have exploded as supernovae (see pp. 26-27). If the remaining core is between about one and a half and three solar masses, it contracts to form a neutron star. If the remaining core is greater than about three solar masses, it contracts to form a black hole. Neutron stars are typically only about 10 kilometres in diameter and consist almost entirely of subatomic particles called neutrons. Such stars are so dense that a teaspoonful would weigh about a billion tonnes. Neutron stars are observed as pulsars, so-called because they rotate rapidly and emit two beams of radio waves, which sweep across the sky and are detected as short pulses. Black holes are characterized by their extremely strong gravity, which is so powerful that not even light can escape; as a result, black holes are invisible. However, they may be detected if they have a close companion star. The gravity of the black hole pulls gas from the other star, forming an accretion disc that spirals around the black hole at high speed, heating up and emitting radiation. Eventually, the matter spirals in to cross the event horizon (the boundary of the black hole), thereby disappearing from the visible Universe.

X-ray emission from pulsar (neutron star rotating 30 times each second)
X-ray emission from centre of nebula

X-RAY IMAGE OF THE CRAB NEBULA (SUPERNOVA REMNANT)

PULSAR (ROTATING NEUTRON STAR)

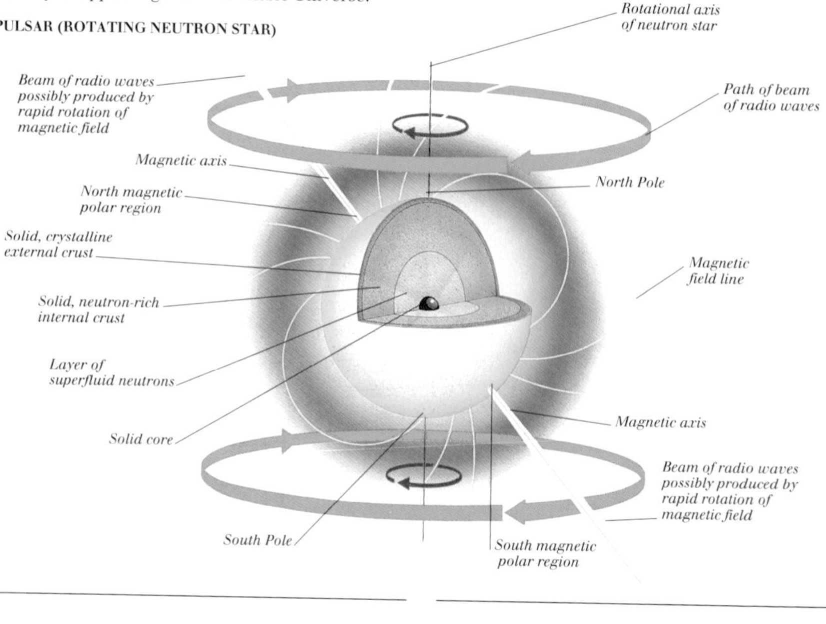
Rotational axis of neutron star
Beam of radio waves possibly produced by rapid rotation of magnetic field
Path of beam of radio waves
Magnetic axis
North Pole
North magnetic polar region
Solid, crystalline external crust
Magnetic field line
Solid, neutron-rich internal crust
Layer of superfluid neutrons
Magnetic axis
Solid core
Beam of radio waves possibly produced by rapid rotation of magnetic field
South Pole
South magnetic polar region

STELLAR BLACK HOLE

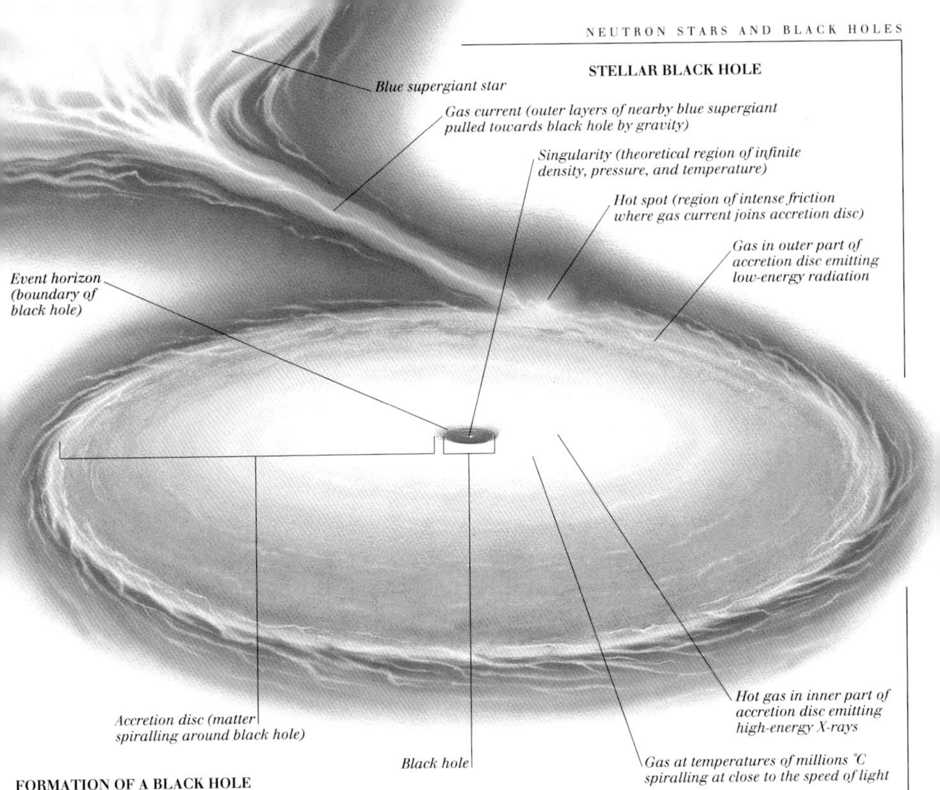
Blue supergiant star
Gas current (outer layers of nearby blue supergiant pulled towards black hole by gravity)
Singularity (theoretical region of infinite density, pressure, and temperature)
Hot spot (region of intense friction where gas current joins accretion disc)
Gas in outer part of accretion disc emitting low-energy radiation
Event horizon (boundary of black hole)
Hot gas in inner part of accretion disc emitting high-energy X-rays
Accretion disc (matter spiralling around black hole)
Black hole
Gas at temperatures of millions °C spiralling at close to the speed of light

FORMATION OF A BLACK HOLE

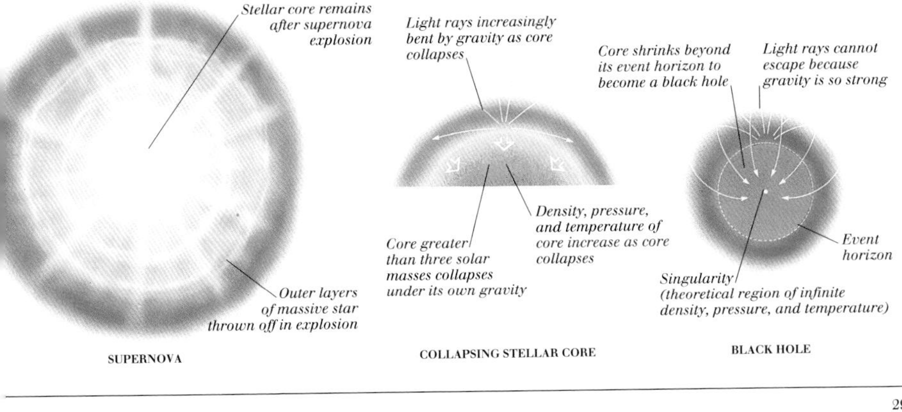
Stellar core remains after supernova explosion
Outer layers of massive star thrown off in explosion
SUPERNOVA
Light rays increasingly bent by gravity as core collapses
Core greater than three solar masses collapses under its own gravity
Density, pressure, and temperature of core increase as core collapses
COLLAPSING STELLAR CORE
Core shrinks beyond its event horizon to become a black hole
Light rays cannot escape because gravity is so strong
Event horizon
Singularity (theoretical region of infinite density, pressure, and temperature)
BLACK HOLE

The Solar System

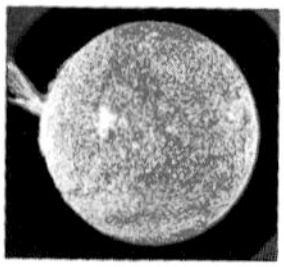

THE SUN

THE SOLAR SYSTEM consists of a central star (the Sun) and the bodies that orbit it. These bodies include nine planets and their 61 known moons; asteroids; comets; and meteoroids. The Solar System also contains interplanetary gas and dust. Most of the planets fall into two groups: four small rocky planets near the Sun (Mercury, Venus, Earth, and Mars); and four planets further out, the gas giants (Jupiter, Saturn, Uranus, and Neptune). Pluto belongs to neither group but is very small, solid, and icy. Pluto is the outermost planet, except when it passes briefly inside Neptune's orbit. Between the rocky planets and gas giants is the asteroid belt, which contains thousands of chunks of rock orbiting the Sun. Most of the bodies in the Solar System move around the Sun in elliptical orbits located in a thin disc around the Sun's equator. All the planets orbit the Sun in the same direction (anticlockwise when viewed from above) and all but Venus, Uranus, and Pluto also spin about their axes in this direction. Moons also spin as they, in turn, orbit their planets. The entire Solar System orbits the centre of our galaxy, the Milky Way (see pp. 14-15).

PLANETARY ORBIT

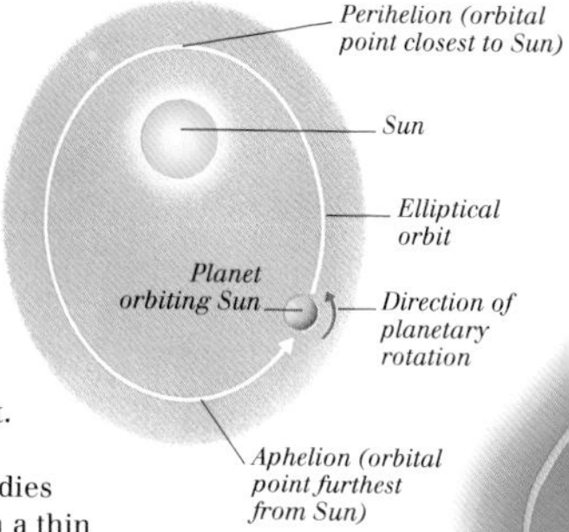
Perihelion (orbital point closest to Sun)
Sun
Elliptical orbit
Planet orbiting Sun
Direction of planetary rotation
Aphelion (orbital point furthest from Sun)

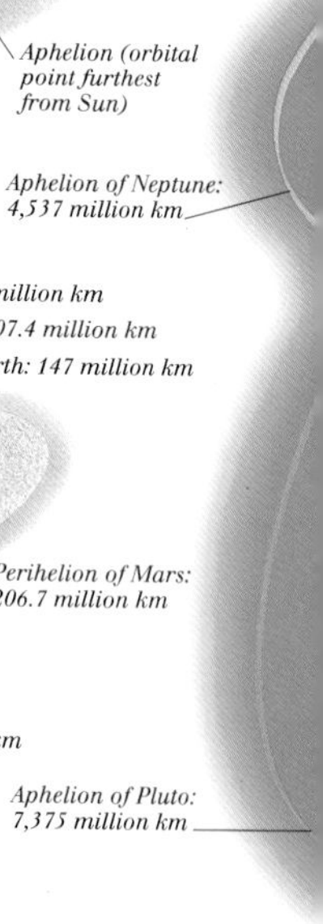
Aphelion of Neptune: 4,537 million km
Aphelion of Pluto: 7,375 million km

ORBITS OF INNER PLANETS

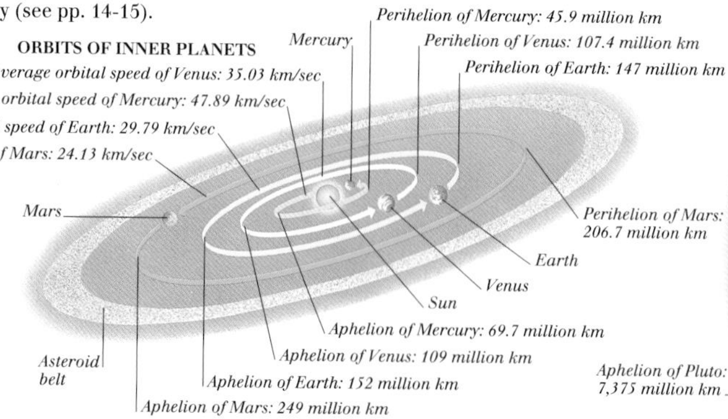
Perihelion of Mercury: 45.9 million km
Mercury
Perihelion of Venus: 107.4 million km
Perihelion of Earth: 147 million km
Average orbital speed of Venus: 35.03 km/sec
Average orbital speed of Mercury: 47.89 km/sec
Average orbital speed of Earth: 29.79 km/sec
Average orbital speed of Mars: 24.13 km/sec
Mars
Perihelion of Mars: 206.7 million km
Earth
Venus
Sun
Aphelion of Mercury: 69.7 million km
Aphelion of Venus: 109 million km
Asteroid belt
Aphelion of Earth: 152 million km
Aphelion of Mars: 249 million km

MERCURY
Year: 87.97 Earth days
Mass: 0.06 Earth masses
Diameter: 4,878 km

VENUS
Year: 224.7 Earth days
Mass: 0.81 Earth masses
Diameter: 12,103 km

EARTH
Year: 365.26 days
Mass: 1 Earth mass
Diameter: 12,756 km

MARS
Year: 1.88 Earth years
Mass: 0.11 Earth masses
Diameter: 6,786 km

JUPITER
Year: 11.86 Earth years
Mass: 317.94 Earth masses
Diameter: 142,984 km

ORBITS OF OUTER PLANETS

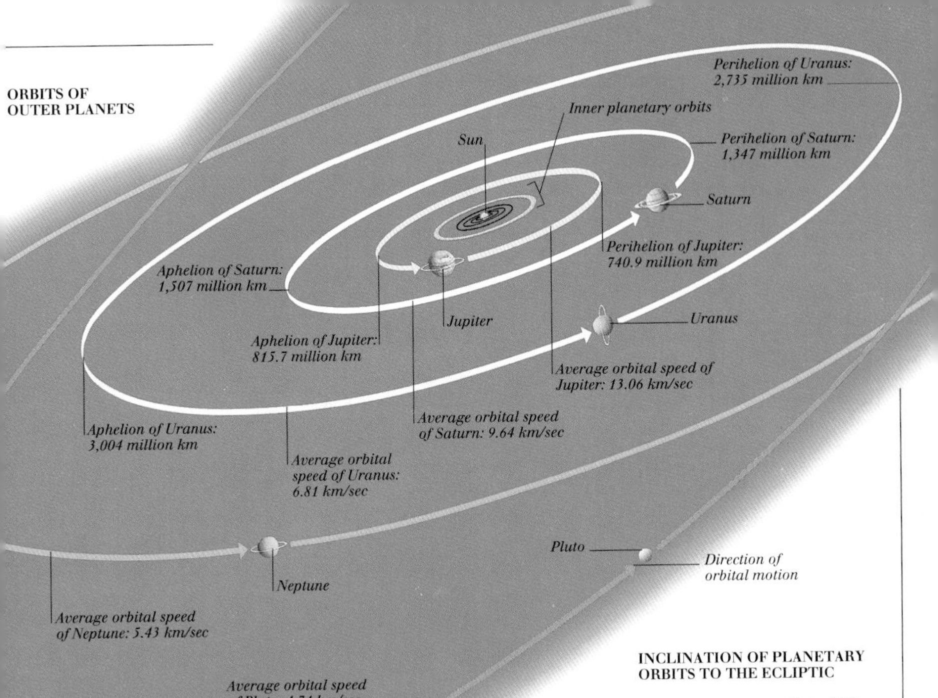

Perihelion of Uranus:
2,735 million km
Inner planetary orbits
Sun
Perihelion of Saturn:
1,347 million km
Saturn
Perihelion of Jupiter:
740.9 million km
Aphelion of Saturn:
1,507 million km
Jupiter
Uranus
Aphelion of Jupiter:
815.7 million km
Average orbital speed of
Jupiter: 13.06 km/sec
Aphelion of Uranus:
3,004 million km
Average orbital speed
of Saturn: 9.64 km/sec
Average orbital
speed of Uranus:
6.81 km/sec
Pluto
Direction of
orbital motion
Neptune
Average orbital speed
of Neptune: 5.43 km/sec
Average orbital speed
of Pluto: 4.74 km/sec

INCLINATION OF PLANETARY ORBITS TO THE ECLIPTIC

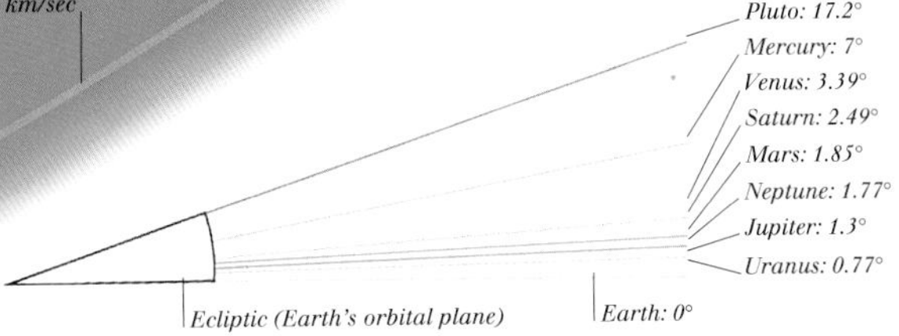

Pluto: 17.2°
Mercury: 7°
Venus: 3.39°
Saturn: 2.49°
Mars: 1.85°
Neptune: 1.77°
Jupiter: 1.3°
Uranus: 0.77°
Ecliptic (Earth's orbital plane)
Earth: 0°

SATURN
Year: 29.46 Earth years
Mass: 95.18 Earth masses
Diameter: 120,536 km

URANUS
Year: 84.01 Earth years
Mass: 14.54 Earth masses
Diameter: 51,118 km

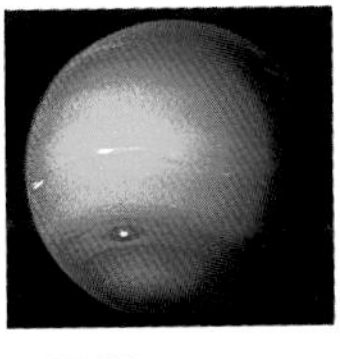

NEPTUNE
Year: 164.79 Earth years
Mass: 17.14 Earth masses
Diameter: 49,528 km

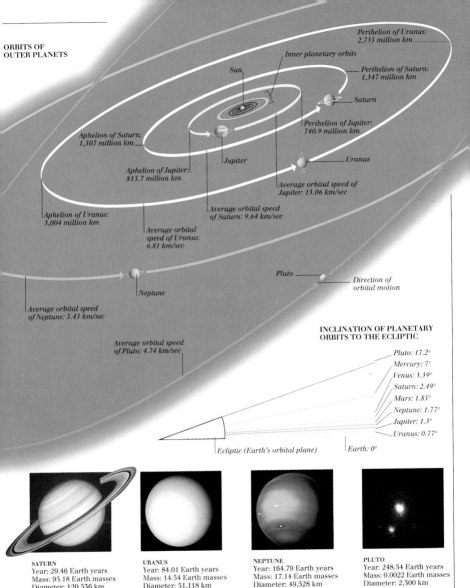

PLUTO
Year: 248.54 Earth years
Mass: 0.0022 Earth masses
Diameter: 2,300 km

The Sun

SOLAR PHOTOSPHERE

THE SUN IS THE STAR AT THE CENTRE of the Solar System. It is about five billion years old and will continue to shine as it does now for about another five billion years. The Sun is a yellow main sequence star (see pp. 22-23) about 1.4 million kilometres in diameter. It consists almost entirely of hydrogen and helium. In the Sun's core, hydrogen is converted to helium by nuclear fusion, releasing energy in the process. The energy travels from the core, through the radiative and convective zones, to the photosphere (visible surface), where it leaves the Sun in the form of heat and light. On the photosphere there are often dark, relatively cool areas called sunspots, which usually appear in pairs or groups and are thought to be caused by magnetic fields. Other types of solar activity are flares, which are usually associated with sunspots, and prominences. Flares are sudden discharges of high-energy radiation and atomic particles. Prominences are huge loops or filaments of gas extending into the solar atmosphere; some last for hours, others for months. Beyond the photosphere is the chromosphere (inner atmosphere) and the extremely rarified corona (outer atmosphere), which extends millions of kilometres into space. Tiny particles that escape from the corona give rise to the solar wind, which streams through space at hundreds of kilometres per second. The chromosphere and corona can be seen from Earth when the Sun is totally eclipsed by the Moon.

HOW A SOLAR ECLIPSE OCCURS

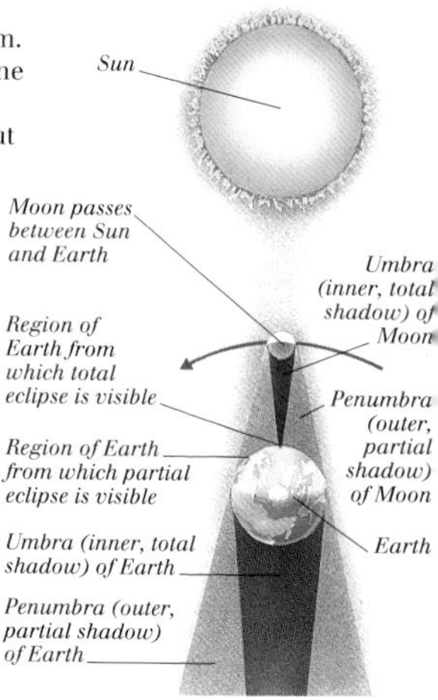
Sun
Moon passes between Sun and Earth
Umbra (inner, total shadow) of Moon
Region of Earth from which total eclipse is visible
Penumbra (outer, partial shadow) of Moon
Region of Earth from which partial eclipse is visible
Earth
Umbra (inner, total shadow) of Earth
Penumbra (outer, partial shadow) of Earth

TOTAL SOLAR ECLIPSE

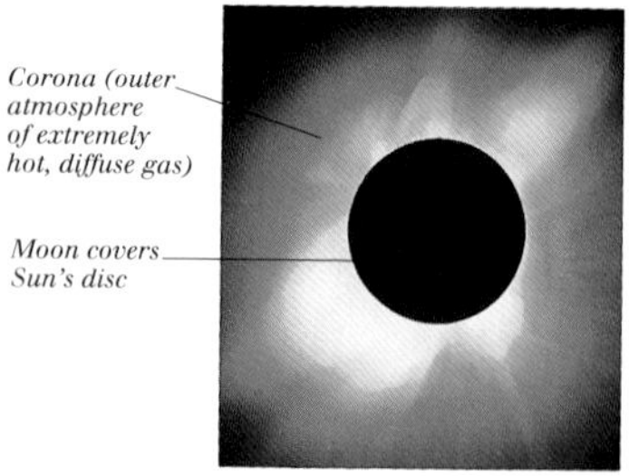
Corona (outer atmosphere of extremely hot, diffuse gas)
Moon covers Sun's disc

SURFACE FEATURES

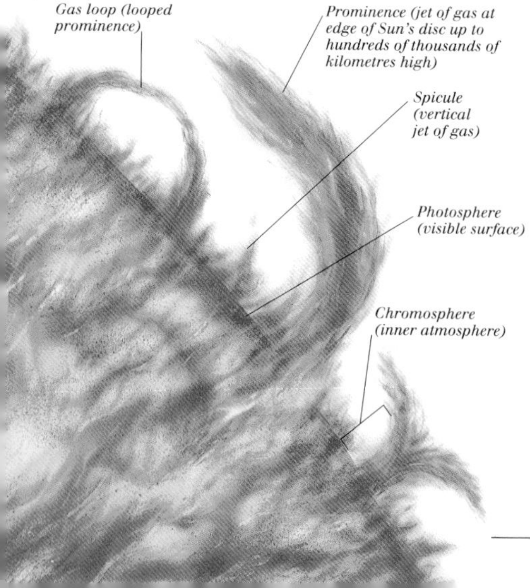
Gas loop (looped prominence)
Prominence (jet of gas at edge of Sun's disc up to hundreds of thousands of kilometres high)
Spicule (vertical jet of gas)
Photosphere (visible surface)
Chromosphere (inner atmosphere)

SUNSPOTS

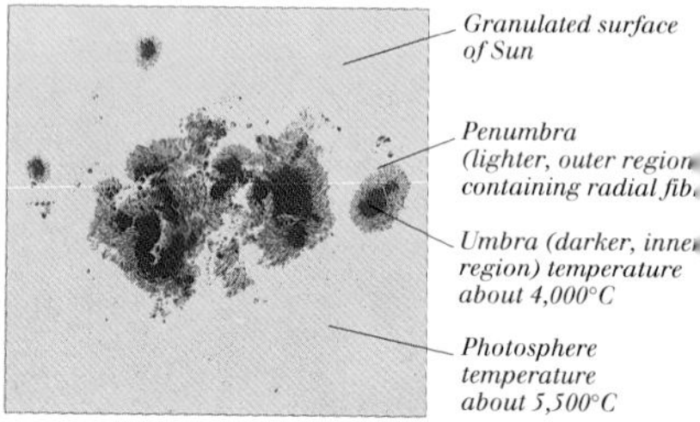
Granulated surface of Sun
Penumbra (lighter, outer region containing radial fib
Umbra (darker, inner region) temperature about 4,000°C
Photosphere temperature about 5,500°C

EXTERNAL FEATURES AND INTERNAL STRUCTURE OF THE SUN

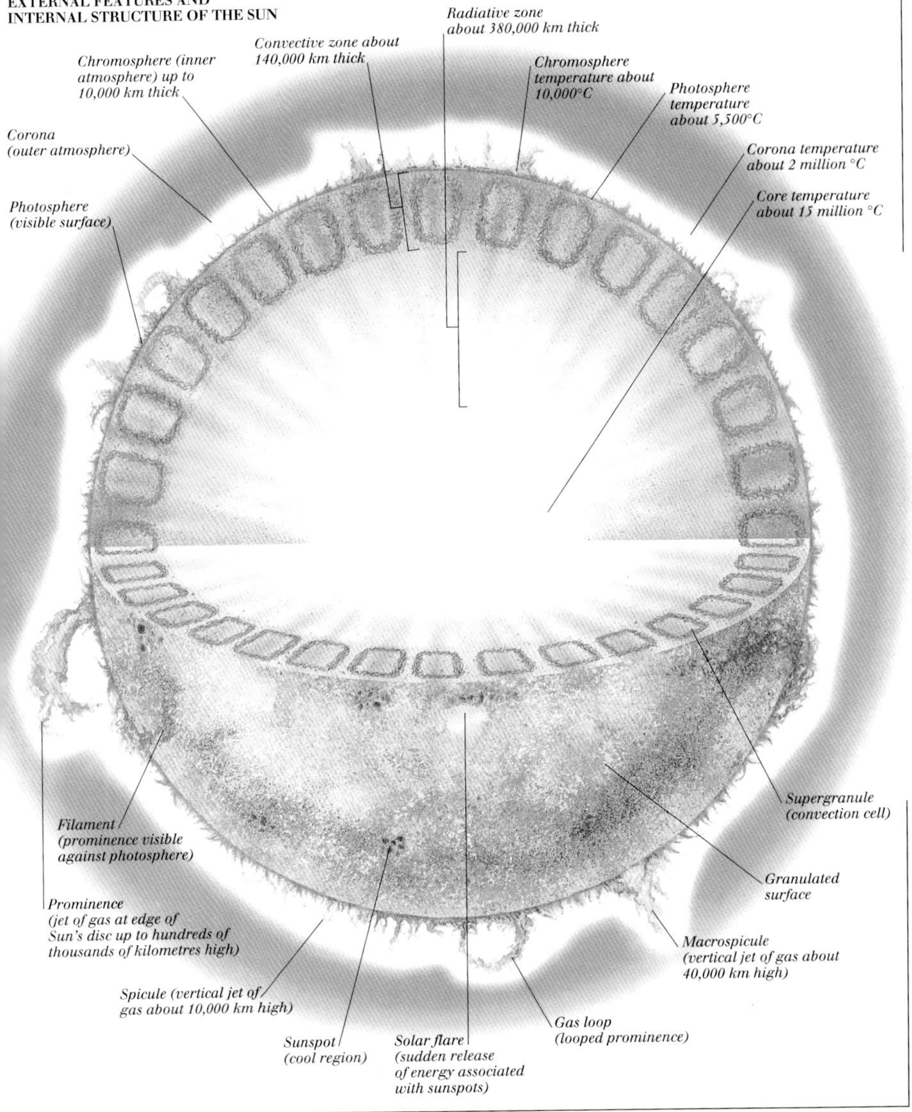
Radiative zone about 380,000 km thick
Convective zone about 140,000 km thick
Chromosphere (inner atmosphere) up to 10,000 km thick
Chromosphere temperature about 10,000°C
Photosphere temperature about 5,500°C
Corona (outer atmosphere)
Corona temperature about 2 million °C
Photosphere (visible surface)
Core temperature about 15 million °C
Supergranule (convection cell)
Filament (prominence visible against photosphere)
Granulated surface
Prominence (jet of gas at edge of Sun's disc up to hundreds of thousands of kilometres high)
Macrospicule (vertical jet of gas about 40,000 km high)
Spicule (vertical jet of gas about 10,000 km high)
Gas loop (looped prominence)
Sunspot (cool region)
Solar flare (sudden release of energy associated with sunspots)

Mercury

MERCURY

MERCURY IS THE NEAREST PLANET to the Sun, orbiting at an average distance of about 58 million kilometres. Because Mercury is the closest planet to the Sun, it moves faster than any other planet, travelling at an average speed of nearly 48 kilometres per second and completing an orbit in just under 88 days. Mercury is very small (only Pluto is smaller) and rocky. Most of the surface has been heavily cratered by the impact of meteorites, although there are also smooth, sparsely cratered plains. The Caloris Basin is the largest crater, measuring about 1,300 kilometres across. It is thought to have been formed when a rock the size of an asteroid hit the planet, and is surrounded by concentric rings of mountains thrown up by the impact. The surface also has many ridges (called rupes) that are thought to have been formed when the hot core of the young planet cooled and shrank about four billion years ago, buckling the planet's surface in the process. The planet rotates about its axis very slowly, taking nearly 59 Earth days to complete one rotation. As a result, a solar day (sunrise to sunrise) on Mercury is about 176 Earth days – twice as long as the 88-day Mercurian year. Mercury has extreme surface temperatures, ranging from a maximum of 430°C on the sunlit side to -170°C on the dark side. At nightfall, the temperature drops very quickly because the planet's atmosphere is almost non-existent. It consists only of minute amounts of helium and hydrogen captured from the solar wind, plus traces of other gases.

TILT AND ROTATION OF MERCURY

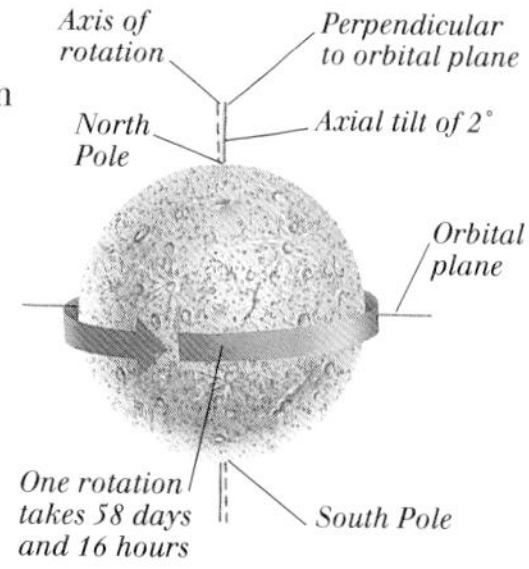

Axis of rotation
Perpendicular to orbital plane
North Pole
Axial tilt of 2°
Orbital plane
One rotation takes 58 days and 16 hours
South Pole

DEGAS AND BRONTË (RAY CRATERS)

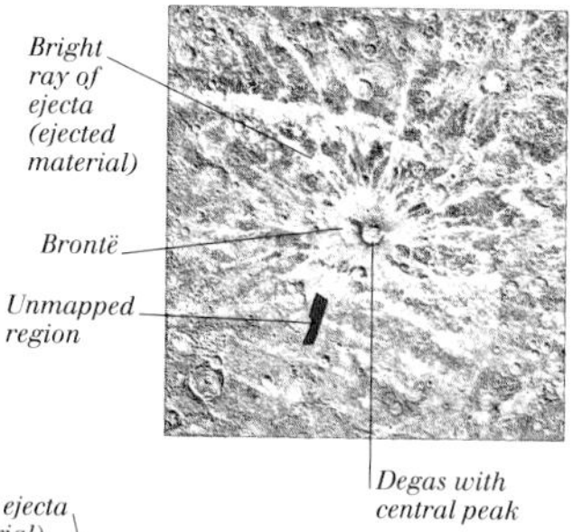

Bright ray of ejecta (ejected material)
Brontë
Unmapped region
Degas with central peak

FORMATION OF A RAY CRATER

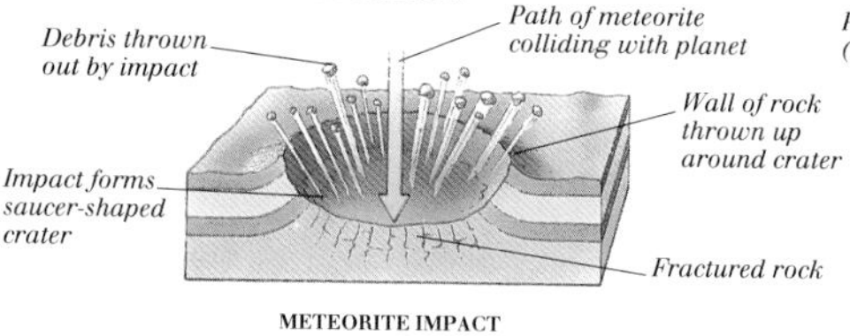

Debris thrown out by impact
Path of meteorite colliding with planet
Wall of rock thrown up around crater
Impact forms saucer-shaped crater
Fractured rock

METEORITE IMPACT

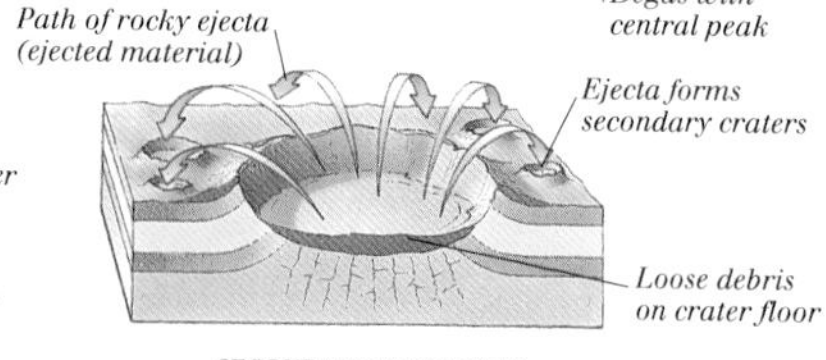

Path of rocky ejecta (ejected material)
Ejecta forms secondary craters
Loose debris on crater floor

SECONDARY CRATERING

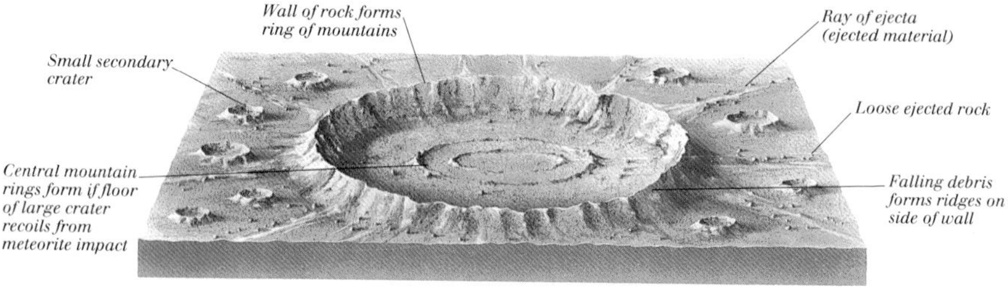

Wall of rock forms ring of mountains
Ray of ejecta (ejected material)
Small secondary crater
Loose ejected rock
Central mountain rings form if floor of large crater recoils from meteorite impact
Falling debris forms ridges on side of wall

RAY CRATER

COMPOSITION OF ATMOSPHERE

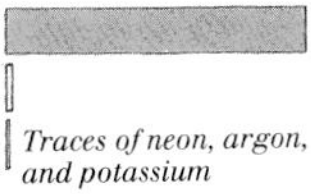
Principal constituents helium and hydrogen
Minor constituents sodium and oxygen
Traces of neon, argon, and potassium

RATERS AND PLAINS NEAR IERCURY'S NORTH POLE

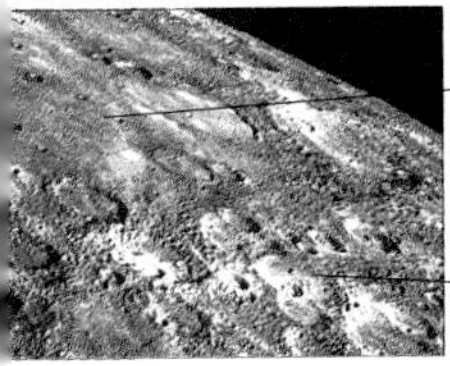
Borealis Planitia (smooth plain with a few young craters)
Terrain with many old craters

EXTERNAL FEATURES AND INTERNAL STRUCTURE OF MERCURY

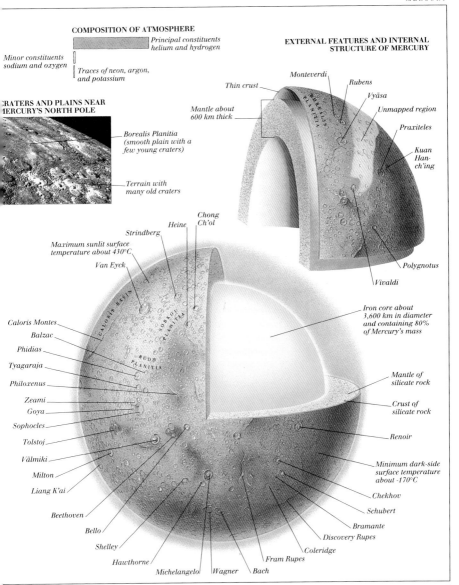

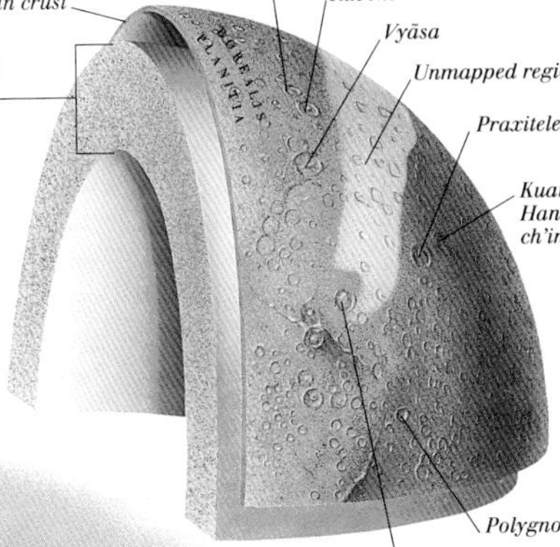
Monteverdi
Rubens
Thin crust
Vyāsa
Borealis Planitia
Mantle about 600 km thick
Unmapped region
Praxiteles
Kuan Han-ch'ing
Polygnotus
Vivaldi

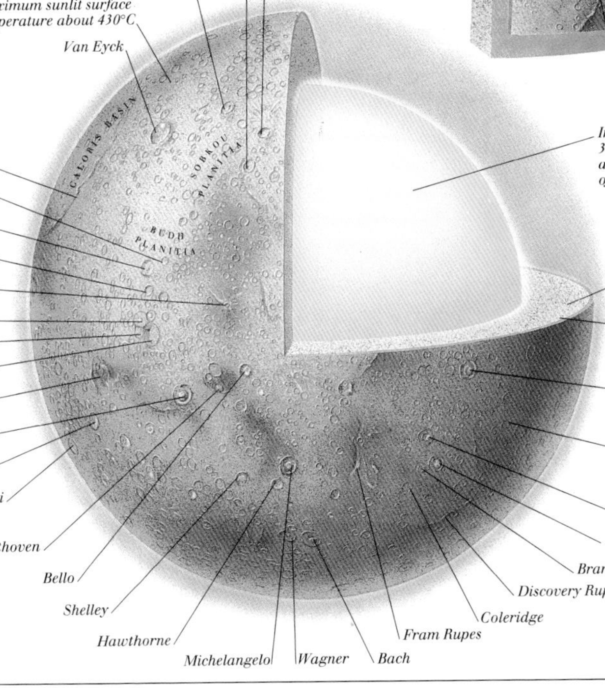
Chong Ch'ol
Heine
Strindberg
Maximum sunlit surface temperature about 430°C
Van Eyck
Caloris Basin
Sobkou Planitia
Budh Planitia
Iron core about 3,600 km in diameter and containing 80% of Mercury's mass
Caloris Montes
Balzac
Phidias
Tyagaraja
Philoxenus
Zeami
Goya
Sophocles
Tolstoj
Vālmiki
Milton
Liang K'ai
Beethoven
Bello
Shelley
Hawthorne
Michelangelo
Wagner
Bach
Fram Rupes
Coleridge
Discovery Rupes
Bramante
Schubert
Chekhov
Minimum dark-side surface temperature about -170°C
Renoir
Crust of silicate rock
Mantle of silicate rock

Venus

RADAR IMAGE OF VENUS

VENUS IS A ROCKY PLANET and the second planet from the Sun. Venus spins slowly backwards as it orbits the Sun, causing its rotational period to be the longest in the Solar System, at about 243 Earth days. It is slightly smaller than Earth and probably has a similar internal structure, consisting of a semi-solid metal core, surrounded by a rocky mantle and crust. Venus is the brightest object in the sky after the Sun and Moon because its atmosphere reflects sunlight strongly. The main component of the atmosphere is carbon dioxide, which traps heat in a greenhouse effect far stronger than that on Earth. As a result, Venus is the hottest planet, with a maximum surface temperature of about 480°C. The thick cloud layers contain droplets of sulphuric acid and are driven around the planet by winds at speeds of up to 360 kilometres per hour. Although the planet takes 243 Earth days to rotate once, the high-speed winds cause the clouds to circle the planet in only four Earth days. The high temperature, acidic clouds, and enormous atmospheric pressure (about 90 times greater at the surface than that on Earth) make the environment extremely hostile. However, space probes have managed to land on Venus and photograph its dry, dusty surface. The Venusian surface has also been mapped by probes with radar equipment that can "see" through the cloud layers. Such radar maps reveal a terrain with craters, mountains, volcanoes, and areas where craters have been covered by plains of solidified volcanic lava. There are two large highland regions called Aphrodite Terra and Ishtar Terra.

TILT AND ROTATION OF VENUS

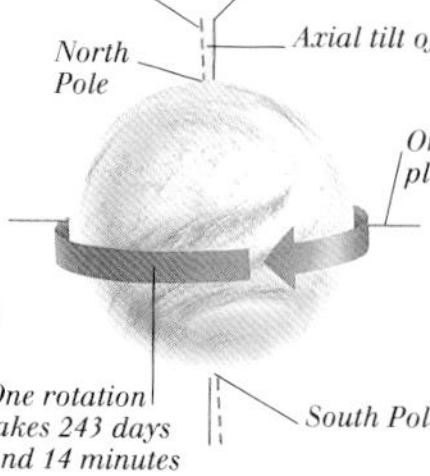
Axis of rotation
Perpendicular to orbital plane
Axial tilt of 2°
North Pole
Orbital plane
One rotation takes 243 days and 14 minutes
South Pole

CLOUD FEATURES

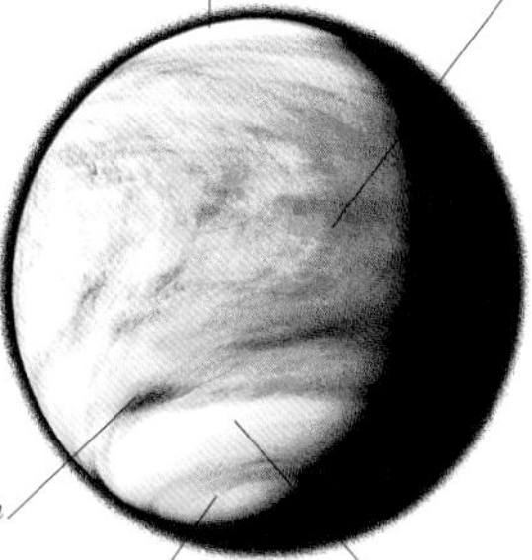
Polar hood
Dark, mid-latitude band
Cloud features swept around planet by winds of up to 360 km/h
Dirty yellow hue due to sulphuric acid in atmosphere
Bright polar band

VENUSIAN CRATERS

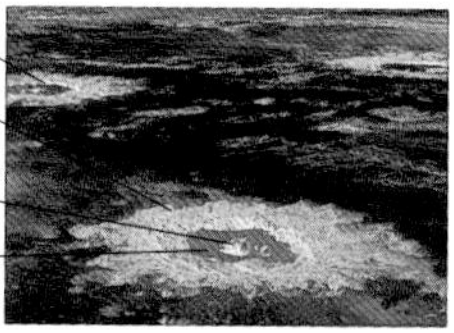
Danilova
Ejecta (ejected material)
Central peak
Howe

FALSE-COLOUR RADAR MAP OF THE SURFACE OF VENUS

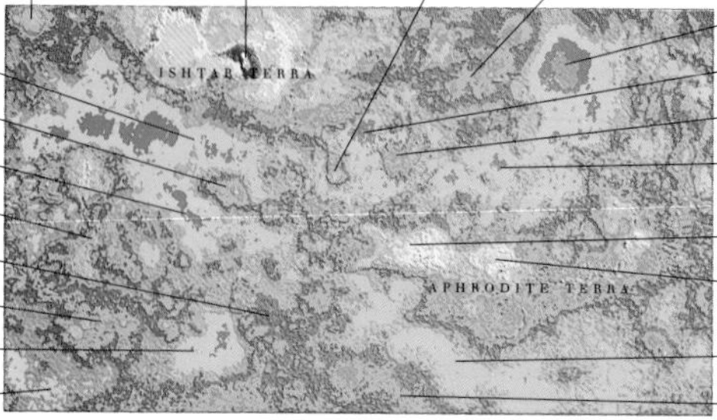
Metis Regio
Maxwell Montes
Bell Regio
Tethus Regio
ISHTAR TERRA
APHRODITE TERRA
Sedna Planitia
Eisila Regio
Guinevere Planitia
Phoebe Regio
Alpha Regio
Themis Regio
Lavinia Planitia
Helen Planitia
Atalanta Planitia
Leda Planitia
Tellus Regio
Niobe Planitia
Ovda Regio
Thetis Regio
Aino Planitia
Lada Terra

EXTERNAL FEATURES AND INTERNAL STRUCTURE OF VENUS

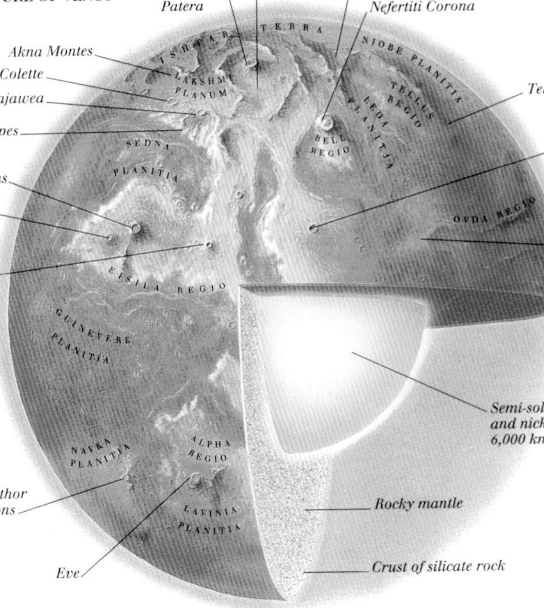
Cleopatra Patera
Maxwell Montes
Dekla Tessera
Nefertiti Corona
Akna Montes
Colette
Sacajawea
Vesta Rupes
Gula Mons
Sif Mons
Sappho Patera
Tellus Tessera
Pavlova
Hestia Rupes
Semi-solid core of iron and nickel about 6,000 km in diameter
Hathor Mons
Rocky mantle
Eve
Crust of silicate rock
ISHTAR TERRA
NIOBE PLANITIA
LAKSHMI PLANUM
TELLUS REGIO
LEDA PLANITIA
BELL REGIO
SEDNA PLANITIA
OVDA REGIO
EISILA REGIO
GUINEVERE PLANITIA
NAVKA PLANITIA
ALPHA REGIO
LAVINIA PLANITIA

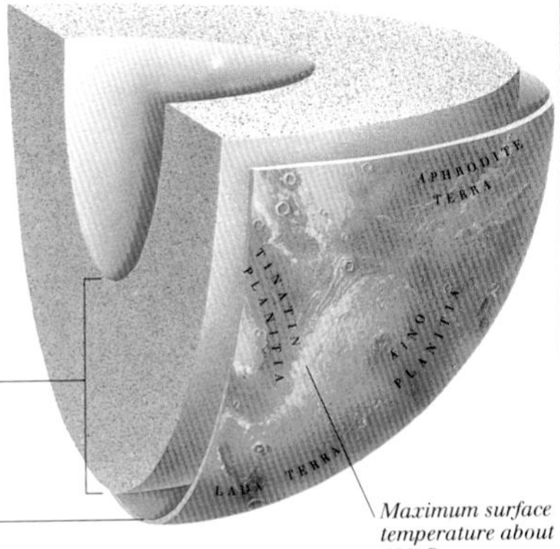
APHRODITE TERRA
TINATIN PLANITIA
AINO PLANITIA
LADA TERRA
Mantle about 3,000 km thick
Crust about 50 km thick
Maximum surface temperature about 480°C

ATMOSPHERE

STRUCTURE

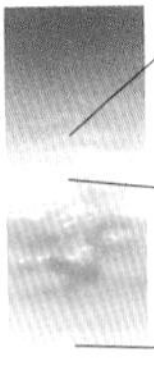
Thermosphere
Haze containing droplets of sulphuric acid
Thick cloud layers containing droplets of sulphuric acid
Lower haze of dust and sulphuric acid aerosol (extremely small droplets)
Troposphere
Clear atmosphere of mainly carbon dioxide

COMPOSITION

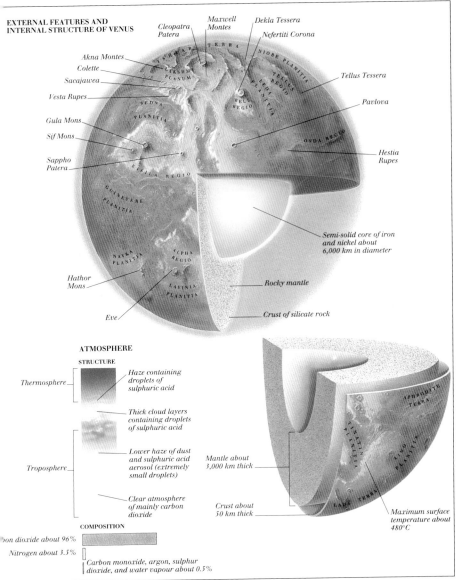

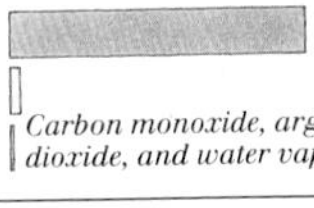
…bon dioxide about 96%
Nitrogen about 3.5%
Carbon monoxide, argon, sulphur dioxide, and water vapour about 0.5%

The Earth

THE EARTH

THE EARTH IS THE THIRD of the nine planets that orbit the Sun. It is the largest and densest rocky planet, and the only one known to support life. About 70 per cent of the Earth's surface is covered by water, which is not found in liquid form on the surface of any other planet. There are four main layers: the inner core, the outer core, the mantle, and the crust. At the heart of the planet the solid inner core has a temperature of about 4,000°C. The heat from this inner core causes material in the molten outer core and mantle to circulate in convection currents. It is thought that these convection currents generate the Earth's magnetic field, which extends into space as the magnetosphere. The Earth's atmosphere helps screen out some of the harmful radiation from the Sun, stops meteorites from reaching the planet's surface, and traps enough heat to prevent extremes of cold. The Earth has one natural satellite, the Moon, which is large enough for both bodies to be considered a double-planet system.

TILT AND ROTATION OF THE EARTH

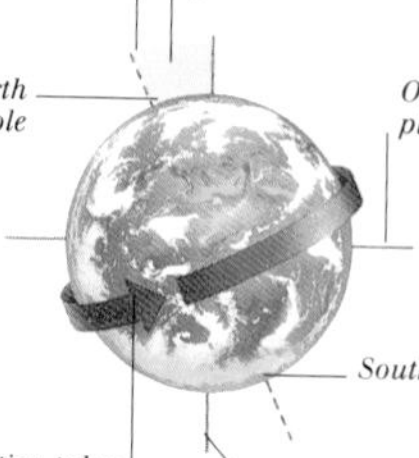
Axis of rotation
Axial tilt of 23.4°
North Pole
Orbital plane
South Pole
One rotation takes 23 hours and 56 minutes
Perpendicular to orbital plane

THE FORMATION OF THE EARTH

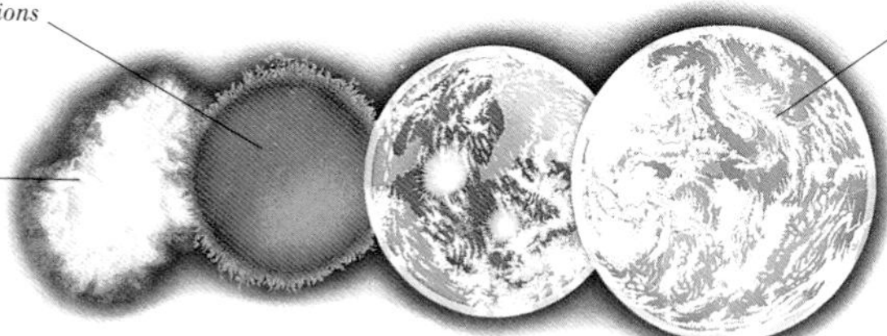
The heat of the collisions caused the planet to glow red
The cloud broke up into particles of ice and rock, which stuck together to form planets
Micro-organisms began to photosynthesize, creating a build up of oxygen

4,600 MILLION YEARS AGO, THE SOLAR SYSTEM FORMED FROM A CLOUD OF GAS AND DUST

THE EARTH WAS FORMED FROM COLLIDING ROCKS

4,500 MILLION YEARS AGO THE SURFACE COOLED TO FORM THE CRUST

THE CONTINENTS BROKE UP AND REFORMED, GRADUALLY TAKING THEIR PRESENT POSITIONS

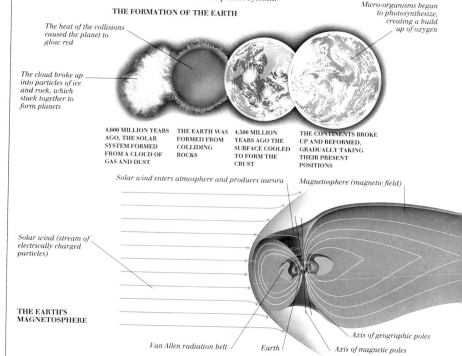

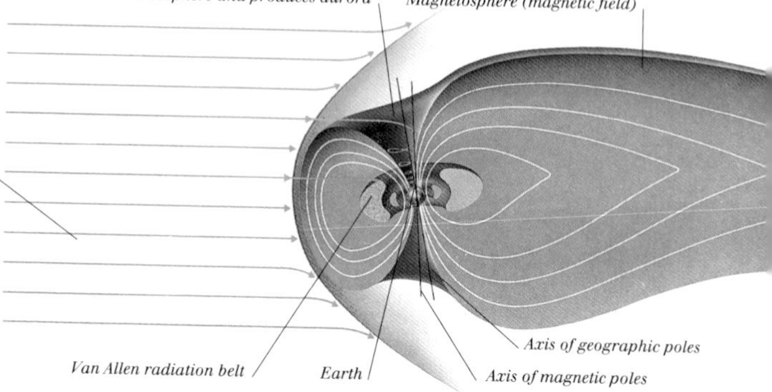
Solar wind enters atmosphere and produces aurora
Magnetosphere (magnetic field)
Solar wind (stream of electrically charged particles)
Van Allen radiation belt
Earth
Axis of geographic poles
Axis of magnetic poles

THE EARTH'S MAGNETOSPHERE

EXTERNAL FEATURES AND INTERNAL STRUCTURE OF THE EARTH

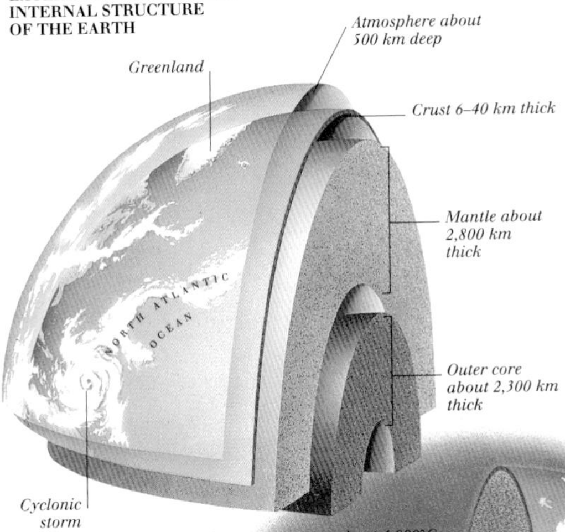

Atmosphere about 500 km deep
Greenland
Crust 6–40 km thick
Mantle about 2,800 km thick
NORTH ATLANTIC OCEAN
Outer core about 2,300 km thick
Cyclonic storm

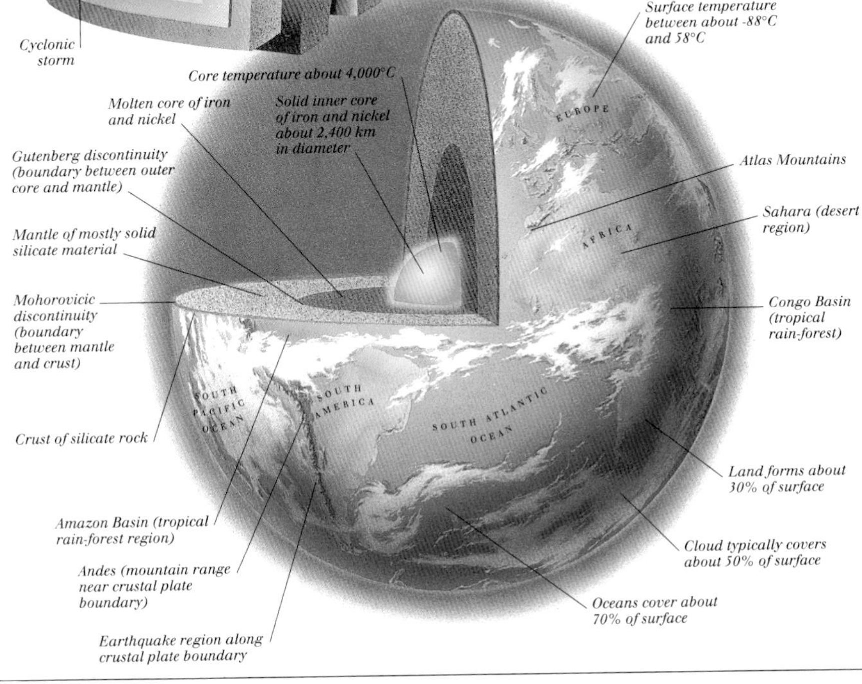

Surface temperature between about -88°C and 58°C
Core temperature about 4,000°C
Molten core of iron and nickel
Solid inner core of iron and nickel about 2,400 km in diameter
EUROPE
Gutenberg discontinuity (boundary between outer core and mantle)
Atlas Mountains
Sahara (desert region)
AFRICA
Mantle of mostly solid silicate material
Mohorovicic discontinuity (boundary between mantle and crust)
Congo Basin (tropical rain-forest)
SOUTH PACIFIC OCEAN
SOUTH AMERICA
SOUTH ATLANTIC OCEAN
Crust of silicate rock
Land forms about 30% of surface
Amazon Basin (tropical rain-forest region)
Cloud typically covers about 50% of surface
Andes (mountain range near crustal plate boundary)
Oceans cover about 70% of surface
Earthquake region along crustal plate boundary

COMPOSITION OF THE EARTH

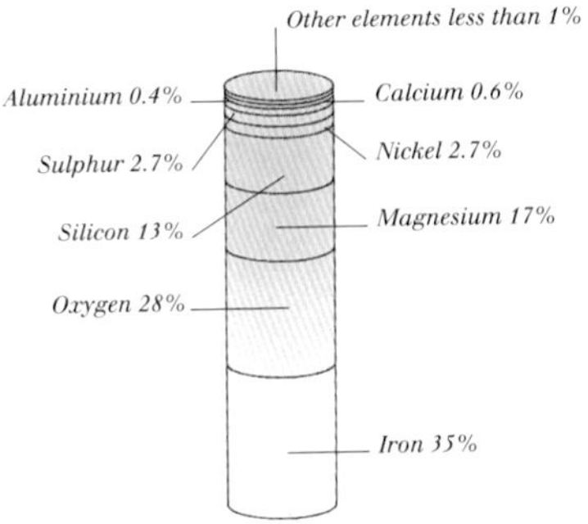

Other elements less than 1%
Aluminium 0.4%
Calcium 0.6%
Sulphur 2.7%
Nickel 2.7%
Silicon 13%
Magnesium 17%
Oxygen 28%
Iron 35%

The Moon

THE MOON FROM EARTH

THE MOON IS THE EARTH'S only natural satellite. It is relatively large for a moon, with a diameter of about 3,470 kilometres – just over a quarter that of the Earth. The Moon takes the same time to rotate on its axis as it takes to orbit the Earth (27.3 days), and so the same side (the near side) always faces us. However, the amount of the surface we can see – the phase of the Moon – depends on how much of the near side is in sunlight. The Moon is dry and barren, with no atmosphere or water. It consists mainly of solid rock, although its core may contain molten rock or iron. The surface is dusty, with highlands covered in craters caused by meteorite impacts, and lowlands in which large craters have been filled by solidified lava to form dark areas called maria or "seas". Maria occur mainly on the near side, which has a thinner crust than the far side. Many of the craters are rimmed by mountain ranges that form the crater walls and can be thousands of metres high.

TILT AND ROTATION OF THE MOON

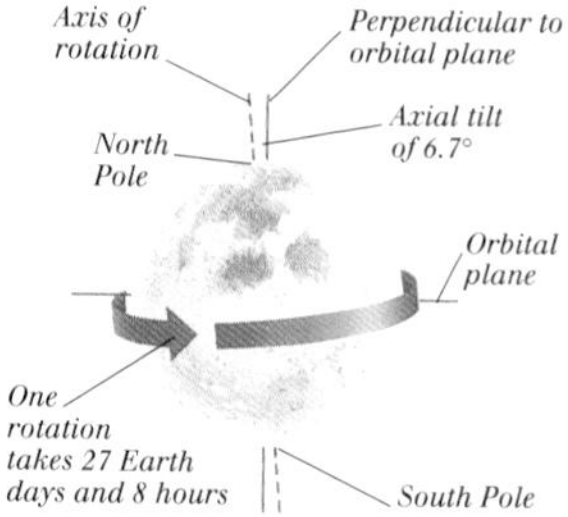
Axis of rotation
Perpendicular to orbital plane
Axial tilt of 6.7°
North Pole
Orbital plane
One rotation takes 27 Earth days and 8 hours
South Pole

CRATERS ON OCEANUS PROCELLARUM

Aristarchus
Cobra Head (head of Schröter's Valley)
Herodotus

NEAR SIDE OF THE MOON

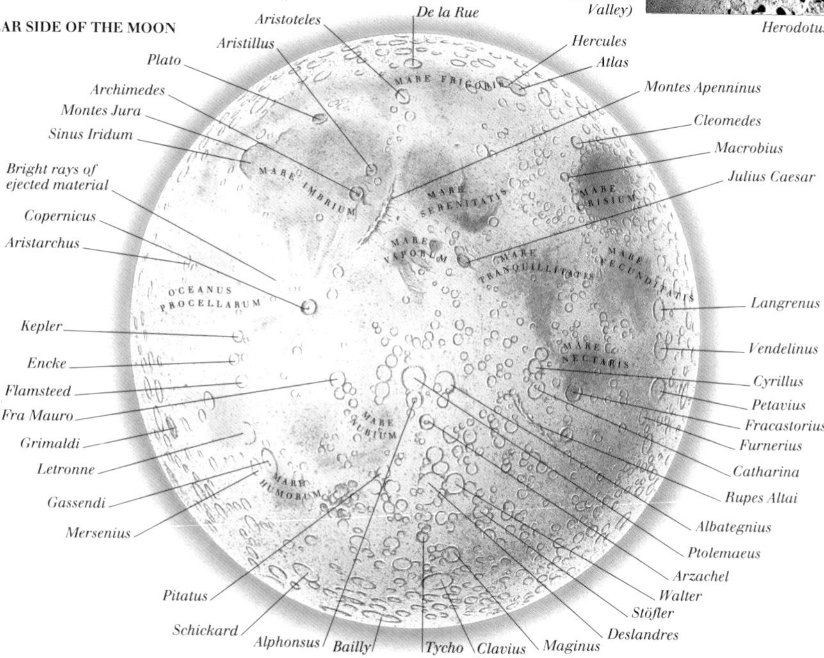
Aristoteles
De la Rue
Aristillus
Plato
Archimedes
Montes Jura
Sinus Iridum
Bright rays of ejected material
Copernicus
Aristarchus
Kepler
Encke
Flamsteed
Fra Mauro
Grimaldi
Letronne
Gassendi
Mersenius
Pitatus
Schickard
Alphonsus
Bailly
Tycho
Clavius
Maginus
Deslandres
Stöfler
Walter
Arzachel
Ptolemaeus
Albategnius
Rupes Altai
Catharina
Furnerius
Fracastorius
Petavius
Cyrillus
Vendelinus
Langrenus
Julius Caesar
Macrobius
Cleomedes
Montes Apenninus
Atlas
Hercules
MARE FRIGORIS
MARE IMBRIUM
MARE SERENITATIS
MARE CRISIUM
MARE VAPORUM
MARE TRANQUILLITATIS
MARE FECUNDITATIS
OCEANUS PROCELLARUM
MARE NECTARIS
MARE NUBIUM
MARE HUMORUM

PHASES OF THE MOON

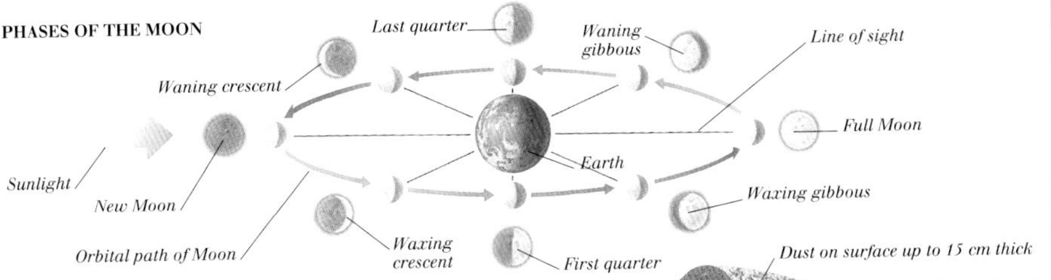
Last quarter
Waning gibbous
Line of sight
Waning crescent
Full Moon
Earth
Sunlight
New Moon
Waxing gibbous
Orbital path of Moon
Waxing crescent
First quarter

FAR SIDE OF THE MOON

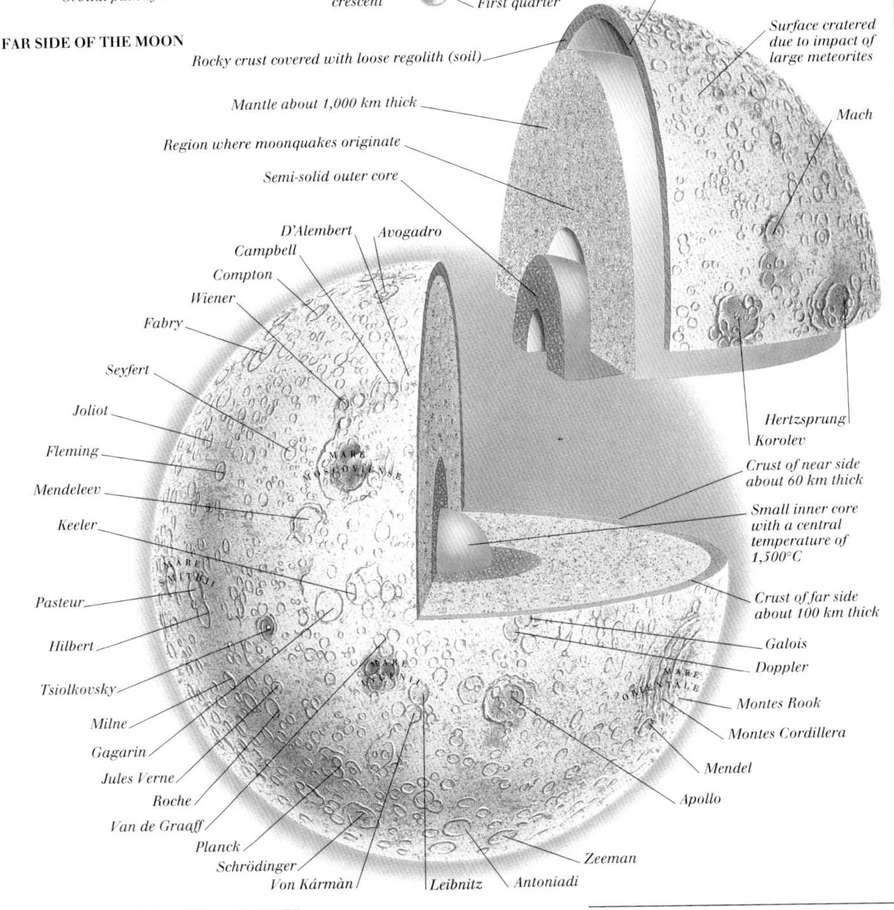
Dust on surface up to 15 cm thick
Surface cratered due to impact of large meteorites
Rocky crust covered with loose regolith (soil)
Mantle about 1,000 km thick
Mach
Region where moonquakes originate
Semi-solid outer core
D'Alembert
Avogadro
Campbell
Compton
Wiener
Fabry
Seyfert
Joliot
Fleming
Mendeleev
Keeler
MARE MOSCOVIENSE
MARE SMYTHII
MARE INGENII
MARE ORIENTALE
Hertzsprung
Korolev
Crust of near side about 60 km thick
Small inner core with a central temperature of 1,500°C
Crust of far side about 100 km thick
Pasteur
Hilbert
Tsiolkovsky
Milne
Gagarin
Jules Verne
Roche
Van de Graaff
Planck
Schrödinger
Von Kármàn
Leibnitz
Antoniadi
Zeeman
Apollo
Mendel
Montes Cordillera
Montes Rook
Doppler
Galois

Mars

MARS

MARS, KNOWN AS THE RED PLANET, is the fourth planet from the Sun and the outermost rocky planet. In the 19th century, astronomers first observed what were thought to be signs of life on Mars. These signs included apparent canal-like markings on the surface, and dark patches that were thought to be vegetation. It is now known that the "canals" are an optical illusion, and the dark patches are areas where the red dust that covers most of the planet has been blown away. The fine dust particles are often whipped up by winds into dust storms that occasionally obscure almost all the surface. Residual dust in the atmosphere gives the Martian sky a pinkish hue. The northern hemisphere of Mars has many large plains formed of solidified volcanic lava, whereas the southern hemisphere has many craters and large impact basins. There are also several huge, extinct volcanoes, including Olympus Mons, which, at 600 kilometres across and 25 kilometres high, is the largest known volcano in the Solar System. The surface also has many canyons and branching channels. The canyons were formed by movements of the surface crust, but the channels are thought to have been formed by flowing water that has now dried up. The Martian atmosphere is much thinner than Earth's, with only a few clouds and morning mists. Mars has two tiny, irregularly shaped moons called Phobos and Deimos. Their small size indicates that they may be asteroids that have been captured by the gravity of Mars.

TILT AND ROTATION OF MARS

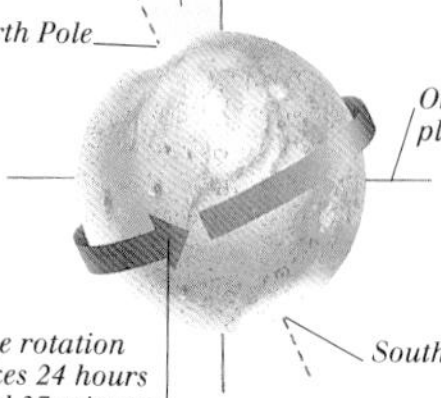
Axial tilt of 24°
Perpendicular to orbital plane
Axis of rotation
North Pole
Orbital plane
One rotation takes 24 hours and 37 minutes
South Pole

SURFACE FEATURES OF MARS

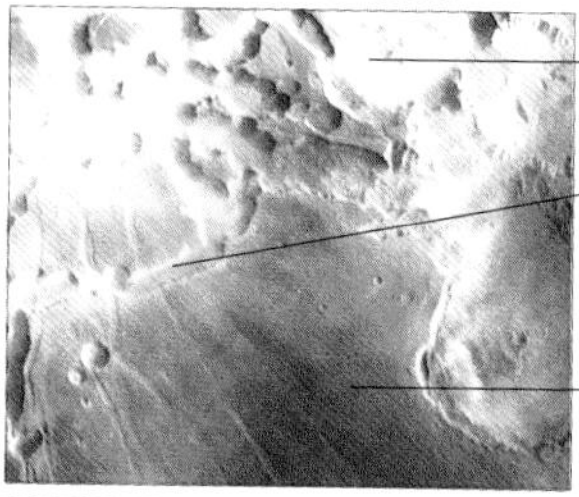
Bright water-ice fog
Fog in canyon about 20 km wide at end of Valles Marineris
Syria Planum

NOCTIS LABYRINTHUS (CANYON SYSTEM)

Summit caldera consisting of overlapping collapsed volcanic craters
Crater
Gentle slope produced by lava flow
Cloud formation

OLYMPUS MONS (EXTINCT SHIELD VOLCANO)

THE SURFACE OF MARS

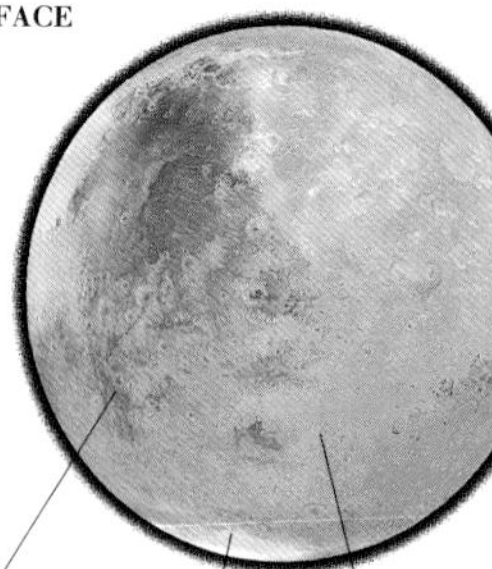
Dark area where dust has been blown away by wind
South polar ice-cap
Surface covered with red-coloured iron oxide dust

MOONS OF MARS

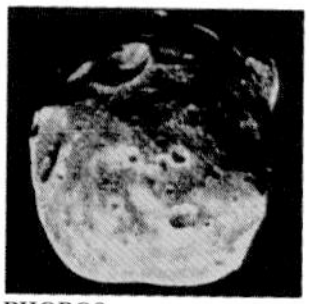

PHOBOS
Average diameter: 22 km
Average distance from planet: 9,400 km

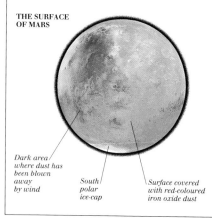

DEIMOS
Average diameter: 13 km
Average distance from planet: 23,500 km

EXTERNAL FEATURES AND INTERNAL STRUCTURE OF MARS

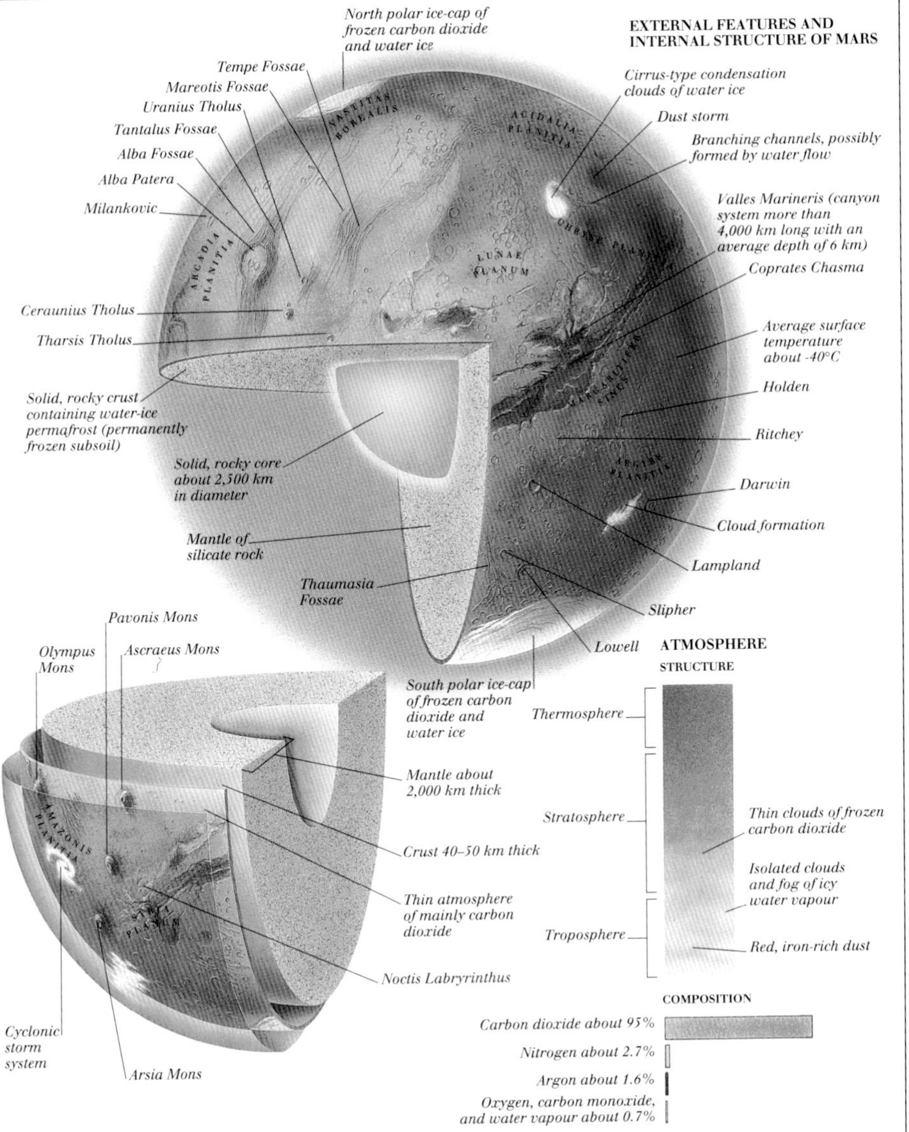
North polar ice-cap of frozen carbon dioxide and water ice
Tempe Fossae
Mareotis Fossae
Uranius Tholus
Tantalus Fossae
Alba Fossae
Alba Patera
Milankovic
VASTITAS BOREALIS
ACIDALIA PLANITIA
ARCADIA PLANITIA
LUNAE PLANUM
CHRYSE PLANITIA
Cirrus-type condensation clouds of water ice
Dust storm
Branching channels, possibly formed by water flow
Valles Marineris (canyon system more than 4,000 km long with an average depth of 6 km)
Coprates Chasma
Ceraunius Tholus
Tharsis Tholus
Average surface temperature about -40°C
MARGARITIFER SINUS
Holden
Ritchey
ARGYRE PLANITIA
Solid, rocky crust containing water-ice permafrost (permanently frozen subsoil)
Solid, rocky core about 2,500 km in diameter
Darwin
Cloud formation
Mantle of silicate rock
Lampland
Thaumasia Fossae
Slipher
Lowell
South polar ice-cap of frozen carbon dioxide and water ice
Pavonis Mons
Olympus Mons
Ascraeus Mons
AMAZONIS PLANITIA
SINAI PLANUM
Mantle about 2,000 km thick
Crust 40–50 km thick
Thin atmosphere of mainly carbon dioxide
Noctis Labryrinthus
Cyclonic storm system
Arsia Mons
ATMOSPHERE
STRUCTURE
Thermosphere
Stratosphere
Troposphere
Thin clouds of frozen carbon dioxide
Isolated clouds and fog of icy water vapour
Red, iron-rich dust
COMPOSITION
Carbon dioxide about 95%
Nitrogen about 2.7%
Argon about 1.6%
Oxygen, carbon monoxide, and water vapour about 0.7%

Jupiter

JUPITER

JUPITER IS THE FIFTH PLANET from the Sun and the first of the four gas giants. It is the largest and the most massive planet, with a diameter about 11 times that of the Earth and a mass about 2.5 times the combined mass of the eight other planets. Jupiter is thought to have a small rocky core surrounded by an inner mantle of metallic hydrogen (liquid hydrogen that acts like a metal). Outside the inner mantle is an outer mantle of liquid hydrogen and helium that merges into the gaseous atmosphere. Jupiter's rapid rate of rotation causes the clouds in its atmosphere to form belts and zones that encircle the planet parallel to the equator. Belts are dark, low-lying, relatively warm cloud layers, and zones are bright, high-altitude, cooler cloud layers. Within the belts and zones, turbulence causes the formation of cloud features such as white ovals and red spots, both of which are huge storm systems. The most prominent cloud feature is a storm called the Great Red Spot, which consists of a spiralling column of clouds three times wider than the Earth that rises about eight kilometres above the upper cloud layer. Jupiter has one thin, faint, main ring, inside which is a tenuous halo ring of tiny particles extending towards the planet. There are 16 known Jovian moons. The four largest moons (called the Galileans) are Ganymede, Callisto, Io, and Europa. Ganymede and Callisto are cratered and probably icy. Europa is smooth and icy and may contain water. Io is covered in bright red, orange, and yellow splotches. This colouring is caused by sulphurous material from active volcanoes that shoot plumes of lava hundreds of kilometres above the surface.

TILT AND ROTATION OF JUPITER

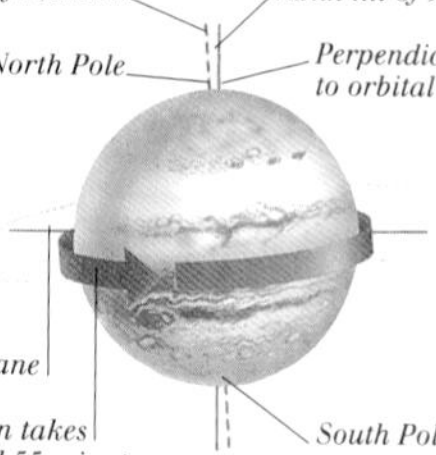
Axis of rotation
Axial tilt of 3.1°
North Pole
Perpendicular to orbital plane
Orbital plane
One rotation takes 9 hours and 55 minutes
South Pole

GREAT RED SPOT AND WHITE OVAL

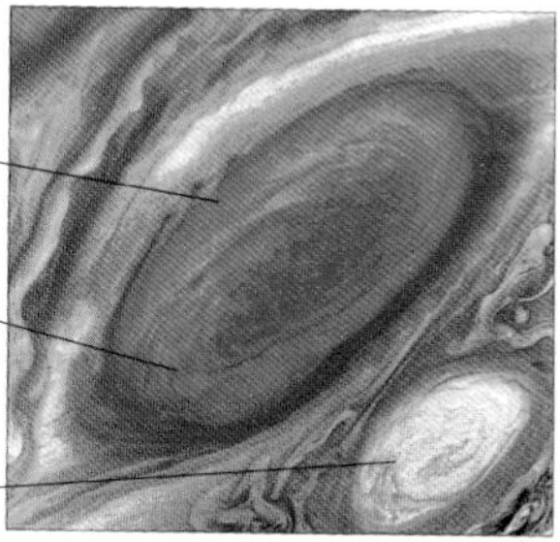
Great Red Spot (anticyclonic storm system)
Red colour probably due to phosphorus
White oval (temporary anticyclonic storm system)

RINGS OF JUPITER

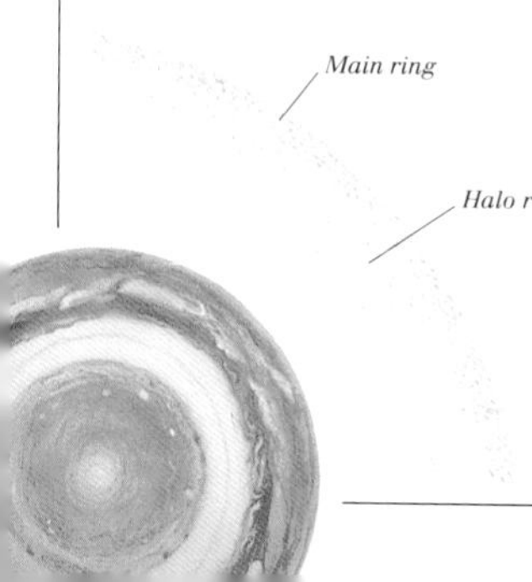
Main ring
Halo ring

GALILEAN MOONS OF JUPITER

EUROPA
Diameter: 3,138 km
Average distance from planet: 670,900 km

CALLISTO
Diameter: 4,800 km
Average distance from planet: 1,880,000 km

GANYMEDE
Diameter: 5,262 km
Average distance from planet: 1,070,000 km

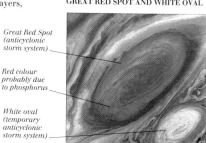

IO
Diameter: 3,642 km
Average distance from planet: 421,800 km

EXTERNAL FEATURES AND INTERNAL STRUCTURE OF JUPITER

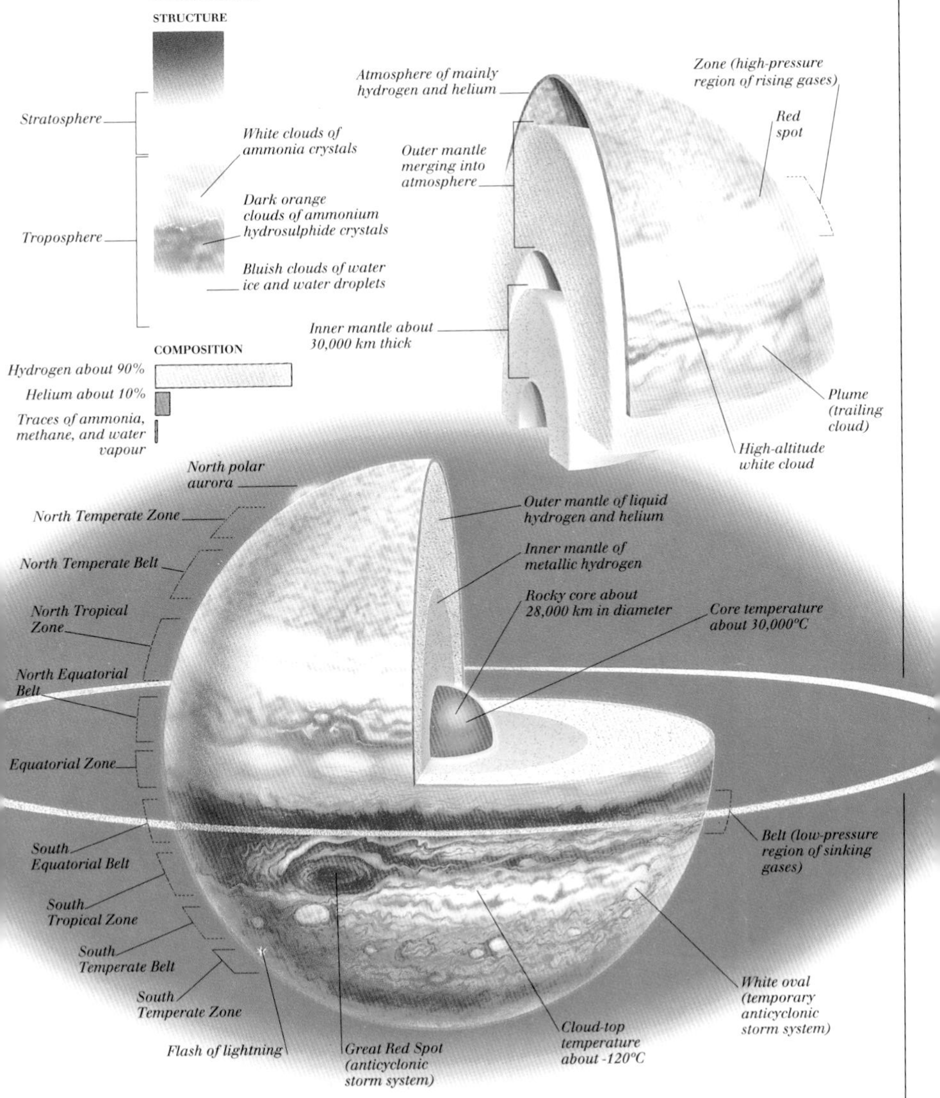
ATMOSPHERE
STRUCTURE
Stratosphere
Troposphere
White clouds of ammonia crystals
Dark orange clouds of ammonium hydrosulphide crystals
Bluish clouds of water ice and water droplets
COMPOSITION
Hydrogen about 90%
Helium about 10%
Traces of ammonia, methane, and water vapour
Atmosphere of mainly hydrogen and helium
Outer mantle merging into atmosphere
Inner mantle about 30,000 km thick
Zone (high-pressure region of rising gases)
Red spot
Plume (trailing cloud)
High-altitude white cloud
North polar aurora
North Temperate Zone
North Temperate Belt
North Tropical Zone
North Equatorial Belt
Equatorial Zone
South Equatorial Belt
South Tropical Zone
South Temperate Belt
South Temperate Zone
Flash of lightning
Great Red Spot (anticyclonic storm system)
Cloud-top temperature about -120°C
White oval (temporary anticyclonic storm system)
Belt (low-pressure region of sinking gases)
Outer mantle of liquid hydrogen and helium
Inner mantle of metallic hydrogen
Rocky core about 28,000 km in diameter
Core temperature about 30,000°C

Saturn

FALSE-COLOUR IMAGE OF SATURN

SATURN IS THE SIXTH PLANET from the Sun. It is a gas giant almost as big as Jupiter, with an equatorial diameter of about 120,500 kilometres. Saturn is thought to consist of a small core of rock and ice surrounded by an inner mantle of metallic hydrogen (liquid hydrogen that acts like a metal). Outside the inner mantle is an outer mantle of liquid hydrogen that merges into a gaseous atmosphere. Saturn's clouds form belts and zones similar to those on Jupiter, but obscured by overlying haze. Storms and eddies, seen as red or white ovals, occur in the clouds. Saturn has an extremely thin but wide system of rings that is less than one kilometre thick but extends outwards to about 420,000 kilometres from the planet's surface. The main rings comprise thousands of narrow ringlets, each made of icy lumps that range in size from tiny particles to chunks several metres across. The D, E, and G rings are very faint, the F ring is brighter, and the A, B, and C rings are bright enough to be seen from Earth with binoculars. Saturn has 18 known moons, some of which orbit inside the rings and are thought to exert a gravitational influence on the shapes of the rings. Unusually, seven of the moons are co-orbital – they share an orbit with another moon. Astronomers believe that such co-orbital moons may have originated from a single satellite that broke up.

TILT AND ROTATION OF SATURN

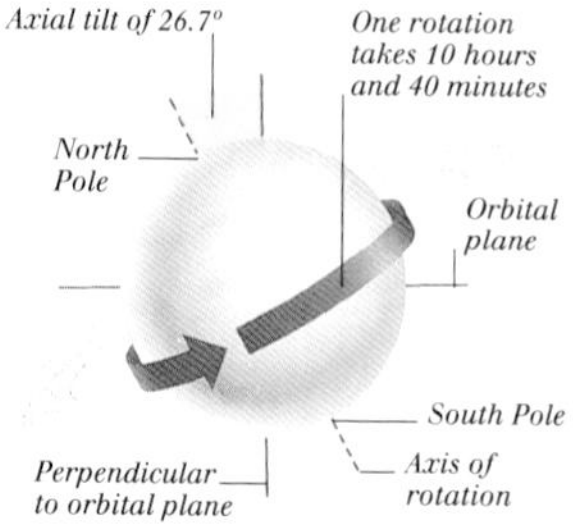
Axial tilt of 26.7°
One rotation takes 10 hours and 40 minutes
North Pole
Orbital plane
South Pole
Perpendicular to orbital plane
Axis of rotation

FALSE-COLOUR IMAGE OF SATURN'S CLOUD FEATURES

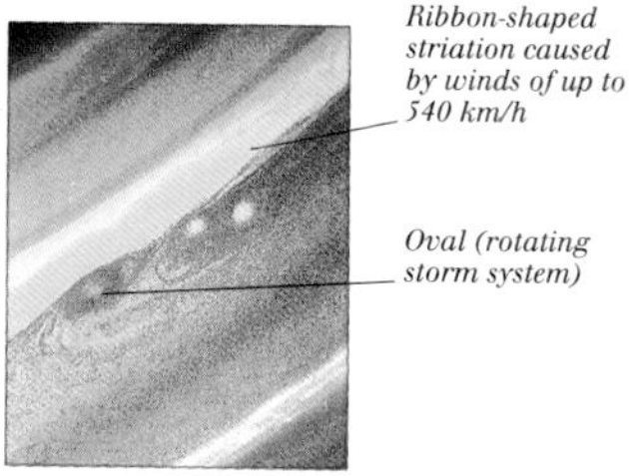
Ribbon-shaped striation caused by winds of up to 540 km/h
Oval (rotating storm system)

INNER RINGS OF SATURN

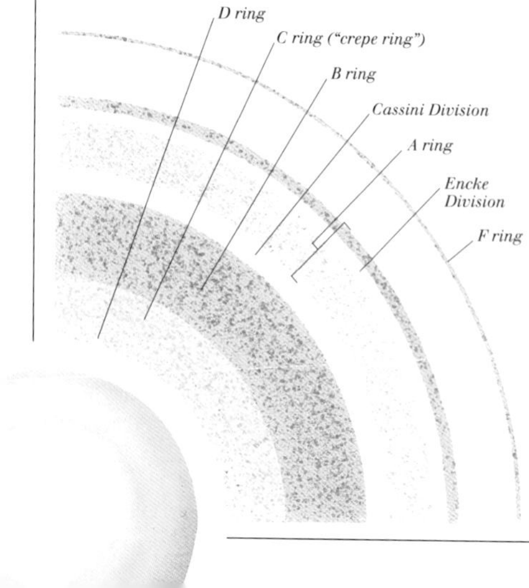
D ring
C ring ("crepe ring")
B ring
Cassini Division
A ring
Encke Division
F ring

MOONS OF SATURN

ENCELADUS
Diameter: 498 km
Average distance from planet: 238,000 km

TETHYS
Diameter: 1,050 km
Average distance from planet: 295,000 km

DIONE
Diameter: 1,118 km
Average distance from planet: 377,000 km

MIMAS
Diameter: 397 km
Average distance from planet: 186,000 km

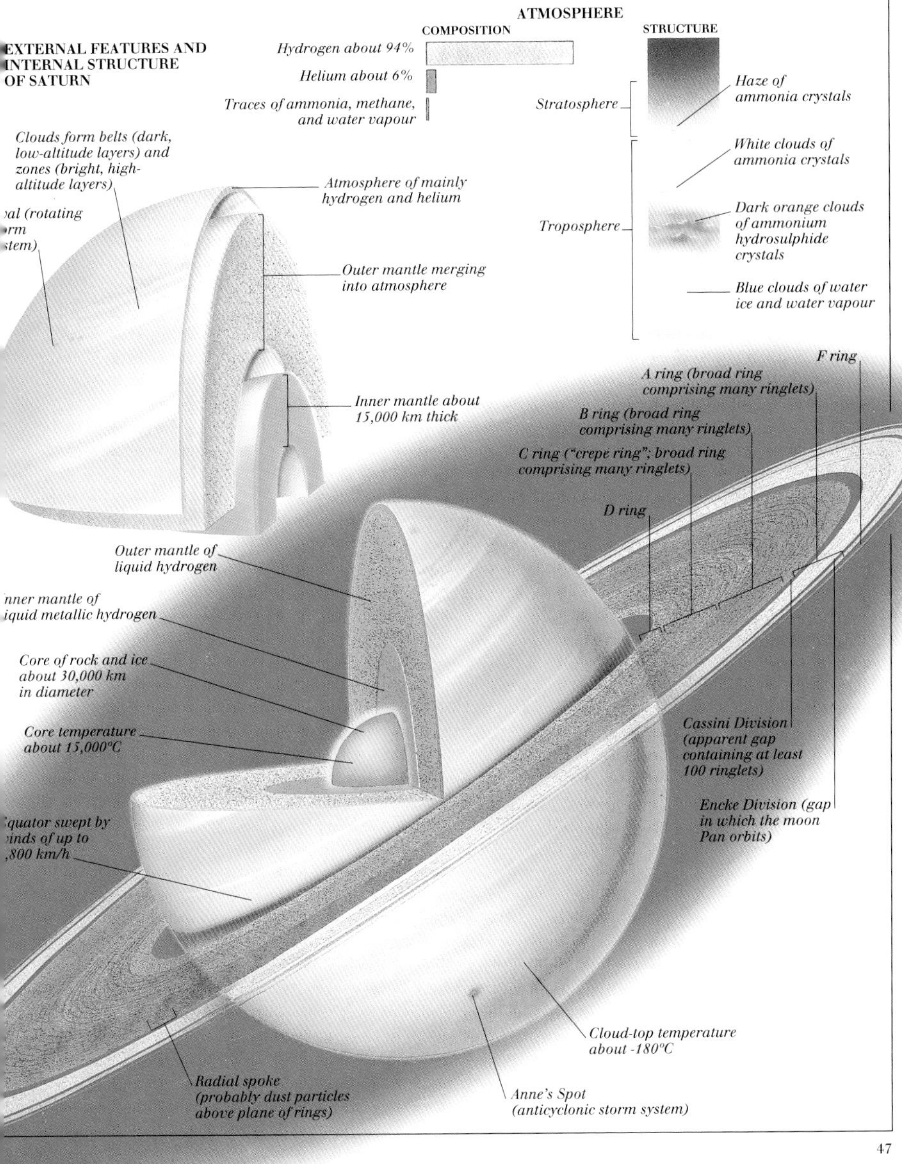

EXTERNAL FEATURES AND INTERNAL STRUCTURE OF SATURN

ATMOSPHERE

COMPOSITION

Hydrogen about 94%

Helium about 6%

Traces of ammonia, methane, and water vapour

STRUCTURE

Stratosphere

Haze of ammonia crystals

Troposphere

White clouds of ammonia crystals

Dark orange clouds of ammonium hydrosulphide crystals

Blue clouds of water ice and water vapour

Clouds form belts (dark, low-altitude layers) and zones (bright, high-altitude layers)

Atmosphere of mainly hydrogen and helium

Outer mantle merging into atmosphere

Inner mantle about 15,000 km thick

...al (rotating ...rm ...stem)

Outer mantle of liquid hydrogen

Inner mantle of liquid metallic hydrogen

Core of rock and ice about 30,000 km in diameter

Core temperature about 15,000°C

...quator swept by ...inds of up to ...800 km/h

F ring

A ring (broad ring comprising many ringlets)

B ring (broad ring comprising many ringlets)

C ring ("crepe ring"; broad ring comprising many ringlets)

D ring

Cassini Division (apparent gap containing at least 100 ringlets)

Encke Division (gap in which the moon Pan orbits)

Cloud-top temperature about -180°C

Radial spoke (probably dust particles above plane of rings)

Anne's Spot (anticyclonic storm system)

Uranus

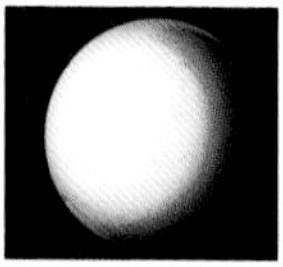

FALSE-COLOUR IMAGE OF URANUS

URANUS IS THE SEVENTH PLANET from the Sun and the third largest, with a diameter of about 51,000 kilometres. It is thought to consist of a dense mixture of different types of ice and gas around a solid core. Its atmosphere contains traces of methane, giving the planet a blue-green hue, and the temperature at the cloud tops is about -210°C. Uranus is the most featureless planet to have been closely observed: only a few icy clouds of methane have been seen so far. Uranus is unique among the planets in that its axis of rotation lies close to its orbital plane. As a result of its strongly tilted rotational axis, Uranus rolls on its side along its orbital path around the Sun, whereas other planets spin more or less upright. Uranus is encircled by 11 rings that consist of rocks interspersed with dust lanes. The rings contain some of the darkest matter in the Solar System and are extremely narrow, making them difficult to detect: nine of them are less than 10 kilometres wide, whereas most of Saturn's rings are thousands of kilometres in width. There are 15 known Uranian moons, all of which are icy and most of which are further out than the rings. The 10 inner moons are small and dark, with diameters of less than 160 kilometres, and the five outer moons are between about 470 and 1,600 kilometres in diameter. The outer moons have a wide variety of surface features. Miranda has the most varied surface, with cratered areas broken up by huge ridges and cliffs 20 kilometres high.

TILT AND ROTATION OF URANUS

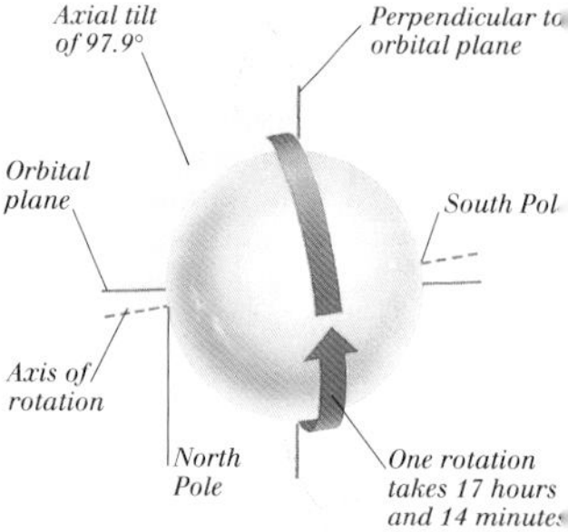

Axial tilt of 97.9°
Perpendicular to orbital plane
Orbital plane
South Pol
Axis of rotation
North Pole
One rotation takes 17 hours and 14 minutes

OUTER MOONS

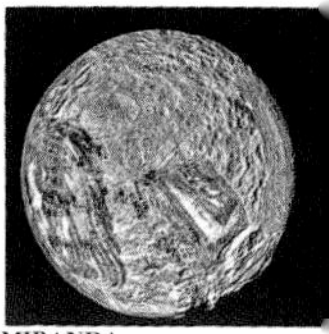

MIRANDA
Diameter: 472 km
Average distance from planet: 129,800 km

RINGS OF URANUS

Epsilon ring
Ring 1986 U1R
Delta ring
Gamma ring
Eta ring
Beta ring
Alpha ring
Rings 4 and 5
Ring 6
Ring 1986 U2R

RINGS AND DUST LANES

ARIEL
Diameter: 1,158 km
Average distance from planet: 191,200 km

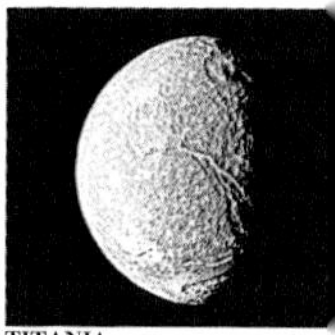

TITANIA
Diameter: 1,578 km
Average distance from planet: 435,900 km

UMBRIEL
Diameter: 1,169 km
Average distance from planet: 266,000 km

OBERON
Diameter: 1,523 km
Average distance from planet: 582,600 km

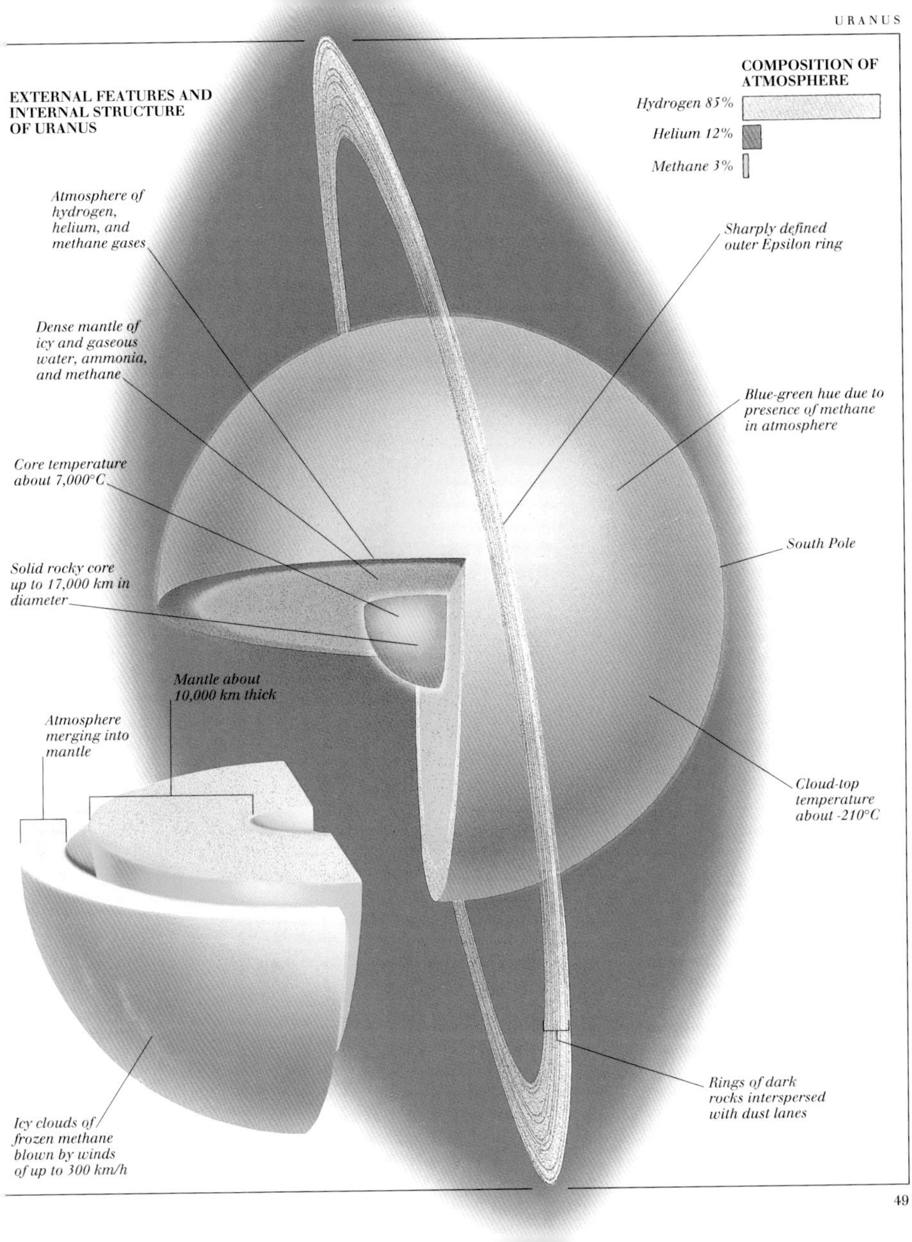
EXTERNAL FEATURES AND INTERNAL STRUCTURE OF URANUS
COMPOSITION OF ATMOSPHERE
Hydrogen 85%
Helium 12%
Methane 3%
Atmosphere of hydrogen, helium, and methane gases
Sharply defined outer Epsilon ring
Dense mantle of icy and gaseous water, ammonia, and methane
Blue-green hue due to presence of methane in atmosphere
Core temperature about 7,000°C
South Pole
Solid rocky core up to 17,000 km in diameter
Mantle about 10,000 km thick
Atmosphere merging into mantle
Cloud-top temperature about -210°C
Rings of dark rocks interspersed with dust lanes
Icy clouds of frozen methane blown by winds of up to 300 km/h

Neptune and Pluto

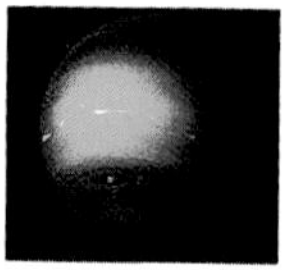

FALSE-COLOUR IMAGE OF NEPTUNE

NEPTUNE AND PLUTO are the two furthest planets from the Sun, at an average distance of about 4,500 million kilometres and 5,900 million kilometres respectively. Neptune is a gas giant and is thought to consist of a small rocky core surrounded by a mixture of liquids and gases. The atmosphere contains several prominent cloud features. The largest of these are the Great Dark Spot, which is as wide as the Earth, the Small Dark Spot, and the Scooter. The Great and Small Dark Spots are huge storms that are swept around the planet by winds of about 2,000 kilometres per hour. The Scooter is a large area of cirrus cloud. Neptune has four tenuous rings and eight known moons. Triton is the largest Neptunian moon and the coldest object in the Solar System, with a temperature of -235°C. Unlike most moons in the Solar System, Triton orbits its mother planet in the opposite direction to the planet's rotation. Pluto is usually the outermost planet but its elliptical orbit causes it to pass inside the orbit of Neptune for 20 years of its 248-year orbit. Pluto is so small and far away that little is known about it. It is a rocky planet, probably covered with ice and frozen methane. Pluto's only known moon, Charon, is large for a moon, at half the size of its parent planet. Because of the small difference in their sizes, Pluto and Charon are sometimes considered to be a double-planet system.

TILT AND ROTATION OF NEPTUNE

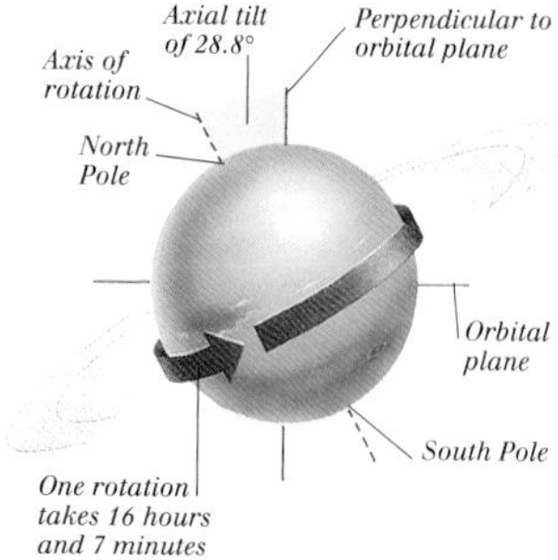
Axial tilt of 28.8°
Perpendicular to orbital plane
Axis of rotation
North Pole
Orbital plane
South Pole
One rotation takes 16 hours and 7 minutes

CLOUD FEATURES OF NEPTUNE

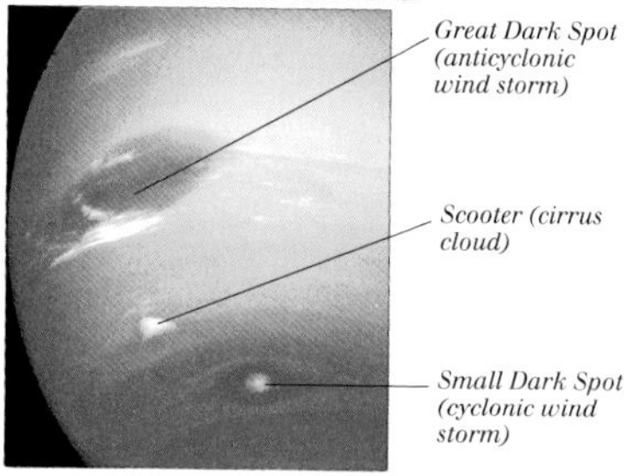
Great Dark Spot (anticyclonic wind storm)
Scooter (cirrus cloud)
Small Dark Spot (cyclonic wind storm)

RINGS OF NEPTUNE

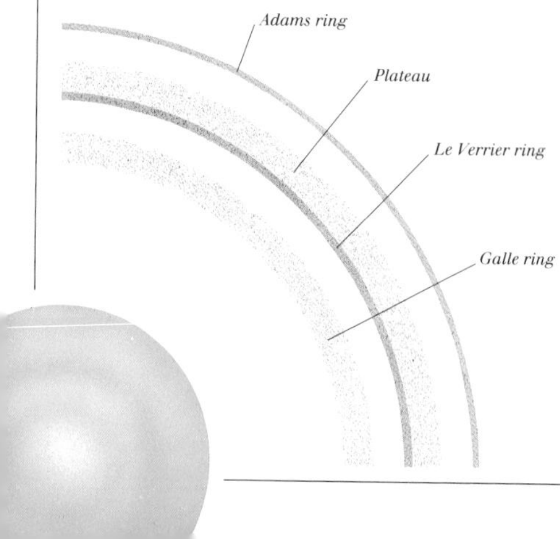
Adams ring
Plateau
Le Verrier ring
Galle ring

HIGH-ALTITUDE CLOUDS

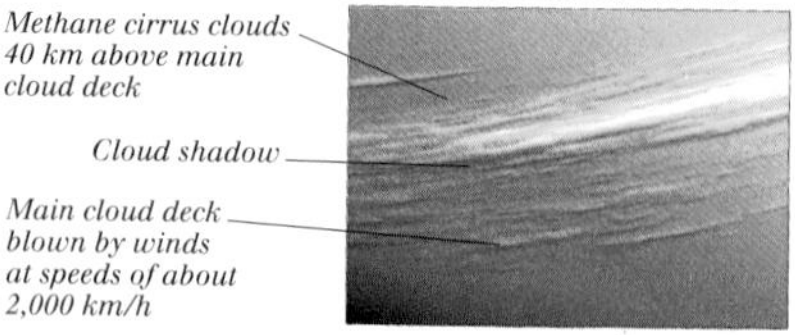
Methane cirrus clouds 40 km above main cloud deck
Cloud shadow
Main cloud deck blown by winds at speeds of about 2,000 km/h

MOONS OF NEPTUNE

TRITON
Diameter: 2,705 km
Average distance from planet: 354,800 km

PROTEUS
Diameter: 416 km
Average distance from planet: 117,600 km

EXTERNAL FEATURES AND INTERNAL STRUCTURE OF NEPTUNE

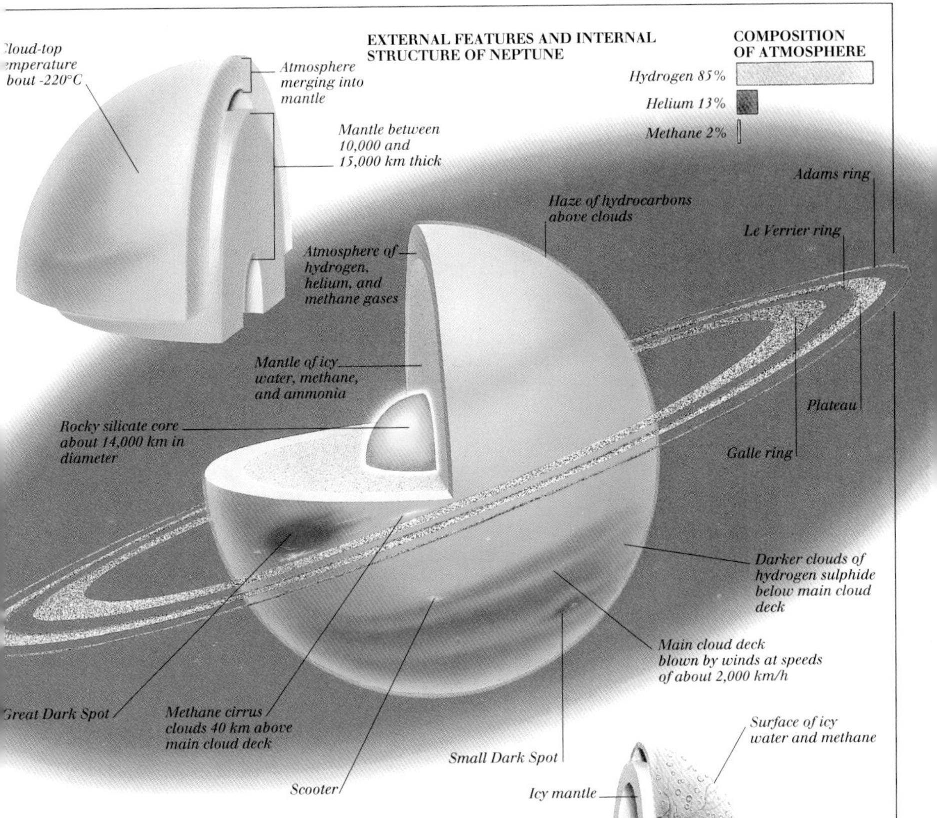
loud-top
mperature
bout -220°C
Atmosphere merging into mantle
Mantle between 10,000 and 15,000 km thick
COMPOSITION OF ATMOSPHERE
Hydrogen 85%
Helium 13%
Methane 2%
Adams ring
Haze of hydrocarbons above clouds
Le Verrier ring
Atmosphere of hydrogen, helium, and methane gases
Mantle of icy water, methane, and ammonia
Rocky silicate core about 14,000 km in diameter
Plateau
Galle ring
Darker clouds of hydrogen sulphide below main cloud deck
Main cloud deck blown by winds at speeds of about 2,000 km/h
reat Dark Spot
Methane cirrus clouds 40 km above main cloud deck
Small Dark Spot
Scooter

TILT AND ROTATION OF PLUTO

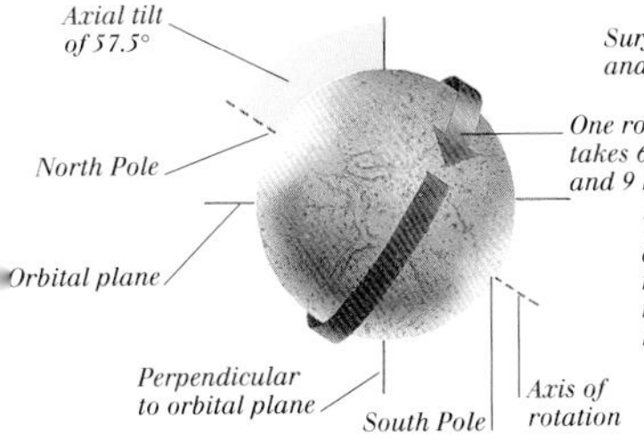
Axial tilt of 57.5°
North Pole
One rotation takes 6 days and 9 hours
Orbital plane
Perpendicular to orbital plane
South Pole
Axis of rotation

EXTERNAL FEATURES AND INTERNAL STRUCTURE OF PLUTO

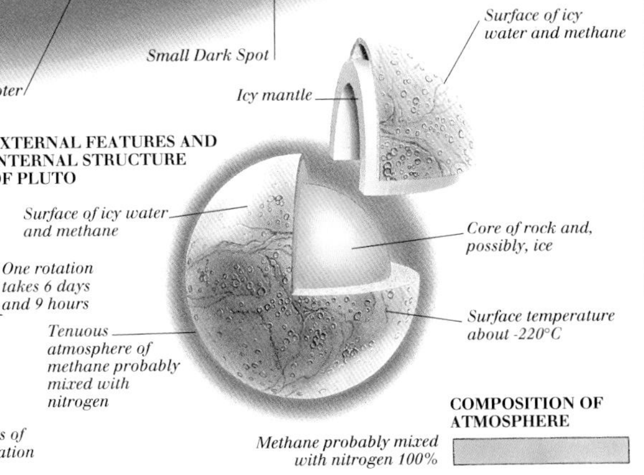
Surface of icy water and methane
Icy mantle
Surface of icy water and methane
Core of rock and, possibly, ice
Surface temperature about -220°C
Tenuous atmosphere of methane probably mixed with nitrogen
COMPOSITION OF ATMOSPHERE
Methane probably mixed with nitrogen 100%

Asteroids, comets, and meteoroids

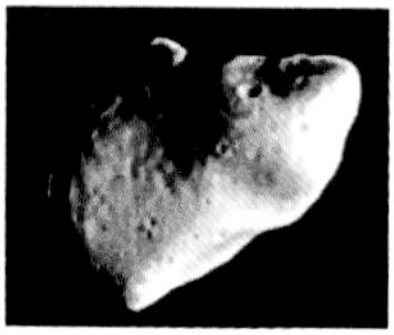

ASTEROID 951 GASPRA

ASTEROIDS, COMETS, AND METEOROIDS are all debris remaining from the nebula in which the Solar System formed 4.6 billion years ago. Asteroids are rocky bodies up to about 1,000 kilometres in diameter, although most are much smaller. Most of them orbit the Sun in the asteroid belt, which lies between the orbits of Mars and Jupiter. Comets may originate in a huge cloud (called the Oort Cloud) that is thought to surround the Solar System. They are made of frozen gases and dust, and are a few kilometres in diameter. Occasionally, a comet is deflected from the Oort Cloud to orbit the Sun in a long, elliptical path. As the comet approaches the Sun, the comet's surface starts to vaporize in the heat, producing a brightly shining coma (a huge sphere of gas and dust around the nucleus), a gas tail, and a dust tail. Meteoroids are small chunks of stone or stone and iron, some of which are fragments of asteroids or comets. Meteoroids range in size from tiny dust particles to objects tens of metres across. If a meteoroid enters the Earth's atmosphere, it is heated by friction and appears as a glowing streak of light called a meteor (also known as a shooting star). Meteor showers occur when the Earth passes through the trail of dust particles left by a comet. Most meteors burn up in the atmosphere. The few that are large enough to reach the Earth's surface are termed meteorites.

OPTICAL IMAGE OF HALLEY'S COMET

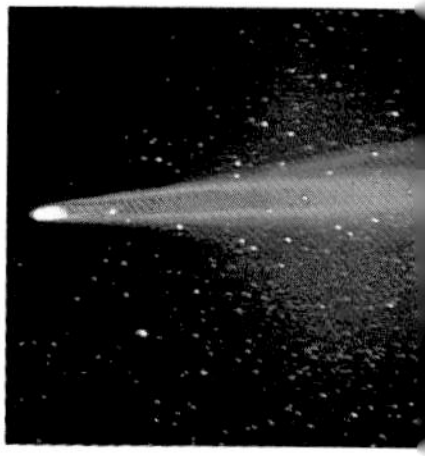

FALSE-COLOUR IMAGE OF HALLEY'S COMET

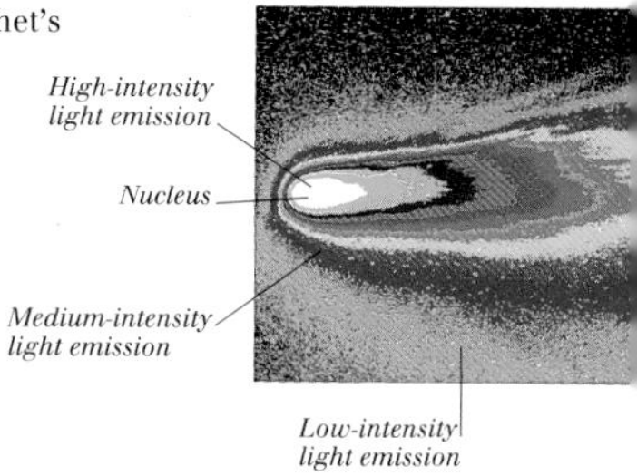
High-intensity light emission
Nucleus
Medium-intensity light emission
Low-intensity light emission

FALSE-COLOUR IMAGE OF A LEONID METEOR SHOWER

METEORITES

STONY METEORITE

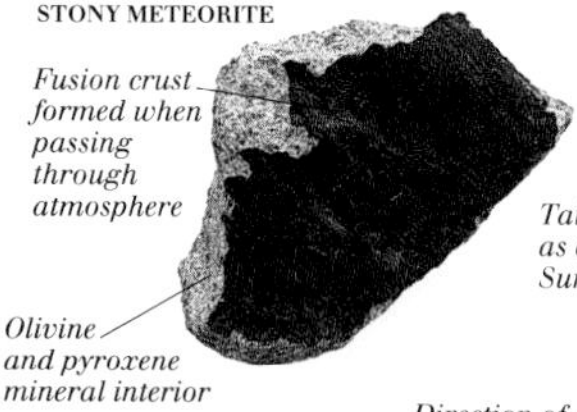
Fusion crust formed when passing through atmosphere
Olivine and pyroxene mineral interior

STONY-IRON METEORITE

Iron
Stone (olivine)

DEVELOPMENT OF COMET TAILS

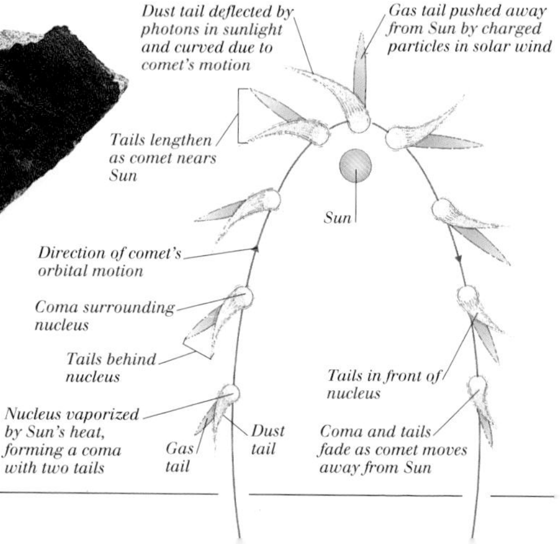
Dust tail deflected by photons in sunlight and curved due to comet's motion
Gas tail pushed away from Sun by charged particles in solar wind
Tails lengthen as comet nears Sun
Sun
Direction of comet's orbital motion
Coma surrounding nucleus
Tails behind nucleus
Tails in front of nucleus
Nucleus vaporized by Sun's heat, forming a coma with two tails
Gas tail
Dust tail
Coma and tails fade as comet moves away from Sun

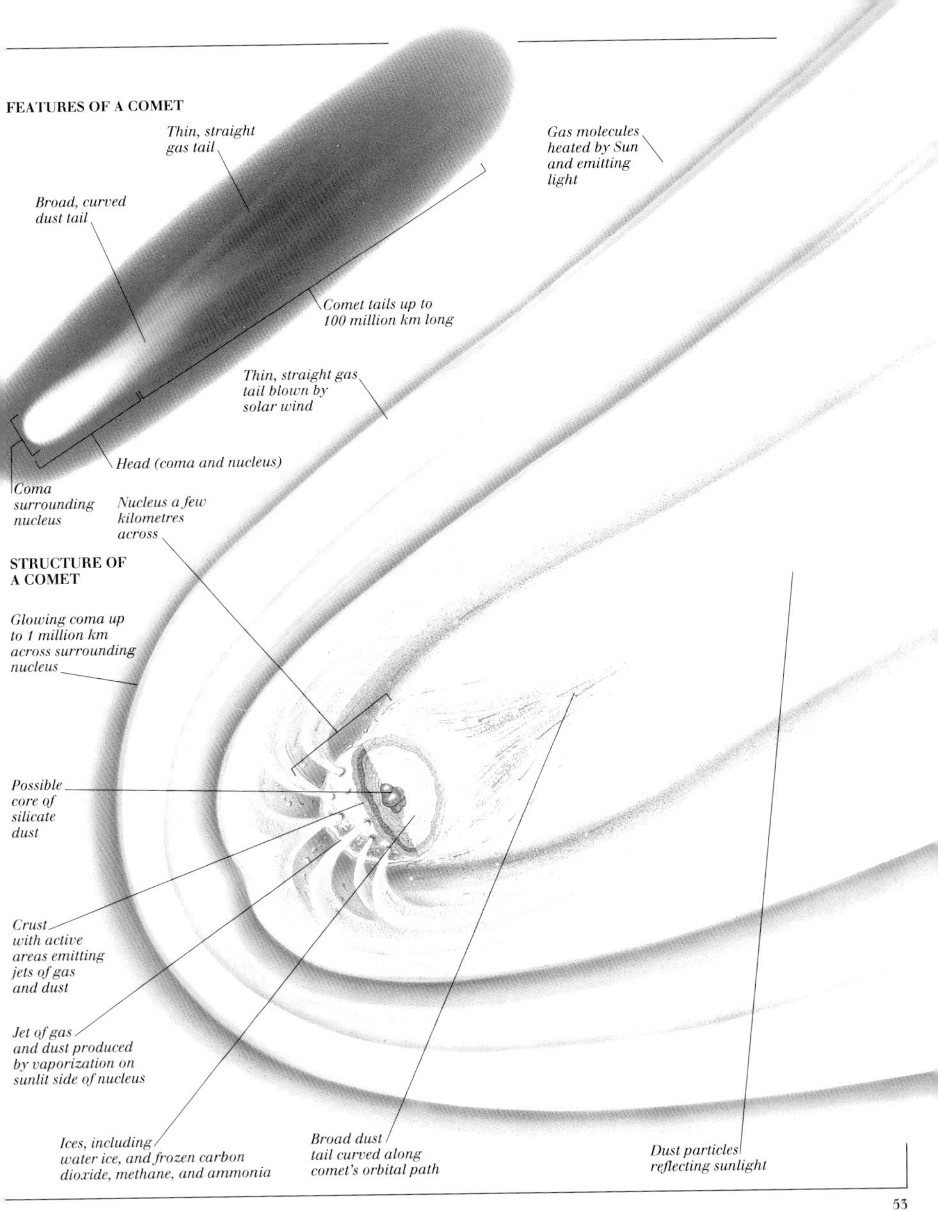
FEATURES OF A COMET
Thin, straight gas tail
Broad, curved dust tail
Gas molecules heated by Sun and emitting light
Comet tails up to 100 million km long
Thin, straight gas tail blown by solar wind
Head (coma and nucleus)
Coma surrounding nucleus
Nucleus a few kilometres across
STRUCTURE OF A COMET
Glowing coma up to 1 million km across surrounding nucleus
Possible core of silicate dust
Crust with active areas emitting jets of gas and dust
Jet of gas and dust produced by vaporization on sunlit side of nucleus
Ices, including water ice, and frozen carbon dioxide, methane, and ammonia
Broad dust tail curved along comet's orbital path
Dust particles reflecting sunlight

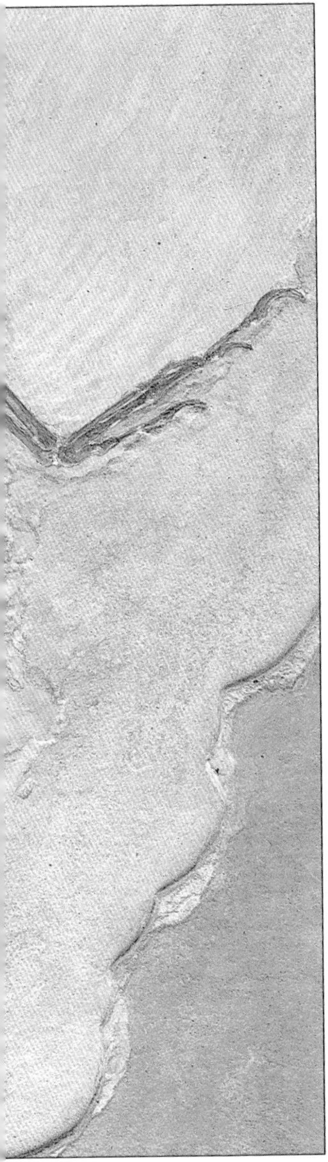

PREHISTORIC EARTH

The changing Earth

THE EARTH FORMED FROM A CLOUD OF DUST and gas drifting through space about 4,600 million years ago. Dense minerals sank to the centre while lighter ones formed a thin rocky crust. However, the first known life-forms – bacteria and blue-green algae – did not appear until about 3,400 million years ago, and it was only about 700 million years ago that more complex plants and animals began to develop. Since then, thousands of animal and plant species have evolved; some, such as the dinosaurs, survived for many millions of years, while others died out quickly. The Earth itself is continually changing. Although continents neared their present locations about 50 million years ago, they are still drifting slowly over the planet's surface, and mountain ranges such as the Himalayas – which began to form 40 million years ago – are continually being built up and worn away. Climate is also subject to change: the Earth has undergone a series of ice ages interspersed with warmer periods (the most recent glacial period was at its height about 20,000 years ago).

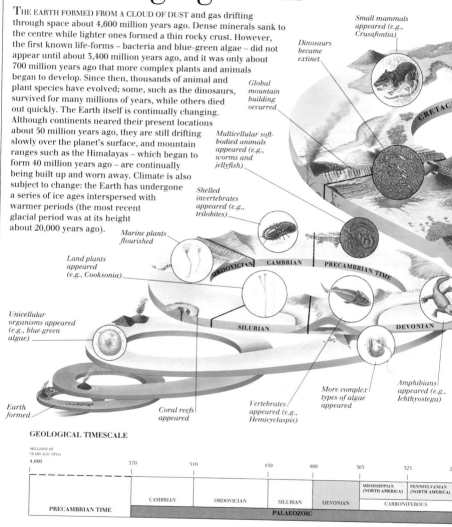

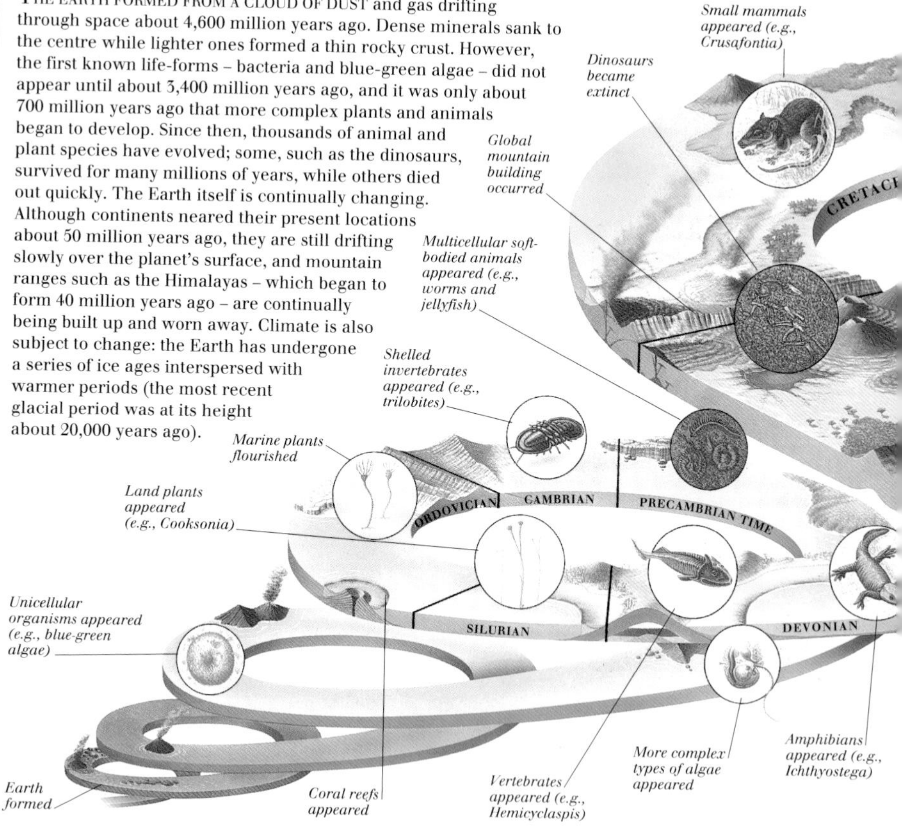

Small mammals appeared (e.g., Crusafontia)
Dinosaurs became extinct
Global mountain building occurred
CRETACE
Multicellular soft-bodied animals appeared (e.g., worms and jellyfish)
Shelled invertebrates appeared (e.g., trilobites)
Marine plants flourished
Land plants appeared (e.g., Cooksonia)
ORDOVICIAN
CAMBRIAN
PRECAMBRIAN TIME
Unicellular organisms appeared (e.g., blue-green algae)
SILURIAN
DEVONIAN
Earth formed
Coral reefs appeared
Vertebrates appeared (e.g., Hemicyclaspis)
More complex types of algae appeared
Amphibians appeared (e.g., Ichthyostega)

GEOLOGICAL TIMESCALE

MILLIONS OF YEARS AGO (MYA)

4,600	570	510	439	409	363	323
					MISSISSIPPIAN (NORTH AMERICA)	PENNSYLVANIAN (NORTH AMERICA)
PRECAMBRIAN TIME	CAMBRIAN	ORDOVICIAN	SILURIAN	DEVONIAN	CARBONIFEROUS	
	PALAEOZOIC					

EVOLUTION OF THE EARTH

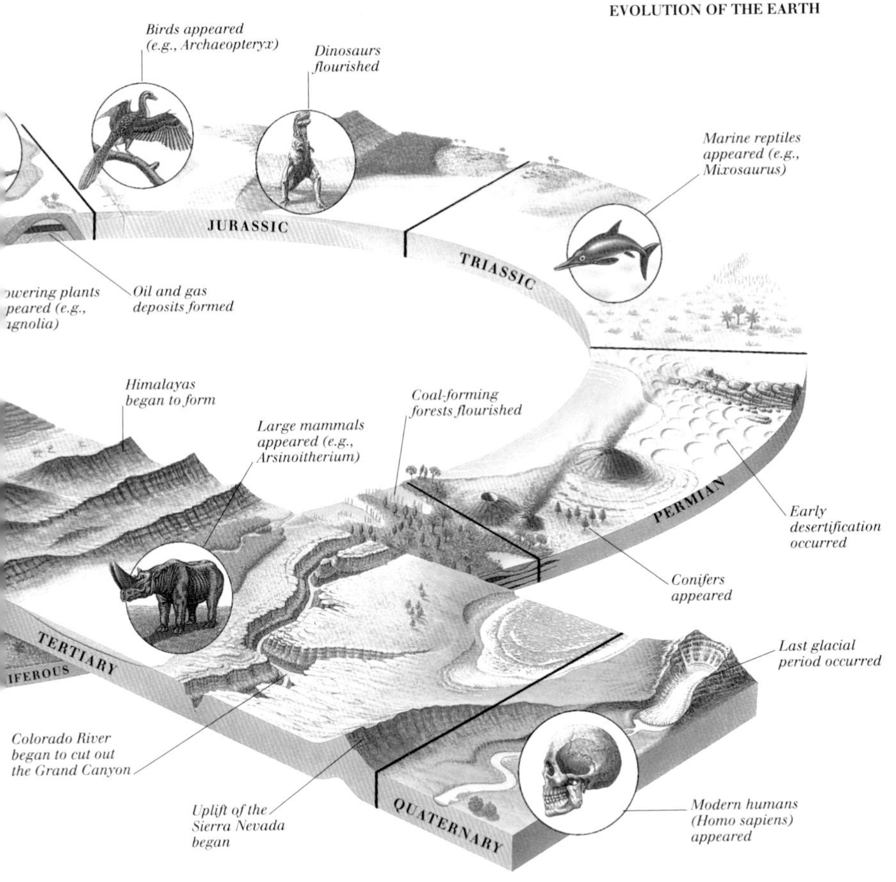
Birds appeared (e.g., Archaeopteryx)
Dinosaurs flourished
Marine reptiles appeared (e.g., Mixosaurus)
JURASSIC
TRIASSIC
owering plants
peared (e.g.,
ıgnolia)
Oil and gas deposits formed
Himalayas began to form
Coal-forming forests flourished
Large mammals appeared (e.g., Arsinoitherium)
PERMIAN
Early desertification occurred
Conifers appeared
TERTIARY
IFEROUS
Last glacial period occurred
Colorado River began to cut out the Grand Canyon
Uplift of the Sierra Nevada began
QUATERNARY
Modern humans (Homo sapiens) appeared

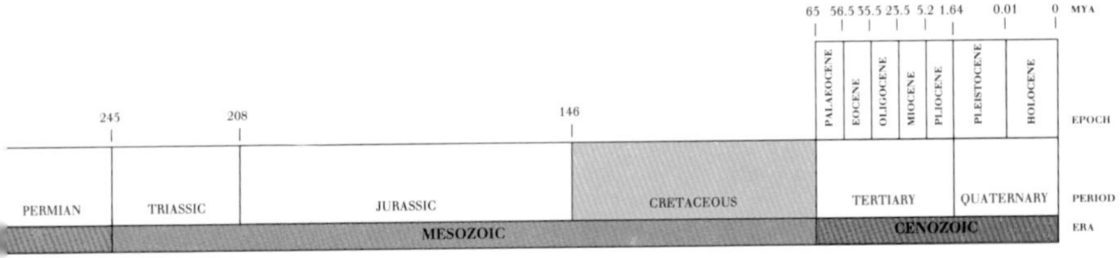
65
56.5
35.5
23.5
5.2
1.64
0.01
0
MYA
PALAEOCENE
EOCENE
OLIGOCENE
MIOCENE
PLIOCENE
PLEISTOCENE
HOLOCENE
EPOCH
245
208
146
PERMIAN
TRIASSIC
JURASSIC
CRETACEOUS
TERTIARY
QUATERNARY
PERIOD
MESOZOIC
CENOZOIC
ERA

The Earth's crust

THE EARTH'S CRUST IS THE SOLID outer shell of the Earth. It includes continental crust (about 40 kilometres thick) and oceanic crust (about six kilometres thick). The crust and the topmost layer of the mantle form the lithosphere. The lithosphere consists of semi-rigid plates that move relative to each other on the underlying asthenosphere (a partly molten layer of the mantle). This process is known as plate tectonics and helps explain continental drift. Where two plates move apart, there are rifts in the crust. In mid-ocean, this movement results in sea-floor spreading and the formation of ocean ridges; on continents, crustal spreading can form rift valleys. When plates move towards each other, one may be subducted beneath (forced under) the other. In mid-ocean, this causes ocean trenches, seismic activity, and arcs of volcanic islands. Where oceanic crust is subducted beneath continental crust or where continents collide, land may be uplifted and mountains formed (see pp. 62–63). Plates may also slide past each other – along the San Andreas fault, for example. Crustal movement on continents may result in earthquakes, while movement under the seabed can lead to tidal waves.

ELEMENTS IN THE EARTH'S CRUST

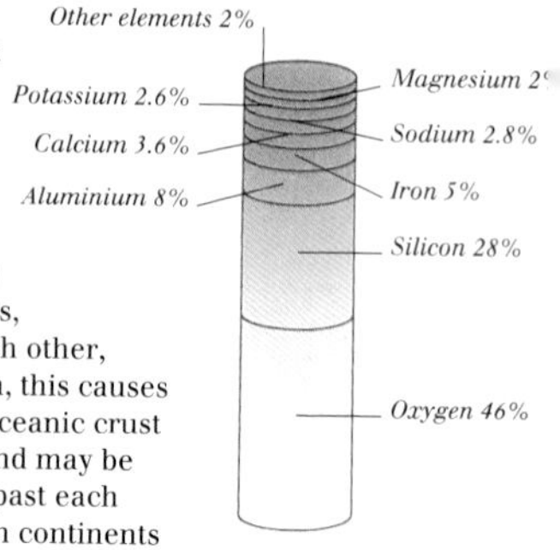

Other elements 2%
Magnesium 2
Potassium 2.6%
Sodium 2.8%
Calcium 3.6%
Iron 5%
Aluminium 8%
Silicon 28%
Oxygen 46%

FEATURES OF PLATE MOVEMENTS

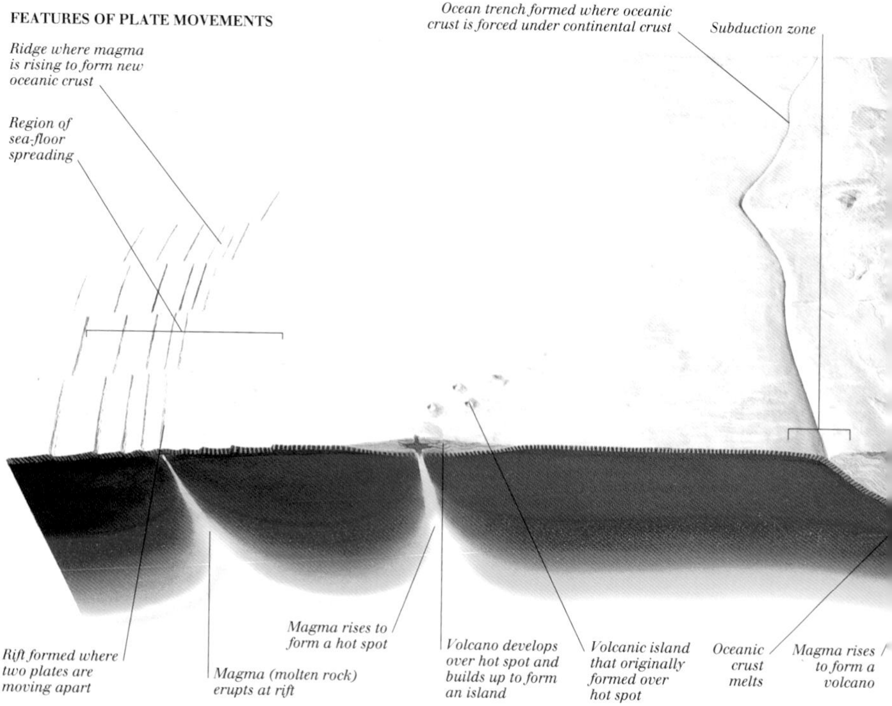

Ocean trench formed where oceanic crust is forced under continental crust
Subduction zone
Ridge where magma is rising to form new oceanic crust
Region of sea-floor spreading
Rift formed where two plates are moving apart
Magma (molten rock) erupts at rift
Magma rises to form a hot spot
Volcano develops over hot spot and builds up to form an island
Volcanic island that originally formed over hot spot
Oceanic crust melts
Magma rises to form a volcano

MAJOR PLATES OF THE EARTH'S CRUST

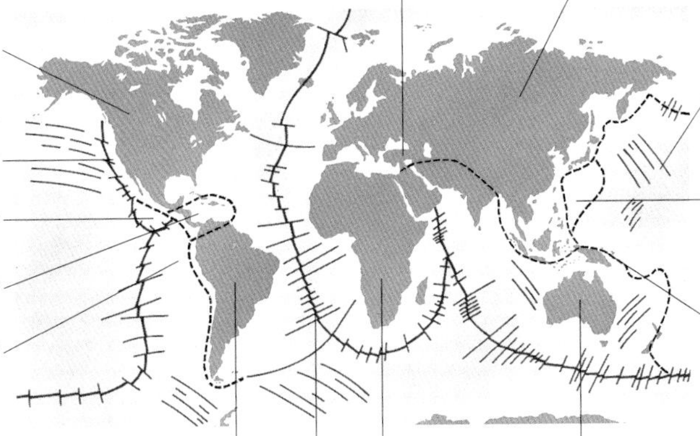
Hellenic plate
Eurasian plate
North American plate
Pacific plate
Plates sliding past each other
Philippine plate
Cocos plate
Caribbean plate
Plates converging
Nazca plate
South American plate
African plate
Indo-Australian plate
Plates moving apart

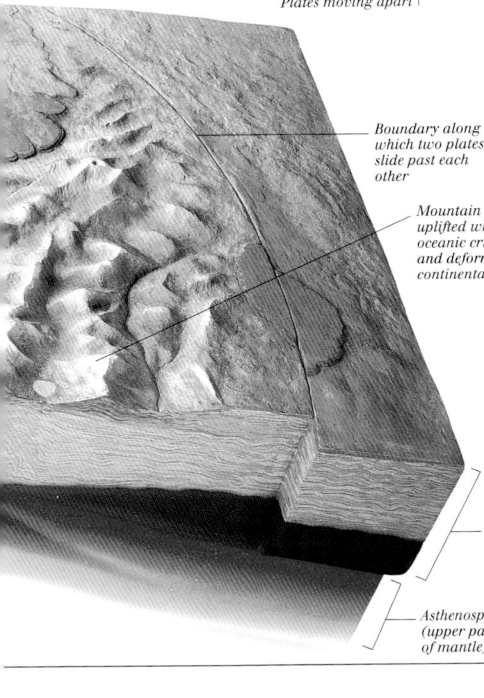
Boundary along which two plates slide past each other
Mountain range uplifted where subducting oceanic crust compresses and deforms edge of continental crust
Lithosphere (crust and topmost layer of mantle)
Asthenosphere (upper part of mantle)

MOVEMENT OF LAND ALONG OCEANIC RIDGES

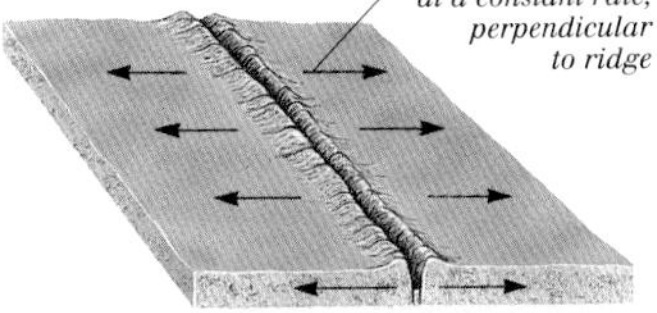
Land moves apart at a constant rate, perpendicular to ridge

STRAIGHT OCEANIC RIDGE

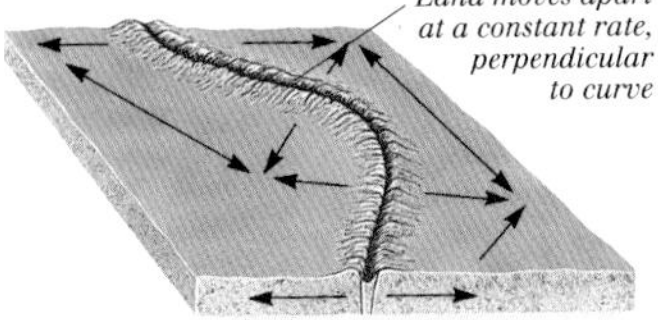
Land moves apart at a constant rate, perpendicular to curve

CURVED OCEANIC RIDGE

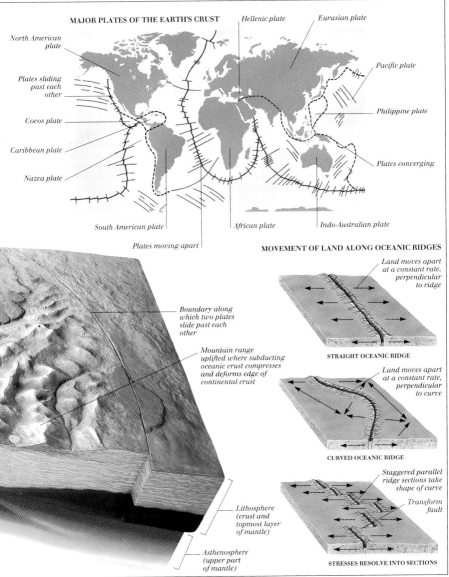

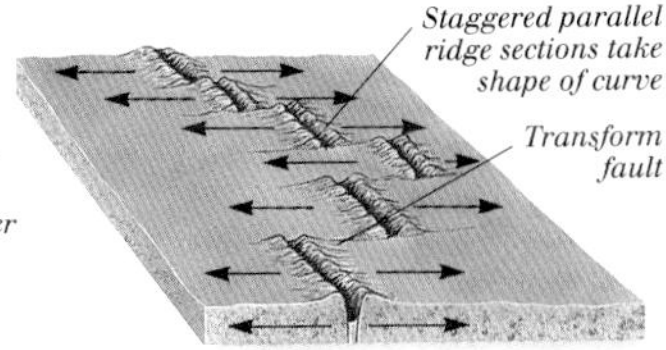
Staggered parallel ridge sections take shape of curve
Transform fault

STRESSES RESOLVE INTO SECTIONS

Faults and folds

THE CONTINUOUS MOVEMENT of the Earth's crustal plates (see pp. 58–59) can squeeze, stretch, or break rock strata, deforming them and producing faults and folds. A fault is a fracture in a rock along which there is movement of one side relative to the other. The movement can be vertical, horizontal, or oblique (vertical and horizontal). Faults develop when rocks are subjected to compression or tension. They tend to occur in hard, rigid rocks, which are more likely to break than bend. The smallest faults occur in single mineral crystals and are microscopically small, whereas the largest – the Great Rift Valley in Africa, which formed between 5 million and 100,000 years ago – is more than 9,000 kilometres long. A fold is a bend in a rock layer caused by compression. Folds occur in elastic rocks, which tend to bend rather than break. The two main types of fold are anticlines (upfolds) and synclines (downfolds). Folds vary in size from a few millimetres long to folded mountain ranges hundreds of kilometres long, such as the Himalayas (see pp. 62–63) and the Alps, which are repeatedly folding. In addition to faults and folds, other features associated with rock deformations include boudins, mullions, and *en échelon* fractures.

STRUCTURE OF A FOLD

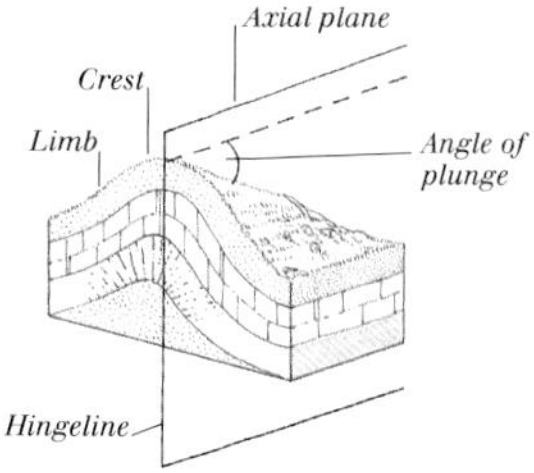

STRUCTURE OF A FAULT

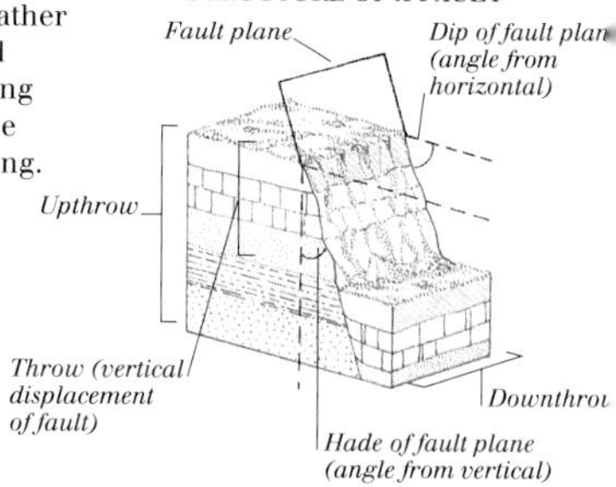
Fault plane
Dip of fault plan
(angle from horizontal)
Upthrow
Throw (vertical displacement of fault)
Downthrou
Hade of fault plane (angle from vertical)

STRUCTURE OF A SLOPE

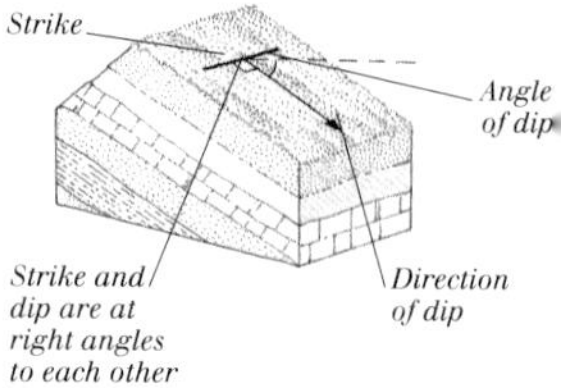
Strike
Angle of dip
Strike and dip are at right angles to each other
Direction of dip

FOLDED ROCK

Steeply dipping limbs
Crest of anticline
Plunge

SECTION THROUGH FOLDED ROCK STRATA THAT HAVE BEEN ERODED

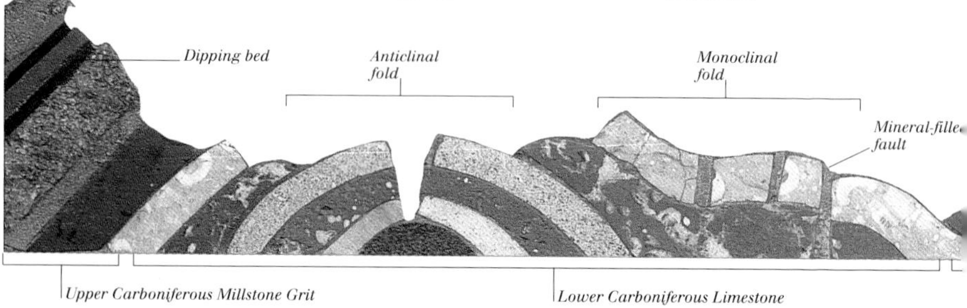
Dipping bed
Anticlinal fold
Monoclinal fold
Mineral-fille fault
Upper Carboniferous Millstone Grit
Lower Carboniferous Limestone

EXAMPLES OF FOLDS

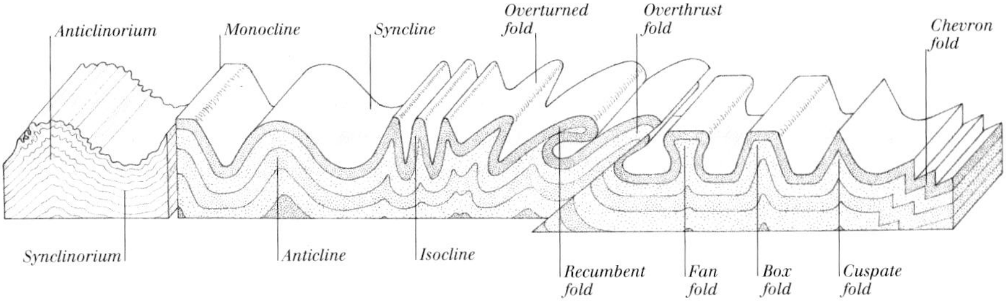
Anticlinorium
Monocline
Syncline
Overturned fold
Overthrust fold
Chevron fold
Synclinorium
Anticline
Isocline
Recumbent fold
Fan fold
Box fold
Cuspate fold

EXAMPLES OF FAULTS

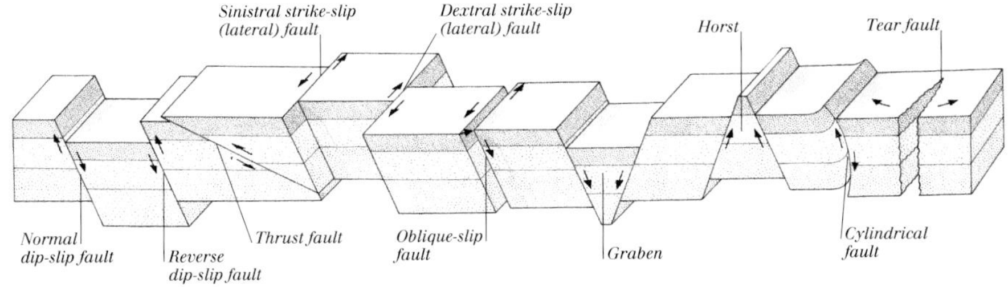
Sinistral strike-slip (lateral) fault
Dextral strike-slip (lateral) fault
Horst
Tear fault
Normal dip-slip fault
Reverse dip-slip fault
Thrust fault
Oblique-slip fault
Graben
Cylindrical fault

SMALL-SCALE ROCK DEFORMATIONS

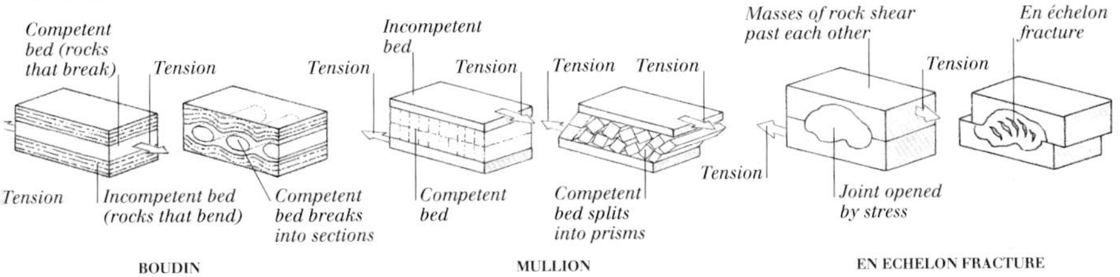
Competent bed (rocks that break)
Tension
Tension
Incompetent bed (rocks that bend)
Competent bed breaks into sections
BOUDIN
Incompetent bed
Tension
Tension
Tension
Tension
Competent bed
Competent bed splits into prisms
MULLION
Masses of rock shear past each other
En échelon fracture
Tension
Tension
Joint opened by stress
EN ECHELON FRACTURE

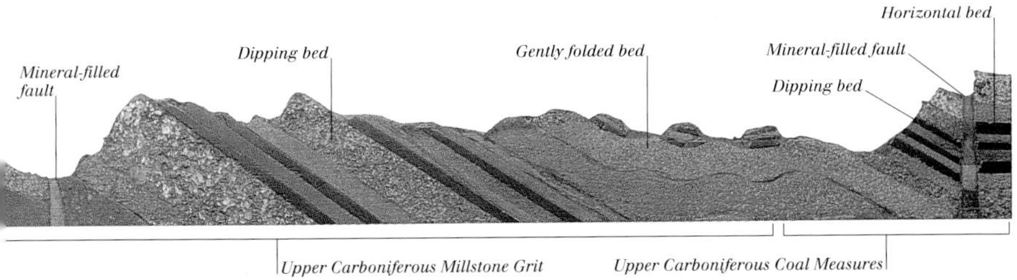
Horizontal bed
Mineral-filled fault
Dipping bed
Gently folded bed
Mineral-filled fault
Dipping bed
Upper Carboniferous Millstone Grit
Upper Carboniferous Coal Measures

Mountain building

THE PROCESSES INVOLVED in mountain building – termed orogenesis – occur as a result of the movement of the Earth's crustal plates (see pp. 58–59). There are three main types of mountains: volcanic mountains, fold mountains, and block mountains. Most volcanic mountains have been formed along plate boundaries where plates have come together or moved apart and lava and other debris have been ejected onto the Earth's surface. The lava and debris may have built up to form a dome around the vent of a volcano. Fold mountains are formed where plates push together and cause the rock to buckle upwards. Where oceanic crust meets less dense continental crust, the oceanic crust is forced under the continental crust. The continental crust is buckled by the impact. This is how folded mountain ranges, such as the Appalachian Mountains in North America, were formed. Fold mountains are also formed where two areas of continental crust meet. The Himalayas, for example, began to form when India collided with Asia, buckling the sediments and parts of the oceanic crust between them. Block mountains are formed when a block of land is uplifted between two faults as a result of compression or tension in the Earth's crust (see pp. 60–61). Often, the movement along faults has taken place gradually over millions of years. However, two plates may cause an earthquake by suddenly sliding past each other along a faultline.

BHAGIRATHI PARBAT, HIMALAYAS

FORMATION OF THE HIMALAYAS

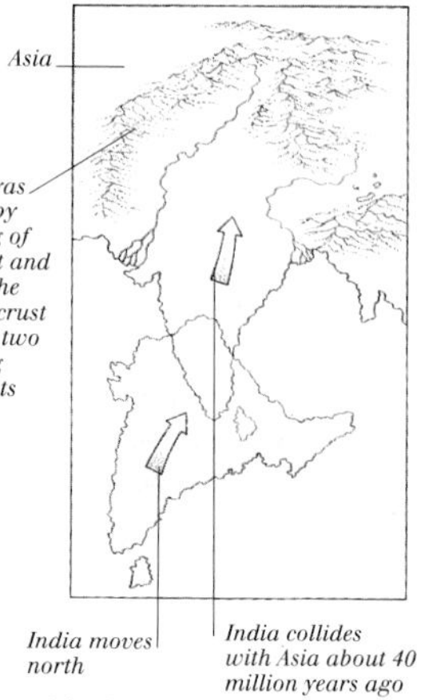

Asia
Himalayas formed by buckling of sediment and part of the oceanic crust between two colliding continents
India moves north
India collides with Asia about 40 million years ago

EXAMPLES OF MOUNTAINS

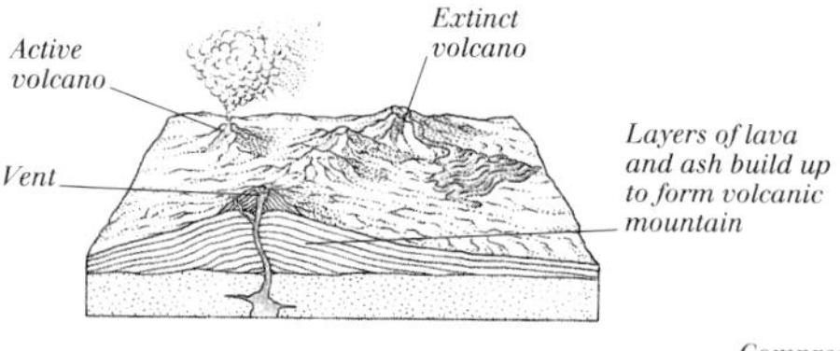

Active volcano
Extinct volcano
Vent
Layers of lava and ash build up to form volcanic mountain

VOLCANIC MOUNTAIN

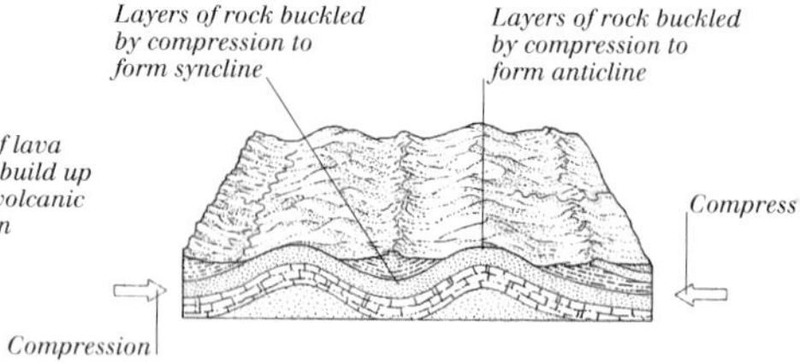

Layers of rock buckled by compression to form syncline
Layers of rock buckled by compression to form anticline
Compress
Compression

FOLD MOUNTAIN

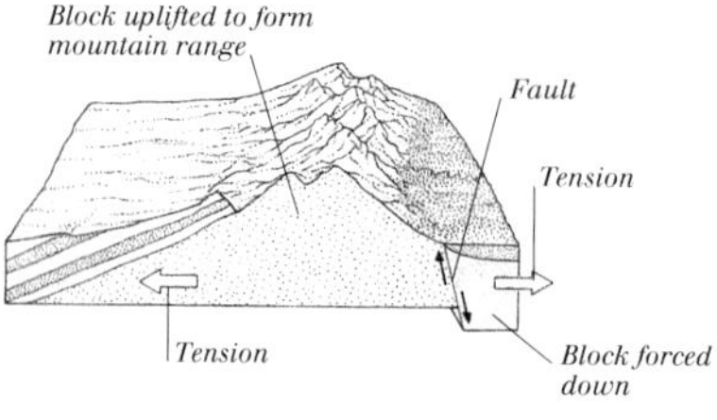

Block uplifted to form mountain range
Fault
Tension
Tension
Block forced down

BLOCK-FAULT MOUNTAIN

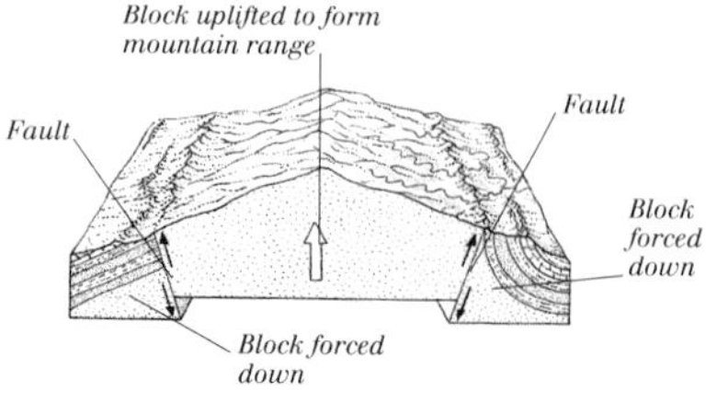

Block uplifted to form mountain range
Fault
Fault
Block forced down
Block forced down

UPLIFTED BLOCK-FAULT MOUNTAIN

STAGES IN THE FORMATION OF THE HIMALAYAS

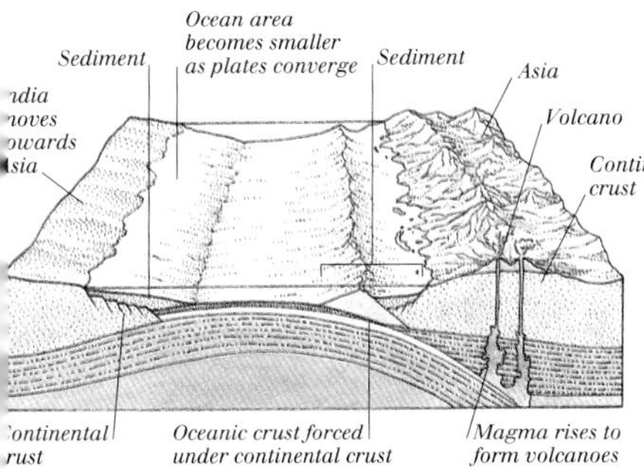
Sediment
Ocean area becomes smaller as plates converge
Sediment
Asia
ndia noves owards sia
Volcano
Continental crust
ontinental rust
Oceanic crust forced under continental crust
Magma rises to form volcanoes

60 MILLION YEARS AGO

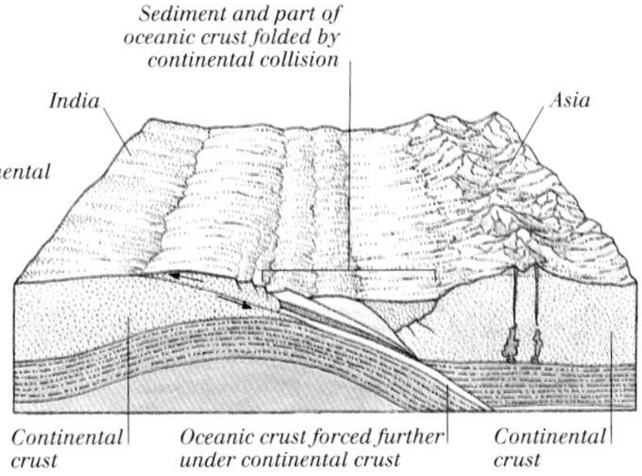
Sediment and part of oceanic crust folded by continental collision
India
Asia
Continental crust
Oceanic crust forced further under continental crust
Continental crust

40 MILLION YEARS AGO

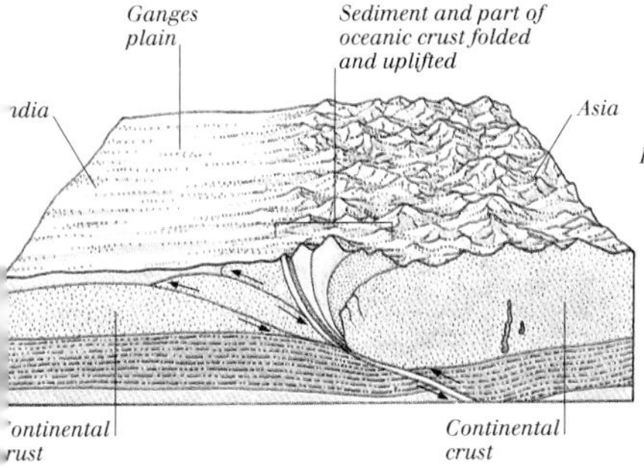
Ganges plain
Sediment and part of oceanic crust folded and uplifted
ndia
Asia
ontinental rust
Continental crust

20 MILLION YEARS AGO

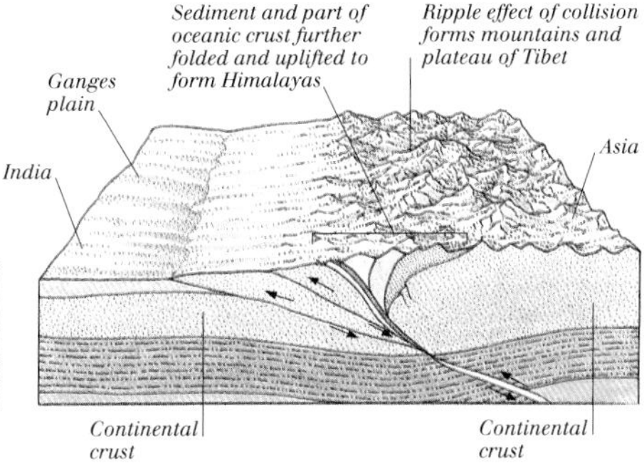
Sediment and part of oceanic crust further folded and uplifted to form Himalayas
Ripple effect of collision forms mountains and plateau of Tibet
Ganges plain
India
Asia
Continental crust
Continental crust

TODAY

SAN ANDREAS FAULT

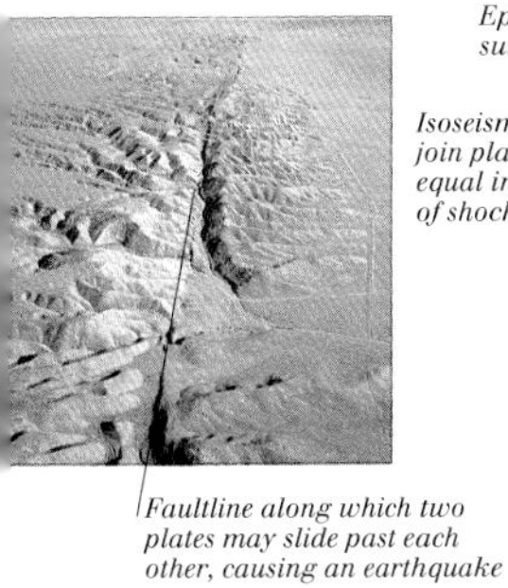
Faultline along which two plates may slide past each other, causing an earthquake

EARTHQUAKES

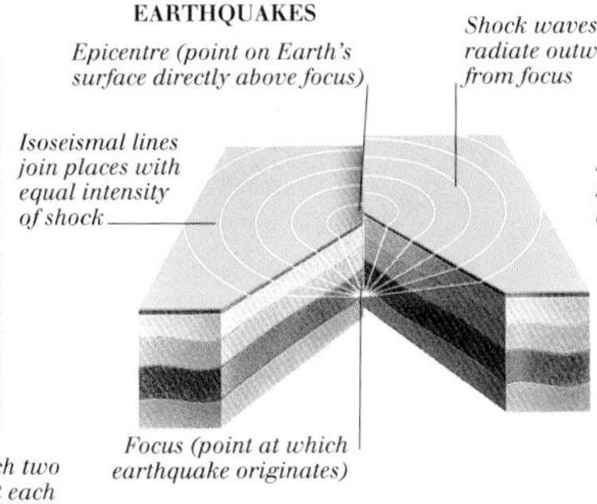
Epicentre (point on Earth's surface directly above focus)
Shock waves radiate outwards from focus
Isoseismal lines join places with equal intensity of shock
Focus (point at which earthquake originates)

ANATOMY OF AN EARTHQUAKE

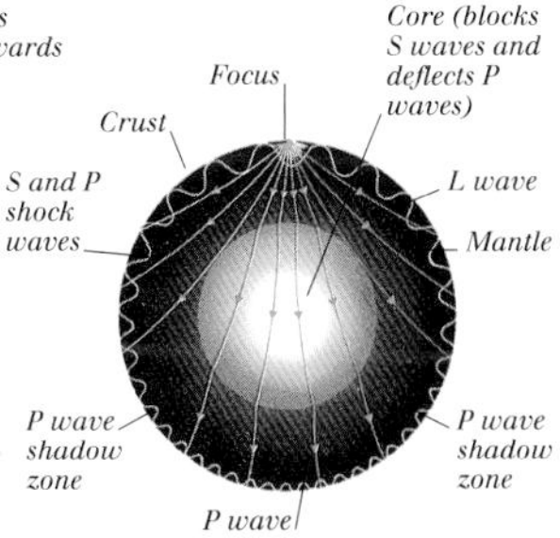
Focus
Core (blocks S waves and deflects P waves)
Crust
S and P shock waves
L wave
Mantle
P wave shadow zone
P wave shadow zone
P wave

PATH OF SHOCK WAVES THROUGH THE EARTH

Precambrian to Devonian periods

MIDDLE ORDOVICIAN POSITIONS OF PRESENT-DAY LAND-MASSES

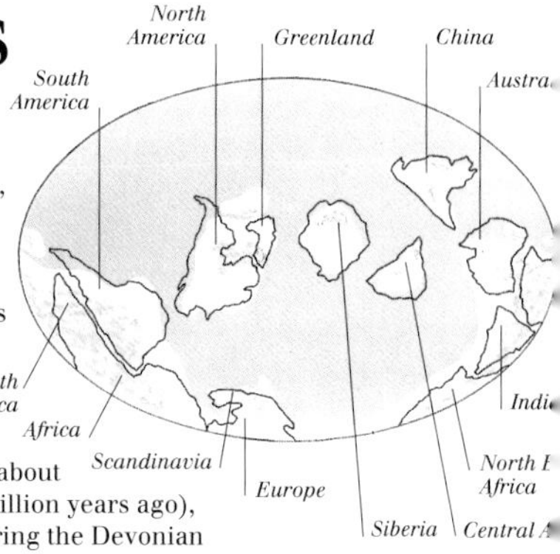
North America
Greenland
China
South America
South Africa
Africa
Scandinavia
Europe
Siberia

WHEN THE EARTH FORMED about 4,600 million years ago, its atmosphere consisted of volcanic gases with little oxygen, making it hostile to most forms of life. One large supercontinent, Gondwanaland, was situated over the southern polar region, while other smaller continents were spread over the rest of the world. Constant movement of the earth's crustal plates carried continents across the earth's surface. The first primitive life-forms emerged around 3,400 million years ago in shallow, warm seas. The build up of oxygen began to form a shield of ozone around the earth, protecting living organisms from the sun's harmful rays and helping to establish an atmosphere in which life could sustain itself. The first vertebrates appeared about 470 million years ago, during the Ordovician period (510–439 million years ago), the first land plants appeared around 400 million years ago during the Devonian period (409–363 million years ago), and the first land animals about 30 million years later.

EXAMPLES OF PRECAMBRIAN TO DEVONIAN PLANT GROUPS

A PRESENT-DAY CLUBMOSS
(Lycopodium sp.)

A PRESENT-DAY LAND PLANT
(Asparagus setaceous)

FOSSIL OF AN EXTINCT LAND PLANT
(Cooksonia hemisphaerica)

FOSSIL OF AN EXTINCT SWAMP PLANT
(Zosterophyllum llanoveranum)

EXAMPLES OF PRECAMBRIAN TO DEVONIAN TRILOBITES

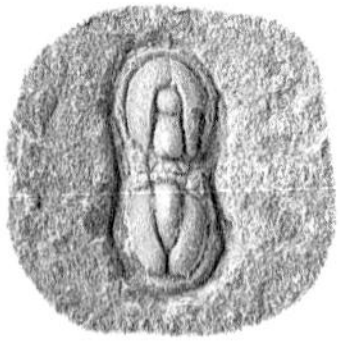

ACADAGNOSTUS
Family: Agnostidae
Length: 8 mm (1/3 in)

PHACOPS
Family: Phacopidae
Length: 4.5 cm (1¾ in)

OLENELLUS
Family: Olenellidae
Length: 6 cm (2½ in)

ELRATHIA
Family: Ptychopariidae
Length: 2 cm (¾ in)

THE EARTH DURING THE MIDDLE ORDOVICIAN PERIOD

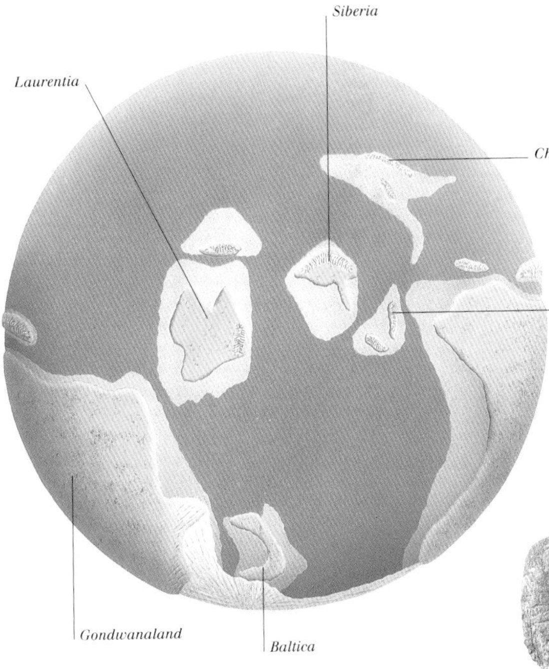

EXAMPLES OF EARLY MARINE INVERTEBRATES

FOSSIL NAUTILOID
(Estonioceras perforatum)

FOSSIL BRACHIOPOD
(Dicoelosia bilobata)

TRACE FOSSIL
(Mawsonites spriggi)

FOSSIL GRAPTOLITE
(Monograptus convolutus)

EXAMPLES OF DEVONIAN FISH

RHAMPHODOPSIS
Family: Ptyctodontidae
Length: 15 cm (6 in)

PTERASPIS
Family: Pteraspidae
Length: 25 cm (10 in)

COCCOSTEUS
Family: Coccosteidae
Length: 35 cm (14 in)

BOTHRIOLEPIS
Family: Bothriolepidae
Length: 40 cm (16 in)

CHEIRACANTHUS
Family: Acanthodidae
Length: 30 cm (12 in)

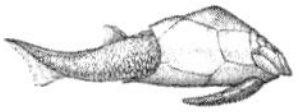

PTERICHTHYODES
Family: Asterolepidae
Length: 15 cm (6 in)

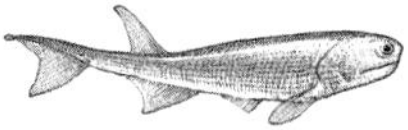

CHEIROLEPIS
Family: Cheirolepidae
Length: 17 cm (6¾ in)

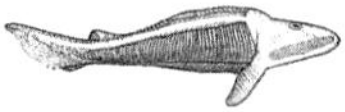

CEPHALASPIS
Family: Cephalaspidae
Length: 22 cm (8¾ in)

Carboniferous to Permian periods

THE CARBONIFEROUS PERIOD (363–290 million years ago) takes its name from the thick, carbon-rich layers – now coal – that were produced during this period as swampy tropical forests were repeatedly drowned by shallow seas. The humid climate across northern and equatorial continents throughout Carboniferous times produced the first dense plant cover on Earth. During the early part of this period, the first reptiles appeared. Their development of a waterproof egg with a protective internal structure ended animal life's dependence on an aquatic environment. Towards the end of Carboniferous times, the earth's continents Laurasia and Gondwanaland collided, resulting in the huge land-mass of Pangaea. Glaciers smothered much of the southern hemisphere during the Permian period (290–245 million years ago), covering Antarctica, parts of Australia, and much of South America, Africa, and India. Ice locked up much of the world's water and large areas of the northern hemisphere experienced a drop in sea-level. Away from the poles, deserts and a hot dry climate predominated. As a result of these conditions, the Permian period ended with the greatest mass extinction of life on earth ever.

LATE CARBONIFEROUS POSITIONS OF PRESENT-DAY LAND-MASSES

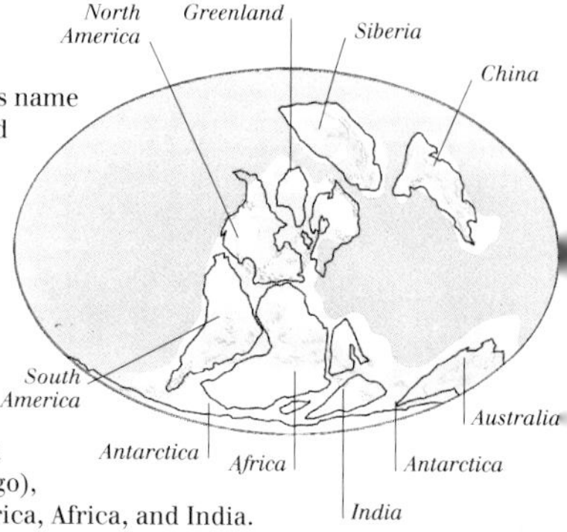
North America
Greenland
Siberia
China
South America
Australia
Antarctica
Africa
Antarctica
India

EXAMPLES OF CARBONIFEROUS AND PERMIAN PLANT GROUPS

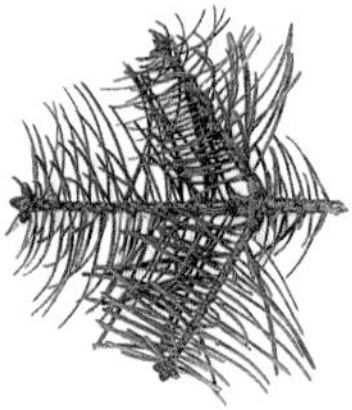

A PRESENT-DAY FIR
(Abies concolor)

FOSSIL OF AN EXTINCT FERN
(Zeilleria frenzlii)

FOSSIL OF AN EXTINCT HORSETAIL
(Equisetites sp.)

FOSSIL OF AN EXTINCT CLUBMOSS
(Lepidodendron sp.)

EXAMPLES OF CARBONIFEROUS AND PERMIAN TREES

PECOPTERIS
Family: Marattiaceae
Height: 4 m (13 ft)

PARIPTERIS
Family: Medullosaceae
Height: 5 m (16 ft 6 in)

MARIOPTERIS
Family: Unclassified
Height: 5 m (16 ft 6 in)

MEDULLOSA
Family: Medullosaceae
Height: 5 m (16 ft 6 in)

THE EARTH DURING THE LATE CARBONIFEROUS PERIOD

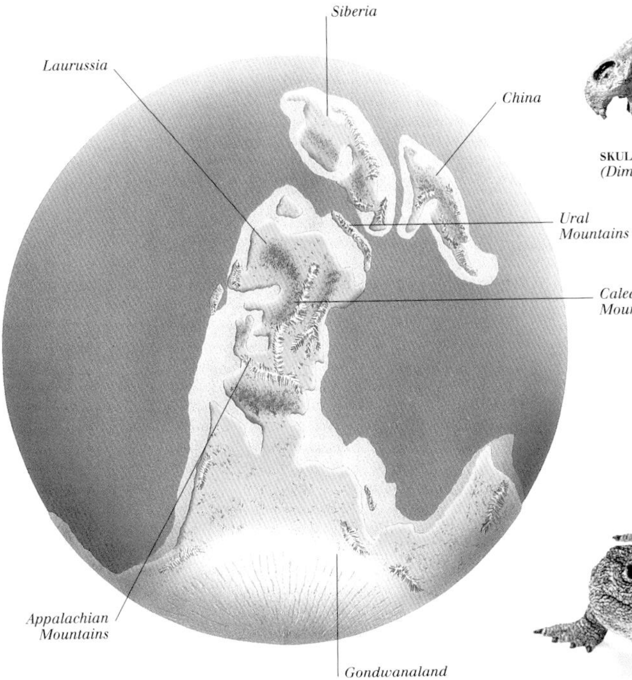
Siberia
Laurussia
China
Ural Mountains
Caledonian Mountains
Appalachian Mountains
Gondwanaland

EXAMPLES OF CARBONIFEROUS AND PERMIAN ANIMALS

SKULL OF AN EXTINCT SYNAPSID REPTILE
(Dimetrodon loomisi)

FOSSIL TEETH OF AN EXTINCT SHARK
(Helicoprion bessonowi)

MODEL OF AN EXTINCT CARBONIFEROUS REPTILE
(Westlothiana lizziae)

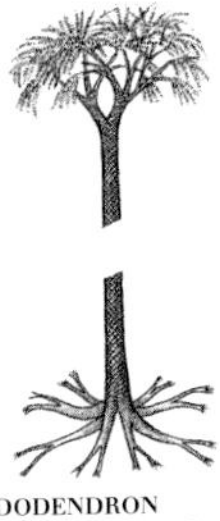

LEPIDODENDRON
Family: Lepidodendraceae
Height: 30 m (100 ft)

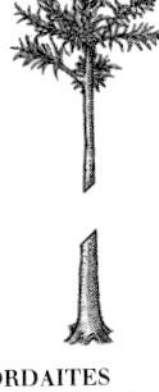

CORDAITES
Family: Cordaitacea
Height: 10 m (33 ft)

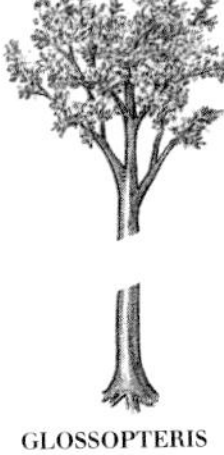

GLOSSOPTERIS
Family: Glossopteridaceae
Height: 8 m (26 ft)

ALETHOPTERIS
Family: Medullosaceae
Height: 5 m (16 ft 6 in)

Triassic period

THE TRIASSIC PERIOD (245–208 million years ago) marked the beginning of what is known as the Age of the Dinosaurs (the Mesozoic era). During this period, the present-day continents were massed together, forming one huge continent known as Pangaea. This land-mass experienced extremes of climate, with lush green areas around the coast or by lakes and rivers, and arid deserts in the interior. The only forms of plant life were non-flowering plants, such as conifers, ferns, cycads, and ginkgos; flowering plants had not yet evolved. The principal forms of animal life included primitive amphibians, rhynchosaurs ("beaked lizards"), and primitive crocodilians. Dinosaurs first appeared about 230 million years ago, at the beginning of the Late Triassic period. The earliest known dinosaurs were the carnivorous (flesh-eating) herrerasaurids and staurikosaurids, such as *Herrerasaurus* and *Staurikosaurus*. Early herbivorous (plant-eating) dinosaurs first appeared in Late Triassic times and included *Plateosaurus* and *Technosaurus*. By the end of the Triassic period, dinosaurs dominated Pangaea, possibly contributing to the extinction of many other reptiles.

TRIASSIC POSITIONS OF PRESENT-DAY LAND-MASSES

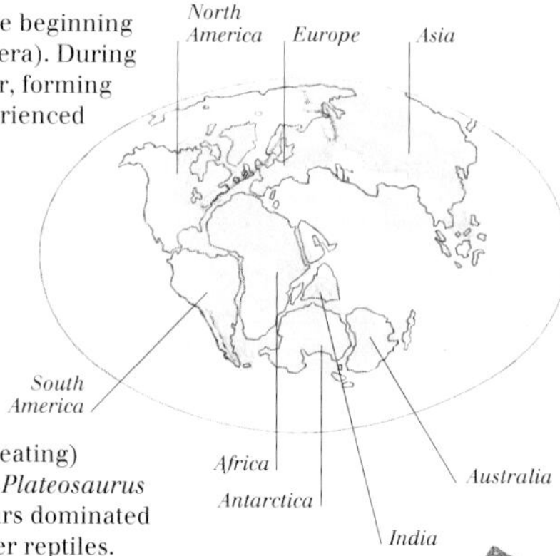
North America
Europe
Asia
South America
Africa
Antarctica
India
Australia

EXAMPLES OF TRIASSIC PLANT GROUPS

A PRESENT-DAY CYCAD *(Cycas revoluta)*

A PRESENT-DAY GINKGO *(Ginkgo biloba)*

A PRESENT-DAY CONIFER *(Araucaria araucana)*

FOSSIL OF AN EXTINCT FERN *(Pachypteris sp.)*

FOSSIL LEAF OF AN EXTINCT CYCAD *(Cycas sp.)*

EXAMPLES OF TRIASSIC DINOSAURS

MELANOROSAURUS
A melanorosaurid
Length: 12.2 m (40 ft)

MUSSAURUS
A plateosaurid
Length: 2–3 m (6 ft 6 in–10 ft)

HERRERASAURUS
A herrerasaurid
Length: 3 m (10 ft)

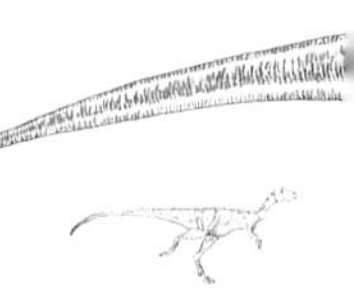

PISANOSAURUS
A primitive ornithischian
Length: 90 cm (3 ft)

THE EARTH DURING THE TRIASSIC PERIOD

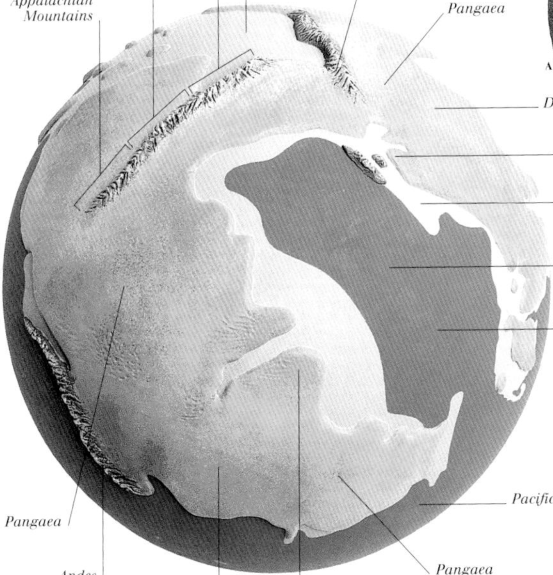
Scandinavian Mountains
Caledonian Mountains
Sinus Borealis
Ural Mountains
Appalachian Mountains
Pangaea
Desert
Vegetation
Continental shelf
Tethys Sea
Deep ocean
Pacific Ocean
Pangaea
Pangaea
Andes
Desert
Vegetation

EXAMPLES OF TRIASSIC ANIMALS

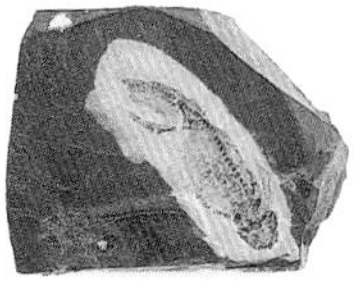

AN EXTINCT AMPHIBIAN

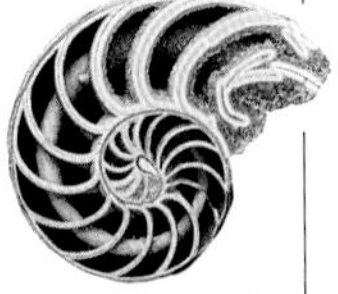

A NAUTILOID MOLLUSC
(Nautilus sp.)

AN EXTINCT CHONDROSTEAN FISH
(Cleithrolepis granulatus)

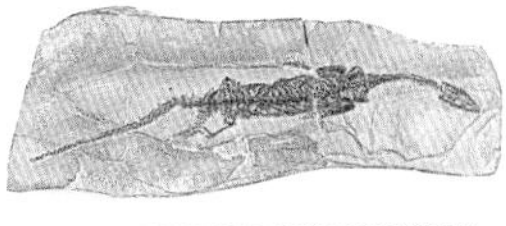

AN EXTINCT NOTHOSAURIAN REPTILE
(Pachypleurosaurus sp.)

AN EXTINCT RHYNCHOSAURIAN REPTILE
(Scaphonyx fischeri)

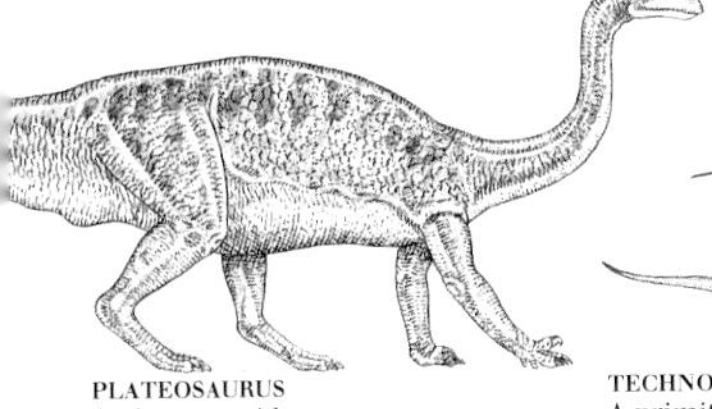

PLATEOSAURUS
A plateosaurid
Length: 7.9 m (26 ft)

TECHNOSAURUS
A primitive ornithischian
Length: 1 m (3 ft 3 in)

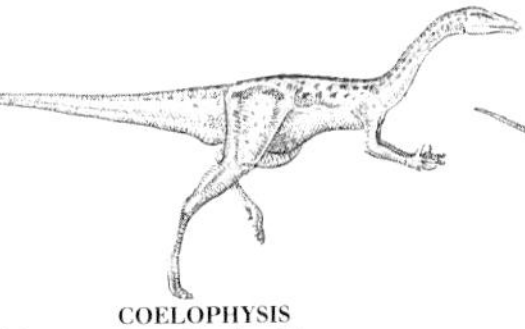

COELOPHYSIS
A coelophysid
Length: 3 m (10 ft)

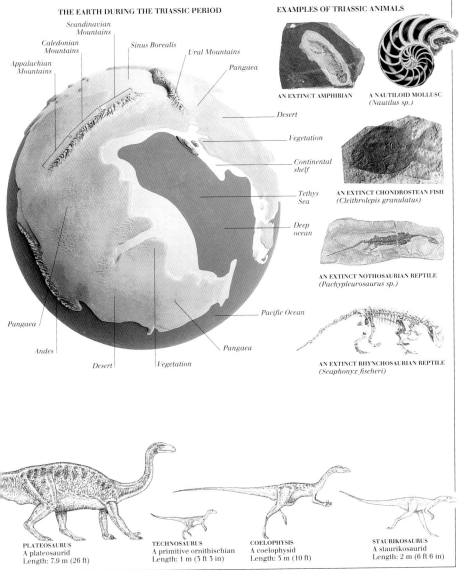

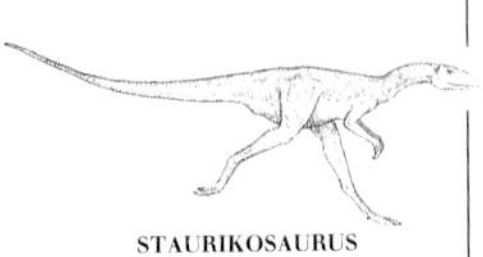

STAURIKOSAURUS
A staurikosaurid
Length: 2 m (6 ft 6 in)

Jurassic period

THE JURASSIC PERIOD, the middle part of the Mesozoic era, lasted from 208 to 146 million years ago. During Jurassic times, the land-mass of Pangaea broke up into the continents of Gondwanaland and Laurasia, and sea-levels rose, flooding areas of lower land. The Jurassic climate was warm and moist. Plants such as ginkgos, horsetails, and conifers thrived, and giant redwood trees appeared, as did the first flowering plants. The abundance of plant food coincided with the proliferation of herbivorous (plant-eating) dinosaurs, such as the large sauropods (e.g., *Diplodocus*) and stegosaurs (e.g., *Stegosaurus*). Carnivorous (flesh-eating) dinosaurs, such as *Compsognathus* and *Allosaurus*, also flourished by hunting the many animals that existed – among them other dinosaurs. Further Jurassic animals included shrew-like mammals, and pterosaurs (flying reptiles), as well as plesiosaurs and ichthyosaurs (both marine reptiles).

JURASSIC POSITIONS OF PRESENT-DAY LAND-MASSES

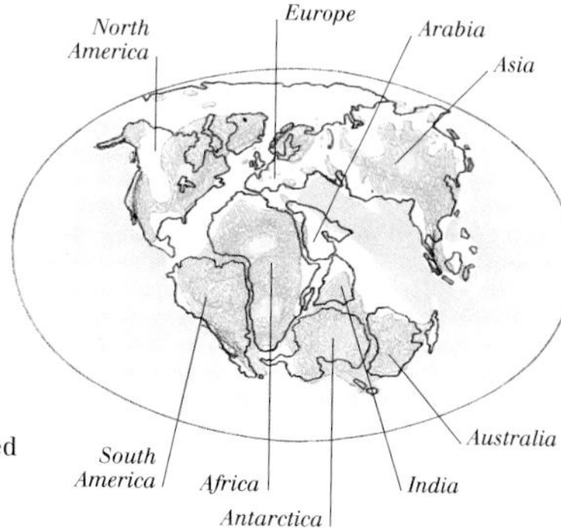
North America
Europe
Arabia
Asia
Australia
South America
Africa
Antarctica
India

EXAMPLES OF JURASSIC PLANT GROUPS

A PRESENT-DAY FERN
(Dicksonia antarctica)

A PRESENT-DAY HORSETAIL
(Equisetum arvense)

A PRESENT-DAY CONIFER
(Taxus baccata)

FOSSIL LEAF OF AN EXTINCT CONIFER
(Taxus sp.)

FOSSIL LEAF OF AN EXTINCT REDWOOD
(Sequoiadendron affinis)

EXAMPLES OF JURASSIC DINOSAURS

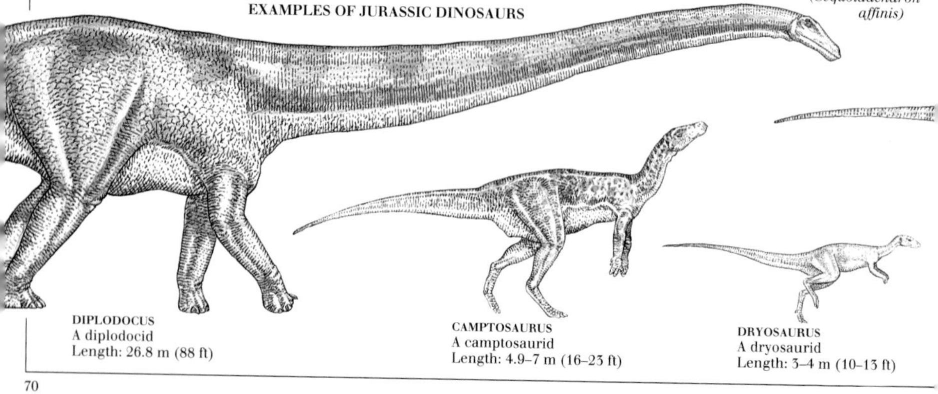

DIPLODOCUS
A diplodocid
Length: 26.8 m (88 ft)

CAMPTOSAURUS
A camptosaurid
Length: 4.9–7 m (16–23 ft)

DRYOSAURUS
A dryosaurid
Length: 3–4 m (10–13 ft)

THE EARTH DURING THE JURASSIC PERIOD

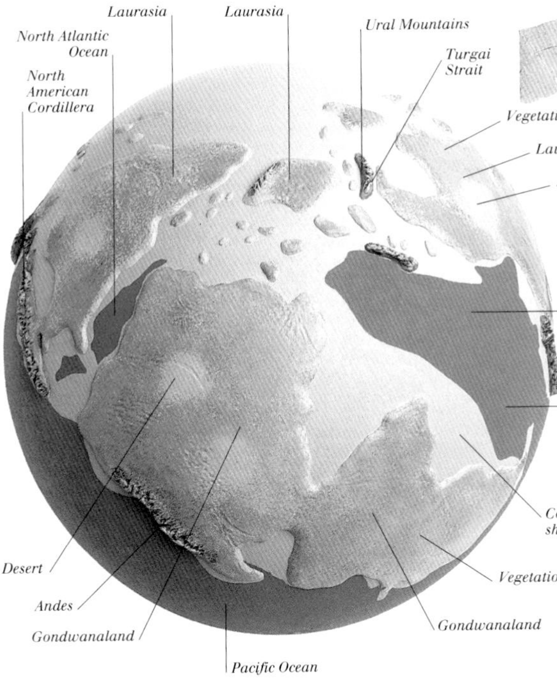
Laurasia
Laurasia
Ural Mountains
North Atlantic Ocean
Turgai Strait
North American Cordillera
Vegetation
Laurasia
Desert
Tethys Sea
Deep ocean
Continental shelf
Desert
Vegetation
Andes
Gondwanaland
Gondwanaland
Pacific Ocean

EXAMPLES OF JURASSIC ANIMALS

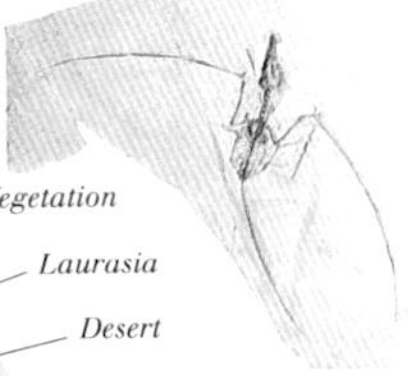

AN EXTINCT PTEROSAUR
(Rhamphorhynchus sp.)

AN EXTINCT BELEMNITE MOLLUSC
(Belemnoteuthis sp.)

AN EXTINCT RHYNCHOSAURIAN REPTILE
(Homeosaurus pulchellus)

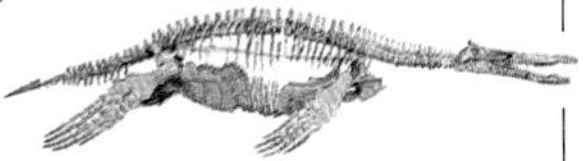

AN EXTINCT PLESIOSAUR
(Peloneustes philarcus)

AN EXTINCT ICHTHYOSAUR
(Ichthyosaurus megacephalus)

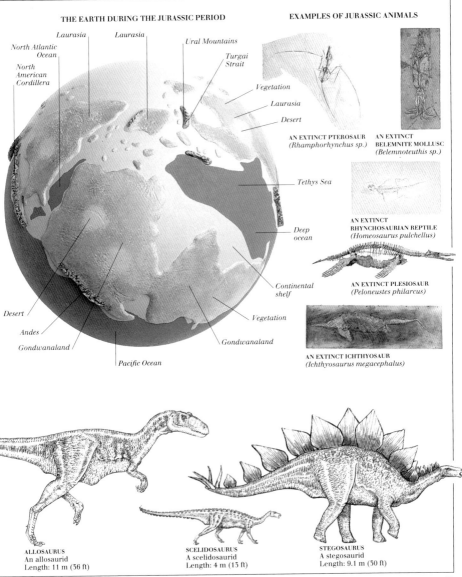

ALLOSAURUS
An allosaurid
Length: 11 m (36 ft)

SCELIDOSAURUS
A scelidosaurid
Length: 4 m (13 ft)

STEGOSAURUS
A stegosaurid
Length: 9.1 m (30 ft)

Cretaceous period

THE MESOZOIC ERA ENDED WITH the Cretaceous period, which lasted from 146 to 65 million years ago. During this period, Gondwanaland and Laurasia were breaking up into smaller land-masses that more closely resembled those of the modern continents. The climate remained mild and moist but the seasons became more marked. Flowering plants, including deciduous trees, replaced many cycads, seed ferns, and conifers. Animal species became more varied, with the evolution of new mammals, insects, fish, crustaceans, and turtles. Dinosaurs evolved into a wide variety of species during Cretaceous times; more than half of all known dinosaurs – including *Iguanodon*, *Deinonychus*, *Tyrannosaurus*, and *Hypsilophodon* – lived during this period. At the end of the Cretaceous period, however, dinosaurs became extinct. The reason for this mass extinction is unknown but it is thought to have been caused by climatic changes due to either a catastrophic meteor impact with the Earth or extensive volcanic eruptions.

CRETACEOUS POSITIONS OF PRESENT-DAY LAND-MASSES

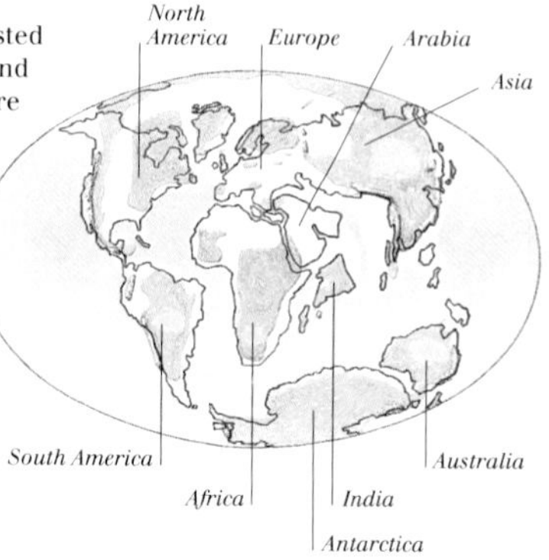
North America
Europe
Arabia
Asia
South America
Africa
India
Antarctica
Australia

EXAMPLES OF CRETACEOUS PLANT GROUPS

A PRESENT-DAY CONIFER
(Pinus muricata)

A PRESENT-DAY DECIDUOUS TREE
(Magnolia sp.)

FOSSIL OF AN EXTINCT FERN
(Sphenopteris latiloba)

FOSSIL OF AN EXTINCT GINKGO
(Ginkgo pluripartita)

FOSSIL LEAVES OF AN EXTINCT DECIDUOUS TREE
(Cercidyphyllum sp.)

EXAMPLES OF CRETACEOUS DINOSAURS

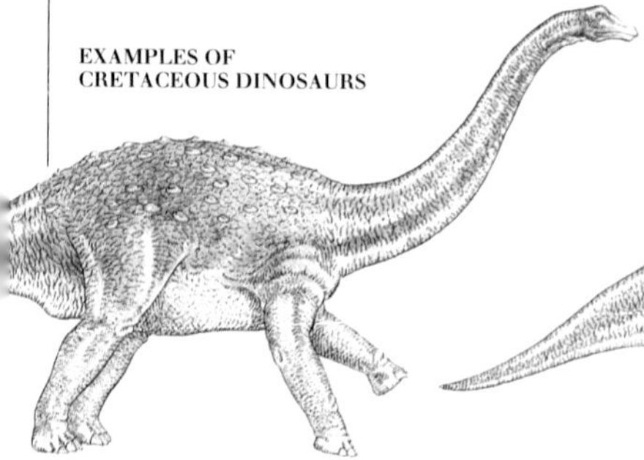
SALTASAURUS
A titanosaurid
Length: 12.2 m (40 ft)

TOROSAURUS
A ceratopsid
Length: 7.6 m (25 ft)

HYPSILOPHODON
A hypsilophodontid
Length: 1.4–2.3 m (4 ft 6 in–7 ft 6 in)

THE EARTH DURING THE CRETACEOUS PERIOD

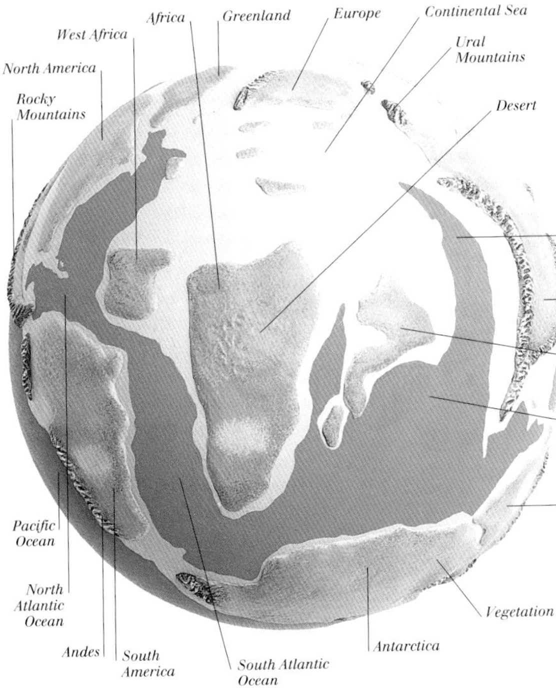
Africa
Greenland
Europe
Continental Sea
West Africa
Ural Mountains
North America
Rocky Mountains
Desert
Tethys Sea
Asia
India
Indian Ocean
Australia
Pacific Ocean
North Atlantic Ocean
Vegetation
Andes
South America
South Atlantic Ocean
Antarctica

EXAMPLES OF CRETACEOUS ANIMALS

AN EXTINCT INSECT
(Libellulium longialatum)

AN EXTINCT MARINE TURTLE
(Plesiochelys latiscutata)

AN EXTINCT CRUSTACEAN
(Homarus sp.)

AN EXTINCT CROCODILIAN

AN EXTINCT HOLOSTEAN FISH
(Lepidotes maximus)

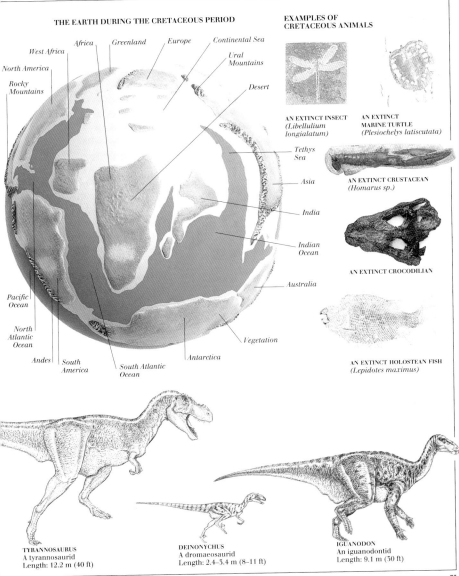

TYRANNOSAURUS
A tyrannosaurid
Length: 12.2 m (40 ft)

DEINONYCHUS
A dromaeosaurid
Length: 2.4–3.4 m (8–11 ft)

IGUANODON
An iguanodontid
Length: 9.1 m (30 ft)

Tertiary period

FOLLOWING THE DEMISE OF THE DINOSAURS at the end of the Cretaceous period, the Tertiary period (65–1.6 million years ago), which formed the first part of the Cenozoic era (65 million years ago–present), was characterized by a huge expansion of mammal life. Placental mammals nourish and maintain the young in the mother's uterus; only three orders of placental mammals existed during Cretaceous times, compared with 25 orders during the Tertiary period. One of these 25 included the first hominid (see pp.108–109), *Australopithecus*, which appeared in Africa. By the beginning of the Tertiary period, the continents had almost reached their present position. The Tethys Sea, which had separated the northern continents from Africa and India, began to close up, forming the Mediterranean Sea and allowing the migration of terrestrial animals between Africa and western Europe. India's collision with Asia led to the formation of the Himalayas. During the middle part of the Tertiary period, the forest-dwelling and browsing mammals were replaced by mammals such as the horse, better suited to grazing the open savannahs that began to dominate. Repeated cool periods throughout the Tertiary period established the Antarctic as an icy island continent.

TERTIARY POSITIONS OF PRESENT-DAY LAND-MASSES

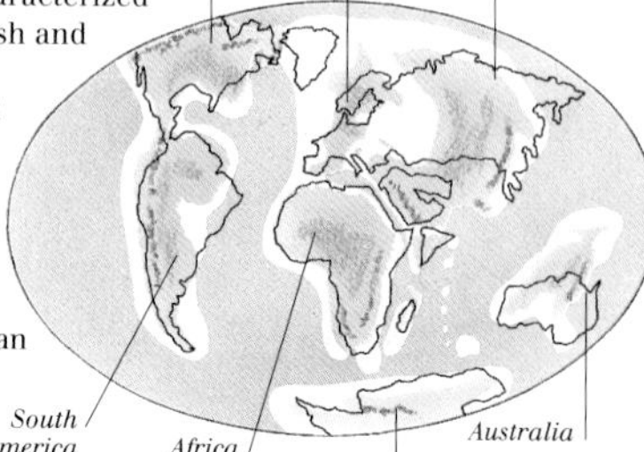
North America
Europe
Asia
South America
Africa
Australia
Antarctica

EXAMPLES OF TERTIARY PLANT GROUPS

A PRESENT-DAY OAK
(Quercus palustris)

A PRESENT-DAY BIRCH
(Betula grossa)

FOSSIL LEAF OF AN EXTINCT BIRCH
(Betulites sp.)

FOSSILIZED STEM OF AN EXTINCT PALM
(Palmoxylon sp.)

EXAMPLES OF TERTIARY ANIMAL GROUPS

HYAENODON
An hyaenodontid
Length: 2 m (6 ft 6 in)

TITANOHYRAX
A pliohyracid
Length: 2 m (6 ft 6 in)

PHORUSRHACUS
A phorusrhacid
Length: 1.5 m (5 ft)

SAMOTHERIUM
A giraffid
Length: 3 m (10 ft)

THE EARTH DURING THE TERTIARY PERIOD

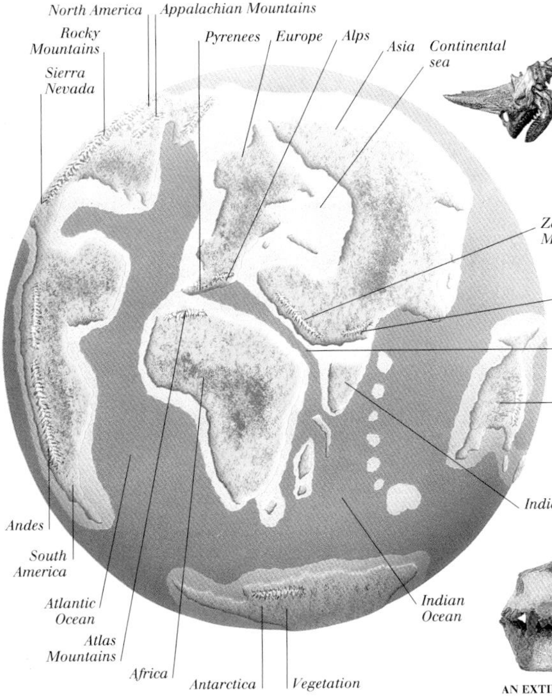
North America
Appalachian Mountains
Rocky Mountains
Pyrenees
Europe
Alps
Asia
Continental sea
Sierra Nevada
Zagros Mountains
Himalayas
Tethys Sea
Australia
India
Andes
South America
Atlantic Ocean
Atlas Mountains
Africa
Antarctica
Vegetation
Indian Ocean

EXAMPLES OF TERTIARY ANIMALS

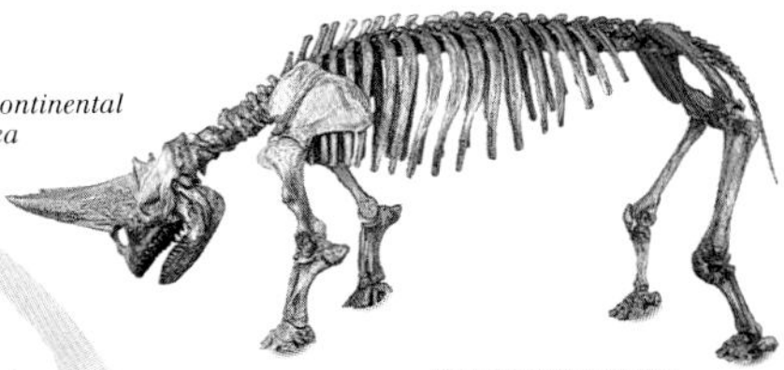

AN EXTINCT MAMMAL
(Arsinoitherium)

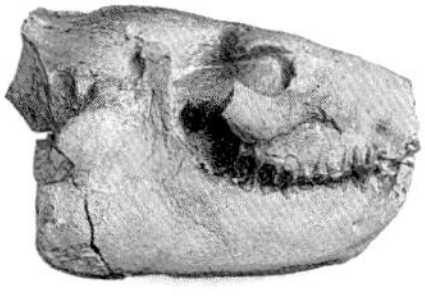

AN EXTINCT MAMMAL
(Merycoidodon culbertsonii)

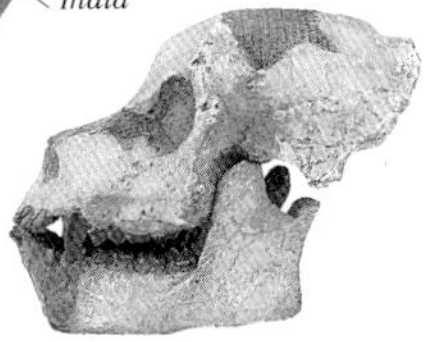

AN EXTINCT HOMINID
(Aegyptopithecus sp.)

AN EXTINCT
GASTROPOD MOLLUSC
(Ecphora quadricostata)

MAMMUT
A mammutid
Length: 2.5 m (8 ft)

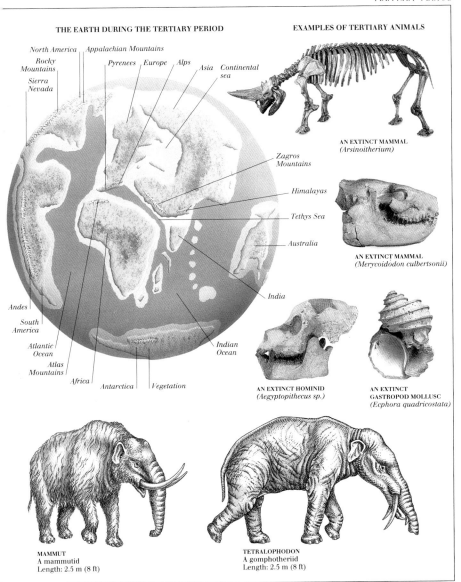

TETRALOPHODON
A gomphotheriid
Length: 2.5 m (8 ft)

Quaternary period

THE QUATERNARY PERIOD (1.6 million years ago–present) forms the second part of the Cenozoic era (65 million years ago–present): it has been characterized by alternating cold (glacial) and warm (interglacial) periods. During cold periods, ice sheets and glaciers have formed repeatedly on northern and southern continents. The cold environments in North America and Eurasia, and to a lesser extent in southern South America and parts of Australia, have caused the migration of many life forms towards the Equator. Only the specialized ice age mammals such as *Mammuthus* and *Coelodonta*, with their thick wool and fat insulation, were suited to life in very cold climates. Humans developed throughout the Pleistocene period (1.6 million–10,000 years ago) in Africa and migrated northward into Europe and Asia. Modern humans, *Homo sapiens*, lived on the cold European continent 30,000 years ago and hunted mammals. The end of the last ice age and the climatic changes that occurred about 10,000 years ago brought extinction to many Pleistocene mammals, but enabled humans to flourish.

QUATERNARY POSITIONS OF PRESENT-DAY LAND-MASSES

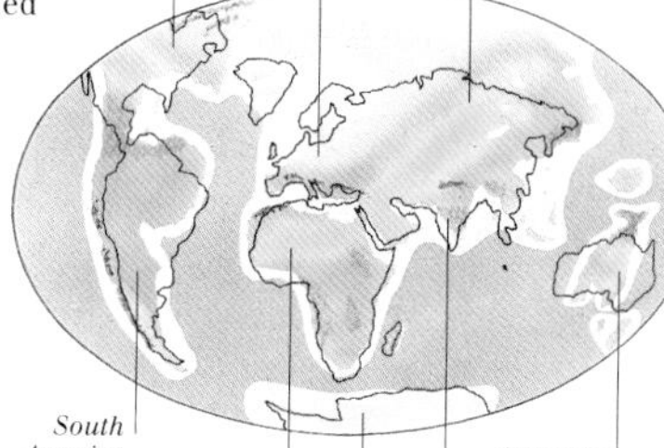
North America
Europe
Asia
South America
Africa
Australia
India
Antarctica

EXAMPLES OF QUATERNARY PLANT GROUPS

A PRESENT-DAY BIRCH
(Betula lenta)

A PRESENT-DAY SWEEETGUM
(Liquidambar styraciflua)

FOSSIL LEAF OF A SWEETGUM
(Liquidambar europeanum)

FOSSIL LEAF OF A BIRCH
(Betula sp.)

EXAMPLES OF QUATERNARY ANIMAL GROUPS

PROCOPTODON
A macropodid
Length: 3 m (10 ft)

DIPROTODON
A diprotodontid
Length: 3 m (10 ft)

TOXODON
A toxodontid
Length: 3 m (10 ft)

MAMMUTHUS
An elephantid
Length: 3 m (10 ft)

THE EARTH DURING THE QUATERNARY PERIOD

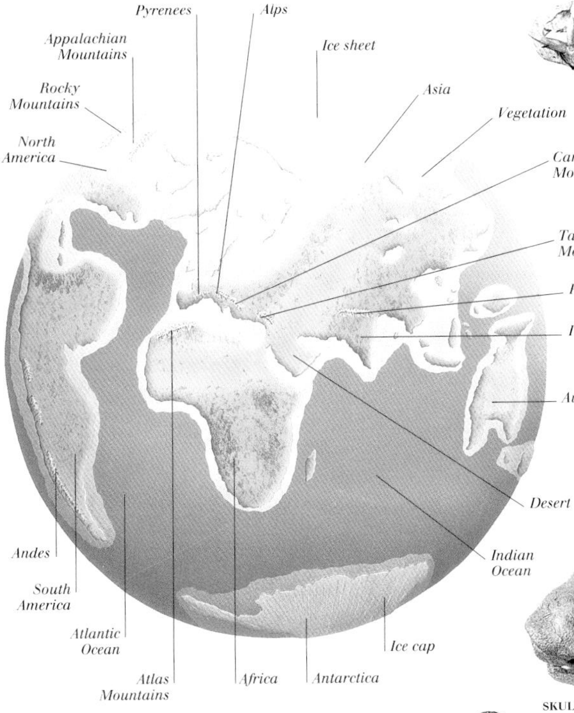
Pyrenees
Alps
Appalachian Mountains
Ice sheet
Rocky Mountains
Asia
Vegetation
North America
Carpathian Mountains
Taurus Mountains
Himalayas
India
Australia
Desert
Andes
Indian Ocean
South America
Atlantic Ocean
Ice cap
Atlas Mountains
Africa
Antarctica

EXAMPLES OF QUATERNARY ANIMALS

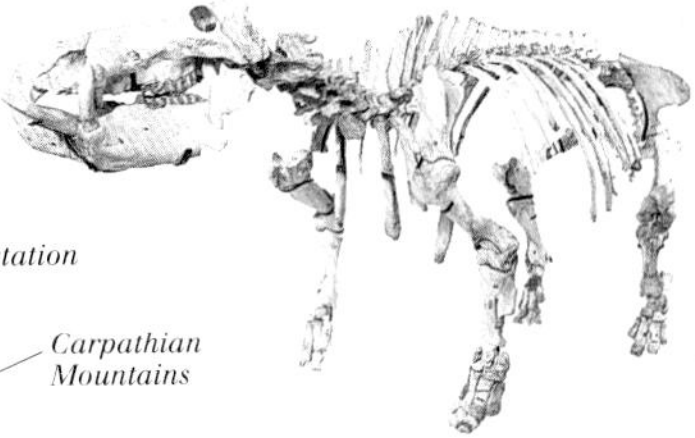

A MAMMAL SKELETON
(Hippopotamus amphibius)

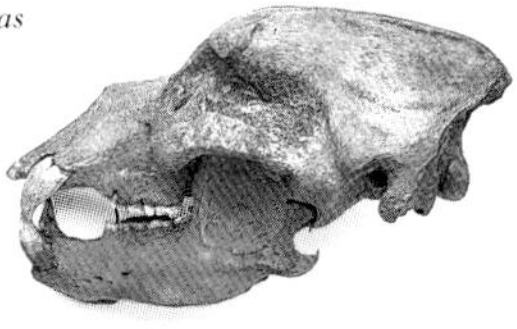

SKULL OF AN EXTINCT CAVE BEAR
(Ursus spelaeus)

SKULL OF AN EXTINCT TORTOISE
(Meiolania platyceps)

A MAMMOTH TOOTH
(Mammuthus primigenius)

DEINOTHERIUM
A deinotheriid
Length: 4 m (13 ft)

COELODONTA
A rhinocerotid
Length: 4 m (13 ft)

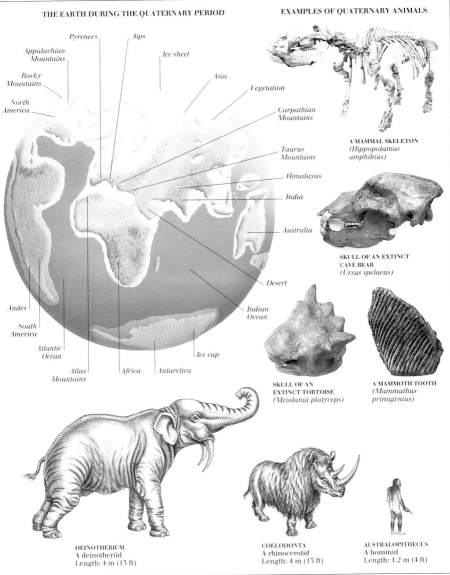

AUSTRALOPITHECUS
A hominid
Length: 1.2 m (4 ft)

Early signs of life

FOR ALMOST A THOUSAND MILLION YEARS after its formation, there was no known life on Earth. The first simple, sea-dwelling organic structures appeared about 3,400 years ago; they may have formed when certain chemical molecules joined together. Prokaryotes, single-celled micro-organisms such as blue-green algae, were able to photosynthesize (see pp. 138–139), and thus produce oxygen. A thousand million years later, sufficient oxygen had built up in the earth's atmosphere to allow multicellular organisms to proliferate in the Precambrian seas (before 570 million years ago). Soft-bodied jellyfish, corals, and seaworms flourished about 700 million years ago. Trilobites, the first animals with hard body frames, developed during the Cambrian period (570–510 million years ago). However, it was not until the beginning of the Devonian period (409–363 million years ago) that early land plants, such as *Asteroxylon*, formed a water-retaining cuticle, which ended their dependence on an aquatic environment. About 363 million years ago, the first amphibians (see pp. 80–81) crawled onto the land, although they still returned to the water to lay their soft eggs. Not until the emergence of the first reptiles would animals appear that were independent of water in this way.

STROMATOLITIC LIMESTONE

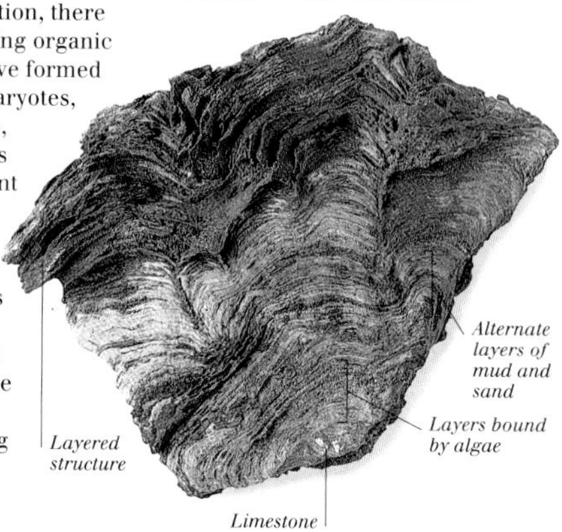
Alternate layers of mud and sand
Layers bound by algae
Layered structure
Limestone

Long, beak-like snout
Growth line
Dorsal plate
Fixed lateral plate
Bony dorsal shield
Dorsal spine base

FOSSILIZED JAWLESS FISH

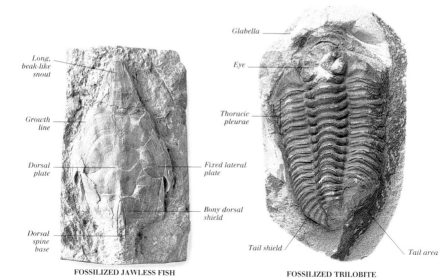

Glabella
Eye
Thoracic pleurae
Tail shield
Tail area

FOSSILIZED TRILOBITE

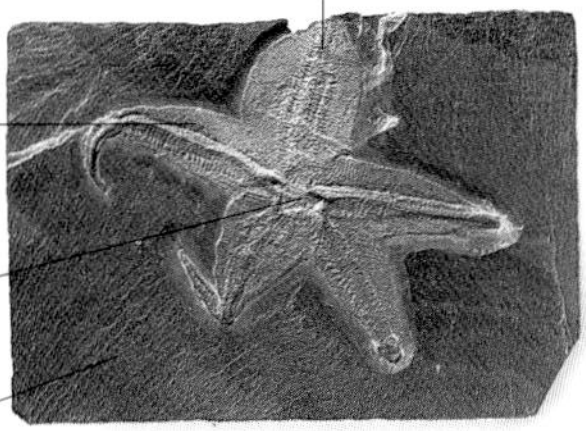
Ambulacral groove
Small ossicles of upper surface
Disc
Iron pyrites

FOSSILIZED STARFISH

Row of ossicles
Broad disc

UPPER SURFACE OF FOSSILIZED STARFISH

Row of ossicles
Short arm

LOWER SURFACE OF FOSSILIZED STARFISH

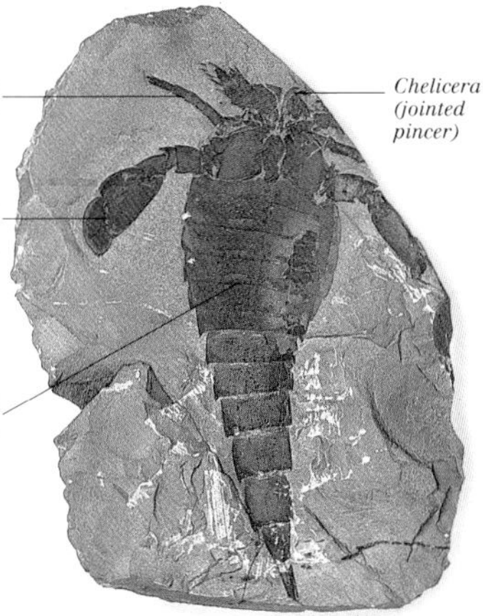
Jointed leg
Chelicera (jointed pincer)
Jointed leg with oar-shaped paddle
Segmented abdomen

UNDERSIDE OF FOSSILIZED EURYPTERID

Telson (tail spine)
ell contains eight somites (thoracic segments)
Abdominal segments
Hingeless, bivalved shell

FOSSIL OF AN EXTINCT SHRIMP

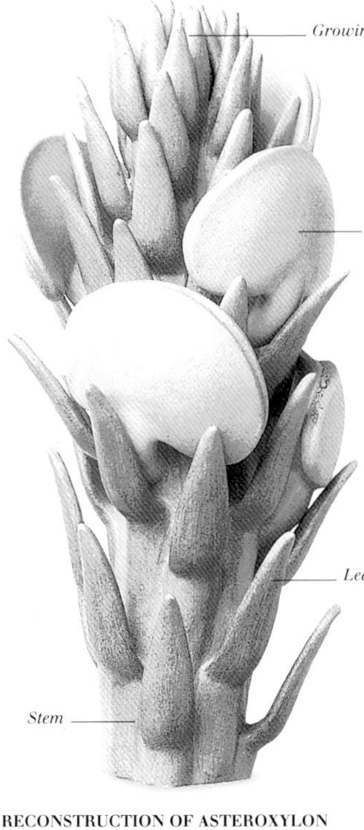
Growing tip
Disc-shaped sporangium (spore-case)
Leaf-like scale
Stem

RECONSTRUCTION OF ASTEROXYLON

Amphibians and reptiles

THE EARLIEST KNOWN AMPHIBIANS, such as *Acanthostega* and *Ichthyostega*, lived about 363 million years ago at the end of the Devonian period (409–363 million years ago). Their limbs may have evolved from the muscular fins of lungfish. These fish can use their fins to push themselves along the bottom of lakes and some can breathe at the water's surface. While amphibians (see pp. 182–183) can exist on land, they are dependent on a wet environment because their skin does not retain moisture and they must return to the water to lay their eggs. Evolving from amphibians, reptiles (see pp. 184–187) first appeared during the Carboniferous period (363–290 million years ago): *Westlothiana*, the earliest known reptile, lived on land 338 million years ago. The development of the amniotic egg, with an embryo enclosed in its own wet environment (the amnion) and protected by a waterproof shell, freed reptiles from the amphibian's dependence on a wet habitat. A scaly skin protected the reptile from desiccation on land and enabled it to exploit ways of life closed to its amphibian ancestors. Reptiles include the dinosaurs, which came to dominate life on land during the Mesozoic era (245–65 million years ago).

Orbit
Pocket enclosing nostril
Sculpted or pitted bone surface
Spiracle to draw in water
Mandible
Small tooth

FOSSIL SKULL OF ACANTHOSTEGA

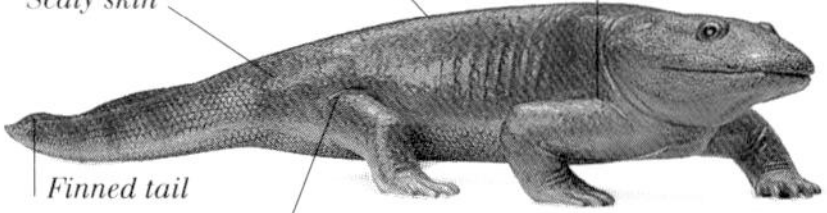
Muscular back
Shoulder girdle
Scaly skin
Finned tail
Hip girdle

MODEL OF ICHTHYOSTEGA

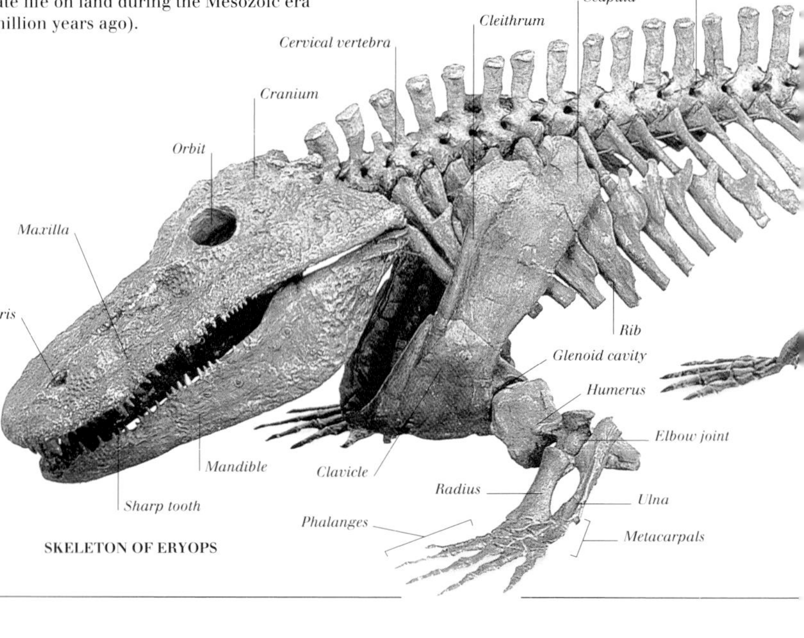
Dorsal vertebra
Scapula
Cleithrum
Cervical vertebra
Cranium
Orbit
Maxilla
Naris
Rib
Glenoid cavity
Humerus
Elbow joint
Mandible
Clavicle
Radius
Ulna
Sharp tooth
Phalanges
Metacarpals

SKELETON OF ERYOPS

FOSSIL SKELETON OF WESTLOTHIANA

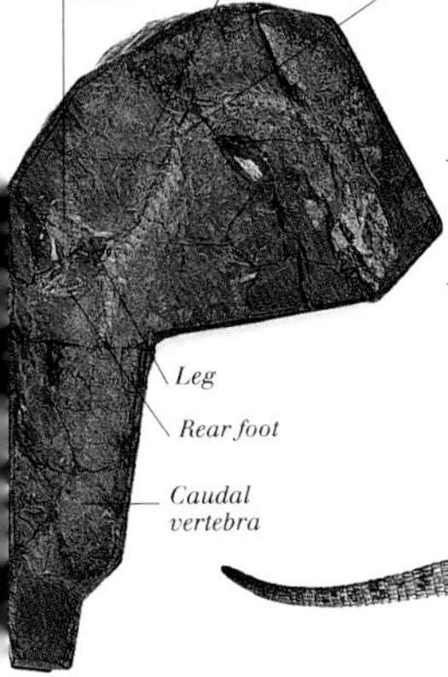
Pelvis
Rib
Vertebra
Flattened skull bones
Leg
Rear foot
Caudal vertebra

FOSSIL SKELETON OF A PAREIASAUR

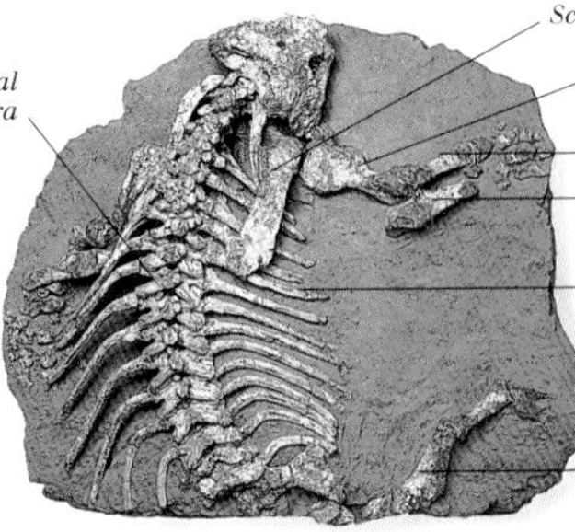
Scapula
Dorsal vertebra
Humerus
Radius
Ulna
Rib
Femur

Tail
Waterproof, scaly skin
Eye
Mouth
Five-toed foot
Semi-sprawling stance

MODEL OF WESTLOTHIANA

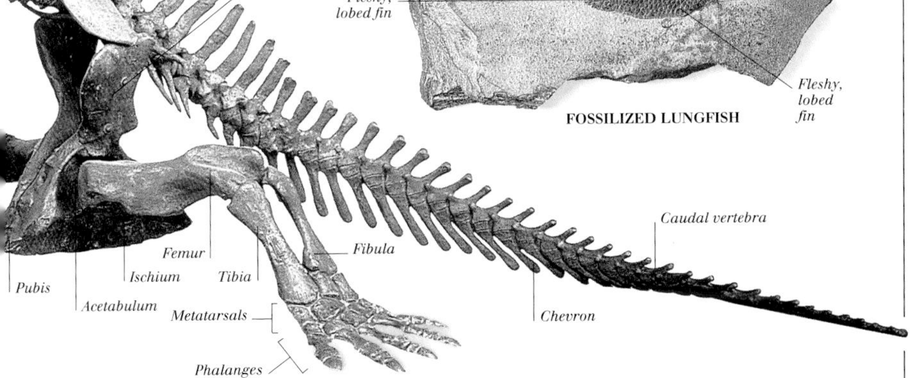
Neural spine
Sacral vertebra
Ilium
Caudal vertebra
Femur
Fibula
Pubis
Ischium
Tibia
Acetabulum
Metatarsals
Chevron
Phalanges

Tri-lobed tail
Fleshy, lobed fin
Fleshy, lobed fin

FOSSILIZED LUNGFISH

The dinosaurs

THE DINOSAURS WERE A LARGE GROUP of reptiles that were the dominant land vertebrates (animals with backbones) for most of the Mesozoic era (245–65 million years ago). They appeared some 230 million years ago and were distinguished from other scaly, egg-laying reptiles by an important feature: dinosaurs had an erect limb stance. This enabled them to keep their bodies well above the ground, unlike the sprawling and semi-sprawling stance of other reptiles. The head of the dinosaur's femur (thigh-bone) fitted into a socket in its pelvis (hip-bone), producing efficient and mobile locomotion. Dinosaurs are categorized into two groups according to the structure of their pelvis: saurischian (lizard-hipped) and ornithischian (bird-hipped) dinosaurs. In the case of most saurischians, the pubis (part of the pelvis) jutted forward, while in ornithischians it slanted back, parallel to the ischium (another part of the pelvis). The enormous variety of dinosaur species equals that of mammals. The Dinosauria were the most successful land vertebrates ever, and survived for 165 million years, until their extinction 65 million years ago.

STRUCTURE OF SAURISCHIAN PELVIS

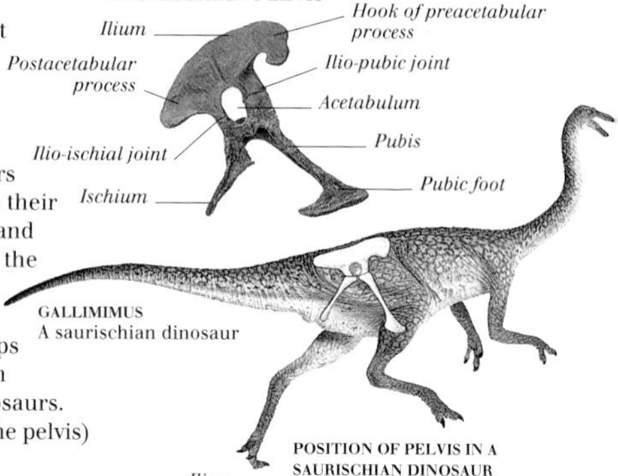
Ilium
Hook of preacetabular process
Postacetabular process
Ilio-pubic joint
Acetabulum
Pubis
Ilio-ischial joint
Pubic foot
Ischium

GALLIMIMUS
A saurischian dinosaur

POSITION OF PELVIS IN A SAURISCHIAN DINOSAUR

STRUCTURE OF ORNTHISCHIAN PELVIS

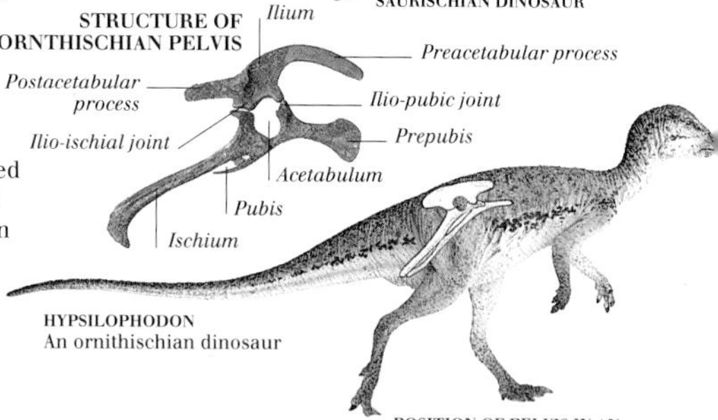
Ilium
Preacetabular process
Postacetabular process
Ilio-pubic joint
Prepubis
Ilio-ischial joint
Acetabulum
Pubis
Ischium

HYPSILOPHODON
An ornithischian dinosaur

POSITION OF PELVIS IN AN ORNITHISCHIAN DINOSAUR

BAROSAURUS
A saurischian dinosaur

COMPARISON OF ANIMAL STANCES

SPRAWLING STANCE
The thighs and upper arms project straight out from the body so that the knees and elbows are bent at right angles.

COMMON IGUANA
(Iguana iguana)
A present-day reptile

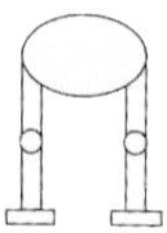

ERECT STANCE
The thighs and upper arms project straight down from the body so that the knees and elbows are straight.

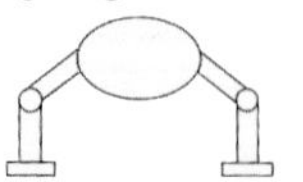

SEMI-SPRAWLING STANCE
The thighs and upper arms project downwards and outwards so that the knees and elbows are slightly bent.

DWARF CROCODILE
(Osteolaemus tetraspis)
A present-day reptile

EXAMPLES OF DINOSAUR CLAWS

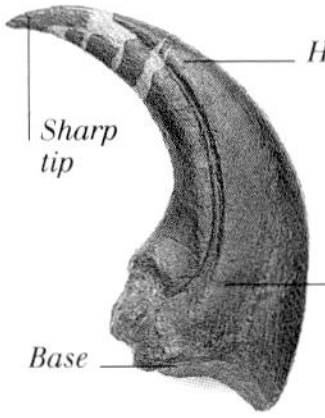
Hook shape
Sharp tip
Claw used for catching fish
Base

BARYONYX THUMB-CLAW

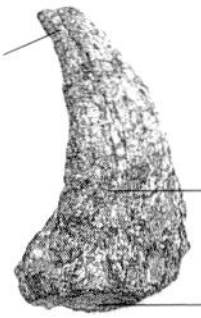
Top part of claw (sharp point missing)
Claw for digging and defence
Base

MASSOSPONDYLUS THUMB-CLAW

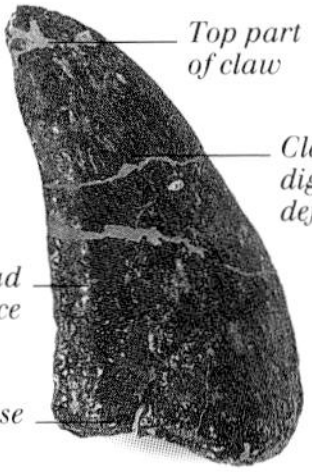
Top part of claw
Claw used for digging and defence
Broad surface
Base

APATOSAURUS THUMB-CLAW

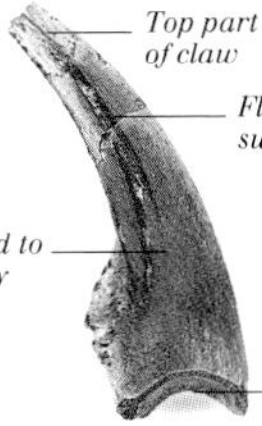
Top part of claw
Flattened surface
law used to
tch prey
Base

ORNITHOMIMUS FINGER-CLAW

DINOSAUR CLADOGRAM

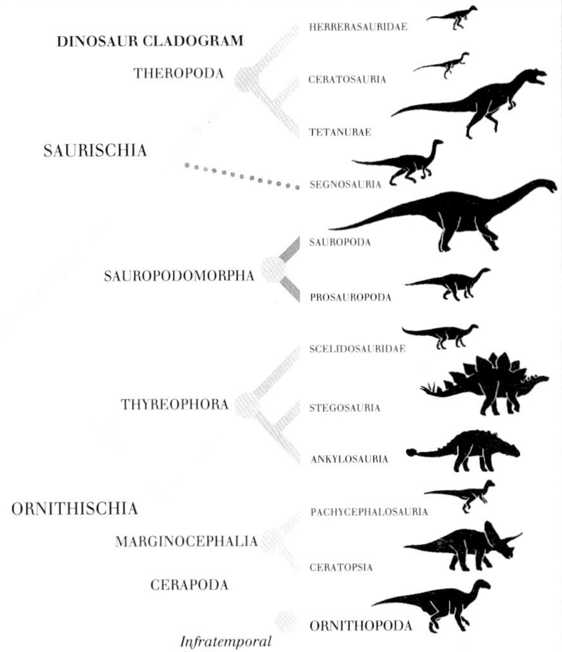
DINOSAURIA
SAURISCHIA
THEROPODA
HERRERASAURIDAE
CERATOSAURIA
TETANURAE
SEGNOSAURIA
SAUROPODOMORPHA
SAUROPODA
PROSAUROPODA
ORNITHISCHIA
THYREOPHORA
SCELIDOSAURIDAE
STEGOSAURIA
ANKYLOSAURIA
MARGINOCEPHALIA
PACHYCEPHALOSAURIA
CERATOPSIA
CERAPODA
ORNITHOPODA
ORDER
SUBORDER
INTERMEDIATE GROUP
RELATIONSHIP UNCERTAIN

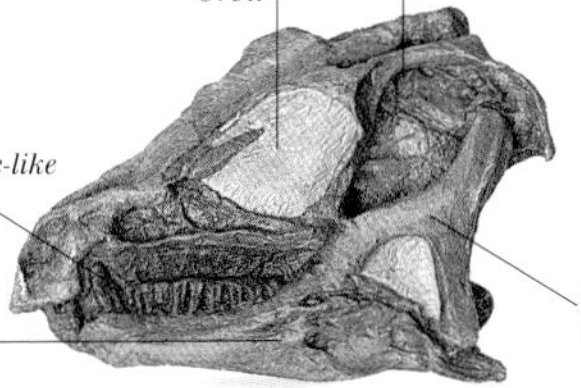
Orbit
Infratemporal fenestra
Canine-like tooth
Quadratojugal bone
Mandible

SKULL AND MANDIBLE OF HETERODONTOSAURUS

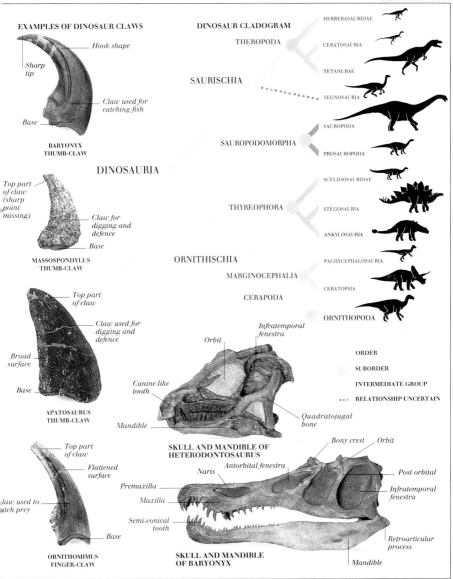

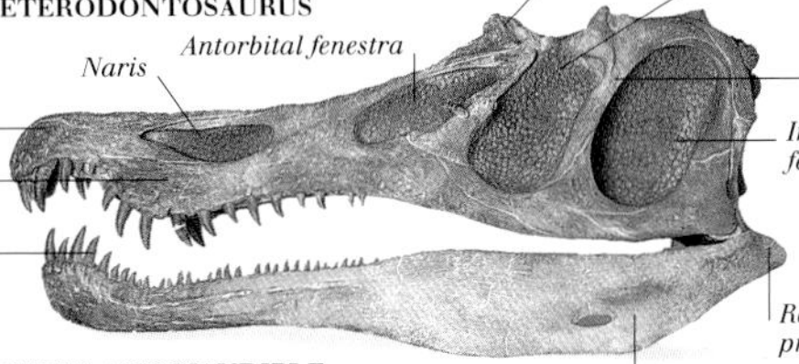
Bony crest
Orbit
Antorbital fenestra
Naris
Post orbital
Premaxilla
Infratemporal fenestra
Maxilla
Semi-conical tooth
Retroarticular process
Mandible

SKULL AND MANDIBLE OF BARYONYX

Theropods 1

AN ENORMOUSLY SUCCESSFUL SUBORDER of the Saurischia, the bipedal (two-footed) theropods ("beast feet") emerged 230 million years ago in Late Triassic times; the oldest known example comes from South America. Theropods spanned the whole of the Age of the Dinosaurs (230–65 million years ago) and included most of the known predatory dinosaurs. The typical theropod had small arms with sharp, clawed fingers; powerful jaws lined with sharp teeth; an S-shaped neck; long, muscular hind limbs; and clawed, usually four-toed feet. Many theropods may have been warm-blooded; most were exclusively carnivorous. Theropods ranged from animals no larger than a chicken to huge creatures, such as *Tyrannosaurus* and *Baryonyx*. The group also included ostrich-like omnivores and herbivores with toothless beaks, such as *Struthiomimus* and *Gallimimus*. Many scientists believe that birds are the closest living relatives to the dinosaurs, and share a common ancestor with the theropods. *Archaeopteryx*, small and feathered, was the first known bird and lived alongside its dinosaur relatives.

INTERNAL ANATOMY OF ALBERTOSAURUS LEG

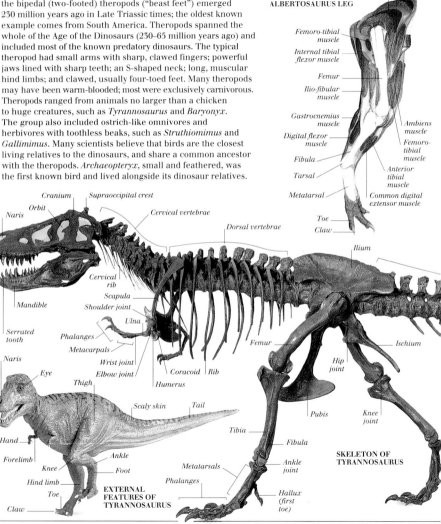

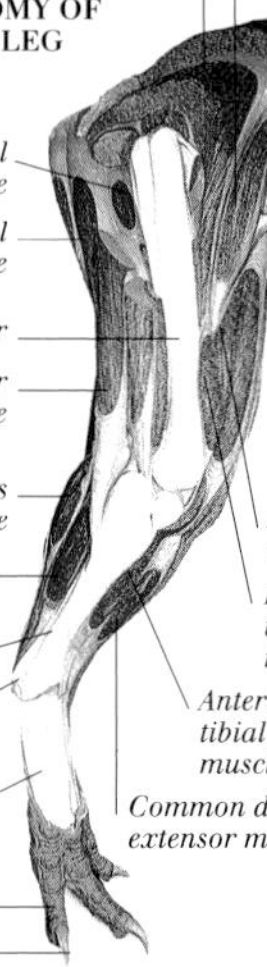
Ilio-tibial muscle
Ilio-femoral muscle
Femoro-tibial muscle
Internal tibial flexor muscle
Femur
Ilio-fibular muscle
Gastrocnemius muscle
Digital flexor muscle
Fibula
Tarsal
Metatarsal
Toe
Claw
Ambiens muscle
Femoro-tibial muscle
Anterior tibial muscle
Common digital extensor muscle

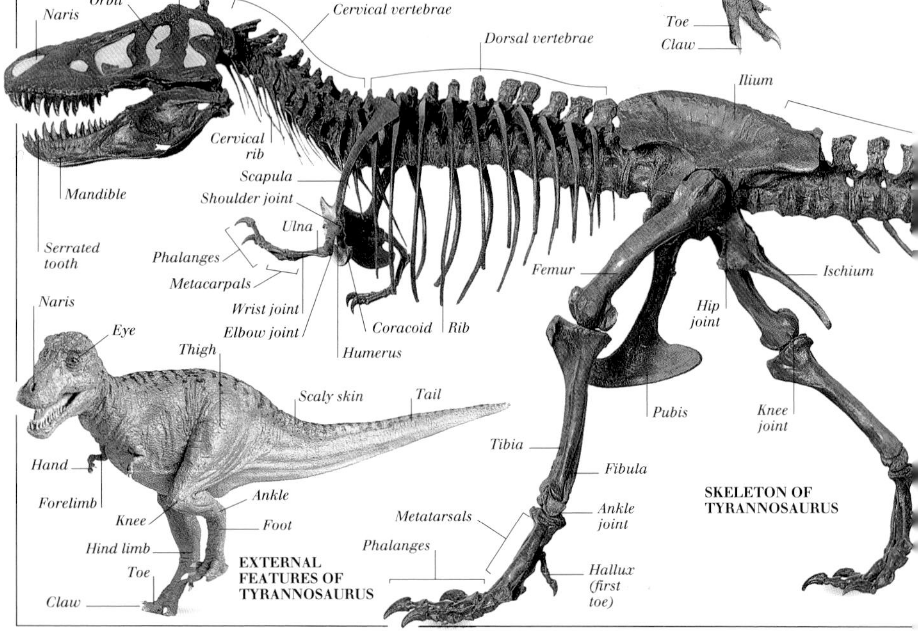
Cranium
Supraoccipital crest
Orbit
Naris
Cervical vertebrae
Dorsal vertebrae
Ilium
Cervical rib
Scapula
Mandible
Shoulder joint
Ulna
Serrated tooth
Phalanges
Metacarpals
Wrist joint
Elbow joint
Coracoid
Rib
Humerus
Femur
Ischium
Hip joint
Pubis
Knee joint
Tibia
Fibula
Metatarsals
Ankle joint
Phalanges
Hallux (first toe)

SKELETON OF TYRANNOSAURUS

Naris
Eye
Thigh
Scaly skin
Tail
Hand
Forelimb
Ankle
Knee
Foot
Hind limb
Toe
Claw

EXTERNAL FEATURES OF TYRANNOSAURUS

FOSSIL SKELETON OF ARCHAEOPTERYX

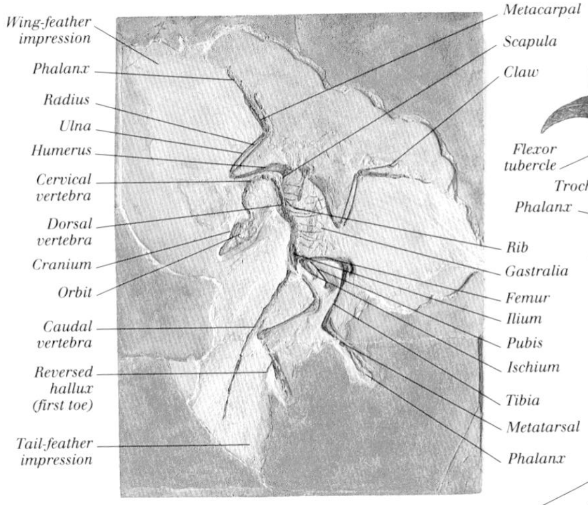
Wing-feather impression
Phalanx
Radius
Ulna
Humerus
Cervical vertebra
Dorsal vertebra
Cranium
Orbit
Caudal vertebra
Reversed hallux (first toe)
Tail-feather impression
Metacarpal
Scapula
Claw
Rib
Gastralia
Femur
Ilium
Pubis
Ischium
Tibia
Metatarsal
Phalanx

SKELETON OF BARYONYX HAND

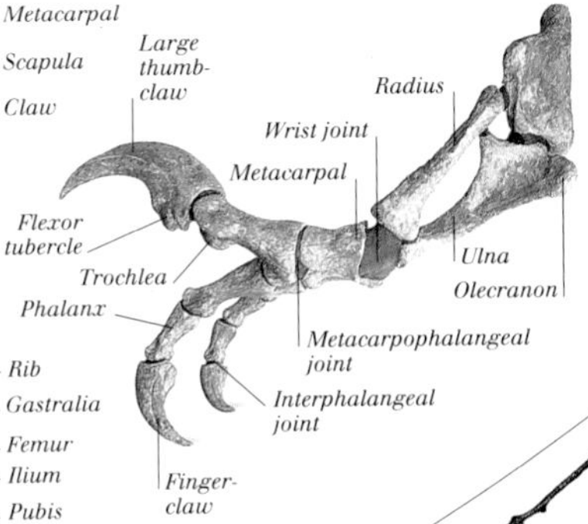
Large thumb-claw
Radius
Wrist joint
Metacarpal
Flexor tubercle
Trochlea
Ulna
Olecranon
Phalanx
Metacarpophalangeal joint
Interphalangeal joint
Finger-claw

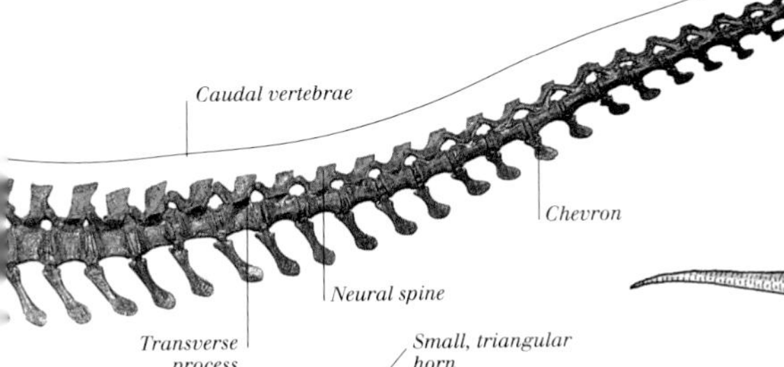
Caudal vertebrae
Chevron
Neural spine
Transverse process

EXAMPLES OF LARGE THEROPODS

EUSTREPTOSPONDYLUS
A megalosaurid
Length: 7 m (23 ft)

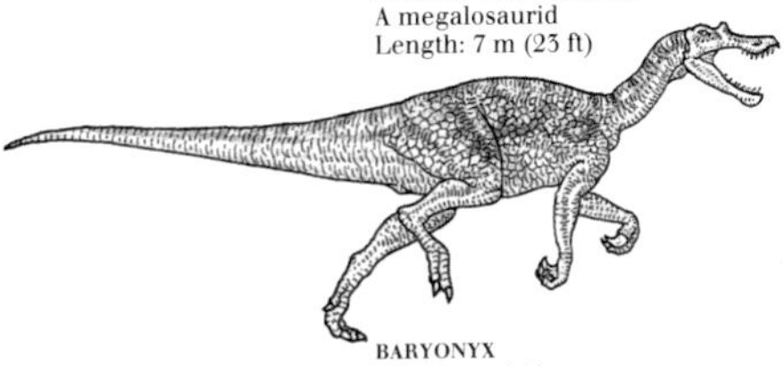

BARYONYX
A baryonychid
Length: 9.1 m (30 ft)

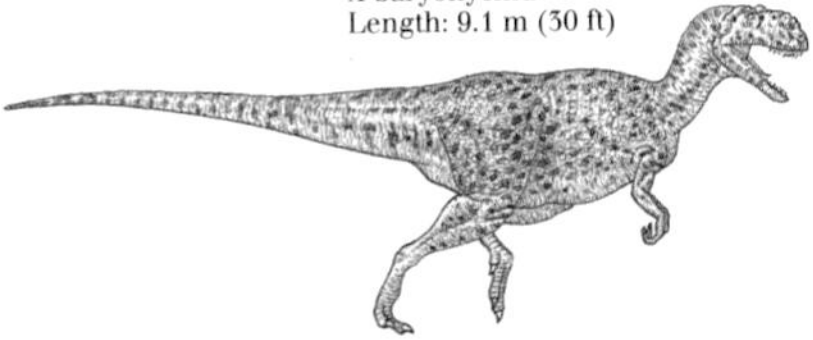

YANGCHUANOSAURUS
A ceratosaurid
Length: 10 m (33 ft)

Small, triangular horn
Eye
Elastic tissue
Curved serrated tooth
Tongue
Large, expansile jaw

HEAD OF ALLOSAURUS

Theropods 2

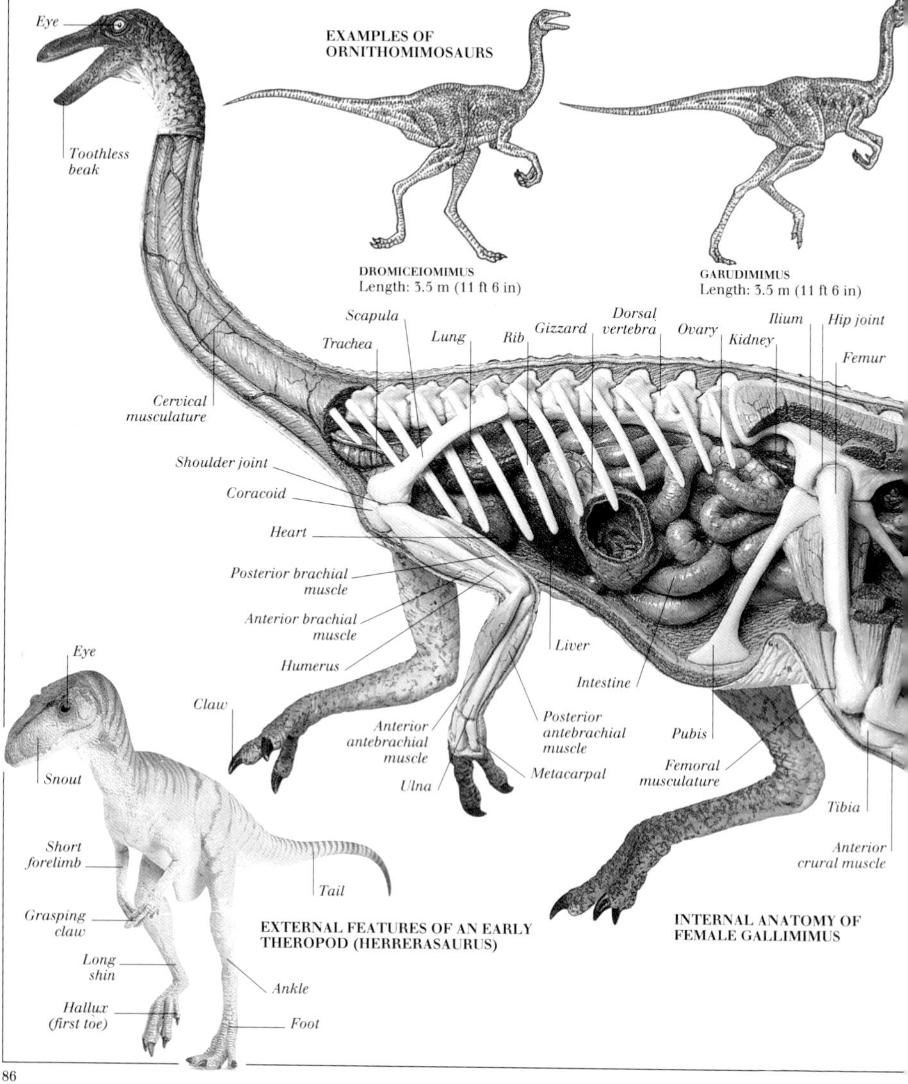
Eye
Toothless beak
Cervical musculature
Scapula
Trachea
Lung
Rib
Gizzard
Dorsal vertebra
Ovary
Kidney
Ilium
Hip joint
Femur
Shoulder joint
Coracoid
Heart
Posterior brachial muscle
Anterior brachial muscle
Humerus
Liver
Intestine
Claw
Anterior antebrachial muscle
Ulna
Posterior antebrachial muscle
Metacarpal
Pubis
Femoral musculature
Tibia
Anterior crural muscle
Eye
Snout
Short forelimb
Tail
Grasping claw
Long shin
Ankle
Hallux (first toe)
Foot

EXAMPLES OF ORNITHOMIMOSAURS

DROMICEIOMIMUS
Length: 3.5 m (11 ft 6 in)

GARUDIMIMUS
Length: 3.5 m (11 ft 6 in)

INTERNAL ANATOMY OF FEMALE GALLIMIMUS

EXTERNAL FEATURES OF AN EARLY THEROPOD (HERRERASAURUS)

EXAMPLES OF SMALL THEROPODS

STRUTHIOMIMUS
Length: 3.5 m (11 ft 6 in)

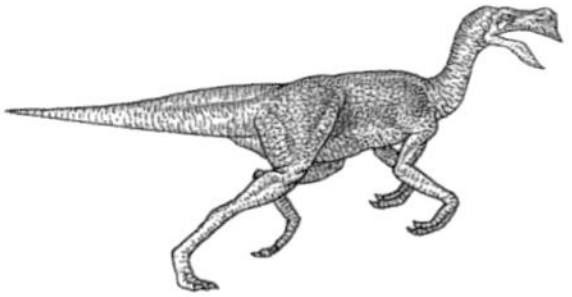

CHIROSTENOTES
Length: 2 m (6 ft 6 in)

AVIMIMUS
Length: 1.5 m (5 ft)

COELURUS
Length: 1.8 m (6 ft)

PROCOMPSOGNATHUS
Length: 1.2 m (4 ft)

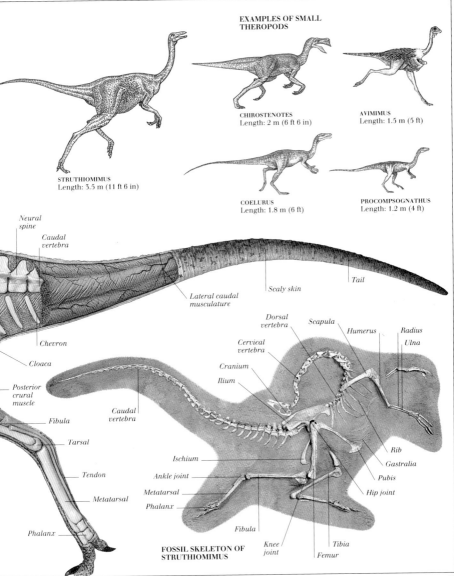

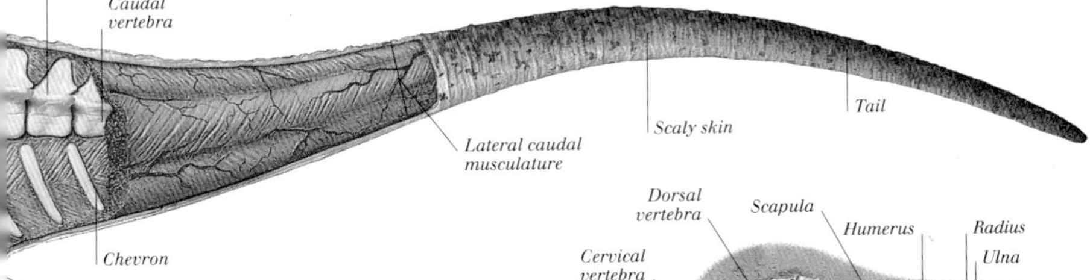
Neural spine
Caudal vertebra
Lateral caudal musculature
Scaly skin
Tail
Chevron
Cloaca

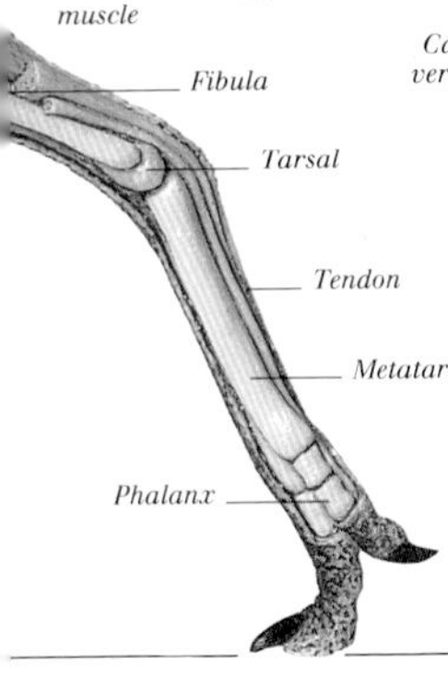
Posterior crural muscle
Fibula
Tarsal
Tendon
Metatarsal
Phalanx

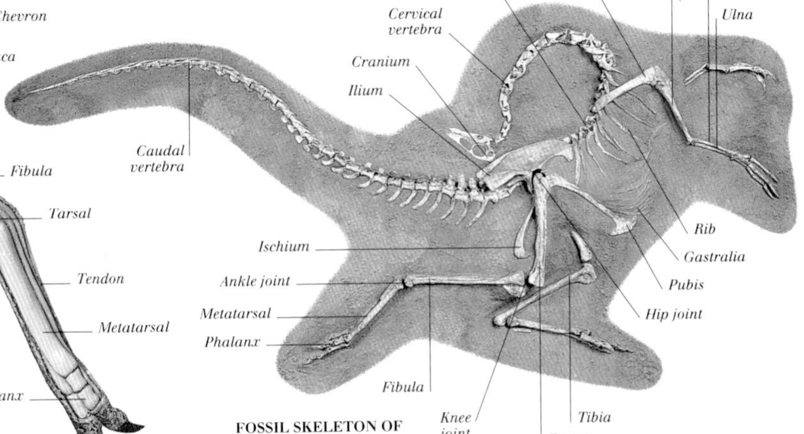
Dorsal vertebra
Scapula
Humerus
Radius
Ulna
Cervical vertebra
Cranium
Ilium
Caudal vertebra
Rib
Gastralia
Ischium
Pubis
Ankle joint
Metatarsal
Hip joint
Phalanx
Fibula
Knee joint
Tibia
Femur

FOSSIL SKELETON OF STRUTHIOMIMUS

Sauropodomorphs 1

THECODONTOSAURUS

THE SAUROPODOMORPHA ("lizard-feet forms") were herbivorous, usually quadrupedal (four-footed) dinosaurs. A suborder of the Saurischia, they were characterized by small heads, bulky bodies, and long necks and tails. There were two infraorders: prosauropods and sauropods. Prosauropods lived from Late Triassic to Early Jurassic times (225–180 million years ago) and included beasts such as the small *Anchisaurus* and one of the first very large dinosaurs, *Melanosaurus*. By Middle Jurassic times (about 165 million years ago), sauropods had replaced prosauropods and spread worldwide. They included the heaviest and longest land animals ever, such as *Diplodocus* and *Brachiosaurus*. Sauropods persisted to the end of the Cretaceous period (65 million years ago). Many of these dinosaurs moved in herds, protected from predatory theropods by their huge bulk and powerful tails, which they could use to lash out at attackers. Sauropodomorphs were the most common large herbivores until Late Jurassic times (about 145 million years ago), and appear to have survived in southern continents long after they had disappeared from the north.

SKULL AND MANDIBLE OF PLATEOSAURUS

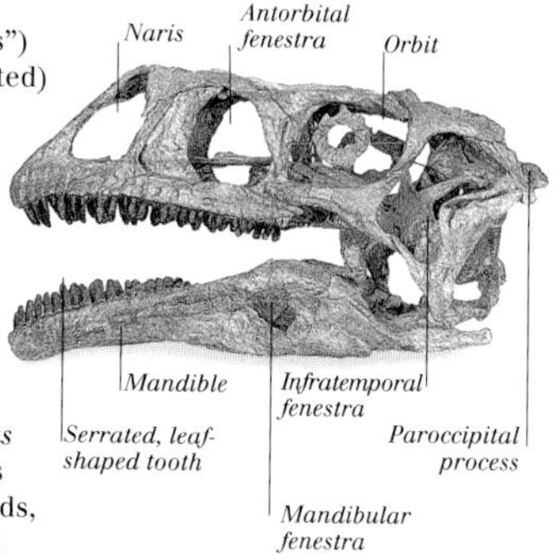
Naris
Antorbital fenestra
Orbit
Mandible
Infratemporal fenestra
Serrated, leaf-shaped tooth
Paroccipital process
Mandibular fenestra

SKELETON OF PLATEOSAURUS

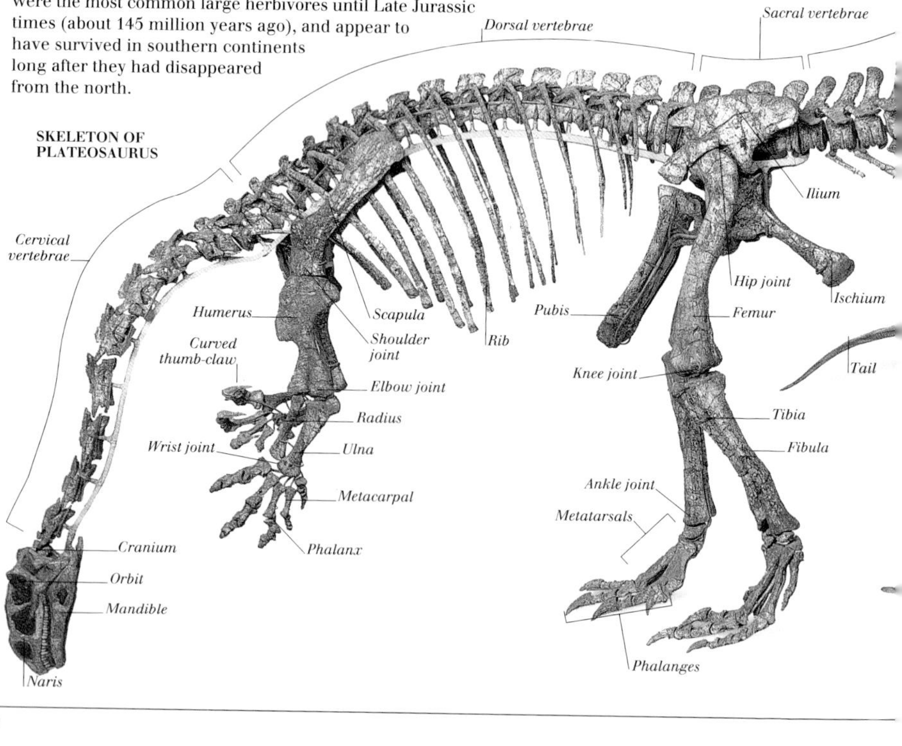
Dorsal vertebrae
Sacral vertebrae
Ilium
Cervical vertebrae
Hip joint
Ischium
Humerus
Scapula
Pubis
Femur
Curved thumb-claw
Shoulder joint
Rib
Tail
Knee joint
Elbow joint
Radius
Tibia
Wrist joint
Ulna
Fibula
Ankle joint
Metacarpal
Metatarsals
Cranium
Phalanx
Orbit
Mandible
Phalanges
Naris

THUMB-CLAW OF MASSOSPONDYLUS

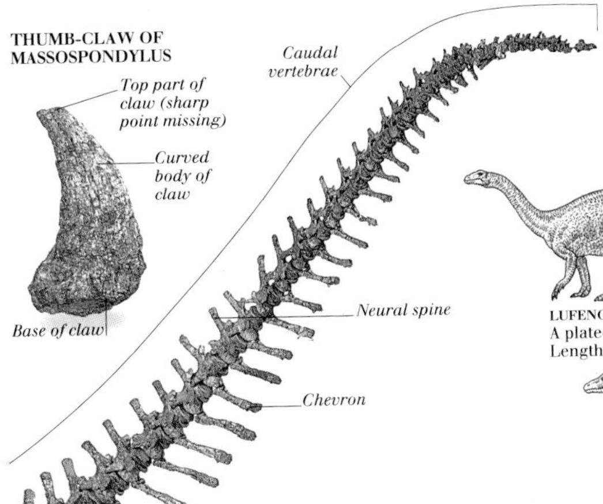
Top part of claw (sharp point missing)
Curved body of claw
Base of claw
Caudal vertebrae
Neural spine
Chevron
Transverse process

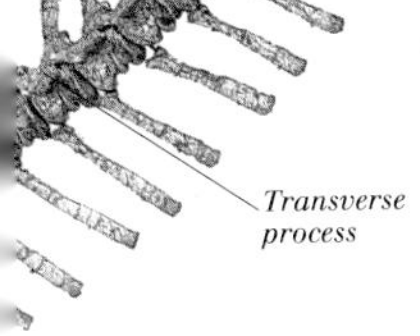

EXAMPLES OF PROSAUROPODS

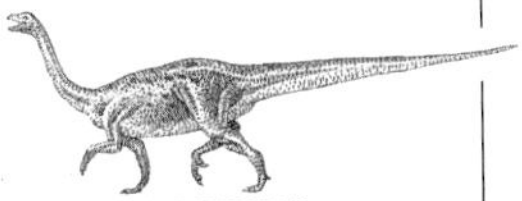

MASSOSPONDYLUS
A massospondylid
Length: 4 m (13 ft)

LUFENGOSAURUS
A plateosaurid
Length: 6.1 m (20 ft)

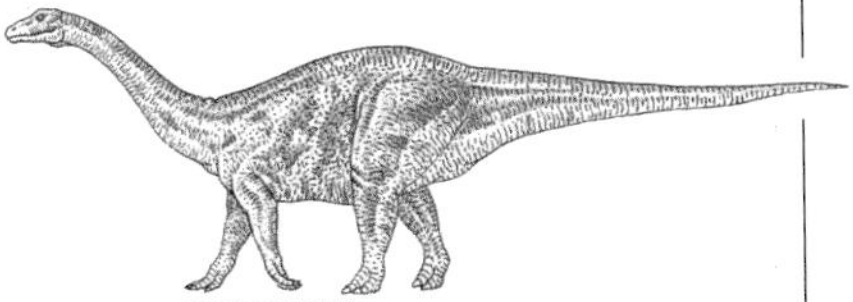

RIOJASAURUS
A melanorosaurid
Length: 11 m (36 ft)

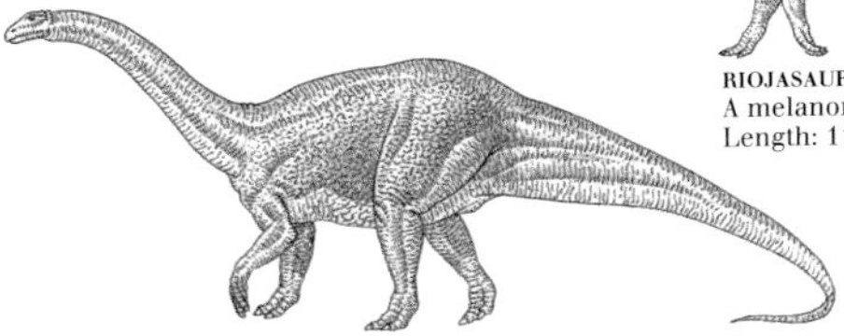

MELANOROSAURUS
A melanorosaurid
Length: 12.2 m (40 ft)

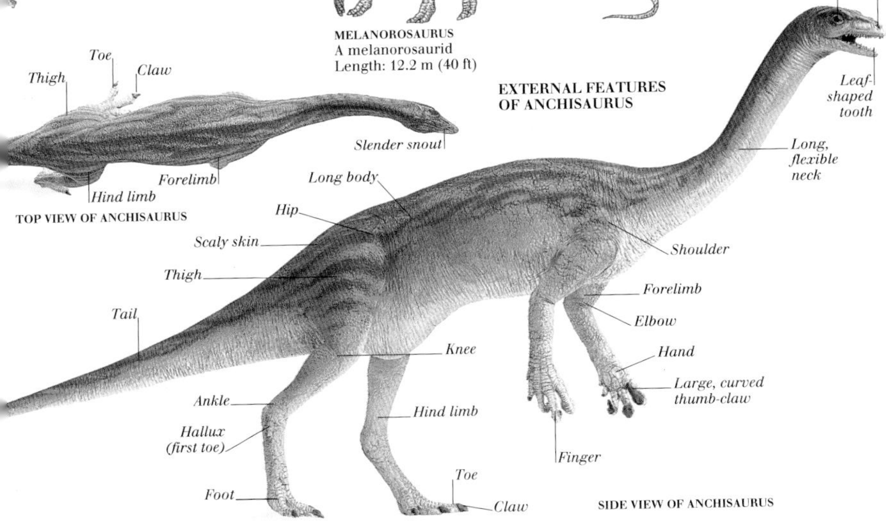
Toe
Claw
Thigh
Slender snout
Forelimb
Hind limb

TOP VIEW OF ANCHISAURUS

EXTERNAL FEATURES OF ANCHISAURUS

Naris
Eye
Leaf-shaped tooth
Long, flexible neck
Long body
Hip
Shoulder
Scaly skin
Thigh
Forelimb
Elbow
Tail
Knee
Hand
Large, curved thumb-claw
Ankle
Hind limb
Hallux (first toe)
Finger
Toe
Foot
Claw

SIDE VIEW OF ANCHISAURUS

Sauropodomorphs 2

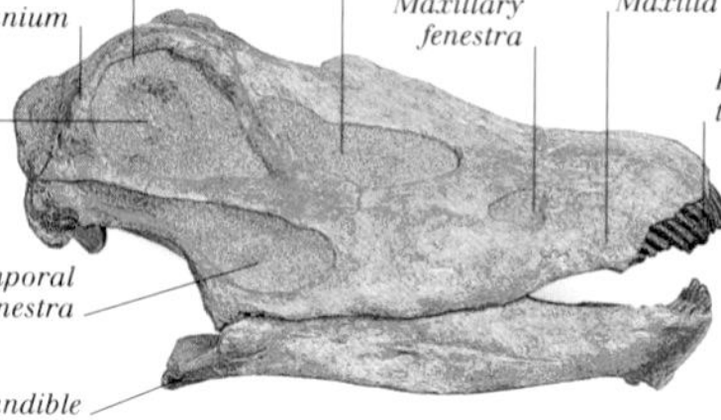
Orbit
Antorbital fenestra
Cranium
Maxillary fenestra
Maxilla
Peg-shaped tooth
Sclerotic ring
Infratemporal fenestra
Mandible

SKULL AND MANDIBLE OF DIPLODOCUS

FOREFOOT OF ELEPHANT

Wrist
Nail

FOREFOOT BONES OF ELEPHANT

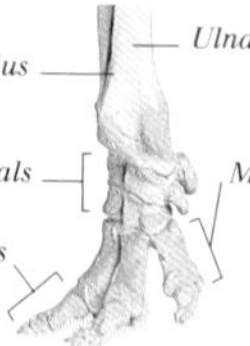
Ulna
Radius
Carpals
Metacarpa
Phalanges

COMPARISON OF THE FOREFEET OF AN ELEPHANT AND DIPLODOCUS

FOREFOOT BONES OF DIPLODOCUS

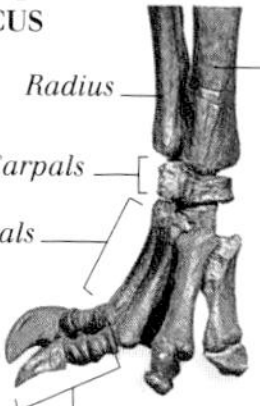
Ulna
Radius
Carpals
Metacarpals
Phalanges

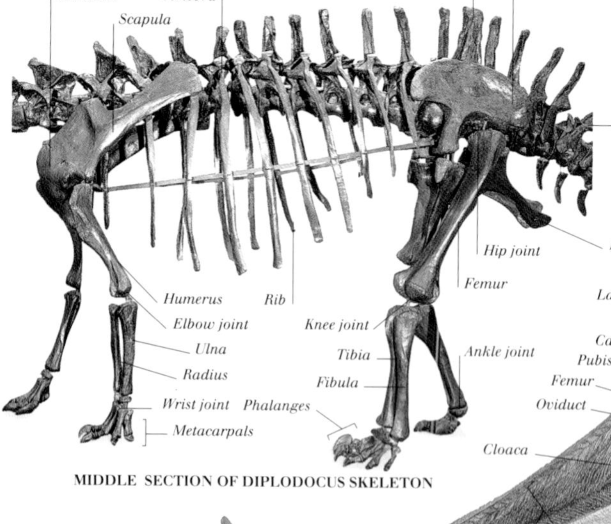
Coracoid
Dorsal vertebra
Scapula
Sacral vertebra
Ilium
Caudal vertebra
Ischium
Hip joint
Femur
Humerus
Rib
Elbow joint
Knee joint
Ulna
Tibia
Ankle joint
Radius
Fibula
Wrist joint
Phalanges
Metacarpals

MIDDLE SECTION OF DIPLODOCUS SKELETON

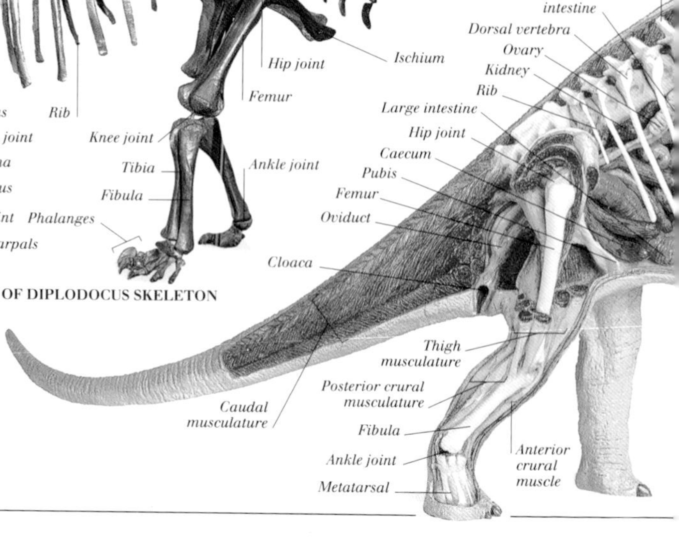
Neural spine
Small intestine
Dorsal vertebra
Ovary
Kidney
Rib
Large intestine
Hip joint
Caecum
Pubis
Femur
Oviduct
Cloaca
Thigh musculature
Posterior crural musculature
Caudal musculature
Fibula
Ankle joint
Metatarsal
Anterior crural muscle

FOSSIL EGG OF TITANOSAURID

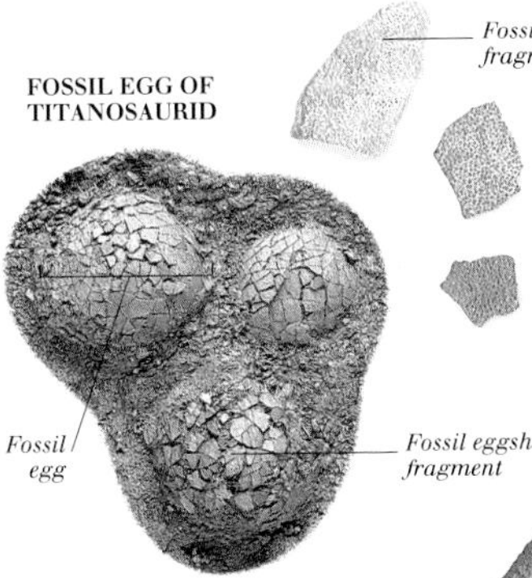
Fossil eggshell fragment
Fossil egg
Fossil eggshell fragment

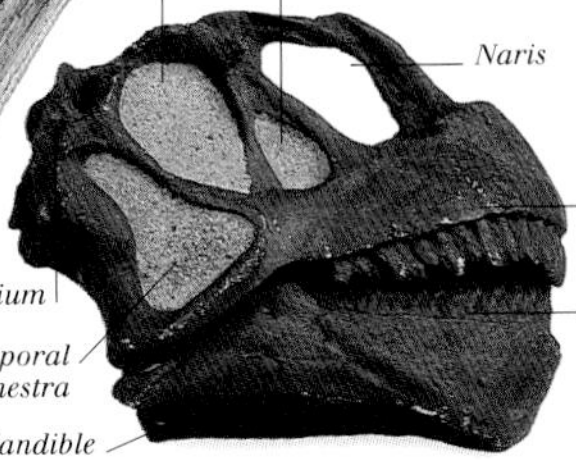
Orbit
Antorbital fenestra
Naris
Maxilla
Cranium
Spoon-shaped tooth
Infratemporal fenestra
Mandible

SKULL AND MANDIBLE OF CAMARASAURUS

INTERNAL ANATOMY OF FEMALE BRACHIOSAURUS

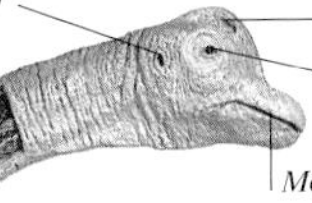
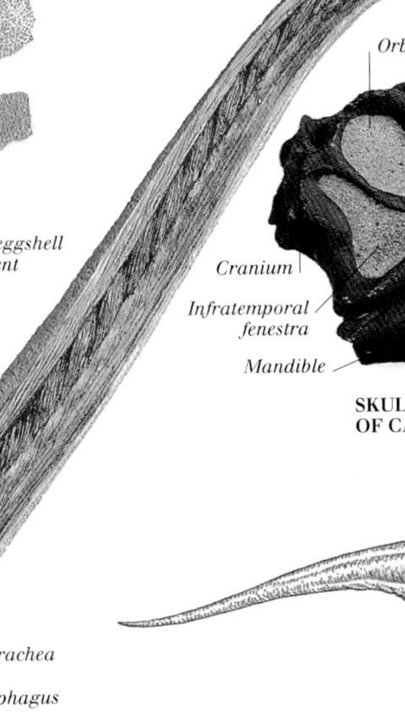
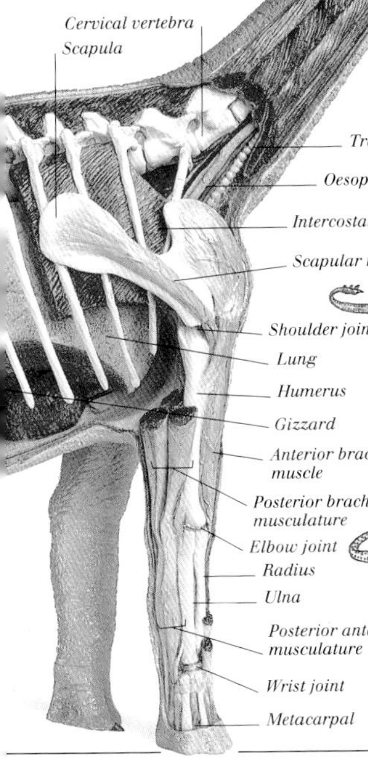
Outer ear
Naris
Eye
Mouth
Cervical vertebra
Scapula
Trachea
Oesophagus
Intercostal muscle
Scapular muscle
Shoulder joint
Lung
Humerus
Gizzard
Anterior brachial muscle
Posterior brachial musculature
Elbow joint
Radius
Ulna
Posterior antebrachial musculature
Wrist joint
Metacarpal

CETIOSAURUS
A cetiosaurid
Length: 18 m (59 ft)

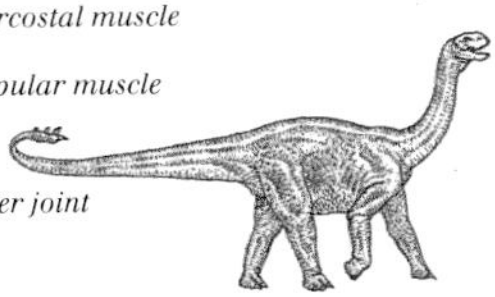

SHUNOSAURUS
A cetiosaurid
Length: 10 m (33 ft)

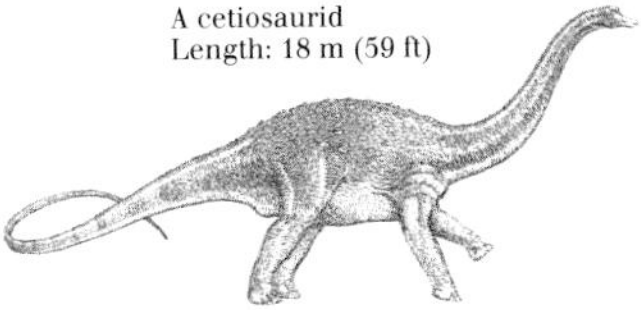

SALTASAURUS
A titanosaurid
Length: 12.2 m (40 ft)

DIPLODOCUS
A diplodocid
Length: 27.4 m (90 ft)

Thyreophorans 1

THYREOPHORANS ("SHIELD BEARERS") were a group of quadrupedal armoured dinosaurs. A sub-order of the Ornithischia (bird-hipped dinosaurs), they were characterized by rows of bony studs, plates, or spikes along the back, which protected some from predators and may have helped others regulate body temperature. Up to 9m (30ft) long, with a small head and small cheek teeth, Thyreophorans had shorter forelimbs than hind limbs and probably browsed on low-level vegetation. The earliest thyreophorans were small and lived in Early Jurassic times (about 200 million years ago) in Europe, North America, and China. Stegosaurs, such as *Stegosaurus* and *Kentrosaurus*, replaced these older forms. The earliest stegosaur remains come from England and China. Several genera of stegosaurs survived into the Early Cretaceous period (146–100 million years ago), but only in India did they persist into Late Cretaceous times (97–65 million years ago). Ankylosaurs, with their toothless beaks and cheek teeth adapted for cropping vegetation, appeared later than stegosaurs. They originated in the Late Jurassic period (155 million years ago) and in North America survived until the extinction of the dinosaurs, 65 million years ago.

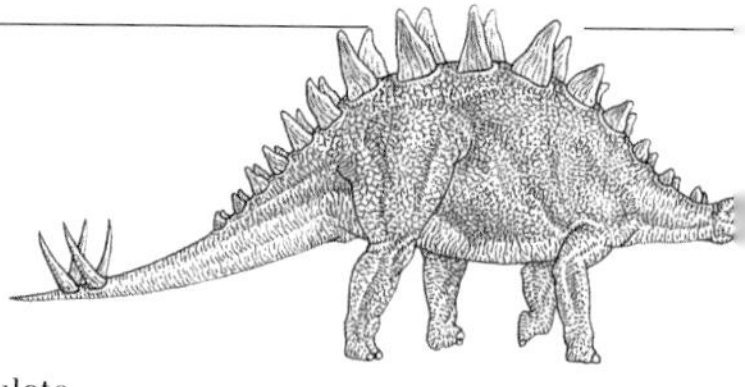

TUOJIANGOSAURUS
A stegosaurid
Length: 7 m (23 ft)

Dorsal plate
Caudal plate
Small head
Caudal spike
Beak
Cervical plate
Hind foot
Scaly skin

TOP VIEW OF STEGOSAURUS

EXTERNAL FEATURES OF STEGOSAURUS

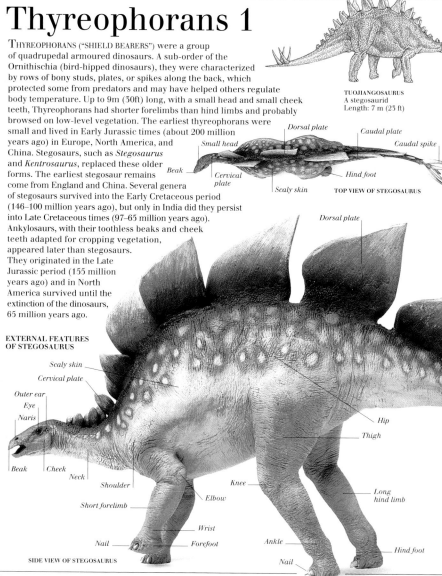

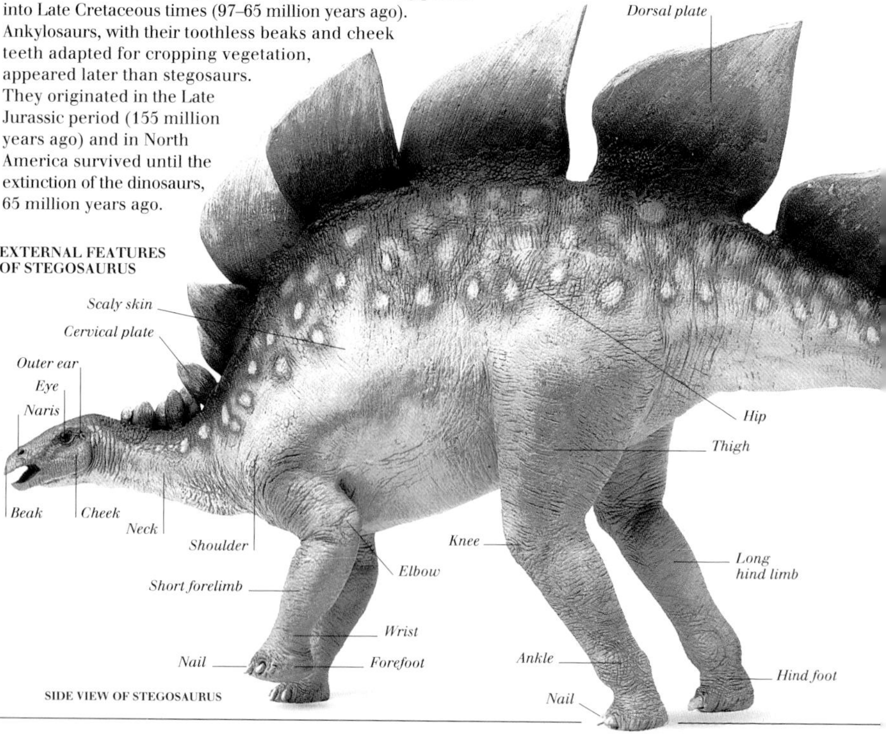

Dorsal plate
Scaly skin
Cervical plate
Outer ear
Eye
Naris
Hip
Thigh
Beak
Cheek
Neck
Shoulder
Knee
Elbow
Long hind limb
Short forelimb
Wrist
Nail
Forefoot
Ankle
Hind foot
Nail

SIDE VIEW OF STEGOSAURUS

EXAMPLES OF STEGOSAURS

HUAYANGOSAURUS
A huayangosaurid
Length: 4 m (13 ft)

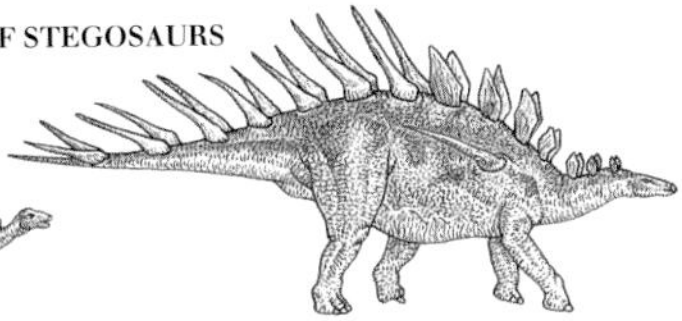

KENTROSAURUS
A stegosaurid
Length: 4.9 m (16 ft)

WUERHOSAURUS
A stegosaurid
Length: 6.1 m (20 ft)

DORSAL PLATE OF STEGOSAURUS

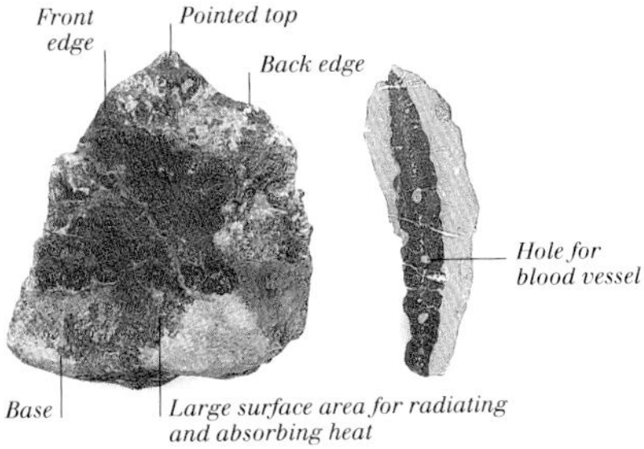
Front edge
Pointed top
Back edge
Hole for blood vessel
Base
Large surface area for radiating and absorbing heat

SIDE VIEW OF DORSAL PLATE

SECTION THROUGH DORSAL PLATE

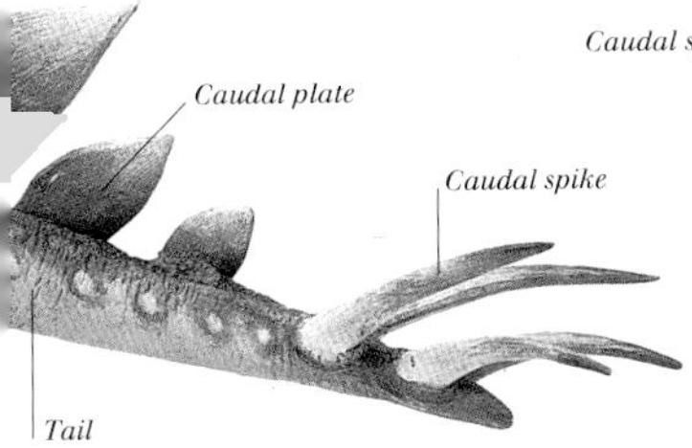
Caudal plate
Caudal spike
Tail

EXAMPLES OF STEGOSAUR SKELETONS

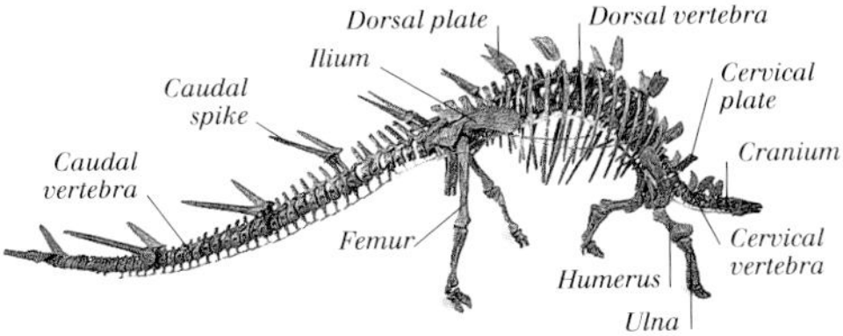
Dorsal plate
Dorsal vertebra
Ilium
Cervical plate
Caudal spike
Cranium
Caudal vertebra
Cervical vertebra
Femur
Humerus
Ulna

KENTROSAURUS

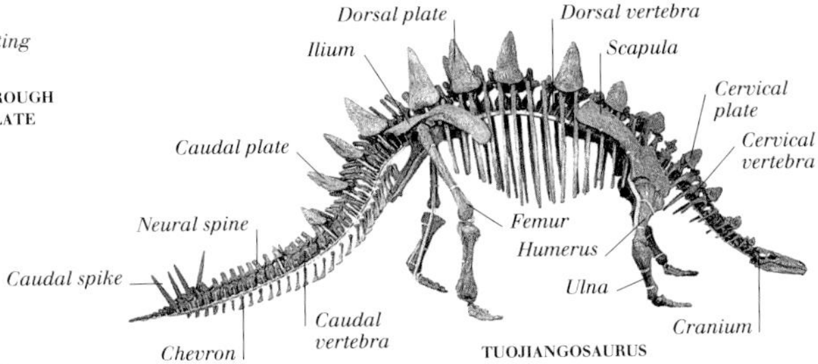
Dorsal plate
Dorsal vertebra
Ilium
Scapula
Cervical plate
Caudal plate
Cervical vertebra
Neural spine
Femur
Humerus
Caudal spike
Ulna
Caudal vertebra
Cranium
Chevron

TUOJIANGOSAURUS

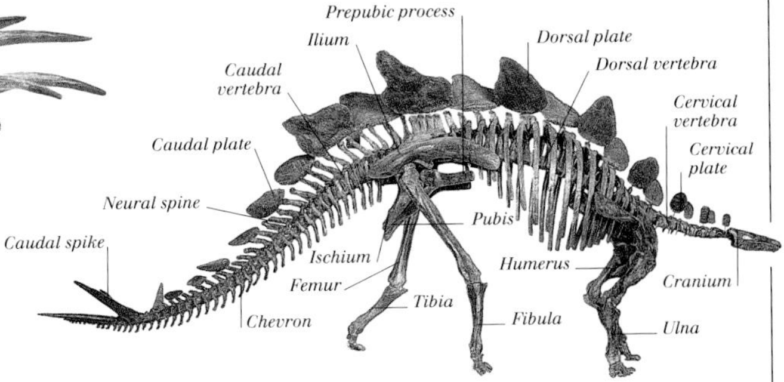
Prepubic process
Ilium
Dorsal plate
Dorsal vertebra
Caudal vertebra
Cervical vertebra
Caudal plate
Cervical plate
Neural spine
Pubis
Caudal spike
Ischium
Humerus
Cranium
Femur
Tibia
Fibula
Chevron
Ulna

STEGOSAURUS

Thyreophorans 2

EXAMPLES OF ANKYLOSAUR SKULLS

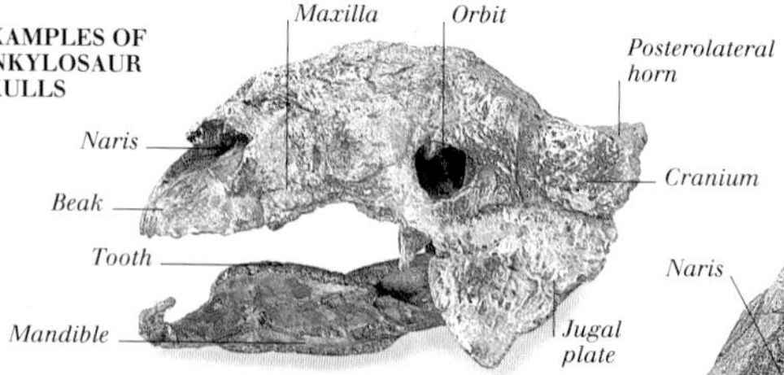
Maxilla
Orbit
Posterolateral horn
Naris
Cranium
Beak
Tooth
Mandible
Jugal plate

SKULL AND MANDIBLE OF EUOPLOCEPHALUS

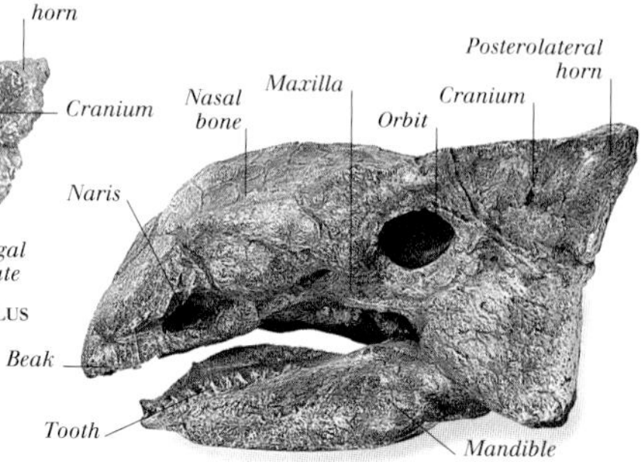
Posterolateral horn
Maxilla
Cranium
Nasal bone
Orbit
Naris
Beak
Tooth
Mandible

SKULL AND MANDIBLE OF ANKYLOSAURUS

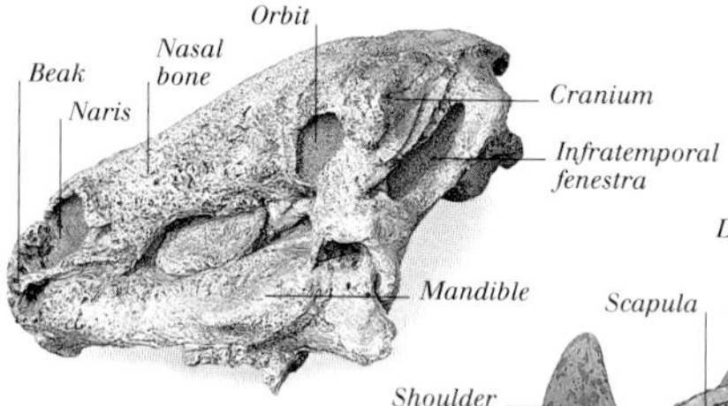
Orbit
Nasal bone
Beak
Naris
Cranium
Infratemporal fenestra
Mandible

SKULL AND MANDIBLE OF PANOPLOSAURUS

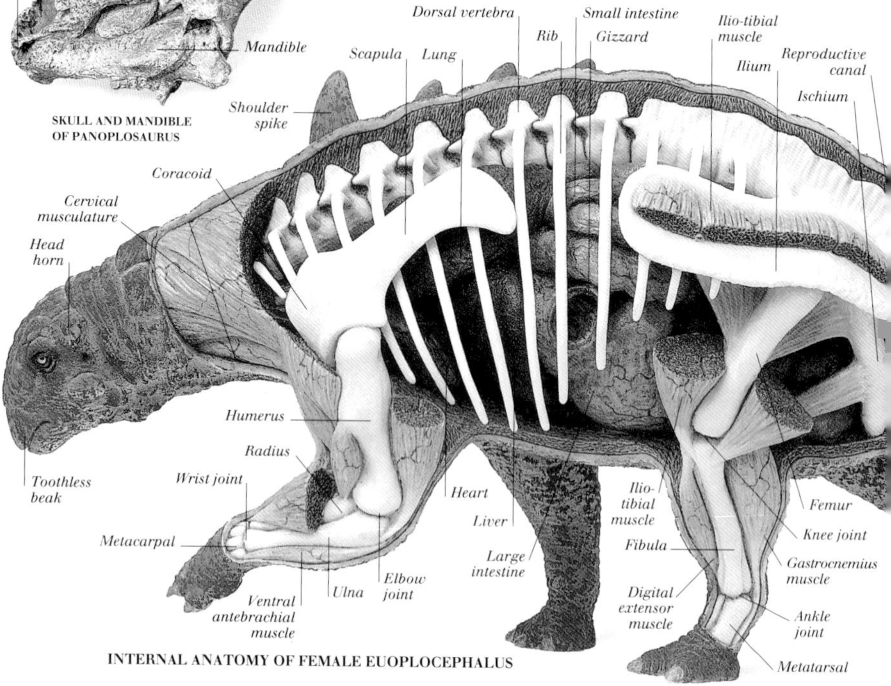
Dorsal vertebra
Small intestine
Rib
Gizzard
Ilio-tibial muscle
Scapula
Lung
Reproductive canal
Ilium
Ischium
Shoulder spike
Coracoid
Cervical musculature
Head horn
Humerus
Radius
Toothless beak
Wrist joint
Heart
Ilio-tibial muscle
Femur
Liver
Knee joint
Metacarpal
Fibula
Large intestine
Gastrocnemius muscle
Elbow joint
Ulna
Ventral antebrachial muscle
Digital extensor muscle
Ankle joint
Metatarsal

INTERNAL ANATOMY OF FEMALE EUOPLOCEPHALUS

EXTERNAL FEATURES OF EDMONTONIA

Hind limb
Flank spike
Dorsal scute
Dermal armour
Scaly skin
Nuchal ring
Shoulder spike
Broad, flat snout
Naris
Ankle
Elbow
Forelimb
Forefoot
Blunt nail

EXAMPLES OF ANKYLOSAURS

PINACOSAURUS
An ankylosaurid
Length: 5 m (16 ft 6 in)

MINMI
A nodosaurid
Length: 2.4 m (8 ft)

POLACANTHUS
A nodosaurid
Length: 4 m (13 ft)

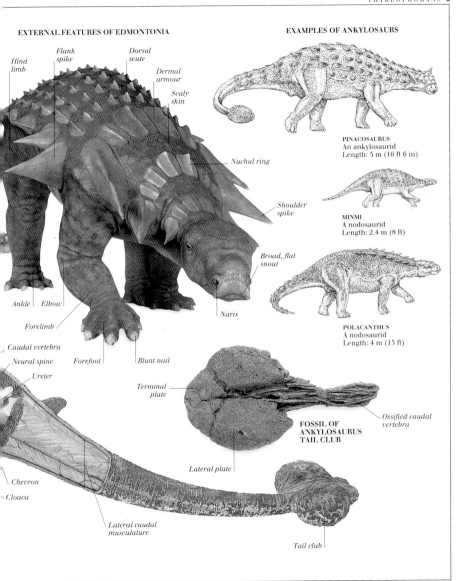

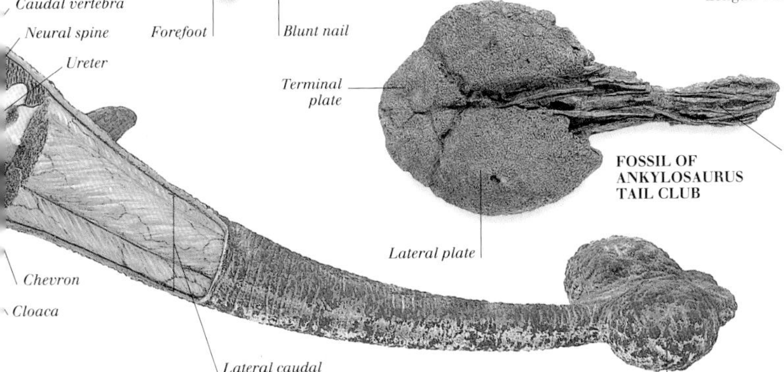
Terminal plate
Ossified caudal vertebra
Lateral plate
Caudal vertebra
Neural spine
Ureter
Chevron
Cloaca
Lateral caudal musculature
Tail club

FOSSIL OF ANKYLOSAURUS TAIL CLUB

Ornithopods 1

IGUANODON TOOTH

ORNITHOPODS ("BIRD FEET") were a group of ornithischian ("bird-hipped") dinosaurs. These bipedal and quadrupedal herbivores had a horny beak, plant-cutting or grinding cheek teeth, and a pelvic and tail region stiffened by bony tendons. They evolved teeth and jaws adapted to pulping vegetation and flourished from the Middle Jurassic to the Late Cretaceous period (165–65 million years ago) in North America, Europe, Africa, China, Australia, and Antarctica. Some ornithopods were no larger than a dog, while others were immense creatures up to 15 m (49 ft) long. Iguanodonts, an ornithopod group, had a broad, toothless beak at the end of a long snout, large jaws with long rows of ridged, closely packed teeth for grinding vegetation, a bulky body, and a heavy tail. *Iguanodon* and some other iguanodonts had large thumb-spikes that were strong enough to stab attackers. Another group, the hadrosaurs, such as *Gryposaurus* and *Hadrosaurus*, lived in Late Cretaceous times (97–65 million years ago) and with their broad beaks are sometimes known as "duckbills". They were characterized by their deep skulls and closely packed rows of teeth, while some, such as *Corythosaurus* and *Lambeosaurus*, had tall, hollow, bony head crests.

SKELETON OF IGUANODON

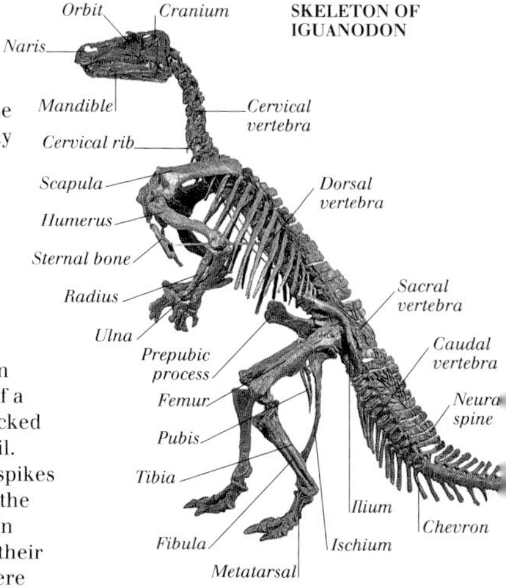
Orbit
Cranium
Naris
Mandible
Cervical vertebra
Cervical rib
Scapula
Dorsal vertebra
Humerus
Sternal bone
Sacral vertebra
Radius
Ulna
Caudal vertebra
Prepubic process
Femur
Neura spine
Pubis
Tibia
Ilium
Chevron
Fibula
Ischium
Metatarsal

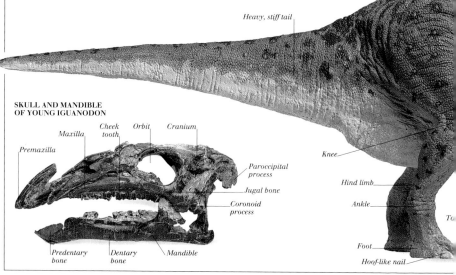

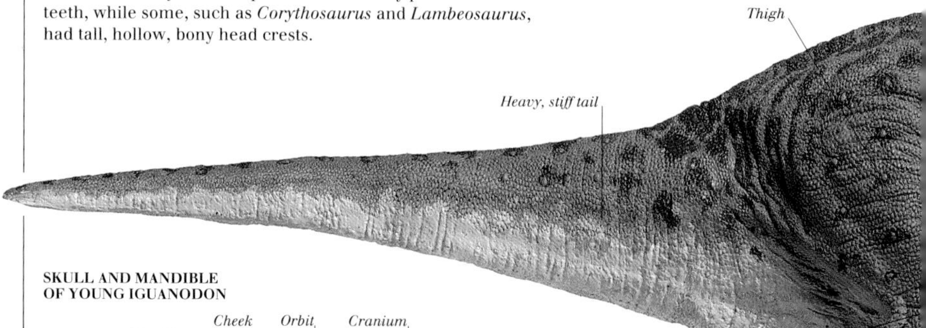
Thigh
Heavy, stiff tail
Knee
Hind limb
Ankle
To
Foot
Hoof-like nail

SKULL AND MANDIBLE OF YOUNG IGUANODON

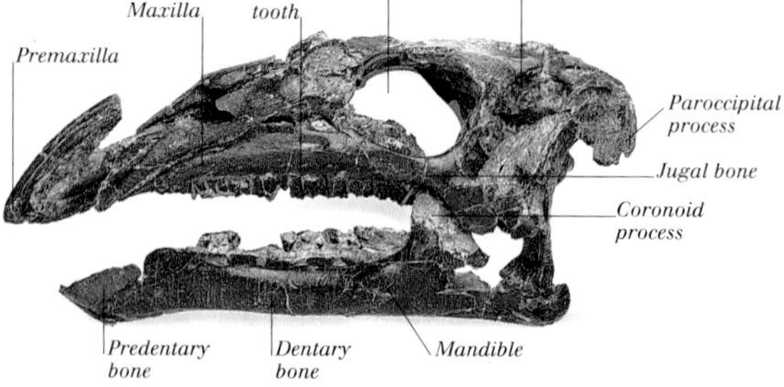
Cheek tooth
Orbit
Cranium
Maxilla
Premaxilla
Paroccipital process
Jugal bone
Coronoid process
Predentary bone
Dentary bone
Mandible

EXAMPLES OF IGUANODONTS

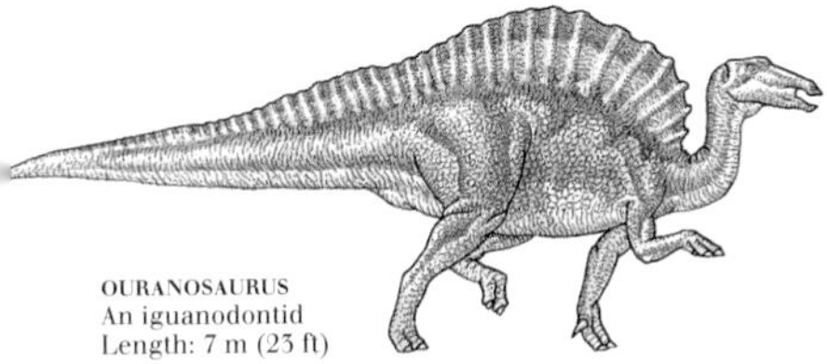

OURANOSAURUS
An iguanodontid
Length: 7 m (23 ft)

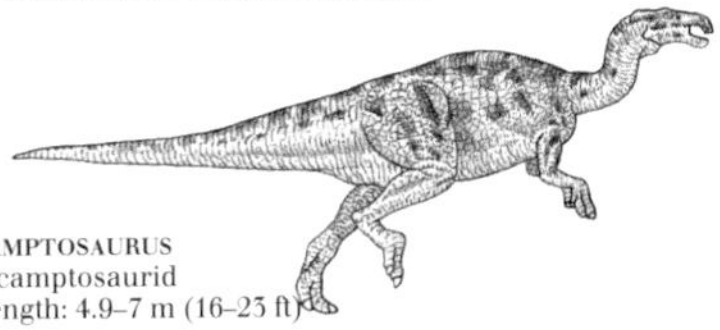

CAMPTOSAURUS
A camptosaurid
Length: 4.9–7 m (16–23 ft)

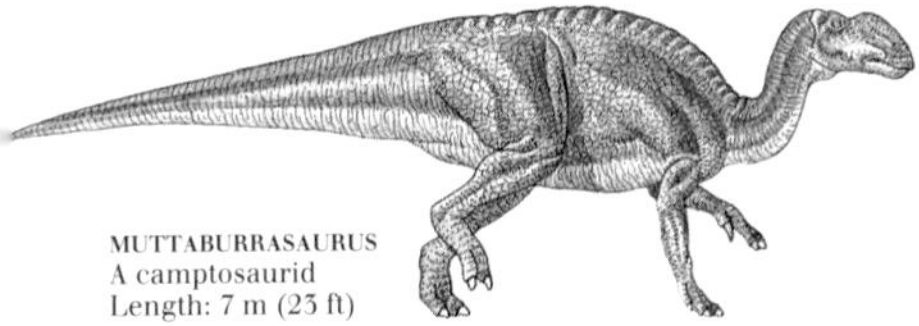

MUTTABURRASAURUS
A camptosaurid
Length: 7 m (23 ft)

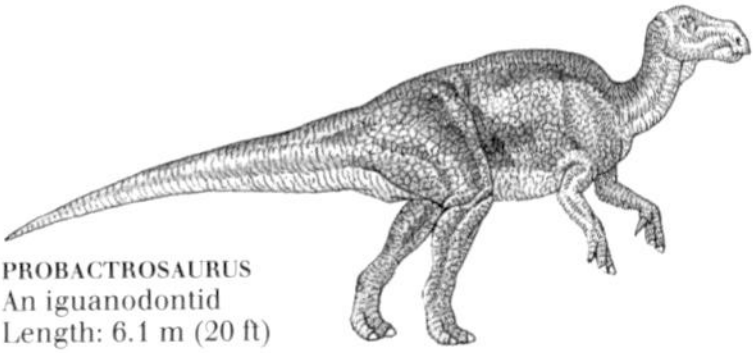

PROBACTROSAURUS
An iguanodontid
Length: 6.1 m (20 ft)

EXTERNAL FEATURES OF IGUANODON

Eye
Naris
Shoulder
Neck
Tongue
Beak
Scaly skin
Forelimb
Elbow
Thumb-spike
Wrist
Hand
Finger
Hoof-like nail

INTERNAL ANATOMY OF HIND LEG OF IGUANODON

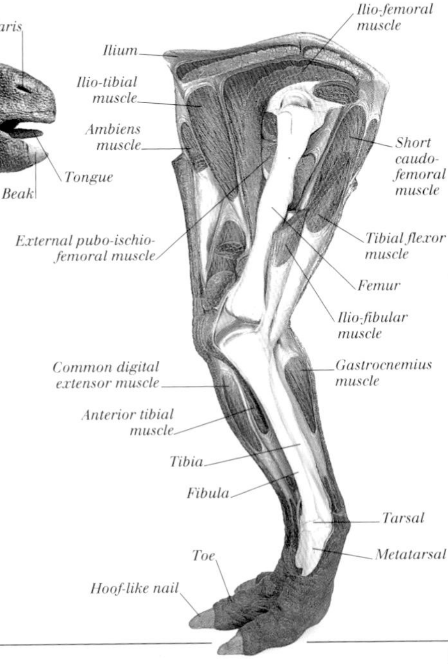
Ilio-femoral muscle
Ilium
Ilio-tibial muscle
Ambiens muscle
Short caudo-femoral muscle
External pubo-ischio-femoral muscle
Tibial flexor muscle
Femur
Ilio-fibular muscle
Common digital extensor muscle
Gastrocnemius muscle
Anterior tibial muscle
Tibia
Fibula
Tarsal
Toe
Metatarsal
Hoof-like nail

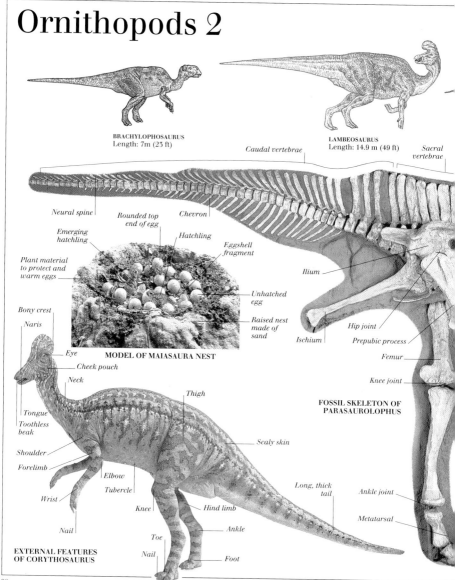

Ornithopods 2

BRACHYLOPHOSAURUS
Length: 7m (23 ft)

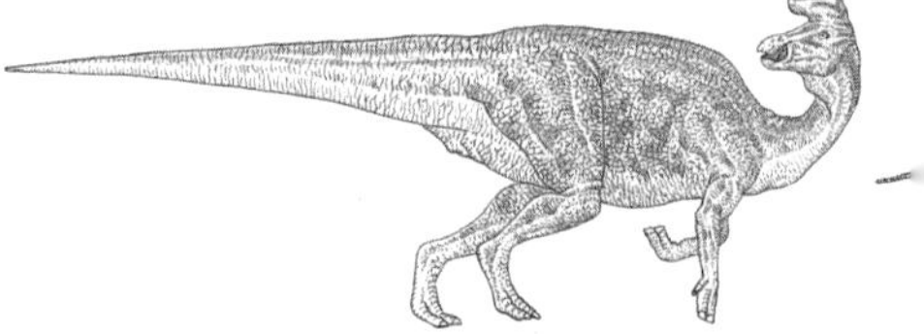

LAMBEOSAURUS
Length: 14.9 m (49 ft)

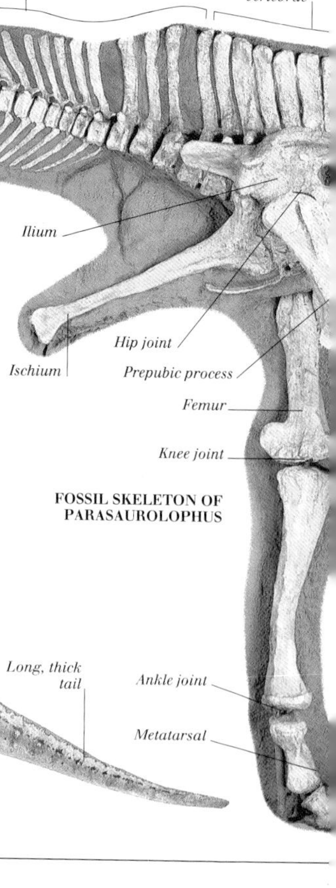
Caudal vertebrae
Sacral vertebrae
Neural spine
Chevron
Ilium
Ischium
Hip joint
Prepubic process
Femur
Knee joint
Ankle joint
Metatarsal

FOSSIL SKELETON OF PARASAUROLOPHUS

Rounded top end of egg
Emerging hatchling
Hatchling
Eggshell fragment
Plant material to protect and warm eggs
Unhatched egg
Raised nest made of sand

MODEL OF MAIASAURA NEST

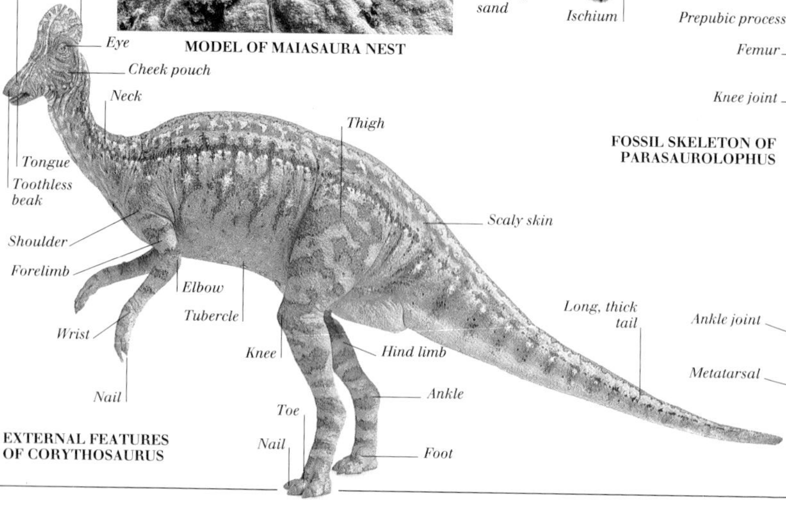
Bony crest
Naris
Eye
Cheek pouch
Neck
Thigh
Tongue
Toothless beak
Scaly skin
Shoulder
Forelimb
Elbow
Tubercle
Wrist
Long, thick tail
Knee
Hind limb
Nail
Ankle
Toe
Nail
Foot

EXTERNAL FEATURES OF CORYTHOSAURUS

EXAMPLES OF HADROSAURS

HYPACROSAURUS
Length: 9.1 m (30 ft)

HADROSAURUS
Length: 7.9–10 m (26–33 ft)

GRYPOSAURUS
Length: 7.9–10 m (26–33 ft)

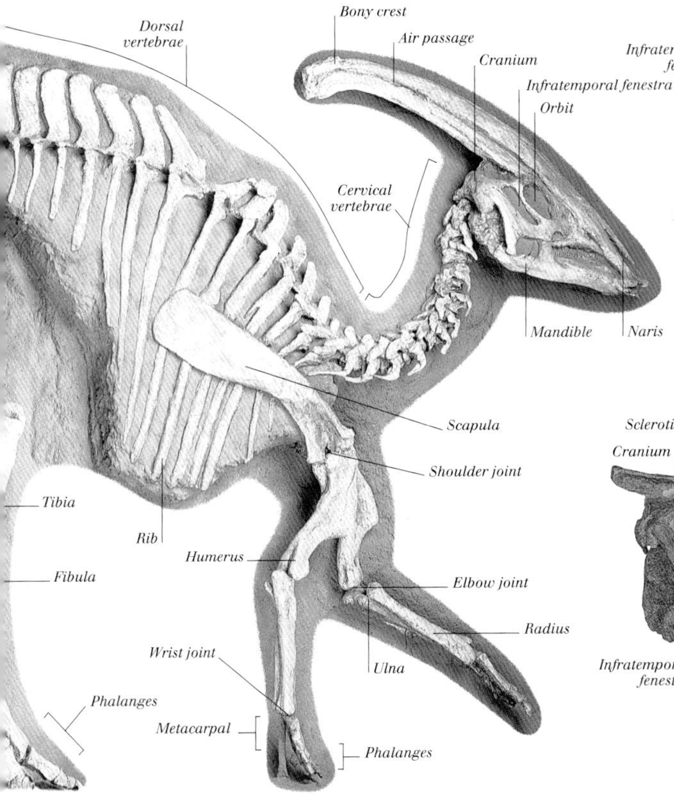
Dorsal vertebrae
Bony crest
Air passage
Cranium
Infratemporal fenestra
Orbit
Cervical vertebrae
Mandible
Naris
Scapula
Shoulder joint
Tibia
Rib
Humerus
Fibula
Elbow joint
Radius
Wrist joint
Ulna
Phalanges
Metacarpal
Phalanges

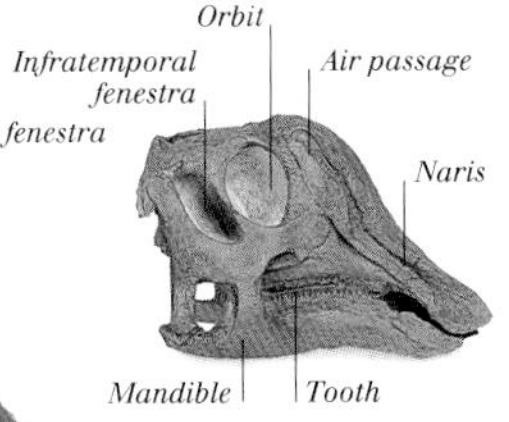
Orbit
Infratemporal fenestra
Air passage
Naris
Mandible
Tooth

SKULL AND MANDIBLE OF JUVENILE LAMBEOSAURUS

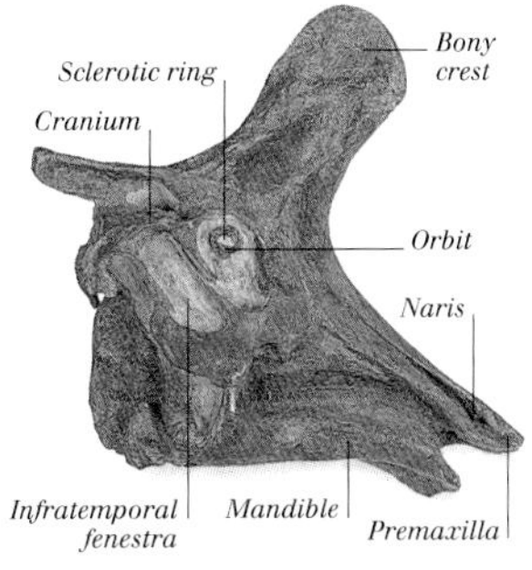
Bony crest
Sclerotic ring
Cranium
Orbit
Naris
Infratemporal fenestra
Mandible
Premaxilla

SKULL AND MANDIBLE OF ADULT LAMBEOSAURUS

Marginocephalians 1

HEAD-BUTTING PRENOCEPHALES

MARGINOCEPHALIA ("margined heads") were a group of bipedal and quadrupedal ornithischian dinosaurs with a narrow shelf or deep, bony frill at the back of the skull. Marginocephalians were probably descended from the same ancestor as the ornithopods and lived in what are now North America, Africa, Asia, and Europe during the Cretaceous period (146–65 million years ago). They were divided into two infraorders: Pachycephalosauria ("thick-headed lizards"), such as *Pachycephalosaurus* and *Stegoceras*, and Ceratopsia ("horned faces"), such as *Triceratops* and *Psittacosaurus*. The thick skulls of Pachycephalosauria protected their brains during head-butting contests fought to win territory and mates; their hips and spines were also strengthened to withstand the shock. The bony frill of Ceratopsia would have added to their frightening appearance when charging; the neck was strengthened for impact and to support the huge head, with its snipping beak and powerful slicing toothed jaws. A charging ceratops would have been a formidable opponent for even the largest predators. Ceratopsia were among the most abundant herbivorous dinosaurs of the Late Cretaceous period (97–65 million years ago).

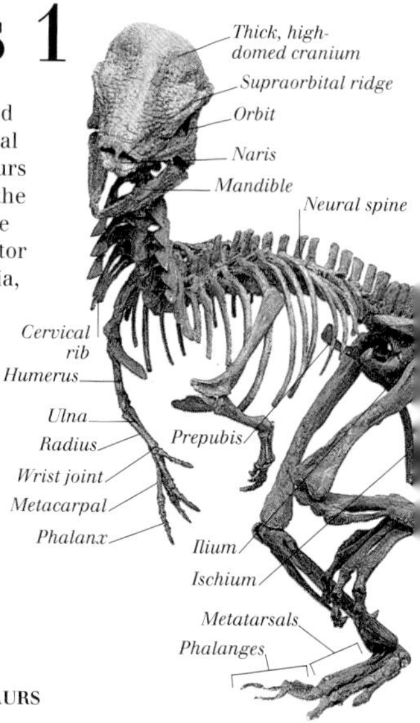
Thick, high-domed cranium
Supraorbital ridge
Orbit
Naris
Mandible
Neural spine
Cervical rib
Humerus
Ulna
Radius
Wrist joint
Metacarpal
Phalanx
Prepubis
Ilium
Ischium
Metatarsals
Phalanges

EXAMPLES OF SKULLS OF PACHYCEPHALOSAURS

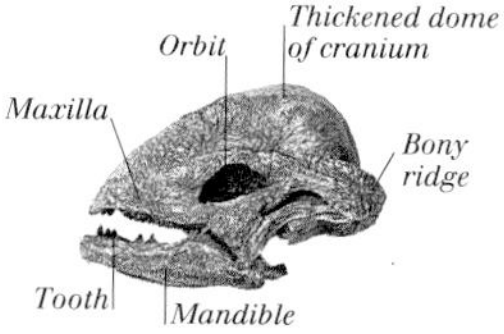
Thickened dome of cranium
Orbit
Maxilla
Bony ridge
Tooth
Mandible

SKULL AND MANDIBLE OF STEGOCERAS

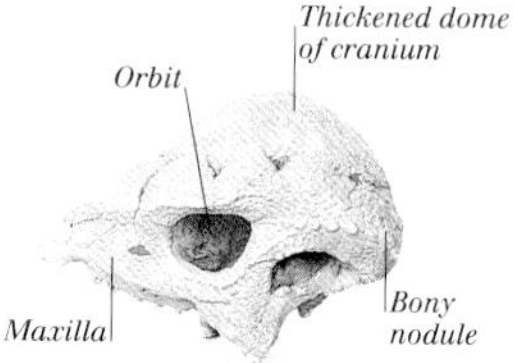
Thickened dome of cranium
Orbit
Maxilla
Bony nodule

SKULL OF PRENOCEPHALE

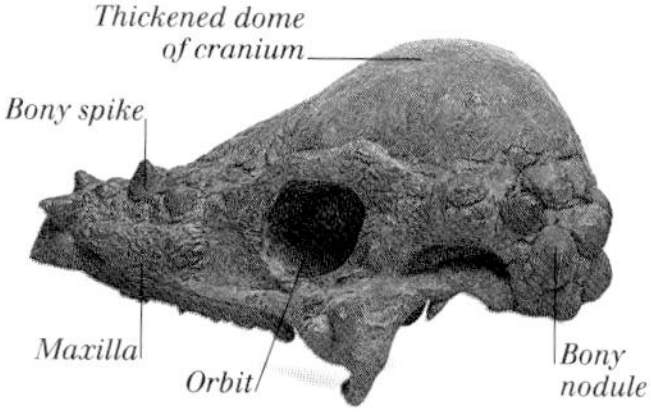
Thickened dome of cranium
Bony spike
Maxilla
Orbit
Bony nodule

SKULL OF PACHYCEPHALOSAURUS

EXTERNAL FEATURES OF PACHYCEPHALOSAURUS

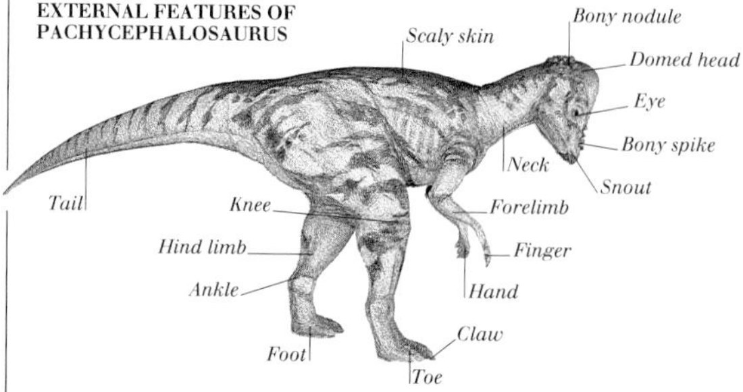
Bony nodule
Scaly skin
Domed head
Eye
Bony spike
Neck
Snout
Tail
Knee
Forelimb
Hind limb
Finger
Ankle
Hand
Claw
Foot
Toe

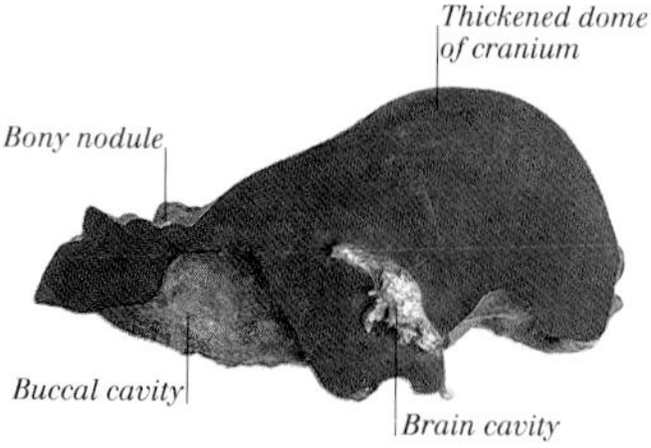
Thickened dome of cranium
Bony nodule
Buccal cavity
Brain cavity

SECTION THROUGH SKULL OF PACHYCEPHALOSAURUS

EXAMPLES OF PACHYCEPHALOSAURS

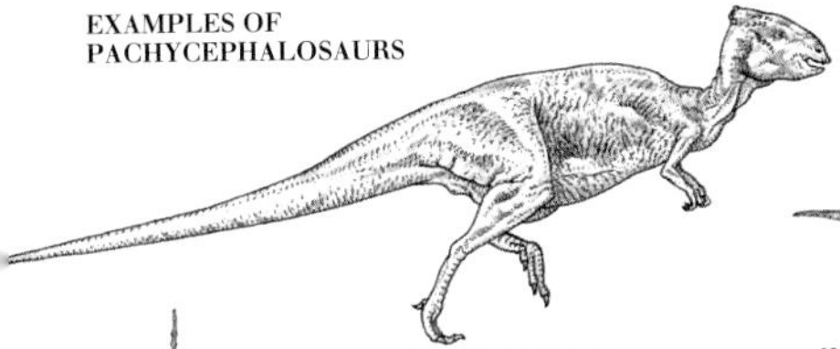

HOMALOCEPHALE
A homalocephalid
Length: 3 m (10 ft)

WANNANOSAURUS
A homalocephalid
Length: 60 cm (2 ft)

PRENOCEPHALE
A pachycephalosaurid
Length: 2.4 m (8 ft)

SKELETONS OF STEGOCERAS

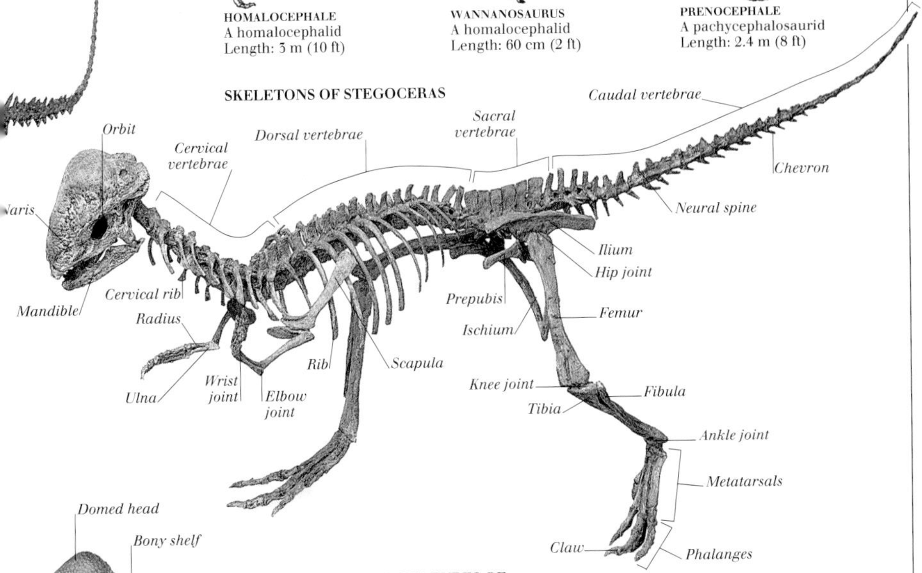
Orbit
Cervical vertebrae
Dorsal vertebrae
Sacral vertebrae
Caudal vertebrae
Chevron
Naris
Neural spine
Ilium
Hip joint
Cervical rib
Mandible
Radius
Prepubis
Femur
Ischium
Rib
Scapula
Ulna
Wrist joint
Elbow joint
Knee joint
Fibula
Tibia
Ankle joint
Metatarsals
Claw
Phalanges

EXTERNAL FEATURES OF STEGOCERAS

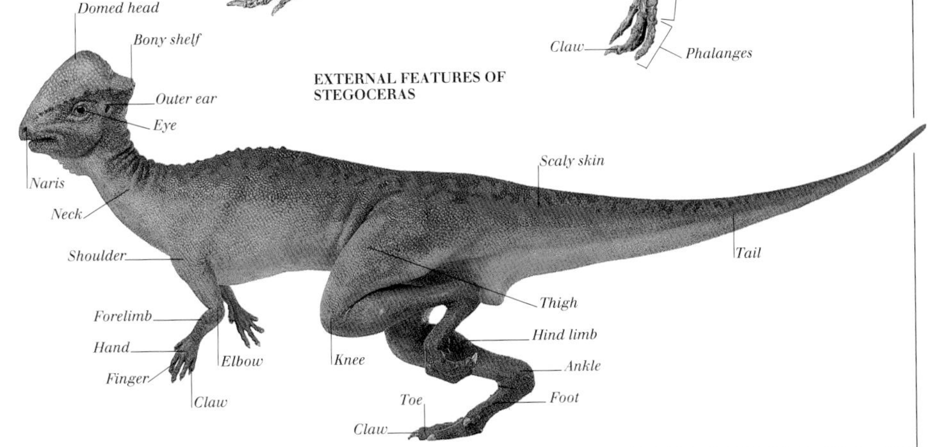
Domed head
Bony shelf
Outer ear
Eye
Naris
Scaly skin
Neck
Shoulder
Tail
Thigh
Forelimb
Hind limb
Hand
Elbow
Knee
Ankle
Finger
Claw
Toe
Foot
Claw

Marginocephalians 2

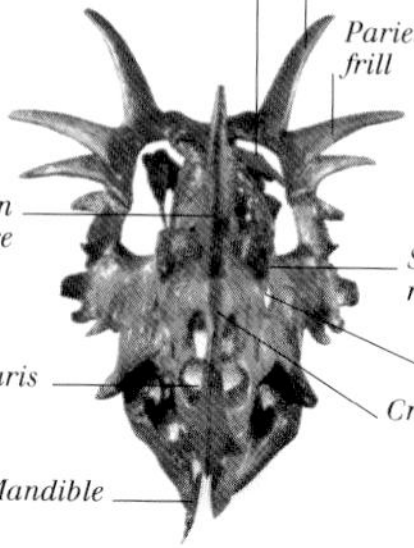
Parietal fenestra
Epoccipital bone
Parietosquamosal frill
Nose horn core
Supraorbital ridge
Orbit
Naris
Cranium
Mandible

SKULL AND MANDIBLE OF STYRACOSAURUS

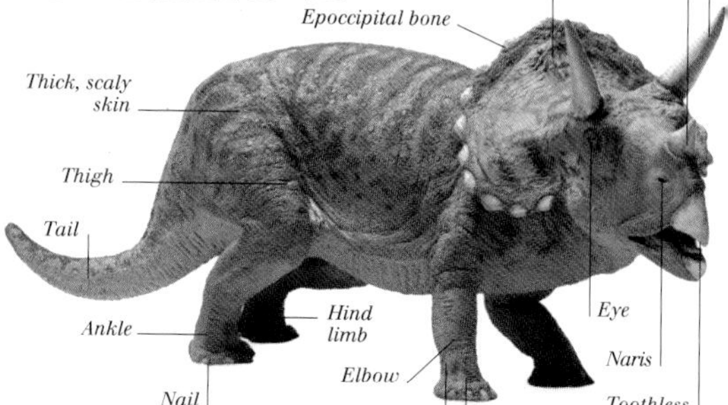
Brow horn
Parietosquamosal frill
Nose horn
Epoccipital bone
Thick, scaly skin
Thigh
Tail
Hind limb
Ankle
Eye
Naris
Elbow
Nail
Toothless beak
Forelimb
Wrist

EXTERNAL FEATURES OF TRICERATOPS

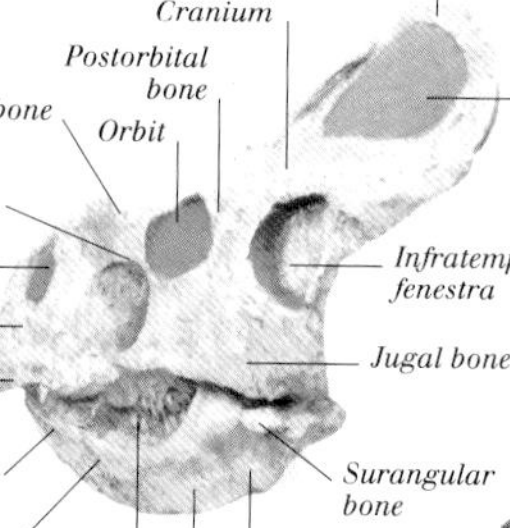
Parietosquamosal frill
Cranium
Postorbital bone
Parietal fenestra
Nasal bone
Orbit
Lacrimal bone
Naris
Infratemporal fenestra
Beak
Jugal bone
Rostral bone
Predentary bone
Surangular bone
Dentary bone
Tooth
Angular bone
Mandible

SKULL AND MANDIBLE OF PROTOCERATOPS

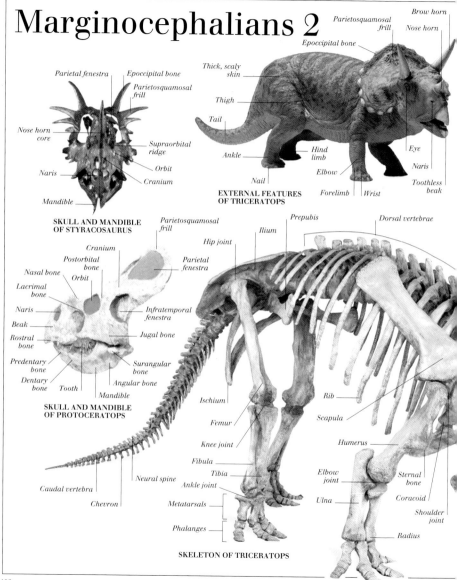

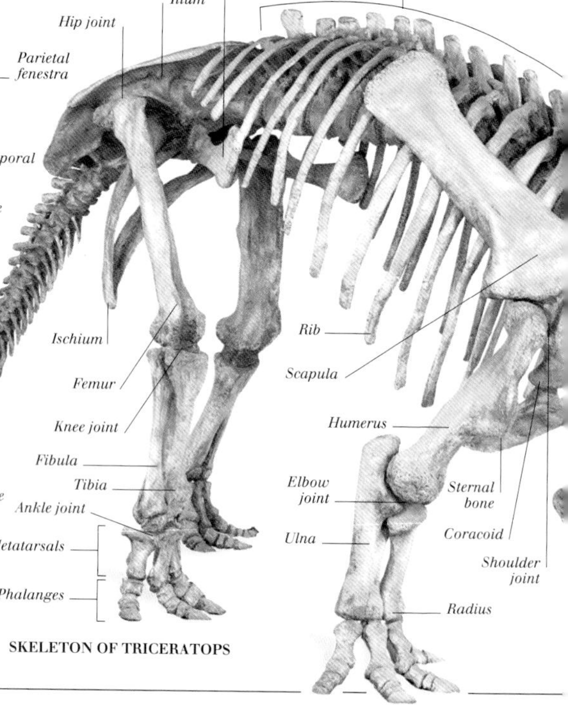
Prepubis
Dorsal vertebrae
Ilium
Hip joint
Ischium
Rib
Femur
Scapula
Knee joint
Humerus
Fibula
Tibia
Neural spine
Elbow joint
Sternal bone
Ankle joint
Caudal vertebra
Metatarsals
Ulna
Coracoid
Chevron
Shoulder joint
Phalanges
Radius

SKELETON OF TRICERATOPS

EXTERNAL FEATURES OF PSITTACOSAURUS

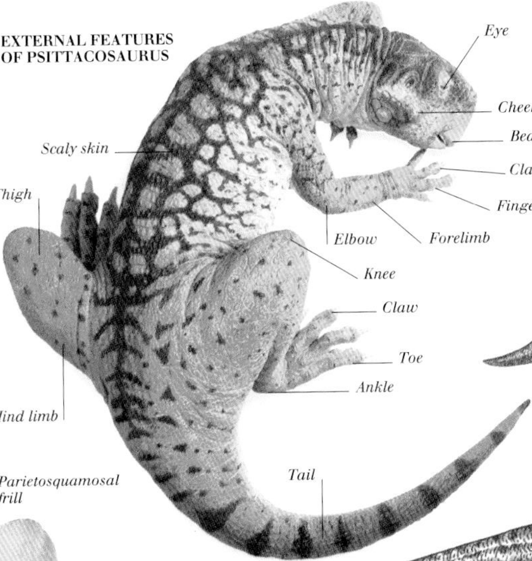
Eye
Cheek horn
Beak
Claw
Finger
Forelimb
Elbow
Scaly skin
Thigh
Knee
Claw
Toe
Ankle
Hind limb
Tail

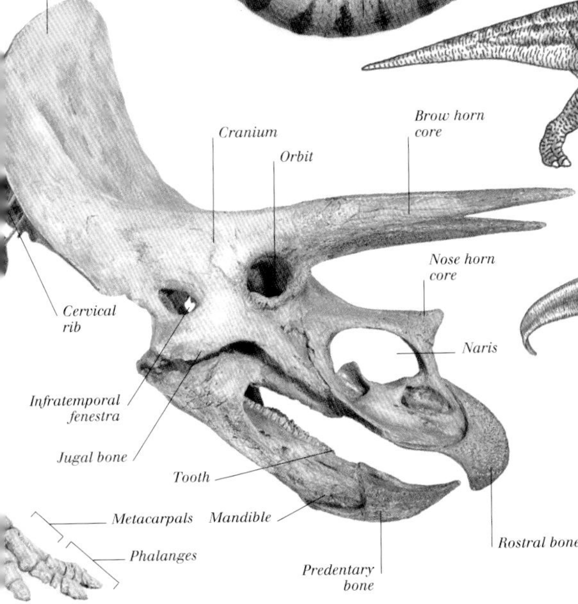
Parietosquamosal frill
Cranium
Orbit
Brow horn core
Nose horn core
Naris
Cervical rib
Infratemporal fenestra
Jugal bone
Tooth
Mandible
Metacarpals
Phalanges
Predentary bone
Rostral bone

EXAMPLES OF CERATOPSIA

PROTOCERATOPS
A protoceratopsid
Length: 2.7 m (9 ft)

STYRACOSAURUS
A ceratopsid
Length: 5.5 m (18 ft)

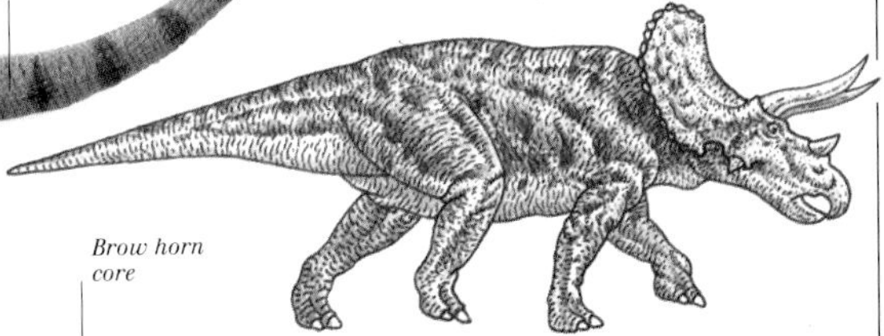

TRICERATOPS
A ceratopsid
Length: 9.1 m (30 ft)

PACHYRHINOSAURUS
A ceratopsid
Length: 5.5 m (18 ft)

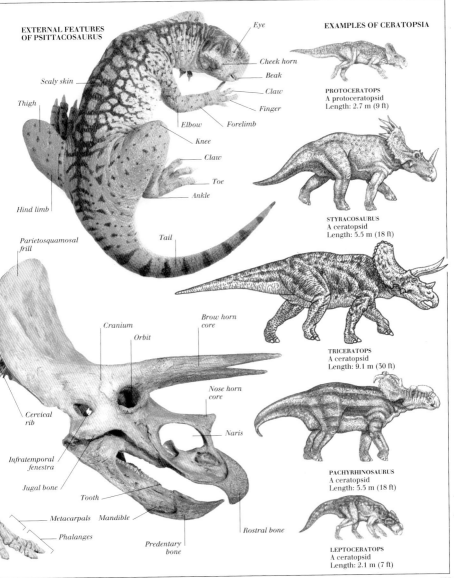

LEPTOCERATOPS
A ceratopsid
Length: 2.1 m (7 ft)

Mammals 1

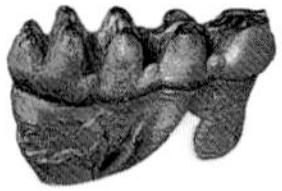

TETRALOPHODON CHEEK TEETH

SINCE THE EXTINCTION of the dinosaurs 65 million years ago, mammals have been the dominant vertebrates on Earth and include terrestrial, aerial, and aquatic forms. Having developed from the reptilian Therapsids, the first true mammals – small, nocturnal, rodent-like creatures, such as *Megazostrodon* – appeared over 200 million years ago during the Triassic period (245–208 million years ago). Mammals had several features that improved on those of their reptilian ancestors: an efficient four-chambered heart allowed these warm-blooded animals to sustain high levels of activity; a covering of hair helped them maintain a constant body temperature; an improved limb structure gave them more efficient locomotion; and the birth of live young and the immediate supply of food from the mother's milk aided their rapid growth. Since the end of the Mesozoic era (65 million years ago), the number of different mammal orders and the abundance of species in each order have varied dramatically. For example, the Perissodactyla (the order that includes *Coelodonta* and modern horses) was the most common group during the Early Tertiary period (about 54 million years ago). Today, the mammalian orders with the most populous species are the Rodentia (rats and mice), the Carnivora (bears, cats, and dogs), and the Artiodactyla (cattle, deer, and pigs), while the Proboscidea order, which included many genera, such as *Phiomia, Moeritherium, Tetralophodon,* and *Mammuthus*, now has only one member: the modern elephant. In Australia and South America, millions of years of continental isolation led to the development of the marsupials, a group of mammals distinct from the placentals (see p. 74) that existed elsewhere.

MODEL OF A MEGAZOSTRODON

Long tail aids balance
Insulating hair

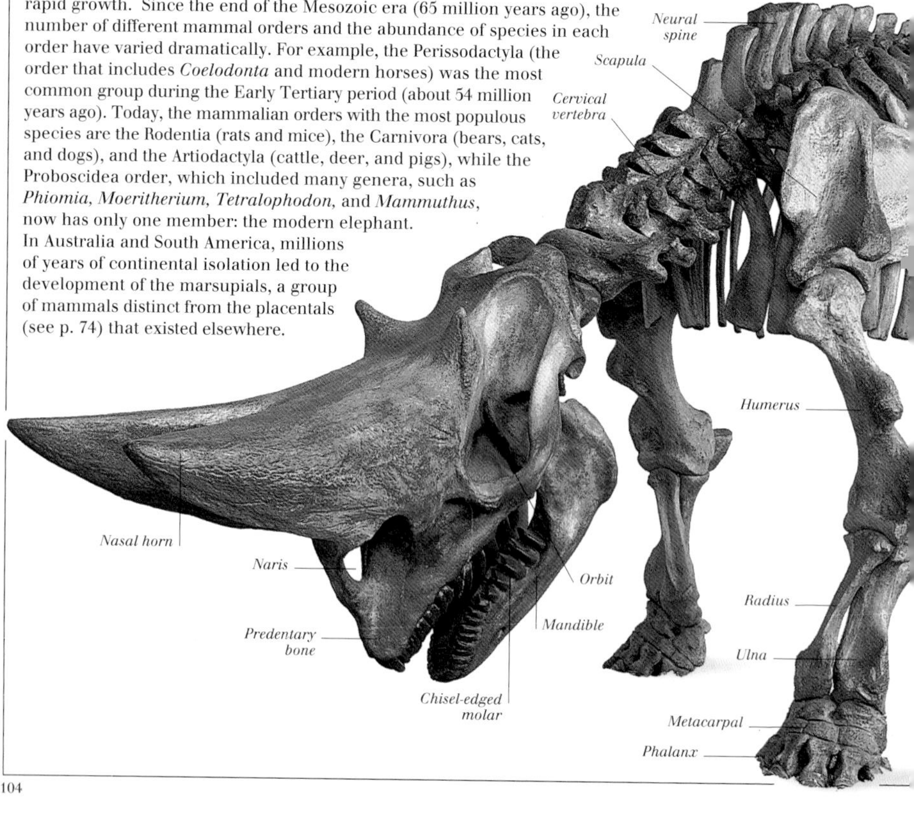
Neural spine
Scapula
Cervical vertebra
Humerus
Nasal horn
Naris
Orbit
Radius
Mandible
Predentary bone
Ulna
Chisel-edged molar
Metacarpal
Phalanx

UPPER JAWBONE (MAXILLA) OF A HORSE

Molars
Premolars

HOOFBONE (THIRD PHALANX) OF A HORSE

Articular surface
Tendon insertion

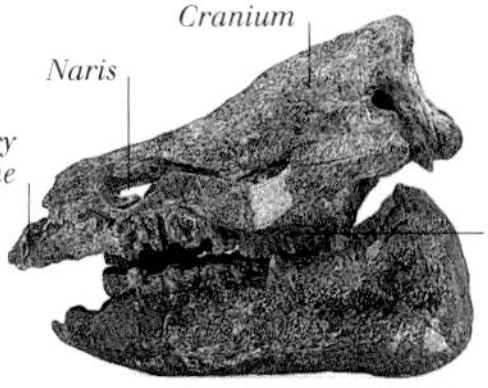
Cranium
Naris
Predentary bone
Molar tooth

SKULL AND MANDIBLE OF A MOERITHERIUM

Nasal tusk
Molar tooth
Shovel-shaped tusk

SKULL AND MANDIBLE OF A PHIOMIA

Trunk
Thick hide
Short tusk used for rooting up plants

MODEL OF A PHIOMIA

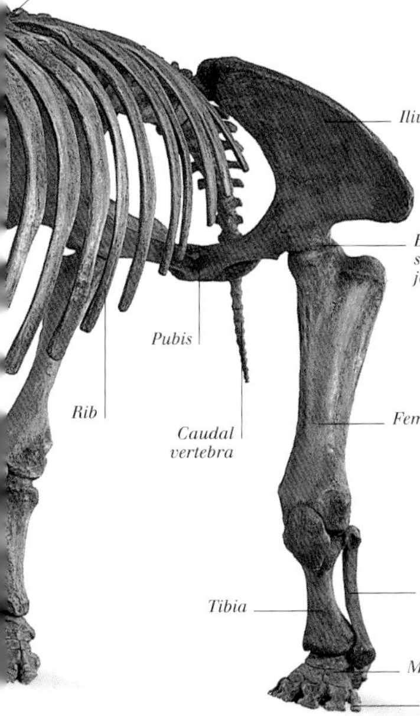
Dorsal vertebra
Ilium
Ball and socket joint
Pubis
Rib
Caudal vertebra
Femur
Fibula
Tibia
Metatarsal
Phalanx

SKELETON OF AN ARSINOITHERIUM

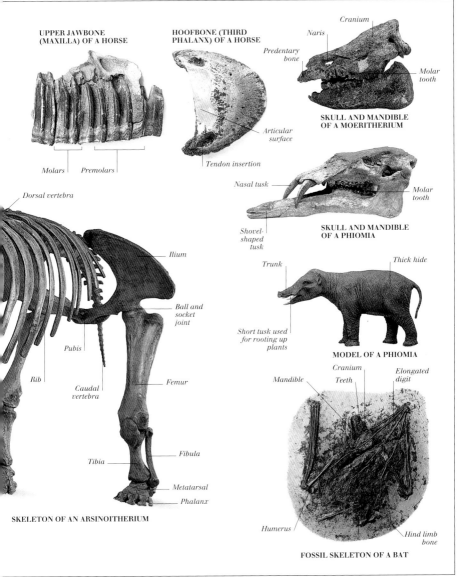

Cranium
Elongated digit
Mandible
Teeth
Humerus
Hind limb bone

FOSSIL SKELETON OF A BAT

Mammals 2

LOWER JAW OF A BEAR

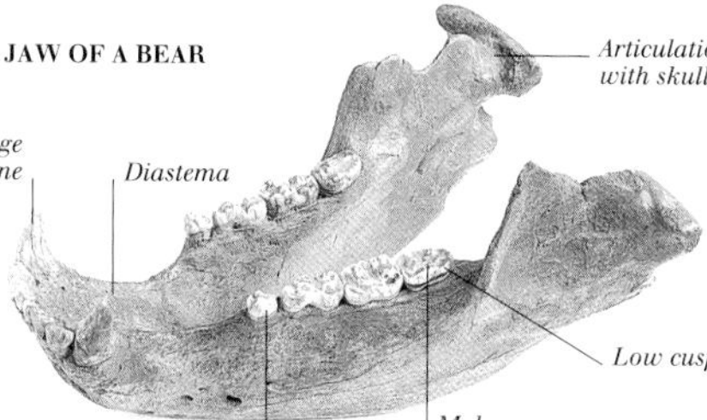
Articulation with skull
Large canine
Diastema
Low cusp
Molar
Premolar

SKELETON OF A TOXODON

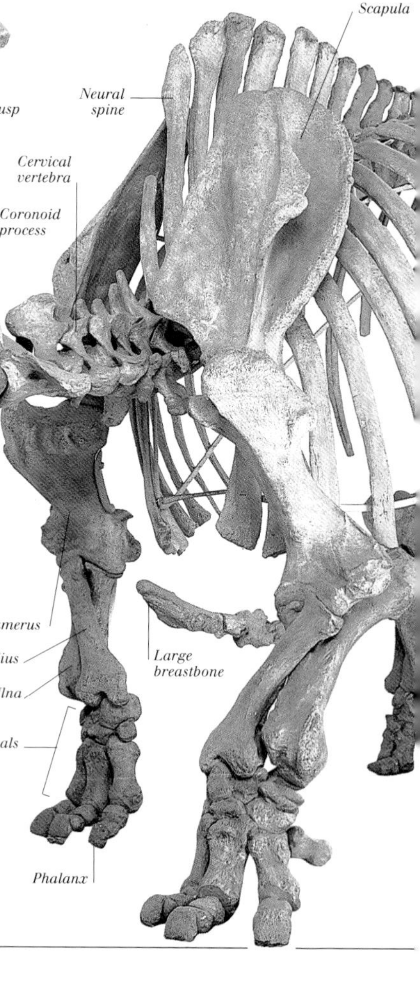
Scapula
Neural spine
Cervical vertebra
Coronoid process
Humerus
Radius
Ulna
Large breastbone
Metacarpals
Phalanx

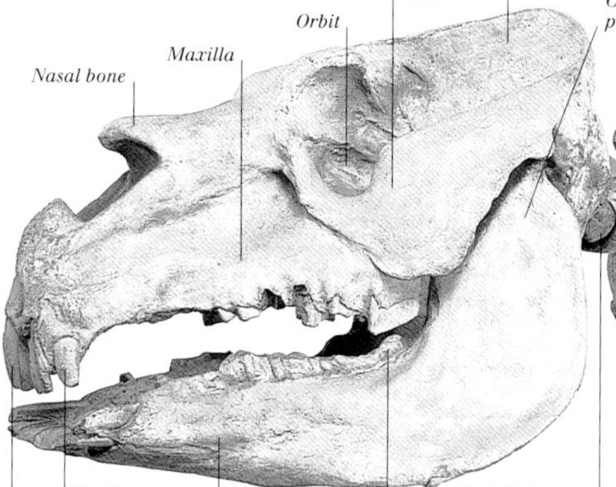
Zygomatic arch
Cranium
Orbit
Maxilla
Nasal bone
Canine
Mandible
Molar
Occipital region
Incisor

SKULL OF AN OPOSSUM

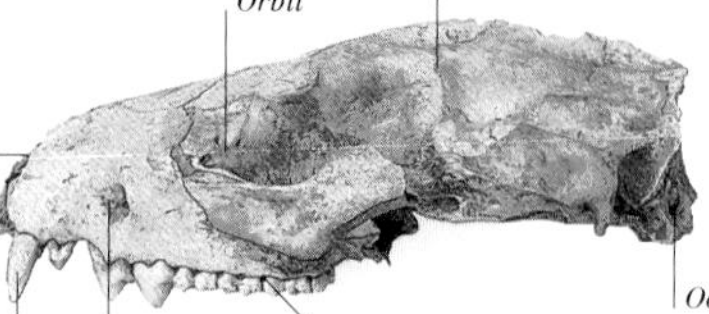
Cranium
Orbit
Naris
Occipital region
Canine
Infraorbital foramen
Molar

FOSSIL SKULL OF AN HYAENODON

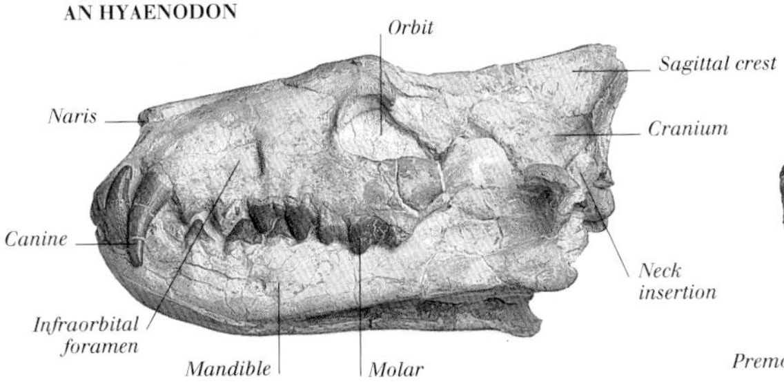
Orbit
Sagittal crest
Naris
Cranium
Canine
Neck insertion
Infraorbital foramen
Mandible
Molar

LOWER JAW OF AN AUSTRALOPITHECUS

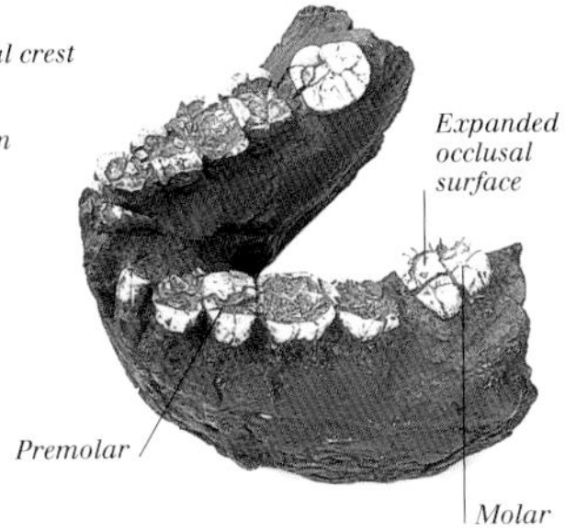
Expanded occlusal surface
Premolar
Molar

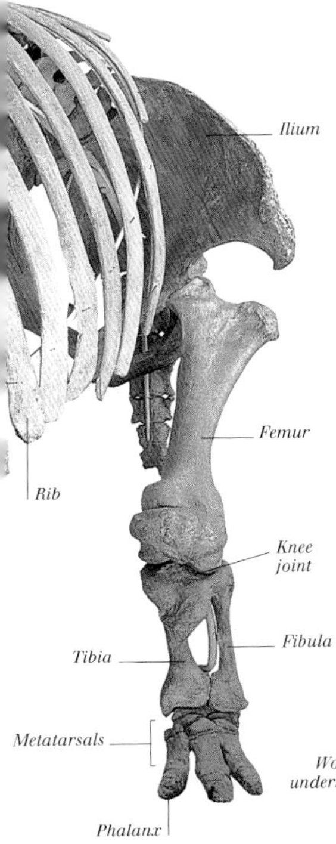
Ilium
Femur
Rib
Knee joint
Fibula
Tibia
Metatarsals
Phalanx

SKULL OF A SMILODON

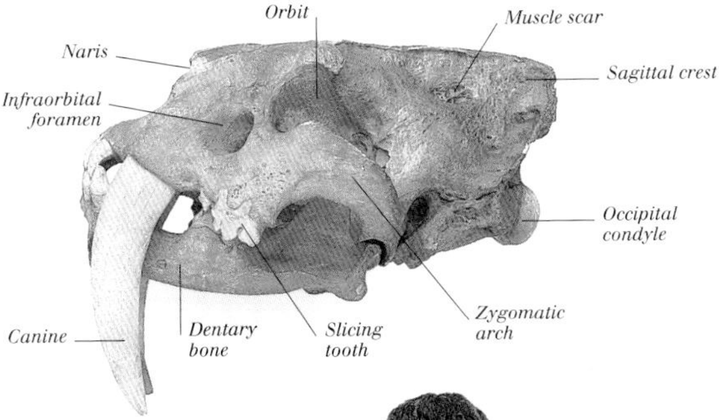
Orbit
Muscle scar
Naris
Sagittal crest
Infraorbital foramen
Occipital condyle
Canine
Dentary bone
Slicing tooth
Zygomatic arch

Thick, insulating coat
Ivory tusk
Woolly underhair
Hairy trunk

RECONSTRUCTION OF A MAMMOTH

The first hominids

MODERN HUMANS BELONG TO THE MAMMALIAN order of primates (see pp. 202–203), which originated about 55 million years ago; they comprise the only extant hominid species. The earliest hominid was *Australopithecus* ("southern ape"), a small-brained intermediate between apes and humans that was capable of standing and walking upright. *Homo habilis*, the first known human appeared at least 2 million years ago. This larger-brained "handy man" began making tools for hunting. *Homo erectus* first appeared in Africa about 1.8 million years ago and spread into Asia about 800,000 years later. Smaller-toothed than *Homo habilis*, it developed fire as a tool, which enabled it to cook food. Neanderthals, a near relative of modern humans, originated about 200,000 years ago, and *Homo sapiens* (modern humans) appeared in Africa about 100,000 years later. The two co-existed for thousands of years, but by 30,000 years ago, *Homo sapiens* had become dominant and the Neanderthals had died out. Classification of *Homo sapiens* in relation to its ancestors is enormously problematic: modern humans must be classified not only by bone structure, but also by specific behaviour – the ability to plan future action; to follow traditions; and to use symbolic communication, including complex language and the ability to use and recognize symbols.

JAWBONE OF AUSTRALOPITHECUS (SOUTHERN APE)

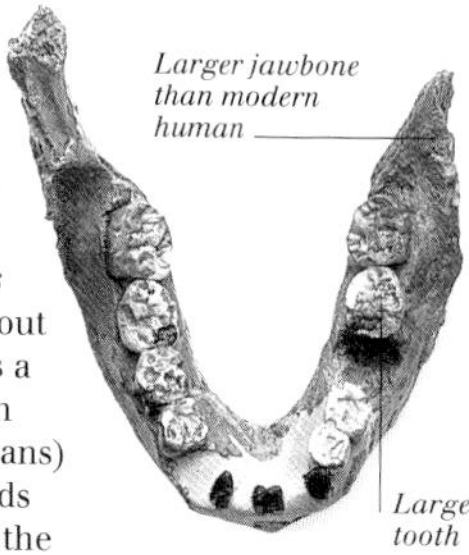

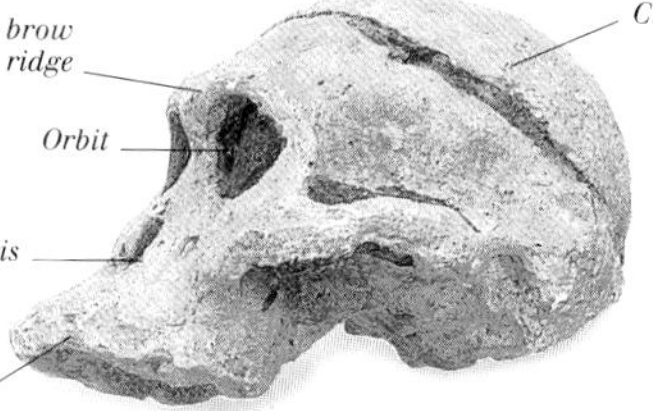

SKULL OF AUSTRALOPITHECUS (SOUTHERN APE)

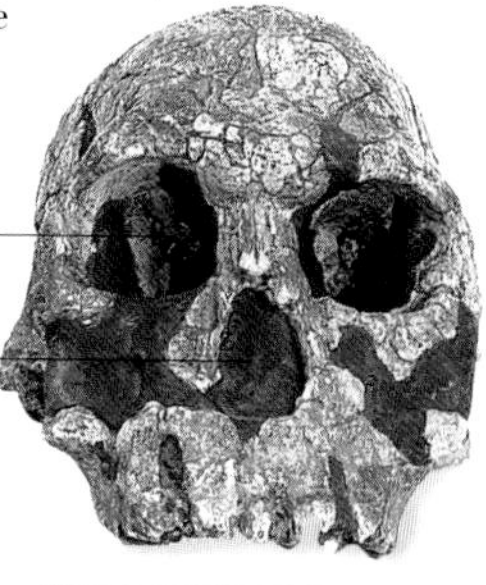

SKULL OF HOMO HABILIS (FIRST KNOWN HUMAN)

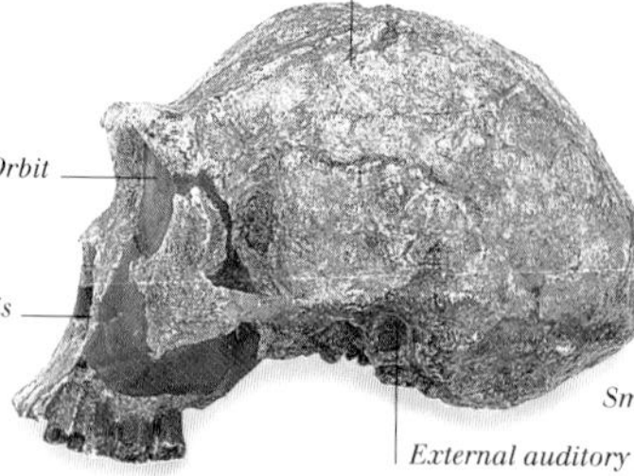

SKULL OF HOMO ERECTUS (UPRIGHT MAN)

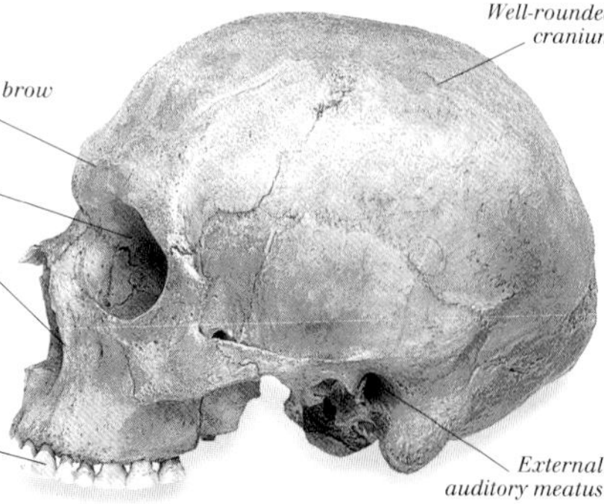

SKULL OF HOMO SAPIENS (MODERN HUMAN)

FLINT TOOL MADE ABOUT 250,000 YEARS AGO

Point
Flint may have been carved by Homo erectus
FLINT HANDAXE

Sharp edge used to cut meat
FLINT FLAKE

Hammer head used to detach chips of flint
Handle
ANTLER HAMMER

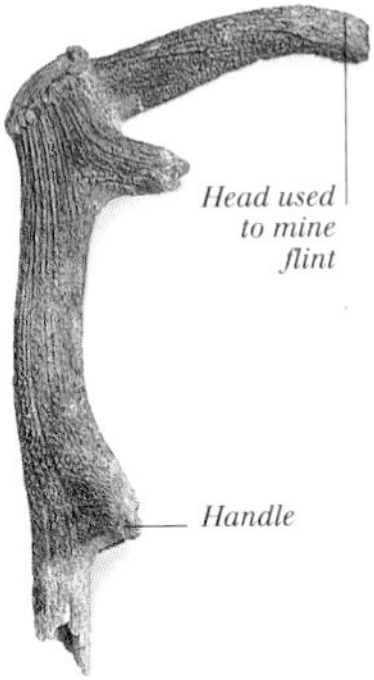
Head used to mine flint
Handle
RED DEER ANTLER HAMMER

EXAMPLES OF TOOLS USED BY HOMO SAPIENS

Axe used to clear land
Leather binding
Handle
FARMING AXE

FIRE-MAKING TOOLS

Wooden mouthpiece held drill securely
WOODEN MOUTHPIECE

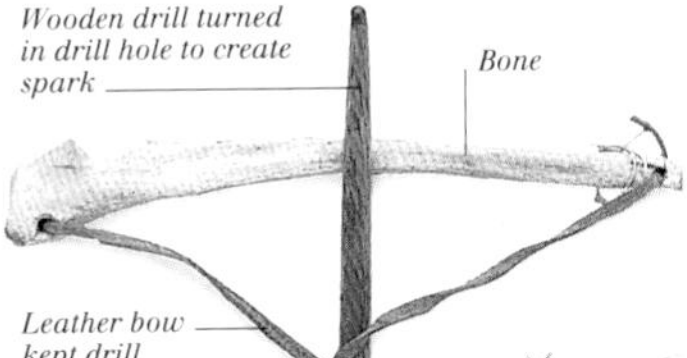
Wooden drill turned in drill hole to create spark
Bone
Leather bow kept drill upright
BOW DRILL

DRY STRAW

Drill hole
WOODEN HEARTH

EXAMPLES OF PREHISTORIC FOODS

MINT

WHEAT GRAINS

SALMON

SPEAR AND ARROW HEADS

Antler
HARPOON POINT

Twine binding
FISHING TACKLE

Wooden point hardened by fire
WOODEN ARROW

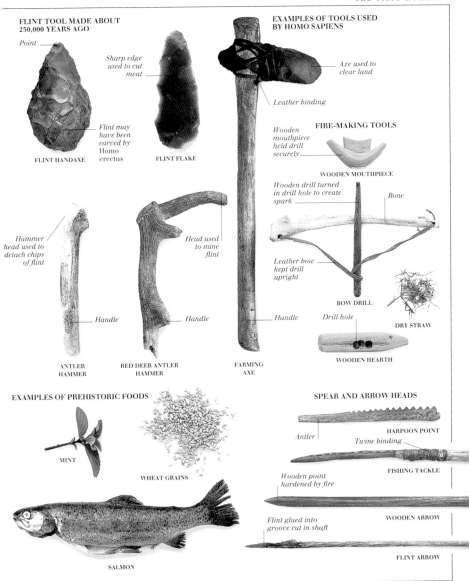

Flint glued into groove cut in shaft
FLINT ARROW

PLANTS

Plant variety

THERE ARE MORE THAN 300,000 SPECIES of plants. They show a wide diversity of forms and life-styles, ranging, for example, from delicate liverworts, adapted for life in a damp habitat, to cacti, capable of surviving in the desert, and from herbaceous plants, such as corn, which completes its life-cycle in one year, to the giant redwood tree, which can live for thousands of years. This diversity reflects the adaptations of plants to survive in a wide range of habitats. This is seen most clearly in the flowering plants (phylum Angiospermophyta), which are the most numerous, with over 250,000 species, and the most widespread, being found from the tropics to the poles. Despite their diversity, plants share certain characteristics: typically, plants are green, and make their food by photosynthesis; and most plants live in or on a substrate, such as soil, and do not actively move. Algae (kingdom Protista) and fungi (kingdom Fungi) have some plant-like characteristics and are often studied alongside plants, although they are not true plants.

FLOWERING PLANT
Bromeliad
(*Acanthostachys strobilacea*)

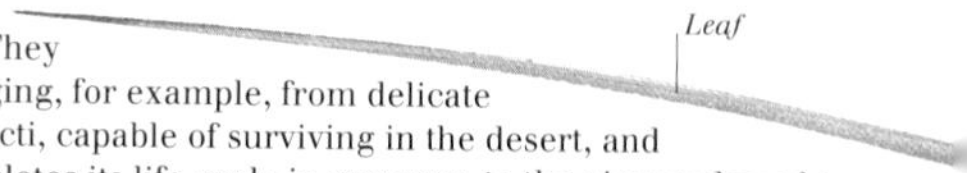
Leaf

GREEN ALGA
Micrograph of desmid
(*Micrasterias sp.*)

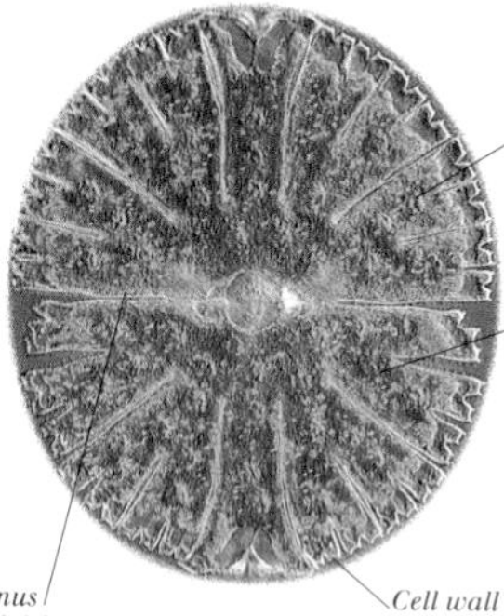
Pyrenoid (small protein body)
Chloroplast
Sinus (division between two halves of cell)
Cell wall

BRYOPHYTE
Moss
(*Bryum sp.*)

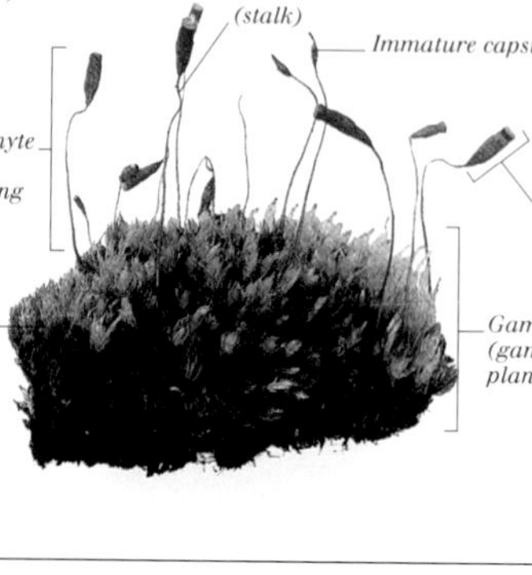
Seta (stalk)
Immature capsule
Sporophyte (spore-producing plant)
Capsule (site of spore production)
"Leaf"
Gametophyte (gamete-producing plant)

FERN
Tree fern
(*Dicksonia antarctica*)

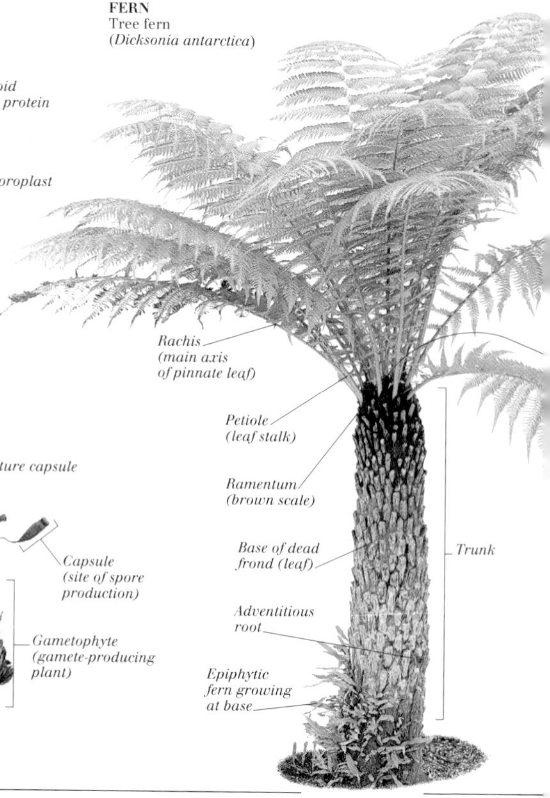
Rachis (main axis of pinnate leaf)
Petiole (leaf stalk)
Ramentum (brown scale)
Base of dead frond (leaf)
Trunk
Adventitious root
Epiphytic fern growing at base

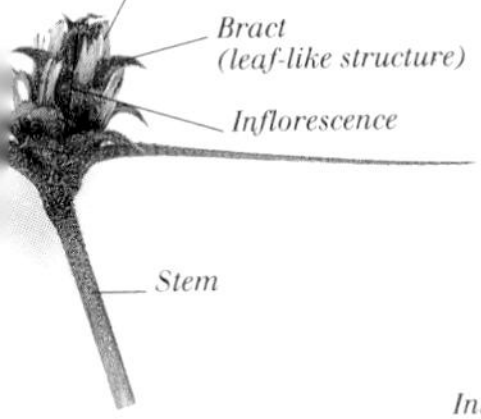

Spine
Flower
Bract
(leaf-like structure)
Inflorescence
Stem

FLOWERING PLANT
Succulent
(*Kedrostis africana*)

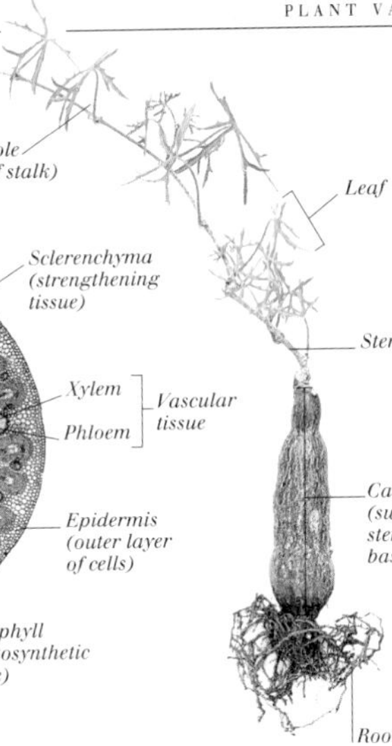

Petiole
(leaf stalk)
Leaf
Stem
Caudex
(swollen
stem
base)
Root

FLOWERING PLANT
Micrograph of cross-section through leaf of marram grass
(*Ammophila arenaria*)

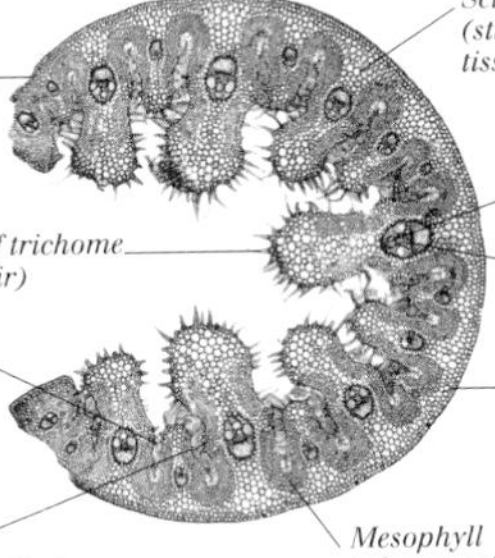

Cuticle
(waterproof
covering)
Sclerenchyma
(strengthening
tissue)
Xylem
Phloem
Vascular
tissue
Stiff trichome
(hair)
Interlocked
trichomes (hairs)
Epidermis
(outer layer
of cells)
Hinge cells
(cause curling of leaf to
reduce water loss)
Mesophyll
(photosynthetic
tissue)

Pinna
(leaflet)
Frond (leaf)
Midrib of
pinna (leaflet)

FLOWERING PLANT
Couch grass
(*Agropyron repens*)

Caryopsis
(type of
dry fruit)
Rachis
(main axis of
grass inflorescence)
Node
Lamina
(blade)
Round, hollow
stem
Sheathing
leaf base
Adventitious
root

FLOWERING PLANT
Pitcher plant
(*Sarracenia purpurea*)

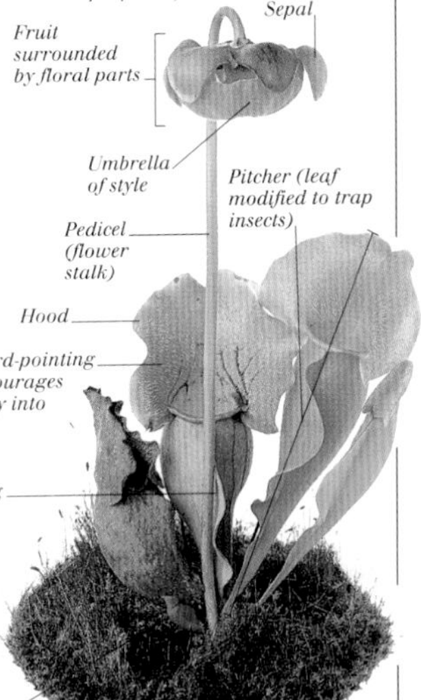

Sepal
Fruit
surrounded
by floral parts
Umbrella
of style
Pitcher (leaf
modified to trap
insects)
Pedicel
(flower
stalk)
Hood
Downward-pointing
hair (encourages
insect prey into
pitcher)
Wing
Immature
pitcher

Fungi and lichens

FUNGI WERE ONCE THOUGHT OF AS PLANTS but are now classified as a separate kingdom. This kingdom includes not only the familiar mushrooms, puffballs, stinkhorns, and moulds, but also yeasts, smuts, rusts, and lichens. Most fungi are multicellular, consisting of a mass of thread-like hyphae that together form a mycelium. However, the simpler fungi (e.g., yeasts) are microscopic, single-celled organisms. Typically, fungi reproduce by means of spores. Most fungi feed on dead or decaying matter, or on living organisms. A few fungi obtain their food from plants or algae, with which they have a symbiotic (mutually advantageous) relationship. Lichens are a symbiotic partnership between algae and fungi. Of the six types of lichens the three most common are crustose (flat and crusty), foliose (leafy), and fruticose (shrub-like). Some lichens (e.g., *Cladonia floerkeana*) are a combination of types. Lichens reproduce by means of spores or soredia (powdery vegetative fragments).

EXAMPLES OF FUNGI

Emerging sporophore (spore-bearing structure)
Pileus (cap) continuous with stipe (stalk)
Bark of dead beech tree
Inrolled margin of pileus (cap)
Gill (site of spore production)
Sporophore (spore-bearing structure)
Stipe (stalk)
Hyphae (fungal filaments)

OYSTER FUNGUS
(Pleurotus pulmonarius)

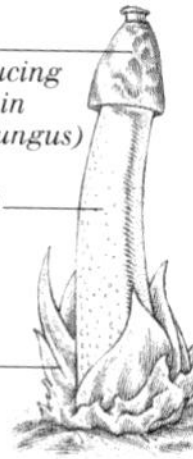

Gleba (spore-producing tissue found in this type of fungus)
Sporophore (spore-bearing structure)
Porous stipe (stalk)
Volva (remains of universal veil)

STINKHORN
(Phallus impudicus)

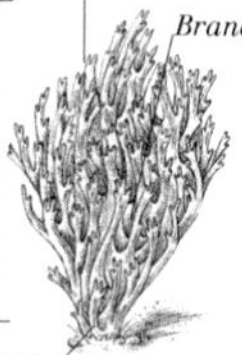

Toothed branchlet
Branch
Sporophore (spore-bearing structure)
Stipe (stalk)

RAMARIA FORMOSA

EXAMPLES OF LICHENS

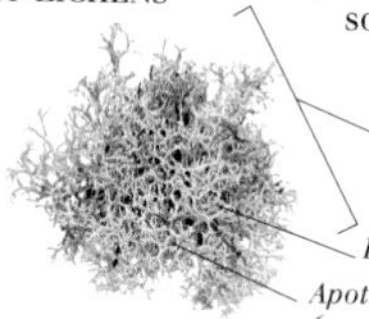

Secondary fruticose thallus
Branched, hollow stem
Apothecium (spore-producing body)

FRUTICOSE
Cladonia portentosa

Soredia (powdery vegetative fragments) produced at end of lobe
Tree bark
Foliose thallus

FOLIOSE
Hypogymnia physodes

Soredia (powdery vegetative fragments) released onto surface of squamulose thallus
Apothecium (spore-producing body)
Basal scale of primary squamulose thallus
Moss
Podetium (granular stalk) of secondary fruticose thallus

SQUAMULOSE (SCALY) AND FRUTICOSE THALLUS
Cladonia floerkeana

SECTION THROUGH FOLIOSE LICHEN SHOWING REPRODUCTION BY SOREDIA

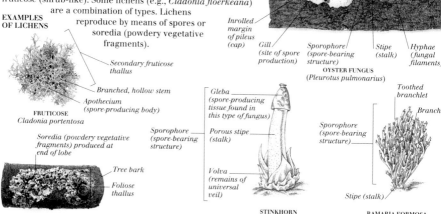

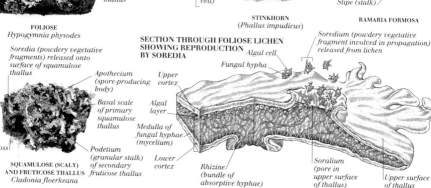

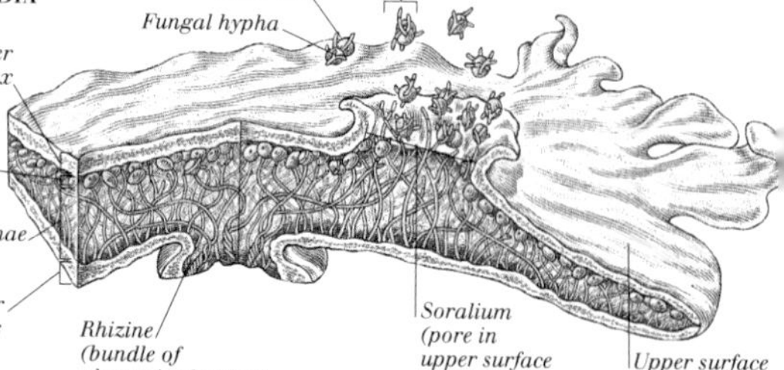

Soredium (powdery vegetative fragment involved in propagation) released from lichen
Algal cell
Fungal hypha
Upper cortex
Algal layer
Medulla of fungal hyphae (mycelium)
Lower cortex
Rhizine (bundle of absorptive hyphae)
Soralium (pore in upper surface of thallus)
Upper surface of thallus

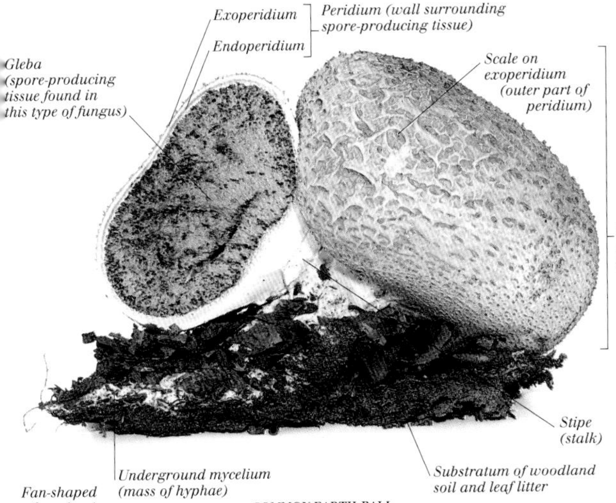
Exoperidium
Endoperidium
Peridium (wall surrounding spore-producing tissue)
Gleba (spore-producing tissue found in this type of fungus)
Scale on exoperidium (outer part of peridium)
Sporophore (spore-bearing structure)
Stipe (stalk)
Underground mycelium (mass of hyphae)
Substratum of woodland soil and leaf litter

COMMON EARTH-BALL
(*Scleroderma citrinum*)

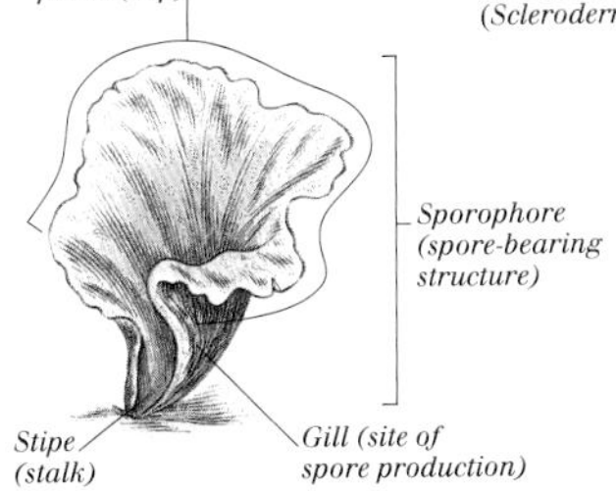
Fan-shaped pileus (cap)
Sporophore (spore-bearing structure)
Stipe (stalk)
Gill (site of spore production)

HOHENBUEHELIA PETALOIDES

Sporophore (spore-bearing structure)
Pileus (cap)
Stipe (stalk)
Substratum of woodland soil and leaf litter
Hyphae (fungal filaments)

FRINGED CRUMBLE CAP
(*Psathyrella candolleana*)

LIFE-CYCLE OF A MUSHROOM

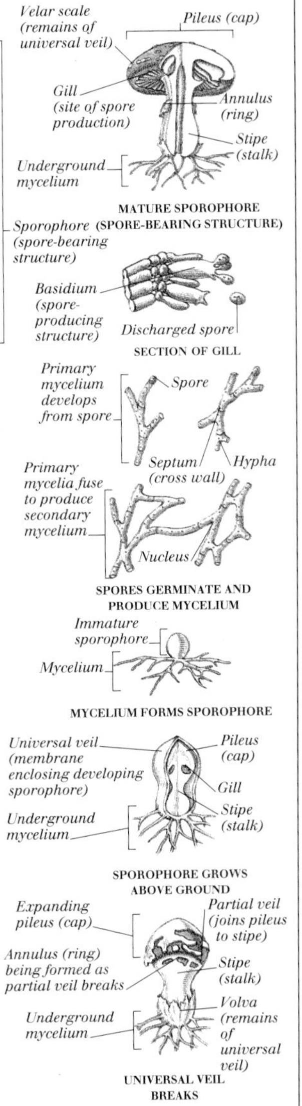
Velar scale (remains of universal veil)
Pileus (cap)
Gill (site of spore production)
Annulus (ring)
Stipe (stalk)
Underground mycelium
MATURE SPOROPHORE (SPORE-BEARING STRUCTURE)
Basidium (spore-producing structure)
Discharged spore
SECTION OF GILL
Primary mycelium develops from spore
Spore
Septum (cross wall)
Hypha
Primary mycelia fuse to produce secondary mycelium
Nucleus
SPORES GERMINATE AND PRODUCE MYCELIUM
Immature sporophore
Mycelium
MYCELIUM FORMS SPOROPHORE
Universal veil (membrane enclosing developing sporophore)
Pileus (cap)
Gill
Stipe (stalk)
Underground mycelium
SPOROPHORE GROWS ABOVE GROUND
Expanding pileus (cap)
Partial veil (joins pileus to stipe)
Annulus (ring) being formed as partial veil breaks
Stipe (stalk)
Volva (remains of universal veil)
Underground mycelium
UNIVERSAL VEIL BREAKS

Algae and seaweeds

ALGAE ARE NOT TRUE PLANTS. They form a diverse group of plant-like organisms that belong to the kingdom Protista. Like plants, algae possess the green pigment chlorophyll and make their own food by photosynthesis (see pp. 138-139). Many algae also possess other pigments by which they can be classified; for example, the brown pigment fucoxanthin is found in the brown algae. Some of the ten phyla of algae are exclusively unicellular (single-celled); others also contain aggregates of cells in filaments or colonies. Three phyla – the Chlorophyta (green algae), Rhodophyta (red algae), and Phaeophyta (brown algae) – contain larger, multicellular, thalloid (flat), marine organisms commonly known as seaweeds.

Most algae can reproduce sexually. For example, in the brown seaweed *Fucus vesiculosus*, gametes (sex cells) are produced in conceptacles (chambers) in the receptacles (fertile tips of fronds); after their release into the sea, antherozoids (male gametes) and oospheres (female gametes) fuse; the resulting zygote settles on a rock and develops into a new seaweed.

Receptacle (fertile tip of frond)
Thallus (plant body)
Apical notch
Margin of lamina (blade) rolled inwards to form channel
Hapteron (holdfast)

BROWN SEAWEED
Channelled wrack
(*Pelvetia canaliculata*)

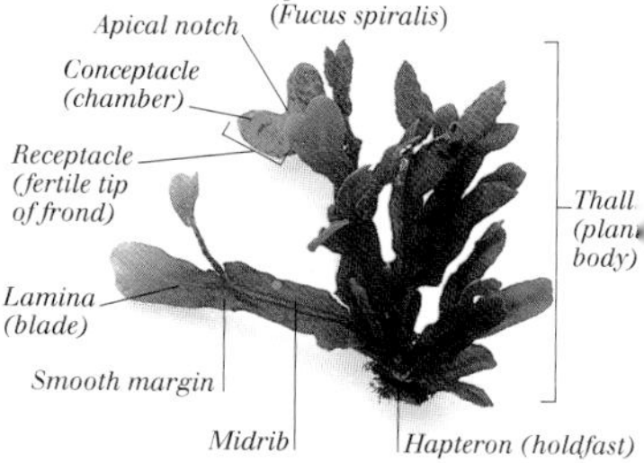

Apical notch
Conceptacle (chamber)
Receptacle (fertile tip of frond)
Thall (plan body)
Lamina (blade)
Smooth margin
Midrib
Hapteron (holdfast)

BROWN SEAWEED
Spiral wrack
(*Fucus spiralis*)

EXAMPLES OF ALGAE

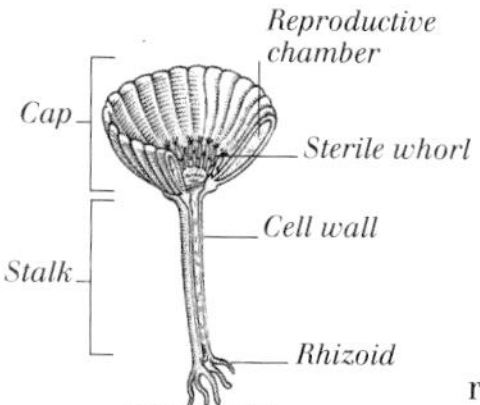

Reproductive chamber
Cap
Sterile whorl
Cell wall
Stalk
Rhizoid

GREEN ALGA
Acetabularia sp.

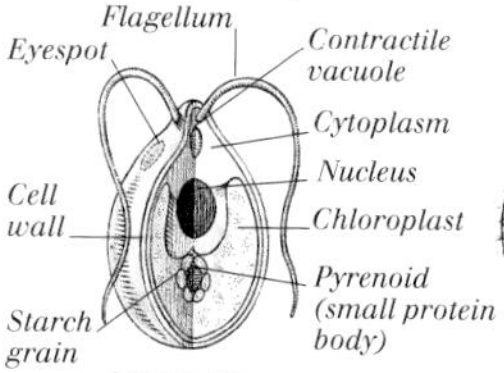

Flagellum
Eyespot
Contractile vacuole
Cytoplasm
Nucleus
Cell wall
Chloroplast
Pyrenoid (small protein body)
Starch grain

GREEN ALGA
Chlamydomonas sp.

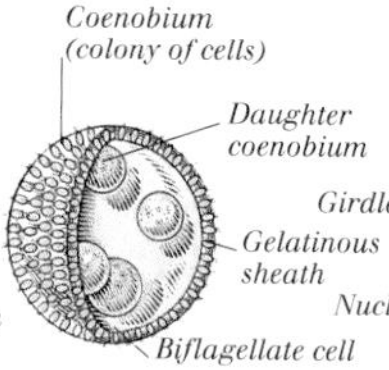

Coenobium (colony of cells)
Daughter coenobium
Gelatinous sheath
Biflagellate cell

GREEN ALGA
Volvox sp.

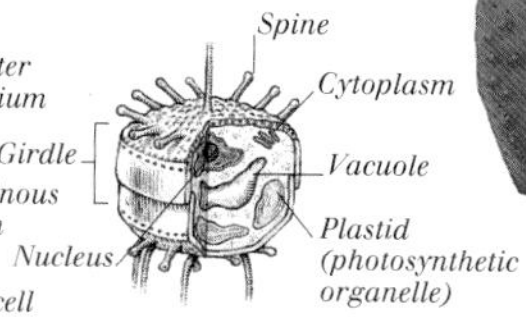

Spine
Cytoplasm
Girdle
Vacuole
Nucleus
Plastid (photosynthetic organelle)

DIATOM
Thalassiosira sp.

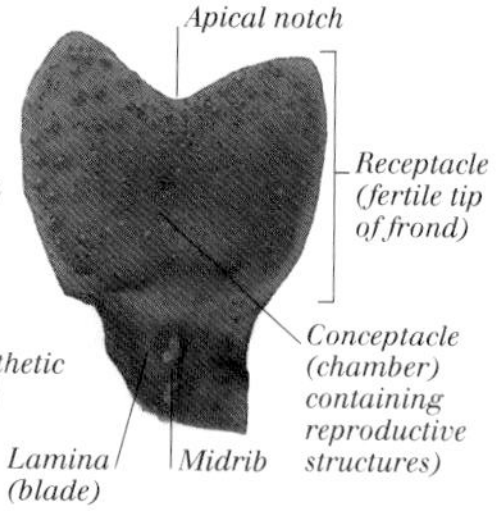

Apical notch
Receptacle (fertile tip of frond)
Conceptacle (chamber) containing reproductive structures)
Lamina (blade)
Midrib

RECEPTACLE
Spiral wrack
(*Fucus spiralis*)

BROWN SEAWEED
Oarweed
(*Laminaria digitata*)

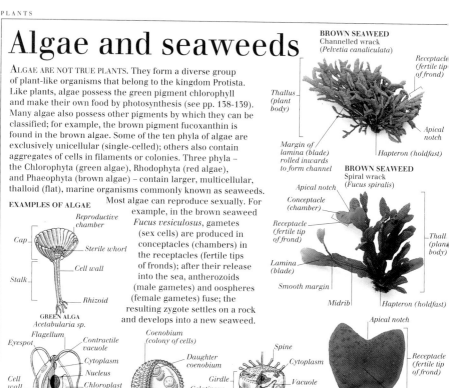

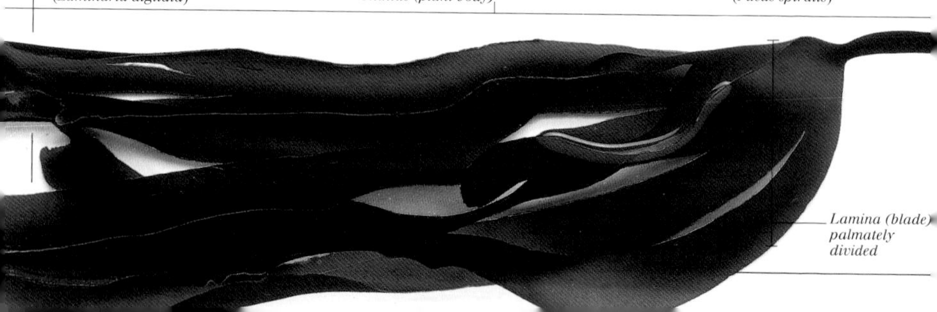

Thallus (plant body)
Lamina (blade) palmately divided

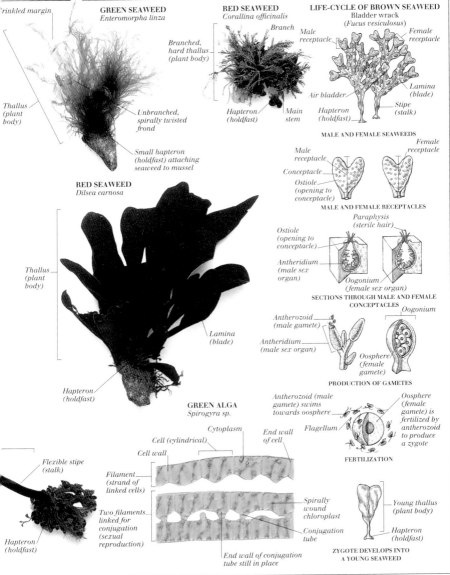

GREEN SEAWEED
Enteromorpha linza

rinkled margin
Thallus (plant body)
Unbranched, spirally twisted frond
Small hapteron (holdfast) attaching seaweed to mussel

RED SEAWEED
Corallina officinalis

Branch
Branched, hard thallus (plant body)
Hapteron (holdfast)
Main stem

LIFE-CYCLE OF BROWN SEAWEED
Bladder wrack
(*Fucus vesiculosus*)

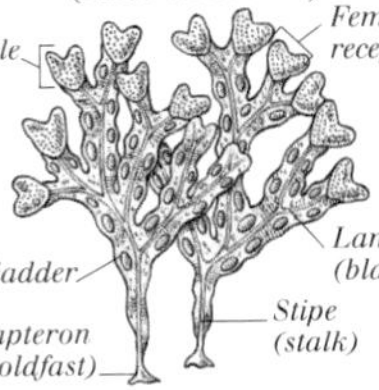
Male receptacle
Female receptacle
Lamina (blade)
Air bladder
Stipe (stalk)
Hapteron (holdfast)

MALE AND FEMALE SEAWEEDS

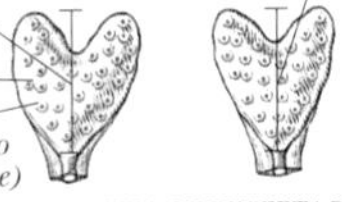
Male receptacle
Female receptacle
Conceptacle
Ostiole (opening to conceptacle)

MALE AND FEMALE RECEPTACLES

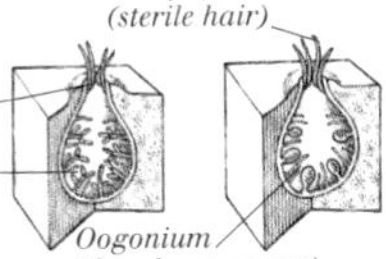
Paraphysis (sterile hair)
Ostiole (opening to conceptacle)
Antheridium (male sex organ)
Oogonium (female sex organ)

SECTIONS THROUGH MALE AND FEMALE CONCEPTACLES

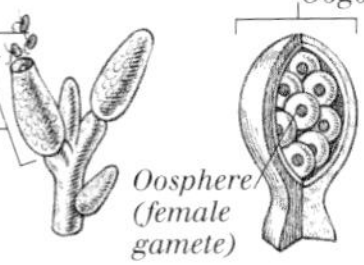
Oogonium
Antherozoid (male gamete)
Antheridium (male sex organ)
Oosphere (female gamete)

PRODUCTION OF GAMETES

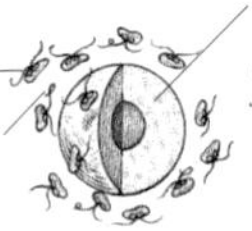
Antherozoid (male gamete) swims towards oosphere
Oosphere (female gamete) is fertilized by antherozoid to produce a zygote
Flagellum

FERTILIZATION

RED SEAWEED
Dilsea carnosa

Thallus (plant body)
Lamina (blade)
Hapteron (holdfast)

Flexible stipe (stalk)
Hapteron (holdfast)

GREEN ALGA
Spirogyra sp.

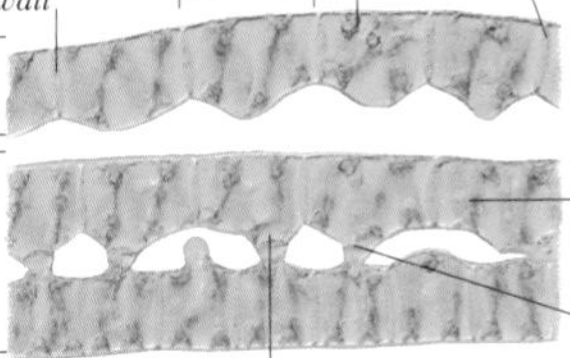
Cytoplasm
End wall of cell
Cell (cylindrical)
Cell wall
Filament (strand of linked cells)
Spirally wound chloroplast
Two filaments linked for conjugation (sexual reproduction)
Conjugation tube
End wall of conjugation tube still in place

Young thallus (plant body)
Hapteron (holdfast)

ZYGOTE DEVELOPS INTO A YOUNG SEAWEED

Liverworts and mosses

LIVERWORTS AND MOSSES ARE SMALL, LOW-GROWING PLANTS that belong to the phylum Bryophyta. Bryophytes do not have true stems, leaves, or roots (they are anchored to the ground by rhizoids), nor do they have the vascular tissues (xylem and phloem) that transport water and nutrients in higher plants. With no outer, waterproof cuticle, bryophytes are susceptible to drying out, and most grow in moist habitats. The bryophyte life-cycle has two stages. In stage one, the green plant (gametophyte) produces male and female gametes (sex cells), which fuse to form a zygote. In stage two, the zygote develops into a sporophyte that remains attached to the gametophyte. The sporophyte produces spores, which are released and germinate into new green plants. Liverworts (class Hepaticae) grow horizontally and may be thalloid (flat and ribbon-like) or "leafy". Mosses (class Musci) typically have an upright "stem" with spirally arranged "leaves".

A LEAFY LIVERWORT
Scapania undulata

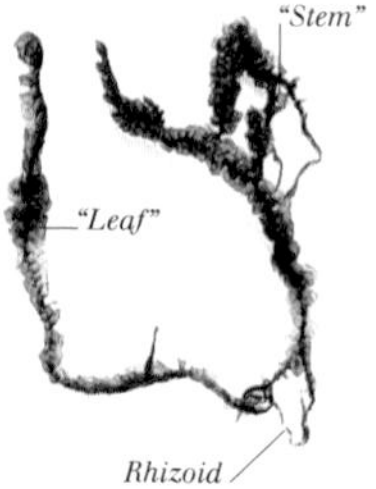
"Stem"
"Leaf"
Rhizoid

A THALLOID LIVERWORT
Marchantia polymorpha

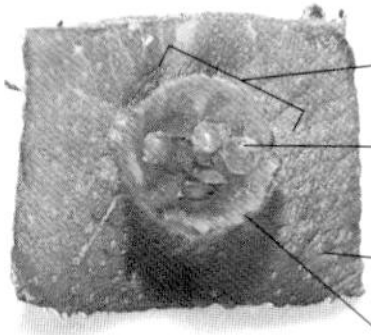
Gemma cup
Gemma (detachable tissue that produces new plants)
Thallus (plant body)
Toothed margin of cup

DETAIL OF GEMMA CUP

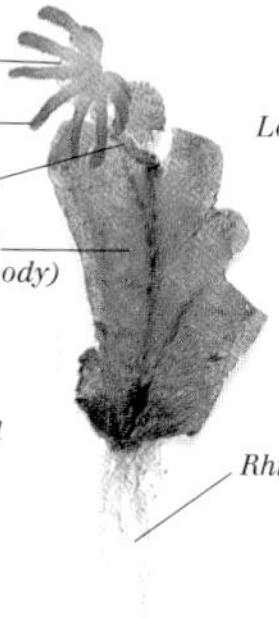
Disc
Archegoniophore (stalked structure carrying archegonia)
Lobe
Stalk
Thallus (plant body)
Rhizoid

FEMALE GAMETOPHYTE

Disc
Lobe
Stalk

SIDE VIEW OF ARCHEGONIOPHORE

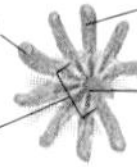
Lobe
Ray (radial groove)
Stalk
Disc

ARCHEGONIOPHORE FROM BELOW

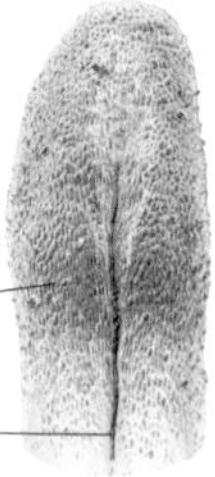
Pore
Ray (radial groove)

MICROGRAPH OF LOBE

Apical notch
Gemma cup
Thallus (plant body)
Midrib
Archegoniophore (stalked structure carrying archegonia)

MICROGRAPH OF THALLUS
Conocephalum conicum

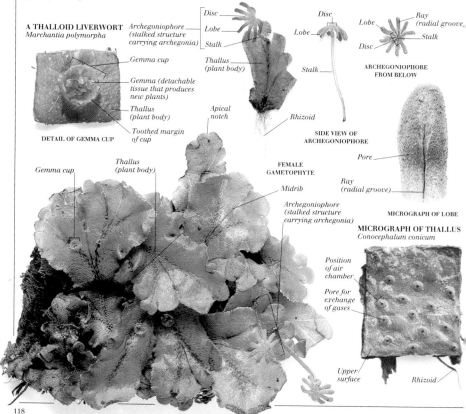

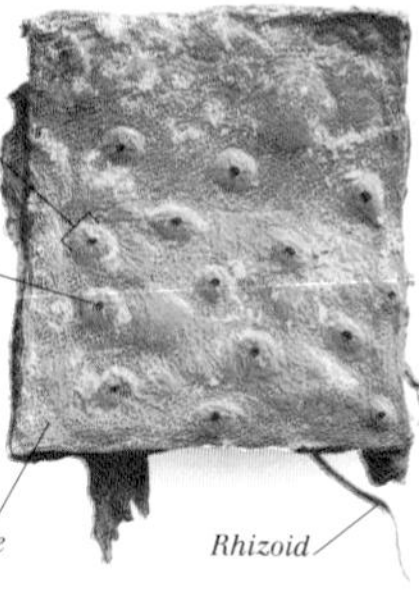
Position of air chamber
Pore for exchange of gases
Upper surface
Rhizoid

A COMMON MOSS
Polytrichum commune

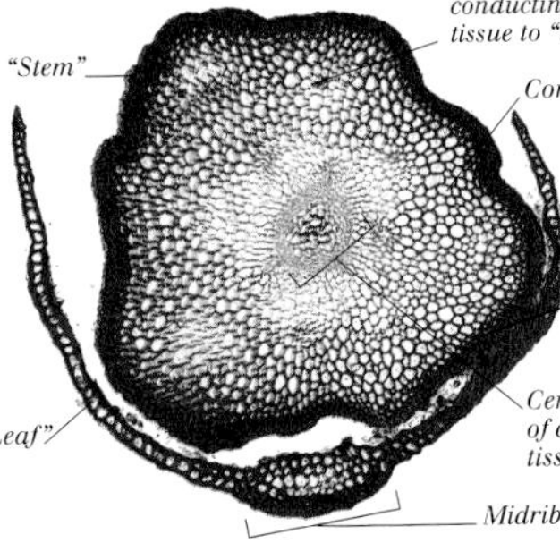
Branch of conducting tissue to "leaf"
"Stem"
Cortex
Epidermis (outer layer of cells)
Central strand of conducting tissue
"Leaf"
Midrib

MICROGRAPH OF CROSS-SECTION THROUGH STEM AND LEAF

MICROGRAPH OF MOSS SPORE
Funaria hygrometrica

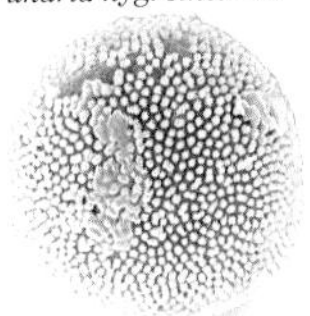

LIFE-CYCLE OF MOSS
Funaria sp.

Male rosette ("leaves" around antheridia)
Female rosette ("leaves" around archegonia)
Main "stem"
Lateral branch of "stem"
Rhizoid

GAMETOPHYTE

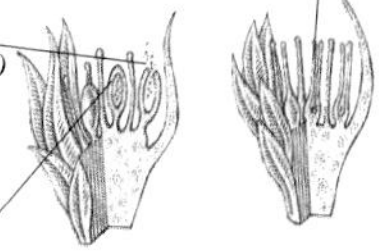
Antherozoids (male gametes) released from antheridium
Antheridium (male sex organ)
Archegonium (female sex organ)

SECTION THROUGH MATURE MALE APEX

SECTION THROUGH MATURE FEMALE APEX

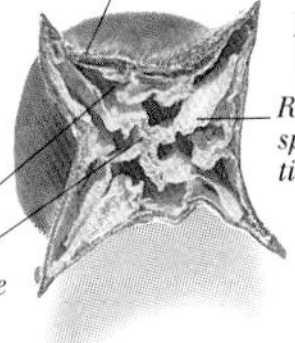
Epidermis of capsule
Remains of spore-forming tissue
Spore-containing space
Columella (central tissue of capsule)

CROSS-SECTION THROUGH CAPSULE

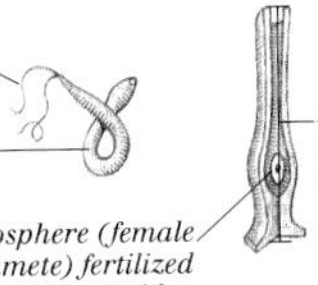
Flagellum
Antherozoid (male gamete) swims to oosphere
Archegonium (female sex organ)
Oosphere (female gamete) fertilized by antherozoid

FERTILIZATION

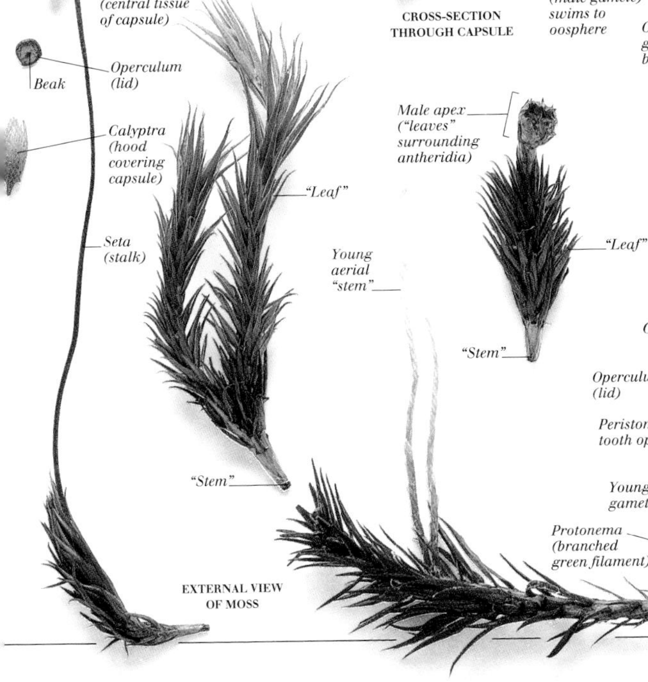
Capsule
Apophysis (swollen area between seta and capsule)
Columella (central tissue of capsule)
Operculum (lid)
Beak
Calyptra (hood covering capsule)
Seta (stalk)
"Leaf"
"Stem"
Young aerial "stem"
Male apex ("leaves" surrounding antheridia)
"Leaf"
"Stem"

EXTERNAL VIEW OF MOSS

Capsule
Seta (stalk)
Sporophyte grows from fertilized oosphere
Gametophyte

SPOROPHYTE

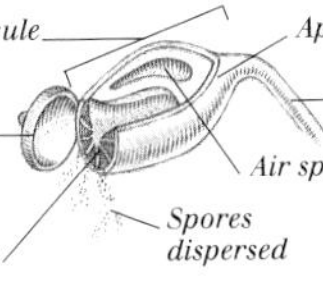
Capsule
Apophysis
Seta (stalk)
Operculum (lid)
Air space
Peristome tooth opens
Spores dispersed

RIPE CAPSULE

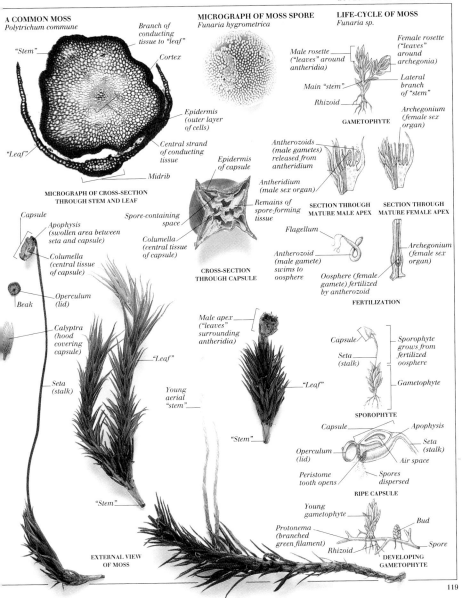

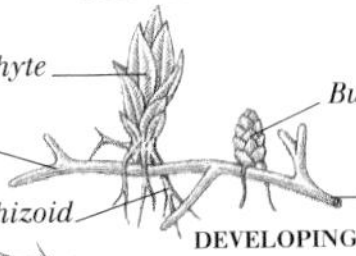
Young gametophyte
Bud
Protonema (branched green filament)
Spore
Rhizoid

DEVELOPING GAMETOPHYTE

Horsetails, clubmosses, and ferns

FROND
Male fern
(*Dryopteris filix-mas*)

HORSETAILS, CLUBMOSSES, AND FERNS are primitive land plants, which, like higher plants, have stems, roots, and leaves, and vascular systems that transport water, minerals, and food. However, unlike higher plants, they do not produce seeds when reproducing. Their life-cycles involve two stages. In stage one, the sporophyte (green plant) produces spores in sporangia. In stage two, the spores germinate, developing into small, short-lived gametophyte plants that produce male and female gametes (sex cells); the gametes fuse to form a zygote from which a new sporophyte plant develops. Horsetails (phylum Sphenophyta) have erect, green stems with branches arranged in whorls; some stems are fertile and have a single spore-producing strobilus (group of sporangia) at the tip. Clubmosses (phylum Lycopodophyta) typically have small leaves arranged spirally around the stem, with spore-producing strobili at the tip of some stems. Ferns (phylum Filicinophyta) typically have large, pinnate fronds (leaves); sporangia, grouped together in sori, develop on the underside of fertile fronds.

CLUBMOSS
Lycopodium sp.

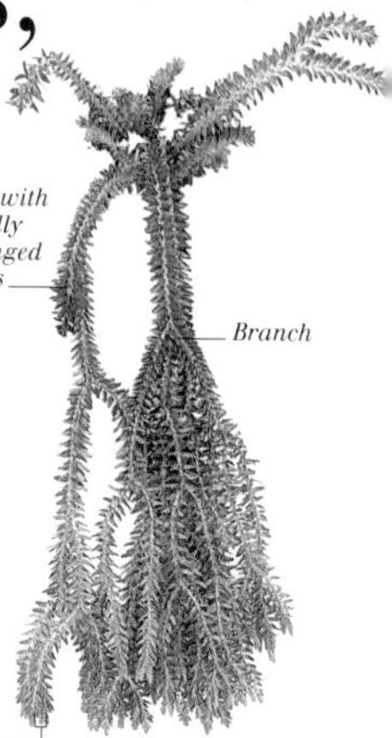
Stem with spirally arranged leaves
Branch
Strobilus (group of sporangia)

CLUBMOSS
Selaginella sp.

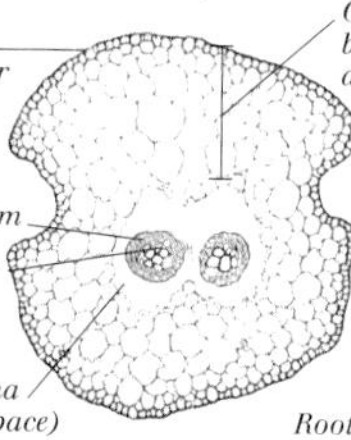
Epidermis (outer layer of cells)
Cortex (layer between epidermis and vascular tissue)
Vascular tissue
Phloem
Xylem
Lacuna (air space)

MICROGRAPH OF CROSS-SECTION THROUGH CLUBMOSS STEM

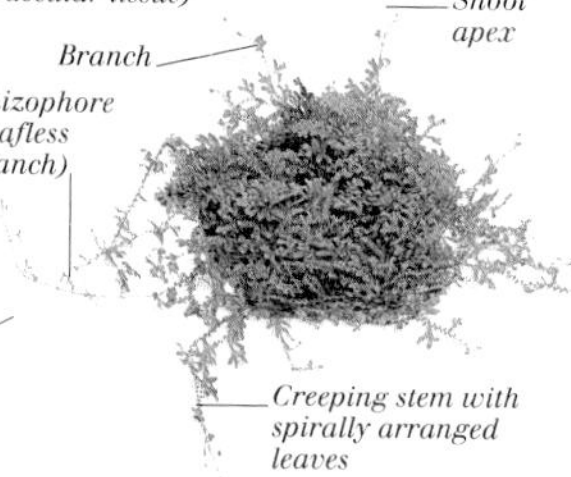
Shoot apex
Branch
Rhizophore (leafless branch)
Root
Creeping stem with spirally arranged leaves

HORSETAIL
Common horsetail
(*Equisetum arvense*)

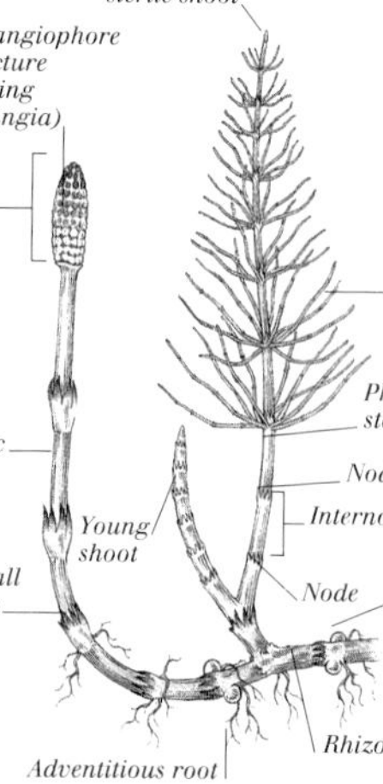
Apex of sterile shoot
Sporangiophore (structure carrying sporangia)
Strobilus (group of sporangia)
Lateral branch
Photosynthetic sterile stem
Non-photosynthetic fertile stem
Node
Internode
Young shoot
Collar of small brown leaves
Node
Tuber
Rhizome
Adventitious root

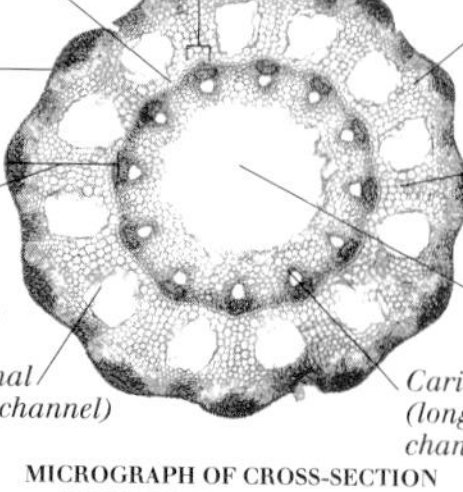
Endodermis (inner layer of cortex)
Vascular tissue
Sclerenchyma (strengthening tissue)
Chlorenchyma (photosynthetic tissue)
Epidermis (outer layer of cells)
Parenchyma (packing tissue)
Cortex (layer between epidermis and vascular tissue)
Hollow pith cavity
Vallecular canal (longitudinal channel)
Carinal canal (longitudinal channel)

MICROGRAPH OF CROSS-SECTION THROUGH HORSETAIL STEM

SPORE PRODUCTION IN FERN

Bracken (*Pteridium aquilinum*)

Apex of pinnule
Sporangium (spore-producing structure)
Pinnule (leaflet of pinna)
Midrib of pinnule
Sorus (group of sporangia)

MICROGRAPH OF LOWER SURFACE OF FERTILE PINNULE

Sporangium (spore-producing structure)
Annulus (ring of cells around sporangium)
Spore
Spore inside dehisced (split open) sporangium
Abaxial (lower) surface of pinnule
Midrib of pinnule

MICROGRAPH OF SPORANGIA ON LOWER SURFACE OF FERTILE PINNULE

FERN

Male fern (*Dryopteris filix-mas*)

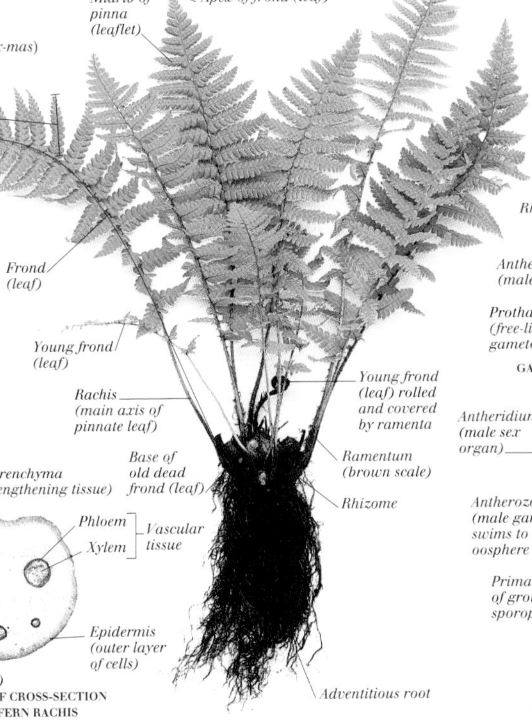
Midrib of pinna (leaflet)
Apex of frond (leaf)
Pinna (leaflet)
Pinnule (leaflet of pinna)
Frond (leaf)
Young frond (leaf)
Rachis (main axis of pinnate leaf)
Young frond (leaf) rolled and covered by ramenta
Base of old dead frond (leaf)
Ramentum (brown scale)
Rhizome
Adventitious root

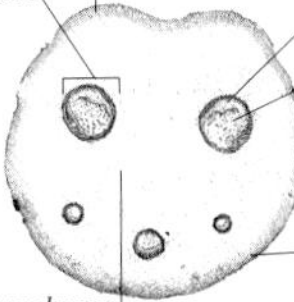
Sclerenchyma (strengthening tissue)
Vascular bundle
Phloem
Xylem
Vascular tissue
Epidermis (outer layer of cells)
Parenchyma (packing tissue)

MICROGRAPH OF CROSS-SECTION THROUGH FERN RACHIS

LIFE-CYCLE OF FERN

Pinna (leaflet)
Pinnule (leaflet of pinna)
Frond (leaf)
Rolled immature frond
Rhizome

SPOROPHYTE

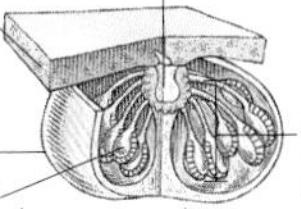
Pinnule (leaflet of pinna)
Placenta
Indusium (flap protecting sorus)
Sorus (group of sporangia)
Sporangium (spore-producing structure)

SECTION THROUGH MATURE PINNULE

Annulus ruptures at weak point
Sporangium splits and releases spores
Spore

RELEASE OF SPORES FROM SPORANGIUM

Spore
Filament develops into prothallus
Rhizoid

GERMINATION OF SPORE

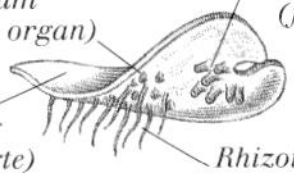
Antheridium (male sex organ)
Archegonium (female sex organ)
Prothallus (free-living gametophyte)
Rhizoid

GAMETOPHYTE PRODUCES GAMETES

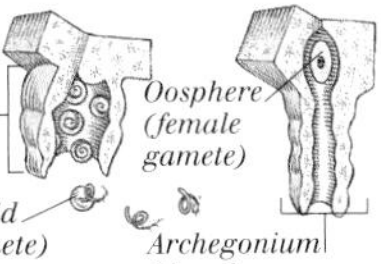
Antheridium (male sex organ)
Oosphere (female gamete)
Antherozoid (male gamete) swims to oosphere
Archegonium (female sex organ)

FERTILIZATION

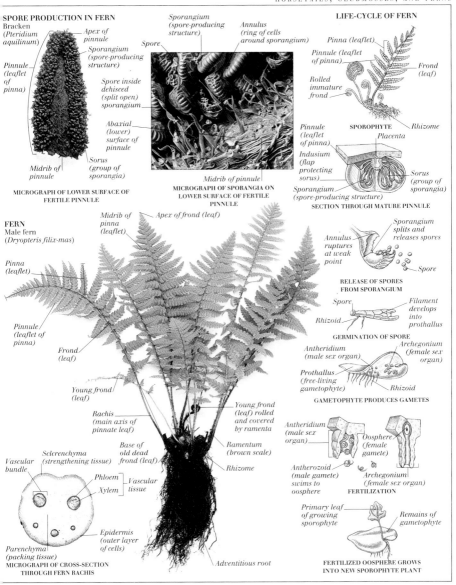

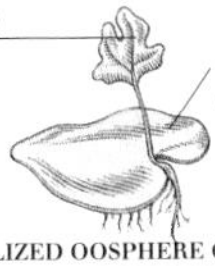
Primary leaf of growing sporophyte
Remains of gametophyte

FERTILIZED OOSPHERE GROWS INTO NEW SPOROPHYTE PLANT

Gymnosperms 1

THE GYMNOSPERMS ARE FOUR RELATED PHYLA of seed-producing plants; their seeds, however, lack the protective, outer covering which surrounds the seeds of flowering plants. Typically, gymnosperms are woody, perennial shrubs or trees, with stems, leaves, and roots, and a well-developed vascular (transport) system. The reproductive structures in most gymnosperms are cones: male cones produce microspores in which male gametes (sex cells) develop; female cones produce megaspores in which female gametes develop. Microspores are blown by the wind to female cones, male and female gametes fuse during fertilization, and a seed develops. The four gymnosperm phyla are the conifers (phylum Coniferophyta), mostly tall trees; cycads (phylum Cycadophyta), small palm-like trees; the ginkgo or maidenhair tree (phylum Ginkgophyta), a tall tree with bilobed leaves; and gnetophytes (phylum Gnetophyta), a diverse group of plants, mainly shrubs, but also including the horizontally growing welwitschia.

LIFE-CYCLE OF SCOTS PINE
(Pinus sylvestris)

Needle (foliage leaf)
Cone

MALE CONES

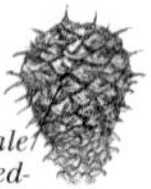

Ovuliferous scale (ovule- then seed-bearing structure)

YOUNG FEMALE CONE

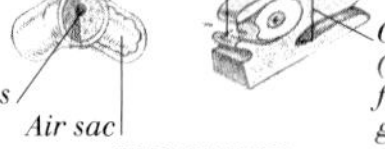

Pollen grain in micropyle (entrance to ovule)
Ovuliferous scale
Pollen grain
Nucleus
Air sac
Ovule (contains female gamete)

POLLINATION

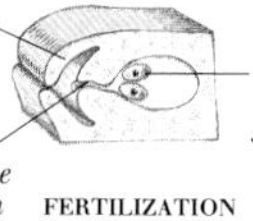

Integument (outer part of ovule)
Archegonium (containing female gamete)
Pollen tube (carries male gamete from pollen grain to ovum)

FERTILIZATION

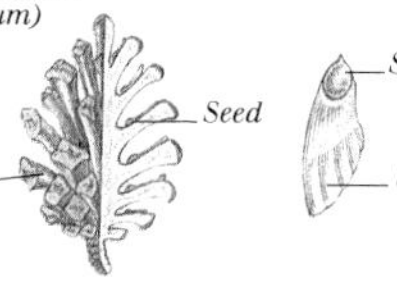

Seed
Ovuliferous scale (ovule- then seed-bearing structure)
Seed
Wing

MATURE FEMALE CONE AND WINGED SEED

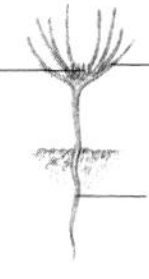

Plumule (embryonic shoot)
Cotyledon (seed leaf)
Root

GERMINATION OF PINE SEEDLING

SCALE AND SEEDS
Pine
(Pinus sp.)

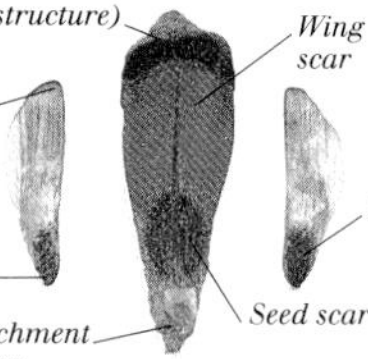

Ovuliferous scale (ovule- then seed-bearing structure)
Wing scar
Wing of seed derived from ovuliferous scale
Seed
Seed
Seed scar
Point of attachment to axis of cone

OVULIFEROUS SCALE FROM THIRD-YEAR FEMALE CONE

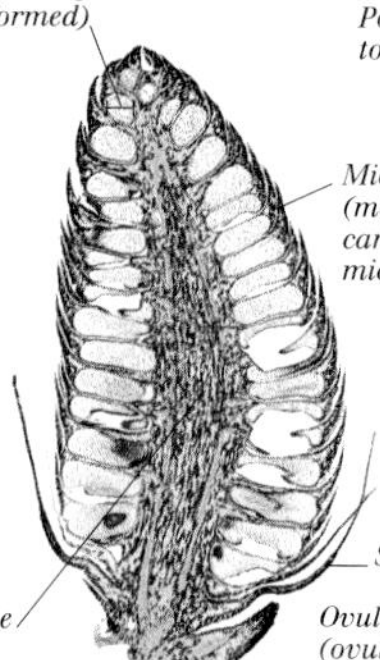

Microsporangium (structure in which pollen grains are formed)
Microsporophyll (modified leaf carrying microsporangia)
Scale leaf
Axis of cone

MICROGRAPH OF LONGITUDINAL SECTION THROUGH YOUNG MALE CONE

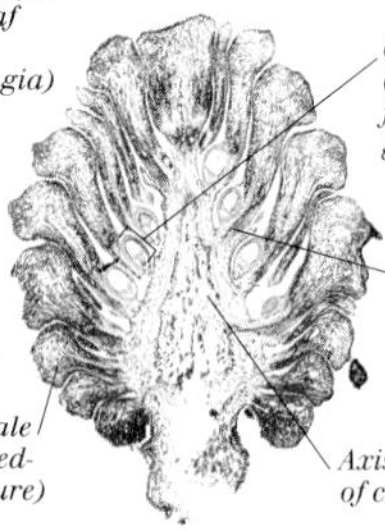

Ovule (contains female gametes)
Bract scale
Ovuliferous scale (ovule- then seed-bearing structure)
Axis of cone

MICROGRAPH OF LONGITUDINAL SECTION THROUGH SECOND-YEAR FEMALE CONE

WELWITSCHIA
(Welwitschia mirabilis)

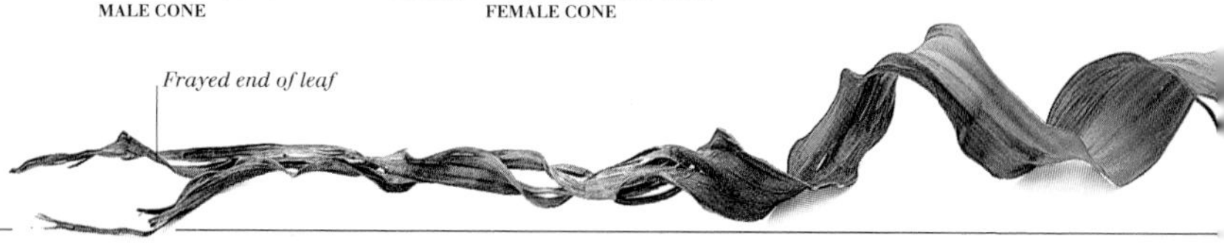

Frayed end of leaf

SMOOTH CYPRESS
(Cupressus glabra)

Immature female cone
Ovuliferous scale (ovule- then seed-bearing structure)
Scale-like leaf
Mature female cone
Immature male cone
Stem

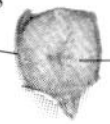
Ovuliferous scale
Ovule (contains female gamete)

CROSS-SECTION THROUGH IMMATURE CONE

Seed
Ovuliferous scale (ovule- then seed-bearing structure)

CROSS-SECTION THROUGH MATURE CONE

Woody scale
Opening between woody scales through which seeds are released

DISCARDED CONE

YEW
(Taxus baccata)

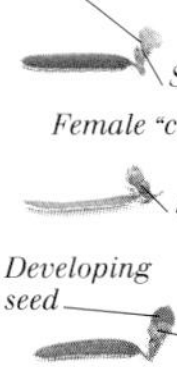
Single ovule (contains female gamete)
Scale
Scale
Developing seed
Scale

FEMALE "CONES" AT VARIOUS STAGES OF DEVELOPMENT

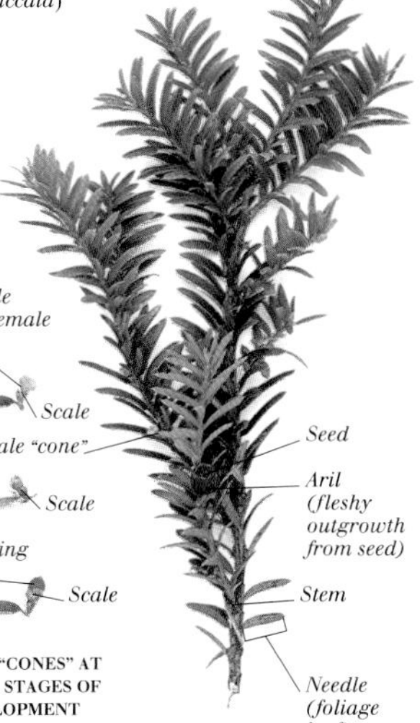
Female "cone"
Seed
Aril (fleshy outgrowth from seed)
Stem
Needle (foliage leaf)

CYCAD
Sago palm
(Cycas revoluta)

Pinna (leaflet)
Pinnate leaf
Scale leaf
Old leaf base
Stem covered by scale leaves

MAIDENHAIR TREE
(Ginkgo biloba)

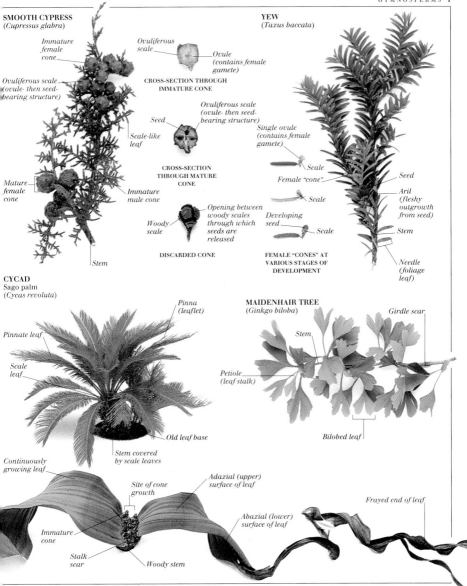

Girdle scar
Stem
Petiole (leaf stalk)
Bilobed leaf

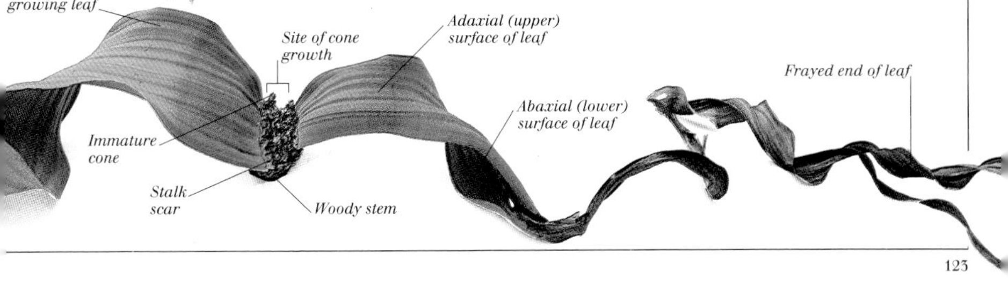
Continuously growing leaf
Site of cone growth
Adaxial (upper) surface of leaf
Frayed end of leaf
Abaxial (lower) surface of leaf
Immature cone
Stalk scar
Woody stem

Gymnosperms 2

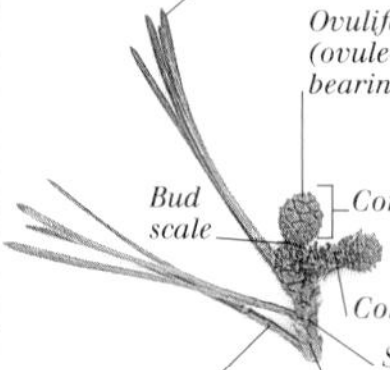
Needle
(foliage leaf)
Ovuliferous scale
(ovule- then seed-
bearing structure)
Bud
scale
Cone
Cone stalk
Stem
Dwarf shoot
Scale leaf scar

FEMALE CONE
(FIRST YEAR)

BRANCH OF BISHOP PINE
(*Pinus muricata*)

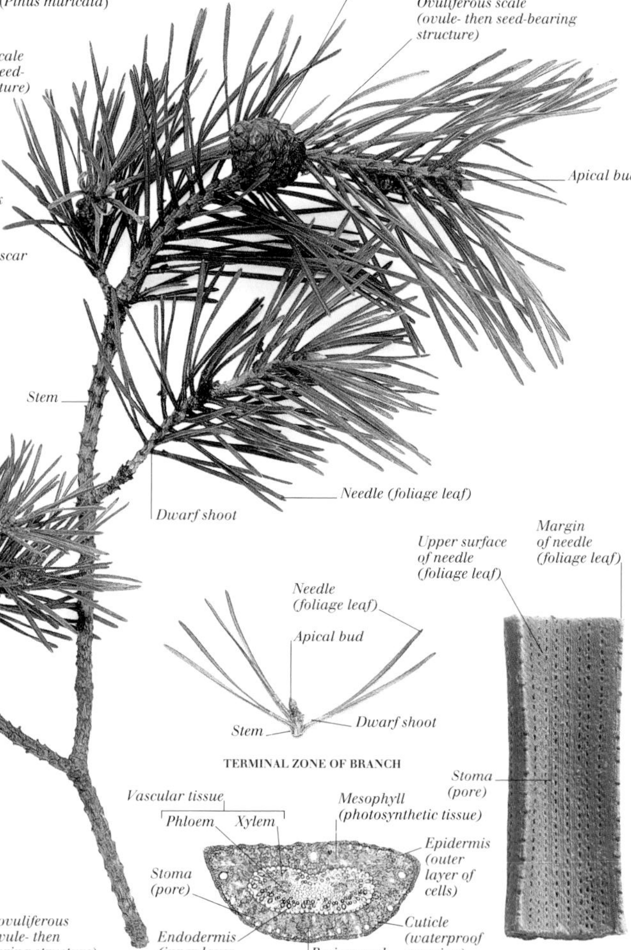
Second-year female cone
Ovuliferous scale
(ovule- then seed-bearing
structure)
Apical bud
Stem
Male cone
Needle (foliage leaf)
Dwarf shoot
Scar of
dwarf shoot
Needle
(foliage leaf)
Apical bud
Stem
Dwarf shoot
Upper surface
of needle
(foliage leaf)
Margin
of needle
(foliage leaf)
Stoma
(pore)
Vascular tissue
Phloem
Xylem
Mesophyll
(photosynthetic tissue)
Epidermis
(outer
layer of
cells)
Stoma
(pore)
Cuticle
(waterproof
covering)
Endodermis
(inner layer
of cortex)
Resin canal

TERMINAL ZONE OF BRANCH

MICROGRAPH OF CROSS-SECTION
THROUGH NEEDLE (FOLIAGE LEAF)

MICROGRAPH OF NEEDLE
(FOLIAGE LEAF) OF PINE
(*Pinus sp.*)

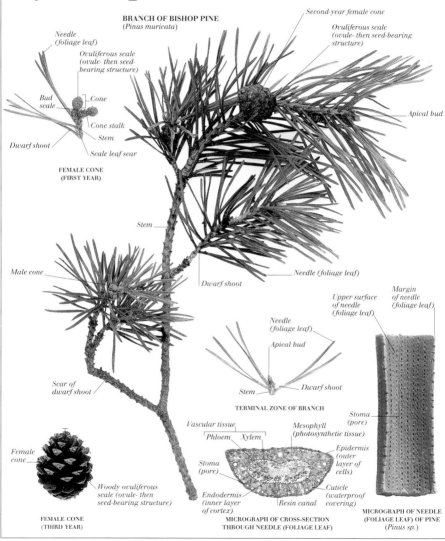

Female
cone
Woody ovuliferous
scale (ovule- then
seed-bearing structure)

FEMALE CONE
(THIRD YEAR)

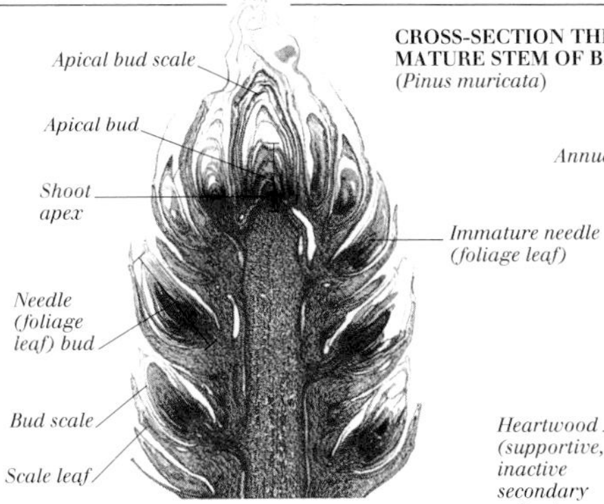

Apical bud scale
Apical bud
Shoot apex
Immature needle (foliage leaf)
Needle (foliage leaf) bud
Bud scale
Scale leaf

MICROGRAPH OF LONGITUDINAL SECTION THROUGH SHOOT APEX OF PINE
(*Pinus sp.*)

CROSS-SECTION THROUGH MATURE STEM OF BISHOP PINE
(*Pinus muricata*)

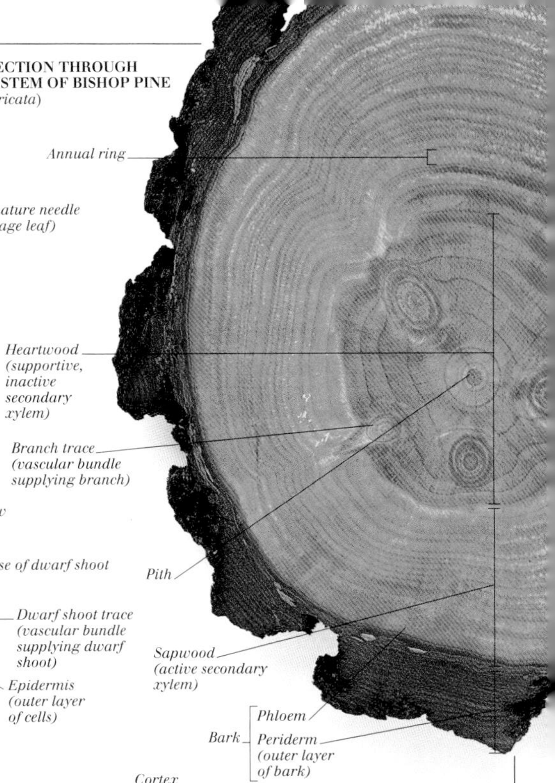

Annual ring
Heartwood (supportive, inactive secondary xylem)
Branch trace (vascular bundle supplying branch)
Pith
Sapwood (active secondary xylem)
Bark
Phloem
Periderm (outer layer of bark)

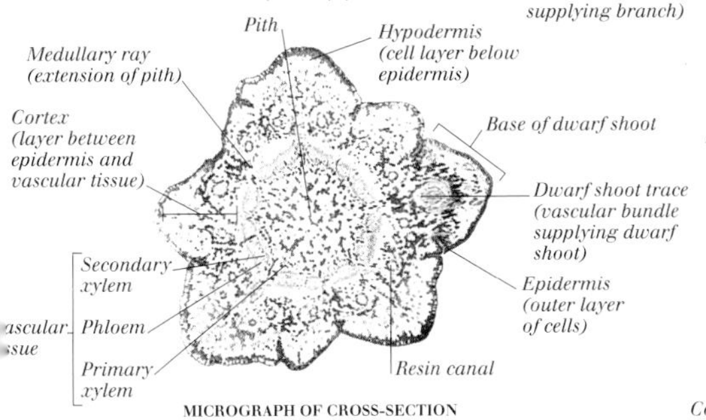

Pith
Hypodermis (cell layer below epidermis)
Medullary ray (extension of pith)
Cortex (layer between epidermis and vascular tissue)
Base of dwarf shoot
Dwarf shoot trace (vascular bundle supplying dwarf shoot)
Secondary xylem
Epidermis (outer layer of cells)
ascular
ssue
Phloem
Primary xylem
Resin canal

MICROGRAPH OF CROSS-SECTION THROUGH YOUNG STEM OF PINE
(*Pinus sp.*)

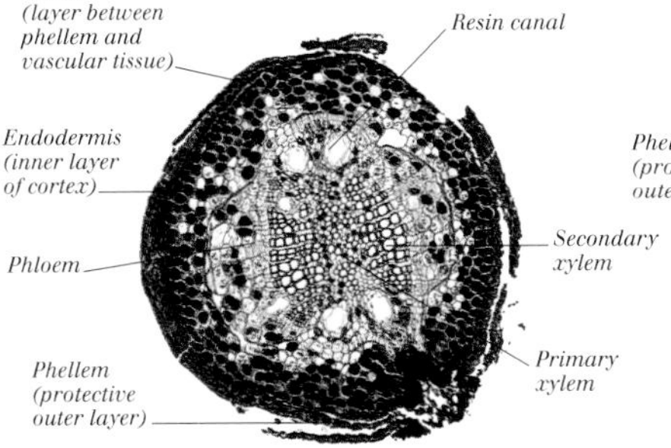

Cortex (layer between phellem and vascular tissue)
Resin canal
Endodermis (inner layer of cortex)
Phloem
Secondary xylem
Primary xylem
Phellem (protective outer layer)

MICROGRAPH OF CROSS-SECTION THROUGH YOUNG ROOT OF PINE
(*Pinus sp.*)

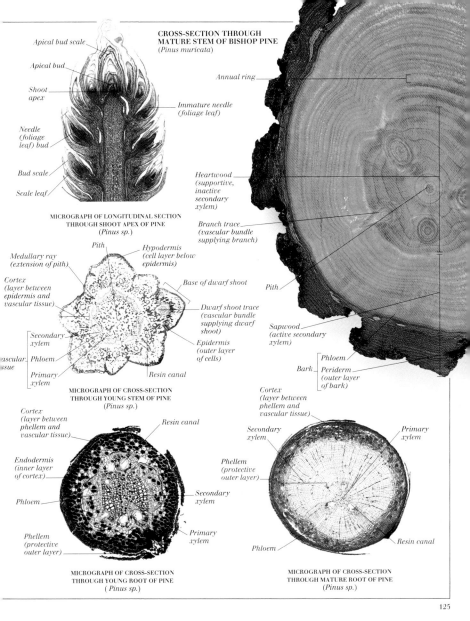

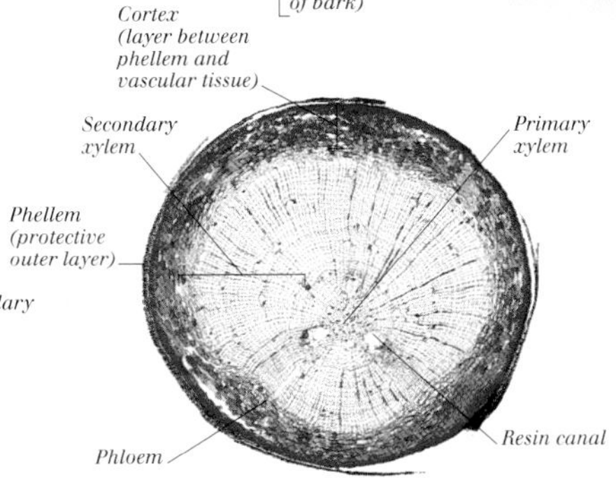

Cortex (layer between phellem and vascular tissue)
Secondary xylem
Primary xylem
Phellem (protective outer layer)
Phloem
Resin canal

MICROGRAPH OF CROSS-SECTION THROUGH MATURE ROOT OF PINE
(*Pinus sp.*)

Monocotyledons and dicotyledons

COMPARISONS BETWEEN MONOCOTYLEDONS AND DICOTYLEDONS

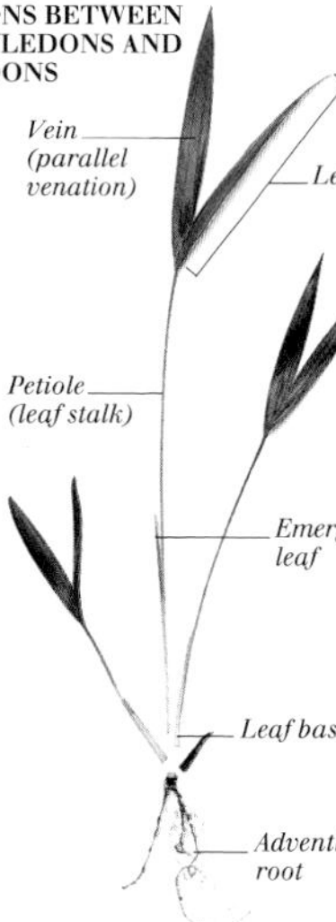

Vein (parallel venation)
Leaflet
Petiole (leaf stalk)
Emerging leaf
Leaf base
Adventitious root

A MONOCOTYLEDON
Paradise palm
(*Howea forsteriana*)

FLOWERING PLANTS (PHYLUM ANGIOSPERMOPHYTA) are divided into two classes: monocotyledons (class Monocotyledoneae) and dicotyledons (class Dicotyledoneae). Typically, monocotyledons have seeds with one cotyledon (seed leaf); their foliage leaves are narrow with parallel veins; the flower components occur in multiples of three; sepals and petals are indistinguishable and are known as tepals; vascular (transport) tissues are scattered in random bundles throughout the stem; and, since they lack stem cambium (actively dividing cells that produce wood), most monocotyledons are herbaceous (see pp. 128-129). Dicotyledons have seeds with two cotyledons; leaves are broad with a central midrib and branched veins; flower parts occur in multiples of four or five; sepals are generally small and green; petals are large and colourful; vascular bundles are arranged in a ring around the edge of the stem; and, because many dicotyledons possess wood-producing stem cambium, there are woody forms (see pp. 130-131) as well as herbaceous ones.

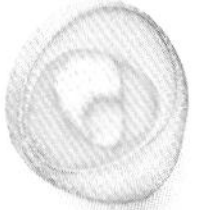

CROSS-SECTION THROUGH MONOCOTYLEDONOUS LEAF BASES

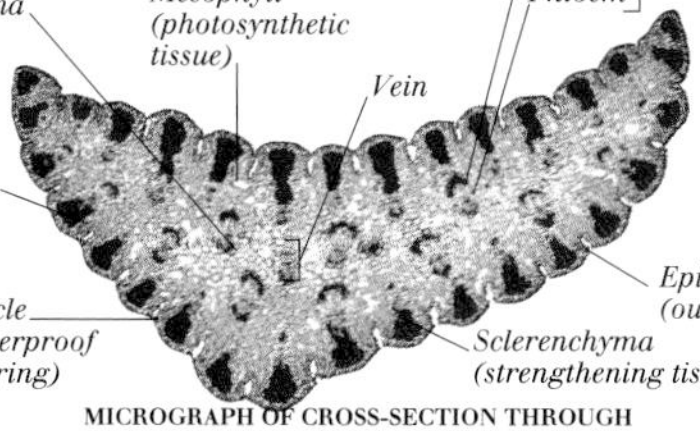

Xylem
Phloem
Vascular tissue
Water-absorbing parenchyma (packing tissue)
Mesophyll (photosynthetic tissue)
Vein
Sunken stoma (pore)
Cuticle (waterproof covering)
Epidermis (outer layer of cells)
Sclerenchyma (strengthening tissue)

MICROGRAPH OF CROSS-SECTION THROUGH A MONOCOTYLEDONOUS LEAF
Yucca (*Yucca sp.*)

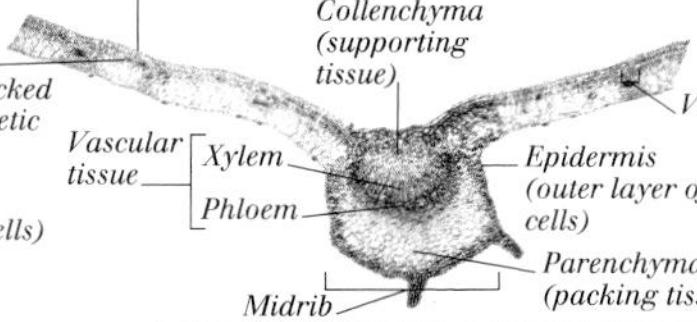

Palisade mesophyll (tightly packed photosynthetic tissue)
Spongy mesophyll (loosely packed photosynthetic tissue)
Collenchyma (supporting tissue)
Vein
Vascular tissue
Xylem
Phloem
Epidermis (outer layer of cells)
Parenchyma (packing tissue)
Midrib

MICROGRAPH OF CROSS-SECTION THROUGH A DICOTYLEDONOUS LEAF
Crab apple (*Malus sp.*)

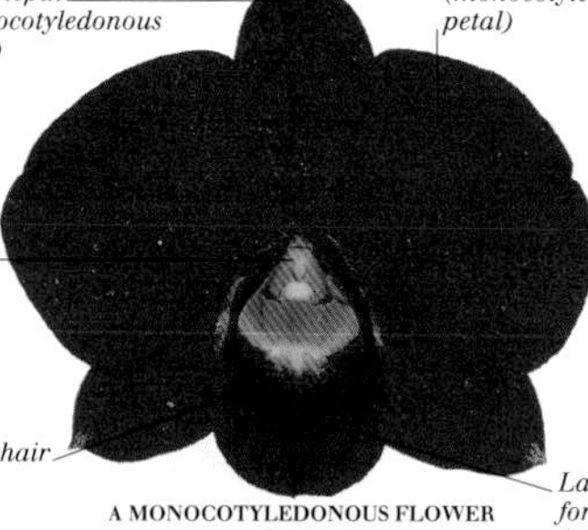

Outer tepal (monocotyledonous sepal)
Lateral, inner tepal (monocotyledonous petal)
Column (stamens and style)
Guide hair
Labellum (lip) forming landing stage for pollinator

A MONOCOTYLEDONOUS FLOWER
Orchid
(*Phalaenopsis sp.*)

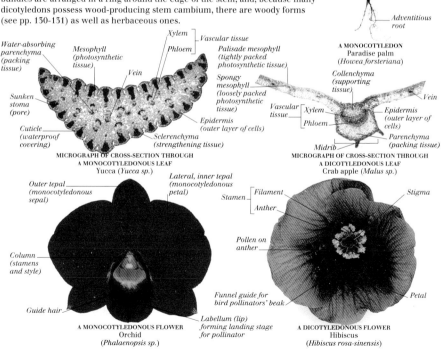

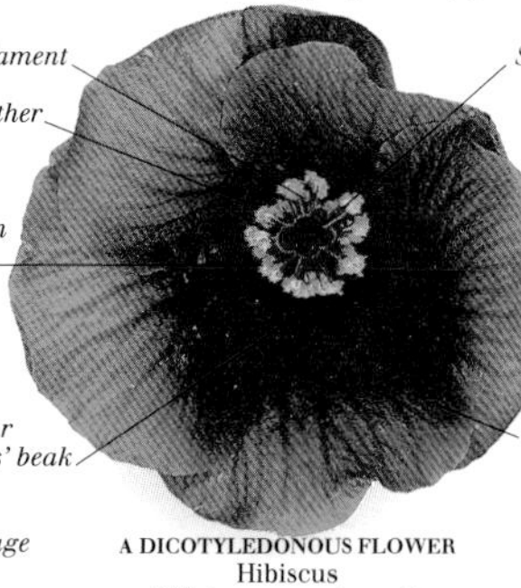

Stamen
Filament
Anther
Stigma
Pollen on anther
Funnel guide for bird pollinators' beak
Petal

A DICOTYLEDONOUS FLOWER
Hibiscus
(*Hibiscus rosa-sinensis*)

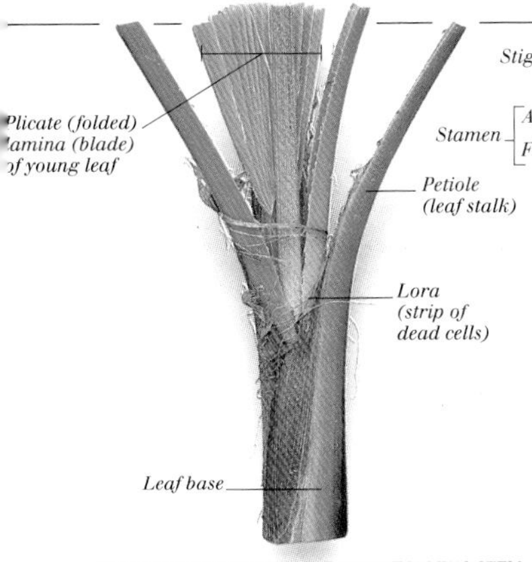
Plicate (folded)
amina (blade)
of young leaf
Petiole
(leaf stalk)
Lora
(strip of
dead cells)
Leaf base

MONOCOTYLEDONOUS LEAF BASES FORMING STEM
Chusan palm
(*Trachycarpus fortunei*)

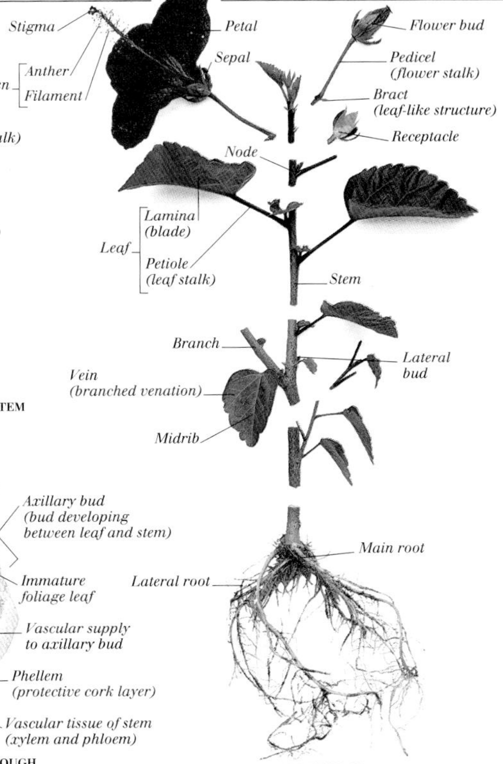
Stigma
Stamen
Anther
Filament
Petal
Sepal
Flower bud
Pedicel
(flower stalk)
Bract
(leaf-like structure)
Receptacle
Node
Leaf
Lamina
(blade)
Petiole
(leaf stalk)
Stem
Branch
Lateral
bud
Vein
(branched venation)
Midrib
Main root
Lateral root

A DICOTYLEDON
Hibiscus (*Hibiscus rosa-sinensis*)

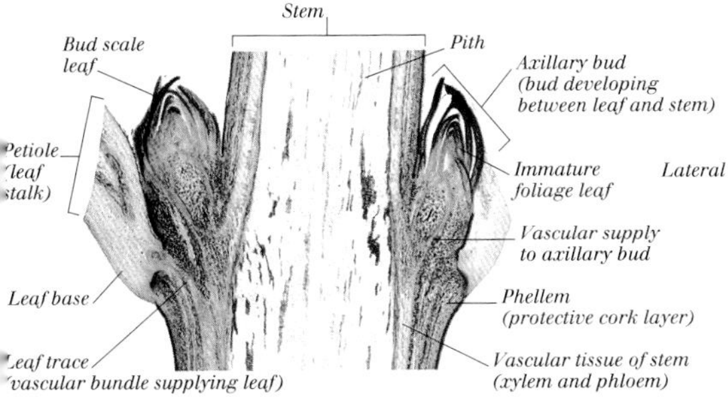
Stem
Bud scale
leaf
Pith
Axillary bud
(bud developing
between leaf and stem)
etiole
leaf
stalk)
Immature
foliage leaf
Vascular supply
to axillary bud
Leaf base
Phellem
(protective cork layer)
eaf trace
vascular bundle supplying leaf)
Vascular tissue of stem
(xylem and phloem)

MICROGRAPH OF LONGITUDINAL SECTION THROUGH A WOODY DICOTYLEDONOUS STEM
Maple (*Acer sp.*)

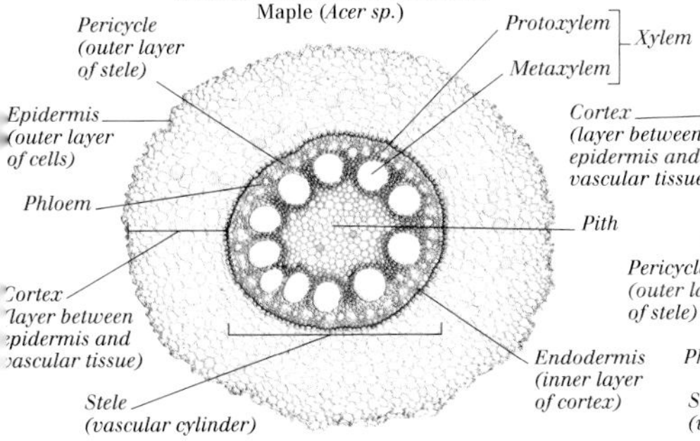
Pericycle
(outer layer
of stele)
Protoxylem
Metaxylem
Xylem
Epidermis
(outer layer
of cells)
Phloem
Pith
ortex
layer between
pidermis and
ascular tissue)
Endodermis
(inner layer
of cortex)
Stele
(vascular cylinder)

MICROGRAPH OF CROSS-SECTION THROUGH A MONOCOTYLEDONOUS ROOT
Maize (*Zea mays*)

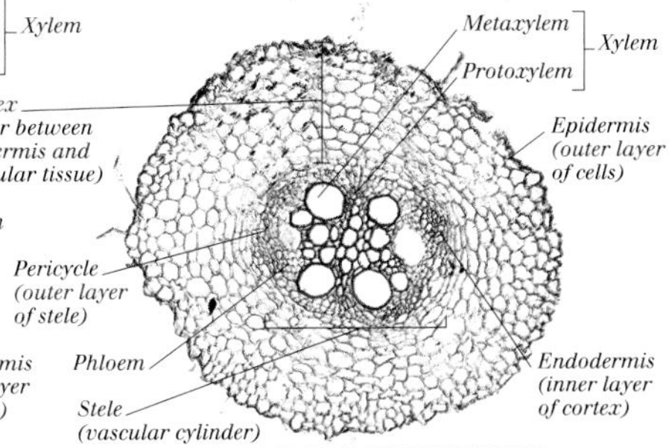
Metaxylem
Protoxylem
Xylem
Cortex
(layer between
epidermis and
vascular tissue)
Epidermis
(outer layer
of cells)
Pericycle
(outer layer
of stele)
Phloem
Endodermis
(inner layer
of cortex)
Stele
(vascular cylinder)

MICROGRAPH OF CROSS-SECTION THROUGH A DICOTYLEDONOUS ROOT
Buttercup (*Ranunculus sp.*)

Herbaceous flowering plants

HERBACEOUS FLOWERING PLANTS TYPICALLY HAVE GREEN, NON-WOODY STEMS, and tend to be relatively short-lived. Many herbaceous plants live for only one or two years. Annuals (e.g., sweet peas) grow from seed, produce flowers and then seeds, and die within a single year. Biennials (e.g., carrots) have a two-year life cycle. In the first year, seeds grow into plants, which produce leaves and store food in underground storage organs; the stems and foliage then die back in winter. In the second year, new stems grow from the storage organs, produce leaves, flowers, and seeds, and then die. Some herbaceous plants (e.g., potatoes) are perennial. They grow back year after year, producing shoots and flowers in spring, storing food in underground tubers or rhizomes during summer, dying back in autumn, and surviving underground during winter.

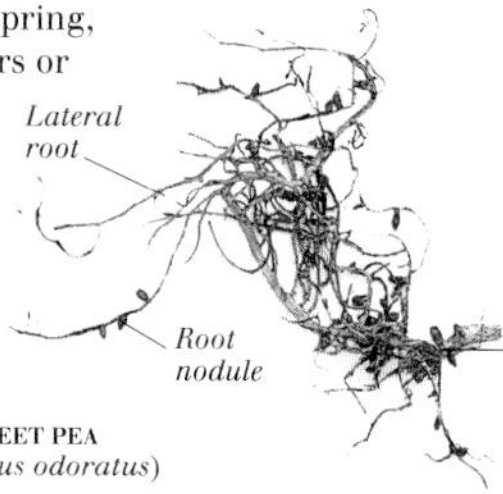
Lateral root
Root nodule
Main root

SWEET PEA
(*Lathyrus odoratus*)

Young plant forming
Petiole (stalk) of young leaf
Stipule (structure at base of leaf)
Trifoliate leaf
Node
Simple ovate leaflet
Runner (creeping stem)

STRAWBERRY
(*Fragaria x ananassa*)

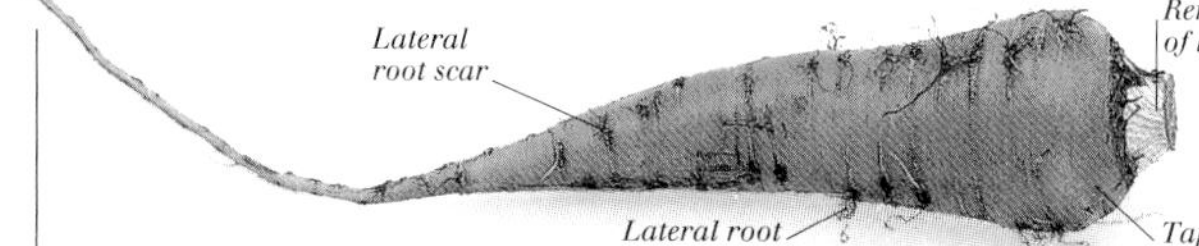
Lateral root scar
Remains of leaves
Lateral root
Tap root

CARROT
(*Daucus carota*)

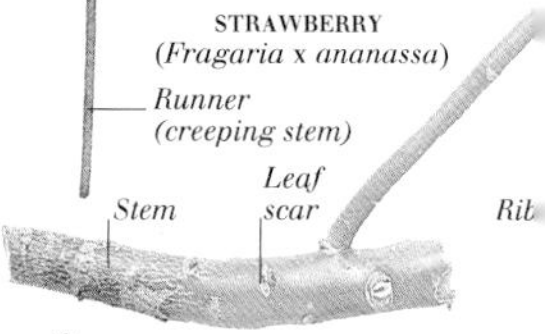
Stem
Leaf scar
Rib

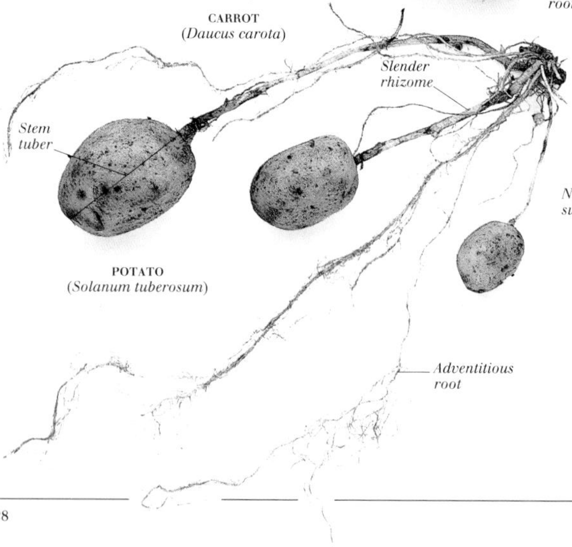
Slender rhizome
Stem tuber
Adventitious root

POTATO
(*Solanum tuberosum*)

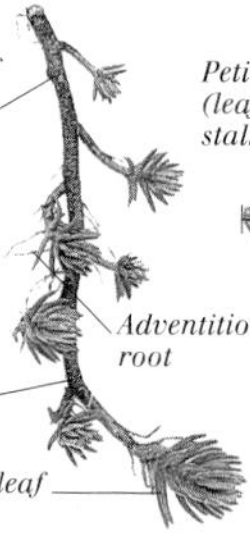
Leaf scar
Adventitious root
Stem
Narrow, succulent leaf

ROCK STONECROP
(*Sedum rupestre*)

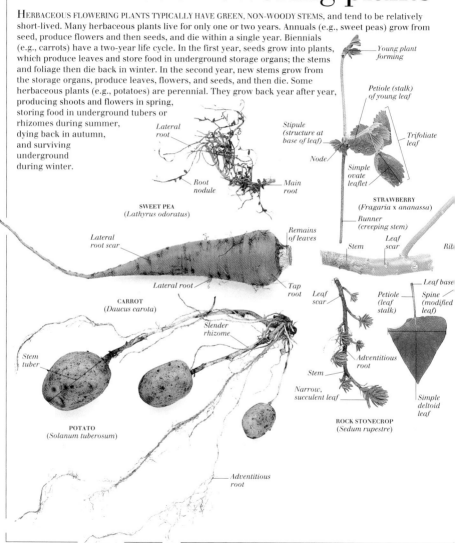

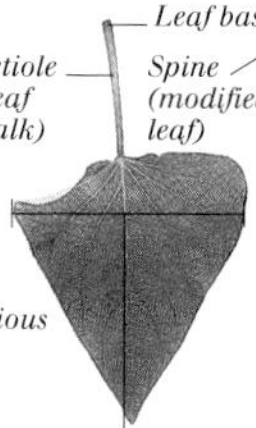
Leaf base
Petiole (leaf stalk)
Spine (modified leaf)
Simple deltoid leaf

ARTS OF HERBACEOUS FLOWERING PLANTS

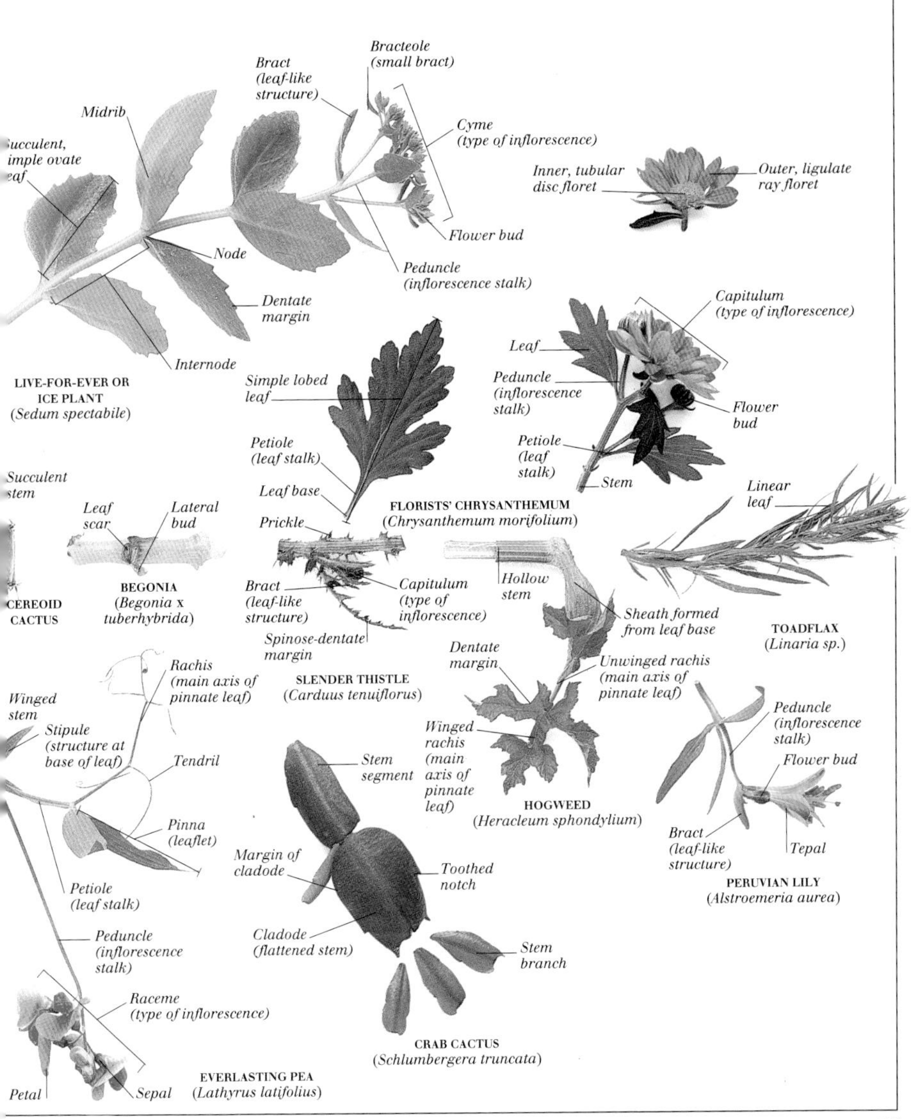
Bracteole
(small bract)
Bract
(leaf-like
structure)
Midrib
ucculent,
imple ovate
eaf
Cyme
(type of inflorescence)
Inner, tubular
disc floret
Outer, ligulate
ray floret
Flower bud
Node
Peduncle
(inflorescence stalk)
Dentate
margin
Internode
LIVE-FOR-EVER OR
ICE PLANT
(Sedum spectabile)
Capitulum
(type of inflorescence)
Leaf
Peduncle
(inflorescence
stalk)
Flower
bud
Petiole
(leaf
stalk)
Stem
Simple lobed
leaf
Petiole
(leaf stalk)
Leaf base
FLORISTS' CHRYSANTHEMUM
(Chrysanthemum morifolium)
Succulent
stem
Leaf
scar
Lateral
bud
Prickle
Linear
leaf
CEREOID
CACTUS
BEGONIA
(Begonia x
tuberhybrida)
Bract
(leaf-like
structure)
Capitulum
(type of
inflorescence)
Hollow
stem
Sheath formed
from leaf base
TOADFLAX
(Linaria sp.)
Spinose-dentate
margin
SLENDER THISTLE
(Carduus tenuiflorus)
Dentate
margin
Unwinged rachis
(main axis of
pinnate leaf)
Rachis
(main axis of
pinnate leaf)
Winged
stem
Stipule
(structure at
base of leaf)
Tendril
Winged
rachis
(main
axis of
pinnate
leaf)
Peduncle
(inflorescence
stalk)
Flower bud
Stem
segment
HOGWEED
(Heracleum sphondylium)
Pinna
(leaflet)
Bract
(leaf-like
structure)
Tepal
Margin of
cladode
Toothed
notch
PERUVIAN LILY
(Alstroemeria aurea)
Petiole
(leaf stalk)
Cladode
(flattened stem)
Stem
branch
Peduncle
(inflorescence
stalk)
Raceme
(type of inflorescence)
CRAB CACTUS
(Schlumbergera truncata)
EVERLASTING PEA
(Lathyrus latifolius)
Petal
Sepal

Woody flowering plants

WOODY FLOWERING PLANTS ARE PERENNIAL, that is, they continue to grow and reproduce for many years. They have one or more permanent stems above ground, and numerous smaller branches. The stems and branches have a strong woody core that supports the plant and contains vascular tissue for transporting water and nutrients. Outside the woody core is a layer of tough, protective bark, which has lenticels (tiny pores) in it to enable gases to pass through. Woody flowering plants may be shrubs, which have several stems arising from the soil; bushes, which are shrubs with dense branching and foliage; or trees, which typically have a single upright stem (the trunk) that bears branches. Deciduous woody plants (e.g., roses) shed all their leaves once a year and remain leafless during winter. Evergreen woody plants (e.g., ivy) shed their leaves gradually, so retaining full leaf cover throughout the year.

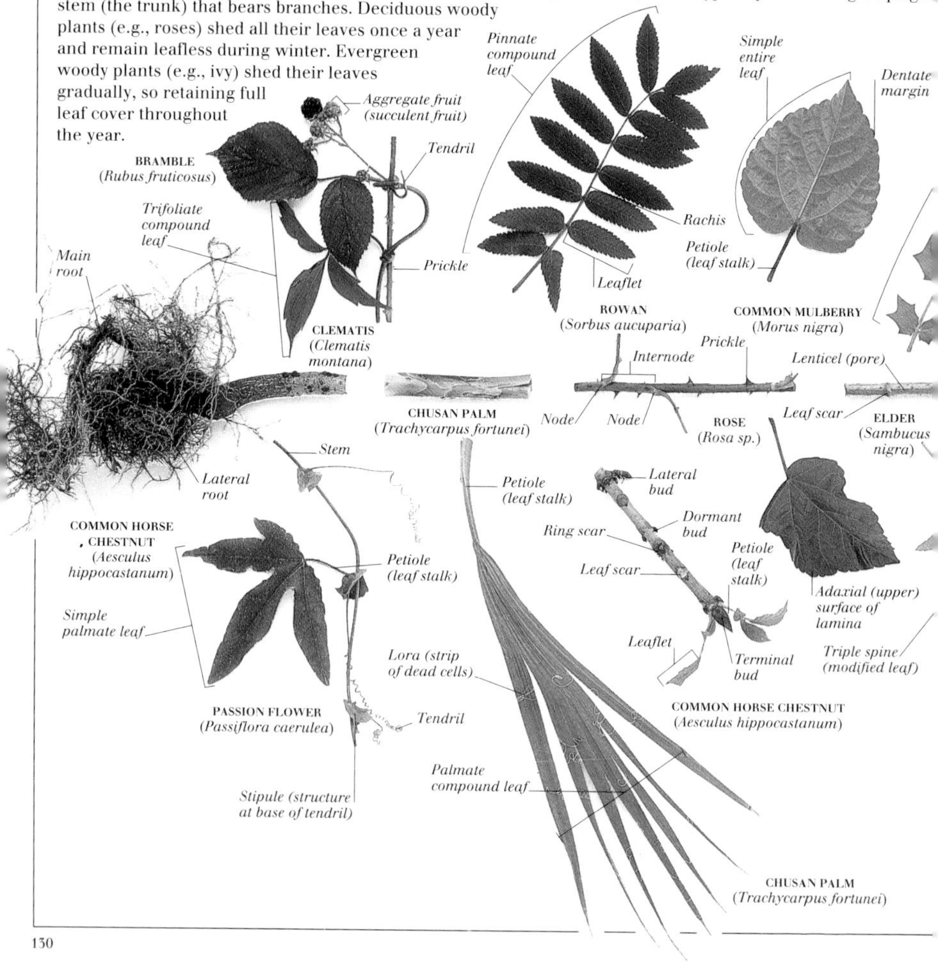
Aggregate fruit (succulent fruit)
Tendril
BRAMBLE (Rubus fruticosus)
Trifoliate compound leaf
Prickle
CLEMATIS (Clematis montana)
Main root
Lateral root
COMMON HORSE CHESTNUT (Aesculus hippocastanum)
Pinnate compound leaf
Rachis
Leaflet
ROWAN (Sorbus aucuparia)
Simple entire leaf
Dentate margin
Petiole (leaf stalk)
COMMON MULBERRY (Morus nigra)
CHUSAN PALM (Trachycarpus fortunei)
Internode
Prickle
Node
Node
ROSE (Rosa sp.)
Lenticel (pore)
Leaf scar
ELDER (Sambucus nigra)
Stem
Petiole (leaf stalk)
Simple palmate leaf
Tendril
Stipule (structure at base of tendril)
PASSION FLOWER (Passiflora caerulea)
Petiole (leaf stalk)
Lora (strip of dead cells)
Palmate compound leaf
CHUSAN PALM (Trachycarpus fortunei)
Lateral bud
Dormant bud
Ring scar
Leaf scar
Petiole (leaf stalk)
Leaflet
Terminal bud
COMMON HORSE CHESTNUT (Aesculus hippocastanum)
Adaxial (upper) surface of lamina
Triple spine (modified leaf)

PARTS OF WOODY FLOWERING PLANTS

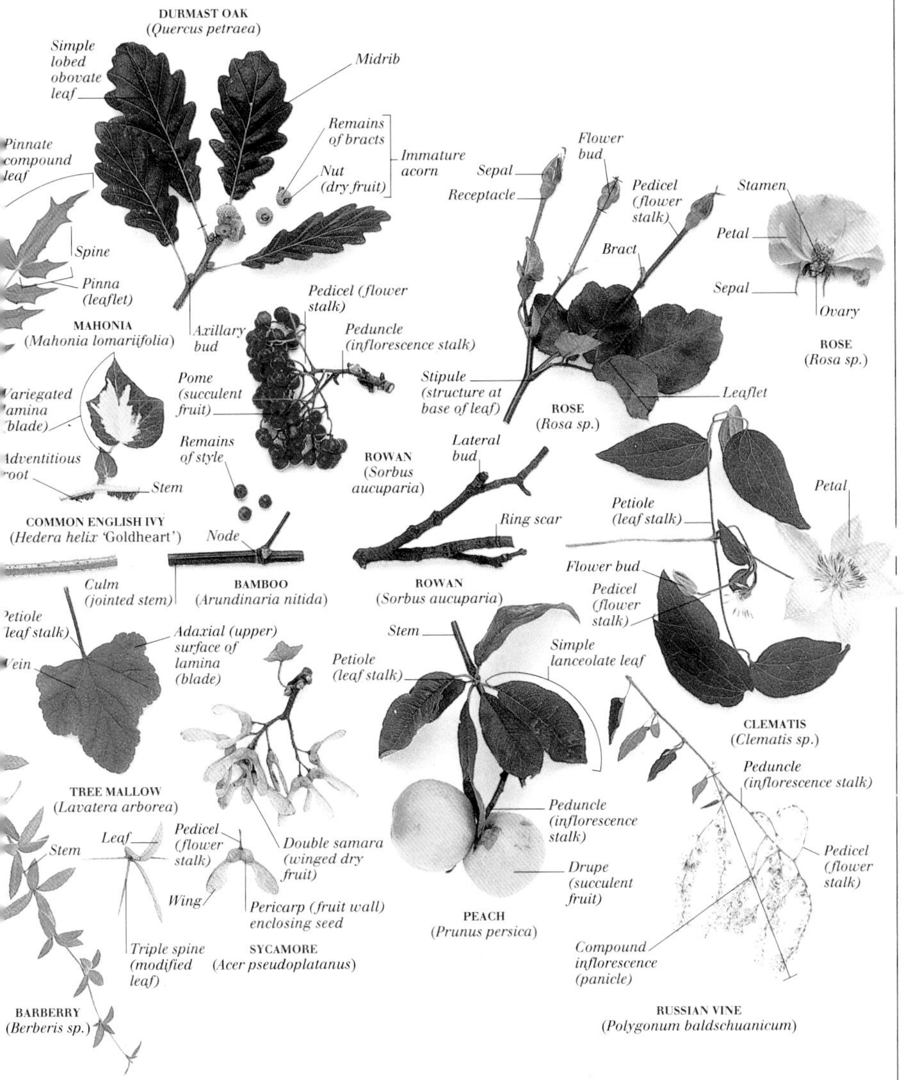
DURMAST OAK
(Quercus petraea)
Simple lobed obovate leaf
Midrib
Remains of bracts
Nut (dry fruit)
Immature acorn
Axillary bud
Pinnate compound leaf
Spine
Pinna (leaflet)
MAHONIA
(Mahonia lomariifolia)
ariegated amina blade)
dventitious oot
Stem
COMMON ENGLISH IVY
(Hedera helix 'Goldheart')
Pedicel (flower stalk)
Peduncle (inflorescence stalk)
Pome (succulent fruit)
Remains of style
ROWAN
(Sorbus aucuparia)
Node
Culm (jointed stem)
BAMBOO
(Arundinaria nitida)
Lateral bud
Ring scar
ROWAN
(Sorbus aucuparia)
Flower bud
Sepal
Receptacle
Pedicel (flower stalk)
Bract
Stipule (structure at base of leaf)
ROSE
(Rosa sp.)
Leaflet
Stamen
Petal
Sepal
Ovary
ROSE
(Rosa sp.)
etiole leaf stalk)
Adaxial (upper) surface of lamina (blade)
ein
TREE MALLOW
(Lavatera arborea)
Stem
Leaf
Pedicel (flower stalk)
Double samara (winged dry fruit)
Wing
Pericarp (fruit wall) enclosing seed
Triple spine (modified leaf)
SYCAMORE
(Acer pseudoplatanus)
BARBERRY
(Berberis sp.)
Stem
Petiole (leaf stalk)
Simple lanceolate leaf
Peduncle (inflorescence stalk)
Drupe (succulent fruit)
PEACH
(Prunus persica)
Petiole (leaf stalk)
Petal
Flower bud
Pedicel (flower stalk)
CLEMATIS
(Clematis sp.)
Peduncle (inflorescence stalk)
Pedicel (flower stalk)
Compound inflorescence (panicle)
RUSSIAN VINE
(Polygonum baldschuanicum)

Roots

ROOTS ARE THE UNDERGROUND PARTS OF PLANTS. They have three main functions. First, they anchor the plant in the soil. Second, they absorb water and minerals from the spaces between soil particles; the roots' absorptive properties are increased by root hairs, which grow behind the root tip, allowing maximum uptake of vital substances. Third, the root is part of the plant's transport system: xylem carries water and minerals from the roots to the stem and leaves, and phloem carries nutrients from the leaves to all parts of the root system. In addition, some roots (e.g., carrots) are food stores. Roots have an outer epidermis covering a cortex of parenchyma (packing tissue), and a central cylinder of vascular tissue. This arrangement helps the roots resist the forces of compression as they grow through the soil.

CARROT
(Daucus carota)

MICROGRAPH OF PRIMARY ROOT DEVELOPMENT
Cabbage (*Brassica sp.*)

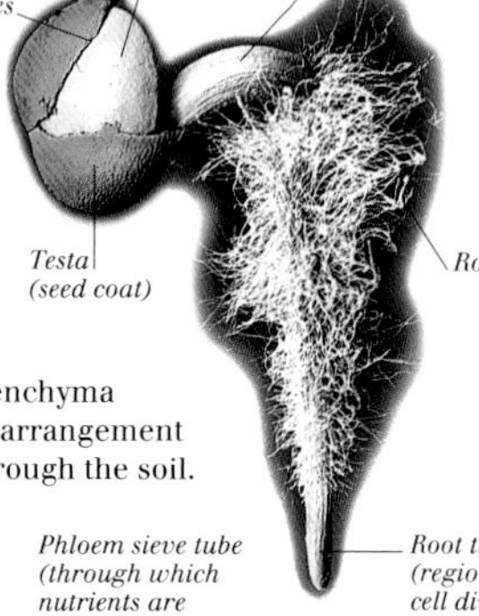

Split in testa as seed germinates
Cotyledon (seed leaf)
Primary root
Root hair
Testa (seed coat)
Root tip (region of cell division)

FEATURES OF A TYPICAL ROOT
Buttercup
(*Ranunculus sp.*)

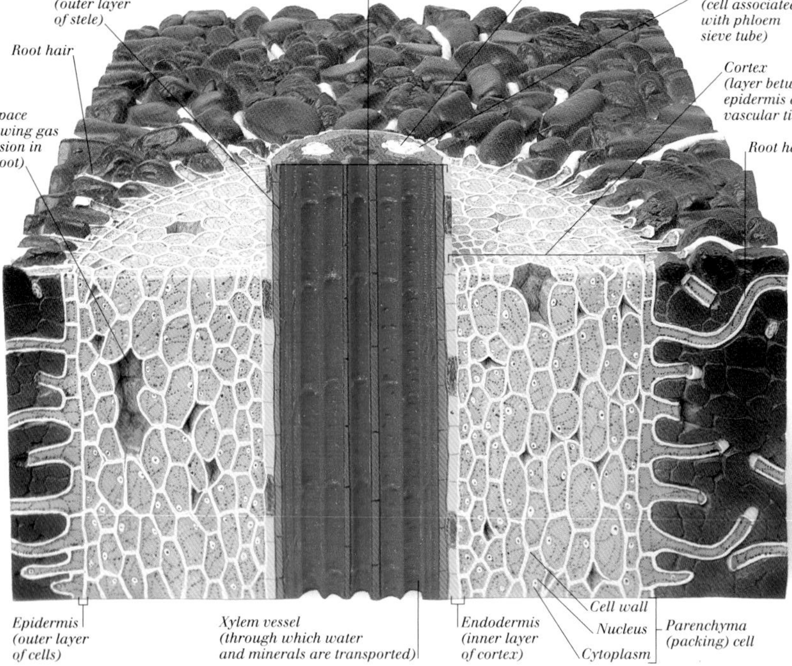

Stele (vascular cylinder)
Phloem sieve tube (through which nutrients are transported)
Pericycle (outer layer of stele)
Companion cell (cell associated with phloem sieve tube)
Root hair
Cortex (layer between epidermis and vascular tissue)
Air space (allowing gas diffusion in the root)
Root hair
Cell wall
Epidermis (outer layer of cells)
Xylem vessel (through which water and minerals are transported)
Endodermis (inner layer of cortex)
Nucleus
Parenchyma (packing) cell
Cytoplasm

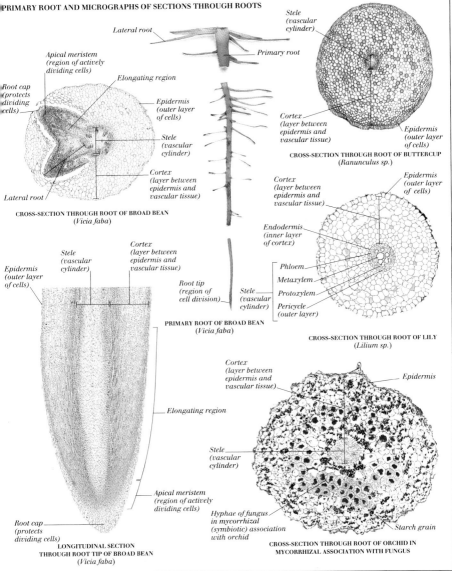

PRIMARY ROOT AND MICROGRAPHS OF SECTIONS THROUGH ROOTS

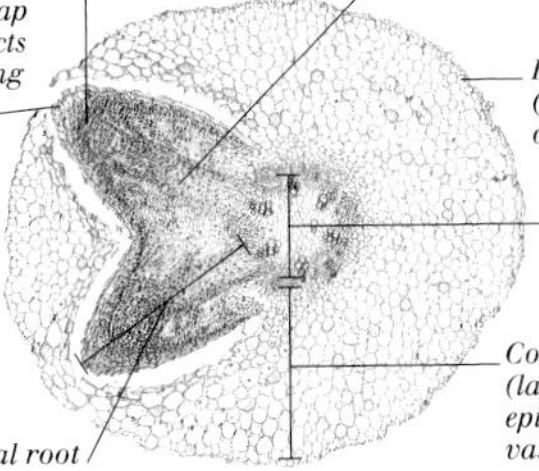
Apical meristem (region of actively dividing cells)
Elongating region
Root cap (protects dividing cells)
Epidermis (outer layer of cells)
Stele (vascular cylinder)
Cortex (layer between epidermis and vascular tissue)
Lateral root

CROSS-SECTION THROUGH ROOT OF BROAD BEAN
(*Vicia faba*)

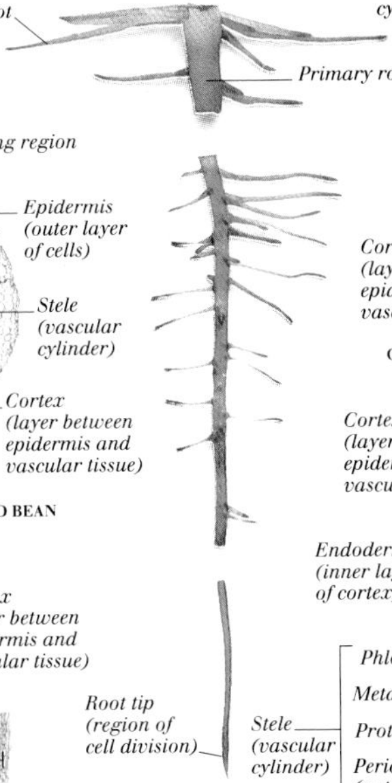
Lateral root
Primary root
Root tip (region of cell division)

PRIMARY ROOT OF BROAD BEAN
(*Vicia faba*)

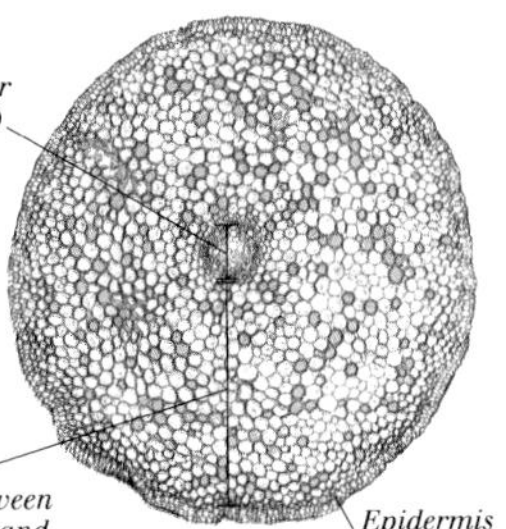
Stele (vascular cylinder)
Cortex (layer between epidermis and vascular tissue)
Epidermis (outer layer of cells)

CROSS-SECTION THROUGH ROOT OF BUTTERCUP
(*Ranunculus sp.*)

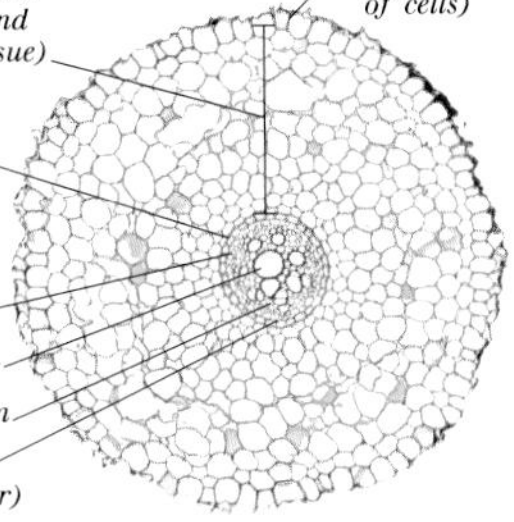
Cortex (layer between epidermis and vascular tissue)
Epidermis (outer layer of cells)
Endodermis (inner layer of cortex)
Phloem
Metaxylem
Stele (vascular cylinder)
Protoxylem
Pericycle (outer layer)

CROSS-SECTION THROUGH ROOT OF LILY
(*Lilium sp.*)

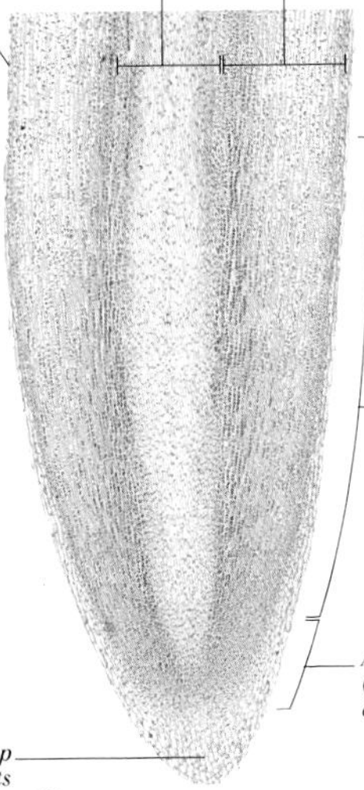
Stele (vascular cylinder)
Cortex (layer between epidermis and vascular tissue)
Epidermis (outer layer of cells)
Elongating region
Apical meristem (region of actively dividing cells)
Root cap (protects dividing cells)

LONGITUDINAL SECTION
THROUGH ROOT TIP OF BROAD BEAN
(*Vicia faba*)

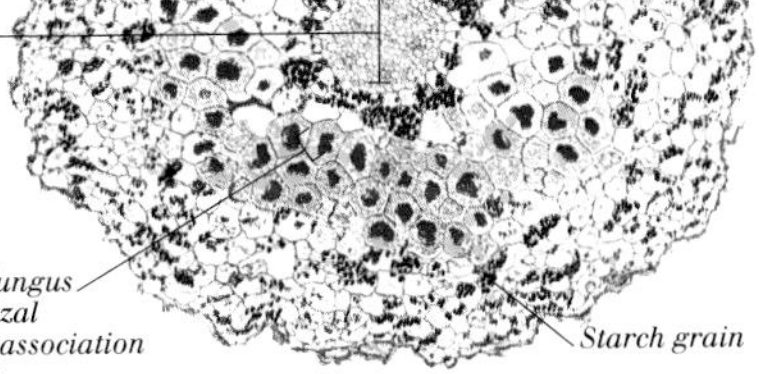
Cortex (layer between epidermis and vascular tissue)
Epidermis
Stele (vascular cylinder)
Hyphae of fungus in mycorrhizal (symbiotic) association with orchid
Starch grain

CROSS-SECTION THROUGH ROOT OF ORCHID IN
MYCORRHIZAL ASSOCIATION WITH FUNGUS

Stems

THE STEM IS THE MAIN SUPPORTIVE PART OF A PLANT that grows above ground. Stems bear leaves (organs of photosynthesis), which grow at nodes; buds (shoots covered by protective scales), which grow at the stem tip (apical or terminal buds) and in the angle between a leaf and the stem (axillary or lateral buds); and flowers (reproductive structures). The stem forms part of the plant's transport system: xylem tissue in the stem transports water and minerals from the roots to the aerial parts of the plant, and phloem tissue transports nutrients manufactured in the leaves to other parts of the plant. Stem tissues are also used for storing water and food. Herbaceous (non-woody) stems have an outer protective epidermis covering a cortex that consists mainly of parenchyma (packing tissue) but also has some collenchyma (supporting tissue). The vascular tissue of such stems is arranged in bundles, each of which consists of xylem, phloem, and sclerenchyma (strengthening tissue). Woody stems have an outer protective layer of tough bark, which is perforated with lenticels (pores) to allow gas exchange. Inside the bark is a ring of secondary phloem, which surrounds an inner core of secondary xylem.

MICROGRAPH OF LONGITUDINAL SECTION THROUGH APEX OF STEM
Coleus sp.

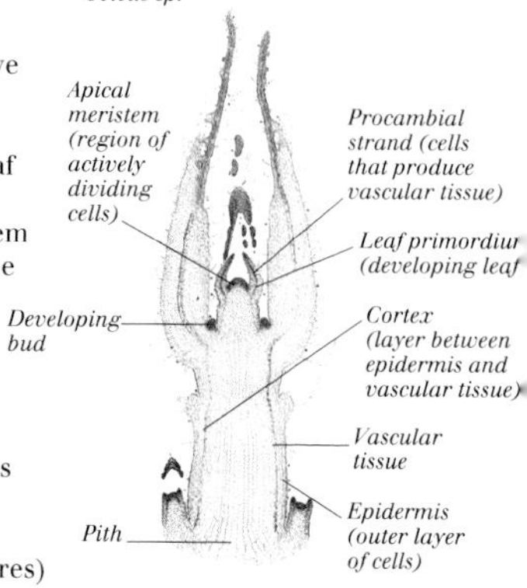

Apical meristem (region of actively dividing cells)
Procambial strand (cells that produce vascular tissue)
Leaf primordium (developing leaf
Developing bud
Cortex (layer between epidermis and vascular tissue)
Vascular tissue
Epidermis (outer layer of cells)
Pith

YOUNG WOODY STEM
Lime
(*Tilia sp.*)

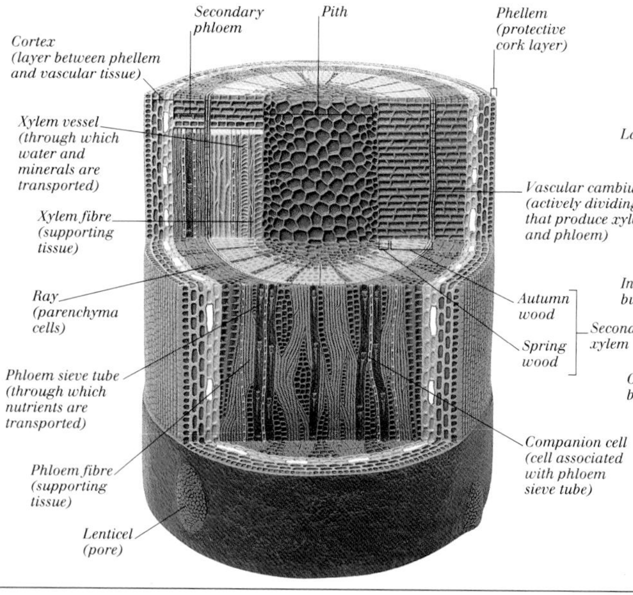

Secondary phloem
Pith
Phellem (protective cork layer)
Cortex (layer between phellem and vascular tissue)
Xylem vessel (through which water and minerals are transported)
Xylem fibre (supporting tissue)
Vascular cambium (actively dividing cells that produce xylem and phloem)
Ray (parenchyma cells)
Autumn wood
Secondary xylem
Spring wood
Phloem sieve tube (through which nutrients are transported)
Phloem fibre (supporting tissue)
Companion cell (cell associated with phloem sieve tube)
Lenticel (pore)

EMERGENT BUDS
London plane
(*Platanus x acerifolia*)

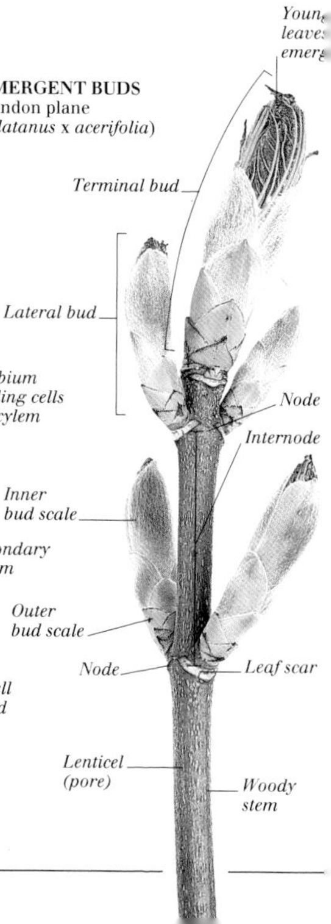

Terminal bud
Lateral bud
Node
Internode
Inner bud scale
Outer bud scale
Node
Leaf scar
Lenticel (pore)
Woody stem

MICROGRAPHS OF CROSS-SECTIONS THROUGH VARIOUS STEMS

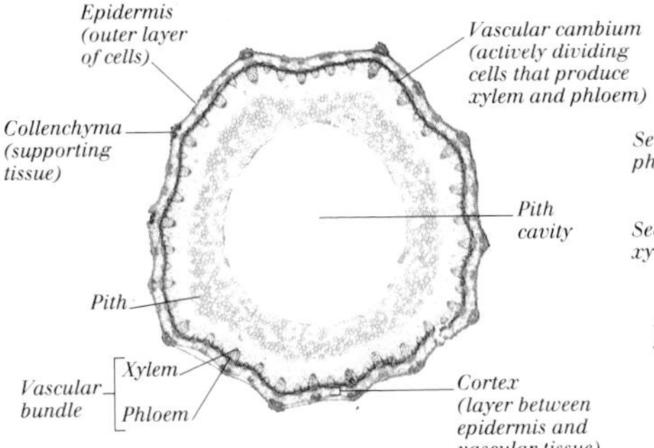
Epidermis (outer layer of cells)
Vascular cambium (actively dividing cells that produce xylem and phloem)
Collenchyma (supporting tissue)
Pith cavity
Pith
Vascular bundle
Xylem
Phloem
Cortex (layer between epidermis and vascular tissue)

CHERVIL
(*Anthriscus sp.*)

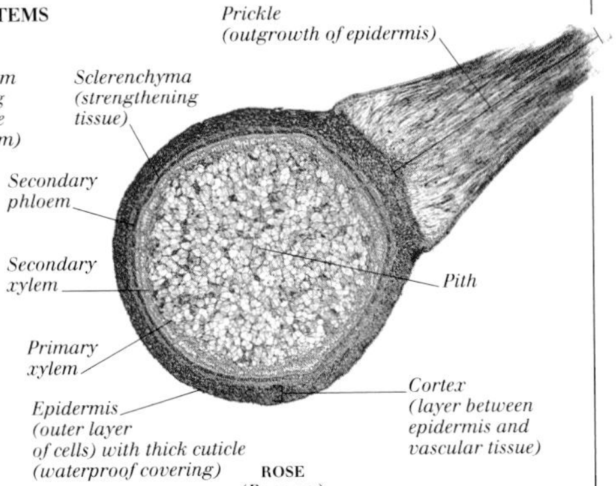
Prickle (outgrowth of epidermis)
Sclerenchyma (strengthening tissue)
Secondary phloem
Secondary xylem
Pith
Primary xylem
Cortex (layer between epidermis and vascular tissue)
Epidermis (outer layer of cells) with thick cuticle (waterproof covering)

ROSE
(*Rosa sp.*)

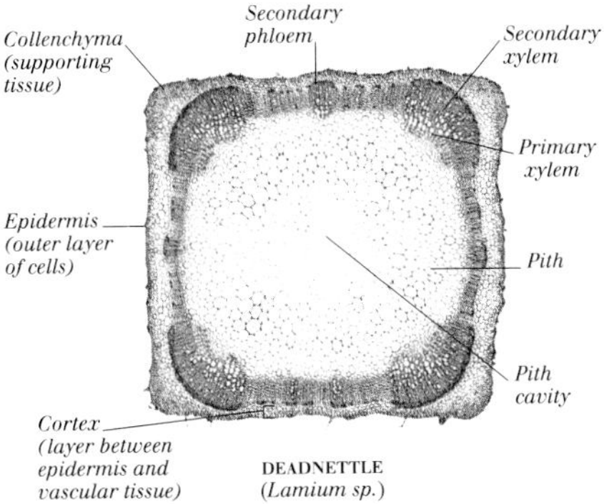
Secondary phloem
Collenchyma (supporting tissue)
Secondary xylem
Primary xylem
Epidermis (outer layer of cells)
Pith
Pith cavity
Cortex (layer between epidermis and vascular tissue)

DEADNETTLE
(*Lamium sp.*)

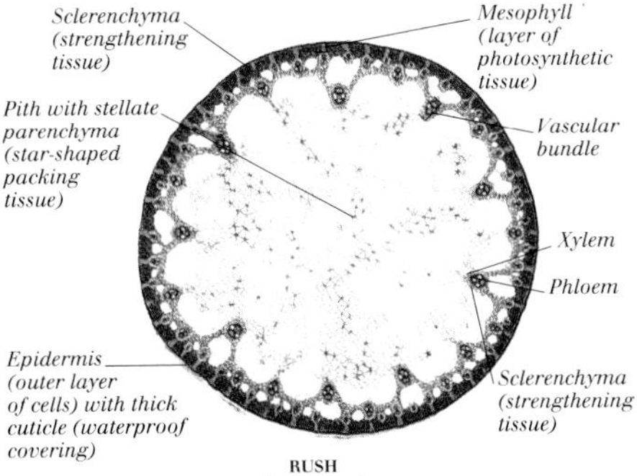
Sclerenchyma (strengthening tissue)
Mesophyll (layer of photosynthetic tissue)
Pith with stellate parenchyma (star-shaped packing tissue)
Vascular bundle
Xylem
Phloem
Epidermis (outer layer of cells) with thick cuticle (waterproof covering)
Sclerenchyma (strengthening tissue)

RUSH
(*Juncus sp.*)

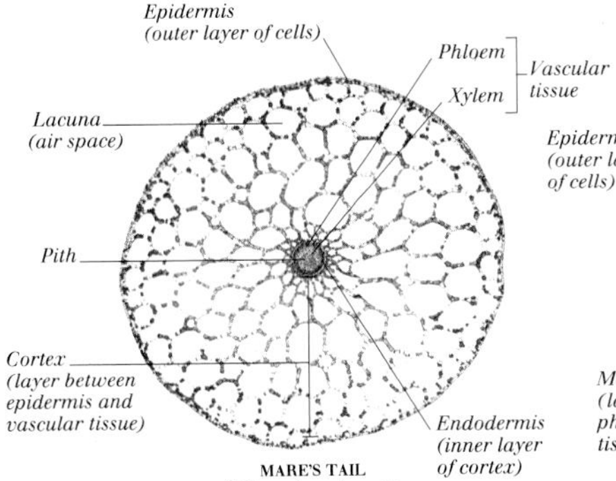
Epidermis (outer layer of cells)
Phloem
Xylem
Vascular tissue
Lacuna (air space)
Pith
Cortex (layer between epidermis and vascular tissue)
Endodermis (inner layer of cortex)

MARE'S TAIL
(*Hippuris vulgaris*)

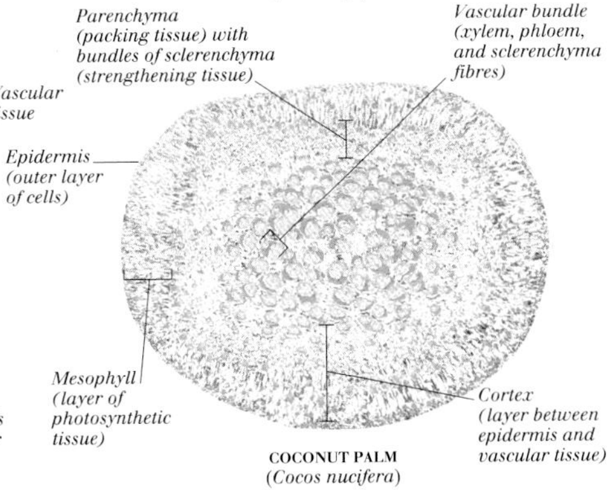
Parenchyma (packing tissue) with bundles of sclerenchyma (strengthening tissue)
Vascular bundle (xylem, phloem, and sclerenchyma fibres)
Epidermis (outer layer of cells)
Mesophyll (layer of photosynthetic tissue)
Cortex (layer between epidermis and vascular tissue)

COCONUT PALM
(*Cocos nucifera*)

Leaves

CHECKERBLOOM
(*Sidalcea malviflora*)

LEAVES ARE THE MAIN SITES OF PHOTOSYNTHESIS (see pp. 138-139) and transpiration (water loss by evaporation) in plants. A typical leaf consists of a thin, flat lamina (blade) supported by a network of veins; a petiole (leaf stalk); and a leaf base, where the petiole joins the stem. Leaves can be classified as simple, in which the lamina is a single unit, or compound, in which the lamina is divided into separate leaflets. Compound leaves may be pinnate, with pinnae (leaflets) on both sides of a rachis (main axis), or palmate, with leaflets arising from a single point at the tip of the petiole. Leaves can be classified further by the overall shape of the lamina, and by the shape of the lamina's apex, margin, and base.

GENERAL LEAF FEATURES

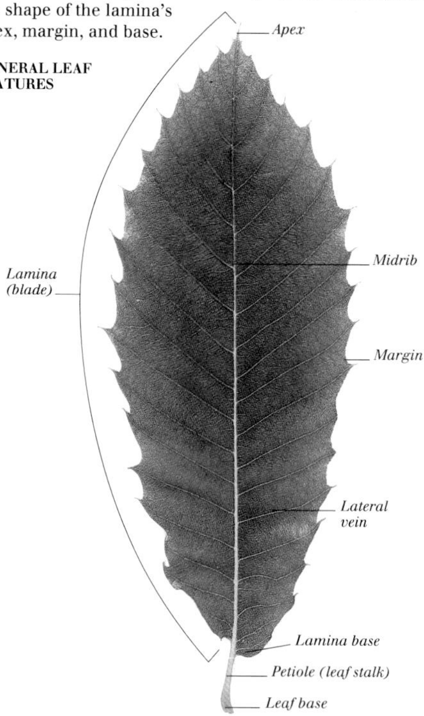

Apex
Midrib
Lamina (blade)
Margin
Lateral vein
Lamina base
Petiole (leaf stalk)
Leaf base

Sweet chestnut
(*Castanea sativa*)

SIMPLE LEAF SHAPES

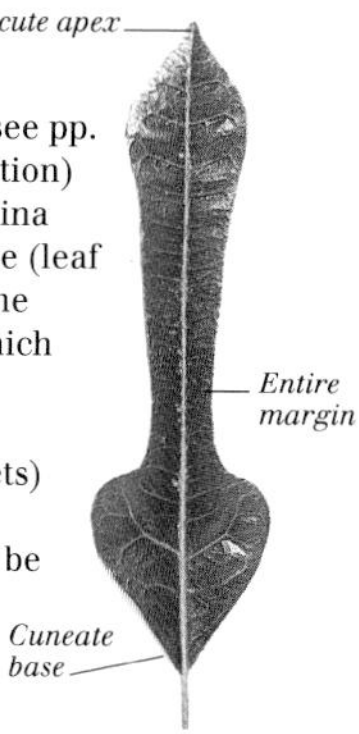

Subacute apex
Entire margin
Cuneate base

PANDURIFORM
Croton
(*Codiaeum variegatum*)

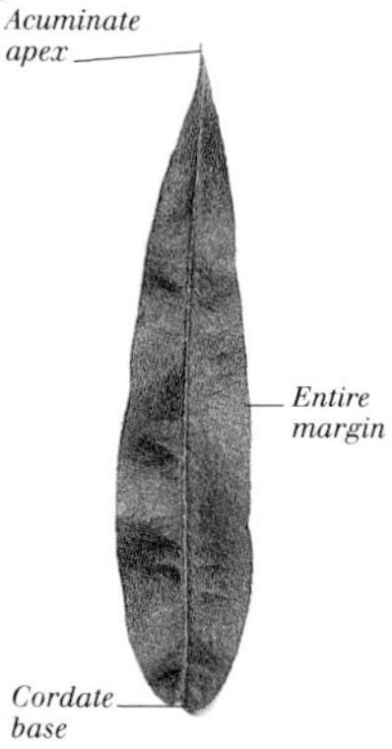

Acuminate apex
Entire margin
Cordate base

LANCEOLATE
Sea buckthorn
(*Hippophae rhamnoides*)

COMPOUND LEAF SHAPES

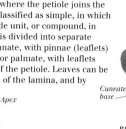

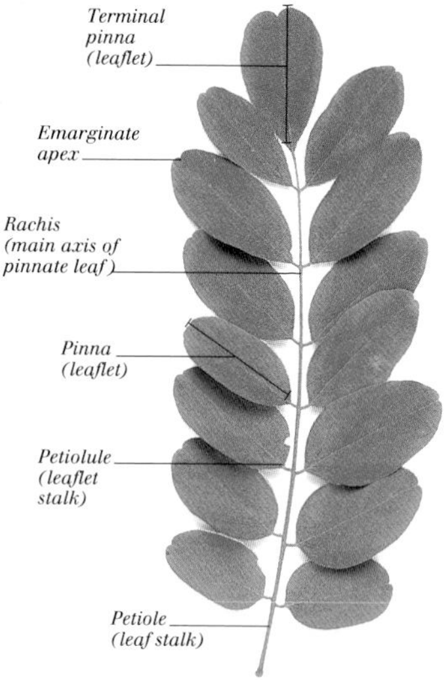

Terminal pinna (leaflet)
Emarginate apex
Rachis (main axis of pinnate leaf)
Pinna (leaflet)
Petiolule (leaflet stalk)
Petiole (leaf stalk)

ODD PINNATE
False acacia
(*Robinia pseudoacacia*)

Subacute apex
Entire margin
Cuneate base

OBOVATE
Tupelo
(*Nyssa sylvatica*)

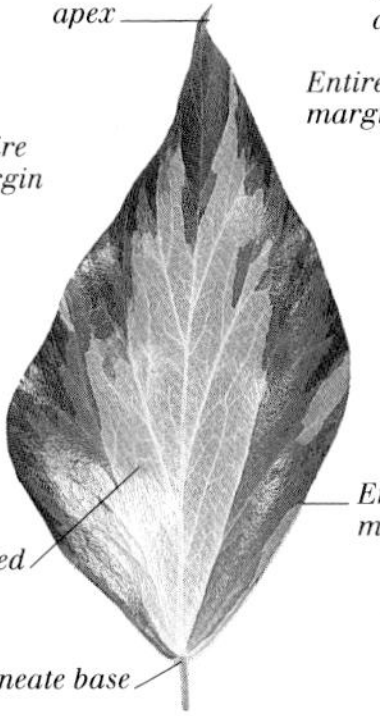
Acuminate apex
Variegated lamina (blade)
Entire margin
Cuneate base

RHOMBOID
Persian ivy
(*Hedera colchica* 'Sulphur Heart')

Subacute apex
Entire margin
Cuneate base

ELLIPTIC
Fig
(*Ficus sp.*)

Mucronate apex
Serrulate margin

ORBICULAR
Camellia
(*Camellia japonica*)

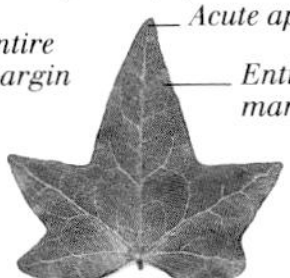
Acute apex
Entire margin
Cordate base

PALMATELY LOBED
Common ivy
(*Hedera helix*)

Cuspidate apex
Entire margin
Truncate base

DELTOID
Persian ivy
(*Hedera colchica*)

Acuminate apex
Entire margin

LINEAR
Iris
(*Iris lazica*)

Pinna (leaflet)
Petiolule (leaflet stalk)
Rachis (main axis of pinnate leaf)
Petiole (leaf stalk)

EVEN PINNATE
Black walnut
(*Juglans nigra*)

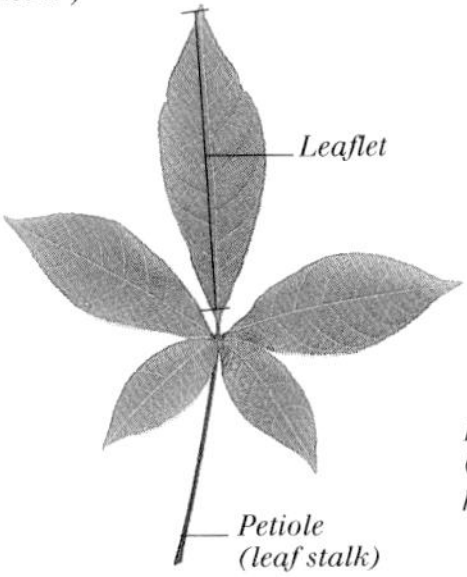
Leaflet
Petiole (leaf stalk)

DIGITATE
Horse chestnut
(*Aesculus parviflora*)

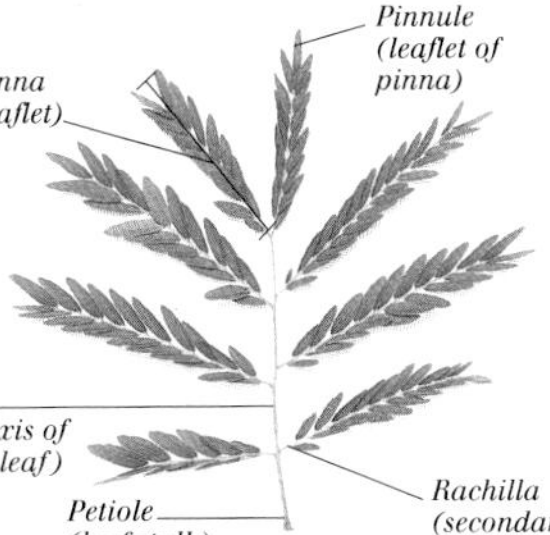
Pinnule (leaflet of pinna)
Pinna (leaflet)
Rachis (main axis of pinnate leaf)
Petiole (leaf stalk)
Rachilla (secondary axis of pinnate leaf)

BIPINNATE
Honey locust
(*Gleditsia triacanthos*)

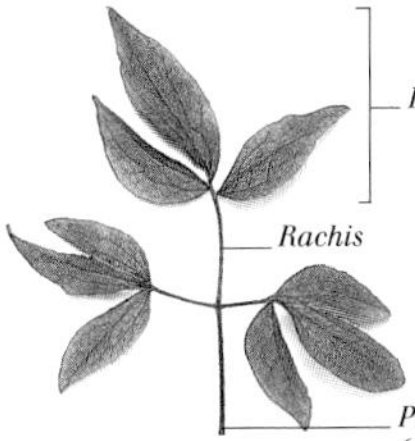
Leaflet
Rachis
Petiole (leaf stalk)

BITERNATE
Clematis
(*Clematis sp.*)

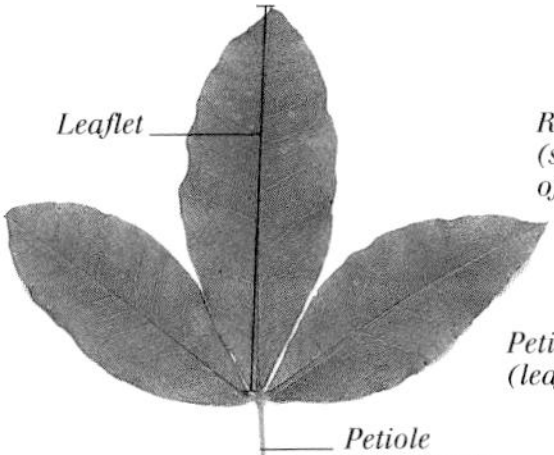
Leaflet
Petiole (leaf stalk)

TRIFOLIATE
Laburnum
(*Laburnum* x *watereri*)

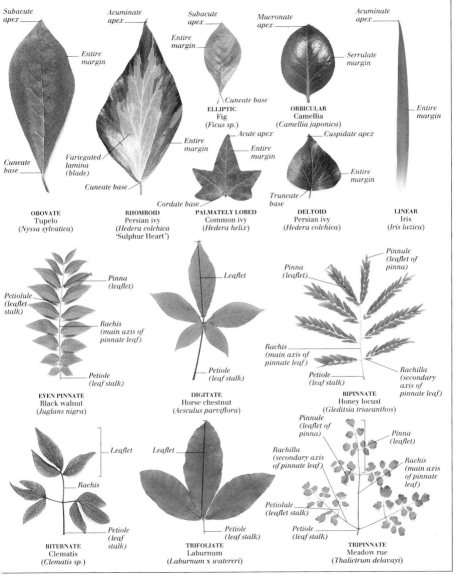

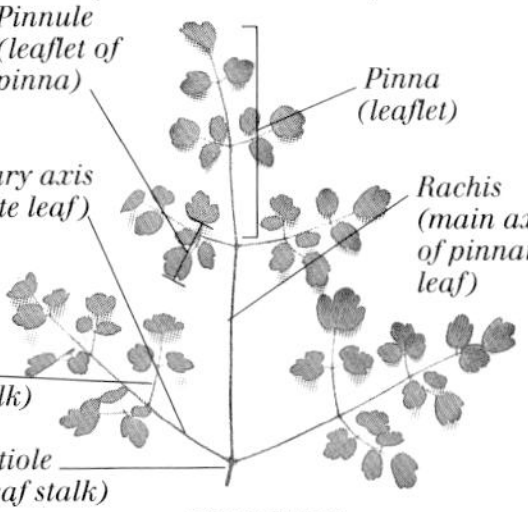
Pinnule (leaflet of pinna)
Pinna (leaflet)
Rachilla (secondary axis of pinnate leaf)
Rachis (main axis of pinnate leaf)
Petiolule (leaflet stalk)
Petiole (leaf stalk)

TRIPINNATE
Meadow rue
(*Thalictrum delavayi*)

Photosynthesis

PHOTOSYNTHESIS IS THE PROCESS by which plants make their food using sunlight, water, and carbon dioxide. It takes place inside special structures in leaf cells called chloroplasts. The chloroplasts contain chlorophyll, a green pigment that absorbs energy from sunlight. During photosynthesis, the absorbed energy is used to join together carbon dioxide and water to form the sugar glucose, which is the energy source for the whole plant; oxygen, a waste product, is released into the air. Leaves are the main sites of photosynthesis, and have various adaptations for that purpose: flat laminae (blades) provide a large surface for absorbing sunlight; stomata (pores) in the lower surface of the laminae allow gases (carbon dioxide and oxygen) to pass into and out of the leaves; and an extensive network of veins brings water into the leaves and transports the glucose produced by photosynthesis to the rest of the plant.

MICROGRAPH OF LEAF
Lily (*Lilium sp.*)

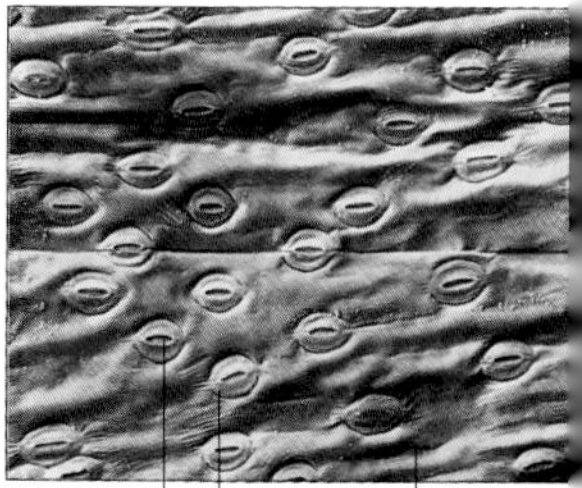
Stoma (pore)
Guard cell (controls opening and closing of stoma)
Lower surface of lamina (blade)

THE PROCESS OF PHOTOSYNTHESIS

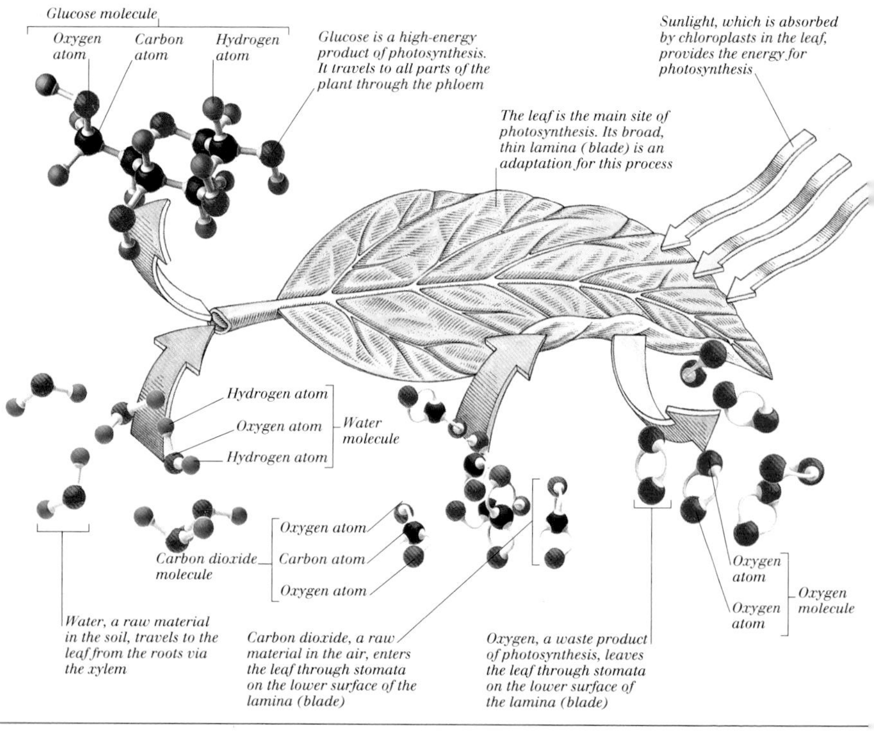
Glucose molecule
Oxygen atom
Carbon atom
Hydrogen atom
Glucose is a high-energy product of photosynthesis. It travels to all parts of the plant through the phloem
Sunlight, which is absorbed by chloroplasts in the leaf, provides the energy for photosynthesis
The leaf is the main site of photosynthesis. Its broad, thin lamina (blade) is an adaptation for this process
Hydrogen atom
Oxygen atom
Hydrogen atom
Water molecule
Oxygen atom
Carbon atom
Oxygen atom
Carbon dioxide molecule
Oxygen atom
Oxygen atom
Oxygen molecule
Water, a raw material in the soil, travels to the leaf from the roots via the xylem
Carbon dioxide, a raw material in the air, enters the leaf through stomata on the lower surface of the lamina (blade)
Oxygen, a waste product of photosynthesis, leaves the leaf through stomata on the lower surface of the lamina (blade)

CROSS-SECTION THROUGH LEAF

Christmas rose
(*Helleborus niger*)

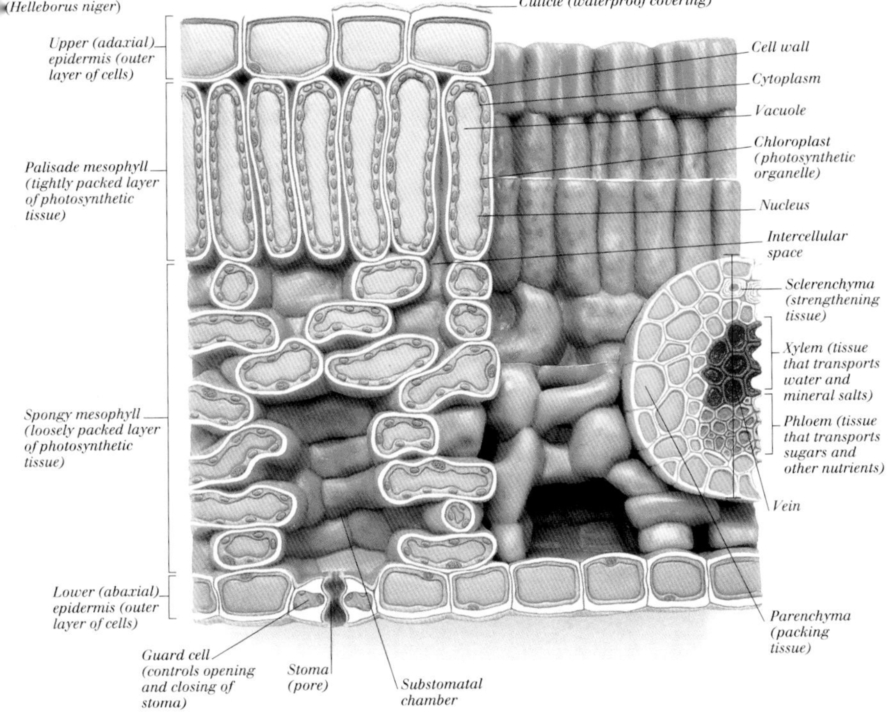
Cuticle (waterproof covering)
Upper (adaxial) epidermis (outer layer of cells)
Cell wall
Cytoplasm
Vacuole
Chloroplast (photosynthetic organelle)
Palisade mesophyll (tightly packed layer of photosynthetic tissue)
Nucleus
Intercellular space
Sclerenchyma (strengthening tissue)
Xylem (tissue that transports water and mineral salts)
Spongy mesophyll (loosely packed layer of photosynthetic tissue)
Phloem (tissue that transports sugars and other nutrients)
Vein
Lower (abaxial) epidermis (outer layer of cells)
Parenchyma (packing tissue)
Guard cell (controls opening and closing of stoma)
Stoma (pore)
Substomatal chamber

INTERNAL VIEW OF CHLOROPLAST

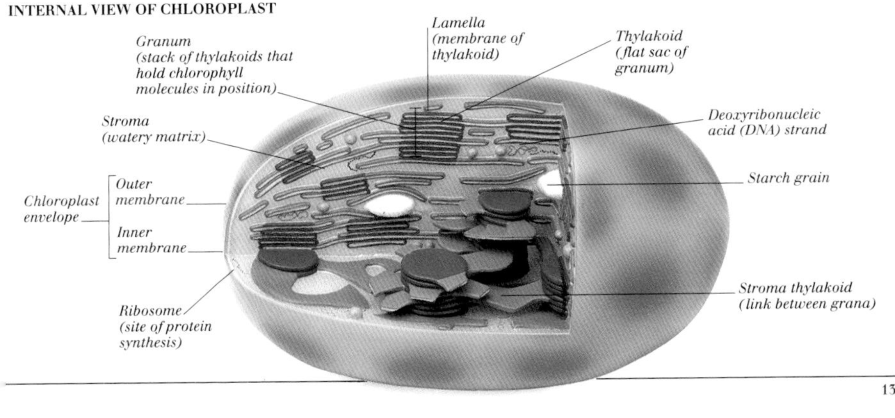
Lamella (membrane of thylakoid)
Granum (stack of thylakoids that hold chlorophyll molecules in position)
Thylakoid (flat sac of granum)
Stroma (watery matrix)
Deoxyribonucleic acid (DNA) strand
Starch grain
Outer membrane
Chloroplast envelope
Inner membrane
Ribosome (site of protein synthesis)
Stroma thylakoid (link between grana)

Flowers 1

FLOWERS ARE THE SITES OF SEXUAL REPRODUCTION in flowering plants. Their component parts are arranged in whorls around the receptacle (tip of the flower stalk). The sepals (collectively called the calyx) are outermost; typically small and green, they protect the developing flower. The petals (collectively called the corolla) are typically large and brightly coloured; they are found inside the sepals. In monocotyledonous flowers (see pp. 126-127), sepals and petals are indistinguishable; individually they are called tepals (collectively called the perianth). The petals surround the male and female reproductive structures (androecium and gynoecium). The androecium consists of stamens (male organs); each stamen is made up of a filament (stalk) and anther. The gynoecium has one or more carpels (female organs); each carpel consists of an ovary, style, and stigma. Some flowers (e.g., lily) occur singly on a pedicel (flower stalk); others (e.g., elder, sunflower) are arranged in a group (inflorescence) on a peduncle (inflorescence stalk).

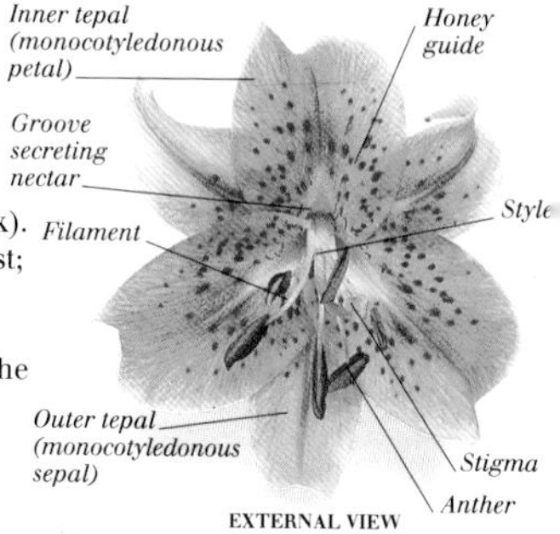

Inner tepal (monocotyledonous petal)
Honey guide
Groove secreting nectar
Style
Filament
Outer tepal (monocotyledonous sepal)
Stigma
Anther

EXTERNAL VIEW

A MONOCOTYLEDONOUS FLOWER
Lily
(*Lilium sp.*)

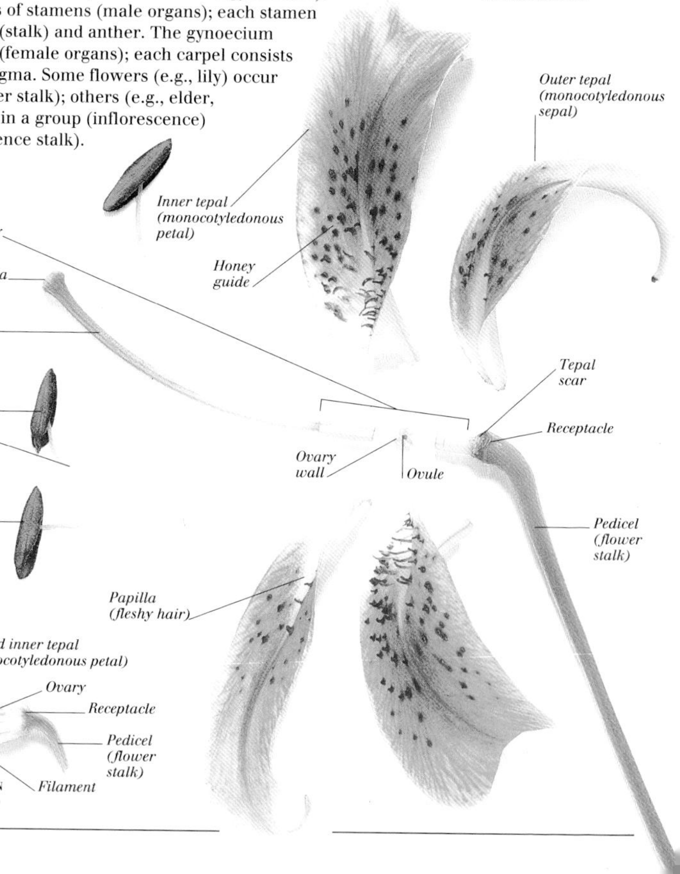

Syncarpous (fused carpels) gynoecium
Ovary
Stigma
Style
Inner tepal (monocotyledonous petal)
Honey guide
Outer tepal (monocotyledonous sepal)
Stamen
Anther
Filament
Pollen on anther
Tepal scar
Receptacle
Ovary wall
Ovule
Pedicel (flower stalk)
Papilla (fleshy hair)

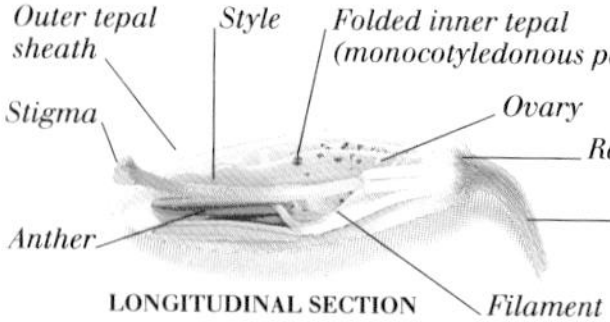

Outer tepal sheath
Style
Folded inner tepal (monocotyledonous petal)
Stigma
Ovary
Receptacle
Anther
Pedicel (flower stalk)
Filament

LONGITUDINAL SECTION THROUGH FLOWER BUD

A DICOTYLEDONOUS FLOWER
Larkspur
(*Delphinium orientalis*)

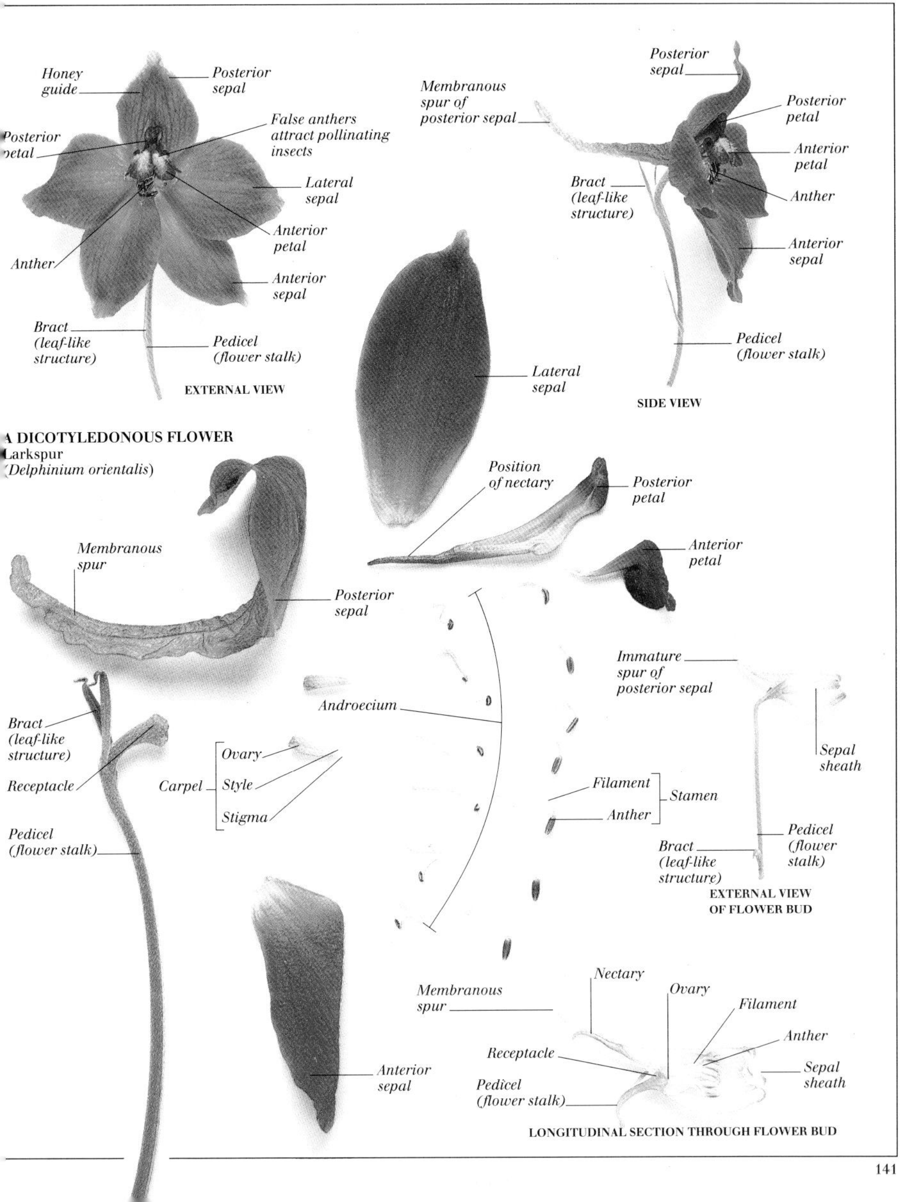
Honey guide
Posterior sepal
Posterior petal
False anthers attract pollinating insects
Lateral sepal
Anterior petal
Anther
Anterior sepal
Bract (leaf-like structure)
Pedicel (flower stalk)
EXTERNAL VIEW
Posterior sepal
Membranous spur of posterior sepal
Posterior petal
Anterior petal
Bract (leaf-like structure)
Anther
Anterior sepal
Pedicel (flower stalk)
SIDE VIEW
Lateral sepal
Position of nectary
Posterior petal
Anterior petal
Membranous spur
Posterior sepal
Immature spur of posterior sepal
Androecium
Bract (leaf-like structure)
Receptacle
Carpel
Ovary
Style
Stigma
Filament
Anther
Stamen
Sepal sheath
Pedicel (flower stalk)
Pedicel (flower stalk)
Bract (leaf-like structure)
EXTERNAL VIEW OF FLOWER BUD
Anterior sepal
Nectary
Membranous spur
Ovary
Filament
Anther
Receptacle
Sepal sheath
Pedicel (flower stalk)
LONGITUDINAL SECTION THROUGH FLOWER BUD

Flowers 2

COMPOUND INFLORESCENCE (CAPITULUM)
Sunflower
(*Helianthus annulus*)

Disc florets
Ray floret
Florets (small flowers) are grouped together to resemble a single large flower

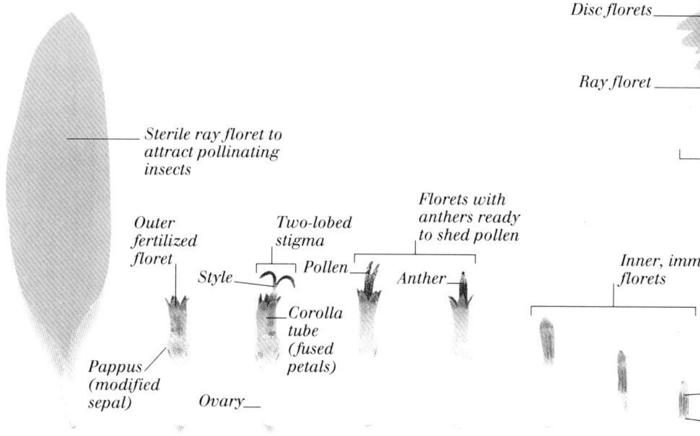
Sterile ray floret to attract pollinating insects
Outer fertilized floret
Two-lobed stigma
Florets with anthers ready to shed pollen
Style
Pollen
Anther
Corolla tube (fused petals)
Pappus (modified sepal)
Ovary
Inner, immature florets
Corolla tube (fused petals)
Ovary

FLORETS FROM SUNFLOWER

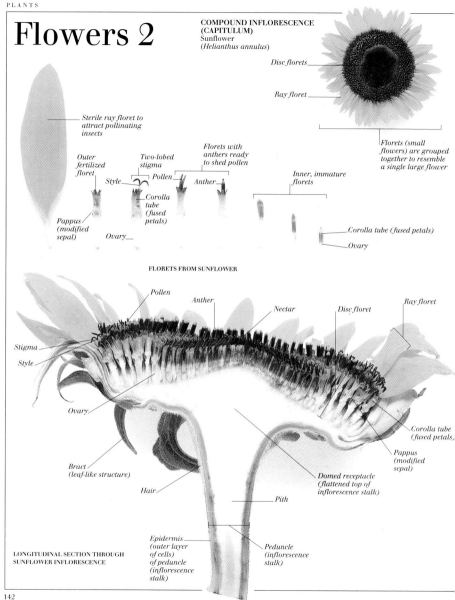

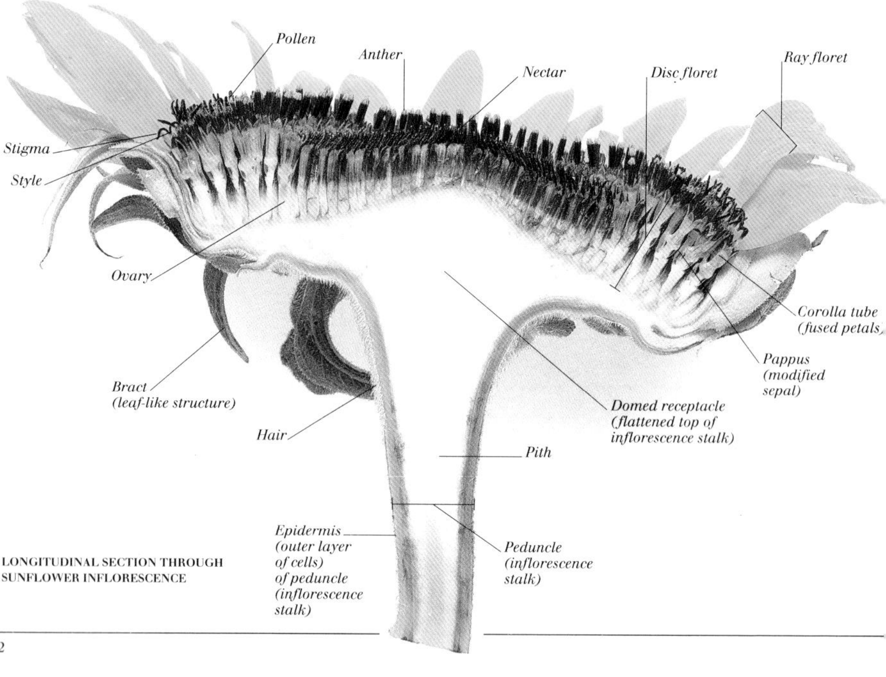
Pollen
Anther
Nectar
Disc floret
Ray floret
Stigma
Style
Ovary
Corolla tube (fused petals)
Pappus (modified sepal)
Bract (leaf-like structure)
Domed receptacle (flattened top of inflorescence stalk)
Hair
Pith
Epidermis (outer layer of cells) of peduncle (inflorescence stalk)
Peduncle (inflorescence stalk)

LONGITUDINAL SECTION THROUGH SUNFLOWER INFLORESCENCE

RRANGEMENT OF FLOWERS ON STEM

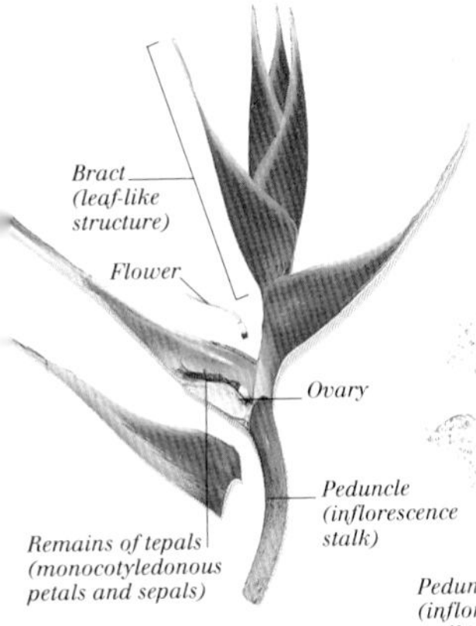
Bract (leaf-like structure)
Flower
Ovary
Peduncle (inflorescence stalk)
Remains of tepals (monocotyledonous petals and sepals)

INFLORESCENCE (SPIKE)
Heliconia peruviana

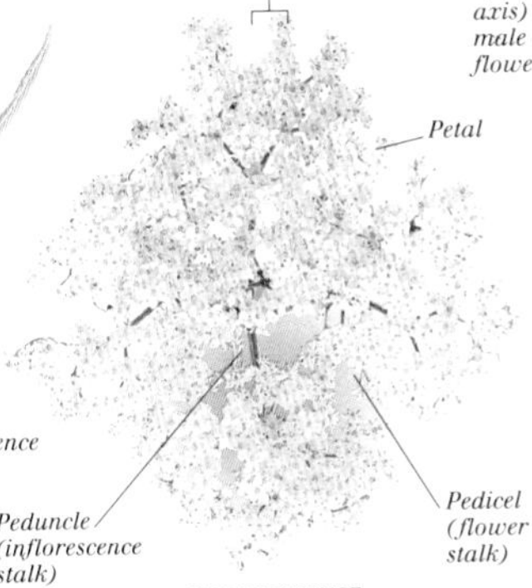
Flower
Petal
Peduncle (inflorescence stalk)
Pedicel (flower stalk)

INFLORESCENCE (COMPOUND UMBEL)
Common elder
(*Sambucus nigra*)

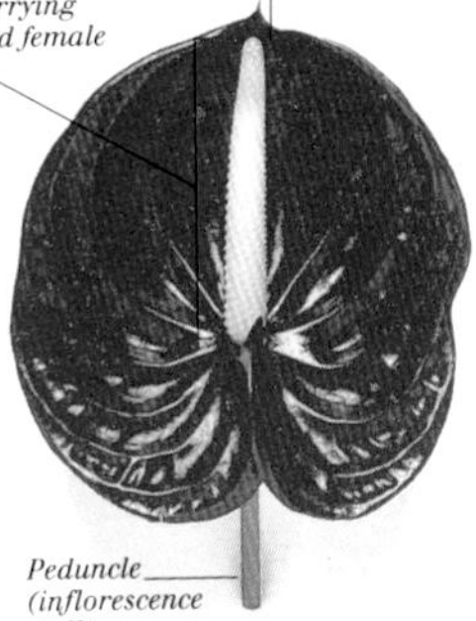
Spathe (large bract) to attract pollinating insects
Spadix (fleshy axis) carrying male and female flowers
Peduncle (inflorescence stalk)

INFLORESCENCE (SPADIX)
Painter's palette
(*Anthurium andreanum*)

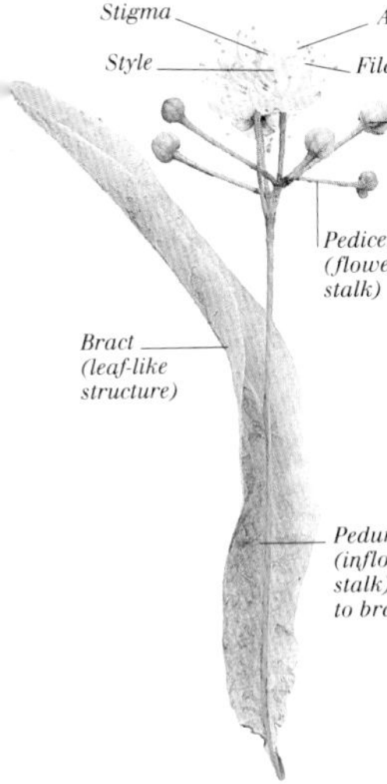
Stigma
Anther
Stamen
Style
Filament
Flower bud
Pedicel (flower stalk)
Bract (leaf-like structure)
Peduncle (inflorescence stalk) fused to bract

INFLORESCENCE (DICHASIAL CYME)
Common lime
(*Tilia x europaea*)

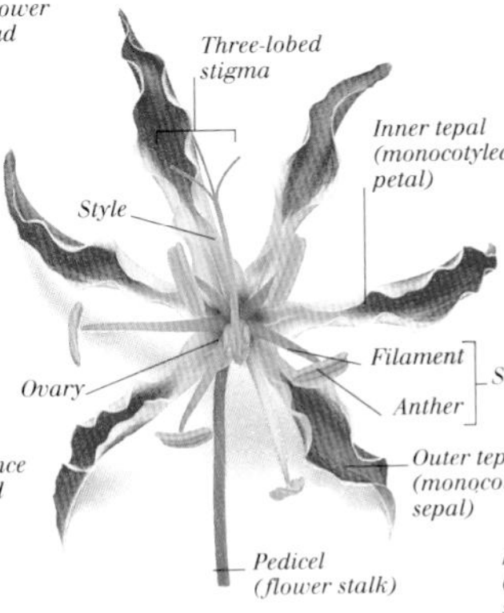
Three-lobed stigma
Inner tepal (monocotyledonous petal)
Style
Filament
Stamen
Anther
Ovary
Outer tepal (monocotyledonous sepal)
Pedicel (flower stalk)

SINGLE FLOWER
Glory lily
(*Gloriosa superba*)

Flower
Corolla
Calyx
Peduncle (inflorescence stalk)
Bract (leaf-like structure)
SINGLE FLOWER

INFLORESCENCE (SPHERICAL UMBEL)
Allium sp.

Pollination

POLLINATION IS THE TRANSFER OF POLLEN (which contains the male sex cells) from an anther (part of the male reproductive organ) to a stigma (part of the female reproductive organ). This process precedes fertilization (see pp. 146-147). Pollination may occur within the same flower (self-pollination), or between flowers on separate plants of the same species (cross-pollination). In most plants, pollination is carried out either by insects (entomophilous pollination) or by the wind (anemophilous pollination). Less commonly, birds, bats, or water are the agents of pollination. Insect-pollinated flowers are typically brightly coloured, scented, and produce nectar, on which insects feed. Such flowers also tend to have patterns that are visible only in ultraviolet light, which many insects can see but which humans cannot. These features attract insects, which become covered with the sticky or hooked pollen grains when they visit one flower, and then transfer the pollen to the next flower they visit. Wind-pollinated flowers are generally small, relatively inconspicuous, and unscented. They produce large quantities of light pollen grains that are easily blown by the wind to other flowers.

REPRODUCTIVE STRUCTURES IN WIND-POLLINATED PLANT
Sweet chestnut
(*Castanea sativa*)

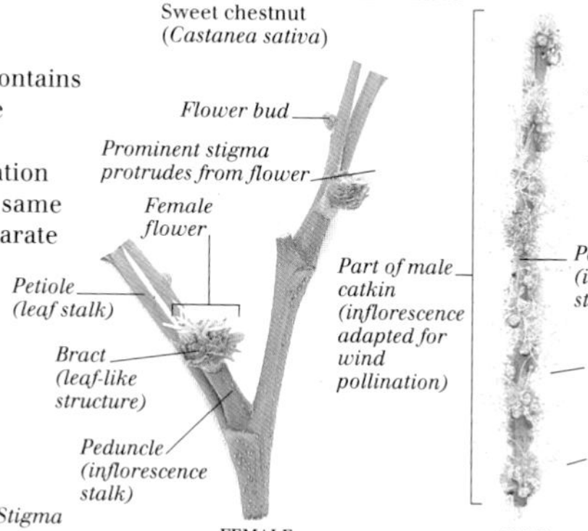
Flower bud
Prominent stigma protrudes from flower
Female flower
Petiole (leaf stalk)
Bract (leaf-like structure)
Peduncle (inflorescence stalk)
Part of male catkin (inflorescence adapted for wind pollination)
Male flower
Peduncle (infloresce
stalk)
Filament
Anther
FEMALE
MALE

REPRODUCTIVE STRUCTURES IN INSECT-POLLINATED PLANTS

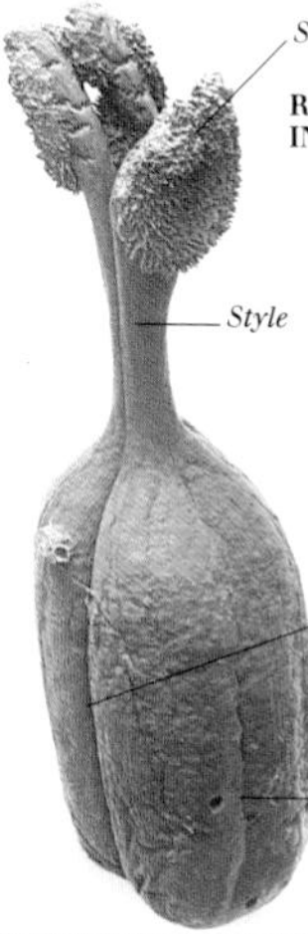
Stigma
Style
Boundary between two fused carpels (each carpel consists of a stigma, style, and ovary)
Ovary

MICROGRAPH OF CARPELS (FEMALE ORGANS)
Yellow-wort
(*Blackstonia perfoliata*)

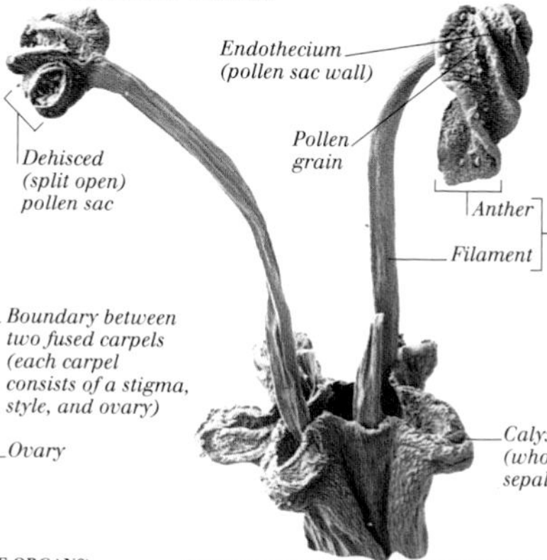
Endothecium (pollen sac wall)
Dehisced (split open) pollen sac
Pollen grain
Anther
Stamen
Filament
Calyx (whorl of sepals)

MICROGRAPH OF STAMENS (MALE ORGANS)
Common centaury
(*Centaurium erythraea*)

MICROGRAPHS OF POLLEN GRAINS

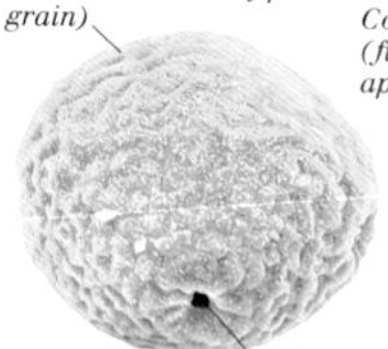
Exine (outer coat of pollen grain)
Pore

EUROPEAN FIELD ELM
(*Ulmus minor*)

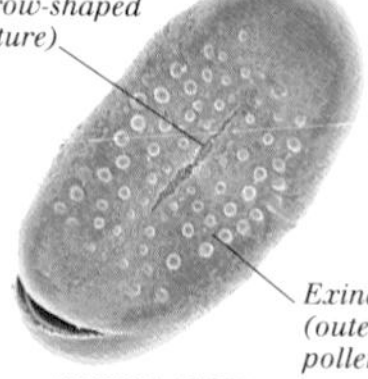
Colpus (furrow-shaped aperture)
Exine (outer coat of pollen grain)

JUSTICIA AUREA

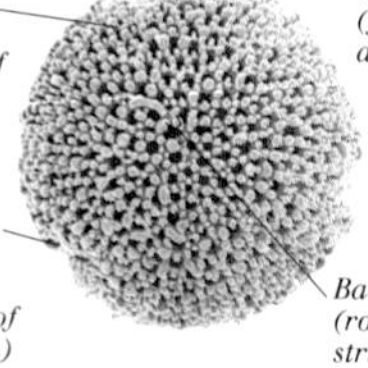
Exine (outer coat of pollen grain)
Pore
Baculum (rod-shaped structure)

MEADOW CRANESBILL
(*Geranium pratense*)

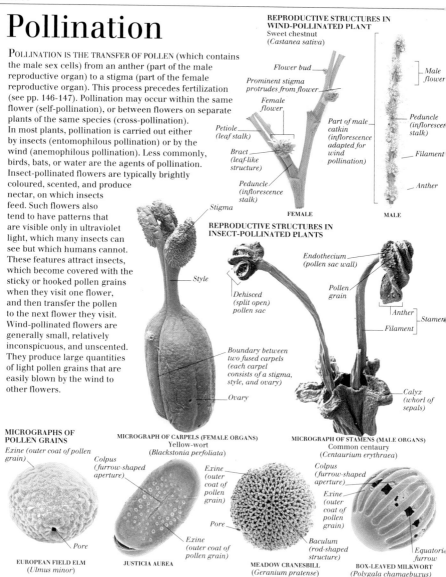

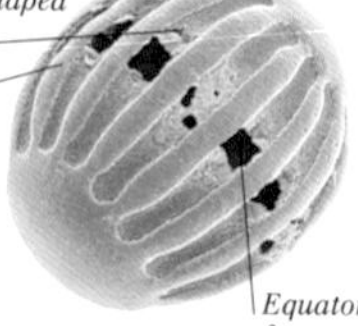
Colpus (furrow-shaped aperture)
Exine (outer coat of pollen grain)
Equatori
furrow

BOX-LEAVED MILKWORT
(*Polygala chamaebuxus*)

INSECT POLLINATION OF MEADOW SAGE

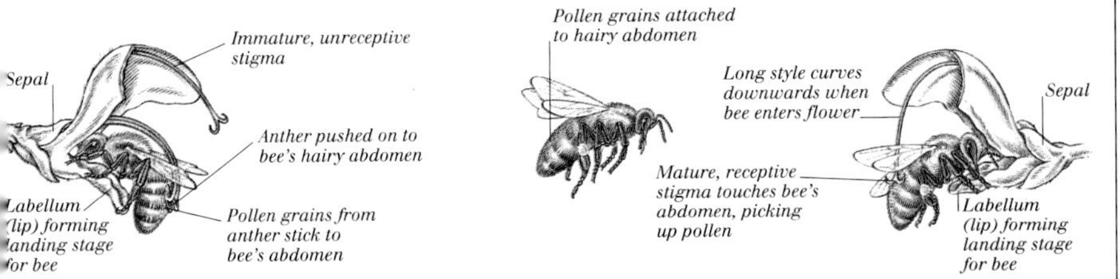
Immature, unreceptive stigma
Sepal
Anther pushed on to bee's hairy abdomen
Labellum (lip) forming landing stage for bee
Pollen grains from anther stick to bee's abdomen
Pollen grains attached to hairy abdomen
Long style curves downwards when bee enters flower
Sepal
Mature, receptive stigma touches bee's abdomen, picking up pollen
Labellum (lip) forming landing stage for bee

1. BEE VISITS FLOWER WITH MATURE ANTHERS BUT IMMATURE STIGMA

2. BEE FLIES TO OTHER FLOWERS

3. BEE VISITS FLOWER WHERE THE ANTHERS HAVE WITHERED AND THE STIGMA IS MATURE

SUNFLOWER UNDER NORMAL AND ULTRAVIOLET LIGHT

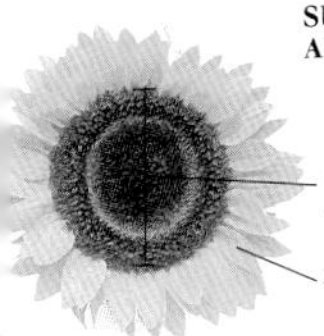
Central area of disc florets
Ray floret

NORMAL LIGHT

Paler, outer part of ray floret
Darker, inner part of ray floret
Insects attracted to darkest, central part of flower, which contains nectaries, anthers, and stigmas

ULTRAVIOLET LIGHT

ST JOHN'S WORT UNDER NORMAL AND ULTRAVIOLET LIGHT

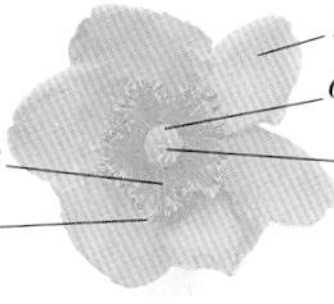
Petal
Ovary
Stigma
Stamen
Filament
Anther

NORMAL LIGHT

Honey guide directs insects to dark, central part of flower
Dark central area containing nectaries, anthers, and stigmas

ULTRAVIOLET LIGHT

Pore
Exine (outer coat of pollen grain)

MIMULOPSIS SOLMSII

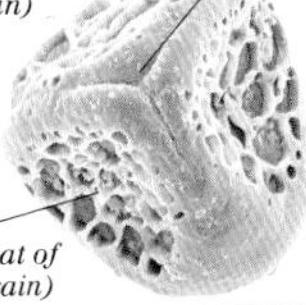
Trilete mark (development scar)
Exine (outer coat of pollen grain)

THESIUM ALPINIUM

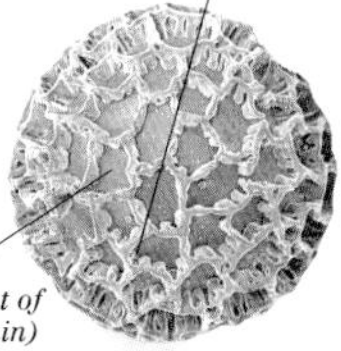
Columella (small column-shaped structure)
Exine (outer coat of pollen grain)

RUELLIA GRANDIFLORA

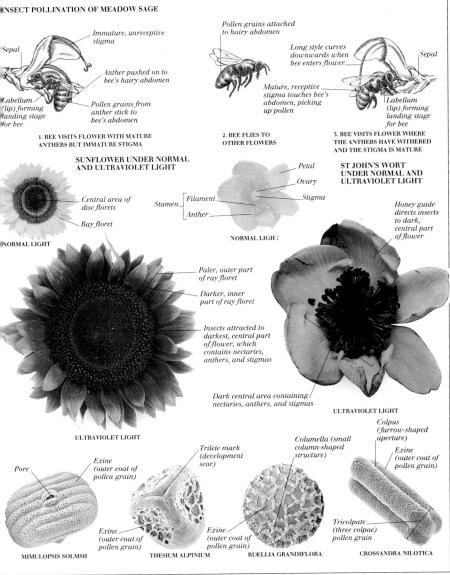

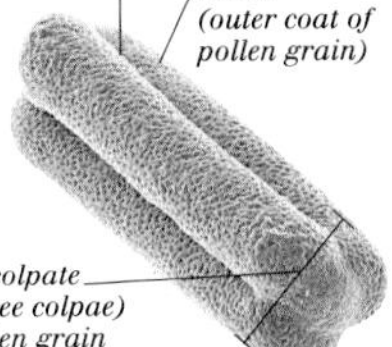
Colpus (furrow-shaped aperture)
Exine (outer coat of pollen grain)
Tricolpate (three colpae) pollen grain

CROSSANDRA NILOTICA

Fertilization

BANANA
(Musa 'lacatan')

FERTILIZATION IS THE FUSION of male and female gametes (sex cells) to produce a zygote (embryo). Following pollination (see pp. 144-145), the pollen grains that contain the male gametes are on the stigma, some distance from the female gamete (ovum) inside the ovule. To enable the gametes to meet, the pollen grain germinates and produces a pollen tube, which grows down and enters the embryo sac (the inner part of the ovule that contains the ovum). Two male gametes, travelling at the tip of the pollen tube, enter the embryo sac. One gamete fuses with the ovum to produce a zygote that will develop into an embryo plant. The other male gamete fuses with two polar nuclei to produce the endosperm, which acts as a food store for the developing embryo. Fertilization also initiates other changes: the integument (outer part of ovule) forms a testa (seed coat) around the embryo and endosperm; the petals fall off; the stigma and style wither; and the ovary wall forms a layer (called the pericarp) around the seed. Together, the pericarp and seed form the fruit, which may be succulent (see pp. 148-149) or dry (see pp. 150-151). In some species (e.g., blackberry), apomixis can occur: the seed develops without fertilization of the ovum by a male gamete but endosperm formation and fruit development take place as in other species.

DEVELOPMENT OF A SUCCULENT FRUIT
Blackberry
(Rubus fruticosus)

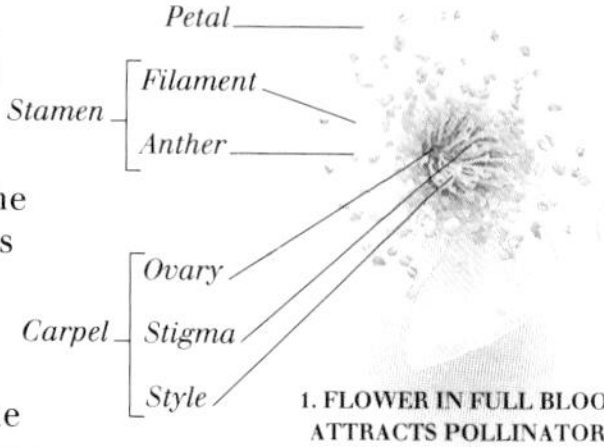
Petal
Stamen
Filament
Anther
Carpel
Ovary
Stigma
Style

1. FLOWER IN FULL BLOOM ATTRACTS POLLINATORS

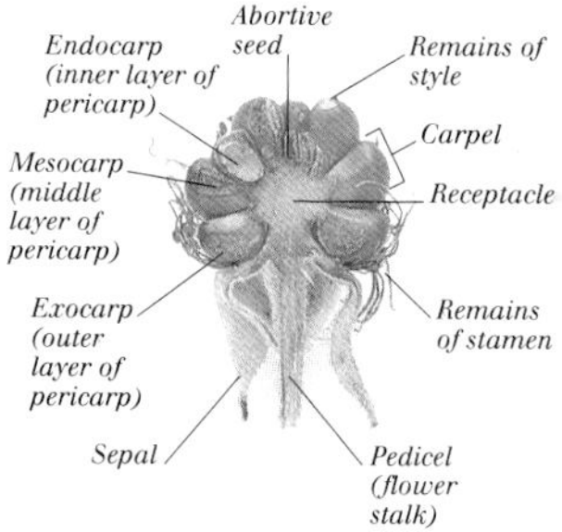
Abortive seed
Endocarp (inner layer of pericarp)
Remains of style
Carpel
Mesocarp (middle layer of pericarp)
Receptacle
Exocarp (outer layer of pericarp)
Remains of stamen
Sepal
Pedicel (flower stalk)

4. PERICARP FORMS FLESH, SKIN, AND A HARD INNER LAYER (SHOWN IN CROSS-SECTION)

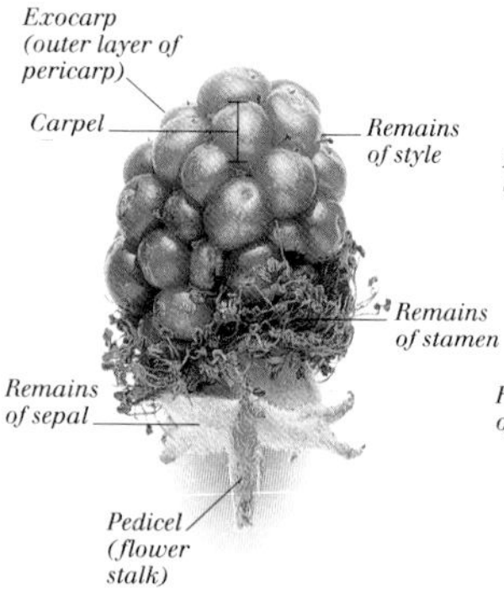
Exocarp (outer layer of pericarp)
Carpel
Remains of style
Remains of stamen
Remains of sepal
Pedicel (flower stalk)

7. MESOCARP (FLESHY PART OF PERICARP) OF EACH CARPEL STARTS TO CHANGE COLOUR

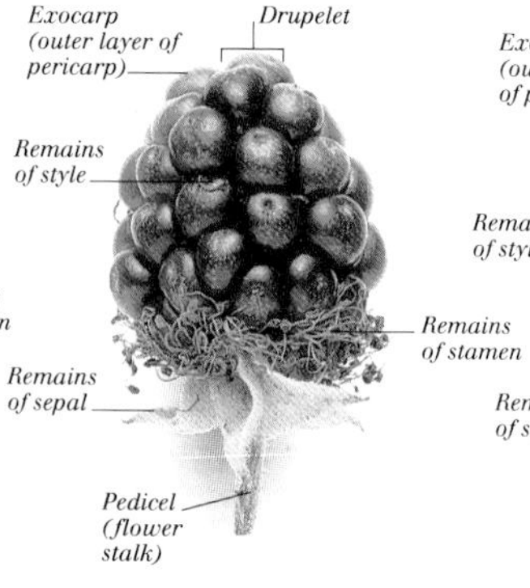
Exocarp (outer layer of pericarp)
Drupelet
Remains of style
Remains of stamen
Remains of sepal
Pedicel (flower stalk)

8. CARPELS MATURE INTO DRUPELETS (SMALL FLESHY FRUITS WITH SINGLE SEEDS SURROUNDED BY HARD ENDOCARP)

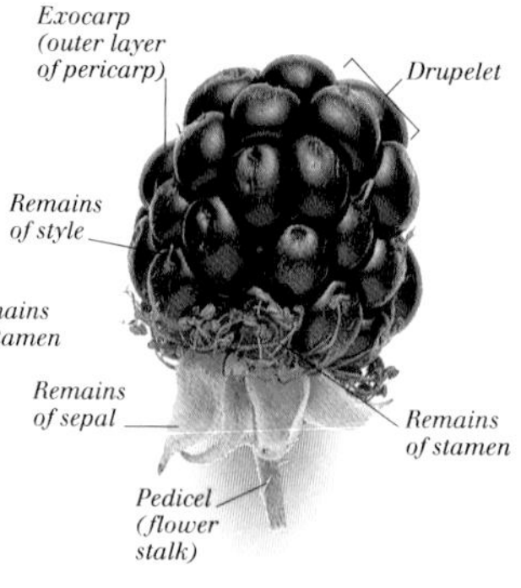
Exocarp (outer layer of pericarp)
Drupelet
Remains of style
Remains of sepal
Remains of stamen
Pedicel (flower stalk)

9. MESOCARP OF DRUPELET BECOMES DARKER AND SWEETER

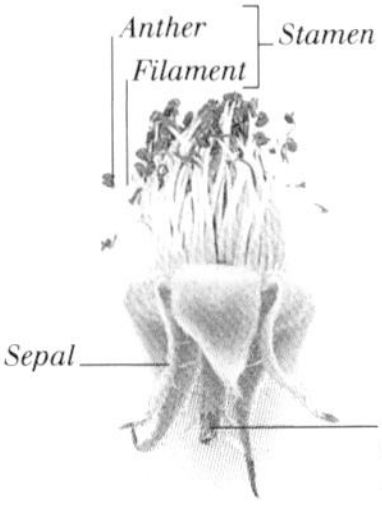
Anther
Filament
Stamen
Sepal
Pedicel (flower stalk)

2. FERTILIZATION HAS TAKEN PLACE; PETALS FALL OFF

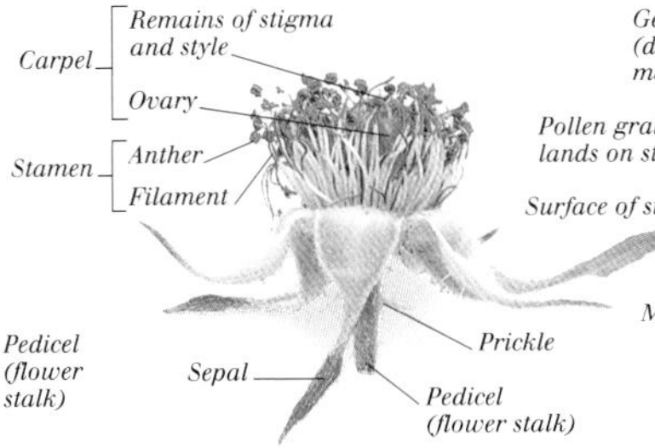
Carpel
Remains of stigma and style
Ovary
Stamen
Anther
Filament
Prickle
Sepal
Pedicel (flower stalk)

3. OVARIES BEGIN TO SWELL; STAMENS WITHER AND DIE

THE PROCESS OF FERTILIZATION

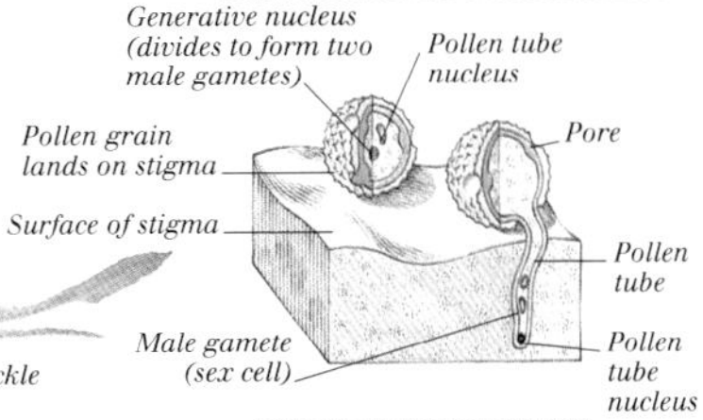
Generative nucleus (divides to form two male gametes)
Pollen tube nucleus
Pore
Pollen grain lands on stigma
Surface of stigma
Pollen tube
Male gamete (sex cell)
Pollen tube nucleus

POLLEN GRAIN GERMINATES

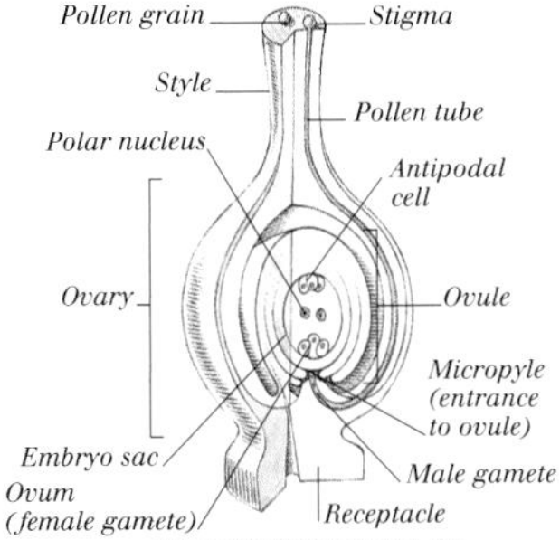
Pollen grain
Stigma
Style
Pollen tube
Polar nucleus
Antipodal cell
Ovary
Ovule
Micropyle (entrance to ovule)
Embryo sac
Male gamete
Ovum (female gamete)
Receptacle

MALE GAMETES TRAVEL TO EMBRYO SAC

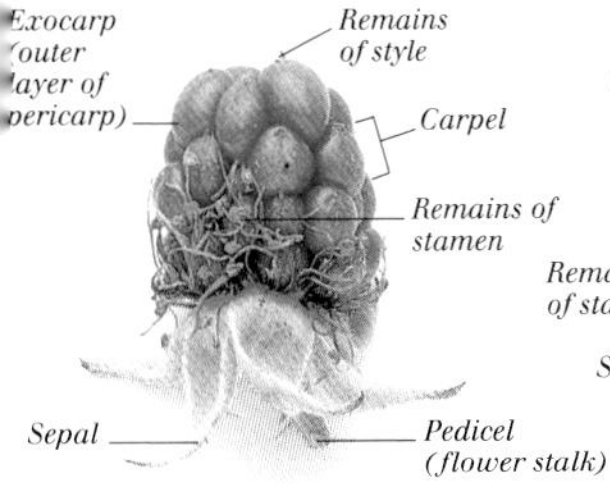
Exocarp (outer layer of pericarp)
Remains of style
Carpel
Remains of stamen
Sepal
Pedicel (flower stalk)

5. CARPELS EXPAND AND BECOME MORE FLESHY

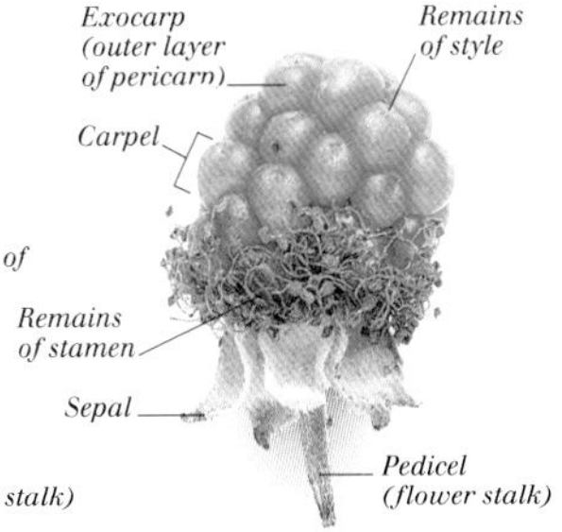
Exocarp (outer layer of pericarp)
Remains of style
Carpel
Remains of stamen
Sepal
Pedicel (flower stalk)

6. CARPELS EXPAND FURTHER

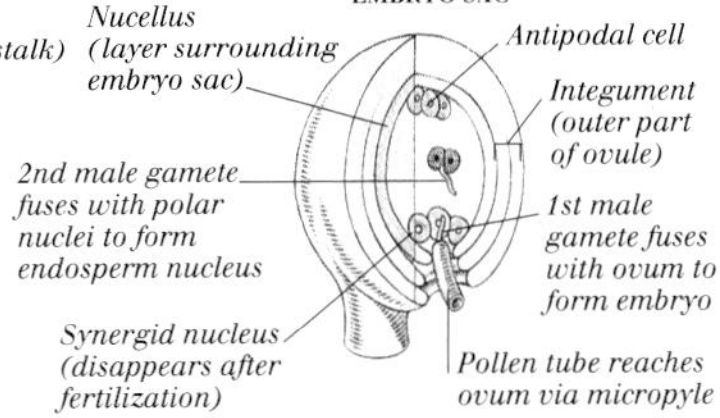
Nucellus (layer surrounding embryo sac)
Antipodal cell
Integument (outer part of ovule)
2nd male gamete fuses with polar nuclei to form endosperm nucleus
1st male gamete fuses with ovum to form embryo
Synergid nucleus (disappears after fertilization)
Pollen tube reaches ovum via micropyle

FERTILIZATION

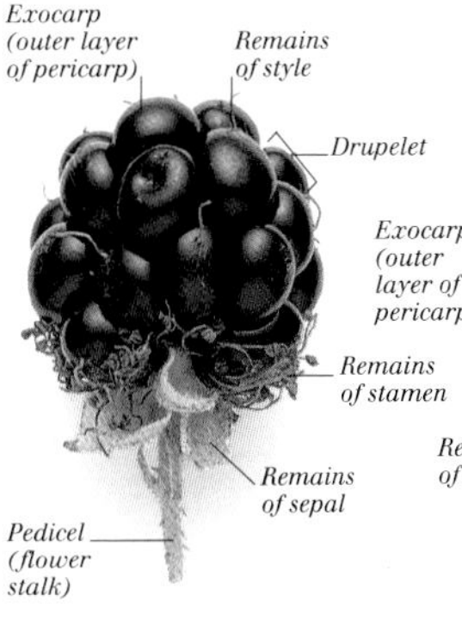
Exocarp (outer layer of pericarp)
Remains of style
Drupelet
Remains of stamen
Remains of sepal
Pedicel (flower stalk)

10. DRUPELETS (COLLECTIVELY AN AGGREGATE FRUIT) EXPAND

Remains of style
Drupelet
Exocarp (outer layer of pericarp)
Remains of stamen
Pedicel (flower stalk)
Remains of sepal

11. DRUPELETS RIPEN FULLY

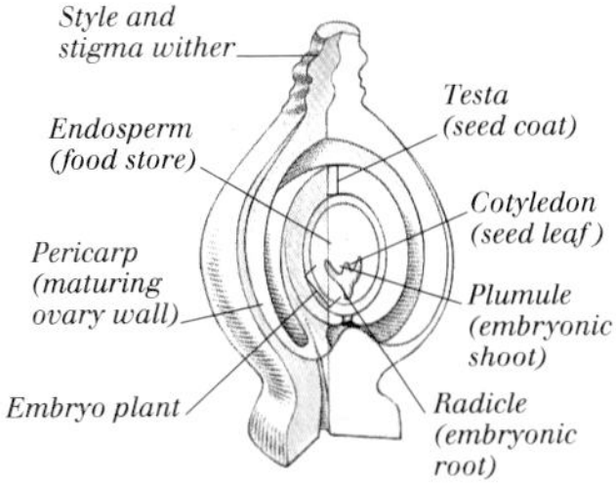
Style and stigma wither
Testa (seed coat)
Endosperm (food store)
Cotyledon (seed leaf)
Pericarp (maturing ovary wall)
Plumule (embryonic shoot)
Embryo plant
Radicle (embryonic root)

DEVELOPMENT OF EMBRYO

Succulent fruits

A FRUIT IS A FULLY DEVELOPED and ripened ovary (seed-producing part of a plant's female reproductive organs). Fruits may be succulent or dry (see pp. 150-151). Succulent fruits are fleshy and brightly coloured, making them attractive to animals, which eat them and so disperse the seeds away from the parent plant. The wall (pericarp) of a succulent fruit has three layers: an outer exocarp, a middle mesocarp, and an inner endocarp. These three layers vary in thickness and texture in different types of fruits and may blend into each other. Succulent fruits can be classed as simple (derived from one ovary) or compound (derived from several ovaries). Simple succulent fruits include berries, which typically have many seeds, and drupes, which typically have a single stone or pip (e.g., cherry and peach). Compound succulent fruits include aggregate fruits, which are formed from many ovaries in one flower, and multiple fruits, which develop from the ovaries of many flowers. Some fruits, known as false fruits or pseudocarps, develop from parts of the flower in addition to the ovaries. For example, the flesh of the apple is formed from the receptacle (the upper end of the flower stalk).

BERRY
Cocoa
(*Theobroma cacao*)

HESPERIDIUM (A TYPE OF BERRY)
Lemon
(*Citrus limon*)

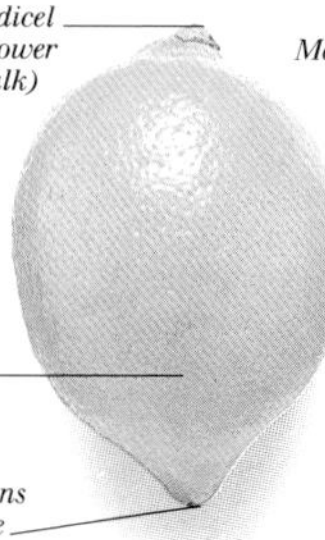

Pedicel (flower stalk)
Leathery exocarp
Remains of style

EXTERNAL VIEW OF FRUIT

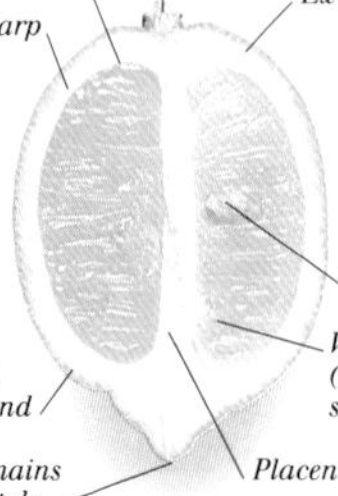

Endocarp
Pedicel (flower stalk)
Exocar
Mesocarp
See
Vesic (juice sac)
Oil gland
Remains of style
Placenta

LONGITUDINAL SECTION THROUGH FRUIT

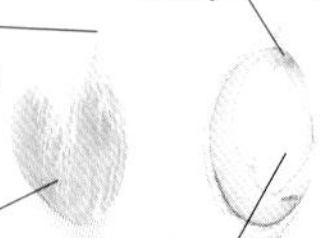

Hilum (point of attachment to ovary)
Embryo
Testa (seed coat)
Cotyledon (seed leaf)

EXTERNAL VIEW AND SECTION THROUGH SEED

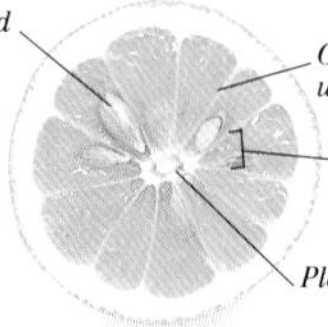

CROSS-SECTION THROUGH FRUIT

SYCONIUM (A TYPE OF FALSE FRUIT)
Fig
(*Ficus carica*)

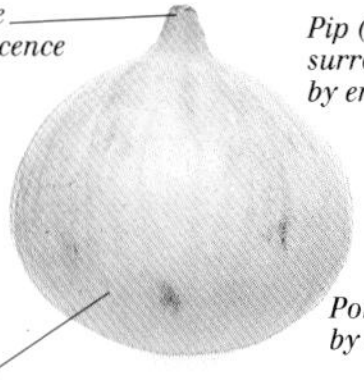

Peduncle (inflorescence stalk)
Skin

EXTERNAL VIEW OF FRUIT

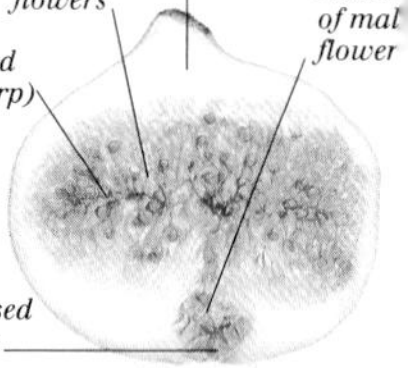

Remains of female flowers
Fleshy infolded receptacle
Remai of mal flower
Pip (seed surrounded by endocarp)
Pore closed by scales

LONGITUDINAL SECTION THROUGH FRUIT

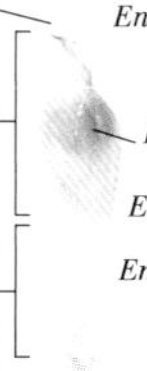

Remains of style
Drupelet
Pip
Pedicel (flower stalk)

REMAINS OF A SINGLE FEMALE FLOWER

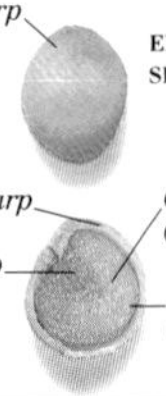

Endocarp
Endocarp
Embryo
Cotyledon (seed leaf)
Testa (seed coat)

EXTERNAL VIEW AND SECTION THROUGH P

FRUIT WITH FLESHY ARIL
Lychee
(*Litchi chinensis*)

Pedicel (flower stalk)
Pericarp (fruit wall)

EXTERNAL VIEW OF FRUIT

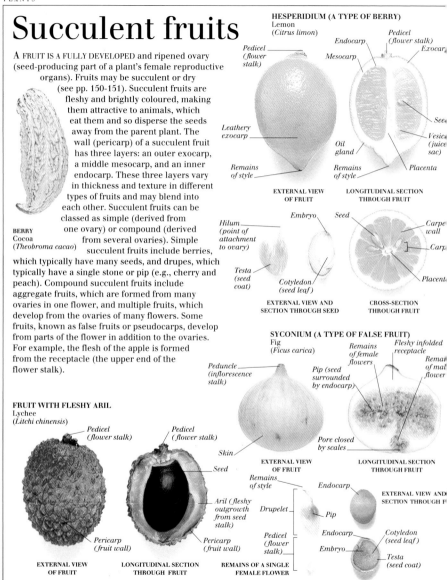

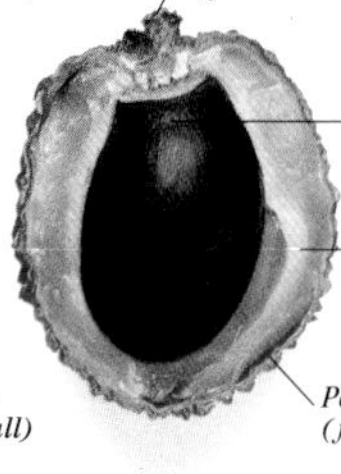

Pedicel (flower stalk)
Seed
Aril (fleshy outgrowth from seed stalk)
Pericarp (fruit wall)

LONGITUDINAL SECTION THROUGH FRUIT

BERRY
Cape gooseberry
(Physalis peruviana)

Calyx
(whorl
of sepals)
Pedicel
(flower
stalk)

EXTERNAL VIEW OF FRUIT

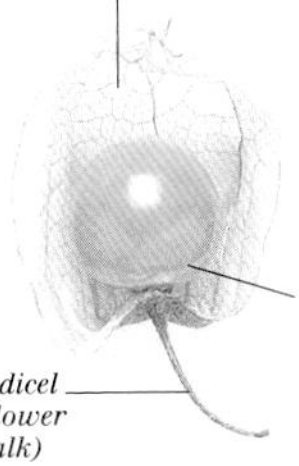
Calyx
(whorl of sepals)
surrounding berry
Exocarp
of berry
Pedicel
(flower
stalk)

INTERNAL VIEW OF FRUIT

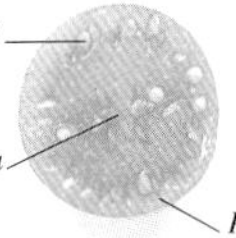
Seed
Placenta
Pericarp

CROSS-SECTION THROUGH FRUIT

Testa
(seed coat)

EXTERNAL VIEW OF SEED

AGGREGATE FRUIT
Raspberry
(Rubus idaeus)

Remains
of stamen
Drupelet
Remains
of style

EXTERNAL VIEW OF FRUIT

Pedicel
(flower
stalk)
Mesocarp
and
exocarp
Pip (seed
surrounded
by endocarp)
Receptacle
Drupelet

LONGITUDINAL SECTION THROUGH FRUIT

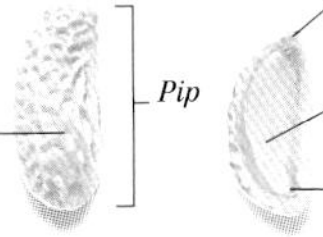
Hard
endocarp
Pip
Hard
endocarp
Cotyledon
(seed leaf)
Seed
Testa
(seed
coat)

EXTERNAL VIEW AND SECTION THROUGH PIP

POME (A TYPE OF FALSE FRUIT)
Apple
(Malus sylvestris)

Pedicel (flower
stalk)
Waxy skin

EXTERNAL VIEW OF FRUIT

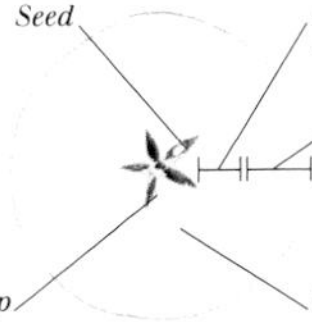
Seed
Mesocarp
and exocarp
Swollen
receptacle
Endocarp
Vascular
strand

CROSS-SECTION THROUGH FRUIT

Hilum (point
of attachment
to ovary)
Testa
(seed coat)
Embryo
Cotyledon
(seed leaf)
Testa
(seed coat)

EXTERNAL VIEW AND SECTION THROUGH SEED

PEPO (A TYPE OF BERRY)
Charentais melon
(Cucumis melo)

Pedicel
(flower stalk)
Rind
(fused receptacle
and exocarp)

EXTERNAL VIEW OF FRUIT

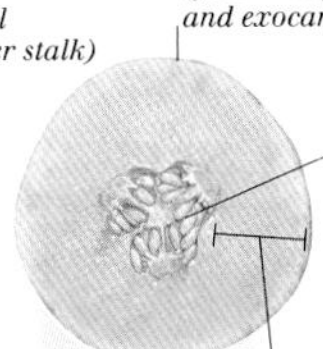
Rind
(fused receptacle
and exocarp)
Seed
Mesocarp
and
endocarp

CROSS-SECTION THROUGH FRUIT

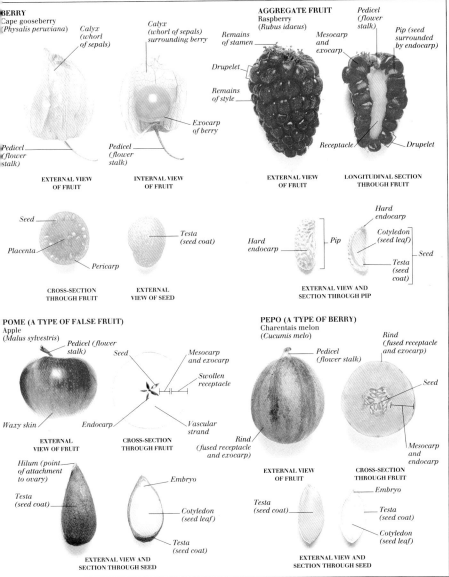

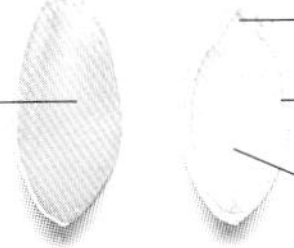
Testa
(seed coat)
Embryo
Testa
(seed coat)
Cotyledon
(seed leaf)

EXTERNAL VIEW AND SECTION THROUGH SEED

Dry fruits

DRY FRUITS HAVE A HARD, DRY PERICARP (fruit wall) around their seeds unlike succulent fruits, which have fleshy pericarps (see pp. 148-149). Dry fruits are divided into three types: dehiscent, in which the pericarp splits open to release the seeds; indehiscent, which do not split open; and schizocarpic, in which the fruit splits but the seeds are not exposed. Dehiscent dry fruits include capsules (e.g., love-in-a-mist), follicles (e.g., delphinium), legumes (e.g., pea), and siliquas (e.g., honesty). Typically, the seeds of dehiscent fruits are dispersed by the wind. Indehiscent dry fruits include nuts (e.g., sweet chestnut), nutlets (e.g., goosegrass), achenes (e.g., strawberry), caryopses (e.g., wheat), samaras (e.g., elm), and cypselas (e.g., dandelion). Some indehiscent dry fruits are dispersed by the wind, assisted by "wings" (e.g., elm) or "parachutes" (e.g., dandelion); others (e.g., goosegrass) have hooked pericarps to aid dispersal on animals' fur. Schizocarpic dry fruits include cremocarps (e.g., hogweed), and double samaras (e.g., sycamore); these are dispersed by the wind.

NUTLET
Goosegrass
(*Galium aparine*)

LEGUME
Pea
(*Pisum sativum*)

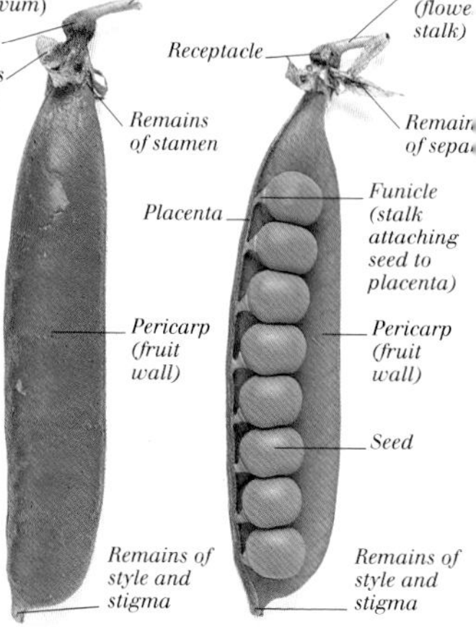

Pedicel (flower stalk)
Receptacle
Remains of sepal
Remains of stamen
Placenta
Funicle (stalk attaching seed to placenta)
Pericarp (fruit wall)
Seed
Remains of style and stigma

EXTERNAL VIEW OF FRUIT

INTERNAL VIEW OF FRUIT

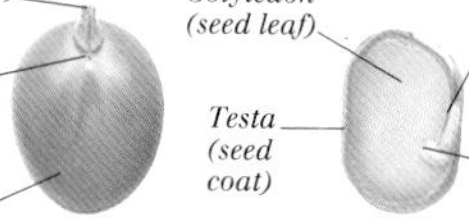

Funicle (stalk attaching seed to placenta)
Micropyle (pore for water absorption)
Testa (seed coat)
Cotyledon (seed leaf)
Radicle (embryonic root)
Testa (seed coat)
Plumule (embryonic shoot)

EXTERIOR VIEW AND SECTION THROUGH SEED

NUT
Sweet chestnut
(*Castanea sativa*)

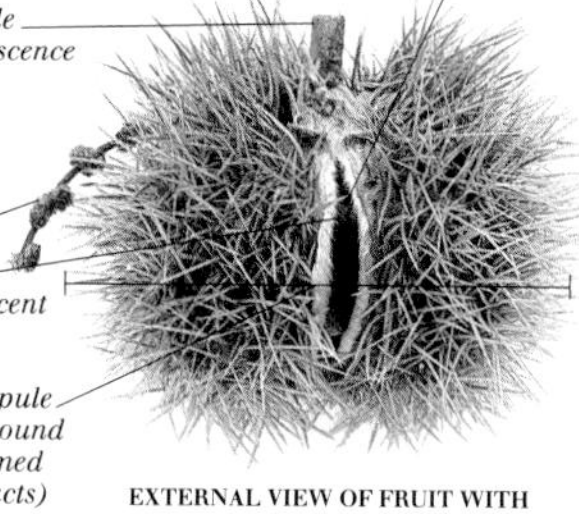

Line of splitting between valves of cupule
Peduncle (inflorescence stalk)
Remains of male inflorescence
Nut (indehiscent fruit)
Spiky cupule (husk around fruit formed from bracts)

EXTERNAL VIEW OF FRUIT WITH SURROUNDING CUPULE

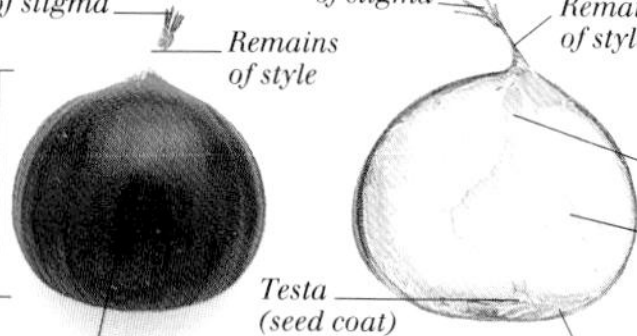

Remains of stigma
Remains of style
Nut (indehiscent fruit)
Woody pericarp (fruit wall)
Remains of stigma
Remains of style
Embryo
Cotyledon (seed leaf)
Testa (seed coat)
Woody pericarp (fruit wall)

EXTERNAL VIEW AND SECTION THROUGH FRUIT

ACHENE
Strawberry
(*Fragaria x ananassa*)

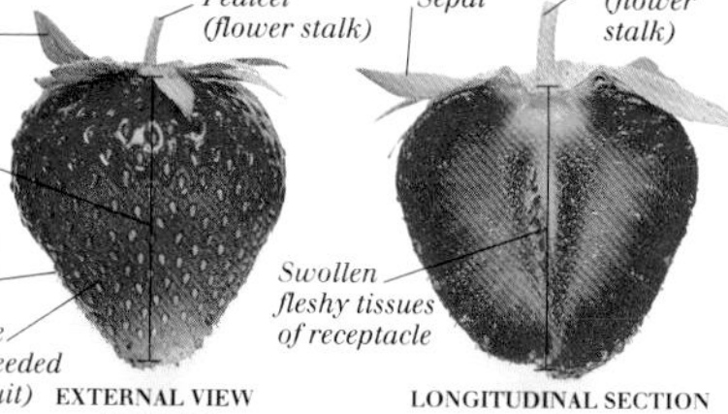

Pedicel (flower stalk)
Sepal
Swollen receptacle
Remains of stigma and style
Achene (one-seeded dry fruit)
Sepal
Pedicel (flower stalk)
Swollen fleshy tissues of receptacle

EXTERNAL VIEW OF FRUIT

LONGITUDINAL SECTION THROUGH FRUIT

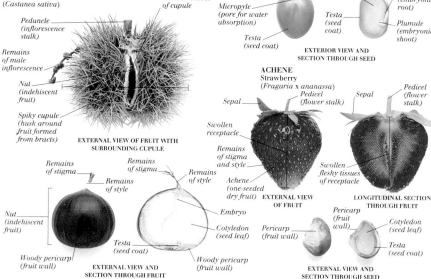

Pericarp (fruit wall)
Pericarp (fruit wall)
Cotyledon (seed leaf)
Testa (seed coat)

EXTERNAL VIEW AND SECTION THROUGH SEED

DOUBLE SAMARA
Sycamore
(Acer pseudoplatanus)

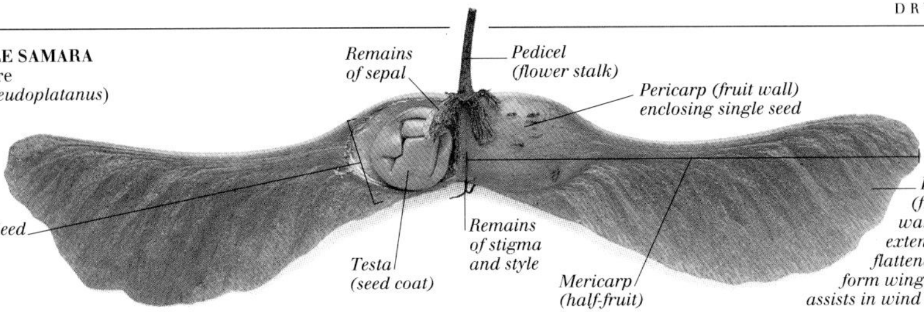
Remains of sepal
Pedicel (flower stalk)
Pericarp (fruit wall) enclosing single seed
Pericarp (fruit wall) extended and flattened to form wing that assists in wind dispersal
Seed
Testa (seed coat)
Remains of stigma and style
Mericarp (half-fruit)

CAPSULE
Love-in-a-mist
(Nigella damascena)

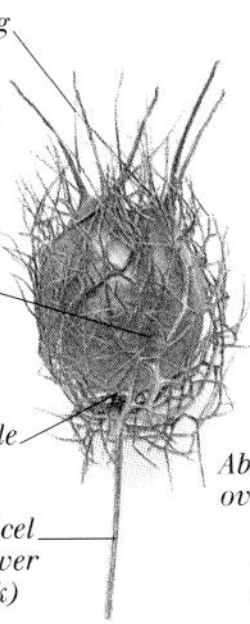
Branching bracteole (leaf-like structure)
Fused edge of carpels
Receptacle
Pedicel (flower stalk)

EXTERNAL VIEW OF FRUIT

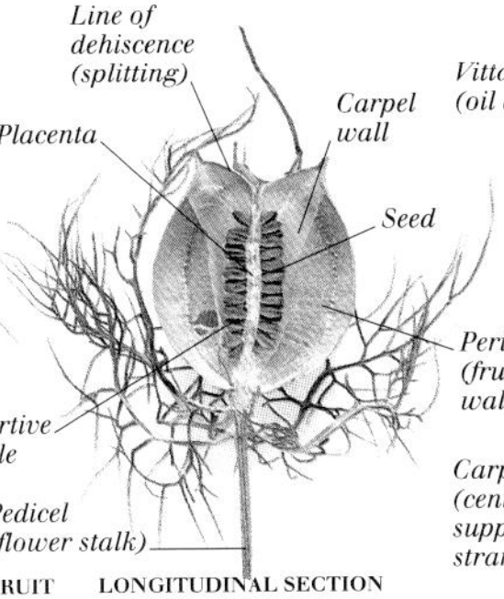
Line of dehiscence (splitting)
Placenta
Carpel wall
Seed
Pericarp (fruit wall)
Abortive ovule
Pedicel (flower stalk)

LONGITUDINAL SECTION THROUGH FRUIT

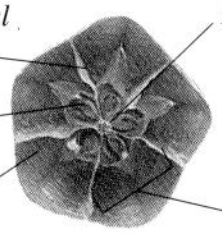
Carpel wall
Placenta
Seed
Pericarp (fruit wall)
Carpel

CROSS-SECTION THROUGH FRUIT

Sculptured testa (seed coat)
Cotyledon (seed leaf)
Testa (seed coat)

EXTERIOR VIEW AND SECTION THROUGH SEED

CREMOCARP
Hogweed
(Heracleum sp.)

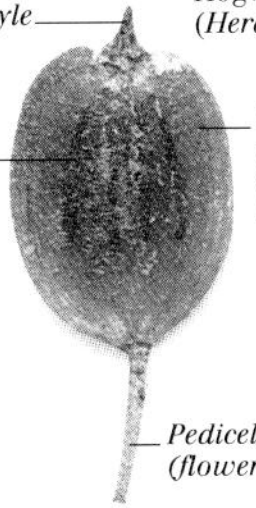
Remains of style
Vitta (oil duct)
Flattened pericarp (fruit wall)
Pedicel (flower stalk)

EXTERNAL VIEW OF FRUIT

Testa (seed coat)

EXTERNAL VIEW OF SEED

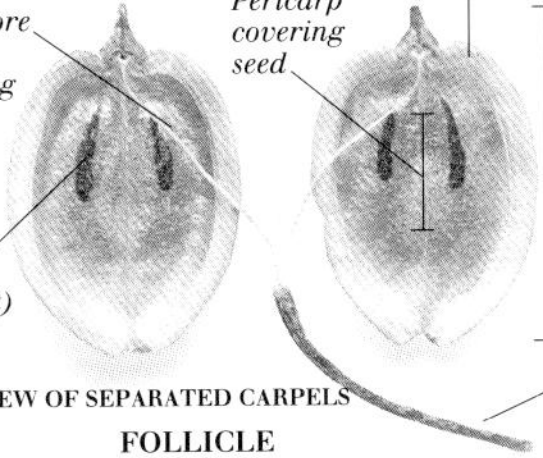
Pericarp (fruit wall)
Carpophore (central supporting strand)
Pericarp covering seed
One-seeded mericarp (half-fruit)
Vitta (oil duct)
Pedicel (flower stalk)

VIEW OF SEPARATED CARPELS

SILIQUA
Honesty
(Lunaria annua)

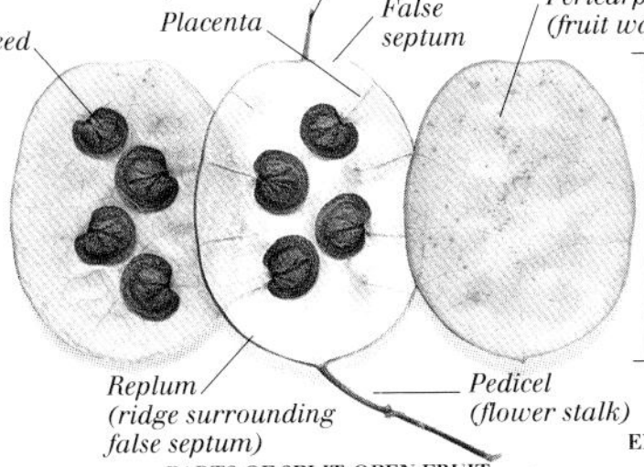
Remains of stigma and style
Seed
Placenta
False septum
Pericarp (fruit wall)
Valve of pericarp
Replum (ridge surrounding false septum)
Pedicel (flower stalk)

PARTS OF SPLIT-OPEN FRUIT

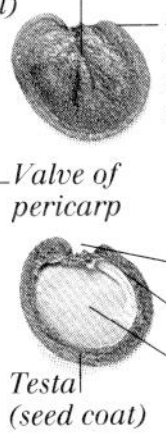
Testa (seed coat)
Flattened edge of testa aids dispersal of seed
Hilum (point of attachment to ovary)
Embryo
Cotyledon (seed leaf)
Testa (seed coat)

EXTERNAL VIEW AND SECTION THROUGH SEED

FOLLICLE
Larkspur
(Delphinium sp.)

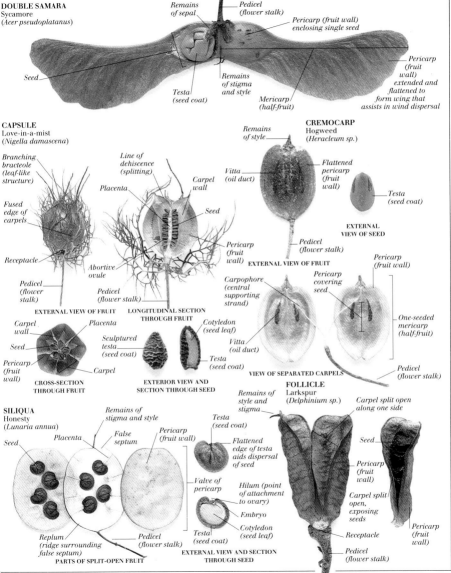

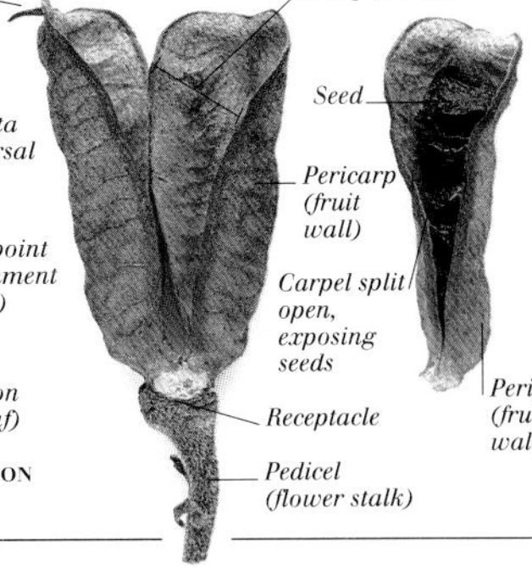
Remains of style and stigma
Carpel split open along one side
Seed
Pericarp (fruit wall)
Carpel split open, exposing seeds
Receptacle
Pericarp (fruit wall)
Pedicel (flower stalk)

Germination

GERMINATION IS THE GROWTH OF SEEDS INTO SEEDLINGS. It starts when seeds become active below ground, and ends when the first foliage leaves appear above ground. A seed consists of an embryo and its food store, surrounded by a testa (seed coat). The embryo is made up of one or two cotyledons (seed leaves) attached to a central axis. The upper part of the axis consists of an epicotyl, which has a plumule (embryonic shoot) at its tip. The lower part of the axis consists of a hypocotyl and a radicle (embryonic root). After dispersal from the parent plant, the seeds dehydrate and enter a period of dormancy. Following this dormant period, germination begins, provided that the seeds have enough water, oxygen, warmth, and, in some cases, light. In the first stages of germination, the seed takes in water; the embryo starts to use its food store; and the radicle swells, breaks through the testa, and grows downwards. Germination then proceeds in one of two ways, depending on the type of seed. In epigeal germination, the hypocotyl lengthens, pulling the plumule and its protective cotyledons out of the soil. In hypogeal germination, the cotyledons remain below ground and the epicotyl lengthens, pushing the plumule upwards.

HYPOGEAL GERMINATION
Broad bean
(*Vicia faba*)

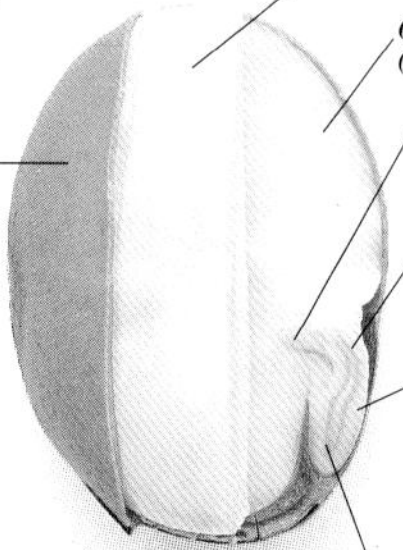
Cotyledon (seed leaf)
Cotyledon (seed leaf)
Plumule (embryonic shoot)
Testa (seed coat)
Epicotyl (upper part of axis)
Hypocotyl (region between epicotyl and radicle)
Radicle (embryonic root)

SEED AT START OF GERMINATION

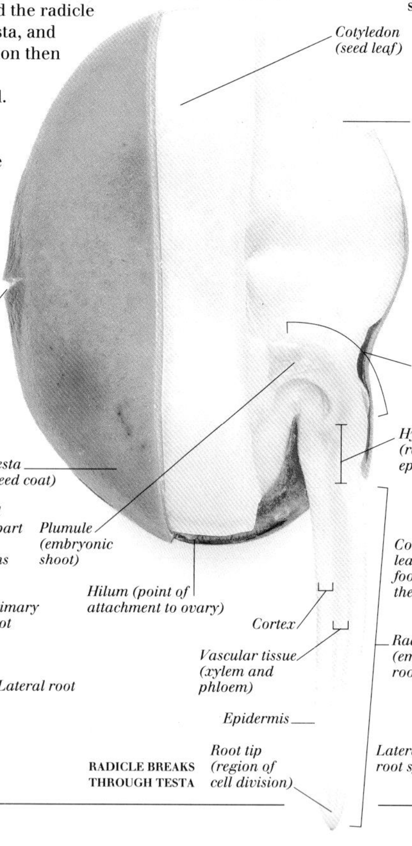
Cotyledon (seed leaf)
Cotyledon (seed leaf)
Split in testa (seed coat) due to expanding cotyledons
Epicotyl (upper part of axis)
Hypocotyl (region between epicotyl and radicle)
Testa (seed coat)
Plumule (embryonic shoot)
Hilum (point of attachment to ovary)
Cortex
Vascular tissue (xylem and phloem)
Epidermis
Root tip (region of cell division)
Radicle (embryonic root)

RADICLE BREAKS THROUGH TESTA

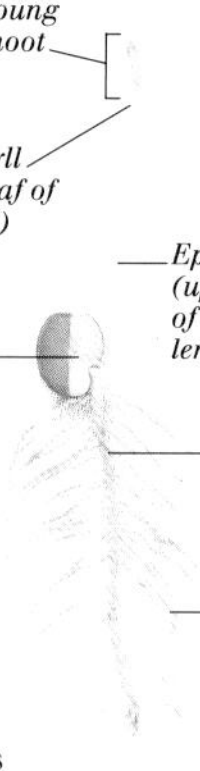
Young shoot
Cataphyll (scale leaf of plumule)
Epicotyl (upper part of axis) lengthens
Cotyledons (seed leaves) remain within testa (seed coat) below soil's surface
Primary root
Lateral root

SHOOT APPEARS ABOVE SOIL

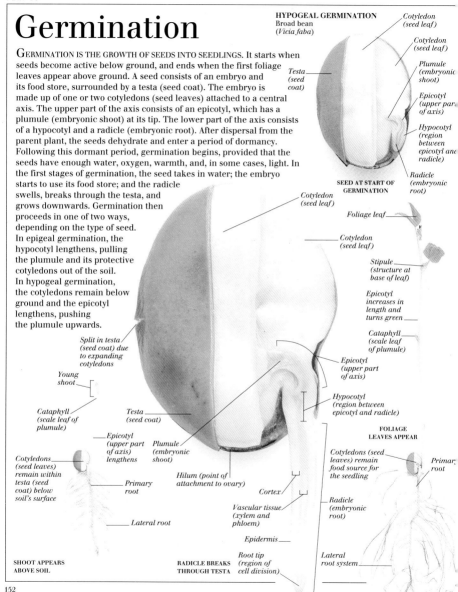

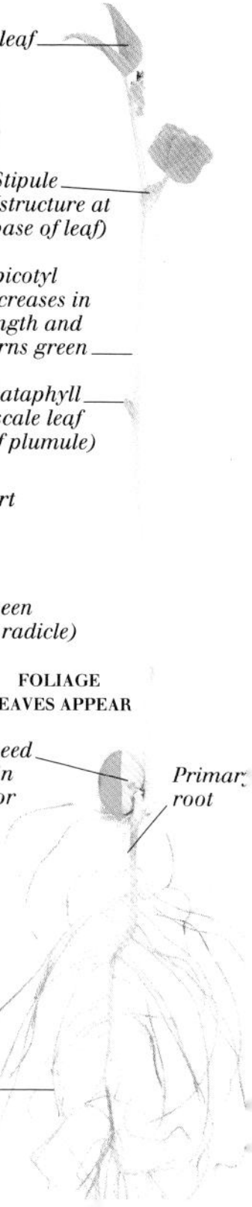
Foliage leaf
Stipule (structure at base of leaf)
Epicotyl increases in length and turns green
Cataphyll (scale leaf of plumule)
Cotyledons (seed leaves) remain food source for the seedling
Primary root
Lateral root system

FOLIAGE LEAVES APPEAR

EPIGEAL GERMINATION
Black bean
(*Phaseolus sp.*)

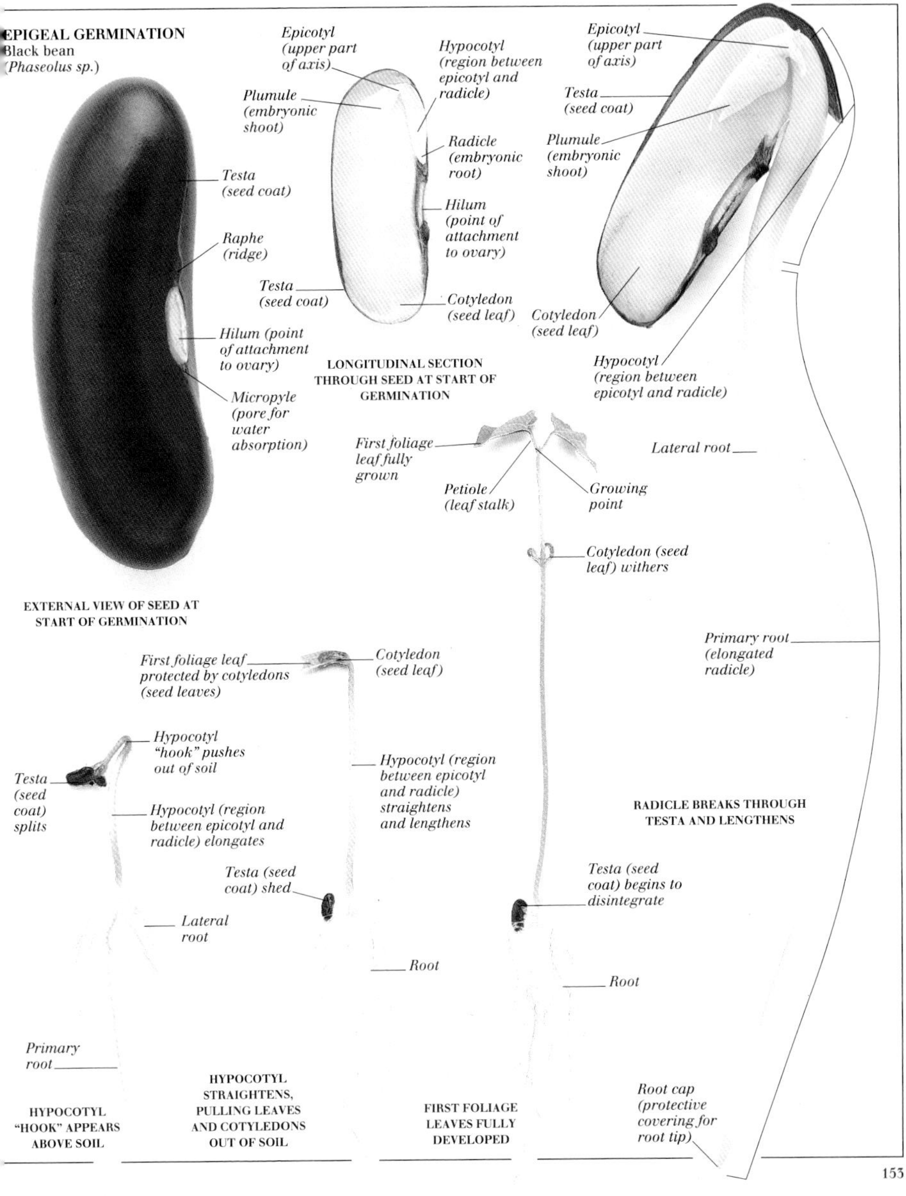
Testa (seed coat)
Raphe (ridge)
Hilum (point of attachment to ovary)
Micropyle (pore for water absorption)
Epicotyl (upper part of axis)
Plumule (embryonic shoot)
Hypocotyl (region between epicotyl and radicle)
Radicle (embryonic root)
Hilum (point of attachment to ovary)
Testa (seed coat)
Cotyledon (seed leaf)
Epicotyl (upper part of axis)
Testa (seed coat)
Plumule (embryonic shoot)
Cotyledon (seed leaf)
Hypocotyl (region between epicotyl and radicle)
First foliage leaf fully grown
Petiole (leaf stalk)
Growing point
Lateral root
Cotyledon (seed leaf) withers
Primary root (elongated radicle)
First foliage leaf protected by cotyledons (seed leaves)
Cotyledon (seed leaf)
Hypocotyl "hook" pushes out of soil
Testa (seed coat) splits
Hypocotyl (region between epicotyl and radicle) elongates
Hypocotyl (region between epicotyl and radicle) straightens and lengthens
Testa (seed coat) shed
Testa (seed coat) begins to disintegrate
Lateral root
Root
Root
Primary root
Root cap (protective covering for root tip)

EXTERNAL VIEW OF SEED AT START OF GERMINATION

LONGITUDINAL SECTION THROUGH SEED AT START OF GERMINATION

RADICLE BREAKS THROUGH TESTA AND LENGTHENS

HYPOCOTYL "HOOK" APPEARS ABOVE SOIL

HYPOCOTYL STRAIGHTENS, PULLING LEAVES AND COTYLEDONS OUT OF SOIL

FIRST FOLIAGE LEAVES FULLY DEVELOPED

Vegetative reproduction

MANY PLANTS CAN PROPAGATE THEMSELVES by vegetative reproduction. In this process, part of a plant separates off, takes root, and grows into a new plant. Vegetative reproduction is a type of asexual reproduction; that is, it involves only one parent, and there is no fusion of gametes (sex cells). Plants use various structures to reproduce vegetatively. Some plants use underground storage organs. Such organs include rhizomes (horizontal, underground stems), the branches of which produce new plants; bulbs (swollen leaf bases) and corms (swollen stems), which produce daughter bulbs or corms that separate off from the parent; and stem tubers (thickened underground stems) and root tubers (swollen adventitious roots), which also separate off from the parent. Other propagative structures include runners and stolons, creeping horizontal stems that take root and produce new plants; bulbils, small bulbs that develop on the stem or in the place of flowers, and then drop off and grow into new plants; and adventitious buds, miniature plants that form on leaf margins before dropping to the ground and growing into mature plants.

CORM
Gladiolus
(*Gladiolus sp.*)

ADVENTITIOUS BUD
Mexican hat plant
(*Kalanchoe daigremontiana*)

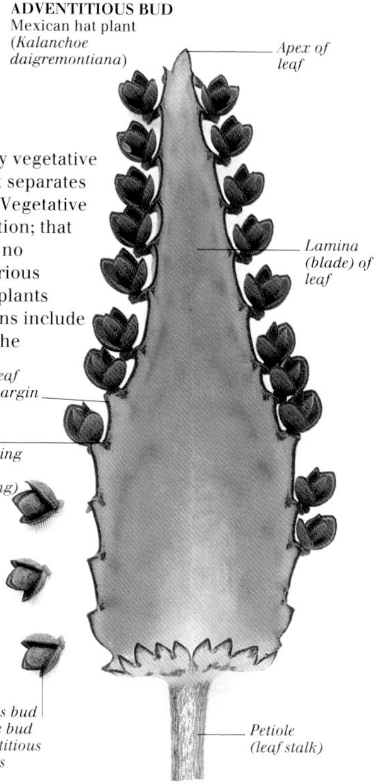

Apex of leaf
Lamina (blade) of leaf
Leaf margin
Notch in leaf margin containing meristematic (actively dividing) cells
Adventitious bud (detachable bud with adventitious roots) drops from leaf
Petiole (leaf stalk)

BULBIL IN PLACE OF FLOWER
Orange lily
(*Lilium bulbiferum*)

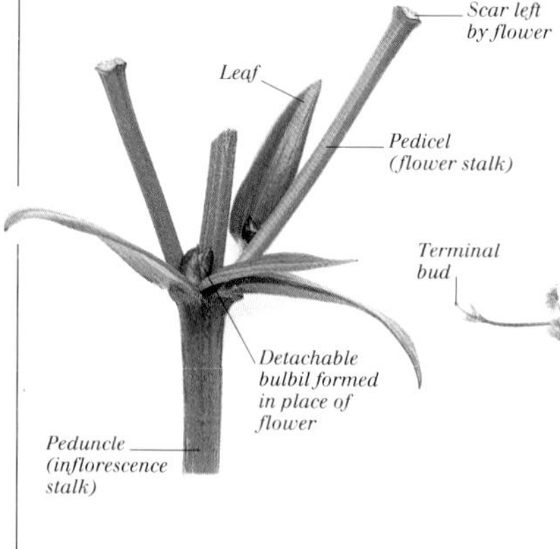

Scar left by flower
Leaf
Pedicel (flower stalk)
Detachable bulbil formed in place of flower
Peduncle (inflorescence stalk)

STOLON
Ground ivy
(*Glechoma hederacea*)

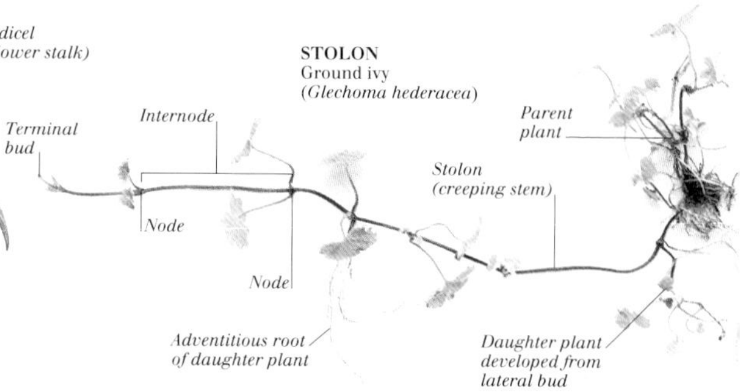

Terminal bud
Internode
Node
Node
Parent plant
Stolon (creeping stem)
Adventitious root of daughter plant
Daughter plant developed from lateral bud

ROOT TUBER
Sweet potato
(*Ipomoea batatas*)

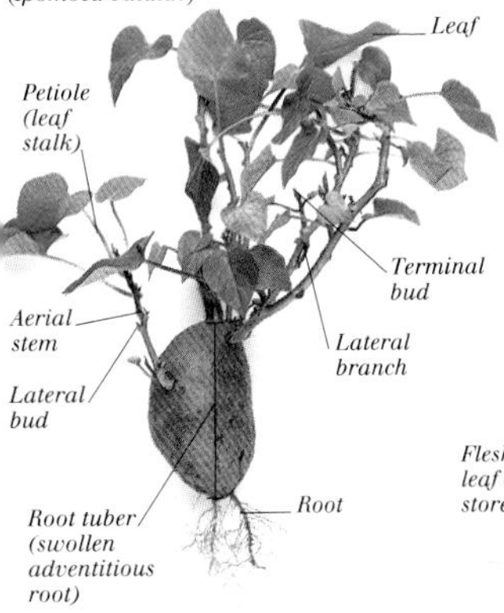
Leaf
Petiole (leaf stalk)
Terminal bud
Aerial stem
Lateral branch
Lateral bud
Root
Root tuber (swollen adventitious root)

STEM BULBIL
Lily
(*Lilium sp.*)

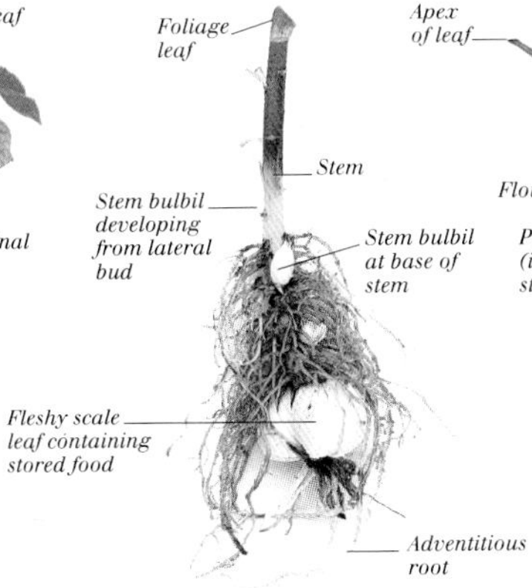
Foliage leaf
Stem
Stem bulbil developing from lateral bud
Stem bulbil at base of stem
Fleshy scale leaf containing stored food
Adventitious root

GROWING BULB
Grape hyacinth
(*Muscari sp.*)

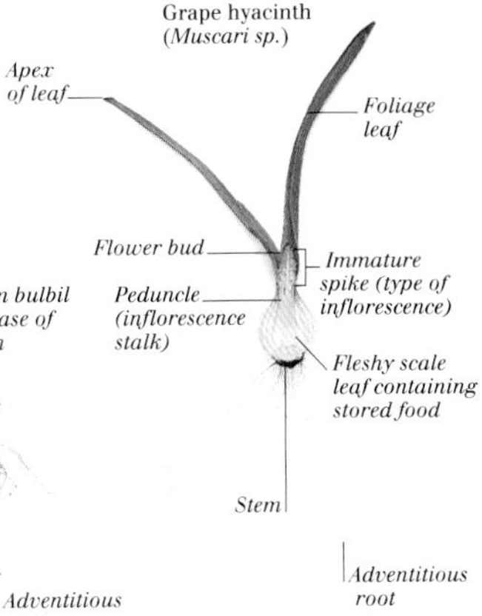
Apex of leaf
Foliage leaf
Flower bud
Immature spike (type of inflorescence)
Peduncle (inflorescence stalk)
Fleshy scale leaf containing stored food
Stem
Adventitious root

ROOT TUBER
Begonia
(*Begonia* x *tuberhybrida*)

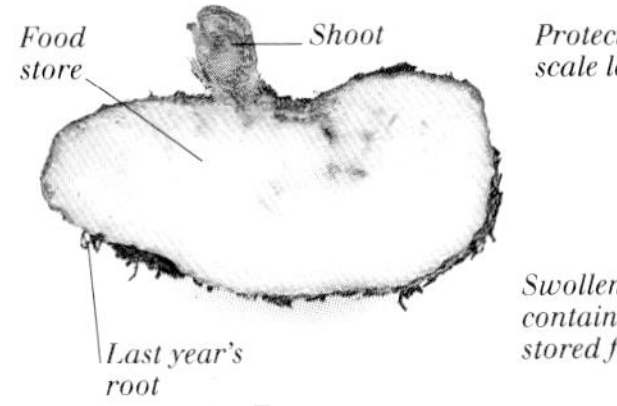
Food store
Shoot
Last year's root

CORM
Gladiolus
(*Gladiolus sp.*)

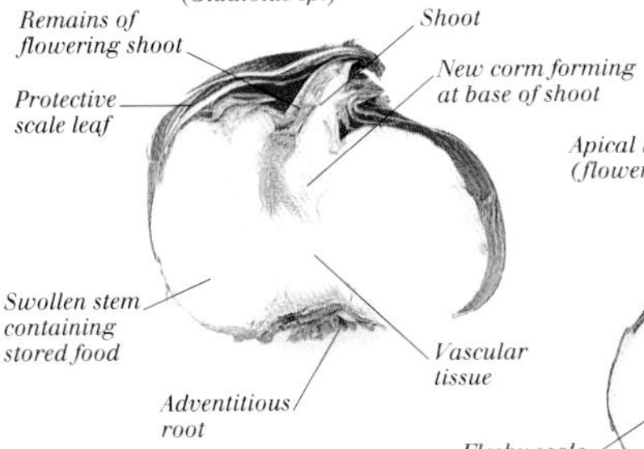
Remains of flowering shoot
Shoot
New corm forming at base of shoot
Protective scale leaf
Swollen stem containing stored food
Vascular tissue
Adventitious root

BULB WITH SHOOT
Amaryllis
(*Hippeastrum sp.*)

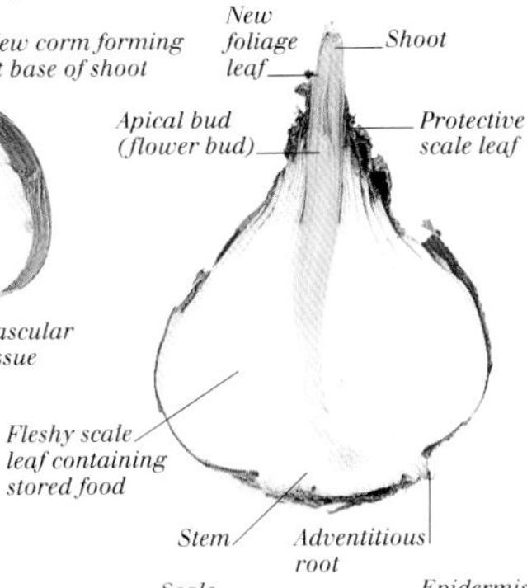
New foliage leaf
Shoot
Apical bud (flower bud)
Protective scale leaf
Fleshy scale leaf containing stored food
Stem
Adventitious root

RHIZOME
Ginger
(*Zingiber officinale*)

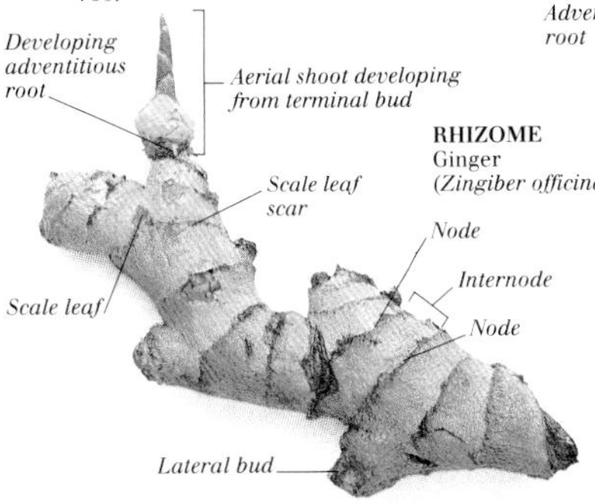
Developing adventitious root
Aerial shoot developing from terminal bud
Scale leaf scar
Node
Internode
Node
Scale leaf
Lateral bud

EXTERNAL VIEW

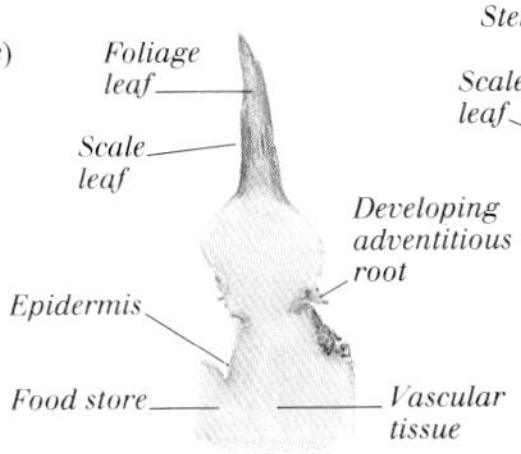
Foliage leaf
Scale leaf
Developing adventitious root
Epidermis
Food store
Vascular tissue

LONGITUDINAL SECTION THROUGH AERIAL SHOOT

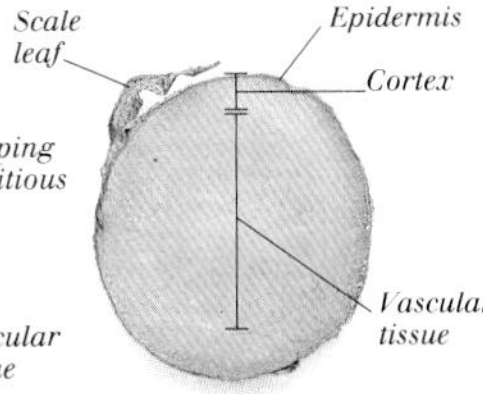
Scale leaf
Epidermis
Cortex
Vascular tissue

CROSS-SECTION THROUGH RHIZOME

Dryland plants

LEAF SUCCULENT
Lithops sp.

DRYLAND PLANTS (XEROPHYTES) are able to survive in unfavourable habitats. All are found in places where little water is available; some live in high temperatures that cause excessive loss of water from the leaves. Xerophytes show a number of adaptations to dry conditions; these include reduced leaf area, rolled leaves, sunken stomata, hairs, spines, and thick cuticles. One group, succulent plants, stores water in specially enlarged spongy tissues found in leaves, roots, or stems. Leaf succulents have enlarged, fleshy, water-storing leaves. Root succulents have a large, underground water-storage organ with short-lived stems and leaves above ground. Stem succulents are represented by the cacti (family Cactaceae). Cacti stems are fleshy, green, and photosynthetic; they are typically ribbed or covered by tubercles in rows, with leaves being reduced to spines or entirely absent.

STEM SUCCULENT
Golden barrel cactus
(Echinocactus grusonii)

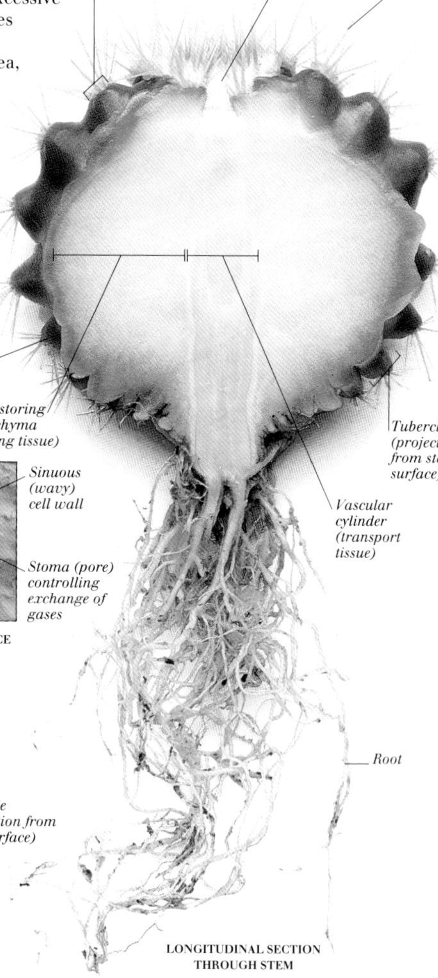
Areole (modified lateral shoot)
Trichome (hair)
Spine (modified leaf)
Waxy cuticle (waterproof covering)
Water-storing parenchyma (packing tissue)
Tubercle (projection from stem surface)
Vascular cylinder (transport tissue)
Root

LONGITUDINAL SECTION THROUGH STEM

Spine (modified leaf)
Tubercle (projection from stem surface)
Root

EXTERNAL VIEW

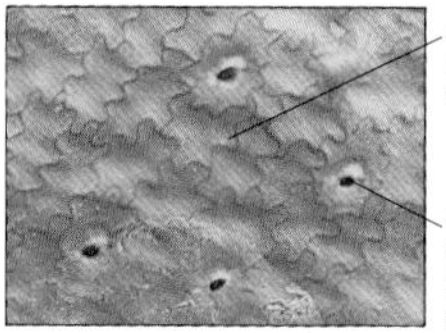
Sinuous (wavy) cell wall
Stoma (pore) controlling exchange of gases

MICROGRAPH OF STEM SURFACE

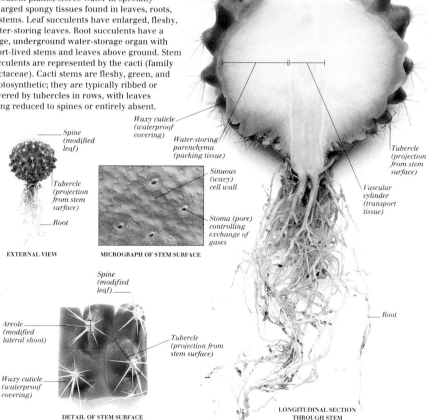

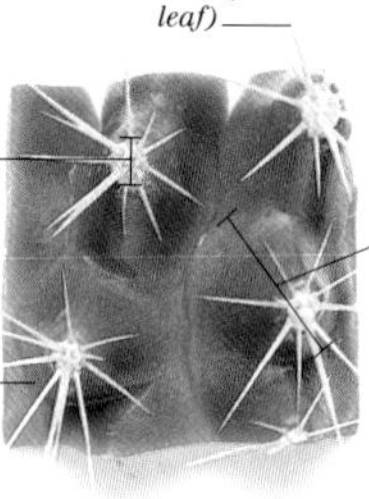
Spine (modified leaf)
Areole (modified lateral shoot)
Tubercle (projection from stem surface)
Waxy cuticle (waterproof covering)

DETAIL OF STEM SURFACE

LEAF SUCCULENT
Haworthia truncata

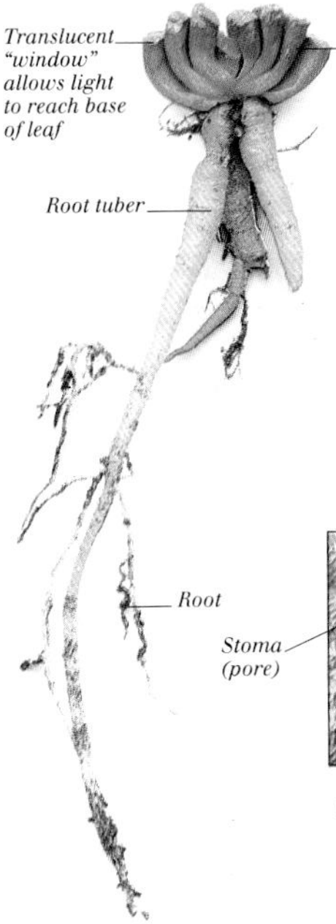
Translucent "window" allows light to reach base of leaf
Succulent leaf
Root tuber
Root

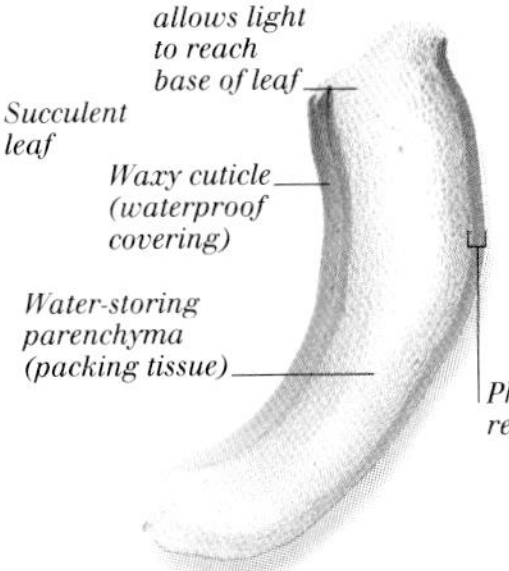
Translucent "window" allows light to reach base of leaf
Waxy cuticle (waterproof covering)
Water-storing parenchyma (packing tissue)
Photosynthetic region

LONGITUDINAL SECTION THROUGH LEAF

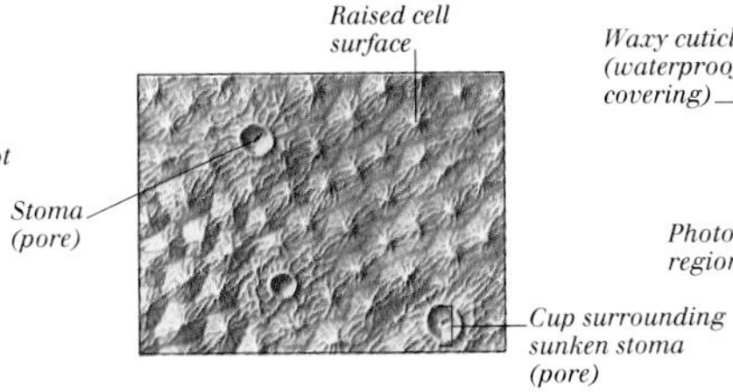
Raised cell surface
Stoma (pore)
Cup surrounding sunken stoma (pore)

MICROGRAPH OF LEAF SURFACE

LEAF SUCCULENT
Lithops bromfieldii

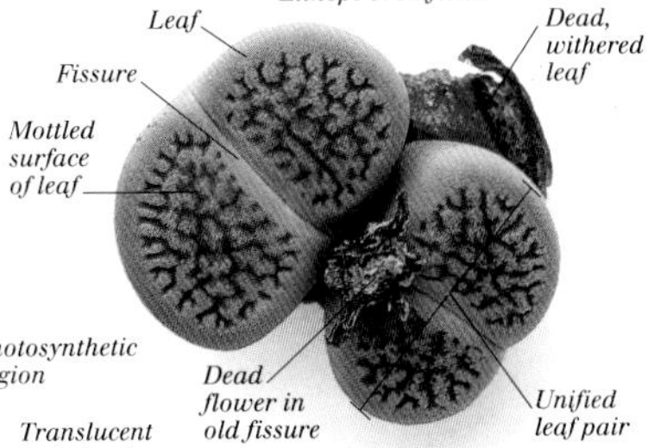
Leaf
Fissure
Mottled surface of leaf
Dead, withered leaf
Dead flower in old fissure
Unified leaf pair

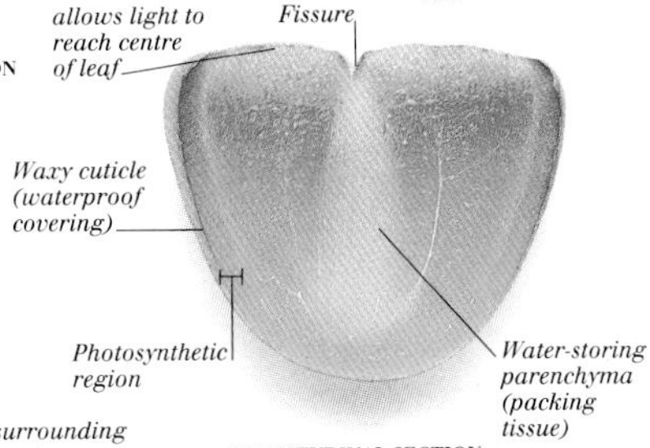
Translucent "window" allows light to reach centre of leaf
Fissure
Waxy cuticle (waterproof covering)
Photosynthetic region
Water-storing parenchyma (packing tissue)

LONGITUDINAL SECTION THROUGH LEAF PAIR

STEM AND ROOT SUCCULENT
String of hearts
(*Ceropegia woodii*)

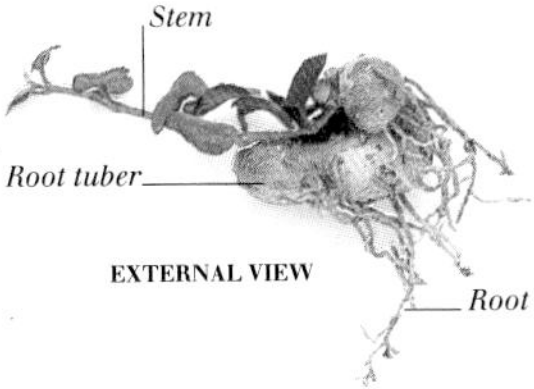
Stem
Root tuber
Root

EXTERNAL VIEW

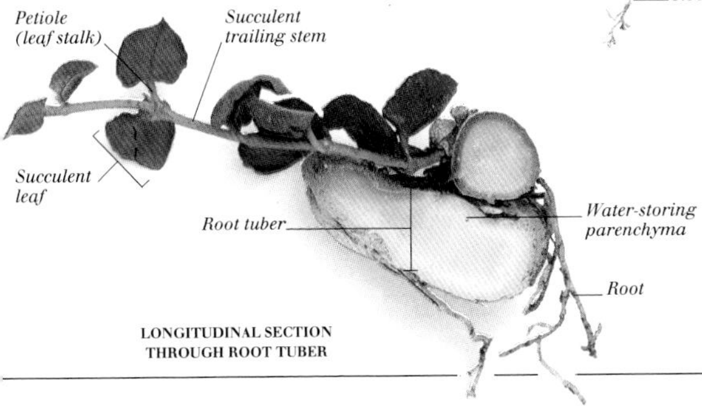
Petiole (leaf stalk)
Succulent trailing stem
Succulent leaf
Root tuber
Water-storing parenchyma
Root

LONGITUDINAL SECTION THROUGH ROOT TUBER

ROOT SUCCULENT
Oxalis sp.

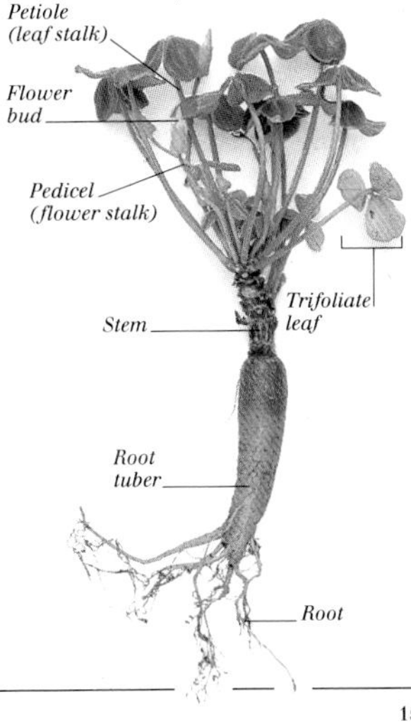
Petiole (leaf stalk)
Flower bud
Pedicel (flower stalk)
Trifoliate leaf
Stem
Root tuber
Root

Wetland plants

WETLAND PLANTS GROW SUBMERGED IN WATER, either partially (e.g., water hyacinth) or completely (e.g., pond weeds), and show various adaptations to this habitat. Typically, there are numerous air spaces inside the stems, leaves, and roots; these aid gas exchange and buoyancy. Submerged parts generally have no cuticle (waterproof covering), enabling the plants to absorb minerals and gases directly from the water; in addition, being supported by the water, they need little of the supportive tissue found in land plants. Stomata, the gas exchange pores, are absent from plants that are completely submerged; in partially submerged plants with floating leaves (e.g., water lilies), stomata are found on the upper leaf surfaces, where they cannot be flooded.

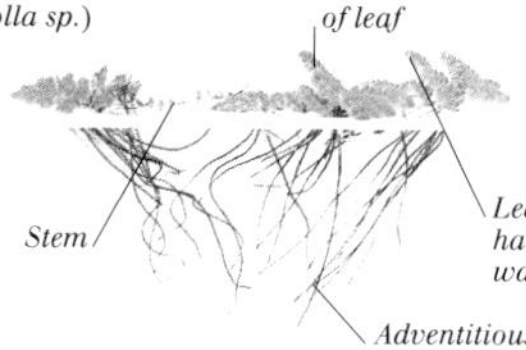
Dorsal lobe of leaf
Stem
Leaf with tiny hairs to prevent waterlogging
Adventitious root

WATER FERN
(Azolla sp.)

Abaxial (lower) surface of lamina (blade)
Adaxial (upper) surface of lamina (blade)
Inflated petiole (leaf stalk) provides buoyancy
Leaf
Isthmus (narrow connecting region)
Orbicular lamina (blade)
Rhizome
Dense, fibrous root system
Adventitious root
Lateral branch of adventitious root

WATER HYACINTH
(Eichhornia crassipes)

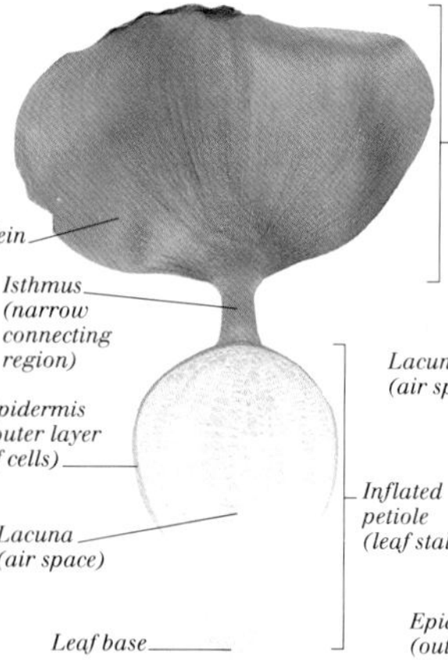
Orbicular lamina (blade)
Vein
Isthmus (narrow connecting region)
Epidermis (outer layer of cells)
Inflated petiole (leaf stalk)
Lacuna (air space)
Leaf base

LAMINA AND SECTION THROUGH INFLATED PETIOLE OF WATER HYACINTH

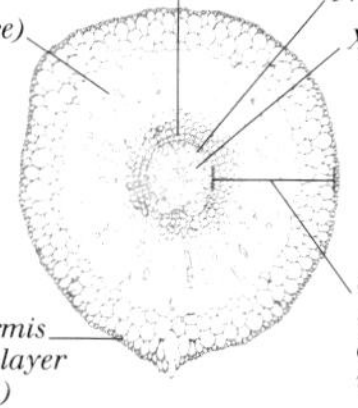
Endodermis (inner layer of cortex)
Lacuna (air space)
Phloem
Xylem
Vascular tissue
Cortex (layer between epidermis and vascular tissue)
Epidermis (outer layer of cells)

MICROGRAPH OF CROSS-SECTION THROUGH ROOT OF WATER HYACINTH

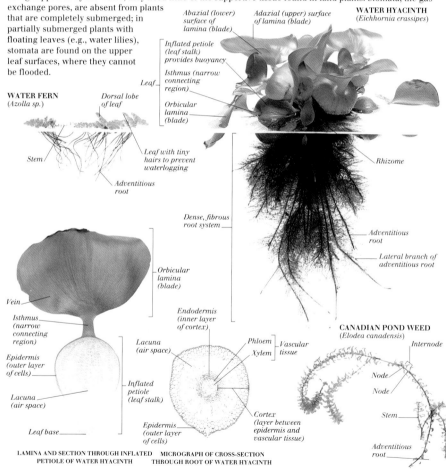

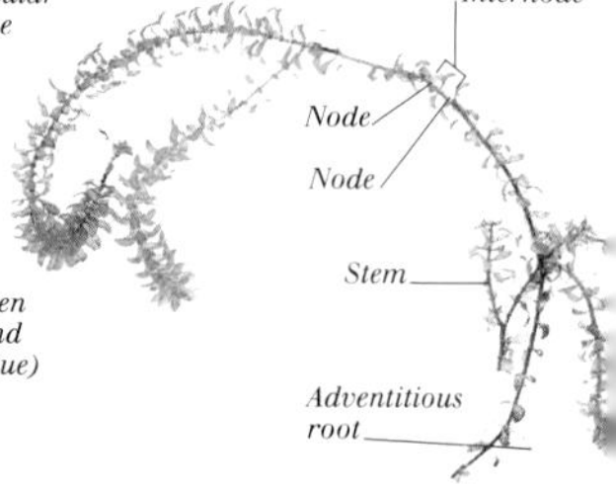
Internode
Node
Node
Stem
Adventitious root

CANADIAN POND WEED
(Elodea canadensis)

VATER LILY

Nymphaea sp.)

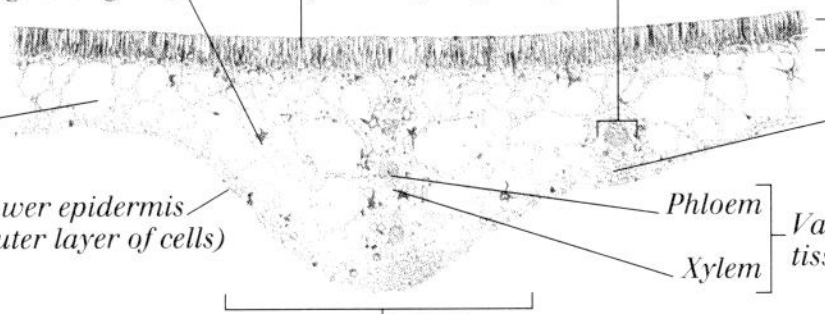
Star-shaped sclereid (short strengthening cell)
Upper epidermis (outer layer of cells)
Vein
Palisade mesophyll (tightly packed photosynthetic tissue)
Lacuna (air space)
Parenchyma (packing tissue)
Lower epidermis (outer layer of cells)
Phloem
Xylem
Vascular tissue
Midrib

MICROGRAPH OF CROSS-SECTION THROUGH LEAF OF WATER LILY

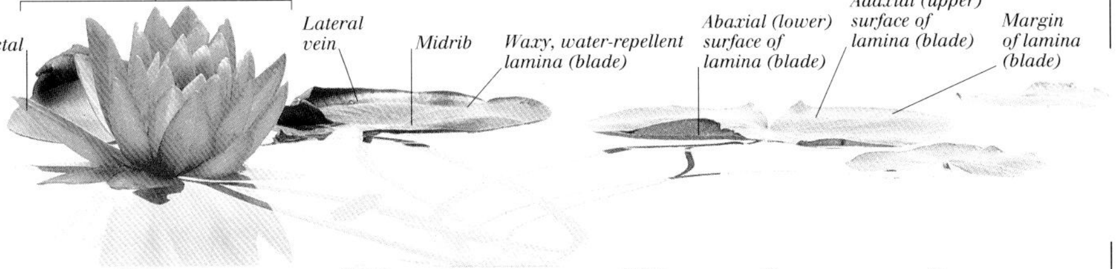
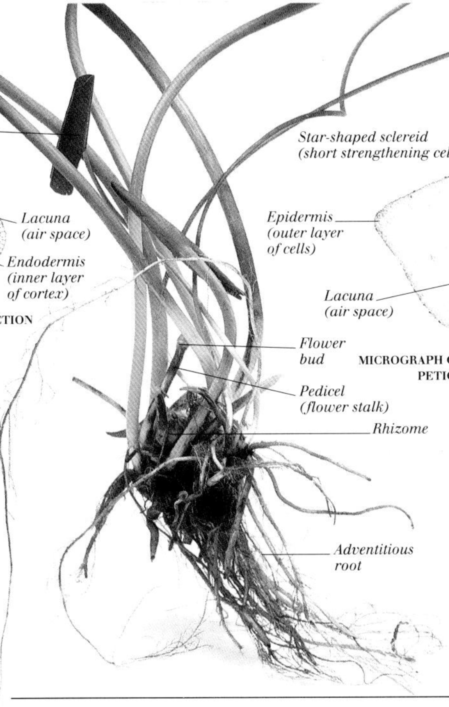
Flower
etal
Lateral vein
Midrib
Waxy, water-repellent lamina (blade)
Abaxial (lower) surface of lamina (blade)
Adaxial (upper) surface of lamina (blade)
Margin of lamina (blade)
Petiole (leaf stalk)
Pedicel (flower stalk)
Developing leaf
Flower bud
Pedicel (flower stalk)
Rhizome
Adventitious root

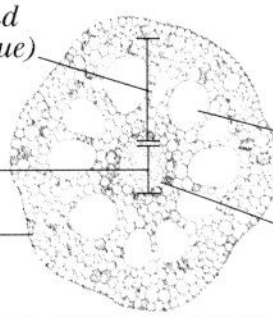
ortex layer between pidermis and ascular tissue)
Vascular bundle
Epidermis outer layer f cells)
Lacuna (air space)
Endodermis (inner layer of cortex)

MICROGRAPH OF CROSS-SECTION THROUGH STEM OF *ELODEA SP.*

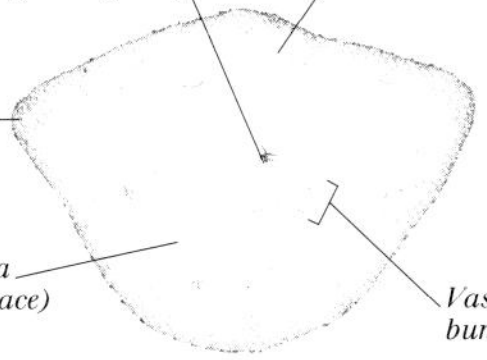
Star-shaped sclereid (short strengthening cell)
Cortex (layer between epidermis and vascular tissue)
Epidermis (outer layer of cells)
Lacuna (air space)
Vascular bundle

MICROGRAPH OF CROSS-SECTION THROUGH PETIOLE OF WATER LILY

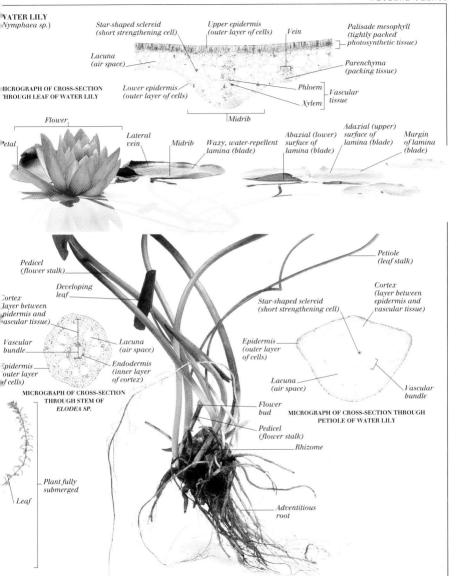

Plant fully submerged
Leaf

Carnivorous plants

CARNIVOROUS (INSECTIVOROUS) PLANTS FEED ON INSECTS and other small animals, in addition to producing food in their leaves by photosynthesis. The nutrients absorbed from trapped insects enable carnivorous plants to thrive in acid, boggy soils that lack essential minerals, especially nitrates, where most other plants could not survive. All carnivorous plants have some leaves modified as traps; many use bright colours and scented nectar to attract prey; and most use enzymes to digest the prey. There are three types of traps. Pitcher plants, such as the monkey cup and cobra lily, have leaves modified as pitcher-shaped pitfall traps, half-filled with water; once lured inside the mouth of the trap, insects lose their footing on the slippery surface, fall into the liquid, and either decompose or are digested. Venus fly traps use a spring-trap mechanism; when an insect touches trigger hairs on the inner surfaces of the leaves, the two lobes of the trap snap shut. Butterworts and sundews entangle prey by sticky droplets on the leaf surface, while the edges of the leaves slowly curl over to envelop and digest the prey.

PITCHER PLANT
Cobra lily (*Darlingtonia californica*)

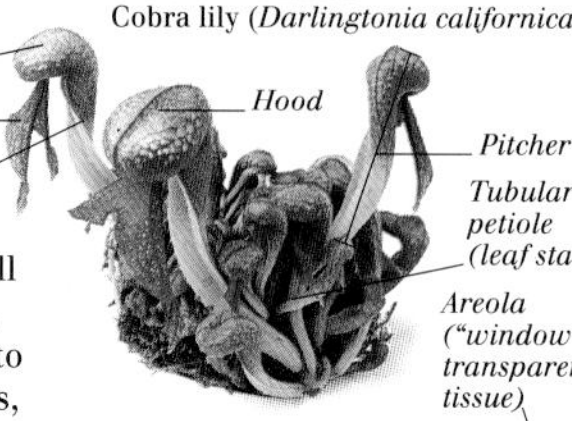
Areola ("window" of transparent tissue)
Fishtail nectary
Wing
Hood
Pitcher
Tubular petiole (leaf stalk)

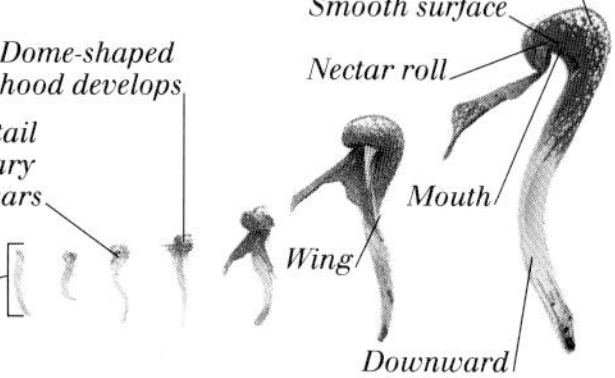
Areola ("window" of transparent tissue)
Smooth surface
Nectar roll
Dome-shaped hood develops
Fishtail nectary appears
Immature pitcher
Wing
Mouth
Downward pointing hair

DEVELOPMENT OF MODIFIED LEAF IN COBRA LILY

VENUS FLY TRAP
(*Dionaea muscipula*)

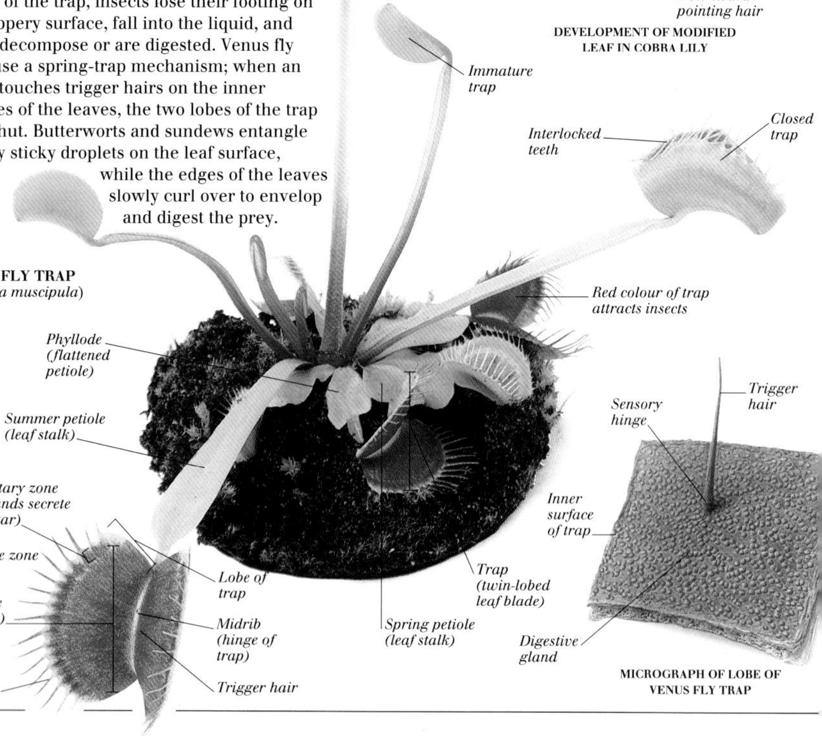
Immature trap
Interlocked teeth
Closed trap
Red colour of trap attracts insects
Phyllode (flattened petiole)
Summer petiole (leaf stalk)
Trap (twin-lobed leaf blade)
Spring petiole (leaf stalk)
Nectary zone (glands secrete nectar)
Digestive zone (glands secrete digestive enzymes)
Lobe of trap
Midrib (hinge of trap)
Tooth
Trigger hair
Trigger hair
Sensory hinge
Inner surface of trap
Digestive gland

MICROGRAPH OF LOBE OF VENUS FLY TRAP

PITCHER PLANT
Monkey cup
(*Nepenthes mirabalis*)

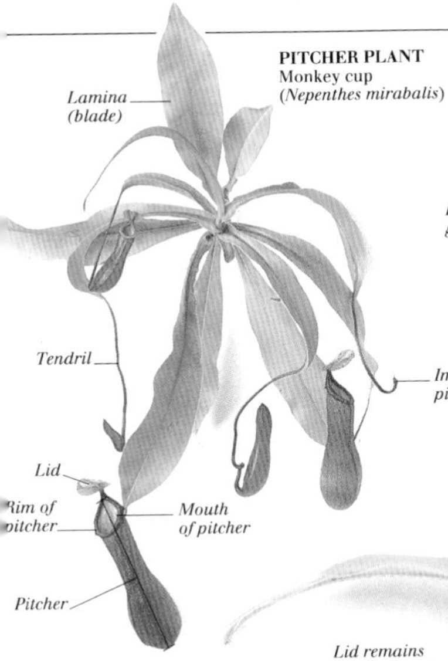
Lamina (blade)
Tendril
Immature pitcher
Lid
Rim of pitcher
Mouth of pitcher
Pitcher

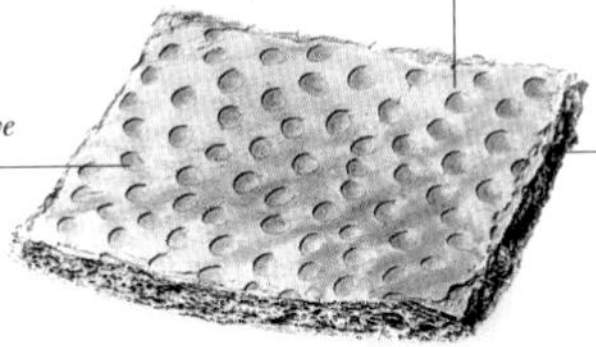
Inner surface of pitcher
Digestive gland
Outer surface of pitcher

MICROGRAPH OF WALL OF PITCHER

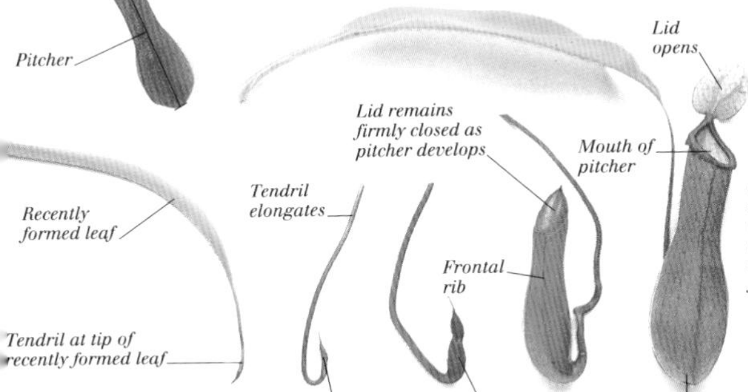
Recently formed leaf
Tendril at tip of recently formed leaf
Tendril elongates
Lid remains firmly closed as pitcher develops
Frontal rib
Lid opens
Mouth of pitcher
Swelling forms at tip of tendril
Immature pitcher fills with air
Mature pitcher

DEVELOPMENT OF MODIFIED LEAF IN PITCHER PLANT

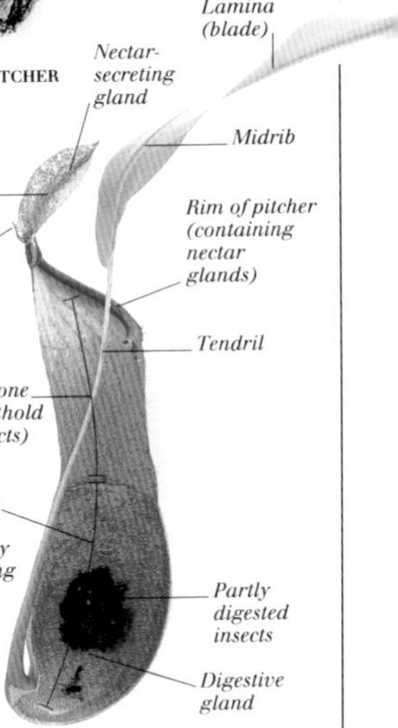
Lamina (blade)
Nectar-secreting gland
Midrib
Lid (attracts insects and stops rainwater flooding pitcher)
Spur
Rim of pitcher (containing nectar glands)
Tendril
Waxy zone (no foothold for insects)
Digestive zone (normally containing digestive fluid)
Partly digested insects
Digestive gland

SECTION THROUGH PITCHER

BUTTERWORT
(*Pinguicula caudata*)

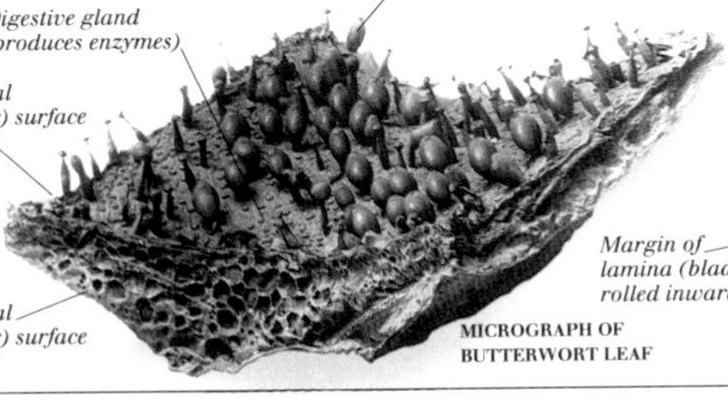
Stalked secretory gland (produces sticky, mucus-like substance)
Digestive gland (produces enzymes)
Adaxial (upper) surface of leaf
Abaxial (lower) surface of leaf

MICROGRAPH OF BUTTERWORT LEAF

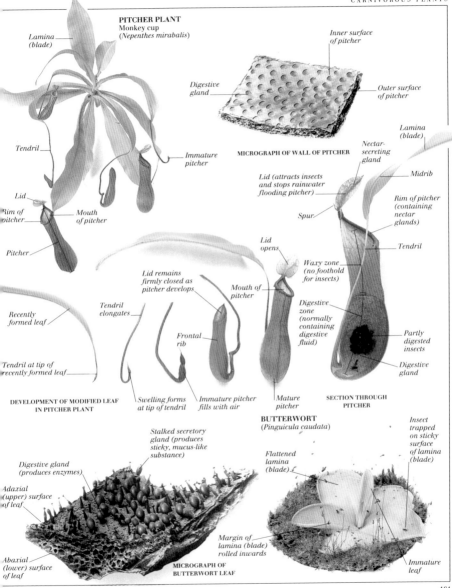

Flattened lamina (blade)
Insect trapped on sticky surface of lamina (blade)
Margin of lamina (blade) rolled inwards
Immature leaf

Epiphytic and parasitic plants

EPIPHYTIC AND PARASITIC PLANTS GROW ON OTHER LIVING PLANTS. Typically, epiphytic plants are not rooted in the soil; instead, they live above ground level on the stems and branches of other plants. Epiphytes obtain water from trapped rainwater and from moisture in the air, and minerals from organic matter that has accumulated on the surface of the plant on which they are growing. Like other green plants, epiphytes produce their food by photosynthesis. Epiphytes include tropical orchids and bromeliads (air plants), and some mosses that live in temperate regions. Parasitic plants obtain all their nutrient requirements from the host plants on which they grow. The parasites produce haustoria, root-like organs that penetrate the stem or roots of the host and grow inwards to merge with the host's vascular tissue, from which the parasite extracts water, minerals, and manufactured nutrients. As they have no need to produce their own food, parasitic plants lack chlorophyll, the green photosynthetic pigment, and they have no foliage leaves. Partial parasitic plants (e.g., mistletoe) obtain water and minerals from the host plant but have green leaves and stems and are therefore able to produce their own food by photosynthesis.

EPIPHYTIC BROMELIAD
Aechmea miniata

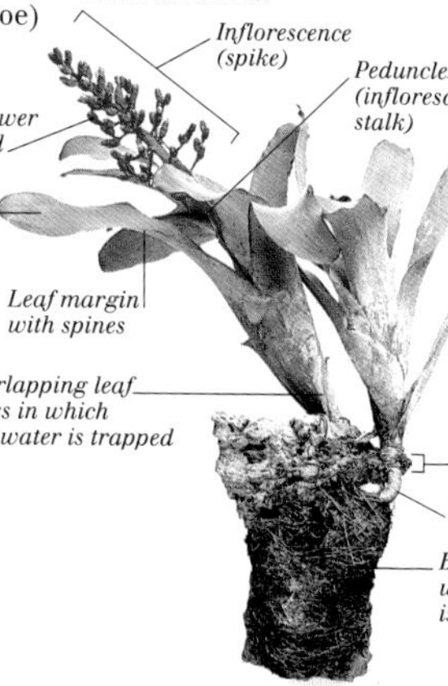
Inflorescence (spike)
Peduncle (inflorescence stalk)
Flower bud
Strap-shaped arching leaf (part of rosette of leaves)
Leaf margin with spines
Overlapping leaf bases in which rainwater is trapped
Mass of adventitious roo
Stem
Bark of tree to which epiphyte is attached

EPIPHYTIC ORCHID
Brassavola nodosa

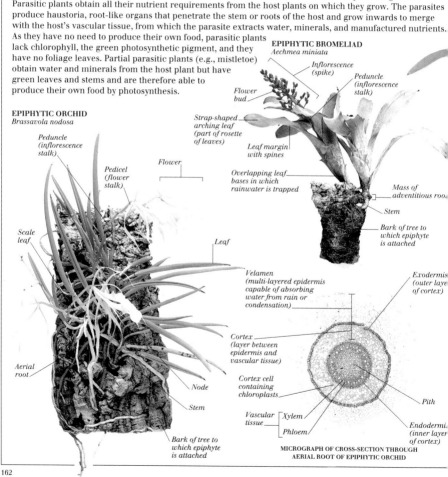

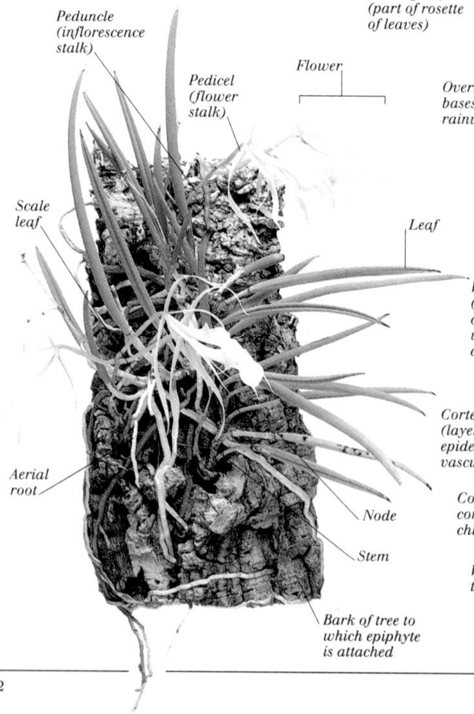
Peduncle (inflorescence stalk)
Flower
Pedicel (flower stalk)
Scale leaf
Leaf
Aerial root
Node
Stem
Bark of tree to which epiphyte is attached

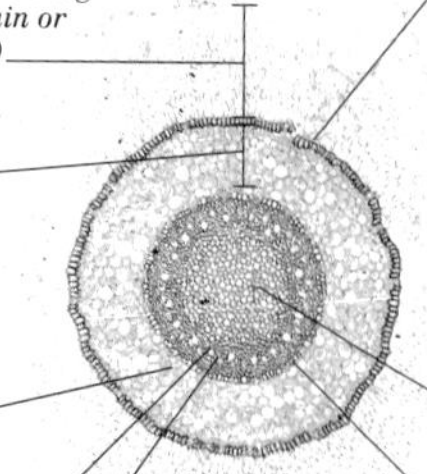
Velamen (multi-layered epidermis capable of absorbing water from rain or condensation)
Exodermis (outer layer of cortex)
Cortex (layer between epidermis and vascular tissue)
Cortex cell containing chloroplasts
Pith
Vascular tissue
Xylem
Phloem
Endodermis (inner layer of cortex)

MICROGRAPH OF CROSS-SECTION THROUGH AERIAL ROOT OF EPIPHYTIC ORCHID

LONGITUDINAL SECTION THROUGH EPIPHYTIC BROMELIAD

Scarlet star
(*Guzmania lingulata*)

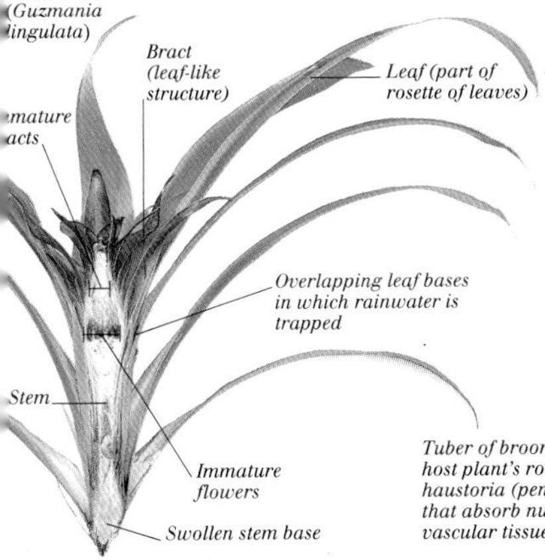
Bract (leaf-like structure)
Leaf (part of rosette of leaves)
mature
acts
Overlapping leaf bases in which rainwater is trapped
Stem
Immature flowers
Swollen stem base

ROOT PARASITE

Broomrape
(*Orobanche sp.*)

Stem of host plant
Flower bud of broomrape
Flower of broomrape
Leaf of host plant
Stem of broomrape
Tuber of broomrape attached to host plant's roots through haustoria (penetrating organs that absorb nutrients from host's vascular tissue)
Shoot of broomrape
Main root of host plant
Lateral root of host plant

STEM PARASITE

Dodder
(*Cuscuta europaea*)

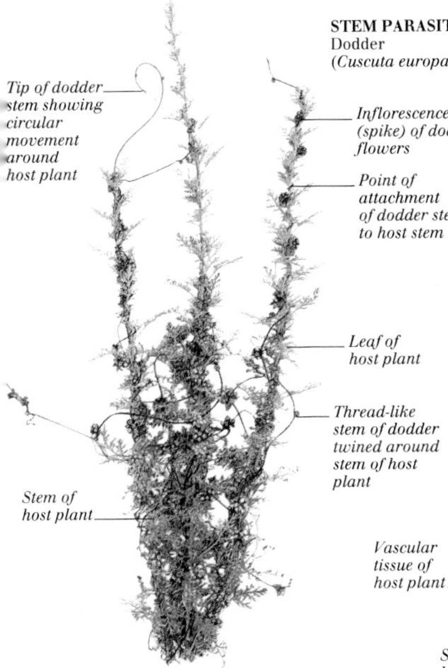
Tip of dodder stem showing circular movement around host plant
Inflorescence (spike) of dodder flowers
Point of attachment of dodder stem to host stem
Leaf of host plant
Thread-like stem of dodder twined around stem of host plant
Stem of host plant

EXTERNAL VIEW OF PLANT PARASITIZED BY DODDER

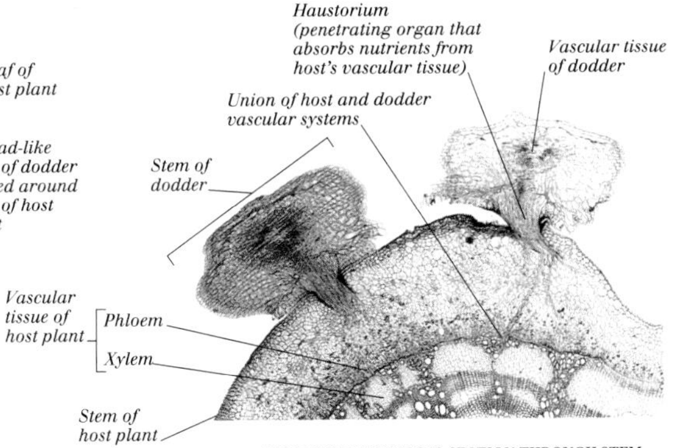
Haustorium (penetrating organ that absorbs nutrients from host's vascular tissue)
Vascular tissue of dodder
Union of host and dodder vascular systems
Stem of dodder
Vascular tissue of host plant
Phloem
Xylem
Stem of host plant

MICROGRAPH OF CROSS-SECTION THROUGH STEM OF PLANT PARASITIZED BY DODDER

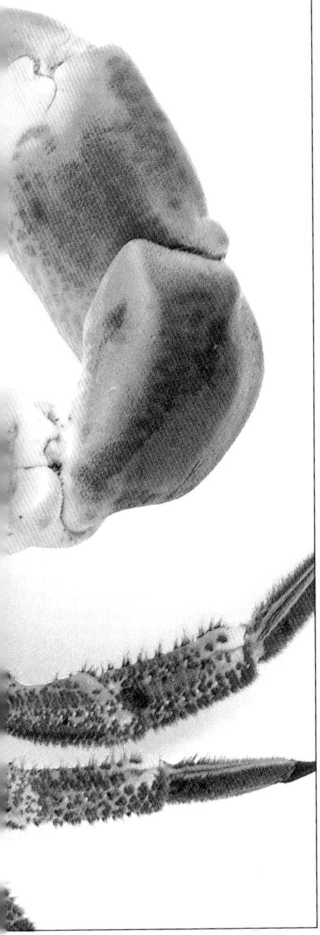

ANIMALS

Sponges, jellyfish, and sea anemones

SPONGES ARE MAINLY MARINE animals that make up the phylum Porifera. They are among the simplest of all animals, having no tissues or organs. Their bodies consist of two layers of cells separated by a jelly-like layer (mesohyal) that is strengthened by mineral spicules or protein fibres. The body is perforated by a system of pores and water channels called the aquiferous system. Special cells (choanocytes) with whip-like structures (flagella) draw water through the aquiferous system, thereby bringing tiny food particles to the sponge's cells. Jellyfish (class Scyphozoa), sea anemones (class Anthozoa), and corals (also class Anthozoa) belong to the phylum Cnidaria, also known as Coelenterata. More complex than sponges, coelenterates have simple tissues, such as nervous tissue; a radially symmetrical body; and a mouth surrounded by tentacles with unique stinging cells (cnidocytes).

INTERNAL ANATOMY OF A SPONGE

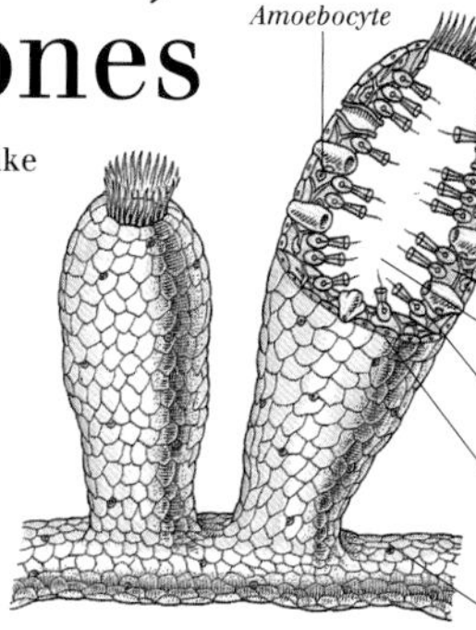

Amoebocyte
Osculum (excurrent pore)
Choanocyte (collar cell)
Ostium (incurrent pore)
Porocyte (pore cel
Mesohyal
Spongocoel (atrium; paragaster
Spicule
Pinacocyte (epidermal cell)
Ostium (incurrent pore)

SKELETON OF A SPONGE

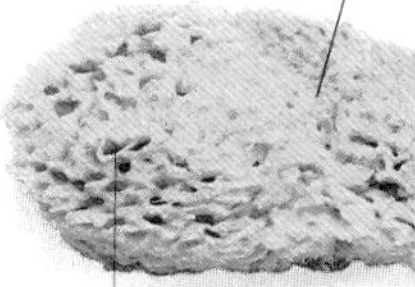

Protein matrix
Pore

EXTERNAL FEATURES OF A SEA ANEMONE

Tentacle

EXAMPLES OF SEA ANEMONES

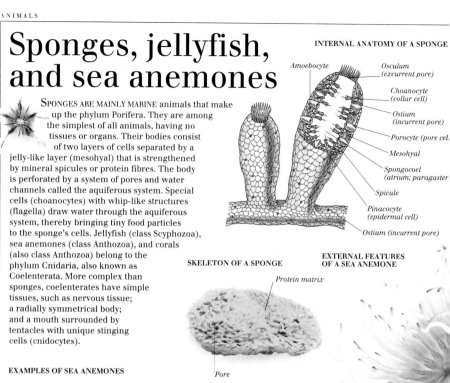

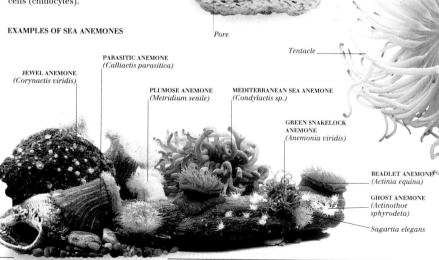

PARASITIC ANEMONE *(Calliactis parasitica)*
JEWEL ANEMONE *(Corynactis viridis)*
PLUMOSE ANEMONE *(Metridium senile)*
MEDITERRANEAN SEA ANEMONE *(Condylactis sp.)*
GREEN SNAKELOCK ANEMONE *(Anemonia viridis)*
BEADLET ANEMONE *(Actinia equina)*
GHOST ANEMONE *(Actinothoe sphyrodeta)*
Sagartia elegans

EXTERNAL APPEARANCE OF A JELLYFISH

INTERNAL ANATOMY OF A JELLYFISH

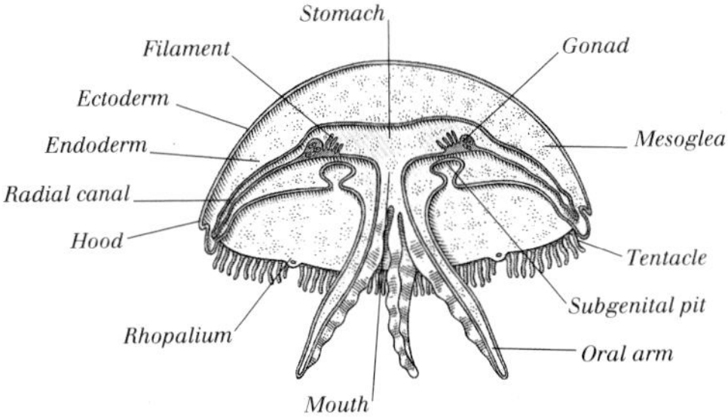
Stomach
Filament
Gonad
Ectoderm
Endoderm
Mesoglea
Radial canal
Hood
Tentacle
Subgenital pit
Rhopalium
Oral arm
Mouth

EXAMPLES OF CORALS

HONEYCOMB CORAL
(Goniastrea aspera)

MUSHROOM CORAL
(Fungia fungites)

STAR CORAL
(Balanophyllia regia)

STRUCTURE OF A CNIDOCYTE

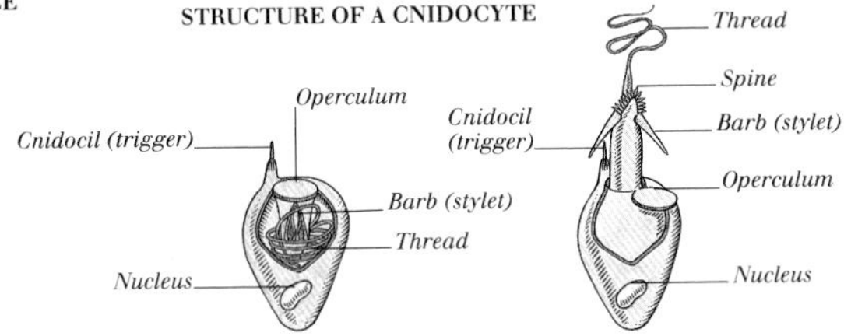
Operculum
Cnidocil (trigger)
Barb (stylet)
Thread
Nucleus
Thread
Spine
Cnidocil (trigger)
Barb (stylet)
Operculum
Nucleus

BEFORE DISCHARGE

AFTER DISCHARGE

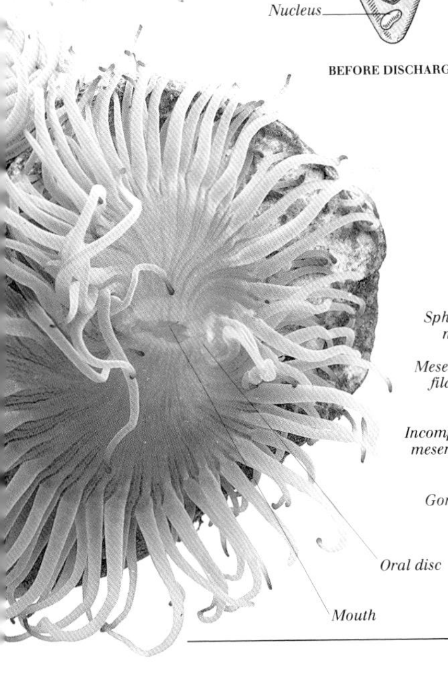
Oral disc
Mouth

INTERNAL ANATOMY OF A SEA ANEMONE

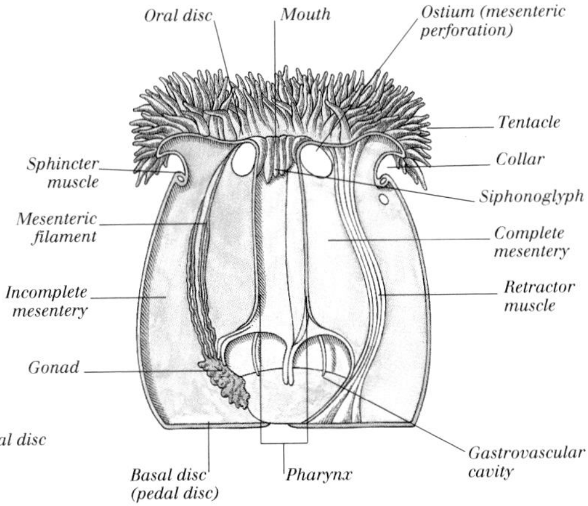
Oral disc
Mouth
Ostium (mesenteric perforation)
Tentacle
Collar
Sphincter muscle
Siphonoglyph
Mesenteric filament
Complete mesentery
Incomplete mesentery
Retractor muscle
Gonad
Gastrovascular cavity
Basal disc (pedal disc)
Pharynx

Insects

PUPA (CHRYSALIS)

THE WORD INSECT REFERS to small invertebrate creatures, especially those with bodies divided into sections. Insects, including beetles, ants, bees, butterflies, and moths, belong to various orders in the class Insecta, which is a division of the phylum Arthropoda. Features common to all insects are an exoskeleton (external skeleton); three pairs of jointed legs; three body sections (head, thorax, and abdomen); and one pair of sensory antennae. Beetles (order Coleoptera) are the biggest group of insects, with about 300,000 species (about 30 per cent of all known insects). They have a pair of hard elytra (wing cases), which are modified front wings. The principal function of the elytra is to protect the hind wings, which are used for flying. Ants, together with bees and wasps, form the order Hymenoptera, which contains about 200,000 species. This group is characterized by a marked narrowing between the thorax and abdomen. Butterflies and moths form the order Lepidoptera, which has about 150,000 species. They have wings covered with tiny scales, hence the name of their order (Lepidoptera means "scale wings"). The separation of lepidopterans into butterflies and moths is largely artificial as there are no features that categorically distinguish one group from the other. In general, however, most butterflies fly by day, whereas most moths are night-flyers. Some insects, including butterflies and moths, undergo complete metamorphosis (transformation) during their life-cycle. A butterfly metamorphoses from an egg to a larva (caterpillar), then to a pupa (chrysalis), and finally to an imago (adult).

EXTERNAL FEATURES OF A BEETLE

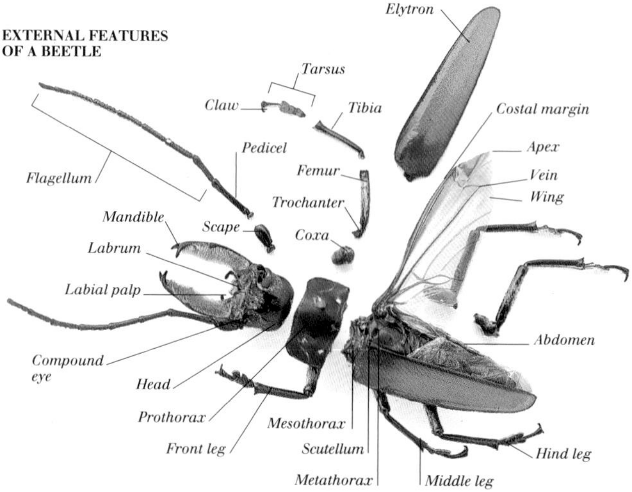
Elytron
Tarsus
Claw
Tibia
Costal margin
Apex
Pedicel
Femur
Vein
Wing
Flagellum
Trochanter
Mandible
Scape
Coxa
Labrum
Labial palp
Abdomen
Compound eye
Head
Prothorax
Mesothorax
Front leg
Scutellum
Hind leg
Metathorax
Middle leg

EXAMPLES OF INSECTS

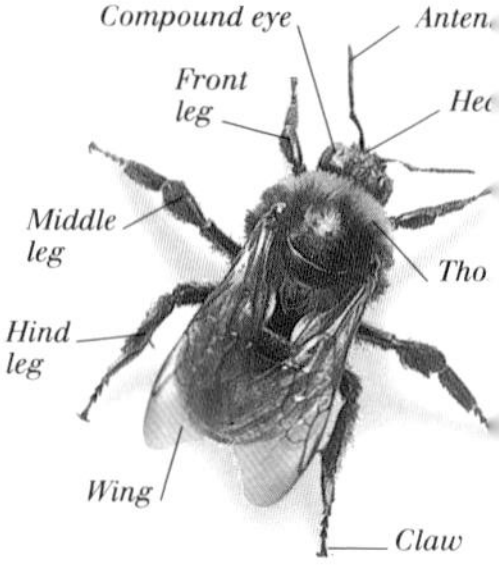
Compound eye
Anten
Front leg
Middle leg
Tho
Hind leg
Wing
Claw

BUMBLEBEE

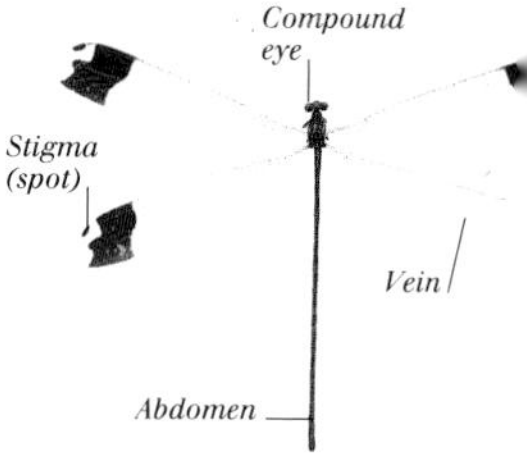
Compound eye
Stigma (spot)
Vein
Abdomen

DAMSELFLY

CRICKET

ANT

FLY

EARWIG

EXTERNAL FEATURES OF A CATERPILLAR

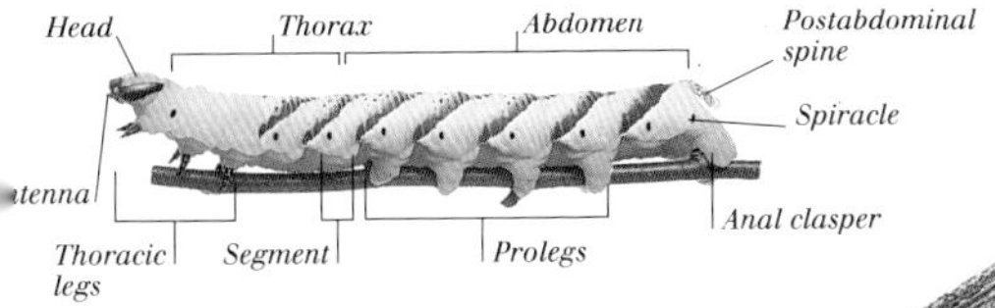
Head
Thorax
Abdomen
Postabdominal spine
Spiracle
tenna
Anal clasper
Thoracic legs
Segment
Prolegs

EXTERNAL FEATURES OF A BUTTERFLY

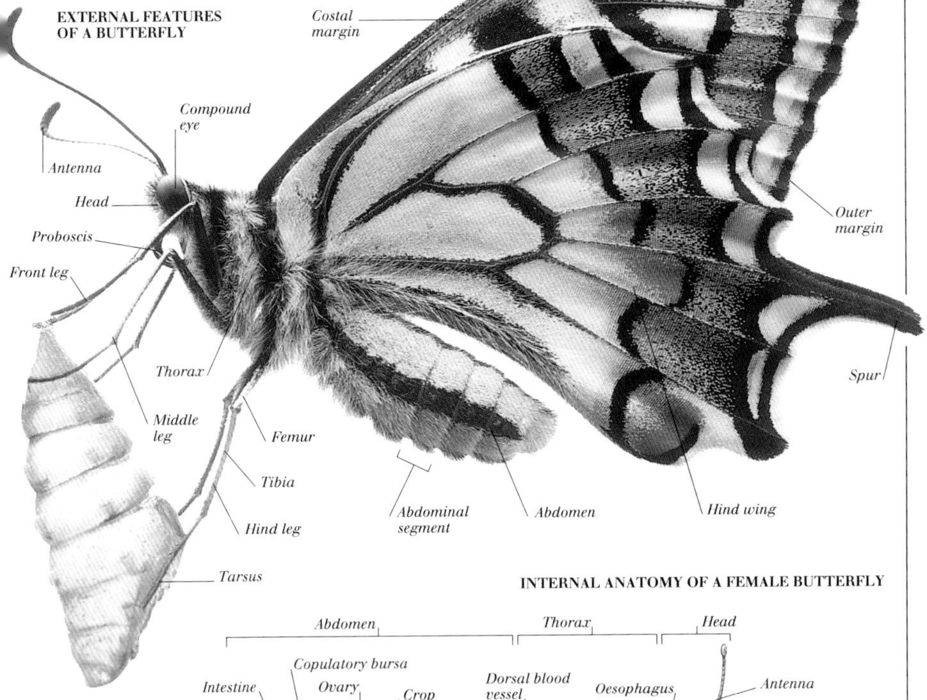
Vein
Apex
Forewing
Costal margin
Compound eye
Antenna
Head
Proboscis
Front leg
Outer margin
Thorax
Spur
Middle leg
Femur
Tibia
Hind leg
Abdominal segment
Abdomen
Hind wing
Tarsus

INTERNAL ANATOMY OF A FEMALE BUTTERFLY

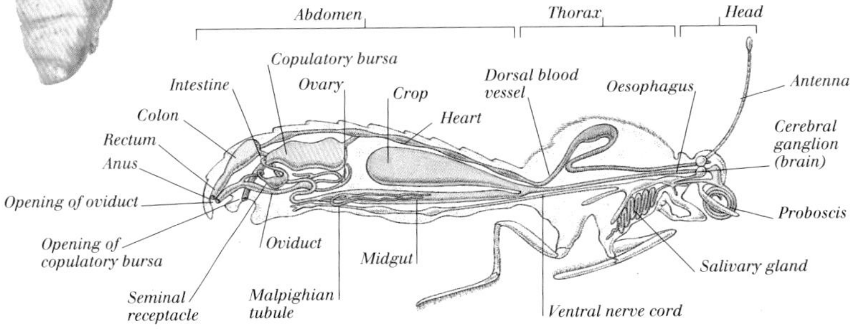
Abdomen
Thorax
Head
Copulatory bursa
Intestine
Ovary
Crop
Dorsal blood vessel
Oesophagus
Antenna
Colon
Heart
Rectum
Cerebral ganglion (brain)
Anus
Opening of oviduct
Proboscis
Opening of copulatory bursa
Oviduct
Midgut
Salivary gland
Seminal receptacle
Malpighian tubule
Ventral nerve cord

Arachnids

THE CLASS ARACHNIDA INCLUDES SPIDERS (order Araneae) and scorpions (order Scorpiones). The class is part of the phylum Arthropoda, which also includes insects and crustaceans. Spiders and scorpions are characterized by having four pairs of walking legs; a pair of pincer-like mouthparts called chelicerae; another pair of frontal appendages called pedipalps, which are sensory in spiders but used for grasping in scorpions; and a body divided into two sections (a combined head and thorax called a cephalothorax or prosoma, and an abdomen or opisthosoma). Unlike other arthropods, spiders and scorpions lack antennae. Spiders and scorpions are carnivorous. Spiders poison prey by biting with the fanged chelicerae, scorpions by stinging with the end of the metasoma (tail).

MEXICAN TRUE RED-LEGGED TARANTULA
(Euathlus emilia)

INTERNAL ANATOMY OF A FEMALE SPIDER

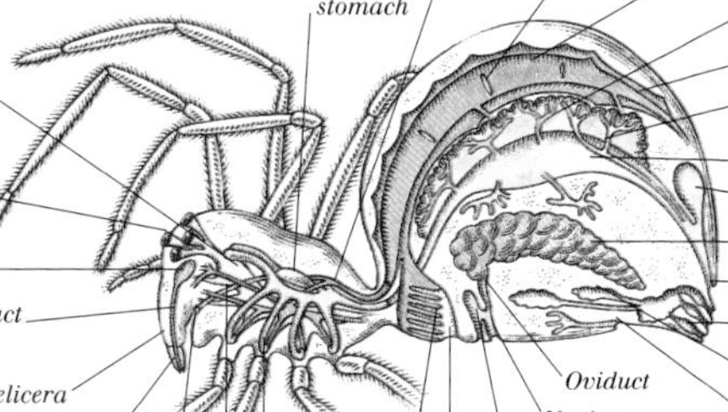
Anterior aorta
Ostium
Heart
Sucking stomach
Digestive gland
Posterior aorta
Malpighian tubule
Brain
Intestine
Simple eye
Cloaca
Ovary
Poison gland
Anus
Poison duct
Spinneret
Chelicera
Oviduct
Silk gland
Vagina
Trachea
Fang
Book lung
Spermatheca (seminal receptacle)
Mouth
Gut caecum
Oesophagus
Spiracle

EXTERNAL FEATURES OF A SCORPION

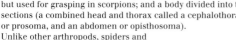

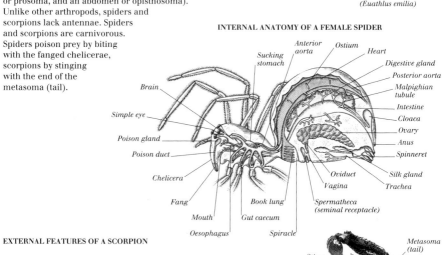

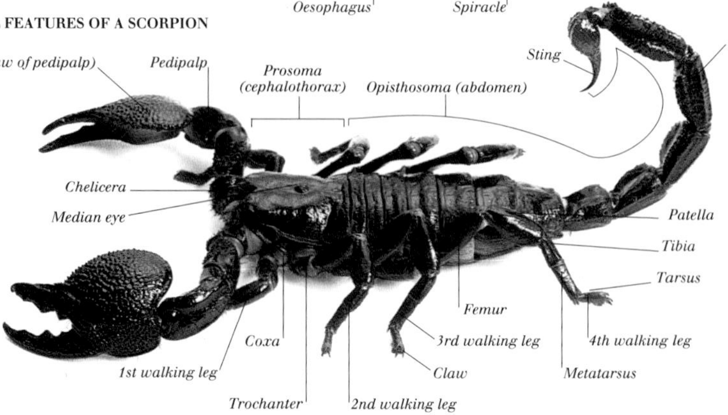
Metasoma (tail)
Sting
Chela (claw of pedipalp)
Pedipalp
Prosoma (cephalothorax)
Opisthosoma (abdomen)
Chelicera
Median eye
Patella
Tibia
Tarsus
Femur
Coxa
3rd walking leg
4th walking leg
1st walking leg
Claw
Metatarsus
Trochanter
2nd walking leg

EXAMPLES OF SPIDERS

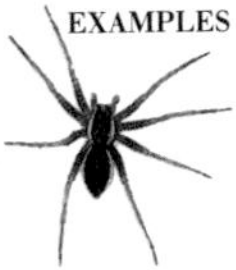

RAFT SPIDER
(Dolomedes fimbriatus)

ORB SPIDER
(Nuctenea umbratica)

HUNTSMAN SPIDER
(Heteropoda venatoria)

BLACK WIDOW SPIDER
(Latrodectus mactans)

HOUSE SPIDER
(Tegenaria gigantea)

EXTERNAL FEATURES OF A SPIDER

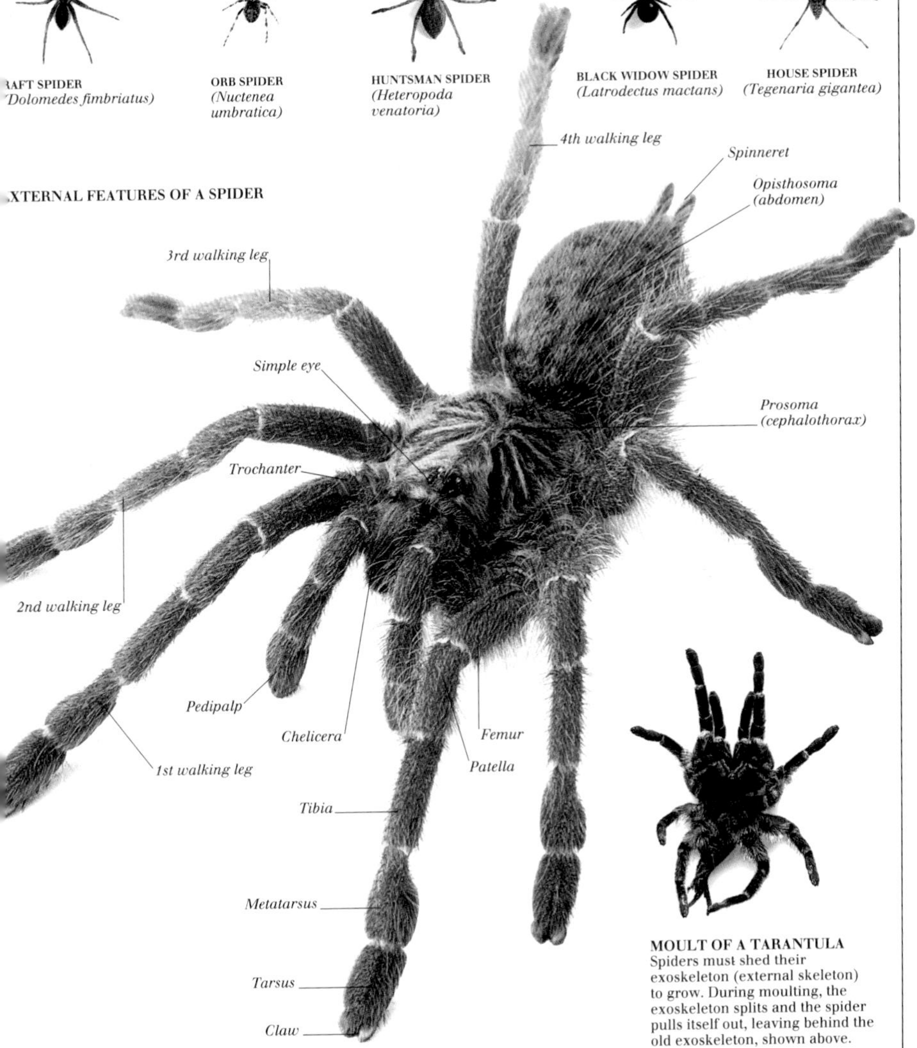

4th walking leg
Spinneret
Opisthosoma (abdomen)
3rd walking leg
Simple eye
Prosoma (cephalothorax)
Trochanter
2nd walking leg
Pedipalp
Chelicera
Femur
Patella
1st walking leg
Tibia
Metatarsus
Tarsus
Claw

MOULT OF A TARANTULA
Spiders must shed their exoskeleton (external skeleton) to grow. During moulting, the exoskeleton splits and the spider pulls itself out, leaving behind the old exoskeleton, shown above.

Crustaceans

THE SUBPHYLUM CRUSTACEA is one of the largest groups in the phylum Arthropoda. The subphylum is divided into several classes, the most important of which are Malacostraca and Cirripedia. The class Malacostraca includes crayfish, crabs, lobsters, and shrimps. Typical features of malacostracans include a body divided into two sections (a combined head and thorax called a cephalothorax, and an abdomen); an exoskeleton (external skeleton) with a large plate (carapace) covering the cephalothorax; stalked, compound eyes; and two pairs of antennae. The class Cirripedia includes barnacles, which, unlike other crustaceans, spend their adult lives attached to a surface, such as a rock. Other characteristics of cirripedes include an exoskeleton of overlapping calcareous plates; a body consisting almost entirely of thorax (the abdomen and head are minute); and six pairs of thoracic appendages (cirri) used for filter feeding.

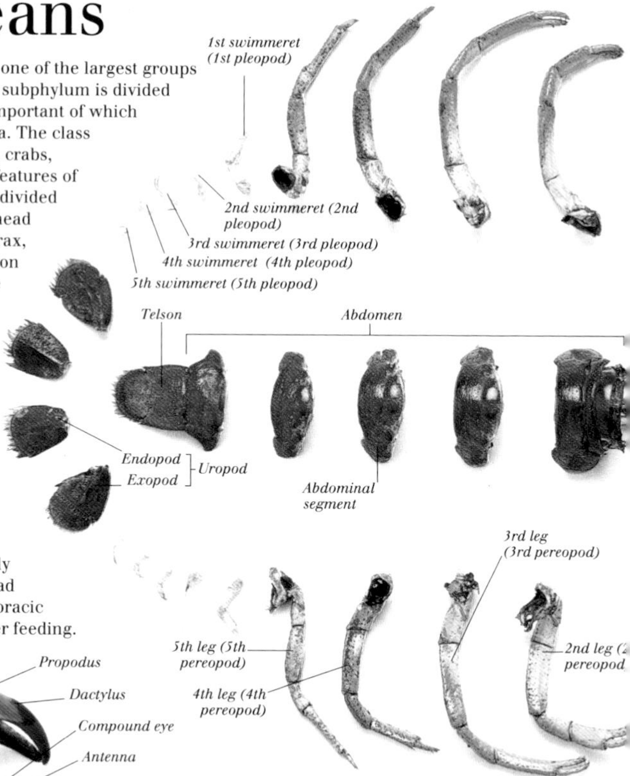
1st swimmeret (1st pleopod)
2nd swimmeret (2nd pleopod)
3rd swimmeret (3rd pleopod)
4th swimmeret (4th pleopod)
5th swimmeret (5th pleopod)
Telson
Abdomen
Endopod
Exopod
Uropod
Abdominal segment
3rd leg (3rd pereopod)
5th leg (5th pereopod)
4th leg (4th pereopod)
2nd leg (2nd pereopod)

EXTERNAL FEATURES OF A CRAB

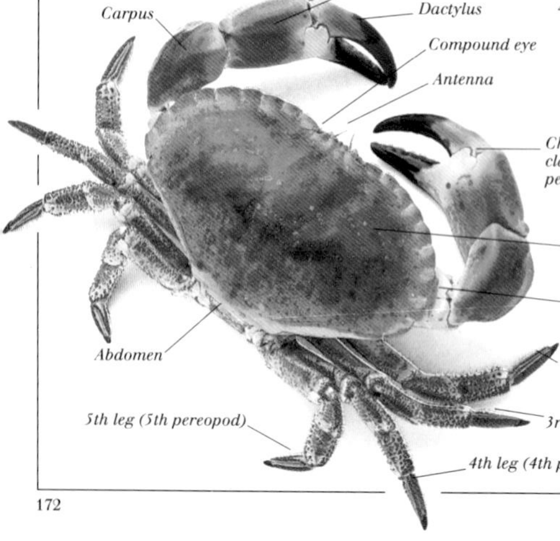
Propodus
Carpus
Dactylus
Compound eye
Antenna
Cheliped (chela; claw; 1st leg; 1st pereopod)
Carapace (shell)
Merus
Abdomen
2nd leg (2nd pereopod)
5th leg (5th pereopod)
3rd leg (3rd pereopod)
4th leg (4th pereopod)

EXTERNAL FEATURES OF A SHRIMP

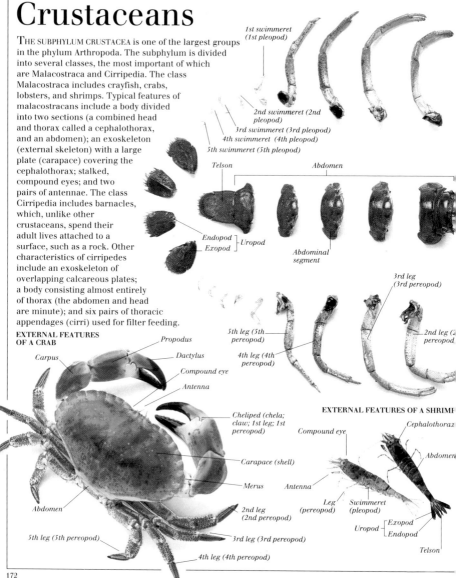

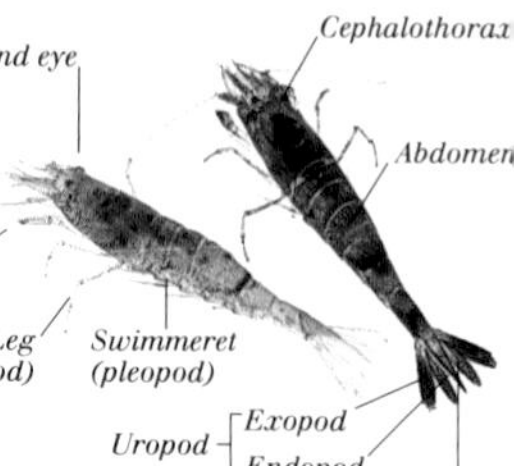
Compound eye
Cephalothorax
Abdomen
Antenna
Leg (pereopod)
Swimmeret (pleopod)
Uropod
Exopod
Endopod
Telson

EXTERNAL FEATURES OF A CRAYFISH

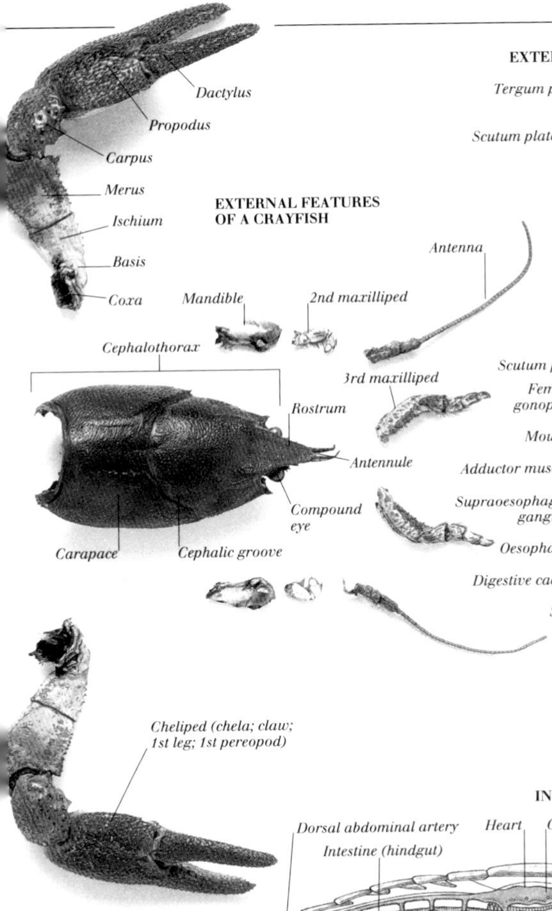
Dactylus
Propodus
Carpus
Merus
Ischium
Basis
Coxa
Mandible
2nd maxilliped
Antenna
Cephalothorax
3rd maxilliped
Rostrum
Antennule
Compound eye
Carapace
Cephalic groove
Cheliped (chela; claw; 1st leg; 1st pereopod)

EXTERNAL FEATURES OF A STALKED BARNACLE

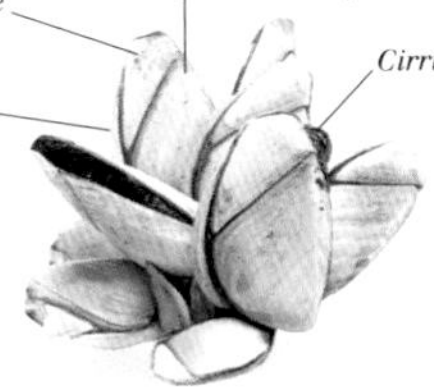
Tergum plate
Carina plate
Cirrus
Scutum plate

INTERNAL ANATOMY OF A STALKED BARNACLE

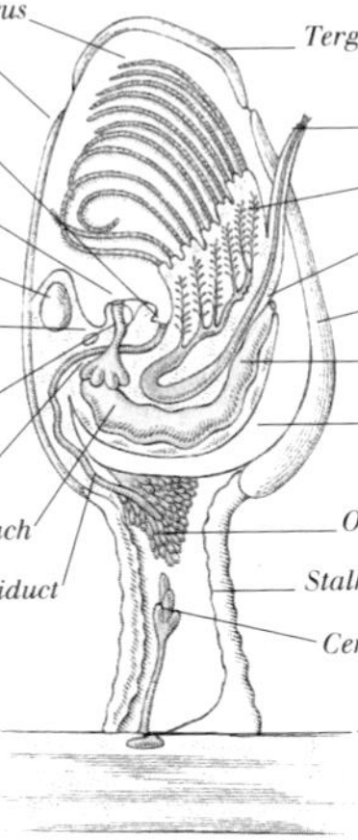
Cirrus
Tergum plate
Scutum plate
Female gonopore
Penis
Testis
Mouth
Anus
Adductor muscle
Carina plate
Supraoesophageal ganglion
Midgut
Oesophagus
Mantle cavity
Digestive caecum
Stomach
Ovary
Oviduct
Stalk (peduncle)
Cement gland
Antennule

INTERNAL ANATOMY OF A FEMALE CRAYFISH

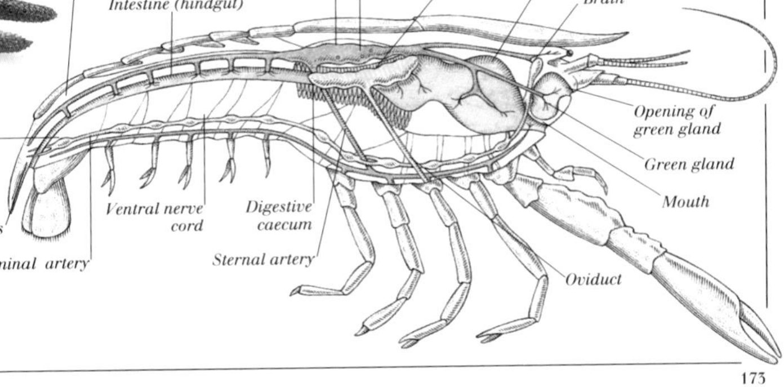
Dorsal abdominal artery
Heart
Ostium
Ovary
Proventriculus (stomach)
Intestine (hindgut)
Brain
Opening of green gland
Ganglion
Green gland
Mouth
Anus
Ventral nerve cord
Digestive caecum
Ventral abdominal artery
Sternal artery
Oviduct

Starfish and sea urchins

STARFISH, SEA URCHINS, AND THEIR relatives (including feather stars, brittle stars, basket stars, sea daisies, sea lilies, and sea cucumbers) make up the phylum Echinodermata. A unique feature of echinoderms is the water vascular system, which consists of a series of water-filled canals from which protrude thousands of tiny tube feet. The tube feet may be used for movement, feeding, or respiration. Other features include pentaradiate symmetry (that is, the body can be divided into five parts radiating from the centre); no head; a diffuse, decentralized nervous system that lacks a brain; and no excretory organs. Typically, echinoderms also have an endoskeleton (internal skeleton) consisting of hard calcite ossicles embedded in the body wall and often bearing protruding spines or tubercles. The ossicles may fit together to form a test (as in sea urchins) or remain separate (as in sea cucumbers).

EXTERNAL FEATURES A STARFISH (UPPER, O ABORAL, SURFACE)

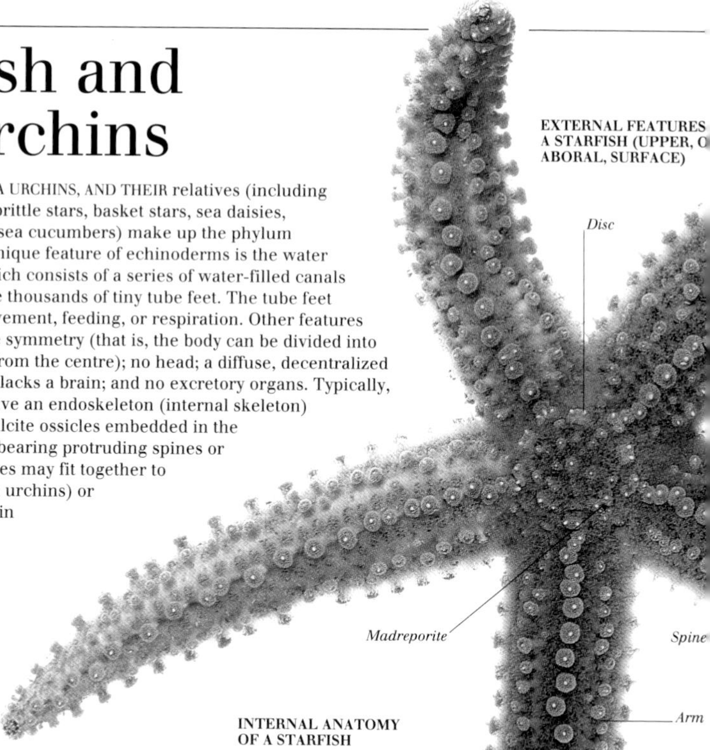

Disc
Madreporite
Spine
Arm

INTERNAL ANATOMY OF A STARFISH

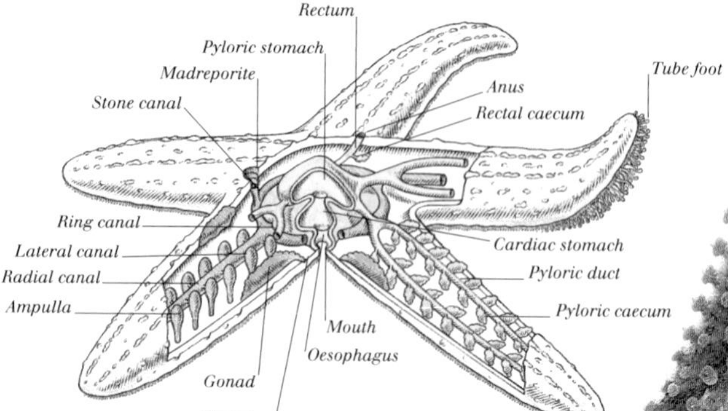
Rectum
Pyloric stomach
Madreporite
Stone canal
Anus
Rectal caecum
Tube foot
Ring canal
Lateral canal
Radial canal
Ampulla
Cardiac stomach
Pyloric duct
Pyloric caecum
Mouth
Oesophagus
Gonad
Gonopore

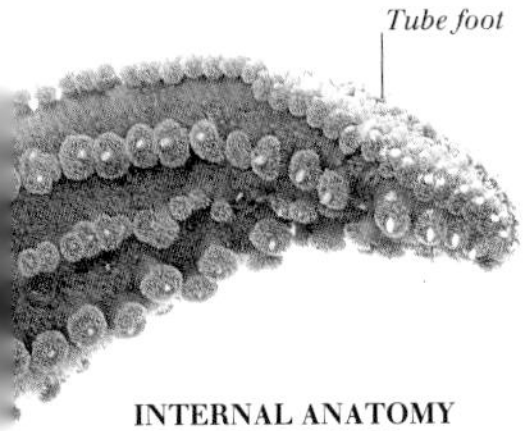
Tube foot

EXAMPLES OF SEA URCHINS

EDIBLE SEA URCHIN
(Echinus escelentus)

CALIFORNIAN PURPLE SEA URCHIN
(Strongylocentrotus purpuratus)

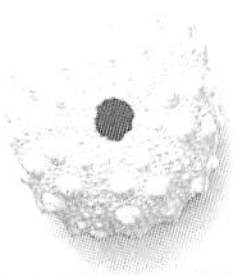

PENCIL SLATE SEA URCHIN
(Heterocentrotus mammillatus)

INTERNAL ANATOMY OF A SEA URCHIN

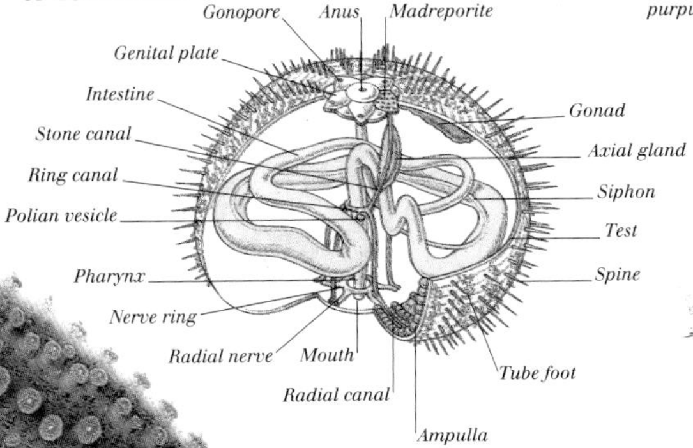
Gonopore
Anus
Madreporite
Genital plate
Intestine
Stone canal
Ring canal
Polian vesicle
Pharynx
Nerve ring
Radial nerve
Mouth
Radial canal
Ampulla
Tube foot
Spine
Test
Siphon
Axial gland
Gonad

EXTERNAL FEATURES OF A SEA URCHIN (UPPER, OR ABORAL, SURFACE)

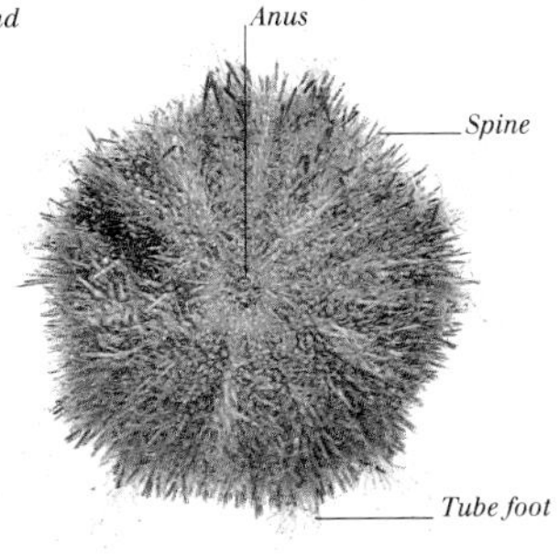
Anus
Spine
Tube foot

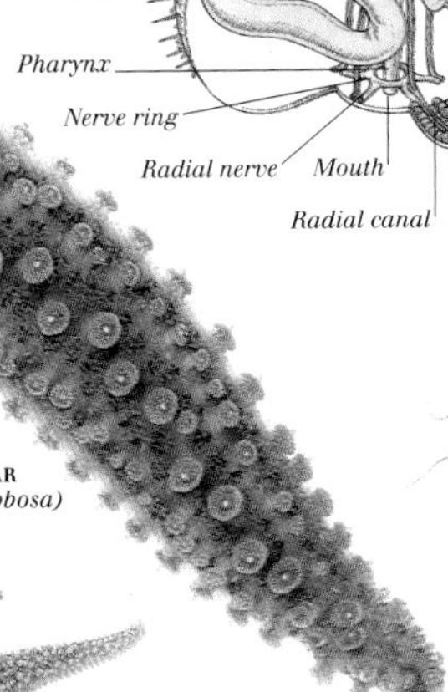

CUSHION STAR
(Asterina gibbosa)

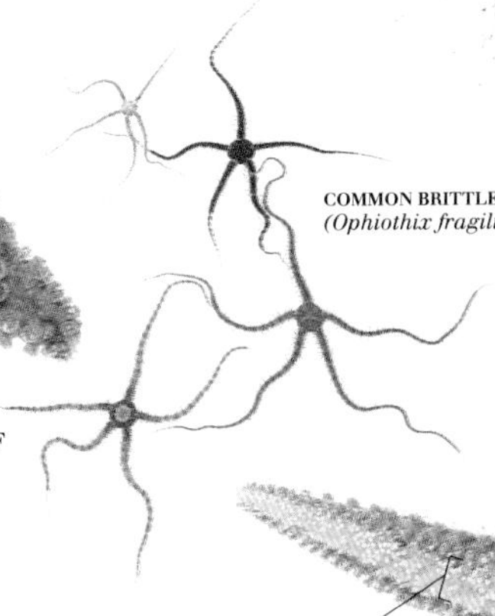

COMMON BRITTLE STAR
(Ophiothix fragilis)

EXAMPLES OF STARFISH

COMMON STARFISH
(Asterias rubens)

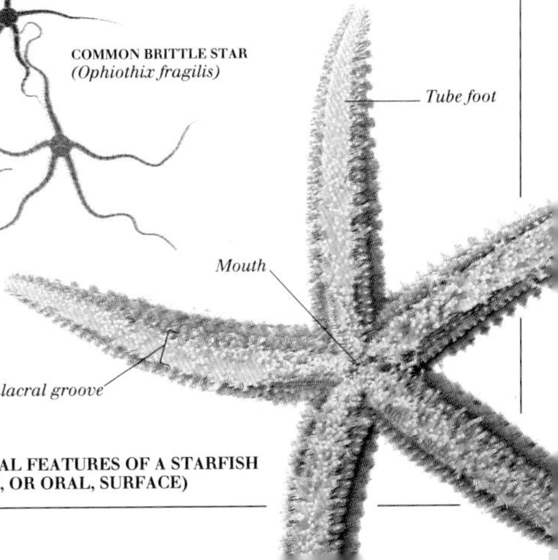
Tube foot
Mouth
Ambulacral groove

EXTERNAL FEATURES OF A STARFISH (LOWER, OR ORAL, SURFACE)

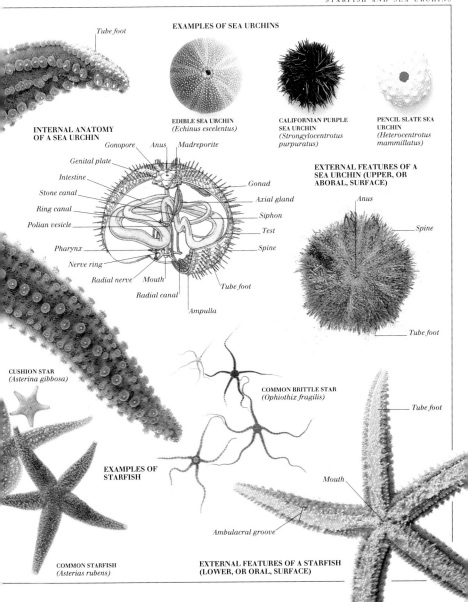

Molluscs

THE PHYLUM MOLLUSCA (MOLLUSCS) is a large group of animals that includes octopuses, snails, and scallops. Octopuses and their relatives—including squid and cuttlefish—form the class Cephalopoda. Cephalopods typically have a head with a radula (a file-like feeding organ) and beak; a well-developed nervous system; sucker-bearing tentacles; a muscular mantle (part of the body wall) that can expel water through the siphon, enabling movement by jet propulsion; and a small shell or no shell. Snails and their relatives—including slugs, limpets, and abalones—make up the class Gastropoda. Gastropods typically have a coiled external shell, although some, such as slugs, have a small internal shell or no shell; a flat foot; and a head with tentacles and a radula. Scallops and their relatives—including clams, mussels, and oysters—make up the class Bivalvia (also called Pelecypoda). Features of bivalves include a shell with two halves (valves); large gills that are used for breathing and filter feeding; and no radula.

EXTERNAL FEATURES OF A SCALLOP

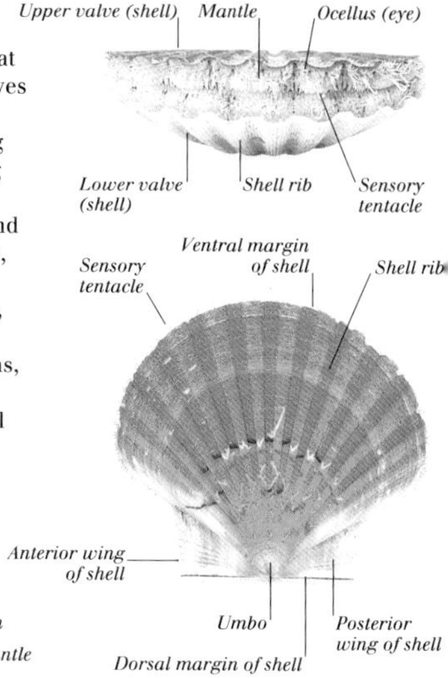
Upper valve (shell)
Mantle
Ocellus (eye)
Lower valve (shell)
Shell rib
Sensory tentacle
Sensory tentacle
Ventral margin of shell
Shell rib
Anterior wing of shell
Umbo
Posterior wing of shell
Dorsal margin of shell

INTERNAL ANATOMY OF AN OCTOPUS

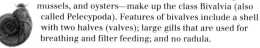

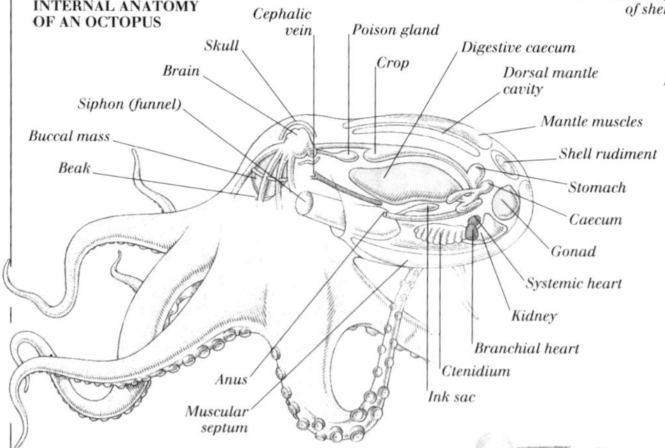
Cephalic vein
Poison gland
Skull
Digestive caecum
Crop
Brain
Dorsal mantle cavity
Siphon (funnel)
Mantle muscles
Buccal mass
Shell rudiment
Beak
Stomach
Caecum
Gonad
Systemic heart
Kidney
Branchial heart
Ctenidium
Anus
Ink sac
Muscular septum

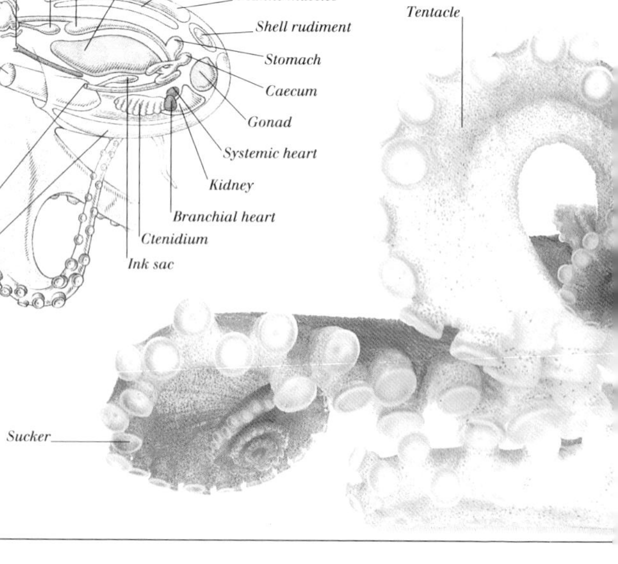
Tentacle
Sucker

XTERNAL FEATURES
F A SNAIL

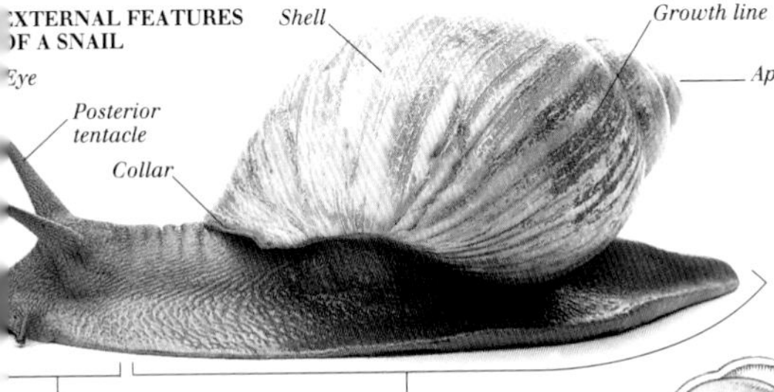
Shell
Growth line
Apex of shell
Eye
Posterior
tentacle
Collar
Head
Foot
erior
acle

INTERNAL ANATOMY
OF A SNAIL

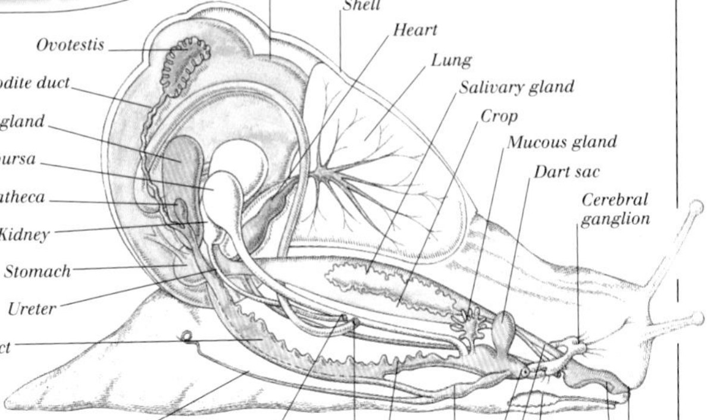
Digestive gland
Shell
Heart
Lung
Ovotestis
Hermaphrodite duct
Salivary gland
Crop
Albumen gland
Mucous gland
Copulatory bursa
Dart sac
Spermatheca
Cerebral
ganglion
Kidney
Stomach
Ureter
Spermoviduct
Flagellum
Excretory
pore
Anus
Penis
Radula
Vagina
Gonopore
Mouth
Oesophagus
Pedal gland

XTERNAL FEATURES
OF AN OCTOPUS

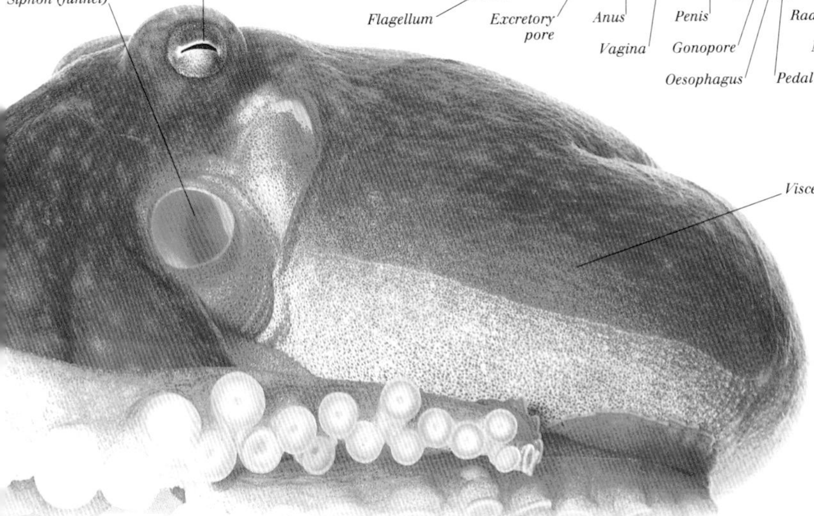
Eye with horizontal iris
Siphon (funnel)
Visceral hump

Sharks and jawless fish

SHARKS, DOGFISH (WHICH ARE actually small sharks), skates, and rays belong to a class of fishes called Chondrichthyes, which is a division of the superclass Gnathostomata (meaning "jawed mouths"). Also sometimes known as elasmobranchs, sharks and their relatives have a skeleton made of cartilage (hence their common name, cartilaginous fish), a characteristic that distinguishes them from bony fish (see pp. 180-181). Other important features of cartilaginous fish are extremely tough, tooth-like scales, and lack of a swim bladder. Jawless fish—lampreys and hagfish—are primitive, eel-like fish that make up the order Cyclostomata (meaning "round mouths"), a division of the superclass Agnatha (meaning "without jaws"). In addition to their characteristic round, sucker-like mouths and lack of jaws, cyclostomes also have smooth, slimy skin without scales, and unpaired fins.

SHARKS' JAWS

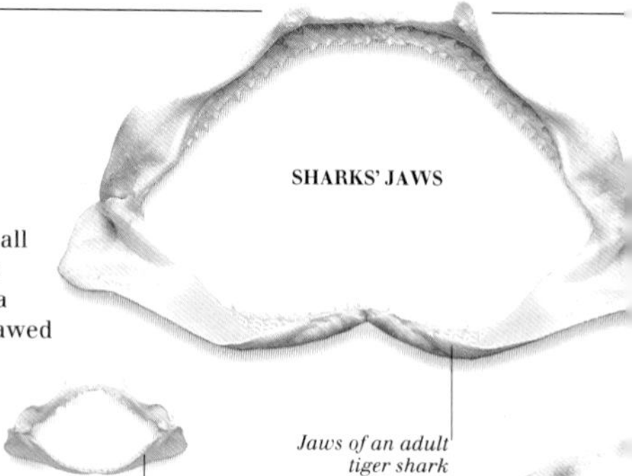
Jaws of an adult tiger shark
Jaws of a young tiger shark

EXTERNAL FEATURES OF A DOGFISH

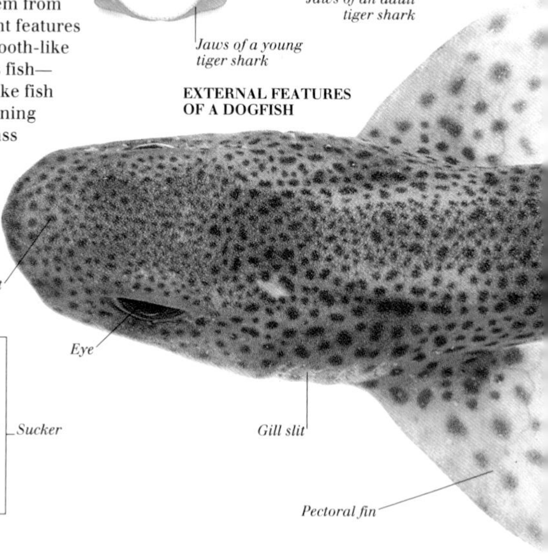
Snout
Eye
Gill slit
Pectoral fin

FEATURES OF A LAMPREY'S HEAD

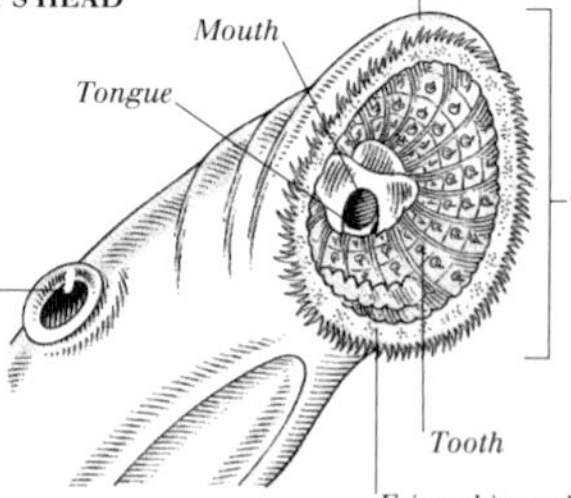
Outer lip
Mouth
Tongue
Sucker
Eye
Tooth
Fringed inner lip

EXTERNAL FEATURES OF A LAMPREY

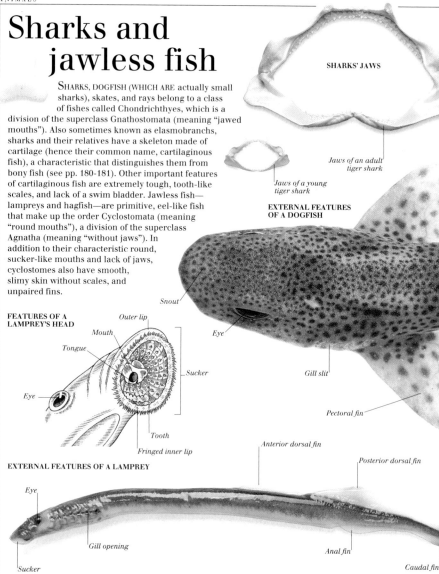

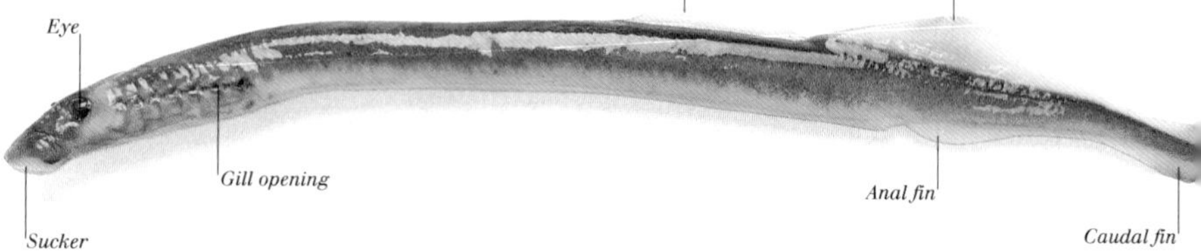
Anterior dorsal fin
Posterior dorsal fin
Eye
Gill opening
Sucker
Anal fin
Caudal fin

EXAMPLES OF CARTILAGINOUS FISH

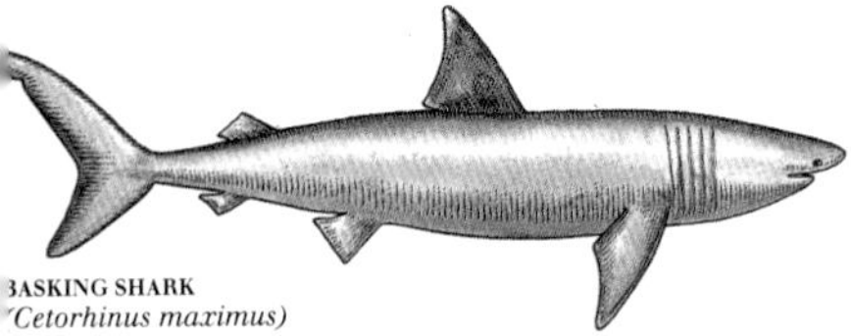

BASKING SHARK
(Cetorhinus maximus)

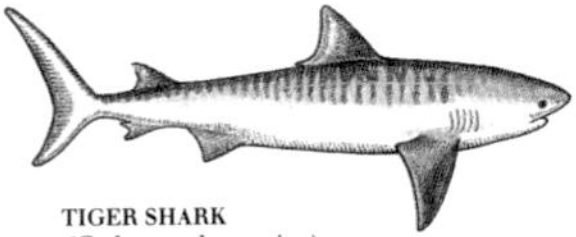

TIGER SHARK
(Galeocerdo cuvier)

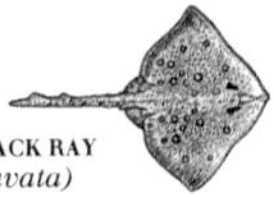

THORNBACK RAY
(Raja clavata)

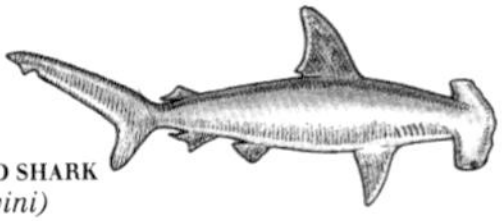

SCALLOPED HAMMERHEAD SHARK
(Sphyrna lewini)

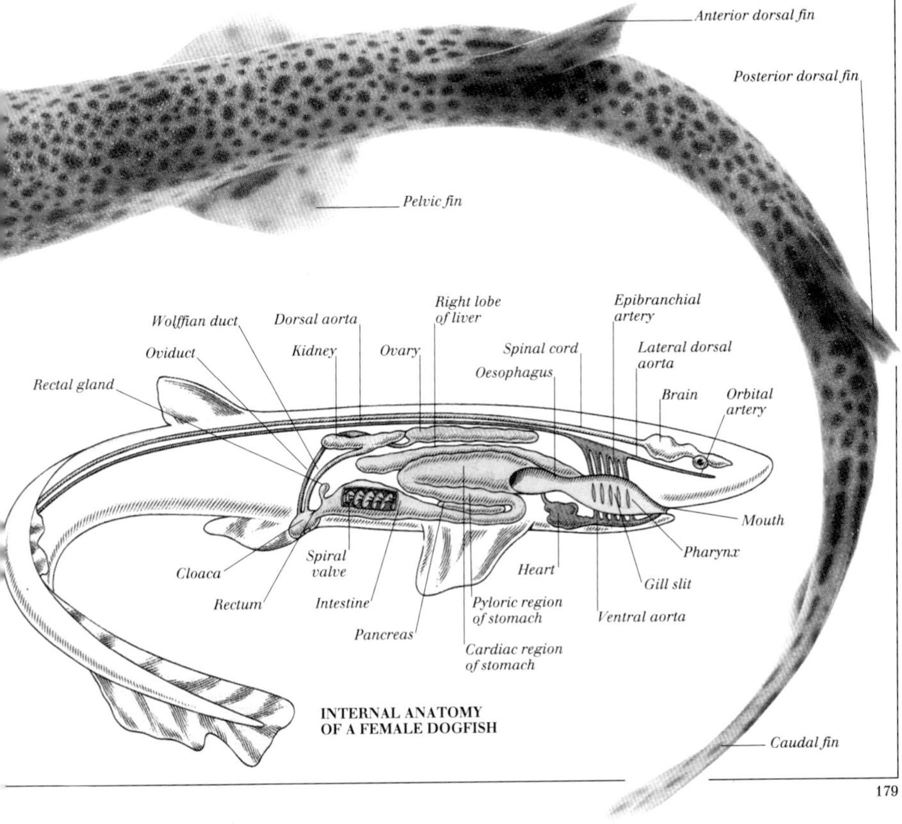
Anterior dorsal fin
Posterior dorsal fin
Pelvic fin
Caudal fin
Wolffian duct
Dorsal aorta
Right lobe of liver
Epibranchial artery
Oviduct
Kidney
Ovary
Spinal cord
Lateral dorsal aorta
Rectal gland
Oesophagus
Brain
Orbital artery
Mouth
Pharynx
Cloaca
Spiral valve
Heart
Gill slit
Rectum
Intestine
Pyloric region of stomach
Ventral aorta
Pancreas
Cardiac region of stomach

INTERNAL ANATOMY OF A FEMALE DOGFISH

Bony fish

BONY FISH, SUCH AS CARP, TROUT, SALMON, perch, and cod, are by far the best known and largest group of fish, with more than 20,000 species (over 95 per cent of all known fish). As their name suggests, bony fish have skeletons made of bone, in contrast to the cartilaginous skeletons of sharks, jawless fish, and their relatives (see pp. 178-179). Other typical features of bony fish include a swim bladder, which functions as a variable-buoyancy organ, enabling a fish to remain effortlessly at whatever depth it is swimming; relatively thin, bone-like scales; a flap (called an operculum) covering the gills; and paired pelvic and pectoral fins. Scientifically, bony fish belong to the class Osteichthyes, which is a division of the superclass Gnathostomata (meaning "jawed mouths").

HOW FISH BREATHE

Fish "breathe" by extracting oxygen from water through their gills. Water is sucked in through the mouth; simultaneously, the opercula close to prevent the water from escaping. The mouth is then closed, and muscles in the walls of the mouth, pharynx, and opercular cavity contract to pump the water inside over the gills and out through the opercula. Some fish rely on swimming with their mouths open to keep water flowing over the gills.

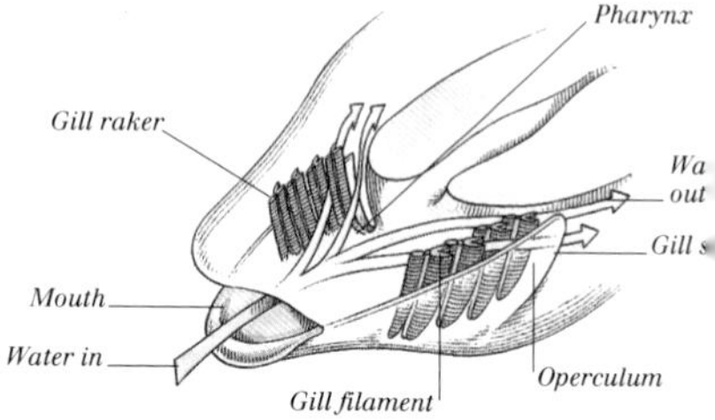
Pharynx
Gill raker
Wa
out
Gill s
Mouth
Water in
Operculum
Gill filament

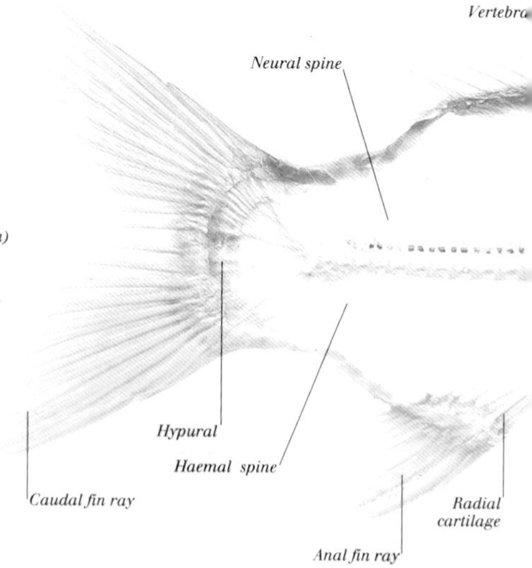
Vertebra
Neural spine
Hypural
Haemal spine
Caudal fin ray
Radial cartilage
Anal fin ray

EXAMPLES OF BONY FISH

MANDARINFISH
(Synchiropus splendidus)

OCEANIC SEAHORSE
(Hippocampus kuda)

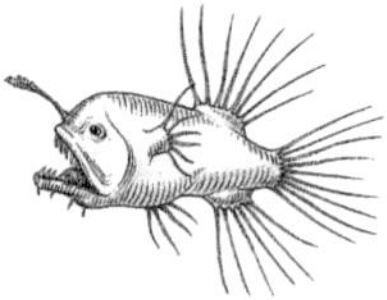

ANGLERFISH
(Caulophryne jordani)

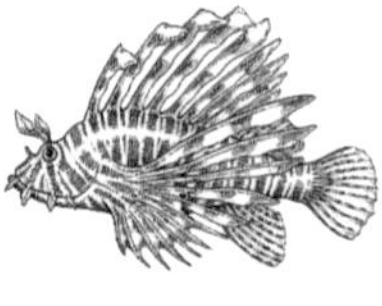

LIONFISH
(Pterois volitans)

STURGEON
(Acipenser sturio)

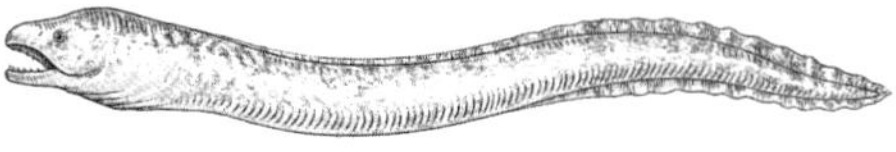

SNOWFLAKE MORAY EEL
(Echidna nebulosa)

INTERNAL ANATOMY OF A FEMALE BONY FISH

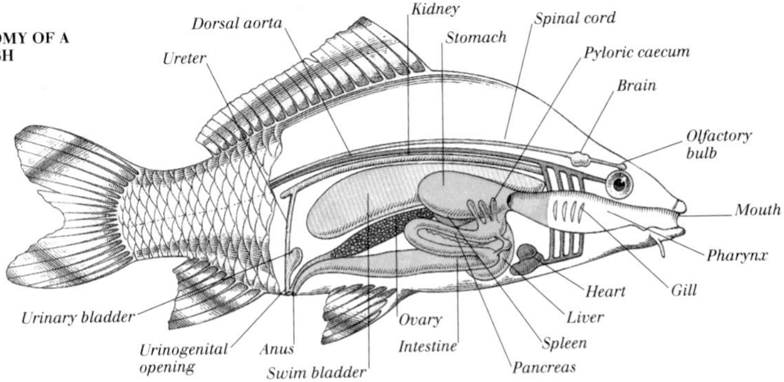
Dorsal aorta
Kidney
Spinal cord
Stomach
Pyloric caecum
Ureter
Brain
Olfactory bulb
Mouth
Pharynx
Gill
Heart
Liver
Spleen
Pancreas
Intestine
Ovary
Swim bladder
Anus
Urinogenital opening
Urinary bladder

SKELETON OF A BONY FISH

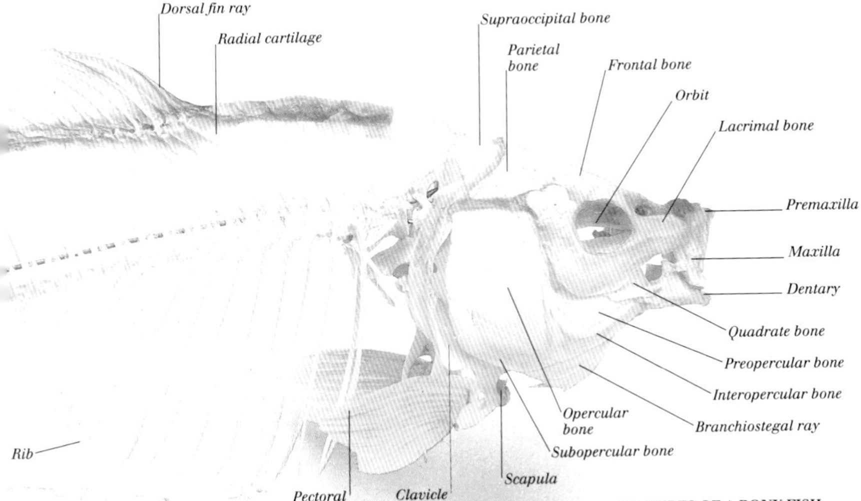
Dorsal fin ray
Radial cartilage
Supraoccipital bone
Parietal bone
Frontal bone
Orbit
Lacrimal bone
Premaxilla
Maxilla
Dentary
Quadrate bone
Preopercular bone
Interopercular bone
Branchiostegal ray
Opercular bone
Subopercular bone
Scapula
Clavicle
Pectoral fin ray
Rib
Pelvis
Pelvic fin ray

EXTERNAL FEATURES OF A BONY FISH

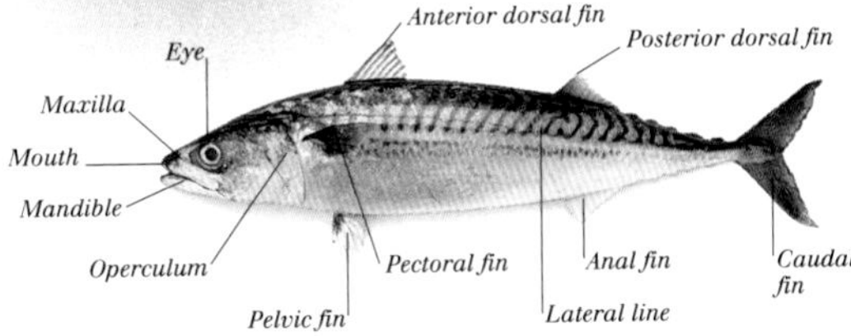
Anterior dorsal fin
Posterior dorsal fin
Eye
Maxilla
Mouth
Mandible
Operculum
Pelvic fin
Pectoral fin
Lateral line
Anal fin
Caudal fin

Amphibians

THE CLASS AMPHIBIA INCLUDES FROGS and toads (which make up the order Anura), and newts and salamanders (which make up the order Urodela). Amphibians typically have moist, scaleless, hairless skin; lungs; and are cold-blooded. They also undergo complete metamorphosis, from eggs laid in water through various water-living larval stages (such as tadpoles) to land-living adults. Typical features of adult frogs and toads include a squat body with no tail; long, powerful hind legs; and large, often bulging, eyes. Adult newts and salamanders typically have a long body with a well-developed tail; and relatively short, equal-sized legs. However, newts and salamanders show considerable variation; for example, in some species the adults have minute legs, external gills rather than lungs, and spend their entire lives in water.

INTERNAL ANATOMY OF A FEMALE FROG

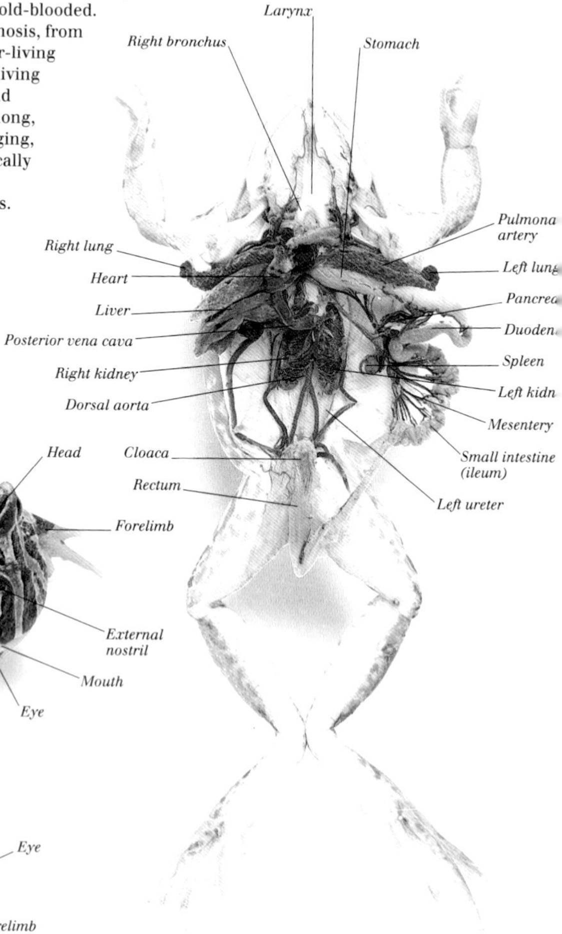
Larynx
Right bronchus
Stomach
Pulmona
artery
Right lung
Left lung
Heart
Pancrea
Liver
Duoden
Posterior vena cava
Spleen
Right kidney
Left kidn
Dorsal aorta
Mesentery
Cloaca
Small intestine
(ileum)
Rectum
Left ureter

EXTERNAL FEATURES OF A FROG

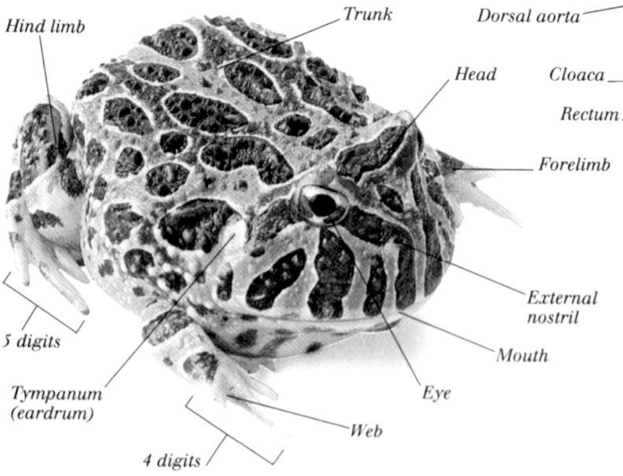
Hind limb
Trunk
Head
Forelimb
5 digits
External
nostril
Mouth
Tympanum
(eardrum)
Eye
Web
4 digits

EXTERNAL FEATURES OF A SALAMANDER

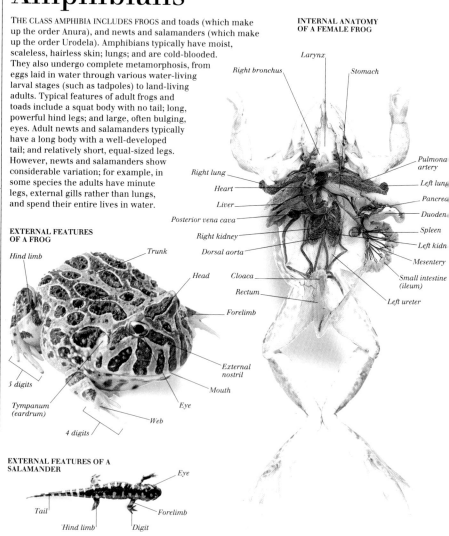

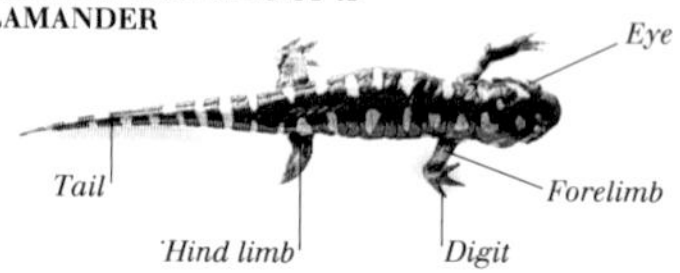
Eye
Tail
Forelimb
Hind limb
Digit

EGGS (SPAWN)
YOUNG TADPOLES
MATURE TADPOLE
YOUNG FROG

METAMORPHOSIS OF FROGS
Frogs undergo complete metamorphosis. Eggs (spawn) are laid in water and hatch into young tadpoles, which have a tail and external gills but no legs. As the tadpoles grow, the gills disappear, back legs develop, then front legs, and the tail shrinks. Eventually the tail disappears, resulting in a young adult frog.

SKELETON OF A FROG

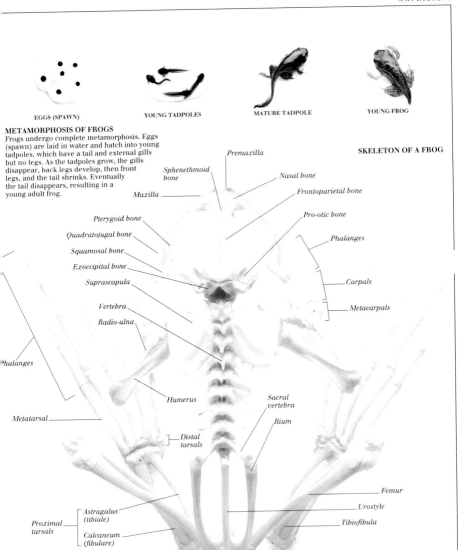

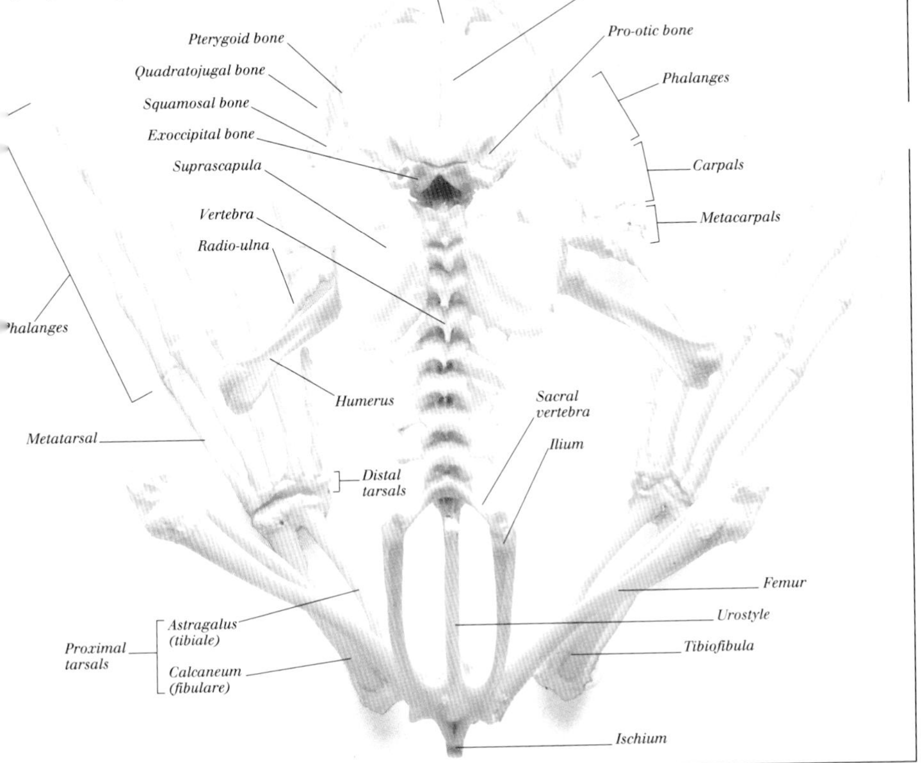
Premaxilla
Sphenethmoid bone
Nasal bone
Maxilla
Frontoparietal bone
Pterygoid bone
Pro-otic bone
Quadratojugal bone
Phalanges
Squamosal bone
Exoccipital bone
Carpals
Suprascapula
Metacarpals
Vertebra
Radio-ulna
halanges
Humerus
Sacral vertebra
Metatarsal
Ilium
Distal tarsals
Femur
Astragalus (tibiale)
Urostyle
Proximal tarsals
Tibiofibula
Calcaneum (fibulare)
Ischium

Lizards and snakes

LIZARDS AND SNAKES BELONG to the order Squamata, a division of the class Reptilia. Characteristic reptilian features include scaly skin, lungs, and cold-bloodedness. Most reptiles lay leathery-shelled eggs, although some hatch the eggs inside their bodies and give birth to live young. Lizards belong to the suborder Lacertilia. Typically, they have long tails, and shed their skin in several pieces. Many lizards can regenerate a tail if it is lost; some can change colour; and some are limbless. Snakes make up the suborder Ophidia (also called Serpentes). All snakes have long, limbless bodies; can dislocate their lower jaw to swallow large prey; and have eyelids that are joined together to form a single transparent covering over the front of the eye. Most snakes shed their skin in a single piece. Constrictor snakes kill their prey by squeezing; venomous snakes poison their prey.

EXAMPLES OF SNAKES

MEXICAN MOUNTAIN KING SNAKE
(Lampropeltis triangulum annulata)
BANDED MILK SNAKE
(Lampropeltis ruthveni)

EXTERNAL FEATURES OF A LIZARD

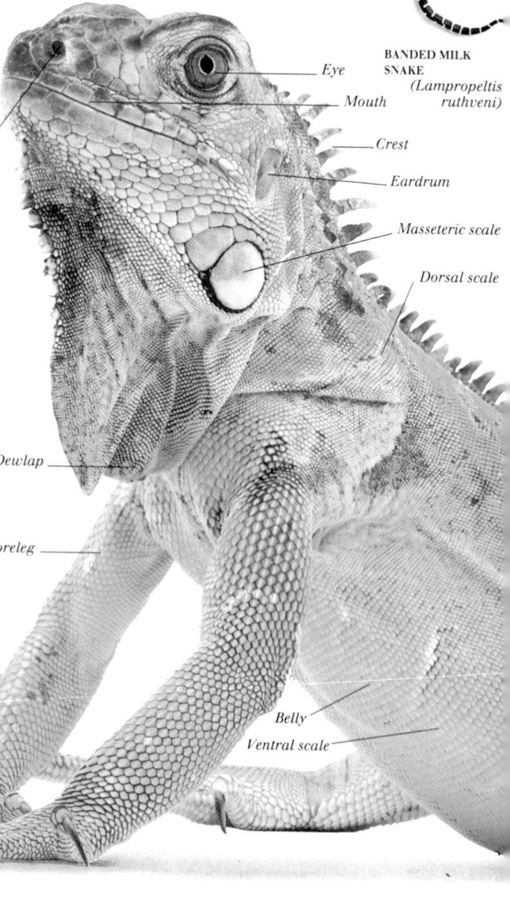
Eye
Mouth
External nostril
Crest
Eardrum
Masseteric scale
Dorsal scale
Dewlap
Foreleg
Belly
Ventral scale
Toe
Claw

SKELETON OF A LIZARD

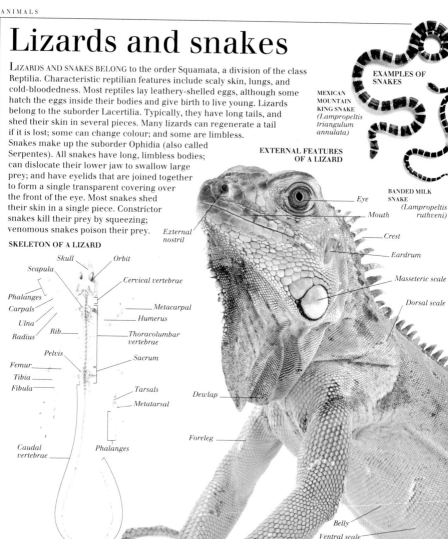

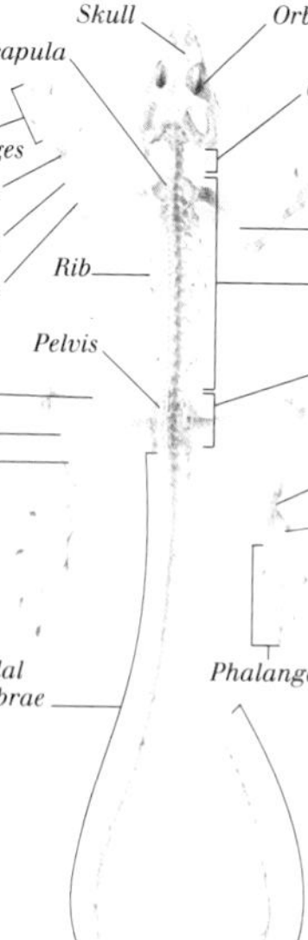
Skull
Orbit
Scapula
Cervical vertebrae
Phalanges
Carpals
Metacarpal
Humerus
Ulna
Rib
Radius
Thoracolumbar vertebrae
Pelvis
Sacrum
Femur
Tibia
Fibula
Tarsals
Metatarsal
Caudal vertebrae
Phalanges

SKELETON OF A SNAKE

Orbit
Skull
Mandible
Vertebra
Rib
Caudal vertebrae

EXTERNAL FEATURES OF A RATTLESNAKE

Scale
Rattle
Abdomen
Tail
Head
Eye
Nostril
Forked tongue

INTERNAL ANATOMY OF A FEMALE LIZARD

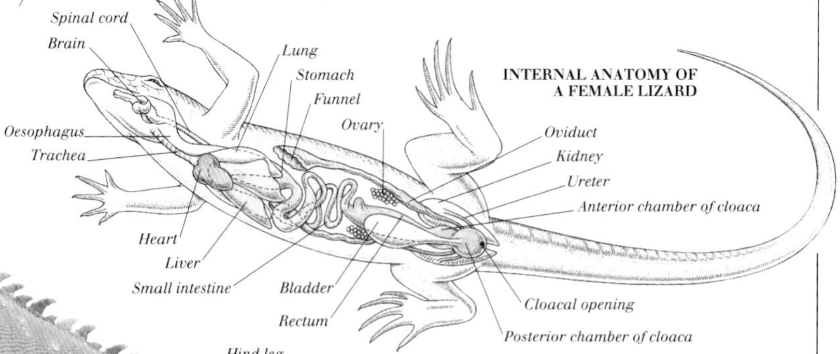
Spinal cord
Brain
Lung
Stomach
Funnel
Ovary
Oesophagus
Trachea
Oviduct
Kidney
Ureter
Anterior chamber of cloaca
Heart
Liver
Small intestine
Bladder
Rectum
Cloacal opening
Posterior chamber of cloaca

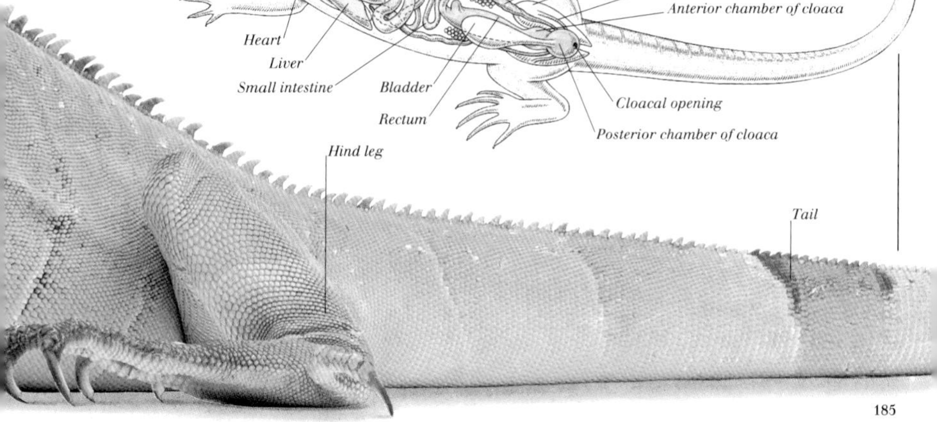
Hind leg
Tail

Crocodilians and turtles

CROCODILIANS AND TURTLES BELONG to different orders in the class Reptilia. The order Crocodilia includes crocodiles, alligators, caimans, and gharials. Typically, crocodilians are carnivores (flesh-eaters), and have a long snout, sharp teeth for gripping prey, and hard, square scales. All crocodilians are adapted to living on land and in water: they have four strong legs for moving on land; a powerful tail for swimming; and their eyes and nostrils are high on the head so that they stay above water while the rest of the body is submerged. The order Chelonia includes marine turtles, terrapins (freshwater turtles), and tortoises (land turtles). Characteristically, chelonians have a short, broad body encased in a bony shell with an outer horny covering, into which the head and limbs can be withdrawn; and a horny beak instead of teeth.

SKULLS OF CROCODILIANS

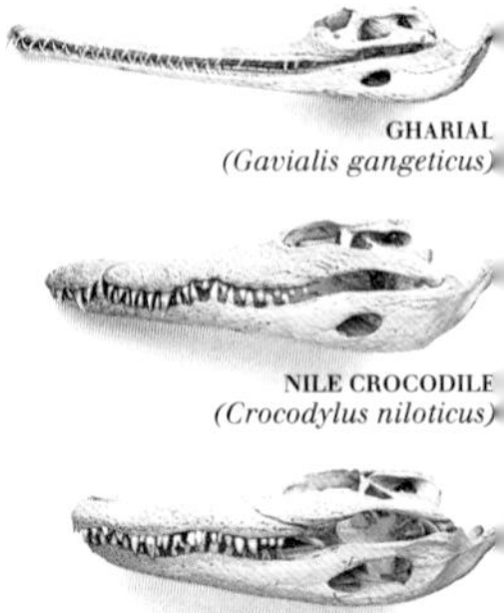
GHARIAL
(Gavialis gangeticus)
NILE CROCODILE
(Crocodylus niloticus)
AMERICAN ALLIGATOR
(Alligator mississippiensis)

SKELETON OF A CROCODILE

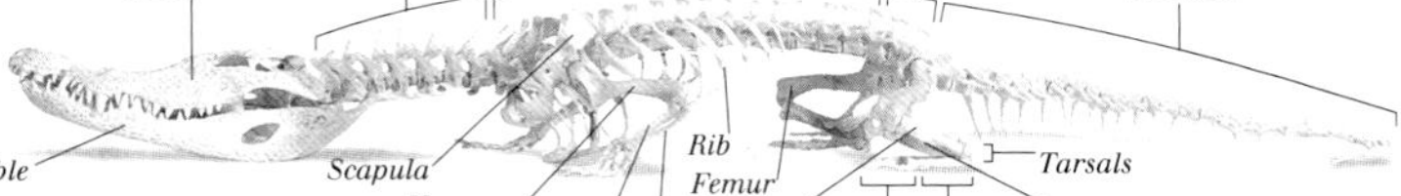
Cervical vertebrae
Thoracic vertebrae
Lumbar vertebrae
Sacrum
Caudal vertebrae
Skull
Mandible
Scapula
Humerus
Radius
Ulna
Rib
Femur
Fibula
Phalanges
Metatarsals
Tarsals
Tibia

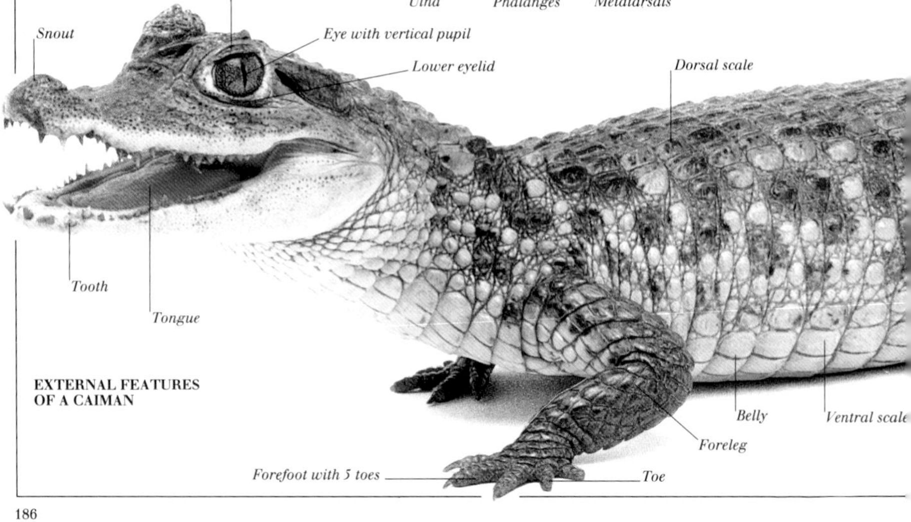
Upper eyelid
Snout
Eye with vertical pupil
Lower eyelid
Dorsal scale
Tooth
Tongue
Belly
Ventral scale
Foreleg
Forefoot with 5 toes
Toe

EXTERNAL FEATURES OF A CAIMAN

EXTERNAL FEATURES OF A TERRAPIN

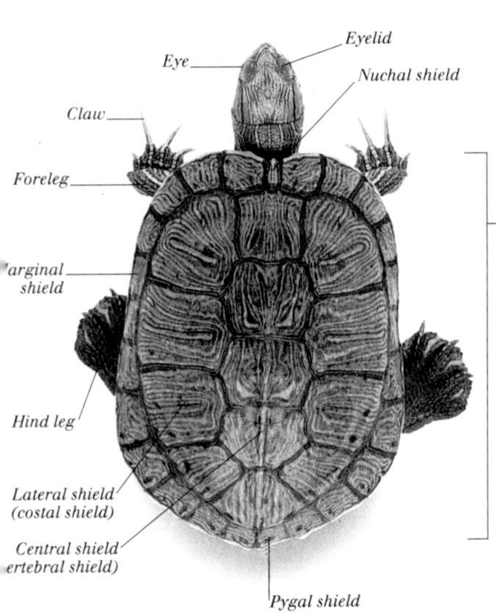
Eyelid
Eye
Nuchal shield
Claw
Foreleg
Carapace
(upper shell)
arginal
shield
Hind leg
Lateral shield
(costal shield)
Central shield
ertebral shield)
Pygal shield

SKELETON OF A TURTLE

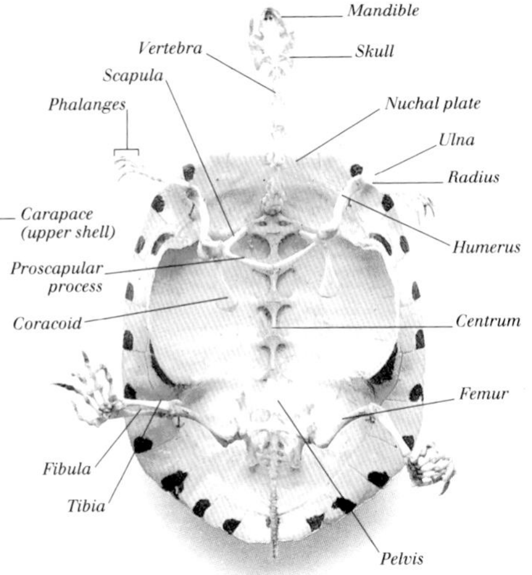
Mandible
Vertebra
Skull
Scapula
Phalanges
Nuchal plate
Ulna
Radius
Humerus
Proscapular
process
Coracoid
Centrum
Femur
Fibula
Tibia
Pelvis

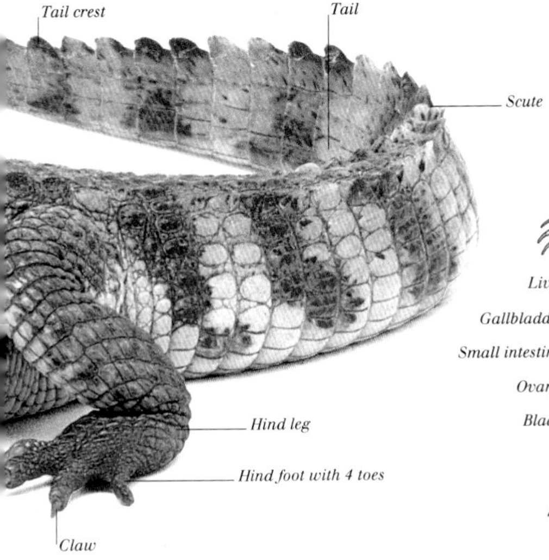
Tail crest
Tail
Scute
Hind leg
Hind foot with 4 toes
Claw

INTERNAL ANATOMY OF A FEMALE TORTOISE

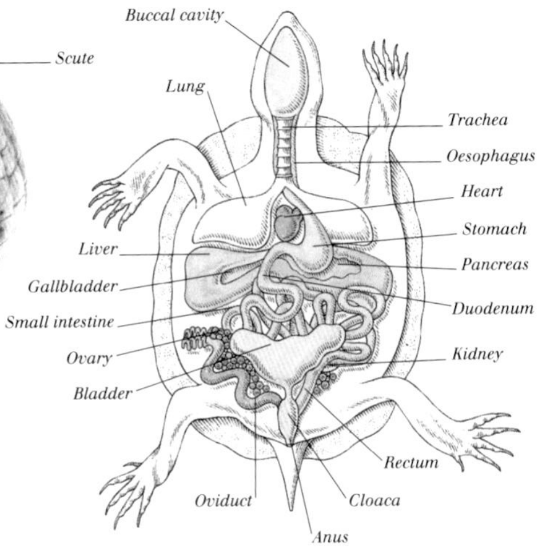
Buccal cavity
Lung
Trachea
Oesophagus
Heart
Stomach
Liver
Pancreas
Gallbladder
Duodenum
Small intestine
Ovary
Kidney
Bladder
Rectum
Oviduct
Cloaca
Anus

Birds 1

BIRDS MAKE UP THE CLASS AVES. There are more than 9,000 species, almost all of which can fly (the only flightless birds are penguins, ostriches, rheas, cassowaries, and kiwis). The ability to fly is reflected in the typical bird features: forelimbs modified as wings; a streamlined body; and hollow bones to reduce weight. All birds lay hard-shelled eggs, which the parents incubate. Birds' beaks and feet vary according to diet and way of life. Beaks range from general-purpose types suitable for a mixed diet (those of thrushes, for example), to types specialized for particular foods (such as the large, curved, sieving beaks of flamingos). Feet range from the webbed "paddles" of ducks, to the talons of birds of prey. Plumage also varies widely, and in many species the male is brightly coloured for courtship display whereas the female is drab.

EXAMPLES OF BIRDS

MALE TUFTED DUCK
(Aythya fuligula)

WHITE STORK
(Ciconia ciconia)

MALE OSTRICH
(Struthio camelus)

EXTERNAL FEATURES OF A BIRD

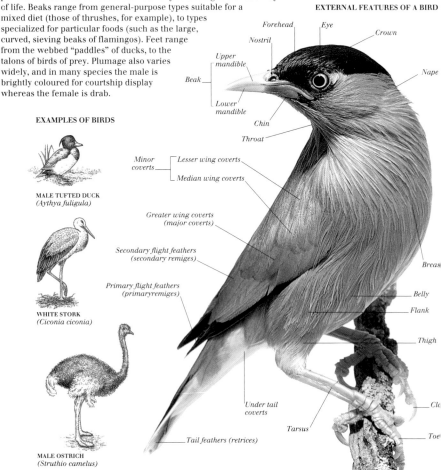

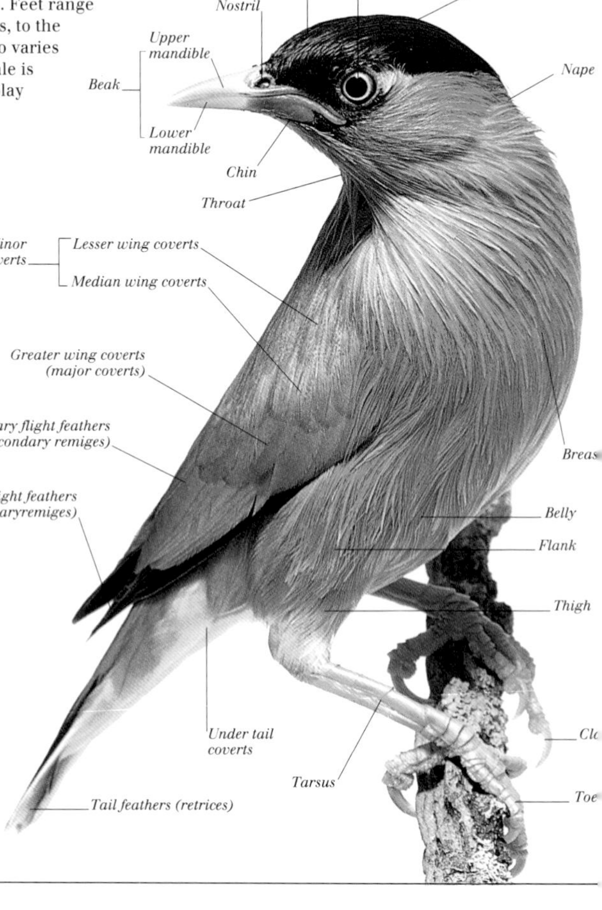
Forehead
Eye
Crown
Nostril
Upper mandible
Beak
Lower mandible
Nape
Chin
Throat
Minor coverts
Lesser wing coverts
Median wing coverts
Greater wing coverts (major coverts)
Secondary flight feathers (secondary remiges)
Primary flight feathers (primaryremiges)
Breas
Belly
Flank
Thigh
Under tail coverts
Cl
Tarsus
Toe
Tail feathers (retrices)

SKELETON OF A BIRD

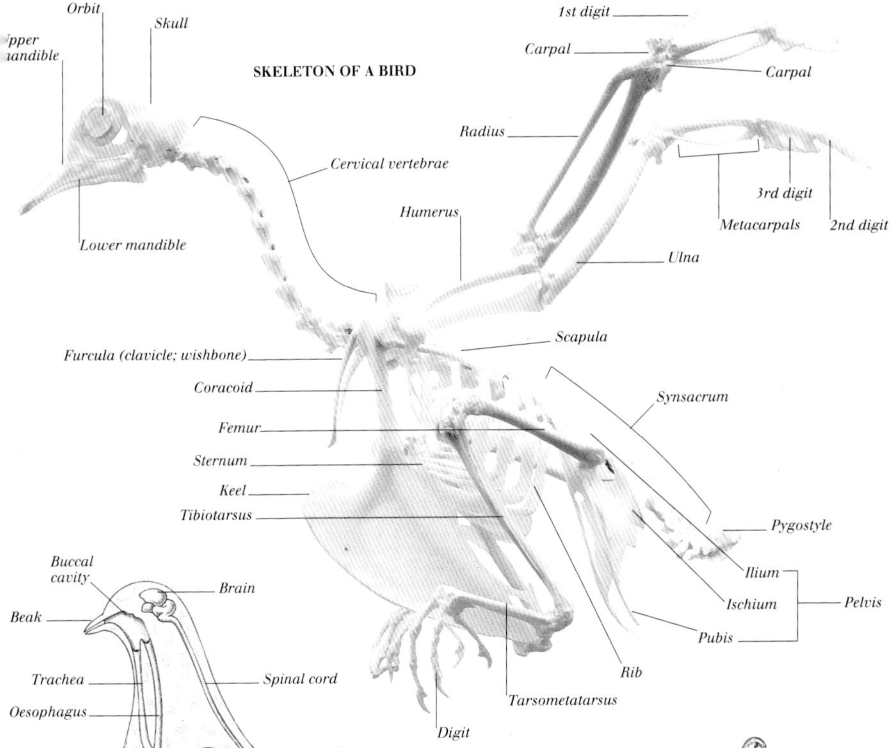

Orbit
Skull
pper andible
Lower mandible
Cervical vertebrae
1st digit
Carpal
Carpal
Radius
3rd digit
Metacarpals
2nd digit
Humerus
Ulna
Scapula
Furcula (clavicle; wishbone)
Coracoid
Synsacrum
Femur
Sternum
Keel
Tibiotarsus
Pygostyle
Ilium
Ischium
Pelvis
Pubis
Rib
Tarsometatarsus
Digit

INTERNAL ANATOMY OF A BIRD

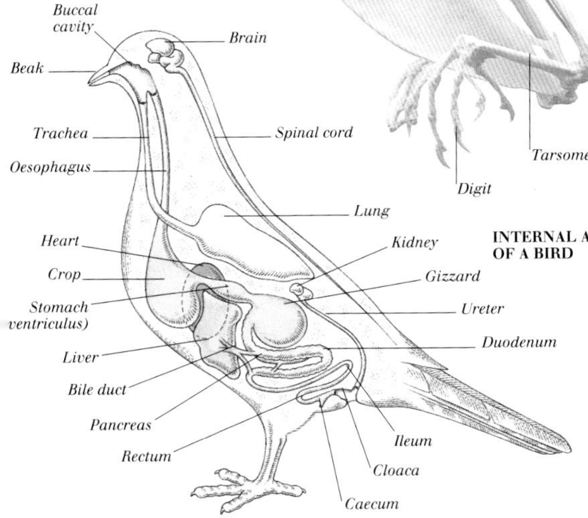

Buccal cavity
Brain
Beak
Trachea
Spinal cord
Oesophagus
Lung
Heart
Kidney
Crop
Gizzard
Stomach ventriculus)
Ureter
Duodenum
Liver
Bile duct
Pancreas
Ileum
Rectum
Cloaca
Caecum

MALE KESTREL
(Falco tinnunculus)

COMMON BLACKHEADED GULL
(Larus ridibundus)

Birds 2

EXAMPLES OF BIRDS' FEET

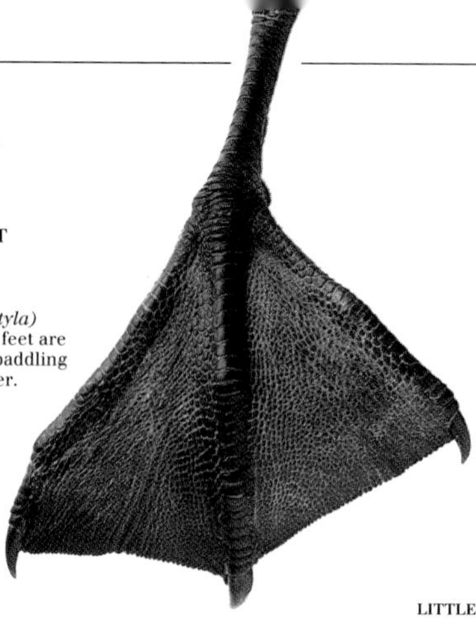

KITTIWAKE
(Rissa tridactyla)
The webbed feet are adapted for paddling through water.

LITTLE GREBE
(Tachybaptus ruficollis)
The lobed, flattened feet are adapted for swimming underwater.

TAWNY OWL
(Strix aluco)
The clawed feet are adapted for gripping prey.

EXAMPLES OF BIRDS' BEAKS

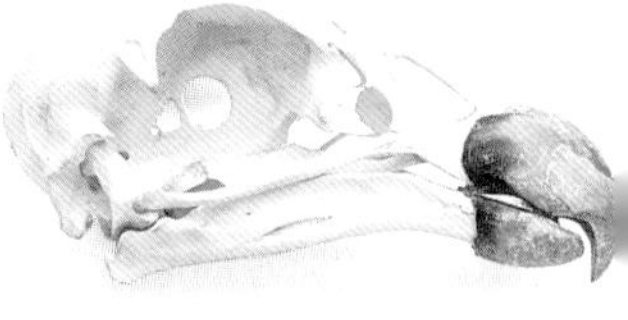

KING VULTURE
(Sarcorhamphus papa)
The hooked beak is adapted for pulling apart flesh.

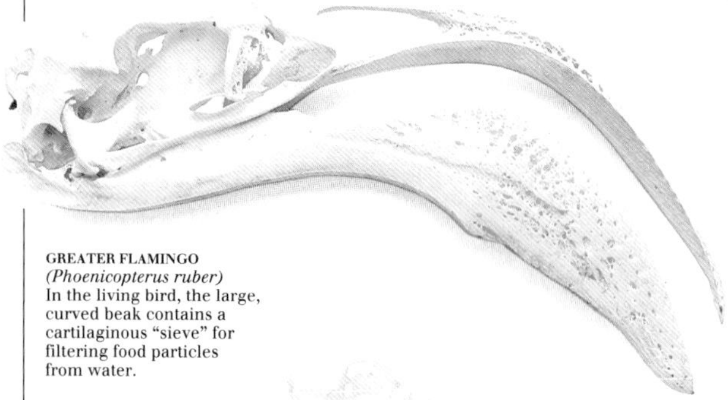

GREATER FLAMINGO
(Phoenicopterus ruber)
In the living bird, the large, curved beak contains a cartilaginous "sieve" for filtering food particles from water.

MISTLE THRUSH
(Turdus viscivorus)
The general-purpose beak is suitable for a wide range of animal and plant foods.

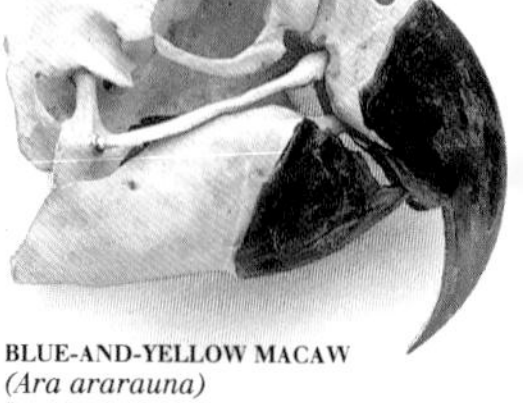

BLUE-AND-YELLOW MACAW
(Ara ararauna)
The broad, powerful, hooked beak is adapted for crushing seeds and eating fruit.

BONES OF A BIRD'S WING

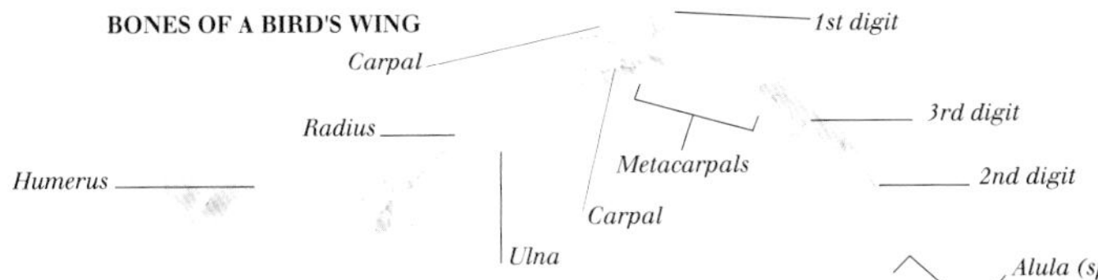
1st digit
Carpal
3rd digit
Radius
Metacarpals
Humerus
2nd digit
Carpal
Ulna

FEATHERS OF A BIRD'S WING

Alula (spurious wing)
Minor coverts
ajor
verts
Secondary flight feathers (secondary remiges)
Primary flight feathers (primary remiges)

STRUCTURE OF A FEATHER

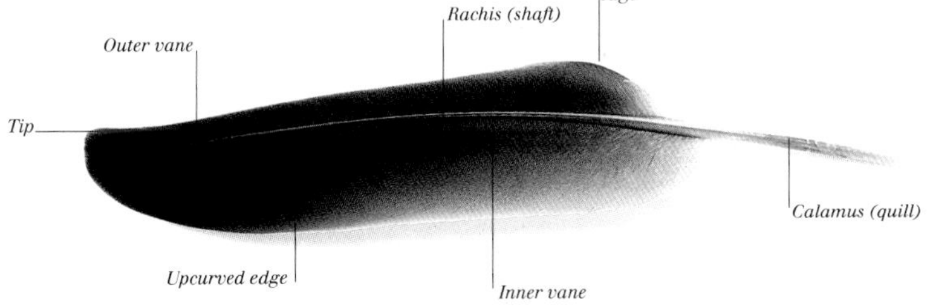
Downcurved edge
Rachis (shaft)
Outer vane
Tip
Calamus (quill)
Upcurved edge
Inner vane

Eggs

AN EGG IS A SINGLE CELL, produced by the female, with the capacity to develop into a new individual. Development may take place inside the mother's body (as in most mammals) or outside, in which case the egg has a protective covering such as a shell. Egg yolk nourishes the growing young. Eggs developing inside the mother generally have little yolk, because the young are nourished from her body. Eggs developing outside may also have little yolk if they are produced by animals whose young go through a larval stage (such as a caterpillar) that feeds itself while developing into the adult form. The shelled eggs of birds and reptiles contain enough yolk to sustain the young until it hatches into a juvenile version of the adult.

SECTION THROUGH A CHICKEN'S EG

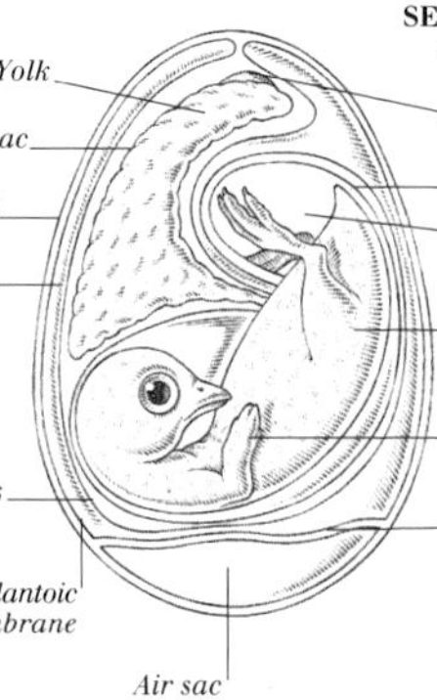
Yolk
Yolk sac
Shell
Allantoic fluid
Allantois
Chorioallantoic membrane
Air sac
Albumen (egg white
Amnion
Amniotic fluid
Developing chic
Developing win
Shell membrane

VARIETY OF EGGS

GIANT STICK INSECT EGGS

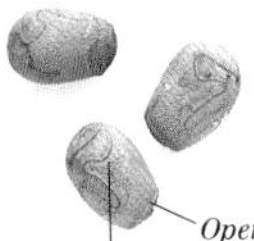
Egg capsule
Operculum

LEAF INSECT EGGS

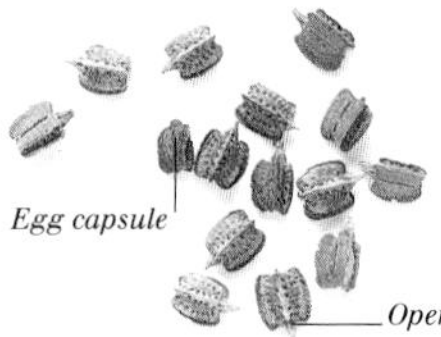
Egg capsule
Operculum

Operculum
Egg capsule

INDIAN STICK INSECT EGGS

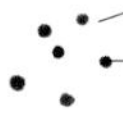
Jelly
Developing tadpole

FROG EGGS (FROG SPAWN)

DOGFISH EGGS (MERMAID'S PURSES

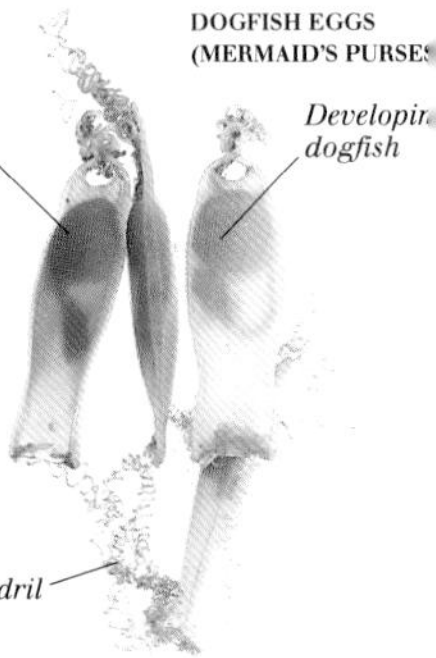
Egg case
Developin dogfish
Tendril

HATCHING OF A QUAIL'S EGG

EGG AT THE POINT OF HATCHING

Rounded end of egg
Shell
Pointed end of egg
Camouflage coloration
Crack caused by chick pecking through the shell

CUTTING THROUGH THE EGG

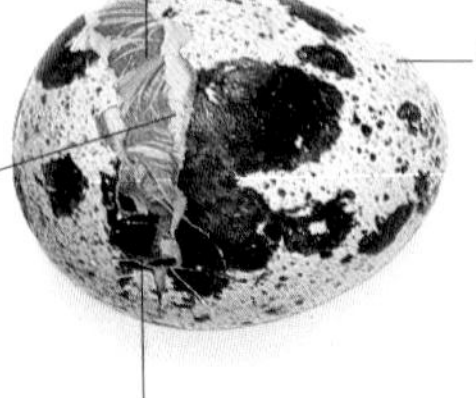
Chick
Shell
Shell membrane
Crack extended by further pecking by the chick

BREAKING OUT OF THE EGG

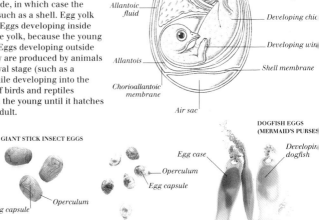

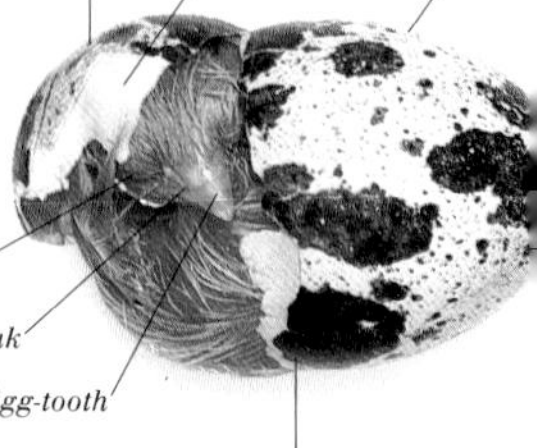
Chick pushes off the top of the shell
Shell membrane
Shel
Eye
Beak
Egg-tooth
Crack runs completely around the shell

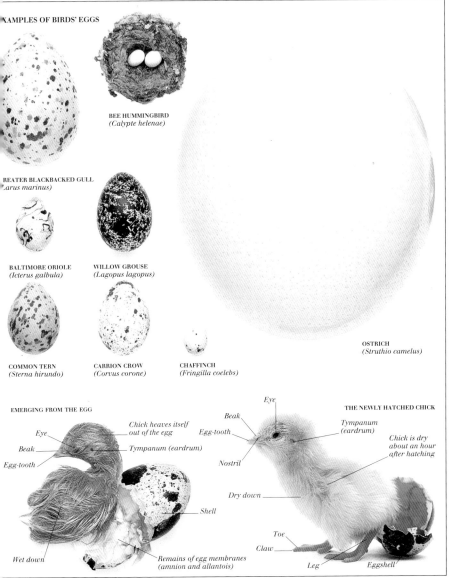

XAMPLES OF BIRDS' EGGS

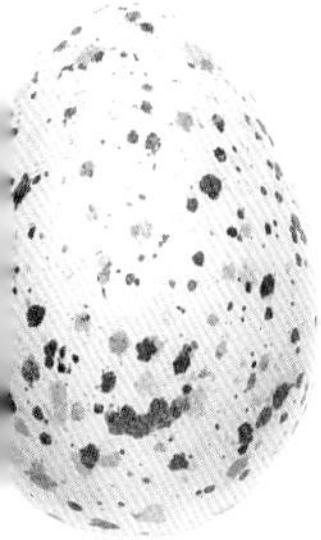

REATER BLACKBACKED GULL
arus marinus)

BEE HUMMINGBIRD
(Calypte helenae)

BALTIMORE ORIOLE
(Icterus galbula)

WILLOW GROUSE
(Lagopus lagopus)

COMMON TERN
(Sterna hirundo)

CARRION CROW
(Corvus corone)

CHAFFINCH
(Fringilla coelebs)

OSTRICH
(Struthio camelus)

EMERGING FROM THE EGG

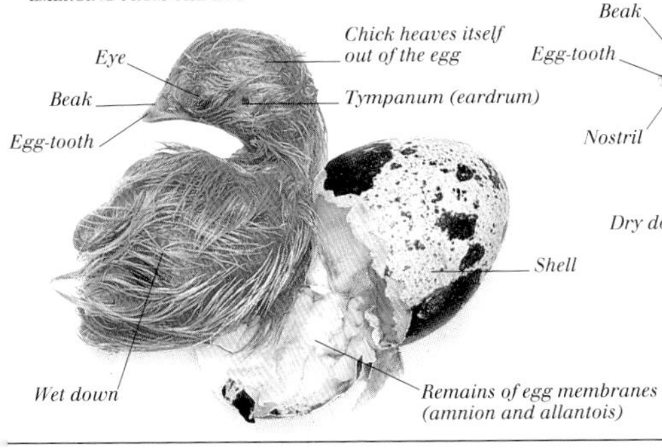
Chick heaves itself out of the egg
Eye
Beak
Egg-tooth
Tympanum (eardrum)
Shell
Wet down
Remains of egg membranes (amnion and allantois)

THE NEWLY HATCHED CHICK

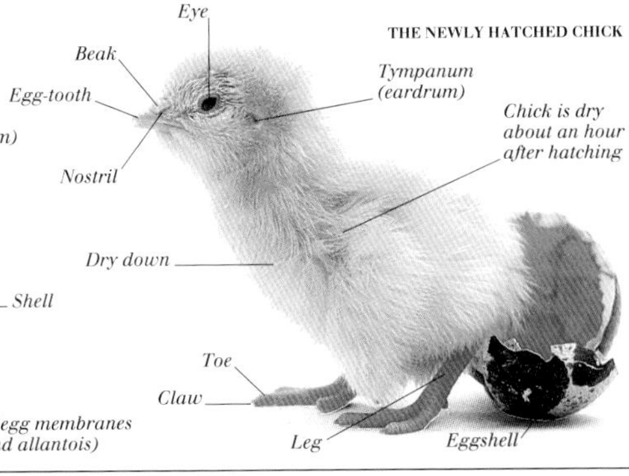
Eye
Beak
Egg-tooth
Nostril
Tympanum (eardrum)
Chick is dry about an hour after hatching
Dry down
Toe
Claw
Leg
Eggshell

Carnivores

THE MAMMALIAN ORDER CARNIVORA includes cats, dogs, bears, raccoons, pandas, weasels, badgers, skunks, otters, civets, mongooses, and hyenas. The order's name is derived from the fact that most of its members are carnivores (flesh-eaters). Typical carnivore features therefore reflect a hunting life-style: speed and agility; sharp claws and well-developed canine teeth for holding and killing prey; carnassial teeth (cheek teeth) for cutting flesh; and forward-facing eyes for good distance judgment. However, some members of the order—bears, badgers, and foxes, for example—have a more mixed diet, and a few are entirely herbivorous (plant-eating), notably pandas. Such animals have no carnassial teeth and tend to be slower-moving than pure flesh-eaters.

SKULL OF A LION

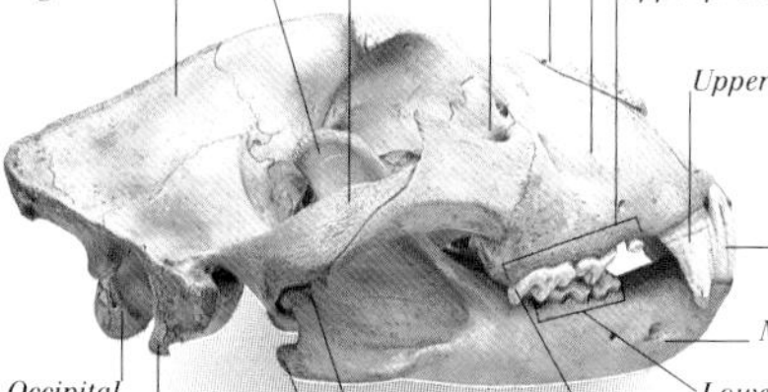
Zygomatic arch
Coronoid process
Sagittal crest
Orbit
Nasal bone
Maxilla
Upper premolars
Upper canine
Lower canine
Mandible
Lower premolars
Occipital condyle
Condyle
Tympanic bulla
Angular process
Upper carnassial tooth (4th upper premolar)

SKULL OF A BEAR

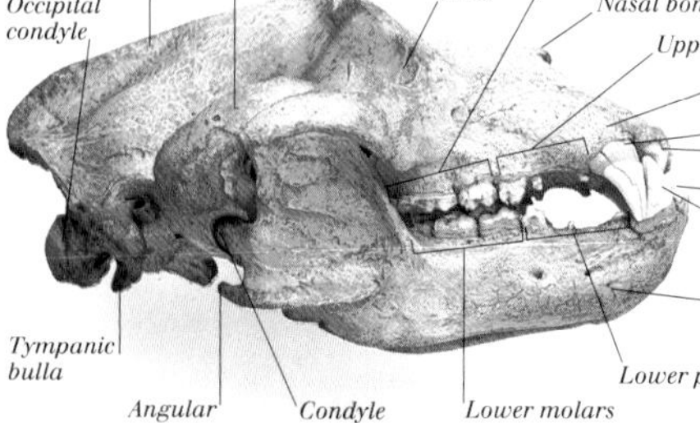
Sagittal crest
Occipital condyle
Zygomatic arch
Orbit
Upper molars
Nasal bone
Upper premolars
Maxilla
Upper canine
Upper incisor
Lower incisor
Lower canine
Mandible
Lower premolars
Tympanic bulla
Angular process
Condyle
Lower molars

EXTERNAL FEATURES OF A MALE LION

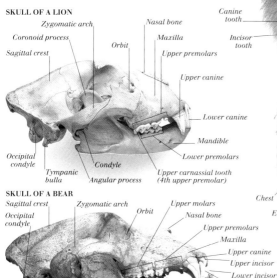

Nose
Eye
Mane
Nostril
Vibrissa (whisker)
Tongue
Canine tooth
Incisor tooth
Chest
Elbow
Lower arm
Toe

EXAMPLES OF CARNIVORES

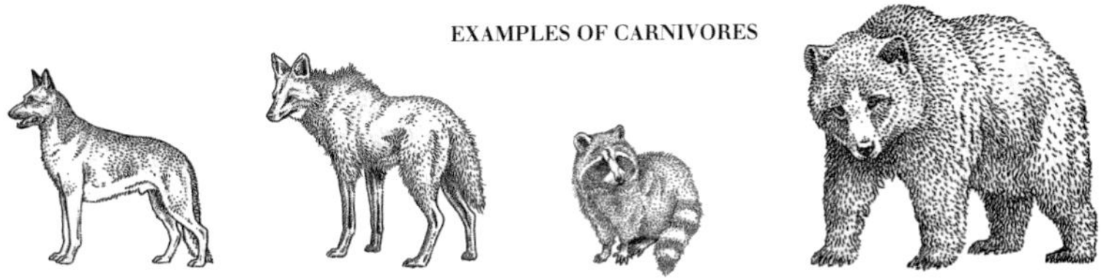

ALSATIAN DOG
(Canis familiaris)

MANED WOLF
(Chrysocyon brachyurus)

RACCOON
(Procyon lotor)

AMERICAN BLACK BEAR
(Ursus americanus)

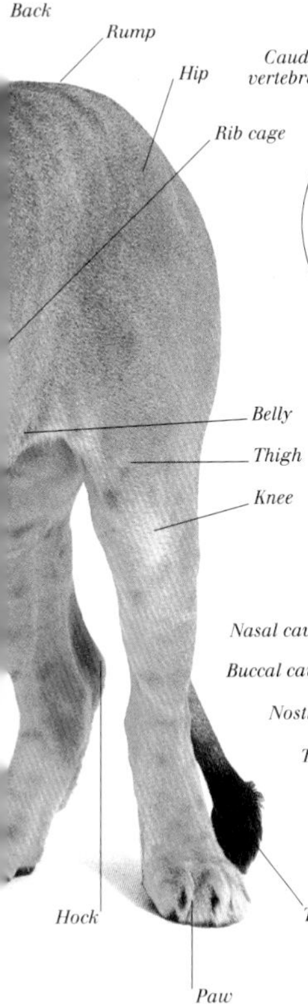
Back
Rump
Hip
Rib cage
Belly
Thigh
Knee
Hock
Paw
Tail

SKELETON OF A DOMESTIC CAT

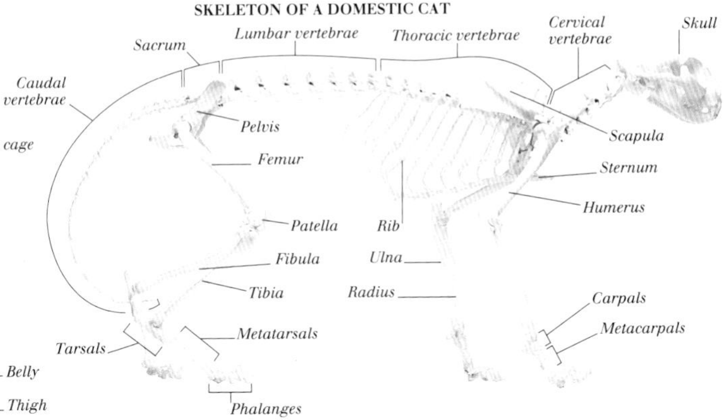
Sacrum
Lumbar vertebrae
Thoracic vertebrae
Cervical vertebrae
Skull
Caudal vertebrae
Pelvis
Scapula
Femur
Sternum
Humerus
Patella
Rib
Fibula
Ulna
Tibia
Radius
Carpals
Metacarpals
Metatarsals
Tarsals
Phalanges

INTERNAL ANATOMY OF A MALE DOMESTIC CAT

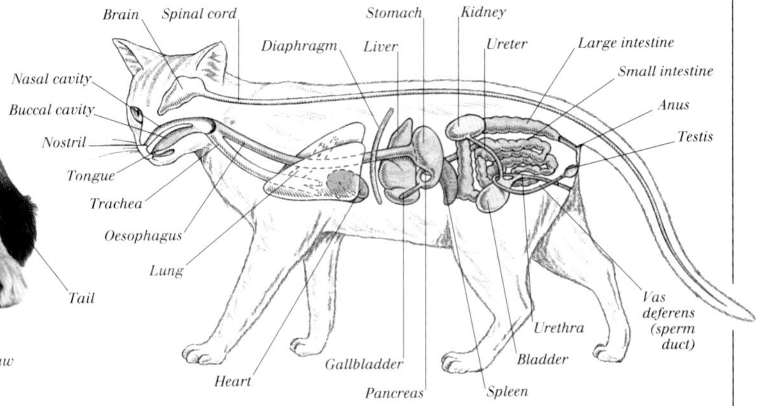
Brain
Spinal cord
Stomach
Kidney
Diaphragm
Liver
Ureter
Large intestine
Small intestine
Nasal cavity
Buccal cavity
Anus
Nostril
Testis
Tongue
Trachea
Oesophagus
Lung
Vas deferens (sperm duct)
Urethra
Bladder
Gallbladder
Heart
Pancreas
Spleen

Rabbits and rodents

ALTHOUGH RABBITS AND RODENTS belong to different orders of mammals, they have some features in common. These features include chisel-shaped incisor teeth that grow continually, and eating their faeces to extract more nutrients from their plant diet. Rabbits and hares belong to the order Lagomorpha. Characteristically, they have four incisors in the upper jaw and two in the lower jaw; powerful hind legs for jumping; forelimbs adapted for burrowing; long ears; and a small tail. Rodents make up the order Rodentia. This is the largest order of mammals, with more than 1,700 species, including squirrels, beavers, chipmunks, gophers, rats, mice, lemmings, gerbils, porcupines, cavies, and the capybara. Typical rodent features include two incisors in each jaw; short forelimbs for manipulating food; and cheek pouches for storing food.

EXTERNAL FEATURES OF A RAT

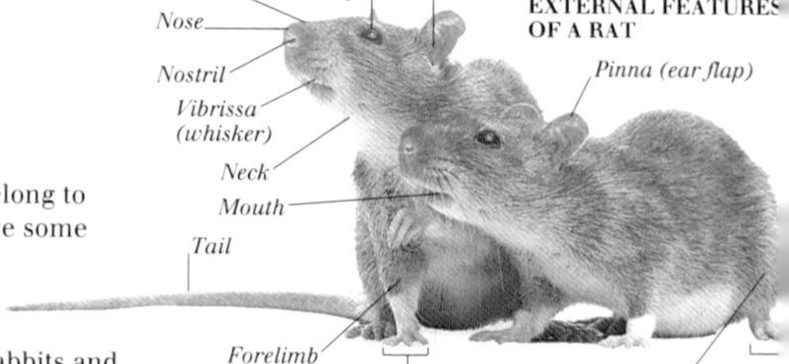
Snout
Eye
Ear
Nose
Nostril
Pinna (ear flap)
Vibrissa (whisker)
Neck
Mouth
Tail
Forelimb
5 digits
Hind limb
5 digits

EXTERNAL FEATURES OF A RABBIT

Pinna (ear flap)
Ear
Shoulder
Eye
Nose
Nostril
Vibrissa (whisker)
Forelimb
5 digits

INTERNAL ANATOMY OF A MALE RABBIT

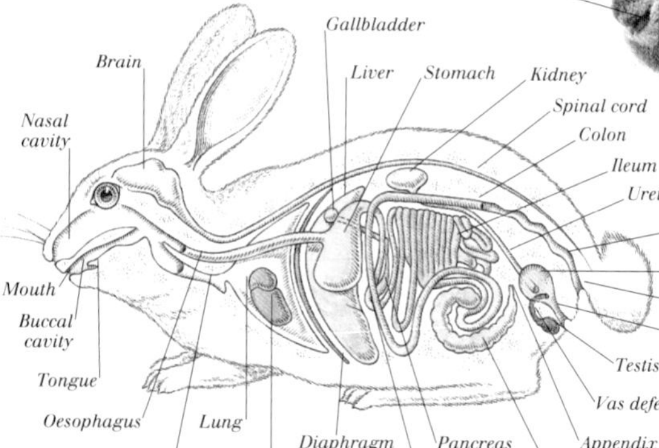
Gallbladder
Brain
Liver
Stomach
Kidney
Spinal cord
Nasal cavity
Colon
Ileum
Ureter
Rectum
Bladder
Mouth
Anus
Buccal cavity
Urethra
Tongue
Testis
Vas deferens
Oesophagus
Lung
Diaphragm
Pancreas
Appendix
Trachea
Heart
Duodenum
Caecum

SKELETON OF A HARE

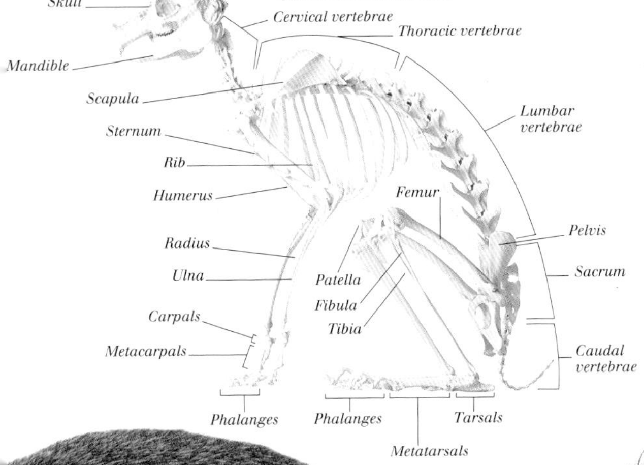
Skull
Cervical vertebrae
Thoracic vertebrae
Mandible
Scapula
Lumbar vertebrae
Sternum
Rib
Humerus
Femur
Pelvis
Radius
Sacrum
Ulna
Patella
Fibula
Tibia
Carpals
Metacarpals
Caudal vertebrae
Phalanges
Phalanges
Tarsals
Metatarsals

Tail
Knee
Hind limb
4 digits

EXAMPLES OF RODENTS

GREY SQUIRREL
(Sciuris carolinensis)

PLAINS VISCACHA
(Lagostomus maximus)

CRESTED PORCUPINE
(Hystrix africaeaustralis)

AMERICAN BEAVER
(Castor canadensis)

CAPYBARA
(Hydrochoerus hydrochaeris)

Ungulates

UNGULATES IS A GENERAL TERM FOR a large, varied group of mammals that includes horses, cattle, and their relatives. The ungulates are divided into two orders on the basis of the number of toes. Members of the order Perissodactyla (odd-toed ungulates) have one or three toes. Perissodactyls include horses, asses, and zebras (all of which are one-toed), and rhinoceroses and tapirs (which are three-toed). Members of the order Artiodactyla (even-toed ungulates) have two or four toes. Most artiodactyls have two toes, which are typically encased in hooves to give the so-called cloven hoof. Two-toed, cloven-hoofed artiodactyls include cows and other cattle, sheep, goats, antelopes, deer, and giraffes. The other main two-toed artiodactyls are camels and llamas. Most two-toed artiodactyls are ruminants; that is, they have a four-chambered stomach and chew the cud. The principal four-toed artiodactyls are pigs, peccaries, and hippopotamuses.

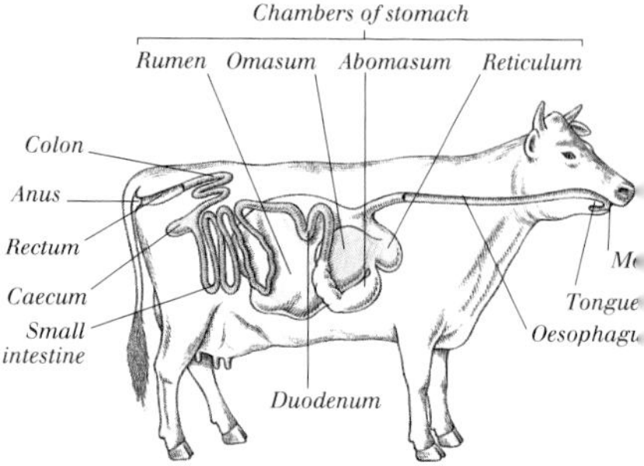

Chambers of stomach
Rumen
Omasum
Abomasum
Reticulum
Colon
Anus
Rectum
Caecum
Small intestine
Duodenum
Tongue

DIGESTIVE SYSTEM OF A COW

COMPARISON OF THE FRONT FEET OF A HORSE AND A COW

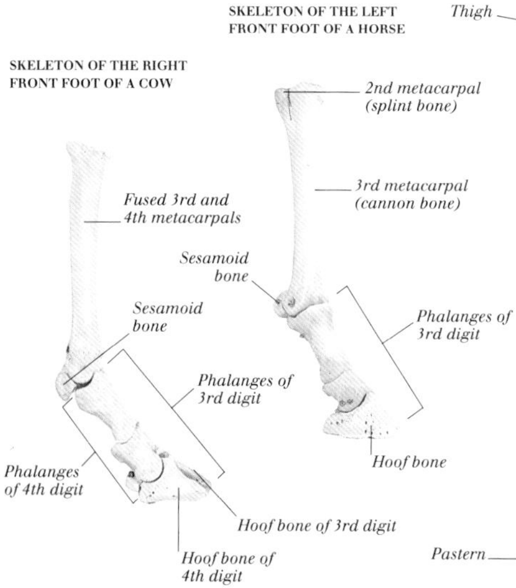

SKELETON OF THE LEFT FRONT FOOT OF A HORSE
SKELETON OF THE RIGHT FRONT FOOT OF A COW
2nd metacarpal (splint bone)
3rd metacarpal (cannon bone)
Fused 3rd and 4th metacarpals
Sesamoid bone
Sesamoid bone
Phalanges of 3rd digit
Phalanges of 3rd digit
Hoof bone
Phalanges of 4th digit
Hoof bone of 3rd digit
Hoof bone of 4th digit

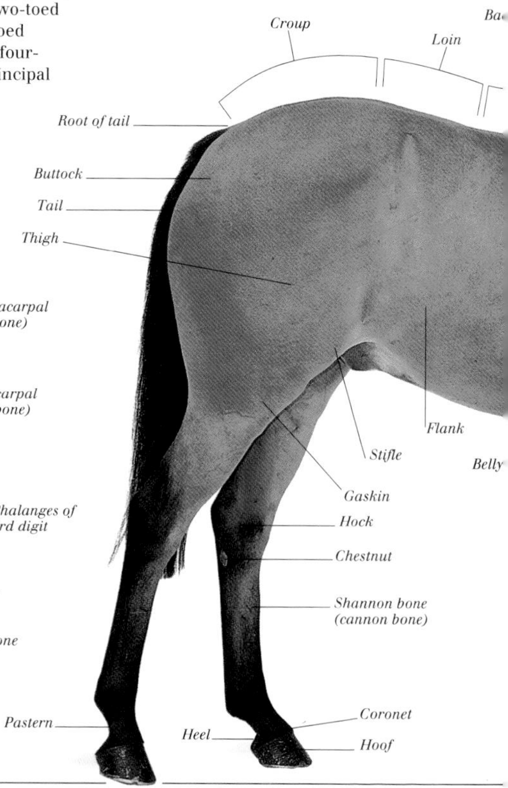

Croup
Loin
Root of tail
Buttock
Tail
Thigh
Flank
Stifle
Gaskin
Hock
Chestnut
Shannon bone (cannon bone)
Pastern
Heel
Coronet
Hoof

EXAMPLES OF UNGULATES

MALE RED DEER
(Cervus elephas)
An even-toed ungulate
(order Artiodactyla)

BACTRIAN CAMEL
(Camelus ferus)
An even-toed ungulate
(order Artiodactyla)

GIRAFFE
(Giraffa camelopardalis)
An even-toed ungulate
(order Artiodactyla)

BLACK RHINOCEROS
(Diceros bicornis)
An odd-toed ungulate
(order Perissodactyla)

EXTERNAL FEATURES OF A HORSE

Mane
Poll
Crest
Ear
Forelock
Forehead
thers
Eye
Muzzle
Nose
Nostril
Cheek
Throatlatch
Mouth
Neck
Chin groove
Shoulder
Breast
lbow
Forearm
Knee
Cannon bone
Fetlock
Pastern

SKELETON OF A HORSE

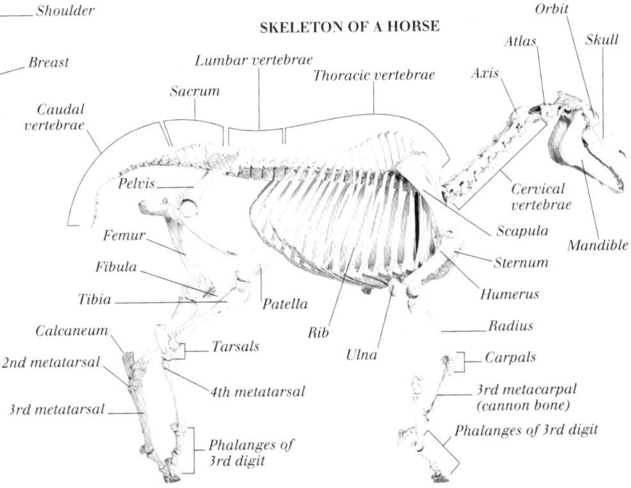
Orbit
Skull
Atlas
Axis
Lumbar vertebrae
Thoracic vertebrae
Sacrum
Caudal vertebrae
Pelvis
Cervical vertebrae
Scapula
Mandible
Femur
Sternum
Fibula
Humerus
Tibia
Patella
Radius
Calcaneum
Rib
Tarsals
Ulna
Carpals
2nd metatarsal
4th metatarsal
3rd metacarpal (cannon bone)
3rd metatarsal
Phalanges of 3rd digit
Phalanges of 3rd digit

Elephants

THE TWO SPECIES OF elephants—African and Asian—are the only members of the mammalian order Proboscidea. The bigger African elephant is the largest land animal: a fully grown male may be up to 4 m (13 ft) tall and weigh as much as 7 tonnes (6.9 tons). A fully grown male Asian elephant may be 3.3 m (11 ft) tall and weigh 5.4 tonnes (5.3 tons). The trunk—an extension of the nose and upper lip—is the elephant's other most obvious feature. It is used for manipulating and lifting, feeding, drinking and spraying water, smelling, touching, and producing trumpeting sounds. Other characteristic features include a pair of tusks, used for defence and for crushing vegetation; thick, pillar-like legs and broad feet to support the massive body; and large ear flaps that act as radiators to keep the elephant cool.

DIFFERENCES BETWEEN AFRICAN AND ASIAN ELEPHANTS

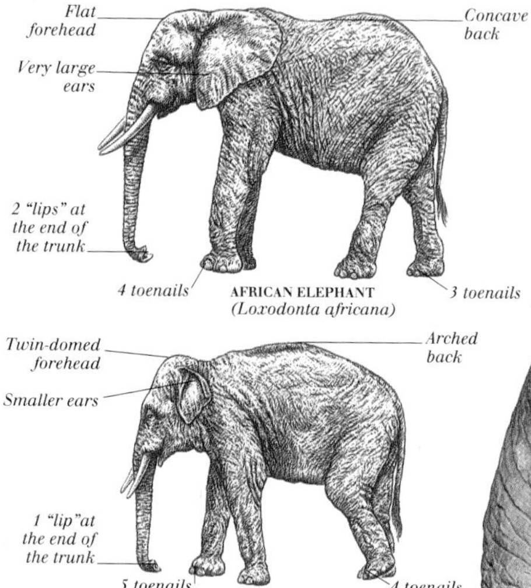

Flat forehead
Concave back
Very large ears
2 "lips" at the end of the trunk
4 toenails
3 toenails
Twin-domed forehead
Arched back
Smaller ears
1 "lip" at the end of the trunk
5 toenails
4 toenails

AFRICAN ELEPHANT *(Loxodonta africana)*

ASIAN ELEPHANT *(Elephas maximus)*

INTERNAL ANATOMY OF A FEMALE ELEPHANT

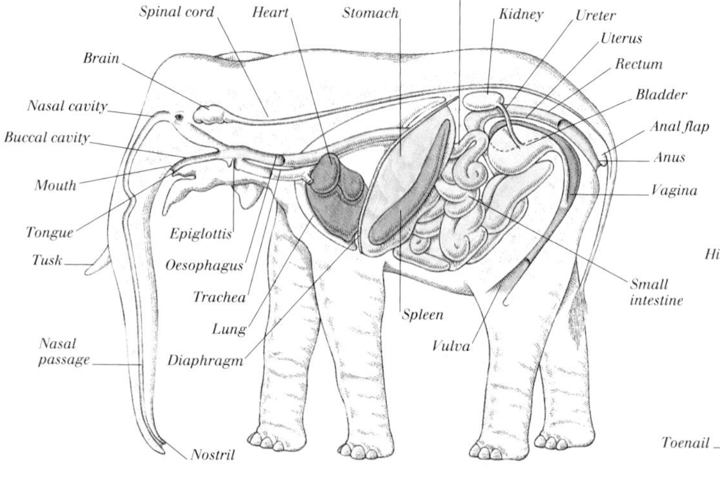

Duodenum
Spinal cord
Heart
Stomach
Kidney
Ureter
Uterus
Rectum
Brain
Bladder
Nasal cavity
Buccal cavity
Anal flap
Anus
Mouth
Vagina
Tongue
Epiglottis
Tusk
Oesophagus
Trachea
Small intestine
Spleen
Lung
Vulva
Nasal passage
Diaphragm
Nostril

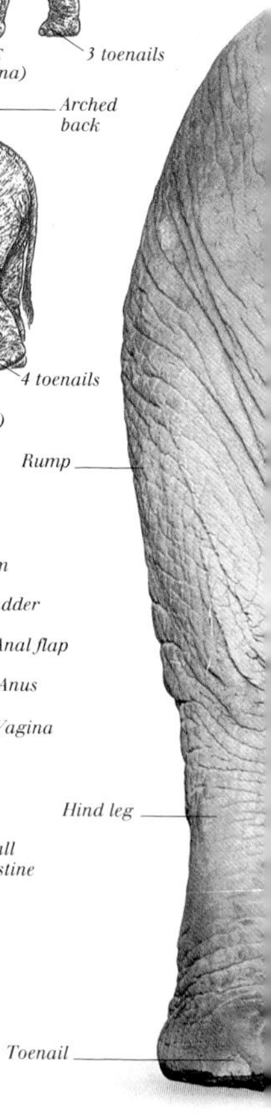

Rump
Hind leg
Toenail

EXTERNAL FEATURES OF A FEMALE AFRICAN ELEPHANT (TUSKS REMOVED)

Flat forehead
Eye
Pinna (ear flap)
Annulus (ring) of trunk
Belly
Foreleg
Trunk (proboscis)
Upper "lip" of trunk
Lower "lip" of trunk

SKULL OF AN ASIAN ELEPHANT

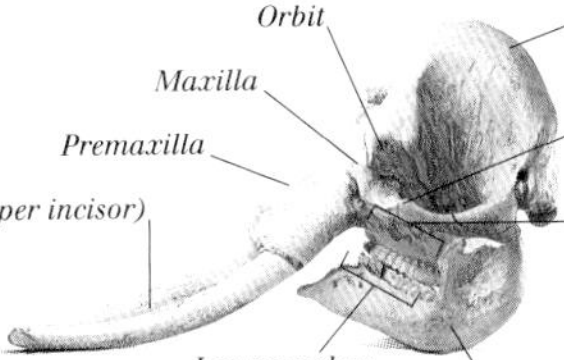
Orbit
Cranium
Maxilla
Jugal bar
Premaxilla
Tusk (upper incisor)
Upper molars
Lower molars
Mandible

SKELETON OF AN AFRICAN ELEPHANT (TUSKS REMOVED)

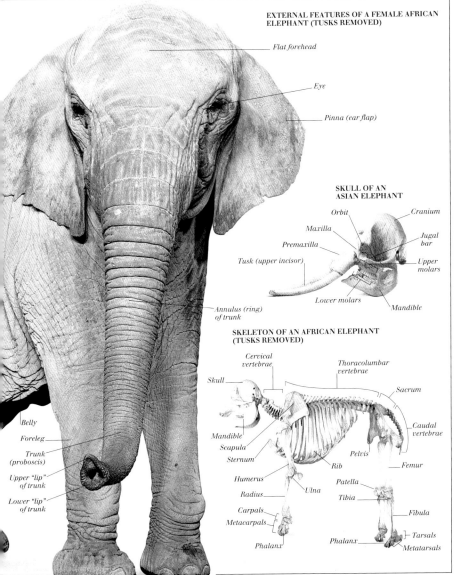

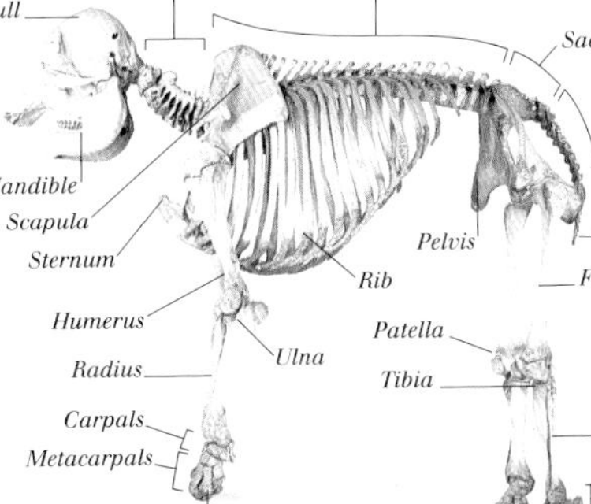
Cervical vertebrae
Thoracolumbar vertebrae
Skull
Sacrum
Caudal vertebrae
Mandible
Scapula
Sternum
Pelvis
Rib
Femur
Humerus
Ulna
Patella
Radius
Tibia
Carpals
Metacarpals
Fibula
Tarsals
Phalanx
Phalanx
Metatarsals

Primates

THE MAMMALIAN ORDER PRIMATES consists of monkeys, apes, and their relatives (including humans). There are two suborders of primates: Prosimii, the primitive primates, which include lemurs, tarsiers, and lorises; and Anthropoidea, the advanced primates, which include monkeys, apes, and humans. The anthropoids are divided into New World monkeys, Old World monkeys, and hominids. New World monkeys typically have wide-apart nostrils that open to the side; and long tails, which are prehensile (grasping) in some species. This group of monkeys lives in South America, and includes marmosets, tamarins, and howler monkeys. Old World monkeys typically have close-set nostrils that open forwards or downwards; and non-prehensile tails. This group of monkeys lives in Africa and Asia, and includes langurs, mandrills, macaques, and baboons. Hominids typically have large brains, and no tail. This group includes the apes—chimpanzees, gibbons, gorillas, and orangutans—and humans.

INTERNAL ANATOMY OF A FEMALE CHIMPANZEE

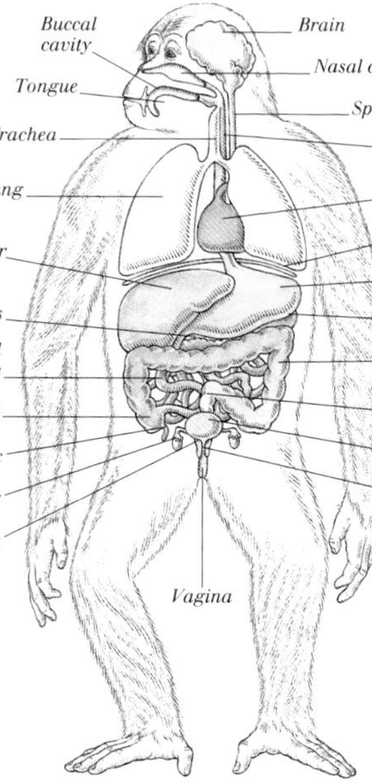
Buccal cavity
Brain
Nasal cavity
Tongue
Spinal cord
Trachea
Oesophagus
Lung
Heart
Diaphrag
Liver
Stomach
Pancreas
Spleen
Small intestine
Large intestine
Caecum
Rectum
Appendix
Bladder
Ovary
Urethra
Uterus
Vagina

SKELETON OF A RHESUS MONKEY

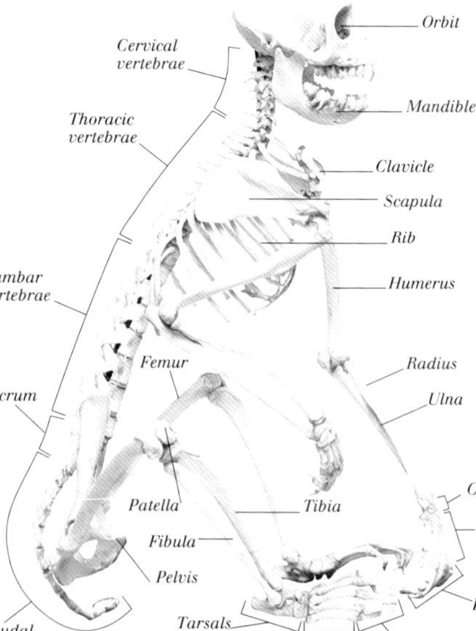
Skull
Orbit
Cervical vertebrae
Mandible
Thoracic vertebrae
Clavicle
Scapula
Rib
Humerus
Lumbar vertebrae
Femur
Radius
Sacrum
Ulna
Carpals
Patella
Tibia
Metacarpals
Fibula
Pelvis
Phalanges
Tarsals
Caudal vertebrae
Metatarsals
Phalanges

SKULL OF A CHIMPANZEE

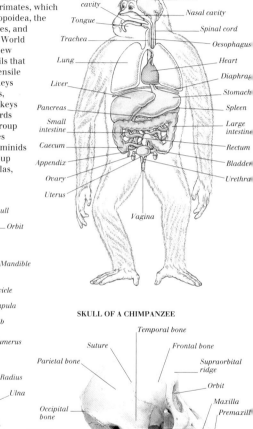

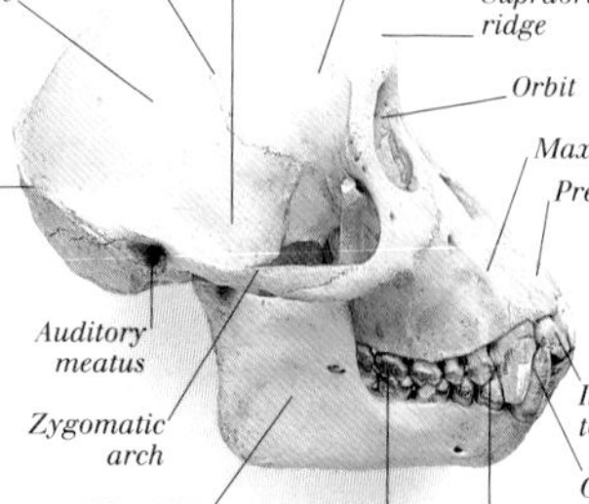
Temporal bone
Suture
Frontal bone
Parietal bone
Supraorbital ridge
Orbit
Maxilla
Premaxill
Occipital bone
Auditory meatus
Incisor tooth
Zygomatic arch
Canine tooth
Mandible
Molar tooth
Premolar tooth

EXAMPLES OF PRIMATES

RING-TAILED LEMUR
(Lemur catta)
A prosimian

MALE RED HOWLER MONKEY
(Alouatta seniculus)
A New World monkey

MALE MANDRILL
(Mandrillus sphinx)
An Old World monkey

CHIMPANZEE
(Pan troglodytes)
An ape

GOLDEN LION TAMARIN
(Leontopithecus rosalia)
A New World monkey

EXTERNAL FEATURES OF A YOUNG GORILLA

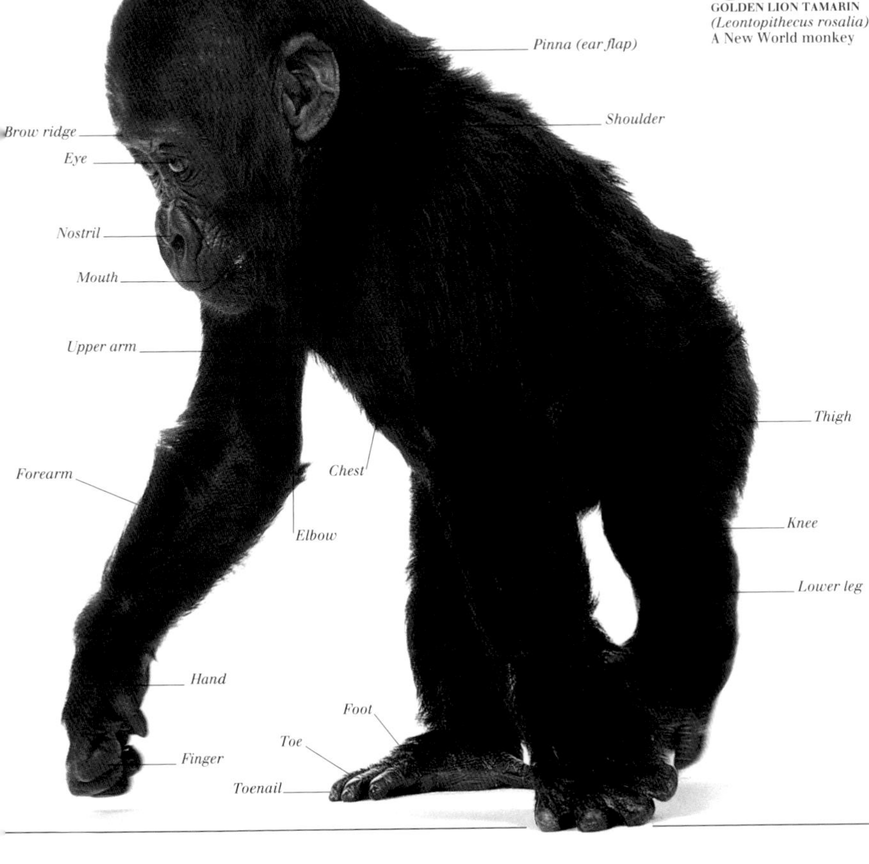
Pinna (ear flap)
Shoulder
Brow ridge
Eye
Nostril
Mouth
Upper arm
Thigh
Forearm
Chest
Elbow
Knee
Lower leg
Hand
Foot
Toe
Finger
Toenail

Dolphins, whales, and seals

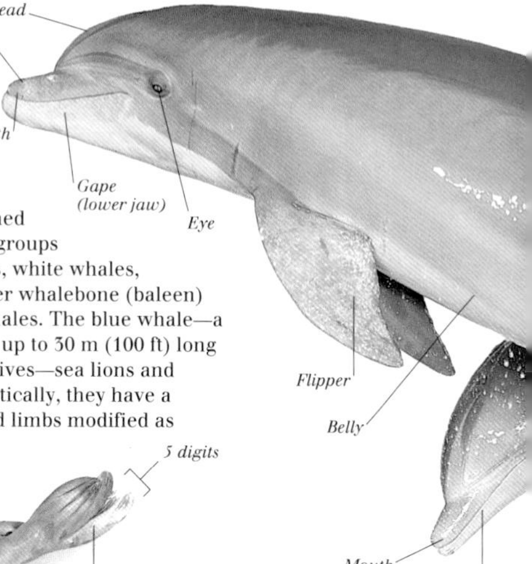
Forehead
Rostrum (beak)
Mouth
Gape (lower jaw)
Eye
Flipper
Belly
Mouth
Gape (lower jaw)

DOLPHINS, WHALES, AND SEALS belong to two orders of mammals adapted to living in water. Dolphins and whales make up the order Cetacea. Typical cetacean features include a streamlined, fish-like shape; forelimbs in the form of flippers; no visible hind limbs; a horizontally flattened tail; and thick blubber under the skin. There are two groups of cetaceans: toothed whales, including sperm whales, white whales, beaked whales, dolphins, and porpoises; and the larger whalebone (baleen) whales, including rorquals, grey whales, and right whales. The blue whale—a rorqual—is the largest living animal: an adult may be up to 30 m (100 ft) long and weigh 130 tonnes (128 tons). Seals and their relatives—sea lions and walruses—make up the order Pinnipedia. Characteristically, they have a streamlined, torpedo-shaped body; forelimbs and hind limbs modified as flippers; thick blubber; and no external ears.

EXTERNAL FEATURES OF A SEAL

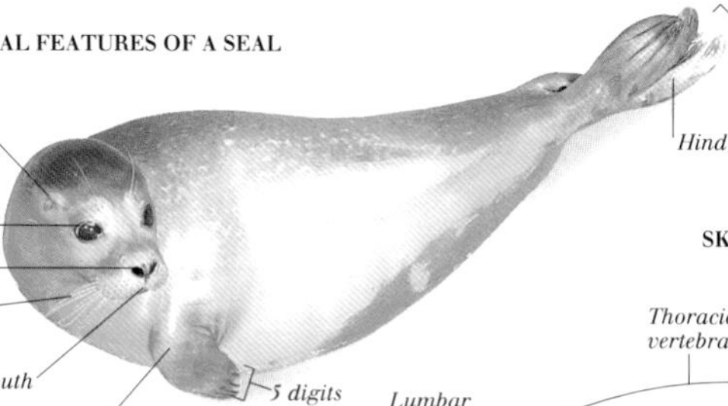
5 digits
Hind flipper
Auditory meatus
Eye
Nostril
Vibrissa (whisker)
Mouth
Front flipper
5 digits

SKELETON OF A SEAL

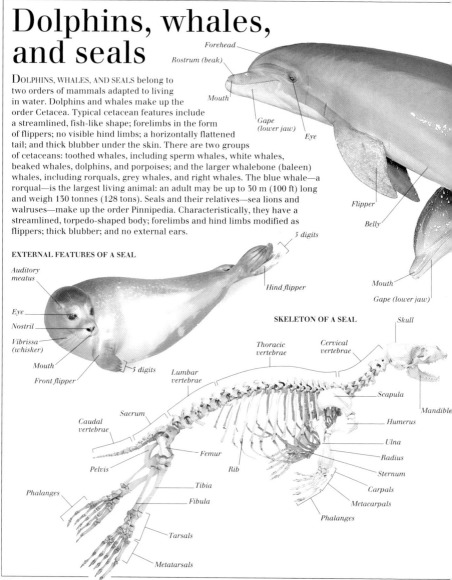

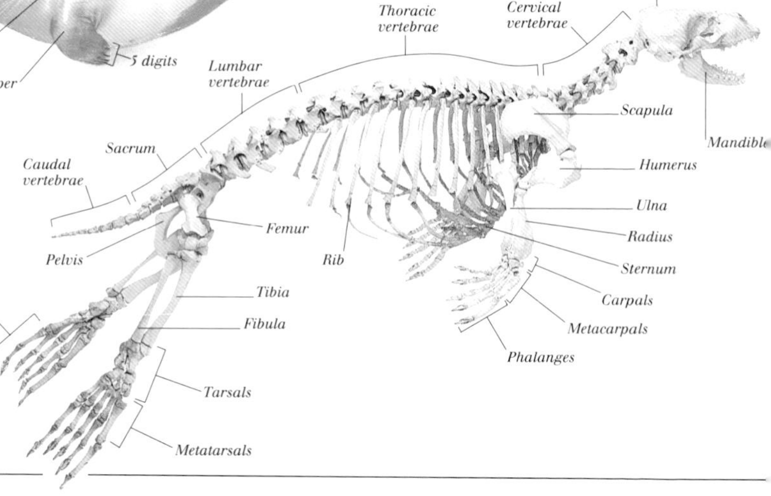
Skull
Cervical vertebrae
Thoracic vertebrae
Lumbar vertebrae
Sacrum
Caudal vertebrae
Scapula
Mandible
Humerus
Ulna
Radius
Sternum
Carpals
Metacarpals
Phalanges
Femur
Pelvis
Rib
Tibia
Fibula
Phalanges
Tarsals
Metatarsals

EXTERNAL FEATURES OF A DOLPHIN

Dorsal fin
Tail
Tail fluke

EXAMPLES OF CETACEANS

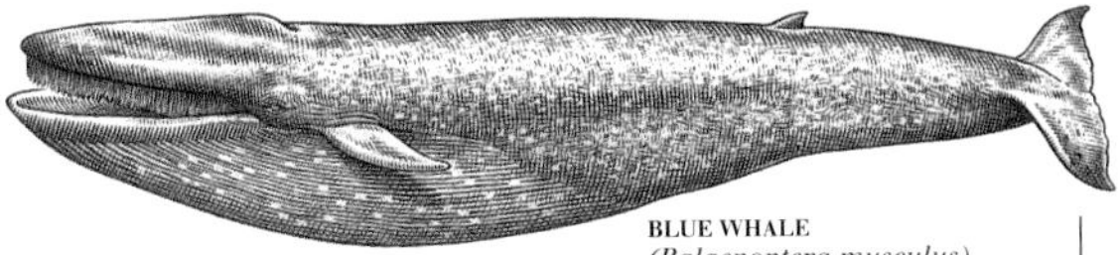

BLUE WHALE
(Balaenoptera musculus)

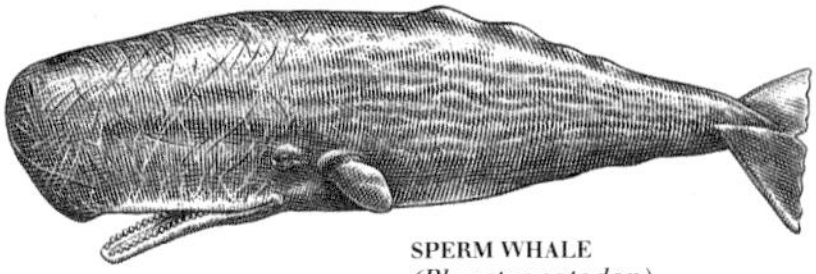

SPERM WHALE
(Physeter catodon)

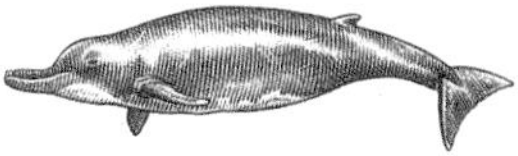

MALE BAIRD'S BEAKED WHALE
(Berardius bairdi)

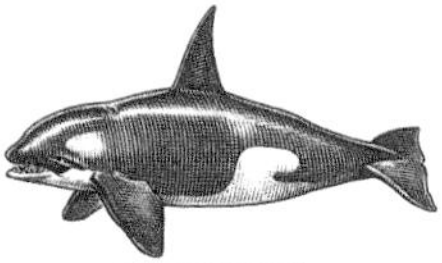

MALE KILLER WHALE
(Orcinus orca)

MALE NARWHAL
(Monodon monoceros)

INTERNAL ANATOMY OF A MALE DOLPHIN

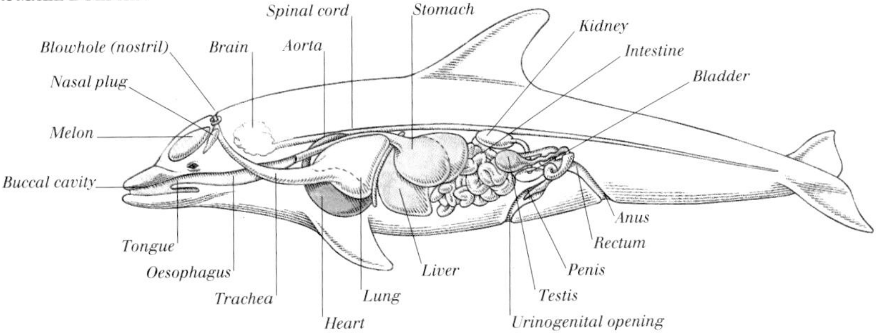
Spinal cord
Stomach
Kidney
Intestine
Bladder
Blowhole (nostril)
Brain
Aorta
Nasal plug
Melon
Buccal cavity
Tongue
Oesophagus
Trachea
Heart
Lung
Liver
Urinogenital opening
Testis
Penis
Rectum
Anus

Marsupials and Monotremes

MARSUPIALS AND MONOTREMES are two orders of mammals that differ from other mammalian groups in the ways that their young develop. The order Marsupalia, the pouched mammals, is made up of kangaroos and their relatives. Typically, marsupials give birth to their young at a very early stage of development. The young then crawls to the mother's pouch (which is on the outside of her abdomen), where it attaches itself to a nipple and remains until fully developed. Most marsupials live in Australia, although the opossums—which are classified as marsupials despite not having a pouch—live in the Americas. The order Monotremata is made up of the platypus and its relatives (the echidnas, or spiny anteaters). The monotremes are primitive mammals that lay eggs, which the mother incubates. The monotremes are found only in Australia and New Guinea.

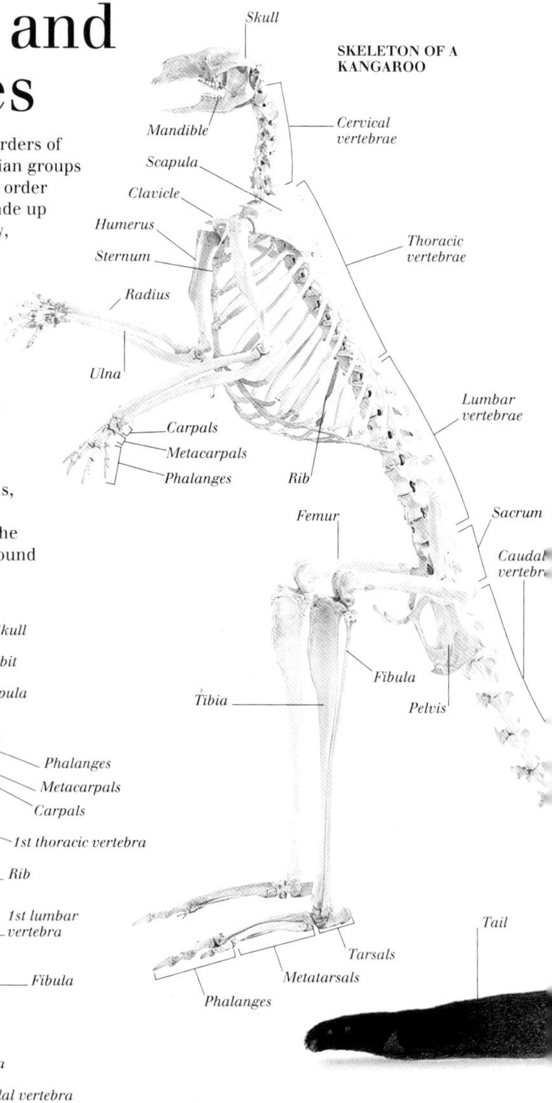
Skull
Mandible
Cervical vertebrae
Scapula
Clavicle
Humerus
Sternum
Thoracic vertebrae
Radius
Ulna
Lumbar vertebrae
Carpals
Metacarpals
Phalanges
Rib
Femur
Sacrum
Caudal vertebr
Fibula
Tibia
Pelvis
Tail
Tarsals
Metatarsals
Phalanges

SKELETON OF A KANGAROO

SKELETON OF A PLATYPUS

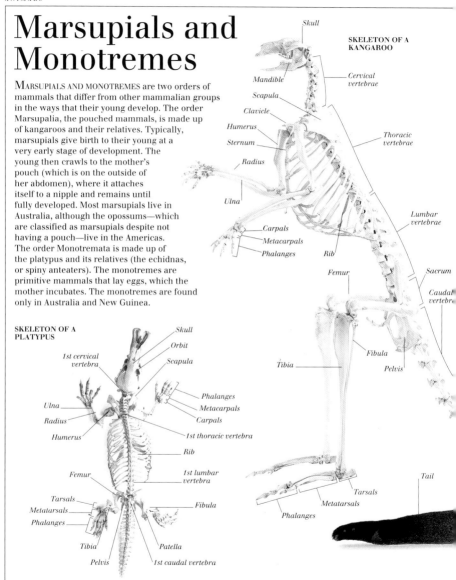

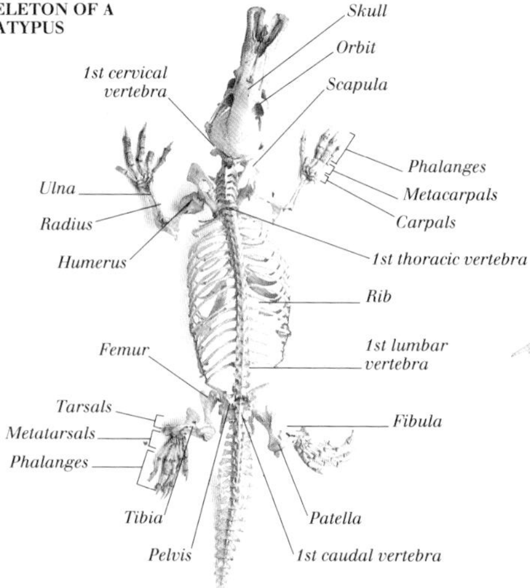
Skull
Orbit
1st cervical vertebra
Scapula
Phalanges
Metacarpals
Carpals
Ulna
Radius
Humerus
1st thoracic vertebra
Rib
Femur
1st lumbar vertebra
Tarsals
Metatarsals
Phalanges
Fibula
Tibia
Patella
Pelvis
1st caudal vertebra

EXAMPLES OF MARSUPIALS AND MONOTREMES

KOALA
(Phascolarctos cinereus)
A marsupial

DUCK-BILLED PLATYPUS
(Ornithorhynchus anatinus)
A monotreme

TASMANIAN DEVIL
(Sarcophilus harrisii)
A marsupial

VIRGINIA OPOSSUM
(Didelphis virginiana)
A marsupial

EXTERNAL FEATURES OF A KANGAROO

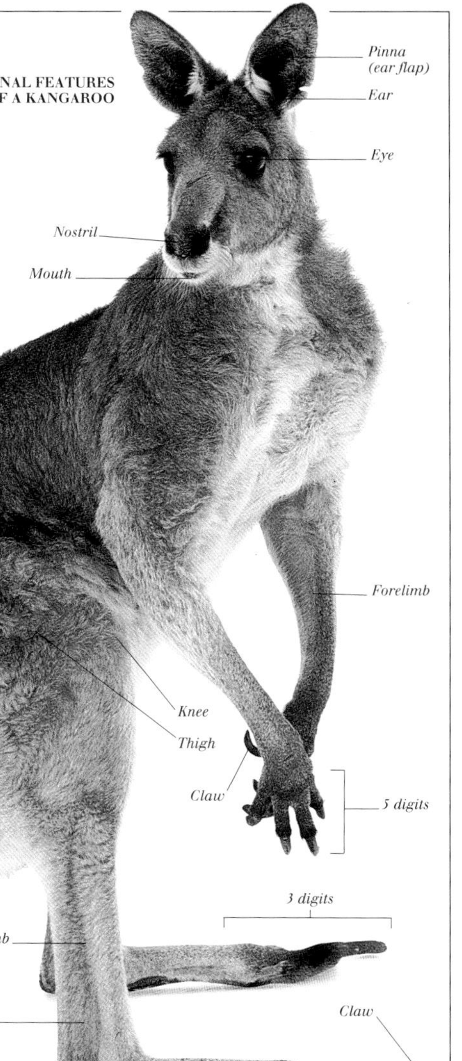
Pinna
(ear flap)
Ear
Eye
Nostril
Mouth
Forelimb
Knee
Thigh
Hip
Claw
5 digits
3 digits
Hind limb
Lower leg
Claw
Foot

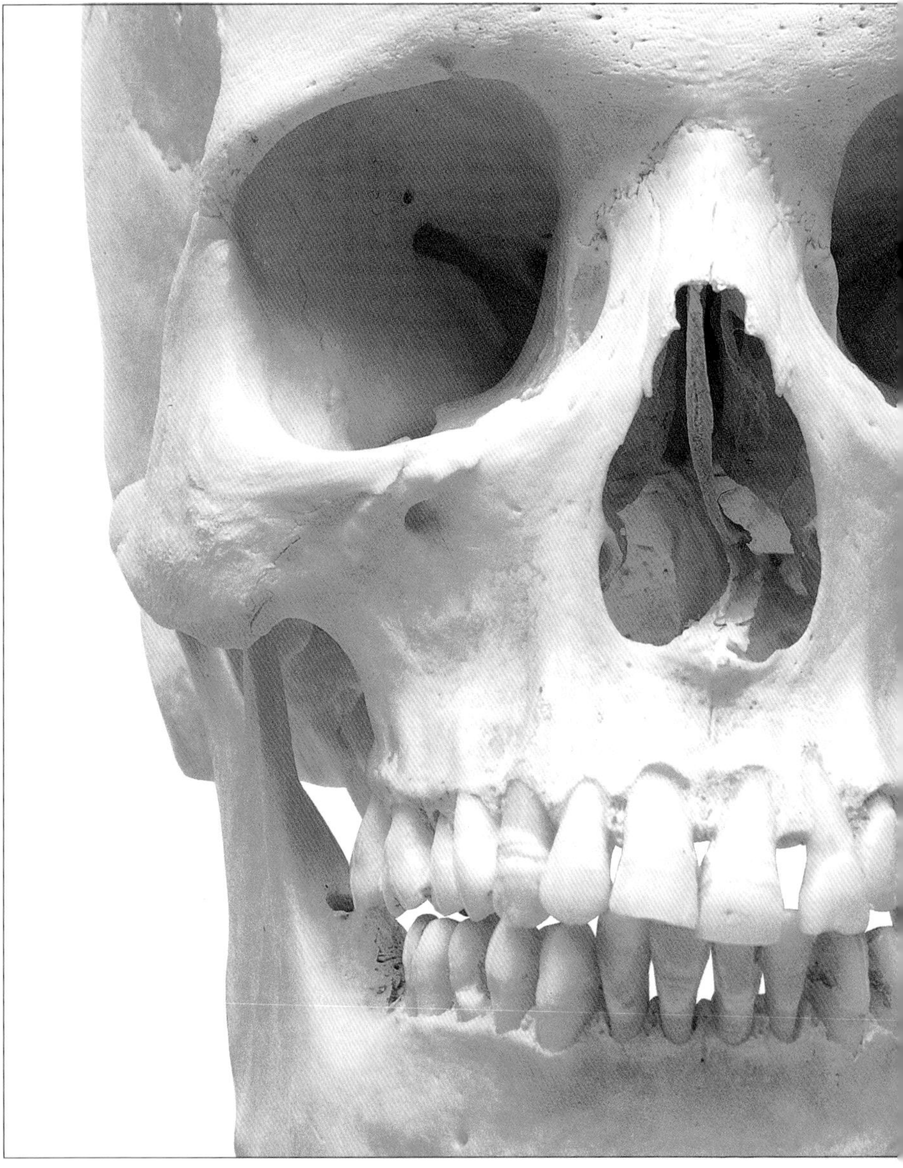

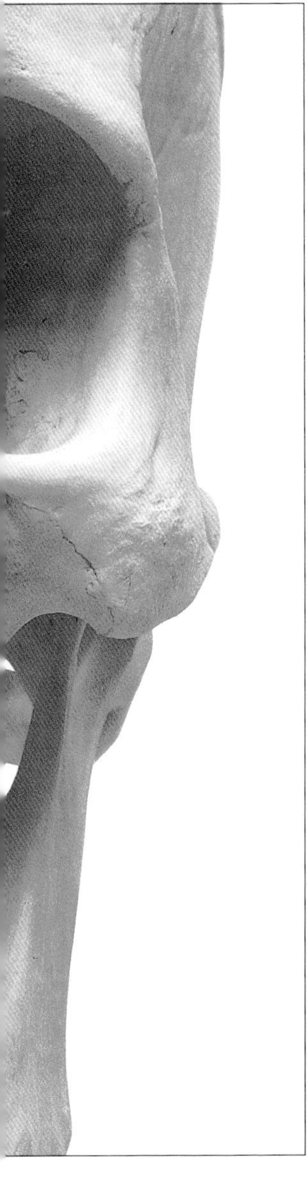

The Human Body

Body features

ALTHOUGH THERE IS enormous variation between the external appearances of humans, all bodies contain the same basic features. The outward form of the human body depends on the size of the skeleton, the shape of the muscles, the thickness of the fat layer beneath the skin, the elasticity or sagginess of the skin, and the person's age and sex. Males tend to be taller than females, with broader shoulders, more body hair, and a different pattern of fat deposits under the skin; the female body tends to be less muscular and has a shallower and wider pelvis to allow for childbirth.

BACK VIEWS OF MALE AND FEMALE

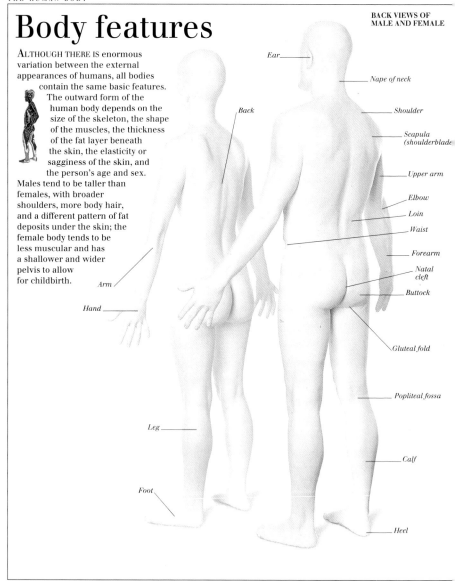

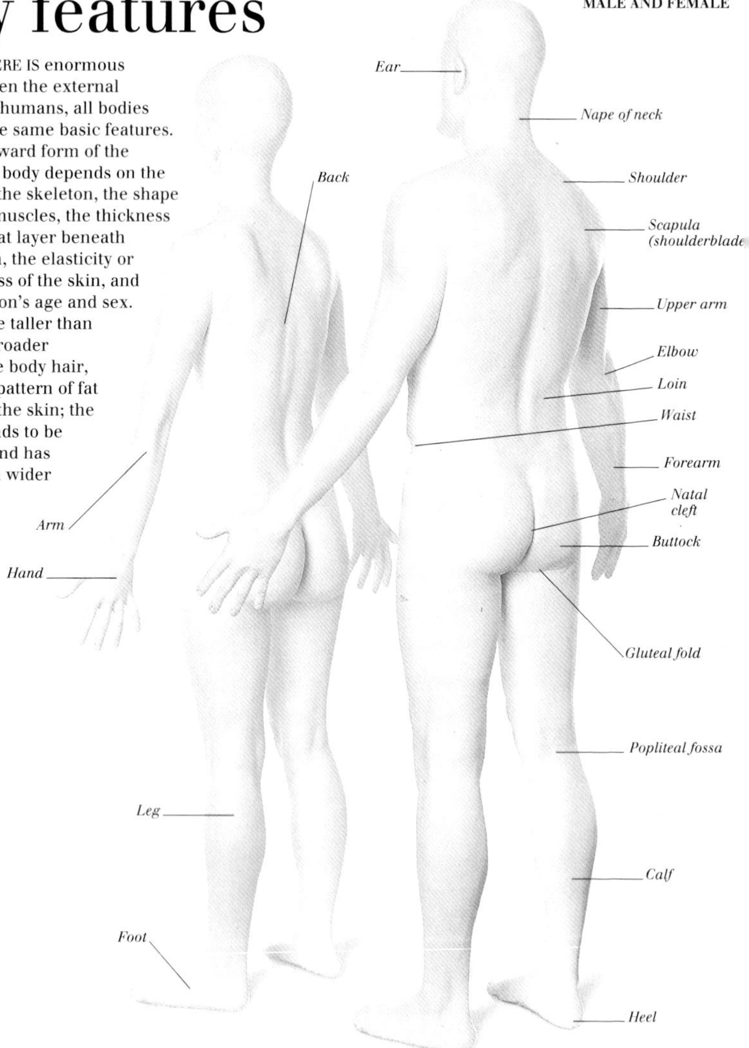
Ear
Nape of neck
Back
Shoulder
Scapula (shoulderblade
Upper arm
Elbow
Loin
Waist
Forearm
Natal cleft
Arm
Buttock
Hand
Gluteal fold
Popliteal fossa
Leg
Calf
Foot
Heel

FRONT VIEWS OF MALE AND FEMALE

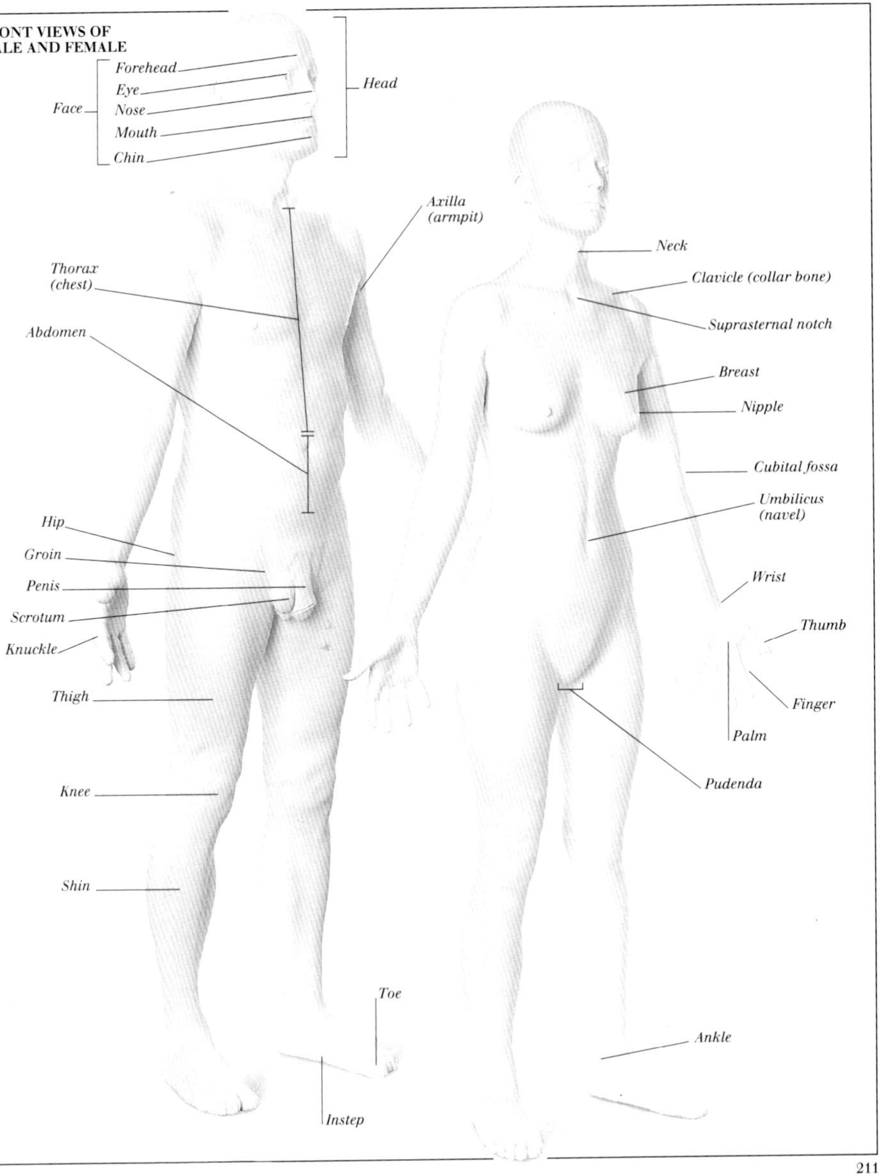
Forehead
Eye
Nose
Mouth
Chin
Face
Head
Axilla (armpit)
Thorax (chest)
Abdomen
Hip
Groin
Penis
Scrotum
Knuckle
Thigh
Knee
Shin
Toe
Instep
Neck
Clavicle (collar bone)
Suprasternal notch
Breast
Nipple
Cubital fossa
Umbilicus (navel)
Wrist
Thumb
Finger
Palm
Pudenda
Ankle

Head

IN A NEWBORN BABY, the head accounts for one-quarter of the total body length; by adulthood, the proportion has reduced to one-eighth. Contained in the head are the body's main sense organs: eyes, ears, olfactory nerves that detect smells, and the taste buds of the tongue. Signals from these organs pass to the body's great coordination centre: the brain, housed in the protective, bony dome of the skull. Hair on the head insulates against heat loss, and adult males also grow thick facial hair. The face has three important openings: two nostrils through which air passes, and the mouth, which takes in nourishment and helps form speech. Although all heads are basically similar, differences in the size, shape, and colour of features produce an infinite variety of appearances.

SIDE VIEW OF EXTERNAL FEATURES OF HEAD

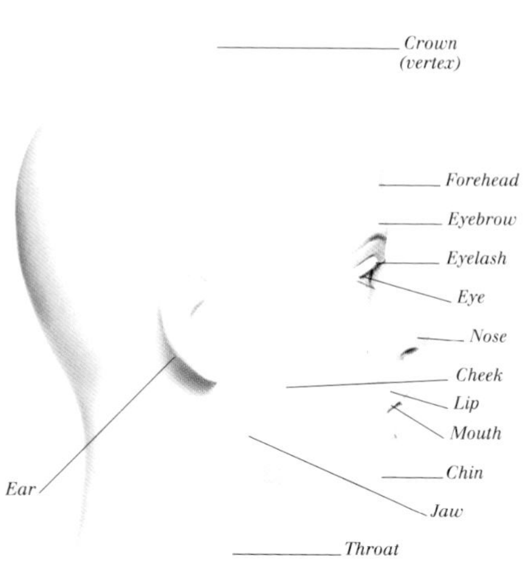
Crown (vertex)
Forehead
Eyebrow
Eyelash
Eye
Nose
Cheek
Lip
Mouth
Chin
Jaw
Throat
Ear

SECTION THROUGH HEAD

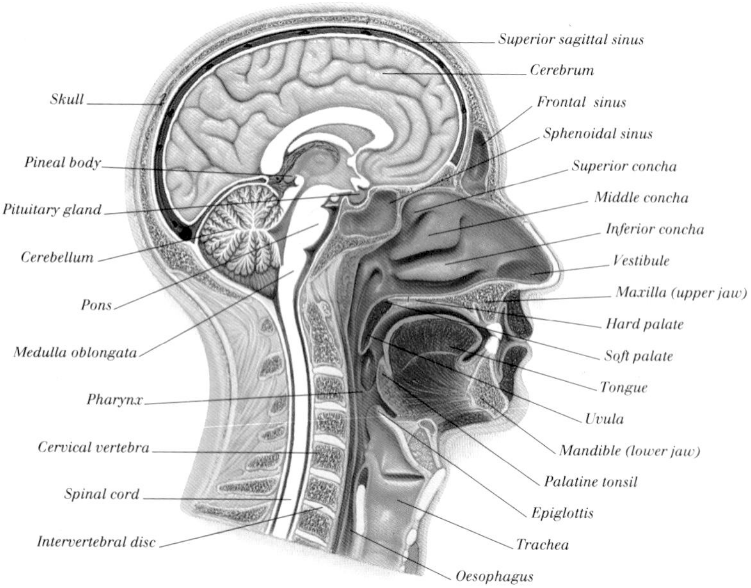
Superior sagittal sinus
Cerebrum
Frontal sinus
Sphenoidal sinus
Superior concha
Middle concha
Inferior concha
Vestibule
Maxilla (upper jaw)
Hard palate
Soft palate
Tongue
Uvula
Mandible (lower jaw)
Palatine tonsil
Epiglottis
Trachea
Oesophagus
Skull
Pineal body
Pituitary gland
Cerebellum
Pons
Medulla oblongata
Pharynx
Cervical vertebra
Spinal cord
Intervertebral disc

FRONT VIEW OF EXTERNAL FEATURES OF HEAD

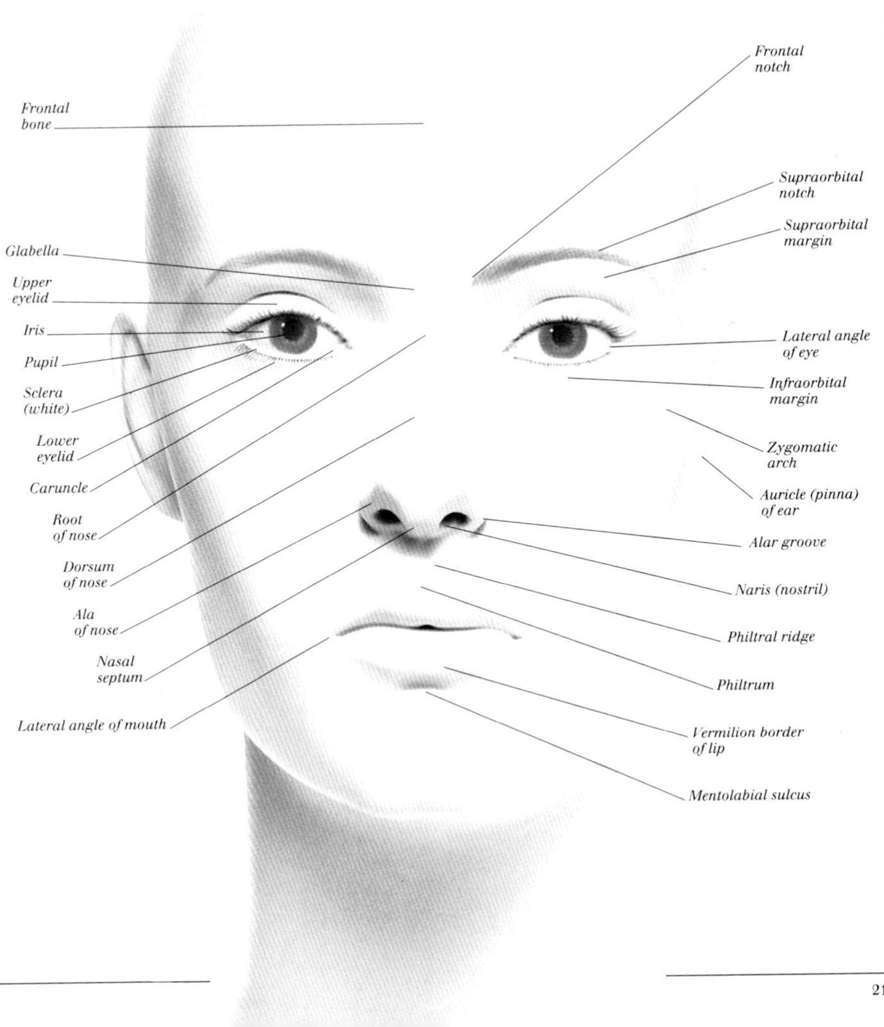

Frontal bone
Glabella
Upper eyelid
Iris
Pupil
Sclera (white)
Lower eyelid
Caruncle
Root of nose
Dorsum of nose
Ala of nose
Nasal septum
Lateral angle of mouth
Frontal notch
Supraorbital notch
Supraorbital margin
Lateral angle of eye
Infraorbital margin
Zygomatic arch
Auricle (pinna) of ear
Alar groove
Naris (nostril)
Philtral ridge
Philtrum
Vermilion border of lip
Mentolabial sulcus

Body organs

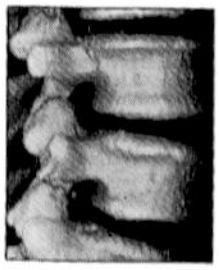

ALL THE VITAL BODY ORGANS except for the brain are enclosed within the trunk or torso (the body apart from the head and limbs). The trunk contains two large cavities separated by a muscular sheet called the diaphragm. The upper cavity, known as the thorax or chest cavity, contains the heart and lungs. The lower cavity, called the abdominal cavity, contains the stomach, intestines, liver, and pancreas, which all play a role in digesting food. Also within the trunk are the kidneys and bladder, which are part of the urinary system, and the reproductive organs, which hold the seeds of new human life. Modern imaging techniques, such as contrast X-rays and different types of scans, make it possible to see and study body organs without the need to cut through their protective coverings of skin, fat, muscle, and bone.

MAJOR INTERNAL STRUCTURES

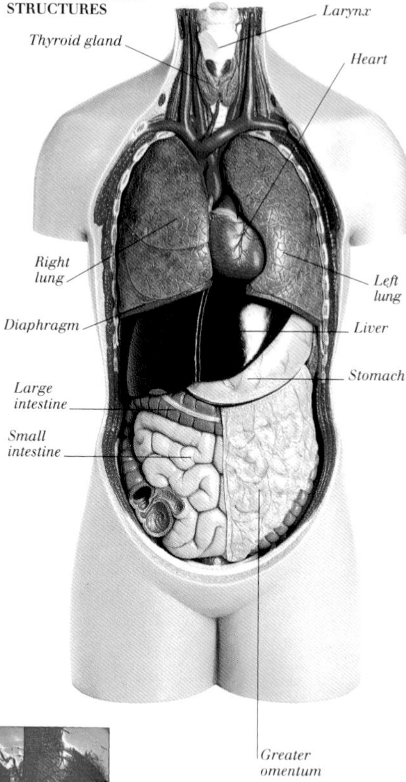
Larynx
Thyroid gland
Heart
Right lung
Left lung
Diaphragm
Liver
Stomach
Large intestine
Small intestine
Greater omentum

IMAGING THE BODY

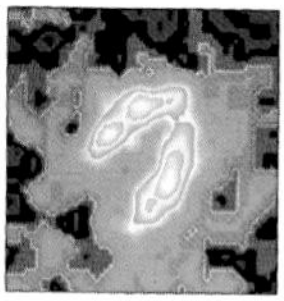

SCINTIGRAM OF HEART CHAMBERS

ANGIOGRAM OF RIGHT LUNG

CONTRAST X-RAY OF GALLBLADDER

SCINTIGRAM OF NERVOUS SYSTEM

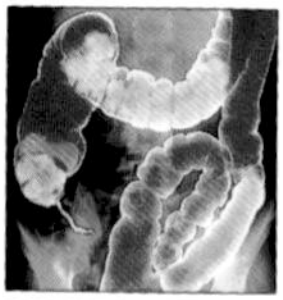

DOUBLE CONTRAST X-RAY OF COLON

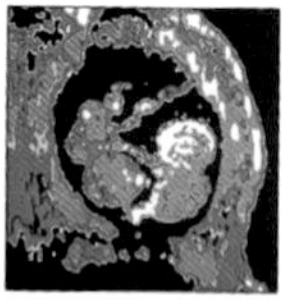

ULTRASOUND SCAN OF TWINS IN UTERUS

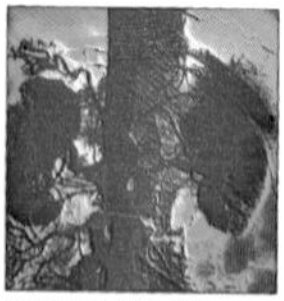

ANGIOGRAM OF KIDNEYS

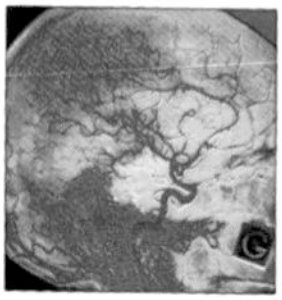

ANGIOGRAM OF ARTERIES OF HEAD

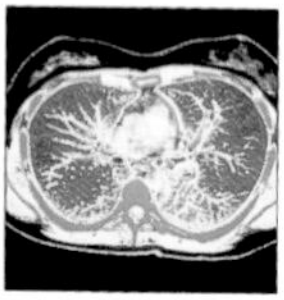

CT SCAN THROUGH FEMALE CHEST

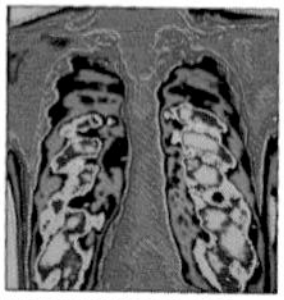

THERMOGRAM OF CHEST REGION

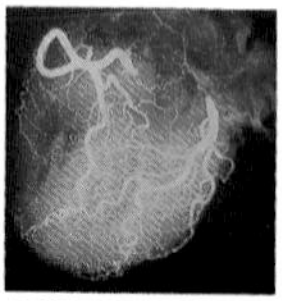

ANGIOGRAM OF ARTERIES OF HEART

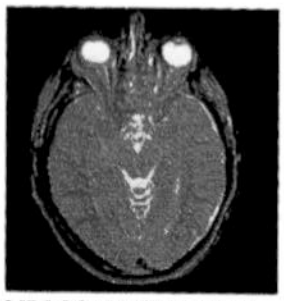

MRI SCAN THROUGH HEAD AT EYE LEVEL

CHEST AND ABDOMINAL CAVITIES WITH SOME ORGANS REMOVED

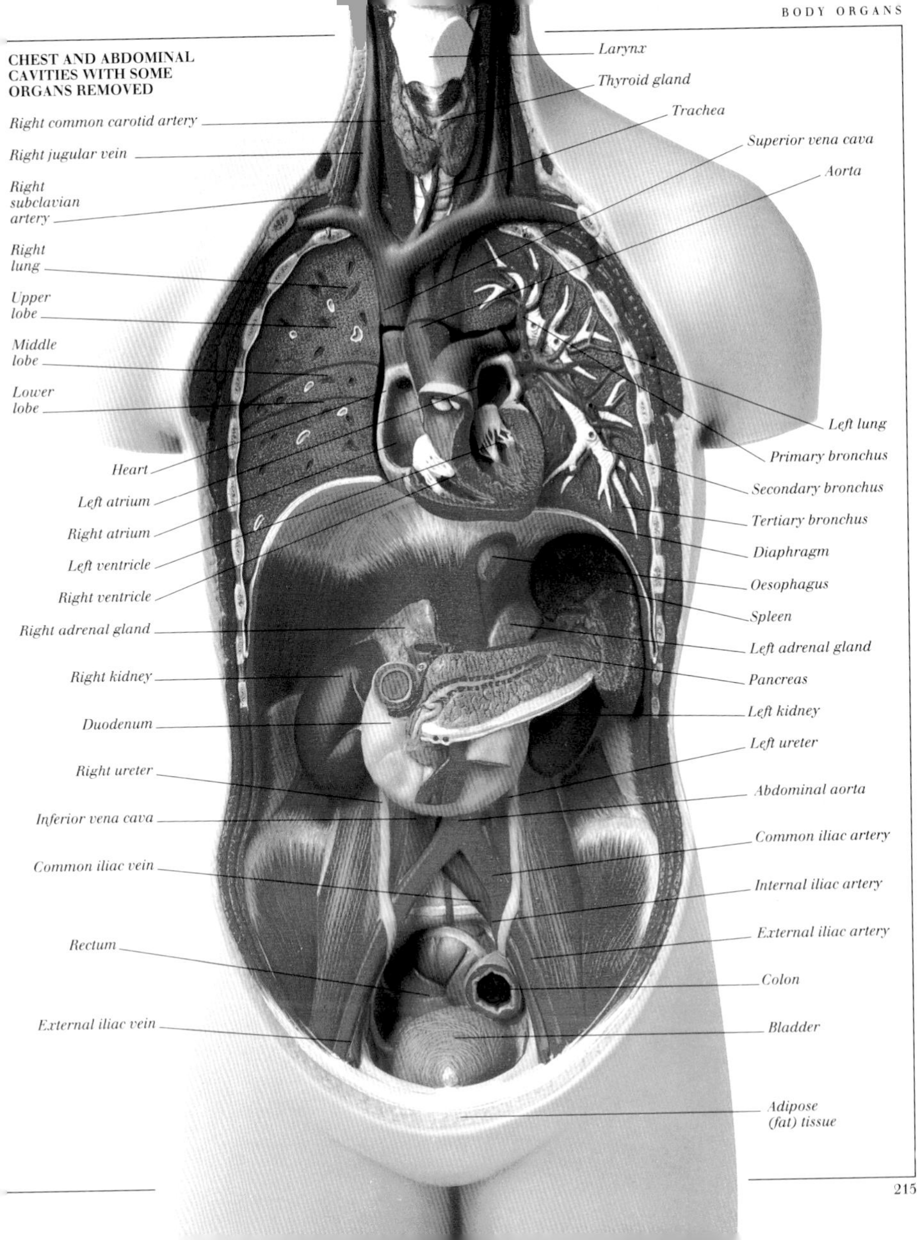
Larynx
Thyroid gland
Trachea
Superior vena cava
Aorta
Right common carotid artery
Right jugular vein
Right subclavian artery
Right lung
Upper lobe
Middle lobe
Lower lobe
Heart
Left atrium
Right atrium
Left ventricle
Right ventricle
Right adrenal gland
Right kidney
Duodenum
Right ureter
Inferior vena cava
Common iliac vein
Rectum
External iliac vein
Left lung
Primary bronchus
Secondary bronchus
Tertiary bronchus
Diaphragm
Oesophagus
Spleen
Left adrenal gland
Pancreas
Left kidney
Left ureter
Abdominal aorta
Common iliac artery
Internal iliac artery
External iliac artery
Colon
Bladder
Adipose (fat) tissue

Body cells

EVERYONE IS MADE UP OF BILLIONS OF CELLS, which are the basic structural units of the body. Bones, muscles, nerves, skin, blood, and all other body tissues are formed from different types of cells. Each cell has a specific function but works with other types of cells to perform the enormous number of tasks needed to sustain life. Most body cells have a similar basic structure. Each cell has an outer layer (called the cell membrane) and contains a fluid material (cytoplasm). Within the cytoplasm are many specialized structures (organelles). The most important organelle is the nucleus, which contains vital genetic material and acts as the cell's control centre.

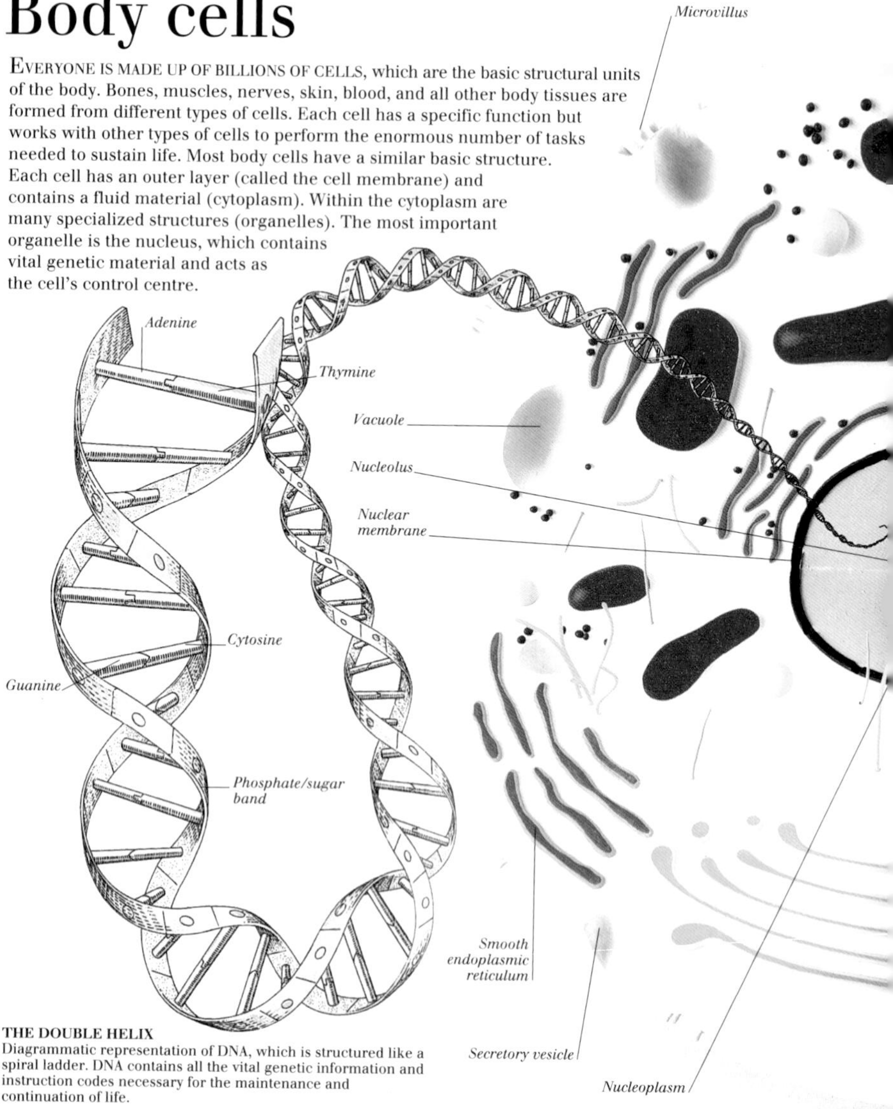
Microvillus
Adenine
Thymine
Vacuole
Nucleolus
Nuclear membrane
Cytosine
Guanine
Phosphate/sugar band
Smooth endoplasmic reticulum
Secretory vesicle
Nucleoplasm

THE DOUBLE HELIX
Diagrammatic representation of DNA, which is structured like a spiral ladder. DNA contains all the vital genetic information and instruction codes necessary for the maintenance and continuation of life.

GENERALIZED HUMAN CELL

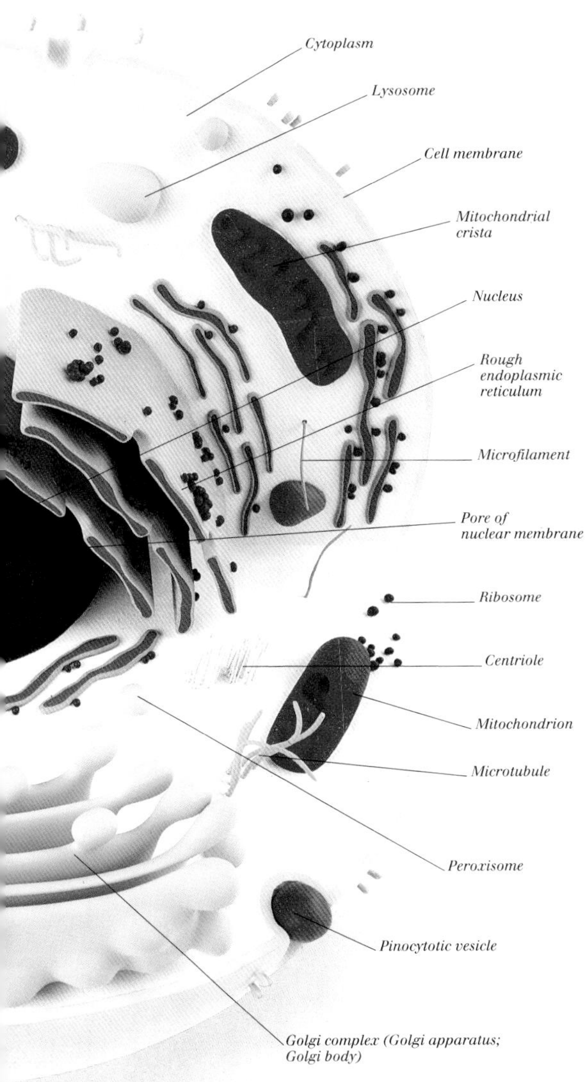
Cytoplasm
Lysosome
Cell membrane
Mitochondrial crista
Nucleus
Rough endoplasmic reticulum
Microfilament
Pore of nuclear membrane
Ribosome
Centriole
Mitochondrion
Microtubule
Peroxisome
Pinocytotic vesicle
Golgi complex (Golgi apparatus; Golgi body)

TYPES OF CELLS

BONE-FORMING CELL

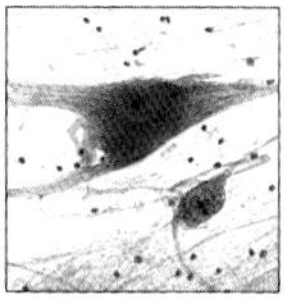
NERVE CELLS IN SPINAL CORD

SPERM CELLS IN SEMEN

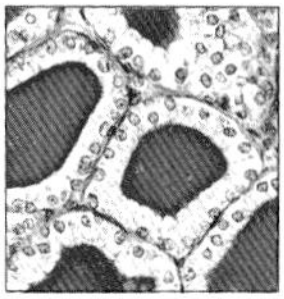
SECRETORY THYROID GLAND CELLS

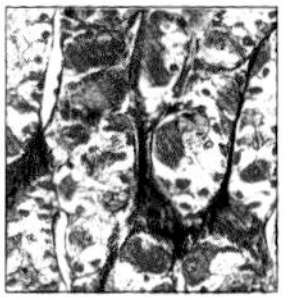
ACID-SECRETING STOMACH CELLS

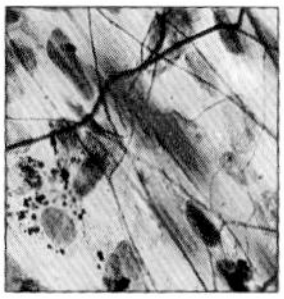
CONNECTIVE TISSUE CELLS

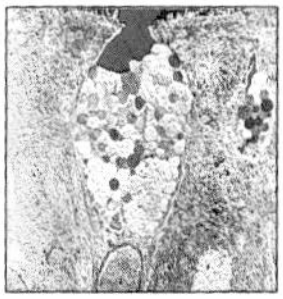
MUCUS-SECRETING DUODENAL CELLS

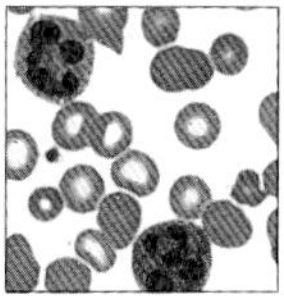
RED AND TWO WHITE BLOOD CELLS

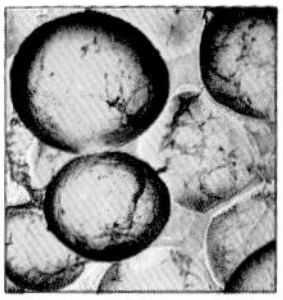
FAT CELLS IN ADIPOSE TISSUE

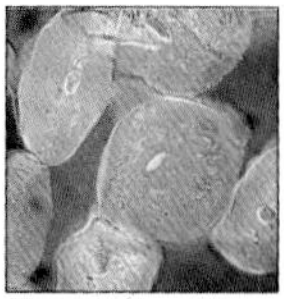
EPITHELIAL CELLS IN CHEEK

Skeleton

THE SKELETON IS A MOBILE FRAMEWORK made up of 206 bones, approximately half of which are in the hands and feet. Although individual bones are rigid, the skeleton as a whole is remarkably flexible and allows the human body a huge range of movement. The skeleton serves as an anchorage for the skeletal muscles, and as a protective cage for the body's internal organs. Female bones are usually smaller and lighter than male bones, and the female pelvis is shallower and has a wider cavity.

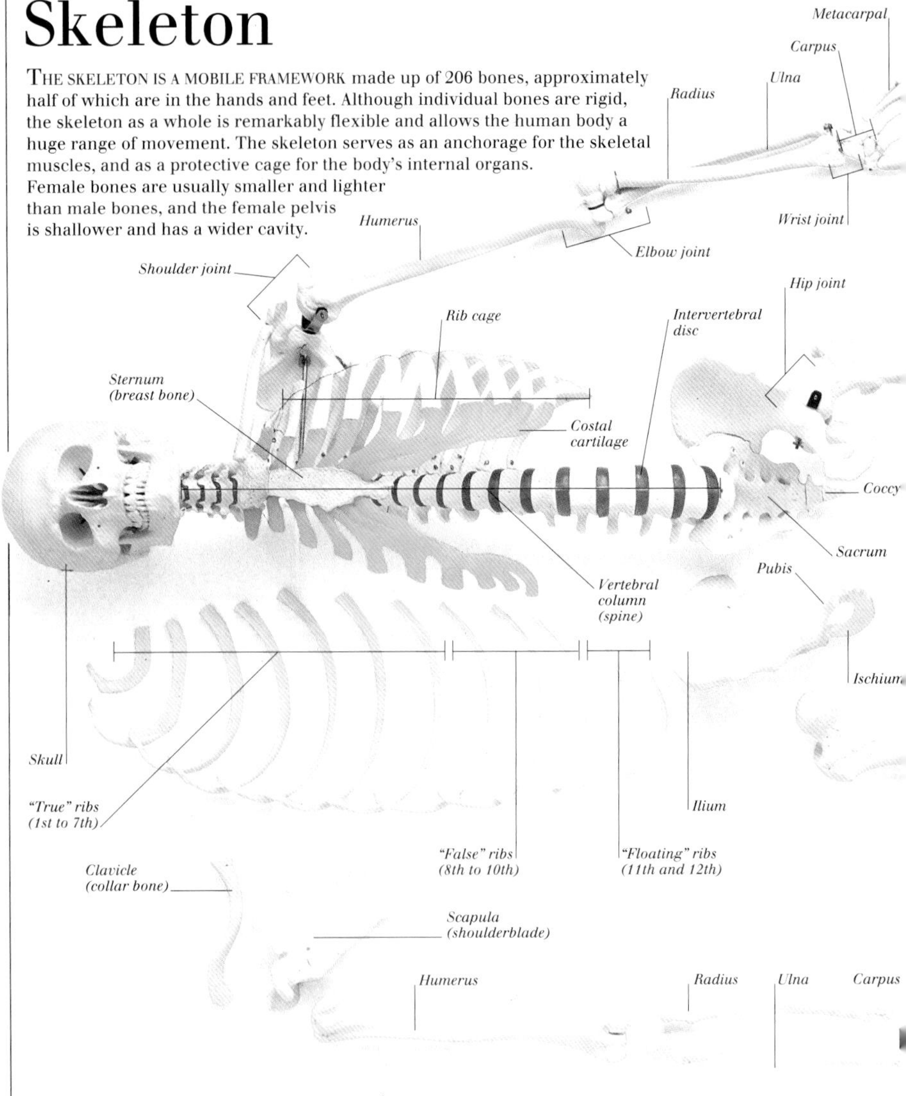

Metacarpal
Carpus
Ulna
Radius
Wrist joint
Humerus
Elbow joint
Shoulder joint
Hip joint
Rib cage
Intervertebral disc
Sternum (breast bone)
Costal cartilage
Coccy
Sacrum
Pubis
Vertebral column (spine)
Ischium
Skull
Ilium
"True" ribs (1st to 7th)
"False" ribs (8th to 10th)
"Floating" ribs (11th and 12th)
Clavicle (collar bone)
Scapula (shoulderblade)
Humerus
Radius
Ulna
Carpus

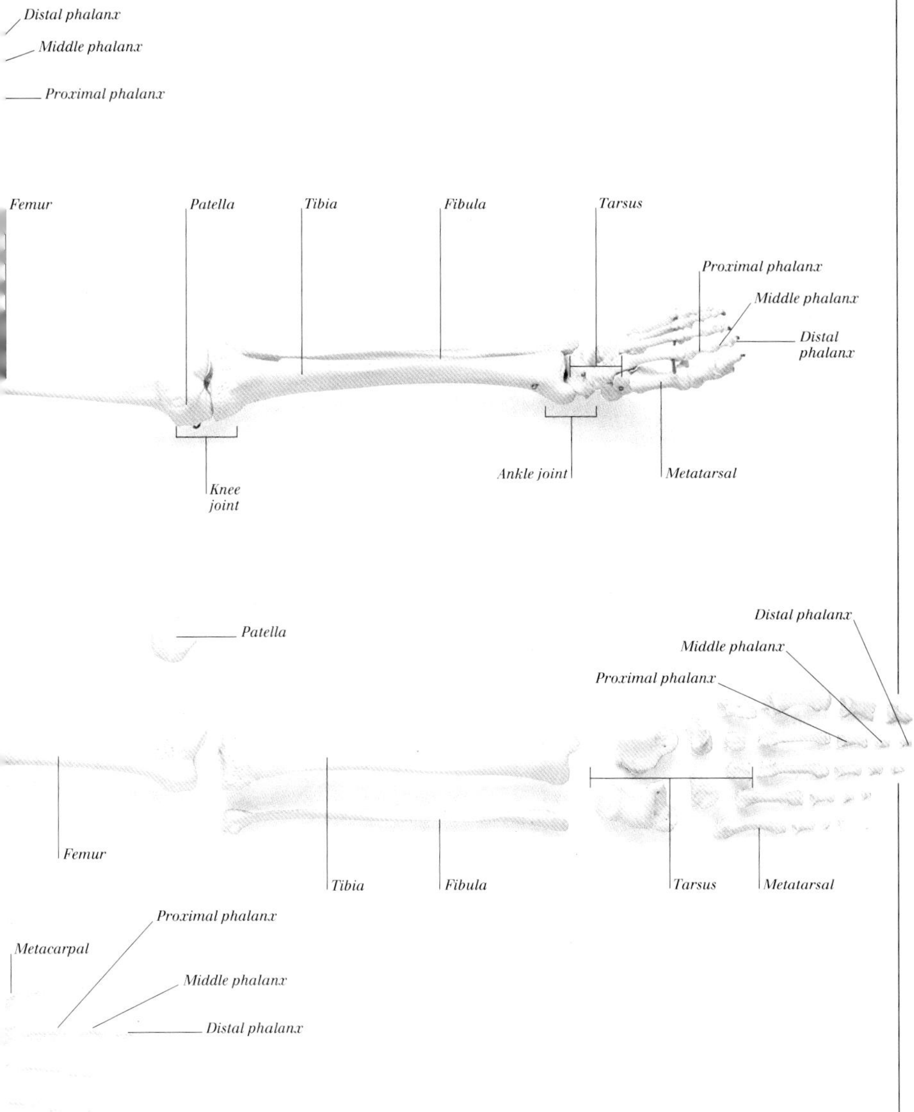
Distal phalanx
Middle phalanx
Proximal phalanx
Femur
Patella
Tibia
Fibula
Tarsus
Proximal phalanx
Middle phalanx
Distal phalanx
Knee joint
Ankle joint
Metatarsal
Patella
Distal phalanx
Middle phalanx
Proximal phalanx
Femur
Tibia
Fibula
Tarsus
Metatarsal
Proximal phalanx
Metacarpal
Middle phalanx
Distal phalanx

Skull

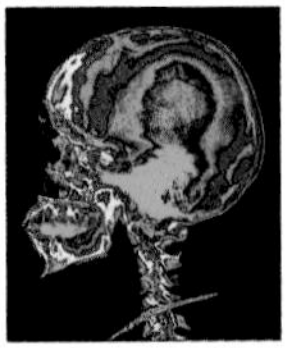

THE SKULL is the most complicated bony structure of the body but every feature serves a purpose. Internally, the main hollow chamber of the skull has three levels that support the brain, with every bump and hollow corresponding to the shape of the brain. Underneath and towards the back of the skull is a large round hole, the foramen magnum, through which the spinal cord passes. To the front of this are many smaller openings through which nerves, arteries, and veins pass to and from the brain. The roof of the skull is formed from four thin, curved bones that are firmly fixed together from the age of about two years. At the front of the skull are the two orbits, which contain the eyeballs, and a central hole for the airway of the nose. The jaw bone hinges on either side at ear level.

RIGHT SIDE VIEW OF A FETAL SKULL

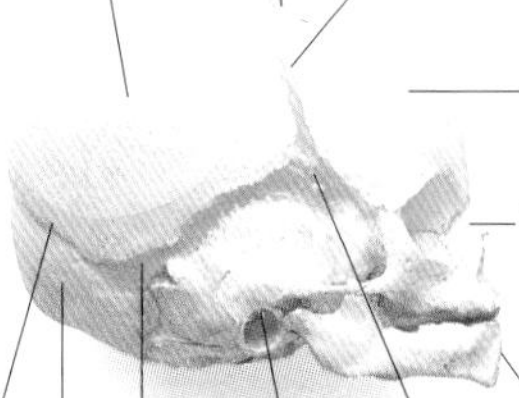
Anterior fontanelle
Parietal bone
Coronal suture
Frontal bone
Nasal bon
Mental symphysi
Lambdoid suture
Occipital bone
Mastoid fontanelle
External auditory meatus
Sphenoidal fontanelle

RIGHT SIDE VIEW OF SKULL

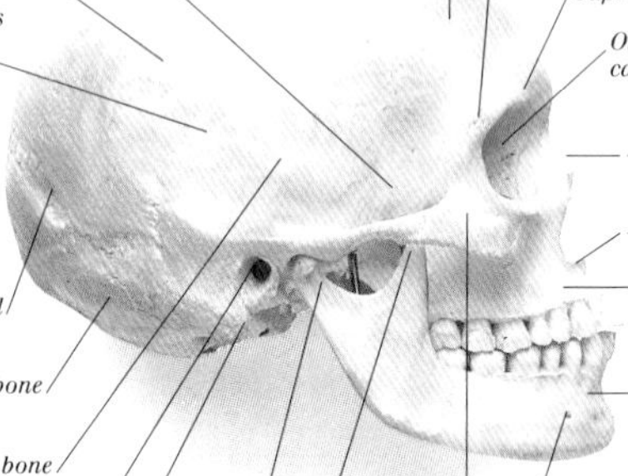
Frontal bone
Coronal suture
Greater wing of sphenoid bone
Frontozygomatic suture
Parietal bone
Supraorbital margin
Squamous suture
Orbital cavity
Nasal bone
Anterior nasal spine
Maxilla (upper jaw)
Lambdoid suture
Occipital bone
Mandible (lower jaw)
Temporal bone
External auditory meatus
Condyle
Mastoid process
Zygomatic bone
Coronoid process
Mental foramen

VIEW OF SKULL FROM BELOW

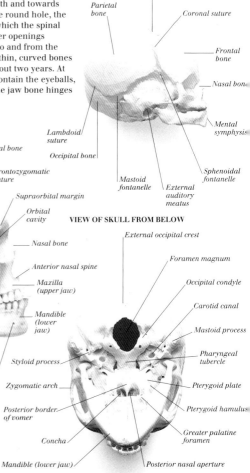

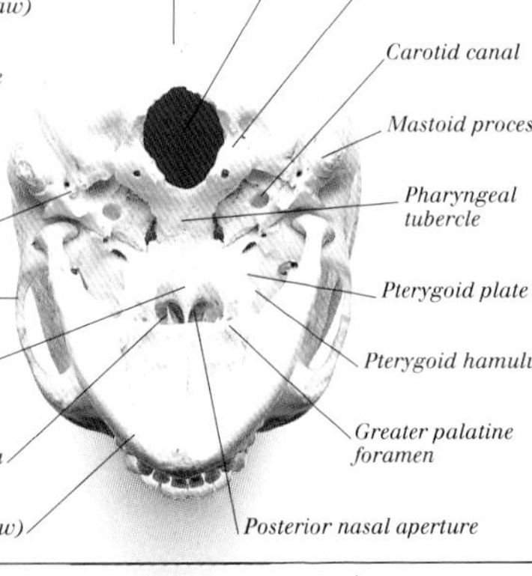
External occipital crest
Foramen magnum
Occipital condyle
Carotid canal
Mastoid process
Styloid process
Pharyngeal tubercle
Zygomatic arch
Pterygoid plate
Posterior border of vomer
Pterygoid hamulus
Greater palatine foramen
Concha
Mandible (lower jaw)
Posterior nasal aperture

FRONT VIEW OF SKULL

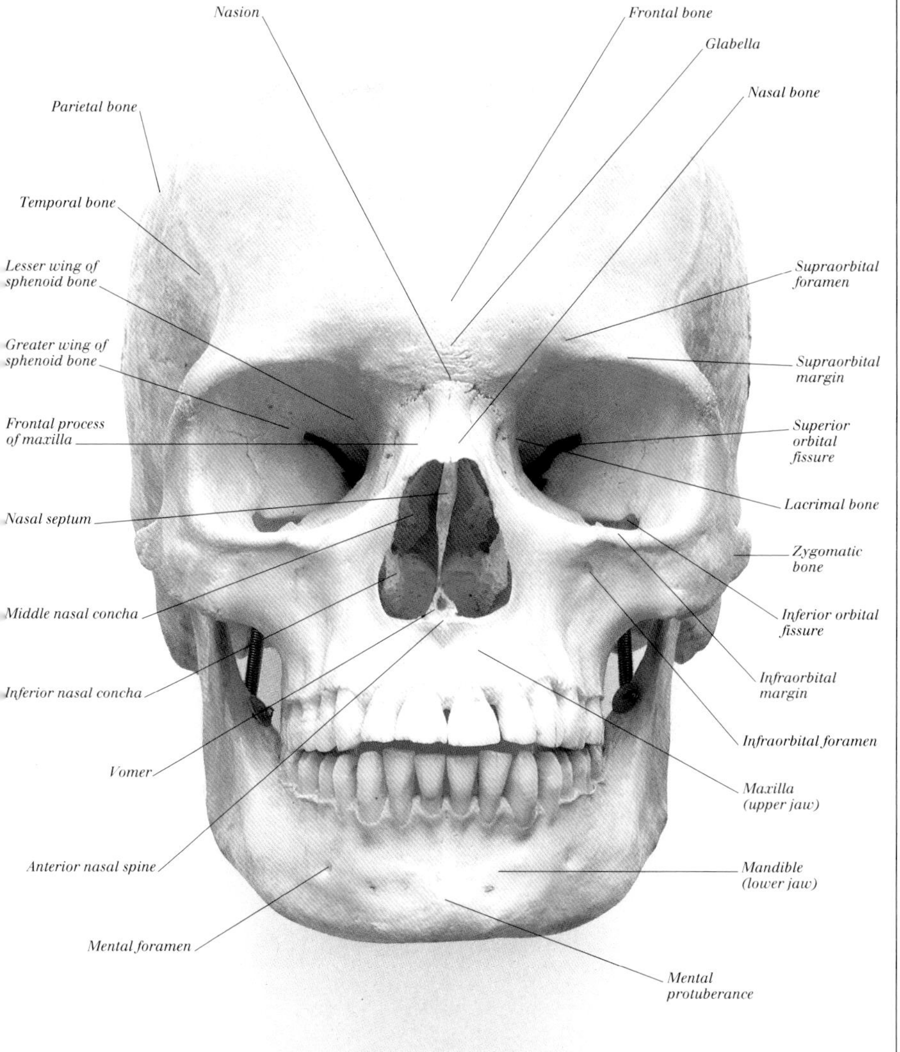
Nasion
Frontal bone
Glabella
Nasal bone
Parietal bone
Temporal bone
Lesser wing of sphenoid bone
Greater wing of sphenoid bone
Frontal process of maxilla
Nasal septum
Middle nasal concha
Inferior nasal concha
Vomer
Anterior nasal spine
Mental foramen
Supraorbital foramen
Supraorbital margin
Superior orbital fissure
Lacrimal bone
Zygomatic bone
Inferior orbital fissure
Infraorbital margin
Infraorbital foramen
Maxilla (upper jaw)
Mandible (lower jaw)
Mental protuberance

Spine

THE SPINE (OR VERTEBRAL COLUMN) has two main functions: it serves as a protective surrounding for the delicate spinal cord and forms the supporting back bone of the skeleton. The spine consists of 24 separate differently shaped bones (vertebrae) with a curved, triangular bone (the sacrum) at the bottom. The sacrum is made up of fused vertebrae; at its lower end is a small tail-like structure made up of tiny bones collectively called the coccyx. Between each pair of vertebrae is a disc of cartilage that cushions the bones during movement. The top two vertebrae differ in appearance from the others and work as a pair: the first, called the atlas, rotates around a stout vertical peg on the second, the axis. This arrangement allows the skull to move freely up and down, and from side to side.

SPINE DIVIDED INTO VERTEBRAL SECTIONS

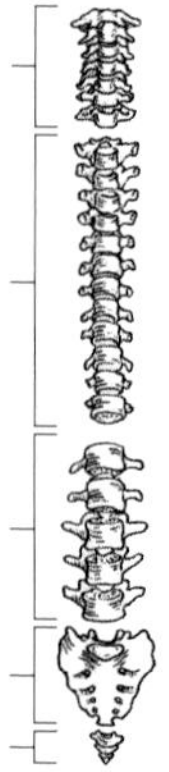
FRONT
Cervical vertebrae
Thoracic vertebrae
Lumbar vertebrae
Sacral vertebrae
Coccygeal vertebrae

TYPES OF VERTEBRAE (VIEWED FROM ABOVE)

ATLAS

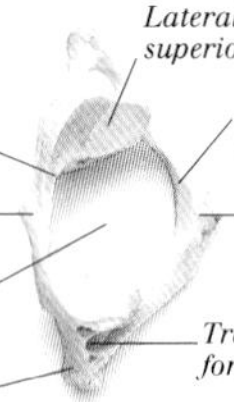
Lateral mass with superior articular facet
Anterior arch
Posterior arch
Anterior tubercle
Posterior tubercle
Vertebral foramen
Transverse foramen
Transverse process

AXIS

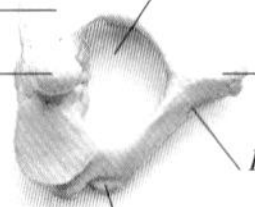
Vertebral foramen
Facet
Dens
Spinous process
Lamina
Transverse process and foramen

CERVICAL VERTEBRA

Superior articular process
Body
Spinous process
Anterior tubercle
Vertebral foramen
Posterior tubercle
Transverse foramen

SKULL AND SPINE

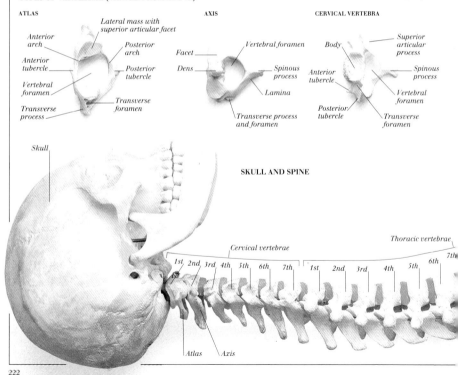

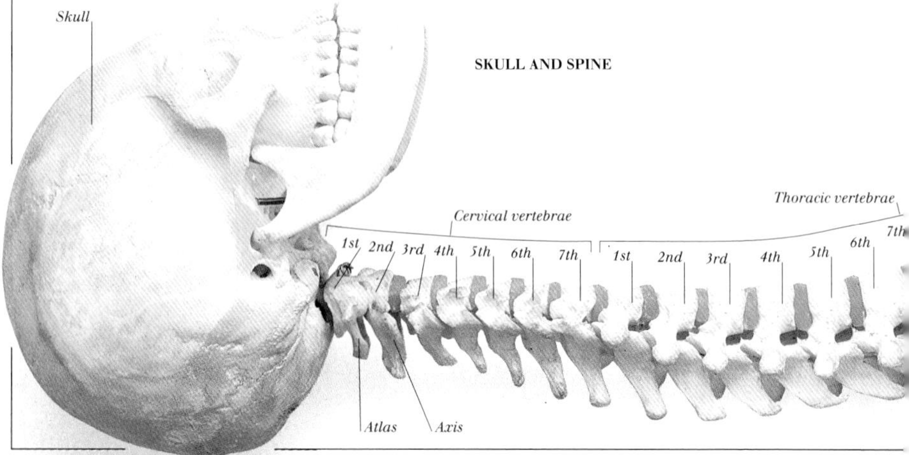
Skull
Cervical vertebrae
Thoracic vertebrae
1st
2nd
3rd
4th
5th
6th
7th
1st
2nd
3rd
4th
5th
6th
7th
Atlas
Axis

RIGHT SIDE

BACK

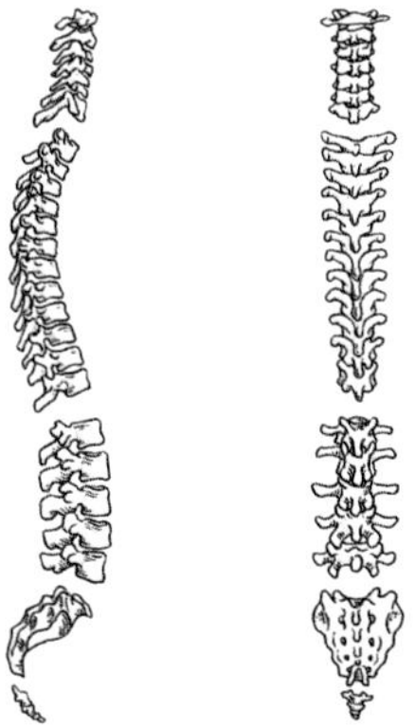

CERVICAL VERTEBRA AND SECTION OF SPINAL CORD

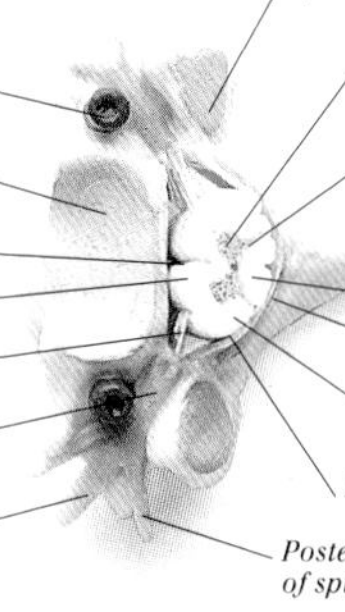
Superior articular process
Vertebral artery
Anterior horn
Vertebral body
Posterior horn
Anterior median fissure
Spinous process of cervical vertebra
Spinal cord
Posterior column
Dura mater
Anterior root
Lateral column
Spinal ganglion
Posterior root
Anterior branch of spinal nerve
Posterior branch of spinal nerve

THORACIC VERTEBRA

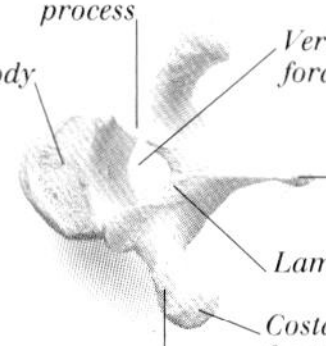
Superior articular process
Vertebral foramen
Body
Spinous process
Lamina
Costal facet
Transverse process

LUMBAR VERTEBRA

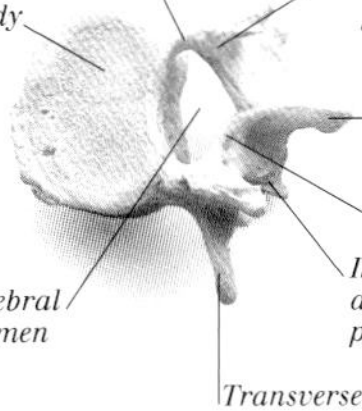
Pedicle
Superior articular process and facet
Body
Spinous process
Lamina
Inferior articular process
Vertebral foramen
Transverse process

SACRUM

COCCYX

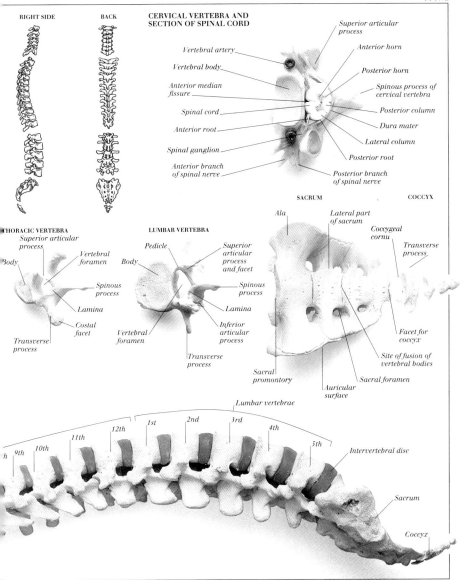

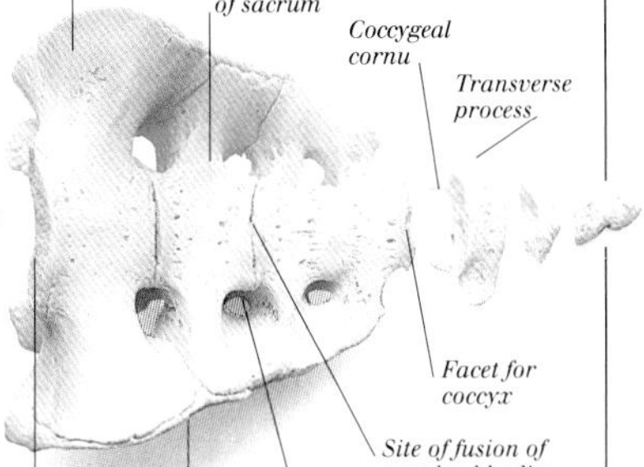
Ala
Lateral part of sacrum
Coccygeal cornu
Transverse process
Facet for coccyx
Site of fusion of vertebral bodies
Sacral promontory
Sacral foramen
Auricular surface

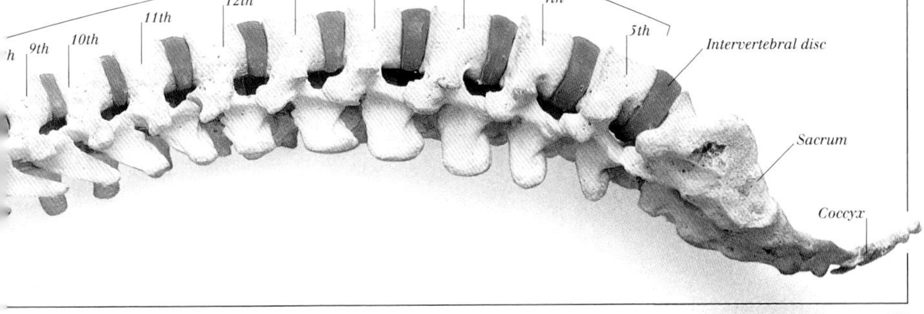
Lumbar vertebrae
1st
2nd
3rd
12th
11th
4th
10th
9th
5th
Intervertebral disc
Sacrum
Coccyx

Bones and joints

BONES FORM the body's hard, strong skeletal framework. Each bone has a hard, compact exterior surrounding a spongy, lighter interior. The long bones of the arms and legs, such as the femur (thigh bone), have a central cavity containing bone marrow. Bones are composed chiefly of calcium, phosphorus, and a fibrous substance known as collagen. Bones meet at joints, which are of several different types. For example, the hip is a ball-and-socket joint that allows the femur a wide range of movement, whereas finger joints are simple hinge joints that allow only bending and straightening. Joints are held in place by bands of tissue called ligaments. Movement of joints is facilitated by the smooth hyaline cartilage that covers the bone ends and by the synovial membrane that lines and lubricates the joint.

LIGAMENTS SURROUNDING HIP JOINT

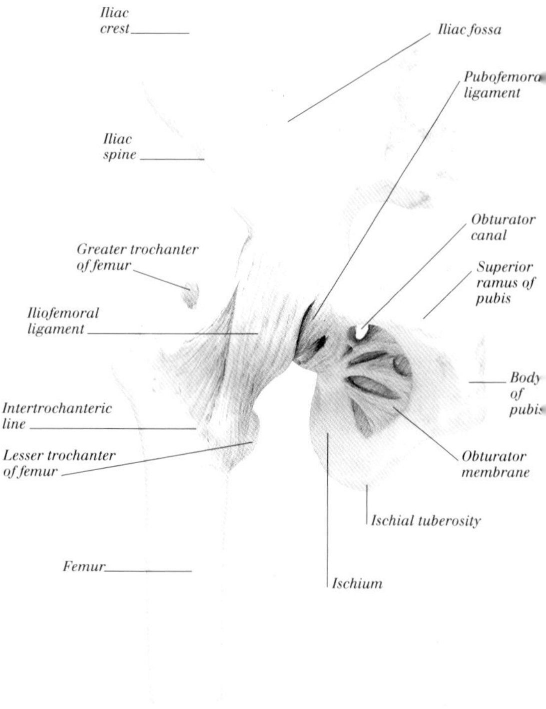

Iliac crest
Iliac fossa
Pubofemora ligament
Iliac spine
Obturator canal
Greater trochanter of femur
Superior ramus of pubis
Iliofemoral ligament
Body of pubis
Intertrochanteric line
Lesser trochanter of femur
Obturator membrane
Ischial tuberosity
Femur
Ischium

SECTION THROUGH LEFT FEMUR

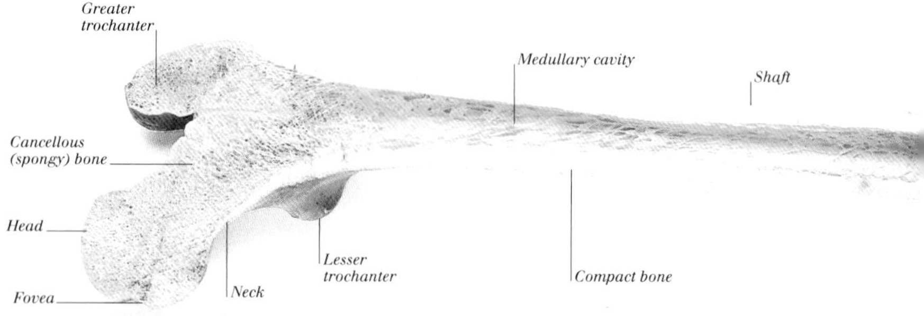

Greater trochanter
Medullary cavity
Shaft
Cancellous (spongy) bone
Head
Lesser trochanter
Compact bone
Neck
Fovea

ECTION THROUGH HIP JOINT

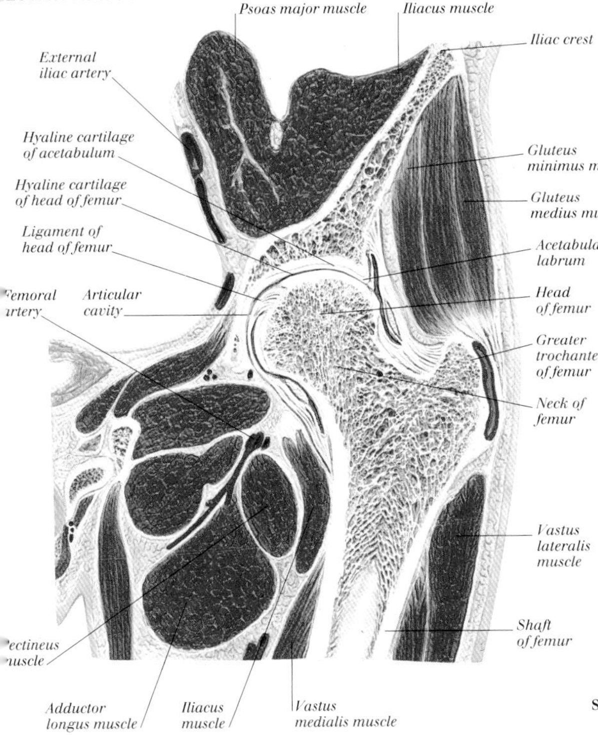
Psoas major muscle
Iliacus muscle
Iliac crest
External iliac artery
Hyaline cartilage of acetabulum
Hyaline cartilage of head of femur
Ligament of head of femur
Femoral artery
Articular cavity
Gluteus minimus muscle
Gluteus medius muscle
Acetabular labrum
Head of femur
Greater trochanter of femur
Neck of femur
Vastus lateralis muscle
Shaft of femur
Pectineus muscle
Adductor longus muscle
Iliacus muscle
Vastus medialis muscle

SECTION OF COMPACT BONE

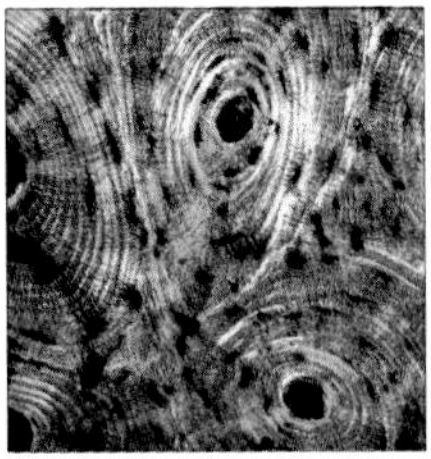

Parallel rows of concentric bony layers make up this strong material.

BONE MARROW SMEAR

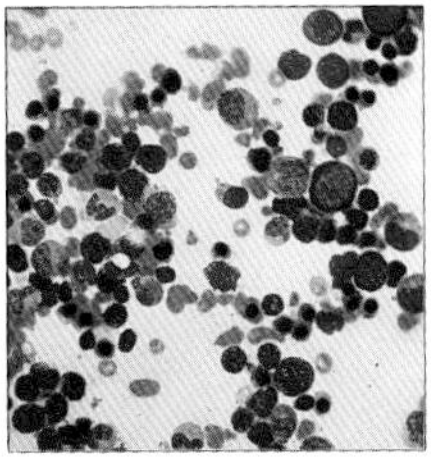

Composed mainly of red and white blood cells, marrow fills the cavities of bones.

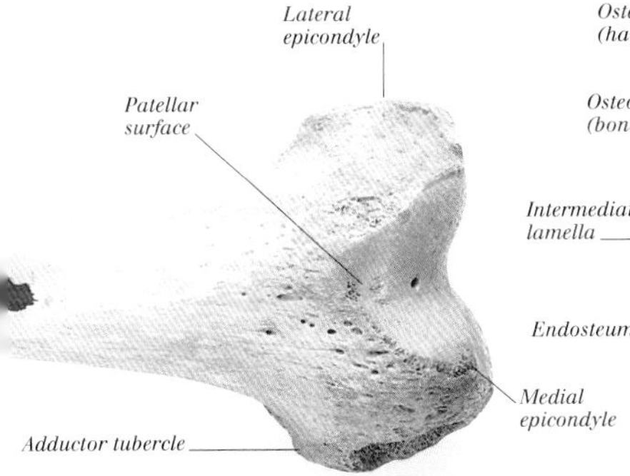
Lateral epicondyle
Patellar surface
Medial epicondyle
Adductor tubercle

SECTION THROUGH LONG BONE

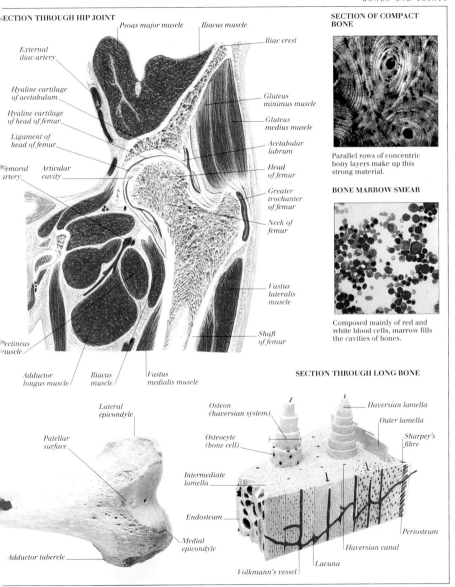

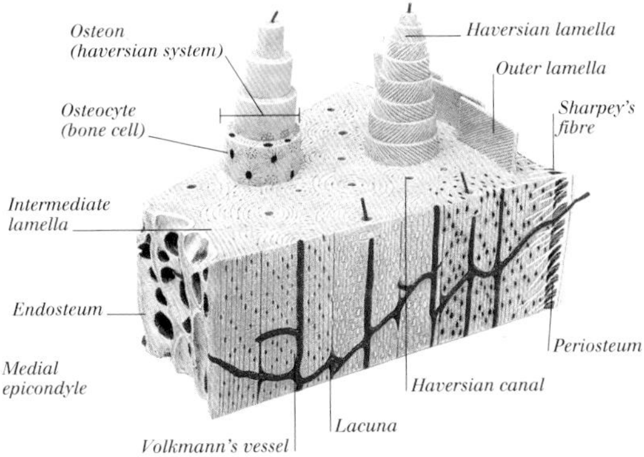
Osteon (haversian system)
Haversian lamella
Outer lamella
Osteocyte (bone cell)
Sharpey's fibre
Intermediate lamella
Endosteum
Periosteum
Haversian canal
Lacuna
Volkmann's vessel

Muscles 1

THERE ARE THREE MAIN TYPES OF MUSCLE: skeletal muscle (also called voluntary muscle because it can be consciously controlled); smooth muscle (also called involuntary muscle because it is not under voluntary control); and the specialized muscle tissue of the heart. Humans have more than 600 skeletal muscles, which differ in size and shape according to the jobs they do. Skeletal muscles are attached either directly or indirectly (via tendons) to bones, and work in opposing pairs (one muscle in the pair contracts while the other relaxes) to produce body movements as diverse as walking, threading a needle, and an array of facial expressions. Smooth muscles occur in the walls of internal body organs and perform actions such as forcing food through the intestines, contracting the uterus (womb) in childbirth, and pumping blood through the blood vessels.

SOME OTHER MUSCLES IN THE BODY

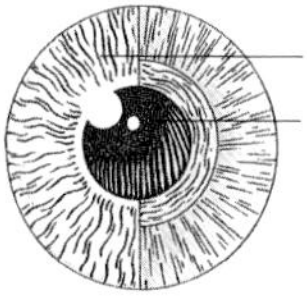
Iris
Pupil

IRIS
The muscle fibres contract and dilate (expand) to alter pupil size.

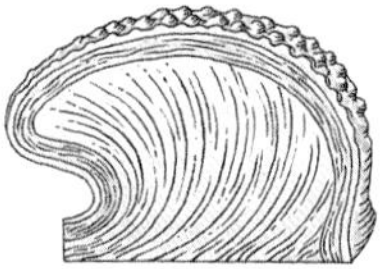

TONGUE
Interlacing layers of muscle allow great mobility.

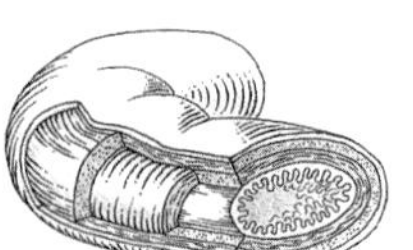

ILEUM
Opposing muscle layers transport semi-digested food.

SUPERFICIAL SKELETAL MUSCLES

FRONT VIEW

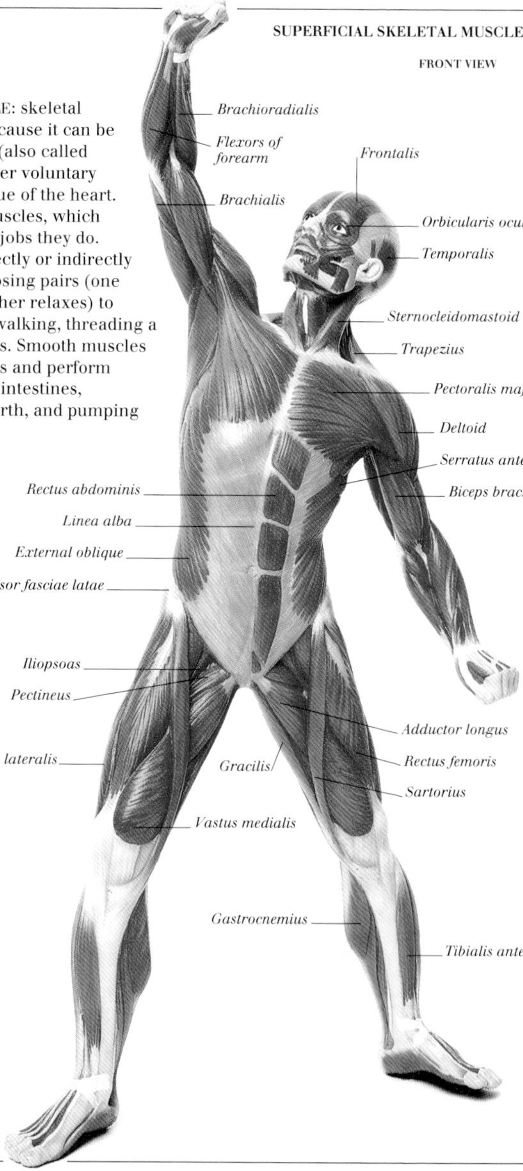
Brachioradialis
Flexors of forearm
Brachialis
Frontalis
Orbicularis oculi
Temporalis
Sternocleidomastoid
Trapezius
Pectoralis major
Deltoid
Serratus anterior
Biceps brachii
Rectus abdominis
Linea alba
External oblique
Tensor fasciae latae
Iliopsoas
Pectineus
Adductor longus
Rectus femoris
Vastus lateralis
Gracilis
Sartorius
Vastus medialis
Gastrocnemius
Tibialis anterior

BACK VIEW

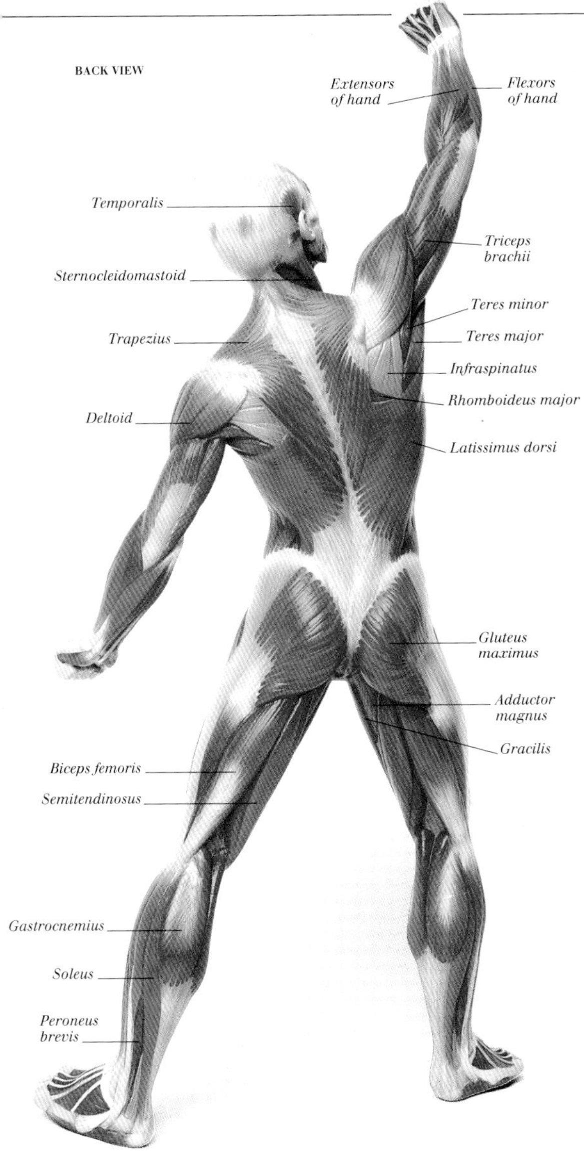
Extensors of hand
Flexors of hand
Temporalis
Triceps brachii
Sternocleidomastoid
Teres minor
Trapezius
Teres major
Infraspinatus
Rhomboideus major
Deltoid
Latissimus dorsi
Gluteus maximus
Adductor magnus
Gracilis
Biceps femoris
Semitendinosus
Gastrocnemius
Soleus
Peroneus brevis

MOVEMENT OF THE FOREARM
Controlled movement of the limbs relies on coordinated relaxation and contraction of opposing muscles. To raise the forearm, the biceps (two-rooted muscle) contracts and shortens while the triceps (three-rooted muscle) relaxes; the reverse occurs when the forearm is lowered.

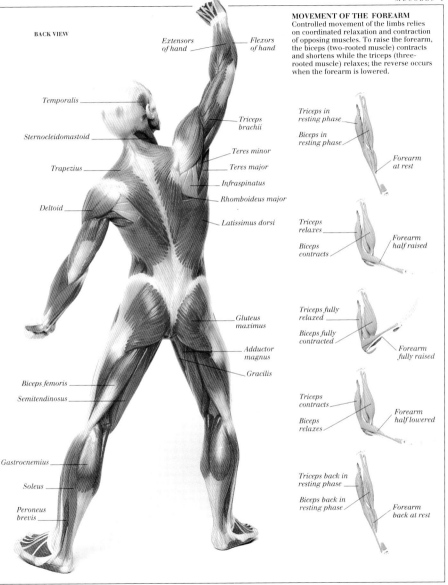

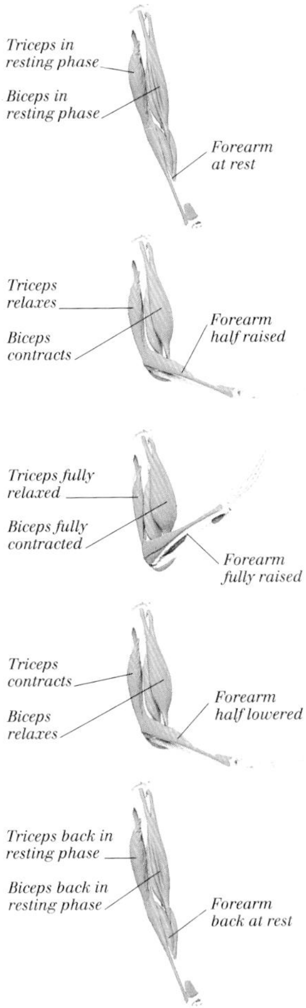
Triceps in resting phase
Biceps in resting phase
Forearm at rest
Triceps relaxes
Biceps contracts
Forearm half raised
Triceps fully relaxed
Biceps fully contracted
Forearm fully raised
Triceps contracts
Biceps relaxes
Forearm half lowered
Triceps back in resting phase
Biceps back in resting phase
Forearm back at rest

Muscles 2

SKELETAL MUSCLE FIBRE

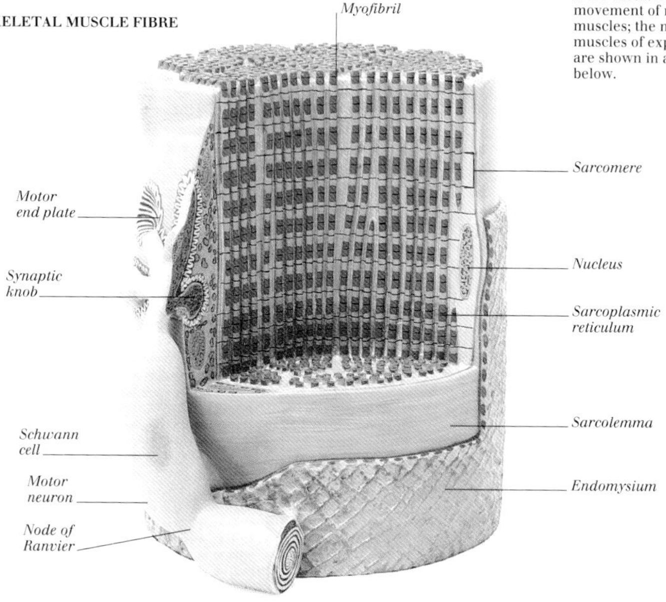
Myofibril
Sarcomere
Motor end plate
Nucleus
Synaptic knob
Sarcoplasmic reticulum
Sarcolemma
Schwann cell
Endomysium
Motor neuron
Node of Ranvier

TYPES OF MUSCLE

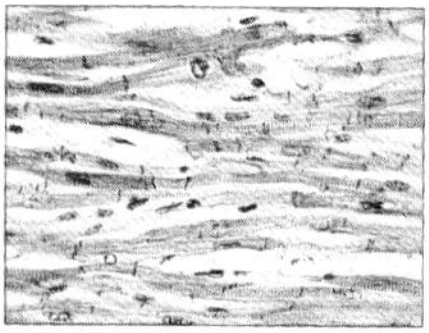
CARDIAC MUSCLE

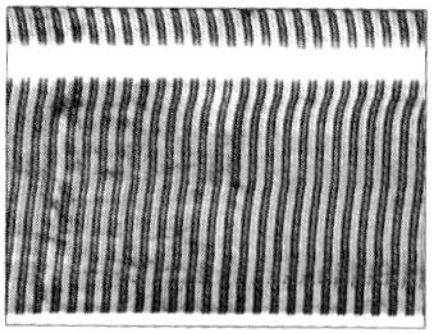
SKELETAL MUSCLE

SMOOTH MUSCLE

CONTRACTION OF SKELETAL MUSCLE

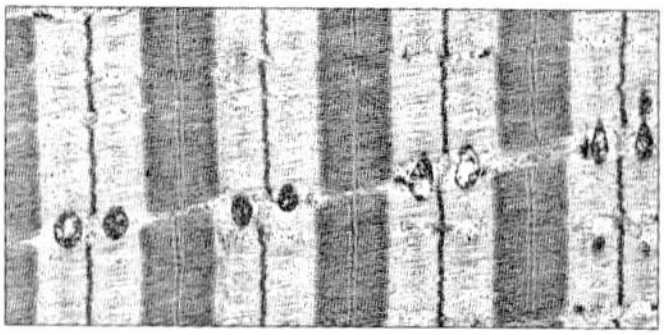
RELAXED STATE

CONTRACTED STATE

MUSCLES OF FACIAL EXPRESSION

A single expression is the result of movement of many muscles; the main muscles of expression are shown in action below.

FRONTALIS

CORRUGATOR SUPERCILII

ORBICULARIS ORIS

ZYGOMATICUS MAJOR

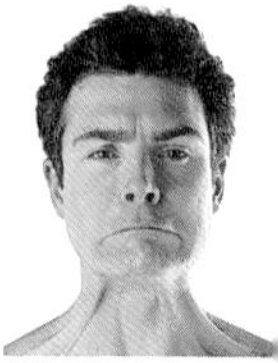
DEPRESSOR ANGULI ORIS

MUSCLES OF HEAD AND NECK

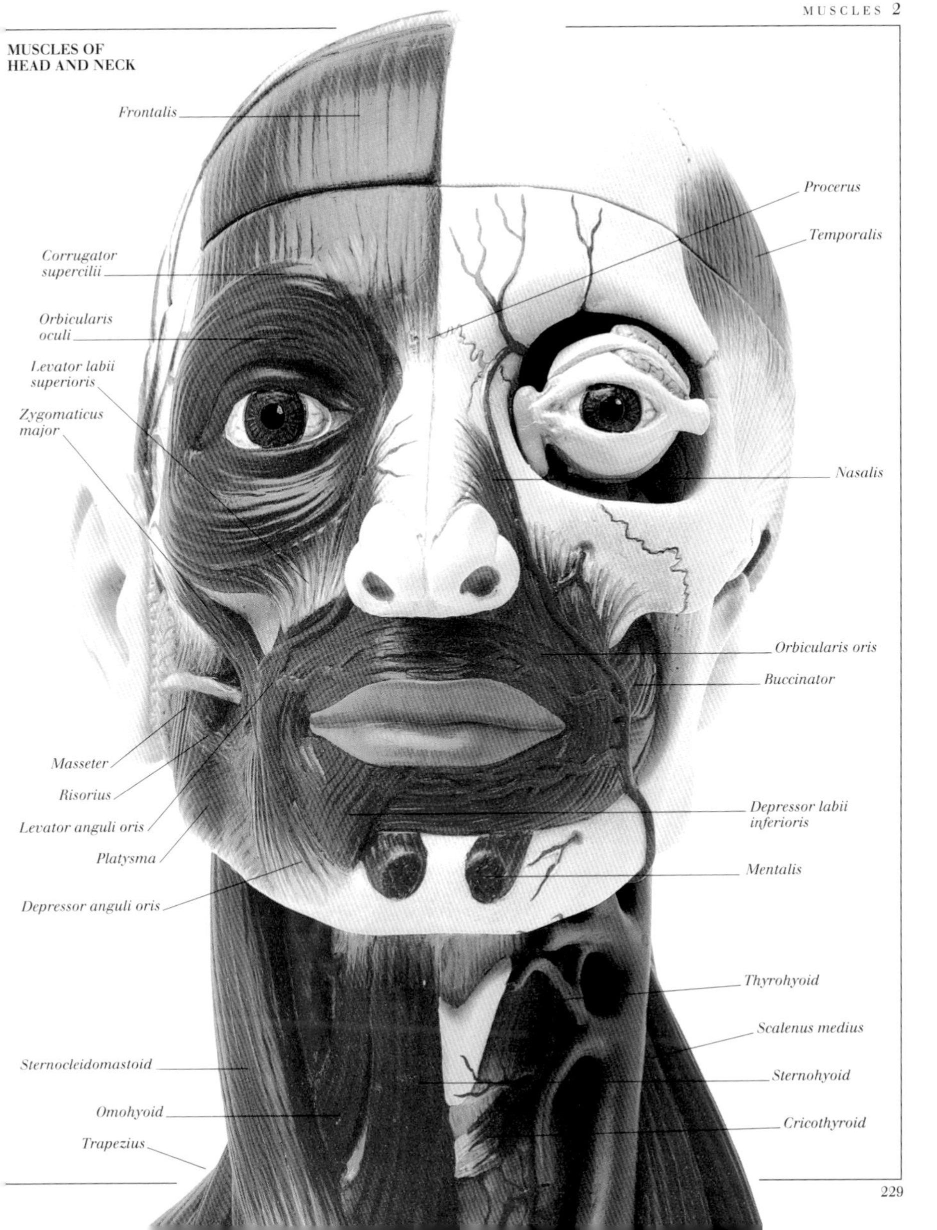

Frontalis
Corrugator supercilii
Orbicularis oculi
Levator labii superioris
Zygomaticus major
Masseter
Risorius
Levator anguli oris
Platysma
Depressor anguli oris
Sternocleidomastoid
Omohyoid
Trapezius
Procerus
Temporalis
Nasalis
Orbicularis oris
Buccinator
Depressor labii inferioris
Mentalis
Thyrohyoid
Scalenus medius
Sternohyoid
Cricothyroid

Hands

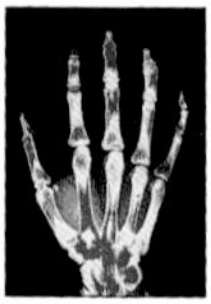

THE HUMAN HAND is an extremely versatile tool, capable of delicate manipulation as well as powerful gripping actions. The arrangement of its 27 small bones, moved by 37 skeletal muscles that are connected to the bones by tendons, allows a wide range of movements. Our ability to bring the tips of our thumbs and fingers together, combined with the extraordinary sensitivity of our fingertips due to their rich supply of nerve endings, makes our hands uniquely dextrous.

X-RAY OF LEFT HAND OF A YOUNG CHILD

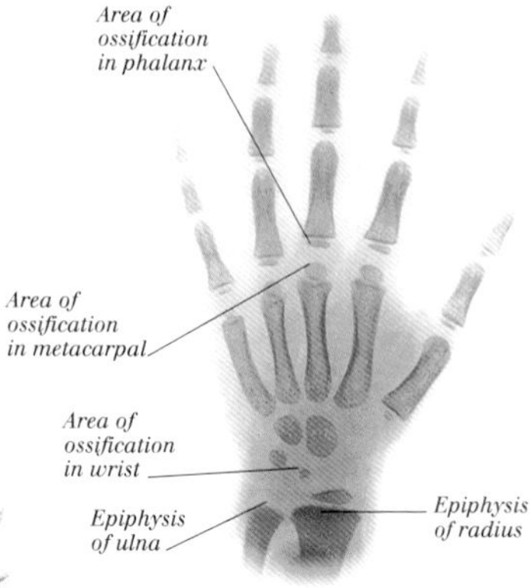

Area of ossification in phalanx
Area of ossification in metacarpal
Area of ossification in wrist
Epiphysis of ulna
Epiphysis of radius

Areas of cartilage in the wrist and at the ends of the finger bones are the sites of growth and have still to ossify.

BONES OF HAND

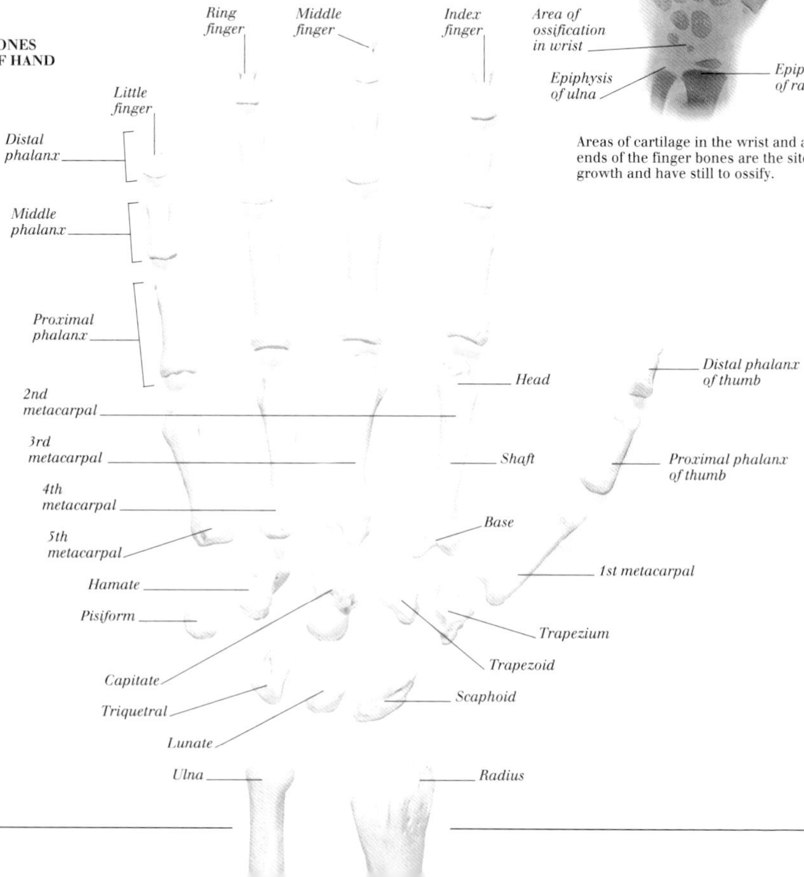

Ring finger
Middle finger
Index finger
Little finger
Distal phalanx
Middle phalanx
Proximal phalanx
Head
2nd metacarpal
3rd metacarpal
Shaft
4th metacarpal
5th metacarpal
Base
Distal phalanx of thumb
Proximal phalanx of thumb
1st metacarpal
Hamate
Pisiform
Trapezium
Trapezoid
Capitate
Scaphoid
Triquetral
Lunate
Ulna
Radius

STRUCTURES UNDERLYING SKIN OF PALM OF HAND

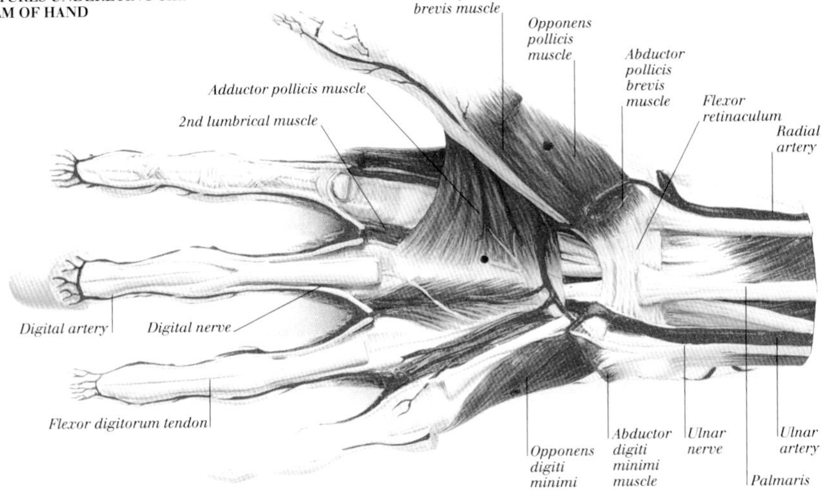

Flexor pollicis brevis muscle
Opponens pollicis muscle
Abductor pollicis brevis muscle
Flexor retinaculum
Radial artery
Adductor pollicis muscle
2nd lumbrical muscle
Digital artery
Digital nerve
Flexor digitorum tendon
Opponens digiti minimi muscle
Abductor digiti minimi muscle
Ulnar nerve
Ulnar artery
Palmaris longus tendon

EXTERNAL FEATURES OF BACK OF HAND

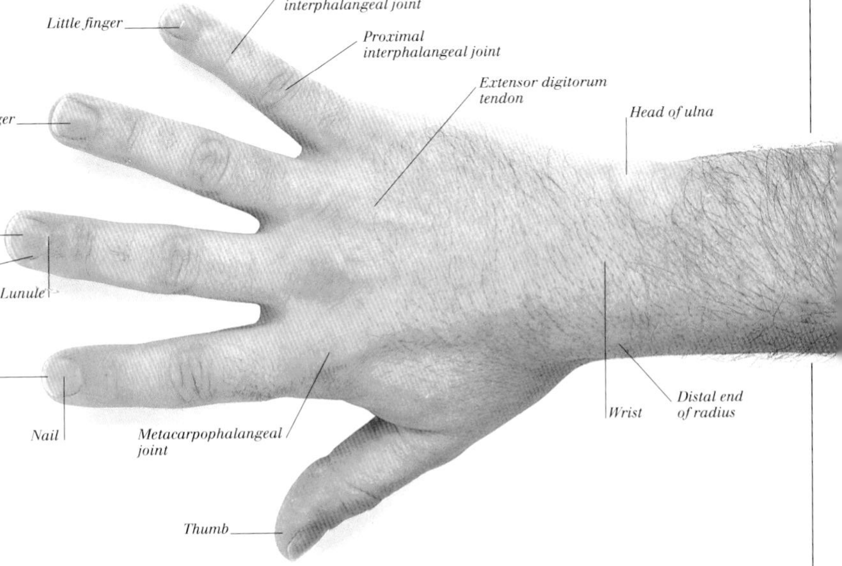

Distal interphalangeal joint
Little finger
Proximal interphalangeal joint
Extensor digitorum tendon
Ring finger
Head of ulna
Middle finger
Cuticle
Lunule
Index finger
Nail
Metacarpophalangeal joint
Wrist
Distal end of radius
Thumb

Feet

THE FEET AND TOES are essential elements in body movement. They bear and propel the weight of the body during walking and running, and also help to maintain balance during changes of body position. Each foot has 26 bones, more than 100 ligaments, and 33 muscles, some of which are attached to the lower leg. The heel pad and the arch of the foot act as shock absorbers, providing a cushion against the jolts that occur with every step.

BONES OF FOOT

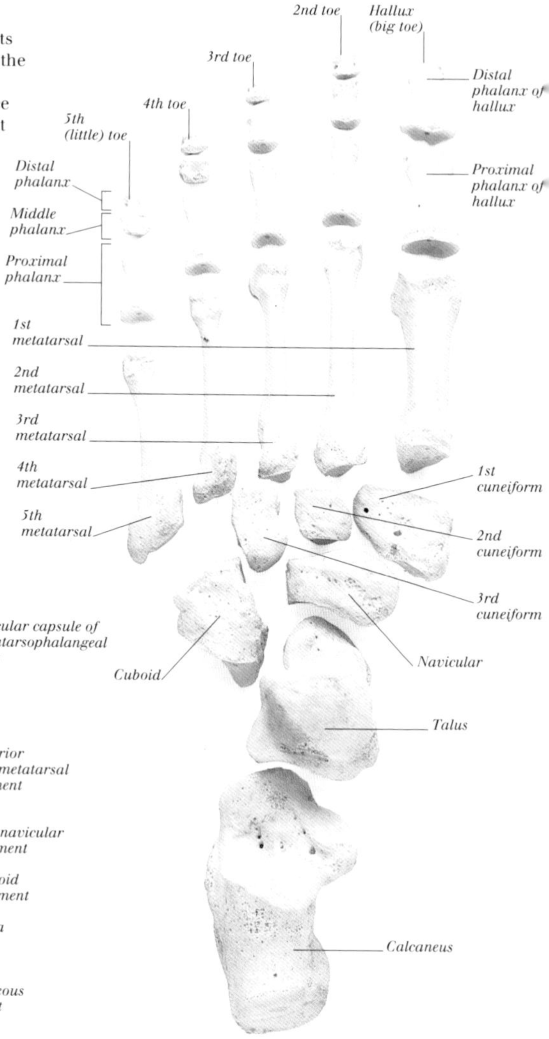

2nd toe
Hallux (big toe)
3rd toe
Distal phalanx of hallux
4th toe
5th (little) toe
Distal phalanx
Proximal phalanx of hallux
Middle phalanx
Proximal phalanx
1st metatarsal
2nd metatarsal
3rd metatarsal
4th metatarsal
1st cuneiform
5th metatarsal
2nd cuneiform
3rd cuneiform
Navicular
Cuboid
Talus
Calcaneus

LIGAMENTS OF FOOT

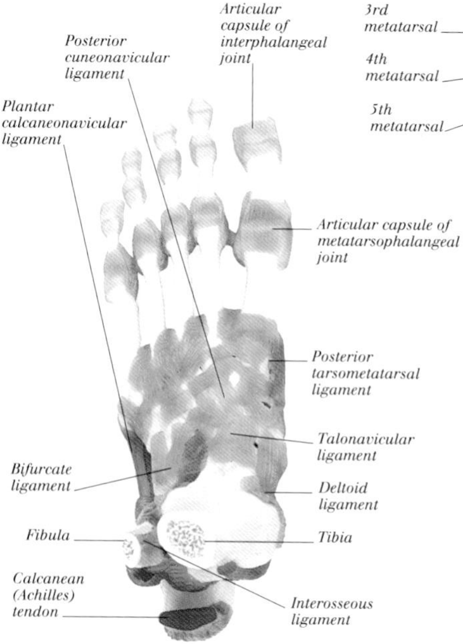

Articular capsule of interphalangeal joint
Posterior cuneonavicular ligament
Plantar calcaneonavicular ligament
Articular capsule of metatarsophalangeal joint
Posterior tarsometatarsal ligament
Talonavicular ligament
Bifurcate ligament
Deltoid ligament
Fibula
Tibia
Calcanean (Achilles) tendon
Interosseous ligament

STRUCTURES UNDERLYING SKIN OF FOOT

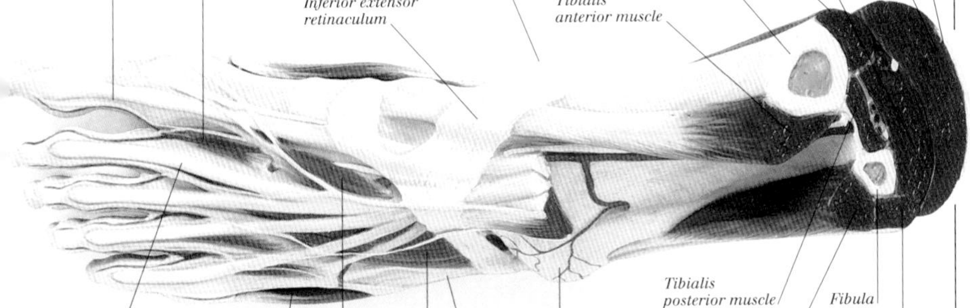

Calcanean (Achilles) tendon
Flexor hallucis longus muscle
Flexor digitorum longus muscle
Soleus muscle
Extensor hallucis longus tendon
1st dorsal interosseous muscle
Medial malleolus
Tibia
Inferior extensor retinaculum
Tibialis anterior muscle
Extensor digitorum longus tendon
Tibialis posterior muscle
Fibula
Lateral malleolus
Peroneus brevis muscle
Abductor digiti minimi muscle
Peroneus brevis tendon
Peroneus longus muscle
Extensor digitorum brevis muscle
Extensor hallucis brevis muscle

EXTERNAL FEATURES OF FOOT

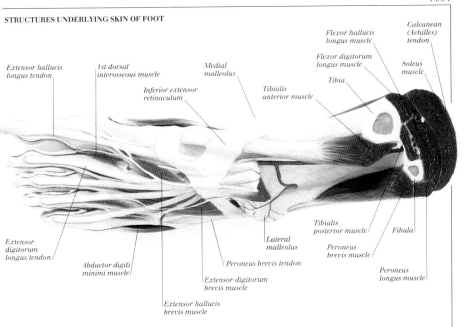

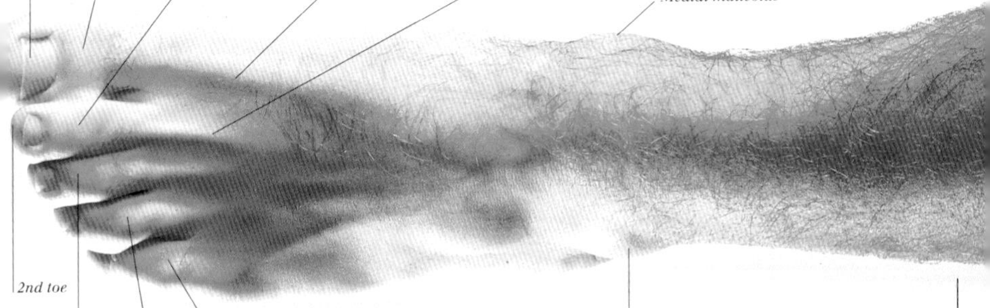

Toenail
Hallux (big toe)
Interphalangeal joint
Extensor hallucis longus tendon
Extensor digitorum longus tendon
Medial malleolus
2nd toe
3rd toe
4th toe
5th (little) toe
Lateral malleolus

Skin and hair

SKIN IS THE BODY'S LARGEST ORGAN, a waterproof barrier that protects the internal organs against infection, injury, and harmful sun rays. The skin is also an important sensory organ and helps to control body temperature. The outer layer of the skin, known as the epidermis, is coated with keratin, a tough, horny protein that is also the chief constituent of hair and nails. Dead cells are shed from the skin's surface and are replaced by new cells from the base of the epidermis, the region that also produces the skin pigment, melanin. The dermis contains most of the skin's living structures, and includes nerve endings, blood vessels, elastic fibres, sweat glands that cool the skin, and sebaceous glands that produce oil to keep the skin supple. Beneath the dermis lies the subcutaneous tissue (hypodermis), which is rich in fat and blood vessels. Hair shafts grow from hair follicles situated in the dermis and subcutaneous tissue. Hair grows on every part of the skin apart from the palms of the hands and soles of the feet.

SECTION OF HAIR

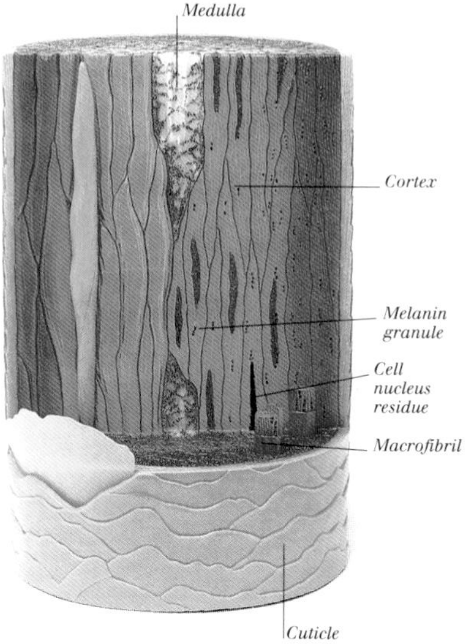
Medulla
Cortex
Melanin granule
Cell nucleus residue
Macrofibril
Cuticle

SECTIONS OF DIFFERENT TYPES OF SKIN

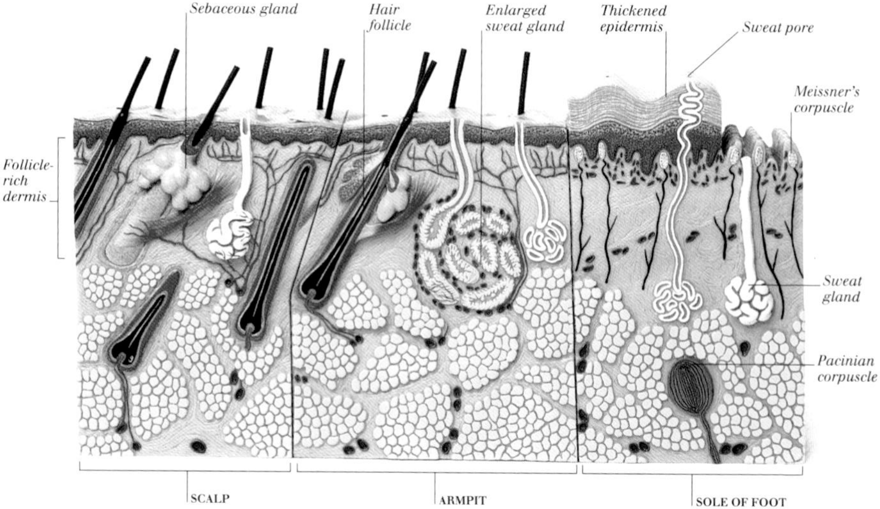
Sebaceous gland
Hair follicle
Enlarged sweat gland
Thickened epidermis
Sweat pore
Meissner's corpuscle
Follicle-rich dermis
Sweat gland
Pacinian corpuscle
SCALP
ARMPIT
SOLE OF FOOT

SECTION OF SKIN

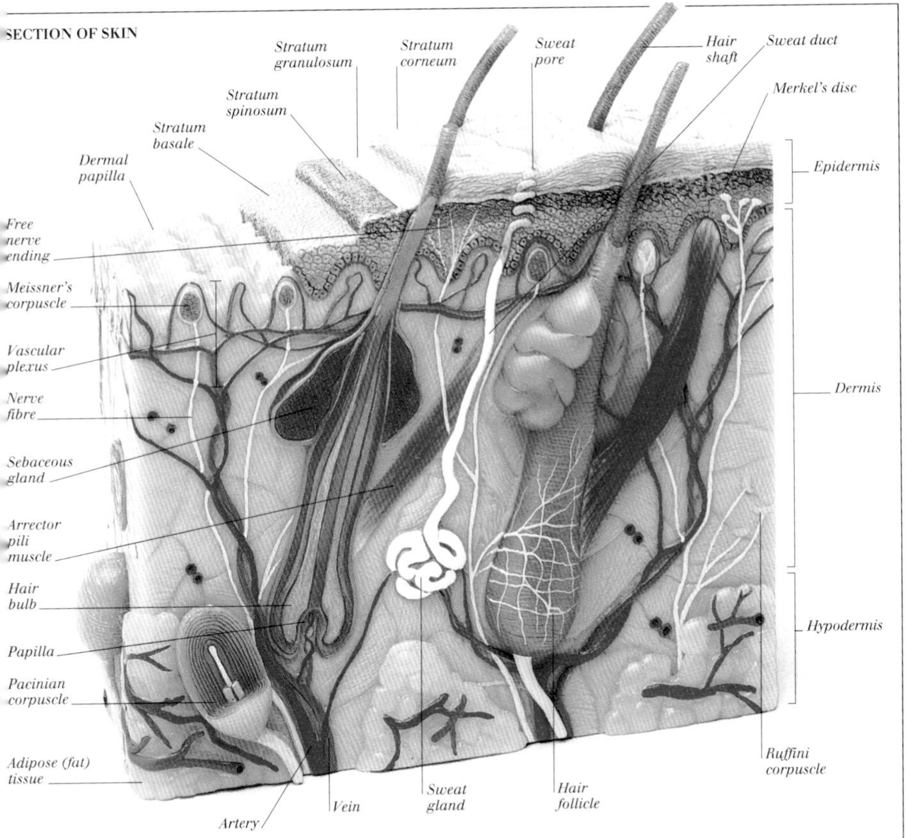
Stratum granulosum
Stratum corneum
Sweat pore
Hair shaft
Sweat duct
Merkel's disc
Stratum spinosum
Stratum basale
Dermal papilla
Epidermis
Free nerve ending
Meissner's corpuscle
Vascular plexus
Nerve fibre
Dermis
Sebaceous gland
Arrector pili muscle
Hair bulb
Hypodermis
Papilla
Pacinian corpuscle
Ruffini corpuscle
Adipose (fat) tissue
Vein
Sweat gland
Hair follicle
Artery

PHOTOMICROGRAPHS OF SKIN AND HAIR

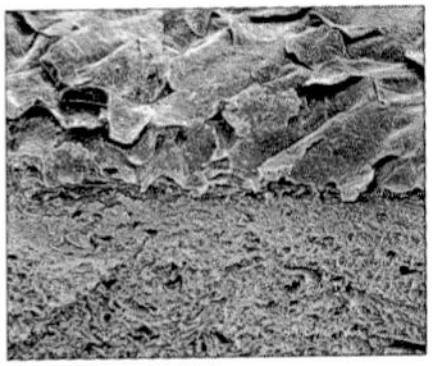

SECTION OF SKIN
The flaky cells at the skin's surface are shed continuously.

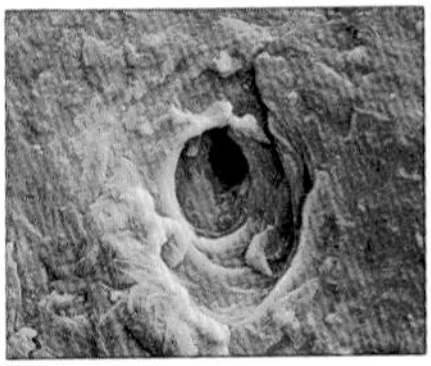

SWEAT PORE
This allows loss of fluid as part of temperature control.

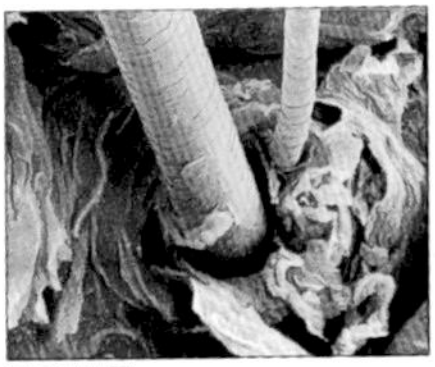

SKIN HAIR
Two hairs pushing through the outer layer of skin.

HEAD HAIR
The root and part of the shaft of a hair from the scalp.

Brain

THE BRAIN IS THE MAJOR ORGAN of the central nervous system and the control centre for all the body's voluntary and involuntary activities. It is also responsible for the complexities of thought, memory, emotion, and language. In adults, this complex organ is a mere 1.4 kg (3 lb) in weight, containing over 10 thousand million nerve cells. Three distinct regions can easily be seen – the brainstem, the cerebellum, and the large cerebrum. The brainstem controls vital body functions, such as breathing and digestion. The cerebellum's main functions are the maintenance of posture and the coordination of body movements. The cerebrum, which consists of the right and left cerebral hemispheres joined by the corpus callosum, is the site of most conscious and intelligent activities.

MRI SCAN OF TRANSVERSE SECTION THROUGH BRAIN

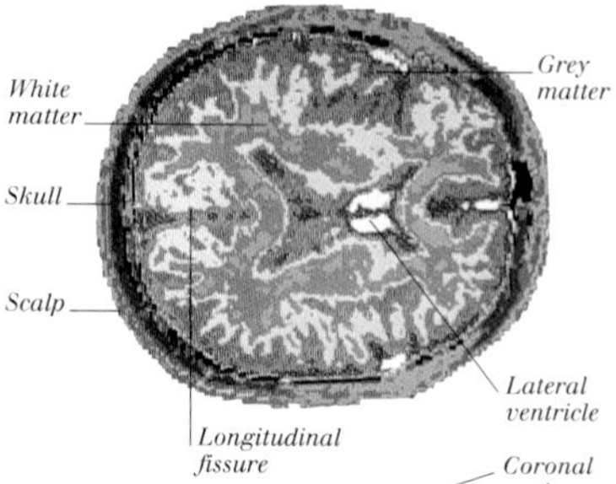
White matter
Skull
Scalp
Grey matter
Lateral ventricle
Longitudinal fissure

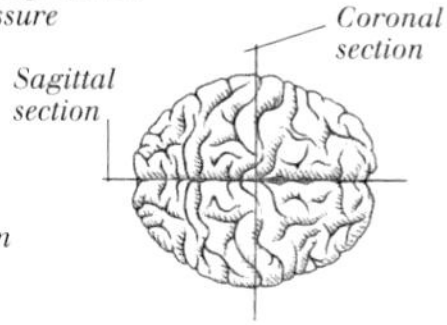
Coronal section
Sagittal section

SAGITTAL SECTION THROUGH BRAIN

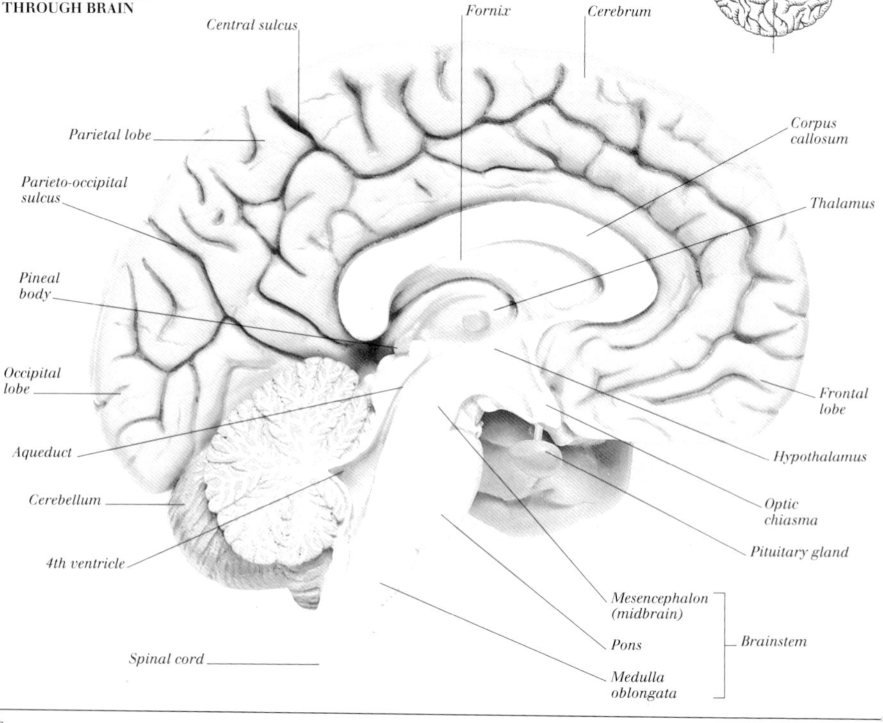
Central sulcus
Fornix
Cerebrum
Parietal lobe
Corpus callosum
Parieto-occipital sulcus
Thalamus
Pineal body
Occipital lobe
Frontal lobe
Aqueduct
Hypothalamus
Cerebellum
Optic chiasma
4th ventricle
Pituitary gland
Mesencephalon (midbrain)
Pons
Brainstem
Spinal cord
Medulla oblongata

SECTION THROUGH SKULL AND BRAIN

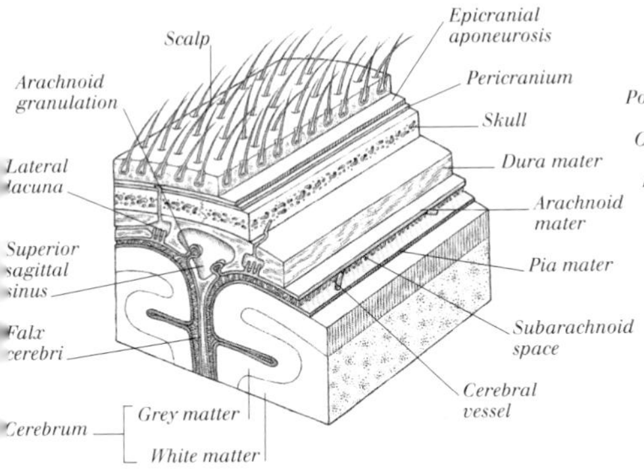
Scalp
Epicranial aponeurosis
Arachnoid granulation
Pericranium
Skull
Lateral lacuna
Dura mater
Arachnoid mater
Superior sagittal sinus
Pia mater
Subarachnoid space
Falx cerebri
Cerebral vessel
Cerebrum
Grey matter
White matter

EXTERNAL ANATOMY OF BRAIN

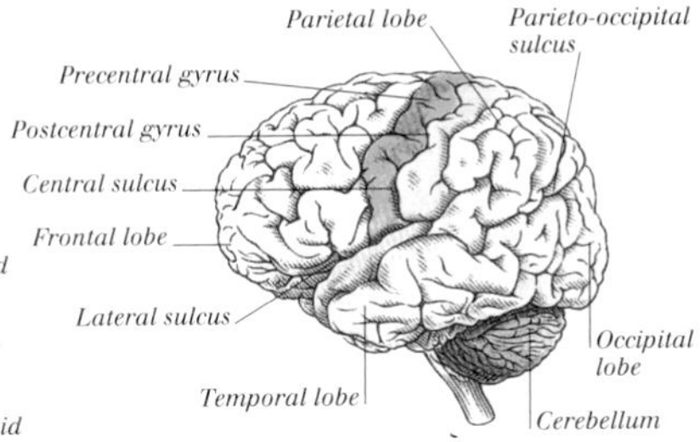
Parietal lobe
Parieto-occipital sulcus
Precentral gyrus
Postcentral gyrus
Central sulcus
Frontal lobe
Lateral sulcus
Occipital lobe
Temporal lobe
Cerebellum

SPECIFIC ROLES OF AREAS OF CEREBRUM

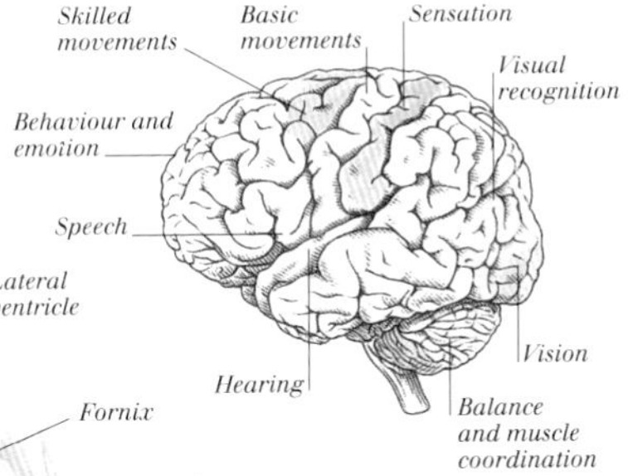
Skilled movements
Basic movements
Sensation
Visual recognition
Behaviour and emotion
Speech
Vision
Hearing
Balance and muscle coordination

CORONAL SECTION THROUGH BRAIN

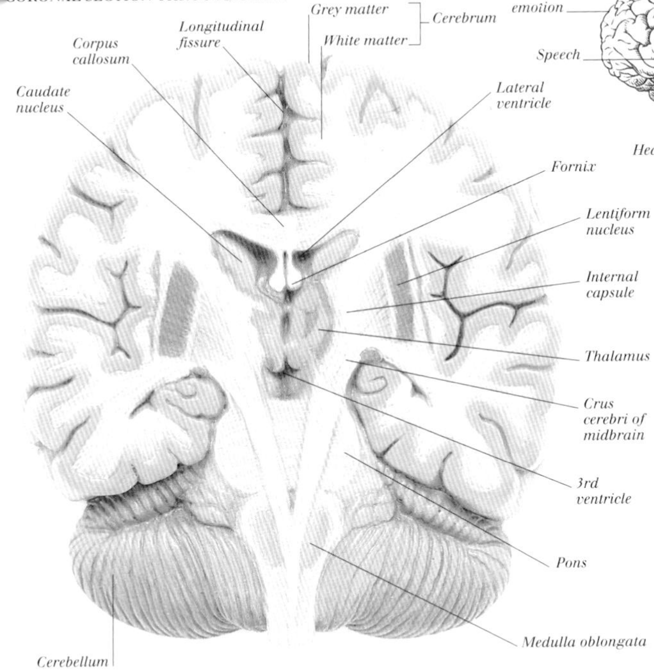
Grey matter
White matter
Cerebrum
Longitudinal fissure
Corpus callosum
Caudate nucleus
Lateral ventricle
Fornix
Lentiform nucleus
Internal capsule
Thalamus
Crus cerebri of midbrain
3rd ventricle
Pons
Medulla oblongata
Cerebellum

NERVE CELLS IN BRAIN

The dark cells are Purkinje's cells, which are among the largest nerve cells in the body.

Nervous system

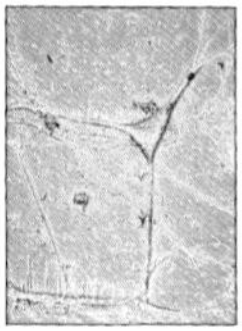

THE NERVOUS SYSTEM IS THE BODY'S internal, electrochemical, communications network. Its main parts are the brain, spinal cord, and nerves. The brain and spinal cord form the central nervous system (CNS), the body's chief controlling and coordinating centres. Billions of long neurons, many grouped as nerves, make up the peripheral nervous system, transmitting nerve impulses between the CNS and other regions of the body. Each neuron has three parts: a cell body, branching dendrites that receive chemical signals from other neurons, and a tube-like axon that conveys these signals as electrical impulses.

CENTRAL AND PERIPHERAL NERVOUS SYSTEMS

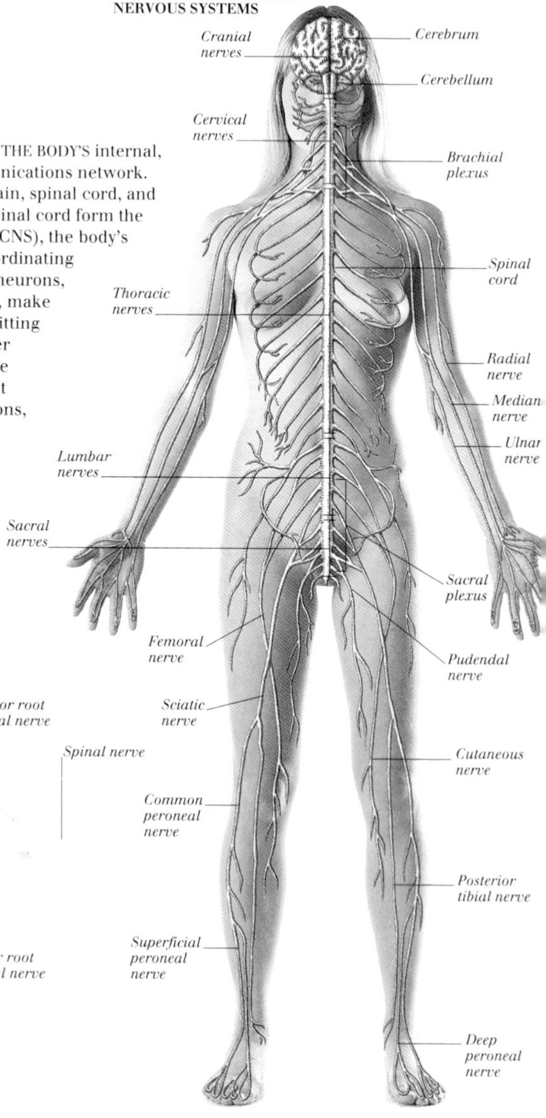
Cranial nerves
Cerebrum
Cerebellum
Cervical nerves
Brachial plexus
Spinal cord
Thoracic nerves
Radial nerve
Median nerve
Ulnar nerve
Lumbar nerves
Sacral nerves
Sacral plexus
Femoral nerve
Pudendal nerve
Sciatic nerve
Cutaneous nerve
Common peroneal nerve
Posterior tibial nerve
Superficial peroneal nerve
Deep peroneal nerve

SECTION THROUGH SPINAL CORD

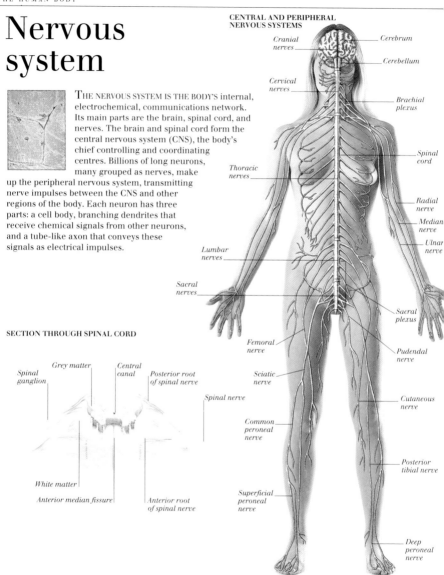

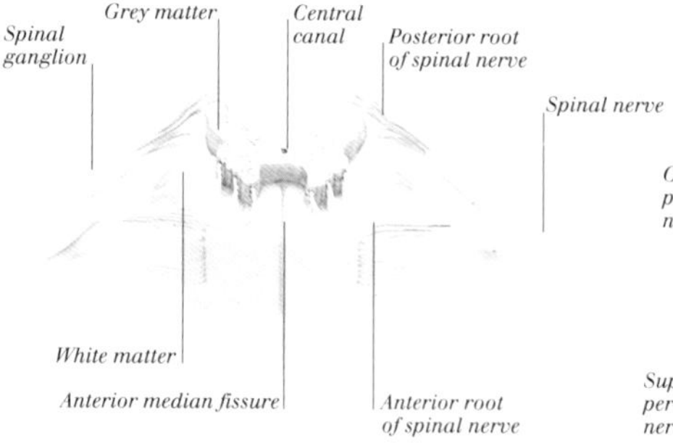
Spinal ganglion
Grey matter
Central canal
Posterior root of spinal nerve
Spinal nerve
White matter
Anterior median fissure
Anterior root of spinal nerve

STRUCTURE OF A MOTOR NEURON

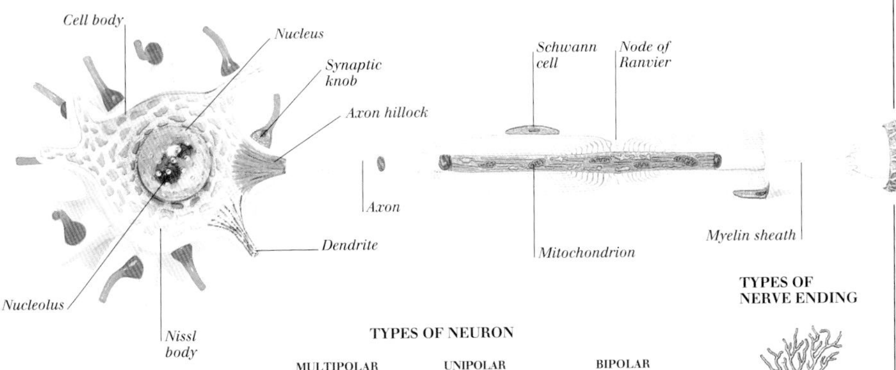
Cell body
Nucleus
Synaptic knob
Axon hillock
Axon
Dendrite
Nucleolus
Nissl body
Schwann cell
Node of Ranvier
Mitochondrion
Myelin sheath

STRUCTURE OF A SYNAPTIC KNOB

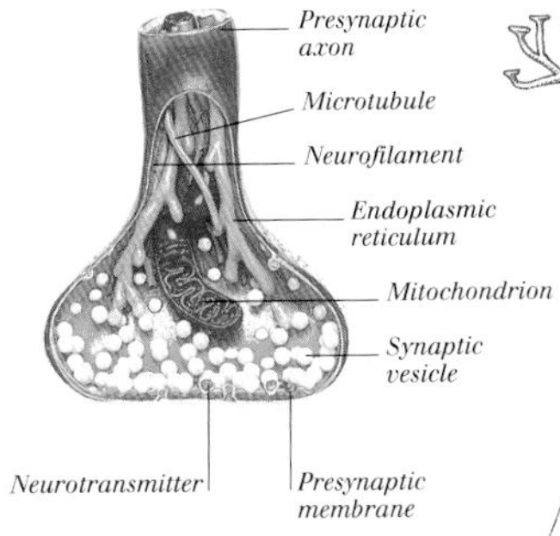
Presynaptic axon
Microtubule
Neurofilament
Endoplasmic reticulum
Mitochondrion
Synaptic vesicle
Neurotransmitter
Presynaptic membrane

TYPES OF NEURON

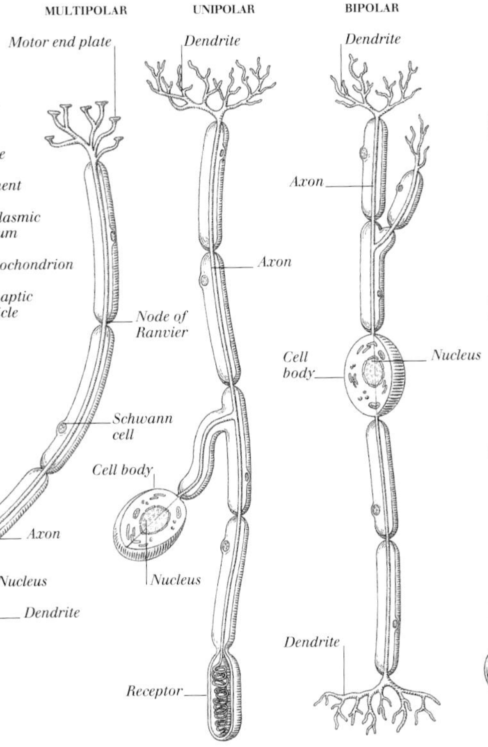
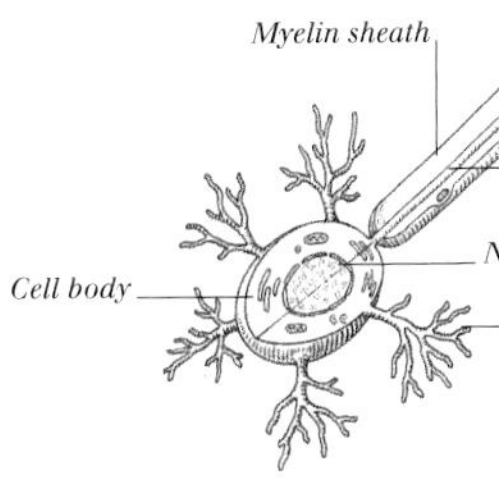
MULTIPOLAR
UNIPOLAR
BIPOLAR
Motor end plate
Node of Ranvier
Schwann cell
Myelin sheath
Axon
Cell body
Nucleus
Dendrite
Dendrite
Axon
Cell body
Nucleus
Receptor
Dendrite
Axon
Cell body
Nucleus
Dendrite

TYPES OF NERVE ENDING

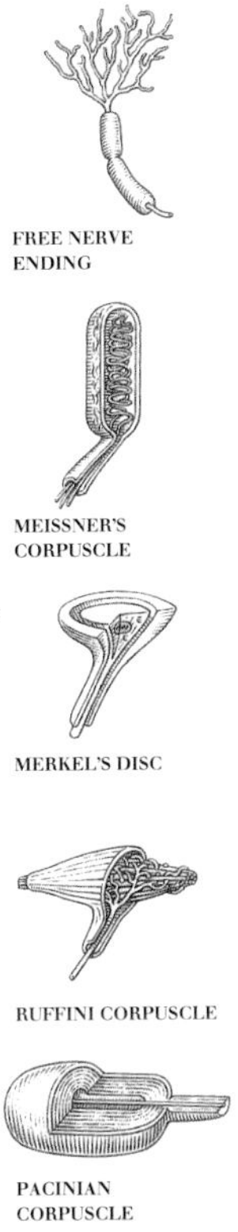
FREE NERVE ENDING
MEISSNER'S CORPUSCLE
MERKEL'S DISC
RUFFINI CORPUSCLE
PACINIAN CORPUSCLE

Eye

THE EYE IS THE ORGAN OF SIGHT. The two eyeballs, protected within bony sockets called orbits and on the outside by the eyelids, eyebrows, and tear film, are directly connected to the brain by the optic nerves. Each eye is moved by six muscles, which are attached around the eyeball. Light rays entering the eye through the pupil are focused by the cornea and lens to form an image on the retina. The retina contains millions of light-sensitive cells, called rods and cones, which convert the image into a pattern of nerve impulses. These impulses are transmitted along the optic nerve to the brain. Information from the two optic nerves is processed in the brain to produce a single coordinated image.

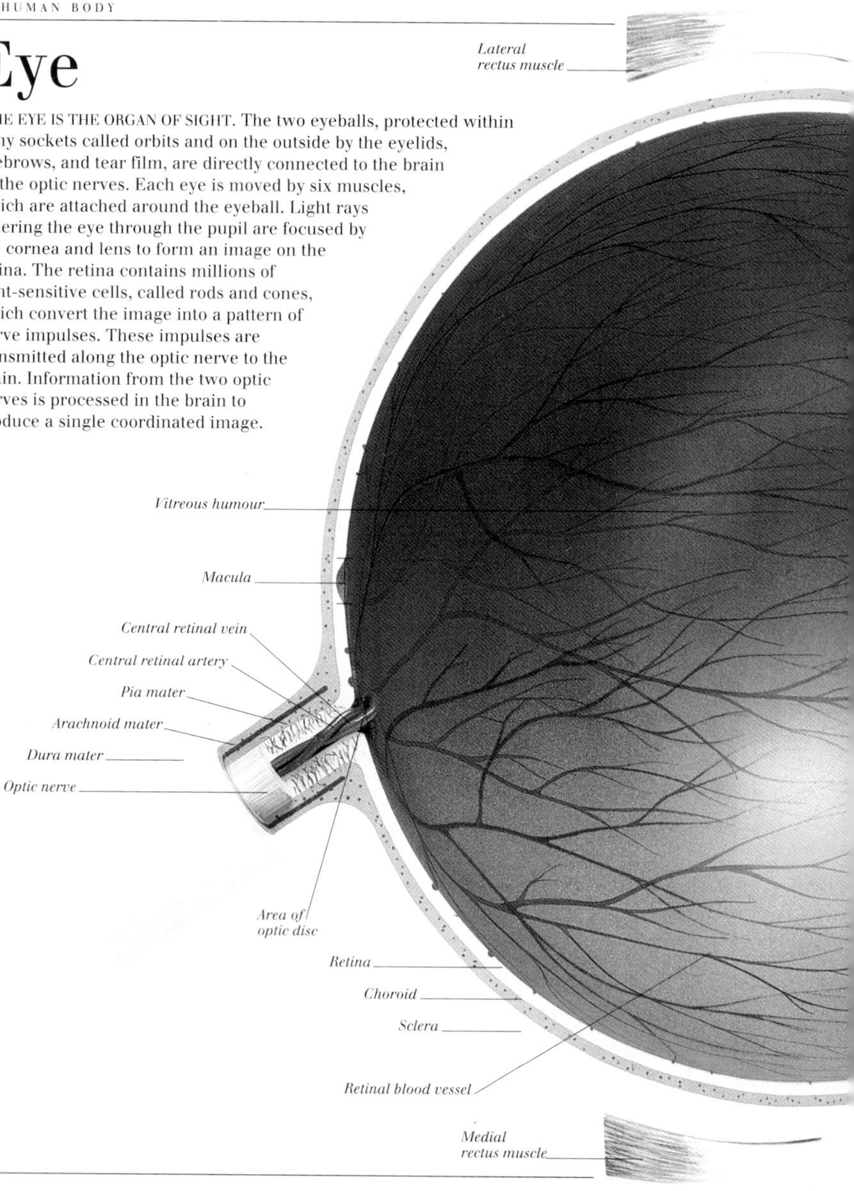
Lateral rectus muscle
Vitreous humour
Macula
Central retinal vein
Central retinal artery
Pia mater
Arachnoid mater
Dura mater
Optic nerve
Area of optic disc
Retina
Choroid
Sclera
Retinal blood vessel
Medial rectus muscle

SECTION THROUGH LEFT EYE

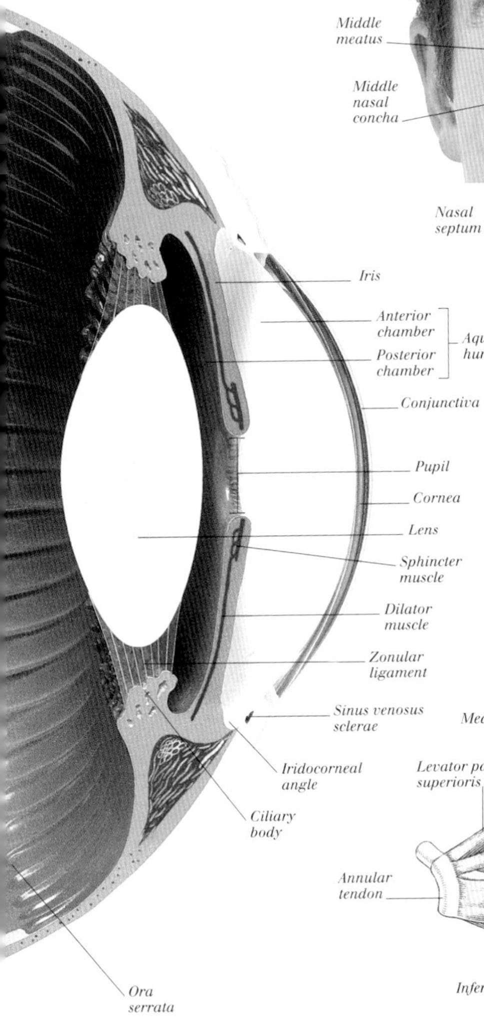
Iris
Anterior chamber
Posterior chamber
Aqueous humour
Conjunctiva
Pupil
Cornea
Lens
Sphincter muscle
Dilator muscle
Zonular ligament
Sinus venosus sclerae
Iridocorneal angle
Ciliary body
Ora serrata

LACRIMAL (TEAR-PRODUCING) APPARATUS

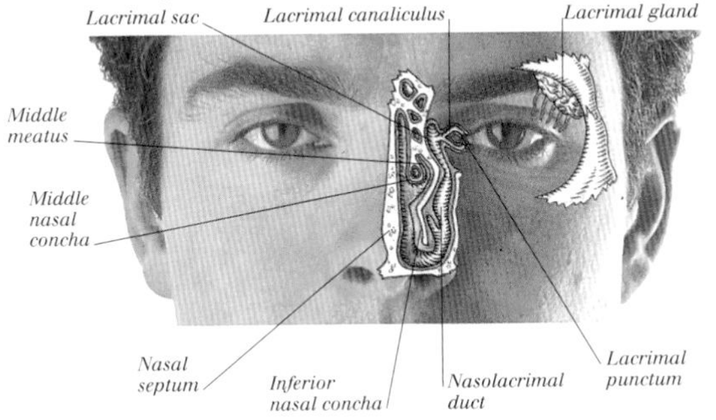
Lacrimal sac
Lacrimal canaliculus
Lacrimal gland
Middle meatus
Middle nasal concha
Nasal septum
Inferior nasal concha
Nasolacrimal duct
Lacrimal punctum

OPHTHALMOSCOPIC VIEW OF RETINA

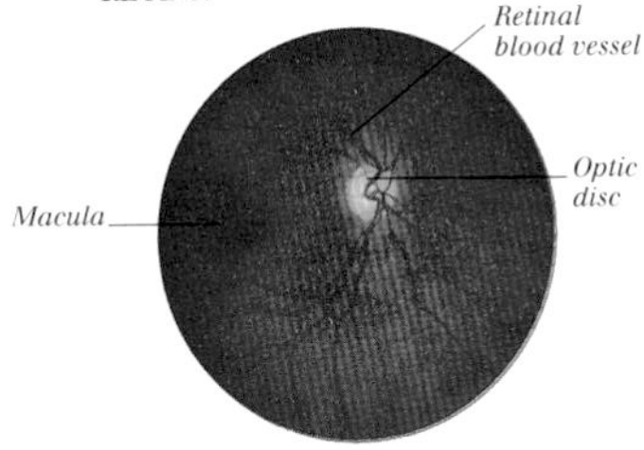
Retinal blood vessel
Optic disc
Macula

The blind spot, where the optic nerve leaves the eye, can be clearly seen as a light circular area towards the centre of the image.

MUSCLES SURROUNDING RIGHT EYE

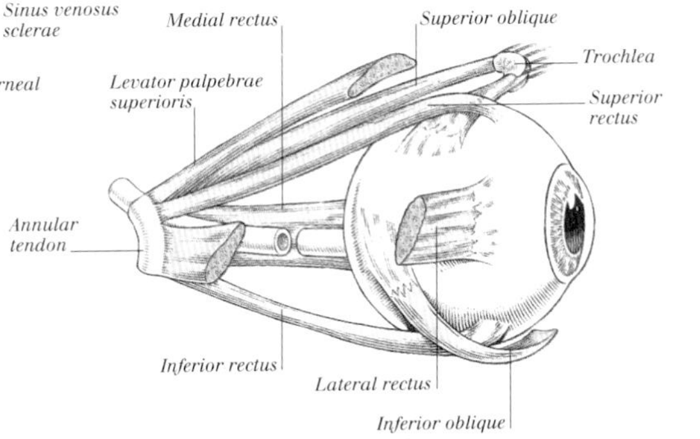
Medial rectus
Superior oblique
Trochlea
Levator palpebrae superioris
Superior rectus
Annular tendon
Inferior rectus
Lateral rectus
Inferior oblique

Ear

THE EAR IS THE ORGAN OF HEARING AND BALANCE. The outer ear consists of a flap called the auricle or pinna and the auditory canal. The main functional parts – the middle and inner ears – are enclosed within the skull. The middle ear consists of three tiny bones, known as auditory ossicles, and the eustachian tube, which links the ear to the back of the nose. The inner ear consists of the spiral-shaped cochlea, and also the semicircular canals and the vestibule, which are the organs of balance. Sound waves entering the ear travel through the auditory canal to the tympanic membrane (eardrum), where they are converted to vibrations that are transmitted via the ossicles to the cochlea. Here, the vibrations are converted by millions of microscopic hairs into electrical nerve signals to be interpreted by the brain.

STRUCTURE OF EAR

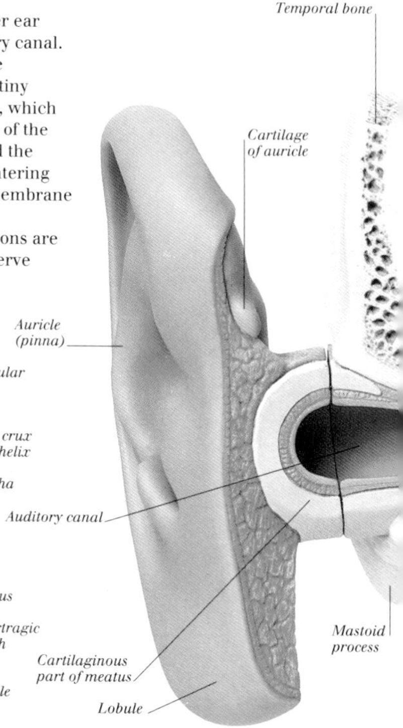
Temporal bone
Cartilage of auricle
Auricle (pinna)
Auditory canal
Mastoid process
Cartilaginous part of meatus
Lobule

RIGHT AURICLE (PINNA)

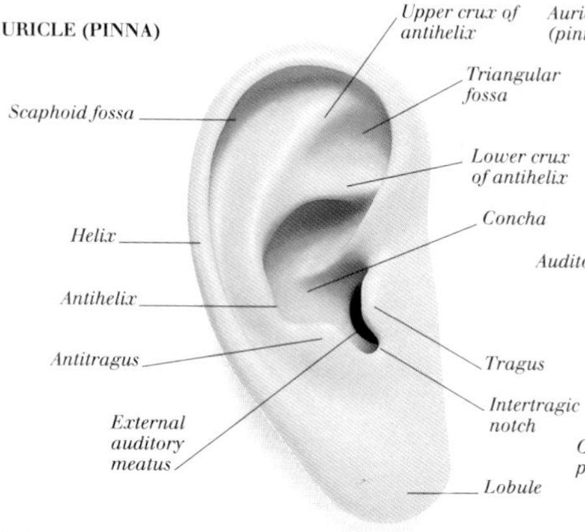
Upper crux of antihelix
Triangular fossa
Scaphoid fossa
Lower crux of antihelix
Concha
Helix
Antihelix
Antitragus
Tragus
Intertragic notch
External auditory meatus
Lobule

OSSICLES OF MIDDLE EAR

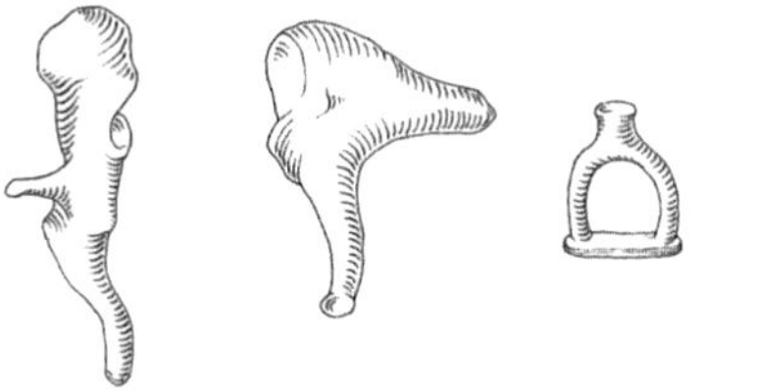

MALLEUS (HAMMER) INCUS (ANVIL) STAPES (STIRRUP)

These three tiny bones connect to form a bridge between the tympanic membrane and the oval window. With a system of membranes they convey sound vibrations to the inner ear.

INTERNAL STRUCTURE OF AMPULLA

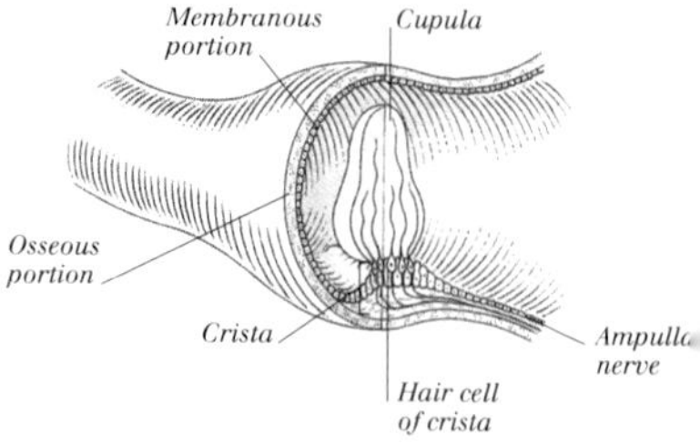
Membranous portion
Cupula
Osseous portion
Crista
Ampulla nerve
Hair cell of crista

LABYRINTH

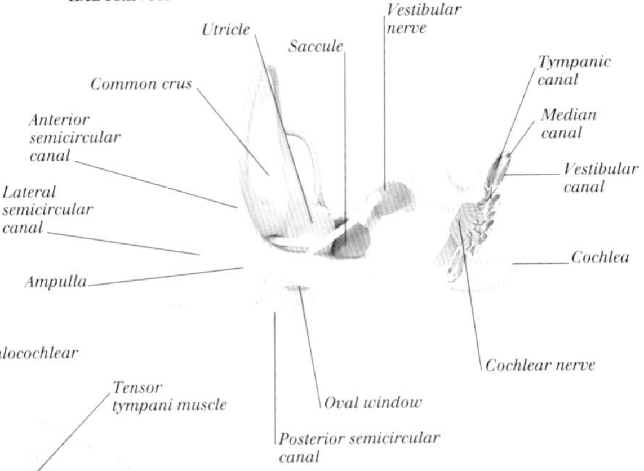
Utricle
Vestibular nerve
Saccule
Tympanic canal
Common crus
Median canal
Anterior semicircular canal
Vestibular canal
Lateral semicircular canal
Cochlea
Ampulla
Cochlear nerve
Oval window
Posterior semicircular canal

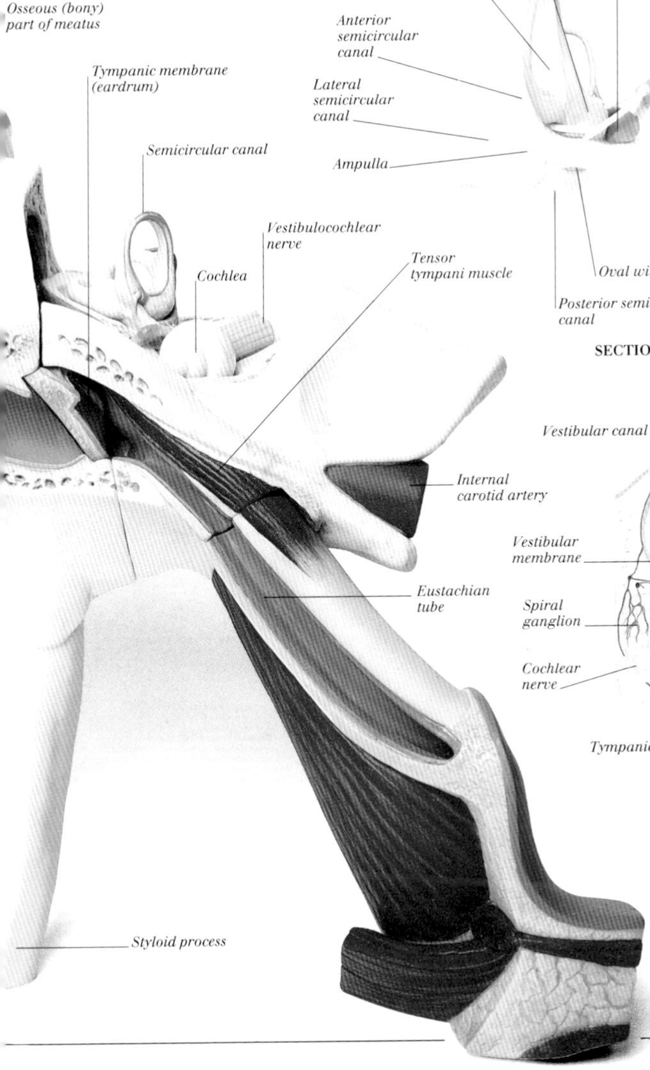
Osseous (bony) part of meatus
Tympanic membrane (eardrum)
Semicircular canal
Vestibulocochlear nerve
Cochlea
Tensor tympani muscle
Internal carotid artery
Eustachian tube
Styloid process

SECTION THROUGH COCHLEA

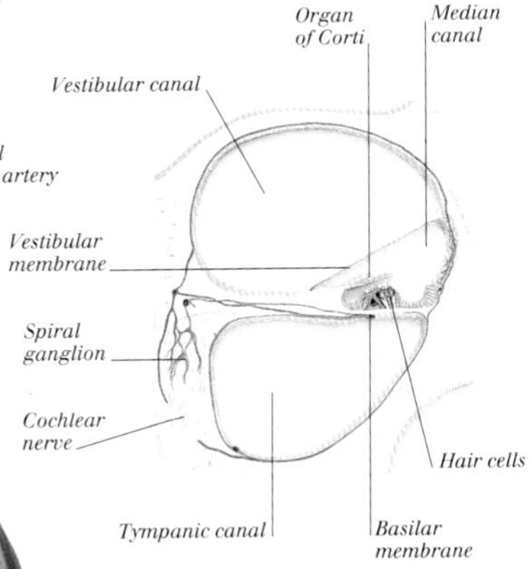
Organ of Corti
Median canal
Vestibular canal
Vestibular membrane
Spiral ganglion
Cochlear nerve
Hair cells
Tympanic canal
Basilar membrane

Nose, mouth, and throat

WITH EVERY BREATH, air passes through the nasal cavity down the pharynx (throat), larynx ("voice box"), and trachea (windpipe) to the lungs. The nasal cavity warms and moistens air, and the tiny layers in its lining protect the airway against damage by foreign bodies. During swallowing, the tongue moves up and back, the larynx rises, the epiglottis closes off the entrance to the trachea, and the soft palate separates the nasal cavity from the pharynx. Saliva, secreted from three pairs of salivary glands, lubricates food to make swallowing easier; it also begins the chemical breakdown of food, and helps to produce taste. The senses of taste and smell are closely linked. Both depend on the detection of dissolved molecules by sensory receptors in the olfactory nerve endings of the nose and in the taste buds of the tongue.

STRUCTURE OF TONGUE

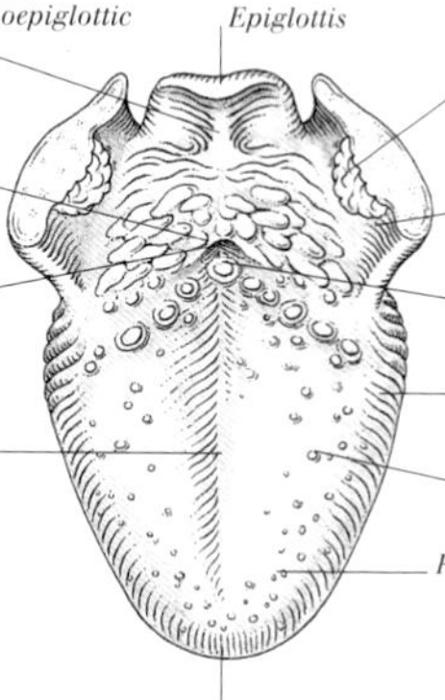
Median glossoepiglottic fold
Epiglottis
Palatine tonsil
Sulcus terminalis
Palatoglossal arch
Foramen caecum
Vallate papilla
Foliate papilla
Median sulcus
Fungiform papilla
Filiform papilla
Apex

TASTE AREAS ON TONGUE

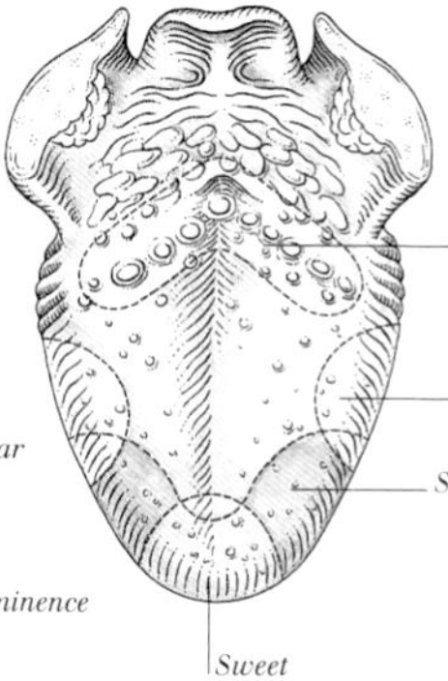
Bitter
Sour
Salt
Sweet

STRUCTURES SURROUNDING PHARYNX

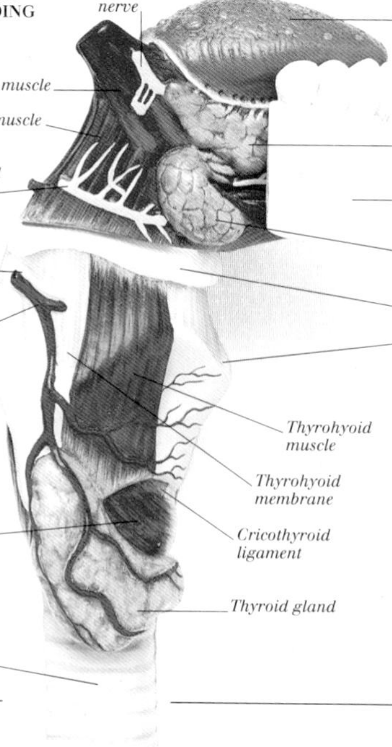
Lingual nerve
Tongue
Styloglossus muscle
Hyoglossus muscle
Sublingual gland
Hypoglossal nerve
Mandible (lower jaw)
Superior laryngeal nerve
Submandibular gland
Hyoid bone
Superior thyroid artery
Laryngeal prominence (Adam's apple)
Thyrohyoid muscle
Thyrohyoid membrane
Cricothyroid muscle
Cricothyroid ligament
Thyroid gland
Trachea

TYPES OF PAPILLAE

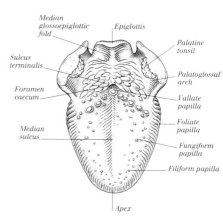

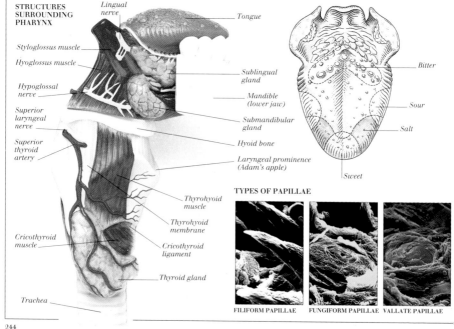

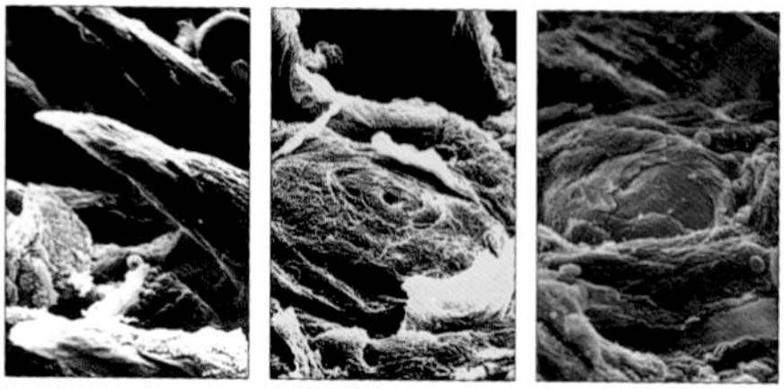

FILIFORM PAPILLAE FUNGIFORM PAPILLAE VALLATE PAPILLAE

SECTION THROUGH NOSE, MOUTH, AND THROAT

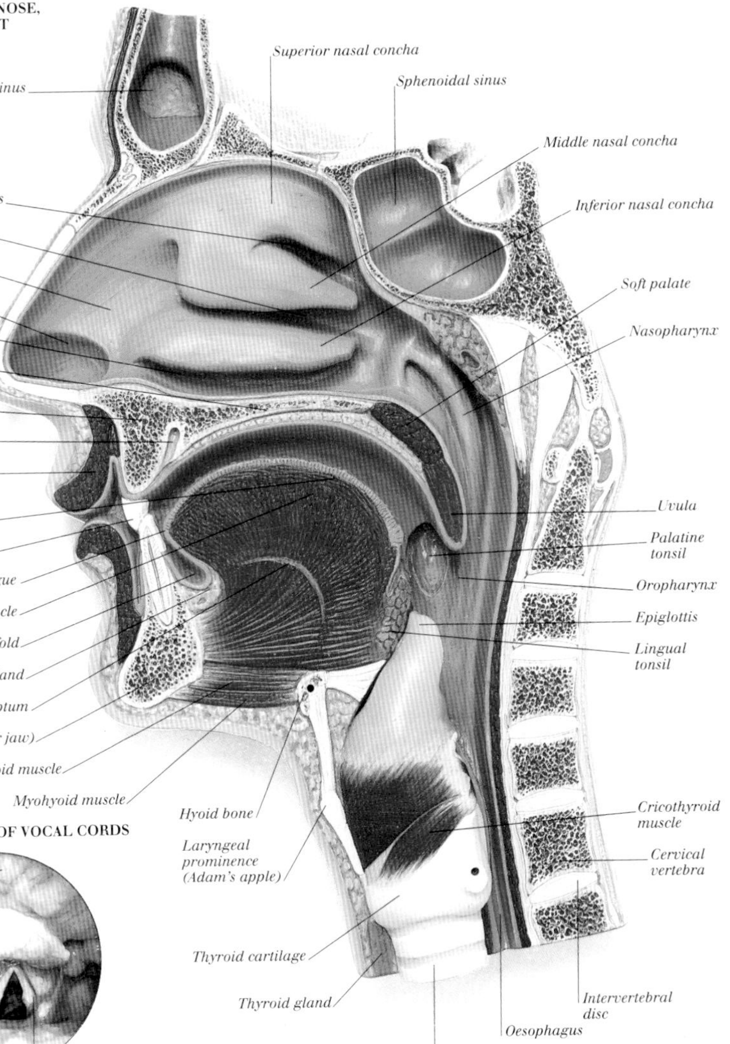

Frontal sinus
Superior nasal concha
Sphenoidal sinus
Middle nasal concha
Superior meatus
Inferior nasal concha
Middle meatus
Nasal cavity
Soft palate
Vestibule
Nasopharynx
Inferior meatus
Hard palate
Maxilla (upper jaw)
Incisive canal
Orbicularis oris muscle
Superior longitudinal muscle
Uvula
Incisor
Palatine tonsil
Apex of tongue
Oropharynx
Genioglossus muscle
Epiglottis
Sublingual fold
Lingual tonsil
Sublingual salivary gland
Fibrous septum
Mandible (lower jaw)
Geniohyoid muscle
Myohyoid muscle
Hyoid bone
Cricothyroid muscle
Laryngeal prominence (Adam's apple)
Cervical vertebra
Thyroid cartilage
Thyroid gland
Intervertebral disc
Oesophagus
Trachea

ENDOSCOPIC VIEW OF VOCAL CORDS

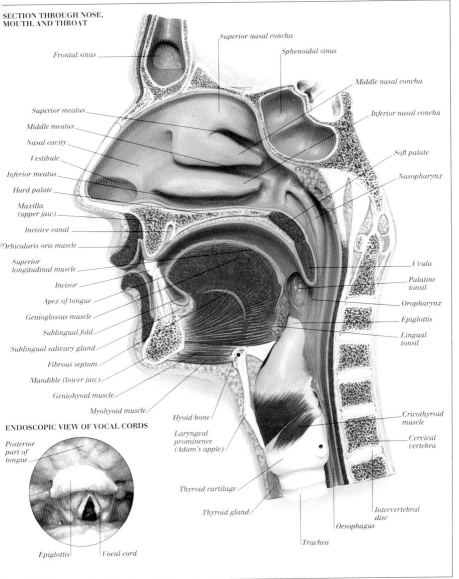

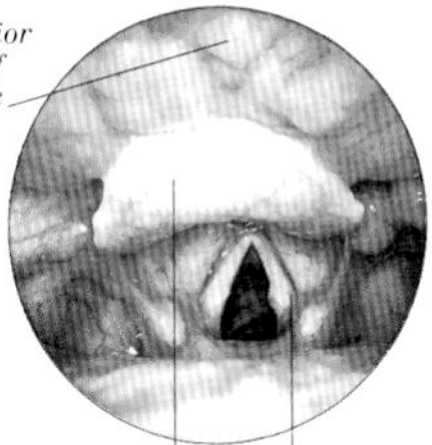

Posterior part of tongue
Epiglottis
Vocal cord

Teeth

THE 20 PRIMARY TEETH (also called deciduous or milk teeth) usually begin to erupt when a baby is about six months old. They start to be replaced by the permanent teeth when the child is about six years old. By the age of 20, most adults have a full set of 32 teeth although the third molars (commonly called wisdom teeth) may never erupt. While teeth help people to speak clearly and give shape to the face, their main function is the chewing of food. Incisors and canines shear and tear the food into pieces; premolars and molars crush and grind it further. Although tooth enamel is the hardest substance in the body, it tends to be eroded and destroyed by acid produced in the mouth during the breakdown of food.

DEVELOPMENT OF TEETH IN A FETUS

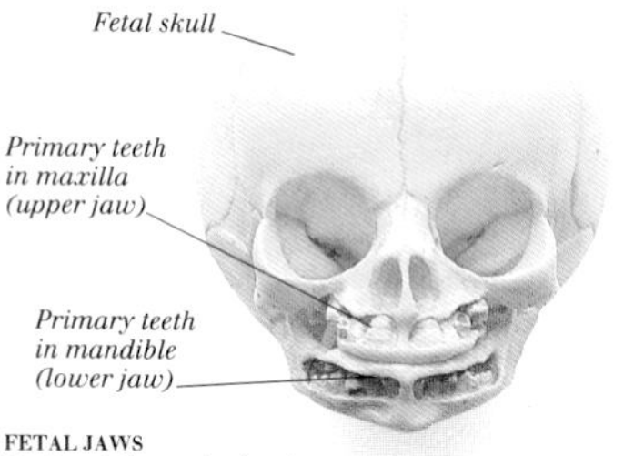
Fetal skull
Primary teeth in maxilla (upper jaw)
Primary teeth in mandible (lower jaw)

FETAL JAWS
By the sixth week of embryonic development areas of thickening occur in each jaw; these areas give rise to tooth buds. By the time the fetus is six months old, enamel has formed on the tooth buds.

DEVELOPMENT OF JAW AND TEETH

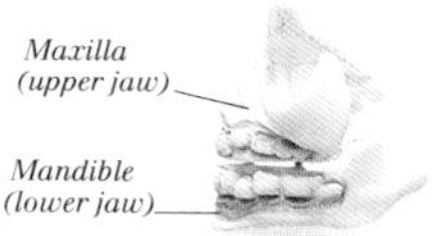
Maxilla (upper jaw)
Mandible (lower jaw)

A NEWBORN BABY'S JAWS
The primary teeth can be seen developing in the jaw bones; they begin to erupt around the age of six months.

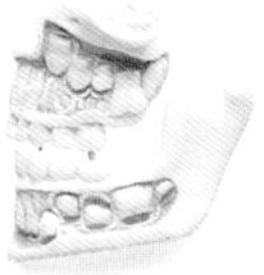

A FIVE-YEAR-OLD CHILD'S TEETH
There is a full set of 20 erupted primary teeth; the permanent teeth can be seen developing in the upper and lower jaws.

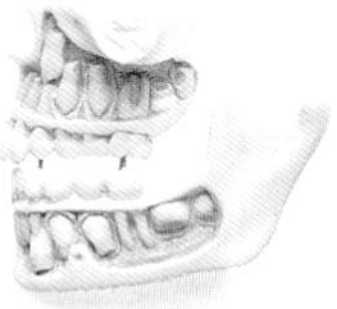

A NINE-YEAR-OLD CHILD'S TEETH
Most of the teeth are primary teeth but the permanent incisors and first molars have now emerged.

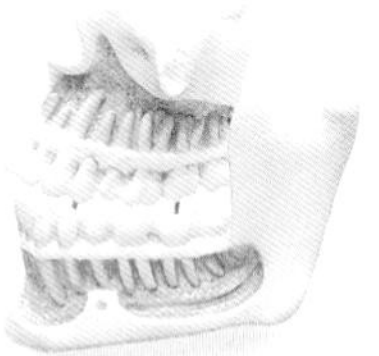

AN ADULT'S TEETH
By the age of 20, the full set of 32 permanent teeth (including the wisdom teeth) should be in position.

THE PERMANENT TEETH

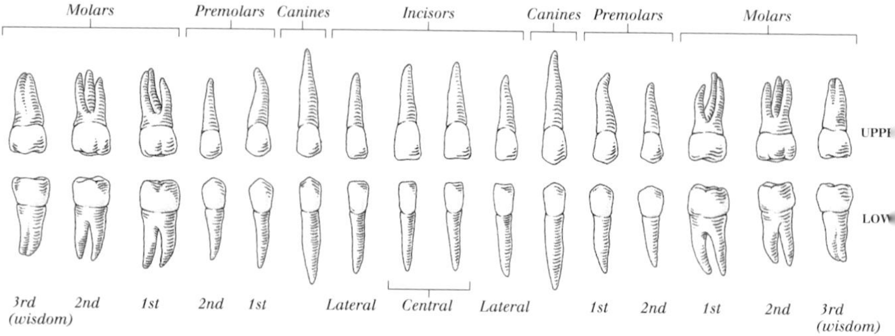
Molars
Premolars
Canines
Incisors
Canines
Premolars
Molars
UPPI
LOW
3rd (wisdom)
2nd
1st
2nd
1st
Lateral
Central
Lateral
1st
2nd
1st
2nd
3rd (wisdom)

STRUCTURE OF A TOOTH

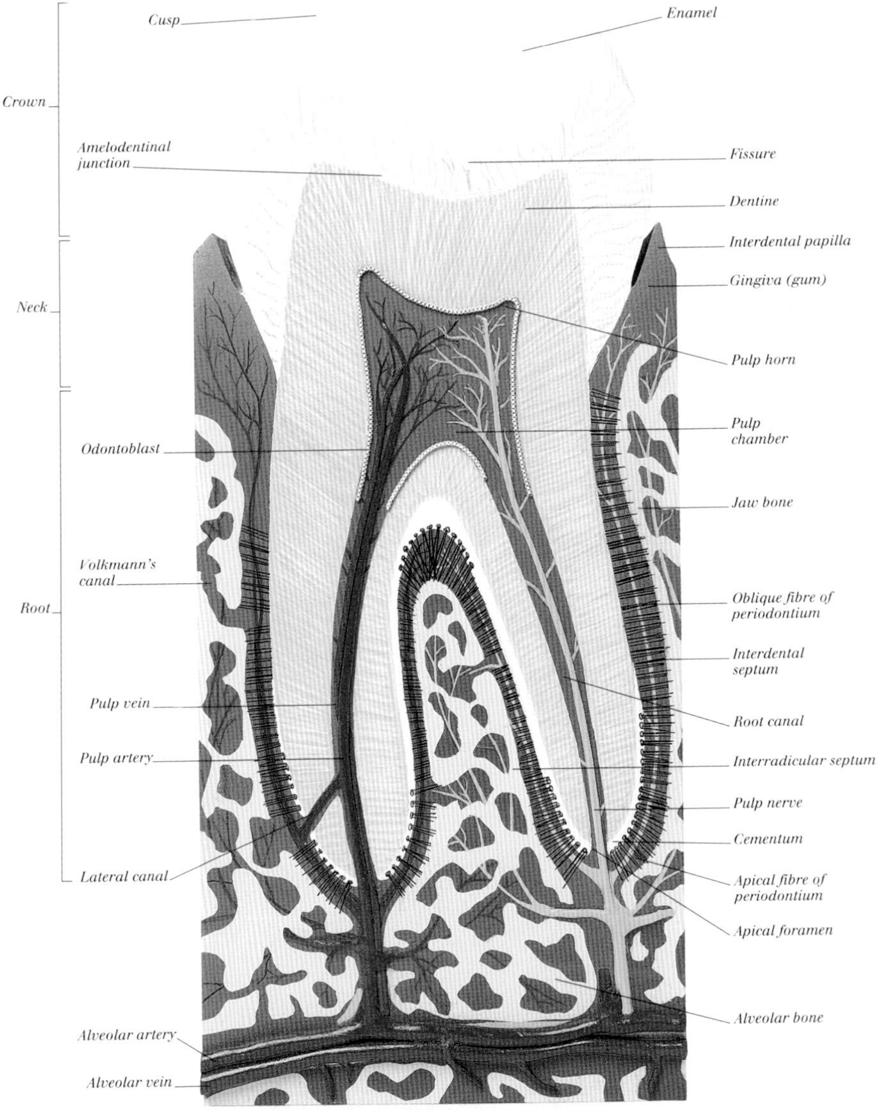
Cusp
Enamel
Crown
Amelodentinal junction
Fissure
Dentine
Interdental papilla
Gingiva (gum)
Neck
Pulp horn
Pulp chamber
Odontoblast
Jaw bone
Volkmann's canal
Root
Oblique fibre of periodontium
Interdental septum
Pulp vein
Root canal
Pulp artery
Interradicular septum
Pulp nerve
Cementum
Lateral canal
Apical fibre of periodontium
Apical foramen
Alveolar bone
Alveolar artery
Alveolar vein

Digestive system

THE DIGESTIVE SYSTEM BREAKS DOWN FOOD into particles so tiny that blood can take nourishment to all parts of the body. The system's main part is a 9 m (30 ft) tube from mouth to rectum; muscles in this alimentary canal force food along. Chewed food first travels through the oesophagus to the stomach, which churns and liquidizes food before it passes through the duodenum, jejunum, and ileum – the three parts of the long, convoluted small intestine. Here, digestive juices from the gallbladder and pancreas break down food particles; many filter out into the blood through tiny fingerlike villi that line the small intestine's inner wall. Undigested food in the colon forms faeces that leave the body through the anus.

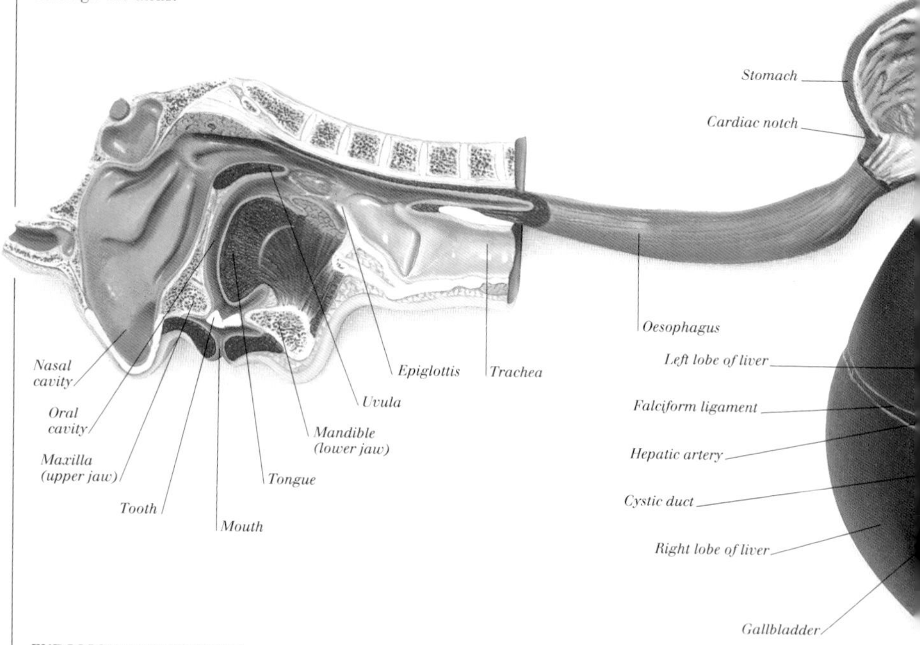
Stomach
Cardiac notch
Oesophagus
Left lobe of liver
Falciform ligament
Hepatic artery
Cystic duct
Right lobe of liver
Gallbladder
Nasal cavity
Oral cavity
Maxilla (upper jaw)
Tooth
Mouth
Tongue
Mandible (lower jaw)
Uvula
Epiglottis
Trachea

ENDOSCOPIC VIEWS INSIDE ALIMENTARY CANAL

OESOPHAGUS

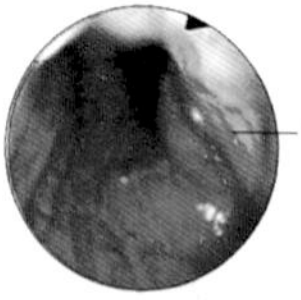
Mucosa

STOMACH ENTRANCE

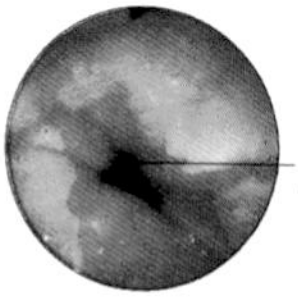
Cardiac orifice

STOMACH

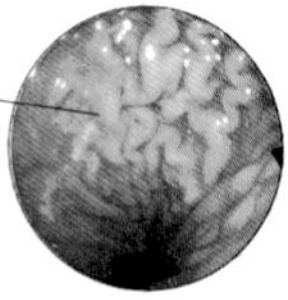
Ruga

STOMACH EXIT

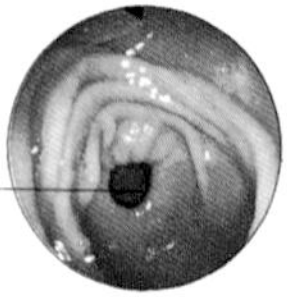
Pylorus

ALIMENTARY CANAL

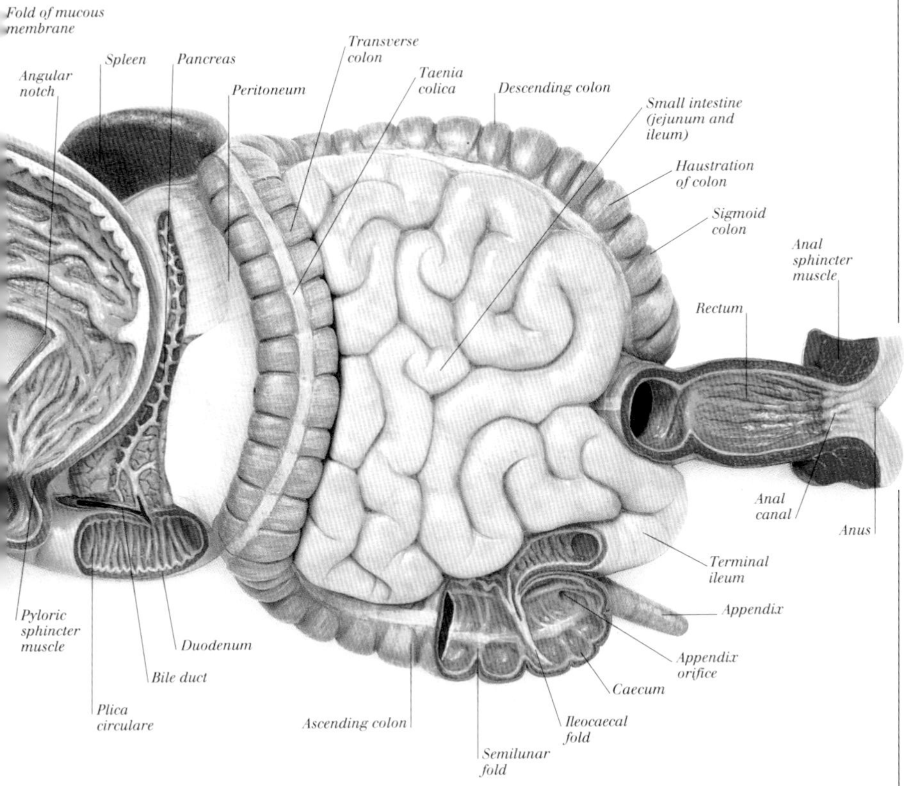
Fold of mucous membrane
Angular notch
Spleen
Pancreas
Peritoneum
Transverse colon
Taenia colica
Descending colon
Small intestine (jejunum and ileum)
Haustration of colon
Sigmoid colon
Anal sphincter muscle
Rectum
Anal canal
Anus
Terminal ileum
Appendix
Appendix orifice
Caecum
Ileocaecal fold
Semilunar fold
Ascending colon
Plica circulare
Bile duct
Duodenum
Pyloric sphincter muscle

DUODENUM

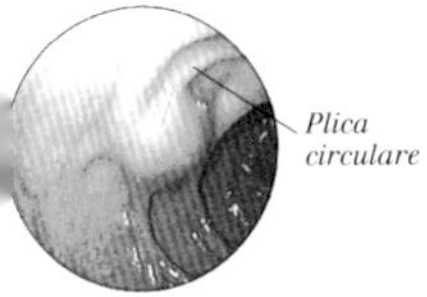
Plica circulare

ILEUM

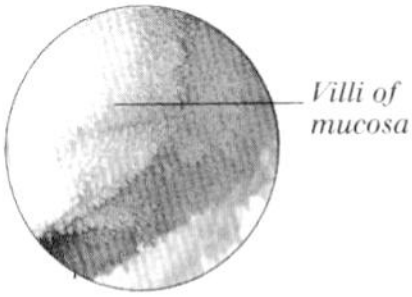
Villi of mucosa

COLON

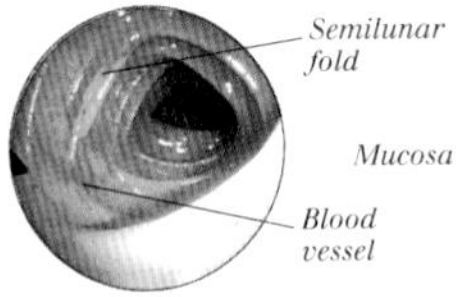
Semilunar fold
Blood vessel

RECTUM

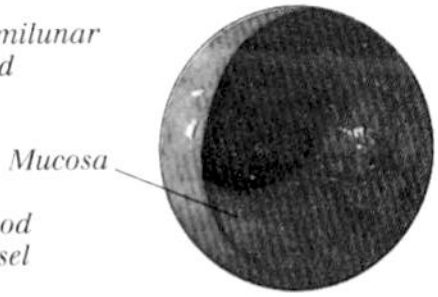
Mucosa

Heart

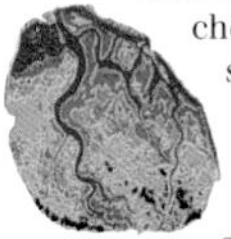

THE HEART IS A HOLLOW MUSCLE in the middle of the chest that pumps blood around the body, supplying cells with oxygen and nutrients. A muscular wall, called the septum, divides the heart lengthways into left and right sides. A valve divides each side into two chambers: an upper atrium and a lower ventricle. When the heart muscle contracts, it squeezes blood through the atria and then through the ventricles. Oxygenated blood from the lungs flows from the pulmonary veins into the left atrium, through the left ventricle, and then out via the aorta to all parts of the body. Deoxygenated blood returning from the body flows from the vena cava into the right atrium, through the right ventricle, and then out via the pulmonary artery to the lungs for reoxygenation. At rest the heart beats between 60 and 80 times a minute; during exercise or at times of stress or excitement the rate may increase to 200 beats a minute.

ARTERIES AND VEINS SURROUNDING HEART

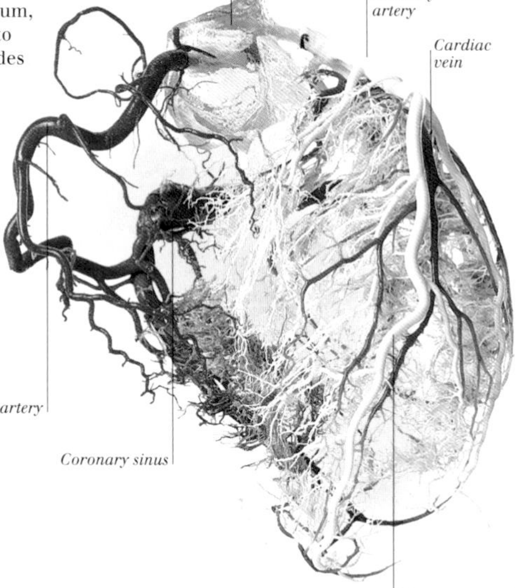
Aorta
Left coronary artery
Cardiac vein
Right coronary artery
Coronary sinus
Main branch of left coronary artery

SECTION THROUGH HEART WALL

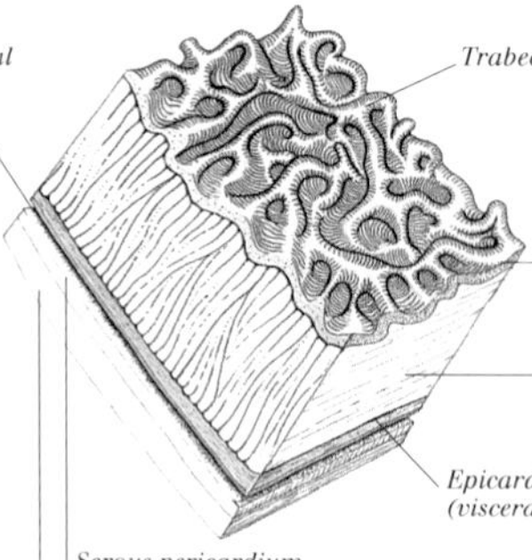
Pericardial cavity
Trabecula
Endocardium
Myocardium
Epicardium (visceral pericardium)
Serous pericardium
Fibrous pericardium

HEARTBEAT SEQUENCE

ATRIAL DIASTOLE

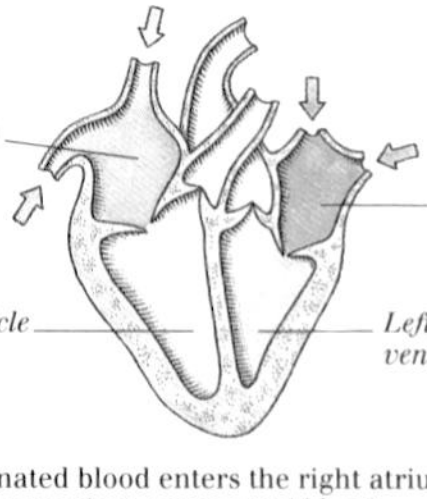
Right atrium
Left atrium
Right ventricle
Left ventricle

Deoxygenated blood enters the right atrium while the left atrium receives oxygenated blood.

STRUCTURE OF HEART

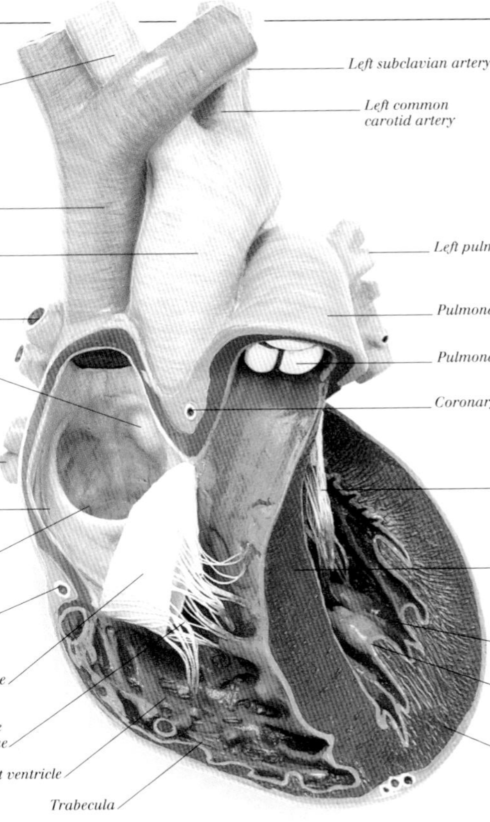
Brachiocephalic trunk
Left subclavian artery
Left common carotid artery
Superior vena cava
Ascending aorta
Left pulmonary vein
Right pulmonary artery
Pulmonary trunk
Fossa ovalis
Pulmonary semilunar valve
Coronary artery
Right pulmonary vein
Chordae tendineae
Right atrium
Opening of inferior vena cava
Muscular part of interventricular septum
Branch of coronary artery
Left ventricle
Tricuspid valve
Papillary muscle
Chordae tendineae
Myocardium of left ventricle
Right ventricle
Trabecula

ATRIAL SYSTOLE (VENTRICULAR DIASTOLE)

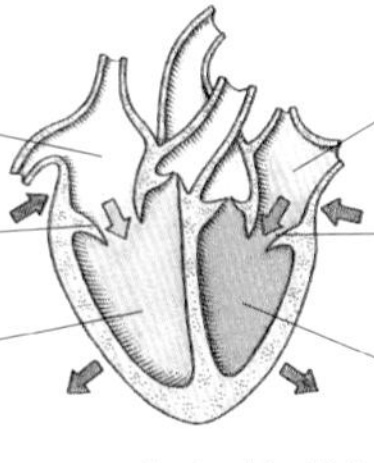
Right atrium contracts
Left atrium contracts
Tricuspid valve opens
Mitral valve opens
Right ventricle dilates
Left ventricle dilates

Left and right atria contract, forcing blood into the relaxed ventricles.

VENTRICULAR SYSTOLE

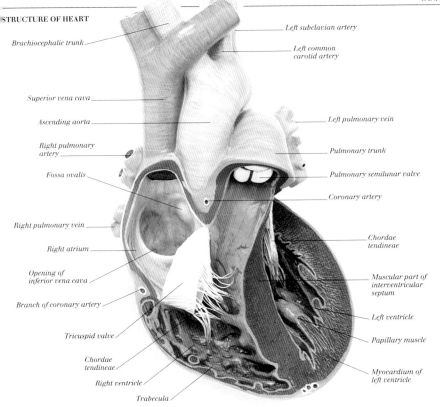

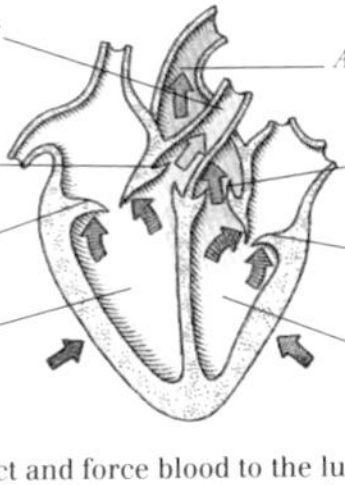
Pulmonary artery
Aorta
Pulmonary valve opens
Aortic valve opens
Tricuspid valve closes
Mitral valve closes
Right ventricle contracts
Left ventricle contracts

Ventricles contract and force blood to the lungs for oxygenation and via the aorta to the rest of the body.

Circulatory system

THE CIRCULATORY SYSTEM consists of the heart and blood vessels, which together maintain a continuous flow of blood around the body. The heart pumps oxygen-rich blood from the lungs to all parts of the body through a network of tubes called arteries, and smaller branches called arterioles. Blood returns to the heart via small vessels called venules, which lead in turn into larger tubes called veins. Arterioles and venules are linked by a network of tiny vessels called capillaries, where the exchange of oxygen and carbon dioxide between blood and body cells takes place. Blood has four main components: red blood cells, white blood cells, platelets, and liquid plasma.

ARTERIAL SYSTEM OF BRAIN

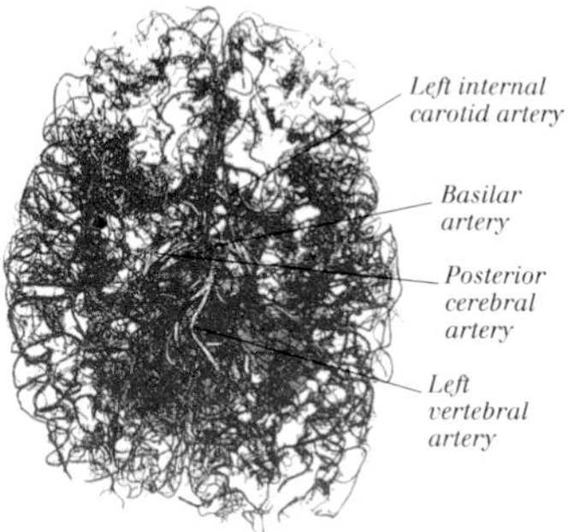
Left internal carotid artery
Basilar artery
Posterior cerebral artery
Left vertebral artery

CIRCULATORY SYSTEM OF LIVER

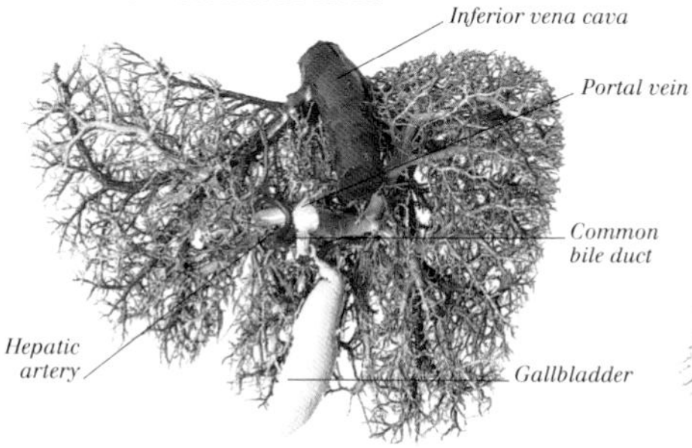
Inferior vena cava
Portal vein
Common bile duct
Hepatic artery
Gallbladder

CIRCULATORY SYSTEM OF HEART AND LUNGS

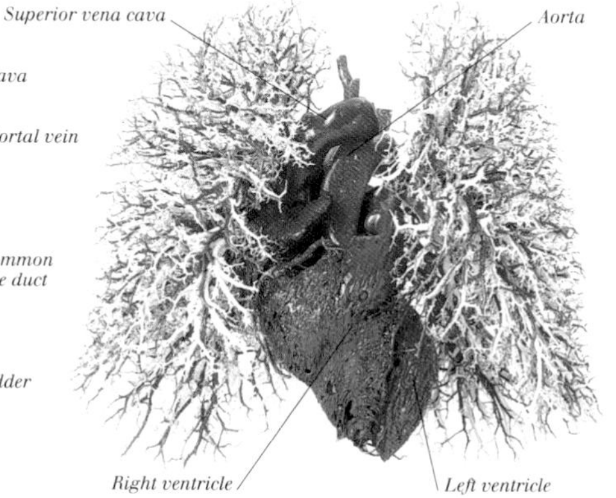
Superior vena cava
Aorta
Right ventricle
Left ventricle

SECTION OF MAIN ARTERY

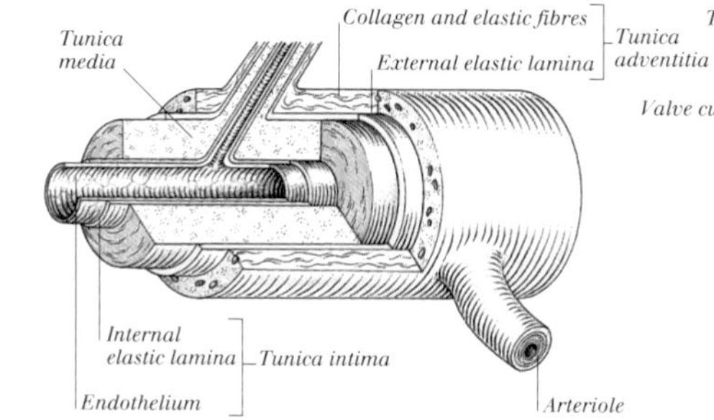
Tunica media
Collagen and elastic fibres
External elastic lamina
Tunica adventitia
Internal elastic lamina
Tunica intima
Endothelium
Arteriole

SECTION OF MAIN VEIN

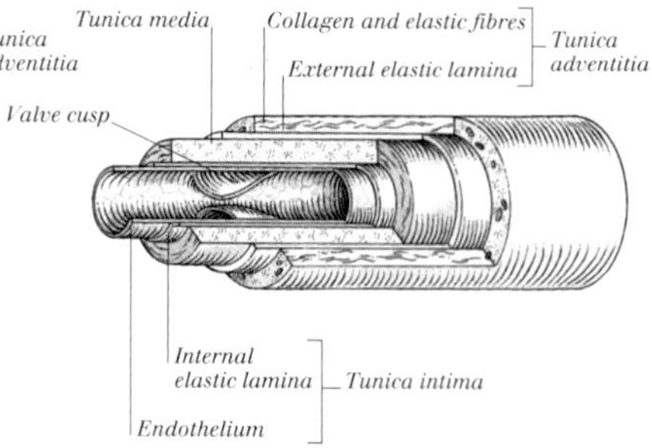
Tunica media
Collagen and elastic fibres
External elastic lamina
Tunica adventitia
Valve cusp
Internal elastic lamina
Tunica intima
Endothelium

PRINCIPAL ARTERIES AND VEINS OF CIRCULATORY SYSTEM

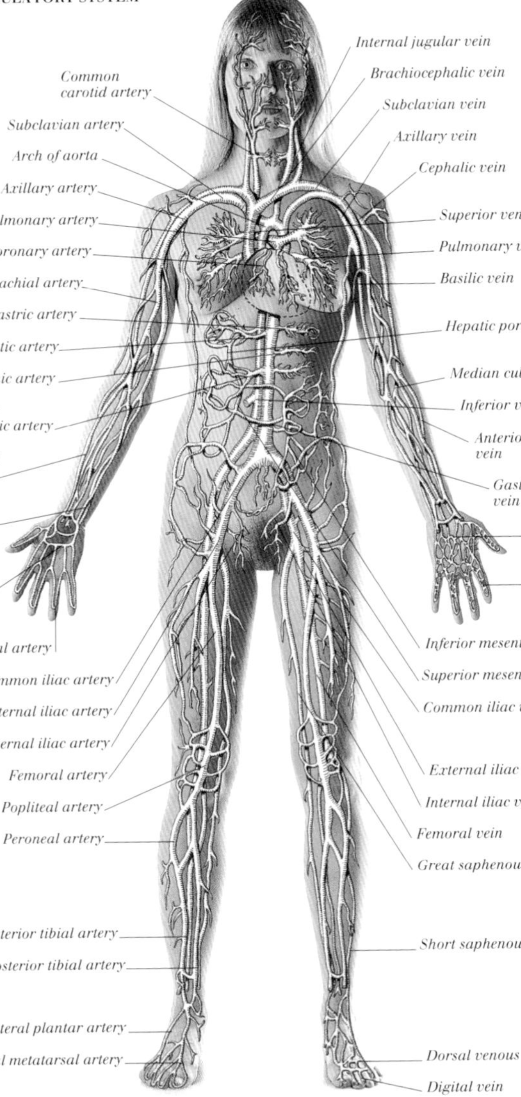
Common carotid artery
Subclavian artery
Arch of aorta
Axillary artery
Pulmonary artery
Coronary artery
Brachial artery
Gastric artery
Hepatic artery
Splenic artery
Superior mesenteric artery
Radial artery
Ulnar artery
Palmar arch
Digital artery
Common iliac artery
External iliac artery
Internal iliac artery
Femoral artery
Popliteal artery
Peroneal artery
Anterior tibial artery
Posterior tibial artery
Lateral plantar artery
Dorsal metatarsal artery
Internal jugular vein
Brachiocephalic vein
Subclavian vein
Axillary vein
Cephalic vein
Superior vena cava
Pulmonary vein
Basilic vein
Hepatic portal vein
Median cubital vein
Inferior vena cava
Anterior median vein
Gastroepiploic vein
Palmar vein
Digital vein
Inferior mesenteric vein
Superior mesenteric vein
Common iliac vein
External iliac vein
Internal iliac vein
Femoral vein
Great saphenous vein
Short saphenous vein
Dorsal venous arch
Digital vein

TYPES OF BLOOD CELLS

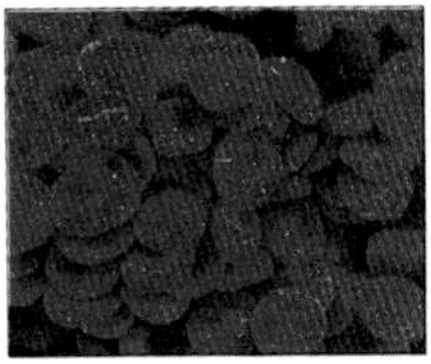

RED BLOOD CELLS
These cells are biconcave in shape to maximize their oxygen-carrying capacity.

WHITE BLOOD CELLS
Lymphocytes are the smallest white blood cells; they form antibodies against disease.

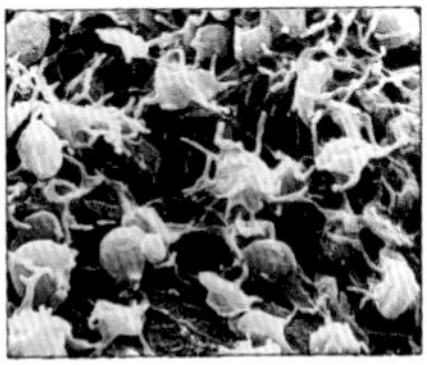

PLATELETS
Tiny cells that are activated whenever blood clotting or repair to vessels is necessary.

BLOOD CLOTTING

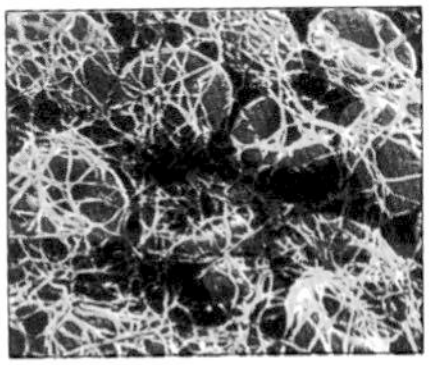

Filaments of fibrin enmesh red blood cells as part of the process of blood clotting.

Respiratory system

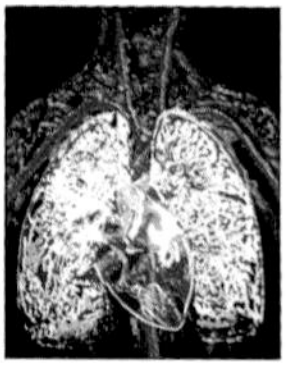

THE RESPIRATORY SYSTEM supplies the oxygen needed by body cells and carries off their carbon dioxide waste. Inhaled air passes via the trachea (windpipe) through two narrower tubes, the bronchi, to the lungs. Each lung comprises many fine, branching tubes called bronchioles that end in tiny clustered chambers called alveoli. Gases cross the thin alveolar walls to and from a network of tiny blood vessels. Intercostal (rib) muscles and the muscular diaphragm below the lungs operate the lungs like bellows, drawing air in and forcing it out at regular intervals.

BRONCHIOLE AND ALVEOLI

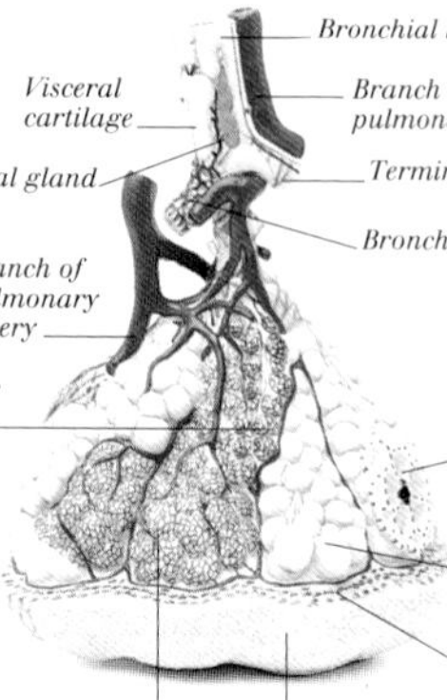
Bronchial nerve
Visceral cartilage
Branch of pulmonary vein
Mucosal gland
Terminal bronchiole
Bronchial vein
Branch of pulmonary artery
Elastic fibres
Interalveolar septum
Alveolus
Connective tissue
Capillary network
Epithelium

SEGMENTS OF BRONCHIAL TREE

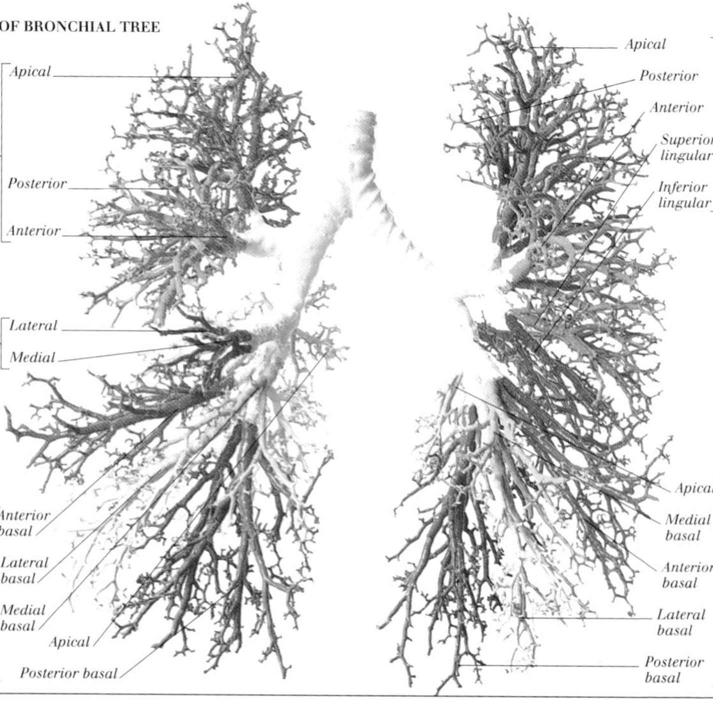
Upper lobe of right lung
Apical
Posterior
Anterior
Middle lobe of right lung
Lateral
Medial
Lower lobe of right lung
Anterior basal
Lateral basal
Medial basal
Apical
Posterior basal
Apical
Posterior
Anterior
Superior lingular
Inferior lingular
Upper lobe of left lung
Apical
Medial basal
Anterior basal
Lateral basal
Posterior basal
Lower lobe of left lung

TRUCTURES OF THORACIC CAVITY

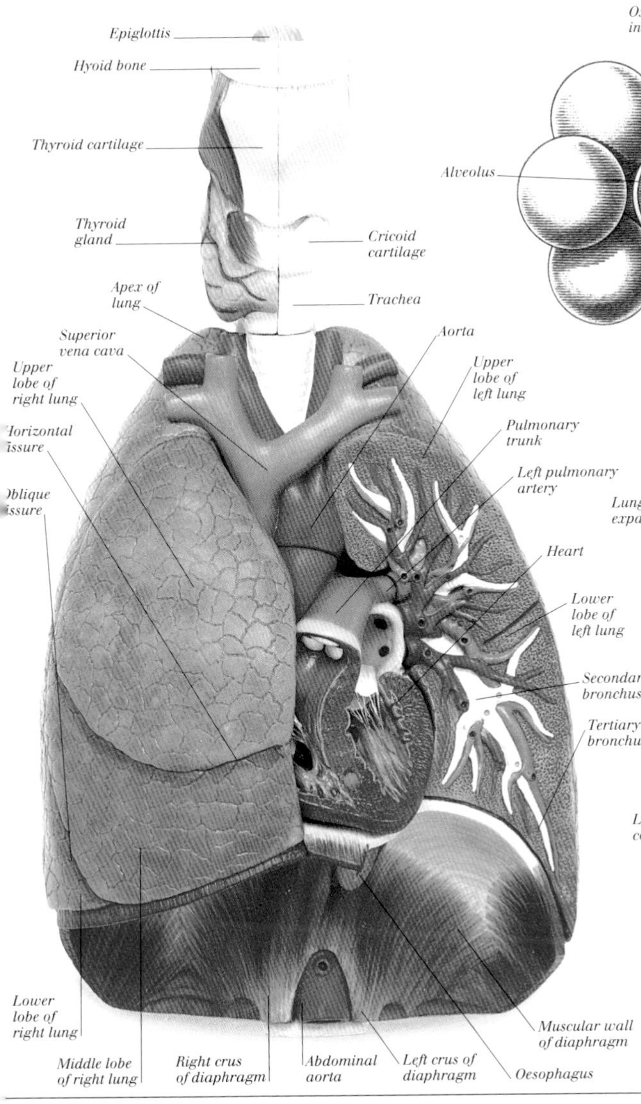
Epiglottis
Hyoid bone
Thyroid cartilage
Thyroid gland
Cricoid cartilage
Apex of lung
Trachea
Superior vena cava
Aorta
Upper lobe of right lung
Upper lobe of left lung
Horizontal fissure
Pulmonary trunk
Oblique fissure
Left pulmonary artery
Heart
Lower lobe of left lung
Secondary bronchus
Tertiary bronchus
Lower lobe of right lung
Middle lobe of right lung
Right crus of diaphragm
Abdominal aorta
Left crus of diaphragm
Oesophagus
Muscular wall of diaphragm

GASEOUS EXCHANGE IN ALVEOLUS

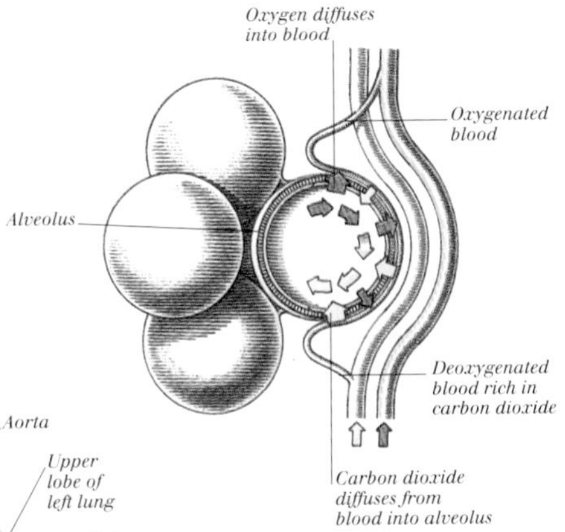
Oxygen diffuses into blood
Oxygenated blood
Alveolus
Deoxygenated blood rich in carbon dioxide
Carbon dioxide diffuses from blood into alveolus

MECHANISM OF RESPIRATION

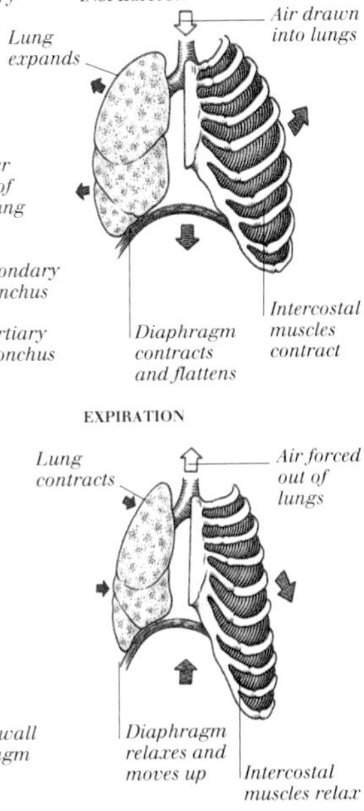
INSPIRATION
Air drawn into lungs
Lung expands
Diaphragm contracts and flattens
Intercostal muscles contract
EXPIRATION
Lung contracts
Air forced out of lungs
Diaphragm relaxes and moves up
Intercostal muscles relax

Urinary system

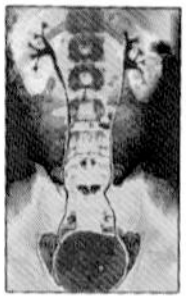

THE URINARY SYSTEM FILTERS WASTE PRODUCTS from the blood and removes them from the body via a system of tubes. Blood is filtered in the two kidneys, which are fist-sized, bean-shaped organs. The renal arteries carry blood to the kidneys; the renal veins remove blood after filtering. Each kidney contains about one million tiny units called nephrons. Each nephron is made up of a tubule and a filtering unit called a glomerulus, which consists of a collection of tiny blood vessels surrounded by the hollow Bowman's capsule. The filtering process produces a watery fluid that leaves the kidney as urine. The urine is carried via two tubes called ureters to the bladder, where it is stored until its release from the body through another tube called the urethra.

ARTERIAL SYSTEM OF KIDNEYS

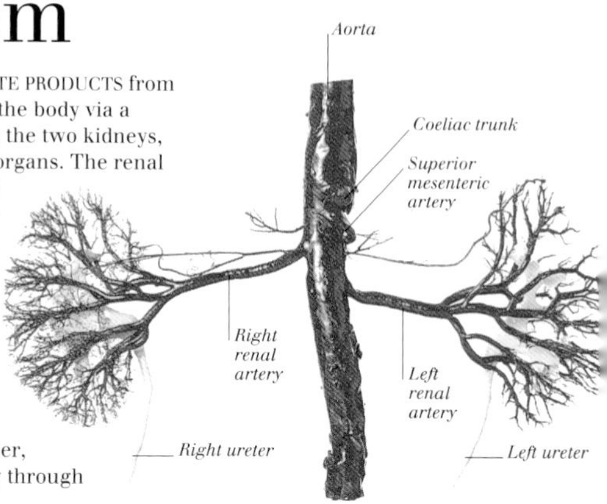
Aorta
Coeliac trunk
Superior mesenteric artery
Right renal artery
Left renal artery
Right ureter
Left ureter

SECTION THROUGH LEFT KIDNEY

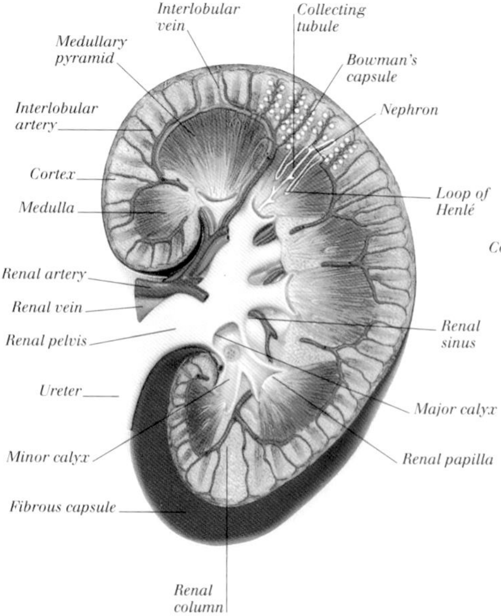
Interlobular vein
Collecting tubule
Medullary pyramid
Bowman's capsule
Nephron
Interlobular artery
Cortex
Medulla
Loop of Henlé
Renal artery
Renal vein
Renal pelvis
Renal sinus
Ureter
Major calyx
Minor calyx
Renal papilla
Fibrous capsule
Renal column

SECTION OF KIDNEY

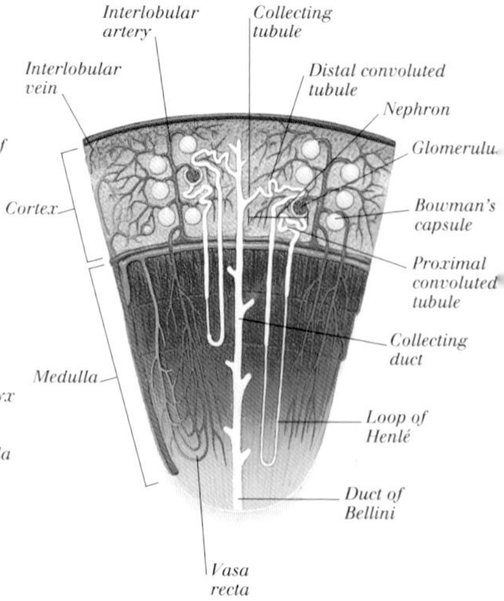
Interlobular artery
Collecting tubule
Interlobular vein
Distal convoluted tubule
Nephron
Glomerulu
Cortex
Bowman's capsule
Proximal convoluted tubule
Collecting duct
Medulla
Loop of Henlé
Duct of Bellini
Vasa recta

MALE URINARY TRACT

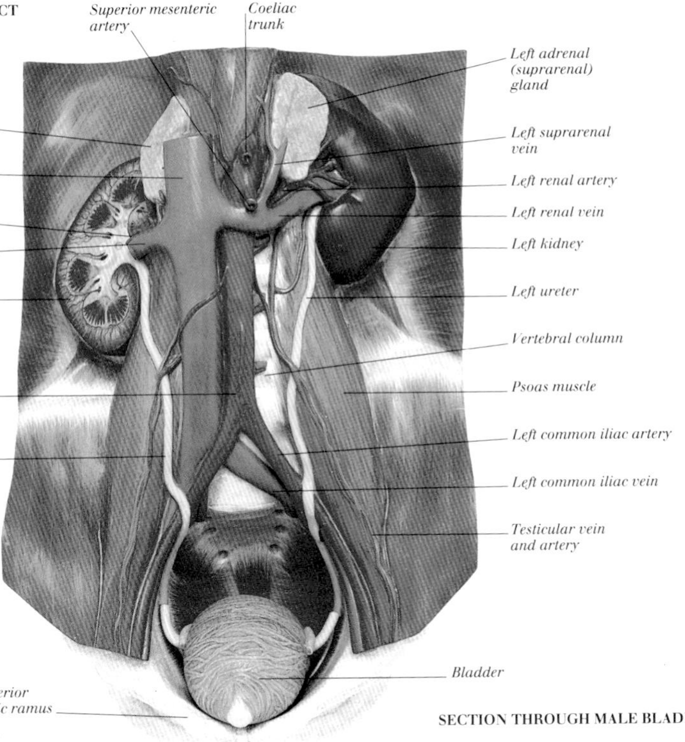
Superior mesenteric artery
Coeliac trunk
Left adrenal (suprarenal) gland
Right adrenal (suprarenal) gland
Left suprarenal vein
Inferior vena cava
Left renal artery
Renal artery
Left renal vein
Renal vein
Left kidney
Right kidney
Left ureter
Vertebral column
Aorta
Psoas muscle
Left common iliac artery
Right ureter
Left common iliac vein
Testicular vein and artery
Bladder
Superior pubic ramus

SECTION THROUGH BOWMAN'S CAPSULE

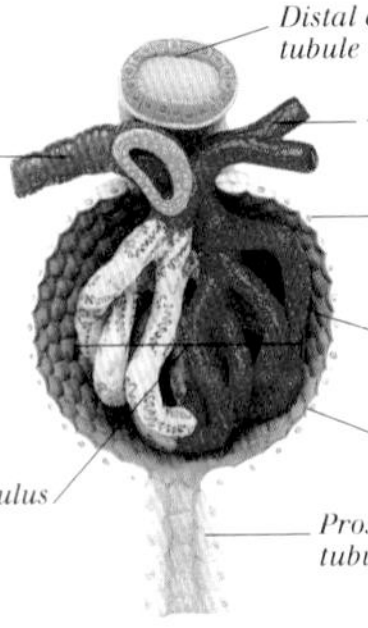
Distal convoluted tubule
Efferent arteriole
Afferent arteriole
Basement membrane of Bowman's capsule
Bowman's space
Bowman's capsule
Glomerulus
Proximal convoluted tubule

SECTION THROUGH MALE BLADDER

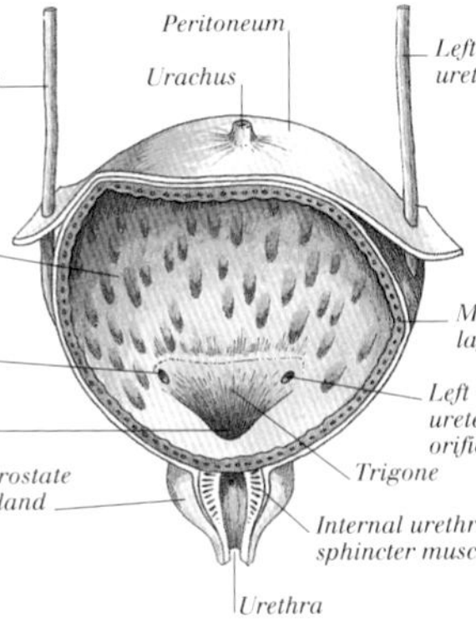
Peritoneum
Right ureter
Urachus
Left ureter
Transitional cell mucosa
Right ureteric orifice
Muscle layer
Internal urethral orifice
Left ureteric orifice
Trigone
Prostate gland
Internal urethral sphincter muscle
Urethra

Reproductive system

SEX ORGANS LOCATED IN THE PELVIS create new human lives. Each month a ripe egg is released from one of the female's ovaries into a fallopian tube leading to the uterus (womb), a muscular pear-sized organ. A male produces minute tadpole-like sperm in two oval glands called testes. When the male is ready to release sperm into the female's vagina, many millions pass into his urethra and leave his body through the fleshy penis. The sperm travel up through the vagina into the uterus and one sperm may enter and fertilize an egg. The fertilized egg becomes embedded in the uterus wall and starts to grow into a new human being.

SECTION THROUGH OVARY

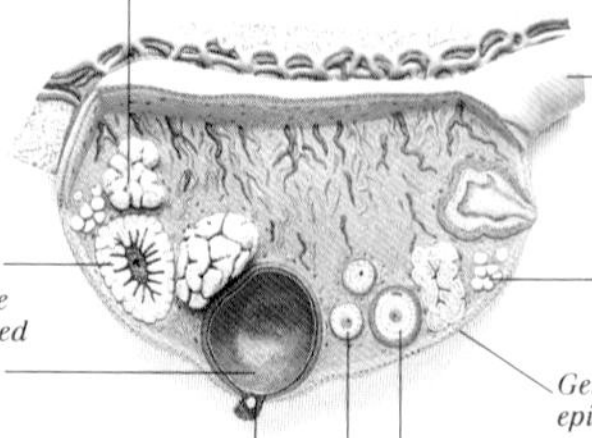
Corpus albicans
Fallopia tube
Corpus luteum
Mature ruptured follicle
Primary follicle
Germinal epithelium
Graffian follicle
Oocyte (egg)
Secondary follicle

SECTION THROUGH FEMALE PELVIC REGION

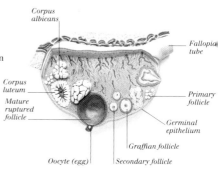

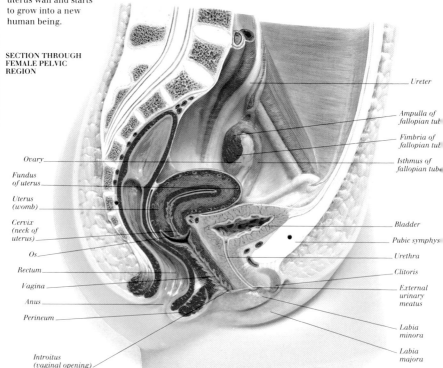

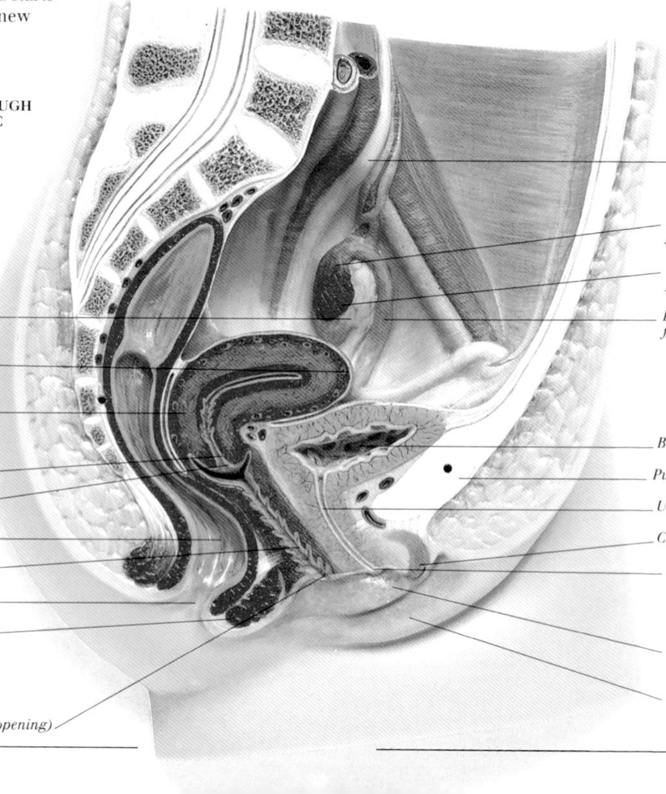
Ureter
Ampulla of fallopian tub
Fimbria of fallopian tub
Ovary
Isthmus of fallopian tub
Fundus of uterus
Uterus (womb)
Cervix (neck of uterus)
Bladder
Pubic symphys
Os
Urethra
Rectum
Clitoris
Vagina
External urinary meatus
Anus
Perineum
Labia minora
Labia majora
Introitus (vaginal opening)

FEMALE REPRODUCTIVE ORGANS

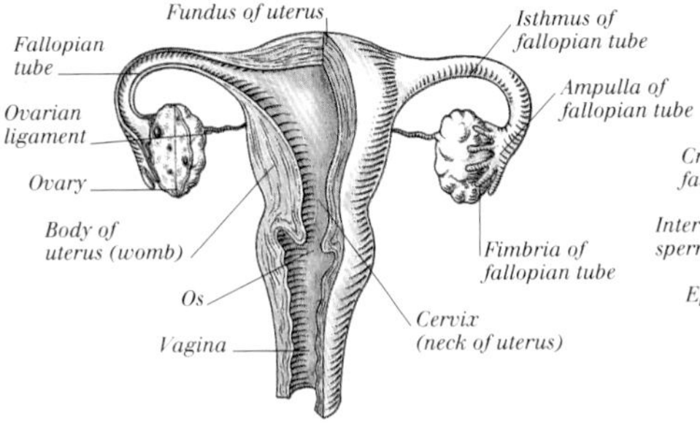
Fundus of uterus
Isthmus of fallopian tube
Fallopian tube
Ampulla of fallopian tube
Ovarian ligament
Ovary
Body of uterus (womb)
Fimbria of fallopian tube
Os
Cervix (neck of uterus)
Vagina

MALE REPRODUCTIVE ORGANS

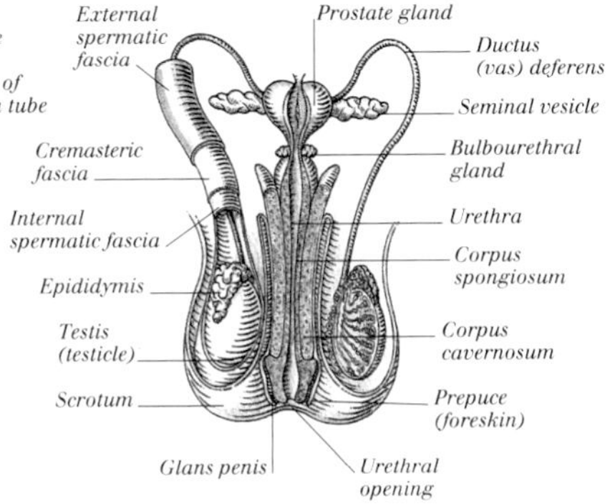
External spermatic fascia
Prostate gland
Ductus (vas) deferens
Seminal vesicle
Cremasteric fascia
Bulbourethral gland
Internal spermatic fascia
Urethra
Corpus spongiosum
Epididymis
Testis (testicle)
Corpus cavernosum
Scrotum
Prepuce (foreskin)
Glans penis
Urethral opening

SECTION THROUGH MALE PELVIC REGION

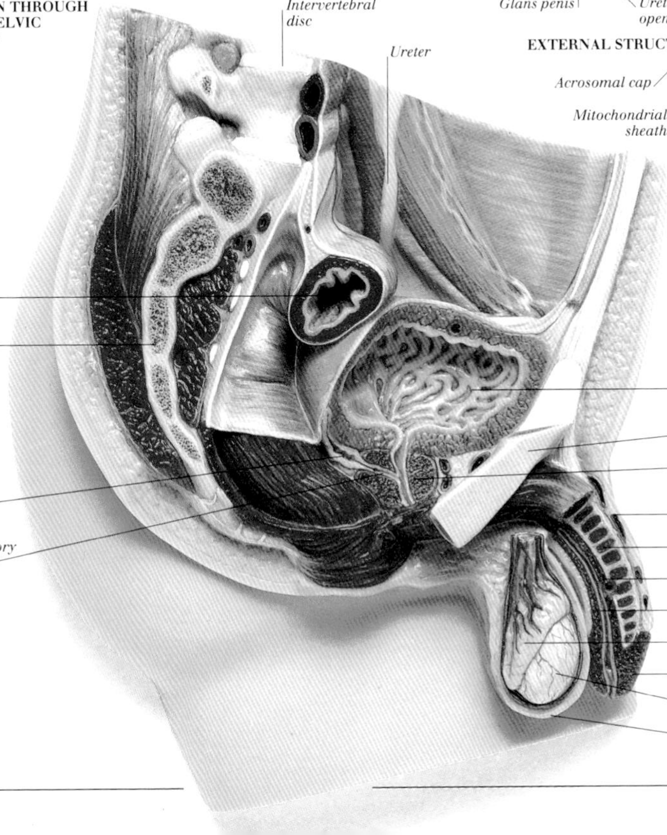
Intervertebral disc
Ureter
Colon
Sacrum
Bladder
Pubis of pelvis
Prostate gland
Seminal vesicle
Penis
Ejaculatory duct
Corpus cavernosum
Corpus spongiosum
Urethra
Epididymis
Glans penis
Testis (testicle)
Scrotum

EXTERNAL STRUCTURE OF SPERM

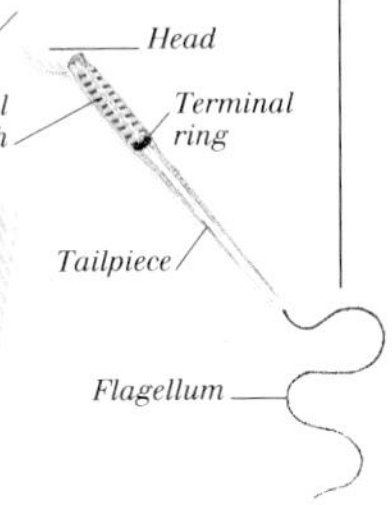
Acrosomal cap
Head
Mitochondrial sheath
Terminal ring
Tailpiece
Flagellum

Development of a baby

A FERTILIZED EGG IS NOURISHED AND PROTECTED as it develops into an embryo and then a fetus during the 40 weeks of pregnancy. The placenta, a mass of blood vessels implanted in the uterus lining, delivers nourishment and oxygen, and removes waste through the umbilical cord. Meanwhile, the fetus lies snugly in its amniotic sac, a bag of fluid that protects it against any sudden jolts. In the last weeks of the pregnancy, the rapidly growing fetus turns head-down: a baby ready to be born.

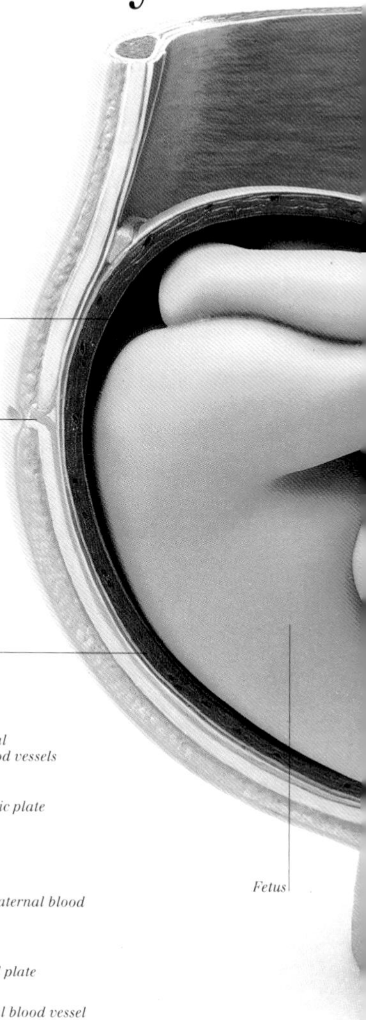
Amniotic fluid
Umbilicus (navel)
Uterine wall
Fetus

EMBRYO AT FIVE WEEKS

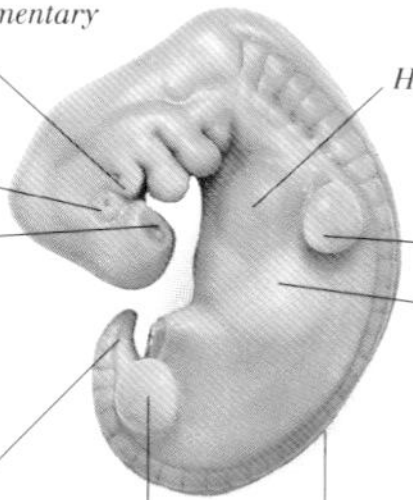
Rudimentary ear
Rudimentary eye
Rudimentary mouth
Heart bulge
Arm bud
Rudimentary liver
Tail bud
Leg bud
Rudimentary vertebra

SECTION THROUGH PLACENTA

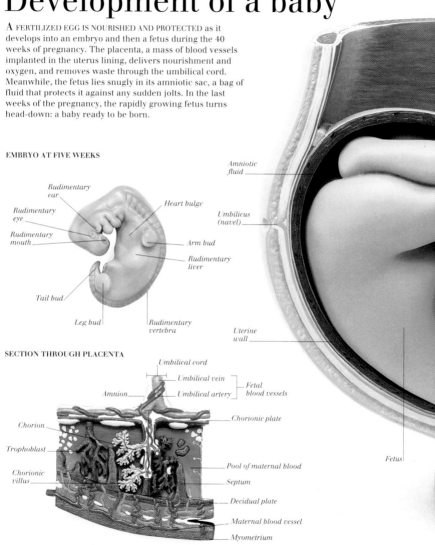

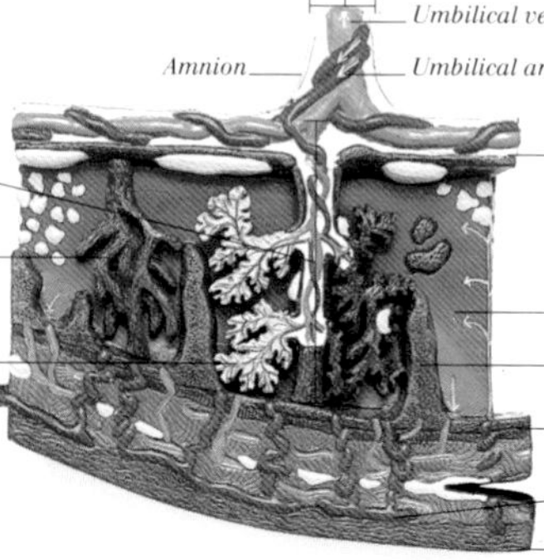
Umbilical cord
Umbilical vein
Umbilical artery
Fetal blood vessels
Amnion
Chorionic plate
Chorion
Trophoblast
Chorionic villus
Pool of maternal blood
Septum
Decidual plate
Maternal blood vessel
Myometrium

SECTION THROUGH PELVIS IN NINTH MONTH OF PREGNANCY

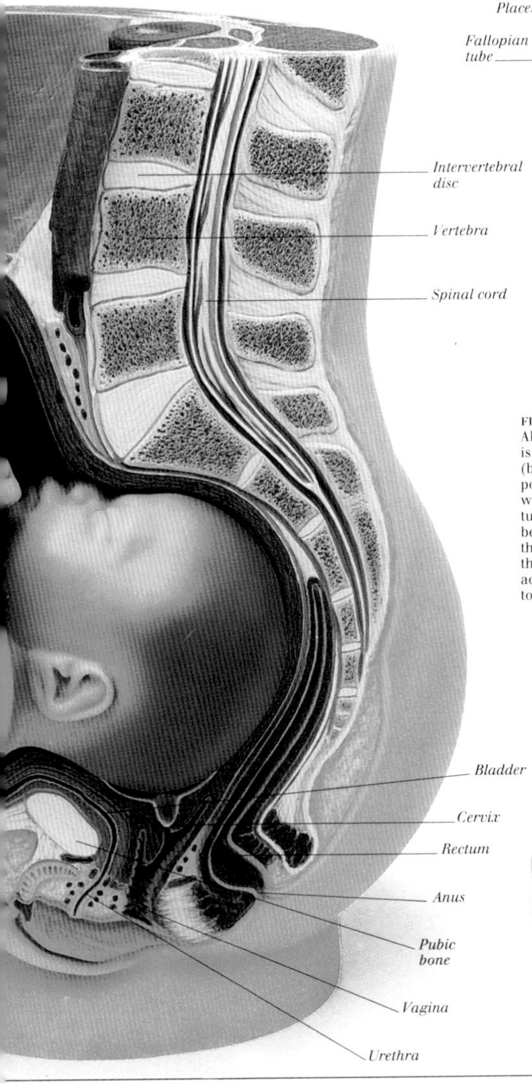
Intervertebral disc
Vertebra
Spinal cord
Bladder
Cervix
Rectum
Anus
Pubic bone
Vagina
Urethra

THE DEVELOPING FETUS

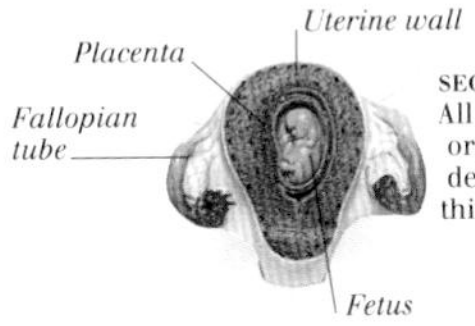
Uterine wall
Placenta
Fallopian tube
Fetus

SECOND MONTH
All the internal organs have developed by this stage.

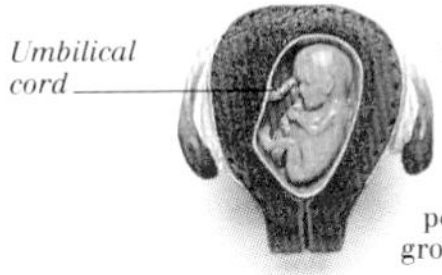
Umbilical cord

THIRD MONTH
The fetus is fully formed and now begins a period of rapid growth.

FIFTH MONTH
Although the fetus is here in breech (bottom down) position, it will probably turn by 180° before birth. By the fifth month the baby is moving actively and responds to sound.

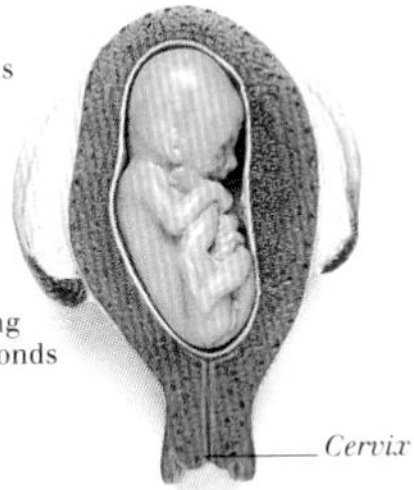
Cervix

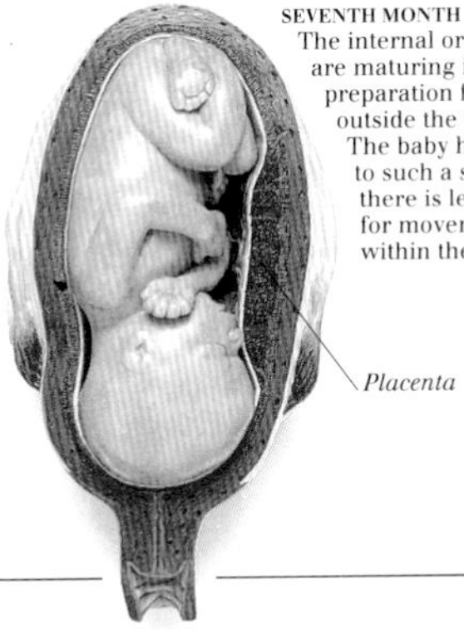
Placenta

SEVENTH MONTH
The internal organs are maturing in preparation for life outside the uterus. The baby has grown to such a size that there is less room for movement within the uterus.

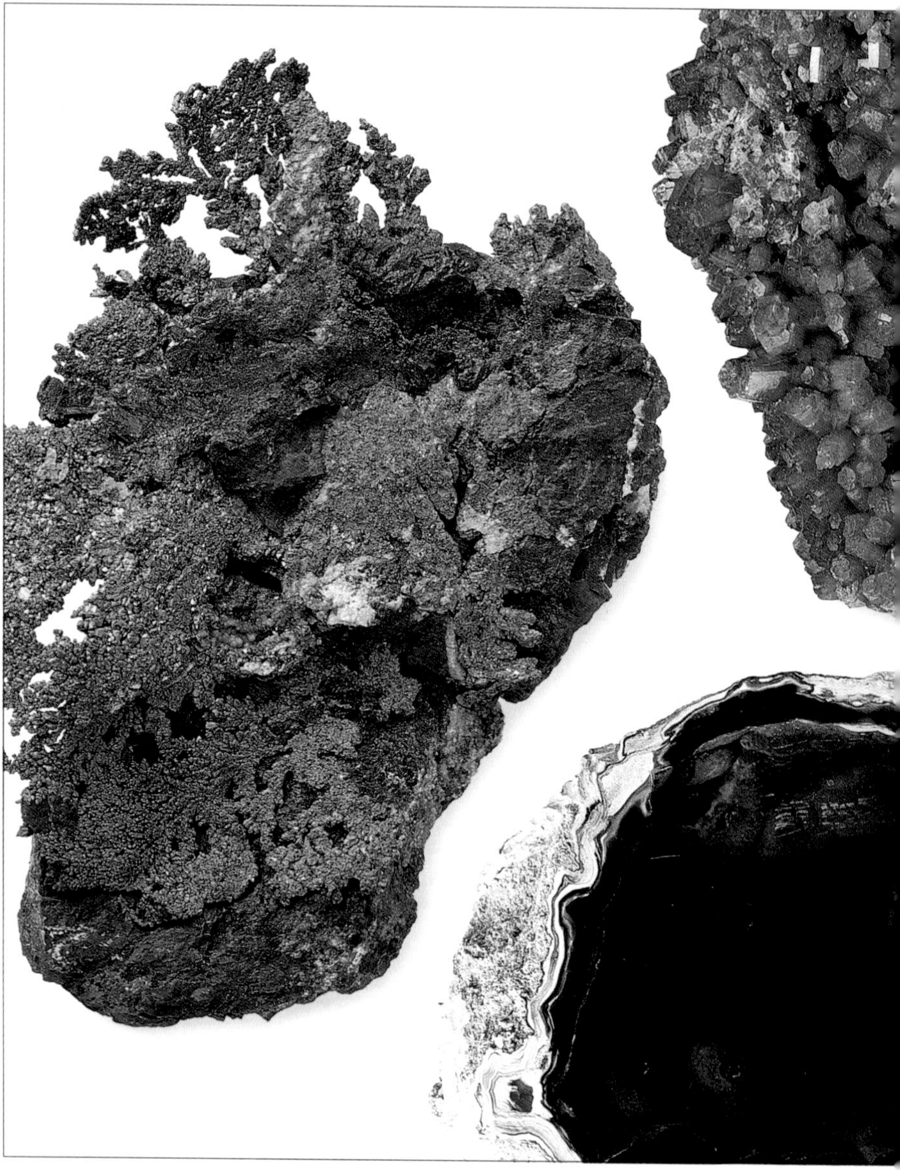

GEOLOGY, GEOGRAPHY, AND METEOROLGY

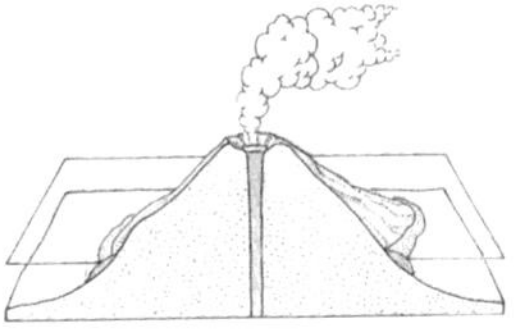

Earth's physical features

MOST OF THE EARTH'S SURFACE (about 70 per cent) is covered with water. The largest single body of water, the Pacific Ocean, alone covers about 30 per cent of the surface. Most of the land is distributed as seven continents; these are (from largest to smallest) Asia, Africa, North America, South America, Antarctica, Europe, and Australasia. The physical features of the land are remarkably varied. Among the most notable are mountain ranges, rivers, and deserts. The largest mountain ranges – the Himalayas in Asia and the Andes in South America – extend for thousands of kilometres. The Himalayas include the world's highest mountain, Mount Everest (8,848 metres). The longest rivers are the River Nile in Africa (6,695 kilometres) and the Amazon River in South America (6,437 kilometres). Deserts cover about 20 per cent of the total land area. The largest is the Sahara, which covers nearly a third of Africa. The Earth's surface features can be represented in various ways. Only a globe can correctly represent areas, shapes, sizes, and directions, because there is always distortion when a spherical surface – the Earth's, for example – is projected on to the flat surface of a map. Each map projection is therefore a compromise: it shows some features accurately but distorts others. Even satellite mapping does not produce completely accurate maps, although they can show physical features with great clarity.

SATELLITE MAPPING OF THE EARTH

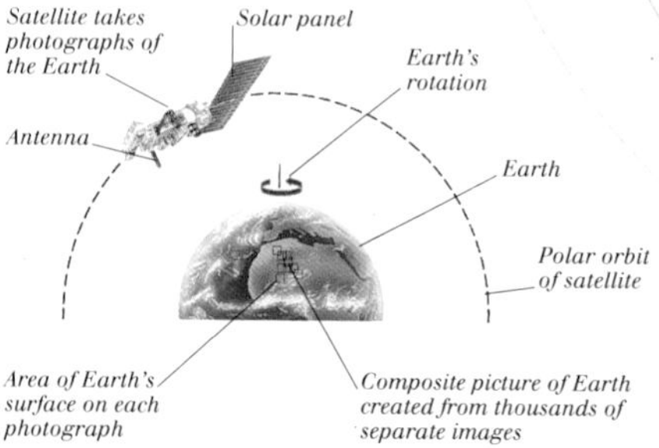
Satellite takes photographs of the Earth
Solar panel
Earth's rotation
Antenna
Earth
Polar orbit of satellite
Area of Earth's surface on each photograph
Composite picture of Earth created from thousands of separate images

EXAMPLES OF MAP PROJECTIONS

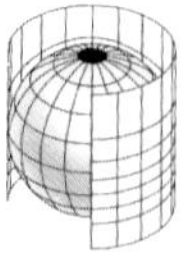

CYLINDRICAL PROJECTION

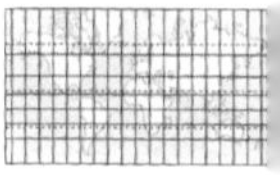

CYLINDRICAL-PROJECTION MAP

180°
160°
120°
80°
Great Slave Lake
Great Bear Lake
Lake Superior
Mackenzie-Peace River
Bering Sea
Hudson Bay
NORTH AMERICA
Rocky Mountains
Sonoran Desert
Sierra Madre
Chihuahuan Desert
Mississippi-Missouri River
Gulf of Mexico
Appalachian Mountains
Lake Michigan
Lake Erie
Lake Ontario
Caribbean Sea
Guiana Highlands
PACIFIC OCEAN
SOUTH AMERICA
Andes
Atacama Desert
Gran Chaco
Parana River
Pampas
Patagonia
WEST OF GREEN MERIDIAN

CONICAL PROJECTION

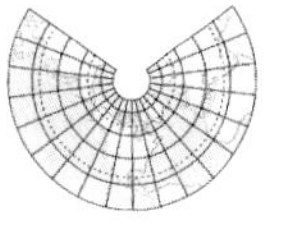

CONICAL-PROJECTION MAP

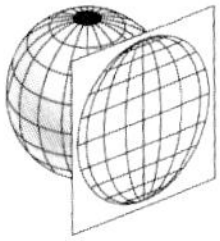

AZIMUTHAL PROJECTION

AZIMUTHAL-PROJECTION MAP

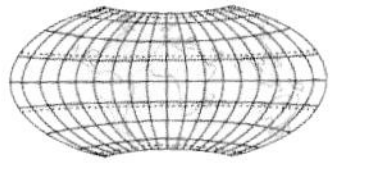

MODIFIED AZIMUTHAL-PROJECTION MAP

SATELLITE MAP OF THE EARTH

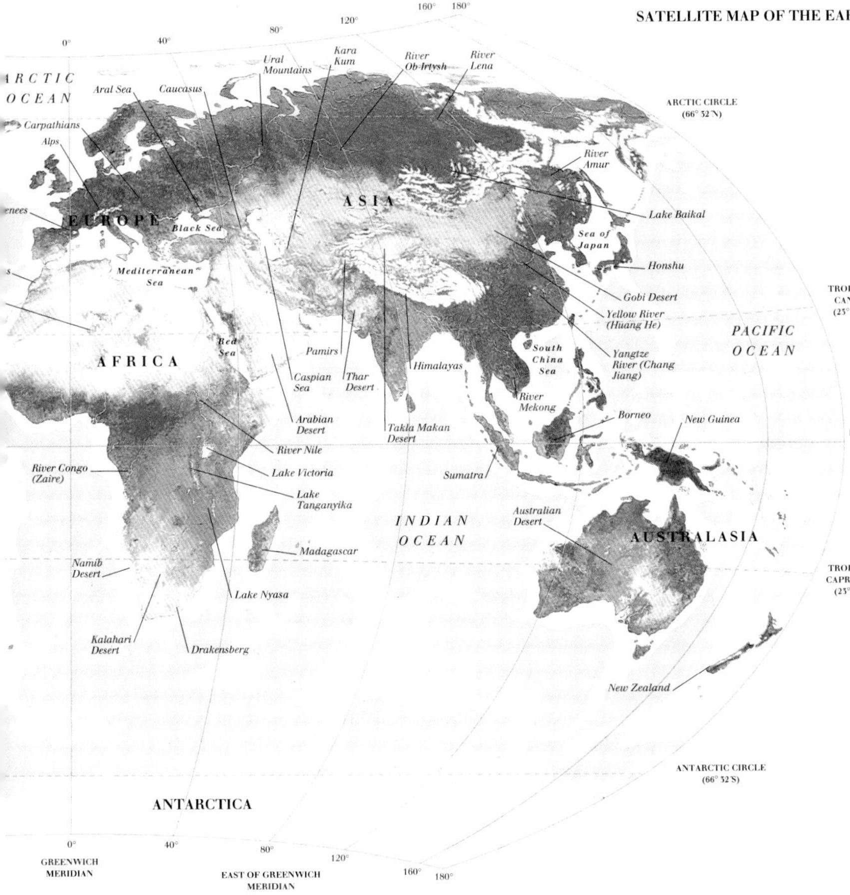

0°
40°
80°
120°
160°
180°
Ural Mountains
Kara Kum
River Ob-Irtysh
River Lena
Aral Sea
Caucasus
Carpathians
Alps
ARCTIC CIRCLE (66° 32'N)
River Amur
ASIA
EUROPE
Black Sea
Lake Baikal
Sea of Japan
Honshu
Mediterranean Sea
Gobi Desert
Yellow River (Huang He)
TROPIC OF CANCER (23° 30'N)
PACIFIC OCEAN
Red Sea
AFRICA
Pamirs
Caspian Sea
Thar Desert
Himalayas
South China Sea
Yangtze River (Chang Jiang)
River Mekong
Arabian Desert
Takla Makan Desert
Borneo
New Guinea
EQUATOR (0°)
River Nile
River Congo (Zaire)
Lake Victoria
Sumatra
Lake Tanganyika
Australian Desert
INDIAN OCEAN
AUSTRALASIA
Madagascar
Namib Desert
TROPIC OF CAPRICORN (23° 30'S)
Lake Nyasa
Kalahari Desert
Drakensberg
New Zealand
ANTARCTIC CIRCLE (66° 32'S)
ANTARCTICA
0°
GREENWICH MERIDIAN
40°
80°
120°
160°
180°
EAST OF GREENWICH MERIDIAN

The rock cycle

HEXAGONAL BASALT COLUMNS, ICELAND

THE ROCK CYCLE IS A CONTINUOUS PROCESS through which old rocks are transformed into new ones. Rocks can be divided into three main groups: igneous, sedimentary, and metamorphic. Igneous rocks are formed when magma (molten rock) from the Earth's interior cools and solidifies (see pp. 274-275). Sedimentary rocks are formed when sediment (rock particles, for example) becomes compressed and cemented together in a process known as lithification (see pp. 276-277). Metamorphic rocks are formed when igneous, sedimentary, or other metamorphic rocks are changed by heat or pressure (see pp. 274-275). Rocks are added to the Earth's surface by crustal movements and volcanic activity. Once exposed on the surface, the rocks are broken down into rock particles by weathering (see pp. 282-283). The particles are then transported by glaciers, rivers, and wind, and deposited as sediment in lakes, deltas, deserts, and on the ocean floor. Some of this sediment undergoes lithification and forms sedimentary rock. This rock may be thrust back to the surface by crustal movements or forced deeper into the Earth's interior, where heat and pressure transform it into metamorphic rock. The metamorphic rock in turn may be pushed up to the surface or may be melted to form magma. Eventually, the magma cools and solidifies – below or on the surface – forming igneous rock. When the sedimentary, igneous, and metamorphic rocks are exposed once more on the Earth's surface, the cycle begins again.

THE ROCK CYCLE

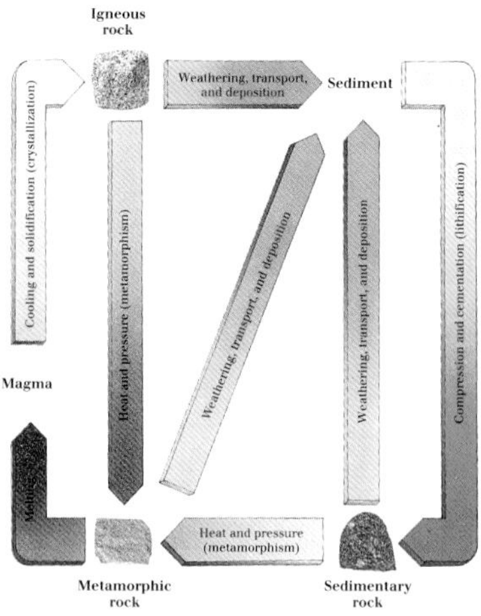
Igneous rock
Weathering, transport, and deposition
Sediment
Cooling and solidification (crystallization)
Heat and pressure (metamorphism)
Weathering, transport, and deposition
Weathering, transport, and deposition
Compression and cementation (lithification)
Magma
Melting
Heat and pressure (metamorphism)
Metamorphic rock
Sedimentary rock

STAGES IN THE ROCK CYCLE

Magma extruded as lava, which solidifies to form igneous rock
Lava flow
Vent
Main conduit
Secondary conduit
Lava
Ash
Rock surrounding magma changed by heat to form metamorphic rock
Intense heat of rising magma melts some of the surrounding rock
Sedimentary rock crushed and folded to form metamorphic rock

IGNEOUS ROCK

Pyroxene crystal
Olivine crystal
Plagioclase feldspar

PHOTOMICROGRAPH OF GABBRO

Coarse-grained texture
Dark pyroxene crystal

PIECE OF GABBRO

SEDIMENTARY ROCK

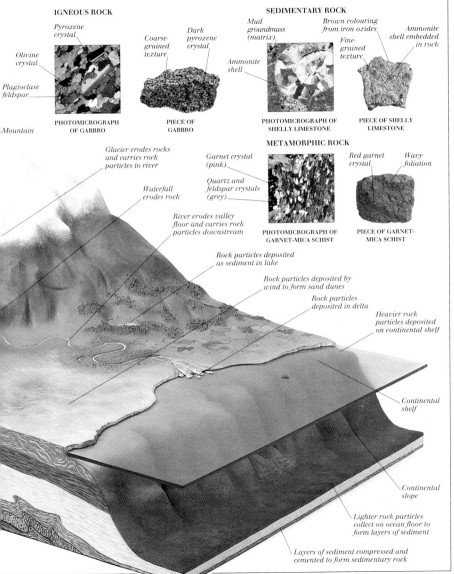

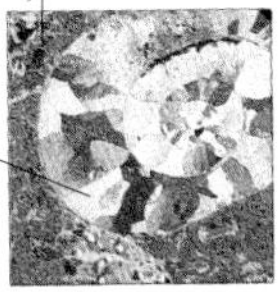
Mud groundmass (matrix)
Ammonite shell

PHOTOMICROGRAPH OF SHELLY LIMESTONE

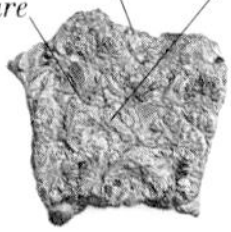
Brown colouring from iron oxides
Fine-grained texture
Ammonite shell embedded in rock

PIECE OF SHELLY LIMESTONE

METAMORPHIC ROCK

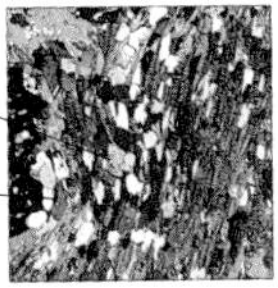
Garnet crystal (pink)
Quartz and feldspar crystals (grey)

PHOTOMICROGRAPH OF GARNET-MICA SCHIST

Red garnet crystal
Wavy foliation

PIECE OF GARNET-MICA SCHIST

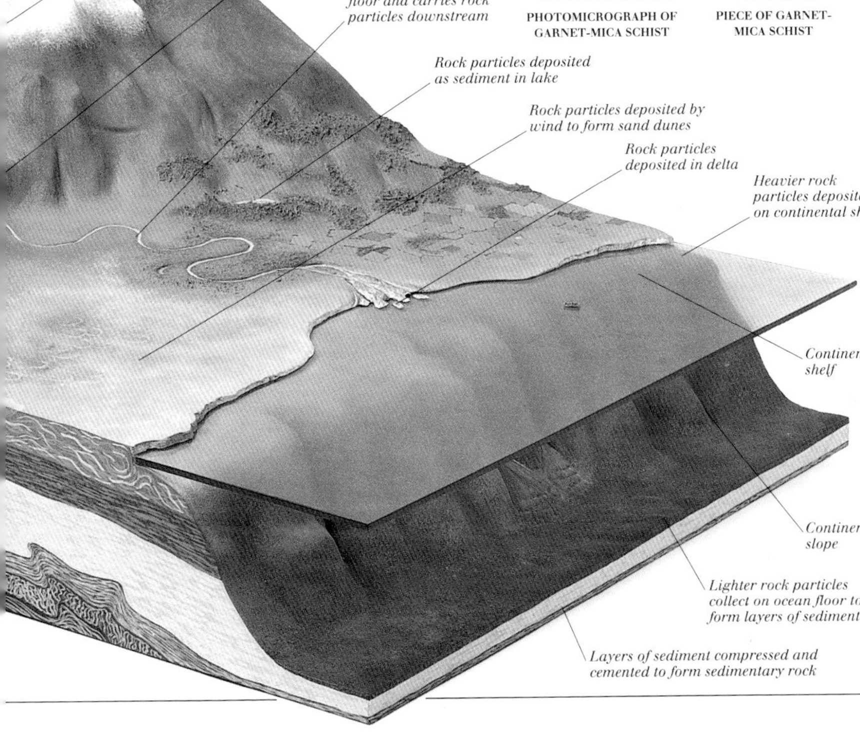
Mountain
Glacier erodes rocks and carries rock particles to river
Waterfall erodes rock
River erodes valley floor and carries rock particles downstream
Rock particles deposited as sediment in lake
Rock particles deposited by wind to form sand dunes
Rock particles deposited in delta
Heavier rock particles deposited on continental shelf
Continental shelf
Continental slope
Lighter rock particles collect on ocean floor to form layers of sediment
Layers of sediment compressed and cemented to form sedimentary rock

Minerals

A MINERAL IS A NATURALLY OCCURRING SUBSTANCE that has a characteristic chemical composition and specific physical properties, such as habit and streak (see pp. 270-271). A rock, by comparison, is an aggregate of minerals and need not have a specific chemical composition. Minerals are made up of elements (substances that cannot be broken down chemically into simpler substances), each of which can be represented by a chemical symbol. Minerals can be divided into two main groups: native elements and compounds. Native elements are made up of a pure element. Examples include gold (chemical symbol Au), silver (Ag), copper (Cu), and carbon (C); carbon occurs as a native element in two forms, diamond and graphite. Compounds are combinations of two or more elements. For example, sulphides are compounds of sulphur (S) and one or more other elements, such as lead (Pb) in the mineral galena, or antimony (Sb) in the mineral stibnite.

NATIVE ELEMENTS

Dendritic (branching) copper
Limonite groundmass (matrix)

COPPER
(Cu)

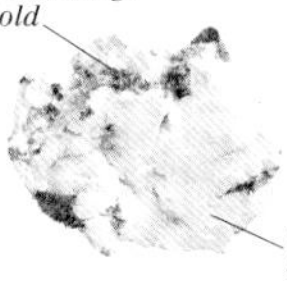
Dendritic (branching) gold
Quartz vein

GOLD
(Au)

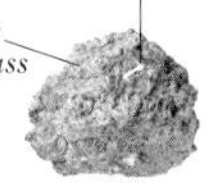
White diamond
Kimberlite groundmass (matrix)

DIAMOND
(C)

Hexagonal graphite crystal

GRAPHITE
(C)

SULPHIDES

Cubic galena crystal

GALENA
(PbS)

Prismatic stibnite crystal
Quartz groundmass (matrix)

STIBNITE
(Sb_2S_3)

Perfect octahedral pyrites crystal
Quartz crystal

PYRITES
(FeS_2)

OXIDES/HYDROXIDES

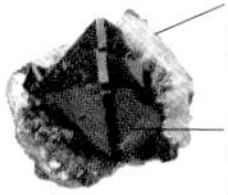
Milky quartz groundmass (matrix)
Smoky quartz crystal

SMOKY QUARTZ
(SiO_2)

Rounded bauxite grains in groundmass (matrix)

BAUXITE
(FeO(OH) and $Al_2O_3.2H_2O$)

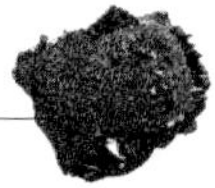
Mass of specular haematite crystals

SPECULAR HAEMATITE
(Fe_2O_3)

Parallel bands of onyx

ONYX
(SiO_2)

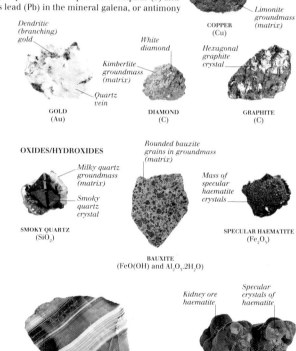

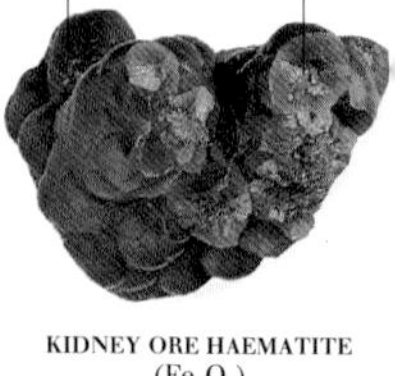
Kidney ore haematite
Specular crystals of haematite

KIDNEY ORE HAEMATITE
(Fe_2O_3)

PHOSPHATES

Limonite groundmass (matrix)
Prismatic pyromorphite crystals

PYROMORPHITE
($Pb_5(PO_4)_3Cl$)

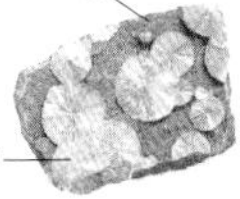
Rock groundmass (matrix)
Radiating wavellite crystals

WAVELLITE
($Al_3(PO_4)_2(OH,F)_3.5H_2O$)

CARBONATES

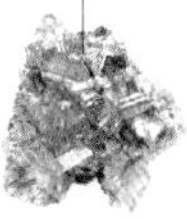
Striated cerussite crystal

CERUSSITE
($PbCO_3$)

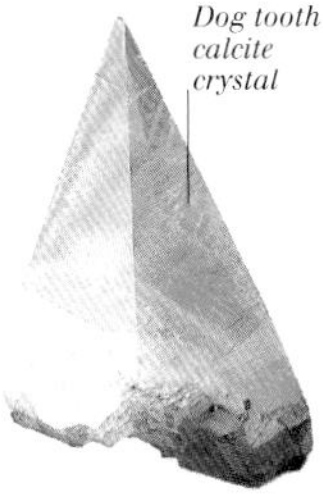
Dog tooth calcite crystal

CALCITE
($CaCO_3$)

SULPHATES

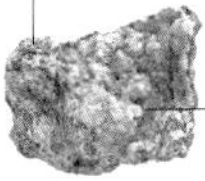
Rock groundmass (matrix)
Radiating cyanotrichite crystals

CYANOTRICHITE
($u_4Al_2(SO_4)(OH)_{12}.2H_2O$)

Radiating crystal mass of daisy gypsum

DAISY GYPSUM
($CaSO_4.2H_2O$)

MOLYBDATE

Tabular wulfenite crystal
Dark rock groundmass (matrix)

WULFENITE
($PbMoO_4$)

SILICATES

Dodecahedral sodalite crystal

SODALITE
($Na_8Al_6Si_6O_{24}Cl_2$)

Feldspar groundmass (matrix)
Transparent bicolored tourmaline crystal

TOURMALINE
($Na(Mg,Fe,Li,Mn,Al)_3Al_6(BO_3)_3Si_6.O_{18}(OH,F)_4$)

Striated surface of olivine crystal

OLIVINE
(Fe_2SiO_4 - Mg_2SiO_4)

Striated prismatic epidote crystal

EPIDOTE
($Ca_2(Al,Fe)_3(SiO_4)_3(OH)$)

Tabular muscovite crystal

MUSCOVITE
($KAl_2(Si_3Al)O_{10}(OH,F)_2$)

Orthoclase crystal

ORTHOCLASE
($KAlSi_3O_8$)

HALIDES

Cubic fluorite crystal

GREEN FLUORITE
(CaF_2)

Cubic rock salt crystal

ORANGE HALITE (ROCK SALT)
($NaCl$)

Mineral features

MINERALS CAN BE IDENTIFIED BY STUDYING features such as fracture, cleavage, crystal system, habit, hardness, colour, and streak. Minerals can break in different ways. If a mineral breaks in an irregular way, leaving rough surfaces, it possesses fracture. If a mineral breaks along well-defined planes of weakness, it possesses cleavage. Specific minerals have distinctive patterns of cleavage; for example, mica cleaves along one plane. Most minerals form crystals, which can be categorized into crystal systems according to their symmetry and number of faces. Within each system, several different but related forms of crystal are possible; for example, a cubic crystal can have six, eight, or twelve sides. A mineral's habit is the typical form taken by an aggregate of its crystals. Examples of habit include botryoidal (like a bunch of grapes) and massive (no definite form). The relative hardness of a mineral may be assessed by testing its resistance to scratching. This property is usually measured using Mohs scale, which increases in hardness from 1 (talc) to 10 (diamond). The colour of a mineral is not a dependable guide to its identity as some minerals have a range of colours. Streak (the colour the powdered mineral makes when rubbed across an unglazed tile) is a more reliable indicator.

FRACTURE

Fire opal with conchoidal (shell-like) fracture

CONCHOIDAL FRACTURE

Nickel-iron with hackly (jagged) fracture

HACKLY FRACTURE

Orpiment with uneven fracture

UNEVEN FRACTURE

Garnierite with splintery fracture

SPLINTERY FRACTURE

CLEAVAGE

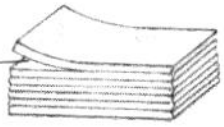
Cleavage in one direction

CLEAVAGE ALONG ONE PLANE

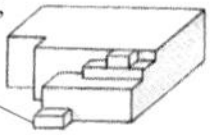
Cleavage in three directions, forming a block cube

CLEAVAGE ALONG THREE PLANES

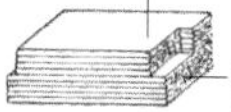
Horizontal cleavage
Vertical cleavage

CLEAVAGE ALONG TWO PLANES

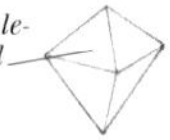
Cleavage in four directions, forming a double-pyramid crystal

CLEAVAGE ALONG FOUR PLANES

CRYSTAL SYSTEMS

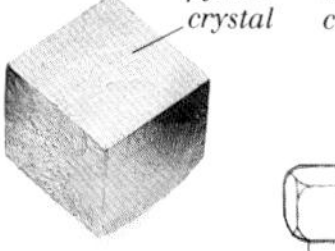
Cubic iron pyrites crystal
Representation of cubic system

CUBIC SYSTEM

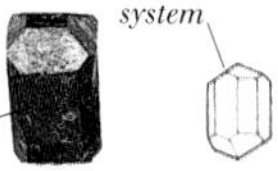
Tetragonal idocrase crystal
Representation of tetragonal system

TETRAGONAL SYSTEM

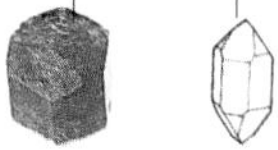
Hexagonal beryl crystal
Representation of hexagonal/ trigonal system

HEXAGONAL/TRIGONAL SYSTEM

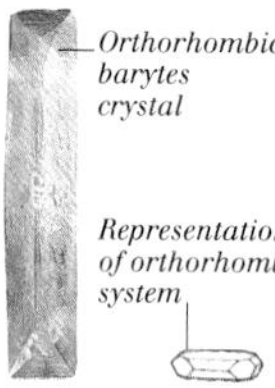
Orthorhombic barytes crystal
Representation of orthorhombic system

ORTHORHOMBIC SYSTEM

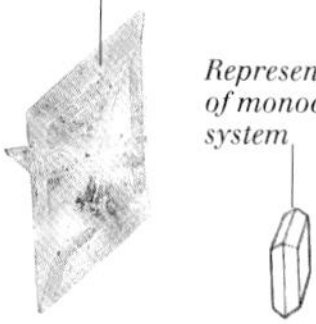
Monoclinic selenite crystal
Representation of monoclinic system

MONOCLINIC SYSTEM

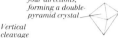

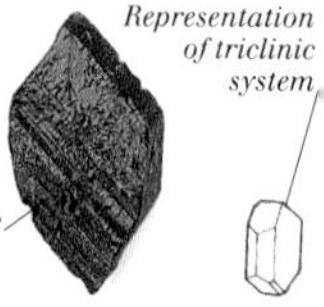
Triclinic axinite crystal
Representation of triclinic system

TRICLINIC SYSTEM

HABIT

Kunzite with prismatic habit

PRISMATIC HABIT

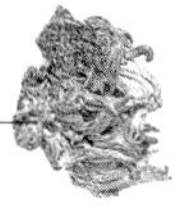
Silver with twisted wire habit

TWISTED WIRE HABIT

Haematite with tabular habit (flattened structure)

TABULAR HABIT

Wollastonite with fibrous habit

FIBROUS HABIT

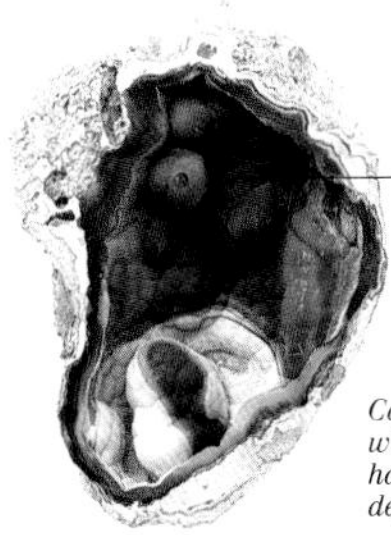
Chalcedony with botryoidal habit (like a bunch of grapes)

BOTRYOIDAL HABIT

Carnallite with massive habit (no definite shape)

MASSIVE HABIT

STREAK

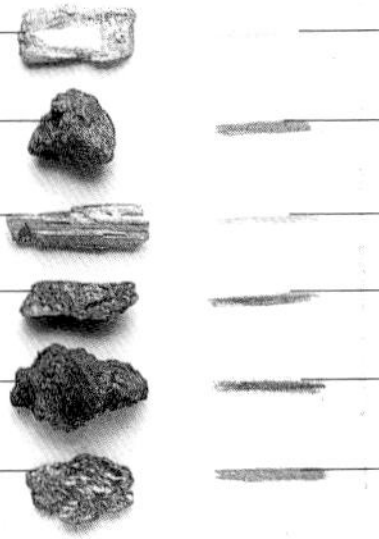
COLOUR OF MINERAL
COLOUR OF STREAK
Yellow orpiment
Golden-yellow
Brown haematite
Red-brown
Red-brown crocoite
Yellow
Gold chalcopyrite
Black
Black-red cinnabar
Red
Silver molybdenite
Grey

COLOUR

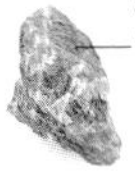
Rose-coloured crystal of rose quartz

ROSE, PINK

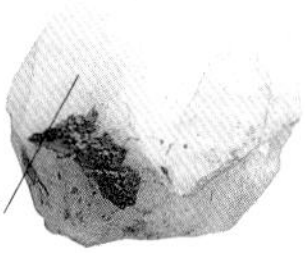
Translucent white-grey crystal of milky quartz

WHITE-GREY

Translucent crystal of orange citrine

ORANGE

Transparent glassy crystal of rock crystal

BEIGE, TRANSPARENT

MOHS SCALE OF HARDNESS

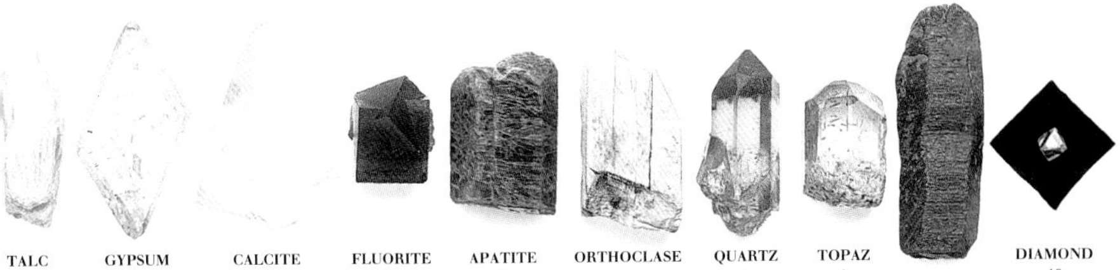

TALC 1 | GYPSUM 2 | CALCITE 3 | FLUORITE 4 | APATITE 5 | ORTHOCLASE 6 | QUARTZ 7 | TOPAZ 8 | CORUNDUM 9 | DIAMOND 10

Volcanoes

Folded, rope-like surface
PAHOEHOE (ROPY LAVA)

VOLCANOES ARE VENTS OR FISSURES in the Earth's crust through which magma (molten rock that originates from deep beneath the crust) is forced on to the surface as lava. They occur most commonly along the boundaries of crustal plates; most volcanoes lie in a belt called the "Ring of Fire", which runs along the edge of the Pacific Ocean. Volcanoes can be classified according to the violence and frequency of their eruptions. Non-explosive volcanic eruptions generally occur where crustal plates pull apart. These eruptions produce runny basaltic lava that spreads quickly over a wide area to form relatively flat cones. The most violent eruptions take place where plates collide. Such eruptions produce thick rhyolitic lava and may also blast out clouds of dust and pyroclasts (lava fragments). The lava does not flow far before cooling and therefore builds up steep-sided, conical volcanoes. Some volcanoes produce lava and ash eruptions, which build up composite volcanic cones. Volcanoes that erupt frequently are described as active; those that erupt rarely are termed dormant; and those that have stopped erupting altogether are termed extinct. As well as the volcanoes themselves, other features associated with volcanic regions include geysers, hot mineral springs, solfataras, fumaroles, and bubbling mud pools.

HORU GEYSER, NEW ZEALAND

VOLCANO TYPES

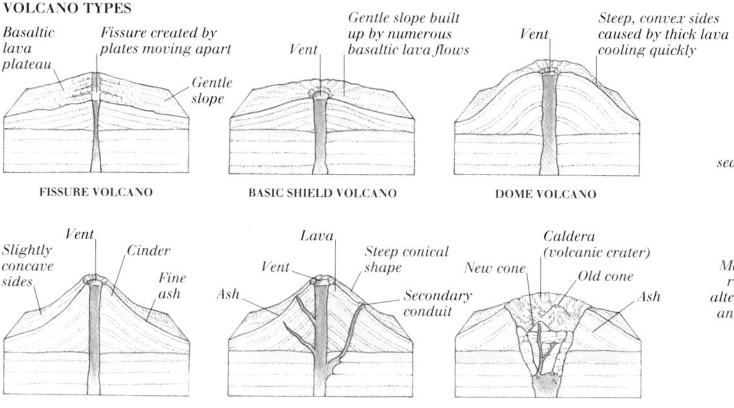
Basaltic lava plateau
Fissure created by plates moving apart
Gentle slope
Vent
Gentle slope built up by numerous basaltic lava flows
Vent
Steep, convex sides caused by thick lava cooling quickly
Vent
Slightly concave sides
Cinder
Fine ash
Lava
Vent
Steep conical shape
Ash
Secondary conduit
Caldera (volcanic crater)
New cone
Old cone
Ash
FISSURE VOLCANO · BASIC SHIELD VOLCANO · DOME VOLCANO · ASH-CINDER VOLCANO · COMPOSITE VOLCANO · CALDERA VOLCANO

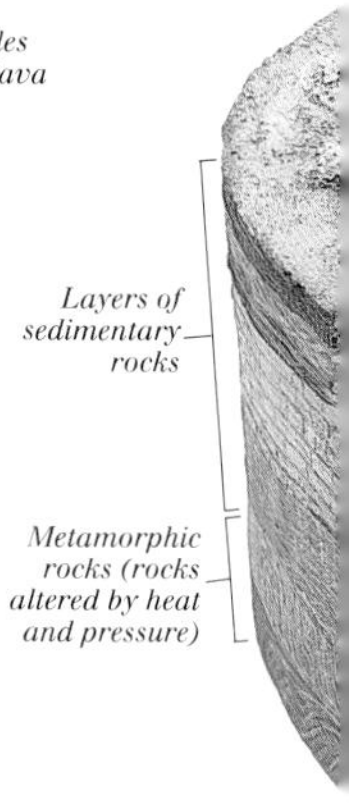
Layers of sedimentary rocks
Metamorphic rocks (rocks altered by heat and pressure)

HOW VOLCANIC PLUGS BECOME EXPOSED

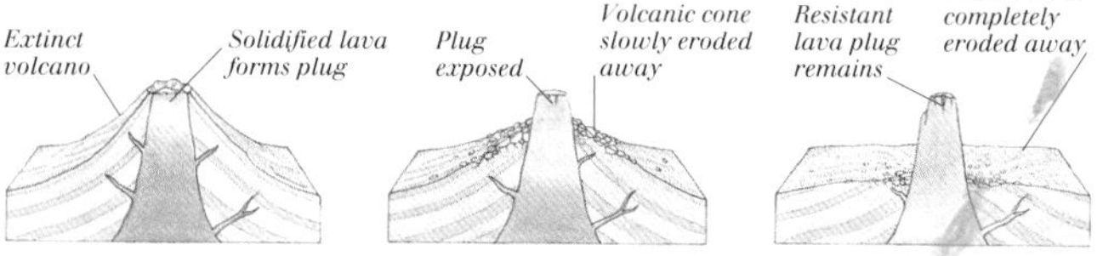
Extinct volcano
Solidified lava forms plug
Plug exposed
Volcanic cone slowly eroded away
Resistant lava plug remains
Volcanic cone completely eroded away
PLUG FORMATION · INITIAL EROSION AROUND PLUG · COMPLETE DENUDATION OF PLUG

LAPILLI (LAVA FRAGMENTS)

Small piece of solidified lava

YPES OF LAVA

AA (BLOCKY LAVA)

Driblets of
lava from roof
of tunnel

REMELTED LAVA

LOCATION OF VOLCANOES

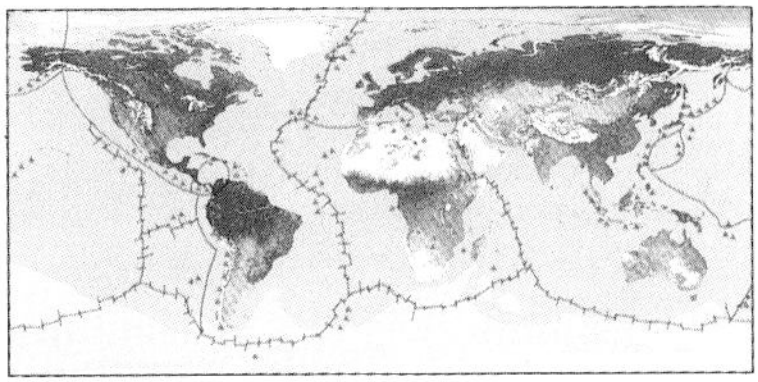

▲ Volcano   Plate boundary

TRUCTURE OF A
OLCANO

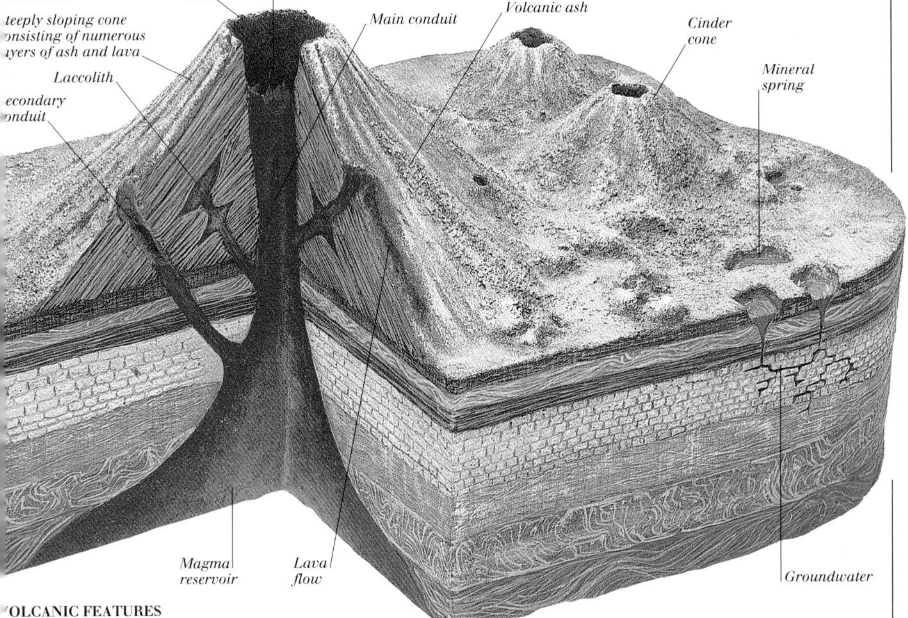
Plug (solidified lava)
Vent
Main conduit
Volcanic ash
Cinder
cone
teeply sloping cone
onsisting of numerous
ayers of ash and lava
Laccolith
econdary
onduit
Mineral
spring
Magma
reservoir
Lava
flow
Groundwater

OLCANIC FEATURES

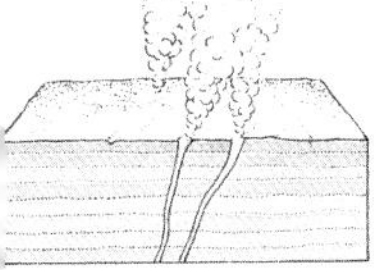
Sulphurous
gases

SOLFATARA

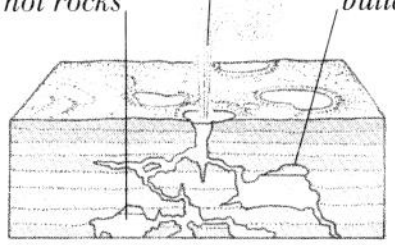
Jet of hot water
and steam
Water heated
by hot rocks
Steam
pressure
builds up

GEYSER

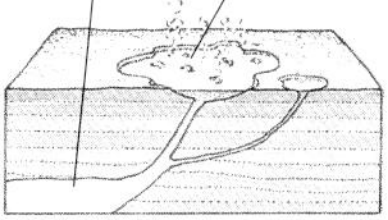
Hot
water
Mud and surface
deposits mixed
with hot water

MUD POOL

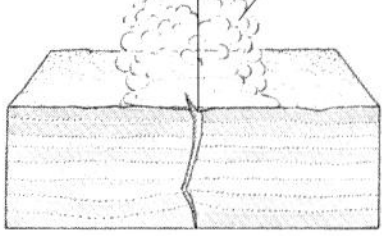
Superheated
water
Steam

FUMAROLE

Igneous and metamorphic rocks

BASALT COLUMNS

IGNEOUS ROCKS ARE FORMED WHEN MAGMA (molten rock that originates from deep beneath the Earth's crust) cools and solidifies. There are two main types of igneous rock: intrusive and extrusive. Intrusive rocks are formed deep underground where magma is forced into cracks or between rock layers to form structures such as sills, dykes, and batholiths. The magma cools slowly to form coarse-grained rocks such as gabbro and pegmatite. Extrusive rocks are formed above the Earth's surface from lava (magma that has been ejected in a volcanic eruption). The molten lava cools quickly, producing fine-grained rocks such as rhyolite and basalt. Metamorphic rocks are those that have been altered by intense heat (contact metamorphism) or extreme pressure (regional metamorphism). Contact metamorphism occurs when rocks are changed by heat from, for example, an igneous intrusion or lava flow. Regional metamorphism occurs when rock is crushed in the middle of a folding mountain range. Metamorphic rocks can be formed from igneous rocks, sedimentary rocks, or even from other metamorphic rocks.

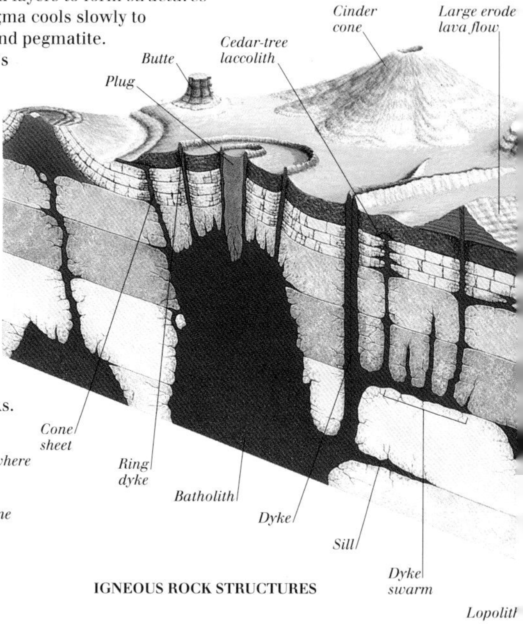

Cinder cone
Large erode lava flow
Cedar-tree laccolith
Butte
Plug
Cone sheet
Ring dyke
Batholith
Dyke
Sill
Dyke swarm
Lopolith

IGNEOUS ROCK STRUCTURES

CONTACT METAMORPHISM

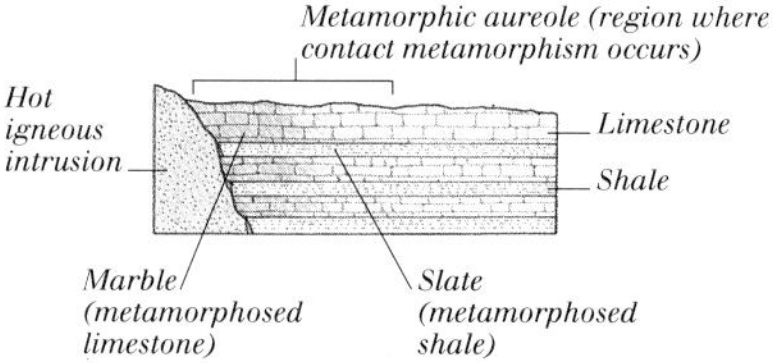

Metamorphic aureole (region where contact metamorphism occurs)
Hot igneous intrusion
Limestone
Shale
Marble (metamorphosed limestone)
Slate (metamorphosed shale)

REGIONAL METAMORPHISM

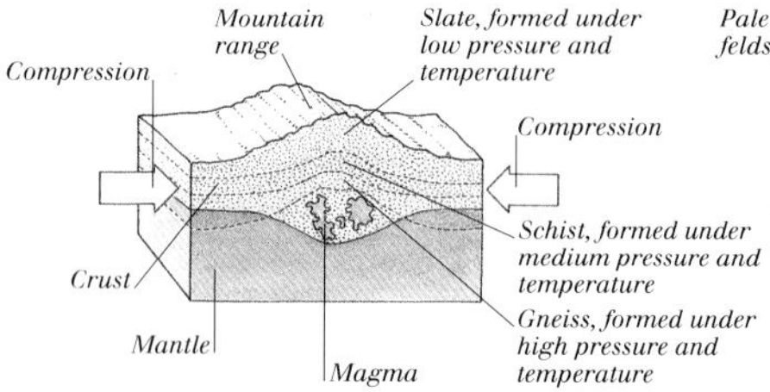

Mountain range
Slate, formed under low pressure and temperature
Compression
Compression
Schist, formed under medium pressure and temperature
Crust
Gneiss, formed under high pressure and temperature
Mantle
Magma

EXAMPLES OF METAMORPHIC ROCKS

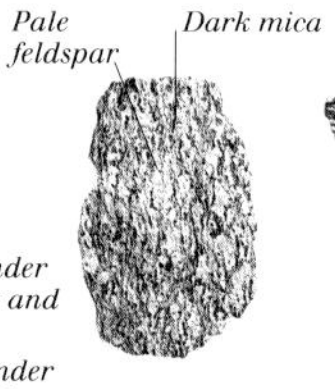

Pale feldspar
Dark mica

GNEISS

Dark mineral band

FOLDED SCHIST

Pale calcite

SKARN

XAMPLES OF EXTRUSIVE IGNEOUS ROCKS

Porphyritic texture

RHYOLITE

Fine-grained crystals

BASALT

Elongated vesicles (gas cavities)

PUMICE

Fine-grained groundmass (matrix)

PORPHYRITIC ANDESITE

Glassy lustre
Conchoidal fracture

OBSIDIAN

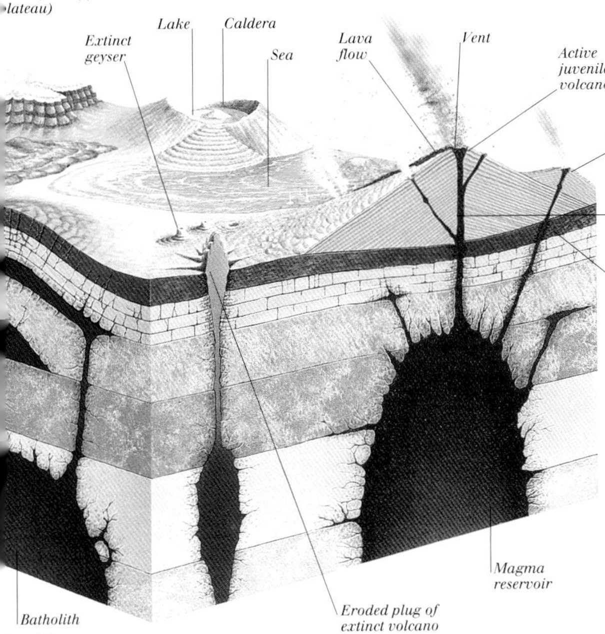
lesa (flat-topped
lateau)
Lake
Caldera
Extinct geyser
Sea
Lava flow
Vent
Active juvenile volcano
Parasitic volcano
Main conduit
Sagging caused by weight of volcano
Magma reservoir
Eroded plug of extinct volcano
Batholith
accolith

EXAMPLES OF INTRUSIVE IGNEOUS ROCKS

Dark groundmass (matrix)

KIMBERLITE

Plagioclase feldspar

OLIVINE GABBRO

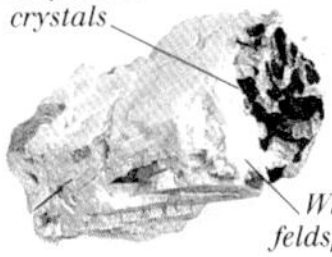
Amphibole crystals
White feldspar

FELDSPAR PEGMATITE

Fine groundmass (matrix)
Pyrites crystal

SLATE WITH PYRITES

Chiastolite crystal

CHIASTOLITE HORNFELS

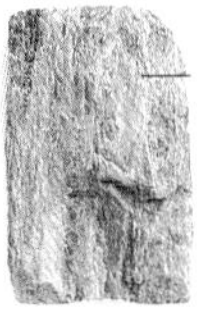
Green calc-silicate mineral

GREEN MARBLE

High quartz content

HALLEFLINTA

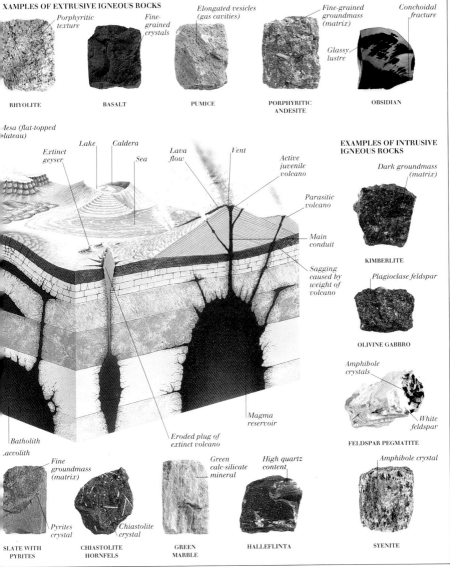

Amphibole crystal

SYENITE

Sedimentary rocks

SEDIMENTARY ROCKS ARE FORMED BY THE ACCUMULATION and consolidation of sediments (see pp. 266-267). There are three main types of sedimentary rock. Clastic sedimentary rocks, such as breccia or sandstone, are formed from other rocks that have been broken down into fragments by weathering (see pp. 282-283), which have then been transported and deposited elsewhere. Organic sedimentary rocks – for example, coal (see pp. 280-281) – are derived from plant and animal remains. Chemical sedimentary rocks are formed by chemical processes. For example, rock salt is formed when salt dissolved in water is deposited as the water evaporates. Sedimentary rocks are laid down in layers, called beds or strata. Each new layer is laid down horizontally over older ones. There are usually some gaps in the sequence, called unconformities. These represent periods in which no new sediments were being laid down, or when earlier sedimentary layers were raised above sea level and eroded away.

THE GRAND CANYON, USA

EXAMPLES OF UNCONFORMITIE

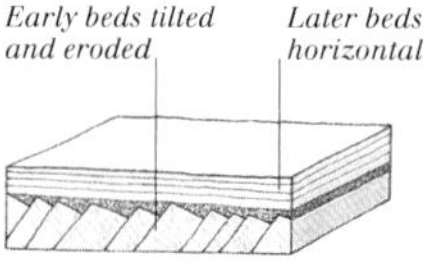
Early beds tilted and eroded
Later beds horizontal

ANGULAR UNCONFORMITY

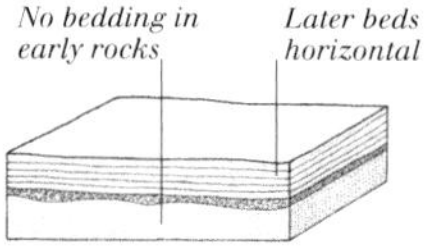
No bedding in early rocks
Later beds horizontal

NONCONFORMITY

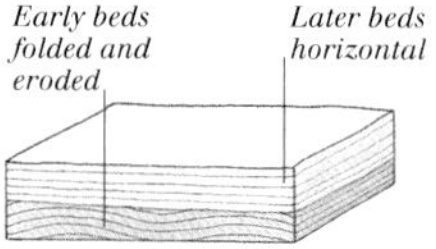
Early beds folded and eroded
Later beds horizontal

DISCONFORMITY

SEDIMENTARY LAYERS OF THE GRAND CANYON REGION

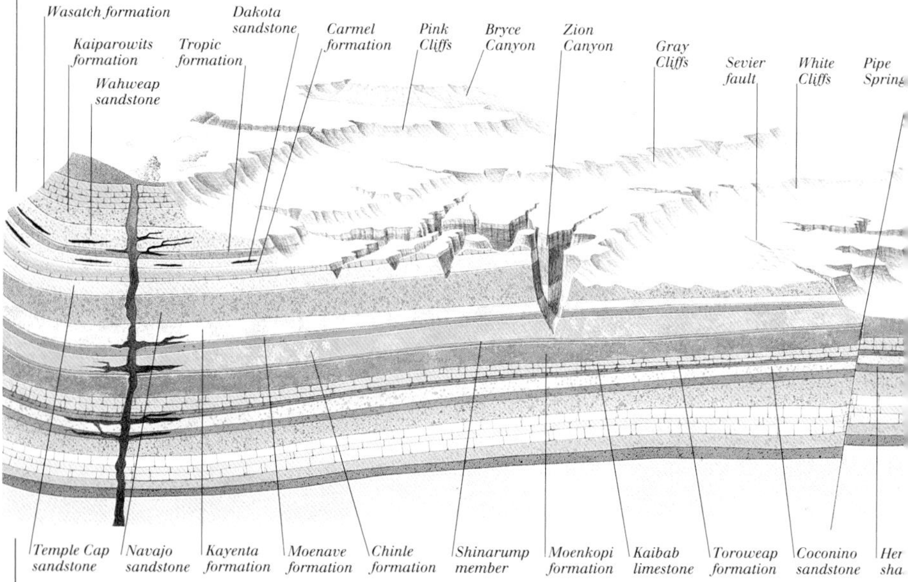
Wasatch formation
Kaiparowits formation
Wahweap sandstone
Tropic formation
Dakota sandstone
Carmel formation
Pink Cliffs
Bryce Canyon
Zion Canyon
Gray Cliffs
Sevier fault
White Cliffs
Pipe Sprin
Temple Cap sandstone
Navajo sandstone
Kayenta formation
Moenave formation
Chinle formation
Shinarump member
Moenkopi formation
Kaibab limestone
Toroweap formation
Coconino sandstone
Her sha

EXAMPLES OF SEDIMENTARY ROCKS

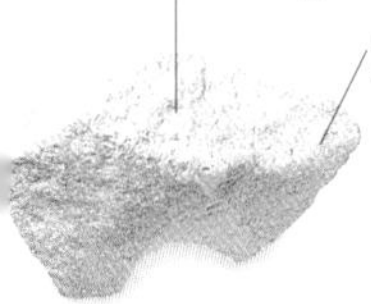

Calcite (composed of minute organic remains)
Powdery texture

CHALK

Band of chert
Band of siderite

BANDED IRONSTONE

Angular rock fragments
Salt or sand groundmass (matrix)

BRECCIA

Red colour due to iron oxide
Millet-seed texture

RED SANDSTONE

Sharp edge
Conchoidal fracture

FLINT

Halite crystals

ORANGE HALITE (ROCK SALT)

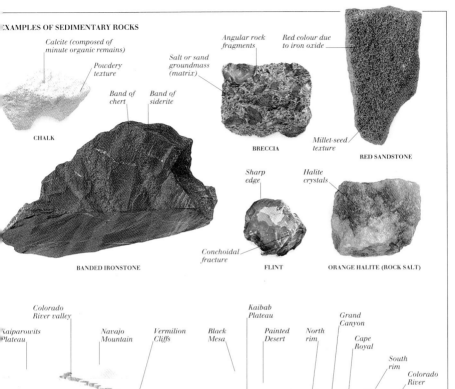

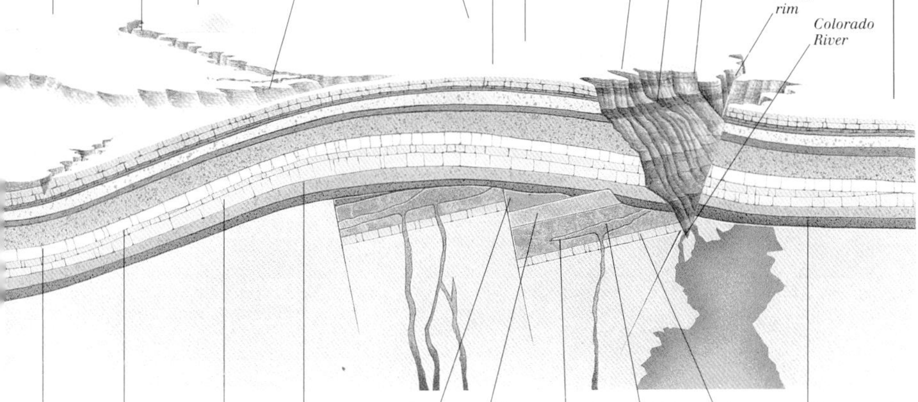

Colorado River valley
Kaiparowits Plateau
Navajo Mountain
Vermilion Cliffs
Black Mesa
Kaibab Plateau
Painted Desert
North rim
Grand Canyon
Cape Royal
South rim
Colorado River
pai oup
Redwall limestone
Temple Butte limestone
Muav limestone
Bright Angel shale
Dox formation
Shinumo quartzite
Hakatai shale
Diabase sill
Bass formation
Tapeats sandstone

Fossils

FOSSILS ARE THE REMAINS of plants and animals that have been preserved in rock. A fossil may be the preserved remains of an organism itself, an impression of it in rock, or preserved traces (known as trace fossils) left by an organism while it was alive, such as organic carbon outlines, fossilized footprints, or droppings. Most dead organisms soon rot away or are eaten by scavengers. For fossilization to occur, rapid burial by sediment is necessary. The organism decays, but the harder parts – bones, teeth, and shells, for example – may be preserved and hardened by minerals from the surrounding sediment. Fossilization may also occur even when the hard parts of an organism are dissolved away to leave an impression called a mould. The mould is filled by minerals, thereby creating a cast of the organism. The study of fossils (palaeontology) can not only show how living things have evolved, but can also help to reveal the Earth's geological history – for example, by aiding in the dating of rock strata.

PROCESS OF FOSSILIZATION

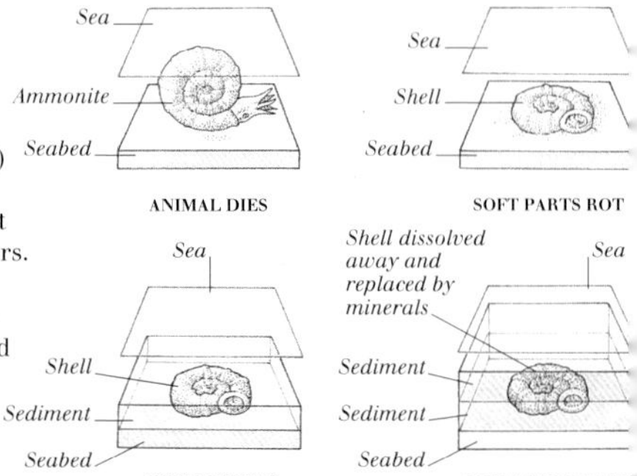

EXAMPLES OF FOSSILS

ALETHOPTERIS (SEED FERN)

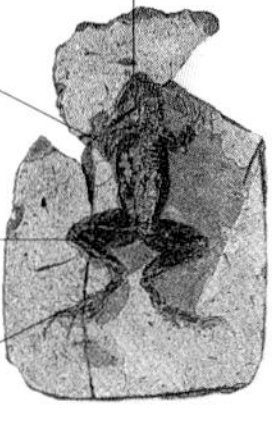

FROG (AMPHIBIAN)

PAVLOVIA (AMMONITE MOLLUSC)

DICYOTHYRIS (BRACHIOPOD)

SCALLOP (BIVALVE MOLLUSC)

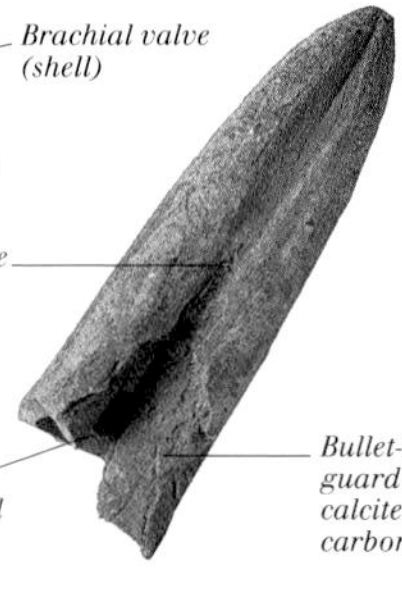

ACROTEUTHIS (BELEMNITE MOLLUSC)

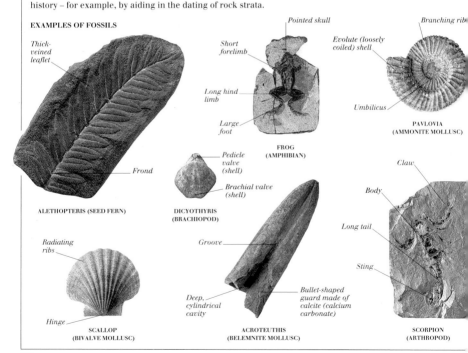

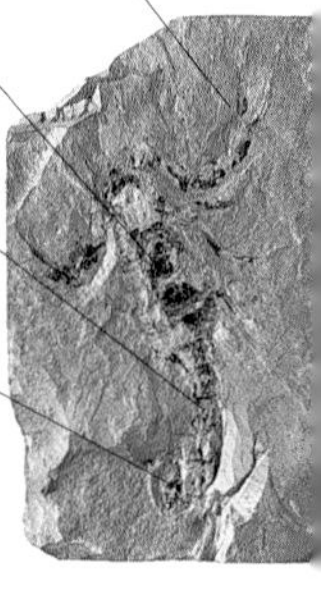

SCORPION (ARTHROPOD)

THE FOSSIL RECORD

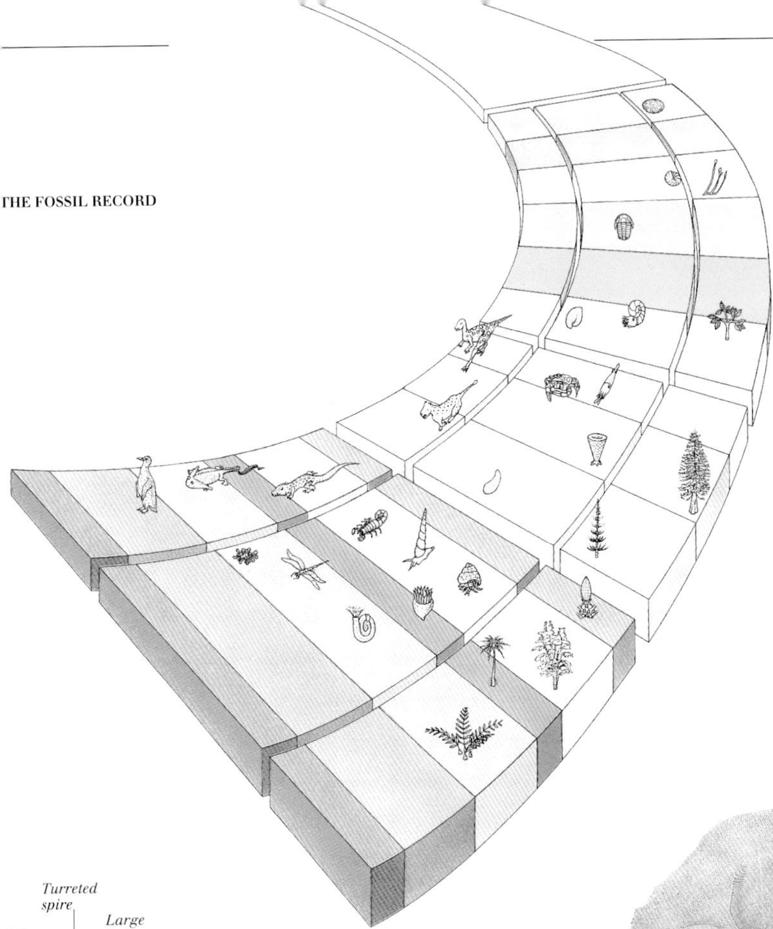

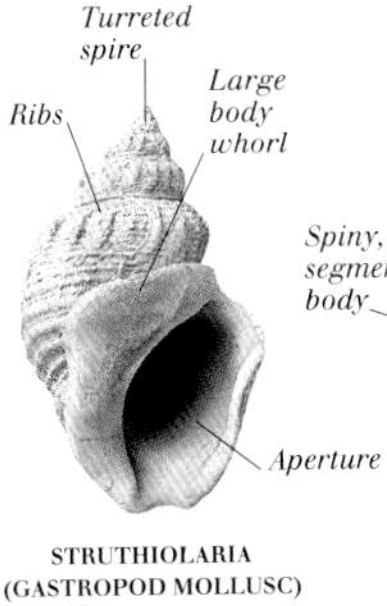
Turreted spire
Ribs
Large body whorl
Aperture

STRUTHIOLARIA (GASTROPOD MOLLUSC)

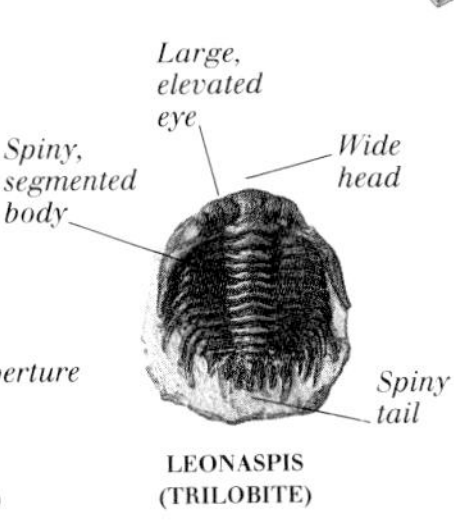
Large, elevated eye
Wide head
Spiny, segmented body
Spiny tail

LEONASPIS (TRILOBITE)

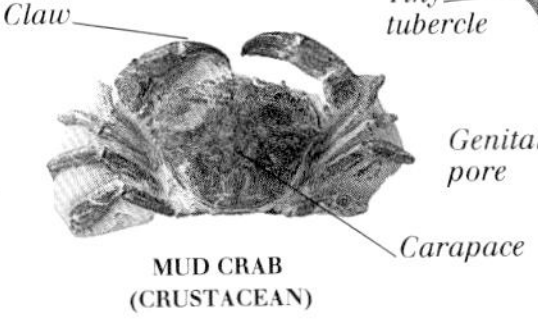
Claw
Carapace

MUD CRAB (CRUSTACEAN)

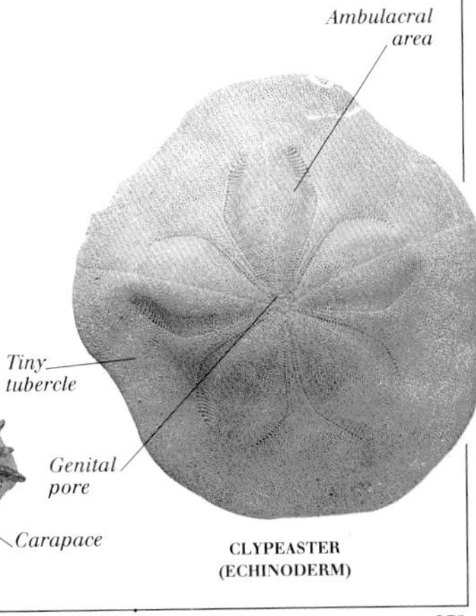
Ambulacral area
Tiny tubercle
Genital pore

CLYPEASTER (ECHINODERM)

Mineral resources

MINERAL RESOURCES CAN BE DEFINED AS naturally occurring substances that can be extracted from the Earth and are useful as fuels and raw materials. Coal, oil, and gas – collectively called fossil fuels – are commonly included in this group, but are not strictly minerals, because they are of organic origin. Coal formation begins when vegetation is buried and partly decomposed to form peat. Overlying sediments compress the peat and transform it into lignite (soft brown coal). As the overlying sediments accumulate, increasing pressure and temperature eventually transform the lignite into bituminous and hard anthracite coals. Oil and gas are usually formed from organic matter that was deposited in marine sediments. Under the effects of heat and pressure, the compressed organic matter undergoes complex chemical changes to form oil and gas. The oil and gas percolate upwards through water-saturated, permeable rocks and they may rise to the Earth's surface or accumulate below an impermeable layer of rock that has been folded or faulted to form a trap – an anticline (upfold) trap, for example. Minerals are inorganic substances that may consist of a single chemical element, such as gold, silver, or copper, or combinations of elements (see pp. 268-269). Some minerals are concentrated in mineralization zones in rock associated with crustal movements or volcanic activity. Others may be found in sediments as placer deposits – accumulations of high-density minerals that have been weathered out of rocks, transported, and deposited (on river-beds, for example).

OIL RIG, NORTH SEA

HOW COAL IS FORMED

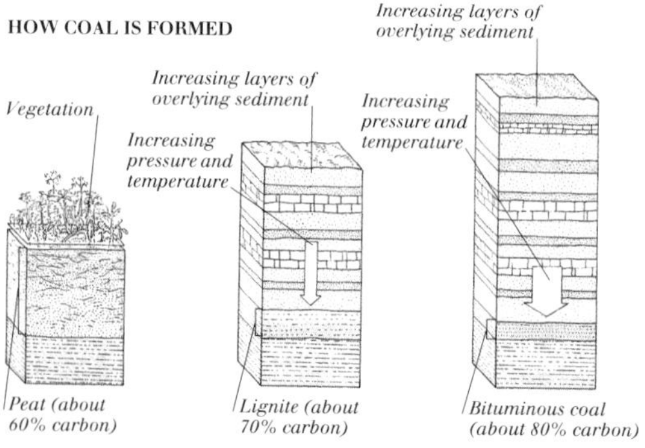
Vegetation
Increasing layers of overlying sediment
Increasing pressure and temperature
Increasing layers of overlying sediment
Increasing pressure and temperature
Peat (about 60% carbon)
Lignite (about 70% carbon)
Bituminous coal (about 80% carbon)

PEAT

LIGNITE (BROWN COAL)

BITUMINOUS COAL

STAGES IN THE FORMATION OF COAL

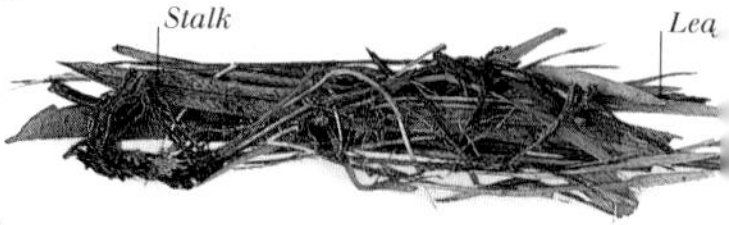

PLANT MATTER

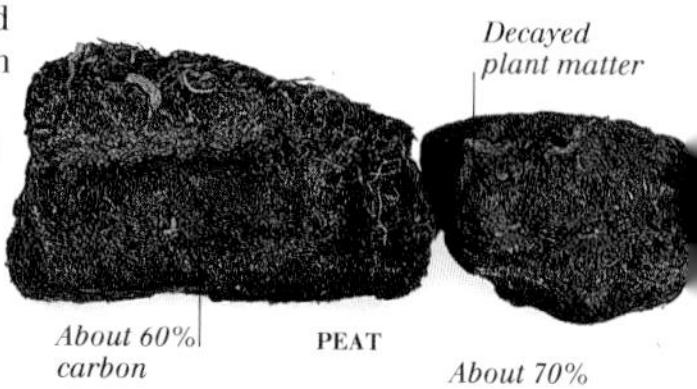
Decayed plant matter
About 60% carbon

PEAT

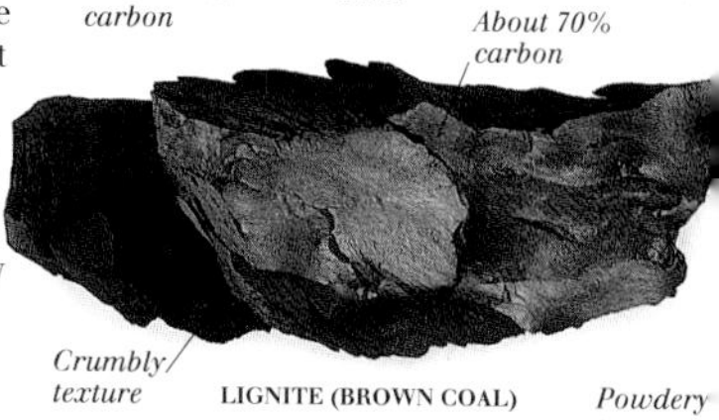
About 70% carbon
Crumbly texture

LIGNITE (BROWN COAL)

Powdery texture
About 80% carbon

BITUMINOUS COAL

Shiny surface
About 95% carbon

ANTHRACITE COAL

EXAMPLES OF OIL AND GAS TRAPS

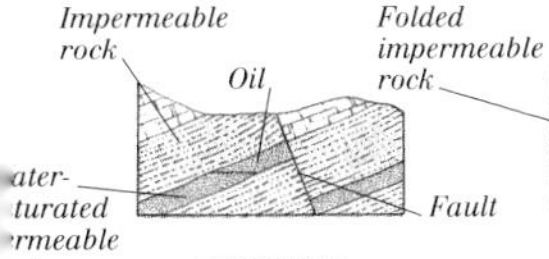

FAULT TRAP

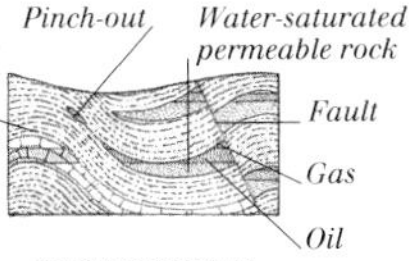

PINCH-OUT TRAP

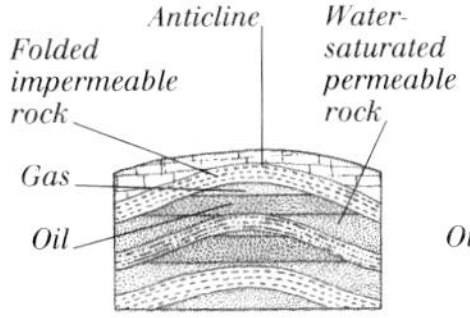

ANTICLINE TRAP

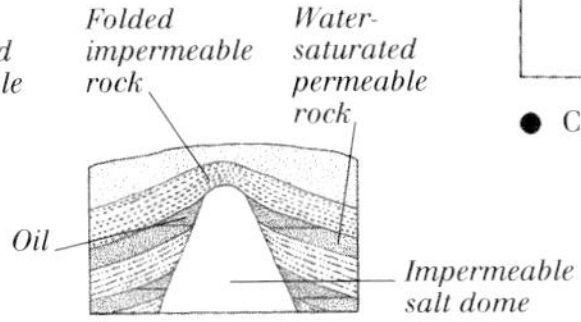

SALT-DOME TRAP

MAJOR COAL, OIL, AND GAS DEPOSITS

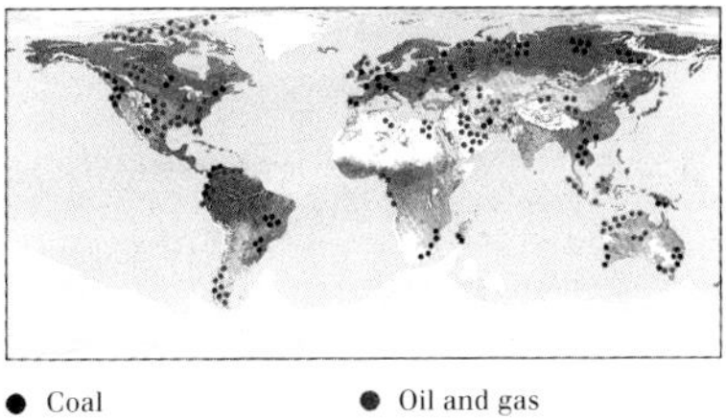

HOW AN ANTICLINE TRAP IS FORMED

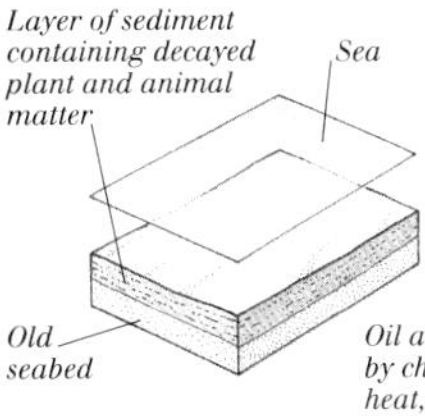

DEPOSITION OF ORGANIC MATERIAL

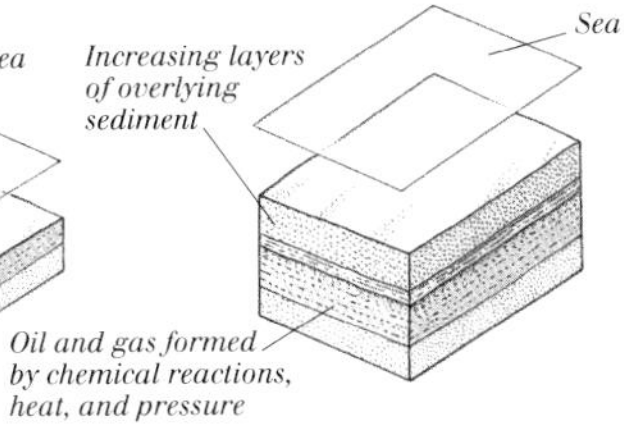

FORMATION OF OIL AND GAS

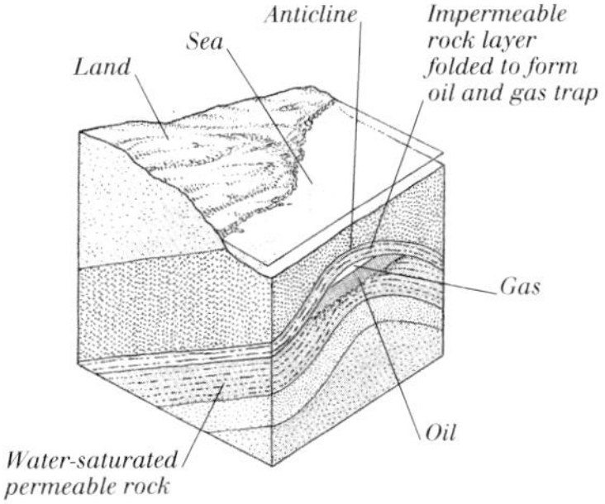

COLLECTION OF OIL AND GAS IN ANTICLINE TRAP

MINERALIZATION ZONES

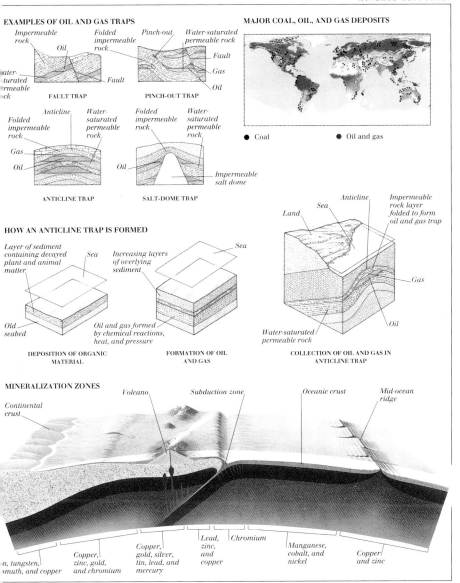

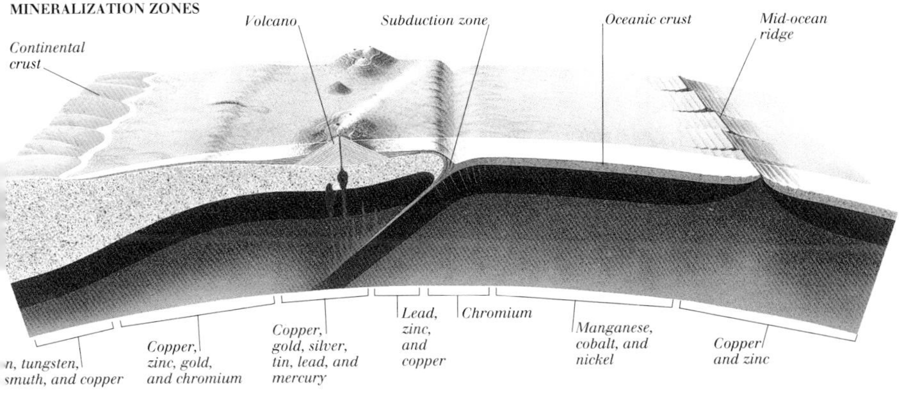

Weathering and erosion

WEATHERING IS THE BREAKING DOWN of rocks on the Earth's surface. There are two main types: physical (or mechanical) and chemical. Physical weathering may be caused by temperature changes, such as freezing and thawing, or by abrasion from material carried by winds, rivers, or glaciers. Rocks may also be broken down by the actions of animals and plants, such as the burrowing of animals and the growth of roots. Chemical weathering causes rocks to decompose by changing their chemical composition – for example, rainwater may dissolve certain minerals in a rock. Erosion is the wearing away and removal of land surfaces by water, wind, or ice. It is greatest in areas of little or no surface vegetation, such as deserts, where sand dunes may form.

FORMATION OF A HAMADA (ROCK PAVEMENT)

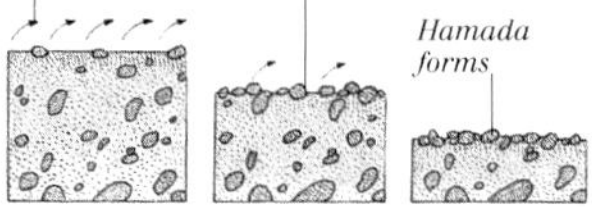
Wind blows away small particles
Larger particles aggregate
Hamada forms

FIRST STAGE
SECOND STAGE
FINAL STAGE

FEATURES OF WEATHERING AND EROSION

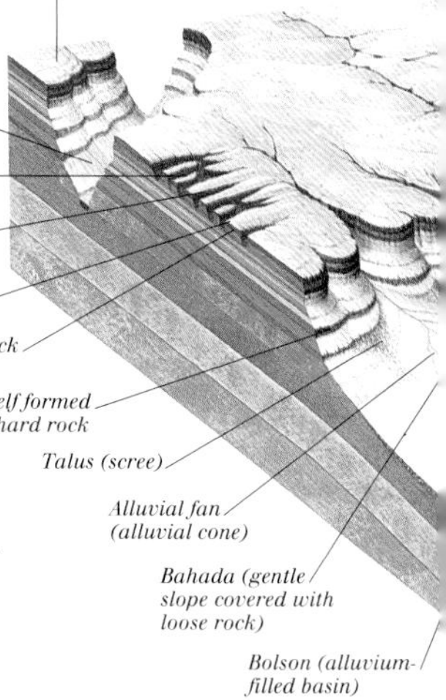
Mesa (flat-topped plateau)
Canyon
Zeugen
Joint
Hard rock
Soft rock
Shelf formed of hard rock
Talus (scree)
Alluvial fan (alluvial cone)
Bahada (gentle slope covered with loose rock)
Bolson (alluvium-filled basin)

FEATURES PRODUCED BY WIND ACTION

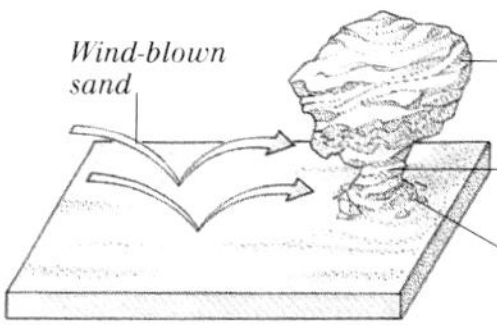
Wind-blown sand
Mushroom-shaped rock
Neck
Rock base eroded by wind-blown sand

ROCK PEDESTAL

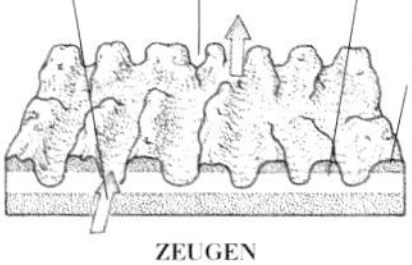
Wind-blown sand
Widened joint
Soft rock
Hard rock

ZEUGEN

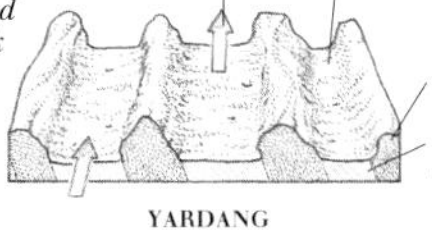
Wind-blown sand
Furrow
Hard rock
Soft rock eroded by wind-blown sand

YARDANG

EXAMPLES OF PHYSICAL WEATHERING PROCESSES

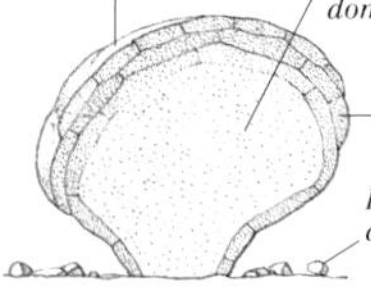
Heated rock surface expands
Exfoliation dome
Flaking rock
Fallen debris

EXFOLIATION (ONION-SKIN WEATHERING)

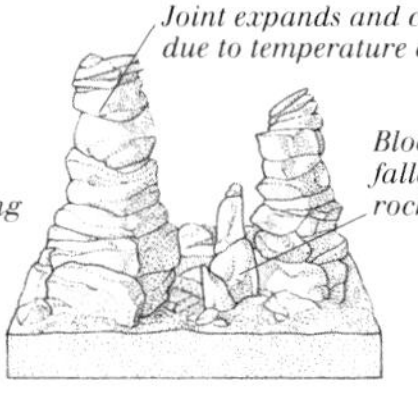
Joint expands and contracts due to temperature changes
Block of fallen rock

BLOCK DISINTEGRATION

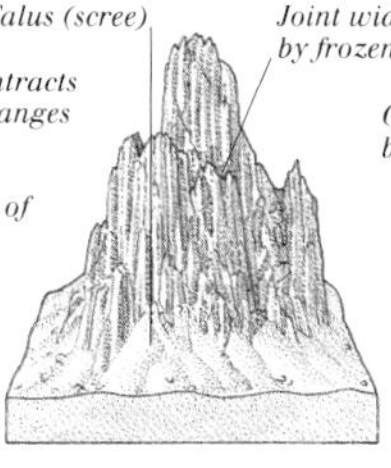
Talus (scree)
Joint widened by frozen water

FROST WEDGING

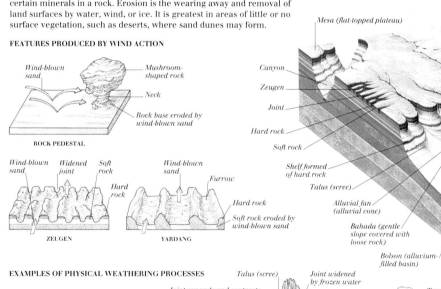

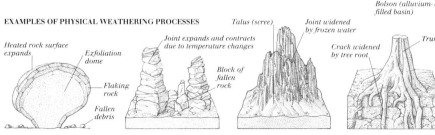

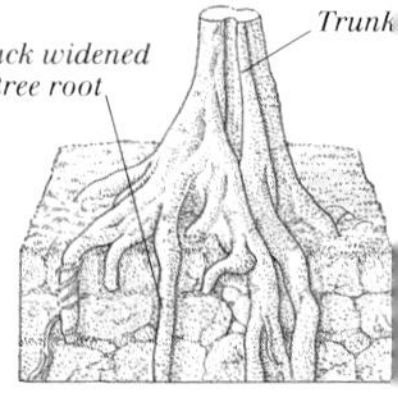
Trunk
Crack widened by tree root

TREE ROOT ACTION

SECTION THROUGH A BARKHAN DUNE

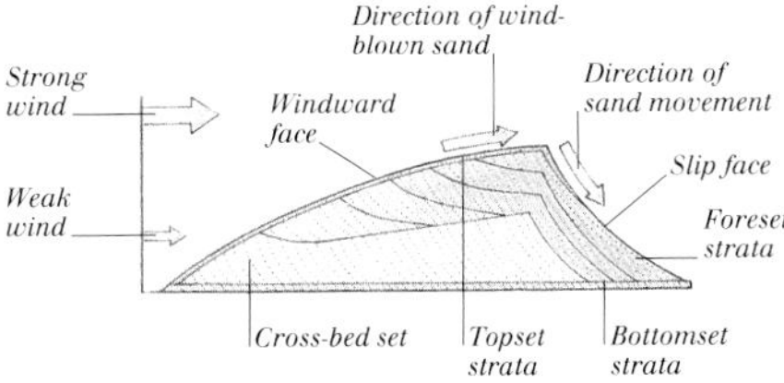
Direction of wind-blown sand
Strong wind
Windward face
Direction of sand movement
Slip face
Weak wind
Foreset strata
Cross-bed set
Topset strata
Bottomset strata

EXAMPLES OF SAND DUNES

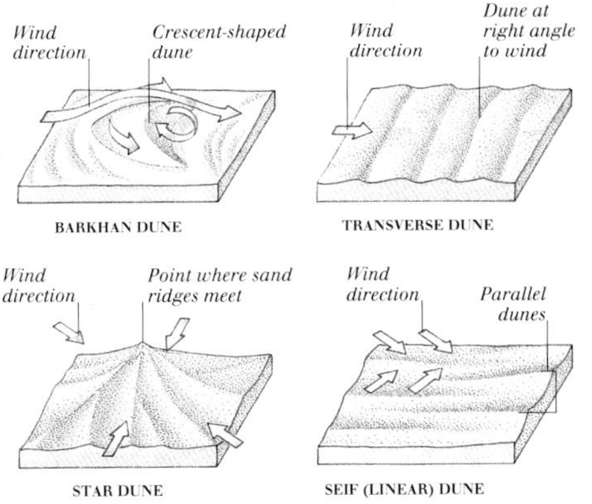
Wind direction
Crescent-shaped dune
BARKHAN DUNE
Wind direction
Dune at right angle to wind
TRANSVERSE DUNE
Wind direction
Point where sand ridges meet
STAR DUNE
Wind direction
Parallel dunes
SEIF (LINEAR) DUNE

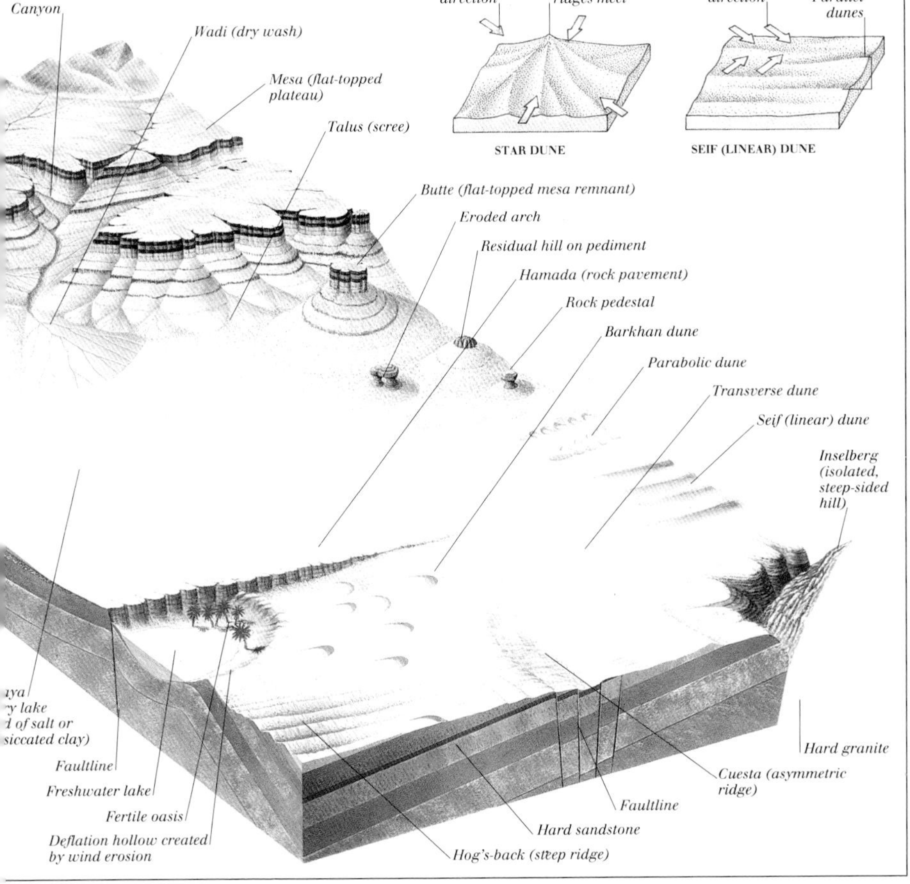
Canyon
Wadi (dry wash)
Mesa (flat-topped plateau)
Talus (scree)
Butte (flat-topped mesa remnant)
Eroded arch
Residual hill on pediment
Hamada (rock pavement)
Rock pedestal
Barkhan dune
Parabolic dune
Transverse dune
Seif (linear) dune
Inselberg (isolated, steep-sided hill)
aya
y lake
d of salt or
siccated clay)
Faultline
Freshwater lake
Fertile oasis
Deflation hollow created by wind erosion
Hog's-back (steep ridge)
Hard sandstone
Faultline
Cuesta (asymmetric ridge)
Hard granite

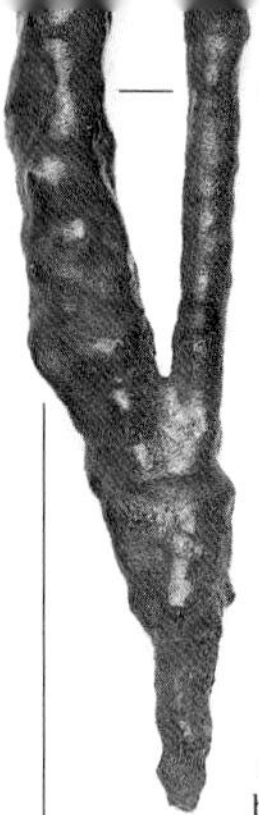

MERGED STALACTITES

Ring mark

STALACTITE WITH RING MARKS

Caves

CAVES COMMONLY FORM in areas of limestone, although on coastlines they also occur in other rocks. Limestone is made of calcite (calcium carbonate), which dissolves in the carbonic acid naturally present in rainwater, and in humic acids from the decay of vegetation. The acidic water trickles down through cracks and joints in the limestone and between rock layers, breaking up the surface terrain into clints (blocks of rock), separated by grikes (deep cracks), and punctuated by sink-holes (also called swallow-holes or potholes) into which surface streams may disappear. Underground, the acidic water dissolves the rock around crevices, opening up a network of passages and caves, which can become large caverns if the roofs collapse. Various features are formed when the dissolved calcite is redeposited; for example, it may be redeposited along an underground stream to form a gour (series of calcite ridges), or in caves and passages to form stalactites and stalagmites. Stalactites develop where calcite is left behind as water drips from the roof; where the drops land, stalagmites build up.

SURFACE TOPOGRAPHY OF A CAVE SYSTEM

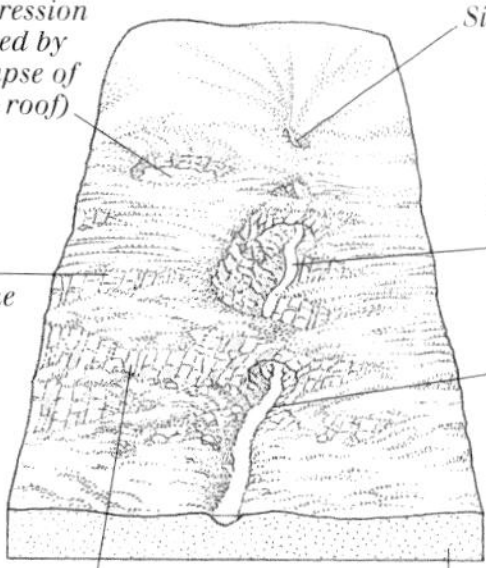
Doline (depression caused by collapse of cave roof)
Sink-hole
Gorge where cave roof has fallen in
Porous limestone
Resurgence
Limestone terrain with clints and grikes
Impermeable rock

Scar of bare rock
Former water table
Permeable limestone
Resurgence
Layer of impermeable rock
Present water table

STALAGMITE FORMATIONS

Calcite (calcium carbonate) crystallized under water

CRYSTALLINE STALAGMITIC FLOOR

Thin encrustations of calcite (calcium carbonate)

CALCAREOUS TUFA

Encrustations on dead stems of small plants
Calcite (calcium carbonate)

STALAGMITIC FLOOR

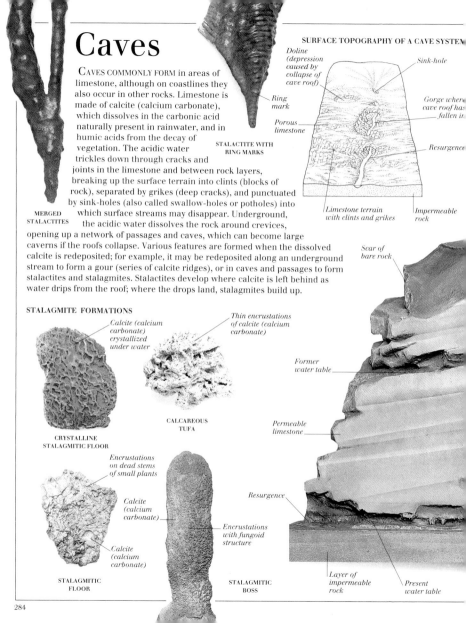

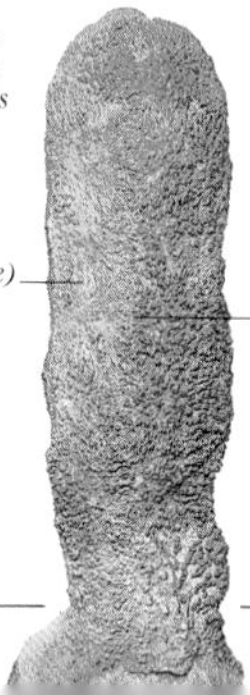
Calcite (calcium carbonate)
Encrustations with fungoid structure

STALAGMITIC BOSS

DEVELOPMENT OF A CAVE SYSTEM

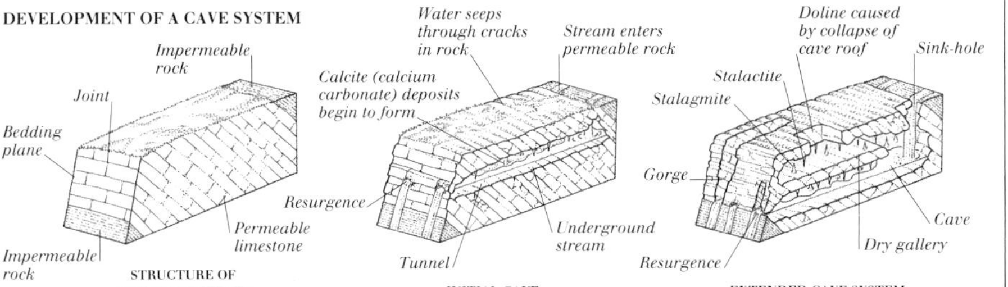
Impermeable rock
Joint
Bedding plane
Permeable limestone
Impermeable rock
STRUCTURE OF LIMESTONE STRATA
Water seeps through cracks in rock
Stream enters permeable rock
Calcite (calcium carbonate) deposits begin to form
Resurgence
Underground stream
Tunnel
INITIAL CAVE
Doline caused by collapse of cave roof
Sink-hole
Stalactite
Stalagmite
Gorge
Cave
Dry gallery
Resurgence
EXTENDED CAVE SYSTEM

INTERCONNECTED CAVE SYSTEM

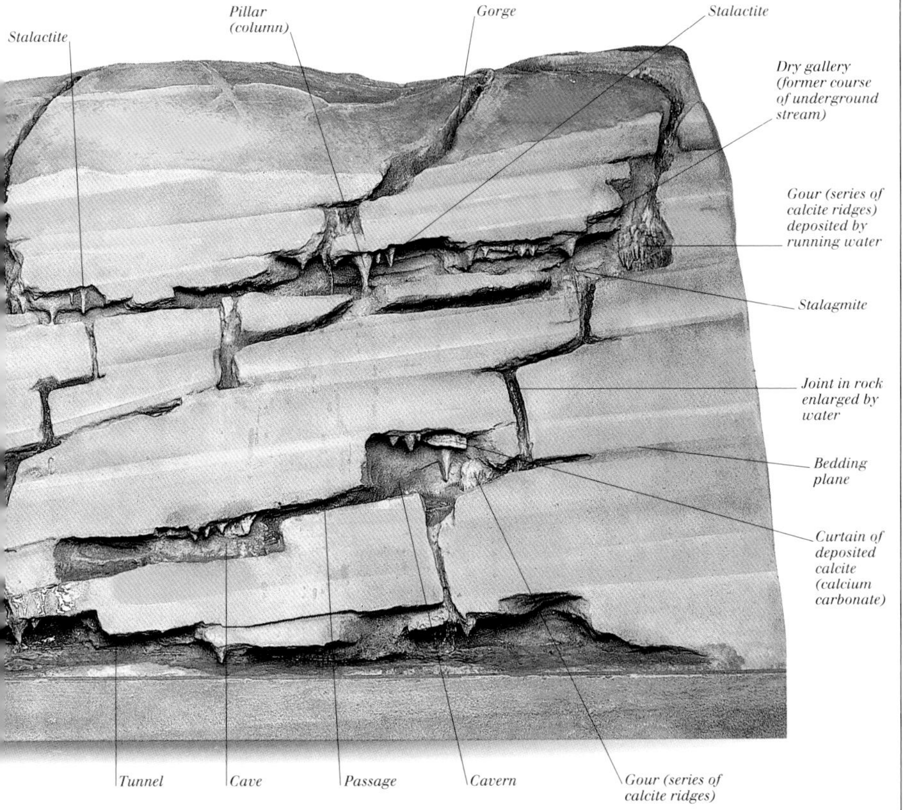
Pillar (column)
Gorge
Stalactite
Stalactite
Dry gallery (former course of underground stream)
Gour (series of calcite ridges) deposited by running water
Stalagmite
Joint in rock enlarged by water
Bedding plane
Curtain of deposited calcite (calcium carbonate)
Tunnel
Cave
Passage
Cavern
Gour (series of calcite ridges)

Glaciers

GLACIER BAY, ALASKA

A VALLEY GLACIER IS A LARGE MASS OF ICE that forms on land and moves slowly downhill under its own weight. It is formed from snow that collects in cirques (mountain hollows also known as corries) and compresses into ice as more and more snow accumulates. The cirque is deepened by frost wedging and abrasion (see pp. 282-283), and arêtes (sharp ridges) develop between adjacent cirques. Eventually, so much ice builds up that the glacier begins to move downhill. As the glacier moves it collects moraine (debris), which may range in size from particles of dust to large boulders. The rocks at the base of the glacier erode the glacial valley, giving it a U-shaped cross-section. Under the glacier, *roches moutonnées* (eroded outcrops of hard rock) and drumlins (rounded mounds of rock and clay) are left behind on the valley floor. The glacier ends at a terminus (the snout), where the ice melts as fast as it arrives. If the temperature increases, the ice melts faster than it arrives, and the glacier retreats. The retreating glacier leaves behind its moraine and also erratics (isolated single boulders). Glacial streams from the melting glacier deposit eskers and kames (ridges and mounds of sand and gravel), but carry away the finer sediment to form a stratified outwash plain. Lumps of ice carried on to this plain melt, creating holes called kettles.

VALLEY GLACIER

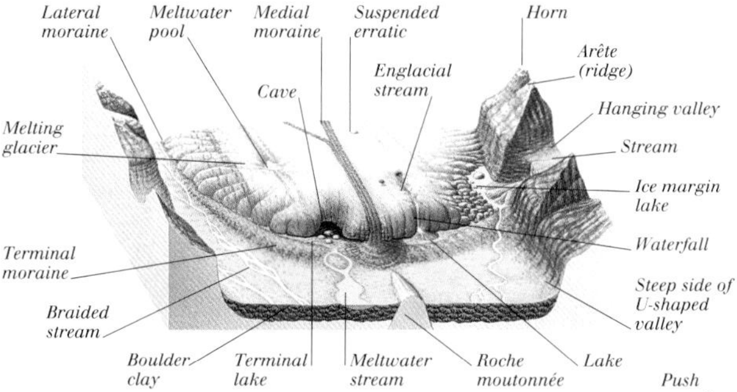

POST-GLACIAL VALLEY

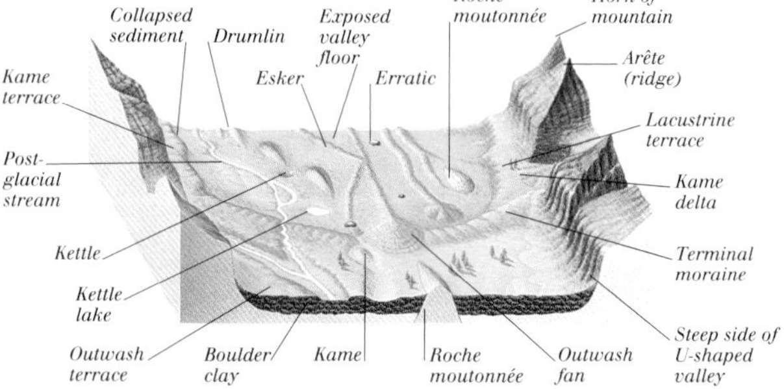

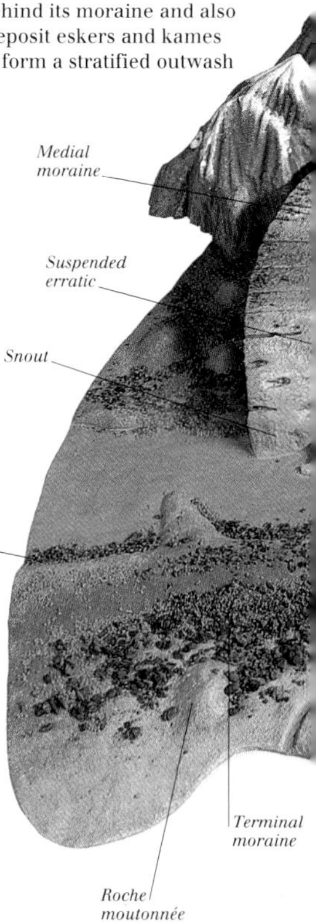

FEATURES OF A GLACIER

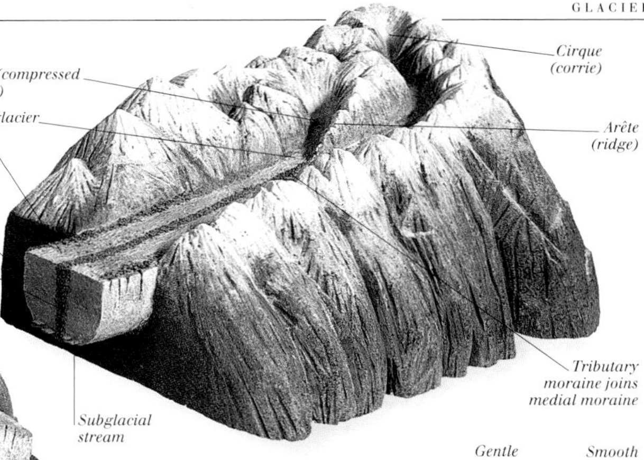

Cirque (corrie)
Firn (compressed snow)
Tributary glacier
Arête (ridge)
Moving ice
U-shaped valley
Medial moraine
Subglacial stream
Tributary moraine joins medial moraine

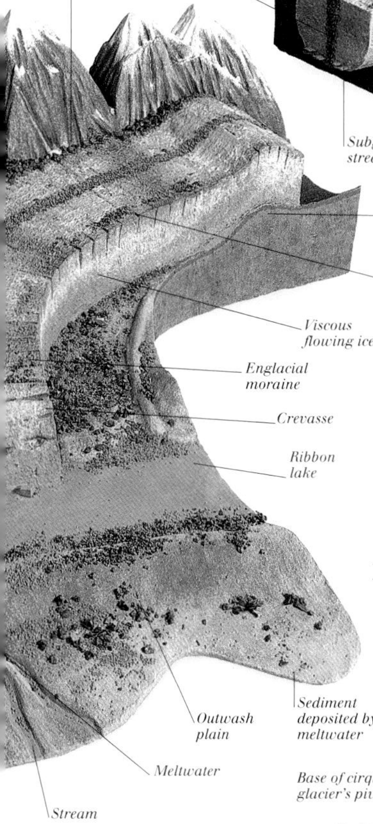

Lateral moraine
Rock being eroded by ice
Brittle surface ice
Viscous flowing ice
Englacial moraine
Crevasse
Ribbon lake
Sediment deposited by meltwater
Outwash plain
Meltwater
Stream

ICE-FALL

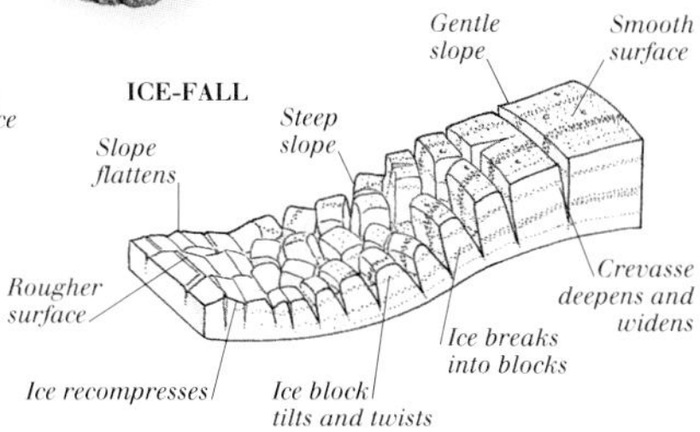

Gentle slope
Smooth surface
Steep slope
Slope flattens
Crevasse deepens and widens
Rougher surface
Ice breaks into blocks
Ice recompresses
Ice block tilts and twists

CIRQUE FORMATION

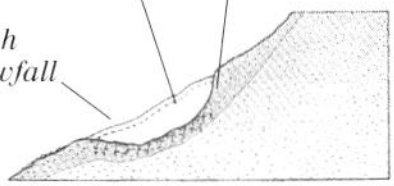

Firn (compressed snow)
Material loosened by frost wedging
Fresh snowfall

EARLY STAGE

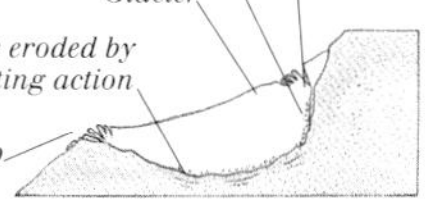

Steep back wall
Moraine pulled from ground
Glacier
Base of cirque eroded by glacier's pivoting action
Rock lip

LATER STAGE

U-SHAPED VALLEY FORMATION

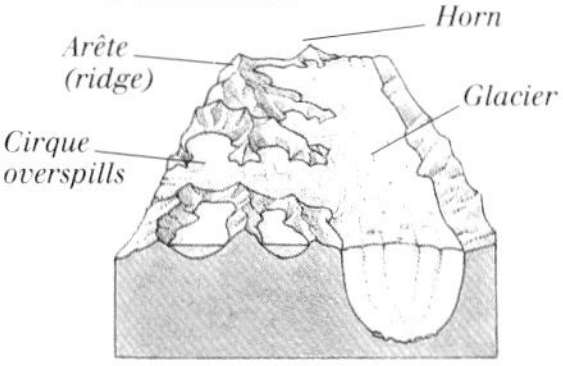

Horn
Arête (ridge)
Glacier
Cirque overspills

DURING GLACIATION

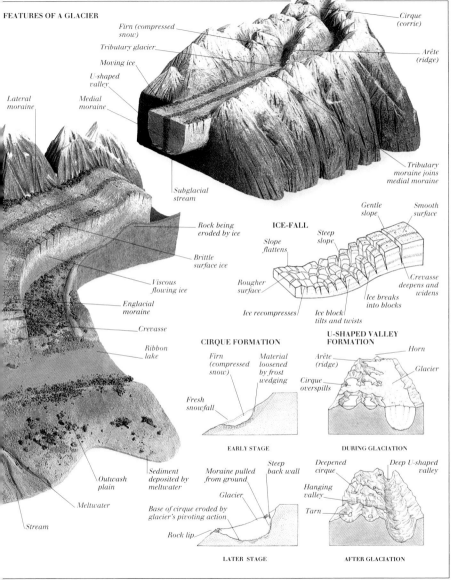

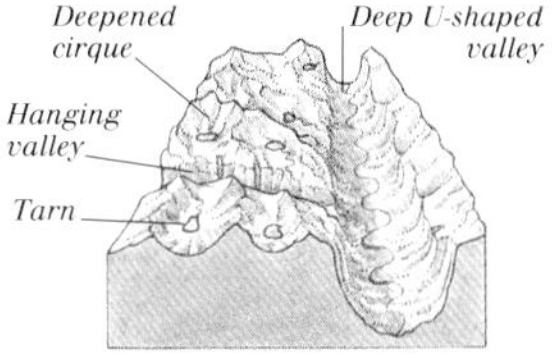

Deepened cirque
Deep U-shaped valley
Hanging valley
Tarn

AFTER GLACIATION

Rivers

RIVERS FORM PART of the water cycle – the continuous circulation of water between the land, sea, and atmosphere. The source of a river may be a mountain spring or lake, or a melting glacier. The course that the river subsequently takes depends on the slope of the terrain and on the rock types and formations over which it flows. In its early, upland stages, a river tumbles steeply over rocks and boulders and cuts a steep-sided V-shaped valley. Farther downstream, it flows smoothly over sediments and forms winding meanders, eroding sideways to create broad valleys and plains. On reaching the coast, the river may deposit sediment to form an estuary or delta (see pp. 290-291).

RIVER CAPTURE

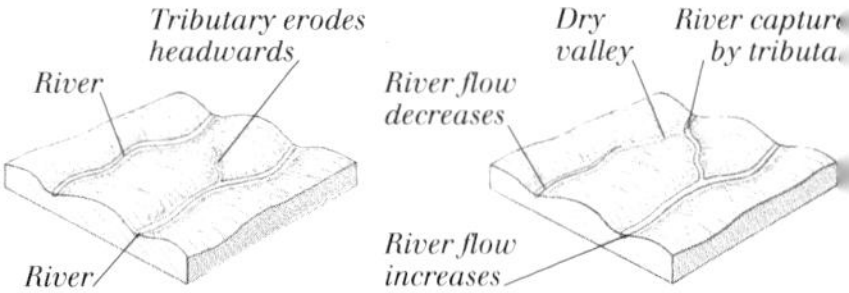
Tributary erodes headwards
River
River
Dry valley
River flow decreases
River flow increases

EARLY STAGE

LATER STAGE

THE WATER CYCLE

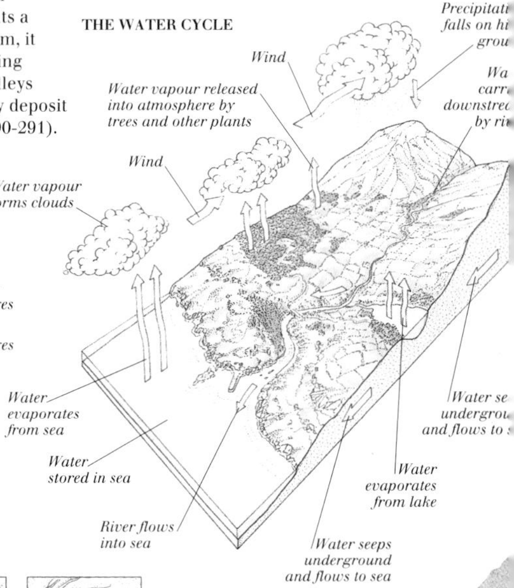
Wind
Water vapour released into atmosphere by trees and other plants
Wind
Water vapour forms clouds
Water evaporates from sea
Water stored in sea
River flows into sea
Water seeps underground and flows to sea
Water evaporates from lake

SATELLITE IMAGE OF GANGES RIVER DELTA, BANGLADESH

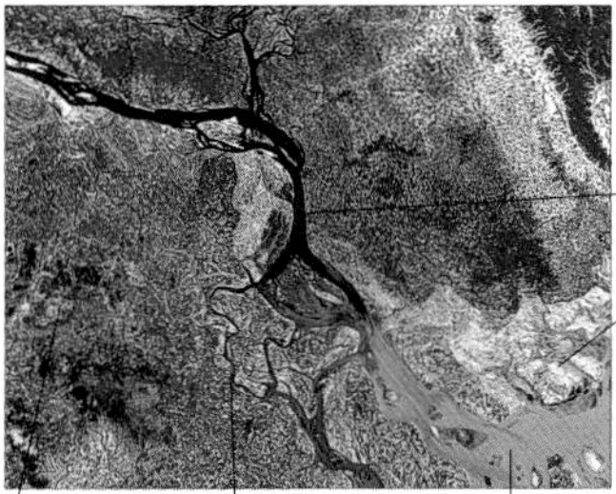
River Ganges
Ganges delta
Infertile swampland
Distributary
Large volume of sediment

RIVER DRAINAGE PATTERNS

RADIAL

CENTRIPETAL

PARALLEL

DENDRITIC

DERANGED

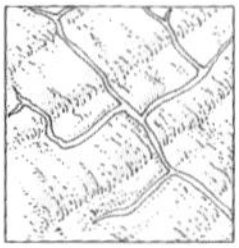

TRELLISED

ANNULAR

RECTANGULAR

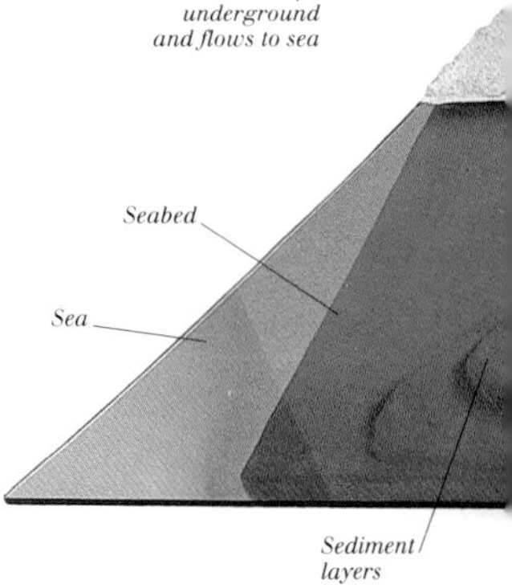
Seabed
Sea
Sediment layers

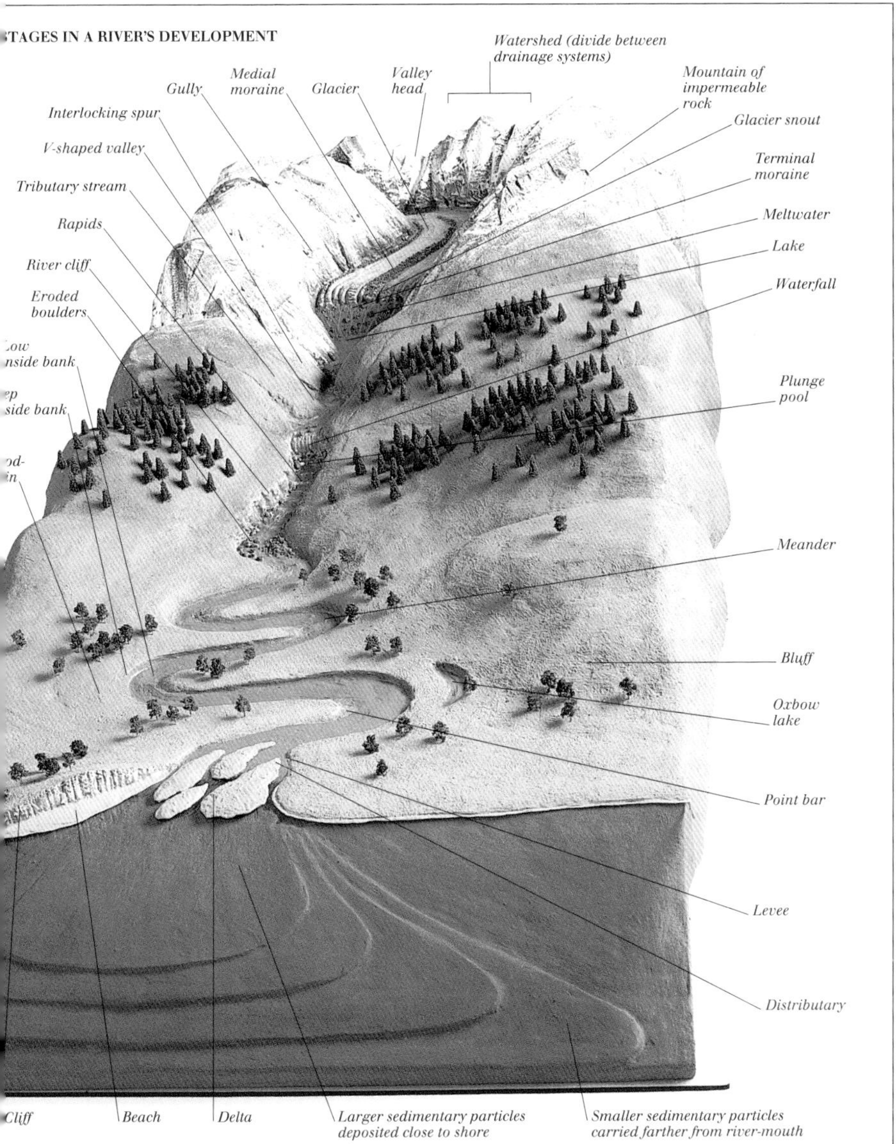

TAGES IN A RIVER'S DEVELOPMENT
Watershed (divide between drainage systems)
Medial moraine
Gully
Glacier
Valley head
Mountain of impermeable rock
Interlocking spur
Glacier snout
V-shaped valley
Terminal moraine
Tributary stream
Meltwater
Rapids
Lake
River cliff
Waterfall
Eroded boulders
ow
nside bank
p
side bank
Plunge pool
od-
in
Meander
Bluff
Oxbow lake
Point bar
Levee
Distributary
Cliff
Beach
Delta
Larger sedimentary particles deposited close to shore
Smaller sedimentary particles carried farther from river-mouth

River features

RIVERS ARE ONE OF THE MAJOR FORCES that shape the landscape. Near its source, a river is steep (see pp. 288-289). It erodes downwards, carving out V-shaped valleys and deep gorges. Waterfalls and rapids are formed where the river flows from hard rock to softer, more easily eroded rock. Farther downstream, meanders may form and there is greater sideways erosion, resulting in a broad river valley. The river sometimes erodes through the neck of a meander to form an oxbow lake. Sediment deposited on the valley floor by meandering rivers and during floods helps to create a flood-plain. Floods may also deposit sediment on the banks of the river to form levees. As a river spills into the sea or a lake, it deposits large amounts of sediment, and may form a delta. A delta is an area of sand-bars, swamps, and lagoons through which the river flows in several channels called distributaries – the Mississippi delta, for example. Often, a rise in sea level may have flooded the river-mouth to form a broad estuary, a tidal section where seawater mixes with fresh water.

HOW WATERFALLS AN RAPIDS ARE FORMED

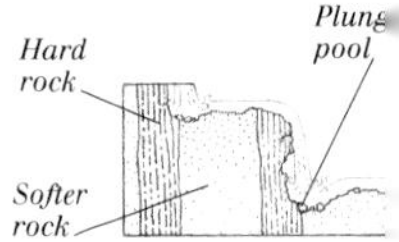
Hard rock
Plung pool
Softer rock

WATERFALL

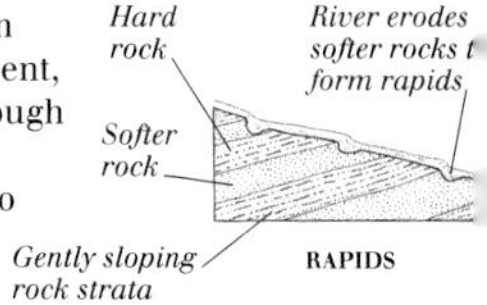
Hard rock
River erodes softer rocks t form rapids
Softer rock
Gently sloping rock strata

RAPIDS

A RIVER VALLEY DRAINAGE SYSTEM

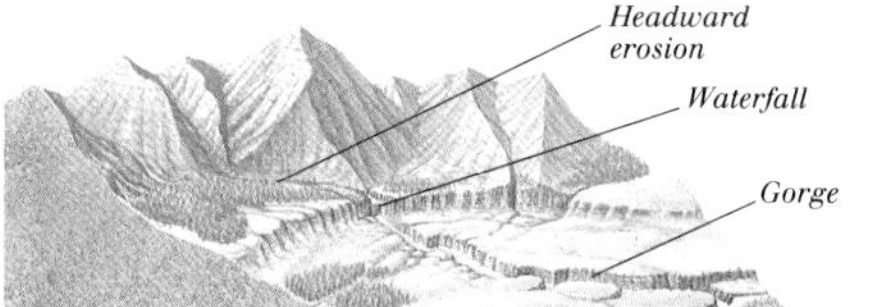
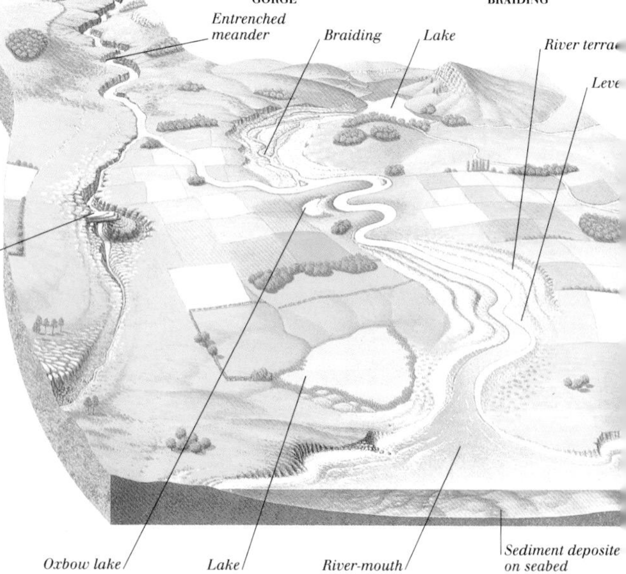
Headward erosion
Waterfall
Gorge
Entrenched meander
Braiding
Lake
River terra
Leve
Natural bridge
Oxbow lake
Lake
River-mouth
Sediment deposite on seabed

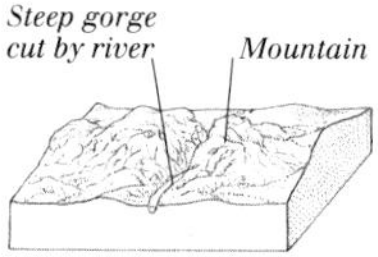
Steep gorge cut by river
Mountain

GORGE

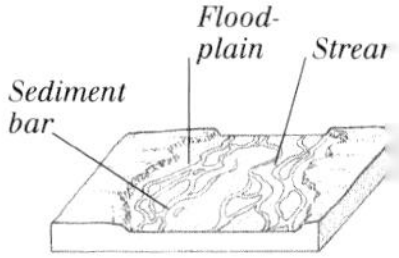
Flood-plain
Strea
Sediment bar
River erodes

BRAIDING

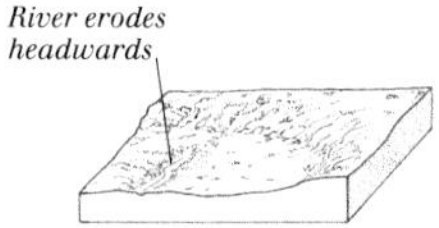
River erodes headwards

HEADWARD EROSION

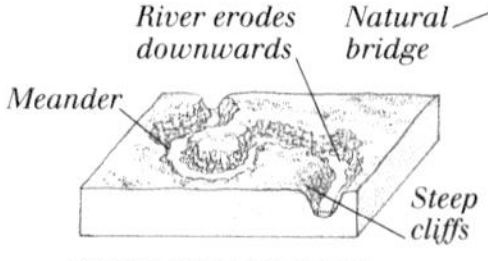
River erodes downwards
Meander
Steep cliffs

ENTRENCHED MEANDER

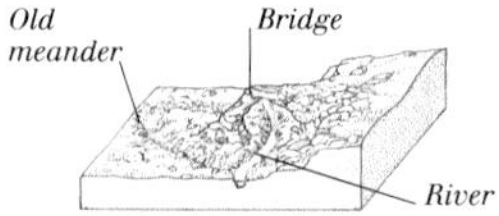

NATURAL BRIDGE

WATERFALL FEATURES

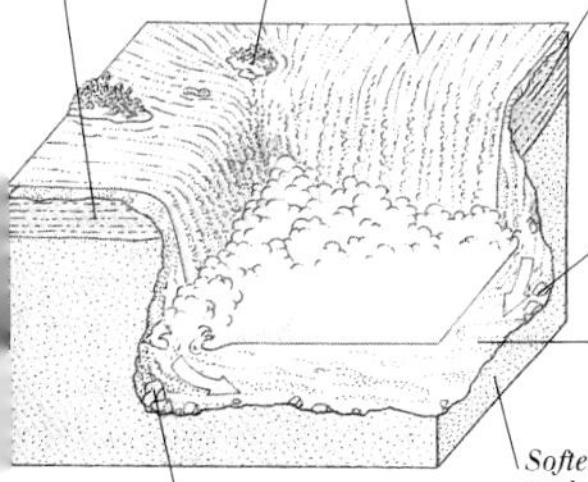
Island
River
Hard rock
Rock undercut by swirling boulders
Plunge pool
Softer rock
Rock undercut by swirling boulders

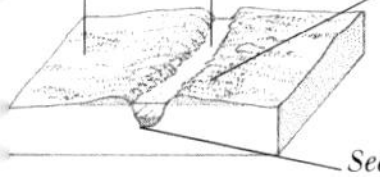
Flood-plain
River
Levee formed from sediment deposited by floods
Sediment

LEVEE

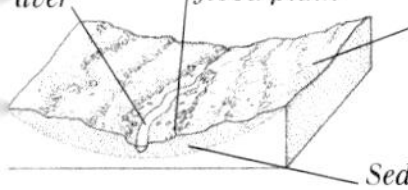
Present flood-plain
Oldest terrace (remnant of previous flood-plain)
Sediment

RIVER TERRACE

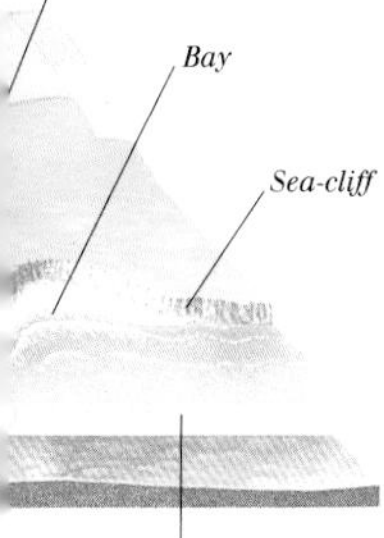
Flood-plain
Bay
Sea-cliff
Sea

THE MISSISSIPPI DELTA

Mississippi River
Levee
Distributary
Point bar
Swamp
Sediment plume
Sea
Levee
Freshwater bay
Spit
Sediment plume

FORMATION OF A DELTA

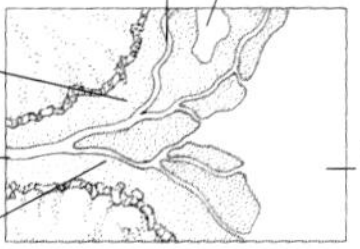
Distributary
Lagoon
Sediment deposited by river
River
Sea
Levee

EARLY STAGE

Earliest deposit of sediment
Bedrock
Latest deposit of sediment
Sea

SECTION THROUGH DELTA

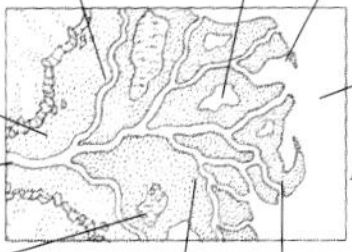
Distributary
Lagoon
Bar
Sediment deposited by river
Sea
River
Swamp formed by deposition of sediment in lagoon
Levee
Spit

MIDDLE STAGE

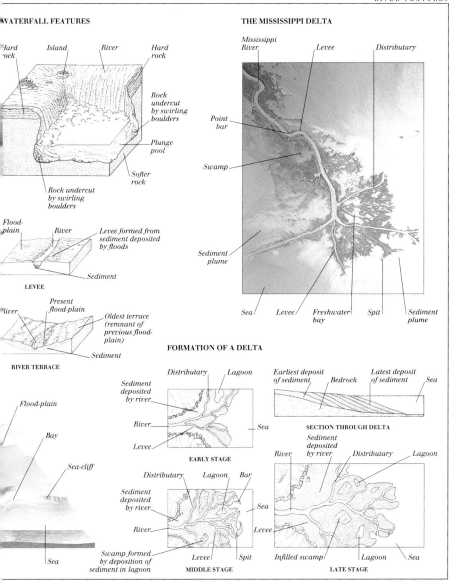

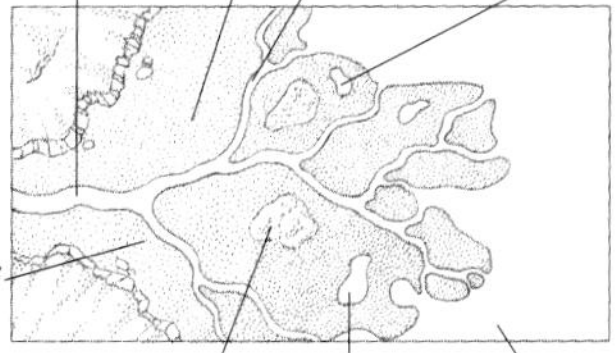
River
Sediment deposited by river
Distributary
Lagoon
Levee
Infilled swamp
Lagoon
Sea

LATE STAGE

Lakes and groundwater

NATURAL LAKES OCCUR WHERE a large quantity of water collects in a hollow in impermeable rock, or is prevented from draining away by a barrier, such as moraine (glacial deposits) or solidified lava. Lakes are often relatively short-lived landscape features, as they tend to become silted up by sediment from the streams and rivers that feed them. Some of the more long-lasting lakes are found in deep rift valleys formed by vertical movements of the Earth's crust (see pp. 58-59) – for example, Lake Baikal in Russia, the world's largest freshwater lake, and the Dead Sea in the Middle East, one of the world's saltiest lakes. Where water is able to drain away, it sinks into the ground until it reaches a layer of impermeable rock, then accumulates in the permeable rock above it; this water-saturated permeable rock is called an aquifer. The saturated zone varies in depth according to seasonal and climatic changes. In wet conditions, the water stored underground builds up, while in dry periods it becomes depleted. Where the upper edge of the saturated zone – the water table – meets the ground surface, water emerges as springs. In an artesian basin, where the aquifer is below an aquiclude (layer of impermeable rock), the water table throughout the basin is determined by its height at the rim. In the centre of such a basin, the water table is above ground level. The water in the basin is thus trapped below the water table and can rise under its own pressure along faultlines or well shafts.

LAKE BAIKAL, RUSSIA

EXAMPLES OF SPRINGS

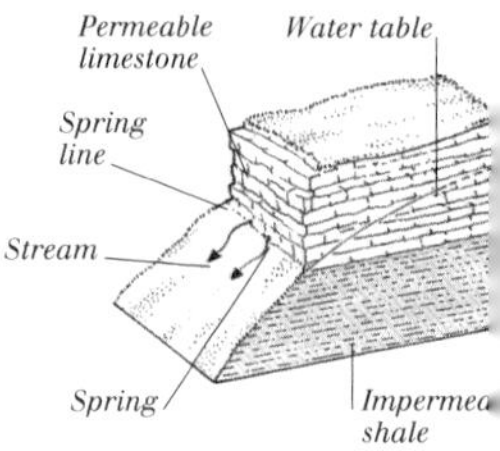
Permeable limestone
Water table
Spring line
Stream
Spring
Impermea
shale

LIMESTONE SPRING

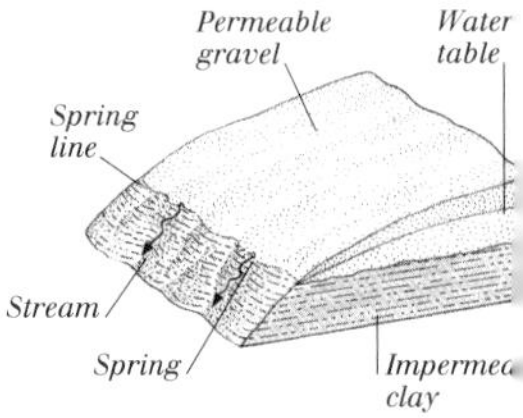
Permeable gravel
Water table
Spring line
Stream
Spring
Impermea
clay

COASTAL (VALLEY) SPRING

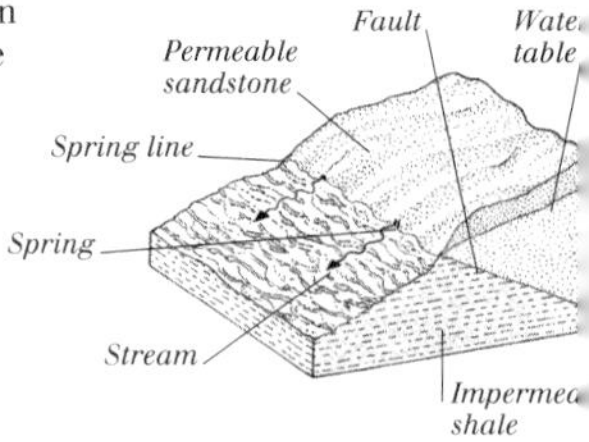
Fault
Wate
table
Permeable sandstone
Spring line
Spring
Stream
Impermea
shale

FAULT SPRING

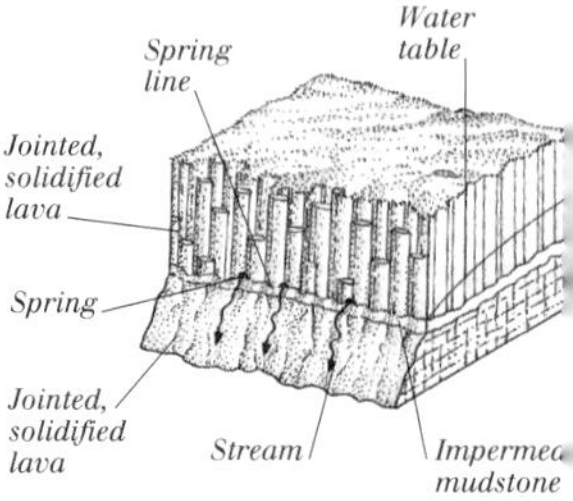
Water table
Spring line
Jointed, solidified lava
Spring
Jointed, solidified lava
Stream
Impermea
mudstone

LAVA SPRING

STRUCTURE OF AN ARTESIAN BASIN

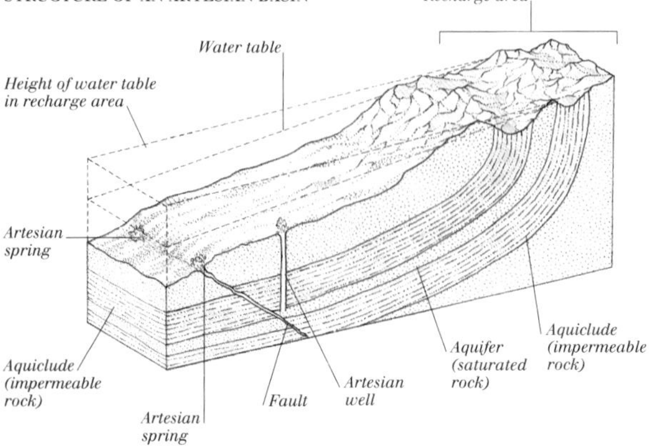
Recharge area
Water table
Height of water table in recharge area
Artesian spring
Aquiclude (impermeable rock)
Aquifer (saturated rock)
Aquiclude (impermeable rock)
Artesian well
Fault
Artesian spring

FEATURES OF A GROUNDWATER SYSTEM

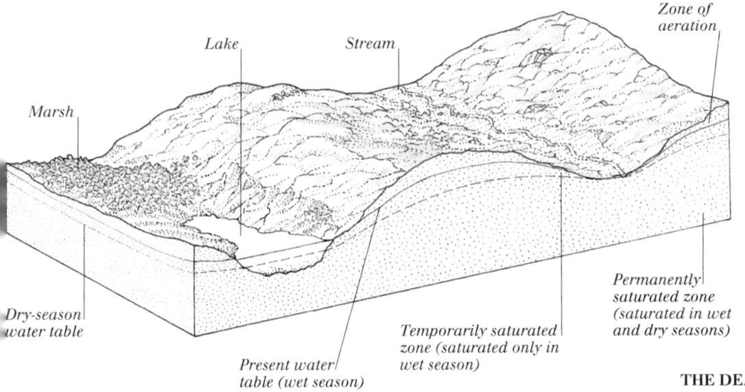
Zone of aeration
Lake
Stream
Marsh
Dry-season water table
Present water table (wet season)
Temporarily saturated zone (saturated only in wet season)
Permanently saturated zone (saturated in wet and dry seasons)

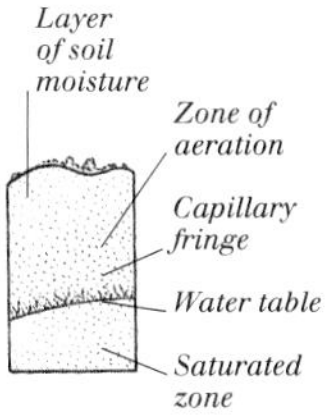
Layer of soil moisture
Zone of aeration
Capillary fringe
Water table
Saturated zone

CLOSE-UP OF SURFACE LAYER

EXAMPLES OF LAKES

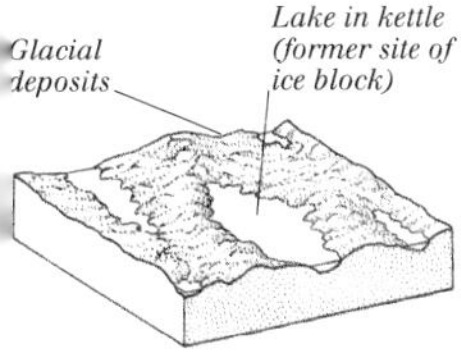
Glacial deposits
Lake in kettle (former site of ice block)

KETTLE LAKE

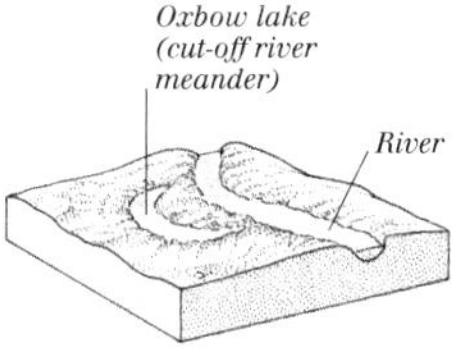
Oxbow lake (cut-off river meander)
River

OXBOW LAKE

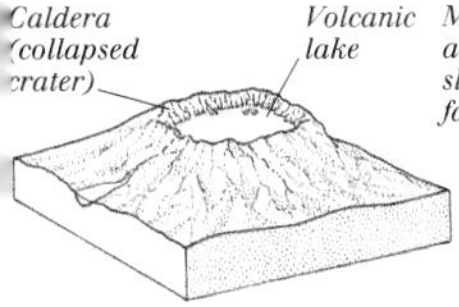
Caldera (collapsed crater)
Volcanic lake

VOLCANIC LAKE

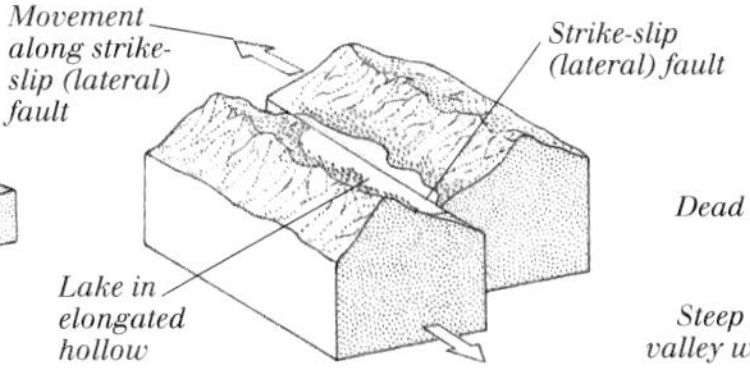
Movement along strike-slip (lateral) fault
Strike-slip (lateral) fault
Lake in elongated hollow

STRIKE-SLIP (LATERAL) FAULT LAKE

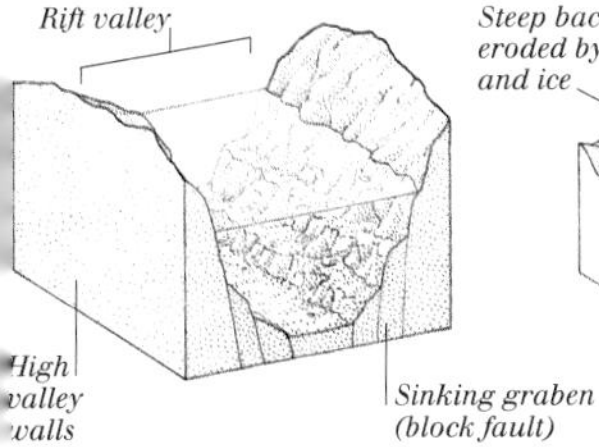
Rift valley
High valley walls
Sinking graben (block fault)

GRABEN (BLOCK-FAULT) LAKE

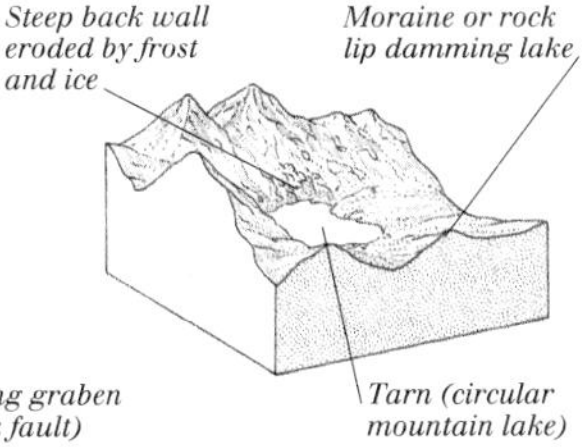
Steep back wall eroded by frost and ice
Moraine or rock lip damming lake
Tarn (circular mountain lake)

TARN

THE DEAD SEA, ISRAEL/JORDAN

River Jordan
Dead Sea
Steep rift-valley walls
Salt left by evaporation
Israel
Shallow flats
Jordan

Coastlines

COASTLINES ARE AMONG THE MOST RAPIDLY changing landscape features. Some are eroded by waves, wind, and rain, causing cliffs to be undercut and caves to be hollowed out of solid rock. Others are built up by waves transporting sand and small rocks in a process known as longshore drift, and by rivers depositing sediment in deltas. Additional influences include the activities of living organisms such as coral, crustal movements, and sea-level variations due to climatic changes. Rising land or a drop in sea level creates an emergent coastline, with cliffs and beaches stranded above the new shoreline. Sinking land or a rise in sea level produces a drowned coastline, typified by fjords (submerged glacial valleys) or submerged river valleys.

FEATURES OF A SEA-CLIFF

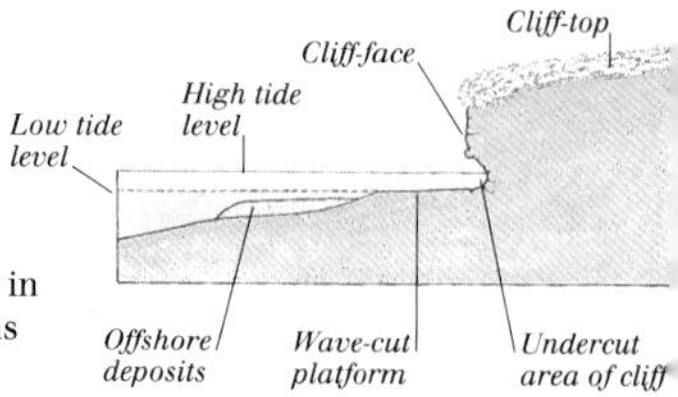
Cliff-top
Cliff-face
High tide level
Low tide level
Offshore deposits
Wave-cut platform
Undercut area of cliff

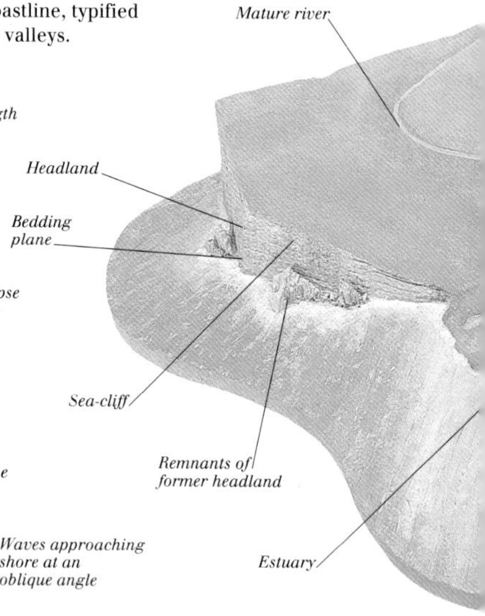
Mature river
Headland
Bedding plane
Sea-cliff
Remnants of former headland
Estuary

FEATURES OF WAVES

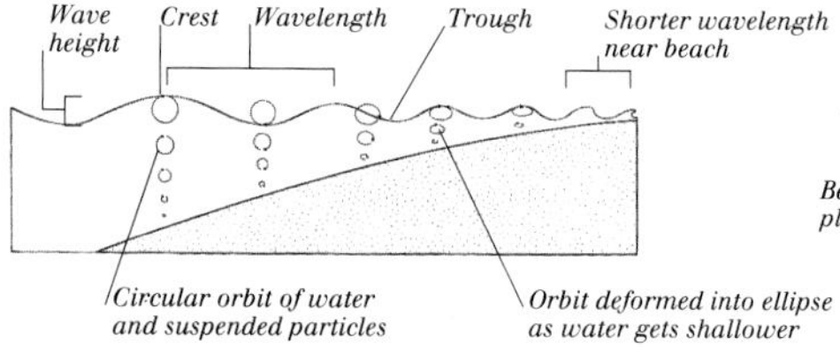
Wave height
Crest
Wavelength
Trough
Shorter wavelength near beach
Circular orbit of water and suspended particles
Orbit deformed into ellipse as water gets shallower

LONGSHORE DRIFT

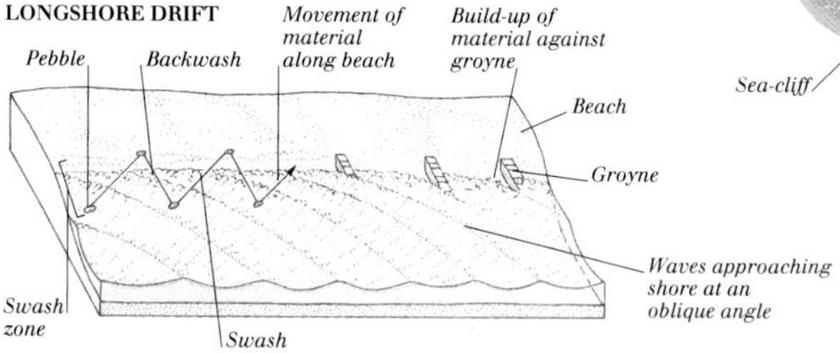
Movement of material along beach
Build-up of material against groyne
Pebble
Backwash
Beach
Groyne
Waves approaching shore at an oblique angle
Swash zone
Swash

DEPOSITIONAL FEATURES OF COASTLINES

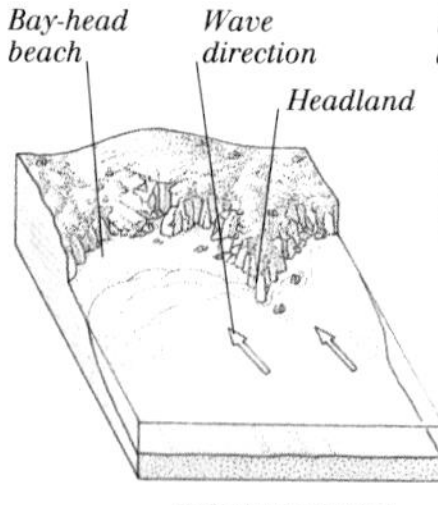
Bay-head beach
Wave direction
Headland

BAY-HEAD BEACH

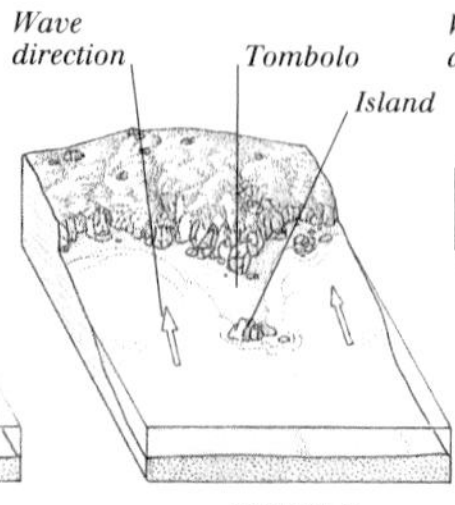
Wave direction
Tombolo
Island

TOMBOLO

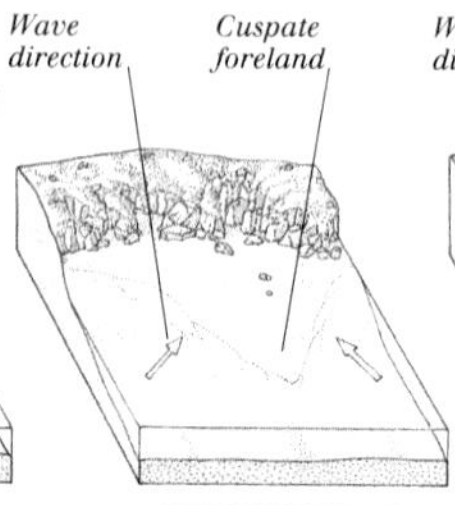
Wave direction
Cuspate foreland

CUSPATE FORELAND

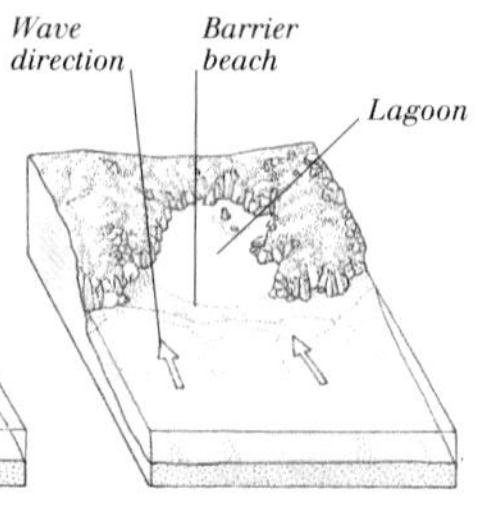
Wave direction
Barrier beach
Lagoon

BARRIER BEACH

FEATURES OF A COASTLINE

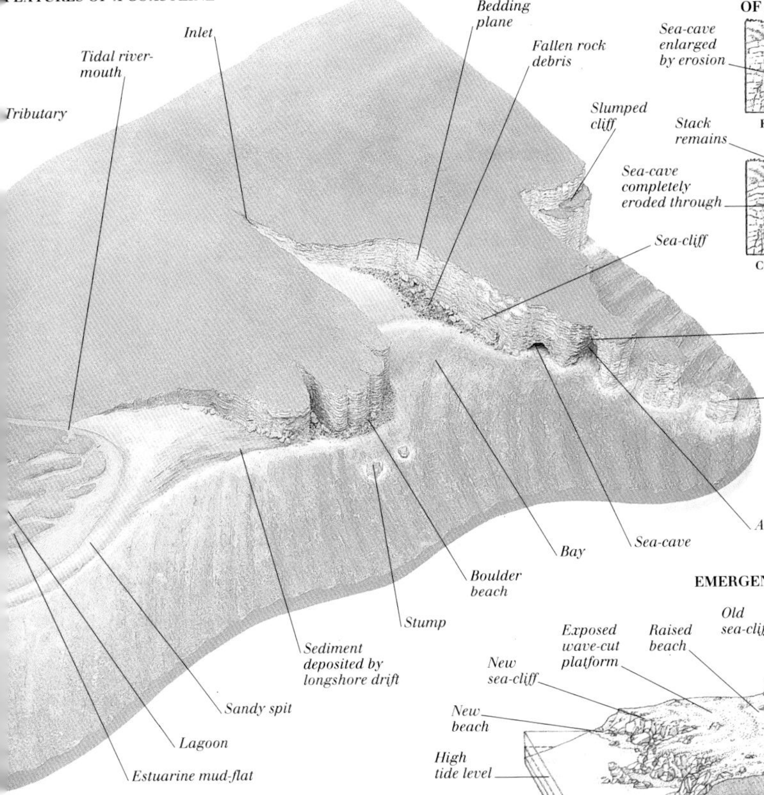
Bedding plane
Inlet
Fallen rock debris
Tidal river-mouth
Tributary
Slumped cliff
Sea-cliff
Lintel
Stack
Arch
Sea-cave
Bay
Boulder beach
Stump
Sediment deposited by longshore drift
Sandy spit
Lagoon
Estuarine mud-flat

FORMATION OF A STACK

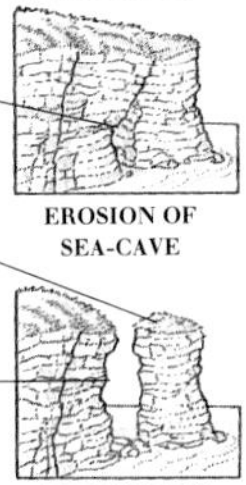
Sea-cave enlarged by erosion
Stack remains
Sea-cave completely eroded through

EROSION OF SEA-CAVE

COLLAPSE OF SEA-CAVE

EMERGENT COASTLINES

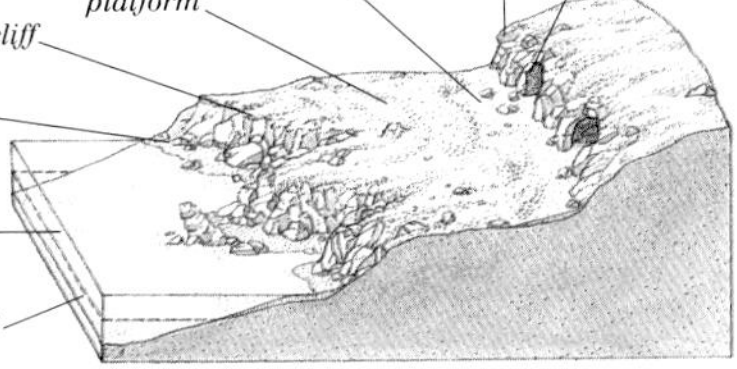
Old sea-cliff
Old sea-cave
Exposed wave-cut platform
Raised beach
New sea-cliff
New beach
High tide level
Low tide level

HIGHLAND COASTLINE

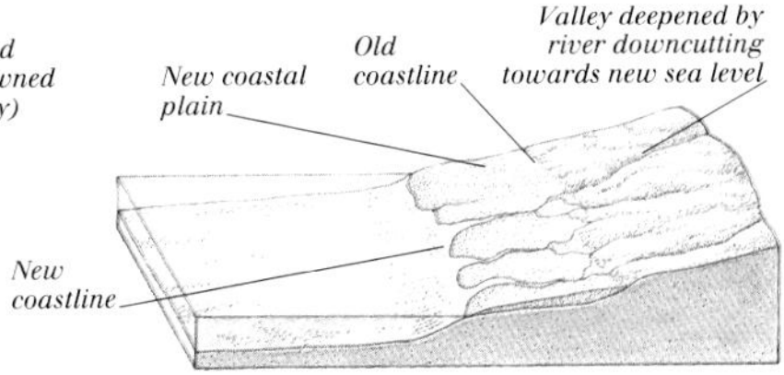
Valley deepened by river downcutting towards new sea level
Old coastline
New coastal plain
New coastline

LOWLAND COASTLINE

DROWNED COASTLINES

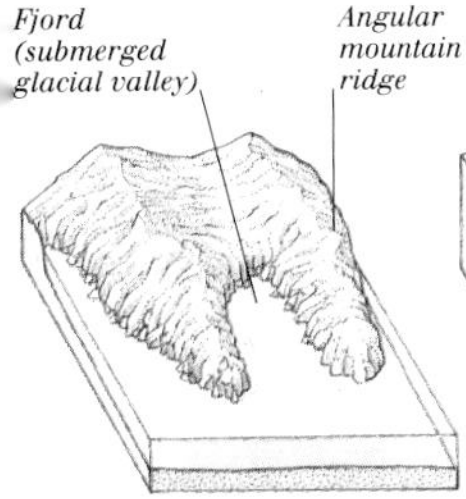
Fjord (submerged glacial valley)
Angular mountain ridge

FJORD COASTLINE

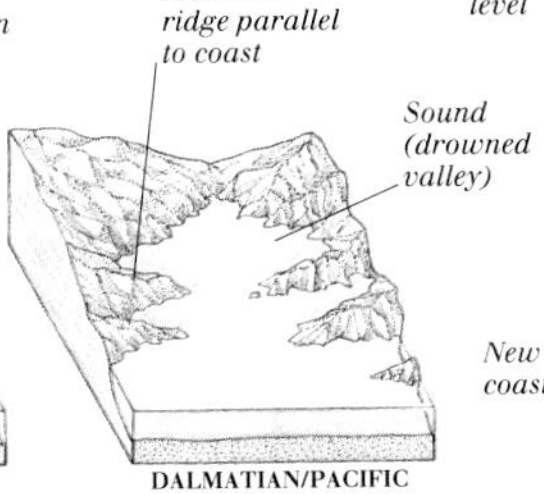
Mountain ridge parallel to coast
Sound (drowned valley)

DALMATIAN/PACIFIC COASTLINE

Oceans and seas

OCEANS AND SEAS COVER ABOUT 70 PER CENT of the Earth's surface and account for about 97 per cent of its total water. These oceans and seas play a crucial role in regulating temperature variations and determining climate. Their waters absorb heat from the Sun, especially in tropical regions, and the surface currents distribute it around the Earth, warming overlying air masses and neighbouring land in winter and cooling them in summer. The oceans are never still. Differences in temperature and salinity drive deep current systems, while surface currents are generated by winds blowing over the oceans. All currents are deflected – to the right in the Northern Hemisphere, to the left in the Southern Hemisphere – as a result of the Earth's rotation. This deflective factor is known as the Coriolis force. A current that begins on the surface is immediately deflected. This current in turn generates a current in the layer of water beneath, which is also deflected. As the movement is transmitted downwards, the deflections form an Ekman spiral. The waters of the oceans and seas are also moved by the constant ebb and flow of tides. These are caused by the gravitational pull of the Moon and Sun. The highest tides (Spring tides) occur at full and new Moon; the lowest tides (neap tides) occur at first and last quarter.

SURFACE CURRENTS

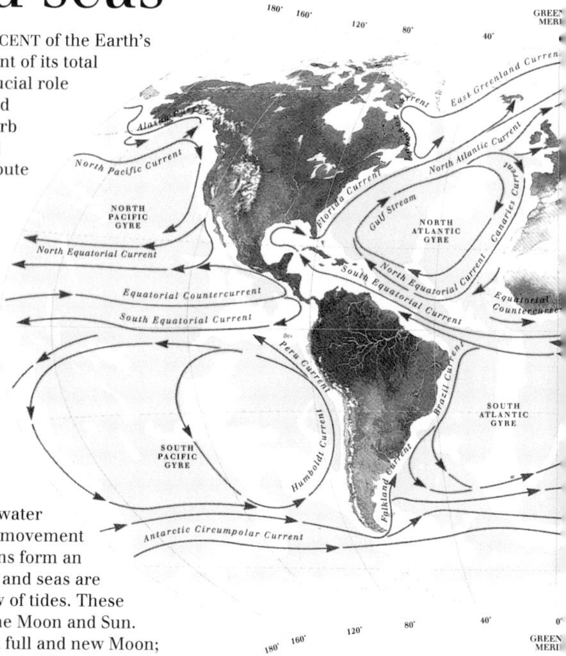

OFFSHORE CURRENTS

SALT CONTENT OF SEAWATER

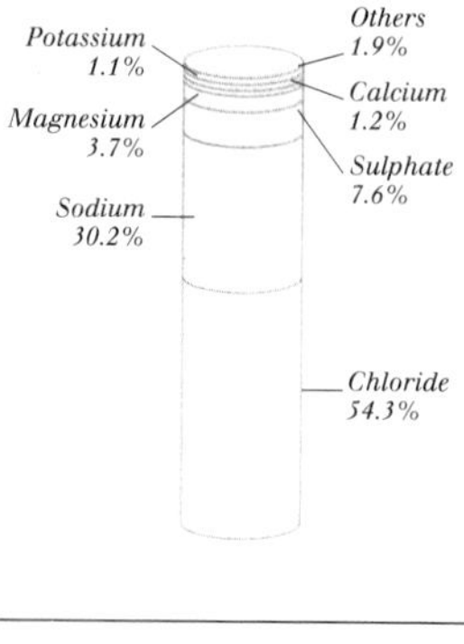

Potassium 1.1%
Others 1.9%
Calcium 1.2%
Magnesium 3.7%
Sulphate 7.6%
Sodium 30.2%
Chloride 54.3%

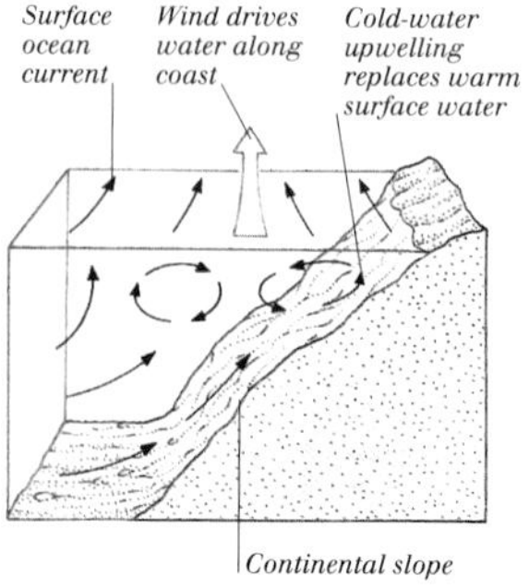

Surface ocean current
Wind drives water along coast
Cold-water upwelling replaces warm surface water
Continental slope

COLD-WATER UPWELLING (SOUTHERN HEMISPHERE)

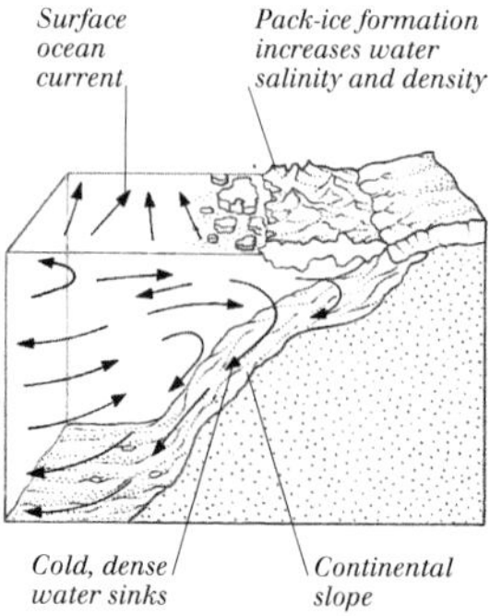

Surface ocean current
Pack-ice formation increases water salinity and density
Cold, dense water sinks
Continental slope

POLAR BOTTOM WATER

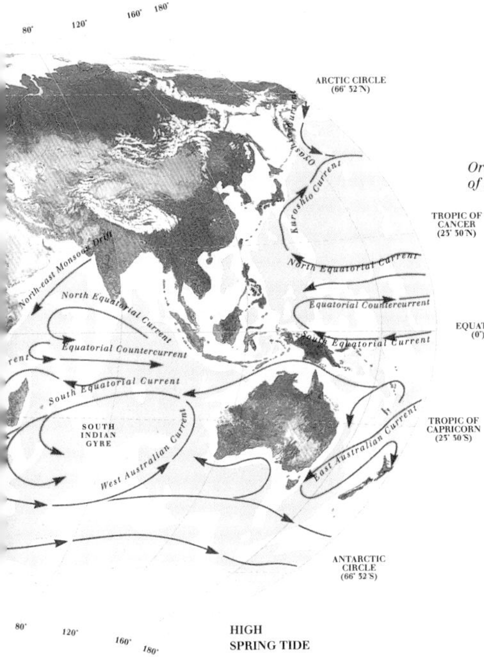
80°
120°
160°
180°
ARCTIC CIRCLE (66° 32'N)
Oyashio Current
Kuroshio Current
TROPIC OF CANCER (23° 30'N)
North-east Monsoon Drift
North Equatorial Current
North Equatorial Current
Equatorial Countercurrent
EQUATOR (0°)
Equatorial Countercurrent
South Equatorial Current
South Equatorial Current
SOUTH INDIAN GYRE
West Australian Current
East Australian Current
TROPIC OF CAPRICORN (23° 30'S)
ANTARCTIC CIRCLE (66° 32'S)
80°
120°
160°
180°

EFFECT OF CORIOLIS FORCE

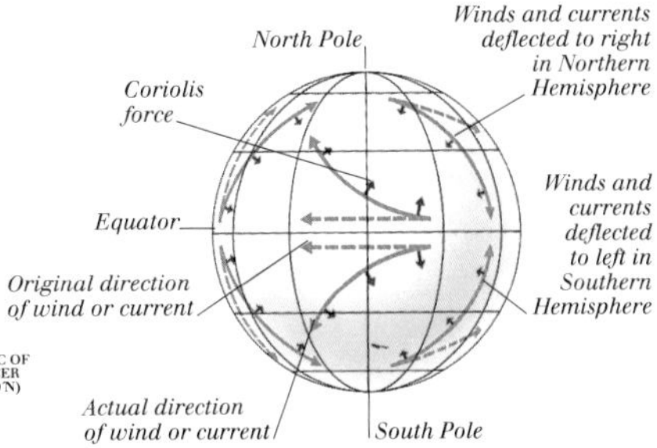
North Pole
Winds and currents deflected to right in Northern Hemisphere
Coriolis force
Winds and currents deflected to left in Southern Hemisphere
Equator
Original direction of wind or current
Actual direction of wind or current
South Pole

EKMAN SPIRAL (NORTHERN HEMISPHERE)

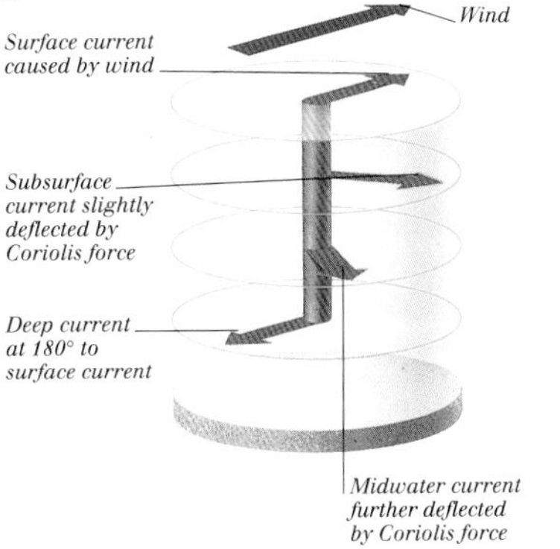
Wind
Surface current caused by wind
Subsurface current slightly deflected by Coriolis force
Deep current at 180° to surface current
Midwater current further deflected by Coriolis force

HOW TIDES ARE CAUSED

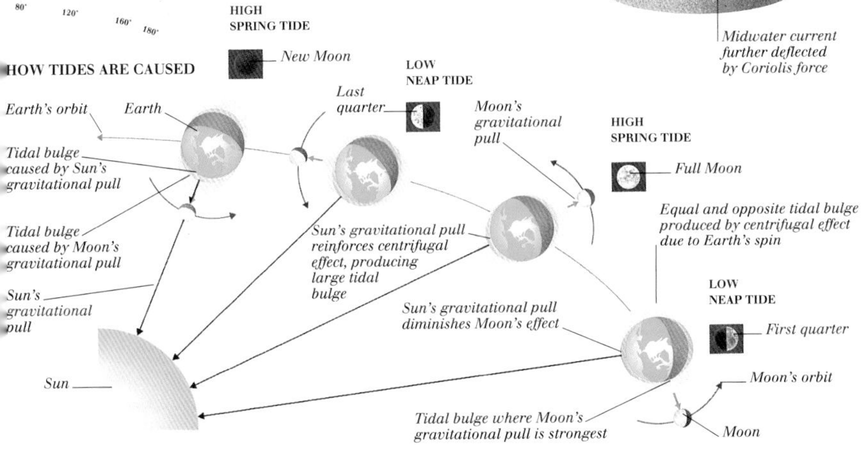
HIGH SPRING TIDE
New Moon
LOW NEAP TIDE
Last quarter
Earth's orbit
Earth
Tidal bulge caused by Sun's gravitational pull
Tidal bulge caused by Moon's gravitational pull
Sun's gravitational pull
Moon's gravitational pull
HIGH SPRING TIDE
Full Moon
Equal and opposite tidal bulge produced by centrifugal effect due to Earth's spin
Sun's gravitational pull reinforces centrifugal effect, producing large tidal bulge
Sun's gravitational pull diminishes Moon's effect
LOW NEAP TIDE
First quarter
Moon's orbit
Sun
Tidal bulge where Moon's gravitational pull is strongest
Moon

The ocean floor

THE OCEAN FLOOR COMPRISES TWO SECTIONS: the continental shelf and slope, and the deep-ocean floor. The continental shelf and slope are part of the continental crust, but may extend far into the ocean. Sloping quite gently to a depth of about 140 metres, the continental shelf is covered in sandy deposits shaped by waves and tidal currents. At the edge of the continental shelf, the seabed slopes down to the abyssal plain, which lies at an average depth of about 3,800 metres. On this deep-ocean floor is a layer of sediment made up of clays, fine oozes formed from the remains of tiny sea creatures, and occasional mineral-rich deposits. Echo-sounding and remote sensing from satellites has revealed that the abyssal plain is divided by a system of mountain ranges, far bigger than any on land – the mid-ocean ridge. Here, magma (molten rock) wells up from the Earth's interior and solidifies, widening the ocean floor (see pp. 58-59). As the ocean floor spreads, volcanoes that have formed over hot spots in the crust move away from their magma source; they become extinct and are increasingly submerged and eroded. Volcanoes eroded below sea level remain as seamounts (underwater mountains). In warm waters, a volcano that projects above the ocean surface often acquires a fringing coral reef, which may develop into an atoll as the volcano becomes submerged.

CONTINENTAL-SHELF FLOOR

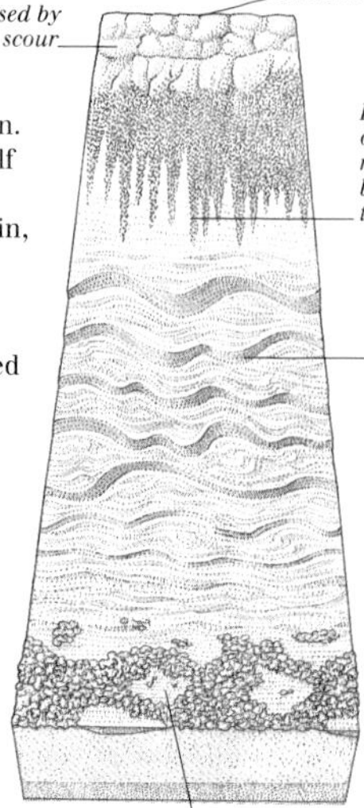
Bedrock exposed by tidal scour
Shoreline
Parallel strip of coarse material left by strong tidal current
Sand deposited in wavy pattern by weaker currents
Irregular patches of fine sand deposited by weakest currents

FEATURES OF THE OCEAN FLOOR

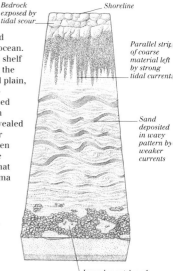

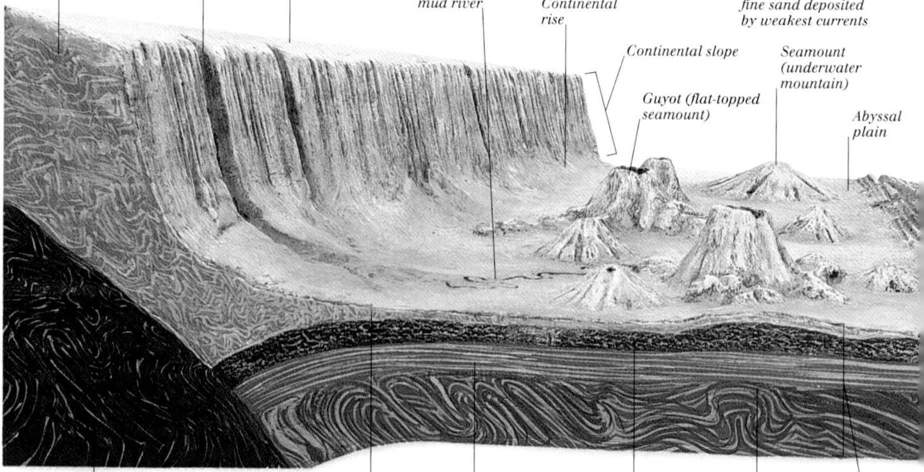
Sediment
Submarine canyon
Continental shelf
Course of mud river
Continental rise
Continental slope
Guyot (flat-topped seamount)
Seamount (underwater mountain)
Abyssal plain
Continental crust
Ooze (sediment consisting of remains of tiny sea creatures)
Layer of volcanic rock
Pillow lava
Volcanic crystalline rock
Oceanic crust

DEEP-OCEAN FLOOR SEDIMENTS

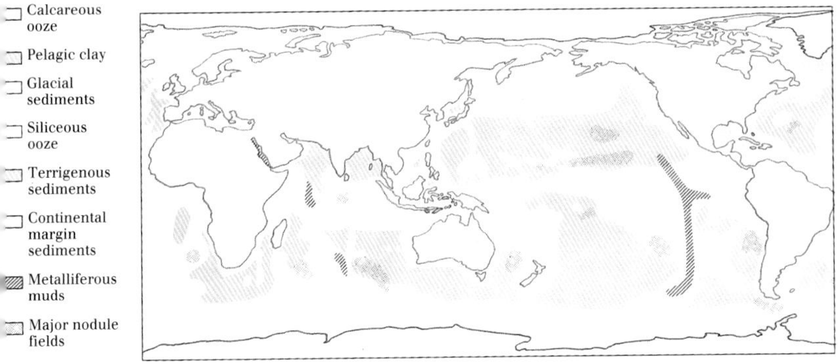
KEY
Calcareous ooze
Pelagic clay
Glacial sediments
Siliceous ooze
Terrigenous sediments
Continental margin sediments
Metalliferous muds
Major nodule fields

ECHO-SOUND PROFILE OF OCEAN FLOOR

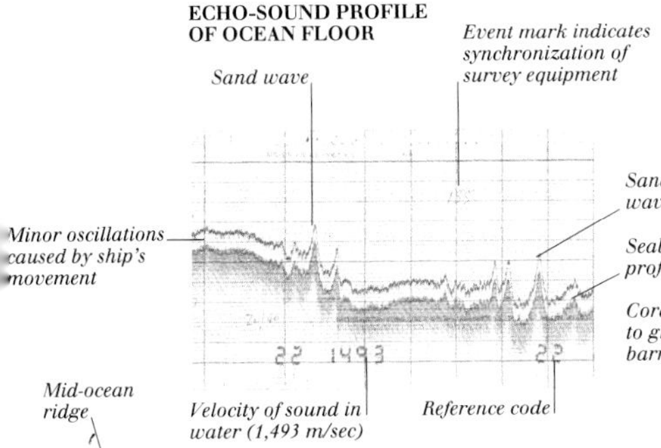
Event mark indicates synchronization of survey equipment
Sand wave
Sand wave
Minor oscillations caused by ship's movement
Seabed profile
22 1493
22
Velocity of sound in water (1,493 m/sec)
Reference code

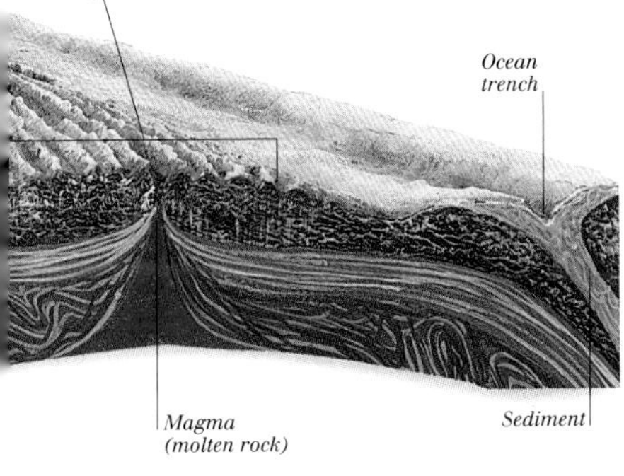
Mid-ocean ridge
Ocean trench
Magma (molten rock)
Sediment

DEVELOPMENT OF AN ATOLL

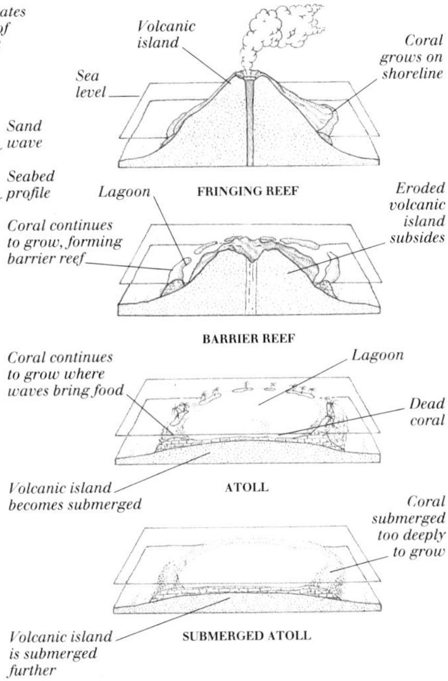
Volcanic island
Coral grows on shoreline
Sea level
FRINGING REEF
Lagoon
Eroded volcanic island subsides
Coral continues to grow, forming barrier reef
BARRIER REEF
Coral continues to grow where waves bring food
Lagoon
Dead coral
Volcanic island becomes submerged
ATOLL
Coral submerged too deeply to grow
Volcanic island is submerged further
SUBMERGED ATOLL

The atmosphere

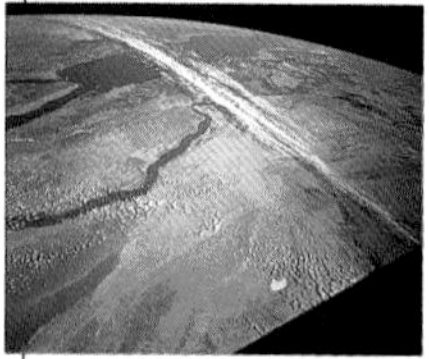
JET STREAM

THE EARTH IS SURROUNDED BY ITS ATMOSPHERE, a blanket of gases that enables life to exist on the planet. This layer has no definite outer edge, gradually becoming thinner until it merges into space, but over 80 per cent of atmospheric gases are held by gravity within about 20 kilometres of the Earth's surface. The atmosphere blocks out much harmful ultraviolet solar radiation, and insulates the Earth against extremes of temperature by limiting both incoming solar radiation and the escape of re-radiated heat into space. This natural balance may be distorted by the greenhouse effect, as gases such as carbon dioxide have built up in the atmosphere, trapping more heat. Close to the Earth's surface, differences in air temperature and pressure cause air to circulate between the equator and poles. This circulation, together with the Coriolis force, gives rise to the prevailing surface winds and the high-level jet streams.

ATMOSPHERIC CIRCULATION AND WINDS

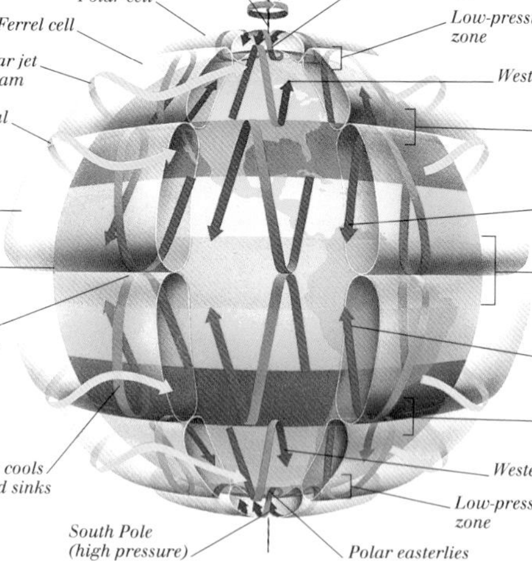
North Pole (high pressure)
Rotation of Earth
Polar cell
Polar easterlies
Ferrel cell
Low-pressure zone
Polar jet stream
Westerlies
Subtropical jet stream
High-pressure zone
Hadley cell
North-east trade winds
Equator
Intertropical convergence zone (low pressure)
Warm equatorial air rises and flows towards pole
South-east trade winds
High-pressure zone
Air cools and sinks
Westerlies
Low-pressure zone
South Pole (high pressure)
Polar easterlies

FORMATION OF ROSSBY WAVES IN THE JET STREAM

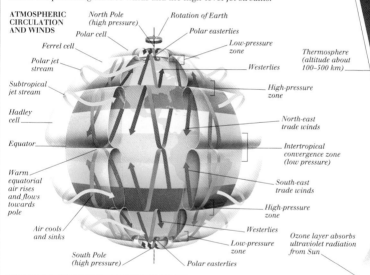

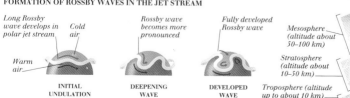

Long Rossby wave develops in polar jet stream
Cold air
Warm air
Rossby wave becomes more pronounced
Fully developed Rossby wave
INITIAL UNDULATION
DEEPENING WAVE
DEVELOPED WAVE

Exosphere (altitude above about 500 km)
Corona
Thermosphere (altitude about 100–500 km)
Ozone layer absorbs ultraviolet radiation from Sun
Mesosphere (altitude about 50–100 km)
Stratosphere (altitude about 10–50 km)
Troposphere (altitude up to about 10 km)

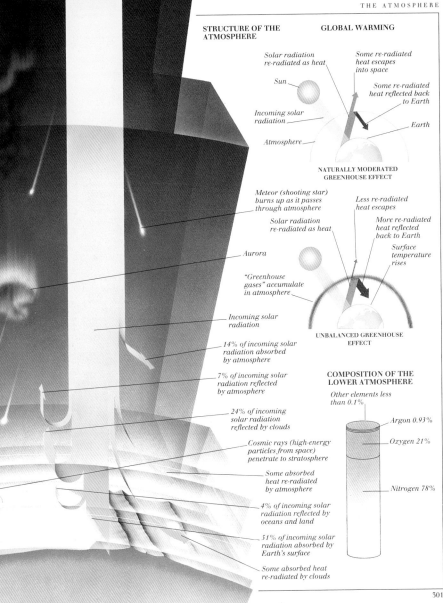

STRUCTURE OF THE ATMOSPHERE

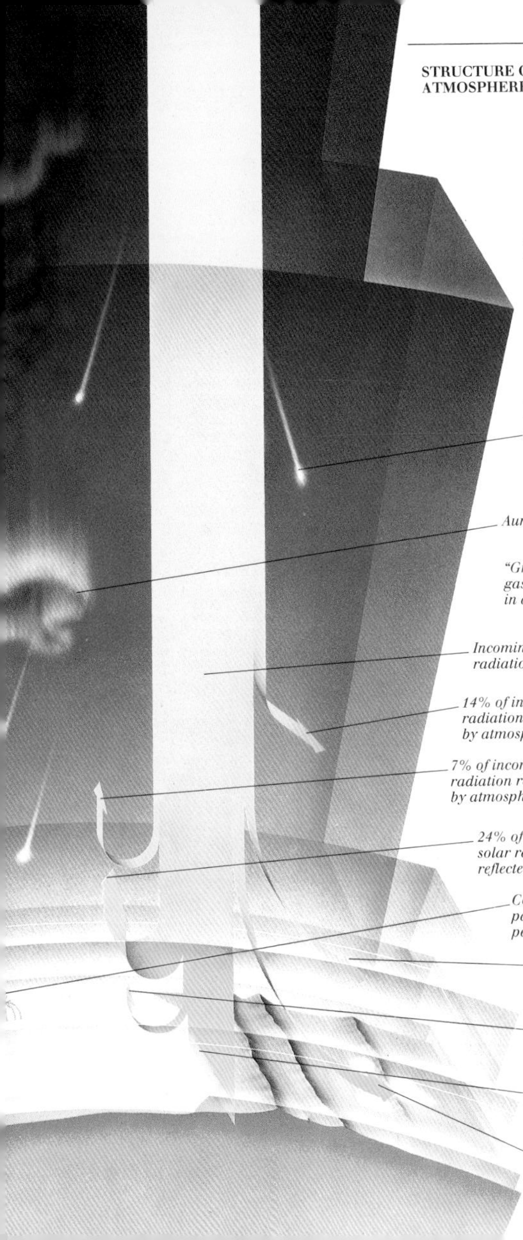

Meteor (shooting star) burns up as it passes through atmosphere
Aurora
Incoming solar radiation
14% of incoming solar radiation absorbed by atmosphere
7% of incoming solar radiation reflected by atmosphere
24% of incoming solar radiation reflected by clouds
Cosmic rays (high-energy particles from space) penetrate to stratosphere
Some absorbed heat re-radiated by atmosphere
4% of incoming solar radiation reflected by oceans and land
51% of incoming solar radiation absorbed by Earth's surface
Some absorbed heat re-radiated by clouds

GLOBAL WARMING

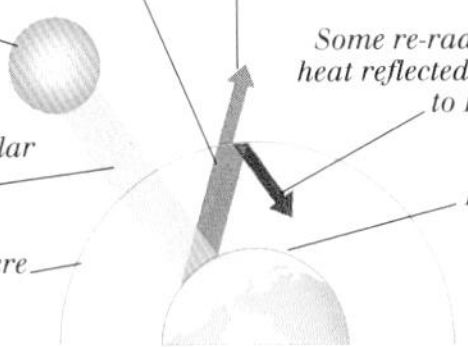

Solar radiation re-radiated as heat
Some re-radiated heat escapes into space
Sun
Some re-radiated heat reflected back to Earth
Incoming solar radiation
Earth
Atmosphere

NATURALLY MODERATED GREENHOUSE EFFECT

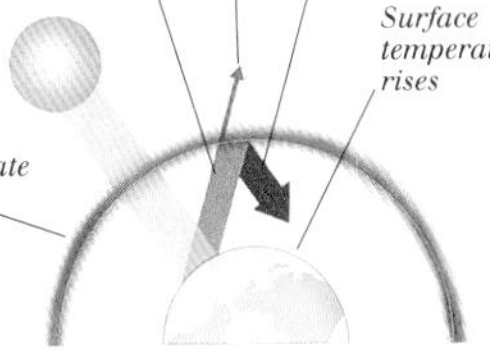

Less re-radiated heat escapes
Solar radiation re-radiated as heat
More re-radiated heat reflected back to Earth
Surface temperature rises
"Greenhouse gases" accumulate in atmosphere

UNBALANCED GREENHOUSE EFFECT

COMPOSITION OF THE LOWER ATMOSPHERE

Other elements less than 0.1%
Argon 0.93%
Oxygen 21%
Nitrogen 78%

Weather

WEATHER IS DEFINED AS THE ATMOSPHERIC CONDITIONS at a particular time and place; climate is the average weather conditions for a given region over time. Weather is assessed in terms of temperature, wind, cloud cover, and precipitation, such as rain or snow. Fine weather is associated with high-pressure areas, where air is sinking. Cloudy, wet, changeable weather is common in low-pressure zones with rising, unstable air. Such conditions occur at temperate latitudes, where warm air meets cool air along the polar fronts. Here, spiralling low-pressure cells known as depressions (mid-latitude cyclones) often form. A depression usually contains a sector of warmer air, beginning at a warm front and ending at a cold front. If the two fronts merge, forming an occluded front, the warm air is pushed upwards. An extreme form of low-pressure cell is a hurricane (also called a typhoon or tropical cyclone), which brings torrential rain and exceptionally strong winds.

TYPES OF CLOUD

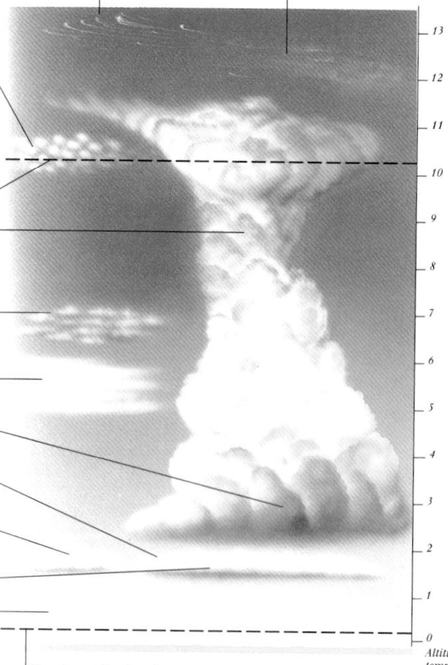
Cirrus
Cirrostratus
Cirrocumulus
Freezing level, above which clouds consist of ice crystals
Cumulonimbus
Altocumulus
Altostratus
Nimbus
Stratocumulus
Cumulus
Nimbostratus
Stratus
Condensation level
13
12
11
10
9
8
7
6
5
4
3
2
1
0
Altitude in temperate regions (km)

TYPES OF OCCLUDED FRONT

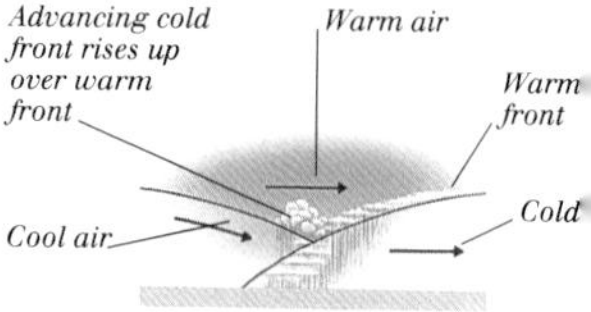
Advancing cold front rises up over warm front
Warm air
Warm front
Cool air
Cold

WARM OCCLUSION

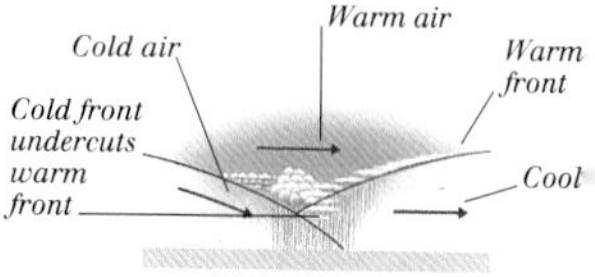
Warm air
Cold air
Warm front
Cold front undercuts warm front
Cool

COLD OCCLUSION

FORMS OF PRECIPITATION

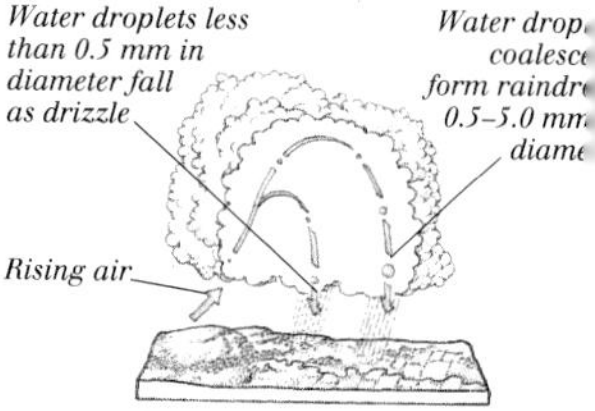
Water droplets less than 0.5 mm in diameter fall as drizzle
Water drop coalesce form raindr 0.5–5.0 mm diame
Rising air

RAIN FROM CLOUDS NOT REACHING FREEZING LEVEL

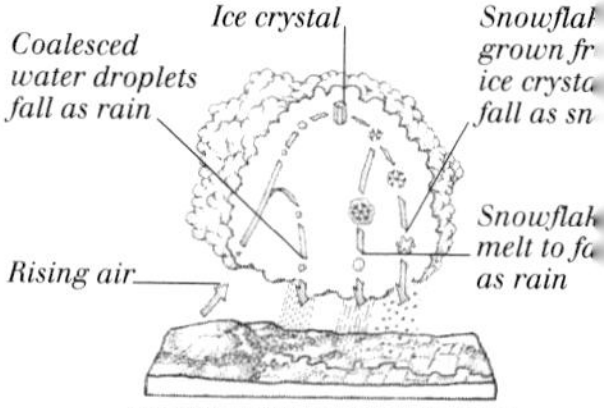
Ice crystal
Coalesced water droplets fall as rain
Snowflak grown fr ice crysta fall as sn
Snowflak melt to fa as rain
Rising air

RAIN AND SNOW FROM CLOUDS REACHING FREEZING LEVEL

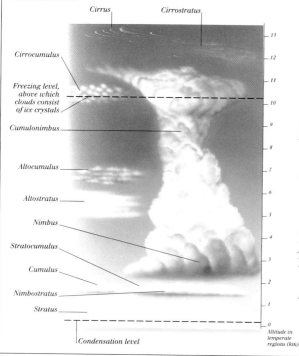

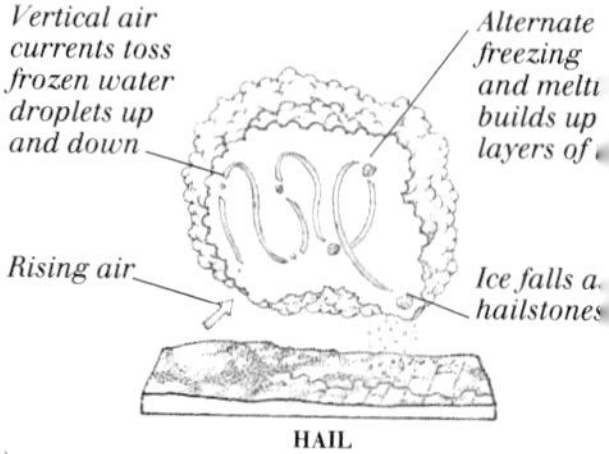
Vertical air currents toss frozen water droplets up and down
Alternate freezing and melti builds up layers of
Rising air
Ice falls a hailstones

HAIL

TRUCTURE OF A HURRICANE

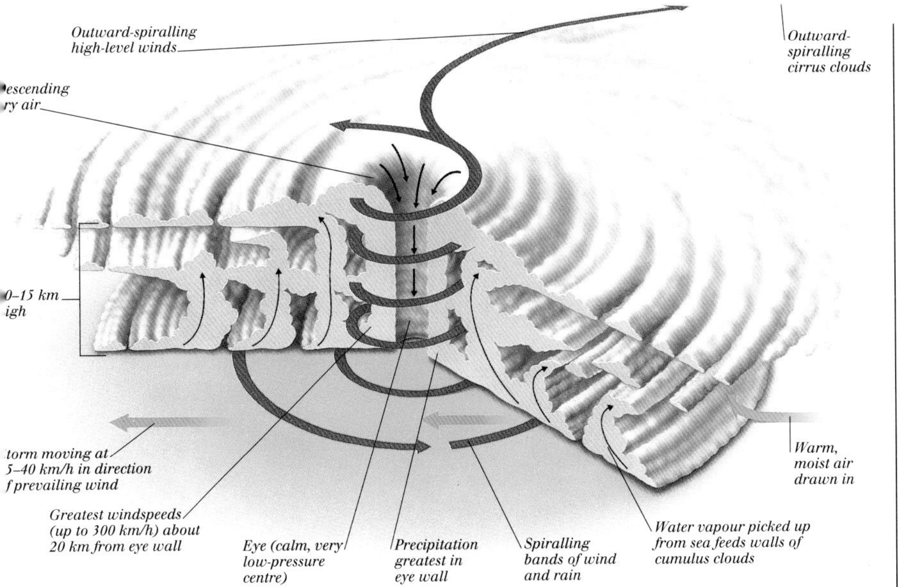
Outward-spiralling high-level winds
Outward-spiralling cirrus clouds
escending ry air
0–15 km igh
torm moving at 5–40 km/h in direction f prevailing wind
Warm, moist air drawn in
Greatest windspeeds (up to 300 km/h) about 20 km from eye wall
Eye (calm, very low-pressure centre)
Precipitation greatest in eye wall
Spiralling bands of wind and rain
Water vapour picked up from sea feeds walls of cumulus clouds

VEATHER MAP

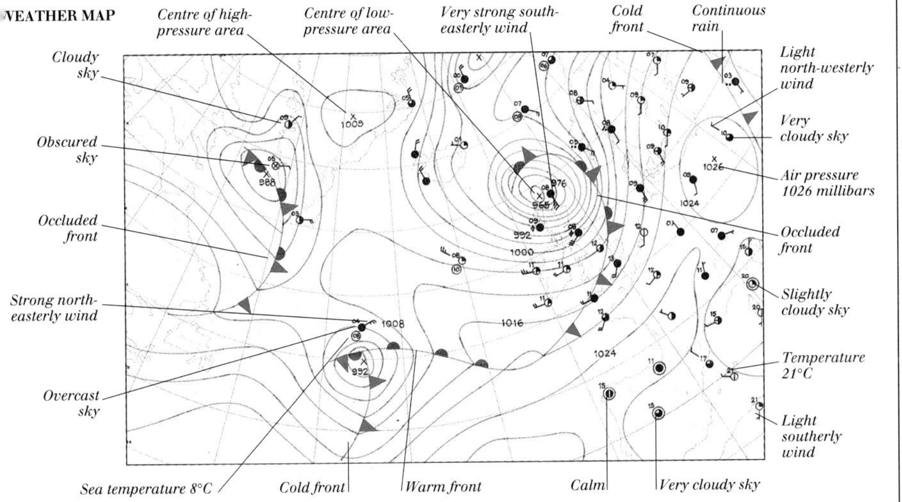
Centre of high-pressure area
Centre of low-pressure area
Very strong south-easterly wind
Cold front
Continuous rain
Cloudy sky
Light north-westerly wind
Obscured sky
Very cloudy sky
Air pressure 1026 millibars
Occluded front
Occluded front
Strong north-easterly wind
Slightly cloudy sky
Temperature 21°C
Overcast sky
Light southerly wind
Sea temperature 8°C
Cold front
Warm front
Calm
Very cloudy sky
1009
988
965
976
992
1000
1008
1016
1024
1026
1024
992

Physics and Chemistry

The variety of matter

PLANT AND INSECT (LIVING MATTER)

MATTER IS ANYTHING THAT OCCUPIES SPACE. It includes everything from natural substances, such as minerals or living organisms, to synthetic materials. Matter can exist in three distinct states – solid, liquid, and gas. A solid is rigid and retains its shape. A liquid is fluid, has a definite volume, and will take the shape of its container. A gas (also fluid) fills a space, so its volume will be the same as the volume of its container. Most substances can exist as a solid, a liquid, or a gas: the state is determined by temperature. At very high temperatures, matter becomes plasma, often considered to be a fourth state of matter. All matter is composed of microscopic particles, such as atoms and molecules (see pp. 308-309). The arrangement and interactions of these particles give a substance its physical and chemical properties, by which matter can be identified. There is a huge variety of matter because particles can arrange themselves in countless ways, in one substance or by mixing with others. Natural glass, for example, seems to be a solid but is, in fact, a supercool liquid: the atoms are not locked into a pattern and can flow. Pure substances known as elements (see p. 310) combine to form compounds or mixtures. Mixtures called colloids are made up of larger particles of matter suspended in a solid, liquid, or gas, while a solution is one substance dissolved in another.

TYPES OF COLLOID

HAIR GEL (SOLID IN LIQUID)

SHAVING FOAM (AIR IN LIQUID)

MIST (LIQUID IN GAS)

EXAMPLES OF MATTER

Polythene is made by combining natural materials in new ways

POLYTHENE (SYNTHETIC POLYMER)

The element silicon in pure crystalline form

PURE SILICON (SEMICONDUCTOR)

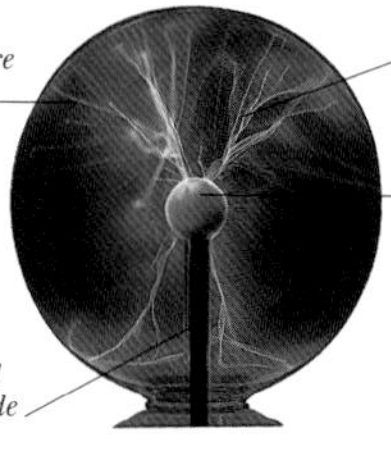
Low pressure gases
Streaks of plasma (mixture of electrons and charged atoms)
Voltage tears electrons from atoms of low pressure gases inside
Central electrode

BALL CONTAINING HIGH-TEMPERATURE GAS (PLASMA)

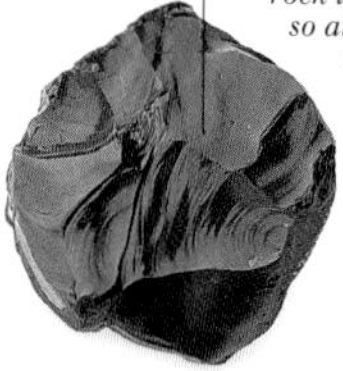
Obsidian is molten volcanic rock that cools quickly, so atoms cannot form a regular pattern

OBSIDIAN (NATURAL GLASS)

Azurite is found naturally with deposits of copper ore

AZURITE (CRYSTALLINE MINERAL)

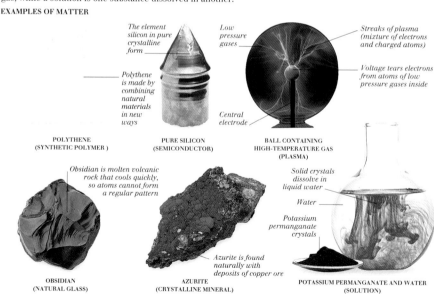

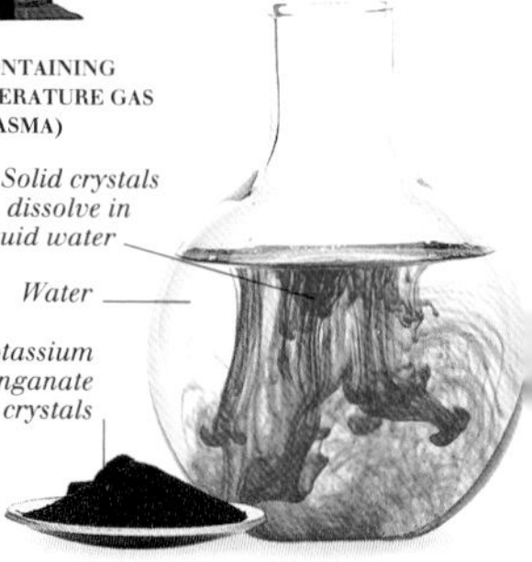
Solid crystals dissolve in liquid water
Water
Potassium permanganate crystals

POTASSIUM PERMANGANATE AND WATER (SOLUTION)

TATES OF MATTER

GAS
There are relatively few bonds between the particles in a gas, allowing for expansion in every direction. The particles move randomly, colliding with the walls of any container and occasionally with each other.

GLASS
A supercooled liquid (glass) is rigid, but its particles are arranged randomly.

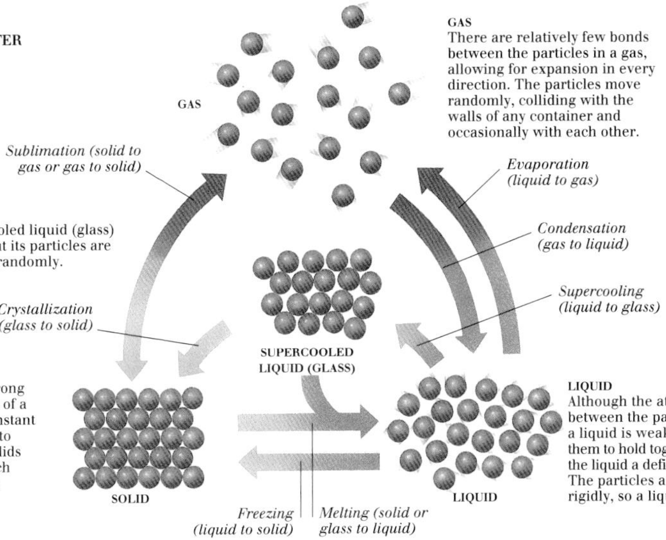
GAS
Sublimation (solid to gas or gas to solid)
Evaporation (liquid to gas)
Condensation (gas to liquid)
Supercooling (liquid to glass)
Crystallization (glass to solid)
SUPERCOOLED LIQUID (GLASS)
SOLID
LIQUID
Freezing (liquid to solid)
Melting (solid or glass to liquid)

OLID
Ield together by strong orces, the particles of a olid maintain a constant osition in relation to ach other. Most solids re crystals, in which articles arrange in epeating patterns.

LIQUID
Although the attraction between the particles of a liquid is weak, it allows them to hold together to give the liquid a definite volume. The particles are not held rigidly, so a liquid flows.

HANGING STATES OF WATER

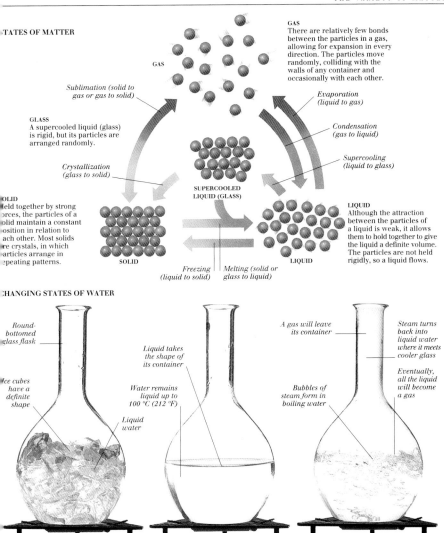

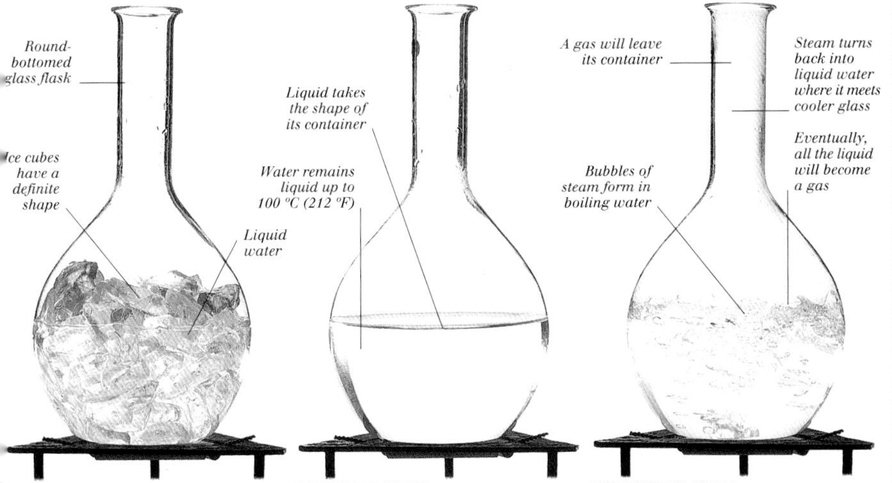
Round-bottomed glass flask
Ice cubes have a definite shape
Liquid water
Liquid takes the shape of its container
Water remains liquid up to 100 °C (212 °F)
A gas will leave its container
Steam turns back into liquid water where it meets cooler glass
Eventually, all the liquid will become a gas
Bubbles of steam form in boiling water

OLID STATE: ICE
he solid state of water, ice, forms when quid water is cooled sufficiently. Ice cubes re rigid, with a definite shape and volume.

LIQUID STATE: WATER
When the temperature of a substance rises above its freezing point, it melts to become a liquid. Ice changes to water.

GASEOUS STATE: STEAM
Above its boiling point, a substance will become a gas. When heated sufficiently, liquid water turns to steam, a colourless gas.

Atoms and molecules

FALSE-COLOUR IMAGE OF ACTUAL GOLD ATOMS

ATOMS ARE THE smallest individual parts of an element (see pp. 310-311). They are tiny, with diameters in the order of one ten-thousand-millionth of a metre (10^{-10} m). Two or more atoms join together (bond) to form a molecule of a substance known as a compound. For example, when atoms of the elements hydrogen and fluorine join together, they form a molecule of the compound hydrogen fluoride. So molecules are the smallest individual parts of a compound. Atoms themselves are not indivisible – they possess an internal structure. At their centre is a dense nucleus, consisting of protons, which have a positive electric charge (see p. 316), and neutrons, which are uncharged. Around the nucleus are the negatively charged electrons. It is the electrons that give a substance most of its physical and chemical properties. They do not follow definite paths around the nucleus. Instead, electrons are said to be found within certain regions, called orbitals. These are arranged around the nucleus in "shells", each containing electrons of a particular energy. For example, the first shell (1) can hold up to two electrons, in a so-called s-orbital (1s). The second shell (2) can hold up to eight electrons, in s-orbitals (2s) and p-orbitals (2p). If an atom loses an electron, it becomes a positive ion (cation). If an electron is gained, an atom becomes a negative ion (anion). Ions of opposite charges will attract and join together, in a type of bonding known as ionic bonding. In covalent bonding, the atoms bond by sharing their electrons in what become molecular orbitals.

ATOMIC ORBITALS

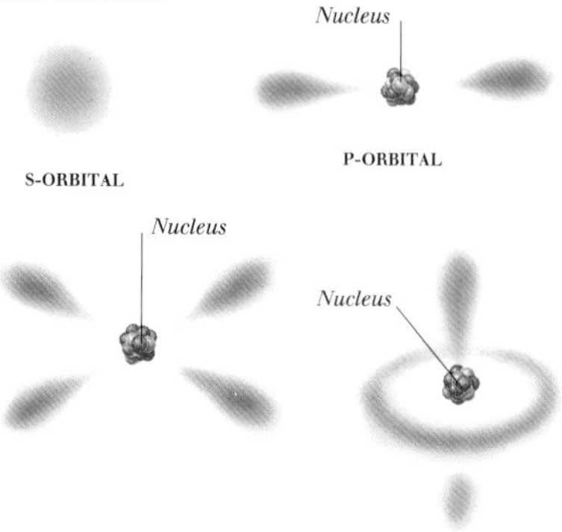

MOLECULAR ORBITALS

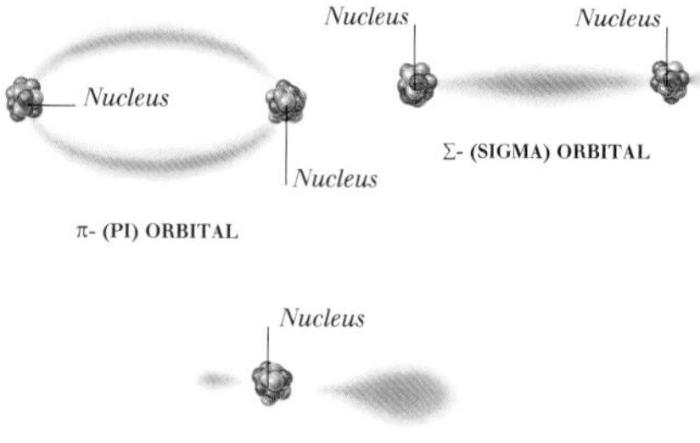

EXAMPLE OF IONIC BONDING

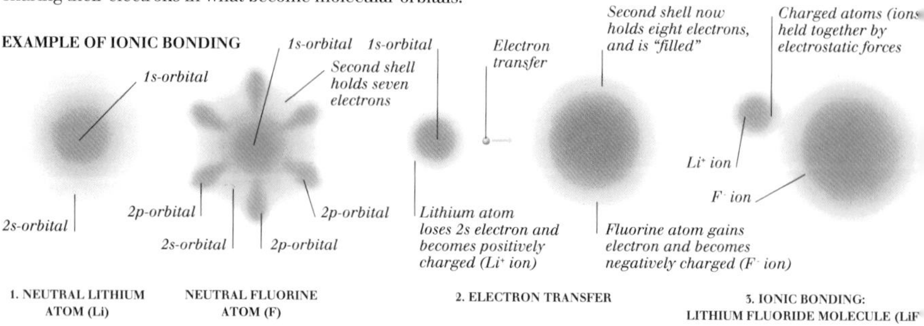
1s-orbital
2s-orbital
1s-orbital
1s-orbital
Second shell holds seven electrons
2p-orbital
2p-orbital
2s-orbital
2p-orbital
Electron transfer
Lithium atom loses 2s electron and becomes positively charged (Li⁺ ion)
Second shell now holds eight electrons, and is "filled"
Fluorine atom gains electron and becomes negatively charged (F⁻ ion)
Charged atoms (ions held together by electrostatic forces
Li⁺ ion
F⁻ ion
1. NEUTRAL LITHIUM ATOM (Li)
NEUTRAL FLUORINE ATOM (F)
2. ELECTRON TRANSFER
3. IONIC BONDING: LITHIUM FLUORIDE MOLECULE (LiF

NATOMY OF A FLUORINE-19 ATOM

ifferent versions (isotopes) f each element exist, with ne same number of protons, ut with different numbers f neutrons. Every atom of ne element fluorine has ine protons in its nucleus, ut the number of neutrons an vary (from eight to leven). Fluorine-19 as ten neutrons.

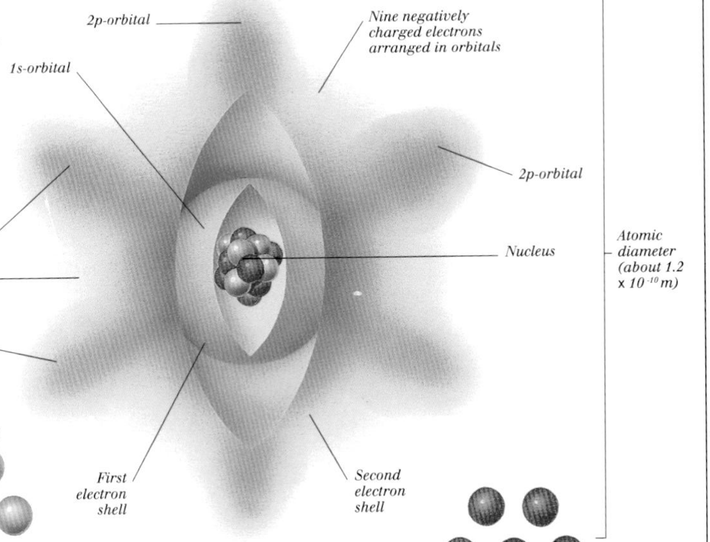

2p-orbital
Nine negatively charged electrons arranged in orbitals
1s-orbital
2p-orbital
2p-orbital
2s-orbital
Nucleus
Atomic diameter (about 1.2 x 10^{-10} m)
Each orbital holds up to two electrons
First electron shell
Second electron shell

NATOMY OF NUCLEUS F A FLUORINE-19 ATOM

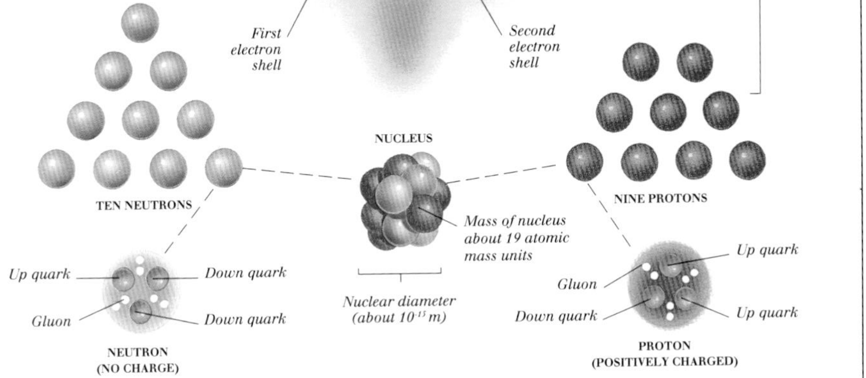

NUCLEUS
TEN NEUTRONS
NINE PROTONS
Mass of nucleus about 19 atomic mass units
Nuclear diameter (about 10^{-15} m)
Up quark
Down quark
Gluon
Down quark
Up quark
Gluon
Down quark
Up quark

NEUTRON (NO CHARGE)

PROTON (POSITIVELY CHARGED)

XAMPLE OF COVALENT BONDING

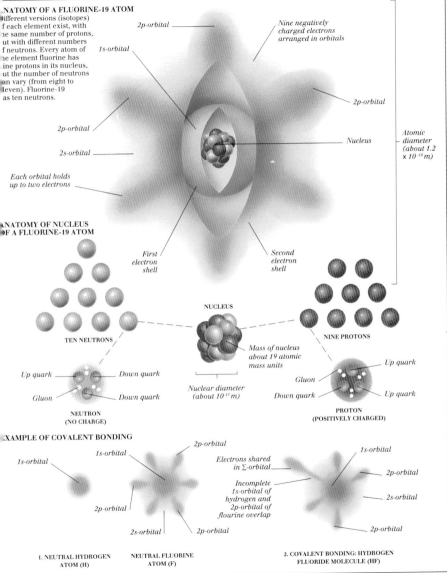

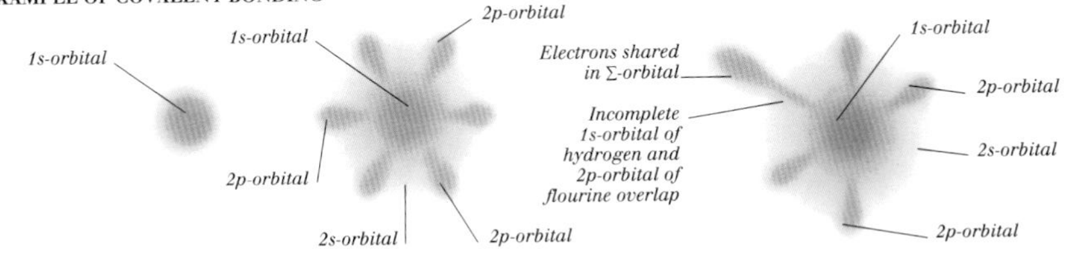

1s-orbital
1s-orbital
2p-orbital
2p-orbital
2s-orbital
2p-orbital
Electrons shared in Σ-orbital
Incomplete 1s-orbital of hydrogen and 2p-orbital of flourine overlap
1s-orbital
2p-orbital
2s-orbital
2p-orbital

1. NEUTRAL HYDROGEN ATOM (H)

NEUTRAL FLUORINE ATOM (F)

2. COVALENT BONDING: HYDROGEN FLUORIDE MOLECULE (HF)

The periodic table

AN ELEMENT is a substance that consists of atoms of one type only. The 92 elements that occur naturally, and the 17 elements created artificially, are often arranged into a chart called the periodic table. Each element is defined by its atomic number – the number of protons in the nucleus of each of its atoms (it is also the number of electrons present). Atomic number increases along each row (period) and down each column (group). The shape of the table is determined by the way in which electrons arrange themselves around the nucleus: the positioning of elements in order of increasing atomic number brings together atoms with a similar pattern of orbiting electrons (orbitals). These appear in blocks. Electrons occupy shells of a certain energy (see pp. 308-309). Periods are ordered according to the filling of successive shells with electrons, while groups reflect the number of electrons in the outer shell (valency electrons). These outer electrons are important – they decide the chemical properties of the atom. Elements that appear in the same group have similar properties because they have the same number of electrons in their outer shell. Elements in Group 0 have "filled shells", where the outer shell holds its maximum number of electrons, and are stable. Atoms of Group I elements have just one electron in their outer shell. This makes them unstable – and ready to react with other substances.

1	*Atomic number*
H	*Chemical symbol*
Hydrogen	*Chemical name*
1.0	*Relative atomic mass*

RELATIVE ATOMIC MASS
Atomic mass (formerly atomic weight) is the mass of each atom of an element. It is equal to the number of protons plus the number of neutrons (electrons have negligible mass). The figures given are the averages for all the different versions (isotopes) of each element, measured relative to the mass of carbon-12.

Atomic number is number of protons in each nucleus

Atomic number goes up by one along each period

Group I	*Group II*	*1st transition metals*				
1 H Hydrogen 1.0						
3 Li Lithium 6.9	4 Be Beryllium 9.0					
11 Na Sodium 23.0	12 Mg Magnesium 24.3					
19 K Potassium 39.1	20 Ca Calcium 40.1	21 Sc Scandium 45.0	22 Ti Titanium 47.9	23 V Vanadium 50.9	24 Cr Chromium 52.0	25 Mn Manganese 54.9
37 Rb Rubidium 85.5	38 Sr Strontium 87.6	39 Y Yttrium 88.9	40 Zr Zirconium 91.2	41 Nb Niobium 92.9	42 Mo Molybdenum 95.9	43 Tc Technetium 99.0
55 Cs Caesium 132.9	56 Ba Barium 137.4	57-71	72 Hf Hafnium 178.5	73 Ta Tantalum 181.0	74 W Tungsten 183.9	75 Re Rhenium 186.2
87 Fr Francium 223.0	88 Ra Radium 226.0	89-103	104 Unq Unnilquadium (261)	105 Unp Unnilpentium (262)	106 Unh Unnilhexium (263)	107 Uns Unnilseptium (262)

s-block | *d-block*

Two series always separated out from the table to give it a coherent shape

SODIUM: GROUP 1 METAL

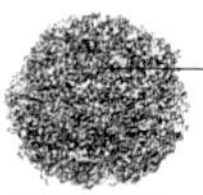

MAGNESIUM: GROUP 2 METAL

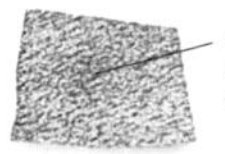

CHROMIUM: 1ST TRANSITION METAL

METALS AND NON-METALS
Elements at the left-hand side of each period are metals. Metals easily lose electrons and form positive ions. Non-metals, on the right of a period, tend to become negative ions. Semi-metals, which have properties of both metals and non-metals, are between the two.

TYPES OF ELEMENT KEY:

- Alkali metals
- Alkaline earth metals
- Transition metals
- Lanthanides (rare earths)
- Actinides
- Poor metals
- Semi-metals
- Non-metals
- Noble gases

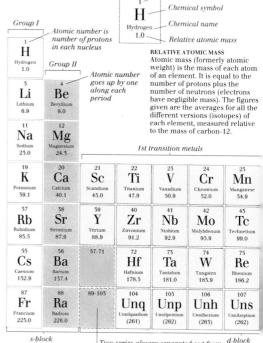

PLUTONIUM: ACTINIDE SERIES METAL

57 La Lanthanum 138.9	58 Ce Cerium 140.1	59 Pr Praseodymium 140.9	60 Nd Neodymium 144.2
89 Ac Actinium 227.0	90 Th Thorium 232.0	91 Pa Protactinium 231.0	92 U Uranium 238.0

DIAMOND

ALLOTROPES OF CARBON
Some elements exist in more than one form – these are known as allotropes. Carbon powder, graphite, and diamond are allotropes of carbon. They all consist of carbon atoms, but have very different physical properties.

GRAPHITE

CARBON POWDER

Bright yellow crystal

SULPHUR: GROUP 6 SOLID NON-METAL

Purple-black solid turns to gas easily

IODINE: GROUP 7 SOLID NON-METAL

2nd transition metals			*3rd transition metals*		*Boron and carbon groups*		*Nitrogen and oxygen groups*		*Halogens*	
					Group III	*Group IV*	*Group V*	*Group VI*	*Group VII*	*Group 0*
										2 He Helium 4.0 (*Period*)
					5 B Boron 10.8	6 C Carbon 12.0	7 N Nitrogen 14.0	8 O Oxygen 16.0	9 F Fluorine 19.0	10 Ne Neon 20.2 (*Short period*)
					13 Al Aluminium 27.0	14 Si Silicon 28.1	15 P Phosphorus 31.0	16 S Sulphur 32.1	17 Cl Chlorine 35.5	18 Ar Argon 40.0
26 Fe Iron 55.9	27 Co Cobalt 58.9	28 Ni Nickel 58.7	29 Cu Copper 63.5	30 Zn Zinc 65.4	31 Ga Gallium 69.7	32 Ge Germanium 72.6	33 As Arsenic 74.9	34 Se Selenium 79.0	35 Br Bromine 79.9	36 Kr Krypton 83.8 (*Long period*)
44 Ru Ruthenium 101.0	45 Rh Rhodium 102.9	46 Pd Palladium 106.4	47 Ag Silver 107.9	48 Cd Cadmium 112.4	49 In Indium 114.8	50 Sn Tin 118.7	51 Sb Antimony 121.8	52 Te Tellurium 127.6	53 I Iodine 126.9	54 Xe Xenon 131.3
76 Os Osmium 190.2	77 Ir Iridium 192.2	78 Pt Platinum 195.1	79 Au Gold 197.0	80 Hg Mercury 200.6	81 Tl Thallium 204.4	82 Pb Lead 207.2	83 Bi Bismuth 209.0	84 Po Polonium 210.0	85 At Astatine 210.0	86 Rn Radon 222.0
108 Uno Unniloctium (265)	109 Une Unnilennium (266)									

d-block — *p-block*

Atomic mass is estimated, as element exists fleetingly

Yellow, unreactive precious metal

GOLD: 3RD TRANSITION METAL

Soft, shiny, reactive metal

TIN: GROUP 4 POOR METAL

Shiny semi-metal

ANTIMONY: GROUP 5 SEMI-METAL

NOBLE GASES
Group 0 contains elements that have a filled (complete) outer shell of electrons, which means the atoms do not need to lose or gain electrons by bonding with other atoms. This makes them stable and they do not easily form ions or react with other elements. Noble gases are also called rare or inert gases.

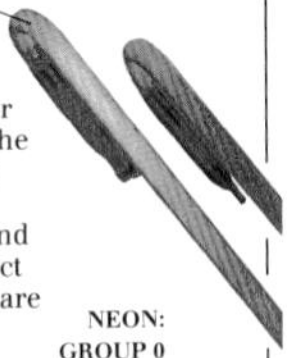

Unreactive, colourless gas glows red in discharge tube

NEON: GROUP 0 COLOURLESS GAS

61 Pm Promethium 147.0	62 Sm Samarium 150.4	63 Eu Europium 152.0	64 Gd Gadolinium 157.3	65 Tb Terbium 158.9	66 Dy Dysprosium 162.5	67 Ho Holmium 164.9	68 Er Erbium 167.3	69 Tm Thulium 168.9	70 Yb Ytterbium 173.0	71 Lu Lutetium 175.0
93 Np Neptunium 237.0	94 Pu Plutonium 242.0	95 Am Americium 243.0	96 Cm Curium 247.0	97 Bk Berkelium 247.0	98 Cf Californium 251.0	99 Es Einsteinium 254.0	100 Fm Fermium 253.0	101 Md Mendelevium 256.0	102 No Nobelium 254.0	103 Lr Lawrencium 257.0

f-block

Chemical reactions

A CHEMICAL REACTION TAKES PLACE whenever bonds between atoms are broken or made. In each case, atoms or groups of atoms rearrange, making new substances (products) from the original ones (reactants). Reactions happen naturally, or can be made to happen; they may take years, or only an instant. Some of the main types are shown here. A reaction usually involves a change in energy (see pp. 314-315). In a burning reaction, for example, the making of new bonds between atoms releases energy as heat and light. This type of reaction, in which heat is given off, is an exothermic reaction. Many reactions, like burning, are irreversible, but some can take place in either direction, and are said to be reversible. Reactions can be used to form solids from solutions: in a double decomposition reaction, two compounds in solution break down and re-form into two new substances, often creating a precipitate (insoluble solid); in displacement, an element (eg. copper) displaces another element (eg. silver) from a solution. The rate (speed) of a reaction is determined by many different factors, such as temperature, and the size and shape of the reactants. To describe and keep track of reactions, internationally recognized chemical symbols and equations are used. Reactions are also used in the laboratory to identify matter. An experiment with candle wax, for example, demonstrates that it contains carbon and hydrogen.

BURNING MATTER

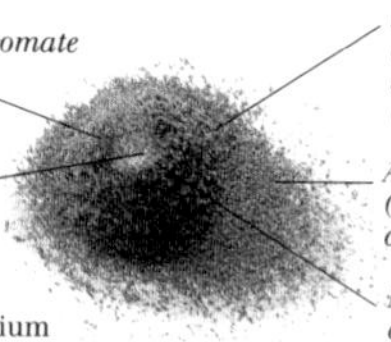
Ammonium dichromate ($(NH_4)_2Cr_2O_7$)
Flame
In this burning reaction, atoms form simpler substances and give off heat and light
Ammonium dichromate ($(NH_4)_2Cr_2O_7$) converts to chromium oxide (Cr_2O_3)
Nitrogen monoxide (NO) and water vapour (H_2O) given off as colourless gases

THE REACTION
When lit, ammonium dichromate combines with oxygen from air.
$(NH_4)_2Cr_2O_7 + O_2 \rightarrow Cr_2O_3 + 4H_2O + 2NO$

SALT FORMATION (ACID ON METAL)

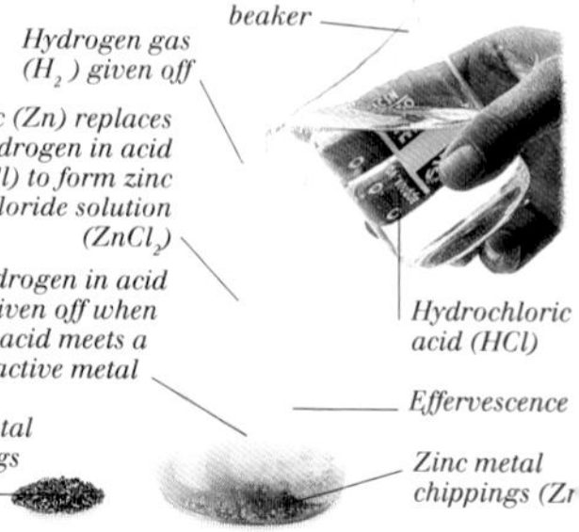
Glass beaker
Hydrogen gas (H_2) given off
Zinc (Zn) replaces hydrogen in acid (HCl) to form zinc chloride solution ($ZnCl_2$)
Hydrogen in acid driven off when acid meets a reactive metal
Hydrochloric acid (HCl)
Effervescence
Zinc metal chippings (Zn)
Zinc metal chippings (Zn

THE REACTION
Hydrochloric acid added to zinc produces zinc chloride and hydrogen.
$Zn + 2HCl \rightarrow ZnCl_2 + H_2$

DISPLACEMENT

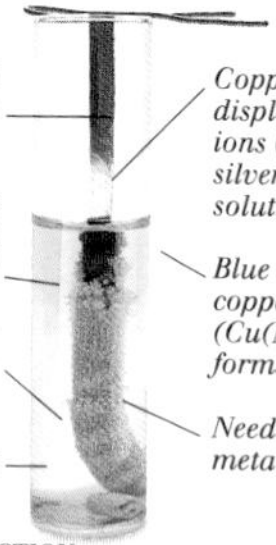
Copper metal (Cu)
Copper (Cu) displaces silver ions (Ag^{2+}) from silver nitrate solution ($AgNO_3$)
Silver nitrate solution ($AgNO_3$)
Blue solution of copper nitrate ($Cu(NO_3)_2$) forms
Two metals compete for nitrate ions
Needles of silver metal (Ag) form
Glass flask

THE REACTION
Copper metal added to silver nitrate solution produces copper nitrate and silver metal.
$Cu + 2AgNO_3 \rightarrow Cu(NO_3)_2 + 2Ag$

A REVERSIBLE REACTION

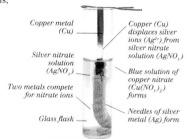

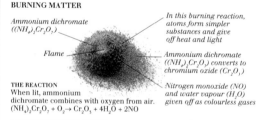

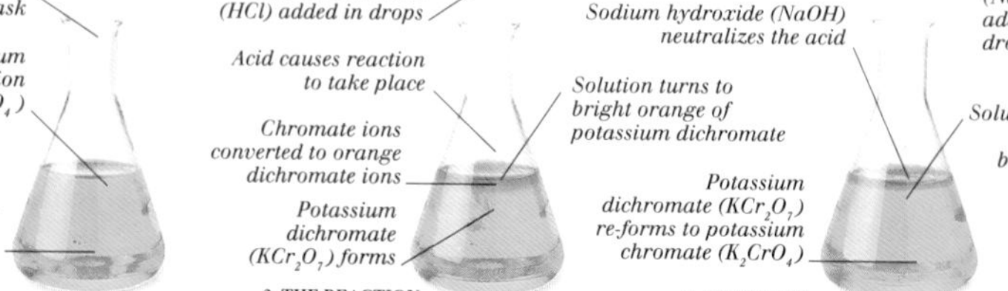
Flat-bottomed glass flask
Potassium chromate solution (K_2CrO_4)
Bright yellow solution contains potassium and chromate ions
Pipette
Hydrochloric acid (HCl) added in drops
Acid causes reaction to take place
Chromate ions converted to orange dichromate ions
Potassium dichromate (KCr_2O_7) forms
Solution turns to bright orange of potassium dichromate
Pipette
Sodium hydroxide (NaOH) added in drops
Sodium hydroxide (NaOH) neutralizes the acid
Solution returns to original bright yellow colour
Potassium dichromate (KCr_2O_7) re-forms to potassium chromate (K_2CrO_4)

1. THE REACTANT
Potassium chromate dissolves in water to form potassium ions and chromate ions.
$K_2CrO_4 \rightarrow 2K^+ + CrO_4^{2-}$

2. THE REACTION
Addition of hydrochloric acid changes chromate ions into dichromate ions.
$2CrO_4^{2-} \rightarrow Cr_2O_7^{2-}$

3. REVERSING
Addition of sodium hydroxide changes dichromate ions back into chromate ions.
$Cr_2O_7^{2-} \rightarrow 2CrO_4^{2-}$

FERMENTATION

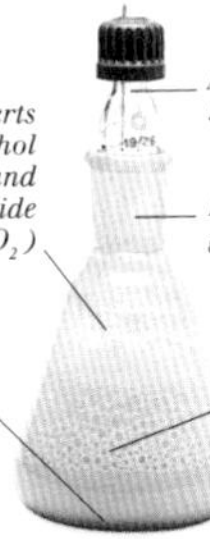

HE REACTION
east converts sugar and warm water
nto alcohol and carbon dioxide.
$C_6H_{12}O_6 \rightarrow 2C_2H_5OH + 2CO_2$

DOUBLE DECOMPOSITION

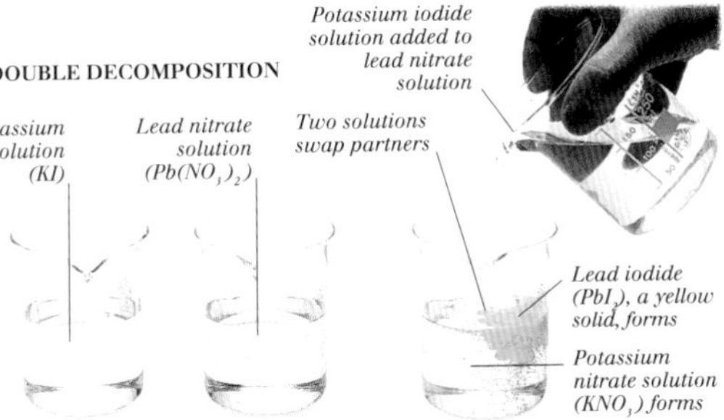

1. THE REACTANTS
Potassium iodide in water (KI) and lead nitrate in water ($Pb(NO_3)_2$) each form colourless solutions.

2. THE REACTION
When the solutions are mixed, lead iodide, a precipitate, and potassium nitrate solution are formed.
$2KI + Pb(NO_3)_2 \rightarrow PbI_2 + 2KNO_3$

TESTING CANDLE WAX, AN ORGANIC COMPOUND

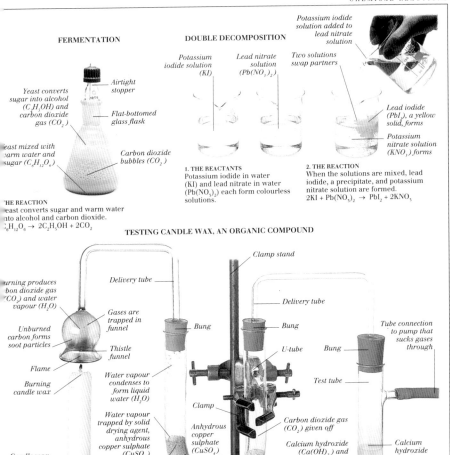

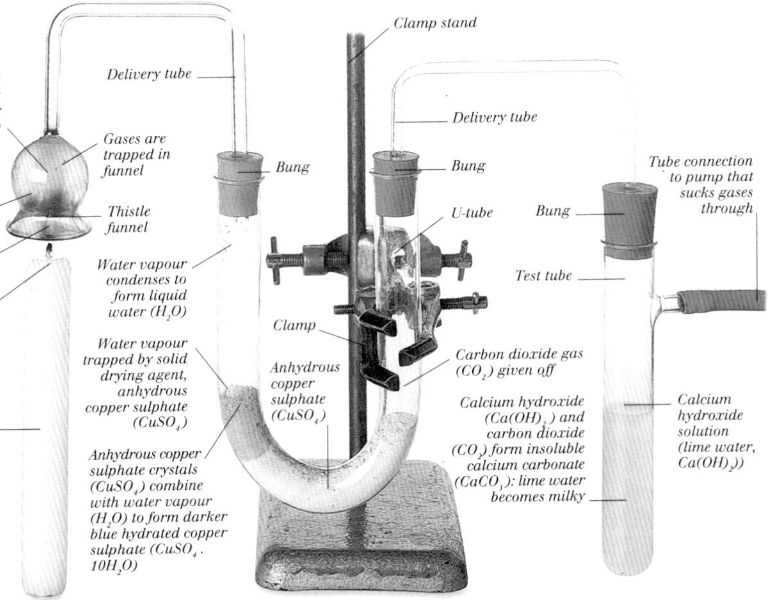

. THE BURNING REACTION
Burning wax produces carbon
dioxide gas and water vapour.
$2C_{18}H_{38} + 55O_2 \rightarrow 36CO_2 + 38H_2O$

2. TESTING FOR WATER VAPOUR
A solid drying agent traps water vapour, proving the presence of hydrogen in the candle wax.
$CuSO_4 + 10H_2O \rightarrow CuSO_4 . 10H_2O$

3. TESTING FOR CARBON DIOXIDE
Calcium hydroxide in solution reacts with carbon dioxide, forming a carbonate and turning milky.
$Ca(OH)_2 + CO_2 \rightarrow CaCO_3 + H_2O$

Energy

ANYTHING THAT HAPPENS – from a pin-drop to an explosion – requires energy. Energy is the capacity for "doing work" (making something happen). Various forms of energy exist, including light, heat, sound, electrical, chemical, nuclear, kinetic, and potential energies. The Law of Conservation of Energy states that the total amount of energy in the Universe is fixed – energy cannot be created or destroyed. It means that energy can only change from one form to another (energy transfer). For example, potential energy is energy that is "stored", and can be used in the future. An object gains potential energy when it is lifted; as the object is released, potential energy changes into the energy of motion (kinetic energy). During transference, some of the energy converts into heat. A combined heat and power station can put some of the otherwise "waste" heat to useful effect in local schools and housing. Most of the Earth's energy is provided by the Sun, in the form of electromagnetic radiation (see pp. 316-317). Some of this energy transfers to plant and animal life, and ultimately to fossil fuels, where it is stored in chemical form. Our bodies obtain energy from the food we eat, while energy needed for other tasks, such as heating and transport, can be obtained by burning fossil fuels – or by harnessing natural forces like wind or moving water – to generate electricity. Another source is nuclear power, where energy is released by reactions in the nucleus of an atom. All energy is measured by the international unit, the joule (J). As a guide, one joule is about equal to the amount of energy needed to lift an apple one metre.

SANKEY DIAGRAM SHOWING ENERGY FLOW IN A COAL-FIRED COMBINED HEAT AND POWER STATION

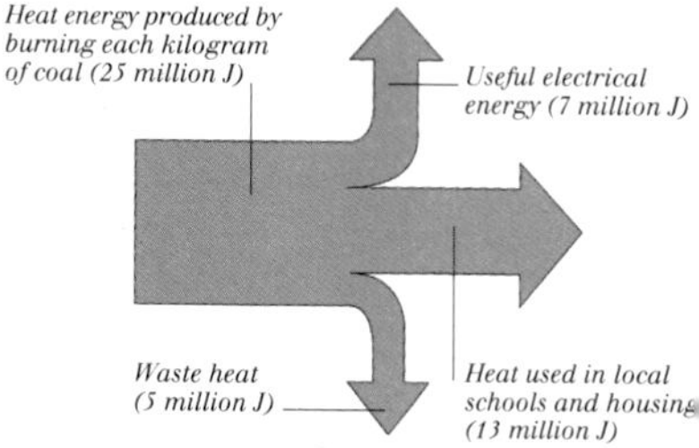
Heat energy produced by burning each kilogram of coal (25 million J)
Useful electrical energy (7 million J)
Waste heat (5 million J)
Heat used in local schools and housing (13 million J)

CROSS-SECTION OF HYDROELECTRIC POWER STATION WITH FRANCIS TURBINE

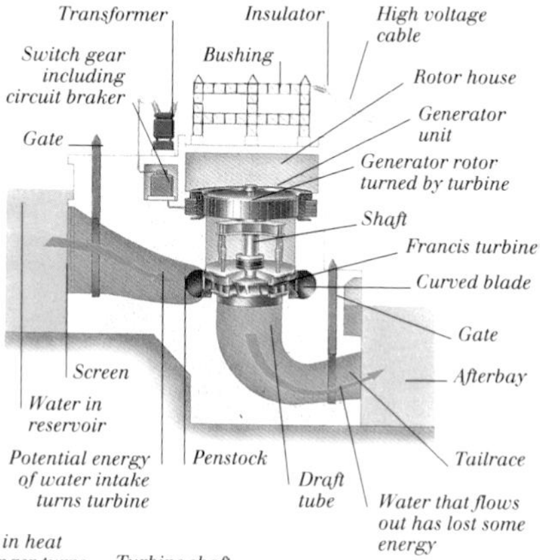
Transformer
Insulator
High voltage cable
Switch gear including circuit braker
Bushing
Rotor house
Generator unit
Gate
Generator rotor turned by turbine
Shaft
Francis turbine
Curved blade
Gate
Screen
Afterbay
Water in reservoir
Potential energy of water intake turns turbine
Penstock
Draft tube
Tailrace
Water that flows out has lost some energy

CROSS-SECTION OF NUCLEAR POWER STATION WITH PRESSURIZED WATER REACTOR

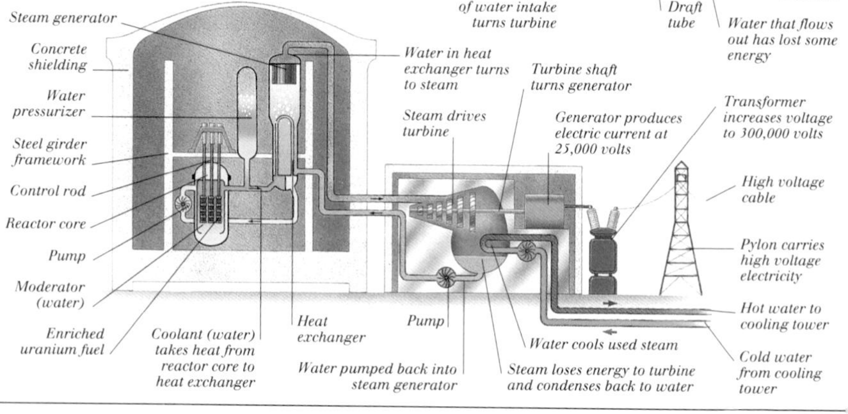
Steam generator
Concrete shielding
Water pressurizer
Steel girder framework
Control rod
Reactor core
Pump
Moderator (water)
Enriched uranium fuel
Coolant (water) takes heat from reactor core to heat exchanger
Heat exchanger
Water in heat exchanger turns to steam
Turbine shaft turns generator
Steam drives turbine
Generator produces electric current at 25,000 volts
Transformer increases voltage to 300,000 volts
High voltage cable
Pylon carries high voltage electricity
Pump
Hot water to cooling tower
Water cools used steam
Water pumped back into steam generator
Steam loses energy to turbine and condenses back to water
Cold water from cooling tower

ENERGY SYSTEMS

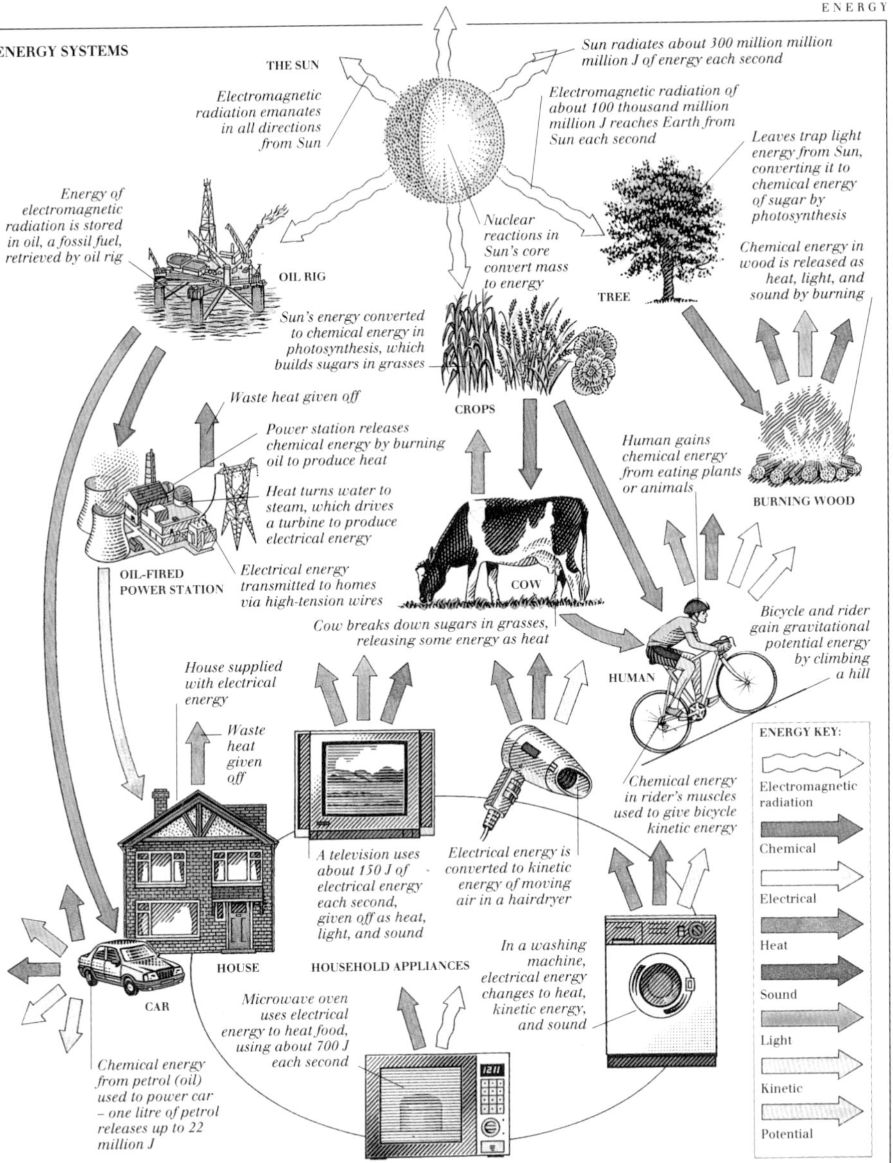
THE SUN
Electromagnetic radiation emanates in all directions from Sun
Sun radiates about 300 million million million J of energy each second
Electromagnetic radiation of about 100 thousand million million J reaches Earth from Sun each second
Nuclear reactions in Sun's core convert mass to energy
Energy of electromagnetic radiation is stored in oil, a fossil fuel, retrieved by oil rig
OIL RIG
Leaves trap light energy from Sun, converting it to chemical energy of sugar by photosynthesis
TREE
Chemical energy in wood is released as heat, light, and sound by burning
Sun's energy converted to chemical energy in photosynthesis, which builds sugars in grasses
CROPS
Waste heat given off
Power station releases chemical energy by burning oil to produce heat
Heat turns water to steam, which drives a turbine to produce electrical energy
OIL-FIRED POWER STATION
Electrical energy transmitted to homes via high-tension wires
Human gains chemical energy from eating plants or animals
BURNING WOOD
COW
Cow breaks down sugars in grasses, releasing some energy as heat
Bicycle and rider gain gravitational potential energy by climbing a hill
HUMAN
House supplied with electrical energy
Waste heat given off
ENERGY KEY:
Electromagnetic radiation
Chemical
Electrical
Heat
Sound
Light
Kinetic
Potential
Chemical energy in rider's muscles used to give bicycle kinetic energy
A television uses about 150 J of electrical energy each second, given off as heat, light, and sound
Electrical energy is converted to kinetic energy of moving air in a hairdryer
In a washing machine, electrical energy changes to heat, kinetic energy, and sound
HOUSE
HOUSEHOLD APPLIANCES
CAR
Microwave oven uses electrical energy to heat food, using about 700 J each second
Chemical energy from petrol (oil) used to power car – one litre of petrol releases up to 22 million J

Electricity and magnetism

ELECTRICAL EFFECTS result from an imbalance of electric charge. There are two types of electric charge, named positive (carried by protons) and negative (carried by electrons). If charges are opposite (unlike), they attract one another, while like charges repel. Forces of attraction and repulsion (electrostatic forces) exist between any two charged particles. Matter is normally uncharged, but if electrons are gained, an object will gain an overall negative charge; if they are removed, it becomes positive. Objects with an overall negative or positive charge are said to have an imbalance of charge, and exert the same forces as individual negative and positive charges. On this larger scale, the forces will always act to regain the balance of charge. This causes static electricity. Lightning, for example, is produced by clouds discharging a huge excess of negative electrons. If charges are "free" – in a wire or material that allows electrons to pass through it – the forces cause a flow of charge called an electric current. Some substances exhibit the strange phenomenon of magnetism – which also produces attractive and repulsive forces. Magnetic substances consist of small regions called domains. Normally unmagnetized, they can be magnetized by being placed in a magnetic field. Magnetism and electricity are inextricably linked, a fact put to use in motors and generators.

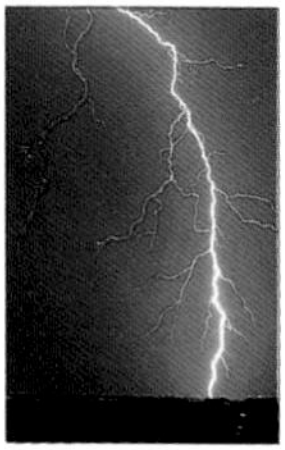

LIGHTNING

VAN DE GRAAFF (ELECTROSTATIC) GENERATOR

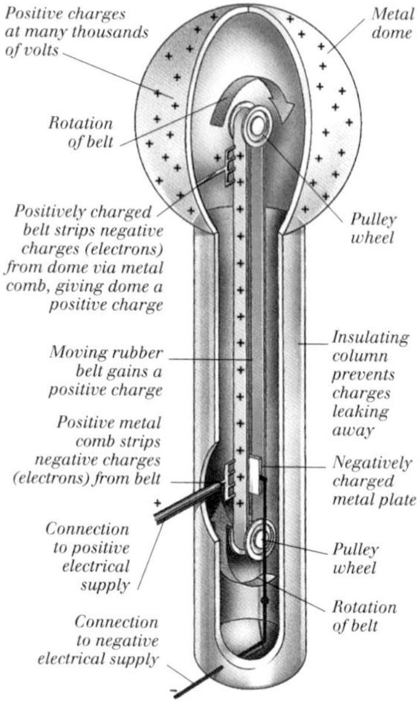
Positive charges at many thousands of volts
Metal dome
Rotation of belt
Positively charged belt strips negative charges (electrons) from dome via metal comb, giving dome a positive charge
Pulley wheel
Moving rubber belt gains a positive charge
Insulating column prevents charges leaking away
Positive metal comb strips negative charges (electrons) from belt
Negatively charged metal plate
Connection to positive electrical supply
Pulley wheel
Rotation of belt
Connection to negative electrical supply

CURRENT ELECTRICITY

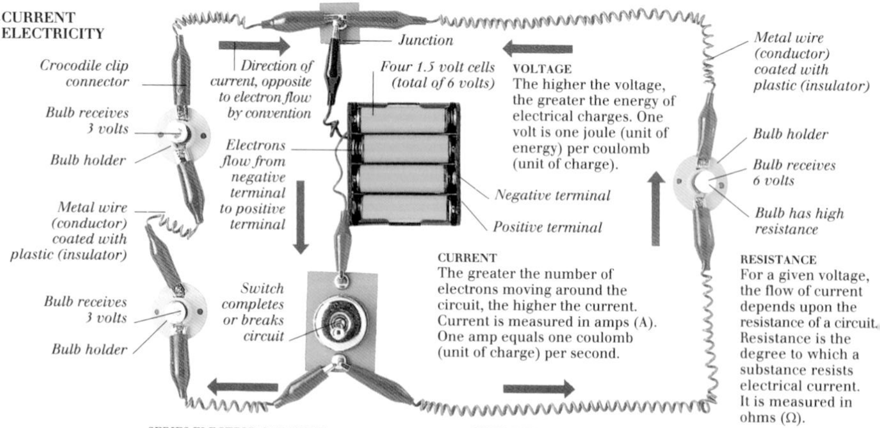
Crocodile clip connector
Bulb receives 3 volts
Bulb holder
Metal wire (conductor) coated with plastic (insulator)
Bulb receives 3 volts
Bulb holder
Direction of current, opposite to electron flow by convention
Junction
Four 1.5 volt cells (total of 6 volts)
Electrons flow from negative terminal to positive terminal
Negative terminal
Positive terminal
Switch completes or breaks circuit
Metal wire (conductor) coated with plastic (insulator)
Bulb holder
Bulb receives 6 volts
Bulb has high resistance

SERIES ELECTRICAL CIRCUIT

SIMPLE ELECTRICAL CIRCUIT

VOLTAGE
The higher the voltage, the greater the energy of electrical charges. One volt is one joule (unit of energy) per coulomb (unit of charge).

CURRENT
The greater the number of electrons moving around the circuit, the higher the current. Current is measured in amps (A). One amp equals one coulomb (unit of charge) per second.

RESISTANCE
For a given voltage, the flow of current depends upon the resistance of a circuit. Resistance is the degree to which a substance resists electrical current. It is measured in ohms (Ω).

MAGNETIC FIELDS AND FORCES

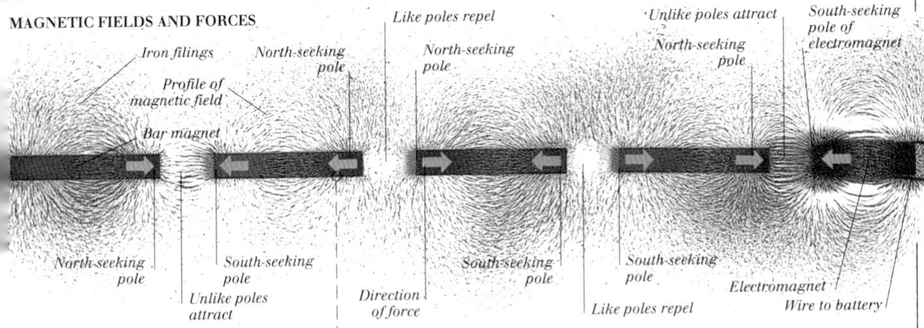
Iron filings
North-seeking pole
Profile of magnetic field
Bar magnet
Like poles repel
North-seeking pole
Unlike poles attract
North-seeking pole
South-seeking pole of electromagnet
North-seeking pole
South-seeking pole
Unlike poles attract
Direction of force
South-seeking pole
Like poles repel
South-seeking pole
Electromagnet
Wire to battery

MAGNETIC DOMAINS

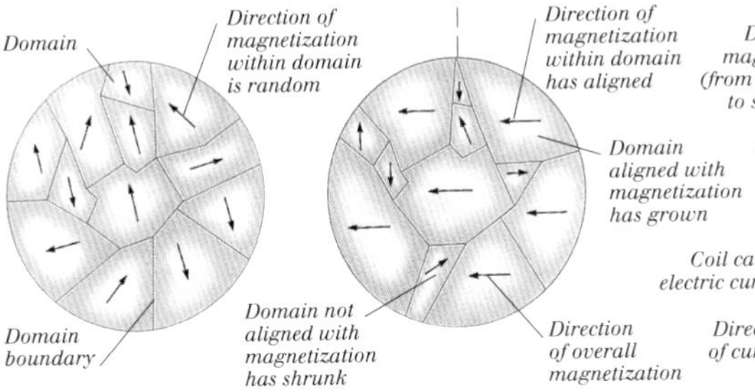
Domain
Direction of magnetization within domain is random
Domain boundary
Direction of magnetization within domain has aligned
Domain aligned with magnetization has grown
Domain not aligned with magnetization has shrunk
Direction of overall magnetization

UNMAGNETIZED IRON

MAGNETIZED IRON IN A MAGNETIC FIELD

GENERATING MAGNETISM FROM ELECTRICITY

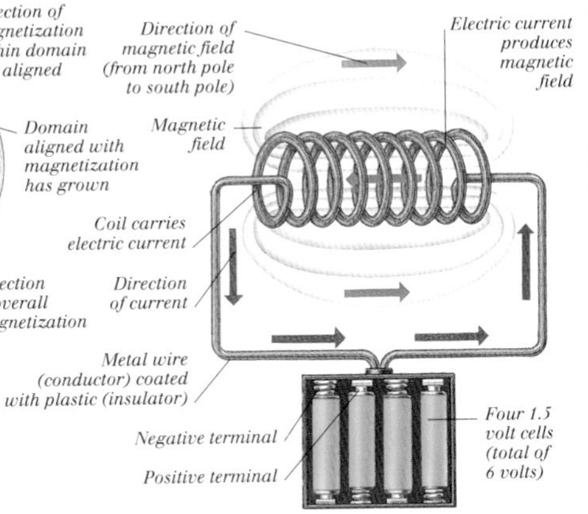
Direction of magnetic field (from north pole to south pole)
Electric current produces magnetic field
Magnetic field
Coil carries electric current
Direction of current
Metal wire (conductor) coated with plastic (insulator)
Negative terminal
Positive terminal
Four 1.5 volt cells (total of 6 volts)

CIRCUIT WITH ELECTROMAGNET

GENERATING ELECTRICITY FROM MAGNETISM

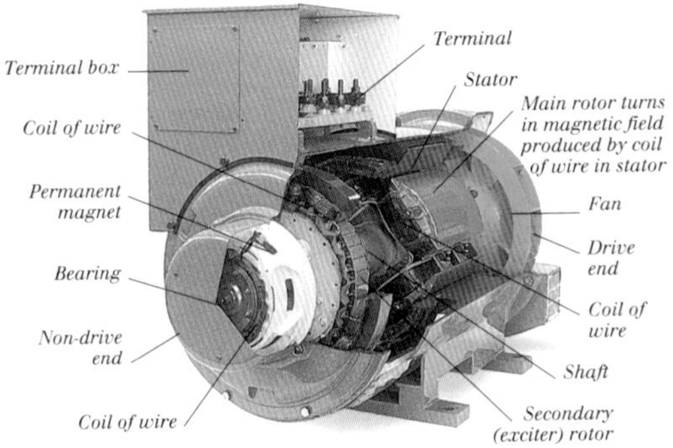
Terminal box
Terminal
Stator
Coil of wire
Main rotor turns in magnetic field produced by coil of wire in stator
Permanent magnet
Fan
Drive end
Bearing
Coil of wire
Non-drive end
Shaft
Coil of wire
Secondary (exciter) rotor

ELECTRIC GENERATOR
In a generator, the rotor rotates within the magnetic field of the stator to produce an electric current.

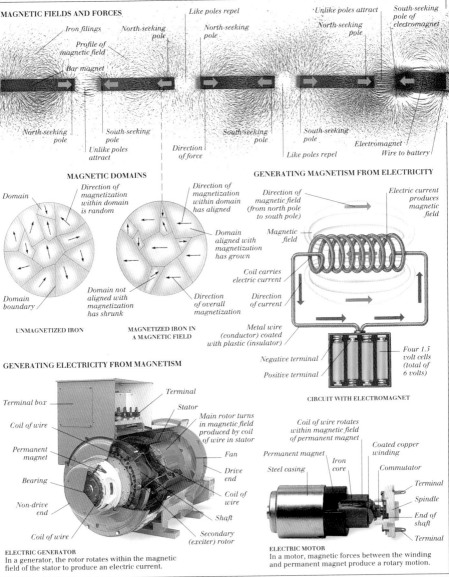

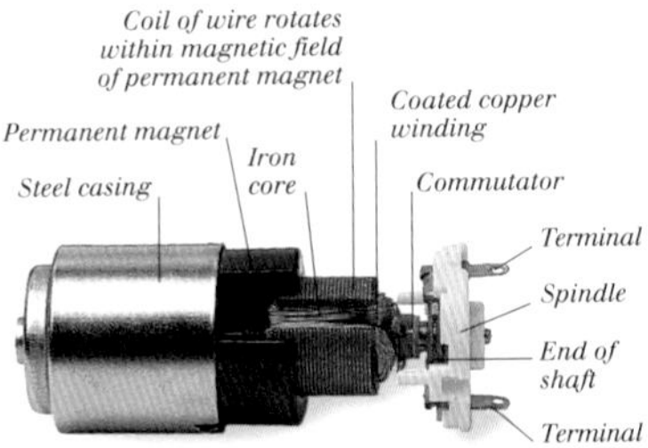
Coil of wire rotates within magnetic field of permanent magnet
Coated copper winding
Permanent magnet
Iron core
Steel casing
Commutator
Terminal
Spindle
End of shaft
Terminal

ELECTRIC MOTOR
In a motor, magnetic forces between the winding and permanent magnet produce a rotary motion.

INFRA-RED IMAGE OF A HOUSE

Light

LIGHT IS A FORM OF ENERGY. It is a type of electromagnetic radiation, like X-rays or radio waves. All electromagnetic radiation is produced by electric charges (see pp. 316-317): it is caused by the effects of oscillating electric and magnetic fields as they travel through space. Electromagnetic radiation is considered to have both wave and particle properties. It can be thought of as a wave of electricity and magnetism. In that case, the difference between the various forms of radiation is their wavelength. Radiation can also be said to consist of particles, or packets of energy, called photons. The difference between light and X-rays, for instance, is the amount of energy that each photon carries. The complete range of radiation is referred to as the electromagnetic spectrum, extending from low energy, long wavelength radio waves to high energy, short wavelength gamma rays. Light is the only part of the electromagnetic spectrum that is visible. White light from the Sun is made up of all the visible wavelengths of radiation, which can be seen when it is separated by using a prism. Light, like all forms of electromagnetic radiation, can be reflected (bounced back) and refracted (bent). Different parts of the electromagnetic spectrum are produced in different ways. Sometimes visible light – and infra-red radiation – is generated by the vibrating particles of warm or hot objects. The emission of light in this way is called incandescence. Light can also be produced by fluorescence, a phenomenon in which electrons gain and lose energy within atoms.

MAXWELLIAN DIAGRAM OF ELECTROMAGNETIC RADIATION AS WAVES

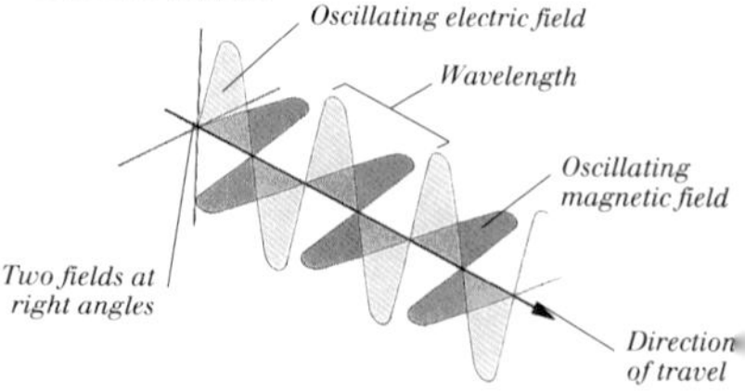
Oscillating electric field
Wavelength
Oscillating magnetic field
Two fields at right angles
Direction of travel

ELECTROMAGNETIC RADIATION AS PARTICLES

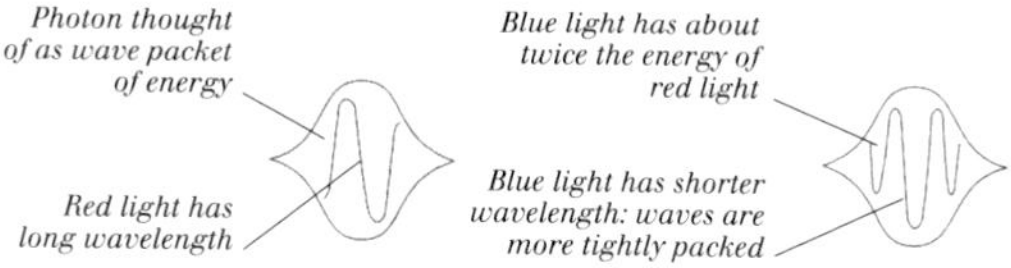
Photon thought of as wave packet of energy
Red light has long wavelength
Blue light has about twice the energy of red light
Blue light has shorter wavelength: waves are more tightly packed

PHOTON OF RED LIGHT

PHOTON OF BLUE LIGHT

SPLITTING WHITE LIGHT INTO THE SPECTRUM

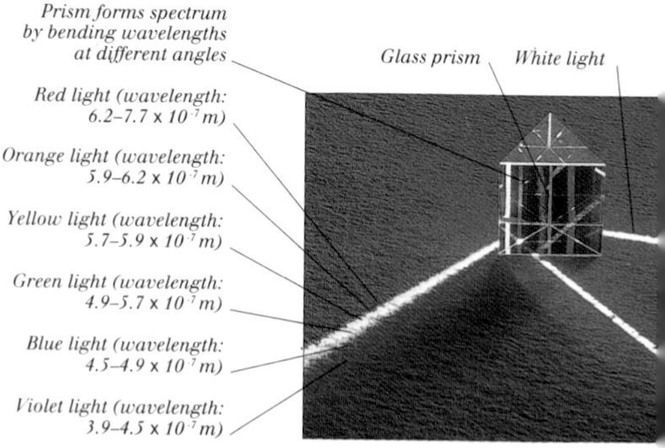
Prism forms spectrum by bending wavelengths at different angles
Glass prism
White light
Red light (wavelength: 6.2–7.7 x 10⁻⁷ m)
Orange light (wavelength: 5.9–6.2 x 10⁻⁷ m)
Yellow light (wavelength: 5.7–5.9 x 10⁻⁷ m)
Green light (wavelength: 4.9–5.7 x 10⁻⁷ m)
Blue light (wavelength: 4.5–4.9 x 10⁻⁷ m)
Violet light (wavelength: 3.9–4.5 x 10⁻⁷ m)

THE ELECTROMAGNETIC SPECTRUM

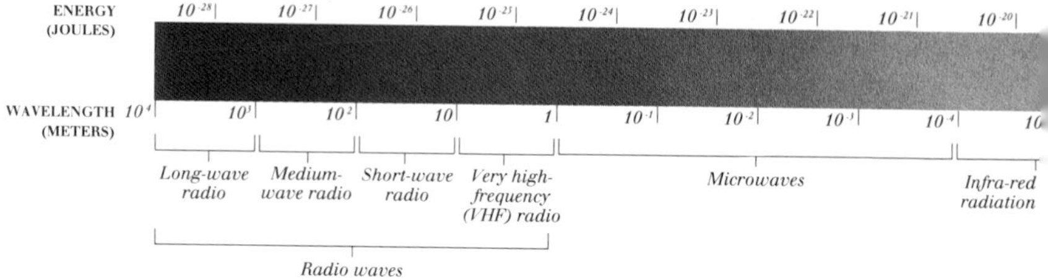
ENERGY (JOULES)
10⁻²⁸ 10⁻²⁷ 10⁻²⁶ 10⁻²⁵ 10⁻²⁴ 10⁻²³ 10⁻²² 10⁻²¹ 10⁻²⁰
WAVELENGTH (METERS)
10⁴ 10³ 10² 10 1 10⁻¹ 10⁻² 10⁻³ 10⁻⁴
Long-wave radio
Medium-wave radio
Short-wave radio
Very high-frequency (VHF) radio
Microwaves
Infra-red radiation
Radio waves

ARTIFICIAL LIGHT SOURCES

FLUORESCENT TUBE

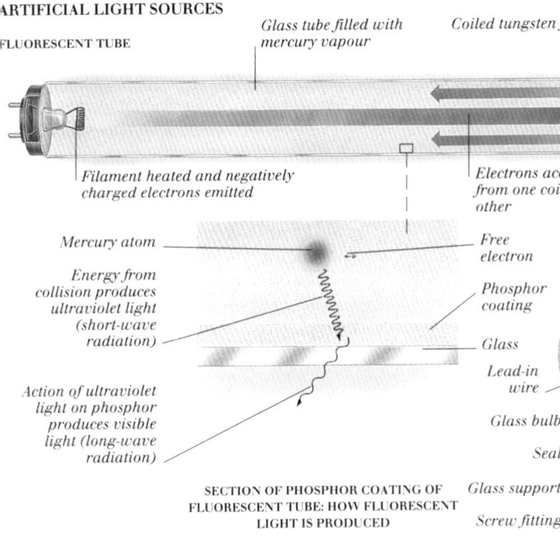

Glass tube filled with mercury vapour
Coiled tungsten filament
Ceramic end-piece
Electrical contact
Glass support
Filament heated and negatively charged electrons emitted
Electrons accelerate from one coil to the other
Electrons collide with mercury atoms
Mercury atom
Free electron
Energy from collision produces ultraviolet light (short-wave radiation)
Phosphor coating
Glass
Action of ultraviolet light on phosphor produces visible light (long-wave radiation)

SECTION OF PHOSPHOR COATING OF FLUORESCENT TUBE: HOW FLUORESCENT LIGHT IS PRODUCED

INCANDESCENT LIGHT BULB

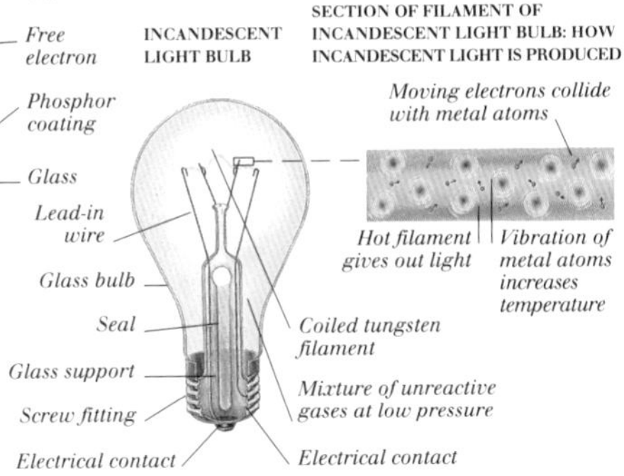

SECTION OF FILAMENT OF INCANDESCENT LIGHT BULB: HOW INCANDESCENT LIGHT IS PRODUCED
Moving electrons collide with metal atoms
Hot filament gives out light
Vibration of metal atoms increases temperature
Lead-in wire
Glass bulb
Seal
Glass support
Screw fitting
Electrical contact
Coiled tungsten filament
Mixture of unreactive gases at low pressure
Electrical contact

REFLECTION OF LIGHT

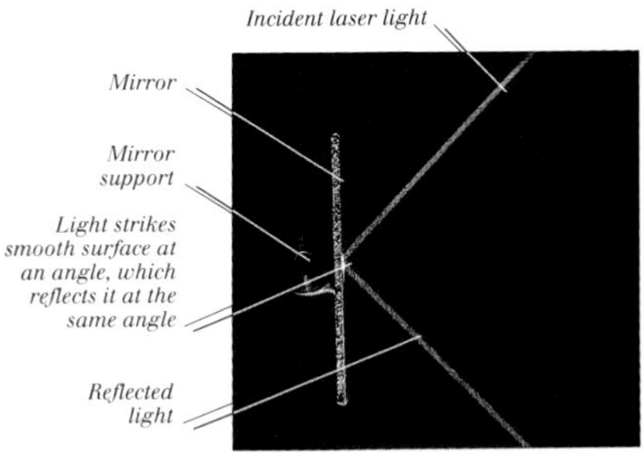

Incident laser light
Mirror
Mirror support
Light strikes smooth surface at an angle, which reflects it at the same angle
Reflected light

REFRACTION OF LIGHT

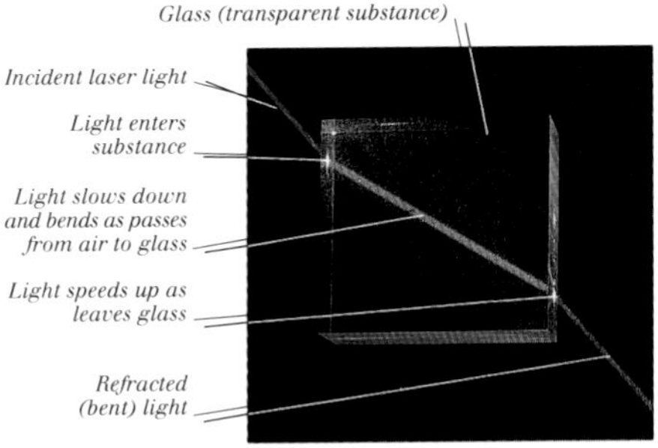

Glass (transparent substance)
Incident laser light
Light enters substance
Light slows down and bends as passes from air to glass
Light speeds up as leaves glass
Refracted (bent) light

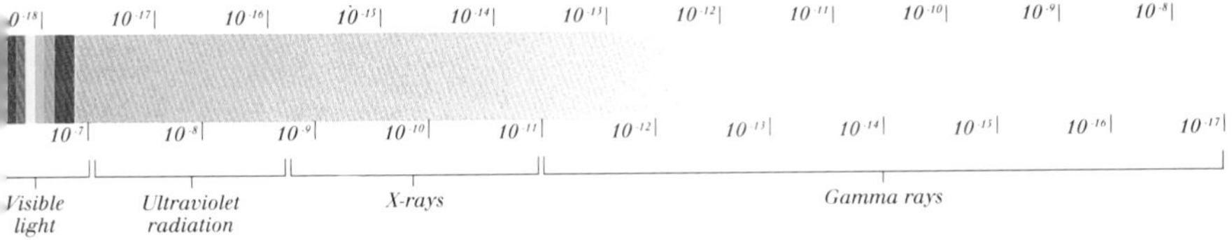

10^{-18} 10^{-17} 10^{-16} 10^{-15} 10^{-14} 10^{-13} 10^{-12} 10^{-11} 10^{-10} 10^{-9} 10^{-8}
10^{-7} 10^{-8} 10^{-9} 10^{-10} 10^{-11} 10^{-12} 10^{-13} 10^{-14} 10^{-15} 10^{-16} 10^{-17}
Visible light
Ultraviolet radiation
X-rays
Gamma rays

Force and motion

FORCES ARE PUSHES OR PULLS that change the motion of objects. To make a stationary object move, or a moving object stop, a force is needed. A force is also required to change the speed or direction of an object. This change in speed or direction is known as acceleration. Acceleration depends on the size (magnitude) of the force, and on the mass of the object. The effects of forces were first summarized by Isaac Newton in his three laws of motion. The international unit of force, named after him, is the newton (N), which is approximately equal to the weight of one apple. Gravity – the force of attraction between any two masses – can be measured using a newton meter (spring balance). Forces are put to useful effect in machines. A simple machine, such as a wheel and axle, is a device that changes the size or direction of an applied force. It allows an applied force (the effort) to produce another force (the load). A lever uses a bar that turns on a fulcrum to exert force. In all simple machines, there is a relationship between force and distance. A small force (in a compound pulley, for instance) moves through a large distance to lift a heavy object a small distance. This is called the Law of Simple Machines.

SIMPLE MACHINES

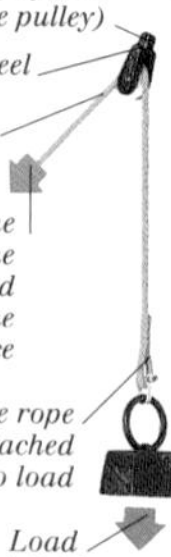
Single-pulley system (simple pulley)
Pulley wheel
Simple pulley only changes direction of a force
Effort is the same size as the load (10 N) and is pulled the same distance
One rope attached to load
Load of 10 N

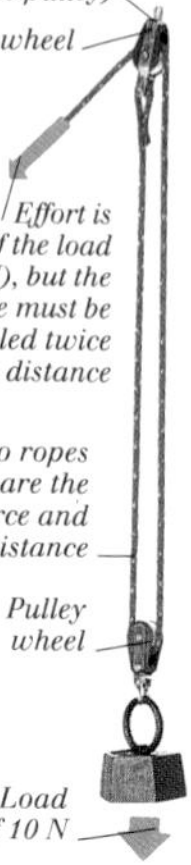
Two-pulley system (simple pulley)
Pulley wheel
Effort is half the load (5 N), but the rope must be pulled twice the distance
Two ropes share the force and distance
Pulley wheel
Load of 10 N

Four-pulley system (compound pulley)
Two pulley wheels
Effort is one quarter of the load (2.5 N), but the rope must be pulled four times the distance
Four ropes share the force and distance
Two pulley wheels
Load of 10 N

SIMPLE AND COMPOUND PULLEYS

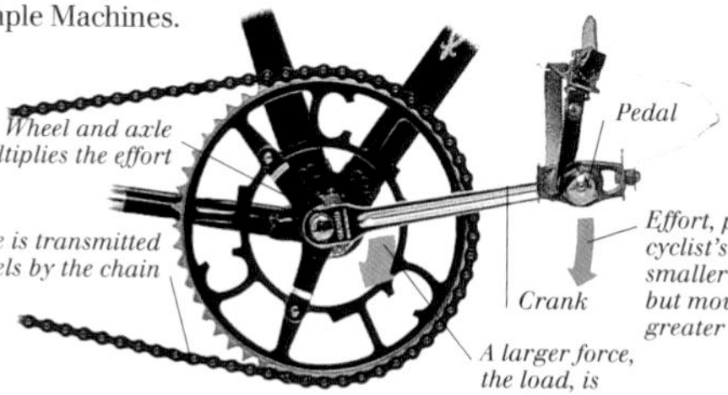
Wheel and axle multiplies the effort
Pedal
Force is transmitted to the wheels by the chain
Crank
Effort, provided by cyclist's muscles, is smaller than the load, but moves through a greater distance
A larger force, the load, is produced at the axle

WHEEL AND AXLE

NEWTON METERS (SPRING BALANCES)

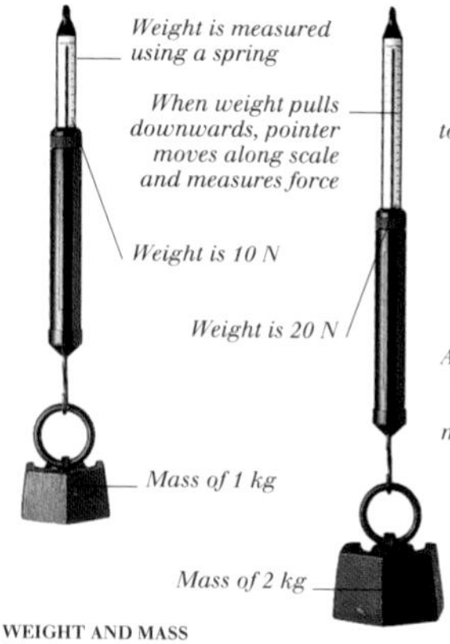
Weight is measured using a spring
When weight pulls downwards, pointer moves along scale and measures force
Weight is 10 N
Weight is 20 N
Mass of 1 kg
Mass of 2 kg

WEIGHT AND MASS
The "mass" of an object is a measure of the quantity of matter that it possesses. Mass is usually measured in grams (g) or kilograms (kg). The "weight" of an object is the force exerted on the object's mass by gravity. Since weight is a force, its unit is the newton (N).

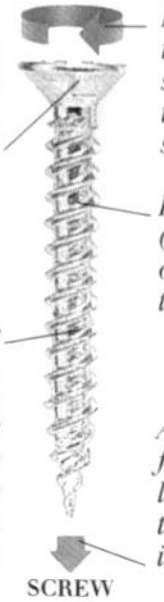
A screw, acting like a wedge wrapped around a shaft, multiplies the effort
Effort, a turning force supplied through a screwdriver
Pitch (the angle of the screw thread)
The smaller the angle of pitch, the less force is required, but more turns are needed to move it through a greater distance
A larger force, the load, pulls the screw into wood

SCREW

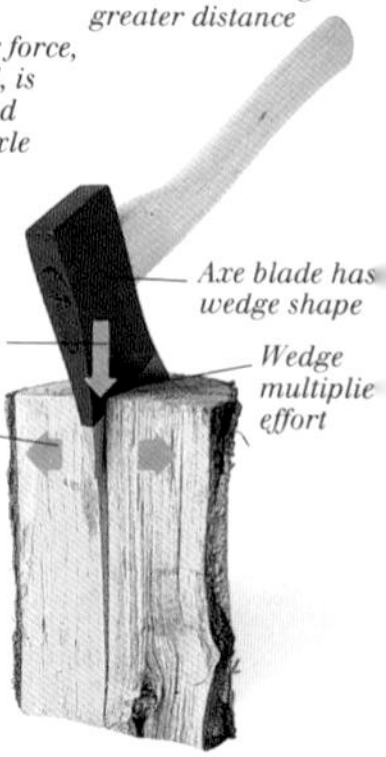
Effort pushes axe into wood
Axe blade has wedge shape
Wedge multiplie effort
A larger force, the load, moves through a smaller distance to push wood apart

WEDGE

NEWTON'S THREE LAWS OF MOTION

EWTON'S FIRST LAW

hen no force acts on a body, it will
ntinue in a state of rest or uniform motion.

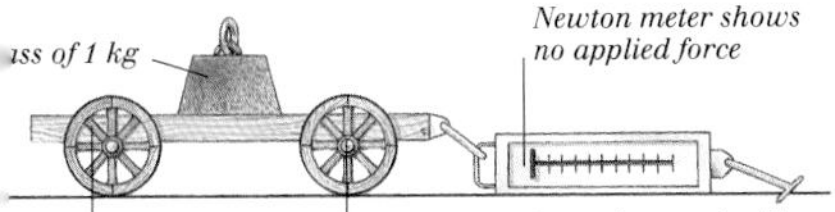
ass of 1 kg
Newton meter shows no applied force
Mass of trolley is negligible
Trolley is not in motion, and will remain at rest until a force acts

NO FORCE, NO ACCELERATION: STATE OF REST

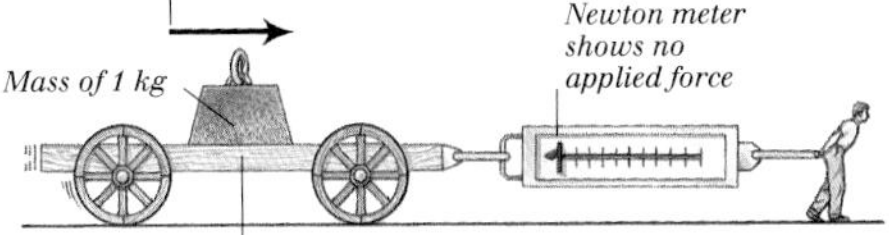
Constant speed
Mass of 1 kg
Newton meter shows no applied force
Trolley is in motion, and will continue at a constant speed in a straight line until a force acts

NO FORCE, NO ACCELERATION: UNIFORM MOTION

EWTON'S SECOND LAW

'hen a force acts on a body, the motion of the body will change. The size of the change
ill depend upon the mass of the object and the magnitude of the applied force.

Acceleration is 2 ms-2
Trolley and mass (1 kg) gain 2 metres per second of speed each second (2 ms-2)
ass of 1 kg
Newton meter registers force of 2 N
Acceleration is 1 ms-2
Trolley and mass (2 kg) gain 1 metre per second of speed each second (1 ms-2)
Mass of 2 kg
Newton meter registers force of 2 N
With the same applied force, an object with 2 kg mass accelerates at half the rate of object with 1 kg mass

FORCE AND ACCELERATION: SMALL MASS, LARGE ACCELERATION

FORCE AND ACCELERATION: LARGE MASS, SMALL ACCELERATION

EWTON'S THIRD LAW

one object exerts a force on another, an equal and opposite force,
alled the reaction force, is applied by the second object on the first.

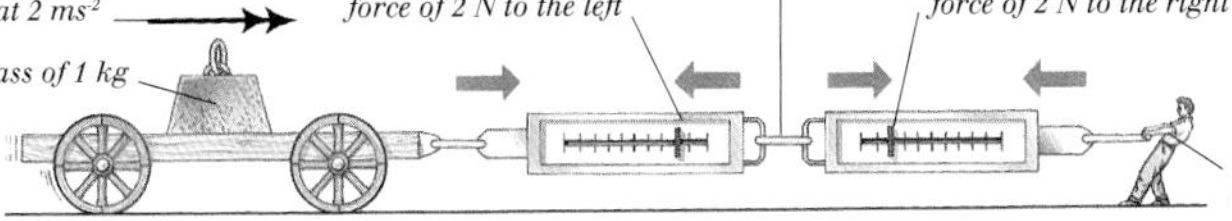
Newton meters pull on each other with equal and opposite forces
Acceleration: the trolley and mass accelerate at 2 ms-2
Newton meter registers force of 2 N to the left
Newton meter registers force of 2 N to the right
Mass of 1 kg
Person experiences a reaction force

ACTION AND REACTION

THREE CLASSES OF LEVER

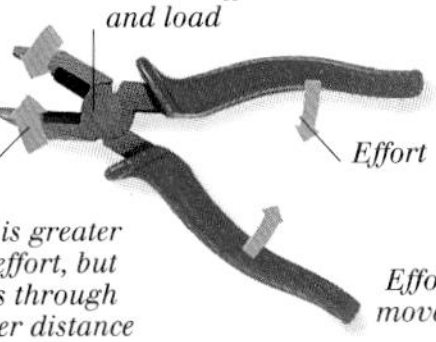
Fulcrum, between effort and load
Effort
Load is greater than effort, but moves through smaller distance

CLASS 1 LEVER

Pliers consist of two class 1 levers.

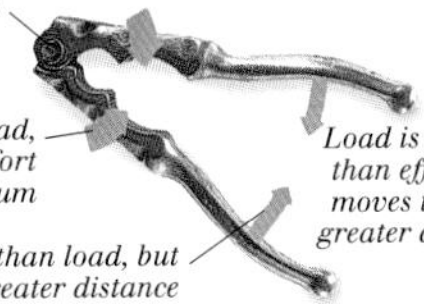
Fulcrum
Load, between effort and fulcrum
Effort is smaller than load, but moves through greater distance
Load is smaller than effort, but moves through greater distance

CLASS 2 LEVER

Nutcrackers consist of two class 2 levers.

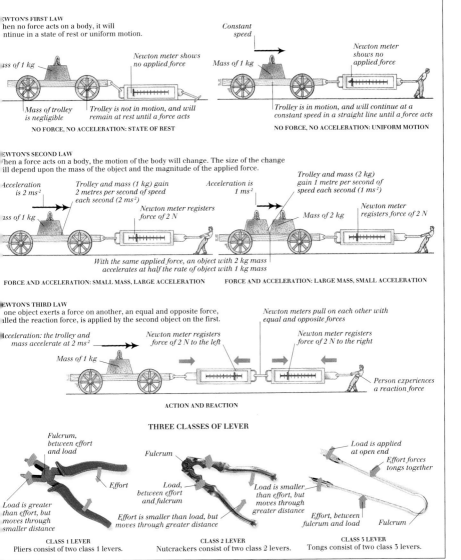

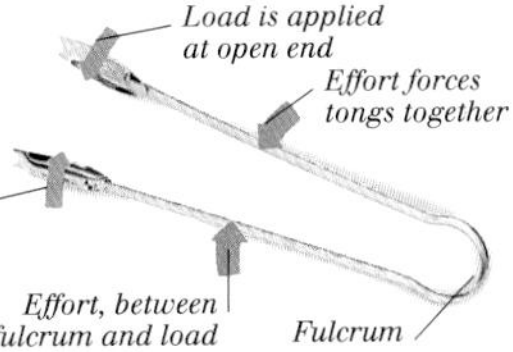
Load is applied at open end
Effort forces tongs together
Effort, between fulcrum and load
Fulcrum

CLASS 3 LEVER

Tongs consist of two class 3 levers.

ELECTRIC

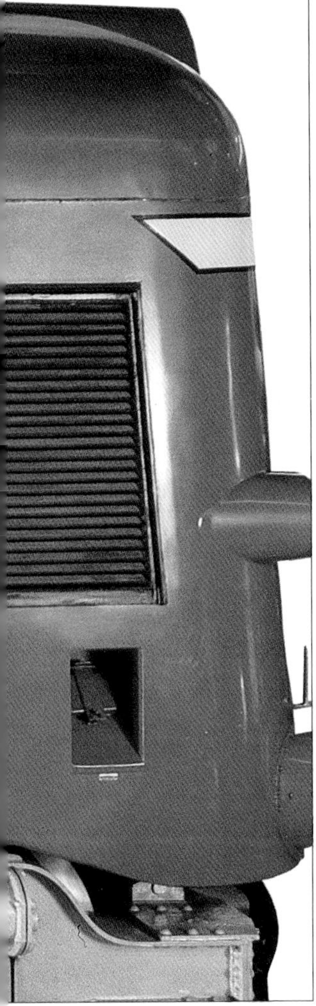

Rail and Road

Steam locomotives

WAGONS THAT ARE PULLED along tracks have been used to transport material since the 16th century, but these trains were drawn by men or horses until the invention of the steam locomotive. Steam locomotives enabled the basic railway system to realize its true potential. In 1804, Richard Trevithick built the world's first working steam locomotive in South Wales. It was not entirely successful, but it encouraged others to develop new designs. By 1829, the British engineer Robert Stephenson had built the "Rocket", considered to be the forerunner of the modern locomotive. The "Rocket" was a self-sufficient unit, carrying coal to heat the boiler and a water supply for generating steam. Steam passed from the boiler to force the pistons back and forth, and this movement turned the driving wheels, propelling the train forwards. Used steam was then expelled in characteristic "chuffs". Later steam locomotives, like "Ellerman Lines" and the "Mallard", worked in a similar way, but on a much larger scale. The simple design and reliability of steam locomotives ensured that they changed very little in 120 years of use, before being replaced from the 1950s by more efficient diesel and electric power (see pp. 326-329).

"ROCKET" STEAM LOCOMOTIVE, 1829

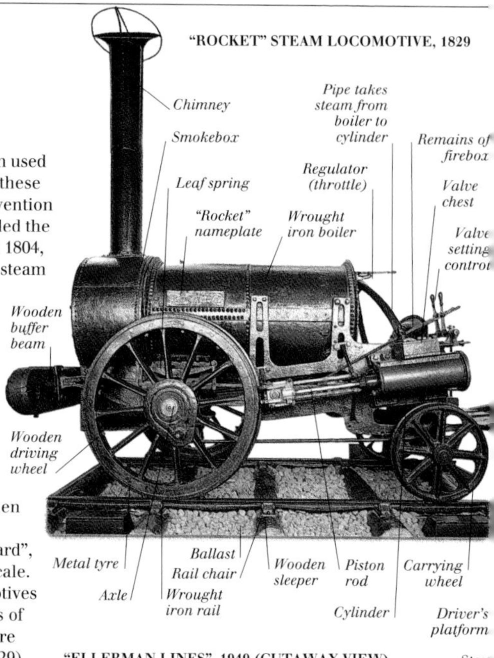
Chimney
Smokebox
Pipe takes steam from boiler to cylinder
Remains of firebox
Regulator (throttle)
Valve chest
Leaf spring
"Rocket" nameplate
Wrought iron boiler
Valve setting control
Wooden buffer beam
Wooden driving wheel
Metal tyre
Axle
Ballast
Rail chair
Wrought iron rail
Wooden sleeper
Piston rod
Cylinder
Carrying wheel
Driver's platform

"ELLERMAN LINES", 1949 (CUTAWAY VIEW)

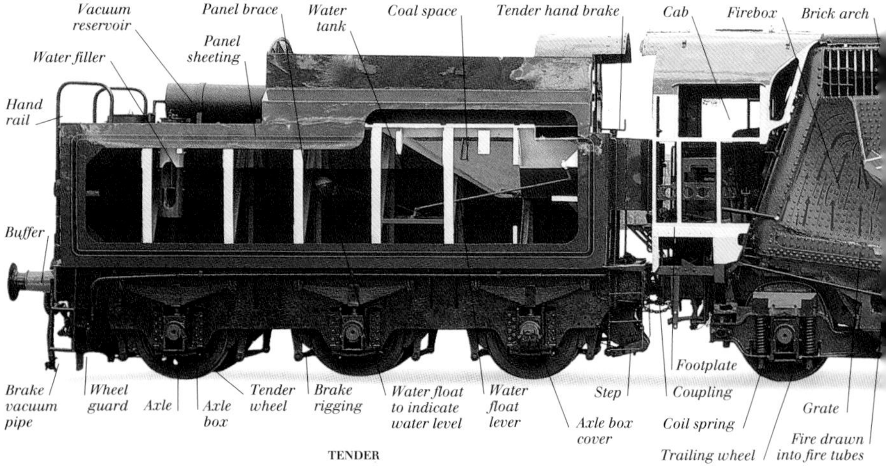
Stay
Vacuum reservoir
Panel brace
Water tank
Coal space
Tender hand brake
Cab
Firebox
Brick arch
Panel sheeting
Water filler
Hand rail
Buffer
Brake vacuum pipe
Wheel guard
Axle
Axle box
Tender wheel
Brake rigging
Water float to indicate water level
Water float lever
Step
Axle box cover
Footplate
Coupling
Coil spring
Trailing wheel
Grate
Fire drawn into fire tubes
TENDER

CAB INTERIOR OF "MALLARD" EXPRESS STEAM LOCOMOTIVE, 1938

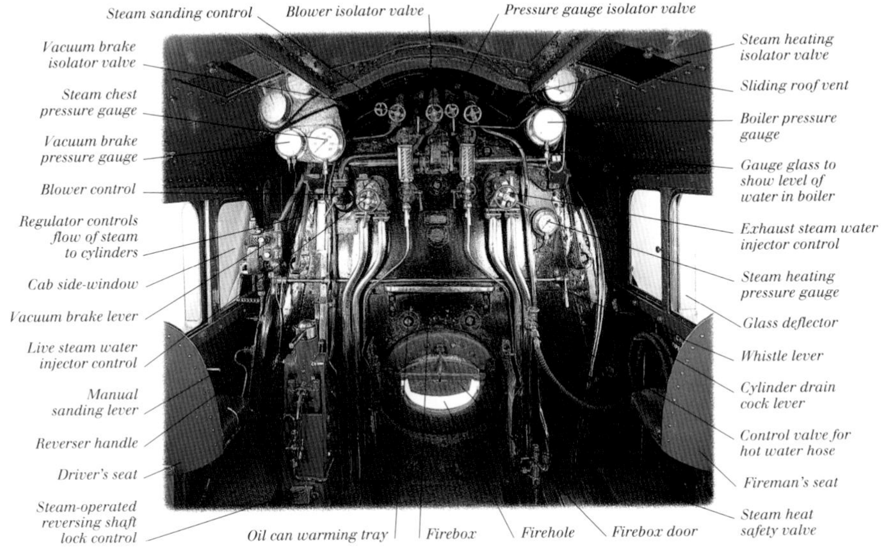

Steam sanding control
Blower isolator valve
Pressure gauge isolator valve
Vacuum brake isolator valve
Steam chest pressure gauge
Vacuum brake pressure gauge
Blower control
Regulator controls flow of steam to cylinders
Cab side-window
Vacuum brake lever
Live steam water injector control
Manual sanding lever
Reverser handle
Driver's seat
Steam-operated reversing shaft lock control
Oil can warming tray
Firebox
Firehole
Firebox door
Steam heating isolator valve
Sliding roof vent
Boiler pressure gauge
Gauge glass to show level of water in boiler
Exhaust steam water injector control
Steam heating pressure gauge
Glass deflector
Whistle lever
Cylinder drain cock lever
Control valve for hot water hose
Fireman's seat
Steam heat safety valve

Fire tube
Steam dome
Thermal siphon
Regulator valve
Mechanical lubricator
Superheater tube inside flue tube
Boiler
Pipe takes steam from boiler to cylinder
Chimney
Blast-pipe
Smokebox
Smokebox door
Lubricating pipe
Piston valve
Buffer
Screw coupling
Leading wheel
Bogie frame
Cylinder
Piston, linked to connecting rod
Slide bar
Combination lever
Connecting rod
Expansion lever
Crank
Driving wheel
Coupling rod
Brake rigging
Brake shoe

STEAM LOCOMOTIVE

Diesel trains

RUDOLF DIESEL FIRST DEMONSTRATED the diesel engine in Germany in 1898, but it was not until the 1940s that diesel locomotives were successfully established on both passenger and freight services, in the US. Early diesel locomotives like the "Union Pacific" were more expensive to build than steam locomotives, but were more efficient and cheaper to operate, especially where oil was plentiful. One feature of diesel engines is that the power output cannot be coupled directly to the wheels. To convert the mechanical energy produced by diesel engines, a transmission system is needed. Almost all diesel locomotives have electric transmissions, and are known as "diesel-electric" locomotives. The diesel engine works by drawing air into the cylinders and compressing it to increase its temperature; a small quantity of diesel fuel is then injected into it. The resulting combustion drives the generator (more recently an alternator) to produce electricity, which is fed to electric motors connected to the wheels. Diesel-electric locomotives are essentially electric locomotives that carry their own power plants, and are used worldwide today. The "Deltic" diesel-electric locomotive, similar to the one shown here, replaced classic express steam locomotives, and ran at speeds up to 160 kph (100 mph).

FRONT VIEW OF "UNION PACIFIC" DIESEL-ELECTRIC LOCOMOTIVE, 1950s

Exhaust vent
Windscreen wiper
Horn
Cab front window
Head-light
Cab door
Name of operating railroad
Illuminate locomotiv unit numb
Railroad crest
Cab step
Step
Motor-driven bogie axle
Air-brake coupling hose
Centre buck eye coupler
UNION PACIFIC
951

PROTOTYPE "DELTIC" DIESEL-ELECTRIC LOCOMOTIVE, 1956

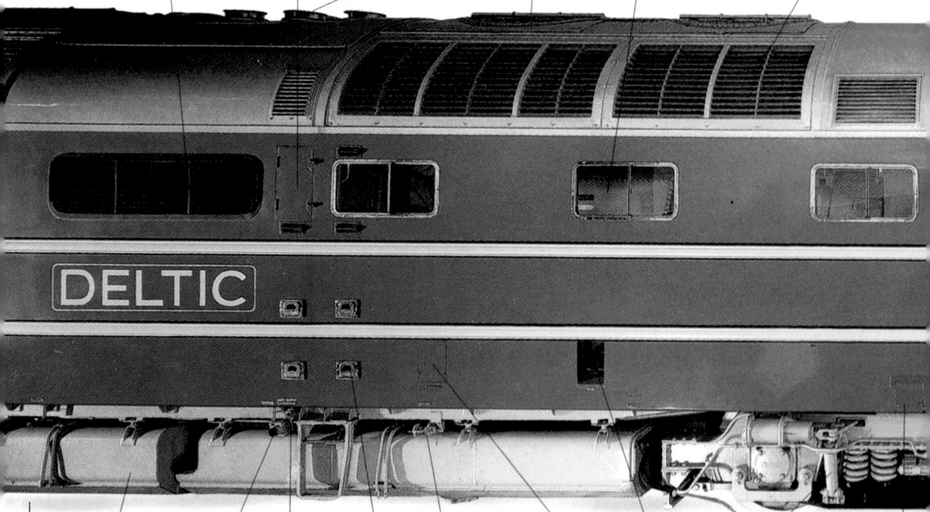
Engine room vent
Inspection hatch
Engine exhaust port
Radiator fan
Engine room window
Engine room vent
DELTIC
Fuel tank
Water for heating boiler
Inspection socket
Folding step
Drain for radiator coolant
Radiator coolant
Sand box
Telescopic damper
Drain for control reservoir

DIESEL ENGINE OF BRITISH RAIL CLASS 20 DIESEL-ELECTRIC LOCOMOTIVE

Exhaust vent
Cylinder head (V-four configuration)
Turbo-charged diesel engine drives generator
Generator cooling fan
Generator compartment vent
Auxiliary generator
ain generator produces lectricity that drives wheels
Main chassis member
Innermost wheel set on cab-end bogie
Air brake pipe
Brake rigging
Battery box
Engine crankcase
Air reservoir and isolator valves
Lubricating oil primary pump and fuel supply pump

Driver's seat
Cab door
Cab
Warning horn
Windscreen
Windscreen wiper
Cab window
Manufacturer's logo
Cab vent
Indicator light
Sand box
Buffer
Brake cylinder
Roller-bearing axle box
Brake shoe
Brake actuating chain
Transverse leaf spring secondary suspension
Coil spring primary suspension

EXAMPLES OF FREIGHT CARS

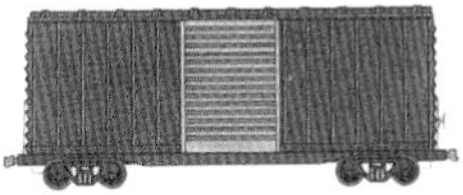

BOX CAR

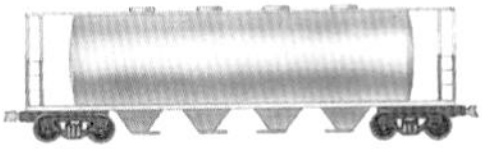

HOPPER CAR

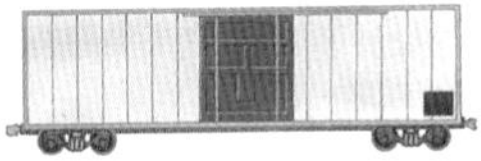

REFRIGERATOR CAR

LIVESTOCK CAR

FLAT CAR WITH BULKHEADS

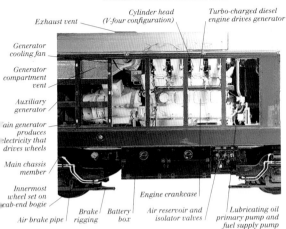

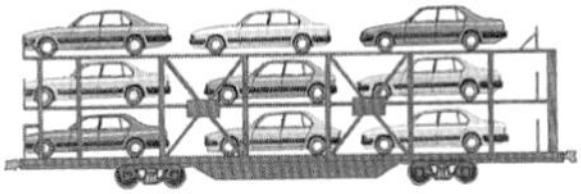

AUTOMOBILE CAR

Electric and high-speed trains

THE FIRST ELECTRIC LOCOMOTIVE ran in 1879 in Berlin, Germany. In Europe, electric trains developed as a more efficient alternative to the steam locomotive and diesel-electric power. Like diesels, electric trains employ electric motors to drive the wheels but, unlike diesels, the electricity is generated externally at a power station. Electric current is picked up either from a catenary (overhead cable) via a pantograph, or from a third rail. Since it does not carry its own power-generating equipment, an electric locomotive has a better power-to-weight ratio and greater acceleration than its diesel-electric equivalent. This makes electric trains suitable for urban routes with many stops. They are also faster, quieter, and less polluting. The latest electric French TGV (Train à Grande Vitesse) reaches 300 kph (186 mph); other trains, like the London to Paris and Brussels "Eurostar", can run at several voltages and operate between different countries. Simpler electric trains perform special duties – the "People Mover" at Gatwick Airport in Britain runs between terminals.

HOW ALTERNATING CURRENT (AC) ELECTRIC TRAINS WORK

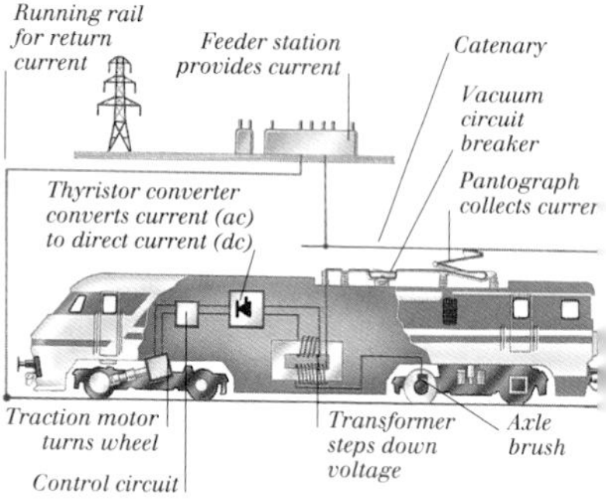
Running rail for return current
Feeder station provides current
Catenary
Vacuum circuit breaker
Pantograph collects current
Thyristor converter converts current (ac) to direct current (dc)
Traction motor turns wheel
Control circuit
Transformer steps down voltage
Axle brush

FRONT VIEW OF PARIS METRO

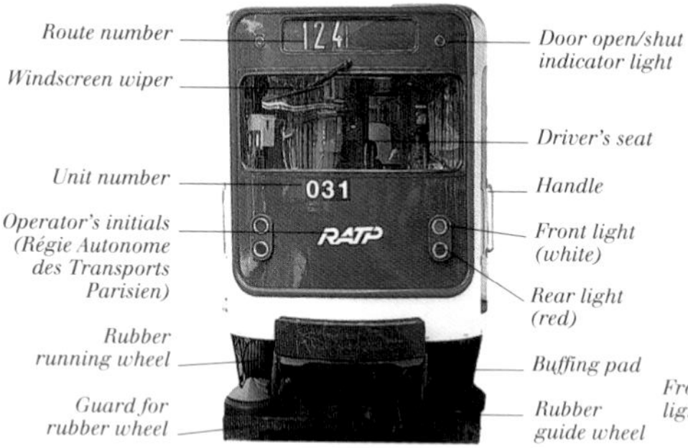
Route number
Windscreen wiper
Unit number
Operator's initials (Régie Autonome des Transports Parisien)
Rubber running wheel
Guard for rubber wheel
Door open/shut indicator light
Driver's seat
Handle
Front light (white)
Rear light (red)
Buffing pad
Rubber guide wheel
124
031
RATP

FRONT VIEW OF ITALIAN STATE RAILWAYS CLASS 402 ELECTRIC LOCOMOTIVE

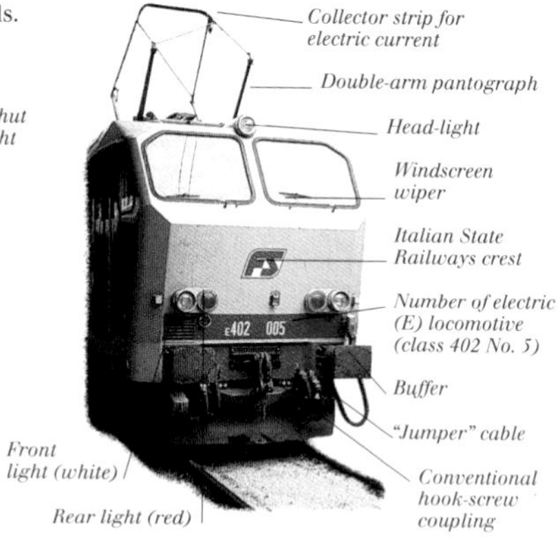
Collector strip for electric current
Double-arm pantograph
Head-light
Windscreen wiper
Italian State Railways crest
Number of electric (E) locomotive (class 402 No. 5)
Buffer
"Jumper" cable
Conventional hook-screw coupling
Front light (white)
Rear light (red)
E402 005

SIDE VIEW OF GATWICK EXPRESS "PEOPLE MOVER"

Gatwick
Gatwick
Pneumatic rubber wheel
Concrete track
Automatic door
No driver (train controlled by central computer)

"EUROSTAR" MULTI-VOLTAGE ELECTRIC TRAIN

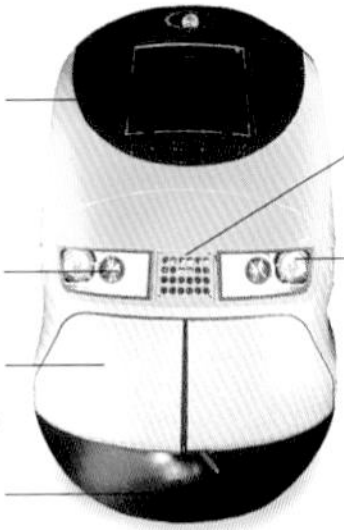
Cab window
Grille over warning horn
Rear light (red)
Head-light (white)
Fibreglass reinforced plastic cover
Aerofoil wheel guard

FRONT VIEW

Cab side-window
Electric equipment compartment
Cab door
Side vent
Cab front window
Fibreglass reinforced plastic cover
Aerofoil wheel guard
Sanding pipe
Leading driven axle
Horizontal telescopic damper
Third (electric) rail collector shoe
Coil spring suspension

SIDE VIEW

TGV ELECTRIC HIGH-SPEED TRAIN

Luggage rack
Reading light
Double-glazed and tinted side-window
Sliding curtain
Seat
Main overhead lighting
Automatic electric carriage end door
Antimacassar
Headrest
Armrest
Centre gangway

INTERIOR OF TGV

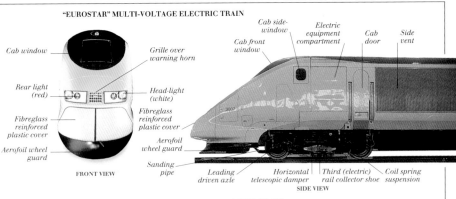

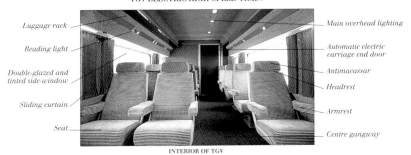

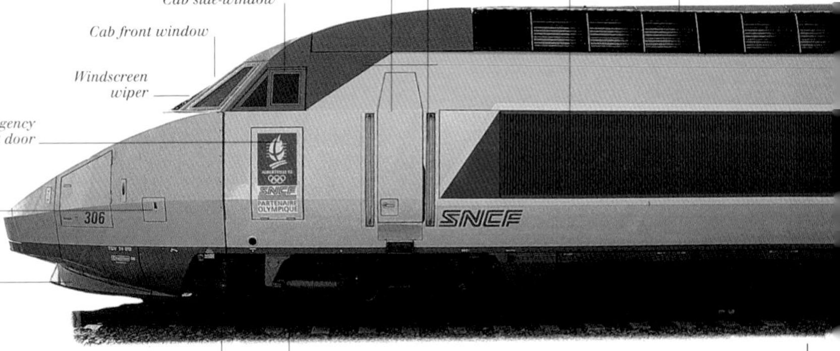
Cab door
Hand rail
Side vent
Roof vent
Cab side-window
Cab front window
Windscreen wiper
Emergency exit door
Access panel for servicing
Nose air deflector dam
Vertical damper
Horizontal damper

SIDE VIEW OF TGV

Train equipment

MODERN RAILWAY TRACK consists of two parallel steel rails clipped on to a support called a sleeper. Sleepers are usually made of reinforced concrete, although wood and steel are still used. The distance between the inside edges of the rails is the track gauge. It evolved in Britain, which uses a gauge of 1,435 mm (4 ft 8½ in), known as the standard gauge. As engineering grew more sophisticated, narrower gauges were adopted because they cost less to build. The loading gauge, which is equally important, determines the size of the largest loaded vehicle that may pass through tunnels and under bridges with adequate clearance. Safe train operation relies on following a signalling system. At first, signalling was based on a simple time interval between trains, but it now depends on maintaining a safe distance between successive trains travelling in the same direction. Most modern signals are colour lights, but older mechanical semaphore signals are still used. On the latest high-speed lines, train drivers receive control instructions by electronic means. Signalling depends on reliable control of the train by effective braking. For fast, modern trains, which have considerable momentum, it is essential that each vehicle in the train can be braked by the driver or by a train control system, such as Automatic Train Protection (ATP). Braking is achieved by the brake shoe acting on the wheel rim (rim brakes), by disc brakes, or, increasingly, by electrical braking.

MECHANICAL SEMAPHORE SIGNAL

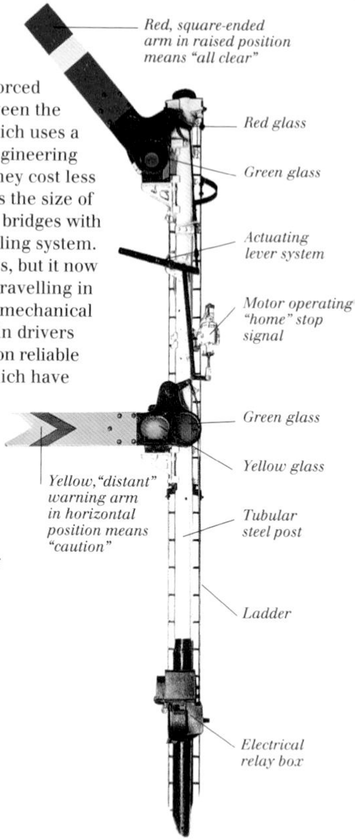
Red, square-ended arm in raised position means "all clear"
Red glass
Green glass
Actuating lever system
Motor operating "home" stop signal
Green glass
Yellow glass
Yellow, "distant" warning arm in horizontal position means "caution"
Tubular steel post
Ladder
Electrical relay box

FOUR-ASPECT COLOUR LIGHT SIGNAL

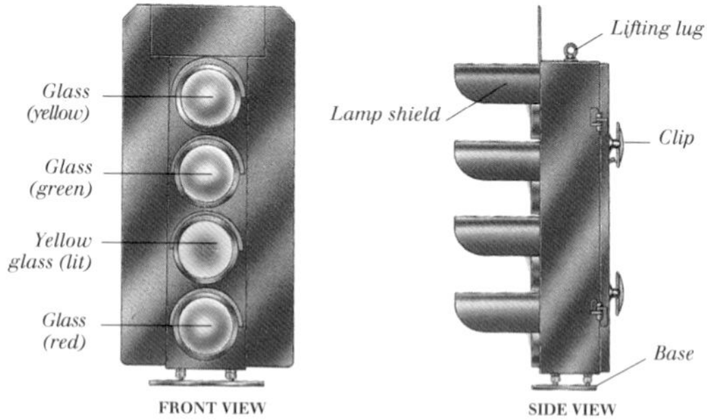
Glass (yellow)
Glass (green)
Yellow glass (lit)
Glass (red)
Lifting lug
Lamp shield
Clip
Base
FRONT VIEW
SIDE VIEW

HOW A MODERN MAIN-LINE SIGNALLING SYSTEM WORKS

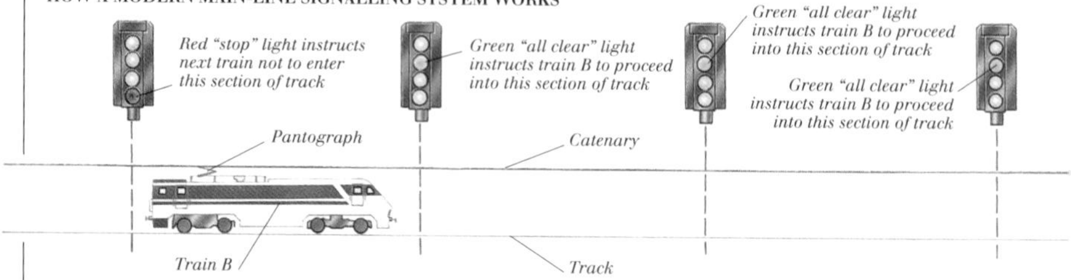
Red "stop" light instructs next train not to enter this section of track
Green "all clear" light instructs train B to proceed into this section of track
Green "all clear" light instructs train B to proceed into this section of track
Green "all clear" light instructs train B to proceed into this section of track
Pantograph
Catenary
Train B
Track

EXAMPLES OF INTERNATIONAL TRACK GAUGES

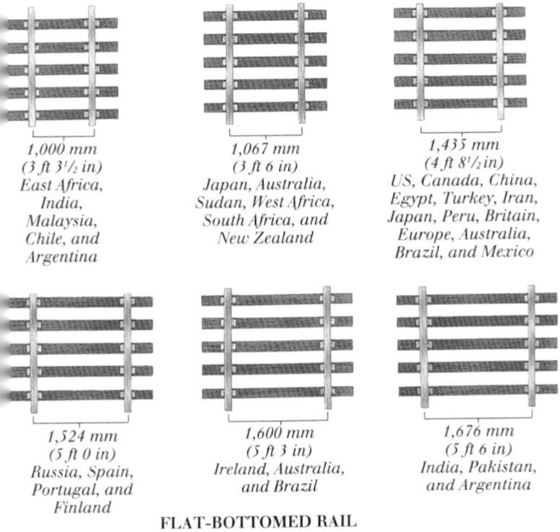
1,000 mm
(3 ft 3½ in)
East Africa, India, Malaysia, Chile, and Argentina
1,067 mm
(3 ft 6 in)
Japan, Australia, Sudan, West Africa, South Africa, and New Zealand
1,435 mm
(4 ft 8½ in)
US, Canada, China, Egypt, Turkey, Iran, Japan, Peru, Britain, Europe, Australia, Brazil, and Mexico
1,524 mm
(5 ft 0 in)
Russia, Spain, Portugal, and Finland
1,600 mm
(5 ft 3 in)
Ireland, Australia, and Brazil
1,676 mm
(5 ft 6 in)
India, Pakistan, and Argentina

EXAMPLES OF INTERNATIONAL LOADING GAUGES

Britain: 2.75 m (9 ft 0 in) x 3.95 m (12 ft 11 in)

Europe: 3.1 m (10 ft 2 in) x 4.5 m (14 ft 9 in)

US: 3.3 m (10 ft 10 in) x 4.9 m (16 ft 2 in)

Russia: 3.4 m (11 ft 2 in) x 5.3 m (17 ft 4 in)

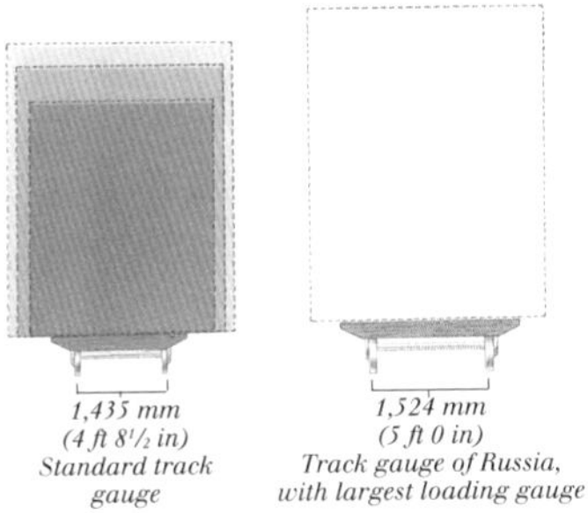
1,435 mm
(4 ft 8½ in)
Standard track gauge
1,524 mm
(5 ft 0 in)
Track gauge of Russia, with largest loading gauge

FLAT-BOTTOMED RAIL

Flat-bottomed steel rail
Steel spring secures rail to sleeper
Synthetic insulating pad
Sleeper supports track and maintains gauge

BULL-HEAD RAIL

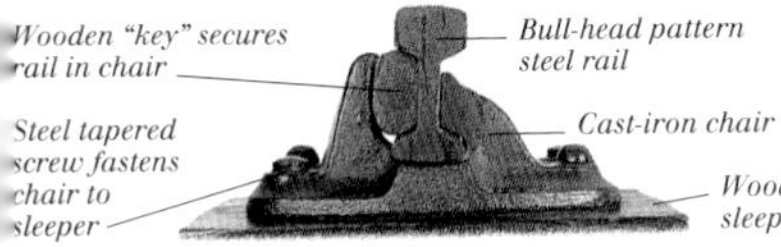
Wooden "key" secures rail in chair
Steel tapered screw fastens chair to sleeper
Bull-head pattern steel rail
Cast-iron chair
Wooden sleeper

DISC BRAKES ON MODERN WAGON BOGIE

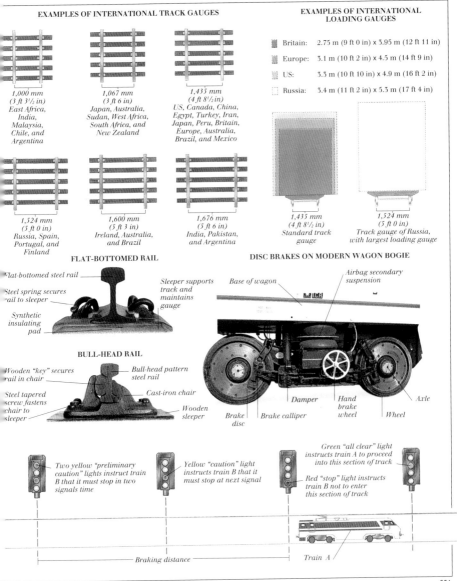

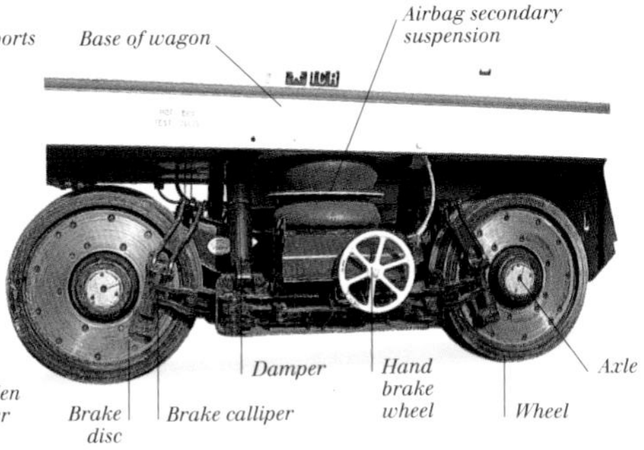
Base of wagon
Airbag secondary suspension
Damper
Hand brake wheel
Axle
Brake disc
Brake calliper
Wheel

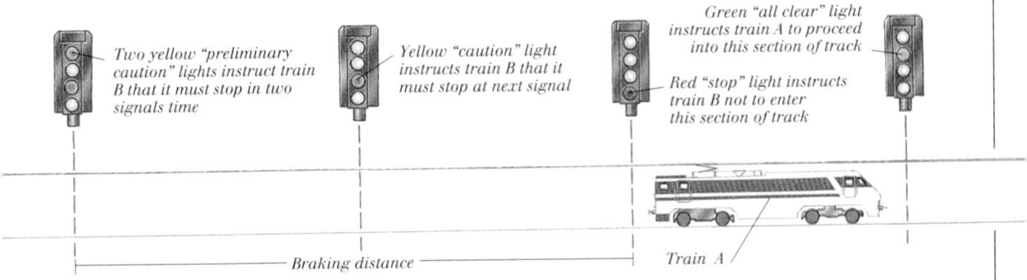
Two yellow "preliminary caution" lights instruct train B that it must stop in two signals time
Yellow "caution" light instructs train B that it must stop at next signal
Green "all clear" light instructs train A to proceed into this section of track
Red "stop" light instructs train B not to enter this section of track
Braking distance
Train A

Trams and buses

METROLINK TRAM, MANCHESTER, BRITAIN

AS CITY POPULATIONS exploded in the 1800s, there was an urgent need for mass transportation. Trams were an early solution. The first trams, like buses, were horse-drawn, but in 1881, electric street tramways appeared in Berlin, Germany. Electric trams soon became widespread throughout Europe and North America. Trams run on rails along a fixed route, using electric motors that receive power from overhead cables. As road networks developed, motorized buses offered a flexible alternative to trams. By the 1930s, they had replaced tram systems in many cities. City buses typically have doors at both front and rear to make loading and unloading easier. Double-decker designs are popular, occupying the same amount of street space as single-decker buses but able to transport twice the number of people. Buses are also commonly used for inter-city travel and touring. Tour buses have reclining seats, large windows, luggage space, and toilets. Recently, as city traffic has become increasingly congested, many city planners have designed new tram routes to run alongside bus routes as part of an integrated transport system.

EARLY TRAM, c.1900

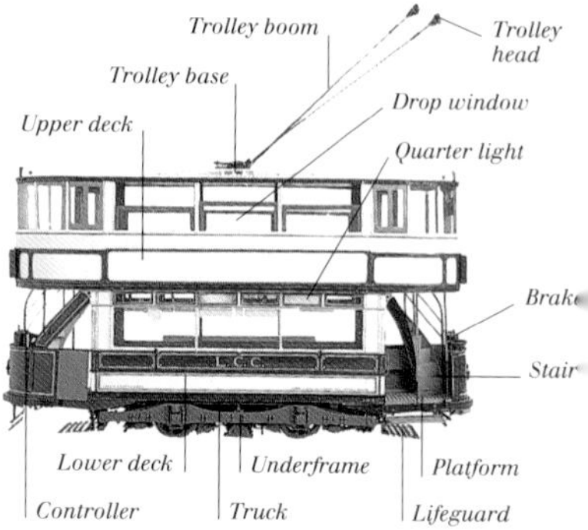
Trolley boom
Trolley head
Trolley base
Drop window
Upper deck
Quarter light
Brake
Stair
L.C.C.
Lower deck
Underframe
Platform
Controller
Truck
Lifeguard

MCW METROBUS, LONDON, BRITAIN

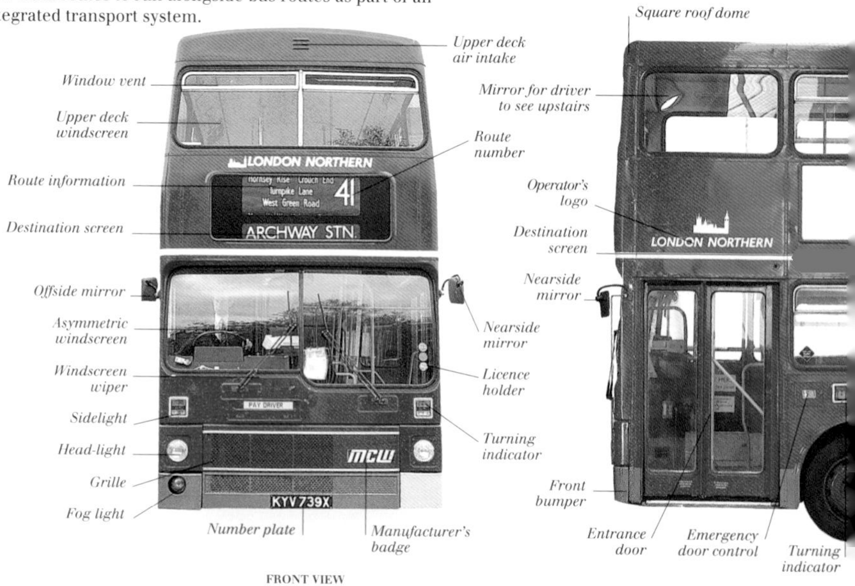
Square roof dome
Upper deck air intake
Window vent
Upper deck windscreen
Mirror for driver to see upstairs
Route number
LONDON NORTHERN
Route information
Hornsey Rise Crouch End
Turnpike Lane
West Green Road
41
Operator's logo
Destination screen
ARCHWAY STN.
Destination screen
LONDON NORTHERN
Offside mirror
Nearside mirror
Asymmetric windscreen
Nearside mirror
Windscreen wiper
Licence holder
PAY DRIVER
Sidelight
Turning indicator
Head-light
mcw
Grille
Front bumper
Fog light
KYV 739X
Number plate
Manufacturer's badge
Entrance door
Emergency door control
Turning indicator

FRONT VIEW

SINGLE-DECKER BUS, NEW YORK, US

Wheelchair access
Sliding window
Sloped roof dome
Tinted glass
Changing the Face of Television
Bumper
Air intake
Tyre
Axle
Exit door
Access panel
Sidelight
Entrance door

SIDE VIEW

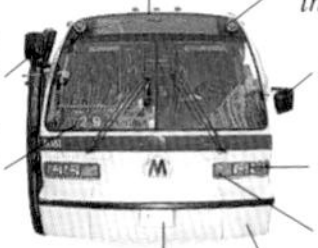
Marker light
Repeater indicator
Entrance door
Side mirror
Route number
Head-light
Turning indicator
Number plate
Bumper

FRONT VIEW

DOUBLE-DECKER TOUR BUS, PARIS, FRANCE

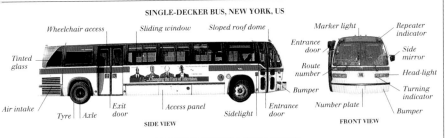

Tinted glass
Raked windscreen
Paris Vision
Air intake
Panoramic window
Access panel
Turning indicator
Skirt
Bumper
Plug-style entrance door
Access door
Twin rear axle
Side entrance
Single front axle
Tyre

Sliding window vent
Upper saloon window
Advertising panel
Air intake
Lower saloon window
Fleet number
M1041
HT
LONDON BUSES
Engine access panel
Rear bumper
Emergency door control
Two-leaf style exit door
Legal lettering
London Buses logo
Tyre
Skirt
Axle

SIDE VIEW

The first cars

THE EARLIEST ROAD VEHICLE powered by an engine, the Cugnot steam traction engine, was built in 1770. More practical steam carriages, such as the Bordino, were available in the early 19th century, but they were heavy and cumbersome. Restrictive laws and the introduction of railways, faster and able to carry more passengers, saw the decline of "cars" powered by steam. It was not until 1860 that the first practical power unit for road vehicles was developed, with the invention of the internal combustion engine by the Belgian Etienne Lenoir. By around 1890, Karl Benz and Gottlieb Daimler in Germany, and Albert de Dion and Armand Peugeot in France were building cars for sale to the public. These early cars, despite being primitive, expensive, and produced in limited numbers, heralded the age of the motor car.

STEAM-POWERED CUGNOT "FARDIER", 1770

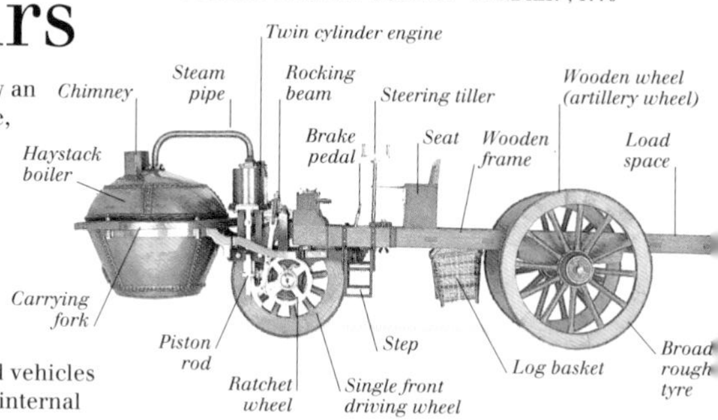

Twin cylinder engine
Chimney
Steam pipe
Rocking beam
Steering tiller
Wooden wheel (artillery wheel)
Haystack boiler
Brake pedal
Seat
Wooden frame
Load space
Carrying fork
Piston rod
Ratchet wheel
Single front driving wheel
Step
Log basket
Broad rough tyre

BORDINO STEAM CARRIAGE, 1854

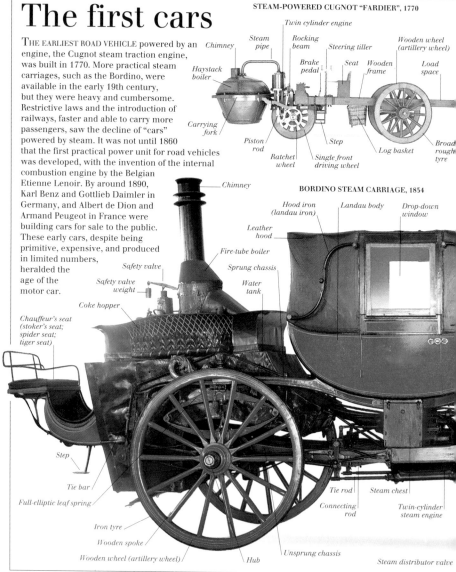

Chimney
Hood iron (landau iron)
Landau body
Drop-down window
Leather hood
Fire-tube boiler
Safety valve
Sprung chassis
Safety valve weight
Water tank
Coke hopper
Chauffeur's seat (stoker's seat; spider seat; tiger seat)
Step
Tie bar
Full-elliptic leaf spring
Iron tyre
Wooden spoke
Wooden wheel (artillery wheel)
Hub
Unsprung chassis
Tie rod
Steam chest
Connecting rod
Twin-cylinder steam engine
Steam distributor valve

SIDE VIEW OF PETROL-DRIVEN BENZ MOTORWAGEN, 1886

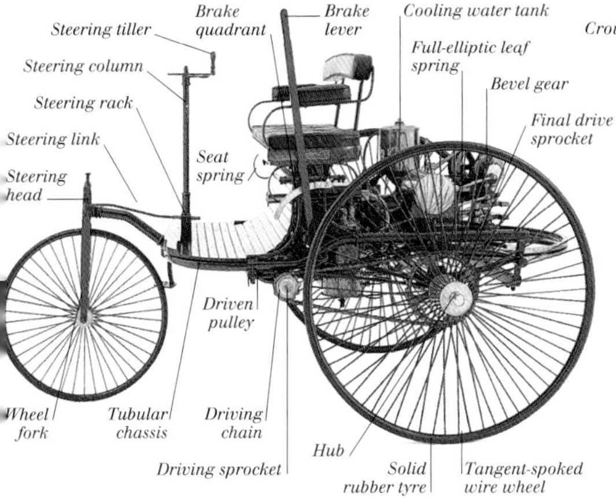
Steering tiller
Brake quadrant
Brake lever
Cooling water tank
Full-elliptic leaf spring
Bevel gear
Final drive sprocket
Steering column
Steering rack
Steering link
Seat spring
Steering head
Driven pulley
Wheel fork
Tubular chassis
Driving chain
Hub
Driving sprocket
Solid rubber tyre
Tangent-spoked wire wheel

REAR VIEW OF BENZ MOTORWAGEN, 1886

Pinion
Lubricator
Cooling tank
Crown wheel
Driving pulley
Fuel tank
Drive belt
Big-end bearing
Groove for rope starter
Crankshaft
Flywheel

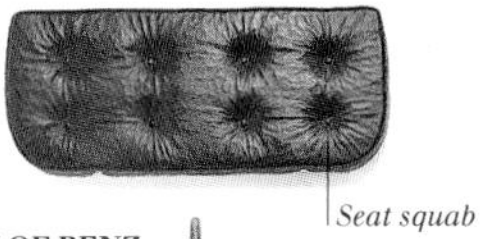
Seat squab

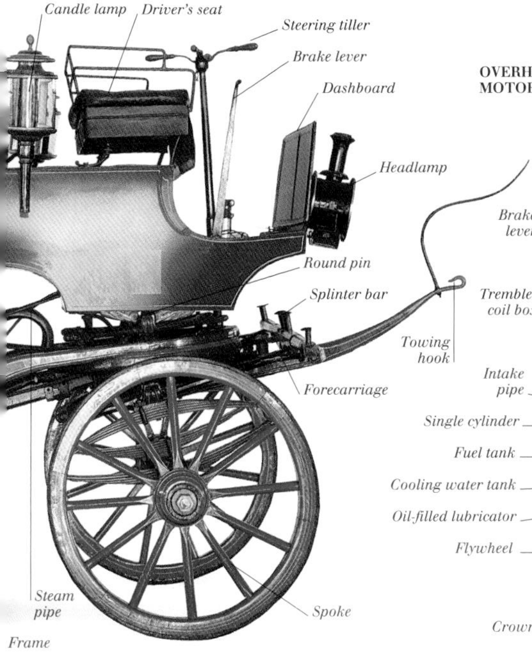
Candle lamp
Driver's seat
Steering tiller
Brake lever
Dashboard
Headlamp
Round pin
Splinter bar
Towing hook
Forecarriage
Steam pipe
Spoke
Frame

OVERHEAD VIEW OF BENZ MOTORWAGEN, 1886

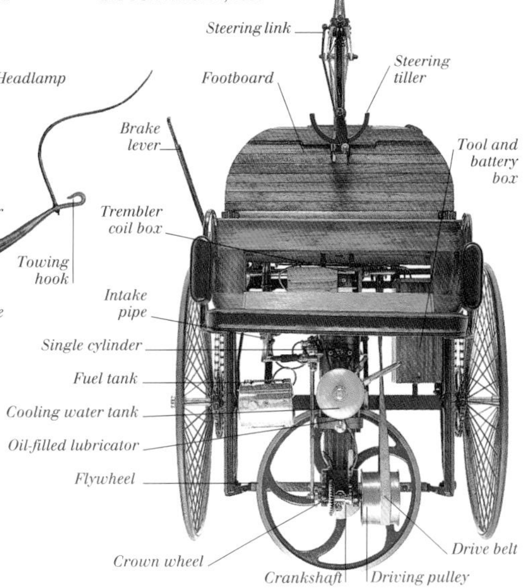
Steering link
Footboard
Steering tiller
Brake lever
Tool and battery box
Trembler coil box
Intake pipe
Single cylinder
Fuel tank
Cooling water tank
Oil-filled lubricator
Flywheel
Drive belt
Crown wheel
Crankshaft
Driving pulley

Elegance and utility

DURING THE FIRST DECADE OF THIS CENTURY, the motorist who could afford it had a choice of some of the finest cars ever made. These handbuilt cars were powerful and luxurious, using the finest woods, leathers, and cloths, and bodywork made to the customer's individual requirements; some had six-cylinder engines as big as 15 litres. The price of such cars was several times that of an average house, and their yearly running costs were also very high. As a result, basic, utilitarian cars became popular. Costing perhaps one-tenth of the price of a luxury car, these cars had very little trim and often had only single-cylinder engines.

1904 OLDSMOBILE SINGLE-CYLINDER ENGINE

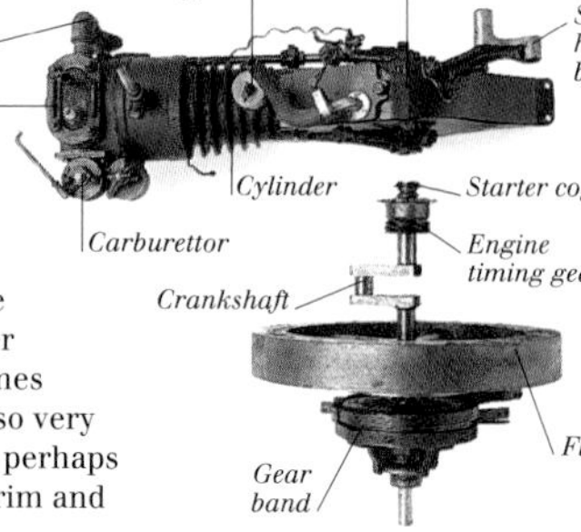
Oil bottle dripfeed
Crankcase
Starting handle bracket
Exhaust pipe
Cylinder head
Cylinder
Starter cog
Carburettor
Engine timing gear
Crankshaft
Flywheel
Gear band

FRONT VIEW OF 1906 RENAULT

Canopy
Mahogany framed windscreen
Cast aluminium wheel spider
British Automobile Association badge
Rear window
Bedford cord upholstery
Window blind
British Royal Automobile Club badge
Blind pull
Window lift strap
Rear-view mirror
Broad lace trim
Lamp bracket
Oil side lamp
Windscreen support
Dashboard radiator
Mudguard (wing)
Brass bevel
Access panel
Bonnet catch
Bail handle
Lifting handle
Mirror reflector
X 825
Acetylene headlamp
Steering spindle
Elliott steering knuckle
Chevron-tread tyre
Front axle
Track rod
Dumb iron
Screwdown greaser
Starting handle

SIDE VIEW OF 1906 RENAULT

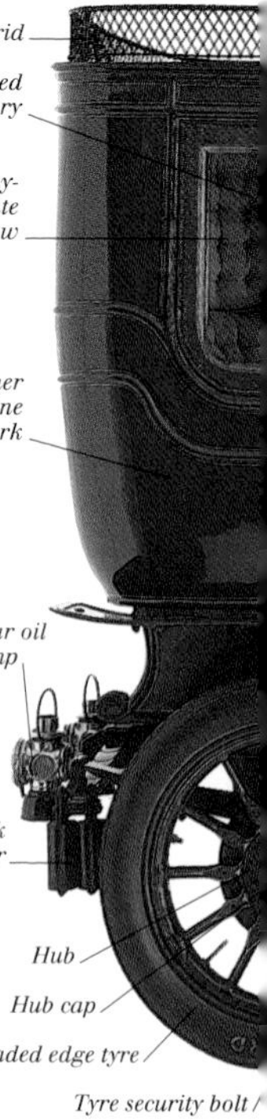
Luggage grid
Button-quilted upholstery
Mahogany-framed plate glass window
Round-corner single limousine coachwork
Rear oil lamp
Shock absorber
Hub
Hub cap
Beaded edge tyre
Tyre security bolt

1904 OLDSMOBILE TRIM AND BODYWORK

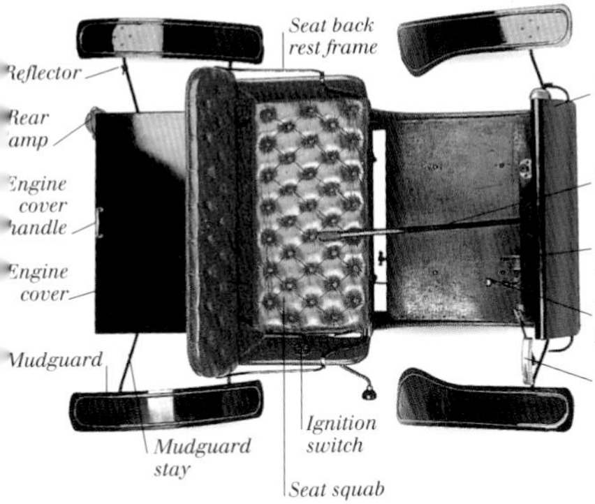
Seat back rest frame
eflector
Rear amp
ngine cover andle
ngine cover
Mudguard
Mudguard stay
Ignition switch
Seat squab
Dashboard
Tiller
Brake pedal
Throttle pedal
Mirror

1904 OLDSMOBILE CHASSIS

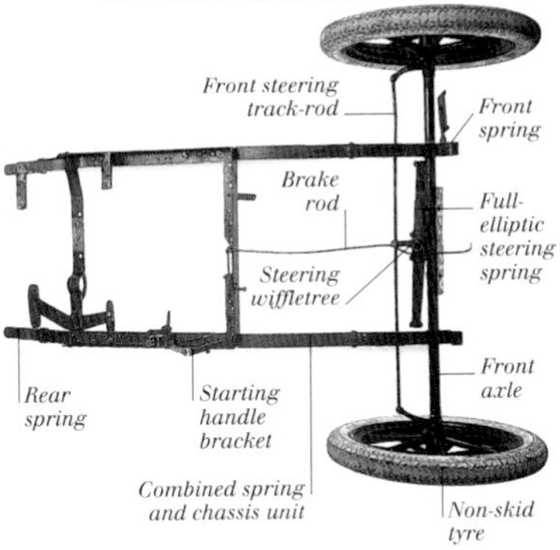
Front steering track-rod
Front spring
Brake rod
Full-elliptic steering spring
Steering wiffletree
Front axle
Rear spring
Starting handle bracket
Combined spring and chassis unit
Non-skid tyre

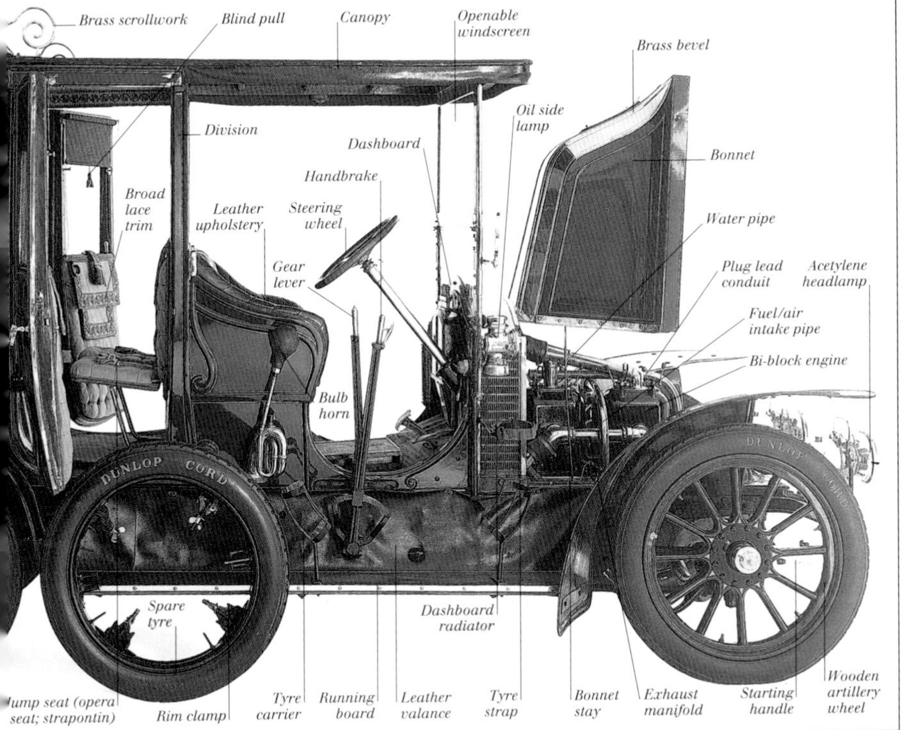
Brass scrollwork
Blind pull
Canopy
Openable windscreen
Brass bevel
Oil side lamp
Division
Dashboard
Bonnet
Handbrake
Broad lace trim
Leather upholstery
Steering wheel
Water pipe
Gear lever
Plug lead conduit
Acetylene headlamp
Fuel/air intake pipe
Bi-block engine
Bulb horn
DUNLOP CORD
DUNLOP
Spare tyre
Dashboard radiator
ump seat (opera seat; strapontin)
Rim clamp
Tyre carrier
Running board
Leather valance
Tyre strap
Bonnet stay
Exhaust manifold
Starting handle
Wooden artillery wheel

Mass-production

THE FIRST CARS WERE HAND-ASSEMBLED from individually built parts, a time-consuming procedure that required skilled mechanics and made cars very expensive. This problem was solved, in America, by a Detroit car manufacturer named Henry Ford; he introduced mass-production by using standardized parts, and later combined these with a moving production line. The work was brought to the workers, each of whom performed one simple task in the construction process as the chassis moved along the line. The first mass-produced car, the Ford Model T, was launched in 1908 and was available in a limited range of body styles and colours. However, when the production line was introduced in 1914, the colour range was cut back; the Model T became available, as Henry Ford said, in "any colour you like, so long as it's black". Ford cut the production time for a car from several days to about 12 hours, and eventually to minutes, making cars much cheaper than before. As a result, by 1920 half the cars in the world were Model T Fords.

FRONT VIEW OF 1913 FORD MODEL T

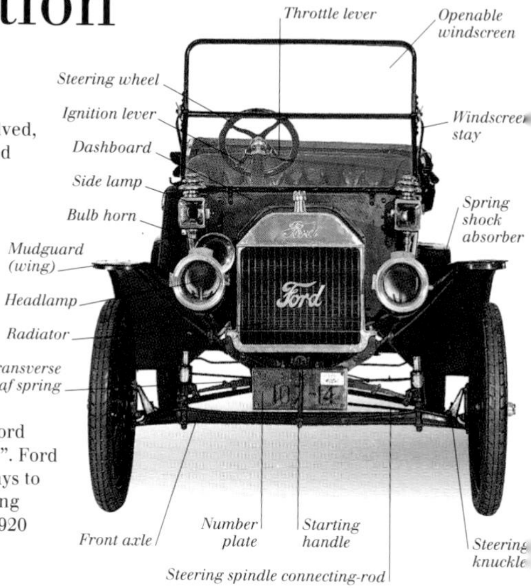

STAGES OF FORD MODEL T PRODUCTION

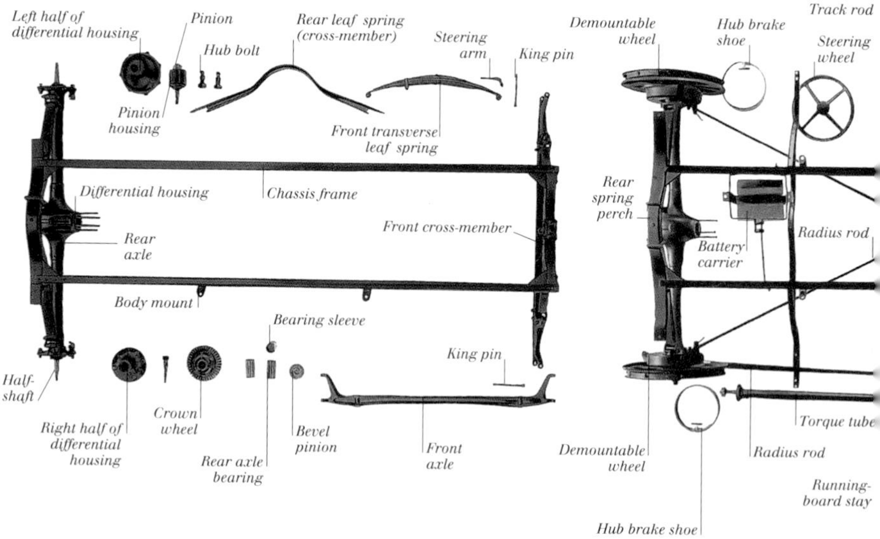

SIDE VIEW OF 1913 FORD MODEL T

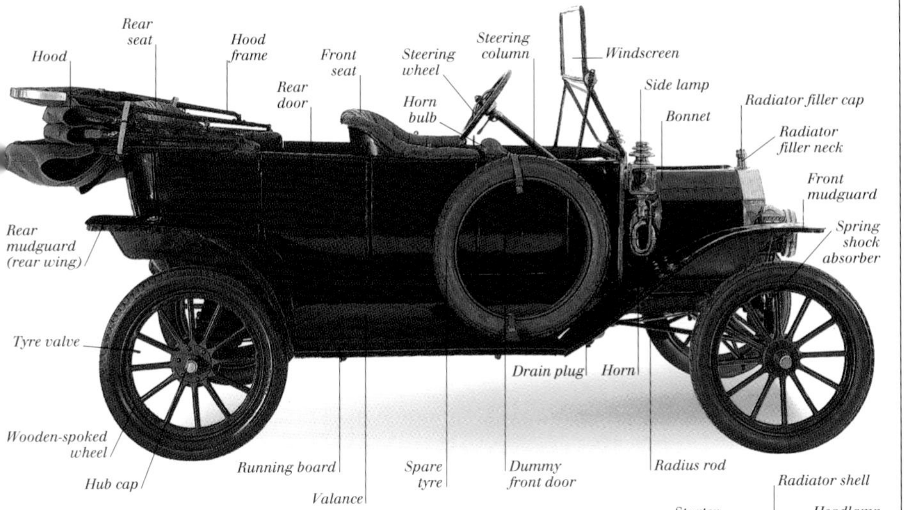
Hood
Rear seat
Hood frame
Front seat
Rear door
Steering wheel
Horn bulb
Steering column
Windscreen
Side lamp
Bonnet
Radiator filler cap
Radiator filler neck
Front mudguard
Spring shock absorber
Rear mudguard (rear wing)
Tyre valve
Wooden-spoked wheel
Hub cap
Running board
Valance
Spare tyre
Dummy front door
Drain plug
Horn
Radius rod

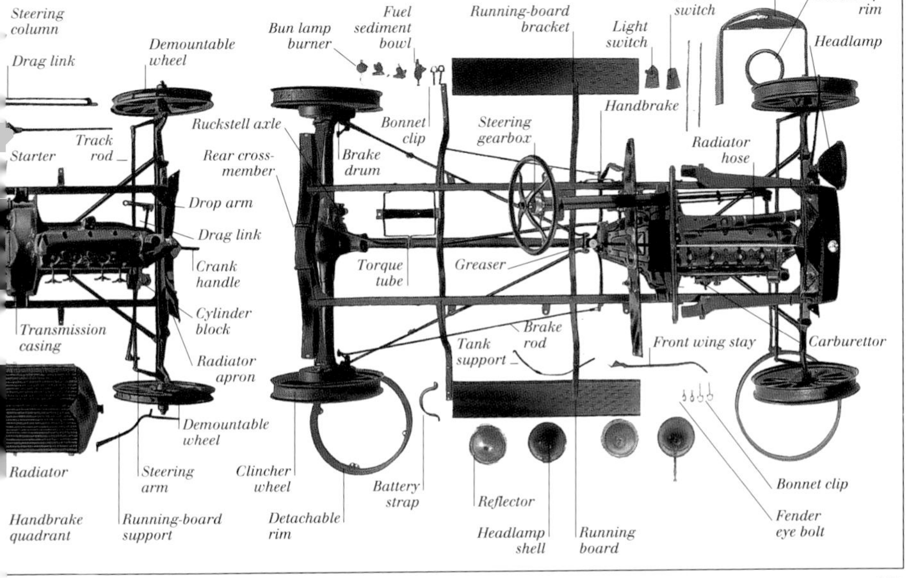
Steering column
Drag link
Starter
Track rod
Demountable wheel
Ruckstell axle
Rear cross-member
Drop arm
Drag link
Crank handle
Cylinder block
Transmission casing
Radiator apron
Demountable wheel
Radiator
Steering arm
Handbrake quadrant
Running-board support
Bun lamp burner
Fuel sediment bowl
Bonnet clip
Brake drum
Torque tube
Clincher wheel
Battery strap
Detachable rim
Running-board bracket
Steering gearbox
Greaser
Brake rod
Tank support
Reflector
Headlamp shell
Running board
Light switch
Starter switch
Handbrake
Radiator hose
Radiator shell
Headlamp rim
Headlamp
Front wing stay
Carburettor
Bonnet clip
Fender eye bolt

The "people's car"

THE MOST POPULAR CAR in the history of car manufacture is the Volkswagen Beetle, originally called the KdF Wagen. The car was developed in Germany in the 1930s by Dr. Ferdinand Porsche. At that time, Germany had only half the number of cars of Britain or France, and Adolf Hitler took a personal interest in the development of the Volkswagen ("people's car"). The intention was to provide a new industry, new jobs, and a car so cheap that anyone in work could afford it. Dr. Porsche designed a car that was cheap to build and run; its rear-mounted, air-cooled engine cut down the number of parts needed and also reduced weight. However, few civilians managed to obtain the Beetle before the outbreak of the Second World War in 1939. After the war, the Beetle proved so popular that eventually more than 20 million were sold.

WORKING PARTS OF VOLKSWAGEN BEETLE

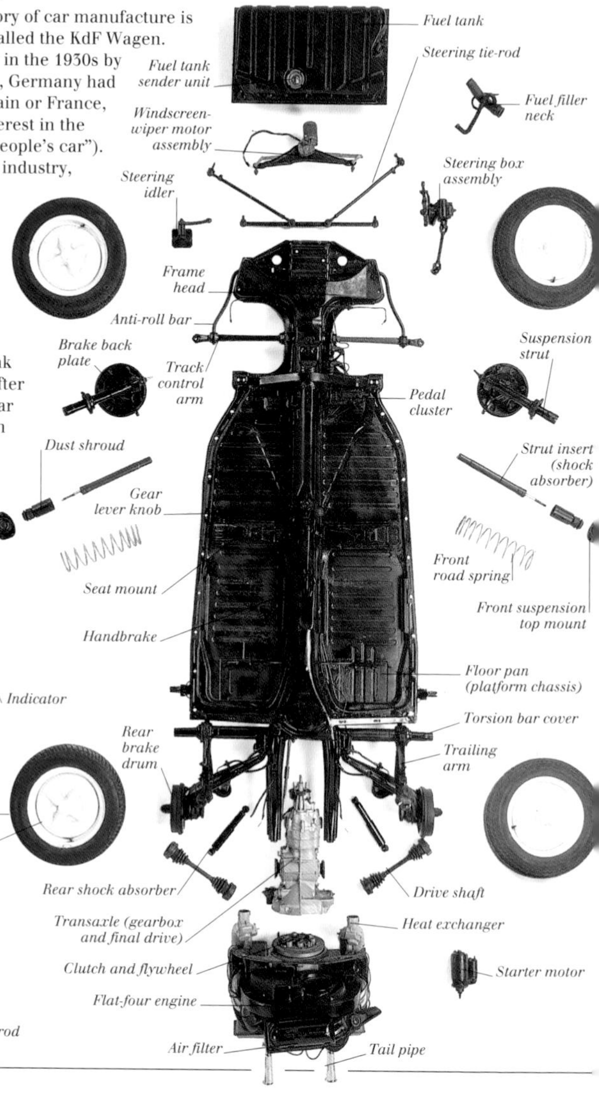
Fuel tank
Steering tie-rod
Fuel tank sender unit
Fuel filler neck
Windscreen-wiper motor assembly
Steering box assembly
Steering idler
Frame head
Anti-roll bar
Suspension strut
Brake back plate
Track control arm
Pedal cluster
Dust shroud
Strut insert (shock absorber)
Front suspension top mount
Gear lever knob
Front road spring
Seat mount
Front suspension top mount
Handbrake
Floor pan (platform chassis)
Torsion bar cover
Rear brake drum
Trailing arm
Tyre
Sports wheel
Rear shock absorber
Drive shaft
Transaxle (gearbox and final drive)
Heat exchanger
Clutch and flywheel
Starter motor
Flat-four engine
Air filter
Tail pipe

CUSTOMIZED VOLKSWAGEN BEETLE

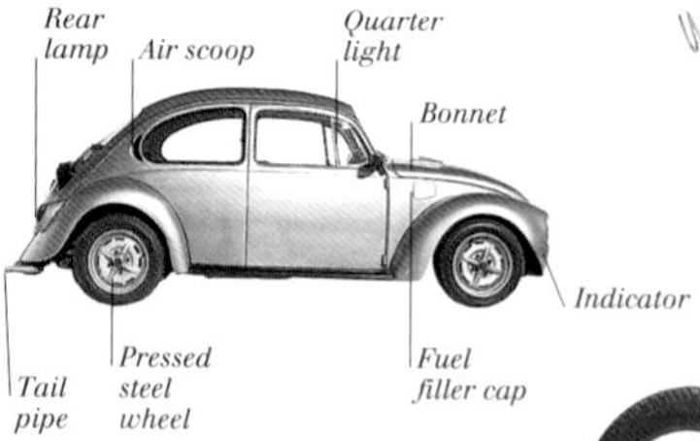
Rear lamp
Air scoop
Quarter light
Bonnet
Indicator
Tail pipe
Pressed steel wheel
Fuel filler cap

FLAT-FOUR CYLINDER ARRANGEMENT

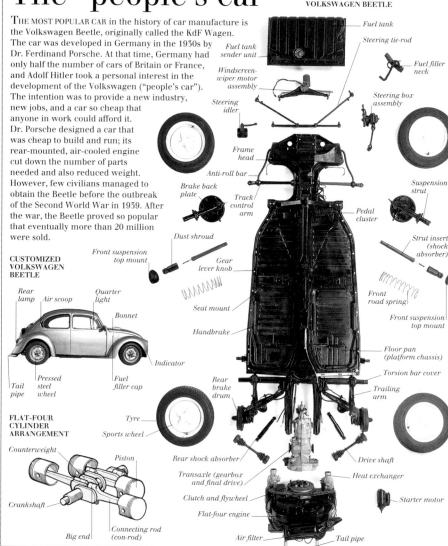

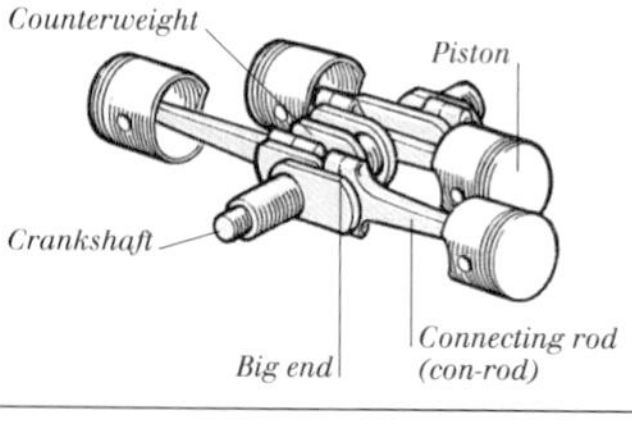
Counterweight
Piston
Crankshaft
Big end
Connecting rod (con-rod)

BODY SHELL OF VOLKSWAGEN BEETLE

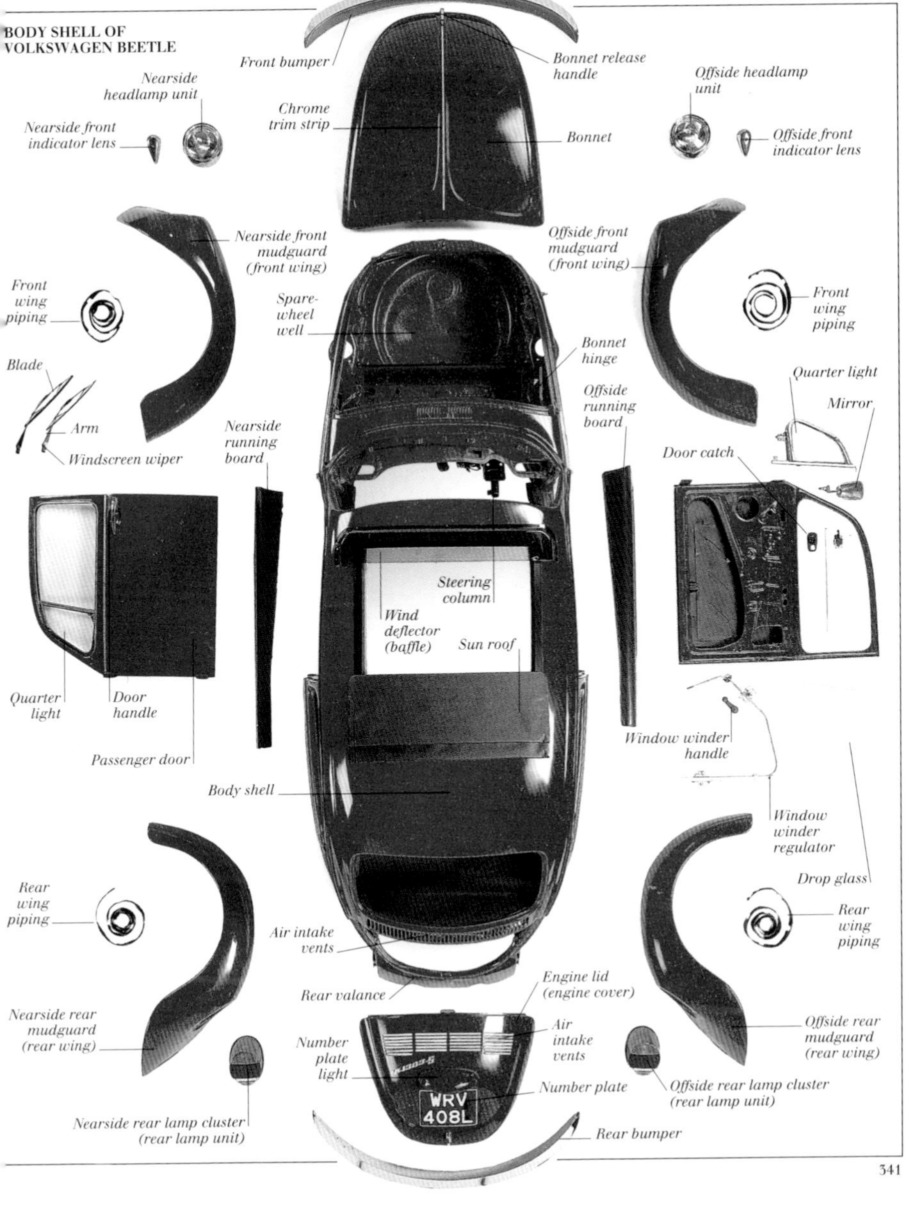
Front bumper
Bonnet release handle
Nearside headlamp unit
Offside headlamp unit
Chrome trim strip
Nearside front indicator lens
Bonnet
Offside front indicator lens
Nearside front mudguard (front wing)
Offside front mudguard (front wing)
Front wing piping
Spare-wheel well
Front wing piping
Bonnet hinge
Blade
Quarter light
Offside running board
Mirror
Arm
Nearside running board
Windscreen wiper
Door catch
Steering column
Wind deflector (baffle)
Sun roof
Quarter light
Door handle
Window winder handle
Passenger door
Body shell
Window winder regulator
Drop glass
Rear wing piping
Rear wing piping
Air intake vents
Rear valance
Engine lid (engine cover)
Nearside rear mudguard (rear wing)
Air intake vents
Offside rear mudguard (rear wing)
Number plate light
Number plate
WRV 408L
Offside rear lamp cluster (rear lamp unit)
Nearside rear lamp cluster (rear lamp unit)
Rear bumper

Early engines

STEAM AND ELECTRICITY were used to power cars until early this century, but neither power source was ideal. Electric cars had to stop frequently to recharge their heavy batteries, and steam cars gave smooth power delivery but were too complicated for the average motorist to use. A rival power source, the internal combustion engine, was invented in 1860 by Etienne Lenoir (see pp. 334-335). This engine converted the force of an explosion into rotary motion, to turn the wheels of a vehicle. Early variations on this basic model included sleeve valves, separately cast cylinders, and the two-stroke combustion cycle. Today, all combustion engines, including the Wankel rotary and diesels (see pp. 346-347), use the four-stroke cycle, first demonstrated by Nikolaus Otto in 1876. The Otto cycle, often described as "suck, squeeze, bang, blow", has proved the best method of ensuring that the engine turns over smoothly and that exhaust emissions are controllable.

TROJAN TWO-STROKE ENGINE, 1927

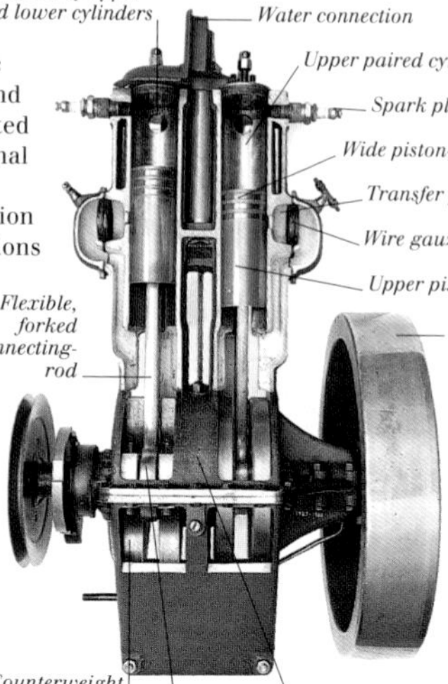
Port linking combustion chambers of upper and lower cylinders
Water connection
Upper paired cylinder
Spark plug
Wide piston-ring
Transfer port
Wire gauze pad
Upper piston
Flywheel
Flexible, forked connecting-rod
Counterweight
Big end
Crankcase

BERSEY ELECTRIC CAB, 1896

Mounting for tray of 40 batteries
Housing for electric motors

SECTIONED WHITE STEAM CAR, 1903

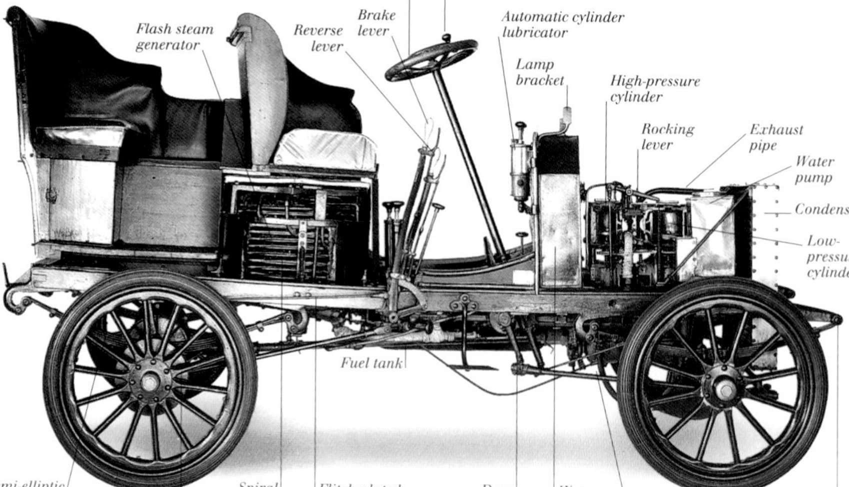
Steering wheel
Throttle wheel
Brake lever
Flash steam generator
Reverse lever
Automatic cylinder lubricator
Lamp bracket
High-pressure cylinder
Rocking lever
Exhaust pipe
Water pump
Condenser
Low-pressure cylinder
Fuel tank
Semi-elliptic spring
Brake drum
Spiral tubes
Flitch-plated wooden chassis
Drop arm
Water tank
Drag link
Dumb iron

CYCLE OF A FOUR-STROKE INTERNAL COMBUSTION ENGINE

INDUCTION STROKE ("SUCK")

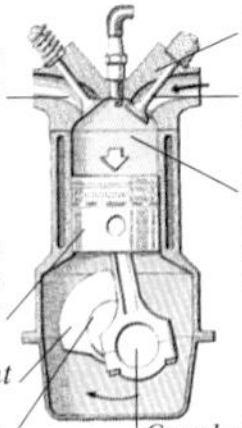
Inlet valve
Exhaust port closed
Inlet port opens
Fuel and air (the "charge") sucked into cylinder
Piston moves downwards
Counterweight
Crankshaft
Crankpin

COMPRESSION STROKE ("SQUEEZE")

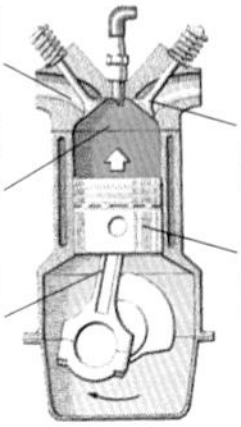
Exhaust port closed
Charge compressed by piston
Inlet port closed
Piston moves upwards
Connecting rod (con-rod)

POWER STROKE ("BANG")

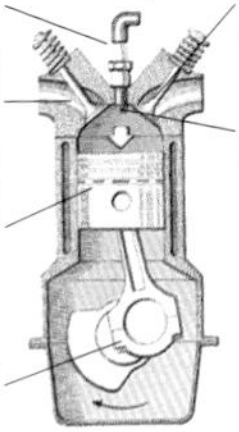
Spark plug
Inlet port closed
Exhaust port closed
Charge ignited by spark plug
Explosion pushes piston downwards
Big end

EXHAUST STROKE ("BLOW")

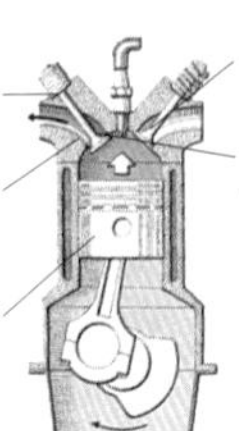
Exhaust valve
Inlet port closed
Exhaust port opens
Burned gases forced out of cylinder
Piston moves upwards

16-HORSEPOWER HUMBER ENGINE, 1911

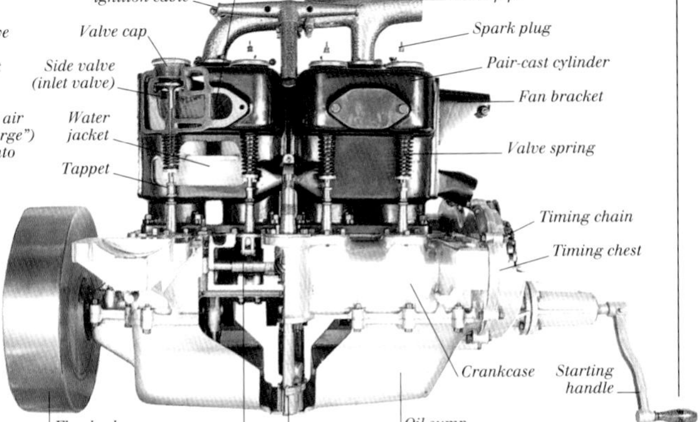
Brass housing for ignition cable
Inlet port
Water pipe
Valve cap
Spark plug
Side valve (inlet valve)
Pair-cast cylinder
Fan bracket
Water jacket
Valve spring
Tappet
Timing chain
Timing chest
Crankcase
Starting handle
Flywheel
Camshaft
Oil pump
Oil sump

DAIMLER DOUBLE-SLEEVE VALVE ENGINE, 1910

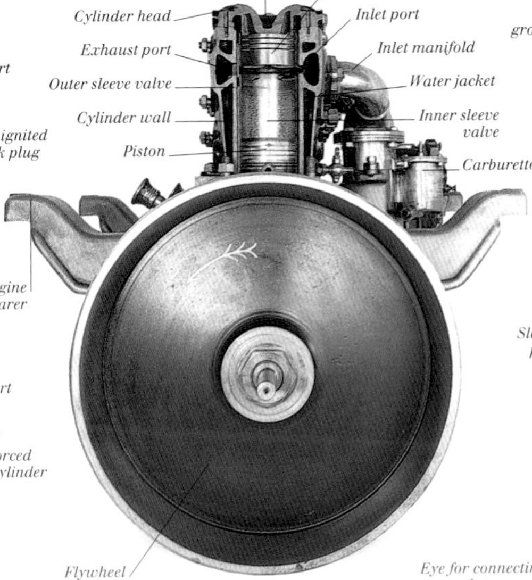
Spark plug socket
Junk ring
Cylinder head
Inlet port
Exhaust port
Inlet manifold
Outer sleeve valve
Water jacket
Cylinder wall
Inner sleeve valve
Piston
Carburettor
Engine bearer
Flywheel

OUTER SLEEVE VALVE

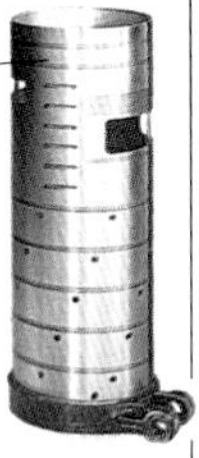
Oil groove

INNER SLEEVE VALVE

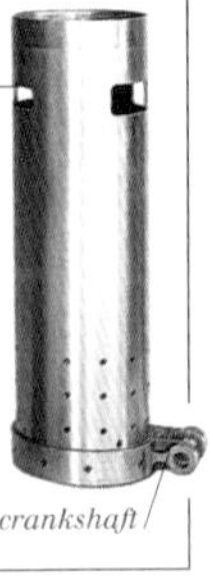
Sleeve port
Eye for connecting con-rods to secondary crankshaft

Modern engines

TODAY'S PETROL ENGINE WORKS on the same basic principles as the first car engines of a century ago, although it has been greatly refined. Modern engines, often made from special metal alloys, are much lighter than earlier engines. Computerized ignition systems, fuel injectors, and multi-valve cylinder heads achieve a more efficient combustion of the fuel/air mixture (the charge) so that less fuel is wasted. As a result of this greater efficiency, the power and performance of a modern engine are increased, and the level of pollution in the exhaust gases is reduced. Exhaust pollution levels today are also lowered by the increasing use of special filters called catalytic converters, which absorb many exhaust pollutants. The need to produce ever more efficient engines means that it can take up to seven years to develop a new engine for a family car, at a cost of many millions of pounds.

FRONT VIEW OF A FORD COSWORTH V6 12-VALVE

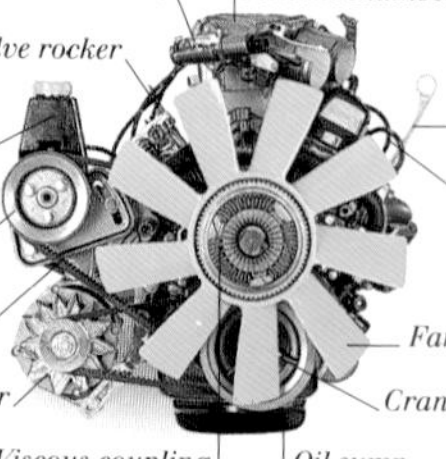

Idle control valve
Plenum chamber
Valve rocker
Power steering pump reservoir
Oil dipstick
High-tension ignition lead (spark plug lead)
Steering pump pulley
Cogged drive belt
Fan
Alternator
Crankshaft pulley
Viscous coupling
Oil sump

FRONT VIEW OF A FORD COSWORTH V6 24-VALVE

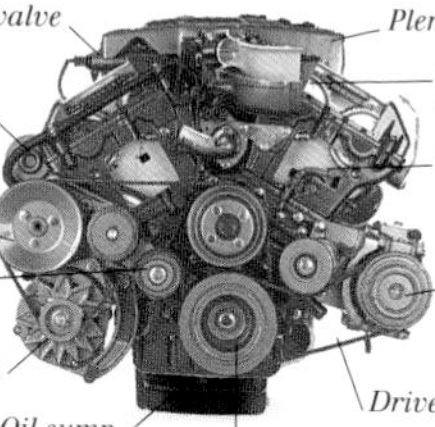

Idle control valve
Plenum chamber
Exhaust gas recirculation valve
Camshaft timing gear
Camshaft chain
Steering pump drive pulley
Belt tensioner
Air conditioning pump
Alternator cooling fan
Drive belt
Oil sump
Crankshaft pulley

SECTIONED VIEW OF A JAGUAR STRAIGHT 6

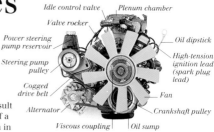

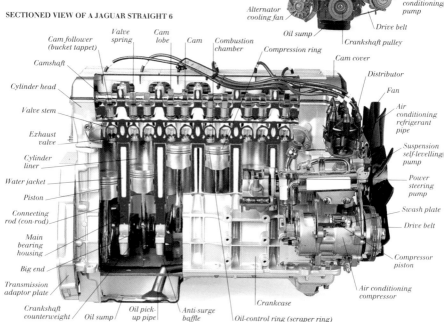

Cam follower (bucket tappet)
Valve spring
Cam lobe
Cam
Combustion chamber
Compression ring
Cam cover
Camshaft
Distributor
Cylinder head
Fan
Valve stem
Air conditioning refrigerant pipe
Exhaust valve
Suspension self-levelling pump
Cylinder liner
Water jacket
Power steering pump
Piston
Swash plate
Connecting rod (con-rod)
Drive belt
Main bearing housing
Compressor piston
Big end
Transmission adaptor plate
Air conditioning compressor
Crankcase
Crankshaft counterweight
Oil sump
Oil pick-up pipe
Anti-surge baffle
Oil-control ring (scraper ring)

FRONT VIEW OF A JAGUAR V12

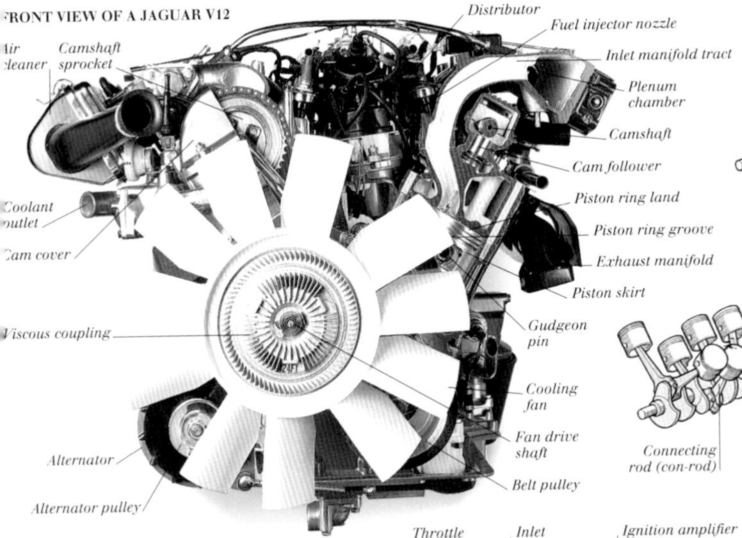
Air cleaner
Camshaft sprocket
Distributor
Fuel injector nozzle
Inlet manifold tract
Plenum chamber
Camshaft
Cam follower
Piston ring land
Piston ring groove
Exhaust manifold
Piston skirt
Gudgeon pin
Coolant outlet
Cam cover
Viscous coupling
Cooling fan
Fan drive shaft
Belt pulley
Alternator
Alternator pulley

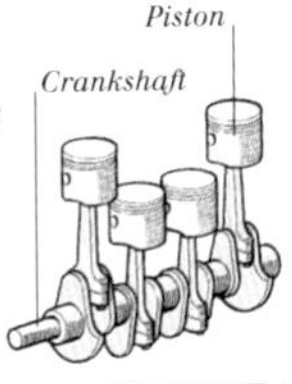
Piston
Crankshaft

STRAIGHT 4 CYLINDER ARRANGEMENT

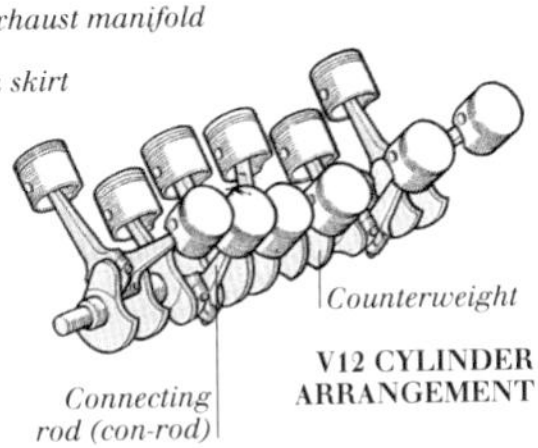
Counterweight
Connecting rod (con-rod)

V12 CYLINDER ARRANGEMENT

SECTIONED VIEW OF A JAGUAR V12

Throttle butterfly
Inlet manifold
Ignition amplifier
Throttle linkage
Fuel pipe
Distributor drive shaft
Air inlet
Exhaust valve
Inlet valve
Cam cover
Timing chain
Oil feed pipe
Piston crown
Cylinder head
Coolant rail (water rail)
Piston ring land
Exhaust heat shield
Water pump
Exhaust manifold
Piston
Oil pipe banjo
Ancillary drive pulley
Drive plate
Timing chain drive sprocket
Starter ring
Connecting rod (con-rod)
Crankcase
Oil filter
Counterweight (balance weight)
Main bearing
Pipe to oil cooler
Sump

Alternative engines

THE MOST COMMON TYPE OF ALTERNATIVE ENGINE is the diesel engine, which, instead of igniting the compressed fuel/air mixture with a spark, uses compression alone, heating the mixture to the point where it explodes. A diesel engine's fuel consumption is low in comparison with similarly sized piston engines, despite its heavier, reinforced moving parts and cylinder block. Another type of engine is the rotary-combustion, first successfully developed by Felix Wankel in the 1950s. Its two trilobate (three-sided) rotors revolve in housings shaped in a fat figure-of-eight. The four sequences of the four-stroke cycle, which occur consecutively in a piston engine, occur simultaneously in a rotary engine, producing power in a continuous stream.

ROTARY-ENGINED MAZDA RX-7

Aerodynamic windscreen
Headrest
Hood bag
Front spoiler (chin spoiler)
Side marker lamp
Rubbing strake
Cast alloy wheel

WANKEL ROTARY ENGINE

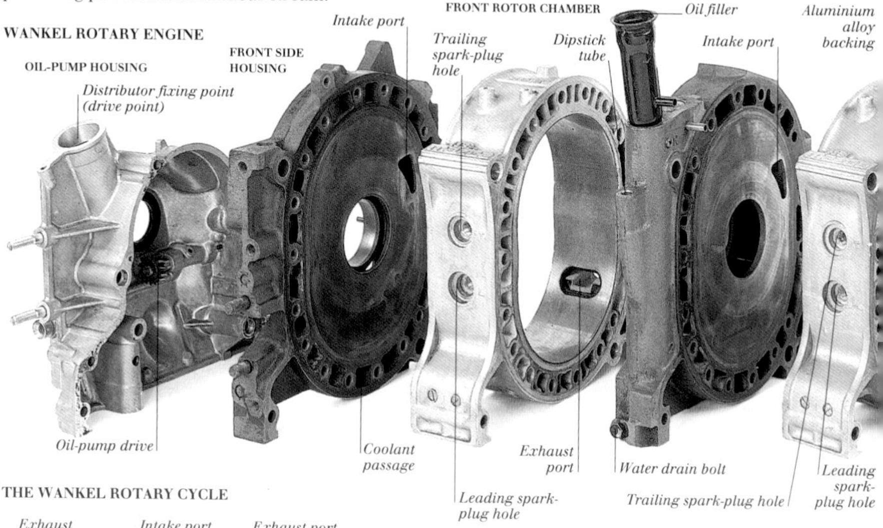

OIL-PUMP HOUSING
FRONT SIDE HOUSING
FRONT ROTOR CHAMBER
INTERMEDIATE HOUSING
REAR ROTOR CHAMBER
Distributor fixing point (drive point)
Intake port
Trailing spark-plug hole
Dipstick tube
Oil filler
Intake port
Aluminium alloy backing
Oil-pump drive
Coolant passage
Exhaust port
Water drain bolt
Leading spark-plug hole
Leading spark-plug hole
Trailing spark-plug hole

THE WANKEL ROTARY CYCLE

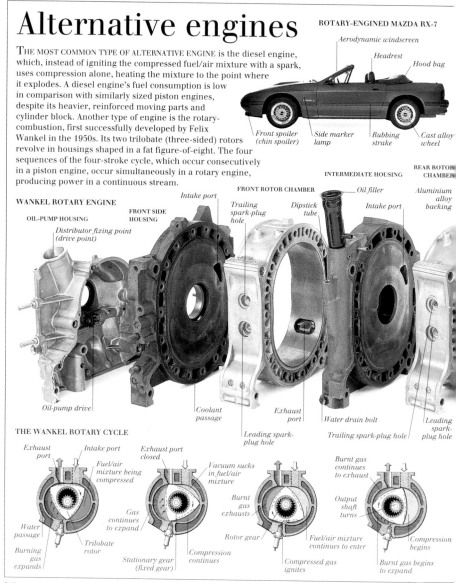

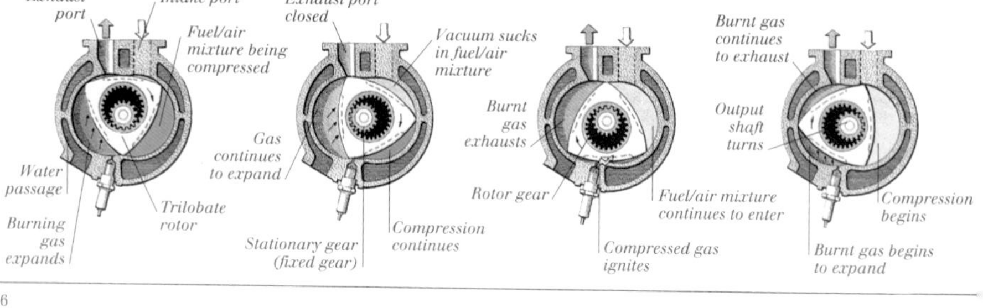

Exhaust port
Intake port
Fuel/air mixture being compressed
Water passage
Burning gas expands
Trilobate rotor
Exhaust port closed
Vacuum sucks in fuel/air mixture
Gas continues to expand
Stationary gear (fixed gear)
Compression continues
Burnt gas exhausts
Rotor gear
Fuel/air mixture continues to enter
Compressed gas ignites
Burnt gas continues to exhaust
Output shaft turns
Compression begins
Burnt gas begins to expand

ORD TURBOCHARGED DIESEL ENGINE

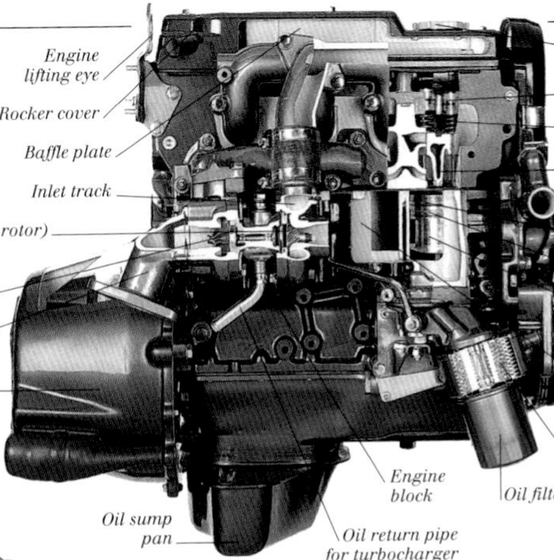
Engine lifting eye
Rocker cover
Baffle plate
Inlet track
Turbo impeller (inlet rotor)
Turbo propeller (exhaust rotor)
Exhaust
Bell housing
Oil sump pan
Oil return pipe for turbocharger
Engine block
Oil filter
Oil cooler matrix
Oil cooler
Water jacket
Ancillary drive belt
Piston
Oil-control ring
Compression ring
Water pump pulley
Water jacket
Valve return spring
Cam follower
Oil filler cap

EAR SIDE HOUSING

Chrome plating
Exhaust port

ROTOR AND SEALS

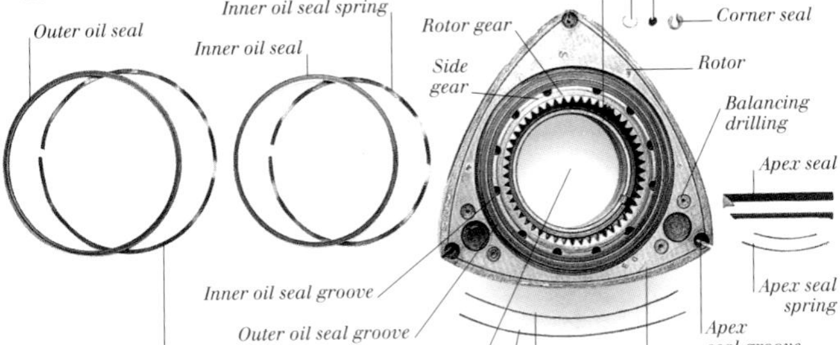
Outer oil seal
Inner oil seal spring
Inner oil seal
Outer oil seal spring
Rotor bearing
Corner seal spring
Corner seal insert
Corner seal
Rotor gear
Side gear
Rotor
Balancing drilling
Apex seal
Apex seal spring
Apex seal groove
Inner oil seal groove
Outer oil seal groove
Hole for output shaft
Side seal
Side seal spring
Side seal groove

OUTPUT SHAFT

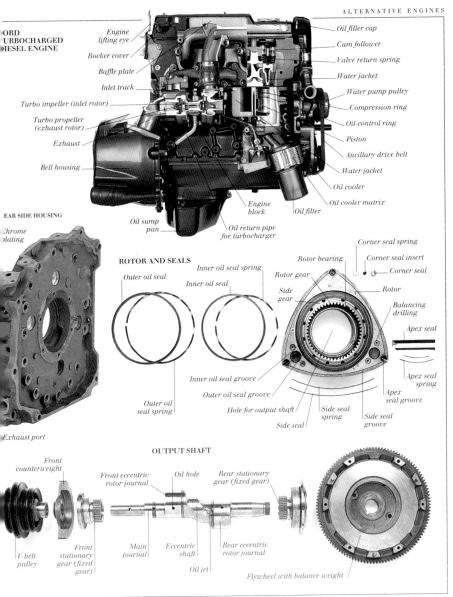

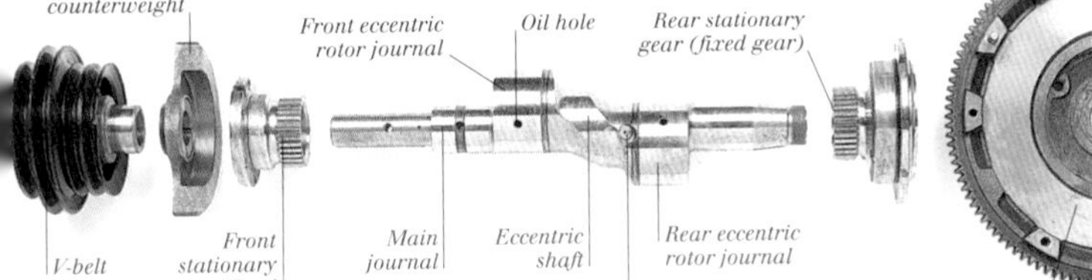
Front counterweight
Front eccentric rotor journal
Oil hole
Rear stationary gear (fixed gear)
V-belt pulley
Front stationary gear (fixed gear)
Main journal
Eccentric shaft
Oil jet
Rear eccentric rotor journal
Flywheel with balance weight

Modern bodywork

RENAULT LOGO

THE BODY OF A MODERN MASS-PRODUCED CAR is built on the monocoque (single-shell) principle, in which the roof, side panels, and floor are welded into a single integral unit. This bodyshell protects and supports the car's internal parts. Steel and glass are used to construct the bodyshell, creating a unit that is both light and strong. Its lightness helps to conserve energy, while its strength protects the occupants. Modern bodywork is designed with the aid of computers, which are used to predict factors such as aerodynamic efficiency and impact-resistance. High-technology is also employed on the production line, where robots are used to assemble, weld, and paint the body.

BODYWORK OF A RENAULT CLI

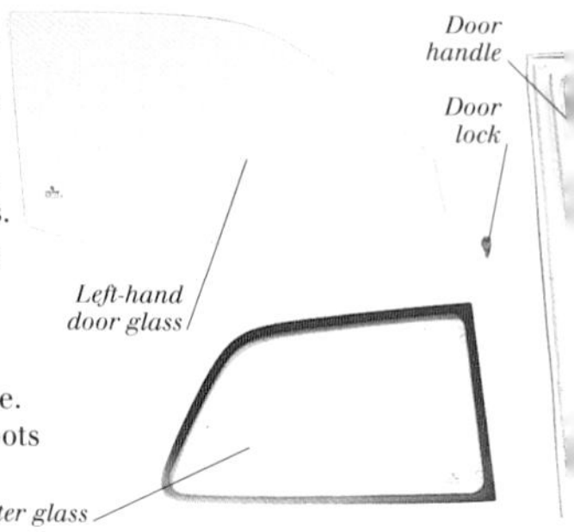
Door handle
Door lock
Left-hand door glass
Left-hand quarter glass

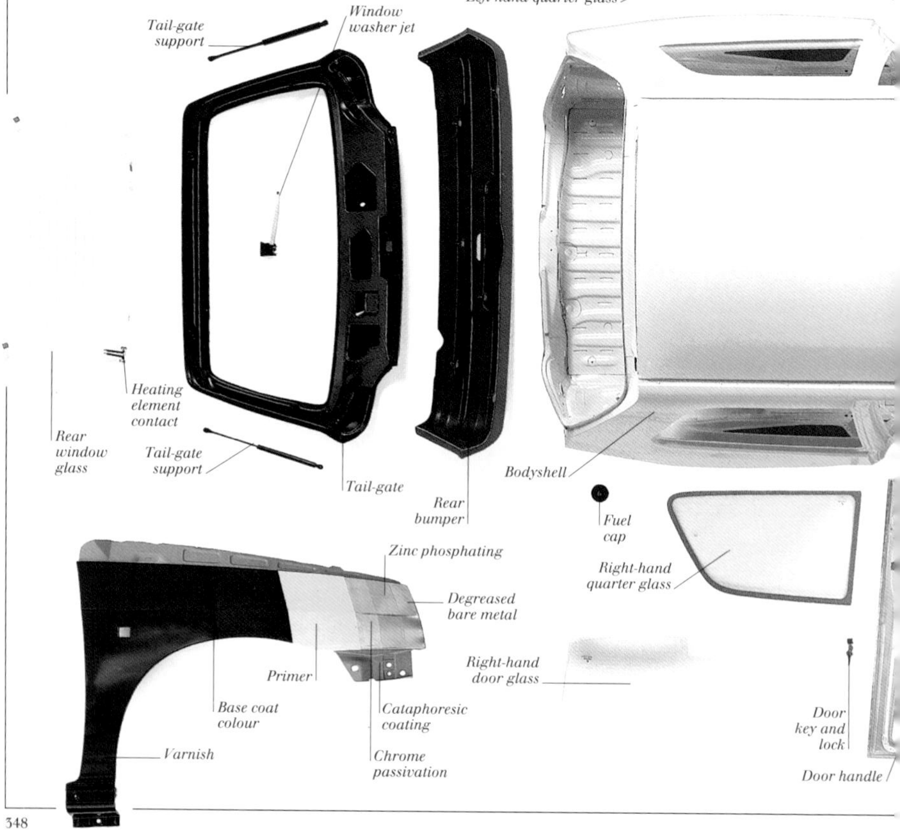
Tail-gate support
Window washer jet
Heating element contact
Rear window glass
Tail-gate support
Tail-gate
Rear bumper
Bodyshell
Fuel cap
Right-hand quarter glass
Zinc phosphating
Degreased bare metal
Right-hand door glass
Primer
Base coat colour
Cataphoresic coating
Varnish
Chrome passivation
Door key and lock
Door handle

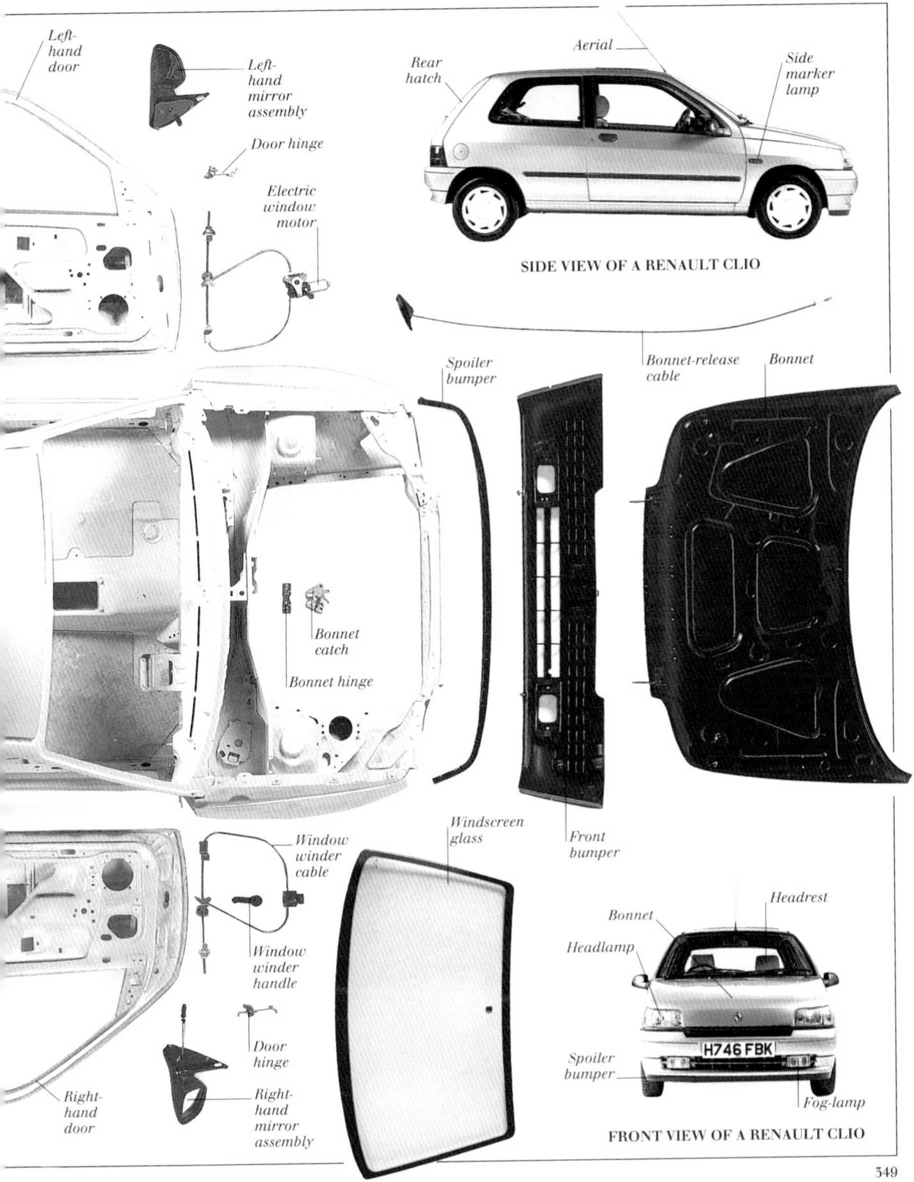
Left-hand door
Left-hand mirror assembly
Door hinge
Electric window motor
Aerial
Rear hatch
Side marker lamp
Bonnet-release cable
Bonnet
Spoiler bumper
Bonnet catch
Bonnet hinge
Windscreen glass
Front bumper
Window winder cable
Window winder handle
Door hinge
Right-hand door
Right-hand mirror assembly
Headrest
Bonnet
Headlamp
H746 FBK
Spoiler bumper
Fog-lamp

SIDE VIEW OF A RENAULT CLIO

FRONT VIEW OF A RENAULT CLIO

Modern mechanics

A TYPICAL MODERN CAR has several thousand individual mechanical components. These are assembled to form the car's various mechanical systems: engine and exhaust, transmission, steering, suspension, and brakes. To ensure that each system functions properly, components are manufactured to extremely fine tolerances – to within a five-hundredth of a millimetre (about one ten-thousandth of an inch) in some cases.

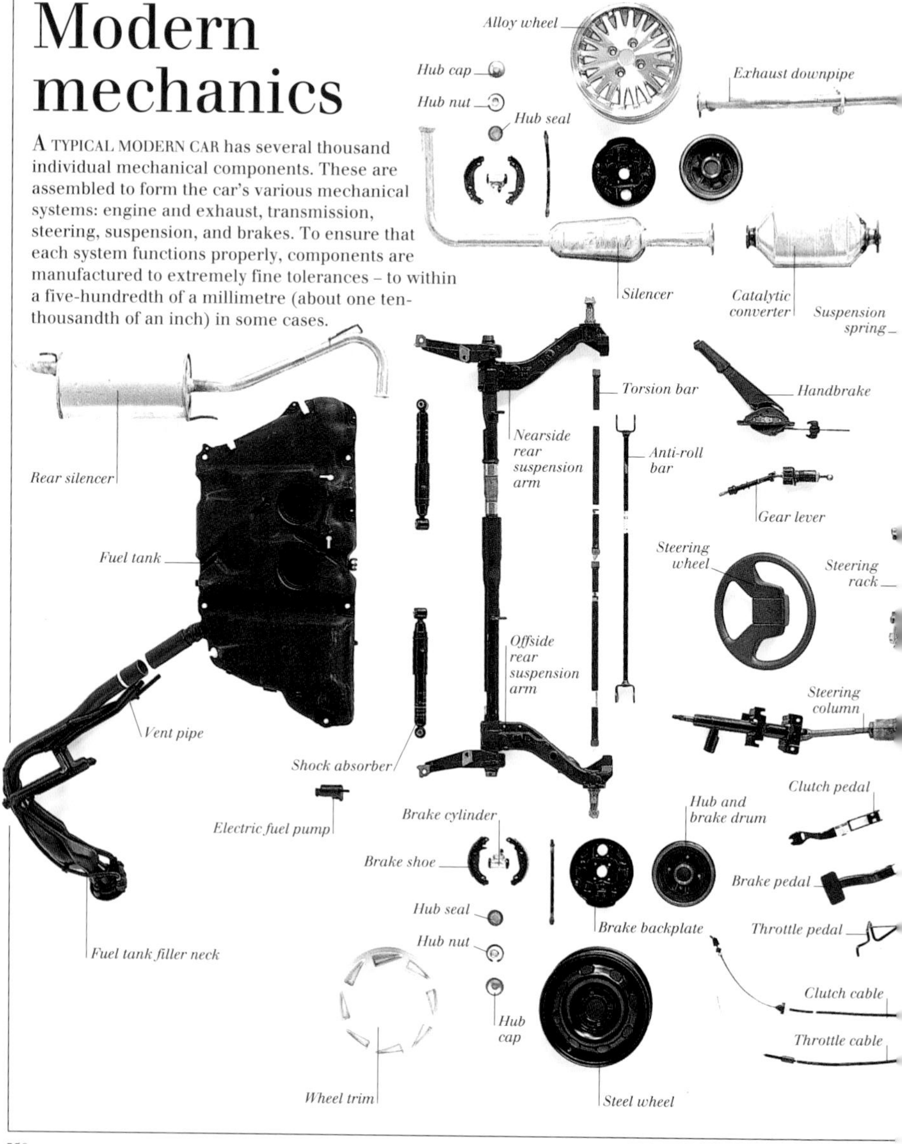
Alloy wheel
Hub cap
Hub nut
Hub seal
Exhaust downpipe
Silencer
Catalytic converter
Suspension spring
Rear silencer
Torsion bar
Handbrake
Nearside rear suspension arm
Anti-roll bar
Gear lever
Fuel tank
Steering wheel
Steering rack
Offside rear suspension arm
Steering column
Vent pipe
Shock absorber
Clutch pedal
Electric fuel pump
Brake cylinder
Hub and brake drum
Brake shoe
Brake pedal
Hub seal
Brake backplate
Throttle pedal
Hub nut
Fuel tank filler neck
Clutch cable
Hub cap
Throttle cable
Wheel trim
Steel wheel

MECHANICAL COMPONENTS OF A RENAULT CLIO, 1991

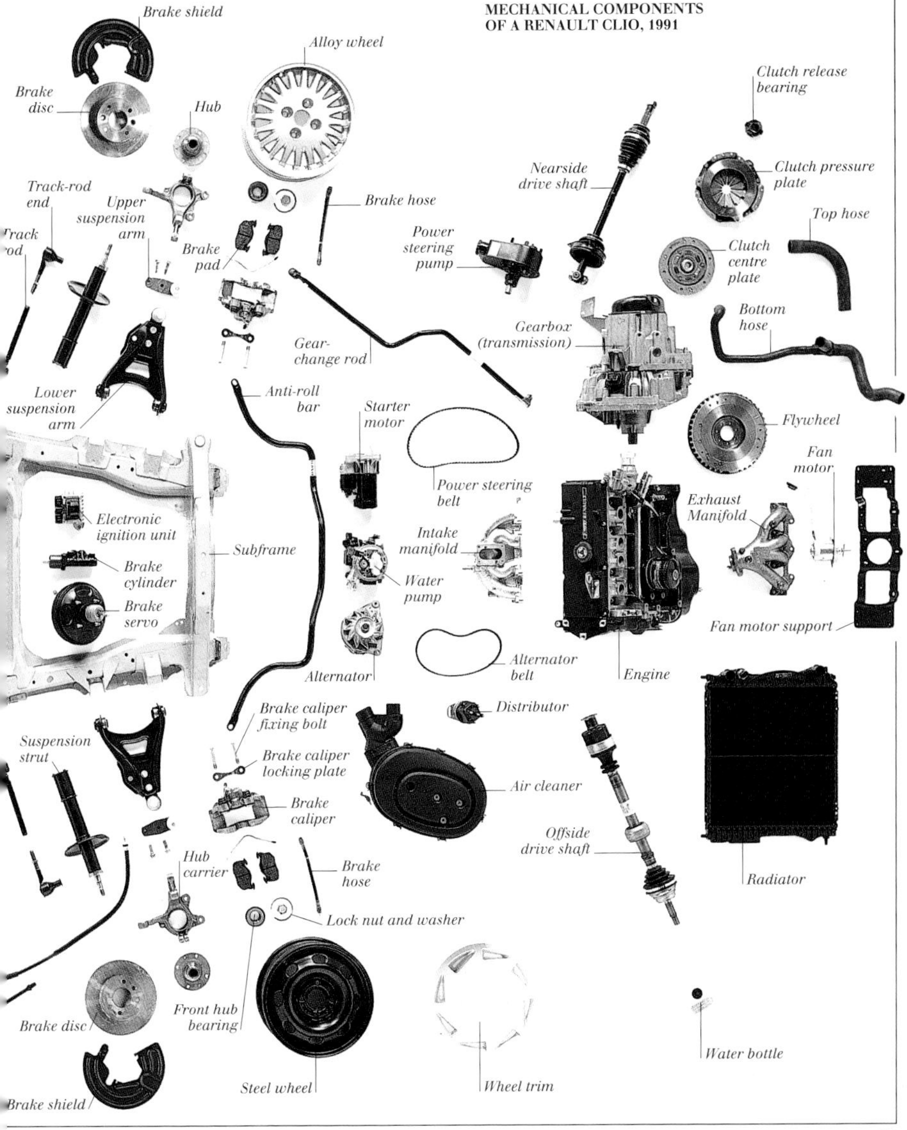
Brake shield
Alloy wheel
Brake disc
Hub
Clutch release bearing
Nearside drive shaft
Clutch pressure plate
Track-rod end
Upper suspension arm
Brake hose
Track rod
Brake pad
Power steering pump
Top hose
Clutch centre plate
Bottom hose
Gearbox (transmission)
Gear-change rod
Lower suspension arm
Anti-roll bar
Starter motor
Flywheel
Fan motor
Power steering belt
Exhaust Manifold
Electronic ignition unit
Intake manifold
Subframe
Brake cylinder
Water pump
Brake servo
Fan motor support
Alternator belt
Alternator
Engine
Distributor
Brake caliper fixing bolt
Suspension strut
Brake caliper locking plate
Air cleaner
Brake caliper
Offside drive shaft
Hub carrier
Brake hose
Radiator
Lock nut and washer
Front hub bearing
Brake disc
Water bottle
Steel wheel
Wheel trim
Brake shield

Modern trim

A MODERN CAR HAS TWO TYPES OF TRIM, according to the materials used: hard (chrome and plastics) and soft (upholstery materials). Safety and comfort are priorities in the trim's design: seats help the occupants to maintain a comfortable posture, rubber seals keep out dirt and moisture, and headlamps light the way. Older cars had interior or leather panelling cut and fitted by craftsmen; modern cars use precisely moulded plastics and seat fabrics cut by robot-controlled lasers to reduce costs and production time. Doors are now trimmed off the production line so that complex wiring can be built in.

TRIM OF A RENAULT CLIO, 1991

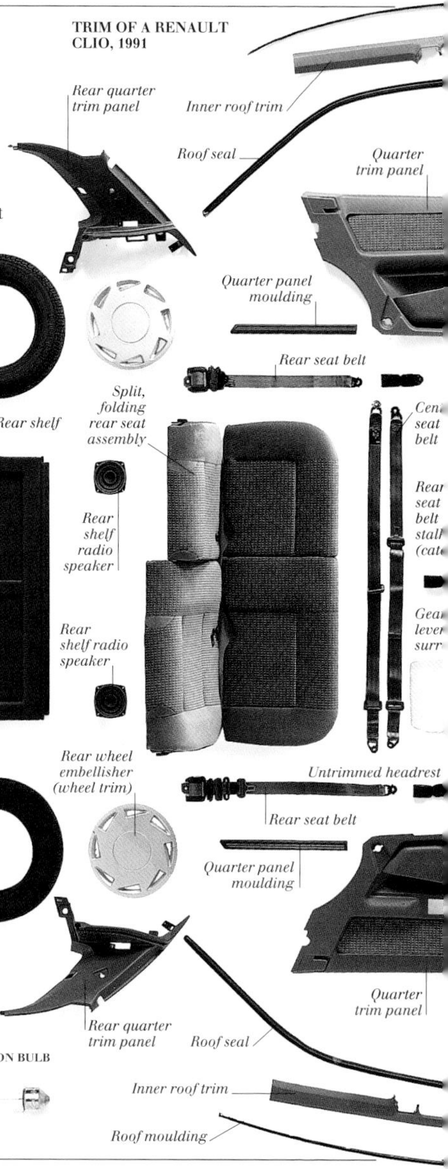
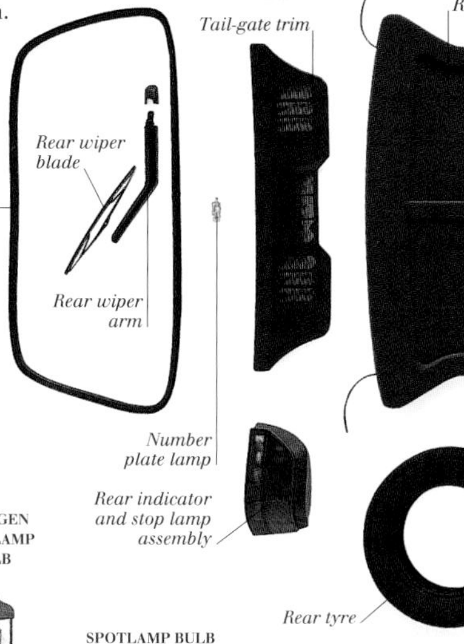
Rear quarter trim panel
Inner roof trim
Roof seal
Quarter trim panel
Quarter panel moulding
Rear seat belt
Rear tyre
Split, folding rear seat assembly
Rear shelf
Tail-gate trim
Rear shelf radio speaker
Rear wiper blade
Tail-gate seal
Rear wiper arm
Rear shelf radio speaker
Number plate lamp
Rear wheel embellisher (wheel trim)
Untrimmed headrest
Rear indicator and stop lamp assembly
Rear seat belt
Quarter panel moulding
Rear tyre
Quarter trim panel
Rear quarter trim panel
Roof seal
Inner roof trim
Roof moulding

HALOGEN HEADLAMP BULB · **SPOTLAMP BULB** · **MARKER LAMP BULB** · **FESTOON BULB**

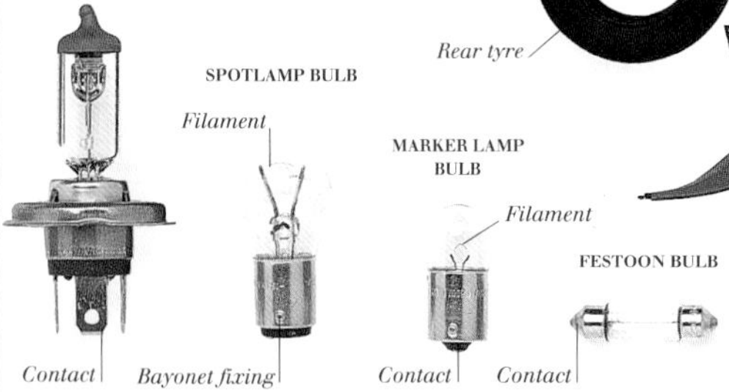
Contact
Filament
Bayonet fixing
Filament
Contact
Contact

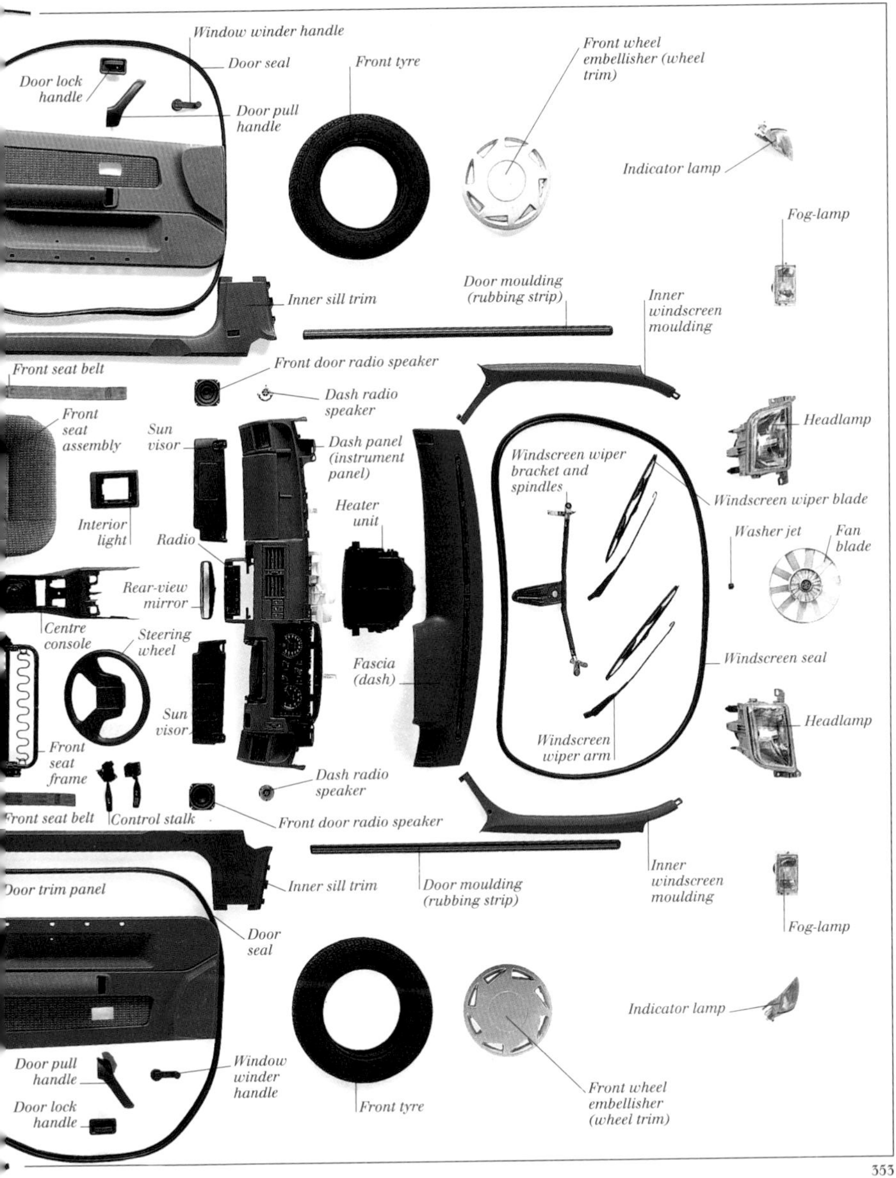
Window winder handle
Door seal
Door lock handle
Door pull handle
Front tyre
Front wheel embellisher (wheel trim)
Indicator lamp
Fog-lamp
Inner sill trim
Door moulding (rubbing strip)
Inner windscreen moulding
Front seat belt
Front door radio speaker
Dash radio speaker
Front seat assembly
Sun visor
Dash panel (instrument panel)
Headlamp
Windscreen wiper bracket and spindles
Windscreen wiper blade
Heater unit
Interior light
Radio
Washer jet
Fan blade
Rear-view mirror
Centre console
Steering wheel
Windscreen seal
Fascia (dash)
Sun visor
Headlamp
Windscreen wiper arm
Front seat frame
Dash radio speaker
ront seat belt
Control stalk
Front door radio speaker
Inner sill trim
Door moulding (rubbing strip)
Inner windscreen moulding
oor trim panel
Fog-lamp
Door seal
Indicator lamp
Door pull handle
Window winder handle
Door lock handle
Front tyre
Front wheel embellisher (wheel trim)

All-terrain vehicles

THE MODERN ALL-TERRAIN VEHICLE has its origins in the US military Jeep of the 1940s and the British Land Rover. Such vehicles have been used for a wide range of purposes, from safari travel to fire-fighting. The principal special features of such cars – including four- or six-wheel drive, high ground clearance, and toughened braking, suspension, and transmission systems – are designed to enable driving under the most difficult off-road conditions. The vehicle shown here is equipped for safari travel and carries a comprehensive range of survival apparatus.

COOKING EQUIPMENT

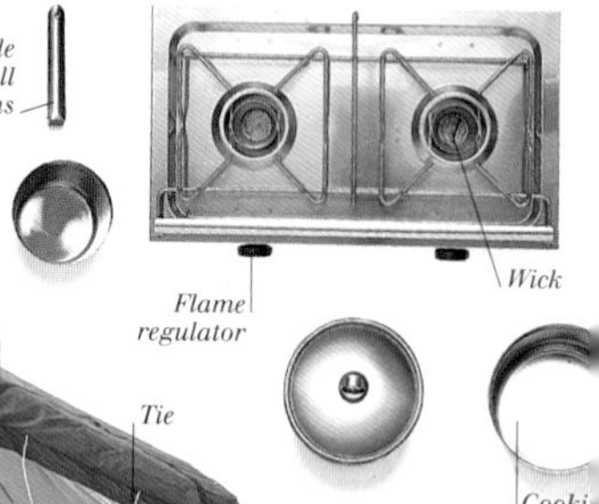
TWO-BURNER ALCOHOL STOVE
Handle for all pans
Flame regulator
Wick
Cooki
pot

HAND WINCH

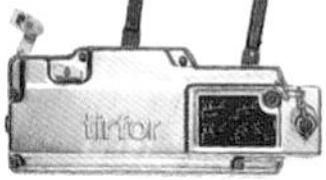

SIDE VIEW OF PINZGAUER TURBO D

Mosquito netting
Zip
Ventilation flap
Tie
Folding rooftop tent
Galvanized roof-rack
Steel body
Jerrycan
Spare wheel and tyre
Rubbing strip (rubbing strake)
Locking fuel filler cap
Dust trap
Raisec air intake
Gua
Heavy-duty shovel
Tubular backbone chassis
Fuel tank
Metal jerrycan for fuel
Plasti jerryca for wate

TYRE PUMP

Pressure gauge

TYRE LEVER

LEFT-HAND TREAD PLATE

RIGHT-HAND TREAD PLATE

TOW STRAP

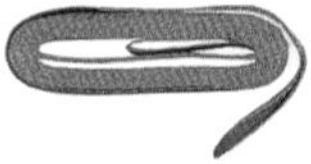

HEAVY-DUTY SHACKLE

SAFETY WINDSCREEN CLAMPS

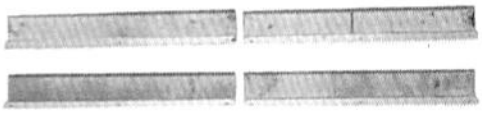

WASHING BUCKET

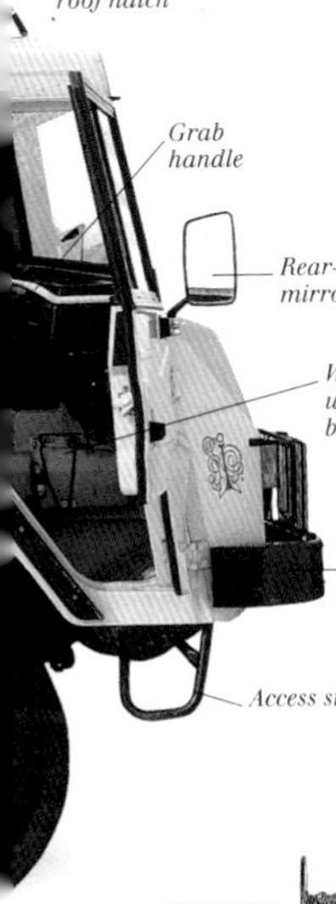

Radio aerial
Observation roof hatch
Grab handle
Rear-view mirror
Windscreen washer bottle
Wrap-around bumper
Access step

SECURITY CHAIN

FRONT VIEW OF PINZGAUER TURBO D

Observation roof hatch
Radio aerial
Galvanized roof-rack
Laminated windscreen
Rear-view mirror
Air vent
Radiator grille
Indicator
Lamp guard
Headlamp
External step
Independent portal swing axle
Locking differential
Towing pintle
Off-road tyre

REAR VIEW OF PINZGAUER TURBO D

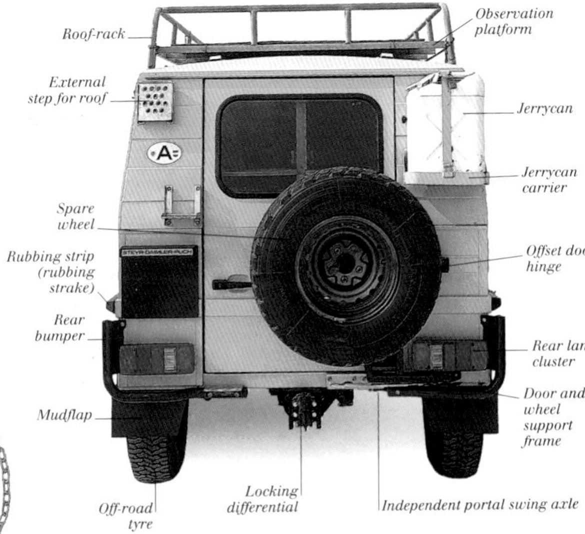

Roof-rack
Observation platform
External step for roof
Jerrycan
Jerrycan carrier
Spare wheel
STEYR-DAIMLER-PUCH
Rubbing strip (rubbing strake)
Offset door hinge
Rear bumper
Rear lamp cluster
Door and wheel support frame
Mudflap
Off-road tyre
Locking differential
Independent portal swing axle

Racing cars

SINCE MOTORING BEGAN, racing cars have been a major focus of innovation in car design. Features that are now commonplace, such as disc brakes, turbochargers, and even safety belts, were used first on competition cars. Research into racing cars has contributed to a new understanding of engine performance, aerodynamics, and tyre adhesion, and has led to the development of ultra-light materials such as carbon-fibre for car bodies. Like the 1937 Bugatti Type 57S below, a modern Williams Formula One car has a low, streamlined body and an open cockpit, but, unlike its forerunner, it also has a front wing that pushes the front wheels firmly on to the track, huge slick tyres for extra grip, and electrical sensors that continually relay information to the pits about the car's performance.

1937 BUGATTI TYPE 57S

Fuel injection trumpet guard (debris guard)
Fuel injector
Cam cover
Cylinder head
Gearbox fixing stud
Mounting point
Electronic control-unit connector
Water outlet
Tail pipe
Stressed cylinder block
Harmonically-tuned exhaust pipe
RENAULT SPORT

RENAULT V10 RS1 ENGINE

OVERHEAD VIEW OF WILLIAMS 1990 FORMULA ONE RACING CA

Diffuser
Bodywork bracket
Heat shield
Forward radius arm
Rear wing upper mainplane
Slot
Upper flap
Half shaft
Rear radius arm
Temperature-sensitive sticker
Aeroquip pipe union
Oil tank
Constant velocity joint cover
Rear wing end-plate
Diffuser
Rear brake duct
Oil feed to engine
Canon

ENGINE COWLING

SIDE FAIRING

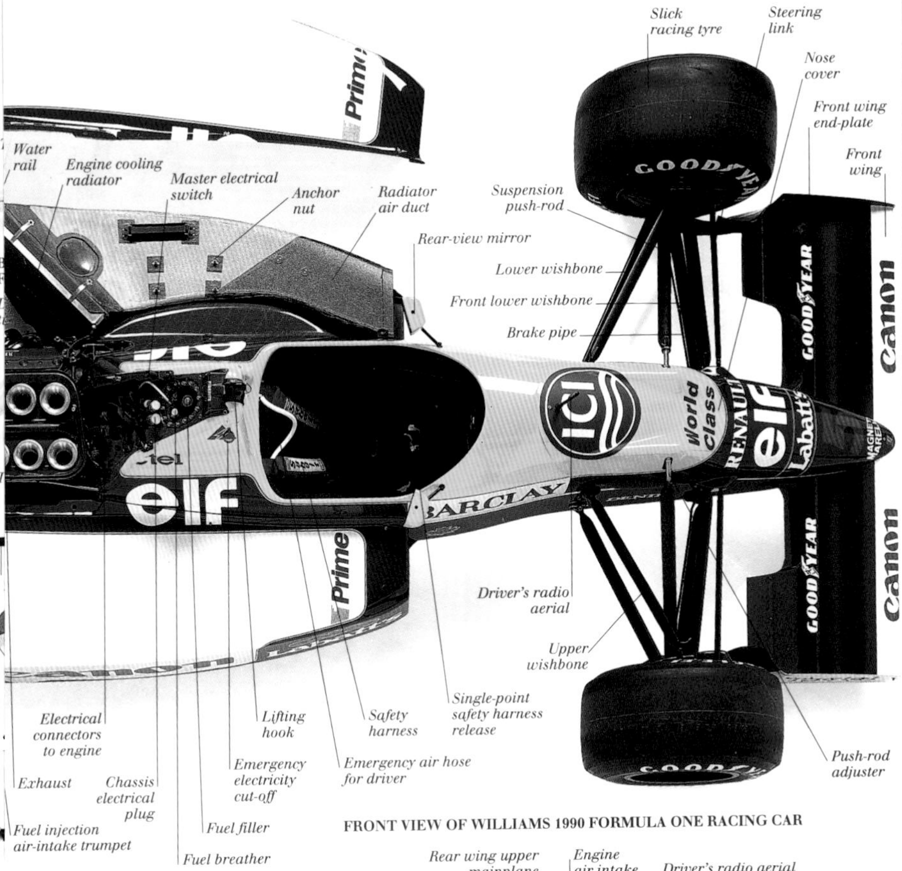
Slick
racing tyre
Steering
link
Nose
cover
Front wing
end-plate
Front
wing
Water
rail
Engine cooling
radiator
Master electrical
switch
Anchor
nut
Radiator
air duct
Suspension
push-rod
Rear-view mirror
Lower wishbone
Front lower wishbone
Brake pipe
Driver's radio
aerial
Upper
wishbone
Electrical
connectors
to engine
Lifting
hook
Safety
harness
Single-point
safety harness
release
Push-rod
adjuster
Exhaust
Chassis
electrical
plug
Emergency
electricity
cut-off
Emergency air hose
for driver
Fuel injection
air-intake trumpet
Fuel filler
Fuel breather

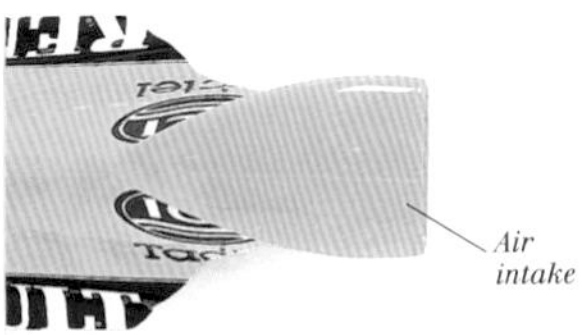
Air
intake

FRONT VIEW OF WILLIAMS 1990 FORMULA ONE RACING CAR

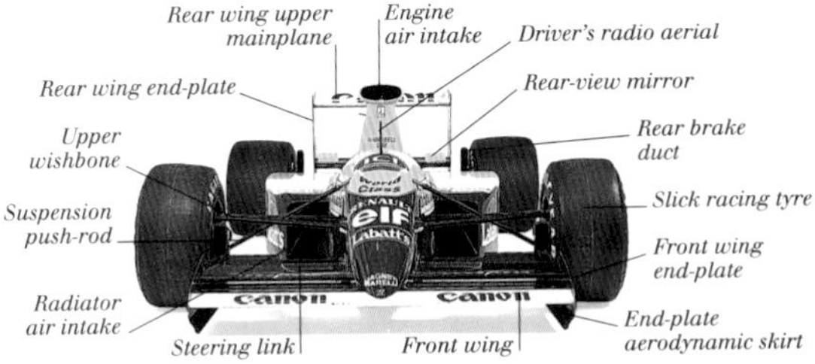
Rear wing upper
mainplane
Engine
air intake
Driver's radio aerial
Rear wing end-plate
Rear-view mirror
Upper
wishbone
Rear brake
duct
Slick racing tyre
Suspension
push-rod
Front wing
end-plate
Radiator
air intake
End-plate
aerodynamic skirt
Steering link
Front wing

Bicycles

ALTHOUGH ALL BICYCLES are made up of the same basic components, they can vary greatly in design. A racing bike, such as the Eddy Merckx model, with its light frame and steep head- and seat-angles, is built for speed. Its design forces the rider to adopt the "aerotuck", a crouched, aerodynamic position. While a touring bike resembles the racing bike in many respects, it is designed for comfort and stability on long-distance journeys. Touring bikes are characterized by more relaxed frame angles, heavy chain stays that support the rear panniers, and a long wheelbase (the distance between the wheel axles) for reliable handling. All-round bicycles, known as "hybrids", combine the light weight and speed of sports bikes with the rugged durability of mountain bikes (see pp. 358-359). Bicycles that are not designed for conventional road use include time-trial bikes, which have a short head tube, sloping top tube, "aero" handlebars, and aerodynamic tubing. Most Human Powered Vehicles (HPVs) are recumbents – the rider has a recumbent position – which maximize power output and minimize drag (resistance). Essential to the safety of all riders are helmets, and both front and rear lights; locks protect against theft.

FRONT AND REAR LIGHTS

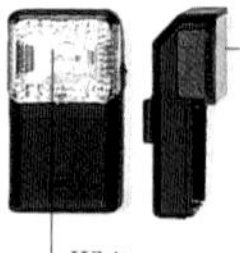
Red rear light
White front light

HELMET

Hard outer shell
Air vent
Polystyrene padding
Quick-release strap

EDDY MERCKX RACING BICYCLE

Saddle
Saddle clamp
Seat post
Cable guide
Seat-post bolt
Rear brake cable
Brake-block bolt
Top tube (crossbar)
Steel frame
Brake block
Seat stay
Seat tube
Down tube
Tyre
Tyre tread
Tyre wall
Wheel rim
Freewheel sprocket
Water-bottle cage
Front derailleur
Chain ring
Crank
Spider
Crank bolt
Pedal
Chain stay
Toe clip
Rear derailleur
Pulley bolt
Tension pulley
Chain

STEEL LOCK

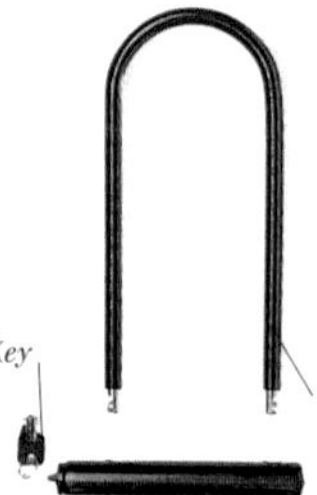
Key
Hardened steel
Pick-proof lock

CANNONDALE SH600 HYBRID BICYCLE

Gel-filled saddle
Light-weight frame
Straight handlebar
Brake bridge
Cantilever brake
All-surface tyre

CANNONDALE ST1000 TOURING BICYCLE

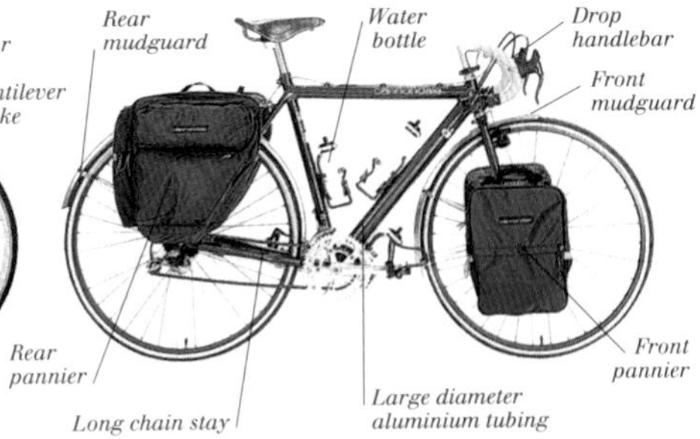
Rear mudguard
Water bottle
Drop handlebar
Front mudguard
Rear pannier
Front pannier
Long chain stay
Large diameter aluminium tubing

Headset
Stem
Binder bolt
Handlebar
Front brake cable
Brake lever
Head tube
Brake pivot bolt
Brake pad
Fork
Hub quick-release lever
Spoke
Spoke nipple
Presta valve
Hub

ROSSIN ITALIAN TIME-TRIAL BICYCLE

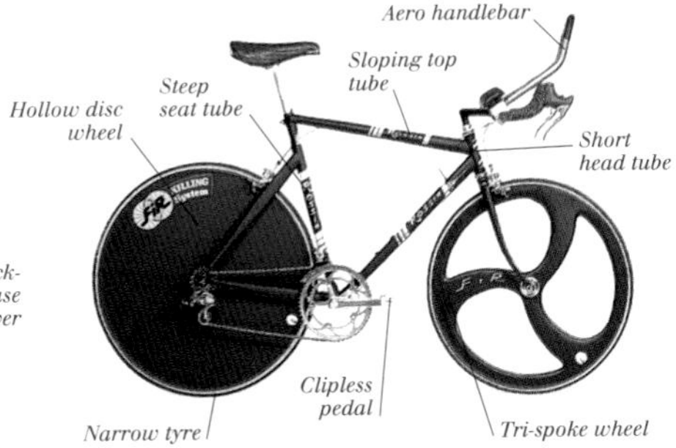
Aero handlebar
Sloping top tube
Steep seat tube
Hollow disc wheel
Short head tube
Clipless pedal
Narrow tyre
Tri-spoke wheel

WINDCHEETAH SL MARK VI "SPEEDY" RACING HPV BICYCLE

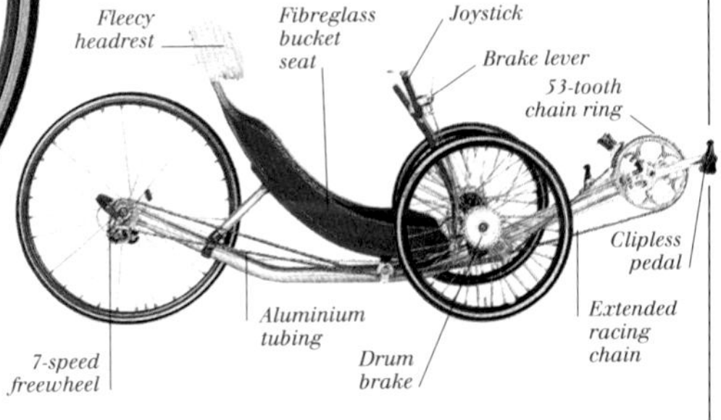
Fleecy headrest
Fibreglass bucket seat
Joystick
Brake lever
53-tooth chain ring
Clipless pedal
Aluminium tubing
Extended racing chain
Drum brake
7-speed freewheel

The motorcycle

THE MOTORCYCLE HAS EVOLVED from a motorized cycle – a basic bicycle with an engine – into a sophisticated, high-performance machine. In 1901, the Werner brothers established the most viable location for the engine by positioning it low in the centre of the chassis (see pp. 364-365): the new Werner became the basis for the modern motorcycle. Motorcycles are used for many purposes – for commuting, delivering messages, touring, and racing – and different machines have been developed according to the demands of different types of riders. The Vespa scooter, for instance, which is small-wheeled, economical, and easy-to-ride, was designed to meet the needs of the commuter. Sidecars provided transport for the family until the arrival of cheap cars caused their popularity to decline. Enthusiast riders generally favour larger capacity machines that are capable of greater performance and offer more comfort. Four-cylinder machines have been common since the Honda CB750 appeared in 1969. Despite advances in motorcycle technology, many riders are attracted to the traditional looks of motorcycles like the twin-cylinder Harley-Davidson. The Harley-Davidson Glides exploit the style of the classic American V-twin engine, where the cylinders are placed in a V-formation.

1901 WERNER MOTORCYCLE

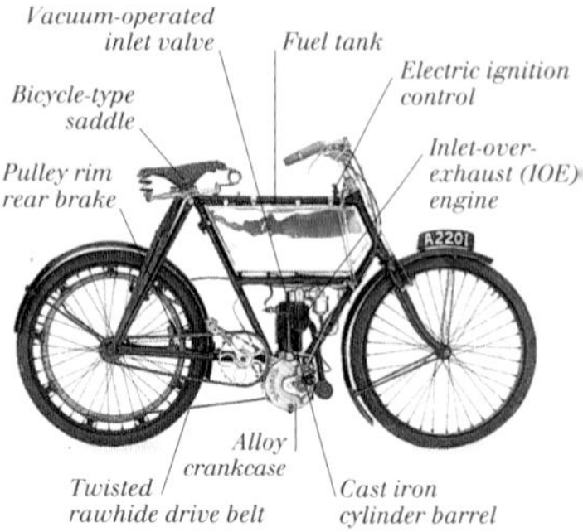
Vacuum-operated inlet valve
Fuel tank
Electric ignition control
Bicycle-type saddle
Inlet-over-exhaust (IOE) engine
Pulley rim rear brake
A2201
Alloy crankcase
Twisted rawhide drive belt
Cast iron cylinder barrel

1988 HARLEY-DAVIDSON FLHS ELECTRA GLIDE

Backrest
Passenger seat
Passenger grab rail
Pannier
Luggage rack
Licence plate
Tail-light
Indicator
Side reflector
Silencer
Silencer bracket
Disc brake
Crash bar
Exhaust clamp

1965 BMW R/60 WITH 1952 STEIB CHAIR

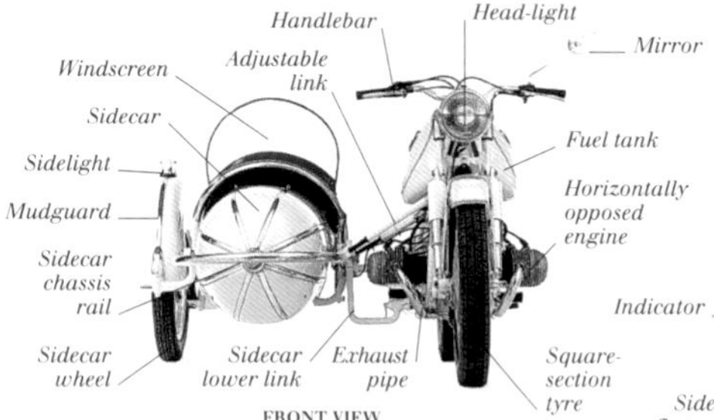
Handlebar
Head-light
Mirror
Windscreen
Adjustable link
Sidecar
Fuel tank
Sidelight
Mudguard
Horizontally opposed engine
Sidecar chassis rail
Sidecar wheel
Sidecar lower link
Exhaust pipe
Square-section tyre

FRONT VIEW

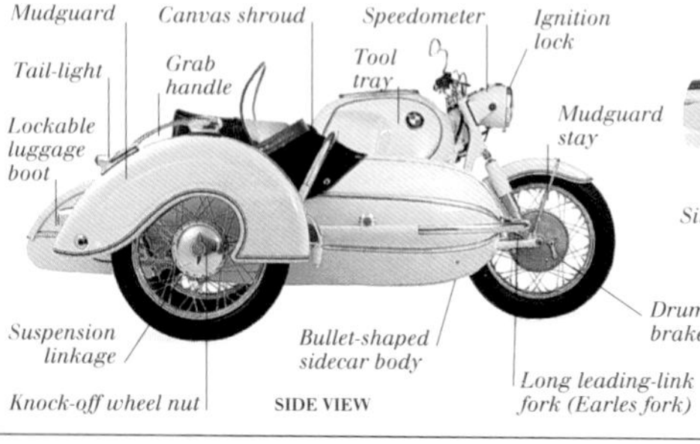
Mudguard
Canvas shroud
Speedometer
Ignition lock
Tail-light
Grab handle
Tool tray
Lockable luggage boot
Mudguard stay
Drum brake
Suspension linkage
Bullet-shaped sidecar body
Knock-off wheel nut
Long leading-link fork (Earles fork)

SIDE VIEW

1969 HONDA CB750

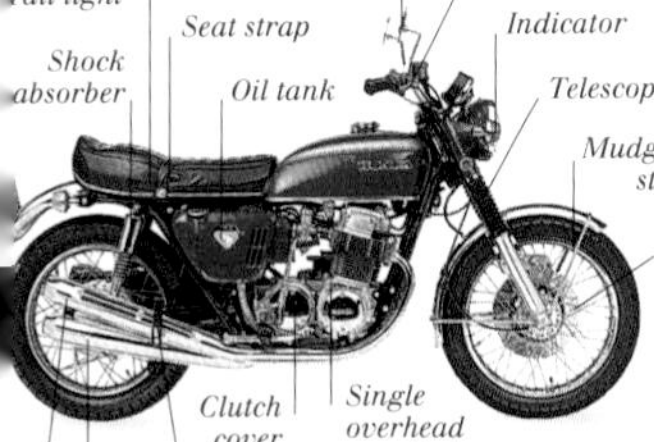
Tail-light
Seat
Mirror
Front brake lever
Seat strap
Indicator
Shock absorber
Oil tank
Telescopic fork
Mudguard stay
Disc brake
Clutch cover
Single overhead camshaft engine
Heat shield
Passenger footrest
Exhaust pipe

1963 VESPA GRAND SPORT 160 MARK 1

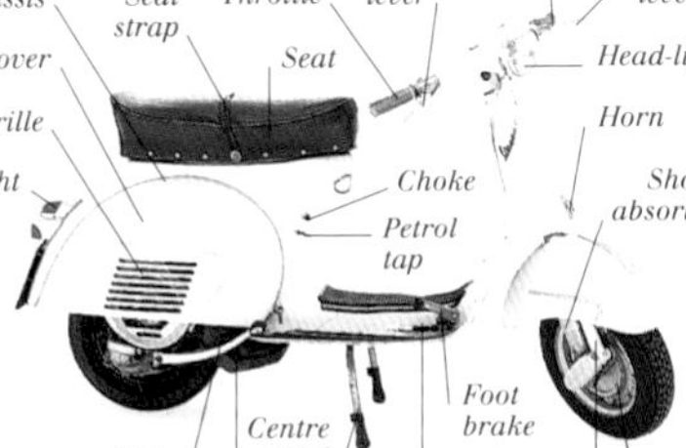
Twist grip gear change
Monocoque chassis
Seat strap
Throttle
Front brake lever
Clutch lever
Engine cover
Seat
Head-light
Cooling grille
Horn
Tail-light
Choke
Shock absorber
Petrol tap
Foot brake
Kick-starter
Centre stand
Silencer
Rubber foot mat
Drum brake
Single-sided trailing-link fork

Mirror
Brake master cylinder
Windscreen
Handgrip
Clutch cable
Front brake lever
Throttle cable
Light switch
added seat
Manufacturer's logo
Windscreen adjustor
Head-light
Oil tank filler cap
Fuel tank
Fog-lamp
Oil tank
Indicator
Telescopic fork
Side reflector
Mudguard
Gearbox
Air filter
Crash bar
45° V-twin engine
assenger
otrest
Exhaust pipe
Duplex tubular cradle frame
Footrest
Brake pedal
Brake calliper
Disc brake
Cast alloy wheel

The motorcycle chassis

THE MOTORCYCLE CHASSIS is the main "body" of the motorcycle, to which the engine is attached. Consisting of the frame, wheels, suspension, and brakes, the chassis performs various functions. The frame, which is built from steel or alloy, keeps the wheels in line to maintain the handling of the motorcycle, and serves as a structure for mounting other components. The engine and gearbox unit is bolted into place, while items such as the seat, the mudguards, and the fairing are more easily removable. Suspension cushions the rider from irregularities in the road surface. In most suspension systems, coil springs controlled by an oil damper separate the main mass of the motorcycle from the wheels. At the front, the spring and damper are usually incorporated in a telescopic fork; the rear employs a pivoted swingarm. The suspension also helps to retain maximum contact between the tyres and the road, necessary to effective braking and steering. Drum brakes were common until the 1970s, but modern motorcycles use disc brakes, which are more powerful.

1985 HONDA VF750 WITH BODYWORK

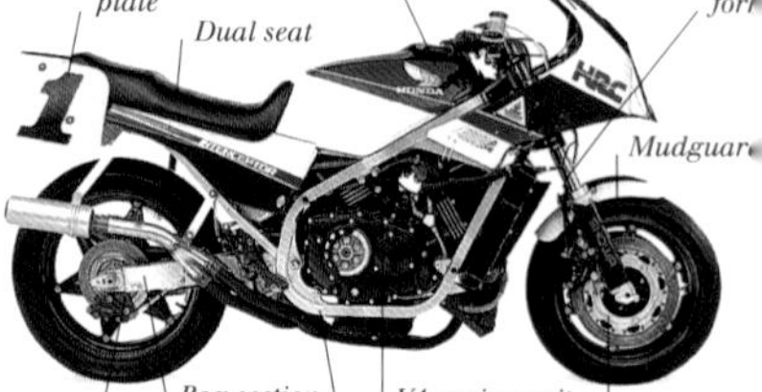
Racing number plate
Dual seat
Fuel tank
Frame-mounted fairing
Telescopi fork
Mudguar
Disc brake
Box-section swingarm
V4 engine unit
Box-section tubular cradle frame
Floating disc brake

1985 HONDA VF750 WITH BODYWORK REMOVED

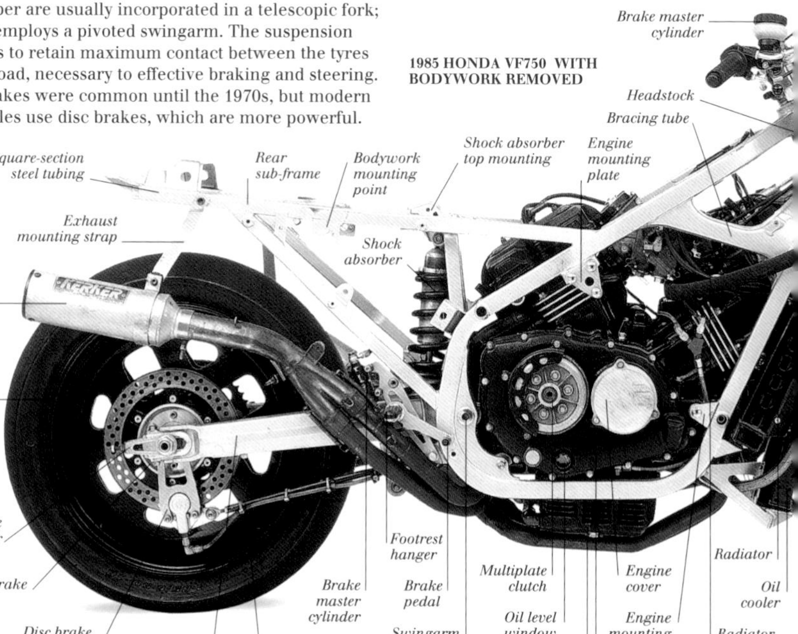
Brake master cylinder
Headstock
Bracing tube
Square-section steel tubing
Rear sub-frame
Bodywork mounting point
Shock absorber top mounting
Engine mounting plate
Exhaust mounting strap
Shock absorber
Exhaust pipe
Light alloy wheel
Axle adjustor
Disc brake
Disc brake calliper
Box-section swingarm
Brake torque arm
Brake master cylinder
Footrest hanger
Brake pedal
Swingarm pivot
Multiplate clutch
Oil level window
Oil sump
V4 engine unit
Engine cover
Engine mounting bolt
Radiator
Oil cooler
Radiator pipe

Clutch cable
Hydraulic brake hose
Telescopic fork leg
Fork slide
Light alloy wheel
Axle
Floating disc brake
Brake calliper

DRUM BRAKE

EXTERIOR OF DRUM BRAKE

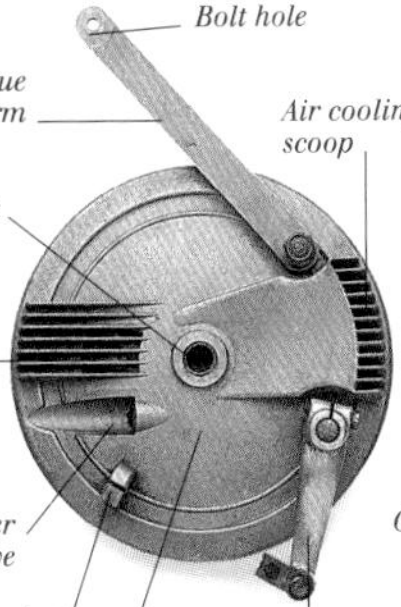
Bolt hole
Torque arm
Air cooling scoop
Axle hole
Cooling fin
Speedometer drive
Cable stop
Brake plate
Operating arm

INTERIOR OF DRUM BRAKE

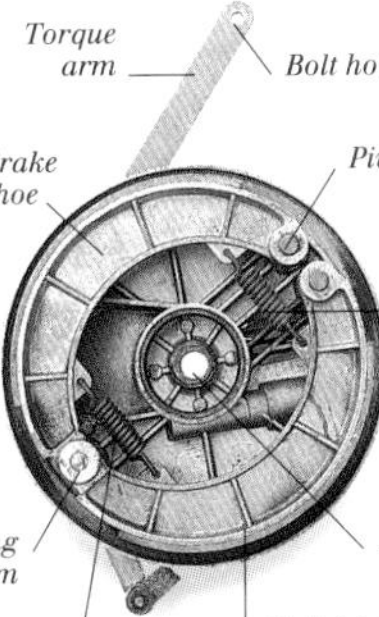
Torque arm
Bolt hole
Brake shoe
Pivot
Brake shoe return spring
Operating cam
Axle hole
Brake shoe return spring
High-friction material

OPERATING PARTS OF DISC BRAKE SYSTEM

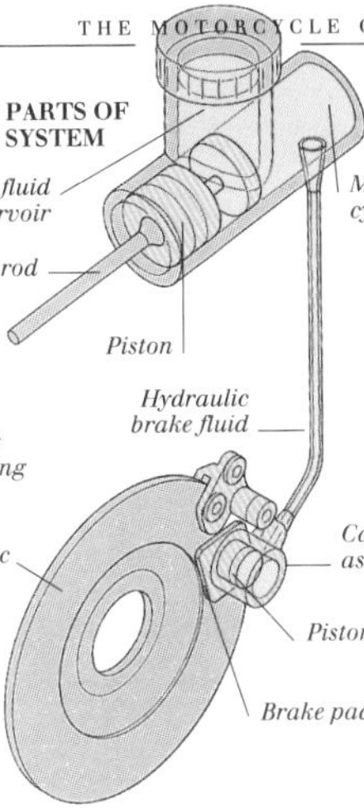
Brake fluid reservoir
Master cylinder
Push-rod
Piston
Hydraulic brake fluid
Wheel disc
Calliper assembly
Piston
Brake pad

SPRING/DAMPER UNIT

Rubber mounting bush
Twin rate spring
Damper rod
Damper body
Pre-load adjustor
Rubber mounting bush

HOW A SPRING/DAMPER UNIT WORKS

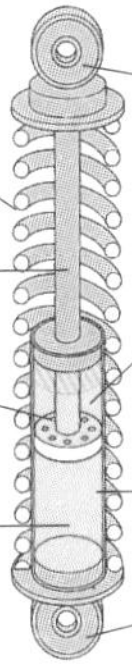
Rubber mounting bush
Spring
Damper rod
Compressible gas
Non-return valve
Hydraulic fluid
Hydraulic fluid chamber
Rubber mounting bush

TYPES OF TYRE

RACING SLICK TYRE

TUBELESS SPORTS TYRE

TRIALS TYRE

GENERAL -USE TYRE

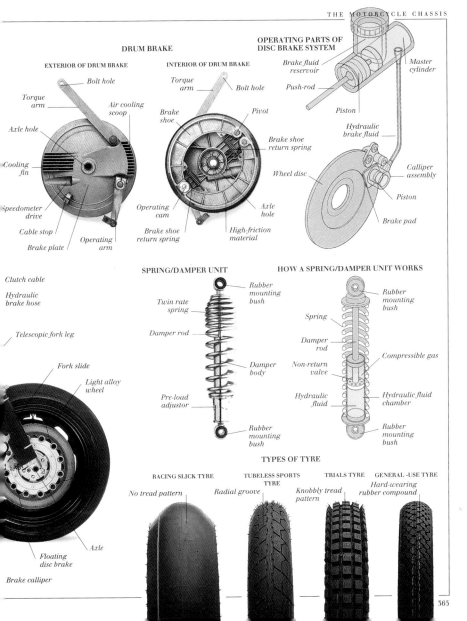

No tread pattern
Radial groove
Knobbly tread pattern
Hard-wearing rubber compound

Motorcycle engines

MOTORCYCLE ENGINES must be light-weight and compact, and have a good power output. They have between one and six cylinders, can be cooled by air or water, and the capacity of the combustion chamber varies from 49cc (cubic centimetres) to 1500cc. Two types of internal combustion engine are common: the four-stroke, which is used in cars (see pp. 342-343), and the two-stroke. A basic two-stroke engine has only three moving parts – the crankshaft, the connecting rod, and the piston – but the power output is high. The engine fires every two strokes (rather than every four), giving a "power stroke" every revolution (see p. 343). Power is conveyed from the engine to the rear wheel by the transmission system. This usually consists of a clutch, a gearbox, and a final drive system. Clutches are multiplate devices, which run in oil. Gearboxes have five or six speeds and are operated by foot pedal. Shaft and belt drive systems are used in some cases, but chain drive to the rear wheel is most common.

EXTERIOR OF STANDARD TWO-STROKE ENGINE

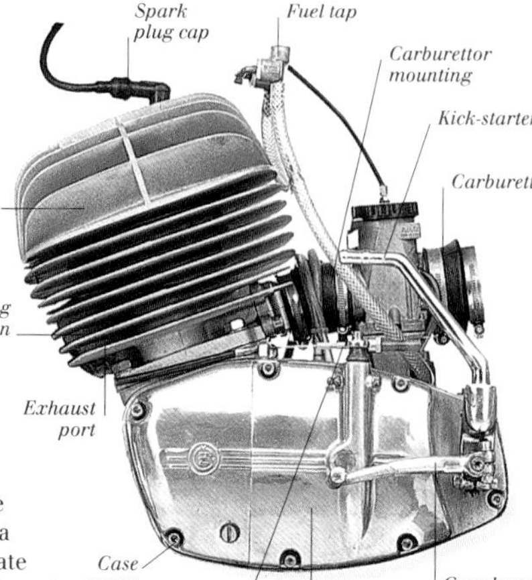
Spark plug cap
Fuel tap
Carburettor mounting
Kick-starter
Carburett
Cylinder head
Cooling fin
Exhaust port
Case screw
Clutch activating arm
Engine cover
Gear lever

TRANSMISSION SYSTEM

GEARBOX

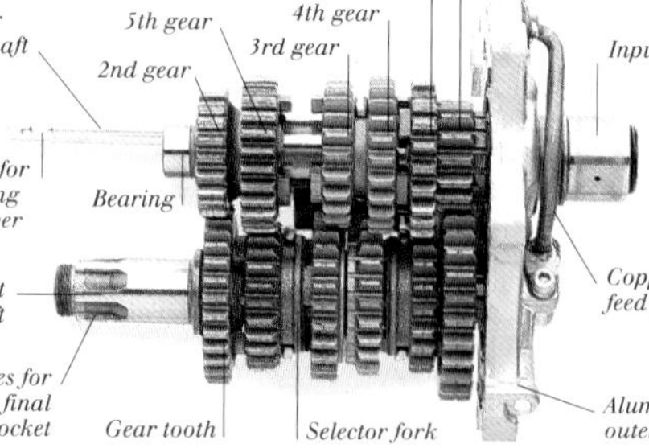
1st gear
6th gear
4th gear
5th gear
3rd gear
2nd gear
Gear lever selector shaft
Input shaft
Splines for mounting gear lever
Bearing
Output shaft
Copper oil feed pipe
Splines for mounting final drive sprocket
Gear tooth
Selector fork
Aluminium outer casing

MULTIPLATE CLUTCH

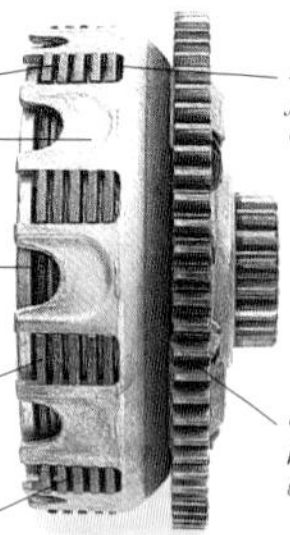
Fibre plate
Key locks fibre plate t outer drum
Outer clutch drum, connected to engine
Pressure plate, connected to inner clutch drum
Springs force plates together
Straight-cut primary-dri gear
Metal plate

MODERN "O RING" DRIVE CHAIN

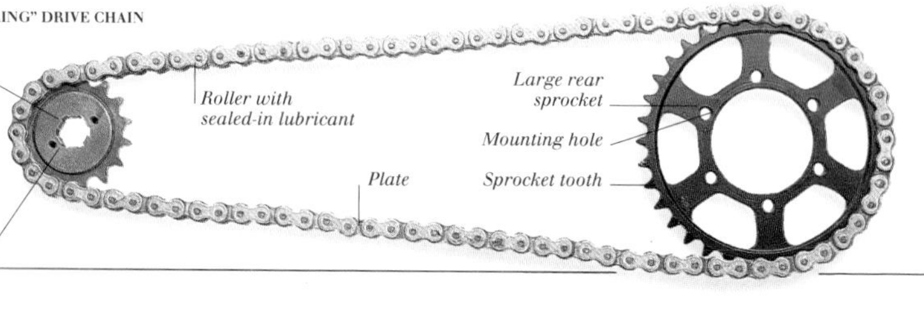
Small front sprocket
Roller with sealed-in lubricant
Large rear sprocket
Mounting hole
Plate
Sprocket tooth
Hole for retaining bolt

VELOCETTE OVERHEAD VALVE (OHV) ENGINE

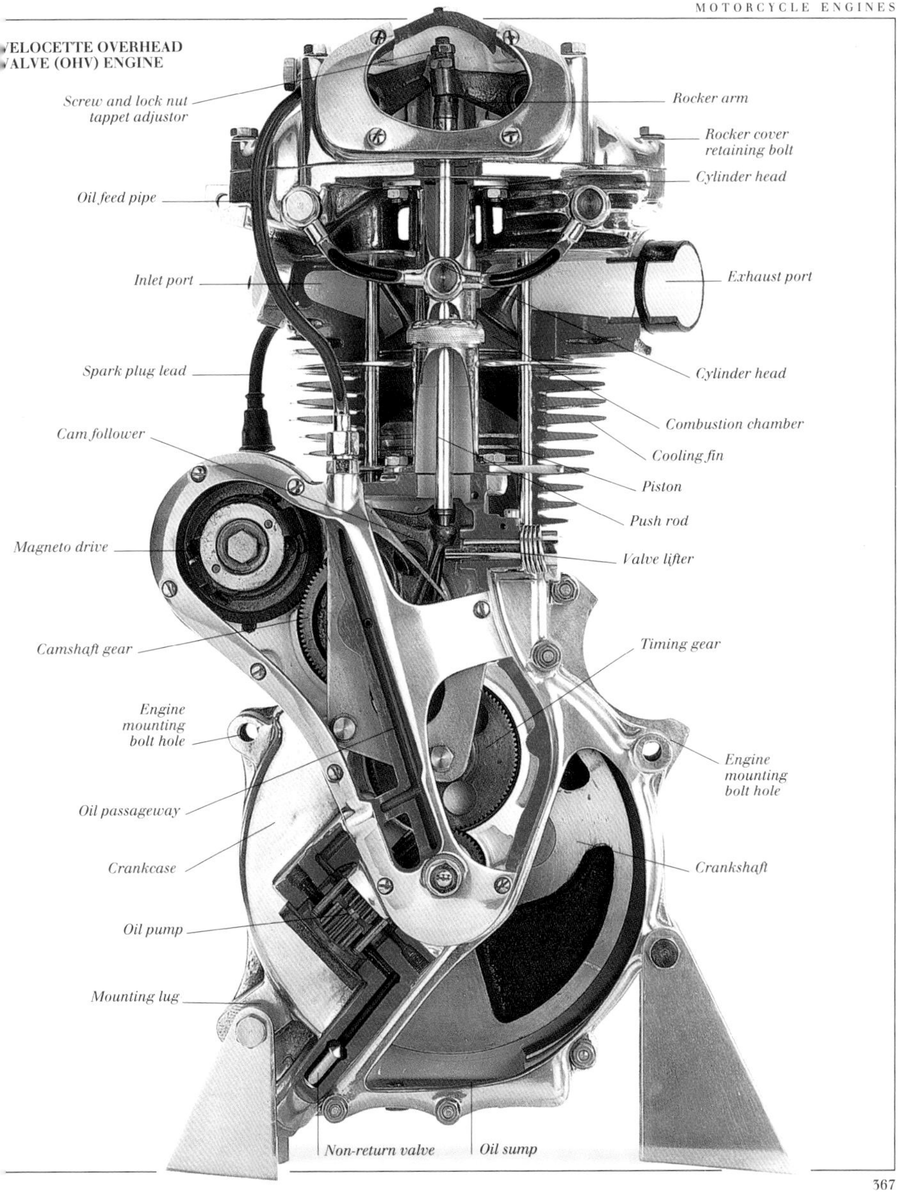
Screw and lock nut tappet adjustor
Rocker arm
Rocker cover retaining bolt
Cylinder head
Oil feed pipe
Inlet port
Exhaust port
Spark plug lead
Cylinder head
Combustion chamber
Cam follower
Cooling fin
Piston
Push rod
Magneto drive
Valve lifter
Camshaft gear
Timing gear
Engine mounting bolt hole
Engine mounting bolt hole
Oil passageway
Crankcase
Crankshaft
Oil pump
Mounting lug
Non-return valve
Oil sump

Competition motorcycles

THERE ARE MANY TYPES of motorcycle sport and in each, a specialist machine has evolved to perform to specific requirements. Races take place on roads or tracks or "off-road", in fields, dirt tracks, and even the desert. "Grand Prix" world championships in road-racing exist for 125cc, 250cc, and 500cc classes, as well as for sidecars. The latest racing sidecars have more in common with racing cars than motorcycles. The rider and passenger operate within an all-enclosing, aerodynamic fairing. The Suzuki RGV500 shown here, like other Grand Prix machines, carries advertising, which promotes the manufacturer and helps to cover the cost of developing motorcycle technology. In Speedway, which originated in the US in 1902, motorcycles operate without brakes or a gearbox. Off-road competition motorcycles have less emphasis on high power output. In Motocross, for example, which is held on rough terrain, they must have high ground clearance, flexible long-travel suspension, and tyres with a chunky tread pattern, to allow them to grip in sand or mud.

1992 HUSQVARNA MOTOCROSS TC610

Throttle cable
Handlebar brace
Long seat
Racing number
Hand protector
Radiator air vent
Flexible plastic mudguard
Light-
weigh
exhaus
system
Telescopic fork
Plastic guard
Axle
Overhead camshaft engine
Gear lever
Shock absorber
Knobbly tyre
Disc brake
Brake calliper
Alloy swingarm
Shock absorber linkage
Disc
brake

1992 SUZUKI RGV500
SIDE VIEW

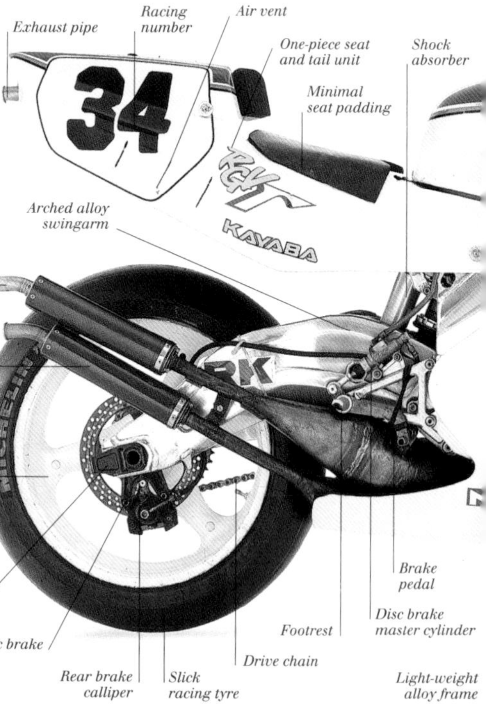
Racing number
Air vent
Exhaust pipe
One-piece seat and tail unit
Shock absorber
Minimal seat padding
Arched alloy swingarm
Exhaust pipe
Silencer
Three-spoke alloy wheel
Brake pedal
Axle adjustor
Disc brake master cylinder
Footrest
Disc brake
Drive chain
Rear brake calliper
Slick racing tyre
Light-weight alloy frame

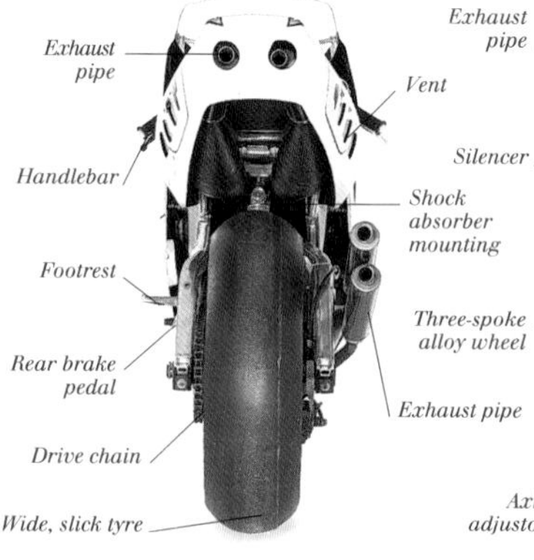
Exhaust pipe
Vent
Handlebar
Shock absorber mounting
Footrest
Rear brake pedal
Exhaust pipe
Drive chain
Wide, slick tyre

REAR VIEW

1981 WESLAKE SPEEDWAY

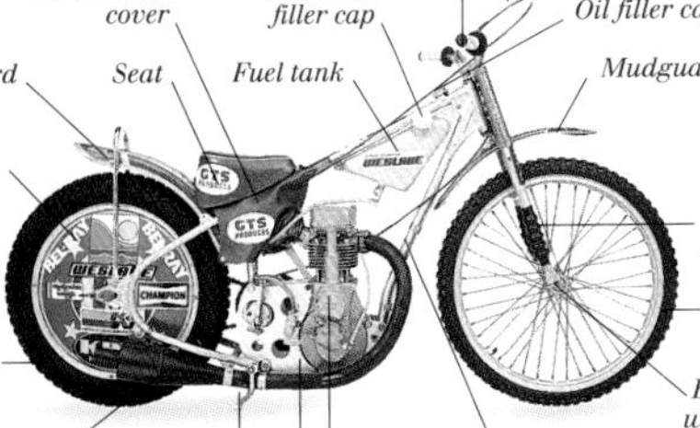
Throttle
Throttle cable
Carburettor cover
Fuel tank filler cap
Oil filler cap
ludguard
Seat
Fuel tank
Mudguard
Wheel cover
Telescopic fork
Narrow tyre
ide tyre
Brakeless wheel hub
Silencer
Footrest
Oil pump
Overhead valve engine
Tubular open cradle frame

1968 KIRBY BSA RACING SIDECAR

FRONT VIEW

Rev counter
Windscreen
All-enclosing fairing
Fuel tank
Wheel guard
Battery
Square-section tyre
Passenger windscreen
Passenger grab rail

SIDE VIEW

Throttle cable
Exhaust pipe
Rev counter
All-enclosing fairing
Sidecar chassis
Engine
Fibreglass wheel guard
Fuel cap

Fairing stay
uel tank
breather
Throttle cable
uel tank
Throttle
Front brake lever
Telescopic fork
Mudguard
Slick tyre
Sponsor's logo
Air vent
Braided steel hydraulic hose
Carbon-fibre disc brake
Three-spoke alloy wheel
uickly detachable
)D) fairing
Brake calliper

Windscreen
Racing number
Clutch lever
Fairing
Radiator
Front brake lever
Hydraulic brake hose
Mudguard
Axle
Slick tyre

FRONT VIEW

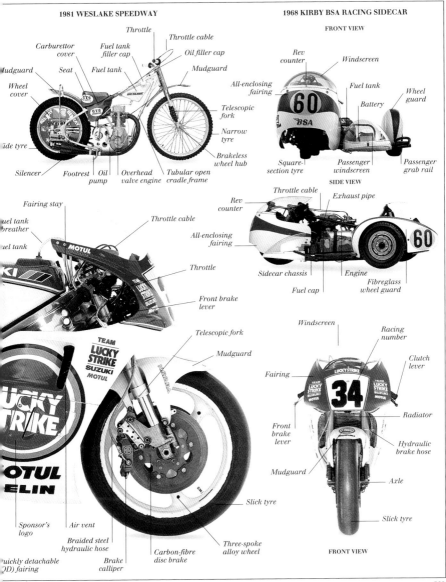

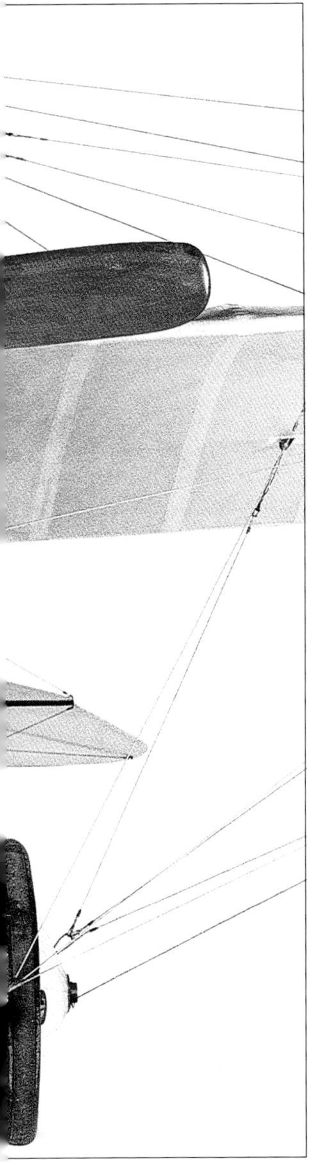

Sea and Air

Ships of Greece and Rome

ROMAN ANCHOR

Stock
Shank
Palm
Acutely angled arm
Ring
Crown

IN THE EXPANSIVE EMPIRES OF GREECE AND ROME, powerful fleets were needed for battle, trade, and communication. Greek galleys were powered by a sail and many oars. A new armament, the embolos (ram), was fitted on to the galley bow. As ramming duels required fast and manoeuvrable boats, extra rows of oarsmen were added, culminating in the trireme. During the fifth and fourth centuries B.C., the trireme dominated the Mediterranean. It was powered by 170 oarsmen, rowing with one oar each. The oarsmen were ranged on three levels, as the model opposite shows. The trireme also carried archers and soldiers for boarding. Galleys were pulled out of the water when not in use, and were kept in dockyard ship-sheds. The merchant ships of the Greeks and Romans were mighty vessels too. The full-bodied Roman corbita, for example, could hold up to 400 tons and carried a cargo of spices, gems, silk, and animals. The construction of these boats was based on a stout hull with planking secured by mortice and tenon. Some of these ships embarked on long voyages, sailing even as far as India. To make them easier to steer, corbitas set a fore sail called an "artemon". It flew from a forward-leaning mast that was a forerunner of the long bowsprits carried by the great clipper ships of the 19th century.

ROMAN CORBITA

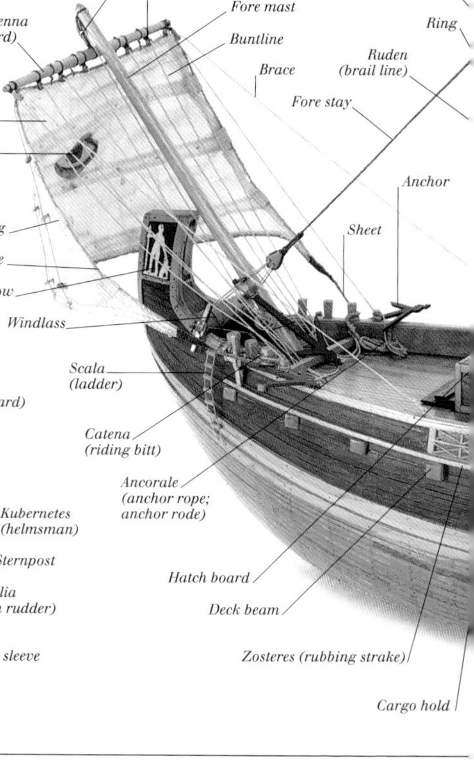
Roband (rope band)
Ceruchi (lift)
Double halyard
Bullseye
Heraldic device
Fore mast
Antenna (yard)
Ring
Buntline
Ruden (brail line)
Brace
Artemon (fore sail)
Fore stay
Oculus (eye)
Anchor
Tabling
Sheet
Bolt rope
Prow
Windlass
Scala (ladder)
Catena (riding bitt)
Ancorale (anchor rope; anchor rode)
Hatch board
Deck beam
Zosteres (rubbing strake)
Cargo hold

ATTIC VASE SHOWING A GALLEY

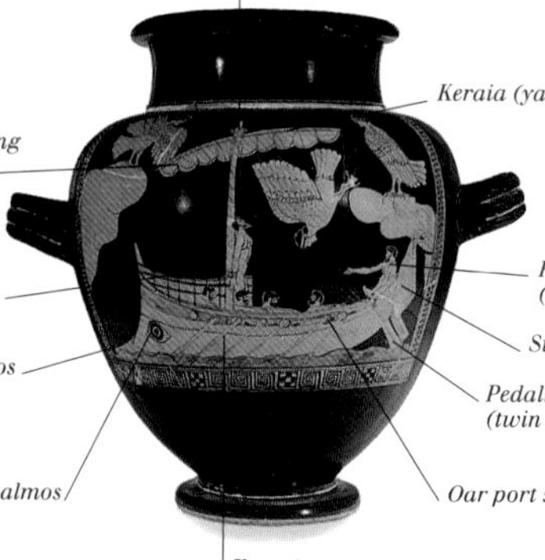
Bronze mast truck
Keraia (yard)
Kalos (brailing rope)
Mast
Kubernetes (helmsman)
Sternpost
Embolos (ram; beak)
Pedalia (twin rudder)
Ophthalmos (eye)
Oar port sleeve
Kope (oar)

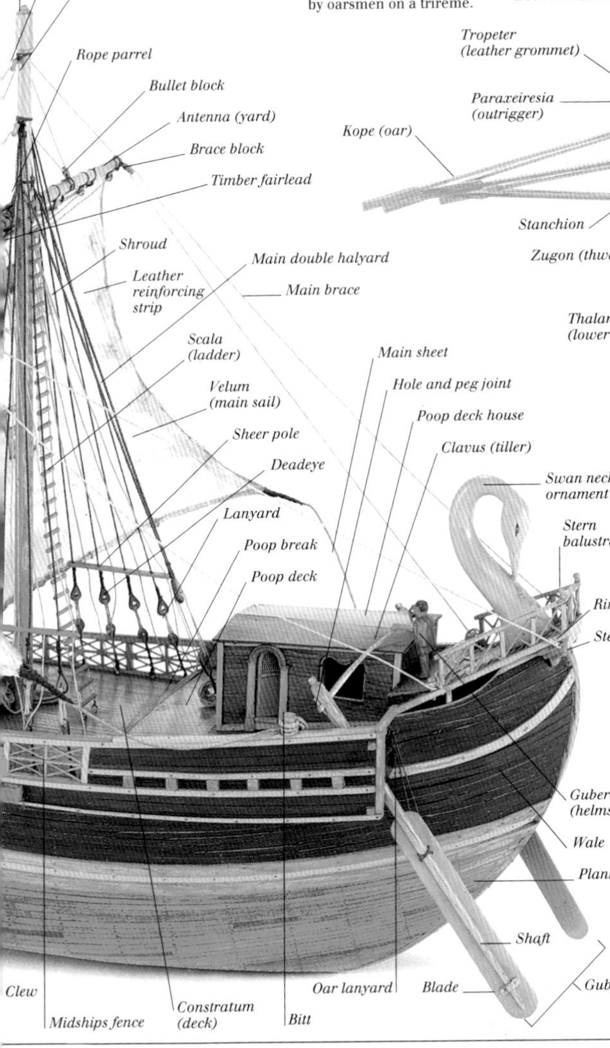
Masthead
Single clump block
Malus (mast)
Rope parrel
Bullet block
Antenna (yard)
Brace block
Timber fairlead
Shroud
Leather reinforcing strip
Main double halyard
Main brace
Scala (ladder)
Velum (main sail)
Sheer pole
Deadeye
Lanyard
Poop break
Poop deck
Main sheet
Hole and peg joint
Poop deck house
Clavus (tiller)
Swan neck ornament
Stern balustrade
Ring bolt
Sternpost
Gubernator (helmsman)
Wale
Planking
Shaft
Blade
Gubernacula (rudders)
Oar lanyard
Bitt
Constratum (deck)
Midships fence
Clew

ROWING POSITIONS ON A GREEK TRIREME (TRIERE)

The katastroma (deck) has been removed from this model to show the positions taken by oarsmen on a trireme.

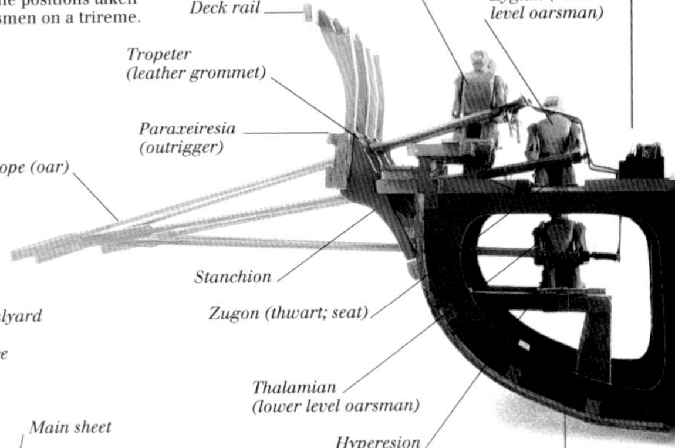
Thranite (upper level oarsman)
Zygian (middle level oarsman)
Deck rail
Tropeter (leather grommet)
Paraxeiresia (outrigger)
Kope (oar)
Stanchion
Zugon (thwart; seat)
Thalamian (lower level oarsman)
Hyperesion (oarsman's cushion)
Pine hull

MORTICE-AND-TENON FASTENINGS FOR HULL PLANKS

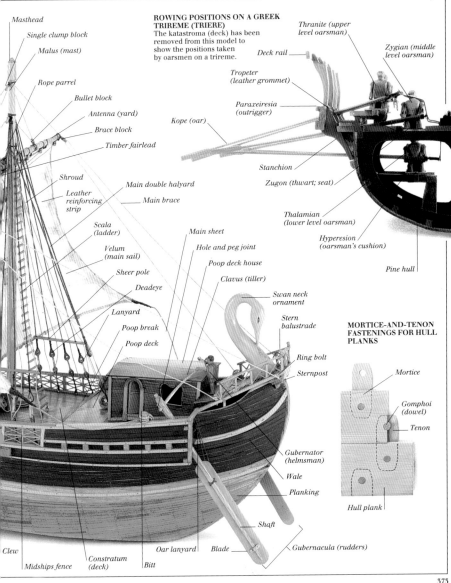

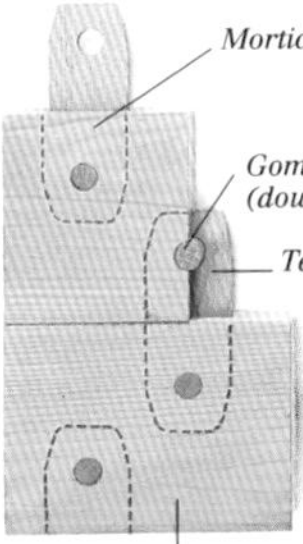
Mortice
Gomphoi (dowel)
Tenon
Hull plank

Viking ships

IN THE DARK AGES and early medieval times, the longships of Scandinavia were one of the most feared sights for people of northern Europe. The Vikings launched raids from Scandinavia every summer in longships equipped with a single steering oar on the right, or "steerboard", side (hence "starboard"). A longship had one row of oars on each side and a single sail. The hull had clinker (overlapping) planks. Prowheads adorned fighting ships during campaigns of war. The sailing longship was also used for local coastal travel. The karv below was probably built as transport for an important family, while the smaller faering (top right) was a rowing boat only. The fleet of William of Normandy that invaded England in 1066 owed much to the Viking boatbuilding tradition, and has been depicted in the Bayeux Tapestry (above). Seals used by port towns and royal courts through the ages provide an excellent record of contemporary ship design. The seal opposite shows how ships changed from the Viking period to the end of the Middle Ages. The introduction of the fighting platform – the castle – and the addition of extra masts and sails changed the character of the medieval ship. Note also that the steering oar has been replaced by a centred rudder.

BOATBUILDERS TOOLS

Shave
Broad axe
Breast auger
Sheer
Master shipwright
Stempost
Hood end
Keel
T-handle auger
Axe
Strake
Tree cut for planking

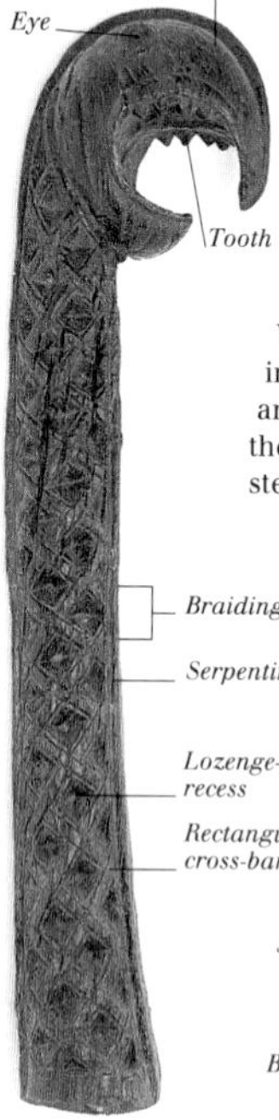
Zoomorphic head
Eye
Tooth
Braiding
Serpentine neck
Lozenge-shaped recess
Rectangular cross-band

DRAGON PROWHEAD

VIKING KARV (COASTER)

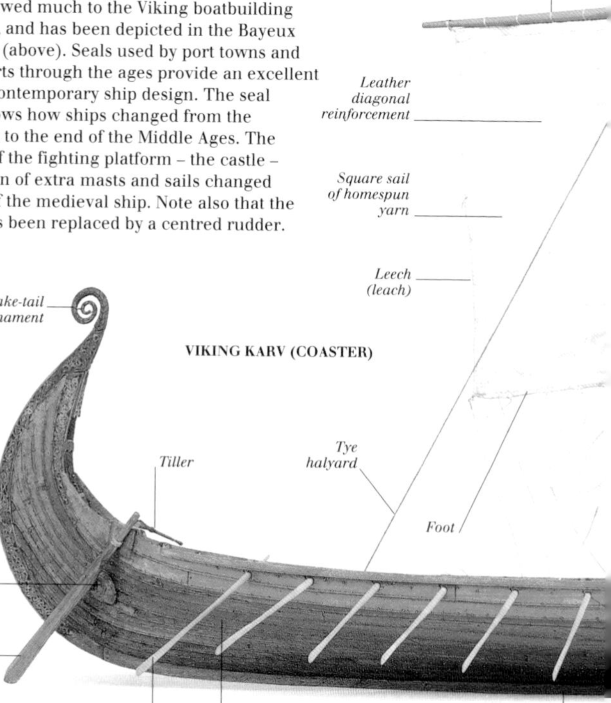
Roband
Leather diagonal reinforcement
Square sail of homespun yarn
Leech (leach)
Snake-tail ornament
Tiller
Tye halyard
Foot
Sternpost
Boss (rudder pivot)
Steering oar (side rudder)
Oar
Starboard (steerboard) side
Keel

FAERING (VIKING ROWING BOAT)

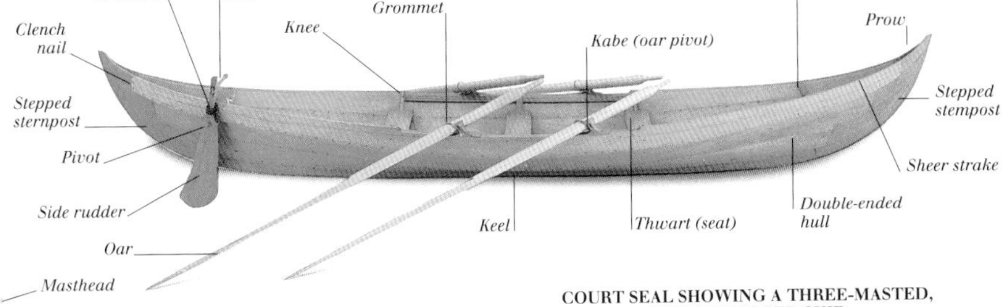
Grommet
Tiller
Clench nail
Knee
Grommet
Kabe (oar pivot)
Plank scarf
Prow
Stepped sternpost
Stepped stempost
Pivot
Sheer strake
Side rudder
Keel
Thwart (seat)
Double-ended hull
Oar

COURT SEAL SHOWING A THREE-MASTED, SQUARE-RIGGED SHIP

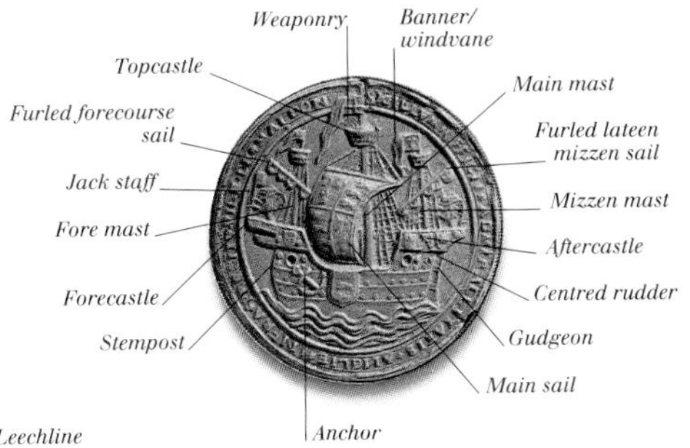
Weaponry
Banner/ windvane
Topcastle
Main mast
Furled forecourse sail
Furled lateen mizzen sail
Jack staff
Mizzen mast
Fore mast
Aftercastle
Forecastle
Centred rudder
Stempost
Gudgeon
Main sail
Anchor

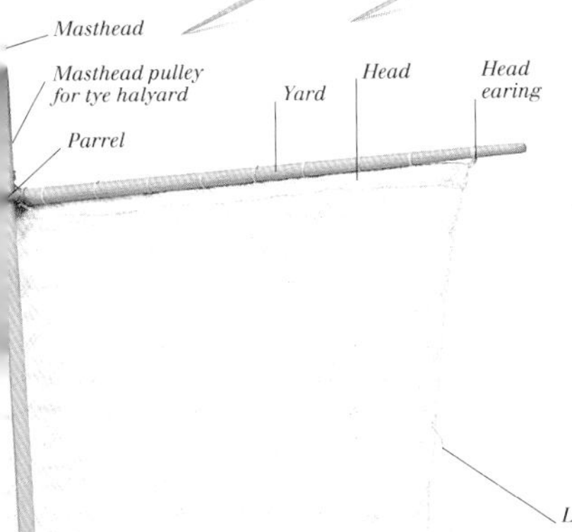
Masthead
Masthead pulley for tye halyard
Yard
Head
Head earing
Parrel
Leechline

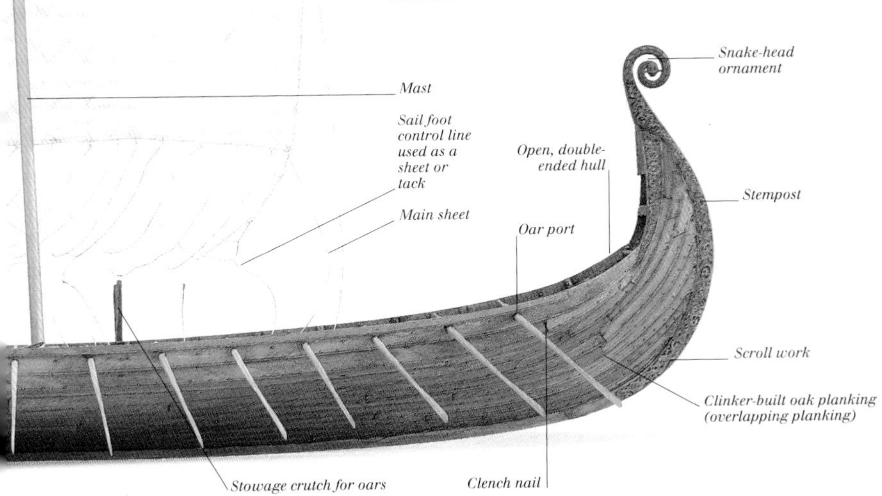
Snake-head ornament
Mast
Sail foot control line used as a sheet or tack
Open, double-ended hull
Stempost
Main sheet
Oar port
Scroll work
Clinker-built oak planking (overlapping planking)
Stowage crutch for oars
Clench nail

Medieval warships and traders

FROM THE 16TH CENTURY, SHIPS WERE BUILT WITH A NEW FORM OF HULL, constructed from carvel (edge-to-edg planking. Warships of the time, like King Henry VIII of England's Mary Rose, boasted awesome fire power. Thi ship carried both long-range cannon in bronze, and short-range, anti-personnel guns in iron. Elsewhere, ships took on a multiformity of shapes. Dhows transported slaves from East Africa to Arabia, their fore-and-aft rigged lateen sails allowing them to sail close to the wind around the lands of the Indian Ocean. The Chinese sailed to East Africa and Arabia in junks, trading goods that were carried in watertight compartments. New astronomical tools helped medieval sailors to find their way. Cross-staves and astrolabes were used to measure the altitude of the sun or stars. One of a choice of four cross-pieces was slid up or down the staff of the cross-stave – which was graduated in degrees of altitude – until its top aligned with the celestial body and its base with the horizon. The sighting rule of the astrolabe was simply lined up with a known body, and its altitude read from marks on the metal disc. With sundials, the sailor could use the shadow of the sun to show the time of day.

DHOW

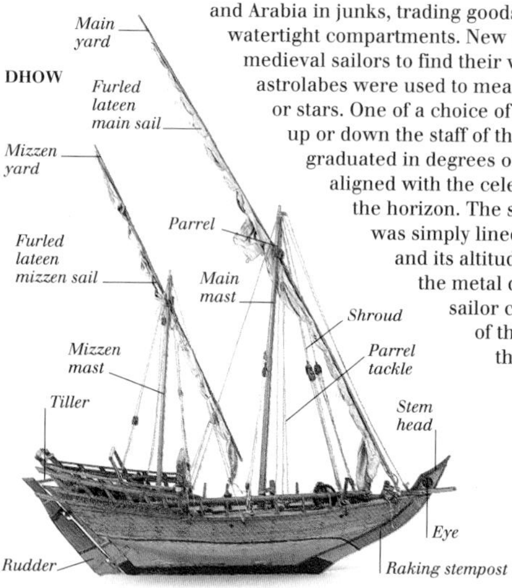
Main yard
Furled lateen main sail
Mizzen yard
Parrel
Furled lateen mizzen sail
Main mast
Shroud
Mizzen mast
Parrel tackle
Tiller
Stem head
Eye
Rudder
Raking stempost

JUNK

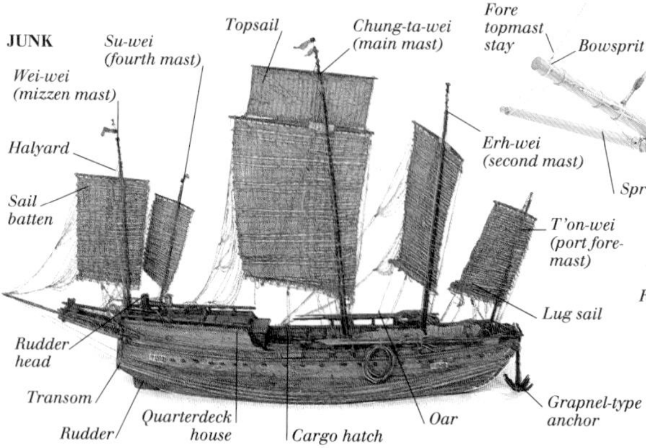
Su-wei (fourth mast)
Topsail
Chung-ta-wei (main mast)
Wei-wei (mizzen mast)
Halyard
Erh-wei (second mast)
Sail batten
T'on-wei (port fore-mast)
Lug sail
Rudder head
Transom
Rudder
Quarterdeck house
Cargo hatch
Oar
Grapnel-type anchor

SAILING WARSHIP

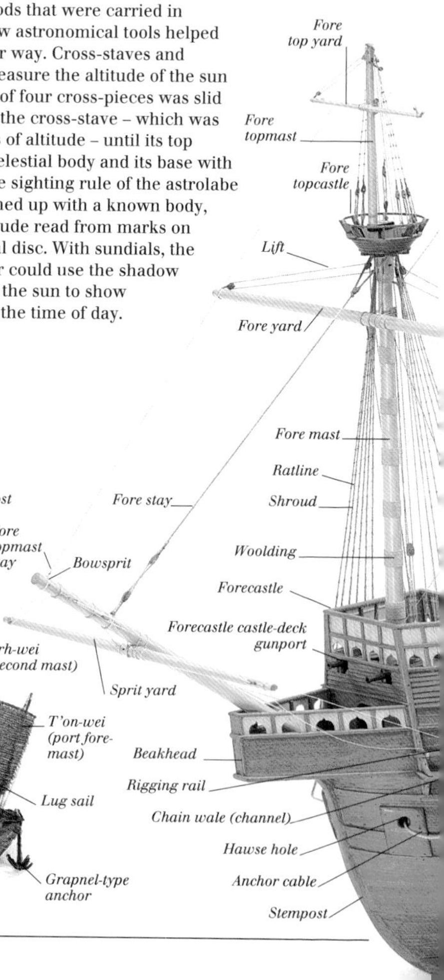
Fore top yard
Fore topmast
Fore topcastle
Lift
Fore yard
Fore mast
Ratline
Shroud
Fore stay
Fore topmast stay
Bowsprit
Woolding
Forecastle
Forecastle castle-deck gunport
Sprit yard
Beakhead
Rigging rail
Chain wale (channel)
Hawse hole
Anchor cable
Stempost

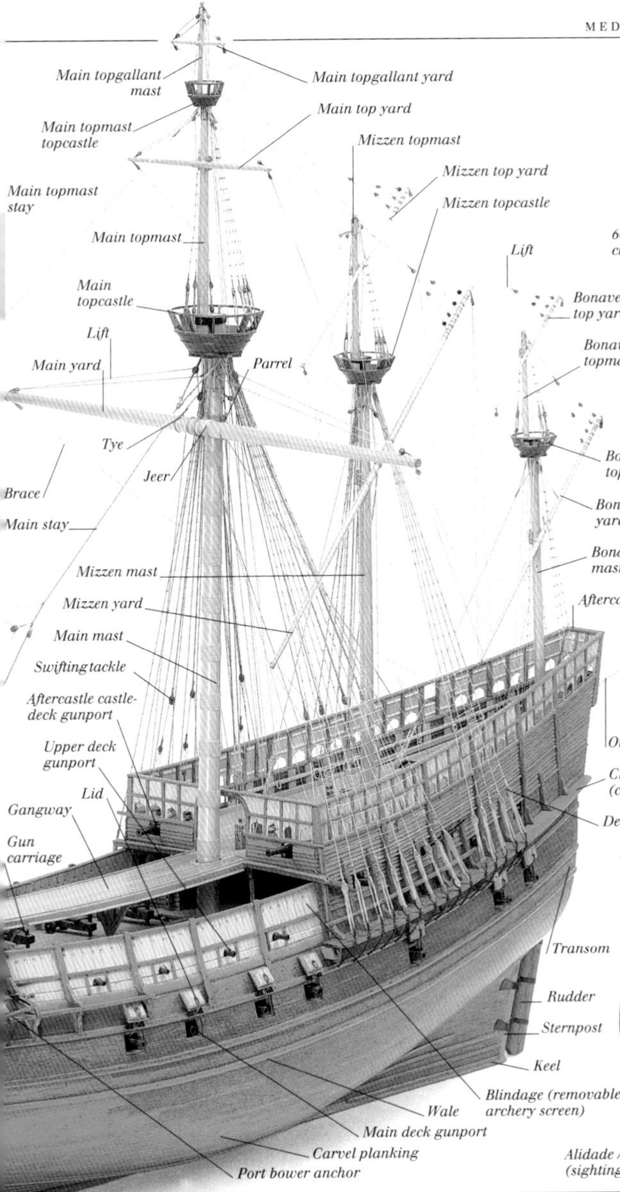
Main topgallant mast
Main topgallant yard
Main top yard
Main topmast topcastle
Mizzen topmast
Mizzen top yard
Main topmast stay
Mizzen topcastle
Main topmast
Lift
Main topcastle
Bonaventure top yard
Lift
Bonaventure topmast
Main yard
Parrel
Tye
Bonaventure topcastle
Jeer
Brace
Bonaventure yard
Main stay
Bonaventure mast
Mizzen mast
Mizzen yard
Aftercastle
Main mast
Swiftingtackle
Aftercastle castle-deck gunport
Outrigger
Upper deck gunport
Chain wale (channel)
Lid
Gangway
Deadeye
Gun carriage
Transom
Rudder
Sternpost
Keel
Blindage (removable archery screen)
Wale
Main deck gunport
Carvel planking
Port bower anchor

CROSS-STAVE (CROSS-STAFF)

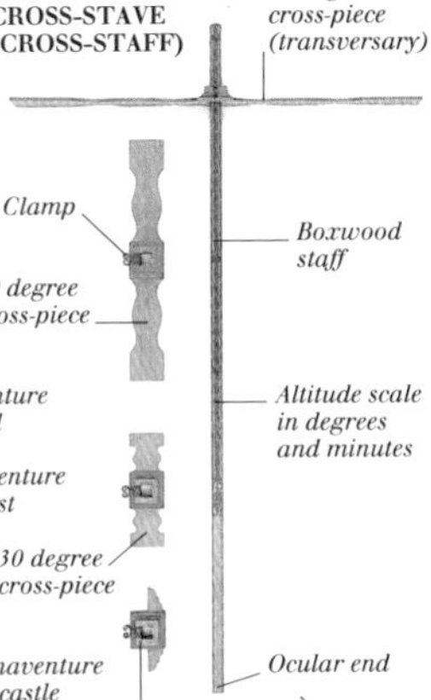
90 degree cross-piece (transversary)
Clamp
Boxwood staff
60 degree cross-piece
Altitude scale in degrees and minutes
30 degree cross-piece
Ocular end
10 degree cross-piece (dutch shoe)

SUNDIAL

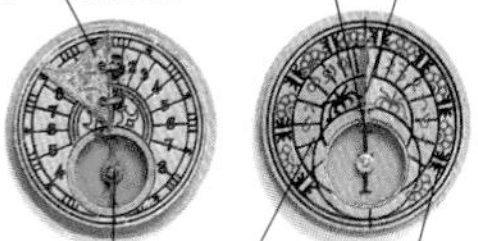
Style of the gnomon (edge)
Needle
Gnomon
Outrigger
Pivot
Hour line
Dial

ASTROLABE

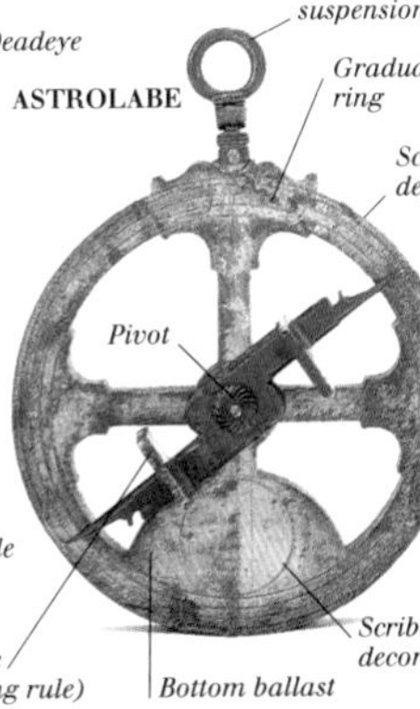
Swivel suspension ring
Graduated ring
Scale of degrees
Pivot
Scribed arc decoration
Alidade (sighting rule)
Bottom ballast

The expansion of sail

BY THE 18TH CENTURY, SAILING SHIPS had become fast and effective floating fortresses. The navies of the north European powers competed with each other by building heavily-armed fighting ships called "men-of-war". The distinctive round stern of the ship below, with its open gallery, balcony, and elaborate wood carving is typical of the period. Hulls around this time were semicircular in cross section, although many boat designers were soon to return to the V-shaped hulls used by the Vikings. Ships of the period carried more sail than ever before. A labyrinth of rigging supported the masts and yards from which the profusion of square sails were set. Ships grew higher, as extra masts were fitted above the lower mast, and the bowsprit became longer to allow the ship to carry staysails, spritsails, and jibsails. Ships went into battle in single file, so that broadsides from the multiple decks of guns would have maximum effect. Ships were classified by rates, the rating of a vessel depending on how many guns it had. A first rate ship had more than 100 guns. The guns fired solid round shot, usually made of iron.

BOW

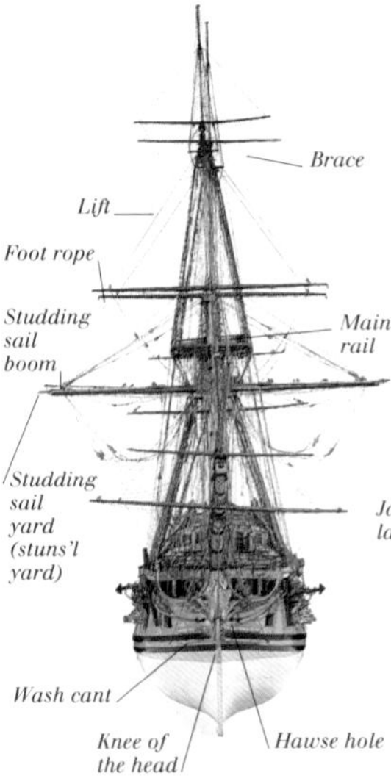
Brace
Lift
Foot rope
Studding sail boom
Main top rail
Studding sail yard (stuns'l yard)
Wash cant
Knee of the head
Hawse hole

WOODEN SAILING SHIP

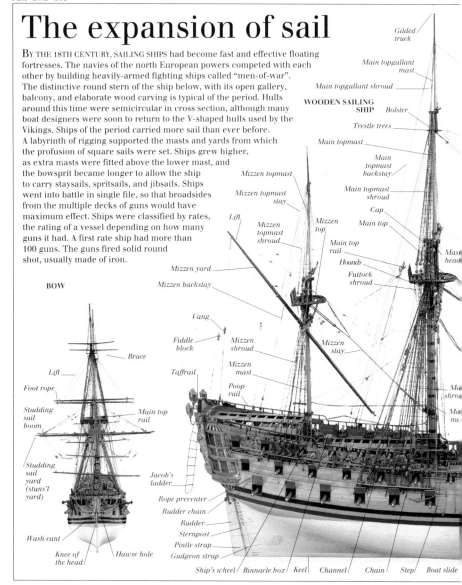

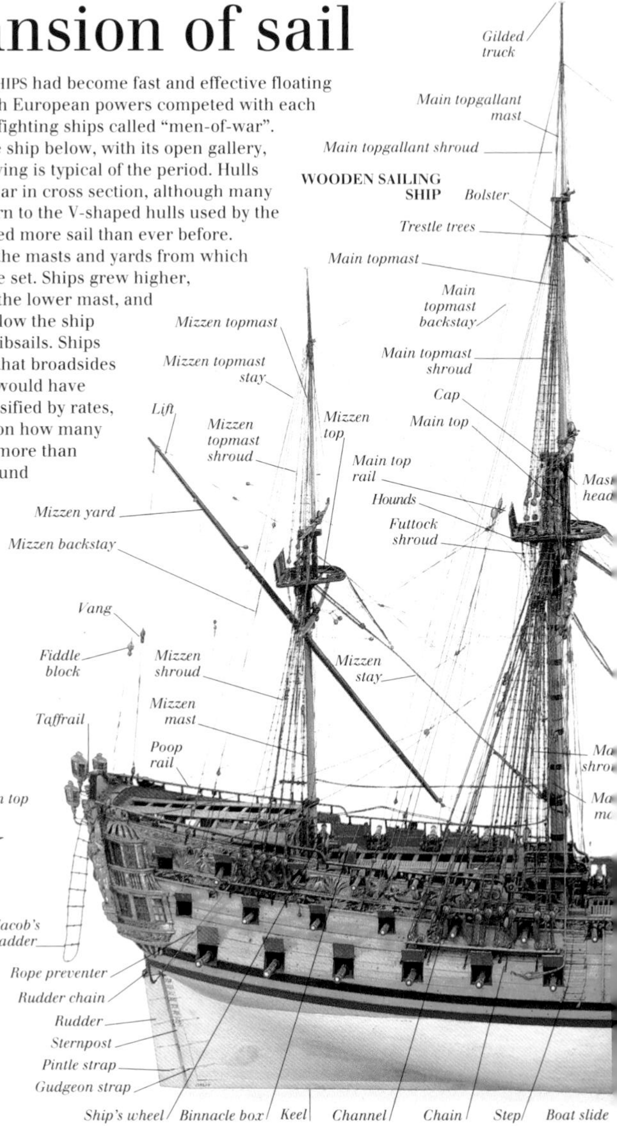
Gilded truck
Main topgallant mast
Main topgallant shroud
Bolster
Trestle trees
Main topmast
Main topmast backstay
Mizzen topmast
Main topmast shroud
Mizzen topmast stay
Cap
Lift
Mizzen topmast shroud
Mizzen top
Main top
Main top rail
Hounds
Futtock shroud
Mizzen yard
Mizzen backstay
Vang
Fiddle block
Mizzen shroud
Mizzen stay
Mizzen mast
Taffrail
Poop rail
Jacob's ladder
Rope preventer
Rudder chain
Rudder
Sternpost
Pintle strap
Gudgeon strap
Ship's wheel
Binnacle box
Keel
Channel
Chain
Step
Boat slide

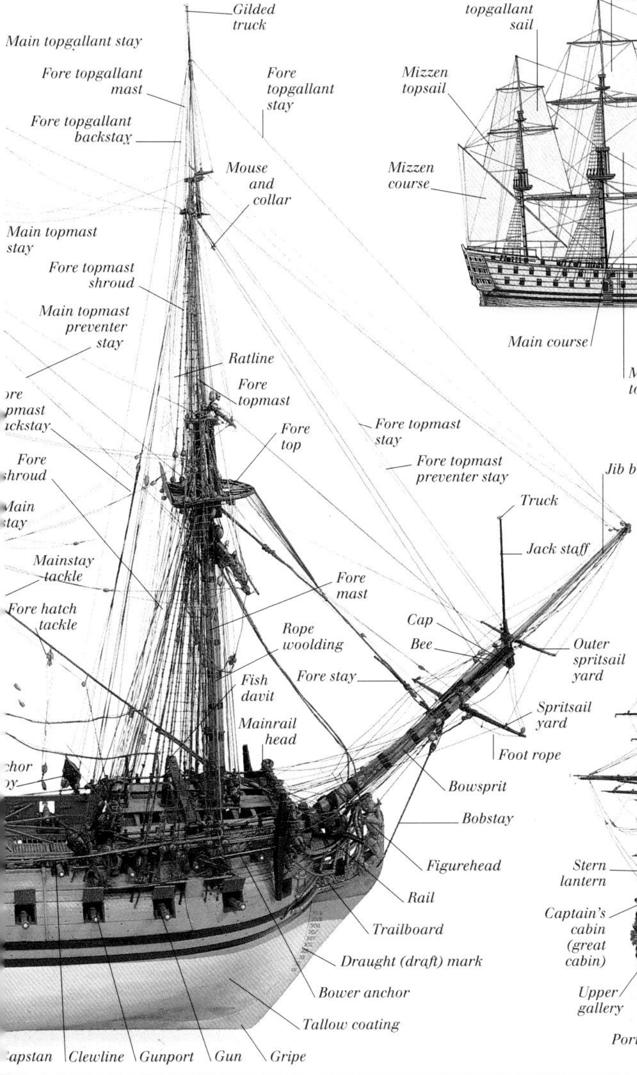

Gilded truck
Main topgallant stay
Fore topgallant mast
Fore topgallant stay
Fore topgallant backstay
Mouse and collar
Main topmast stay
Fore topmast shroud
Main topmast preventer stay
Ratline
Fore topmast
ore topmast ackstay
Fore top
Fore topmast stay
Fore topmast preventer stay
Fore shroud
Main stay
Jib boom
Truck
Jack staff
Mainstay tackle
Fore mast
Fore hatch tackle
Cap
Rope woolding
Bee
Outer spritsail yard
Fore stay
Fish davit
Spritsail yard
Mainrail head
Foot rope
chor oy
Bowsprit
Bobstay
Figurehead
Rail
Trailboard
Draught (draft) mark
Bower anchor
Tallow coating
apstan
Clewline
Gunport
Gun
Gripe

SAIL PATTERN OF A 74-GUN SHIP

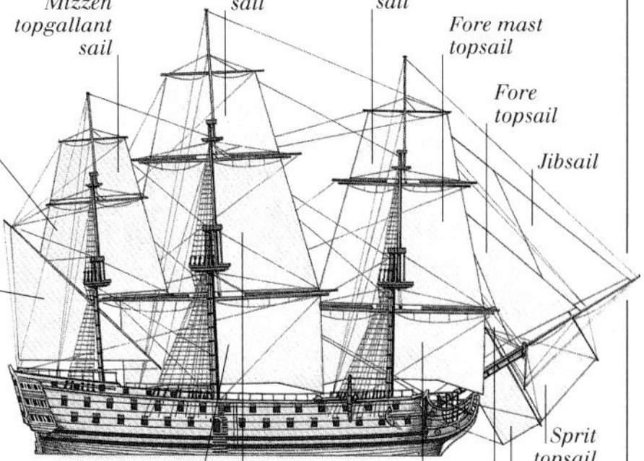

Main topgallant sail
Fore mast topgallant sail
Mizzen topgallant sail
Fore mast topsail
Fore topsail
Mizzen topsail
Jibsail
Mizzen course
Sprit topsail
Main course
Fore mast course
Spritsail course
Main topsail
Fore staysail

STERN

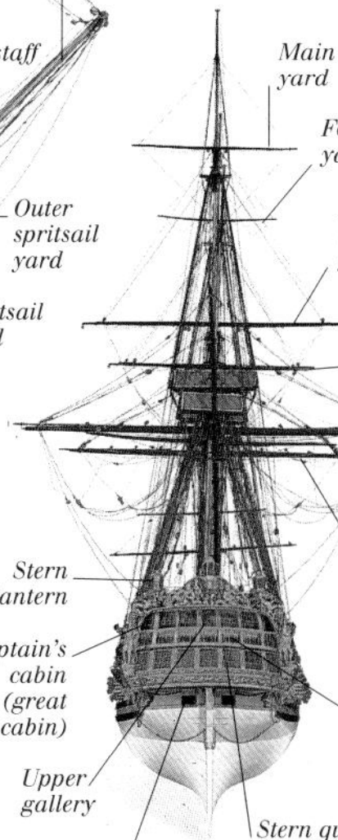

Main topgallant yard
Fore topgallant yard
Main topsail yard
Yardarm
Fore topsail yard
Main yard
Fore yard
Mizzen topmast yard
Stern lantern
Captain's cabin (great cabin)
Balcony
Upper gallery
Port
Stern quarter gallery

A ship of the line

THE 74-GUN WOODEN SHIP WAS A MAINSTAY of British and French battlefleets in the late 18th and early 19th centuries. This "ship of the line" was heavy enough to fight with the most potent of rivals, yet nimble too. The length of such a ship was determined by the number of guns required for each deck, allowing enough room for crews to man them. The gun deck was about 52 m (170 ft) long. The decks had to be very strong to carry the weight of the guns. The deck planks have been removed on the vessel pictured below, to show just how close together the beams had to be to make the hull strong enough. Only timber with a perfect grain was used. The upper deck was open at the waist, but afore and abaft were officers' cabins. The forecastle and quarterdeck carried light guns and acted as platforms for working rigging and for reconnaissance. The ship's longboats (launches) were carried on booms between the gangways.

LONGBOAT

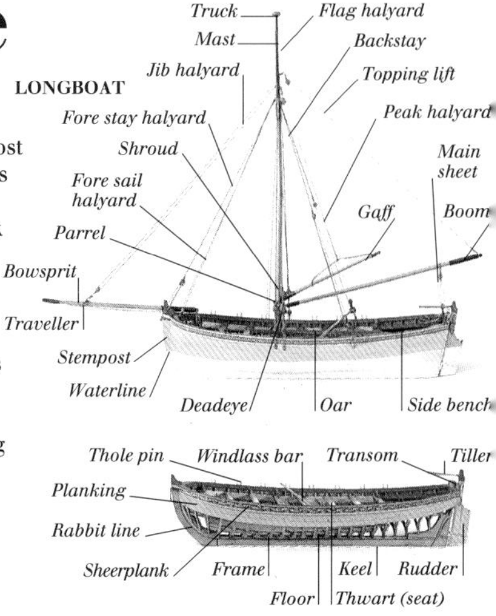

UPPER DECK OF A 74-GUN SHIP

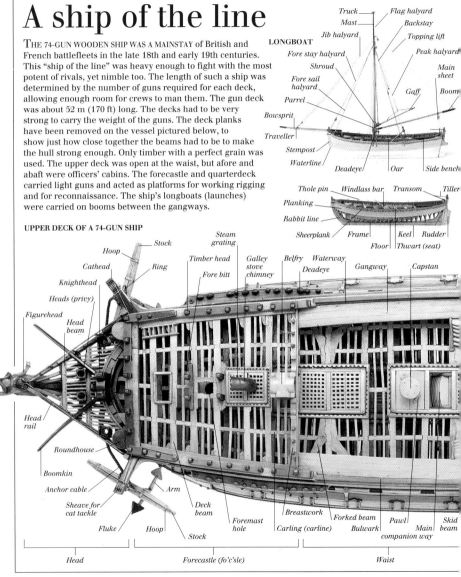

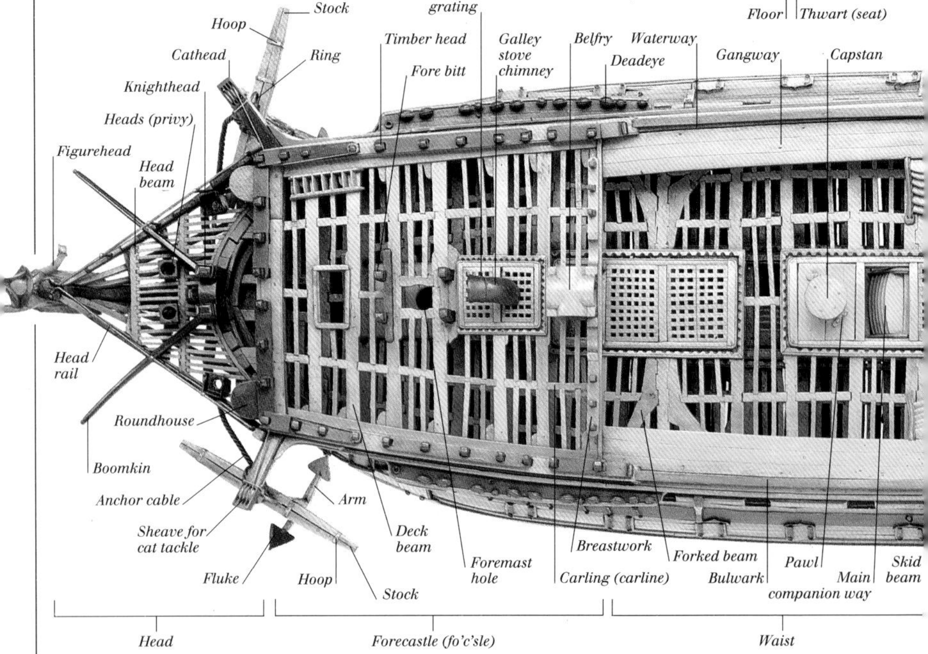

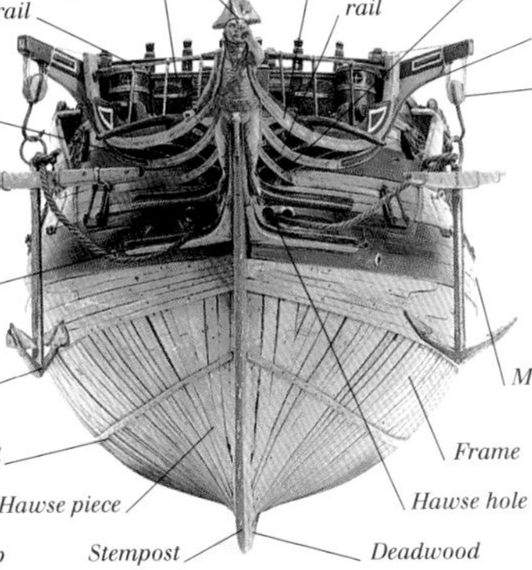
BOW
Figurehead
Main rail
Headboard
Middle rail
Lower rail
Head rail
Supporter
Cat block
Ekeing
Cheek
Catted anchor
Main wale
Riband
Frame
Hawse piece
Hawse hole
Side step
Stempost
Deadwood

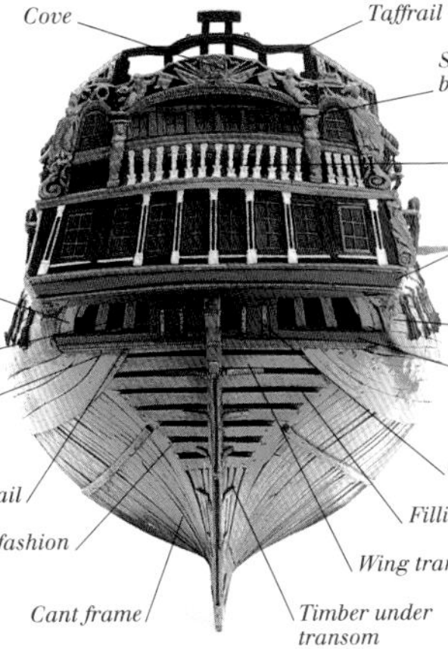
STERN
Cove
Taffrail
Screen bulkhead
Balcony
Side counter timber
Upper counter rail
Drop
Counter timber
Tuck
Lower counter rail
Gunport lid
Tuck rail
Filling transom
After fashion piece
Wing transom
Cant frame
Timber under transom

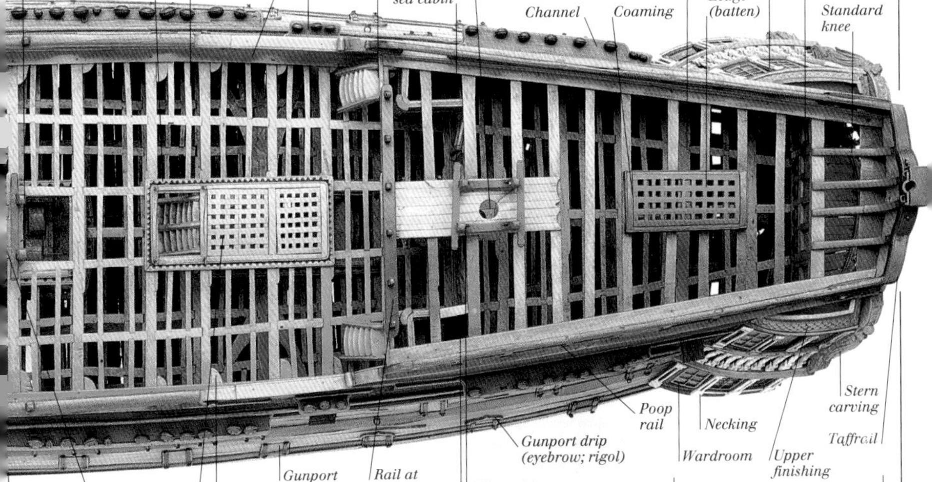
Eye bolt
Main bitt
Ledge
Companion ladder
Hatch coaming/ shot garland
Spirketting
Backstay stool
Master's sea cabin
Mizzen mast hole
Great cabin (captain's cabin)
Pilaster
Screen bulkhead
Channel
Coaming
Ledge (batten)
Standard knee
Stern carving
Poop rail
Necking
Taffrail
Gunport drip (eyebrow; rigol)
Wardroom
Upper finishing
Grating
Gunport lid
Rail at break of poop deck
Mizzen bitt
Main mast hole
Mast partner
Lodging knee
Clerk's cabin
Quarter gallery
Quarterdeck
Poop deck

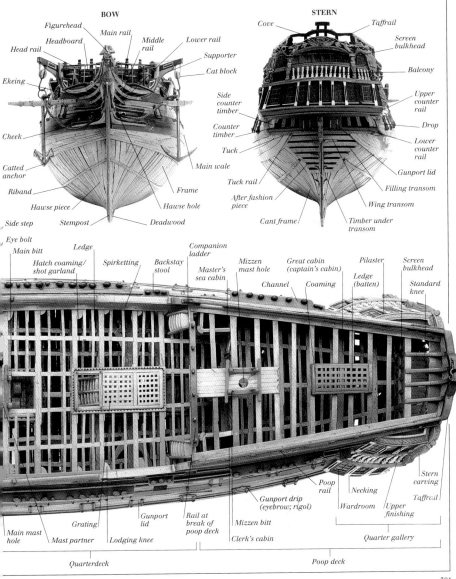

Rigging

MOST SAILING SHIPS HAVE TWO TYPES OF RIGGING. Standing rigging – kept taut by rigging screws or old-fashioned lanyards and deadeyes – refers to the ropes, wires, and chains that support the masts and yards (horizontal spars). Running rigging, which includes types of block and tackle, halyards, and sheets, is used to hoist, lower, or trim sails.

BOWSPRIT AND JIB BOOM

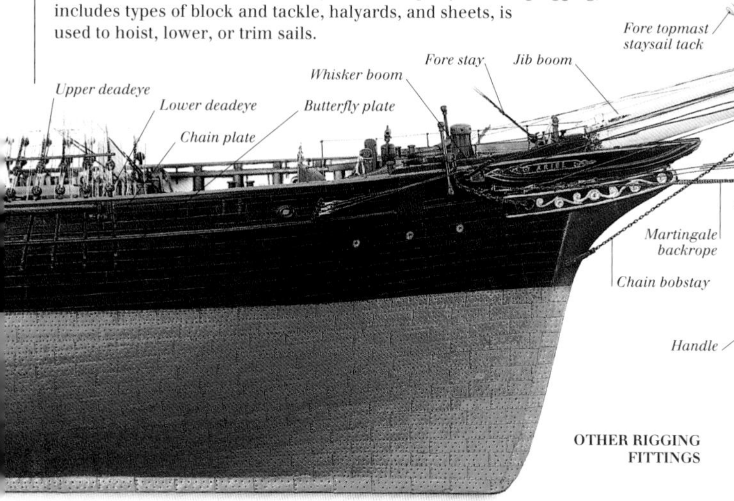
Outer jib stay
Inner jib stay
Inner jib tack
Bowsprit cap
Fore topmast staysail tack
Fore stay
Jib boom
Whisker boom
Upper deadeye
Lower deadeye
Butterfly plate
Chain plate
Bowsprit
Foot rope
Boom guy block
Spear
Martingale backrope
Martingale (dolphin striker)
Lizard
Chain bobstay

OTHER RIGGING FITTINGS

Handle
Parallel shaft

BELAYING PIN

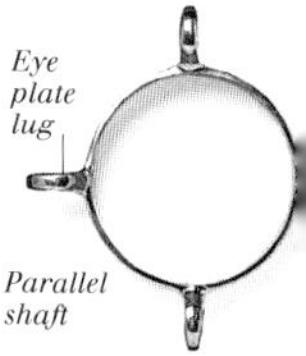
Eye plate lug

MAST BAND

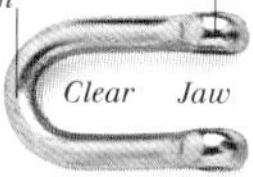
Lug
Crown
Clear
Jaw

SHACKLE

Screw thread
Shank
Shoulder
Eye

SHACKLE PIN

STANDING BLOCK

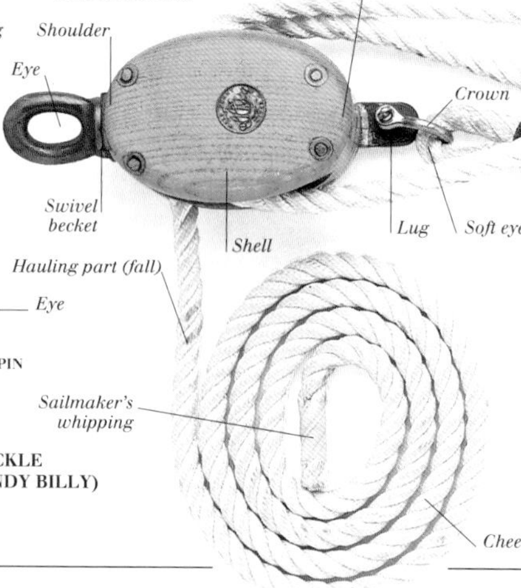
Arse (tail)
Running part
Shoulder
Eye
Crown
Swivel becket
Shell
Lug
Soft eye
Served eye splice
Standing part
Hauling part (fall)
Sailmaker's whipping
Cheese (cheesing)

BLOCK AND TACKLE (PURCHASE; HANDY BILLY)

RIGGING TOOLS

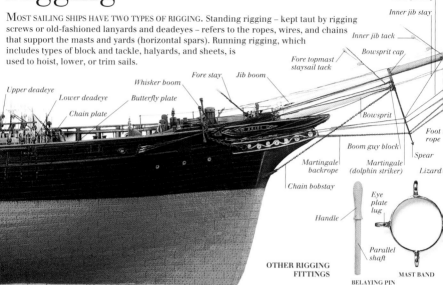

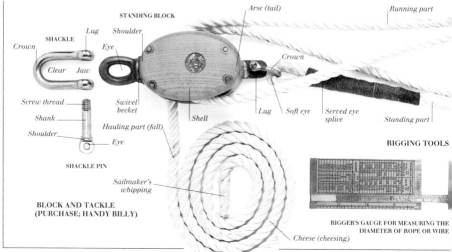

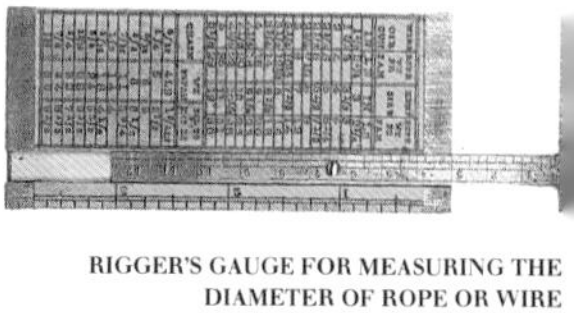

RIGGER'S GAUGE FOR MEASURING THE DIAMETER OF ROPE OR WIRE

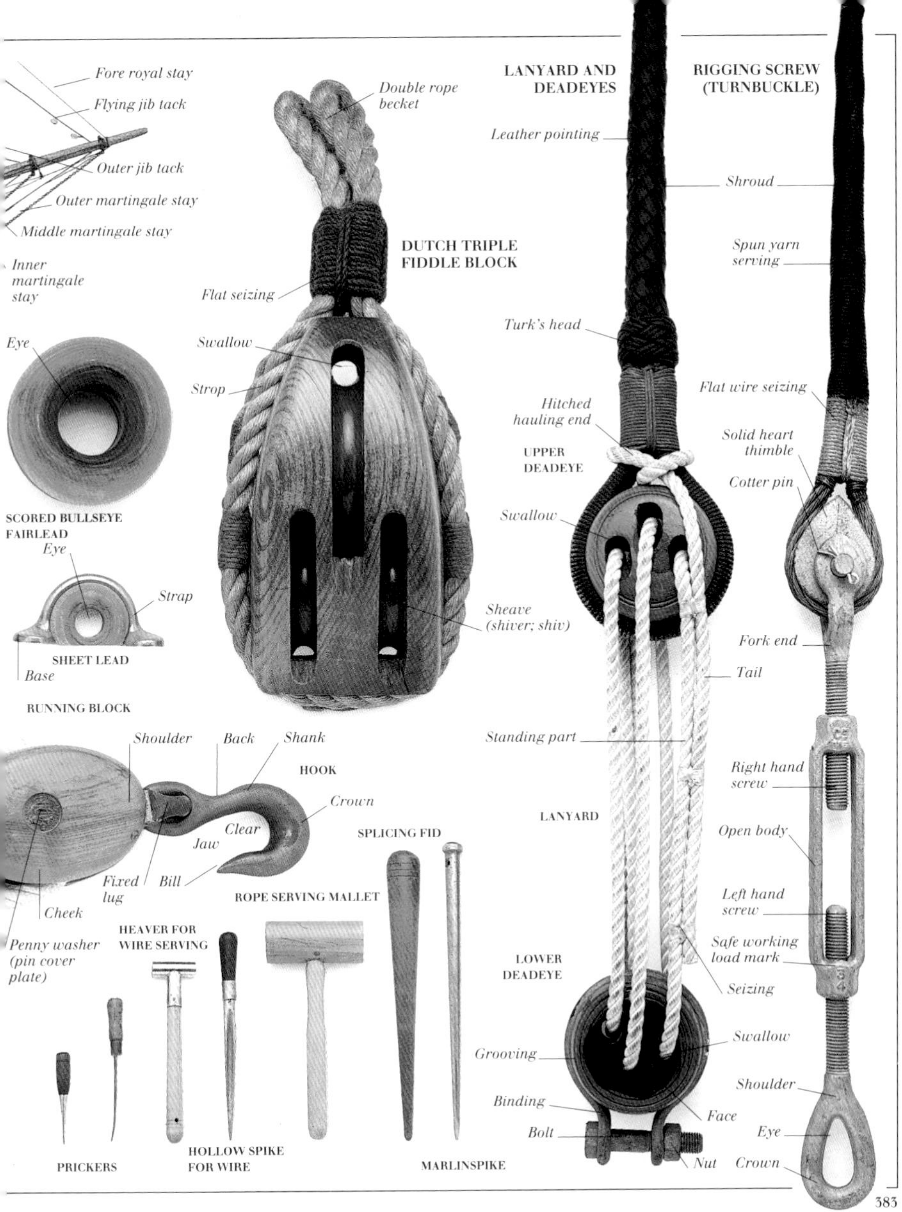

Fore royal stay
Flying jib tack
Outer jib tack
Outer martingale stay
Middle martingale stay
Inner martingale stay
Eye
SCORED BULLSEYE FAIRLEAD
Eye
Strap
SHEET LEAD
Base
RUNNING BLOCK
Double rope becket
DUTCH TRIPLE FIDDLE BLOCK
Flat seizing
Swallow
Strop
Sheave (shiver; shiv)
Shoulder
Back
Shank
HOOK
Crown
Clear
Jaw
Fixed lug
Bill
Cheek
Penny washer (pin cover plate)
SPLICING FID
ROPE SERVING MALLET
HEAVER FOR WIRE SERVING
PRICKERS
HOLLOW SPIKE FOR WIRE
MARLINSPIKE
LANYARD AND DEADEYES
Leather pointing
Shroud
Turk's head
Hitched hauling end
UPPER DEADEYE
Swallow
Tail
Standing part
LANYARD
LOWER DEADEYE
Seizing
Swallow
Grooving
Binding
Face
Bolt
Nut
RIGGING SCREW (TURNBUCKLE)
Spun yarn serving
Flat wire seizing
Solid heart thimble
Cotter pin
Fork end
Right hand screw
Open body
Left hand screw
Safe working load mark
Shoulder
Eye
Crown

PARREL
BEADS

Sails

THERE ARE TWO MAIN TYPES OF SAIL, often used in combination. Square sails are driving sails. They are usually attached by parrels to yards, square to the mast to catch the following wind. On fore-and-aft sails, such as lateen and lug sails, the luff (leading edge) usually abuts a mast or a stay. The head of the sail may abut a gaff, and the foot a boom. Around the world, a great range of rigs (sail patterns), such as the ketch, lugger, and schooner, have evolved to suit local needs. Sails are made from strips of cloth, cut to give the sail a belly and strong enough to resist the most violent of winds. Cotton and flax are the traditional sail materials, but synthetic fabrics are now commonly used

SECTION OF A SAIL

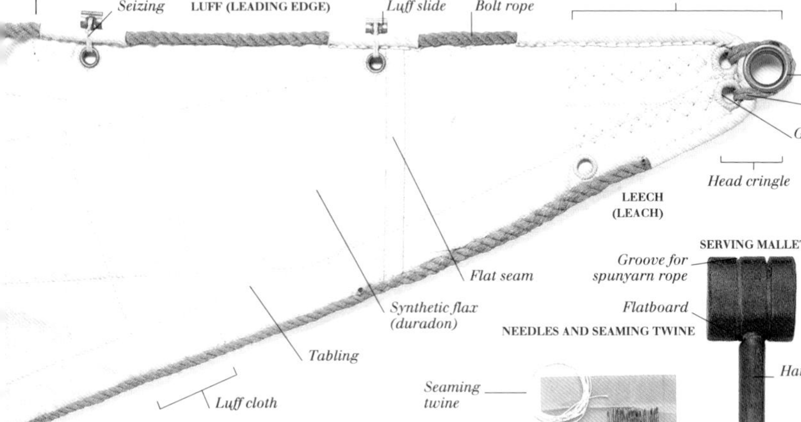
Seizing
LUFF (LEADING EDGE)
Luff slide
Bolt rope
Head
Round thimble
Rope strand
Grommet
Head cringle
LEECH
(LEACH)
Flat seam
Synthetic flax
(duradon)
Tabling
Luff cloth
Rat's tail

SERVING MALLET

Groove for
spunyarn rope
Flatboard
Handle

Sharp
point
Grip

SAILMAKER'S FID

NEEDLES AND SEAMING TWINE

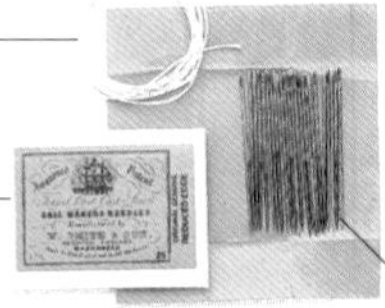
Seaming
twine
Needle packet
Needle

SAILCLOTHS

KEVLAR
ON FLEX
FILM
HEAVYWEIGHT
NYLON CLOTH
MYLAR
NYLON
AND
SILICON
CLOTH
SYNTHETIC
FLAX
(DURADON)
WOVEN
DACRON

SAIL HOOK

Crown
Bill
Shank

SAILMAKER'S PALM

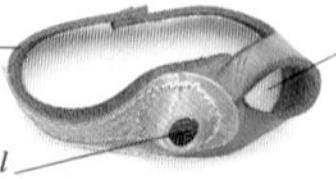
Strap
Thumbhole
Metal
needle pad

BEESWAX

Groove made
by thread

SAILMAKER'S MALLET

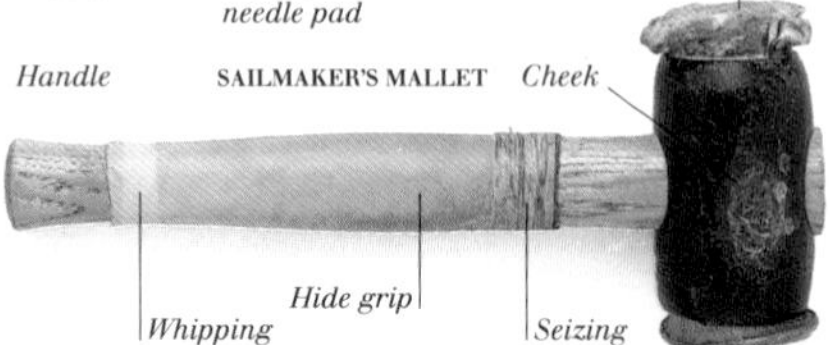
Cowhide
face
Handle
Cheek
Whipping
Hide grip
Seizing
Copper
face

SAILMAKING TOOLS

SAILING RIGS

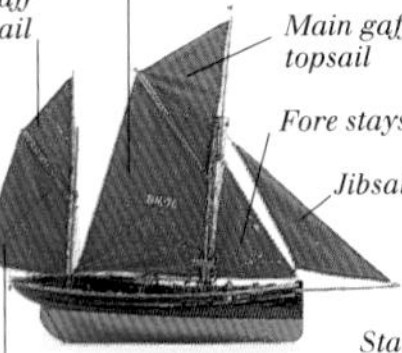
Mizzen gaff topsail
Main sail
Main gaff topsail
Fore staysail
Jibsail
Mizzen sail

KETCH

Mizzen yard topsail
Dipping lug foresail
Standing lug mizzen

LUGGER

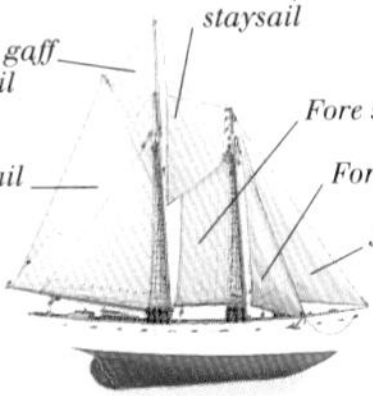
Fore topmast staysail
Main gaff topsail
Fore sail
Main sail
Fore staysail
Jibsail

FISHERMAN'S SCHOONER (FORE-AND-AFT SCHOONER)

SAILS AND RUNNING RIGGING OF A DOUBLE TOPSAIL SCHOONER

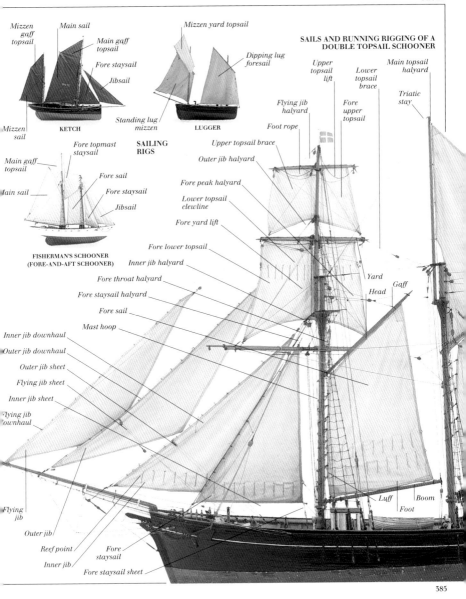

Upper topsail lift
Main topsail halyard
Lower topsail brace
Triatic stay
Flying jib halyard
Fore upper topsail
Foot rope
Upper topsail brace
Outer jib halyard
Fore peak halyard
Lower topsail clewline
Fore yard lift
Fore lower topsail
Inner jib halyard
Yard
Gaff
Fore throat halyard
Head
Fore staysail halyard
Fore sail
Mast hoop
Inner jib downhaul
Outer jib downhaul
Outer jib sheet
Flying jib sheet
Inner jib sheet
Flying jib downhaul
Luff
Boom
Foot
Flying jib
Outer jib
Reef point
Fore staysail
Inner jib
Fore staysail sheet

Mooring and anchoring

FOR LARGE VESSELS IN OPEN WATER, ANCHORAGE IS ESSENTIAL. By holding a ship securely to the seabed, an anchor prevents the vessel from being at the mercy of wave, tide, and current. The earliest anchors were nothing more than stones. In later years, many anchors had a standard design, much like the Admiralty pattern anchor shown on this page. The Danforth anchor is somewhat different. It has particularly deep flukes to give it great holding power. On large sailing ships, anchors were worked by teams of sailors. They turned the drum of a capstan by pushing on bars slotted into the revolving cylinder. This, in turn, lifted or lowered the anchor chain. In calm harbours and estuaries, ships can moor (make fast) without using anchors. Berthing ropes can be attached to bollards both inboard and on the quayside. Berthing ropes are joined to each other by bends, like those opposite.

STONE ANCHOR (KILLICK)

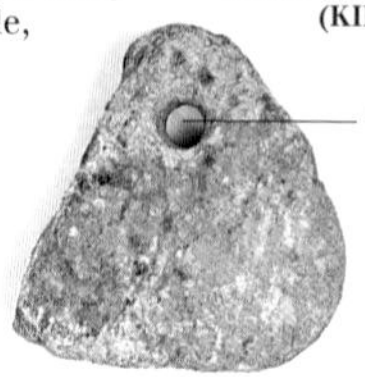
Rope hole

TYPES OF ANCHOR

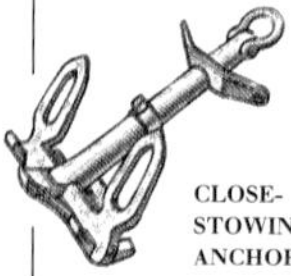

CLOSE-STOWING ANCHOR

End link
Common link
Patent link

ANCHOR CHAIN

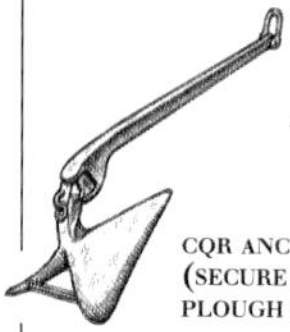

CQR ANCHOR (SECURE ANCHOR; PLOUGH ANCHOR)

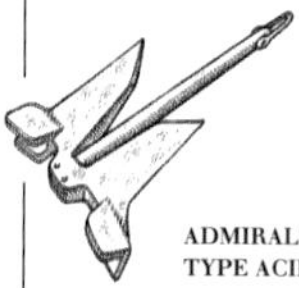

ADMIRALTY ANCHOR TYPE ACII

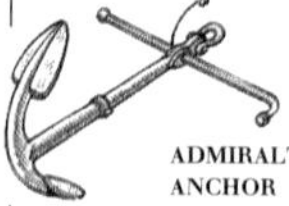

ADMIRALTY PATTERN ANCHOR

STOCKLESS ANCHOR

MUSHROOM ANCHOR (PERMANENT MOORING ANCHOR)

DANFORTH ANCHOR

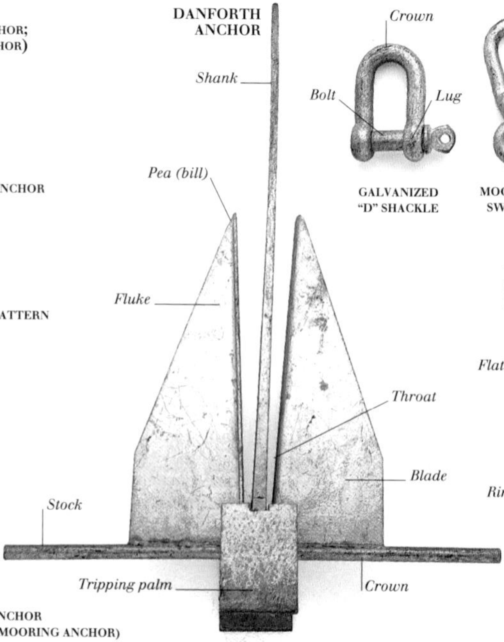
Shank
Pea (bill)
Fluke
Throat
Blade
Stock
Tripping palm
Crown

SHACKLE, SWIVELS, AND LINK

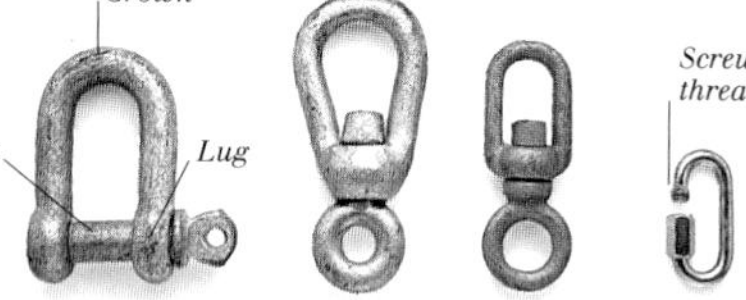
Crown
Bolt
Lug
Screw thread

GALVANIZED "D" SHACKLE

MOORING SWIVEL

CHAIN SWIVEL

MAILLOT (SCREW LINK)

TWIN BOLLARDS WITH RAKED PILLARS AND A HAWSER (HEAVY ROPE)

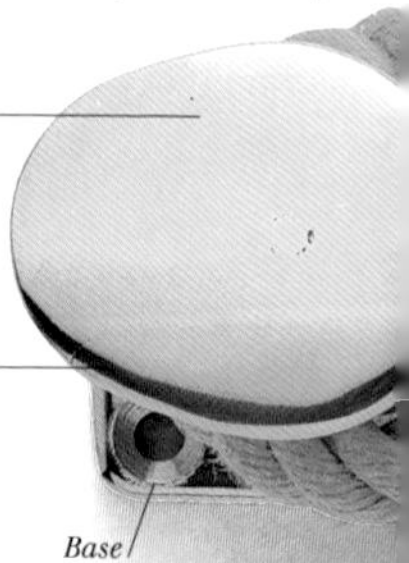
Flat
Rim
Base

ERTHING ROPES (HAWSERS)

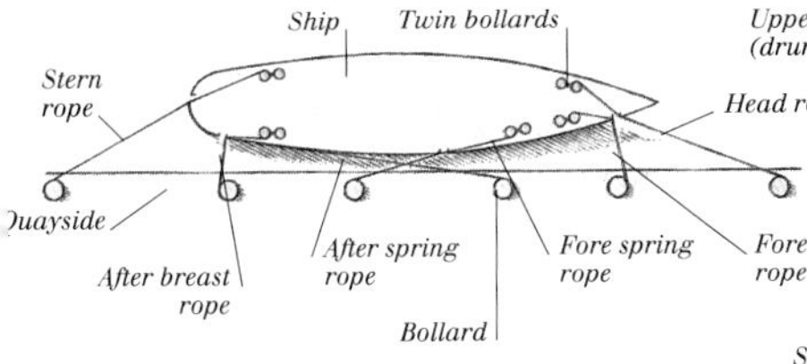
Ship
Twin bollards
Stern rope
Head rope
Quayside
After breast rope
After spring rope
Bollard
Fore spring rope
Fore breast rope

MOORING ROPE BENDS

IAWSER BEND TWO DOUBLE ROUND TURNS AND DOUBLE HALF HITCHES)

Standing part
Seizing

CARRICK BEND

Seizing

SINGLE SHEET BEND SWAB HITCH)

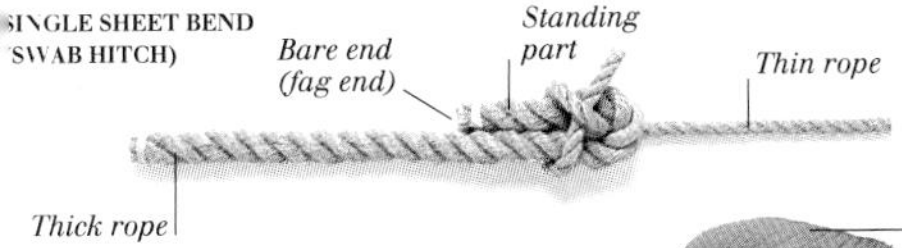
Bare end (fag end)
Standing part
Thin rope
Thick rope

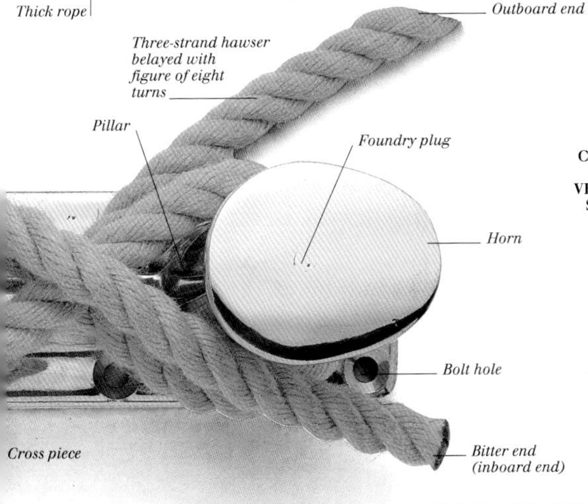
Outboard end
Three-strand hawser belayed with figure of eight turns
Pillar
Foundry plug
Horn
Bolt hole
Cross piece
Bitter end (inboard end)

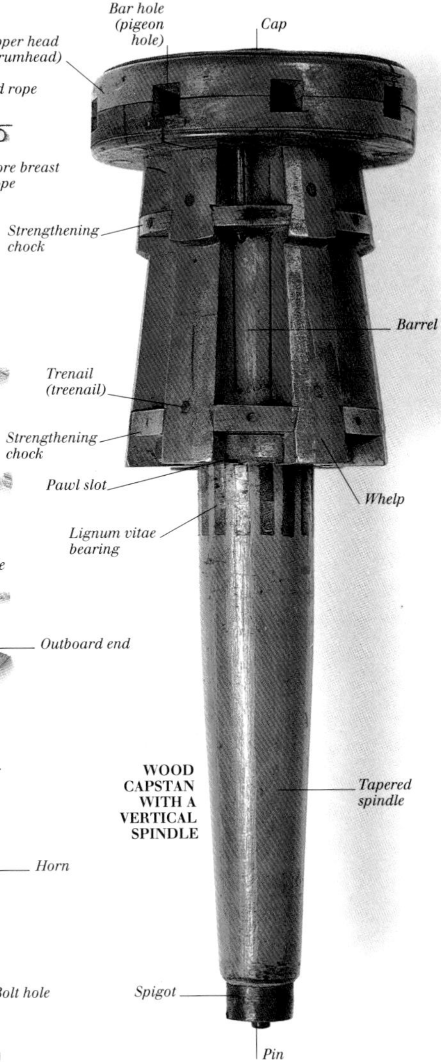
Bar hole (pigeon hole)
Cap
Upper head (drumhead)
Strengthening chock
Barrel
Trenail (treenail)
Strengthening chock
Pawl slot
Whelp
Lignum vitae bearing
Tapered spindle
Spigot
Pin

WOOD CAPSTAN WITH A VERTICAL SPINDLE

Ropes and knots

ALL KINDS OF ROPES ARE USED AT SEA, from thin twines and yarns to thick hawsers. Synthetic fibres have been developed specifically for use at sea. Nylon ropes stretch, and so are ideal for anchoring; polypropylene has little stretch, so is ideal for halyards and sheets. Different types of knots are used for different purposes. Knots that join two ropes are called bends; hitches join a rope to another object; and bowlines produce an eye (loop) in the end of a rope. Ropes can be joined by splicing (unravelling the ends and weaving them together) or seizing (lashing the ropes together side by side).

FRENCH BOWLINE (PORTUGUESE BOWLINE)

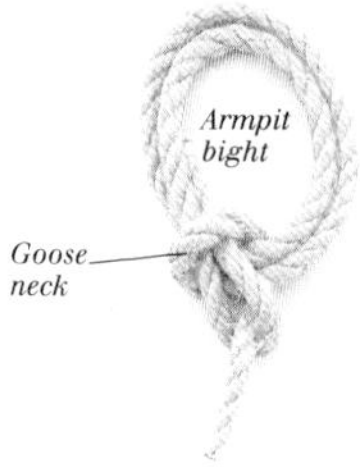
Armpit bight
Goose neck

SYNTHETIC ROPES

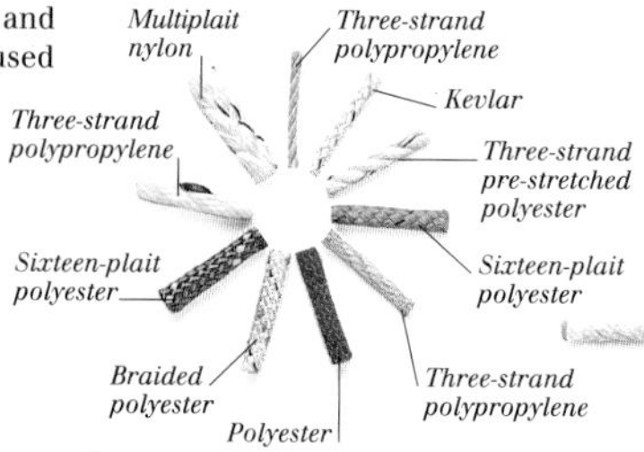
Multiplait nylon
Three-strand polypropylene
Kevlar
Three-strand pre-stretched polyester
Sixteen-plait polyester
Three-strand polypropylene
Polyester
Braided polyester
Sixteen-plait polyester
Three-strand polypropylene

Seizing

HALF HITCH WITH SEIZING

ROPEWORK

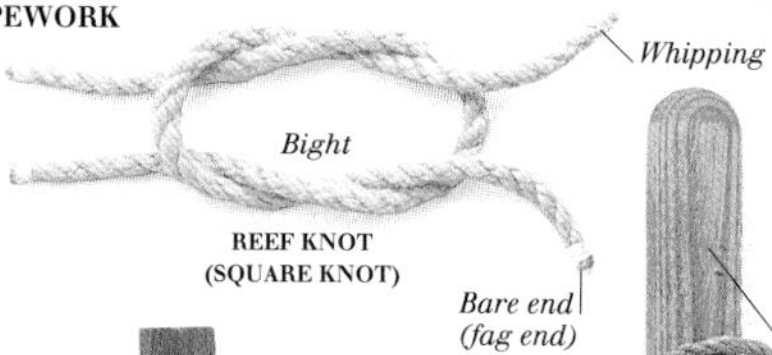
Whipping
Bight
Bare end (fag end)

REEF KNOT (SQUARE KNOT)

Eye

OVERHAND KNOT (HALF HITCH)

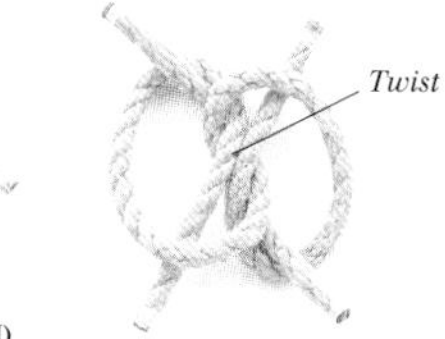
Twist

HUNTER'S BEND

End
Standing part

ROLLING HITCH

End
Standing part

CLOVE HITCH

MARLINSPIKE HITCH

BOWLINE

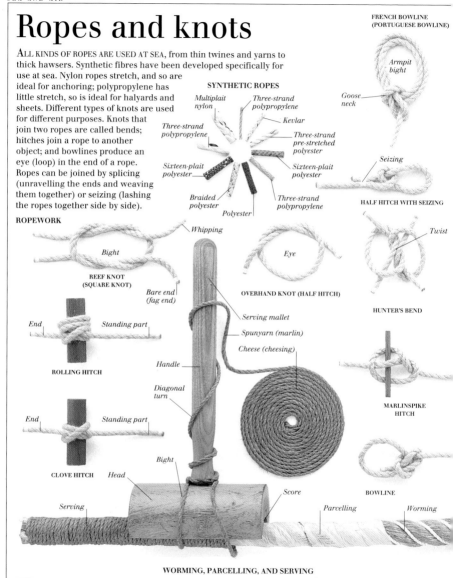

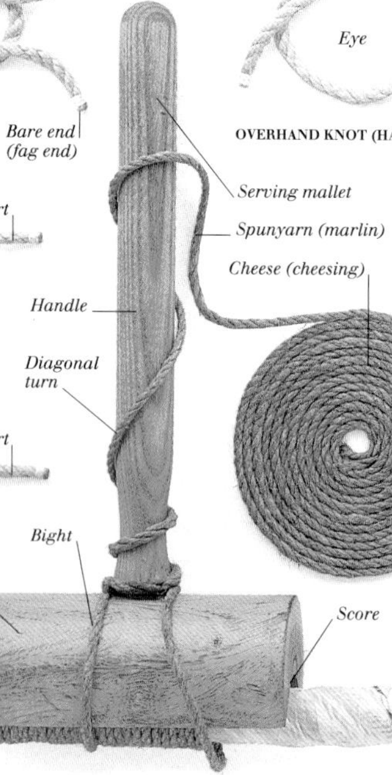
Serving mallet
Spunyarn (marlin)
Cheese (cheesing)
Handle
Diagonal turn
Bight
Head
Score
Serving
Parcelling
Worming

WORMING, PARCELLING, AND SERVING

THUMB KNOT

SPANISH BOWLINE

FLAT SEIZING (ROUND SEIZING)

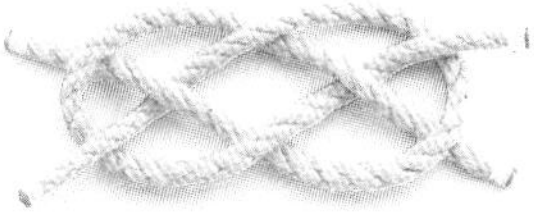

DOUBLE CARRICK BEND

LIGHTERMAN'S HITCH

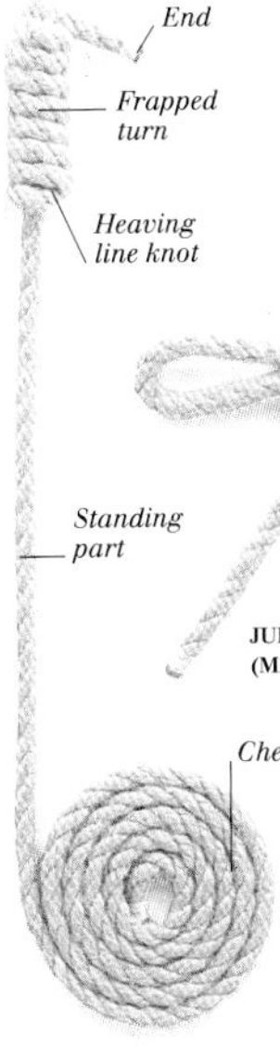
End
Frapped turn
Heaving line knot
Standing part
Cheese (cheesing)

HEAVING LINE

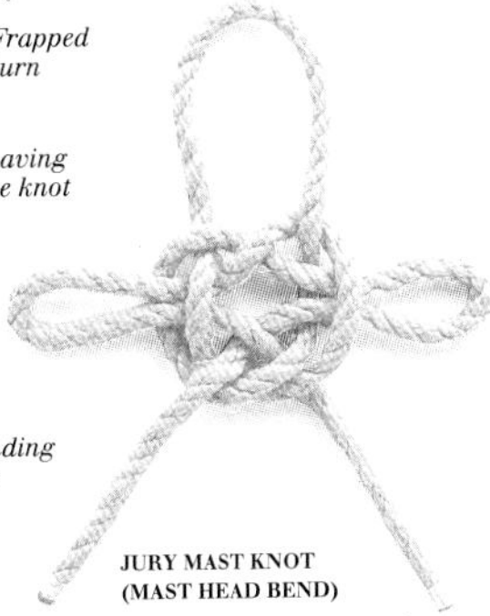

JURY MAST KNOT (MAST HEAD BEND)

SHEET BEND (SWAB HITCH)

HEAVING LINE BEND

MANHARNESS KNOT (BUTTERFLY KNOT; ARTILLERY LOOP)

Marlinspike

PINNED SHEEPSHANK

Rat tail
Jaw
Hawser laid three-strand manilla rope with right-handed lay

Paddle wheels and propellers

THE INVENTION OF THE STEAM ENGINE IN THE 18TH CENTURY made mechanically driven ships fitted with padd wheels or propellers a viable alternative to sails. Paddle wheels have fixed or feathered floats, and the model shown below features both types. Feathered floats give more propulsive power than fixed floats because they are almost upright at all times in the water. Paddle wheels were superseded by the propeller on ocean-going vessels in the mid-19th century. Propellers are more efficient, work better in rough water, and are less vulnerable in collisions. The first propellers were two-bladed but later three- and four-bladed versions are more powerful; the shape and pitch of blades have also been refined over the years. At the beginning of the 18th century, tillers were superseded on many larger ships by the ship's wheel as a means of steering.

SHIP'S WHEEL

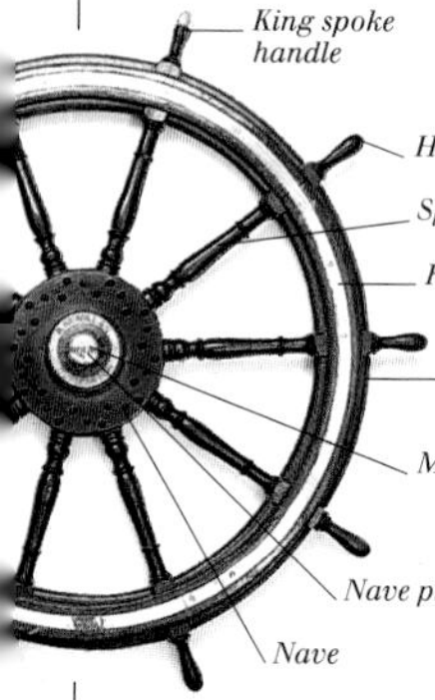
King spoke handle
Handle
Spoke
Rim plate
Felloe (rim section)
Maker's name
Nave plate
Nave

THREE-BLADED PROPELLER

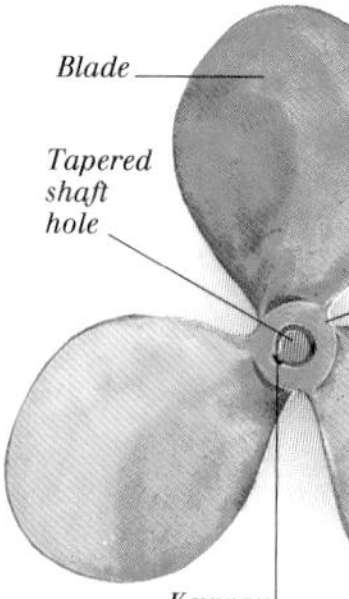
Blade
Tapered shaft hole
Hub
Keyway

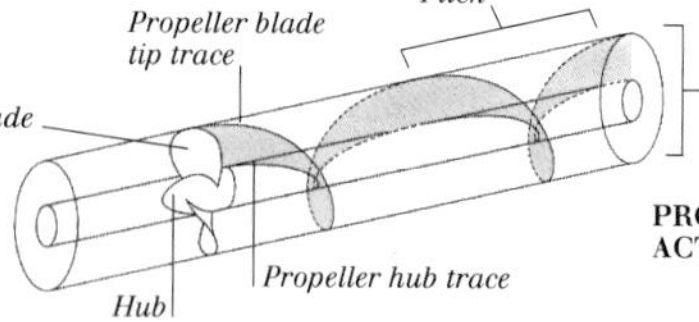
Pitch
Propeller blade tip trace
Propeller diameter
Blade
Propeller hub trace
Hub

PROPELLER ACTION

PADDLE WHEEL WITH FIXED FLOATS

OSCILLATING STEAM ENGINE

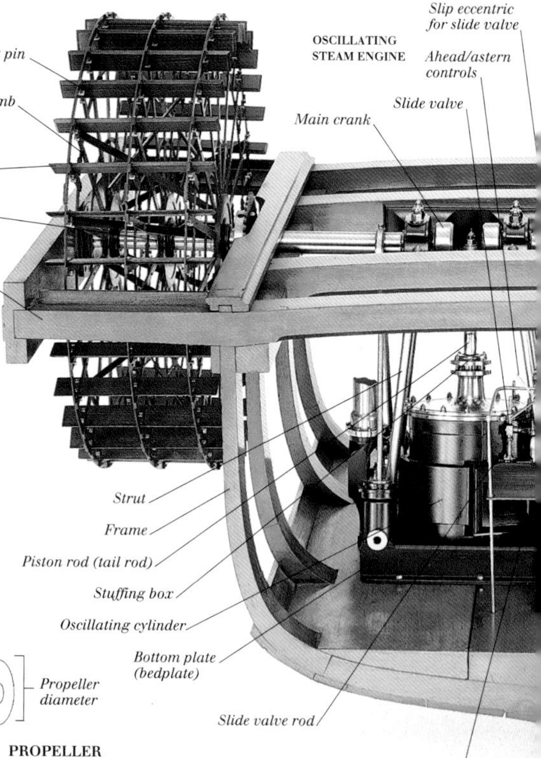
Wrist pin
Limb
Fixed float
Hub
Deck beam
Slip eccentric for slide valve
Ahead/astern controls
Slide valve
Main crank
Strut
Frame
Piston rod (tail rod)
Stuffing box
Oscillating cylinder
Bottom plate (bedplate)
Slide valve rod
Control platform

DESIGN FOR A STEAMBOAT WITH PADDLE WHEELS

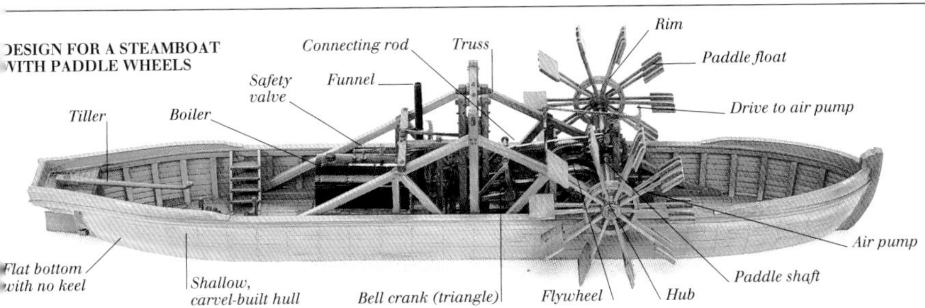
Rim
Connecting rod
Truss
Paddle float
Safety valve
Funnel
Drive to air pump
Tiller
Boiler
Air pump
Flat bottom with no keel
Shallow, carvel-built hull
Bell crank (triangle)
Flywheel
Hub
Paddle shaft

TYPES OF PROPELLER

FROUDE'S EARLY TEST PROPELLER

TUG PROPELLER

THREE-BLADED PROPELLER

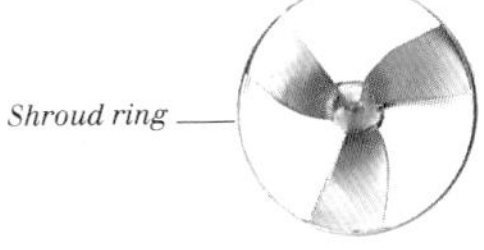
Shroud ring

SHROUD RING PROPELLER

PADDLE WHEEL WITH FEATHERED FLOATS

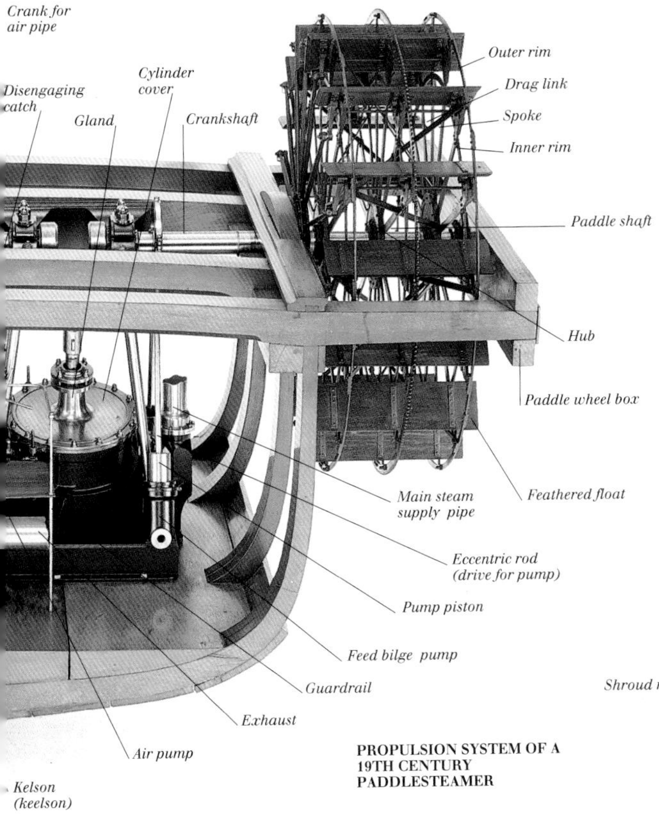
Crank for air pipe
Outer rim
Drag link
Cylinder cover
Disengaging catch
Gland
Crankshaft
Spoke
Inner rim
Paddle shaft
Hub
Paddle wheel box
Main steam supply pipe
Feathered float
Eccentric rod (drive for pump)
Pump piston
Feed bilge pump
Guardrail
Exhaust
Air pump
Kelson (keelson)

PROPULSION SYSTEM OF A 19TH CENTURY PADDLESTEAMER

Anatomy of an iron ship

IRON PARTS WERE USED IN THE HULLS OF WOODEN SHIPS AS EARLY AS 1675, often in the same form as the wooden parts that they replaced. Eventually, as on the tea clipper Cutty Sark (below), iron rigging was found to be stronger than the traditional rope. The first "ironclads" were warships whose wooden hulls were protected by iron armour plates. Later ironclads actually had iron hulls. The model opposite is based on the British warship HMS Warrior, launched in 1860, the first battleship built entirely of iron. The plan of the iron paddlesteamer (bottom), built somewhat later, shows that this vessel was a sailing ship; but it also boasted a steam propulsion plant amidships that turned two side paddlewheels. Early iron hulls were made from plates that were painstakingly rivetted together (as below), but by the 20th century vessels began to be welded together, whole sections at a time. The Second World War "liberty ship" was one of the first of these "production-line vessels".

TEA CLIPPER

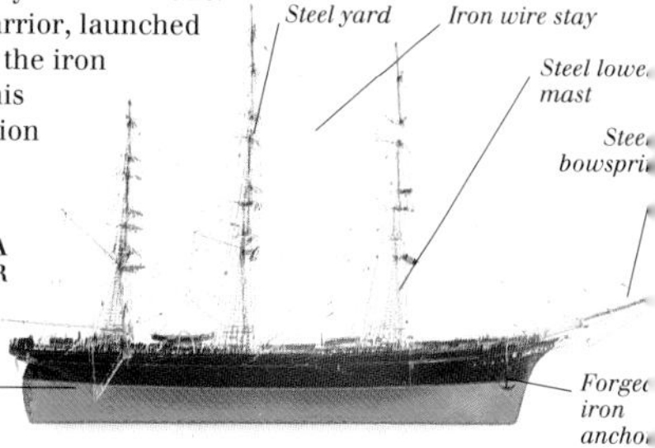
Steel yard
Iron wire stay
Steel lowe
mast
Stee
bowspri
Wooden planking with copper sheathing
Forge
iron
ancho

RIVETTED PLATES

Pan head rivet
Plate
Button head rivet (snap head)
Seam

LIBERTY SHIP

Accommodation section
Cargo derrick
Weld line
Gun section
Stern section
Midships section
Cargo hold
Bow section

PLAN OF AN IRON PADDLESTEAMER

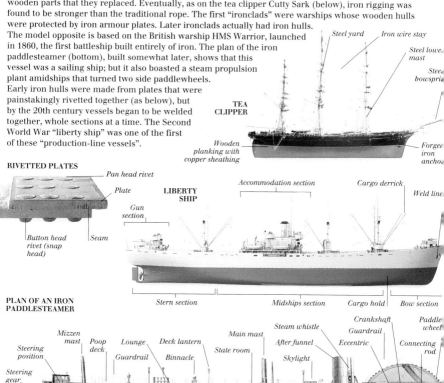

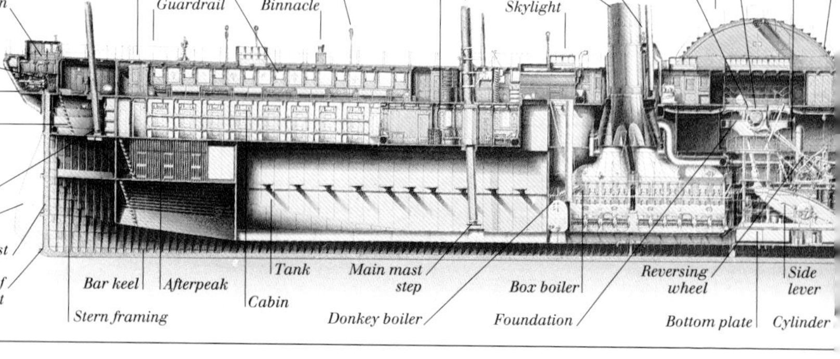
Mizzen mast
Poop deck
Lounge
Deck lantern
Main mast
Steam whistle
Crankshaft
Paddle
wheel
Guardrail
Steering position
Guardrail
Binnacle
State room
After funnel
Eccentric
Connecting rod
Skylight
Steering gear
Stern
Vertical frame ladder
Mast step
Rudder
Rudder post
Heel of rudder post
Bar keel
Afterpeak
Tank
Main mast step
Box boiler
Reversing wheel
Side lever
Stern framing
Cabin
Donkey boiler
Foundation
Bottom plate
Cylinder

NUCLEAR "HUNTER-KILLER" SUBMARINE

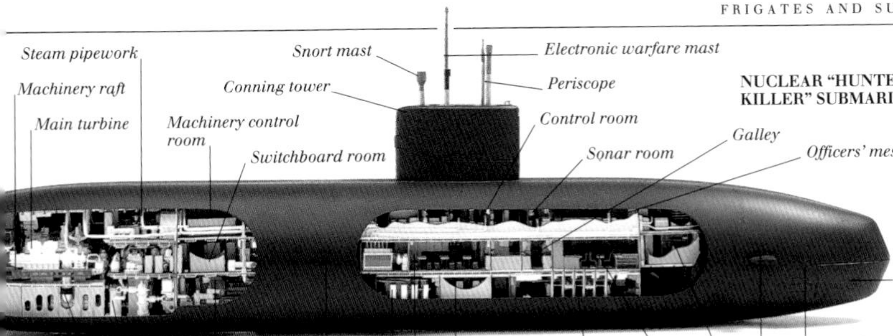
Steam pipework
Machinery raft
Main turbine
Machinery control room
Switchboard room
Snort mast
Conning tower
Electronic warfare mast
Periscope
Control room
Sonar room
Galley
Officers' mess
SONAR transducer array
Torpedo tube
Forward hydroplane
Junior ratings' bunk space
Senior ratings' mess
Torpedo compartment
Wireless office
Junior ratings' mess
Carbon dioxide scrubber compartment
Reactor space
Diesel motor compartment
Distiller
Main engine team condenser

Muzzle

Barrel

15 cm (6 in) SHELL
This shell is designed to burst in the air above its target.

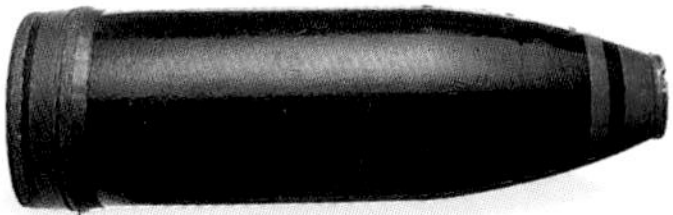
Driving band

SHELL CASE

Bursting charge (explosive)
Flash tube
Body
Wooden packing
Transit plug
Bullet
Expelling plate

CROSS-SECTION OF THE SHELL

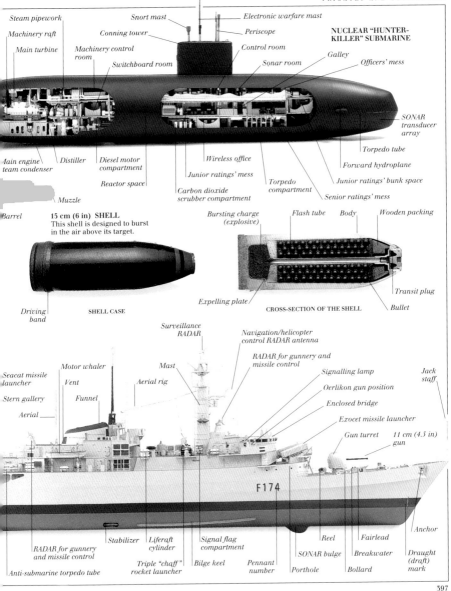

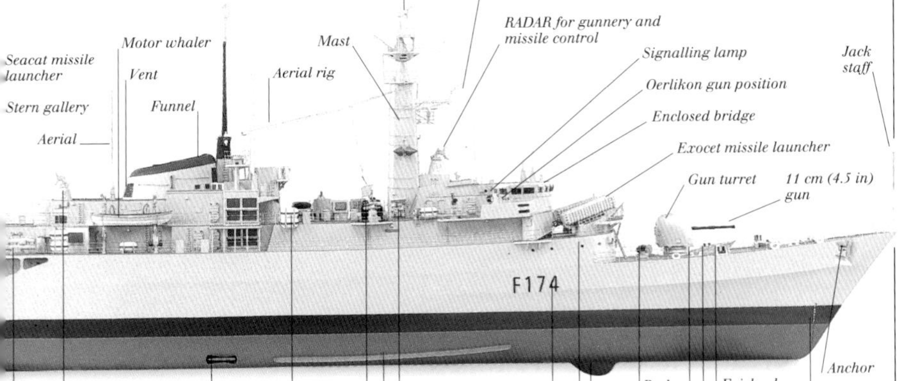
Surveillance RADAR
Navigation/helicopter control RADAR antenna
RADAR for gunnery and missile control
Mast
Motor whaler
Seacat missile launcher
Vent
Aerial rig
Stern gallery
Funnel
Aerial
Signalling lamp
Oerlikon gun position
Enclosed bridge
Exocet missile launcher
Gun turret
11 cm (4.5 in) gun
Jack staff
F174
Anchor
Fairlead
Reel
Draught (draft) mark
Breakwater
SONAR bulge
Bollard
Porthole
Pennant number
Bilge keel
Signal flag compartment
Liferaft cylinder
Triple "chaff" rocket launcher
Stabilizer
RADAR for gunnery and missile control
Anti-submarine torpedo tube

Pioneers of flight

FLIGHT HAS FASCINATED MANKIND for centuries, and countless unsuccessful flying machines have been designed. The first successful flight was made by the French Montgolfier brothers in 1783, when they flew a balloon over Paris. The next major advance was the development of gliders, notably by the Englishman Sir George Cayley, who in 1845 designed the first glider to make a sustained flight, and by the German Otto Lilienthal, who became known as the world's first pilot because he managed to achieve controlled flights. However, powered flight did not become a practical possibility until the invention of lightweight, petrol-driven internal combustion engines at the end of the 19th century. Then, in 1903, the American brothers Orville and Wilbur Wright made the first powered flight in their Wright Flyer biplane, which used a four-cylinder, petrol-driven engine. Aircraft design advanced rapidly, and in 1909 the Frenchman Louis Blériot made his pioneering flight across the English Channel (see pp. 400-401). The American Glenn Curtiss also achieved several "firsts" in his Model-D Pusher and its variants, most notably winning the world's first competition for airspeed at Reims in 1909.

FRONT VIEW OF WRIGHT FLYER, 1903

Pusher propeller (rear
mounted propeller
Biplane elevator
Chain drive to starboard propeller
Fuel tank
Propeller-shaft bracing strut
Offset pilot's cradle
Take-off and landing skid
Side-mounted engine to balance pilot's weight

SIDE VIEW OF CURTISS MODEL-D PUSHER, 1911

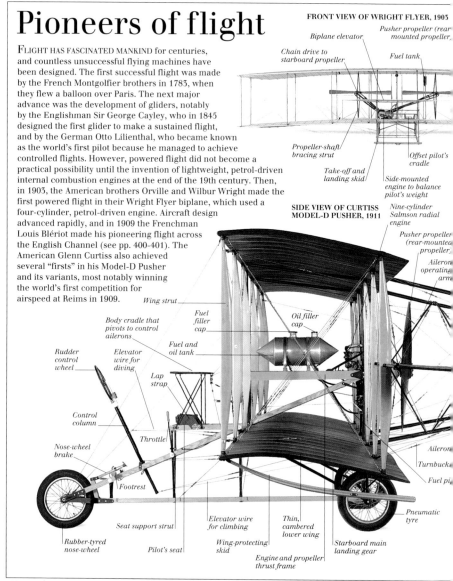

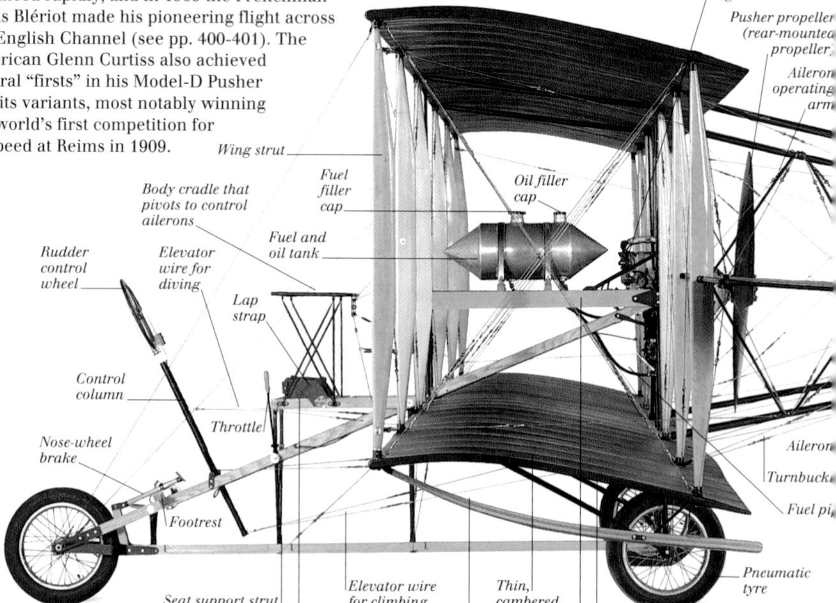
Nine-cylinder Salmson radial engine
Pusher propeller
(rear-mounte
propeller
Aileron
operating
arm
Wing strut
Fuel filler cap
Oil filler cap
Body cradle that pivots to control ailerons
Fuel and oil tank
Rudder control wheel
Elevator wire for diving
Lap strap
Control column
Throttle
Nose-wheel brake
Aileron
Turnbuck
Fuel pi
Footrest
Pneumatic tyre
Seat support strut
Elevator wire for climbing
Thin, cambered lower wing
Rubber-tyred nose-wheel
Pilot's seat
Wing-protecting skid
Starboard main landing gear
Engine and propeller thrust frame

SIDE VIEW OF WRIGHT FLYER, 1903

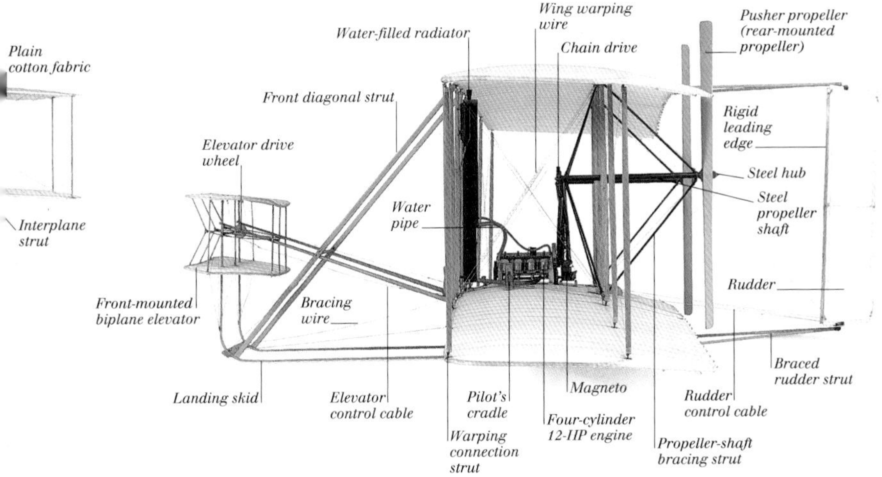
Plain cotton fabric
Interplane strut
Water-filled radiator
Wing warping wire
Chain drive
Pusher propeller (rear-mounted propeller)
Front diagonal strut
Rigid leading edge
Elevator drive wheel
Steel hub
Steel propeller shaft
Water pipe
Rudder
Front-mounted biplane elevator
Bracing wire
Braced rudder strut
Landing skid
Elevator control cable
Pilot's cradle
Magneto
Rudder control cable
Warping connection strut
Four-cylinder 12-HP engine
Propeller-shaft bracing strut

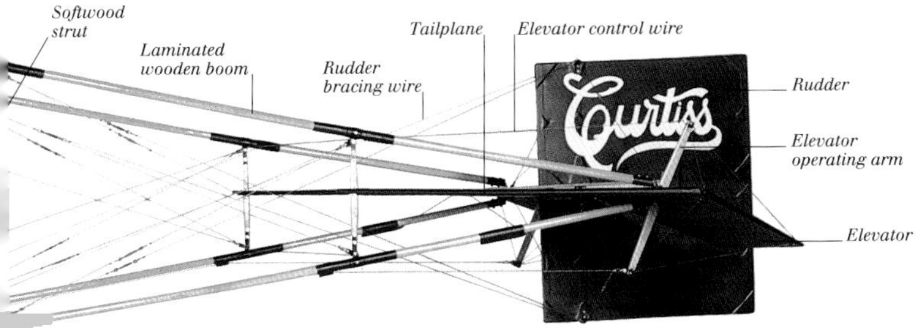
Softwood strut
Laminated wooden boom
Rudder bracing wire
Tailplane
Elevator control wire
Curtiss
Rudder
Elevator operating arm
Elevator

FRONT VIEW OF CURTISS MODEL-D PUSHER, 1911

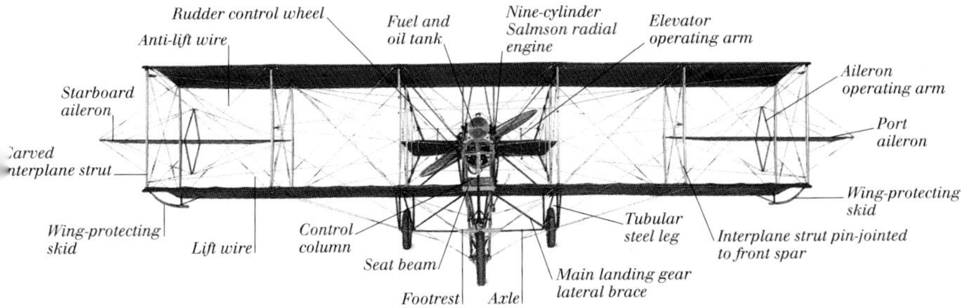
Rudder control wheel
Fuel and oil tank
Nine-cylinder Salmson radial engine
Elevator operating arm
Anti-lift wire
Aileron operating arm
Starboard aileron
Port aileron
Carved interplane strut
Wing-protecting skid
Wing-protecting skid
Lift wire
Control column
Seat beam
Tubular steel leg
Interplane strut pin-jointed to front spar
Main landing gear lateral brace
Footrest
Axle

Early monoplanes

RUMPLER MONOPLANE, 1908

MONOPLANES HAVE ONE WING on each side of the fuselage. The principal disadvantage of this arrangement in early, wooden-framed aircraft was that single wings were weak and required strong wires to brace them to king-posts above and below the fuselage. However, single wings also had advantages: they experienced less drag than multiple wings, allowing greater speed; they also made aircraft more manoeuvrable because single wings were easier to warp (twist) than double wings, and warping the wings was how pilots controlled the roll of early aircraft. By 1912, the French pilot Louis Blériot had used a monoplane to make the first flight across the English Channel, and the Briton Robert Blackburn and the Frenchman Armand Deperdussin had proved the greater speed of monoplanes. However, a spate of crashes caused by broken wings discouraged monoplane production, except in Germany, where all-metal monoplanes were developed in 1917. The wings of all-metal monoplanes did not need strengthening by struts or bracing wires, but despite this, such planes were not widely adopted until the 1930s.

FRONT VIEW OF BLACKBURN MONOPLANE, 1912

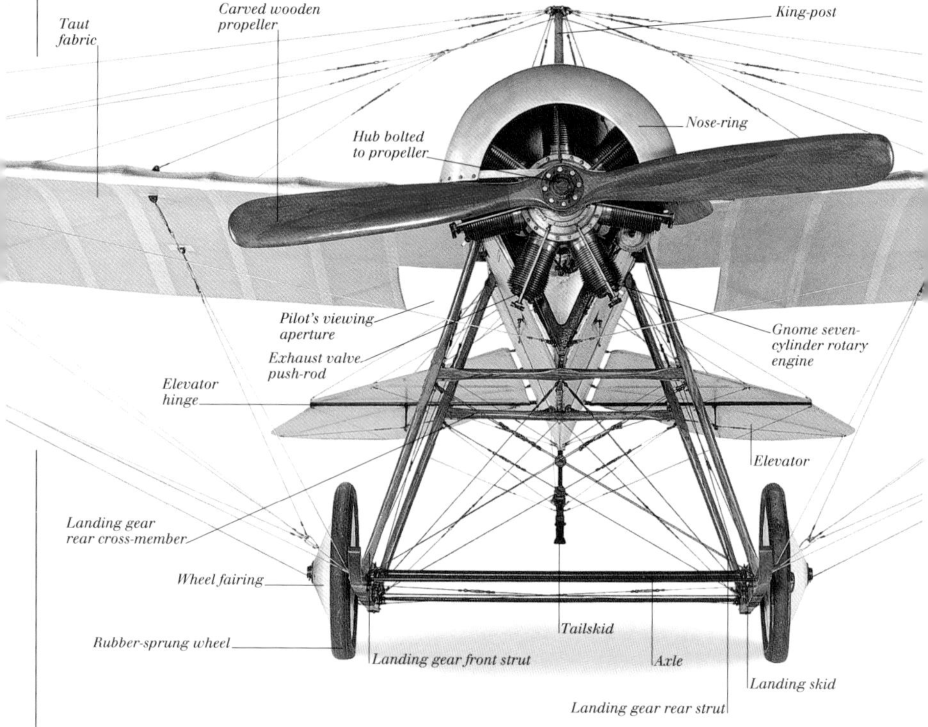

Taut fabric
Carved wooden propeller
King-post
Nose-ring
Hub bolted to propeller
Pilot's viewing aperture
Gnome seven-cylinder rotary engine
Exhaust valve push-rod
Elevator hinge
Elevator
Landing gear rear cross-member
Wheel fairing
Rubber-sprung wheel
Tailskid
Landing gear front strut
Axle
Landing skid
Landing gear rear strut

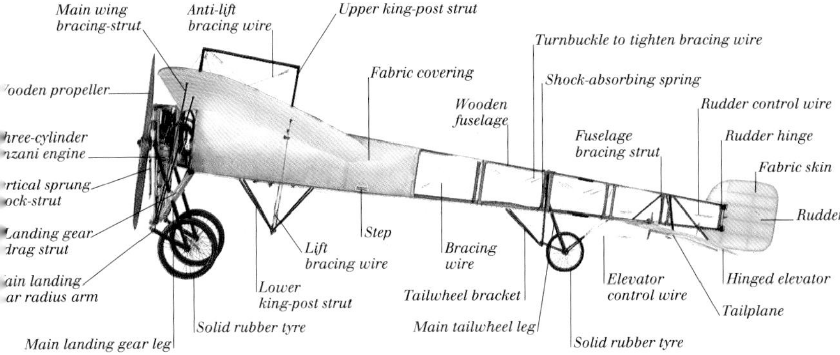
Main wing bracing-strut
Anti-lift bracing wire
Upper king-post strut
Turnbuckle to tighten bracing wire
Fabric covering
Shock-absorbing spring
ooden propeller
Wooden fuselage
Rudder control wire
hree-cylinder
nzani engine
Fuselage bracing strut
Rudder hinge
Fabric skin
rtical sprung
ock-strut
Rudder
Landing gear
drag strut
Step
Lift bracing wire
Bracing wire
ain landing
ar radius arm
Lower king-post strut
Tailwheel bracket
Elevator control wire
Hinged elevator
Tailplane
Solid rubber tyre
Main tailwheel leg
Solid rubber tyre
Main landing gear leg

SIDE VIEW OF BLÉRIOT XI, 1909

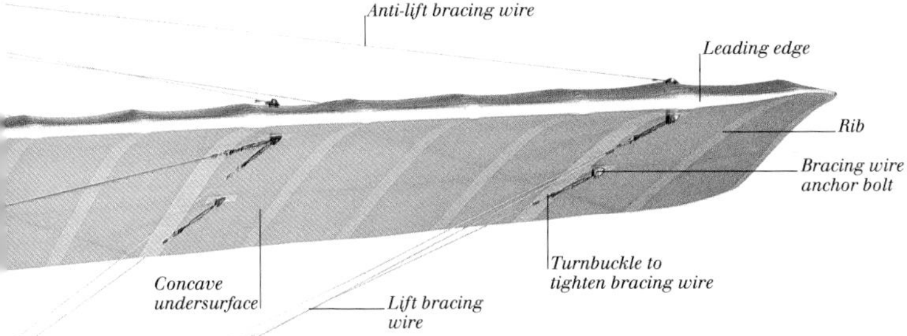
Anti-lift bracing wire
Leading edge
Rib
Bracing wire anchor bolt
Turnbuckle to tighten bracing wire
Concave undersurface
Lift bracing wire

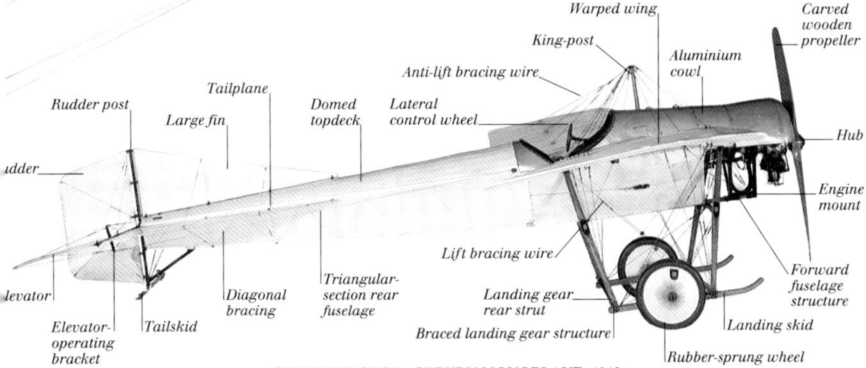
Warped wing
Carved wooden propeller
King-post
Aluminium cowl
Anti-lift bracing wire
Tailplane
Rudder post
Domed topdeck
Lateral control wheel
Large fin
Hub
udder
Engine mount
Lift bracing wire
Forward fuselage structure
Triangular-section rear fuselage
levator
Diagonal bracing
Landing gear rear strut
Landing skid
Elevator-operating bracket
Tailskid
Braced landing gear structure
Rubber-sprung wheel

SIDE VIEW OF BLACKBURN MONOPLANE, 1912

Biplanes and triplanes

LAMINATED PROPELLER

BIPLANES DOMINATED AIRCRAFT DESIGN until the 1930s, largely because some early monoplanes (see pp. 400-401) were too fragile to withstand the stresses of flight. The struts between biplanes' wings made the wings strong compared with those of early monoplanes, although the greater surface area of biplanes' wings increased drag and reduced speed. Many aircraft designers also developed triplanes, which had a particular advantage over biplanes: more wings meant a shorter wingspan to achieve the same lifting power, and a shorter wingspan gave greater manoeuvrability. Triplanes were most successful as fighters during World War I, the German Fokker triplane being a notable example. However, the greater manoeuvrability of triplanes was no advantage for normal flying and so most manufacturers continued to make biplanes. Many other aircraft designs were attempted. Some were quadruplanes, with four pairs of wings. Some had tandem wings (two pairs of monoplane wings, one behind the other). One of the most bizarre designs was by the Englishman Horatio Phillips: it had 20 sets of narrow wings and looked rather like a Venetian blind.

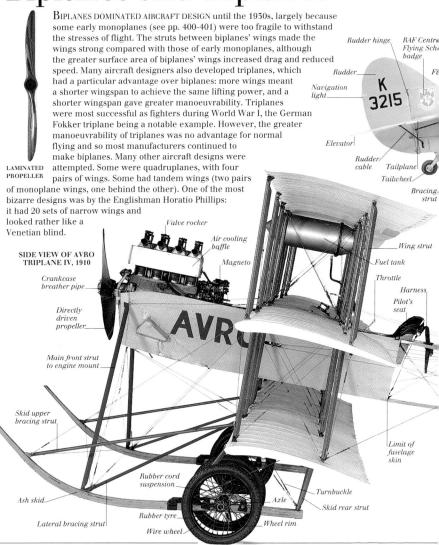

Rudder hinge
Rudder
Navigation light
K
3215
Elevator
Rudder cable
Tailplane
Tailwheel
Bracing strut

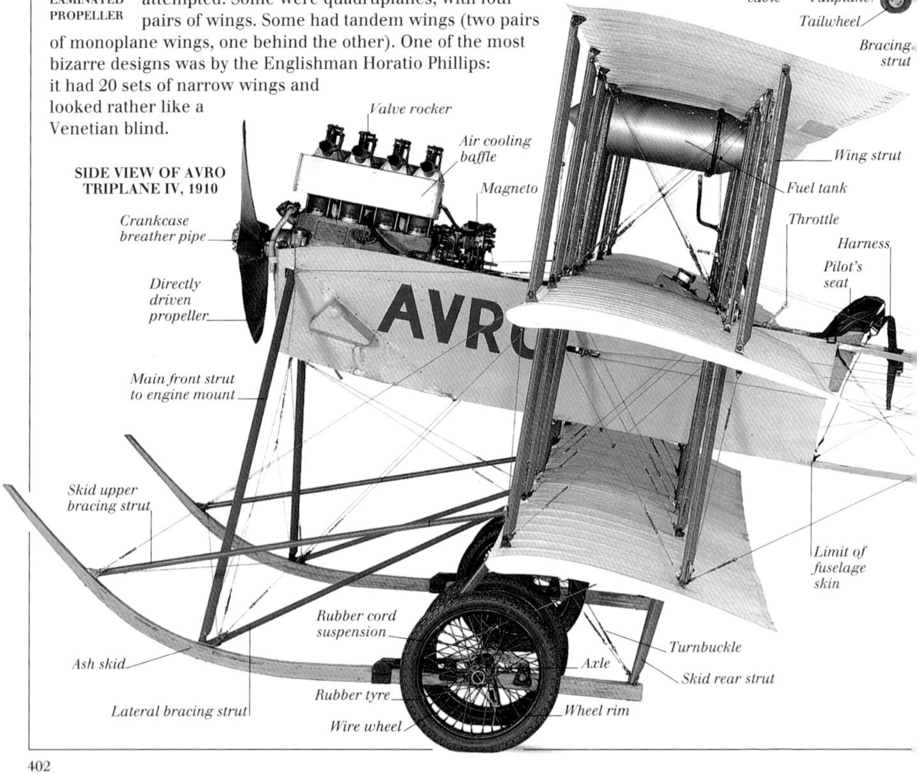
Valve rocker
Air cooling baffle
Magneto
Wing strut
Fuel tank
Throttle
Harness
Pilot's seat
Crankcase breather pipe
Directly driven propeller
AVRO
Main front strut to engine mount
Skid upper bracing strut
Limit of fuselage skin
Rubber cord suspension
Turnbuckle
Axle
Skid rear strut
Ash skid
Rubber tyre
Wheel rim
Lateral bracing strut
Wire wheel

SIDE VIEW OF AVRO TRIPLANE IV, 1910

AVRO TUTOR BIPLANE, 1931

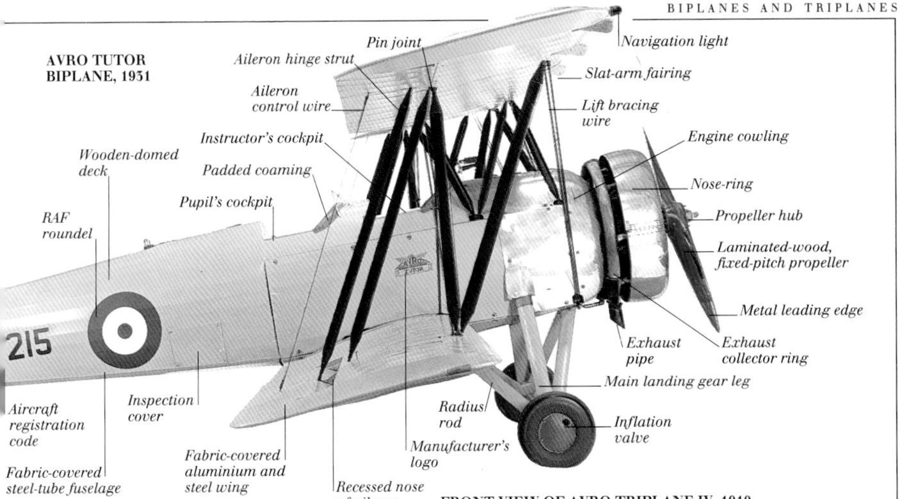
Pin joint
Aileron hinge strut
Navigation light
Slat-arm fairing
Aileron control wire
Lift bracing wire
Instructor's cockpit
Engine cowling
Wooden-domed deck
Padded coaming
Nose-ring
Pupil's cockpit
Propeller hub
RAF roundel
Laminated-wood, fixed-pitch propeller
215
Metal leading edge
Exhaust pipe
Exhaust collector ring
Main landing gear leg
Radius rod
Inflation valve
Inspection cover
Aircraft registration code
Fabric-covered steel-tube fuselage
Fabric-covered aluminium and steel wing
Manufacturer's logo
Recessed nose of aileron

FRONT VIEW OF AVRO TRIPLANE IV, 1910

Unpainted, varnished fabric
Leading edge
Fuel filler and vent
Fixed-pitch wooden propeller
Anti-lift bracing wire
Top wing
Wing strut
Middle wing
Rib
Bottom wing
Landing skid
Lift bracing wire
Axle
Elevator
Tailplane
Triangular-section fuselage
Lateral bracing strut

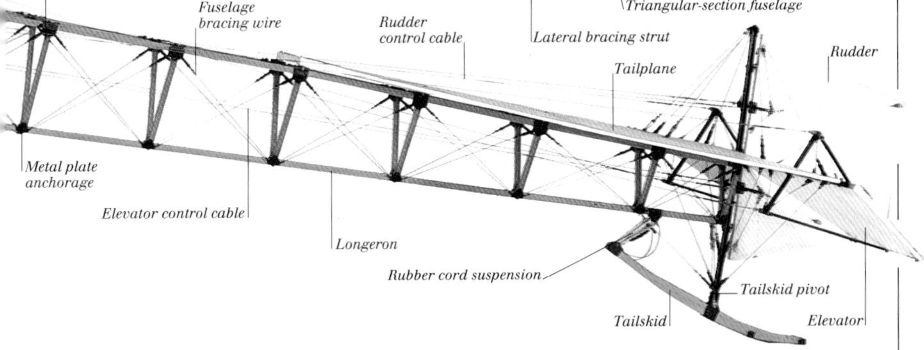
Triangular-section fuselage
Fuselage bracing wire
Rudder control cable
Rudder
Tailplane
Metal plate anchorage
Elevator control cable
Longeron
Rubber cord suspension
Tailskid pivot
Tailskid
Elevator

World War I aircraft

FLYING HELMET

WHEN WORLD WAR I STARTED in 1914, the main purpose of military aircraft was reconnaissance. The British-built BE 2, of which the BE 2B was a variant, was well-suited to this duty; it was very stable in flight, allowing the occupants to study the terrain, take photographs, and make notes. The BE 2 was also one of the first aircraft to drop bombs. One of the biggest problems for aircraft designers during the war was mounting machine-guns. On aircraft that had front-mounted propellers, the field of fire was restricted by the propeller and other parts of the aircraft. The problem was solved in 1915 by the Dutchman Anthony Fokker, who designed an interrupter gear that prevented a machine-gun from firing when a propeller blade passed in front of the barrel. The German LVG CVI had a forward-firing gun to the right of the engine, as well as a rear-cockpit gun, and a bombing capability. It was one of the most versatile aircraft of the war.

PORT WINGS FROM A BE 2B

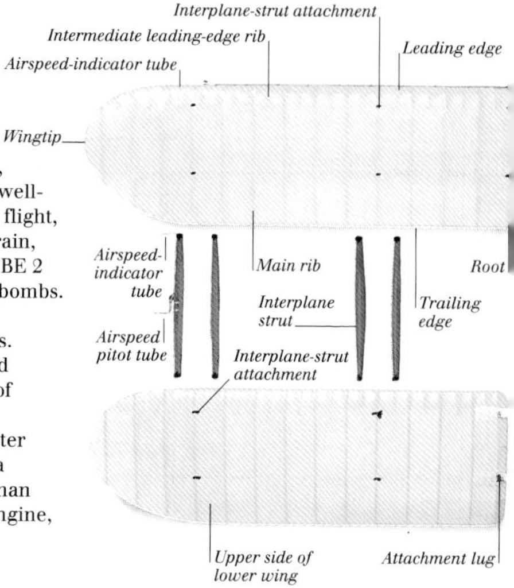
Interplane-strut attachment
Intermediate leading-edge rib
Leading edge
Airspeed-indicator tube
Wingtip
Airspeed-indicator tube
Main rib
Root
Interplane strut
Trailing edge
Airspeed pitot tube
Interplane-strut attachment
Upper side of lower wing
Attachment lug

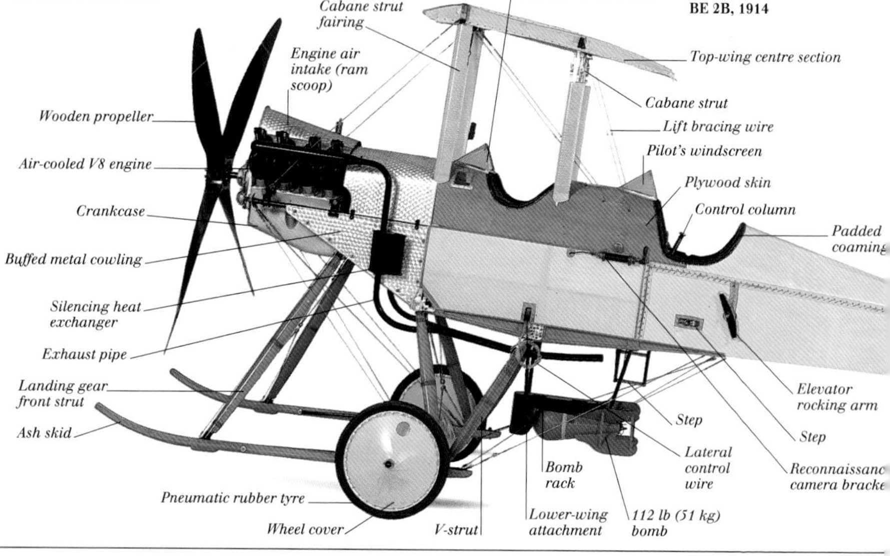
Observer's windscreen
Cabane strut fairing
Engine air intake (ram scoop)
Top-wing centre section
Cabane strut
Lift bracing wire
Pilot's windscreen
Wooden propeller
Air-cooled V8 engine
Plywood skin
Control column
Crankcase
Padded coaming
Buffed metal cowling
Silencing heat exchanger
Exhaust pipe
Landing gear front strut
Elevator rocking arm
Ash skid
Step
Step
Lateral control wire
Bomb rack
Reconnaissance camera bracket
Pneumatic rubber tyre
Wheel cover
V-strut
Lower-wing attachment
112 lb (51 kg) bomb

BE 2B, 1914

SIDE VIEW OF LVG CVI, 1917

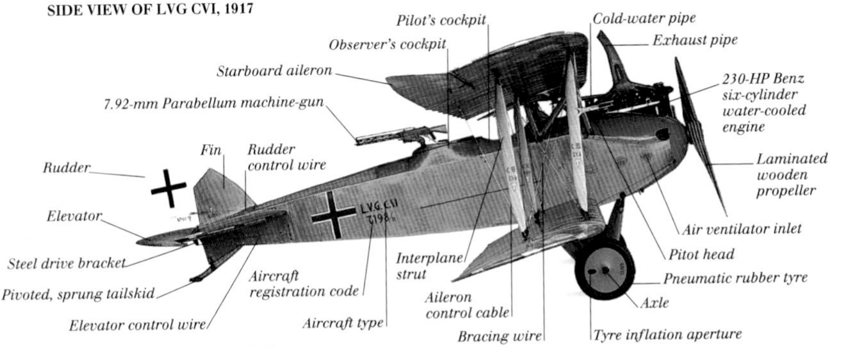
Pilot's cockpit
Cold-water pipe
Exhaust pipe
Observer's cockpit
Starboard aileron
230-HP Benz six-cylinder water-cooled engine
7.92-mm Parabellum machine-gun
Fin
Rudder control wire
Rudder
Laminated wooden propeller
Elevator
LVG.CVI
Air ventilator inlet
Steel drive bracket
Interplane strut
Pitot head
Pivoted, sprung tailskid
Aircraft registration code
Pneumatic rubber tyre
Aileron control cable
Axle
Elevator control wire
Aircraft type
Bracing wire
Tyre inflation aperture

FRONT VIEW OF LVG CVI, 1917

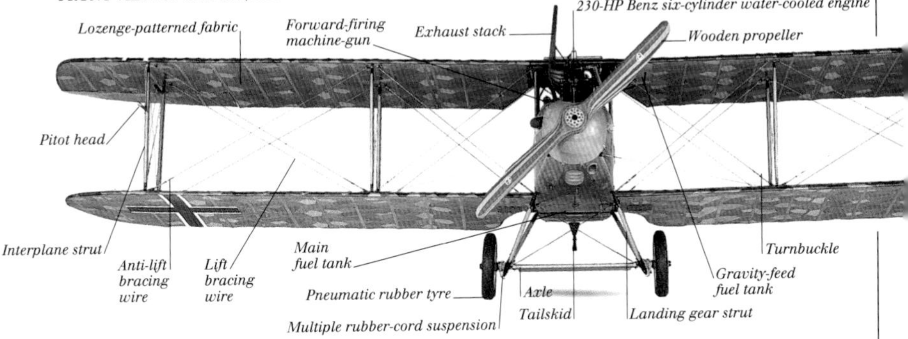
230-HP Benz six-cylinder water-cooled engine
Lozenge-patterned fabric
Forward-firing machine-gun
Exhaust stack
Wooden propeller
Pitot head
Interplane strut
Anti-lift bracing wire
Lift bracing wire
Main fuel tank
Turnbuckle
Gravity-feed fuel tank
Pneumatic rubber tyre
Axle
Multiple rubber-cord suspension
Tailskid
Landing gear strut

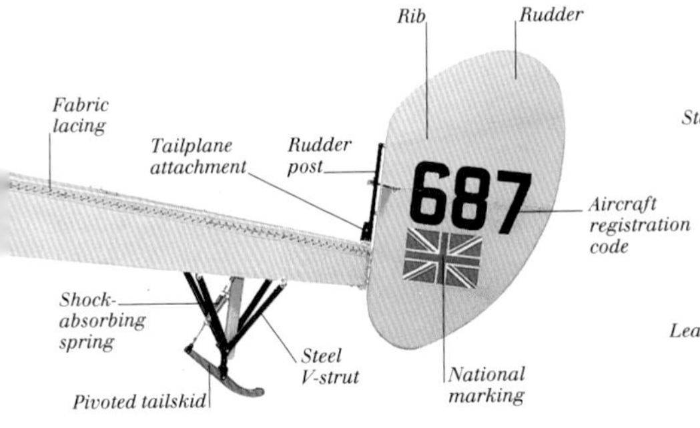
Rib
Rudder
Fabric lacing
Tailplane attachment
Rudder post
687
Aircraft registration code
Shock-absorbing spring
Steel V-strut
National marking
Pivoted tailskid

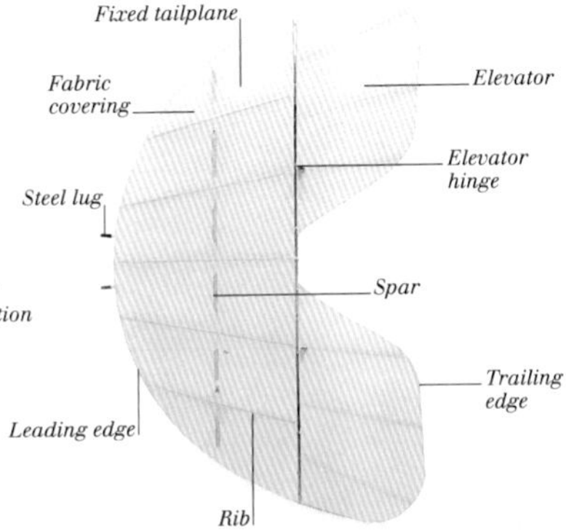
Fixed tailplane
Fabric covering
Elevator
Elevator hinge
Steel lug
Spar
Trailing edge
Leading edge
Rib

HORIZONTAL TAIL OF A BE 2B

Early passenger aircraft

UNTIL THE 1930s, most passenger aircraft were biplanes, with two pairs of wings and a wooden or metal framework covered with fabric or, sometimes, plywood. Such aircraft were restricted to low speeds and low altitudes because of the drag on their wings. Many had an open cockpit, situated behind or in front of an enclosed – but unpressurized – cabin that carried a maximum of ten people. The passengers usually sat in wicker chairs that were not bolted to the floor, and the journey could be bumpy when flying through turbulence. Warm clothing, and ear plugs to reduce the effects of prolonged noise, were often required. During the 1930s, powerful, streamlined, all-metal monoplanes, such as the Lockheed Electra shown here, became widespread. By 1939, the advent of pressurized cabins allowed fast flights at high altitudes, where there is less turbulence. Flying boats were still necessary on many routes until 1945 because of inadequate runways and the frequency of emergency sea-landings. World War II, however, resulted in enough good runways being built for land-planes to become standard on all major airline routes.

FRONT VIEW OF LOCKHEED ELECTRA, 1934

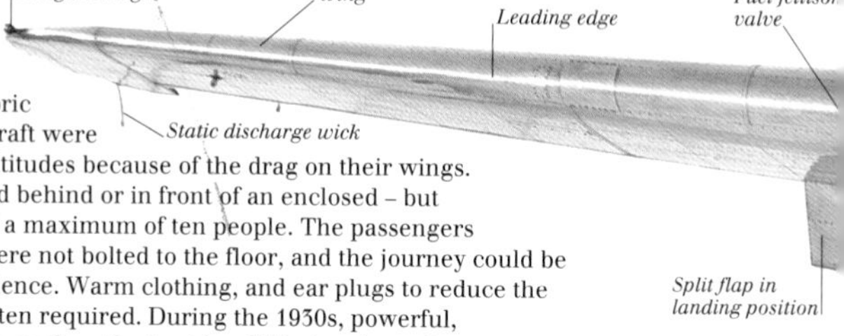
Green starboard navigation light
Flush-riveted metal-skinned wing
Leading edge
Fuel-jettison valve
Static discharge wick
Split flap in landing position

PASSENGER CABIN TRIM PANELS

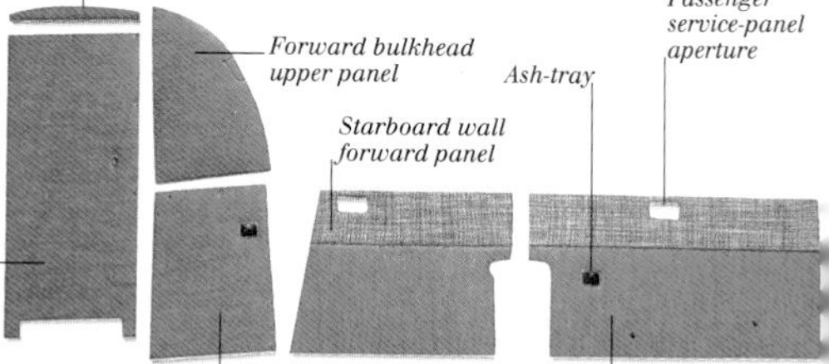
Roof trim panel
Forward bulkhead upper panel
Passenger service-panel aperture
Ash-tray
Starboard wall forward panel
Cockpit door panel
Forward bulkhead lower panel
Starboard wall mid-forward panel

SIDE VIEW OF LOCKHEED ELECTRA, 1934

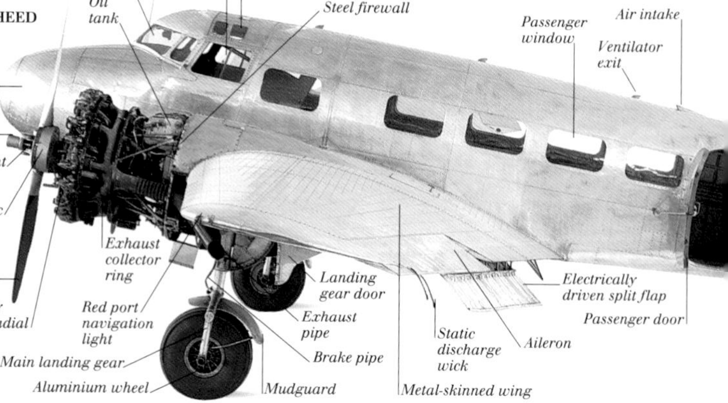
Cockpit windscreen
Sliding window
Emergency escape hatch
Oil tank
Steel firewall
Passenger window
Air intake
Ventilator exit
Nose
Propeller pitch-change cylinder
Blade counterweight
Spinner mounting disc
Exhaust collector ring
Variable-pitch propeller
Landing gear door
Electrically driven split flap
Pratt & Whitney nine-cylinder radial engine
Red port navigation light
Exhaust pipe
Passenger door
Static discharge wick
Aileron
Brake pipe
Main landing gear
Aluminium wheel
Mudguard
Metal-skinned wing

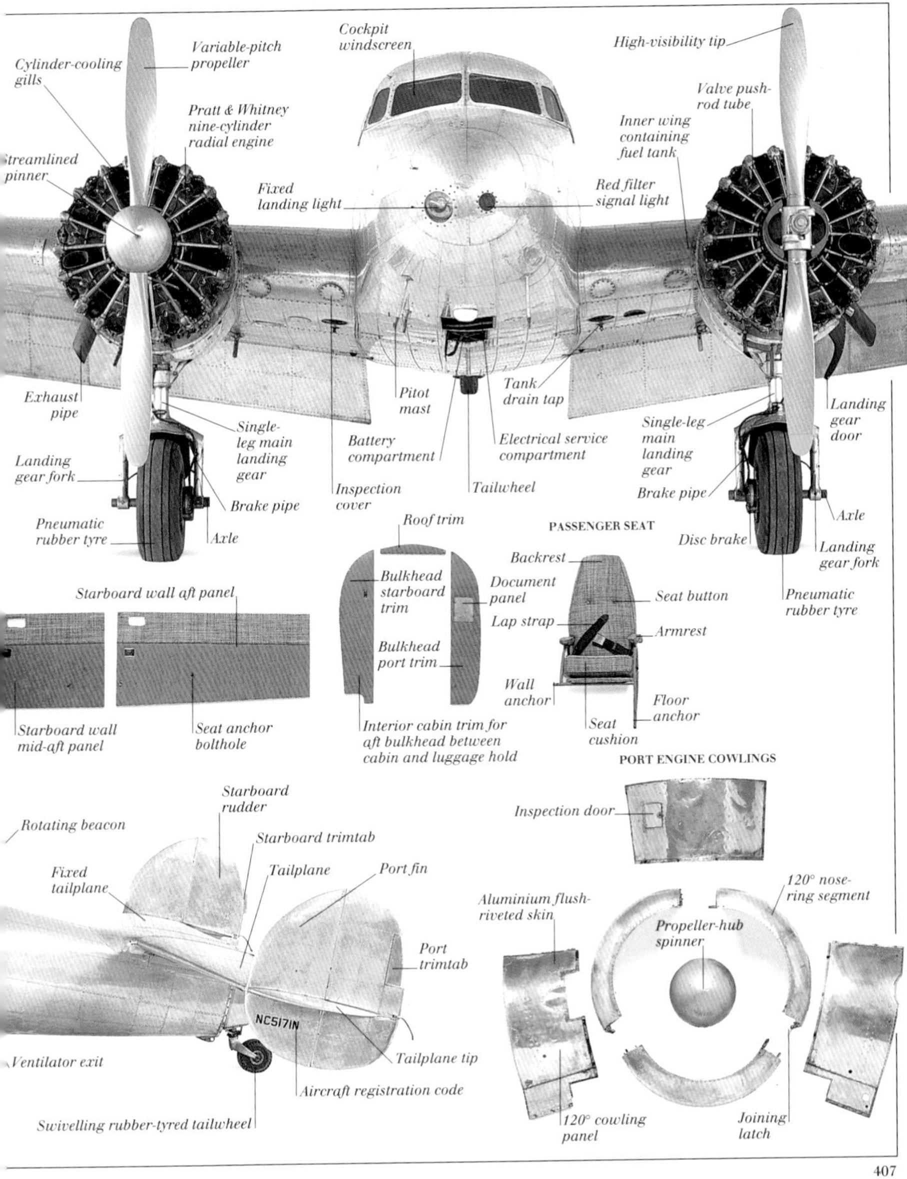
Cockpit windscreen
Variable-pitch propeller
Cylinder-cooling gills
High-visibility tip
Valve push-rod tube
Pratt & Whitney nine-cylinder radial engine
Inner wing containing fuel tank
Streamlined spinner
Fixed landing light
Red filter signal light
Exhaust pipe
Pitot mast
Tank drain tap
Landing gear door
Single-leg main landing gear
Battery compartment
Electrical service compartment
Single-leg main landing gear
Landing gear fork
Inspection cover
Tailwheel
Brake pipe
Brake pipe
Axle
Pneumatic rubber tyre
Axle
Roof trim
PASSENGER SEAT
Disc brake
Landing gear fork
Backrest
Bulkhead starboard trim
Document panel
Starboard wall aft panel
Seat button
Pneumatic rubber tyre
Lap strap
Armrest
Bulkhead port trim
Wall anchor
Floor anchor
Starboard wall mid-aft panel
Seat anchor bolthole
Interior cabin trim for aft bulkhead between cabin and luggage hold
Seat cushion
PORT ENGINE COWLINGS
Starboard rudder
Inspection door
Rotating beacon
Starboard trimtab
Fixed tailplane
Tailplane
Port fin
120° nose-ring segment
Aluminium flush-riveted skin
Propeller-hub spinner
Port trimtab
NC5171N
Ventilator exit
Tailplane tip
Aircraft registration code
Swivelling rubber-tyred tailwheel
120° cowling panel
Joining latch

World War II aircraft

WHEN WORLD WAR II began in 1939, air forces had already replaced most of their fabric-skinned biplanes with all-metal, stressed-skin monoplanes. Aircraft played a far greater role in military operations during World War II than ever before. The wide range of aircraft duties, and the introduction of radar tracking and guidance systems, put pressure on designers to improve aircraft performance. The main areas of improvement were speed, range, and engine power. Bombers became larger and more powerful – converting from two to four engines – in order to carry a heavier bomb load; the US B-17 Flying Fortress could carry up to 6.2 tonnes (6.1 tons) of bombs over a distance of about 3,200 km (2,000 miles). Some aircraft increased their range by using drop tanks (fuel tanks that were jettisoned when empty to reduce drag). Fighters needed speed and manoeuvrability: the Hawker Tempest shown here had a maximum speed of 700 kph (435 mph), and was one of the few Allied aircraft capable of catching the German jet-powered V1 "flying bomb". By 1944, Britain had introduced its first turbojet-powered aircraft, the Gloster Meteor fighter, and Germany had introduced the fastest fighter in the world, the turbojet-powered Me 262, which had a maximum speed of 868 kph (540 mph).

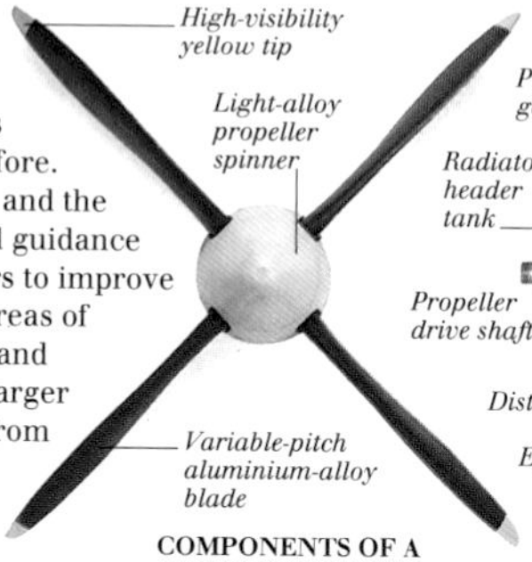
PROPELLER
High-visibility yellow tip
Light-alloy propeller spinner
Variable-pitch aluminium-alloy blade

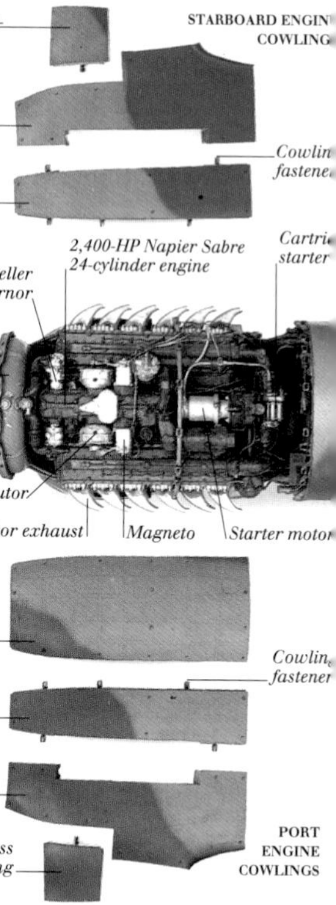
STARBOARD ENGINE COWLING
Radiator-access cowling
Lower side-cowling
Upper side-cowling
Cowling fastener
Cartridge starter
2,400-HP Napier Sabre 24-cylinder engine
Propeller governor
Radiator header tank
Propeller drive shaft
Distributor
Ejector exhaust
Magneto
Starter motor
Engine top cowling
Cowling fastener
Upper side-cowling
Lower side-cowling
Radiator-access cowling
PORT ENGINE COWLINGS

COMPONENTS OF A HAWKER TEMPEST MARK V, c.1943

SECTIONED B-17G FLYING FORTRESS BOMBER, c.1943

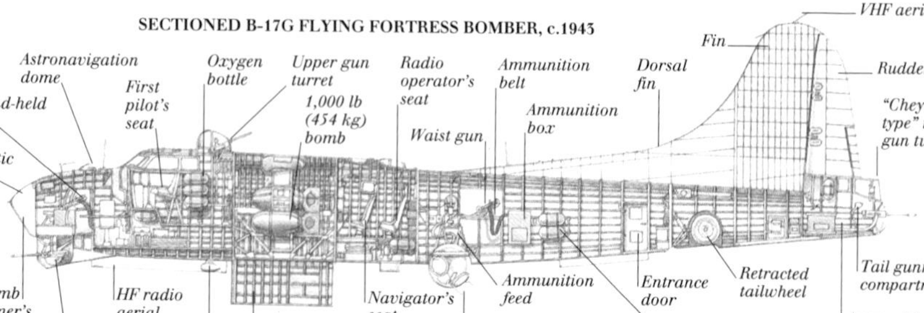
VHF aerial
Fin
Rudder
Dorsal fin
Astronavigation dome
Oxygen bottle
Upper gun turret
Radio operator's seat
Ammunition belt
Hand-held gun
First pilot's seat
1,000 lb (454 kg) bomb
Ammunition box
"Cheyenne type" tail-gun turret
Waist gun
Plastic nose
Bomb aimer's viewing panel
HF radio aerial
Chin gun turret
Bomb door
Direction-finding-aerial fairing
Navigator's seat
Sperry ball gun turret
Ammunition feed
Entrance door
Oxygen bottle
Retracted tailwheel
Tail gunner's compartment
Ammunition feed

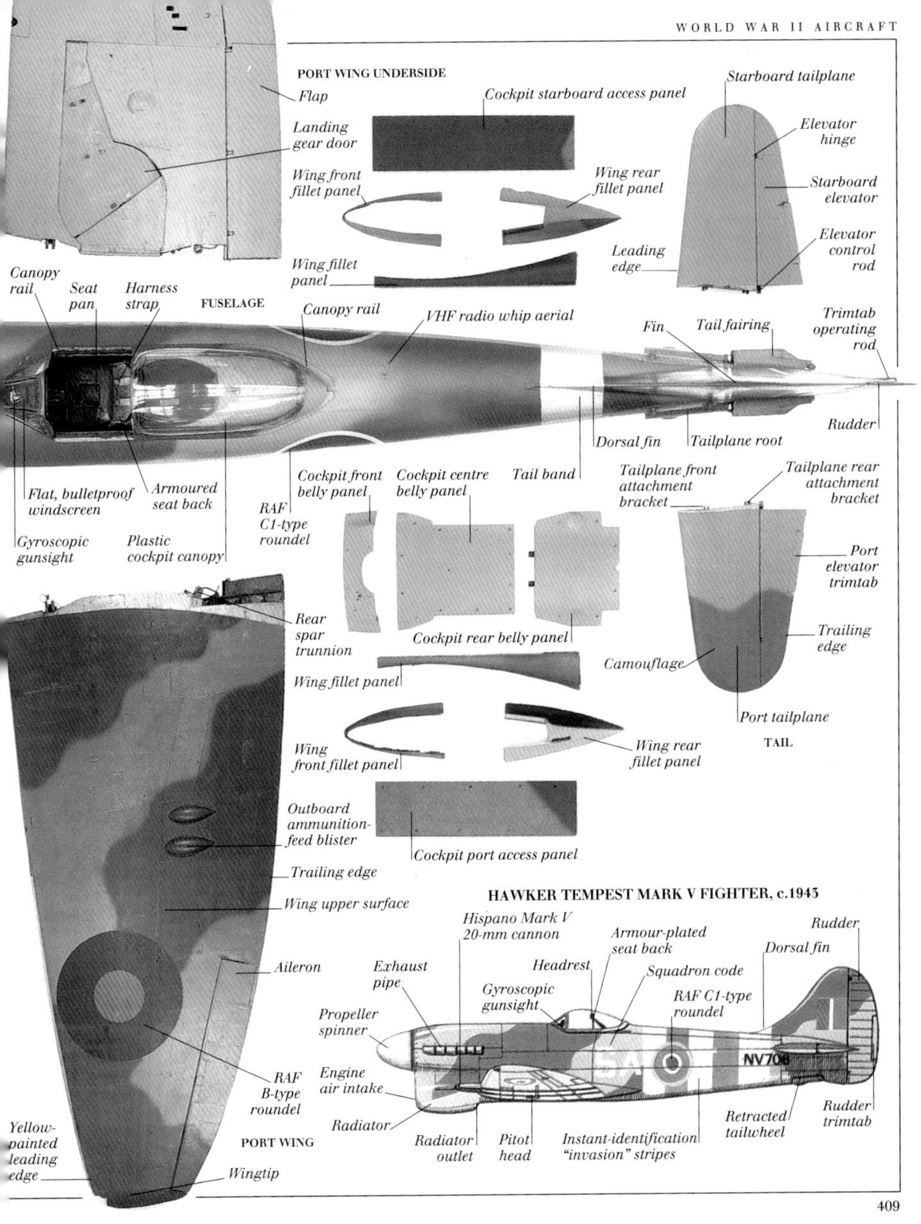
PORT WING UNDERSIDE
Flap
Landing gear door
Cockpit starboard access panel
Wing front fillet panel
Wing rear fillet panel
Wing fillet panel
Starboard tailplane
Elevator hinge
Starboard elevator
Elevator control rod
Leading edge
Canopy rail
Seat pan
Harness strap
FUSELAGE
Canopy rail
VHF radio whip aerial
Fin
Tail fairing
Trimtab operating rod
Rudder
Dorsal fin
Tailplane root
Tail band
Flat, bulletproof windscreen
Armoured seat back
Gyroscopic gunsight
Plastic cockpit canopy
RAF C1-type roundel
Cockpit front belly panel
Cockpit centre belly panel
Tailplane front attachment bracket
Tailplane rear attachment bracket
Port elevator trimtab
Rear spar trunnion
Cockpit rear belly panel
Trailing edge
Camouflage
Wing fillet panel
Port tailplane
TAIL
Wing front fillet panel
Wing rear fillet panel
Outboard ammunition-feed blister
Cockpit port access panel
Trailing edge
Wing upper surface
Aileron
RAF B-type roundel
Yellow-painted leading edge
PORT WING
Wingtip
HAWKER TEMPEST MARK V FIGHTER, c.1943
Hispano Mark V 20-mm cannon
Armour-plated seat back
Rudder
Dorsal fin
Exhaust pipe
Headrest
Squadron code
Gyroscopic gunsight
RAF C1-type roundel
Propeller spinner
NV706
Engine air intake
Radiator
Radiator outlet
Pitot head
Instant-identification "invasion" stripes
Retracted tailwheel
Rudder trimtab

Modern piston aero-engines

MID WEST TWO-STROKE, THREE-CYLINDER ENGINE

PISTON ENGINES today are used mainly to power the vast numbers of light aircraft and microlights, as well as crop-sprayers and crop-dusters, small helicopters, and fire-bombers (which dump water on large fires). Virtually all heavier aircraft are now powered by jet engines. Modern piston aero-engines work on the same basic principles as the engine used by the Wright brothers in the first powered flight in 1903. However, today's engines are more sophisticated than earlier engines. For example, modern aero-engines may use a two-stroke or a four-stroke combustion cycle; they may have from one to nine air- or water-cooled cylinders, which may be arranged horizontally, in-line, in V formation, or radially; and they may drive the aircraft's propeller either directly or through a reduction gearbox. One of the more unconventional types of modern aero-engine is the rotary engine shown here, which has a trilobate (three-sided) rotor spinning in a chamber shaped like a fat figure-of-eight.

MID WEST 75-HP TWO-STROKE, THREE-CYLINDER ENGINE

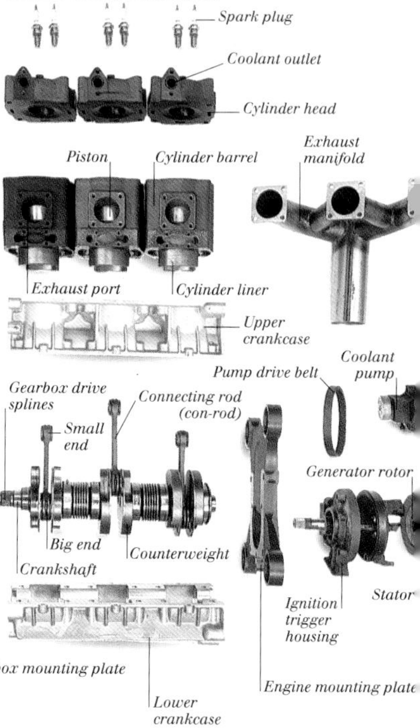
Spark plug
Coolant outlet
Cylinder head
Piston
Cylinder barrel
Exhaust manifold
Exhaust port
Cylinder liner
Upper crankcase
Coolant pump
Pump drive belt
Gearbox drive splines
Connecting rod (con-rod)
Small end
Generator rotor
Big end
Counterweight
Crankshaft
Stator
Ignition trigger housing
Lower crankcase
Engine mounting plate

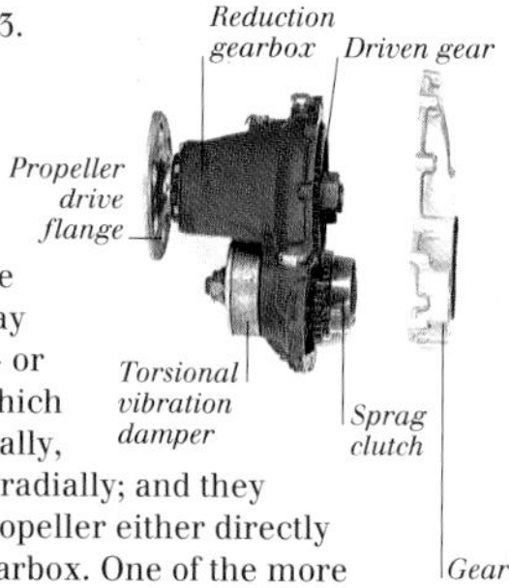
Reduction gearbox
Driven gear
Propeller drive flange
Torsional vibration damper
Sprag clutch
Gearbox mounting plate

ROTOR AND HOUSINGS OF A MID WEST SINGLE-ROTOR ENGINE

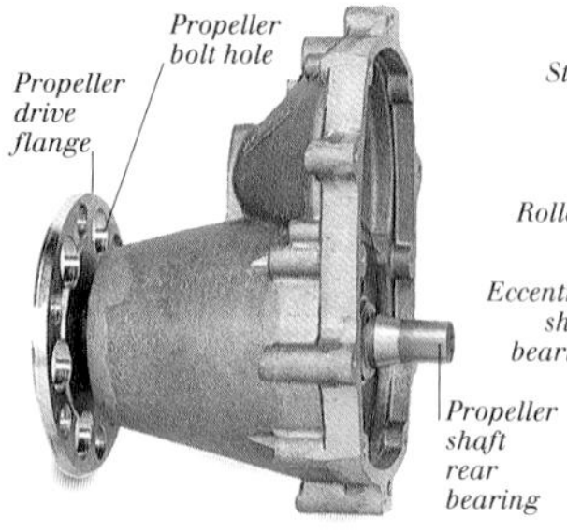
Propeller bolt hole
Propeller drive flange
Propeller shaft rear bearing

GEARBOX CASE

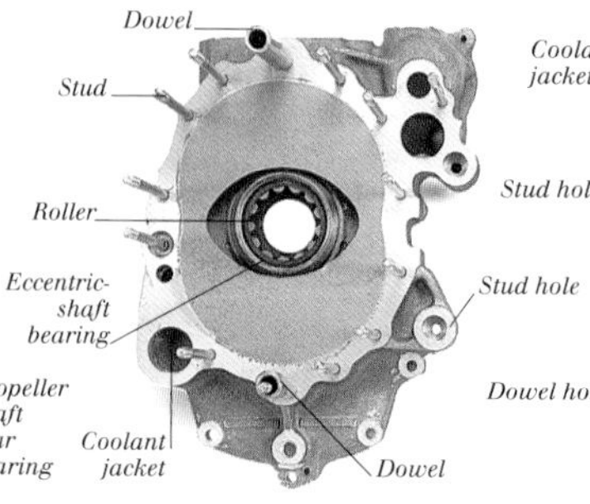
Dowel
Stud
Roller
Eccentric-shaft bearing
Stud hole
Coolant jacket
Dowel

FRONT HOUSING (FRONT END-PLATE)

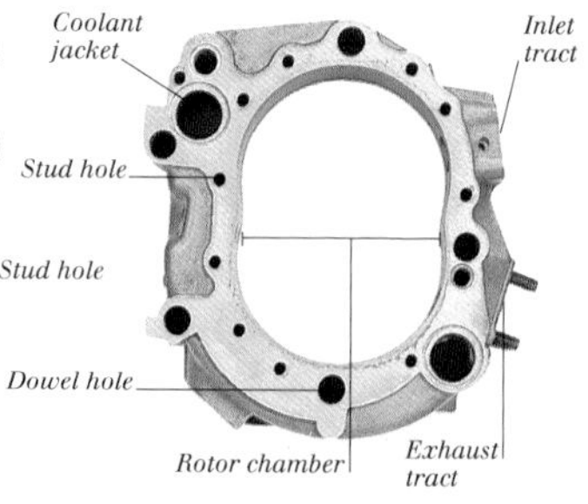
Coolant jacket
Inlet tract
Stud hole
Dowel hole
Rotor chamber
Exhaust tract

TROCHOID HOUSING

MID WEST 90-HP TWIN-ROTOR ENGINE

Propeller-bolt collar
Lubricating oil feed
Engine front mounting plate
Propeller drive flange
Reduction gearbox
Blanking plate over air inlet
Upper rubber anti-vibration engine mount
Carburettor
Rotor-cooling air duct
Pipe clamp joint
Rotor-cooling air pump
Upper rotor-cooling air duct
Generator housing
Electric cable
Starter motor
Flywheel
Front bearing mount
Oil pump drive shaft cover
Torsional vibration damper
Fuel drip tray
Fuel pipe inlet connection
Blanking plate over exhaust port
Exhaust pipe flange
Engine rear mounting plate
Lower rubber anti-vibration engine mount

OUTPUT SHAFT OF A MID WEST ROTARY ENGINE

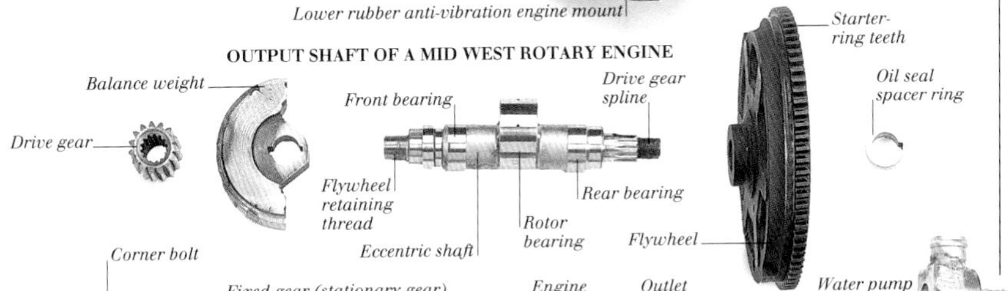
Balance weight
Drive gear
Front bearing
Drive gear spline
Starter-ring teeth
Oil seal spacer ring
Flywheel retaining thread
Rear bearing
Rotor bearing
Eccentric shaft
Flywheel

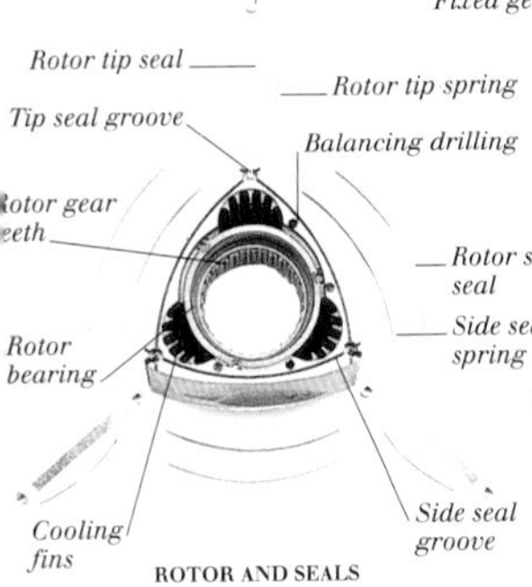
Corner bolt
Rotor tip seal
Rotor tip spring
Tip seal groove
Balancing drilling
otor gear
eeth
Rotor side seal
Side seal spring
Rotor bearing
Cooling fins
Side seal groove
ROTOR AND SEALS

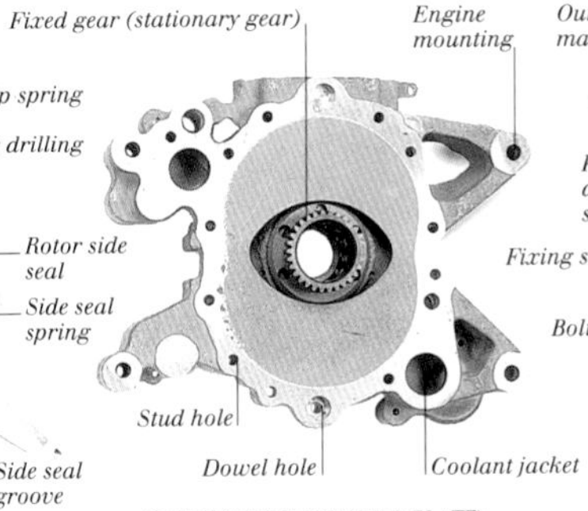
Fixed gear (stationary gear)
Engine mounting
Stud hole
Dowel hole
Coolant jacket
REAR HOUSING (REAR END-PLATE)

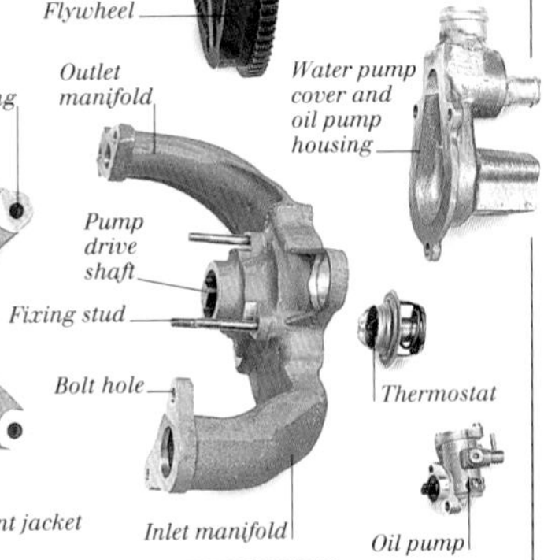
Outlet manifold
Water pump cover and oil pump housing
Pump drive shaft
Fixing stud
Bolt hole
Thermostat
Inlet manifold
Oil pump
WATER PUMP HOUSING

Modern jetliners 1

BAE-146 JETLINER

MODERN JETLINERS HAVE ENABLED ordinary people to travel to places where once only the wealthy could afford to go. Compared with the first jetliners (which were introduced in the 1940s), modern ones are much quieter, burn fuel more efficiently, and produce less air pollution. These advances are largely due to the replacement of turbojet engines with turbofan engines (see pp. 418-419). The greater power of turbofan engines at low speeds enables modern jetliners to carry more fuel and passengers than turbojet aircraft; a modern Boeing 747-400 (popularly known as a "jumbo jet") can fly 400 people for 13,700 km (8,500 miles) without needing to refuel. Jetliners fly at high altitudes, typically cruising at 8,000-11,000 m (26,000-36,000 ft), where they can use fuel efficiently and usually avoid bad weather. The pilot always controls the aircraft during take-off and landing, but at other times the aircraft is usually controlled by an autopilot. Autopilots are complex on-board mechanisms that detect deviations from an aircraft's route and make appropriate adjustments to the flight controls. Flight decks are also equipped with radars that warn pilots of approaching hazards, such as mountain ranges, bad weather, and other aircraft.

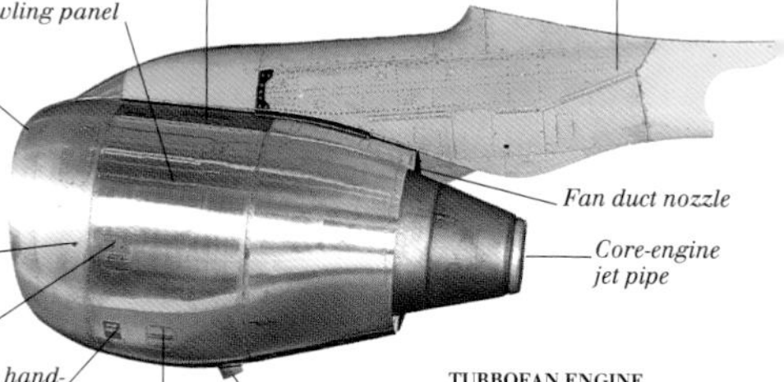
Shoulder cowling
Engine pylon
Hinged cowling panel
Nose cowling
Fan duct nozzle
Fire extinguisher discharge indicator
Core-engine jet pipe
Oil-filler door
Push-in door for hand-held fire extinguisher
Drain mast
Oil-filler door for integrated-drive generator

TURBOFAN ENGINE COWLING

STRUCTURAL COMPONENTS OF A BAE-146 JETLINER

FUSELAGE NOSE-SECTION

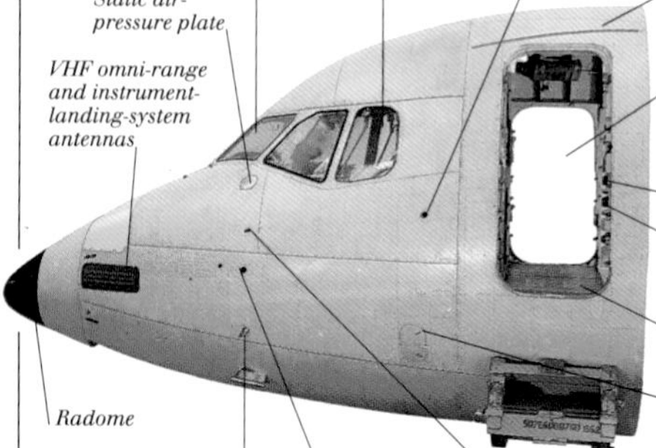
Electrically heated, birdproof windshield
Side window
Anchor for open door
Rain gutter
Static air-pressure plate
Forward main door aperture
VHF omni-range and instrument-landing-system antennas
Light-alloy door frame
Multiple-pinned lock
Floor level
Toilet service connector
Radome
Air temperature probe
Stall warning vane
Pitot head for dynamic air pressure

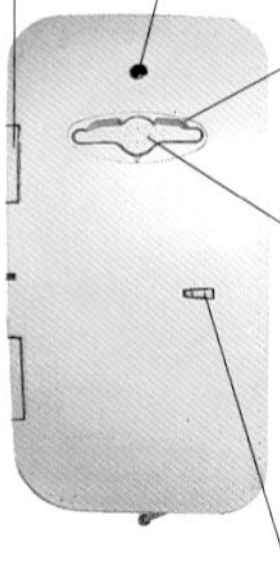
Hinge
Peephole
Finger recess
Main external operating handle
Anchor for open door

FORWARD MAIN DOOR

FUSELAGE MID-SECTIC

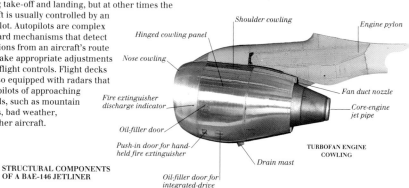

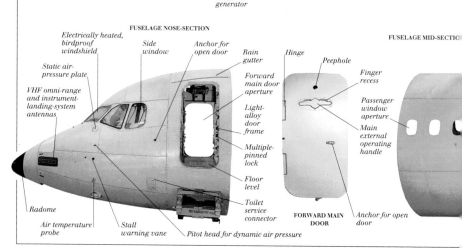

Passenger window aperture

STARBOARD WING ASSEMBLY

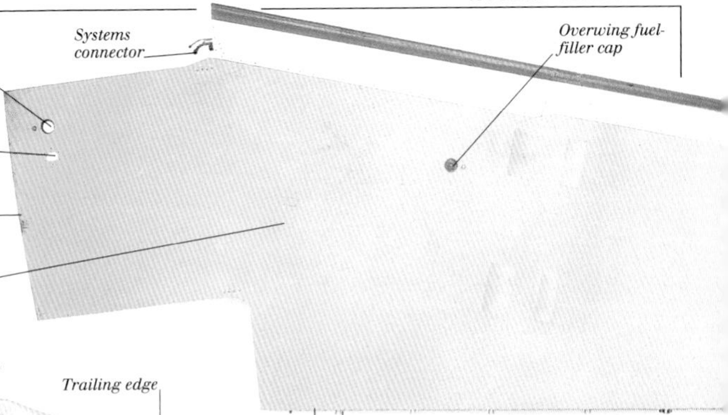
Systems connector
Overwing fuel-filler cap
Overwing fuel-filler cap
Fuel contents indicator
Centre-line (spine) of aircraft
Single-piece skin over inboard wing
Trailing edge of fixed wing
Spoiler anchorage
Hydraulic actuator attachment

Rubber sealing strip
Rubber sealing strip
Trailing edge
Pivot point
Flap-track fairing
Screw joint
Aft section

MOVABLE FLAP TRACK AND FAIRING

Hinge
Stainless-steel flap seal

INBOARD LIFT SPOILERS

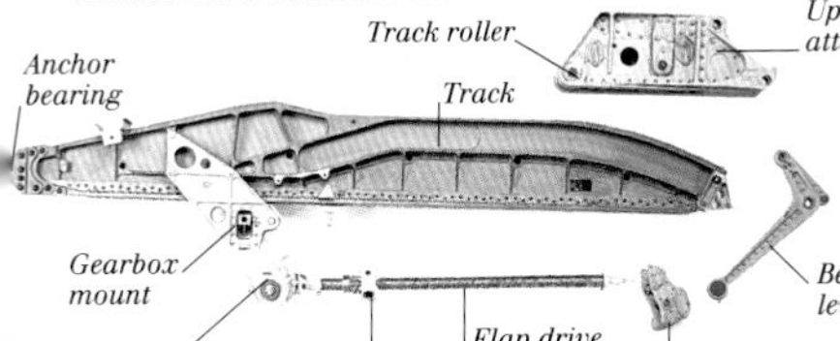
Track roller
Upper carriage attached to flap
Anchor bearing
Track
Gearbox mount
Bellcrank lever
Gearbox unit
Carriage drive nut
Flap drive screw
Lower carriage

FOWLER FLAP

Tab-hinge line
Leading edge
Root
Inboard tab

Skin lap-joint
Leading edge
Main spar bridge
Root rib
Wing-root mount containing central fuel tank
Attachment structure for wing-to-fuselage fairing
Cabin air-pressure discharge valve
Floor level
Fairing of landing gear bay
Fairing of landing gear pivot
Yellow anti-corrosion paint

Modern jetliners 2

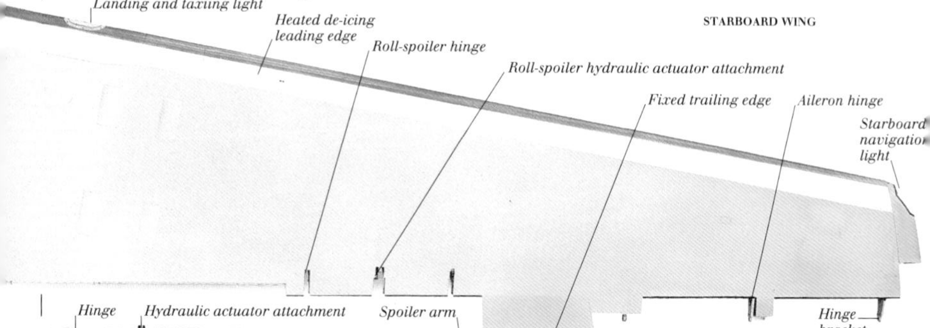
Landing and taxiing light
Heated de-icing leading edge
Roll-spoiler hinge
Roll-spoiler hydraulic actuator attachment
Fixed trailing edge
Aileron hinge
Starboard navigation light

STARBOARD WING

Hinge
Hydraulic actuator attachment
Flap seal

INTERMEDIATE LIFT SPOILER

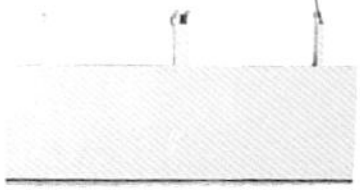
Spoiler arm

OUTBOARD ROLL SPOILER

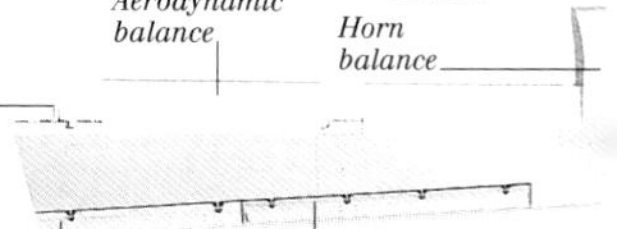
Hinge bracket
Aerodynamic balance
Horn balance
Recessed hinge
Trimtab
Servo-tab
Static discharge wick attachment

AILERON

MAIN FOWLER FLAP

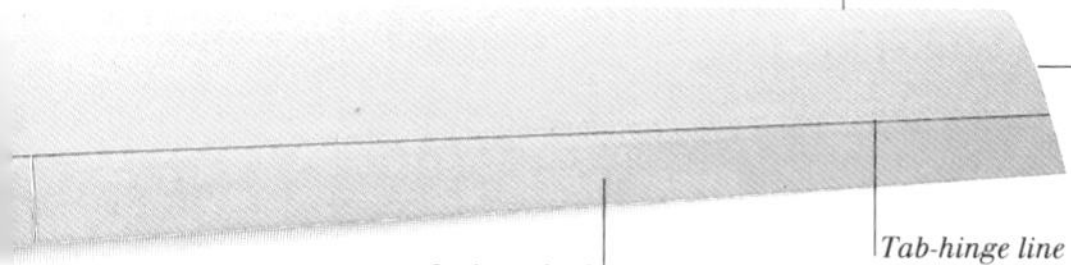
Leading edge
Flap tip
Tab-hinge line
Outboard tab

FUSELAGE SPINE FAIRING

Landing gear door
Hinge

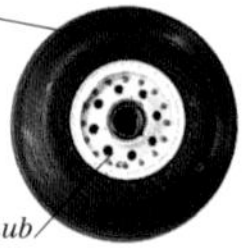

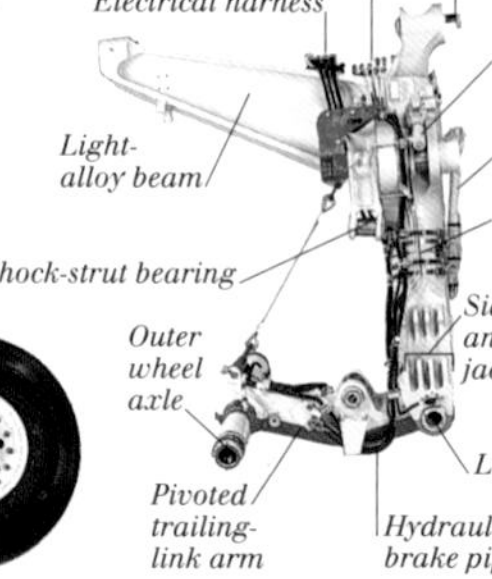
Hydraulic brake pipe
Main pivot
Electrical harness
Oleo lock-jack
Direction bar
Light-alloy beam
Brake pipe
Shock-strut bearing
Side brace and retraction jack trunnions
Outer wheel axle
Lower pivot
Pneumatic tyre
Wheel hub
Pivoted trailing-link arm
Hydraulic brake pipe

STARBOARD TWIN-WHEEL MAIN LANDING GEAR

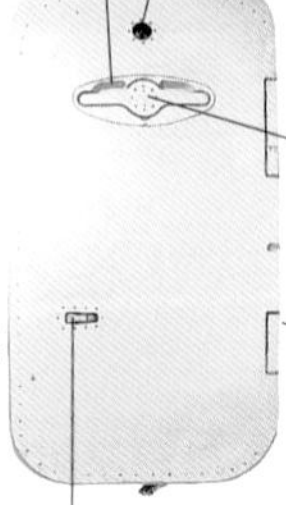
Finger recess
Peephole
Main external operating handle
Hinge
Anchor for open door

AFT MAIN DOOR

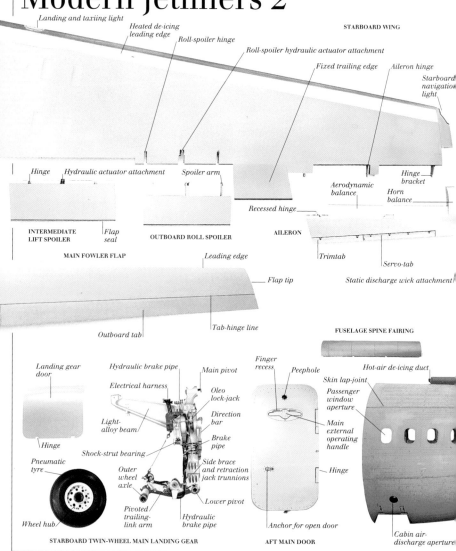

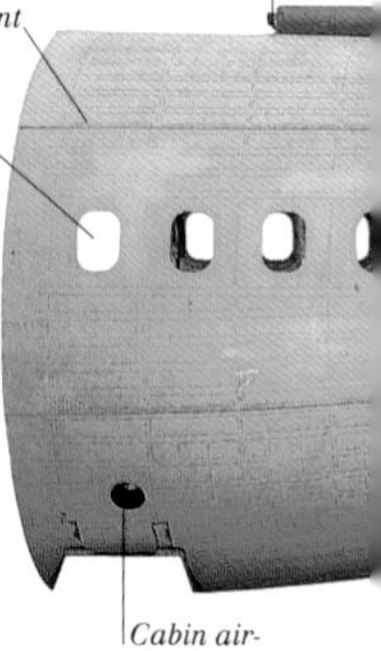
Hot-air de-icing duct
Skin lap-joint
Passenger window aperture
Cabin air-discharge aperture

BAE-146 MODERN JETLINER

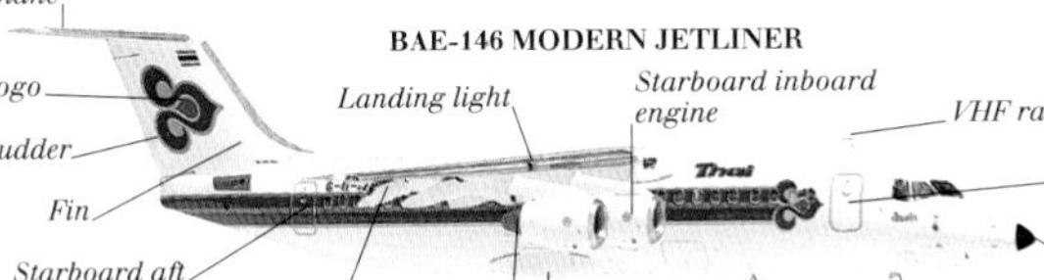
Tailplane
Logo
Rudder
Fin
Starboard aft service door
Flap-track fairing
Core-engine jet pipe
Main landing gear fairing
Landing light
Starboard inboard engine
VHF radio aerial
Forward door for crew and service
Radome
VHF aerial
Water-drain mast

STARBOARD ELEVATOR

Horn balance
Tab hinge
Aerodynamic balance
Recessed hinge
Root
Trimtab
Servo-tab

TAILPLANE FAIRINGS

Intermediate fairing (fin tip)
Aft fairing
Fin trailing edge
Forward fairing
Side fairing
Elevator chassis box

FIN

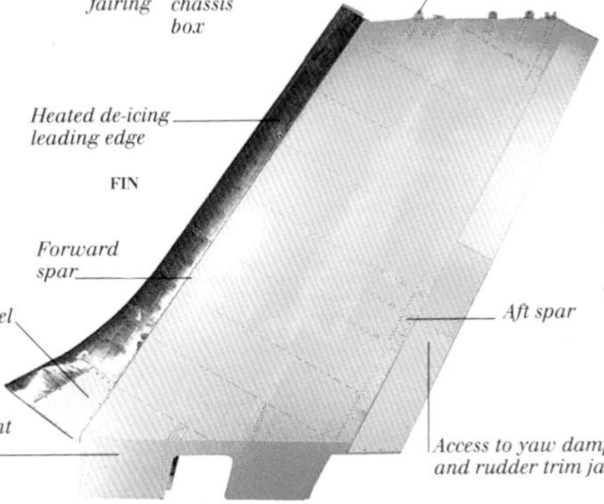
Tailplane attachment bracket
Heated de-icing leading edge
Forward spar
Fairing panel
Aft spar
Fin-attachment skin
Access to yaw dampers and rudder trim jack

TAILPLANE

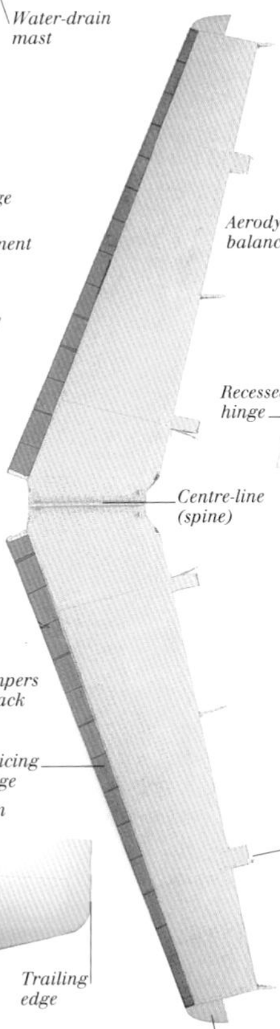
Centre-line (spine)
Heated de-icing leading edge
Elevator hinge
Tailplane tip

FUSELAGE TAIL-SECTION

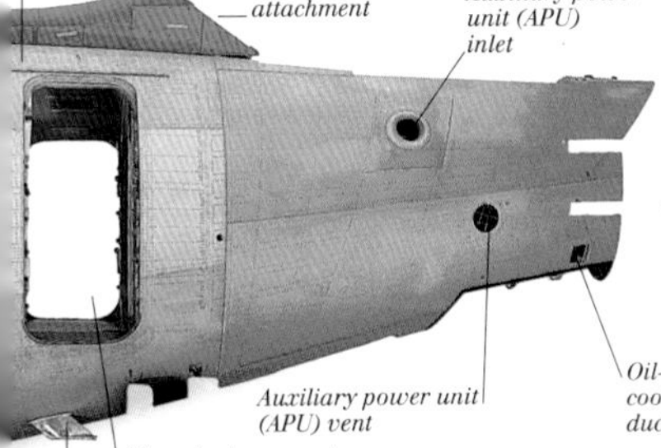
Rain gutter
Fin leading-edge attachment
Auxiliary power unit (APU) inlet
Auxiliary power unit (APU) vent
Oil-cooler duct
Aft main door aperture
Heated drain mast

STARBOARD AIR-BRAKE

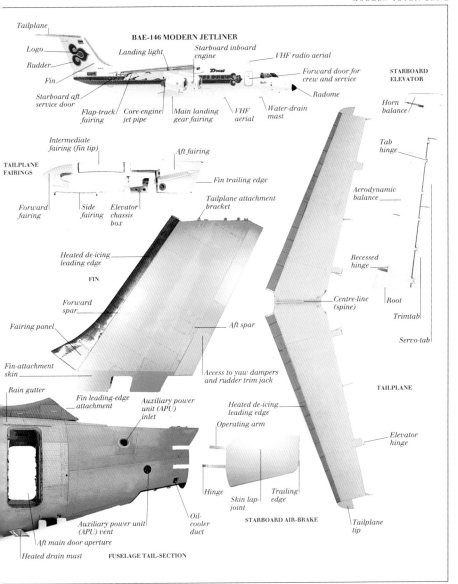

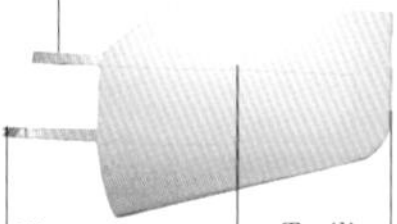
Operating arm
Hinge
Skin lap-joint
Trailing edge

Supersonic jetliners

COMPUTER-DESIGNED SST

SUPERSONIC AIRCRAFT FLY FASTER than the speed of sound (Mach 1). There are many supersonic military aircraft, but only two supersonic passenger-carrying aircraft (also called SSTs, or supersonic transports) have been produced: the Russian Tu-144, and Concorde, produced jointly by Britain and France. The Tu-144 had a greater maximum speed than Concorde but was withdrawn in 1978, after only seven months in service. Concorde has remained in service since 1976. It features many innovations, including a droop nose, which is lowered during take-off and landing to aid visibility from the cockpit, and the pumping of fuel between forward and aft trim tanks to help stabilize the aircraft. Concorde has a narrow fuselage and short-span wings to reduce drag during supersonic flight. Its noisy turbojet engines with afterburners enable it to carry 100 passengers at a cruising speed of Mach 2 at 15,000-18,000 m (50,000-60,000 ft). Once an aircraft is flying faster than Mach 1, it produces a continuous air-pressure wave, which is heard as a "sonic boom".

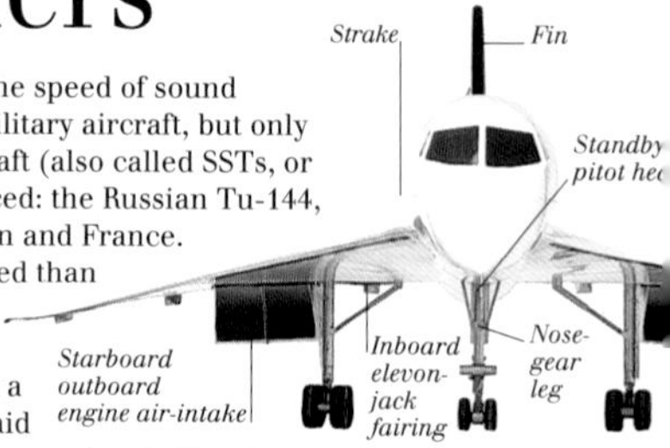
Strake
Fin
Inboard elevon-jack fairing
Nose-gear leg
Starboard outboard engine air-intake

FRONT VIEW OF CONCORDE

OVERHEAD VIEW OF CONCORDE

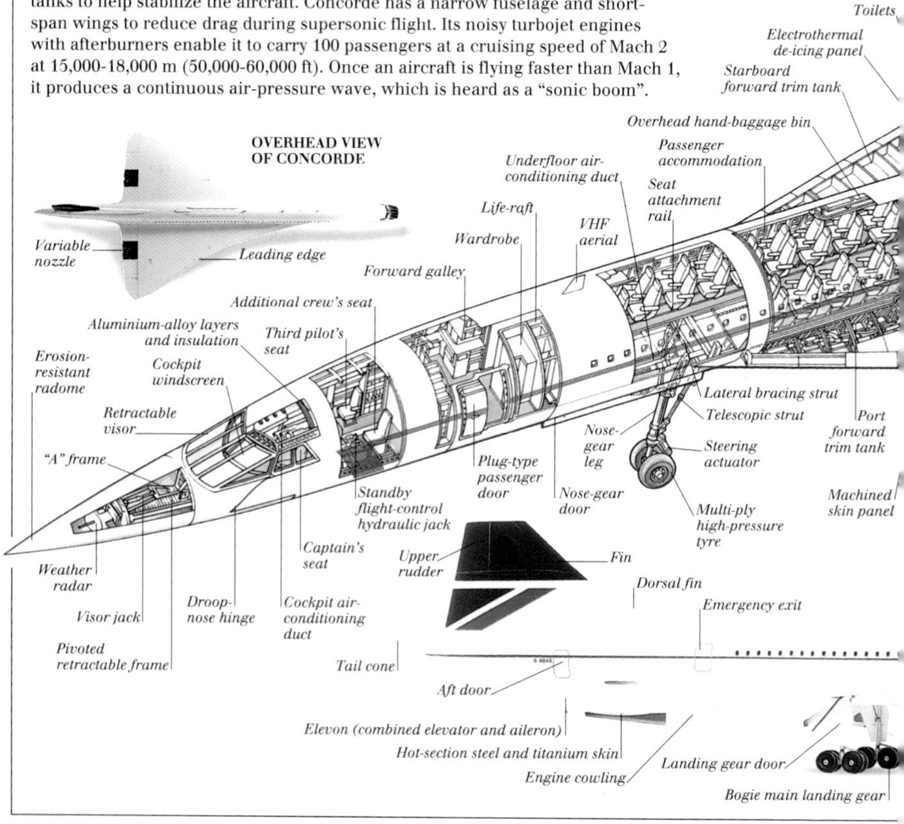
Variable nozzle
Leading edge
Toilets
Electrothermal de-icing panel
Starboard forward trim tank
Overhead hand-baggage bin
Passenger accommodation
Underfloor air-conditioning duct
Seat attachment rail
Life-raft
VHF aerial
Wardrobe
Forward galley
Additional crew's seat
Aluminium-alloy layers and insulation
Third pilot's seat
Erosion-resistant radome
Cockpit windscreen
Retractable visor
"A" frame
Lateral bracing strut
Telescopic strut
Port forward trim tank
Nose-gear leg
Steering actuator
Plug-type passenger door
Standby flight-control hydraulic jack
Nose-gear door
Multi-ply high-pressure tyre
Machined skin panel
Captain's seat
Weather radar
Visor jack
Droop-nose hinge
Cockpit air-conditioning duct
Pivoted retractable frame
Upper rudder
Fin
Dorsal fin
Emergency exit
Tail cone
Aft door
Elevon (combined elevator and aileron)
Hot-section steel and titanium skin
Engine cowling
Landing gear door
Bogie main landing gear

SECTIONED VIEW OF CONCORDE

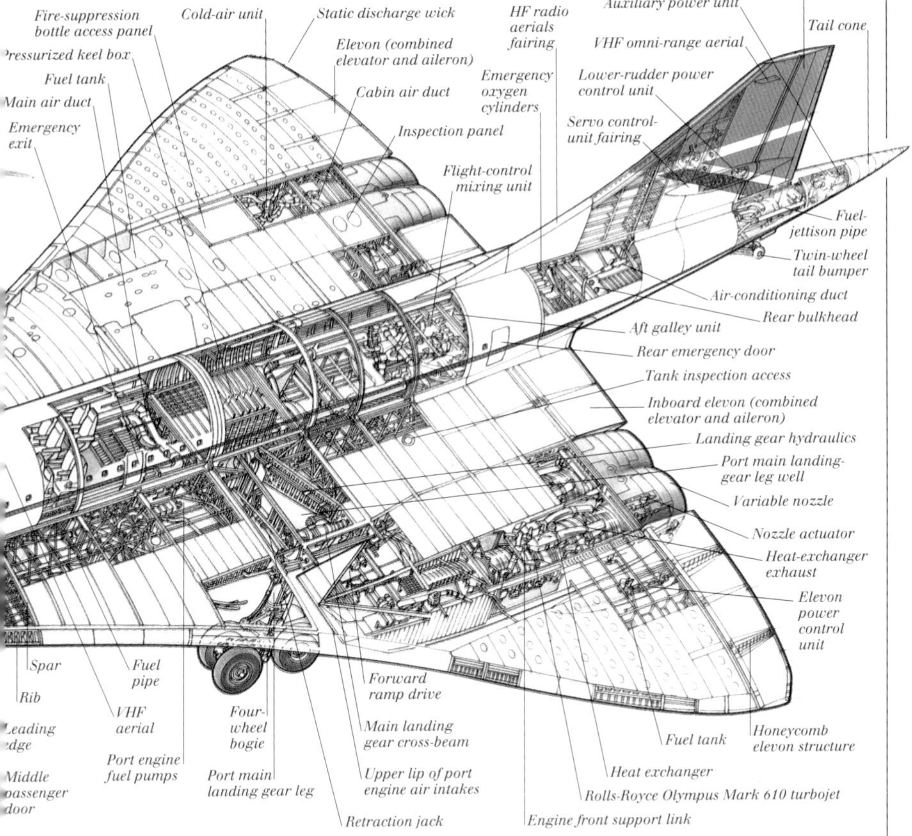
Upper rudder
Cold-air unit
Static discharge wick
HF radio aerials fairing
Auxiliary power unit
Fire-suppression bottle access panel
Tail cone
VHF omni-range aerial
Pressurized keel box
Elevon (combined elevator and aileron)
Emergency oxygen cylinders
Lower-rudder power control unit
Fuel tank
Cabin air duct
Main air duct
Servo control-unit fairing
Emergency exit
Inspection panel
Flight-control mixing unit
Fuel-jettison pipe
Twin-wheel tail bumper
Air-conditioning duct
Rear bulkhead
Aft galley unit
Rear emergency door
Tank inspection access
Inboard elevon (combined elevator and aileron)
Landing gear hydraulics
Port main landing-gear leg well
Variable nozzle
Nozzle actuator
Heat-exchanger exhaust
Elevon power control unit
Spar
Fuel pipe
Forward ramp drive
Rib
VHF aerial
Four-wheel bogie
Leading edge
Main landing gear cross-beam
Fuel tank
Honeycomb elevon structure
Port engine fuel pumps
Middle passenger door
Port main landing gear leg
Upper lip of port engine air intakes
Heat exchanger
Rolls-Royce Olympus Mark 610 turbojet
Retraction jack
Engine front support link

SIDE VIEW OF CONCORDE

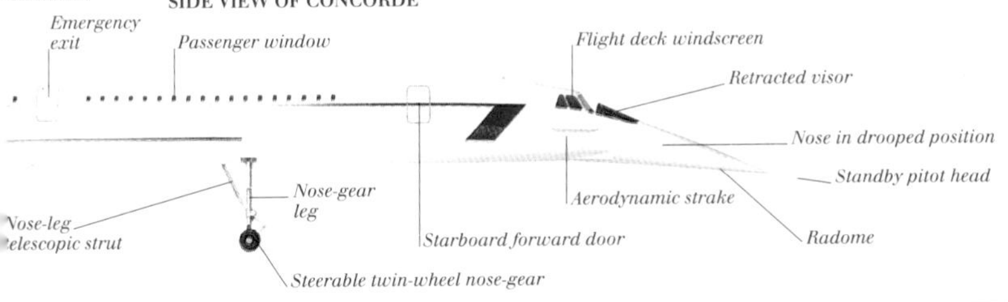
VHF aerial
Emergency exit
Passenger window
Flight deck windscreen
Retracted visor
Nose in drooped position
Standby pitot head
Nose-gear leg
Aerodynamic strake
Nose-leg telescopic strut
Starboard forward door
Radome
Steerable twin-wheel nose-gear

Jet engines

JET ENGINES ARE USED BY MOST MILITARY and heavy aircraft, and by many helicopters. The simplest type of jet engine, or gas turbine, is the turbojet. It works by continuously burning a mixture of fuel and air in a combustion chamber to produce a jet of hot exhaust gas that is expelled through a nozzle to produce thrust. The hot gas also spins turbine blades, which, in turn, spin the blades of an air compressor; the compressor forces air into the combustion chamber. Many of the fastest aircraft use turbojets, with additional booster units called afterburners, but their use is restricted by their high noise emission. Most jetliners use turbofan jet engines, which are quieter. An enormous fan, driven by a low-pressure turbine, feeds some air into the compressor but feeds most of it through bypass ducts to join the exhaust jetstream in the tail cone. The bypass stream produces most of the thrust. Many smaller, propeller-driven aircraft use turboprop jet engines, in which the engine powers a propeller.

NPT 301 MODERN TURBOJET

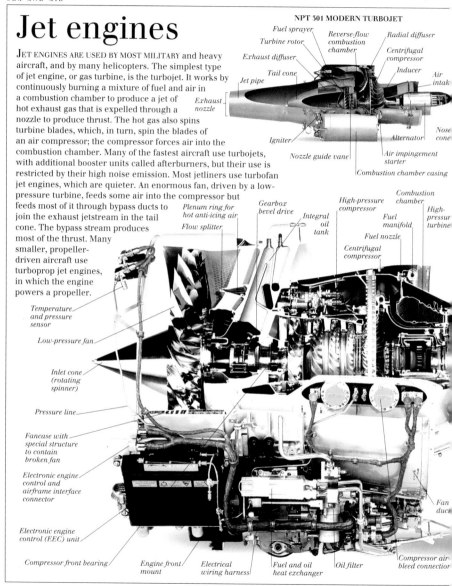

Fuel sprayer
Turbine rotor
Reverse-flow combustion chamber
Radial diffuser
Centrifugal compressor
Exhaust diffuser
Inducer
Tail cone
Jet pipe
Air intak
Exhaust nozzle
Igniter
Alternator
Nose cone
Nozzle guide vane
Air impingement starter
Combustion chamber casing

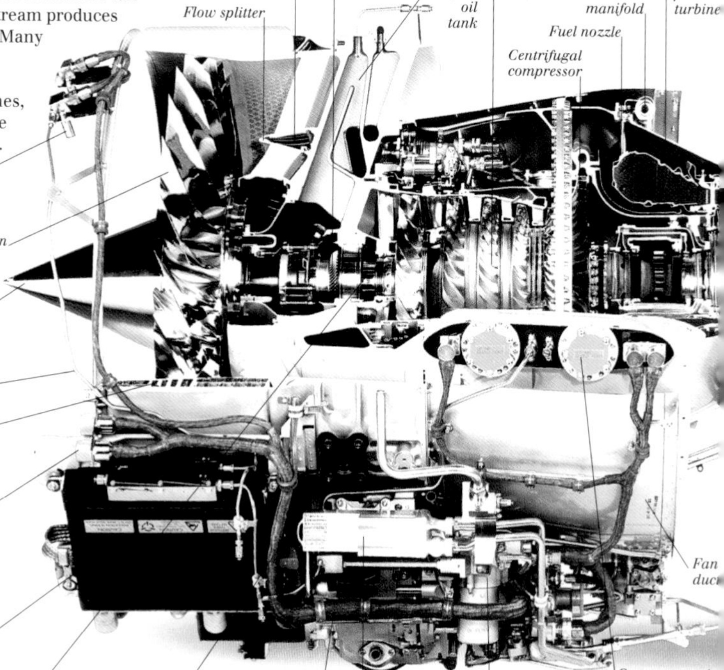
Plenum ring for hot anti-icing air
Gearbox bevel drive
Integral oil tank
High-pressure compressor
Combustion chamber
High-pressur turbine
Fuel manifold
Flow splitter
Fuel nozzle
Centrifugal compressor
Temperature and pressure sensor
Low-pressure fan
Inlet cone (rotating spinner)
Pressure line
Fancase with special structure to contain broken fan
Electronic engine control and airframe interface connector
Fan duc
Electronic engine control (EEC) unit
Compressor front bearing
Engine front mount
Electrical wiring harness
Fuel and oil heat exchanger
Oil filter
Compressor air-bleed connectio

PRATT & WHITNEY CANADA PW120 SERIES MODERN TURBOPROP

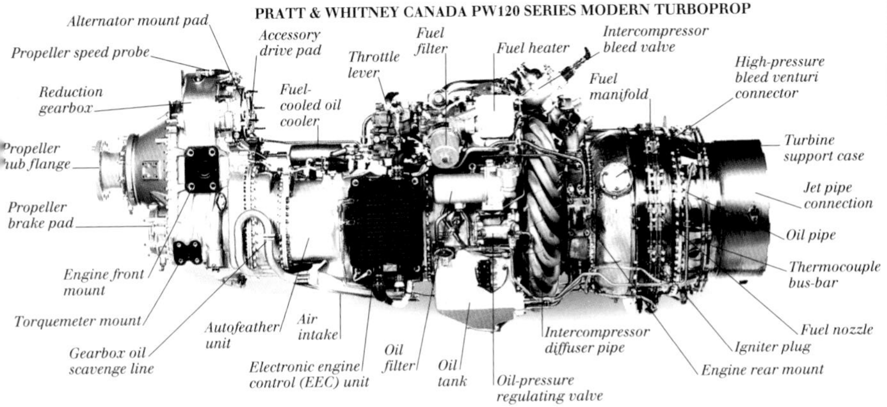
Alternator mount pad
Propeller speed probe
Reduction gearbox
Propeller hub flange
Propeller brake pad
Engine front mount
Torquemeter mount
Gearbox oil scavenge line
Accessory drive pad
Fuel-cooled oil cooler
Autofeather unit
Air intake
Electronic engine control (EEC) unit
Throttle lever
Fuel filter
Oil filter
Oil tank
Fuel heater
Oil-pressure regulating valve
Intercompressor bleed valve
Fuel manifold
Intercompressor diffuser pipe
High-pressure bleed venturi connector
Turbine support case
Jet pipe connection
Oil pipe
Thermocouple bus-bar
Fuel nozzle
Igniter plug
Engine rear mount

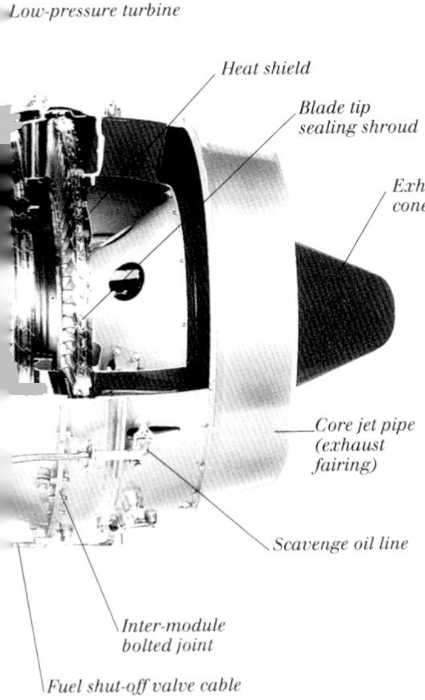
Low-pressure turbine
Heat shield
Blade tip sealing shroud
Exhaust cone
Core jet pipe (exhaust fairing)
Scavenge oil line
Inter-module bolted joint
Fuel shut-off valve cable

ECTIONED PRATT & WHITNEY
ANADA PW305 MODERN TURBOFAN

HOW JET ENGINES WORK

TURBOFAN

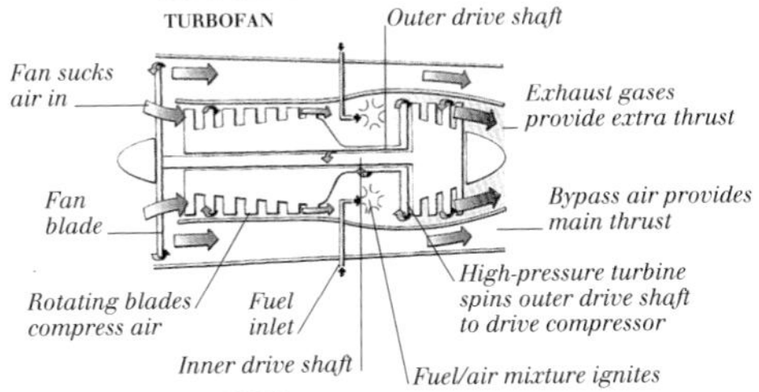
Outer drive shaft
Fan sucks air in
Exhaust gases provide extra thrust
Fan blade
Bypass air provides main thrust
Rotating blades compress air
Fuel inlet
High-pressure turbine spins outer drive shaft to drive compressor
Inner drive shaft
Fuel/air mixture ignites

TURBOPROP

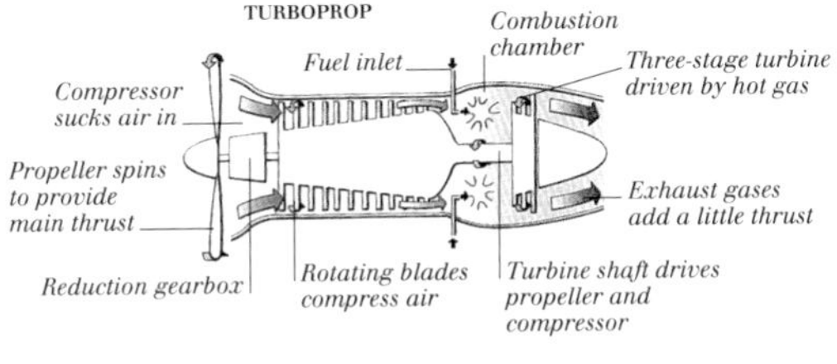
Combustion chamber
Fuel inlet
Three-stage turbine driven by hot gas
Compressor sucks air in
Propeller spins to provide main thrust
Exhaust gases add a little thrust
Reduction gearbox
Rotating blades compress air
Turbine shaft drives propeller and compressor

TURBOJET

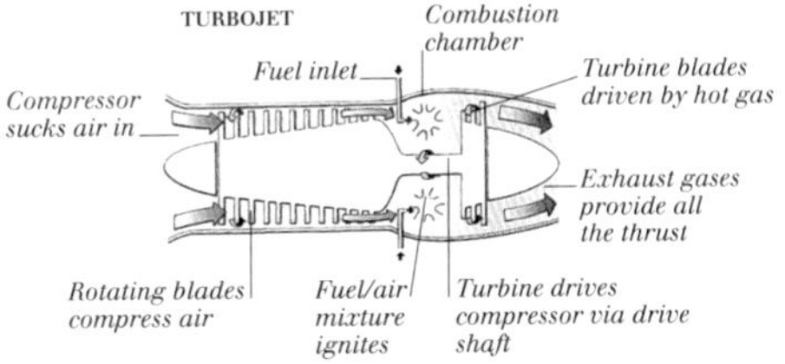
Combustion chamber
Fuel inlet
Turbine blades driven by hot gas
Compressor sucks air in
Exhaust gases provide all the thrust
Rotating blades compress air
Fuel/air mixture ignites
Turbine drives compressor via drive shaft

Modern military aircraft

MODERN MILITARY AIRCRAFT ARE AMONG THE MOST SOPHISTICATED and expensive products of the 20th century. Fighters need computer-operated controls for manoeuvrability, powerful engines, and effective air-to-air weapons. Most modern fighters also have guided missiles, radar, and passive, infra-red sensors. These developments enable today's fighters to engage in combat with adversaries that are outside visual range. Bombers carry a large weapon load and enough fuel for long-range flights. A few military aircraft, such as the Tornado and the F-14 Tomcat, have variable-sweep ("swing") wings. During take-off and landing their wings are fully extended, but for high-speed flight and low-level attacks the wings are pivoted fully back. A recent development is the "stealth" bomber, which is designed to absorb or deflect enemy radar in order to remain undetected. Earlier bombers, such as the Tornado, use terrain-following radars to fly so close to the ground that they avoid enemy radar detection.

FRONT VIEW OF A PANAVIA TORNADO

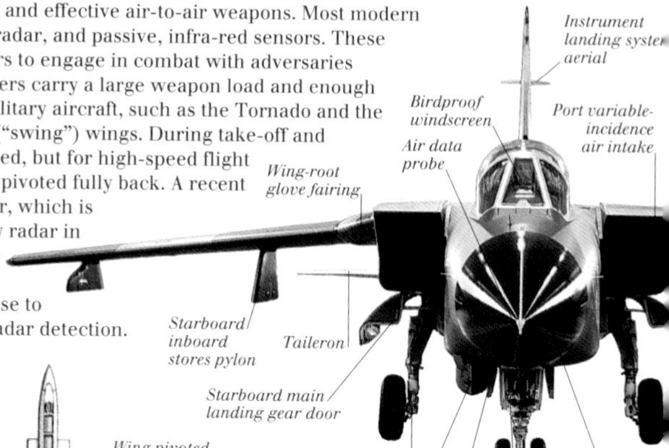

Instrument landing syste aerial
Port variable-incidence air intake
Birdproof windscreen
Air data probe
Wing-root glove fairing
Starboard inboard stores pylon
Taileron
Starboard main landing gear door
Main landing gear leg
Laser ranger and marked-target seeker
Starboard nose-gear door
Steerable twin-wheel nose-gear
Taxiing light
Radom containin ground-mapping attack, and terrain following radar

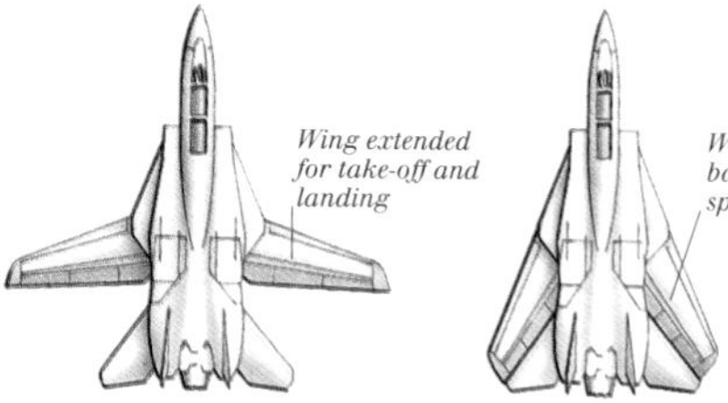

Wing extended for take-off and landing
Wing pivoted back for high-speed flight

SWING-WING F-14 TOMCAT FIGHTER

SIDE VIEW OF A PANAVIA TORNADO GR1A (RECONNAISSANCE VERSION), 1986

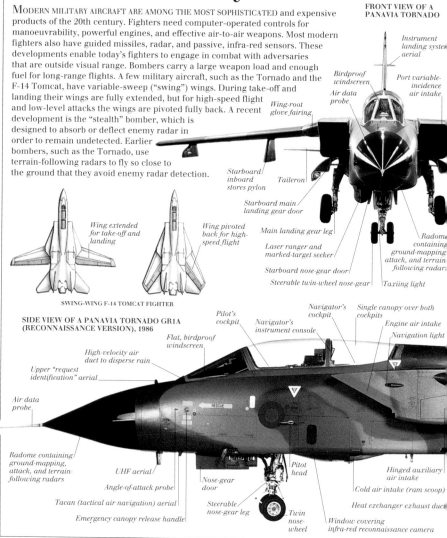

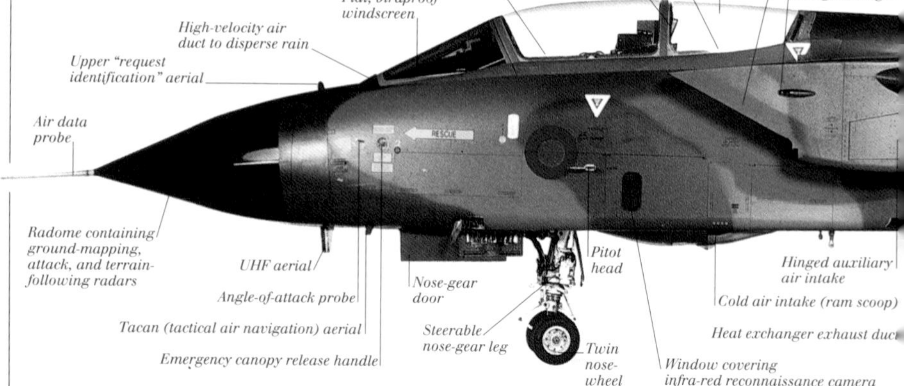

Pilot's cockpit
Navigator's cockpit
Single canopy over both cockpits
Navigator's instrument console
Engine air intake
Navigation light
Flat, birdproof windscreen
High-velocity air duct to disperse rain
Upper "request identification" aerial
Air data probe
RESCUE
Radome containing ground-mapping, attack, and terrain-following radars
UHF aerial
Angle-of-attack probe
Tacan (tactical air navigation) aerial
Emergency canopy release handle
Nose-gear door
Steerable nose-gear leg
Pitot head
Twin nose-wheel
Window covering infra-red reconnaissance camera
Cold air intake (ram scoop)
Hinged auxiliary air intake
Heat exchanger exhaust duc

NORTHROP B-2 ("STEALTH" BOMBER), 1989

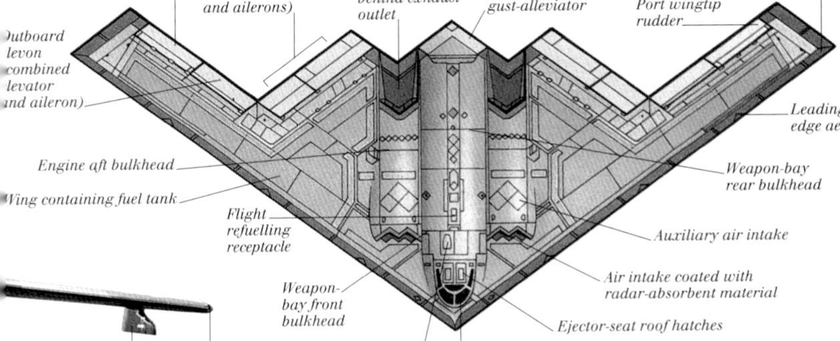
Starboard split rudder
Inboard elevons (combined elevators and ailerons)
Refractory (heat-resistant) skin behind exhaust outlet
Variable-incidence gust-alleviator
Wing leading edge coated with radar-absorbent material
Port wingtip rudder
utboard levon combined levator nd aileron)
Leading-edge aerial
Engine aft bulkhead
Weapon-bay rear bulkhead
Ving containing fuel tank
Flight refuelling receptacle
Auxiliary air intake
Air intake coated with radar-absorbent material
Weapon-bay front bulkhead
Ejector-seat roof hatches
Space for extra crew member
Two-seater cockpit
Port outboard stores pylon
Port navigation light

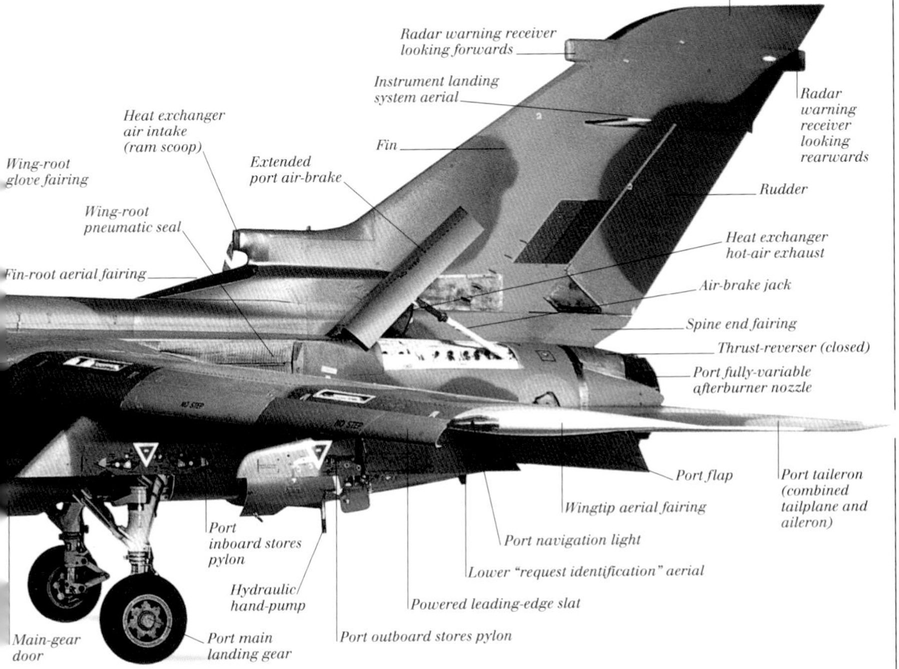
Fin-tip aerial fairing
Radar warning receiver looking forwards
Instrument landing system aerial
Radar warning receiver looking rearwards
Heat exchanger air intake (ram scoop)
Fin
Wing-root glove fairing
Extended port air-brake
Rudder
Wing-root pneumatic seal
Heat exchanger hot-air exhaust
Fin-root aerial fairing
Air-brake jack
Spine end fairing
Thrust-reverser (closed)
Port fully-variable afterburner nozzle
Port flap
Port taileron (combined tailplane and aileron)
Wingtip aerial fairing
Port inboard stores pylon
Port navigation light
Lower "request identification" aerial
Hydraulic hand-pump
Powered leading-edge slat
Main-gear door
Port main landing gear
Port outboard stores pylon

Helicopters

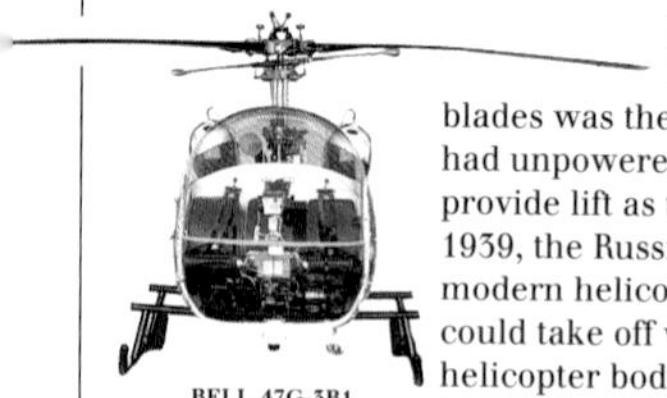

BELL 47G-3B1

HELICOPTERS USE ROTATING BLADES for lift, propulsion, and steering. The first machine to achieve sustained, controlled flight using rotating blades was the autogiro built in the 1920s by the Spaniard Juan de la Cierva. His machine had unpowered blades above the fuselage that relied on the flow of air to rotate them and provide lift as the autogiro was driven forwards by a conventional propeller. Then, in 1939, the Russian-born American Igor Sikorsky produced his VS-300, the forerunner of modern helicopters. Its engine-driven blades provided lift, propulsion, and steering. It could take off vertically, hover, and fly in any direction, and had a tail rotor to prevent the helicopter body from spinning. The introduction of gas turbine jet engines to helicopters in 1955 produced quieter, safer, and more powerful machines. Because of their versatility in flight, helicopters are today used for many purposes, including crop-spraying, traffic surveillance, and transporting crews to deep-sea oil rigs, as well as acting as gunships, air ambulances, and air taxis.

BELL 47G-3B1

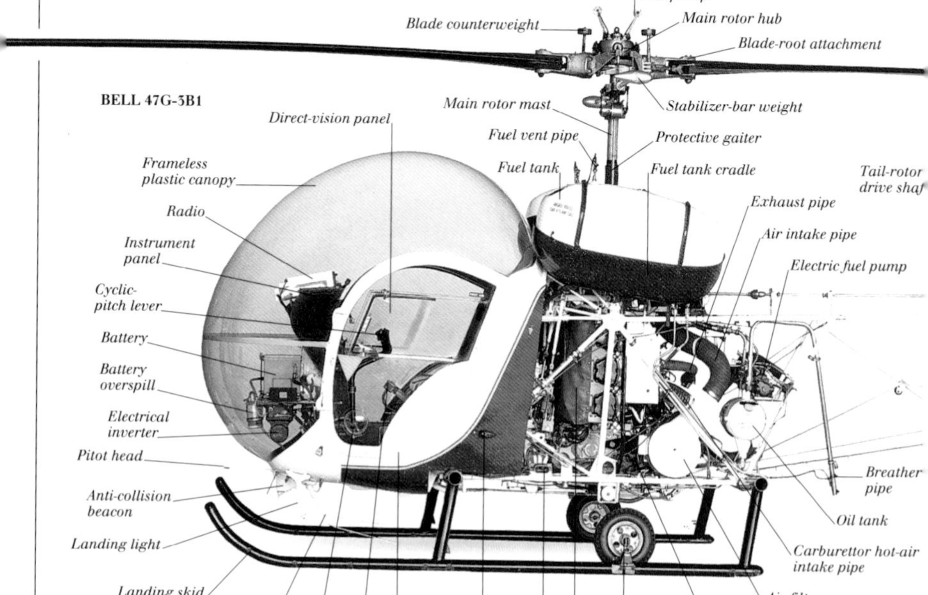
Droop stop
Blade counterweight
Main rotor hub
Blade-root attachment
Main rotor mast
Stabilizer-bar weight
Direct-vision panel
Fuel vent pipe
Protective gaiter
Frameless plastic canopy
Fuel tank
Fuel tank cradle
Tail-rotor drive shaf
Radio
Exhaust pipe
Instrument panel
Air intake pipe
Electric fuel pump
Cyclic-pitch lever
Battery
Battery overspill
Electrical inverter
Pitot head
Breather pipe
Anti-collision beacon
Oil tank
Landing light
Carburettor hot-air intake pipe
Landing skid
Air filter
Navigation light
Ground handling wheel
Valve-rocker cover
VHF omni-range aerial
Ventilator
Electric power socket
Lycoming six-cylinder engine
Collective-pitch lever
Riveted light-alloy forward fuselage section

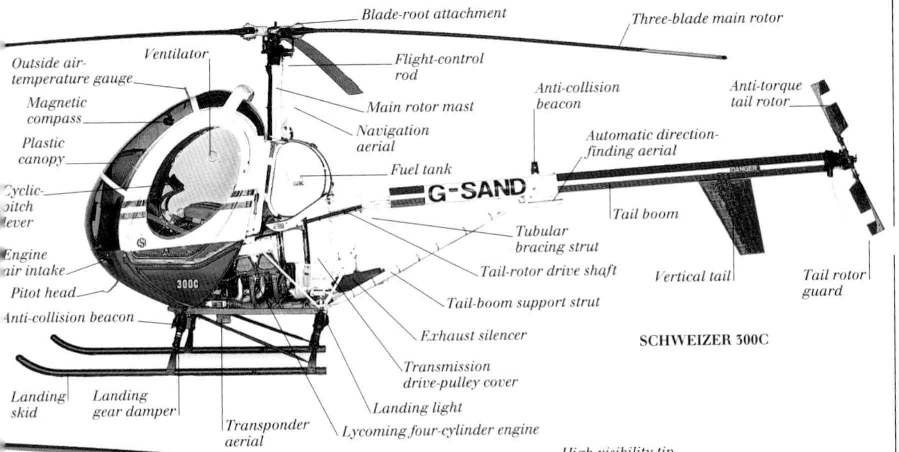
Blade-root attachment
Three-blade main rotor
Ventilator
Outside air-temperature gauge
Flight-control rod
Magnetic compass
Main rotor mast
Anti-collision beacon
Anti-torque tail rotor
Plastic canopy
Navigation aerial
Automatic direction-finding aerial
Fuel tank
yclic-
itch
ever
G-SAND
DANGER
Tail boom
Tubular bracing strut
Engine
air intake
Tail-rotor drive shaft
Vertical tail
Tail rotor guard
300C
Pitot head
Tail-boom support strut
Anti-collision beacon
Exhaust silencer
Transmission drive-pulley cover
Landing skid
Landing gear damper
Landing light
Transponder aerial
Lycoming four-cylinder engine

SCHWEIZER 300C

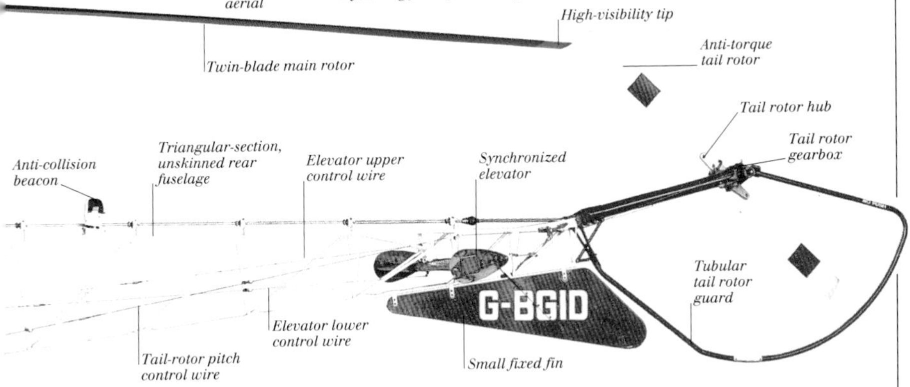
High-visibility tip
Twin-blade main rotor
Anti-torque tail rotor
Tail rotor hub
Tail rotor gearbox
Anti-collision beacon
Triangular-section, unskinned rear fuselage
Elevator upper control wire
Synchronized elevator
Tubular tail rotor guard
G-BGID
Elevator lower control wire
Tail-rotor pitch control wire
Small fixed fin

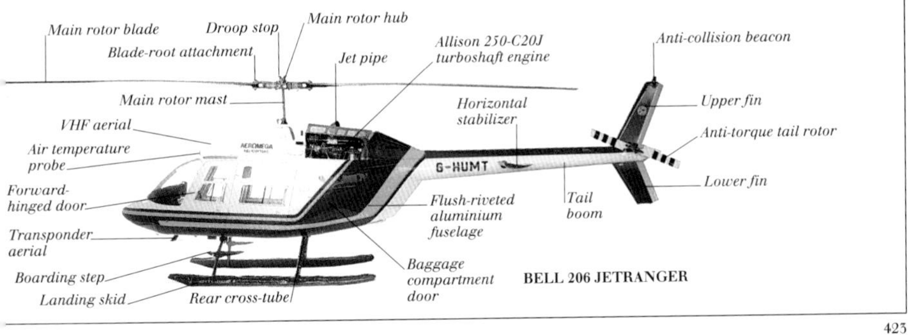
Main rotor blade
Droop stop
Main rotor hub
Blade-root attachment
Jet pipe
Allison 250-C20J turboshaft engine
Anti-collision beacon
Main rotor mast
Upper fin
Horizontal stabilizer
VHF aerial
Anti-torque tail rotor
Air temperature probe
AEROMEGA
G-HUMT
Forward-hinged door
Lower fin
Flush-riveted aluminium fuselage
Tail boom
Transponder aerial
Baggage compartment door
Boarding step
Landing skid
Rear cross-tube

BELL 206 JETRANGER

Light aircraft

LIGHT AIRCRAFT, SUCH AS THE ARV SUPER 2 shown here, are small, lightweight, and of simple construction. More than a million have been built since World War I, mainly for recreational use by private owners. Virtually all light aircraft have piston engines, most of which are air-cooled, although some are liquid-cooled. Open cockpits, almost universal in the 1920s, have today been replaced by enclosed cabins. The cabins of high-wing aircraft have one or two doors, whereas those of low-wing aircraft usually have a sliding or hinged canopy. Most modern light aircraft are made of aluminium alloy, although some are made of wood or of fibre-reinforced materials. Light aircraft today also usually have navigational instruments, an electrical system, cabin heating, wheel brakes, and a two-way radio.

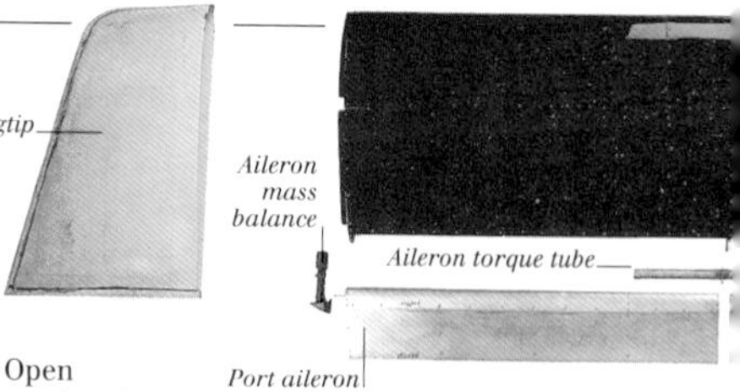
Port wingtip
Aileron mass balance
Aileron torque tube
Port aileron

PORT MAIN LANDING GEAR

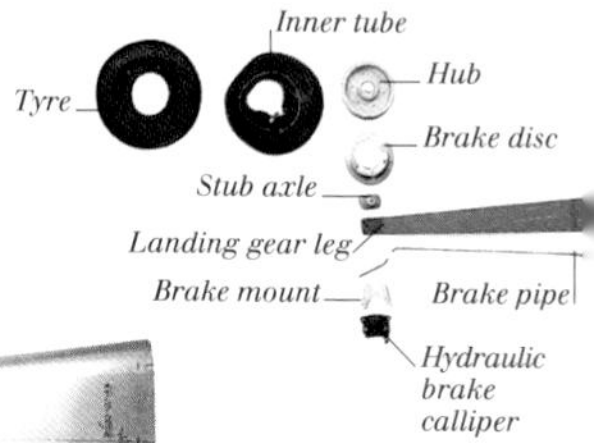
Inner tube
Hub
Tyre
Brake disc
Stub axle
Landing gear leg
Brake mount
Brake pipe
Hydraulic brake calliper

TAILPLANE AND RUDDER

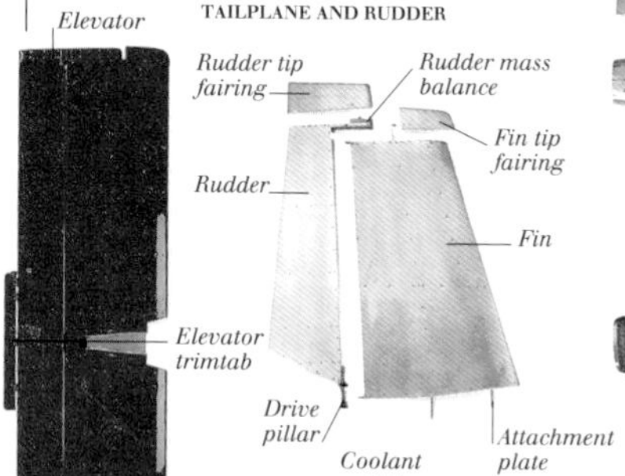
Elevator
Rudder tip fairing
Rudder mass balance
Fin tip fairing
Rudder
Fin
Elevator trimtab
Drive pillar
Attachment plate
Tailplane

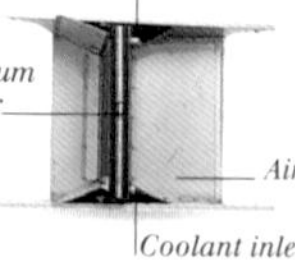
Coolant outlet
Aluminium radiator
Air scoop
Coolant inlet

REAR FUSELAGE

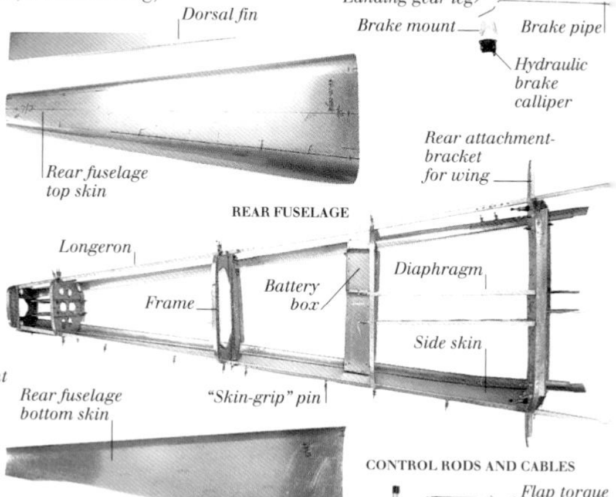
Dorsal fin
Rear fuselage top skin
Rear attachment-bracket for wing
Longeron
Diaphragm
Battery box
Frame
Side skin
"Skin-grip" pin
Rear fuselage bottom skin

CONTROL RODS AND CABLES

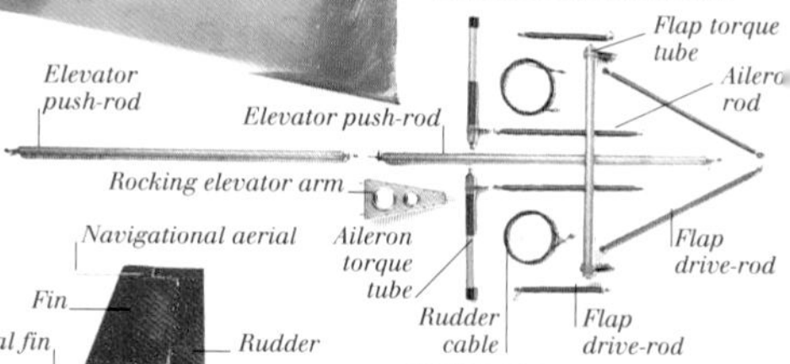
Flap torque tube
Aileron rod
Elevator push-rod
Elevator push-rod
Rocking elevator arm
Aileron torque tube
Flap drive-rod
Rudder cable
Flap drive-rod

SIDE VIEW OF ARV SUPER 2

Navigational aerial
Canopy
Wing
Communications aerial
Fin
Spinner
Engine cowling
Dorsal fin
Rudder
Super 2
G-BNHB
Elevator
Radiator
Tailplane
Nose-gear
Tailskid
Step
Wing strut
Venturi for instruments
Main landing gear
Aircraft registration code

STARBOARD MAIN LANDING GEAR

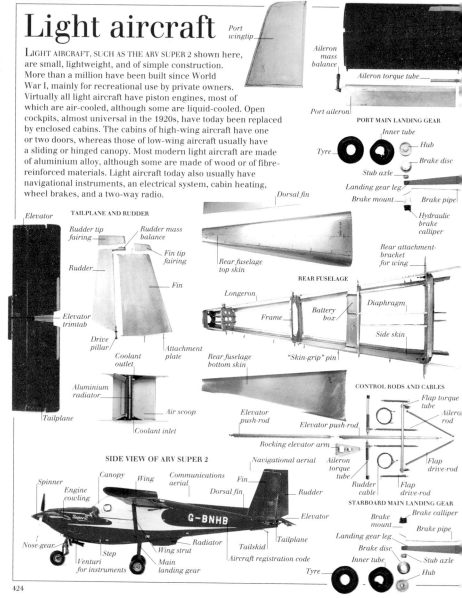

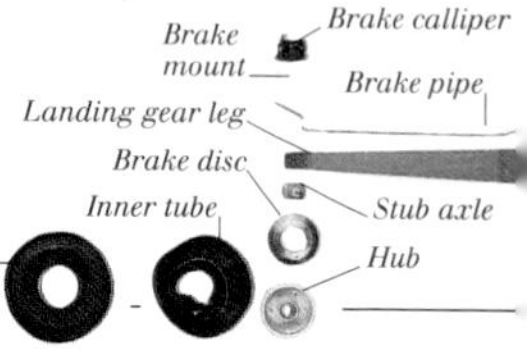
Brake calliper
Brake mount
Brake pipe
Landing gear leg
Brake disc
Stub axle
Inner tube
Tyre
Hub

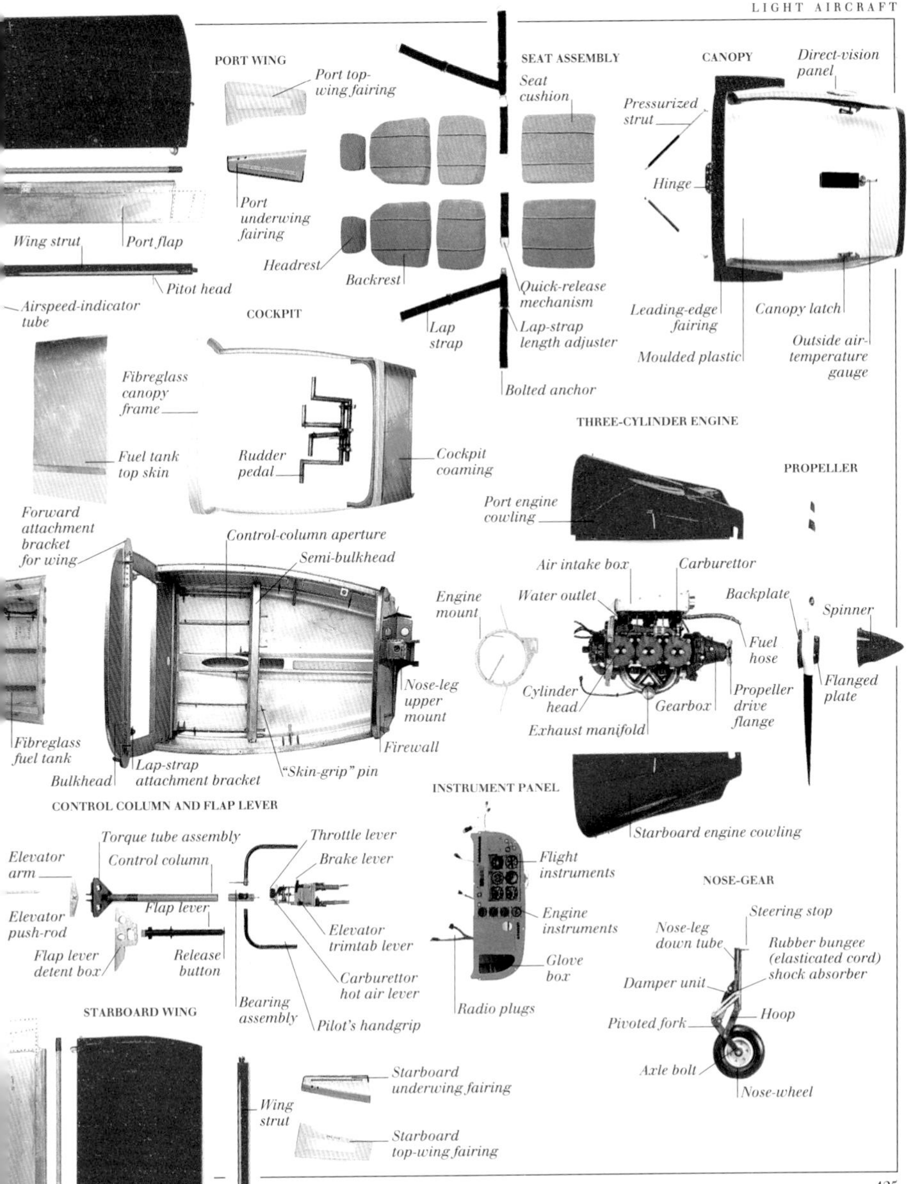
PORT WING
Port top-wing fairing
Port underwing fairing
Wing strut
Port flap
Pitot head
Airspeed-indicator tube
SEAT ASSEMBLY
Seat cushion
Headrest
Backrest
Quick-release mechanism
Lap strap
Lap-strap length adjuster
Bolted anchor
CANOPY
Direct-vision panel
Pressurized strut
Hinge
Leading-edge fairing
Canopy latch
Moulded plastic
Outside air-temperature gauge
COCKPIT
Fibreglass canopy frame
Fuel tank top skin
Rudder pedal
Cockpit coaming
Forward attachment bracket for wing
Control-column aperture
Semi-bulkhead
Nose-leg upper mount
Firewall
Fibreglass fuel tank
Bulkhead
Lap-strap attachment bracket
"Skin-grip" pin
THREE-CYLINDER ENGINE
Port engine cowling
Air intake box
Carburettor
Water outlet
Engine mount
Fuel hose
Cylinder head
Gearbox
Propeller drive flange
Exhaust manifold
Starboard engine cowling
PROPELLER
Backplate
Spinner
Flanged plate
CONTROL COLUMN AND FLAP LEVER
Torque tube assembly
Elevator arm
Control column
Flap lever
Elevator push-rod
Flap lever detent box
Release button
Bearing assembly
Throttle lever
Brake lever
Elevator trimtab lever
Carburettor hot air lever
Pilot's handgrip
INSTRUMENT PANEL
Flight instruments
Engine instruments
Glove box
Radio plugs
NOSE-GEAR
Steering stop
Nose-leg down tube
Rubber bungee (elasticated cord) shock absorber
Damper unit
Hoop
Pivoted fork
Axle bolt
Nose-wheel
STARBOARD WING
Wing strut
Starboard underwing fairing
Starboard top-wing fairing

Gliders, hang-gliders, and microlights

HANG-GLIDER

MODERN GLIDERS ARE AMONG the most graceful and aerodynamically efficient of all aircraft. Unpowered but with a large wingspan (up to about 25 m, or 82 ft), gliders use currents of hot, rising air (thermals) to stay aloft, and a rudder, elevators, and ailerons for control. Modern gliders have achieved flights of more than 1,450 km (900 miles) and altitudes above 15,000 m (49,000 ft). Hang-gliders consist of a simple frame across which rigid or flexible material is stretched to form the wings. The pilot is suspended below the wings in a harness or body-bag and, gripping a triangular A-frame, steers by shifting weight from side to side. Like gliders, hang-gliders rely on thermals for lift. Microlights are basically powered hang-gliders. A small engine and an open fibreglass car (trike), which can hold a crew of two, are suspended beneath a stronger version of a hang-glider frame; the frame may have rigid or flexible wings. Microlight pilots, like hang-glider pilots, steer by shifting their weight against an A-frame. Microlights can reach speeds of up to 160 kph (100 mph).

NOSE SHELL

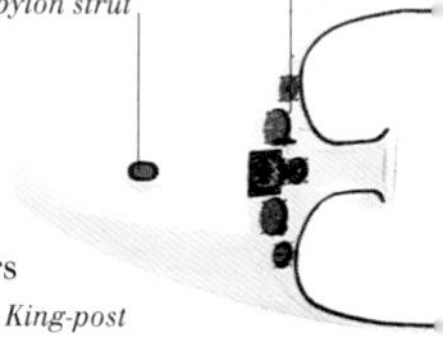
Grommet for front pylon strut
Instrumen panel

PEGASUS XL SE MICROLIGHT

King-post
Apex
Stiffening rib
Centre-line beam
Apex wire
Main suspension
Nose shell
Rear-mounted propeller (pusher propeller)
Fuel tank
Main wheel
Spat (wheel fairing)
Trike nacelle
Fixed nose-wheel

Nose-gear mount

HANG-GLIDER BODY-BAG

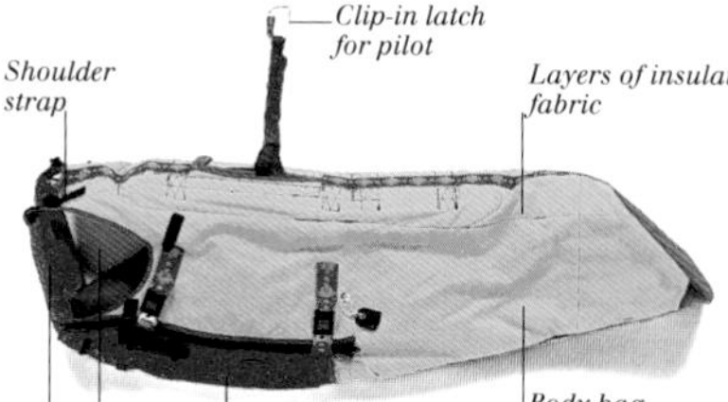
Clip-in latch for pilot
Shoulder strap
Layers of insulating fabric
Body-bag
Camera pouch
Armhole
Shoulder pad

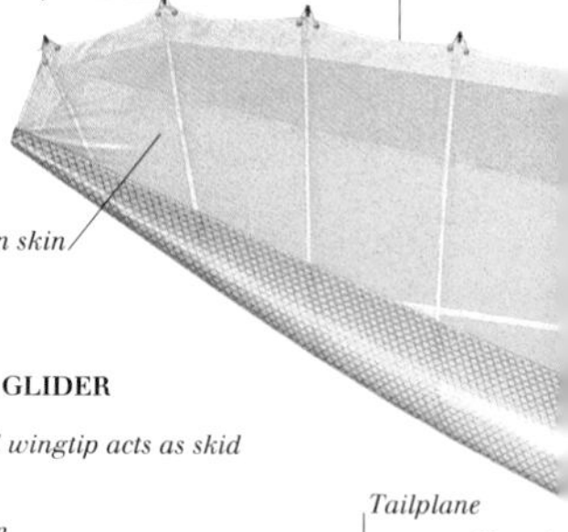
End of rib
Trailing edge
Dacron skin

SCHLEICHER K23 GLIDER

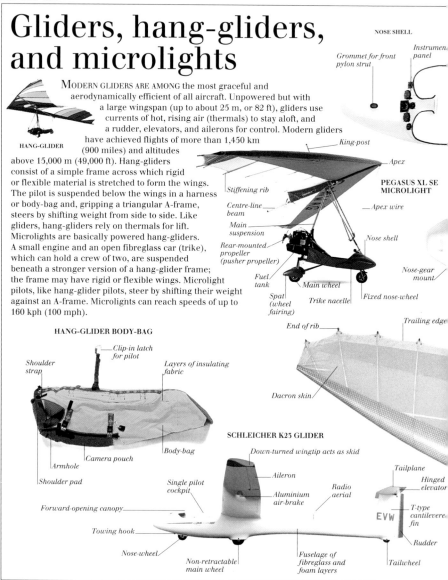

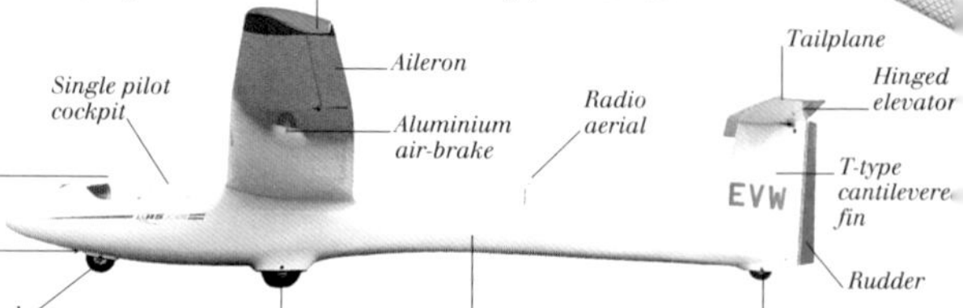
Down-turned wingtip acts as skid
Aileron
Aluminium air-brake
Single pilot cockpit
Radio aerial
Tailplane
Hinged elevator
Forward-opening canopy
EVW
T-type cantilevere fin
Towing hook
Rudder
Nose-wheel
Non-retractable main wheel
Fuselage of fibreglass and foam layers
Tailwheel

SOLAR WINGS PEGASUS QUASAR MICROLIGHT

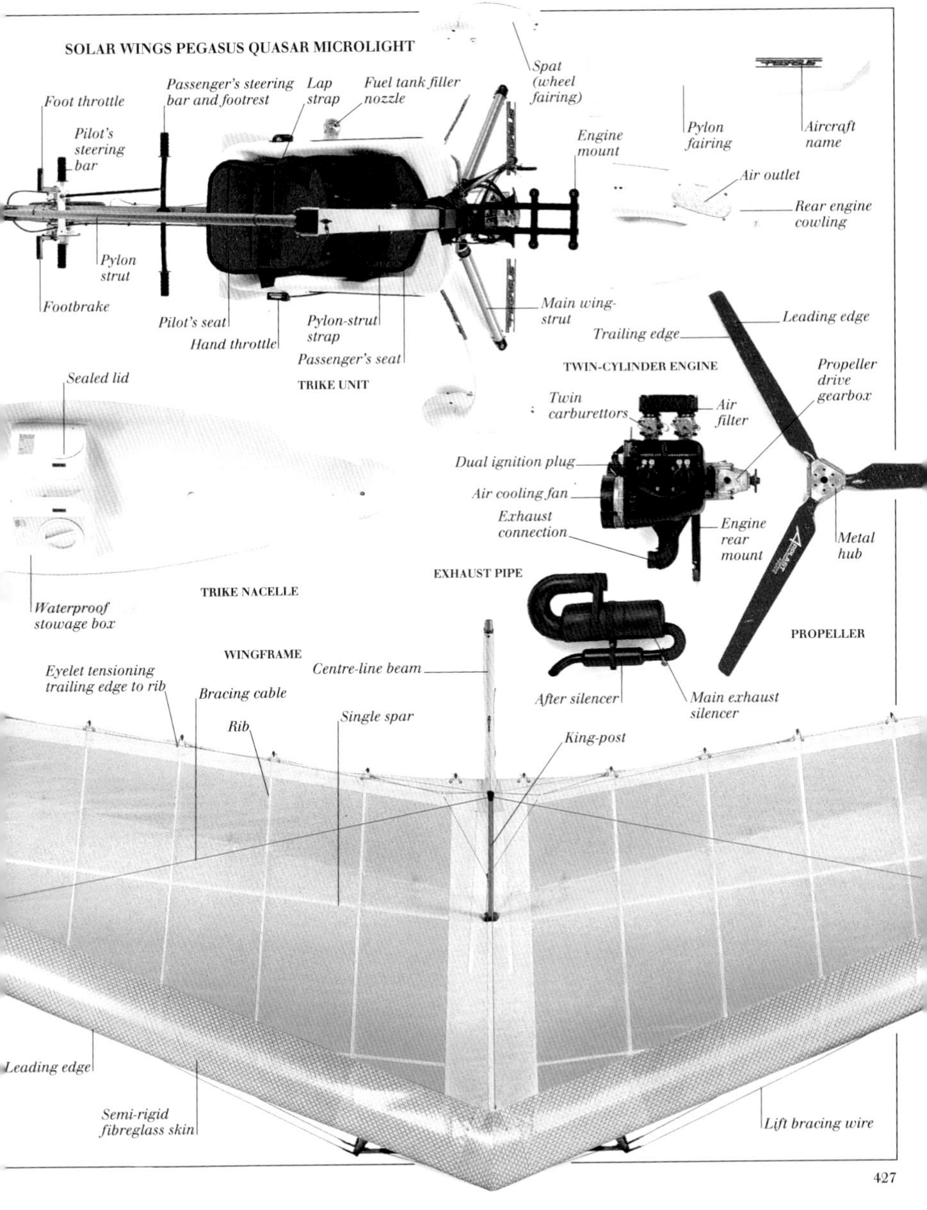

Foot throttle
Pilot's steering bar
Passenger's steering bar and footrest
Lap strap
Fuel tank filler nozzle
Spat (wheel fairing)
Pylon fairing
Aircraft name
Engine mount
Air outlet
Rear engine cowling
Pylon strut
Footbrake
Pilot's seat
Hand throttle
Pylon-strut strap
Passenger's seat
Main wing-strut
TRIKE UNIT
Sealed lid
Waterproof stowage box
TRIKE NACELLE
TWIN-CYLINDER ENGINE
Twin carburettors
Air filter
Dual ignition plug
Air cooling fan
Exhaust connection
Engine rear mount
EXHAUST PIPE
After silencer
Main exhaust silencer
Leading edge
Trailing edge
Propeller drive gearbox
Metal hub
PROPELLER
WINGFRAME
Eyelet tensioning trailing edge to rib
Bracing cable
Rib
Single spar
Centre-line beam
King-post
Leading edge
Semi-rigid fibreglass skin
Lift bracing wire

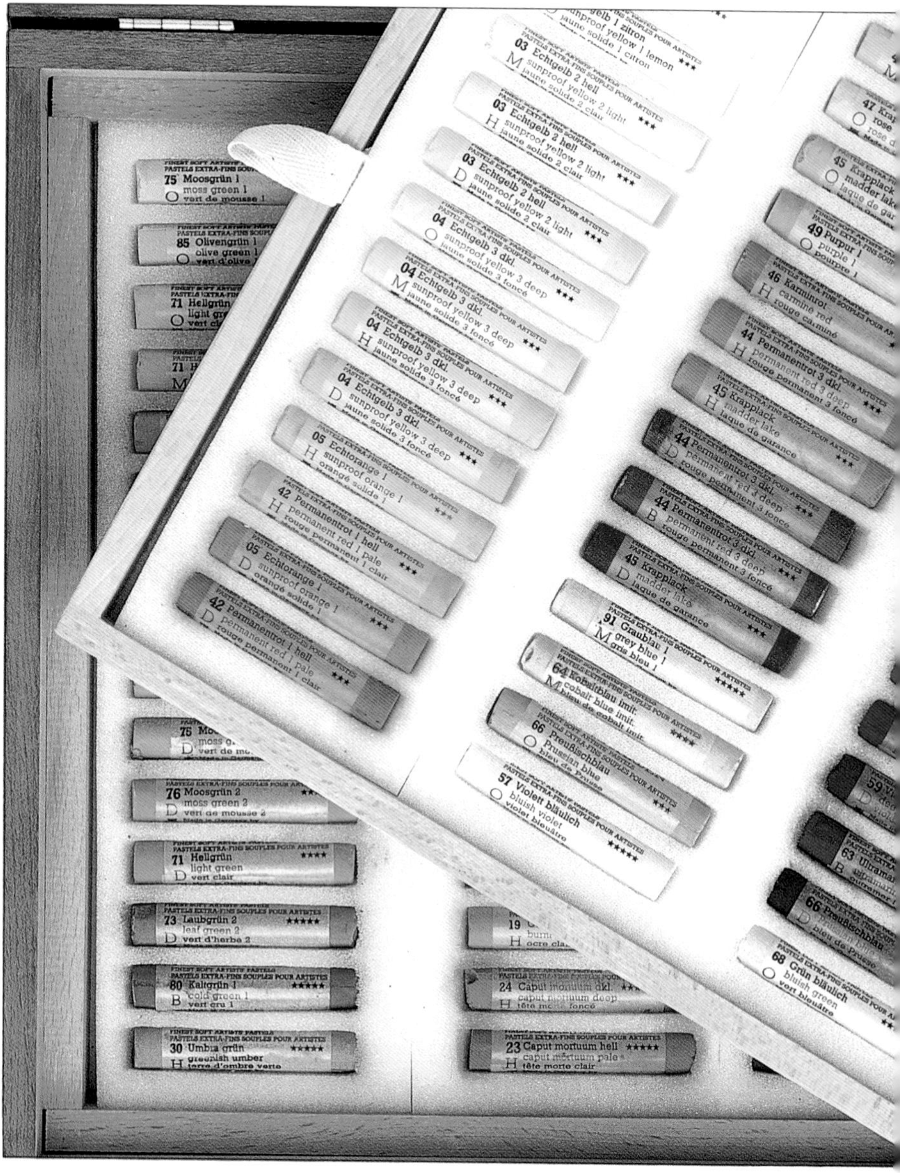
FINEST SOFT ARTISTS' PASTELS
PASTELS EXTRA-FINS SOUPLES POUR ARTISTES
03 Echtgelb 1 zitron
sunproof yellow 1 lemon
jaune solide 1 citron
03 Echtgelb 2 hell
sunproof yellow 2 light
jaune solide 2 clair
04 Echtgelb 3 dkl.
sunproof yellow 3 deep
jaune solide 3 foncé
05 Echtorange 1
sunproof orange 1
orangé solide 1
42 Permanentrot 1 hell
permanent red 1 pale
rouge permanent 1 clair
49 Purpur 1
purpur 1
pourpre 1
46 Karminrot
carmine red
rouge carminé
44 Permanentrot 3 dkl.
permanent red 3 deep
rouge permanent 3 foncé
45 Krapplack
madder lake
laque de garance
91 Graublau 1
grey blau 1
gris bleu 1
64 Kobaltblau imit.
cobalt blue imit.
bleu de cobalt imit.
66 Preußischblau
Prussian blue
bleu de Prusse
57 Violett bläulich
bluish violet
violet bleuâtre
68 Grün bläulich
bluish green
vert bleuâtre
75 Moosgrün 1
moss green 1
vert de mousse 1
85 Olivengrün 1
olive green 1
76 Moosgrün 2
moss green 2
vert de mousse 2
71 Hellgrün
light green
vert clair
73 Laubgrün 2
leaf green 2
vert d'herbe 2
80 Kaltgrün 1
cold green 1
vert gru 1
30 Umbra grün
greenish umber
terre d'ombre verte
24 Caput mortuum dkl.
caput mortuum deep
23 Caput mortuum hell
caput mortuum pale
tête morte clair

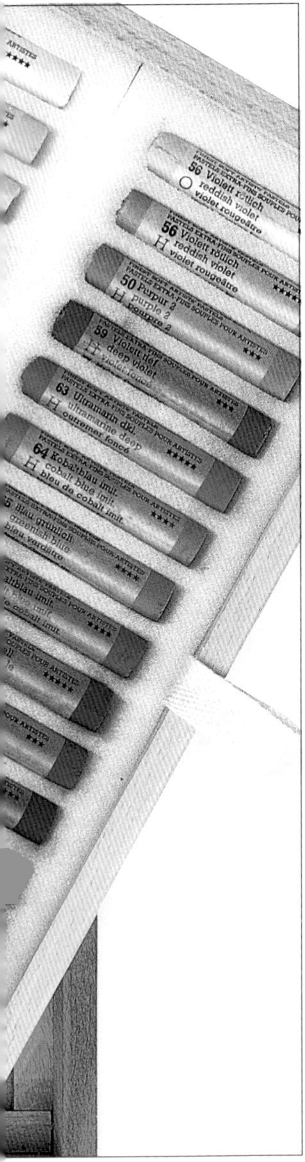

THE VISUAL ARTS

Drawing

DRAWINGS CAN BE FINISHED WORKS OF ART, or preparatory studies for paintings and other visual arts. They can be made using a wide variety of drawing instruments such as pencils, graphite sticks, chalks, charcoal, pens and inks, and silver wires. The most common drawing instrument is the graphite pencil. A graphite pencil consists of a thin rod of graphite mixed with clay, encased in wood. Charcoal is one of the oldest drawing instruments. It is produced by firing twigs of willow, vine, or other woods at high temperatures in airtight containers. Erasers can be used to rub out marks made by drawing materials such as graphite pencils or charcoal, or to achieve a particular effect – such as smudging. Fixative is often applied – using a mouth diffuser or aerosol spray fixative – to prevent smudging once a drawing is finished. Silver lines can be produced by drawing silver wire across specially prepared paper – a technique known as silverpoint. The lines are permanent and cannot be erased. In time the silver lines oxidize and turn brown.

FIXATIVE AND MOUTH DIFFUSER

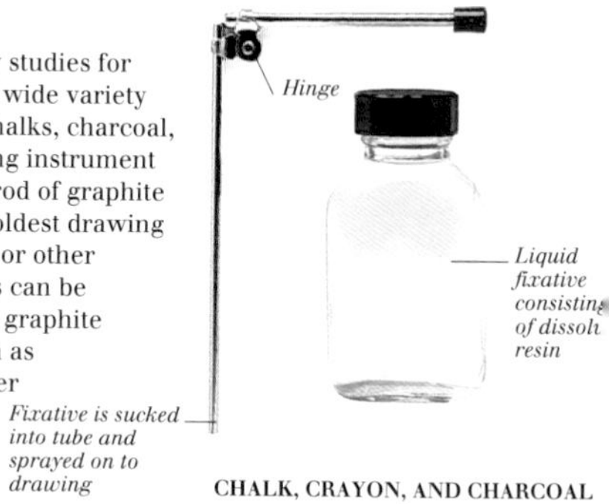
Hinge
Liquid
fixative
consistin
of dissol
resin
Fixative is sucked
into tube and
sprayed on to
drawing

CHALK, CRAYON, AND CHARCOAL

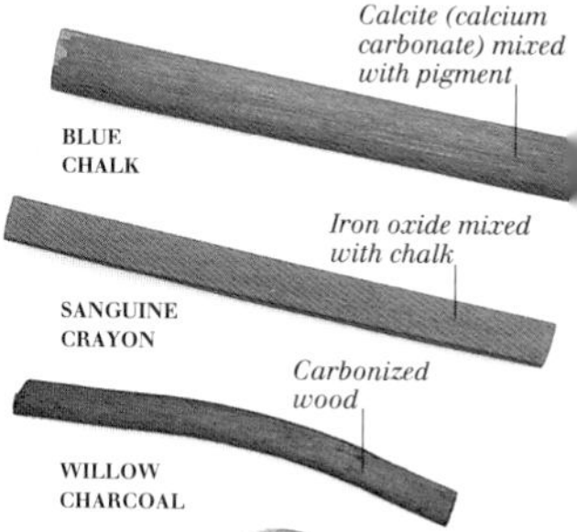
Calcite (calcium
carbonate) mixed
with pigment
BLUE
CHALK
Iron oxide mixed
with chalk
SANGUINE
CRAYON
Carbonized
wood
WILLOW
CHARCOAL

ERASERS

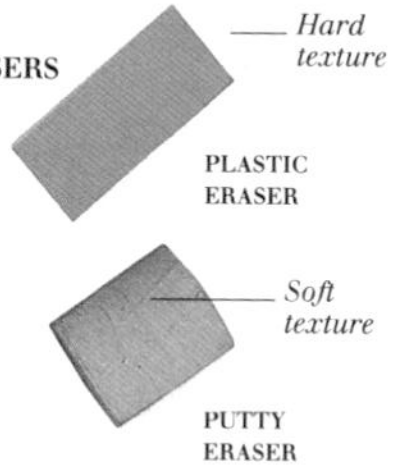
Hard
texture
PLASTIC
ERASER
Soft
texture
PUTTY
ERASER

DRAWING INSTRUMENTS

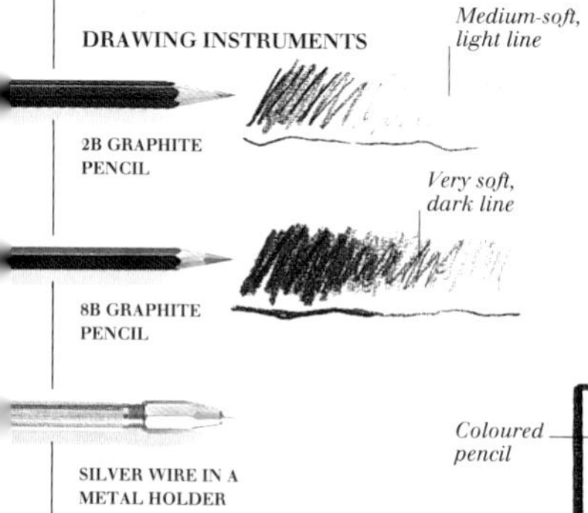
Medium-soft,
light line
2B GRAPHITE
PENCIL
Very soft,
dark line
8B GRAPHITE
PENCIL
SILVER WIRE IN A
METAL HOLDER

DRAWING BOARD

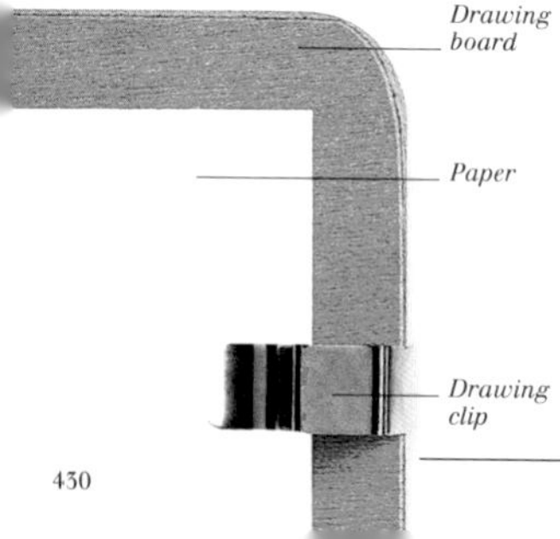
Drawing
board
Paper
Drawing
clip

DRAWING MATERIALS

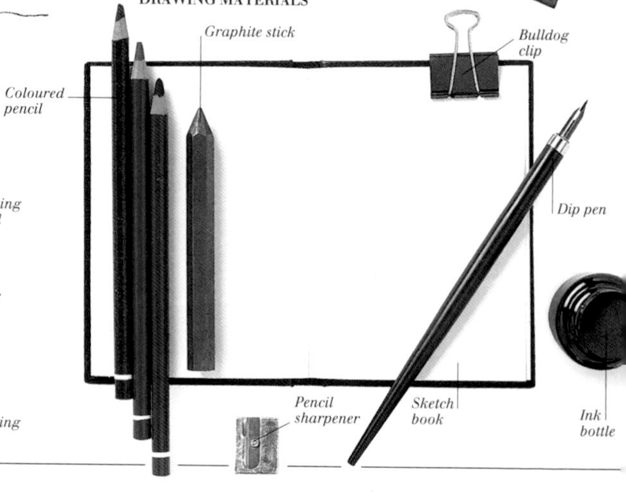
Graphite stick
Bulldog
clip
Coloured
pencil
Dip pen
Pencil
sharpener
Sketch
book
Ink
bottle

Silver lines oxidize to a light brown colour
Figures drawn in ink on top of lines
Line drawn in silverpoint using a rule
Complex perspective drawing done as a preparatory study for a painting
Vanishing point located on head of man riding rearing horse
Lines of squared pavement slabs recede toward a single vanishing point
Paper prepared with size (glue) and pigment

EXAMPLE OF A SILVERPOINT DRAWING
The Adoration of the Magi, Leonardo da Vinci, 1481
Pen and ink over silverpoint on paper
16.5 x 29.2 cm (6½ x 11½ in)

Handmade, tinted paper
One of a series of drawings recording London during 1944–1945
Charcoal lines softened by rubbing and smudging
Broad charcoal mark
Charcoal gives strong, expressive lines
Lines rapidly drawn on site

EXAMPLE OF A CHARCOAL DRAWING
St. Paul's and the River, David Bomberg, 1945
Charcoal on paper
50.8 x 65.8 cm (20 x 25⅞ in)

Tempera

ILLUMINATED MANUSCRIPT

THE TERM TEMPERA is applied to any paint in which pigment is tempered (mixed) with a water-based binding medium – usually egg yolk. Egg tempera is applied to a smooth surface such as vellum (for illuminated manuscripts) or more commonly to hardwood panels prepared with gesso – a mixture of chalk and size (glue). Hog hair brushes are used to apply the gesso. A layer of gesso grosso (coarse gesso) is followed by successive layers of gesso sotile (fine gesso) that are sanded between coats to provide a smooth, yet absorbent ground. The paint is applied with fine sable brushes in thin layers, using light brushstrokes. Tempera dries quickly to form a tough skin with a satin sheen. The luminous white surface of the gesso combined with the overlaid paint produces the brilliant crispness and rich colours particular to this medium. Egg tempera paintings are frequently gilded with gold. Leaves of finely beaten gold are applied to a bole (reddish-brown clay) base and polished by burnishing.

MATERIALS FOR GILDING

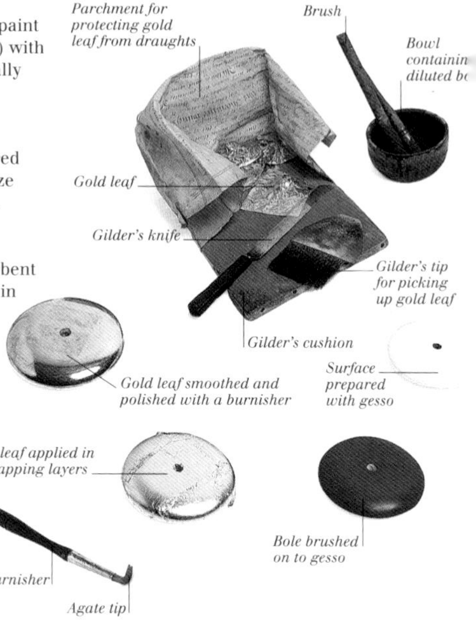
Parchment for protecting gold leaf from draughts
Brush
Bowl containin
diluted b
Gold leaf
Gilder's knife
Gilder's tip for picking up gold leaf
Gilder's cushion
Gold leaf smoothed and polished with a burnisher
Surface prepared with gesso
Gold leaf applied in overlapping layers
Bole brushed on to gesso
Burnisher
Agate tip

MATERIALS FOR TEMPERA PANEL PAINTING

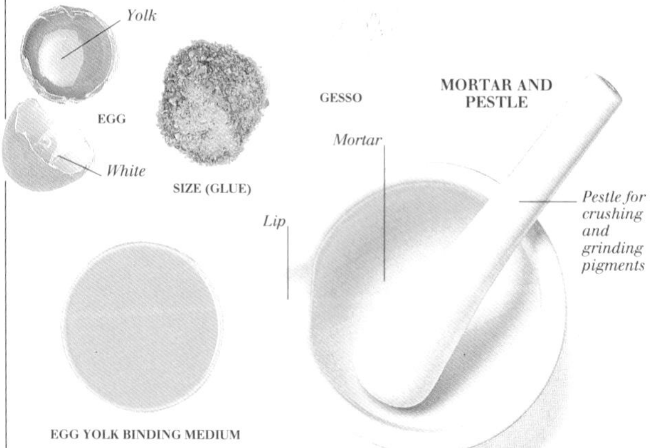
Yolk
EGG
White
SIZE (GLUE)
GESSO
MORTAR AND PESTLE
Mortar
Lip
Pestle for crushing and grinding pigments
EGG YOLK BINDING MEDIUM

EXAMPLES OF BRUSHES

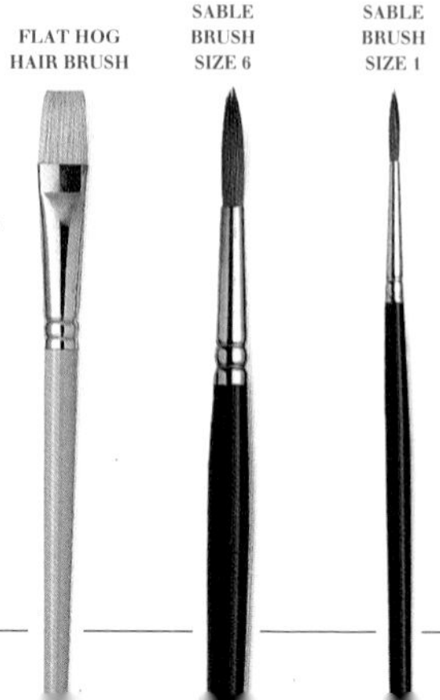
FLAT HOG HAIR BRUSH
SABLE BRUSH SIZE 6
SABLE BRUSH SIZE 1

EXAMPLE OF A TEMPERA PAINTING

Presentation in the Temple, Ambrogio Lorenzetti, 1342
Tempera on wood, 257 x 168 cm (8 ft 5⅛ in x 5 ft 6⅛ in)

Altarpiece commissioned for Siena Cathedral, Italy
Textured gold ornament made by punching motifs into the gilded surface
The red tinge of the bole is just visible beneath the gold
Edge of a sheet of gold leaf
Crisp edge characteristic of tempera painting
Vine black used to create the dim cathedral interior
Highlights on the beard made by applying thin layers of white over dried paint
Red drapery painted in vermilion
Raised right hand and pointing finger is the gesture of prophecy
Receding floor tiles create the impression of depth
Patch of discoloured varnish, left from last cleaning

PIGMENTS FOR FLESH-COLOUR PAINTING

VERDACCIO

VERMILION AND LEAD WHITE

VERMILION

RED EARTH (IRON OXIDE)

EXAMPLES OF PIGMENTS

MALACHITE

ULTRAMARINE LAPIS LAZULI

VINE BLACK

LEAD TIN YELLOW

Warm flesh tones achieved by layering vermilion and white over an undercoat of verdaccio
Patterned gold halo glitters in candlelight
Ultramarine lapis lazuli, as costly as gold, was reserved for significant figures such as the Virgin Mary
Craquelure (pattern of cracks in the paint)

DETAIL FROM "PRESENTATION IN THE TEMPLE"

Fresco

FRESCO IS A METHOD OF WALL PAINTING. In buon fresco (true fresco), pigments are mixed with water and applied to an intonaco (layer of fresh, damp lime-plaster). The intonaco absorbs and binds the pigments as it dries making the picture a permanent part of the wall surface. The intonaco is applied in sections called giornate (daily sections). The size of each giornata depends on the artist's estimate of how much can be painted before the plaster sets. The junctions between giornate are sometimes visible on a finished fresco. The range of colours used in buon fresco are limited to lime-resistant pigments such as earth colours (below). Slaked lime (burnt lime mixed with water), bianco di San Giovanni (slaked lime that has been partly exposed to air), and chalk can be used to produce fresco whites. In fresco secco (dry fresco), pigments are mixed with a binding medium and applied to dry plaster. The pigments are not completely absorbed into the plaster and may flake off over time.

CROSS-SECTION SHOWING FRESCO LAYERS

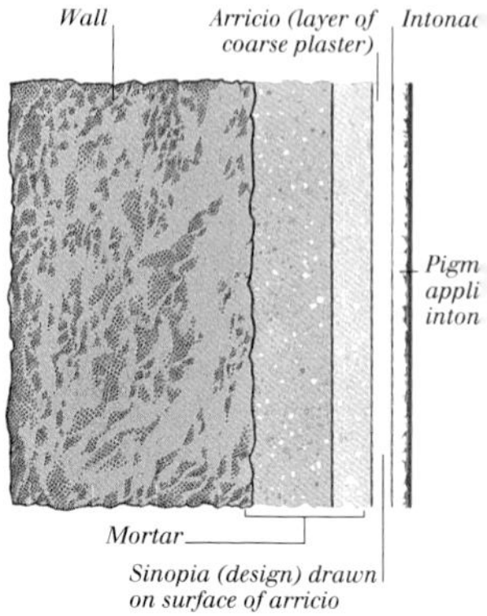
Wall
Arricio (layer of coarse plaster)
Mortar
Sinopia (design) drawn on surface of arricio

EXAMPLES OF EARTH COLOUR PIGMENTS

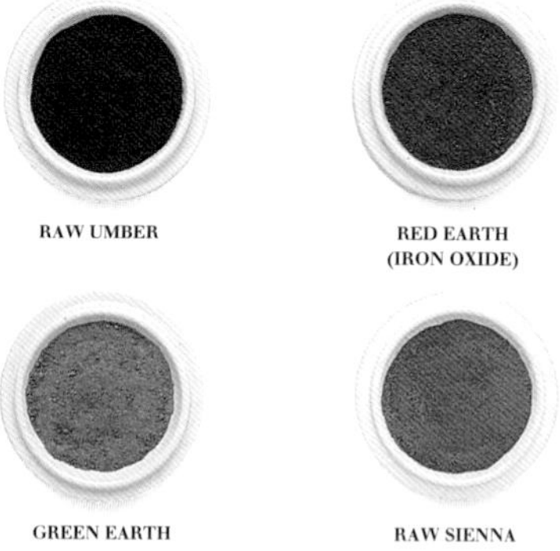
RAW UMBER
RED EARTH (IRON OXIDE)
GREEN EARTH
RAW SIENNA

EXAMPLES OF FRESCO BRUSHES

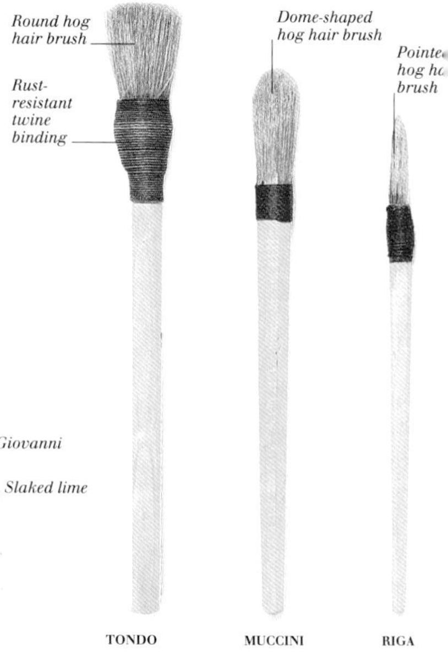
Round hog hair brush
Rust-resistant twine binding
Dome-shaped hog hair brush
TONDO
MUCCINI
RIGA

INGREDIENTS FOR FRESCO WHITES

Marble slab for mixing ingredients
Bianco di San Giovanni
Slaked lime
Chalk

EXAMPLE OF A FRESCO

The Expulsion of the Merchants from the Temple, Giotto, c.1306
Fresco, 200 x 185 cm (78 x 72 in)

One of a series of frescoes in the Arena Chapel, Padua, Italy
Temple acts as a backdrop for the action
Patches of azurite blue have turned green due to reaction with carbon dioxide
Bianco di San Giovanni often used for fresco whites
Gold leaf applied to apostle's halo
Hairline junction between giornate is visible
Green earth pigment applied to robe
Red earth pigment applied in buon fresco has retained rich hue
Child painted on top of apostle's robe
Azurite blue applied in fresco secco has flaked off to reveal the plaster beneath
Dry, matt surface characteristic of buon fresco

Paint applied in buon fresco to child's face
White dove represents the Holy Ghost
Paint applied in fresco secco to child's body has flaked off
Sinopia (design) sketched in red earth

DETAIL FROM "THE EXPULSION"

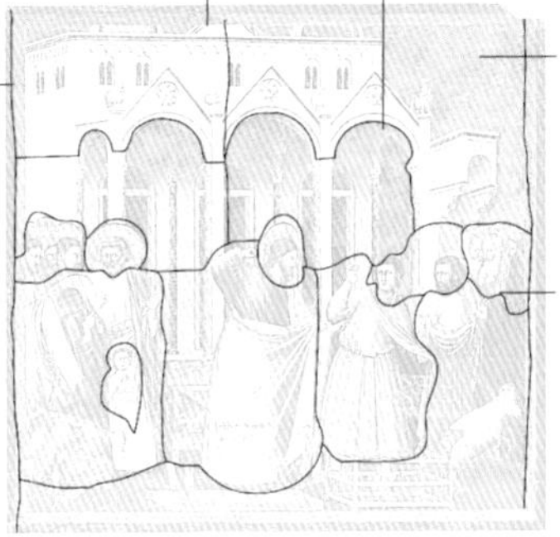
Artist has to finish giornata before plaster dries
Junction between giornate
A fresco was generally worked in zones from the top down
Area with little detail can be painted quickly, allowing a larger giornata to be completed
Highly detailed area takes a longer time to paint, restricting the size of the giornata

GIORNATE (DAILY SECTIONS) IN "THE EXPULSION"

Oils

KIDNEY-SHAPED PALETTE

OIL PAINTS ARE MADE BY MIXING and grinding pigment with a drying vegetable oil such as linseed oil. The paint can be applied to many different surfaces and textures – the most common being canvas. Before painting, the canvas is stretched on a wooden frame and its surface is prepared with layers of size (glue) and primer. The two main types of brushes used in oil painting are stiff hog hair bristle brushes – generally used for covering large areas; and soft hair brushes made from sable or synthetic material – generally used for fine detail. Other tools, including painting knives, can also be used to achieve different effects. Oil paint can be applied thickly (a technique known as impasto), or can be thinned down using a solvent – such as turpentine or white spirit. Varnishes are sometimes applied to finished paintings to protect their surface and to give them a matt or gloss finish.

DAMMAR RESIN VARNISH

Crystals are dissolved and applied to painting to protect its surface

COMMERCIAL OIL PAINTS

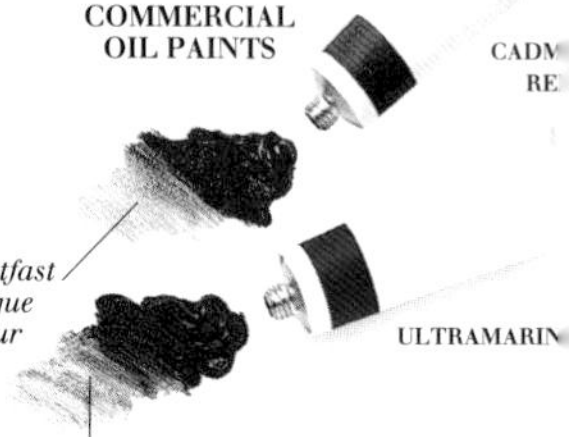
CADM
RE
Lightfast opaque colour
ULTRAMARIN
Transparent colour

LINSEED OIL

Oil derived from seeds of flax plant

EXAMPLES OF PIGMENTS

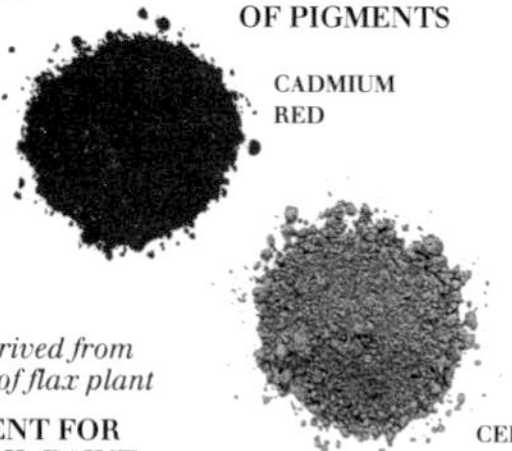
CADMIUM RED
CERULEAN BLUE

DOUBLE DIPPER (PALETTE ATTACHMENT)

Screw-top lid
Container for storing solvent or drying oil

EQUIPMENT FOR MAKING OIL PAINT

Airtight jar for storing paint
Palette knife for mixing drying oil and pigment
Glass muller for grinding drying oil and pigment
Glass slab with abrasive surface

PAINTING KNIVES

TROWEL-SHAPED PAINTING KNIFE
DIAMOND-SHAPED PAINTING KNIFE
Blade
Blade
Cranked, steel shank
Cranked, steel shank

EXAMPLES OF BRUSHES

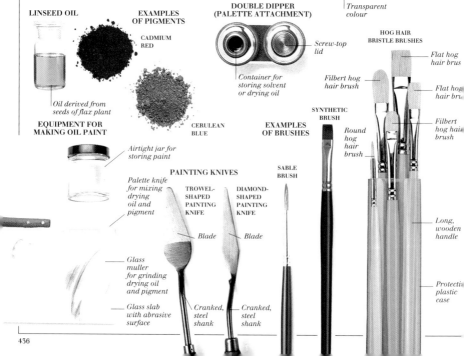

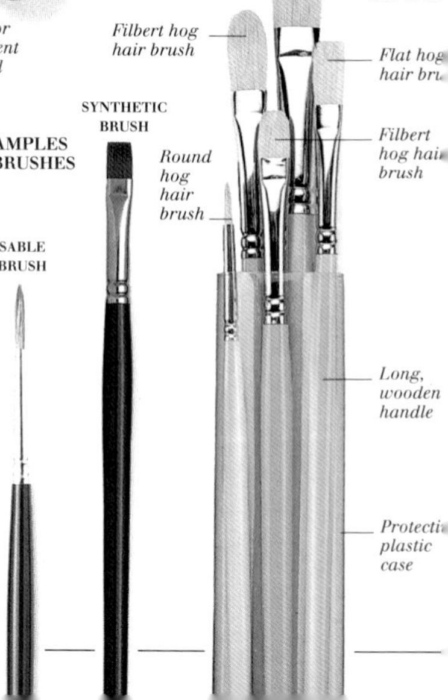
SABLE BRUSH
SYNTHETIC BRUSH
HOG HAIR BRISTLE BRUSHES
Flat hog hair brus
Filbert hog hair brush
Flat hog hair bru
Round hog hair brush
Filbert hog hai brush
Long, wooden handle
Protecti plastic case

EXAMPLE OF AN OIL PAINTING

Fritillarias, Vincent van Gogh, 1886
Oil on canvas, 73.5 x 60.5 cm (29 x 24 in)

Artist's signature scratched in wet paint with the end of the brush
Each leaf painted in a single, rapid stroke
Impasto (deep ridges of paint applied in thick strokes)
Strong directional brushstrokes on table draw attention to the vase
Background enlivened by dabs of white and green
Orange and blue (complementary colours) placed together to give maximum contrast and enhance one another to appear brighter
Features of vase highlighted by generous touches of yellow

RADIAL STUDIO EASEL

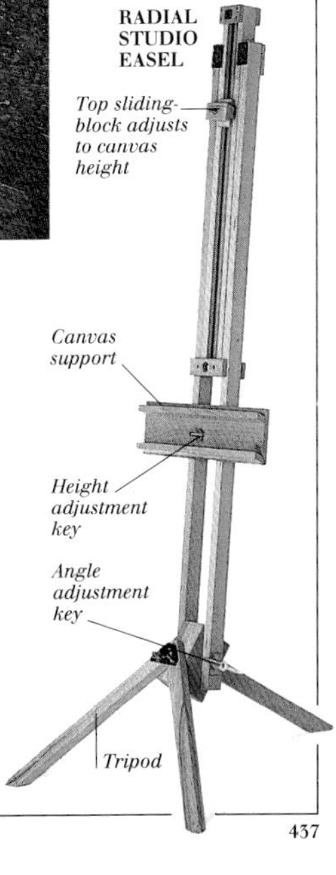
Top sliding-block adjusts to canvas height
Canvas support
Height adjustment key
Angle adjustment key
Tripod

CANVAS STRETCHED ON WOODEN FRAME (VIEWED FROM THE BACK)

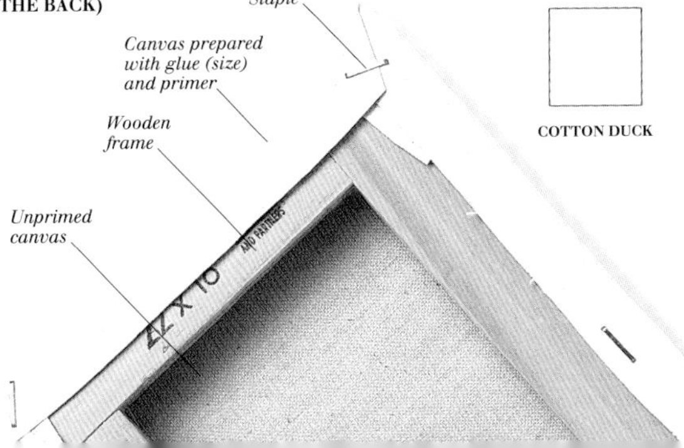
Staple
Canvas prepared with glue (size) and primer
Wooden frame
Unprimed canvas
22 X 10

EXAMPLES OF CANVASES

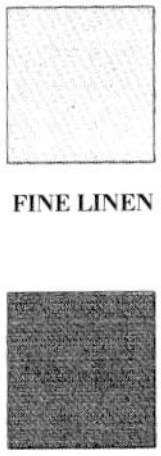
COTTON DUCK
FINE LINEN
COARSE LINEN

Watercolour

WATERCOLOUR PAINT IS MADE OF GROUND PIGMENT mixed with a water-soluble binding medium, usually gum arabic. It is usually applied to paper using soft hair brushes such as sable, goat hair, squirrel, and synthetic brushes. Watercolours are often diluted and applied as overlaying washes (thin, transparent layers) to build up depth of colour. Washes can be laid in a variety of ways to create a range of different effects. For example, a wet-in-wet wash can be achieved by laying a wash on top of another wet wash. The two washes blend together to give a fused effect. Sponges are used to modify washes by soaking up paint so that areas of pigment are lightened or removed from the paper. Watercolours can also be applied undiluted – a technique known as dry brush – to create a broken-colour effect. Watercolours are generally transparent and allow light to reflect from the surface of the paper through the layers of paint to give a luminous effect. They can be thickened and made opaque by adding body colour (Chinese white).

GUM ARABIC

NATURAL SPONGE

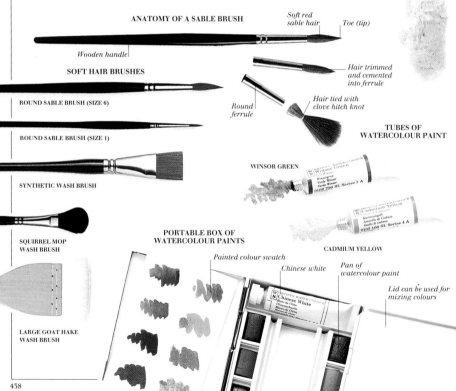

ANATOMY OF A SABLE BRUSH

SOFT HAIR BRUSHES

ROUND SABLE BRUSH (SIZE 6)

ROUND SABLE BRUSH (SIZE 1)

SYNTHETIC WASH BRUSH

SQUIRREL MOP WASH BRUSH

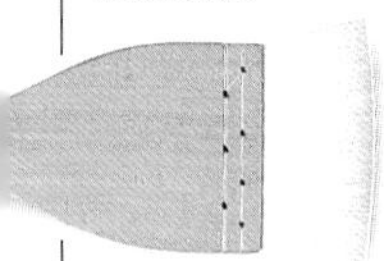

LARGE GOAT HAKE WASH BRUSH

TUBES OF WATERCOLOUR PAINT

WINSOR GREEN

CADMIUM YELLOW

PORTABLE BOX OF WATERCOLOUR PAINTS

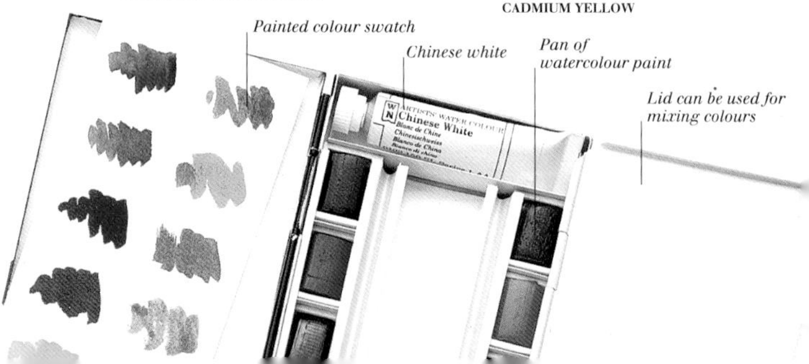

EXAMPLE OF A WATERCOLOUR

Burning of the Houses of Parliament, Turner, 1834
Watercolour on paper, 29.2 x 44.5 cm (11½ x 17½ in)

Transparent washes laid on top of each other to create tonal depth
Transparent washes allow light to reflect off the surface of the paper to give a luminous effect
Highlight scratched out with a scalpel
Paper shows through thin wash to give flames added highlight
Crowd painted with thin strokes laid over a pale wash
Undiluted paint applied, then partly washed out, to create the impression of water

EXAMPLES OF WATERCOLOUR PAPERS

SMOOTH-TEXTURED PAPER

MEDIUM-TEXTURED PAPER

ROUGH-TEXTURED PAPER

EXAMPLES OF WASHES

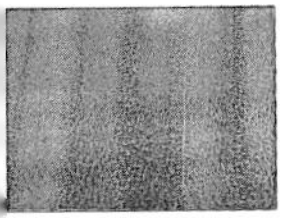

VASH OVER DRY BRUSH
Vash laid over paint
.pplied with dry brush
;ives two-tone effect

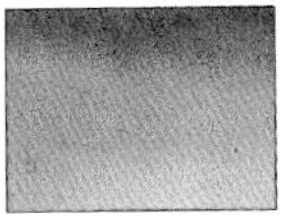

GRADED WASH
Strong wash applied to tilted paper gives graded effect

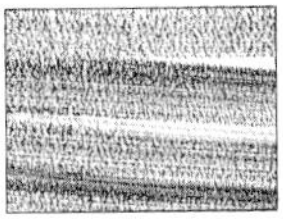

DRY BRUSH
Undiluted paint dragged across surface of paper gives broken effect

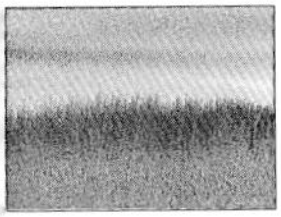

VET-IN-WET
Two diluted washes
eft to run together
:o give fused effect

COLOUR WHEEL OF WATERCOLOUR PAINTS

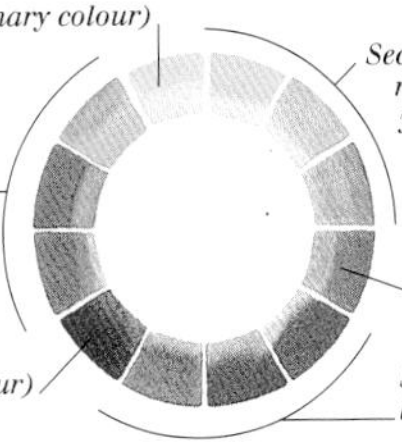
Yellow (primary colour)
Secondary colours made by mixing yellow and blue
Secondary colours made by mixing red and yellow
Blue (primary colour)
Red (primary colour)
Secondary colours made by mixing blue and red

Pastels

PASTELS ARE STICKS OF PIGMENT made by mixing ground pigment with chalk and a binding medium, such as gum arabic. They vary in hardness depending on the proportion of the binding medium to the chalk. Soft pastel – the most common form of pastel – contains just enough binding medium to hold the pigment in stick form. Pastels can be applied directly to any support (surface) with sufficient tooth (texture). When a pastel is drawn over a textured surface, the pigment crumbles and lodges in the fibres of the support. Pastel marks have a particular soft, matt quality and are suitable for techniques such as blending, scumbling, and feathering. Blending is a technique of rubbing and fusing two or more colours on the support using fingers or various tools such as tortillons (paper stumps), soft hair brushes, putty erasers, and soft bread. Scumbling is a technique of building up layers of pastel colours. The side or blunted tip of a soft pastel is lightly drawn over an underpainted area so that patches of the colour beneath show through. Feathering is a technique of applying parallel strokes of colour with the point of a pastel, usually over an existing layer of pastel colour. A thin spray of fixative can be applied – using a mouth diffuser (see pp. 430-431) or aerosol spray fixative – to a finished pastel painting, or in between layers of colour, to prevent smudging.

EQUIPMENT FOR MAKING PASTELS

Glass muller
Chalk
Glass slab with abrasive surface
Gum arabic
Ivory-black pigment
Cobalt-b pigment

EXAMPLES OF SOFT PASTELS

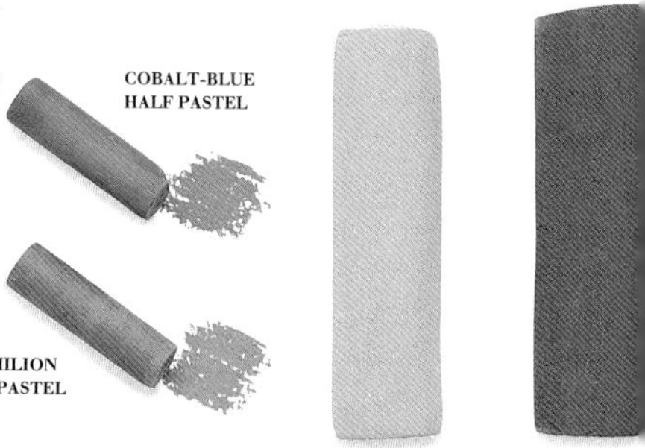
COBALT-BLUE HALF PASTEL
VERMILION HALF PASTEL
OLIVE-GREEN FULL PASTEL
MAUVE FULL PASTEL

BOXED PASTEL SET

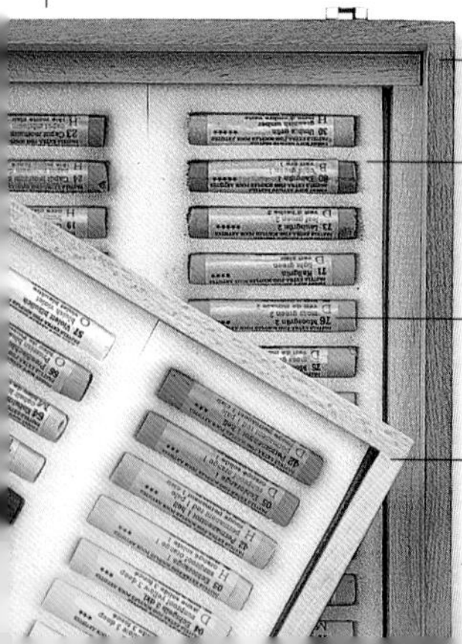
Boxed set containing a mixture of portrait and landscape colours
Foam compartments protect the pastels
Soft pastel
Wooden tray

EQUIPMENT USED WITH PASTELS

PUTTY ERASER

BREAD

AEROSOL SPRAY FIXATIVE

SOFT HAIR BRUSH

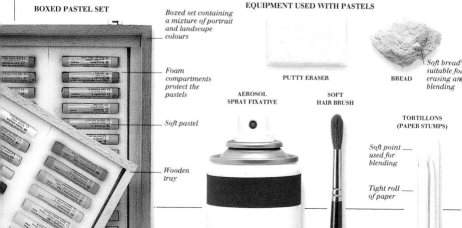

Soft point used for blending
Tight roll of paper
TORTILLONS (PAPER STUMPS)

EXAMPLE OF A PASTEL PAINTING

Woman Drying her Neck, Edgar Degas, c.1898
Pastel on cardboard, 62.5 x 65.5 cm (24½ x 25½ in)

Degas
Pastels applied directly to support
Colours are blended together using fingers or tools such as tortillons
Built up layers of pastel
Pure bright colours laid side by side produce strong contrasts
Rich colour of fabric created by overlaying yellows and oranges
Broken colours, characteristic of scumbling technique
Toned colour of paper visible beneath thinly applied pastels

DETAIL FROM "WOMAN DRYING HER NECK"

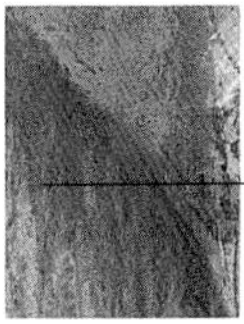
Feathering technique used to produce skin tones

EXAMPLES OF TEXTURED PAPERS AND PASTEL BOARDS

WATERCOLOUR PAPER (ROUGH TEXTURE)

GLASS PAPER

WATERCOLOUR PAPER (MEDIUM TEXTURE)

INGRES PAPER

FLOCKED PASTEL BOARD

CANSON PAPER

EXAMPLES OF COLOURED AND TINTED PAPERS

Acrylics

ACRYLIC PAINT IS MADE BY MIXING PIGMENT with a synthetic resin. It can be thinned with water but dries to become water insoluble. Acrylics are applied to many surfaces, such as paper and acrylic-primed board and canvas. A variety of brushes, painting knives, rollers, air-brushes, plastic scrapers, and other tools are used in acrylic painting. The versatility of acrylics makes them suitable for a wide range of techniques. They can be used opaquely or – by adding water – in a transparent, watercolour style. Acrylic mediums can be added to the paint to adjust its consistency for special effects such as glazing and impasto (ridges of paint applied in thick strokes) or to make it more matt or glossy. Acrylics are quick-drying, which allows layers of paint to be applied on top of each other almost immediately.

EXAMPLES OF BRUSHES

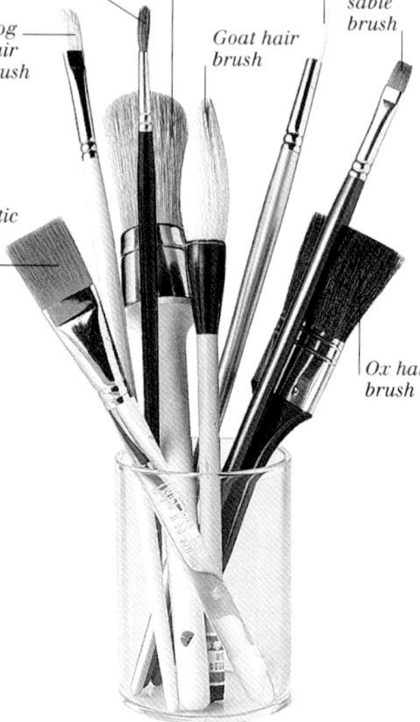
Sable brush
Hog hair sash brush
Synthetic hog hair brush
Synthetic sable brush
Hog hair brush
Goat hair brush
Synthetic wash brush
Ox hair brush

EXAMPLES OF PAINTS USED IN ACRYLICS

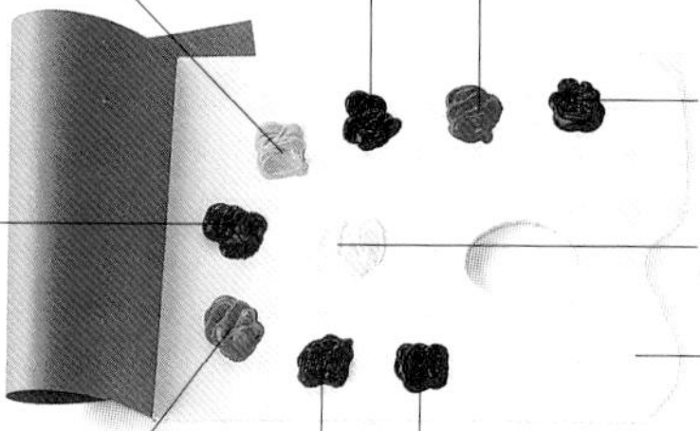
Azo yellow
Phthalo green
Cerulean blue
Phthalo blue
Quinacridone red
Titanium white
Pad of disposable paper palettes
Yellow ochre
Burnt umber
Burnt sienna

PAINTING TOOLS

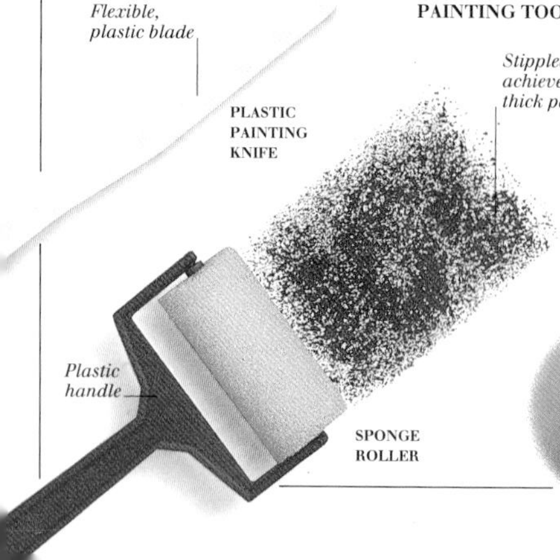
Flexible, plastic blade
PLASTIC PAINTING KNIFE
Stippled effect achieved using thick paint
Plastic handle
SPONGE ROLLER

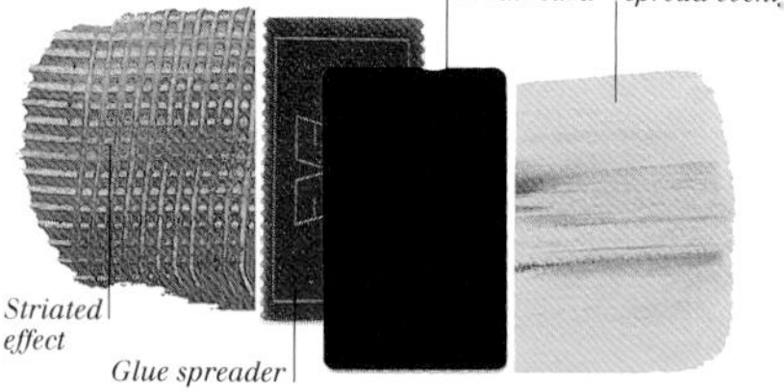
Credit card
Paint spread evenl
Striated effect
Glue spreader

PLASTIC SCRAPERS

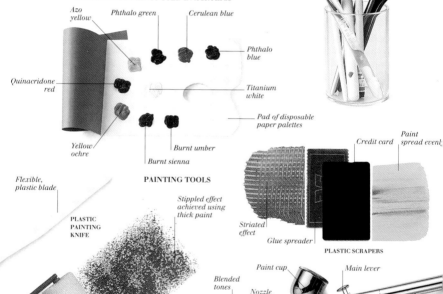

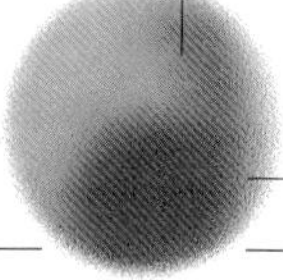
Blended tones
Uniform tone

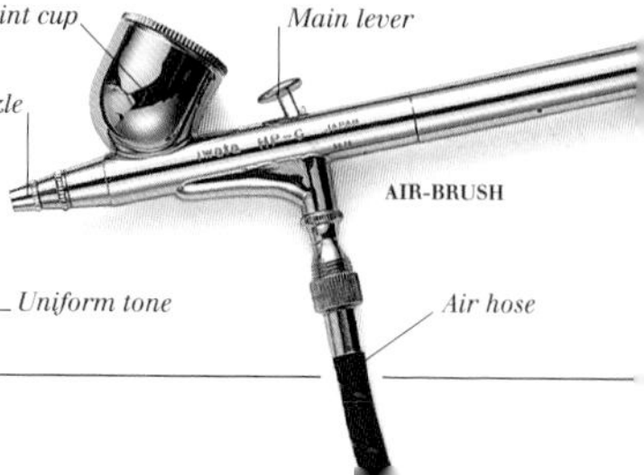
Paint cup
Main lever
Nozzle
Air hose

AIR-BRUSH

EXAMPLE OF AN ACRYLIC PAINTING

A Bigger Splash, David Hockney, 1967
Acrylic on canvas, 242.5 x 243.8 cm (95½ x 96 in)

Paint applied evenly using a roller
Cotton duck canvas support (surface)
Flatness of rollered areas enhanced by adding gel medium to the paint
Masking tape stuck on to canvas to define main shapes, and paint applied within these areas using a roller
Thin strip of pool edge left unpainted
Splash painted using thicker paint and small brush
Imprecise edge on end of spring board where paint has seeped under masking tape

EXAMPLES OF ACRYLIC PAINTS AND TECHNIQUES

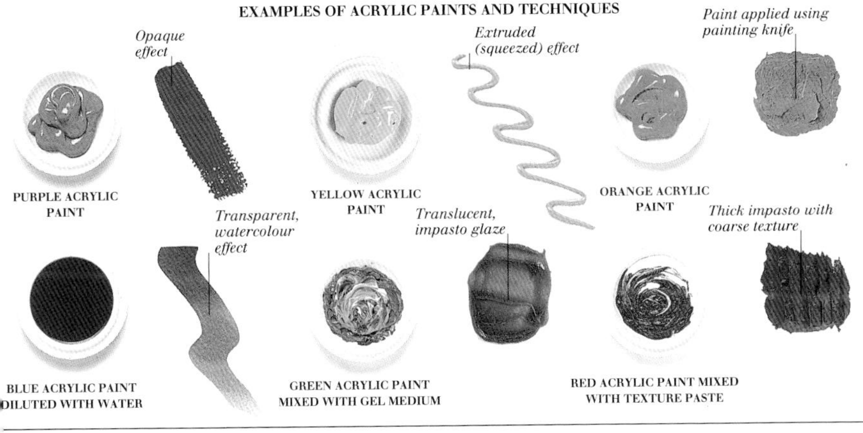
Opaque effect
Extruded (squeezed) effect
Paint applied using painting knife
PURPLE ACRYLIC PAINT
YELLOW ACRYLIC PAINT
ORANGE ACRYLIC PAINT
Transparent, watercolour effect
Translucent, impasto glaze
Thick impasto with coarse texture
BLUE ACRYLIC PAINT DILUTED WITH WATER
GREEN ACRYLIC PAINT MIXED WITH GEL MEDIUM
RED ACRYLIC PAINT MIXED WITH TEXTURE PASTE

Calligraphy

CALLIGRAPHY IS BEAUTIFULLY FORMED LETTERING. The term applies to written text and illumination (the decoration of manuscripts using gold leaf and colour). The essential materials needed to practise calligraphy are a writing tool, ink, and a writing surface. Quills are among the oldest writing tools. They are usually made from goose or turkey feathers, and are noted for their flexibility and ability to produce fine lines. A quill point, however, is not very durable and constant recutting and trimming is required. The most commonly used writing instrument in western calligraphy is a detachable, metal nib held in a penholder. The metal nib is very durable, and there are a wide range of different types. Particular types of nibs – such as copperplate, speedball, and roundhand nibs – are used for specific styles of lettering. Some nibs have integral ink reservoirs and others have reservoirs that are detachable. Brushes are also used for writing, and for filling in outlined letters and painting decoration. Other writing tools used in calligraphy are fountain pens, felt-tip pens, rotring pens, and reed pens. Calligraphy inks may come in liquid form, or as a solid ink stick. Ink sticks are ground down in distilled water to form a liquid ink. The most common writing surfaces for calligraphy are good quality, smooth -surfaced papers. To achieve the best writing position, the calligrapher places the paper on a drawing board set at an angle.

EQUIPMENT USED IN BRUSH LETTERING

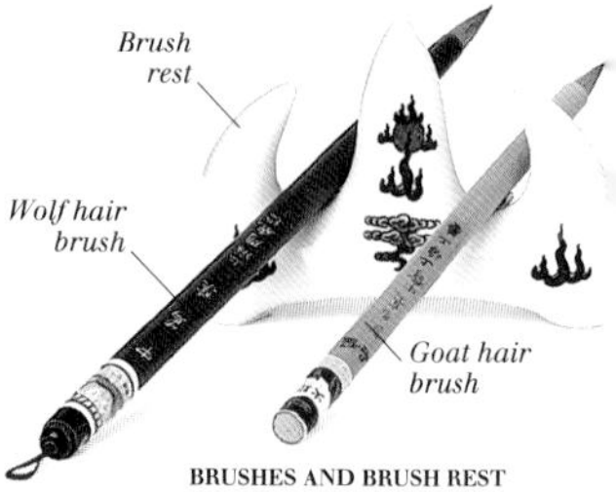
Brush rest
Wolf hair brush
Goat hair brush

BRUSHES AND BRUSH REST

Liquid ink made by grinding down ink stick in distilled water
Solid carbon ink stick
Ink stone
千秋光

INK STICK AND STONE

PENS, NIBS, AND BRUSHES USED IN CALLIGRAPHY

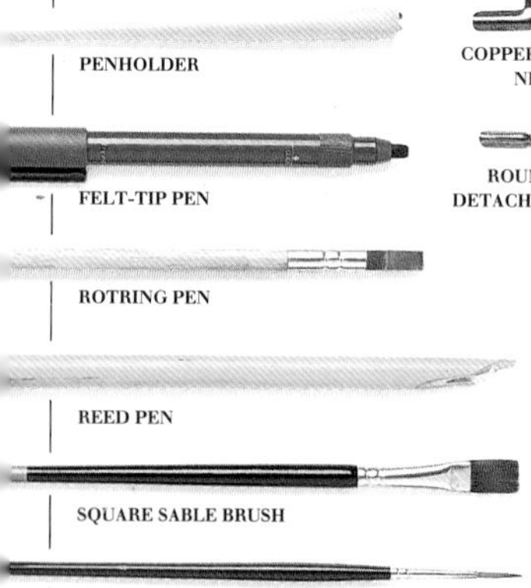

PENHOLDER

FELT-TIP PEN

ROTRING PEN

REED PEN

SQUARE SABLE BRUSH

POINTED SABLE BRUSH

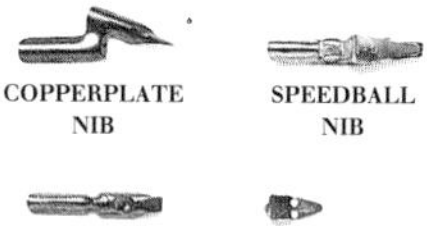

COPPERPLATE NIB

SPEEDBALL NIB

ROUNDHAND NIB AND DETACHABLE INK RESERVOIR

Feather
Feather stripped for better handling
Barrel
Hand-cut point

GOOSE-FEATHER QUILL

GOAT HAIR BRUSH

WOLF HAIR BRUSH

FOUNTAIN PEN AND INK

EXAMPLES OF LETTERING STYLES

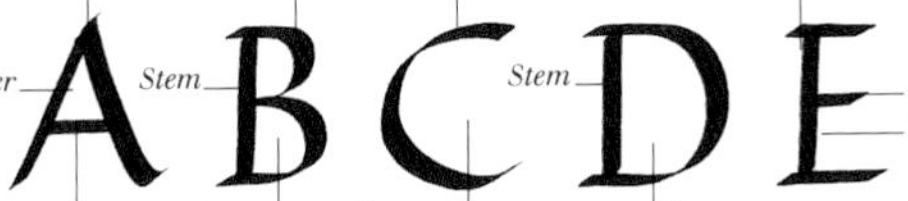
Apex
Bowl
Curved stroke
Stem
Inner counter
Stem
Stem
Arm
Counter
Crossbar
Inner counter
Counter
Inner counter

ROMAN CAPITALS

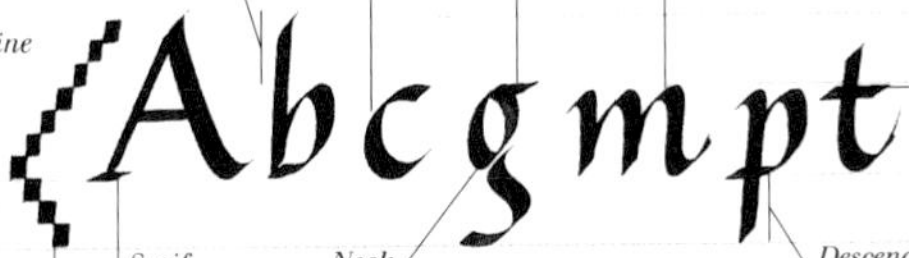
Cap line
X line
'ase
'ine
Descender
'ne
Ascender
Curved stroke
Ear
Arch
Crossbar
Serif
Neck
Descender
'ight of letter
'termined by
'dder of nib
'dths

ITALIC ROMAN

Slightly pinched (curved) vertical stroke
Letter filled in using brush
Inner counter
Tail
Spine
Pointed apex

VERSAL

AN ILLUMINATED MANUSCRIPT

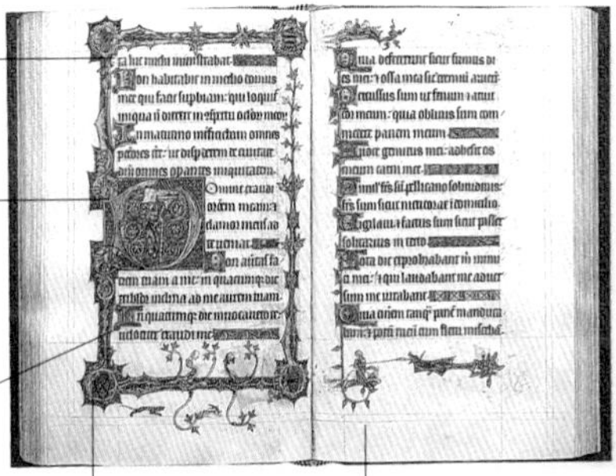
'e of lettering
'alled Gothic
book script
'ge decorative
'letter used to
mark the
opening of
a chapter
'ords written
carefully by
hand
Gold leaf
Grid lines provide guide to position of words and pictures

CHINESE LETTERING

Rice paper
Broad brush stroke
Chinese character meaning long life
Artist's stamped signature

ARTIST'S STAMP

Stamp
Stamped signature of the artist
Ink pad

DRAWING BOARD

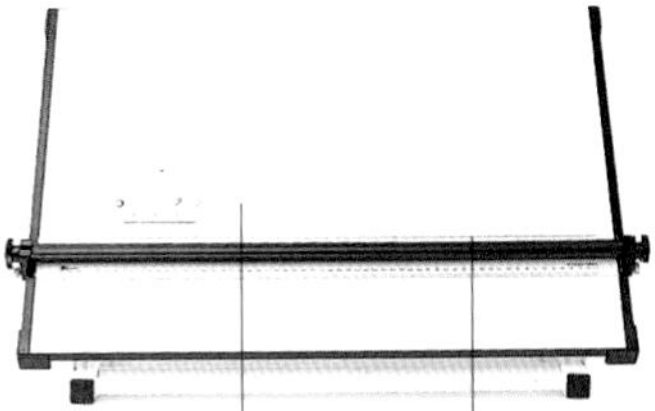
Adjustable set square
Blade with parallel motion

EXAMPLES OF CALLIGRAPHY PAPERS

Standard European paper
Indian handmade paper
Flecked, tinted paper
Imitation parchment paper

Printmaking 1

PRINTS ARE MADE BY FOUR BASIC printing processes – intaglio, lithographic, relief, and screen. In intaglio printing, lines are engraved or etched into the surface of a metal plate. Lines are engraved by hand using sharp metal tools. They are etched by corroding the metal plate with acid, using acid-resistant ground to protect the areas not to be etched. The plate is then inked and wiped, leaving the grooves filled with ink and the surface clean. Dampened paper is laid over the plate, and both paper and plate are passed through the rollers of an etching press. The pressure of the rollers forces the paper into the grooves, so that it takes up the ink, leaving an impression on the paper. Lithographic printing is based on the antipathy between grease and water. An image is drawn on a surface – usually a stone or metal plate – with a greasy medium, such as tusche (lihographic ink). The greasy drawing is fixed on to the plate by applying an acidic solution, such as gum arabic. The surface is then dampened and rolled with ink. The ink adheres only to the greasy areas and is repelled by the water. Paper is laid on the plate and pressure is applied by means of a press. In relief printing, the non-printing areas of a wood or linoleum block are cut away using gouges, knives, and other tools. The printing areas are left raised in relief and are rolled with ink. Paper is laid on the inked block and pressure is applied by means of a press or by burnishing (rubbing) the back of the paper. The most common forms of relief printing are woodcut, wood engraving, and linocut. In screen printing, the printing surface is a mesh stretched across a wooden frame. A stencil is applied to the mesh to seal the non-printing areas and ink is scraped through the mesh to produce an image.

THE FOUR MAIN PRINTING PROCESSES

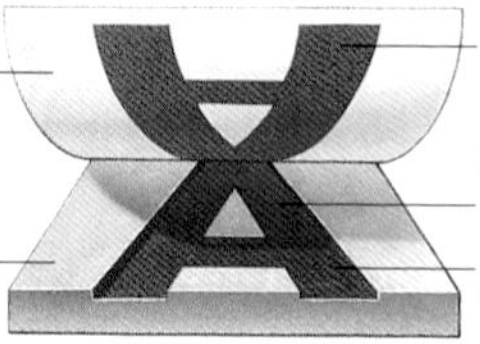
Paper
Printed image
Engraved or etched image
Metal plate
Inked area

INTAGLIO

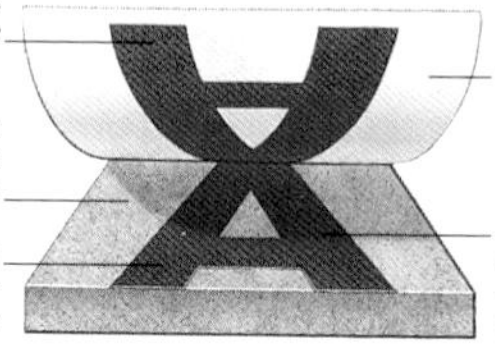
Printed image
Paper
Damp surface rejects ink
Image drawn on stone with greasy medium
Ink adheres to greasy image

LITHOGRAPHIC

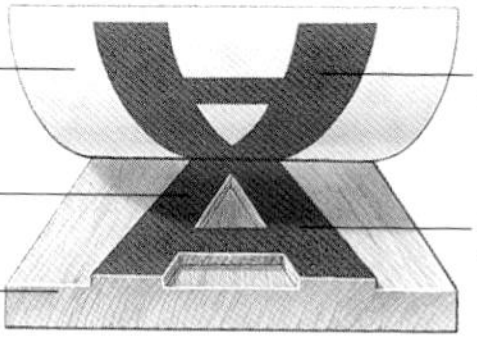
Paper
Printed image
Raised figure
Inked surface
Wood block

RELIEF

Wooden frame
Stencil
Ink forced through mesh
Printed image
Paper

SCREEN

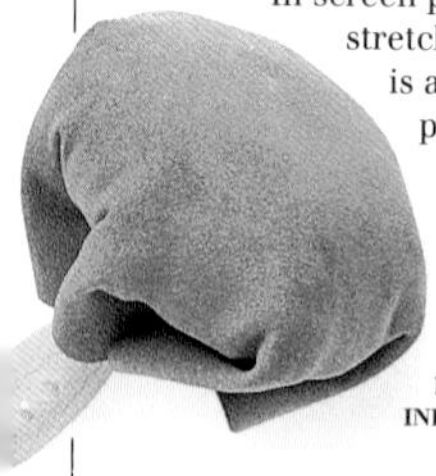

LEATHER INK DABBER

EQUIPMENT USED IN INTAGLIO PRINTING

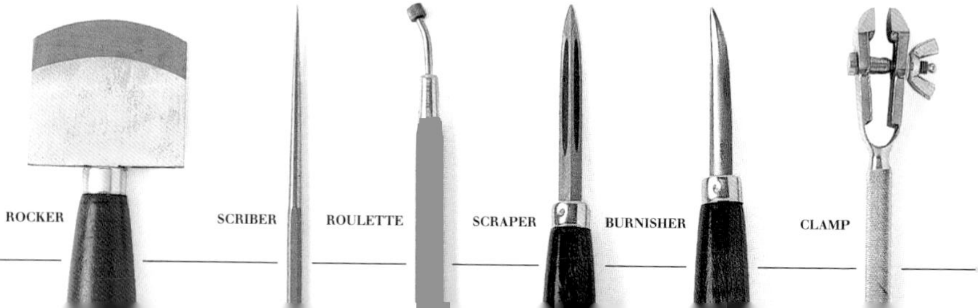
ROCKER
SCRIBER
ROULETTE
SCRAPER
BURNISHER
CLAMP

ETCHING PRESS USED FOR INTAGLIO PRINTMAKING

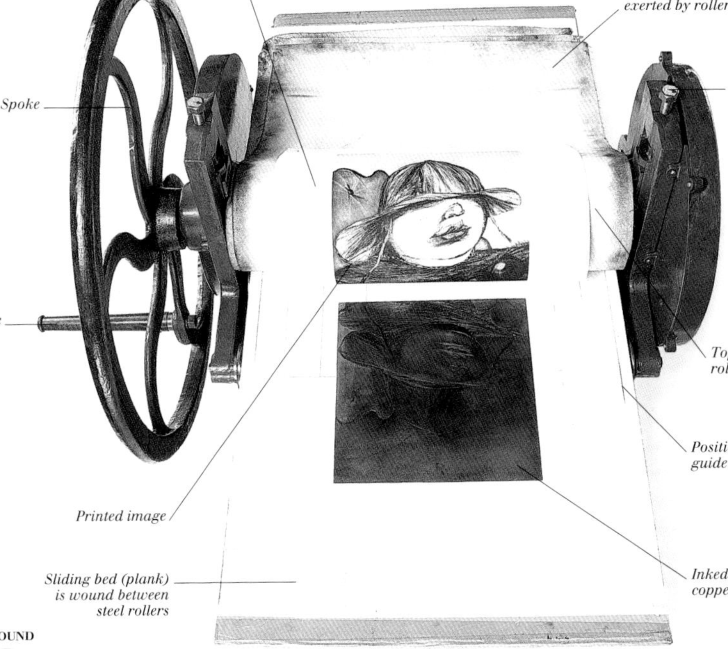
Flywheel
Paper
Felt blanket cushions and distributes pressure exerted by rollers
Spoke
Screw pressure adjustor
Handle
Top roller
Position guide
Printed image
Sliding bed (plank) is wound between steel rollers
Inked-up copper plate

GROUND

Acid-resistant ground rolled on to metal plate before etching

EXAMPLES OF PRINTING PAPERS

GROUND ROLLER

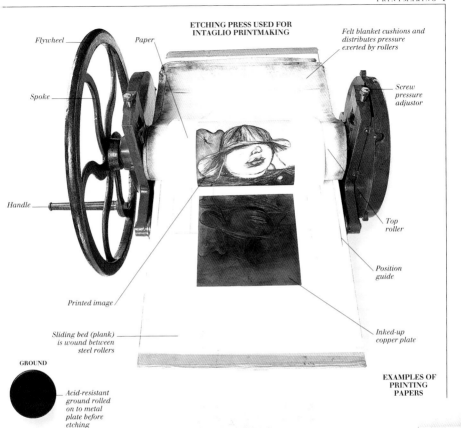

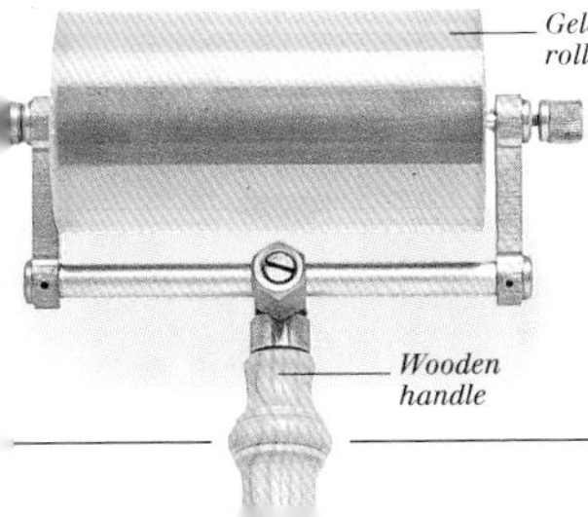
Gelatine roller
Wooden handle

EXAMPLE OF AN INTAGLIO PRINT
Annie with a Sun Hat, Jock McFadyen, 1993
Etched copper plate, 41 x 40 cm (16 x 15¾ in)

Printmaking 2

EXAMPLE OF A LITHOGRAPHIC STONE AND PRINT

Crown Gateway 2, Mandy Bonnell, 1987
Lithograph, 50 x 40 cm (19½ x 15¾ in)

IMAGE DRAWN ON STONE

LITHOGRAPIC PRINT

EXAMPLE OF A SCREEN PRINT

Sea Change, Patrick Hughes, 1992
Screen print, 77 x 94.5 cm (30 x 37 in)

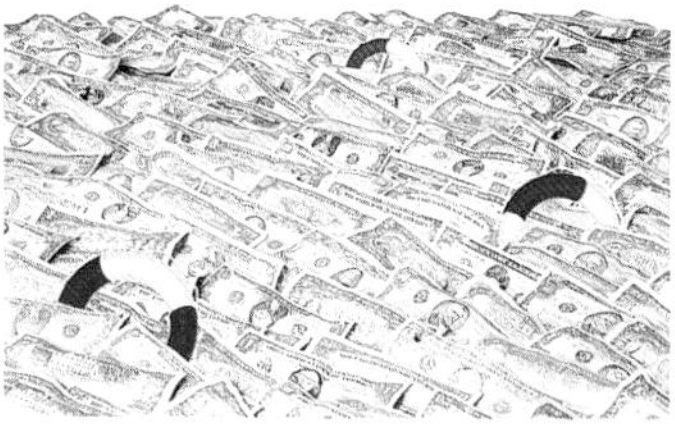

SCREEN AND SQUEEGEE

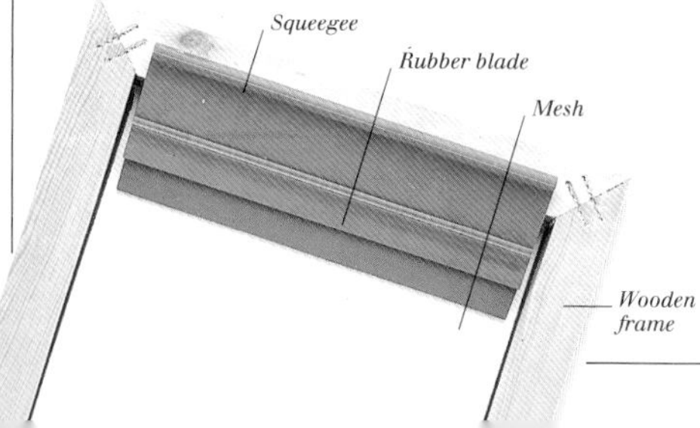
Squeegee
Rubber blade
Mesh
Wooden frame

EQUIPMENT USED IN LITHOGRAPHIC PRINTING

CRAYON AND HOLDER

LITHOGRAPHIC PENCIL

TUSCHE (LITHOGRAPHIC INK) PEN

ERASING STICK

EXPANDABLE SPONGE

TUSCHE (LITHOGRAPHIC INK) STICK

INK ROLLER

RUBBING INK

MILD ACIDIC SOLUTION

GUM ARABIC SOLUTION

WATER-BASED SCREEN PRINTING INKS

BLUE ACRYLIC INK

RED ACRYLIC INK

BROWN TEXTILE INK

EQUIPMENT USED IN RELIEF PRINTING

V-SHAPED GOUGE

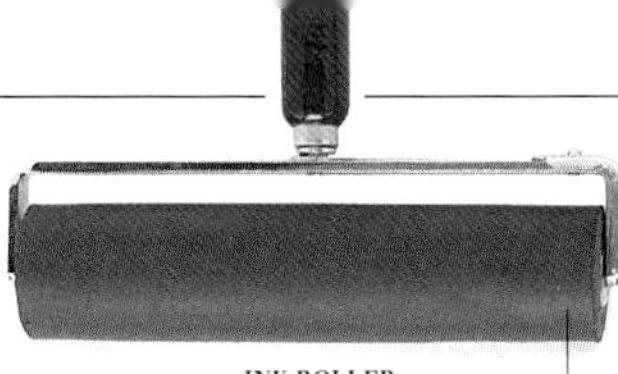
Rubber roller

INK ROLLER

LINOLEUM AND WOODCUT BLOCK

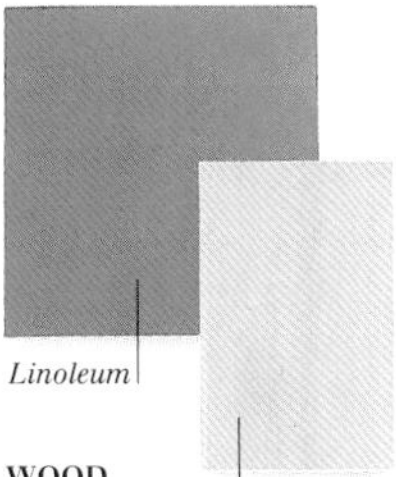
Linoleum
Side-grain wood block

U-SHAPED GOUGE

GRAVER

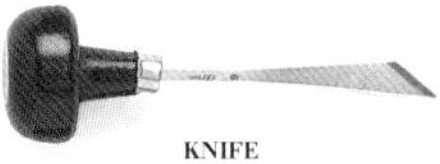

KNIFE

SCORPER

WOOD ENGRAVING

END-GRAIN WOOD BLOCK

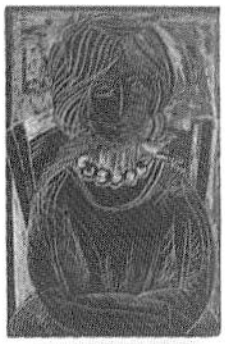

INKED-UP ENGRAVED BLOCK

WOOD ENGRAVING PRINT

RELIEF-PRINTING PRESS

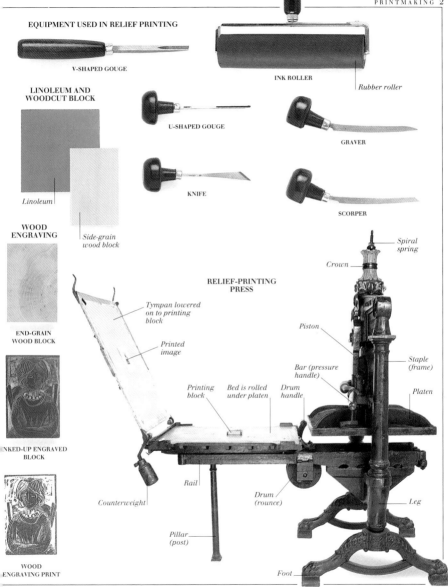

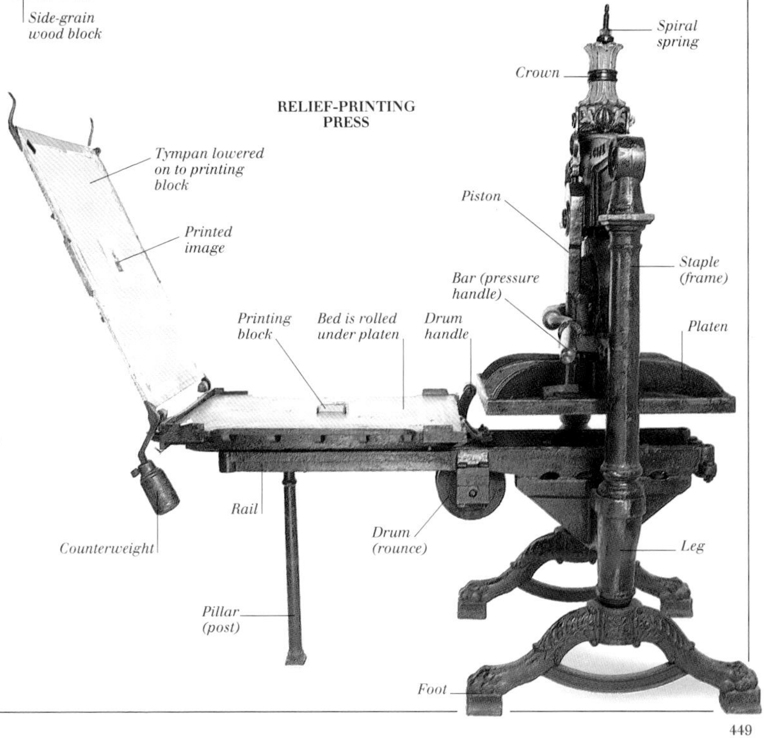
Spiral spring
Crown
Tympan lowered on to printing block
Printed image
Piston
Staple (frame)
Bar (pressure handle)
Printing block
Bed is rolled under platen
Drum handle
Platen
Rail
Counterweight
Drum (rounce)
Leg
Pillar (post)
Foot

Mosaic

MOSAIC IS THE ART OF MAKING patterns and pictures from tesserae (small, coloured pieces of glass, marble, and other materials). Different materials are cut into tesserae using different tools. Smalti (glass enamel) and marble are cut into pieces using a hammer and a hardy (a pointed blade) embedded in a log. Vitreous glass is cut into pieces using a pair of nippers. Mosaics can be made using a direct or indirect method. In the direct method, the tesserae are laid directly into a bed of cement–based adhesive. In the indirect method, the design is drawn in reverse on paper or cloth. The tesserae are then stuck face-down on the paper or cloth using water-soluble glue. Adhesive is spread with a trowel on to a solid surface – such as a wall – and the back of the mosaic is laid into the adhesive. Finally, the paper or cloth is soaked off to reveal the mosaic. Gaps between tesserae can be filled with grout. Grout is forced into gaps by dragging a grouting squeegee across the face of the mosaic. Mosaics are usually used to decorate walls and floors, but they can also be applied to smaller objects.

EQUIPMENT FOR BREAKING MARBLE

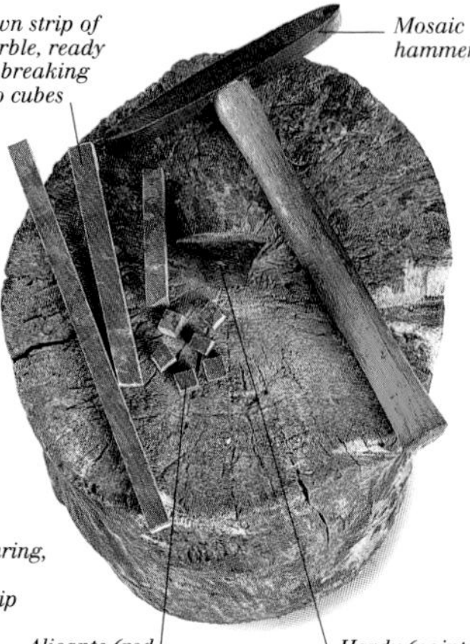
Sawn strip of marble, ready for breaking into cubes
Mosaic hammer
Alicante (red marble) pieces
Hardy (pointe[d] blade) embed[ded] in a log

NIPPERS

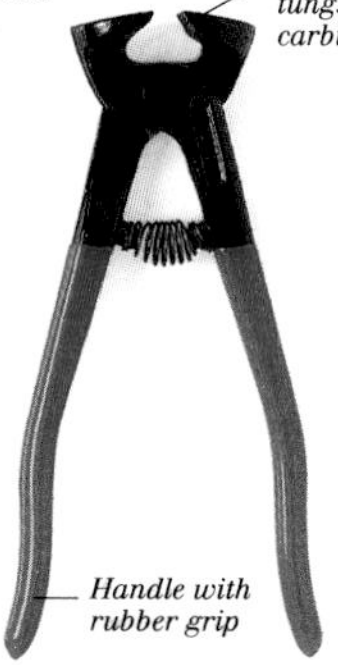
Hardwearing, tungsten carbide tip
Handle with rubber grip

MOSAIC TOOLS

CEMENT-BASED ADHESIVE

GROUT

SMALTI (GLASS ENAMEL)

RED SMALTI

EXAMPLE OF A MOSAIC (DIRECT METHOD)
Seascape, Tessa Hunkin, 1993
Smalti mosaic on board
80 cm (31½ in) diameter

Gold-leaf smalti

YELLOW SMALTI

BLUE SMALTI

TROWEL

Notch
Steel blade
Wooden handle

GROUTING SQUEEGEE

STAGES IN THE CREATION OF A MOSAIC (INDIRECT METHOD)

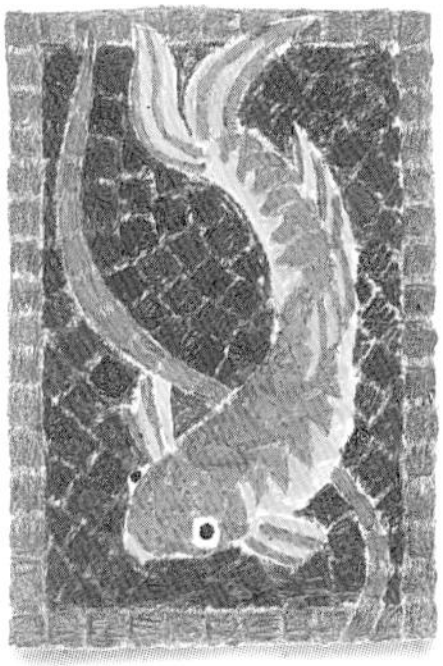

COLOUR SKETCH
A colour sketch is drawn in oil pastel to give a clear impression of how the finished mosaic will look.

REVERSE IMAGE
Tesserae are glued face-down on reverse image on paper. Mosaic is then attached to solid surface and paper is removed.

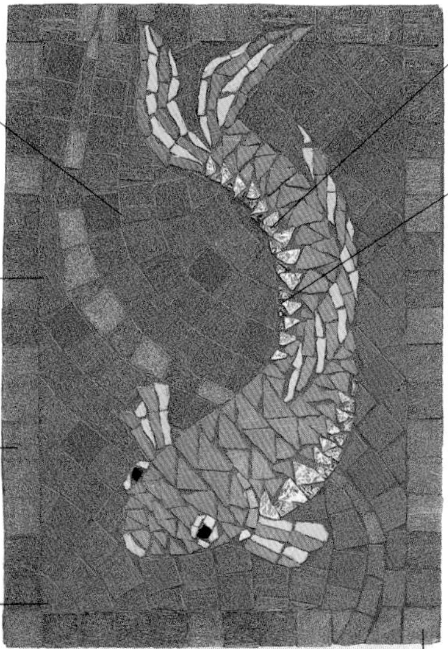
Andamenti (line along hich tesserae are laid)
Gold tessera with ripple finish
Gold tessera placed upside-down
Grout fills the gaps between the tesserae
Mosaic mounted on board
Vitreous glass cut into triangular shape with nippers
Border of square vitreous glass

FINISHED MOSAIC
Goldfish, Tessa Hunkin, 1993
Vitreous glass mosaic on board
35.5 x 25.5 cm (14 x 10 in)

MOSAIC POT

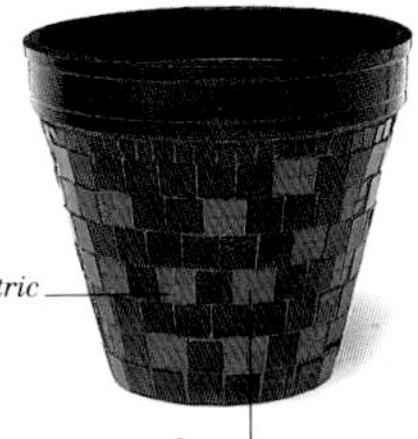
Geometric design
Grout

MOSAIC MOSQUE DESIGN

Floral design
Geometric border

VITREOUS GLASS

GREEN VITREOUS GLASS WITH GOLD LEAF

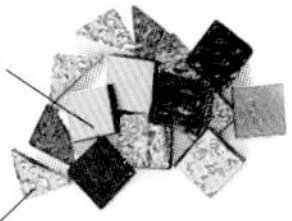
Plain finish
Ripple finish

RED VITREOUS GLASS

BLUE VITREOUS GLASS

SHEETS OF VITREOUS GLASS

Sculpture 1

THE TWO TRADITIONAL METHODS OF MAKING SCULPTURE are carving and modelling. A carved sculpture is made by cutting away the surplus from a block of hard material such as stone, marble, or wood. The tools used for carving vary according to the material being carved. Heavy steel points, claws, and chisels that are struck with a lump hammer are generally used for stone and marble. Sharp gouges and chisels that are struck with a wooden mallet are used for wood. Sculptures formed from hard materials are generally finished by filing with rasps, rifflers, and other abrasive implements. Modelling is a process by which shapes are built up, using malleable materials such as clay, plaster, and wax. The material is cut with wire-ended tools and modelled with the fingers or a variety of hardwood and metal implements. For large or intricate modelled sculptures an armature (frame), made from metal or wood, is used to provide internal support. Sculptures formed in soft materials may harden naturally or can be made more durable by firing in a kiln. Modelled sculptures are often first designed in wax or another material to be cast later in a metal (see pp. 454-455) such as bronze. The development of many new materials in the 20th century has enabled sculptors to experiment with new techniques such as construction (joining preformed pieces of material such as machine components, mirrors, and furniture) and kinetic (mobile) sculpture.

EXAMPLES OF MARBLE CARVING TOOLS

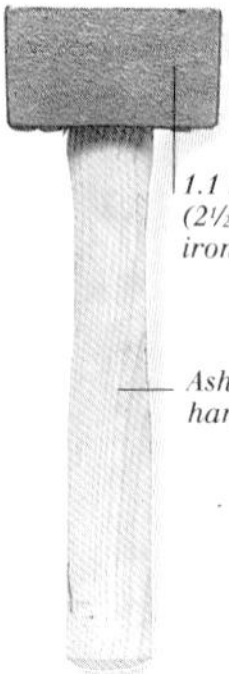
1.1 kg
(2½ lb)
iron head
Ash
handle

LUMP HAMMER

WIDE MARBLE CLAW

NARROW MARBLE CLAW

POINT

FLAT CHISEL

BULLNOSE CHISEL

Surface for
sharpening
stonecarving
tools

DIAMOND WHETSTONE

CALLIPERS

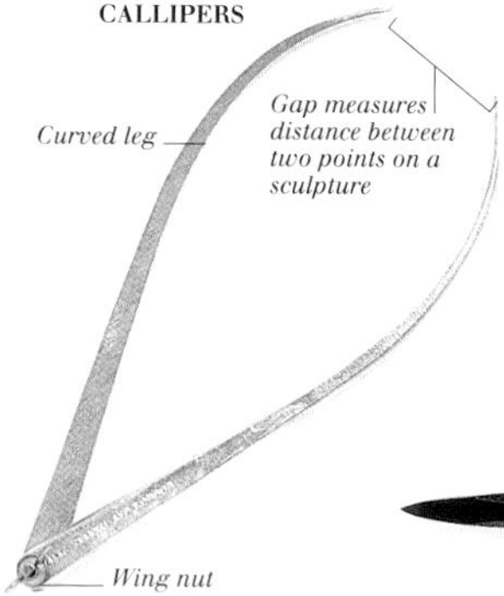
Curved leg
Gap measures
distance between
two points on a
sculpture
Wing nut

EXAMPLES OF WOODCARVING TOOLS

CABINET RASP

STRAIGHT GOUGE

SALMON BEND GOUGE

CHISEL

Stone for
sharpening
woodcarving
tools
Cedar
box

ARKANSAS HONE-STONE

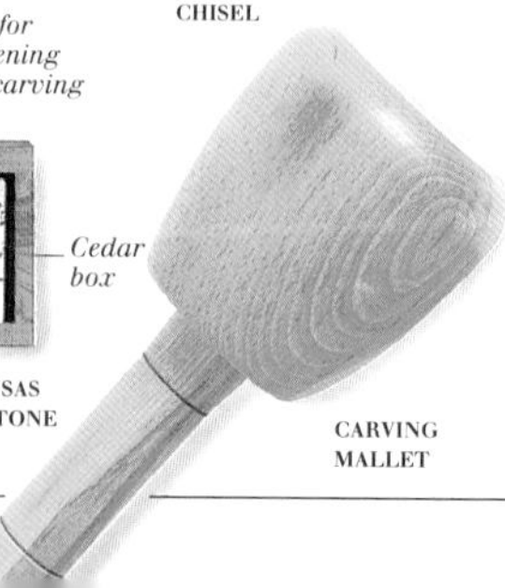

CARVING MALLET

EXAMPLES OF RIFFLERS (FOR STONE, MARBLE, AND WOOD)

30 CM (12 IN) RIFFLER

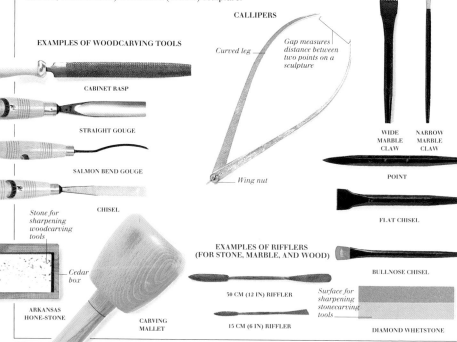

15 CM (6 IN) RIFFLER

EXAMPLE OF A CARVED MARBLE SCULPTURE
The Rebel Slave, Michelangelo, 1513-1516
Marble, height 213 cm (7ft)

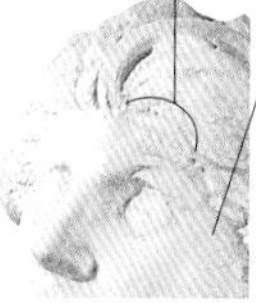
Tiny holes along the hairline made with a point
Soft skin texture tooled with a fine-toothed marble claw

DETAIL OF SLAVE'S HEAD

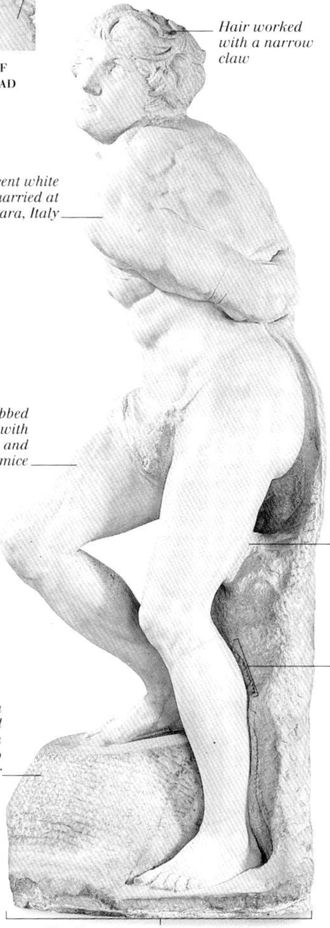
Hair worked with a narrow claw
Translucent white marble, quarried at Carrara, Italy
Surface rubbed smooth with rifflers and pumice
Strut gives added support to long slender limb
Series of tiny punch holes, made with a fine point, outline the form
ase scored with jagged parallel cuts made with oint and lump hammer

The dimensions of the marble block determine the size of the sculpture

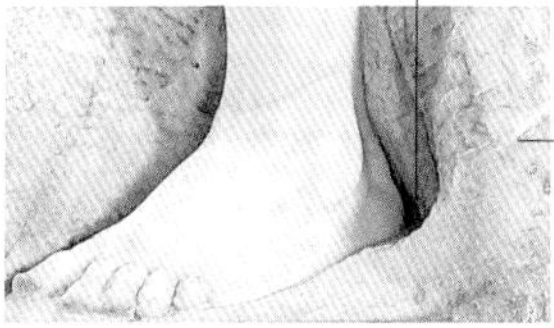
Foot carved in deep relief
Rough surface made by driving a point into the marble at an oblique angle

DETAIL OF SLAVE'S FOOT

EXAMPLE OF A CARVED WOOD SCULPTURE
Mary Magdalene, Donatello, 1454-1455
Poplar wood, height 188 cm (6 ft 2 in)

Delicately modelled hand carved with a chisel
Hair highlighted with gold leaf
Figure cut from single length of poplar
Deep ridges of hair cut with a gouge
Wood prepared with gesso (chalk and glue) and painted

Sculpture 2

EXAMPLES OF MODELLING TOOLS

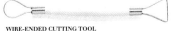

WIRE-ENDED CUTTING TOOL

CURVED MOULDING TOOL

SPATULA-ENDED WAX MODELLING TOOL

ROUNDED WAX MODELLING TOOL

EXAMPLES OF BRONZE FINISHING TOOLS

HOOKED RIFFLER

POINTED RIFFLER

SPIRIT LAMP (FOR HEATING WAX MODELLING TOOLS)

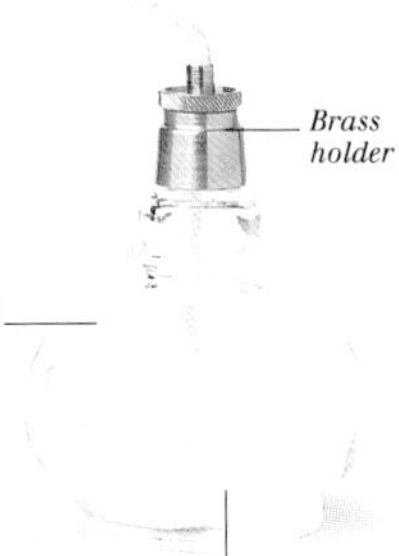
Wick
Brass holder
Glass bowl
Methylated spirit

STAGES IN THE LOST-WAX METHOD OF CASTING

Based on Mars, Giambologna, c.1546

Wax-covered wire armature

ORIGINAL MODEL
An original, solid wax model is made and preserved so that numerous replicas can be cast.

Wax riser (vertical, hollow rod)
Chaplet (iron nail)
Wax runner (horizontal, hollow rod)

HOLLOW WAX FIGURE IS CAST
A new, hollow wax model is cast from the original model. It is filled with a plaster core that is held in place with nails. Wax runners and risers are attached.

Fire-resistant clay

FIGURE IS BAKED IN CASTING MOULD
The model is encased in clay and baked. The wax melts away (through the channels made by the wax rods) and is replaced by molten bronze.

MODELLING STAND AND ARMATURE

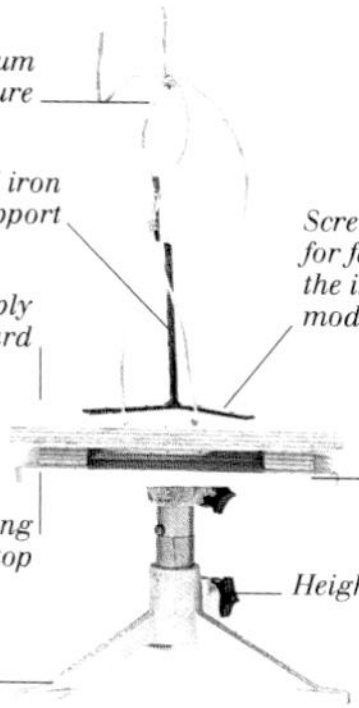
Aluminium wire figure
Fixed iron armature support
Screw-hole for fastening the iron to modelling board
Marine ply modelling board
Aluminium table stand
Rotating table top
Height adjustor
Tripod

EXAMPLE OF A CLAY MODEL
Madonna and Child, Henry Moore, 1943
Terracotta, height 18.4 cm (7¼ in)

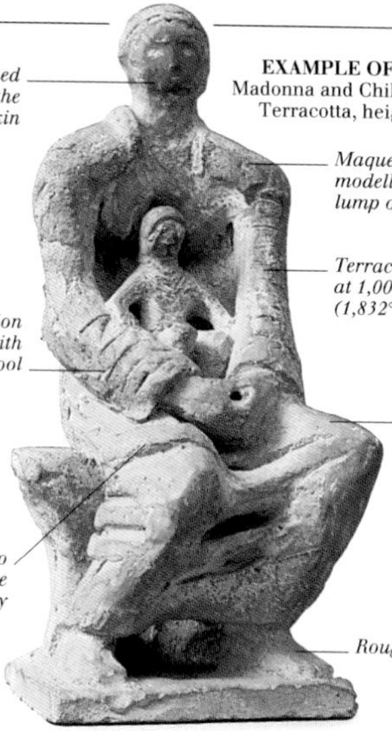
Clay smoothed to create the effect of soft skin
Maquette (small sketch) modelled from a solid lump of clay
Terracotta clay, fires at 1,000°C to 1,050°C (1,832°F to 1,922°F)
Incision made with serrated tool
Model for a much larger bronze sculpture
Strips of clay, added to the model, give the effect of folded drapery
Roughly worked clay

Metal riser
Metal runner

STATUE IS STRIPPED OF CLAY
When the bronze has cooled, the clay mould is broken open to reveal the bronze statue with solid metal runners and risers.

Golden brown colour of untreated bronze
Stump left by rod will be filed down
Hole left by nail will be plugged with bronze

STATUE IS FINISHED
The nails are pulled out and a large hole is made to remove the plaster core. When the metal rods have been sawn off, the sculpture is filed to refine the surface.

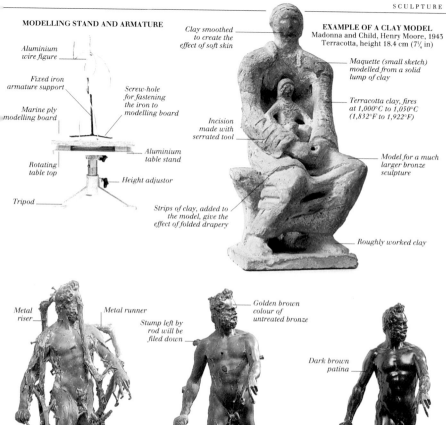

Dark brown patina

STATUE IS CLEANED
Finally the work is cleaned and polished. An artificial patina (colouring) is achieved by treating the surface with chemicals.

ARCHITECTURE

Ancient Egypt

THE CIVILIZATION OF THE ANCIENT EGYPTIANS (which lasted from about 3100 BC until it was finally absorbed into the Roman empire in 30 BC) is famous for its temples and tombs. Egyptian temples were often huge and geometric, like the Temple of Amon-Re (below and right). They were usually decorated with hieroglyphs (sacred characters used for picture-writing) and painted reliefs depicting gods, Pharaohs (kings), and queens. Tombs were particularly important to the Egyptians, who believed that the dead were resurrected in the after-life. The tombs were often decorated – as, for example, the surround of the false door opposite – in order to give comfort to the dead. The best-known ancient Egyptian tombs are the pyramids, which were designed to symbolize the rays of the sun. Many of the architectural forms used by the ancient Egyptians were later adopted by other civilizations; for example, columns and capitals were later used by the ancient Greeks (see pp. 460-461) and ancient Romans (see pp. 462-465).

FRONT VIEW OF HYPOSTYLE HALL, TEMPLE OF AMON-RE

Cornice decorated with cavetto moulding
Campaniform (open papyrus) capital
Architrave
Papyrus bud capital
Socle
Side aisle
Central nave
Side aisle

SIDE VIEW OF HYPOSTYLE HALL, TEMPLE OF AMON-RE, KARNAK, EGYPT, c.1290 BC

Horus, the sun-god
Architrave
Stone slab forming flat roof of side aisle
Kepresh crown with disc
Chons, the moon-god
Amon-Re, king of the gods
Hathor, the sky-goddess
Papyrus motif
Cartouche (oval border) containing the titles of the Pharaoh (king)
Socle
Aisle running north-south

LIMESTONE FALSE DOOR WITH HIEROGLYPHS, TOMB OF KING TJETJI, GIZA, EGYPT, c.2400 BC

Hieroglyph representing a house
intel
Disc representing sun or light
Eroded
nage of
Tjetji
Limestone stela (slab)
Hoe-shaped hieroglyph representing "mr" sound
Head of false door
Image of Tjetji's wife
Image of Tjetji's daughter

PLANT CAPITAL OF THE PTOLEMAIC-ROMAN PERIOD, EGYPT, 332-30 BC

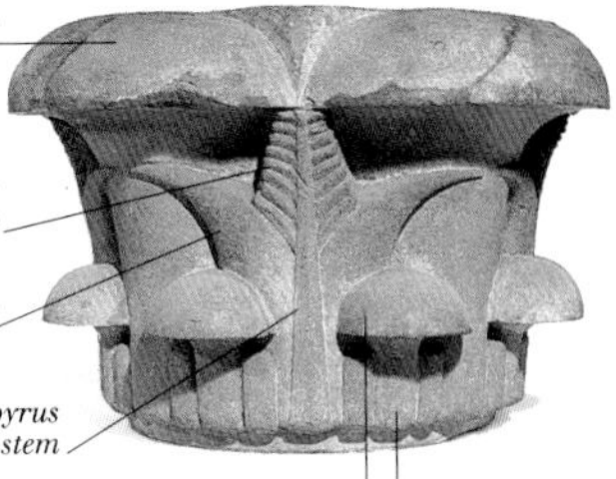

Palm leaf
Papyrus flower
Papyrus leaf
Papyrus stem
Lotus bud
Lotus stem

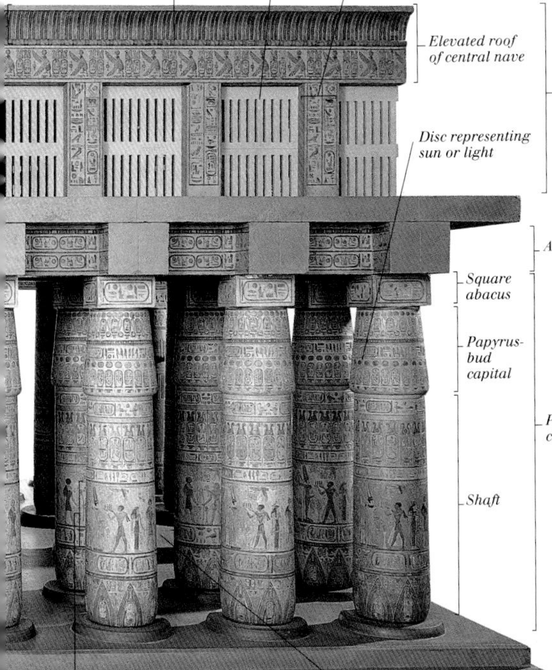

Cornice decorated with cavetto moulding
Bead moulding
Trellis window
Rectangular pier decorated with hieroglyphs
Elevated roof of central nave
Clerestory
Disc representing sun or light
Architrave
Square abacus
Papyrus-bud capital
Papyriform column
Shaft
Scene depicting a Pharaoh (king) paying homage to the god Amon-Re
Central nave

ANCIENT EGYPTIAN BUILDING DECORATION

DECORATED WINDOW, MEDINET HABU, EGYPT, C.1198 BC

ROPE AND PATERAE DECORATION

CAPITAL WITH THE HEAD OF THE SKY-GODDESS HATHOR, TEMPLE OF ISIS, PHILAE, EGYPT, 283-47 BC

LOTUS AND PAPYRUS FRIEZE DECORATION

Ancient Greece

THE CLASSICAL TEMPLES OF ANCIENT GREECE were built according to the belief that certain forms and proportions were pleasing to the gods. There were three main ancient Greek architectural orders (styles), which can be distinguished by the decoration and proportions of their columns, capitals (column tops), and entablatures (structures resting on the capitals). The oldest is the Doric order, which dates from the seventh century BC and was used mainly on the Greek mainland and in the western colonies, such as Sicily and southern Italy. The Temple of Neptune, shown here, is a classic example of this order. It is hypaethral (roofless) and peripteral (surrounded by a single row of columns). About a century later, the more decorative Ionic order developed on the Aegean Islands. Features of this order include volutes (spiral scrolls) on capitals and acroteria (pediment ornaments). The Corinthian order was invented in Athens in the fifth century BC and is typically identified by an acanthus leaf on the capitals. This order was later widely used in ancient Roman architecture.

CAPITALS OF THE THREE ORDERS OF ANCIENT GREEK ARCHITECTURE

Abacus
Echinus
Annulet
Trachelion (neck)

DORIC CAPITAL, THE PROPYLAEUM (GATEWAY), THE ACROPOLIS, ATHENS, GREECE, 449 BC

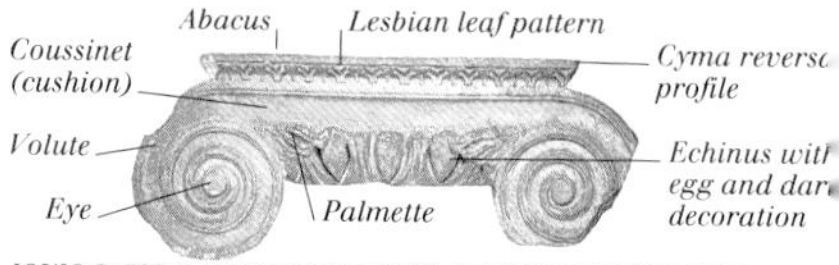
Abacus
Lesbian leaf pattern
Coussinet (cushion)
Cyma reversa profile
Volute
Echinus with egg and dart decoration
Eye
Palmette

IONIC CAPITAL, THE PROPYLAEUM (GATEWAY), TEMPLE OF ATHENA POLIAS, PRIENE, GREECE, c.334 BC

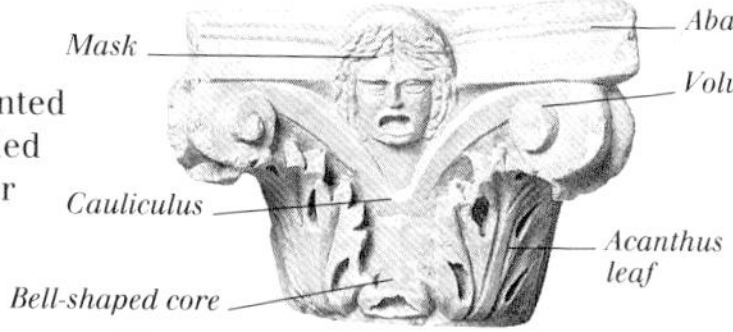
Mask
Abacus
Volute
Cauliculus
Acanthus leaf
Bell-shaped core

CORINTHIAN CAPITAL FROM A STOA (PORTICO), PROBABLY FROM ASIA MINOR

TEMPLE OF NEPTUNE, PAESTUM, ITALY, c.460 BC

Raking cornice
Pediment
Trachelion (neck)
Taenia
Triglyph
Metope
Glyph (channel)
Doric entablature
Pteron (external colonnade)
Euthynteria
Drum
Stylobate
Column of the Doric order

PLAN OF THE TEMPLE OF NEPTUNE, PAESTUM

Pronaos (vestibule)
Naos wall
Anta (pilaster terminating naos wall)
Naos (cella)
Peristyle
Opisthodomos (rear portico)
Pteron (external colonnade)
Hexastyle pteron (colonnade of six columns)

ANCIENT GREEK BUILDING DECORATION

Volute

FACADE, TREASURY OF ATREUS, MYCENAE, GREECE, 1350-1250 BC

Meander

FRETWORK, PARTHENON, ATHENS, GREECE, 447-436 BC

ACROTERION, TEMPLE OF APHAIA, AEGINA, GREECE, 490 BC

Griffon (gryphon)
Raking cornice

ANTEFIXA, TEMPLE OF APHAIA, AEGINA, GREECE, 490 BC

Palmette
Volute

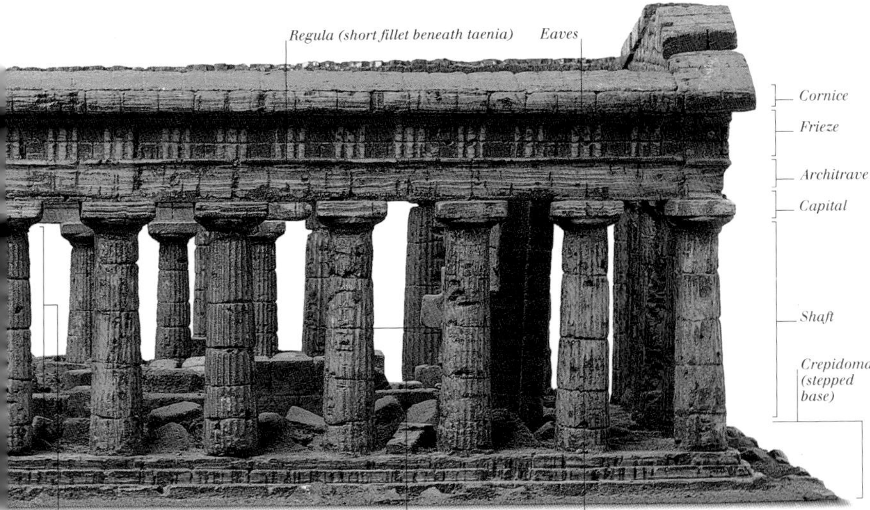
Regula (short fillet beneath taenia)
Eaves
Cornice
Frieze
Architrave
Capital
Shaft
Crepidoma (stepped base)
Entasis (slight curve of a column)
Intercolumniation
Fluting

Ancient Rome 1

IN THE EARLY PERIOD OF THE ROMAN EMPIRE extensive use was made of ancient Greek architectural ideas, particularly those of the Corinthian order (see pp. 460-461). As a result, many early Roman buildings – such as the Temple of Vesta (opposite) – closely resemble ancient Greek buildings. A distinctive Roman style began to evolve in the first century AD. This style developed the interiors of buildings (the Greeks had concentrated on the exterior) by using arches, vaults, and domes inside the buildings, and by ornamenting internal walls. Many of these features can be seen in the Pantheon. Exterior columns were often used for decorative, rather than structural, purposes, as in the Colosseum and the Porta Nigra (see pp. 464-465). Smaller buildings had timber frames with wattle-and-daub walls, as in the mill (see pp. 464-465). Roman architecture remained influential for many centuries, with some of its principles being used in the 11th century in Romanesque buildings (see pp. 468-469) and also in the 15th and 16th centuries in Renaissance buildings (see pp. 474-477).

ANCIENT ROMAN BUILDING DECORATION

FESTOON, TEMPLE OF VESTA, TIVOLI, ITALY, C.80 BC

RICHLY DECORATED ROMAN OVUM

INTERIOR OF THE PANTHEON, ROME, ITALY, 118-c.128

Inner dome, following the curve of a depressed arch
Outer saucer dome
Entablature
Curved cornice
Lesene
Cornice
Triangular pediment
Concave niche
Marble veneer
Segmental pediment
Pedestal

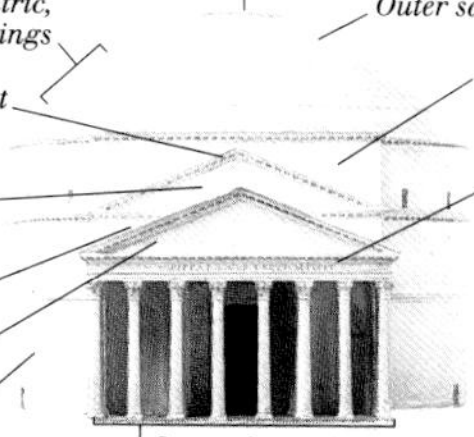
Oculus
Series of concentric, step-like rings
Outer saucer dome
Dentil ornament
Intermediate block
Engaged pediment
Entablature with inscription
Raking cornice
Pediment
Rotunda
Octastyle portico (eight-column portico)

FRONT VIEW OF THE PANTHEON

SIDE VIEW OF THE PANTHEON

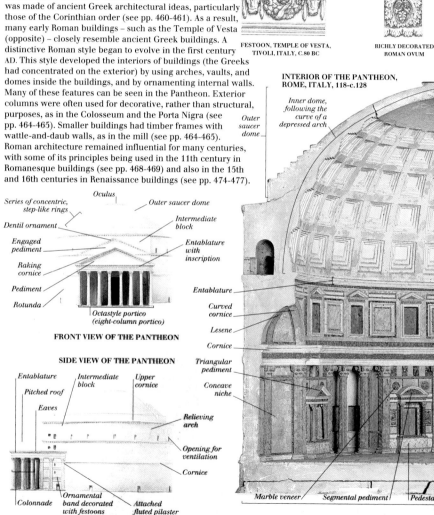

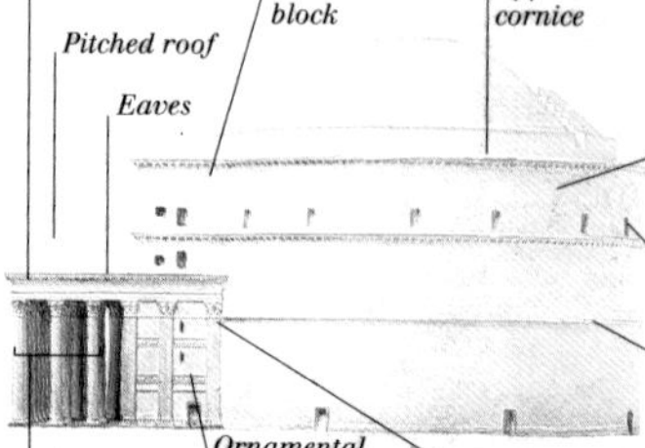
Entablature
Intermediate block
Upper cornice
Pitched roof
Eaves
Relieving arch
Opening for ventilation
Cornice
Colonnade
Ornamental band decorated with festoons
Attached fluted pilaster

FRIEZE, FORUM OF TRAJAN, ROME, ITALY, 98-113

KEYSTONE, ARCH OF TITUS, ROME, ITALY, 81

TEMPLE OF VESTA, TIVOLI, ITALY, c.80 BC

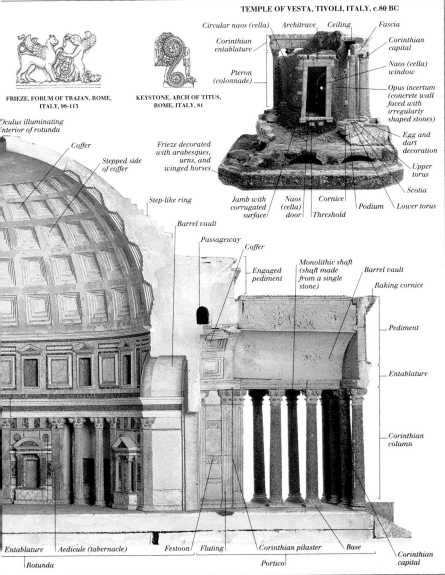

Circular naos (cella)
Architrave
Ceiling
Fascia
Corinthian entablature
Corinthian capital
Naos (cella) window
Pteron (colonnade)
Opus incertum (concrete wall faced with irregularly shaped stones)
Egg and dart decoration
Frieze decorated with arabesques, urns, and winged horses
Upper torus
Scotia
Jamb with corrugated surface
Naos (cella) door
Cornice
Threshold
Podium
Lower torus

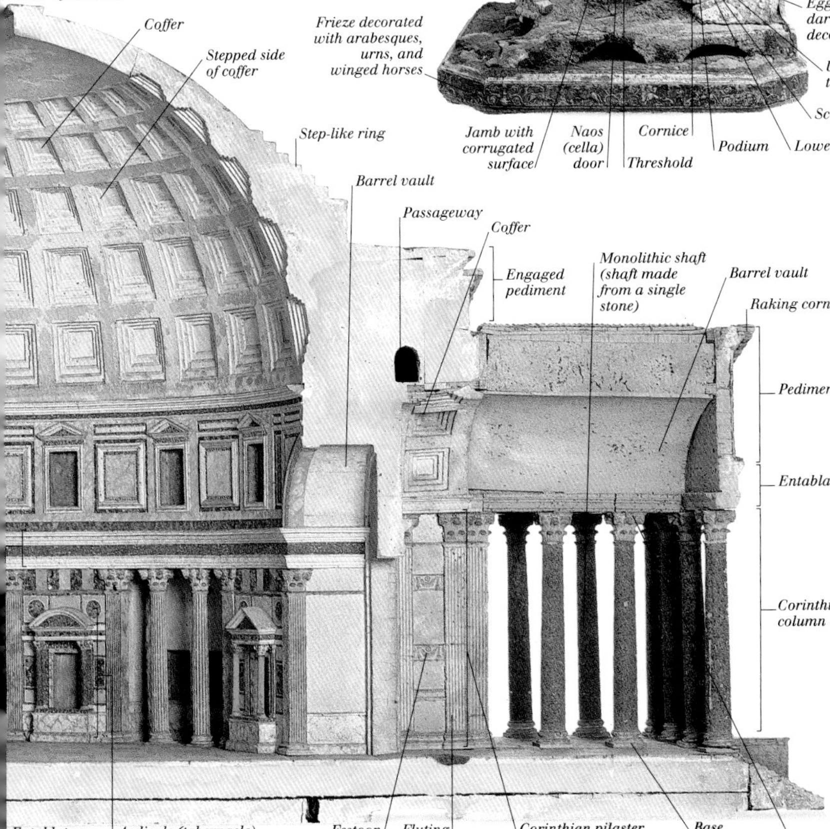
Oculus illuminating interior of rotunda
Coffer
Stepped side of coffer
Step-like ring
Barrel vault
Passageway
Coffer
Engaged pediment
Monolithic shaft (shaft made from a single stone)
Barrel vault
Raking cornice
Pediment
Entablature
Corinthian column
Entablature
Aedicule (tabernacle)
Festoon
Fluting
Corinthian pilaster
Base
Corinthian capital
Rotunda
Portico

Ancient Rome 2

SIDE VIEW OF A ROMAN MILL

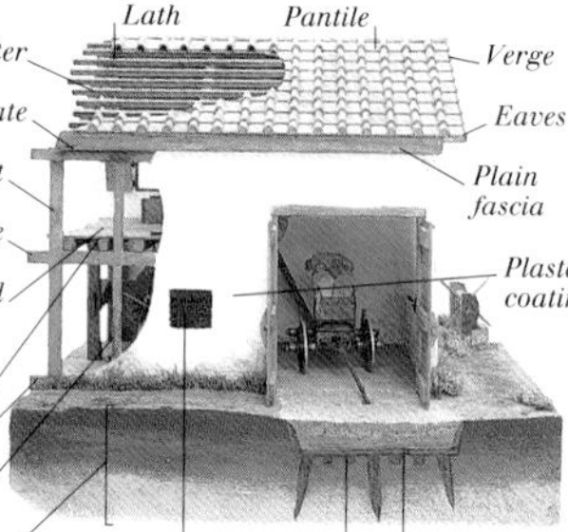
Lath
Pantile
Principal rafter
Verge
Wall-plate
Eaves
Wall-post
Plain fascia
Top-plate
Floorboard
Plaster coating
Intermediate floor-joist
Sill
Stud
Foundation
Grille
Joist
Boarding

FRONT VIEW OF A ROMAN MILL, 1ST CENTURY BC

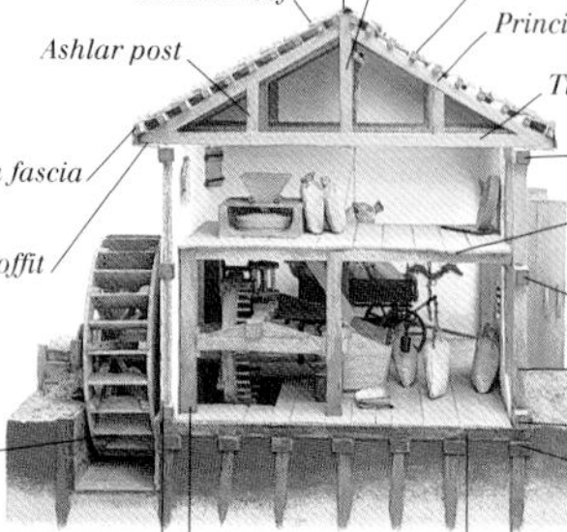
Half-round ridge tile
King-strut
Lath
Pitched roof
Principal rafter
Ashlar post
Tie-beam
Wall-plate
Plain fascia
Intermedia floor-joist
Flat soffit
Top-plate
Wall-pos
Mill wheel
Sill
Binde
Wattle-and-daub wall with plaster coating
Supporting post
Floor-joist
Foundation post

THE COLOSSEUM (FLAVIAN AMPHITHEATRE), ROME, ITALY, 70-82

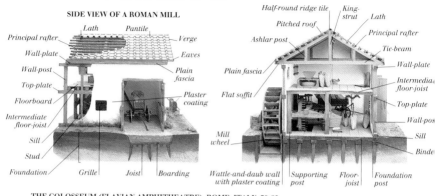

Bracket for velarium (awning)
Crowning cornice
Barrel vault
Horizontal gangway
Arcac
Third floor
Corinthian pilaster
Round arch
Second floor
Corinthian half-column
Entablature
Ionic half-column
First floor
Doric half-column
Ground floor
External travertine shell
Intermediate shell
Inner shel

ORTA NIGRA, TRIER, GERMANY, c.240-260

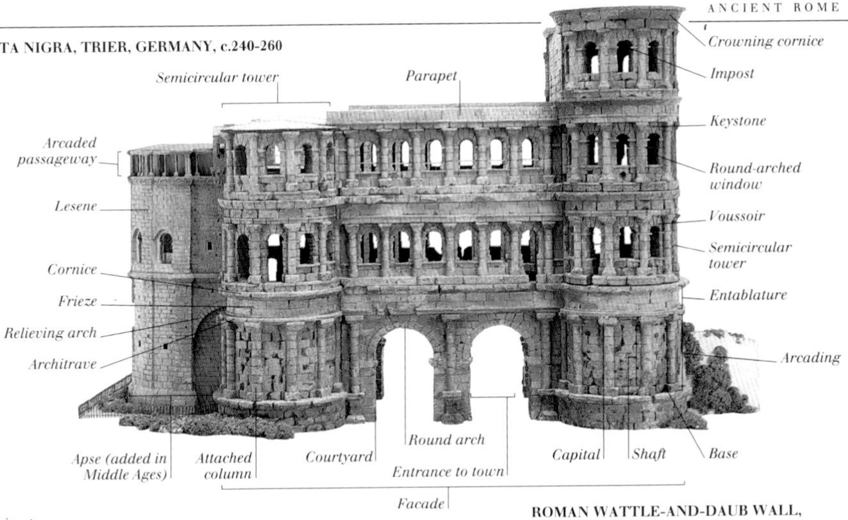
Semicircular tower
Parapet
Crowning cornice
Impost
Keystone
Arcaded passageway
Round-arched window
Lesene
Voussoir
Semicircular tower
Cornice
Entablature
Frieze
Relieving arch
Arcading
Architrave
Round arch
Courtyard
Capital
Shaft
Base
Apse (added in Middle Ages)
Attached column
Entrance to town
Facade

ROMAN WATTLE-AND-DAUB WALL, 1ST CENTURY BC

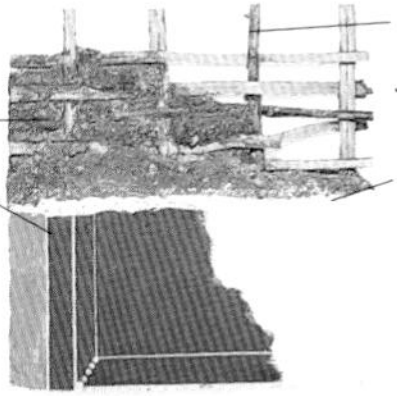
Hazel twig framework
Clay mixture
Paintwork
Plaster

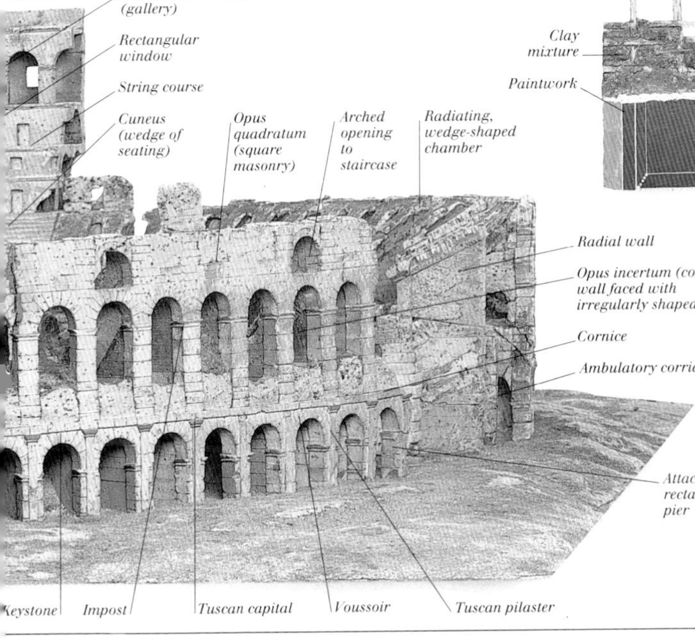
pening to aircase
Maenianum summum (gallery)
Rectangular window
String course
Cuneus (wedge of seating)
Opus quadratum (square masonry)
Arched opening to staircase
Radiating, wedge-shaped chamber
Radial wall
Opus incertum (concrete wall faced with irregularly shaped stones)
Cornice
Ambulatory corridor
Attached rectangular pier
eystone
Impost
Tuscan capital
Voussoir
Tuscan pilaster

Medieval castles and houses

WARFARE WAS COMMON IN EUROPE in the Middle Ages, and many monarchs and nobles built castles as a form of defence. Typical medieval castles have outer walls surrounding a moat. Inside the moat is a bailey (courtyard), protected by a chemise (jacket-wall). The innermost and strongest part of a medieval castle is the keep. There are two main types of keep: towers called donjons, such as the Tour de César and Coucy-le-Château, and rectangular keeps ("hall-keeps"), such as the Tower of London. Castles were often guarded by salients (projecting fortifications), like those of the Bastille. Medieval houses typically had timber cruck (tent-like) frames, wattle-and-daub walls, and pitched roofs, like those on medieval London Bridge (opposite).

DONJON, TOUR DE CESAR, PROVINS, FRANCE, 12TH CENTURY

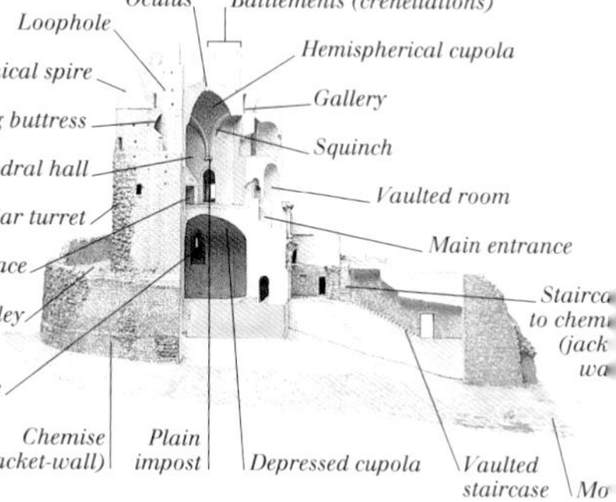
Oculus
Battlements (crenellations)
Loophole
Hemispherical cupola
Conical spire
Gallery
Flying buttress
Squinch
Hexahedral hall
Vaulted room
Semicircular turret
Main entrance
Fireplace
Bailey
Embrasure
Chemise (jacket-wall)
Plain impost
Depressed cupola
Vaulted staircase

Loophole

SALIENT, CAERNARVON CASTLE, BRITAIN, 1283–1323

Timber cruck frame

CRUCK-FRAMED HOUSE, BRITAIN, c.1200

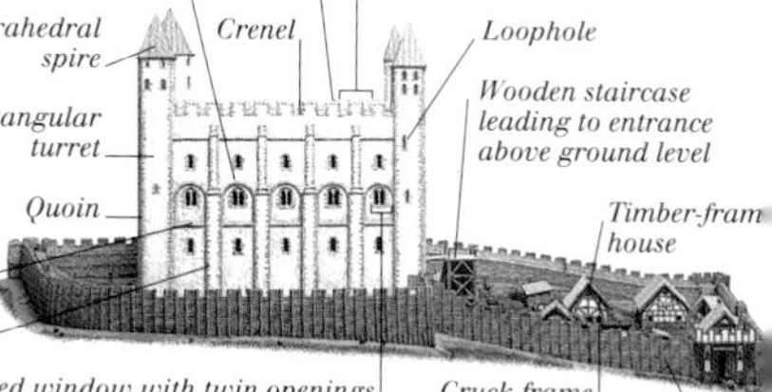
Blind, rounded relieving arch
Merlon
Battlements (crenellations)
Tetrahedral spire
Crenel
Loophole
Wooden staircase leading to entrance above ground level
Rectangular turret
Quoin
Timber-fram
house
Cornice
Buttress
Round-arched window with twin openings
Cruck frame

TOWER OF LONDON, BRITAIN, FROM 1070

Curtain wall
Pointed relieving arch
Semicircular relieving arch
Plain string course
Rectangular window
Sunken rectangular panel
Round-arched window
Semicircular salient
Loophole
Lateral circular salient

THE BASTILLE, PARIS, FRANCE, 14TH CENTURY

MEDIEVAL LONDON BRIDGE, BRITAIN, 1176 (WITH 14TH-CENTURY BATTLEMENTED BUILDING, NONESUCH HOUSE, AND TWO-TOWERED GATE)

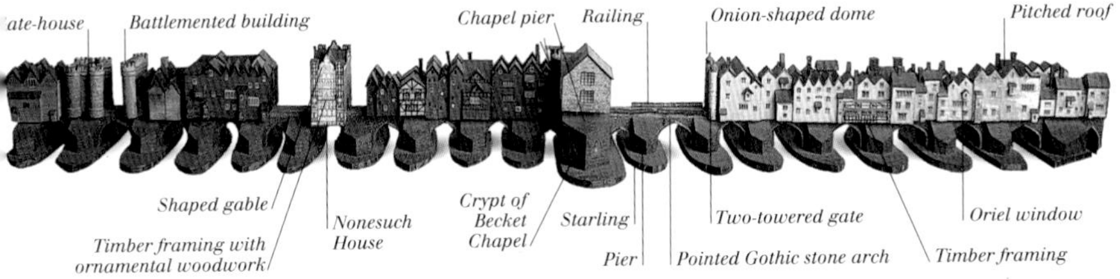

ate-house
Battlemented building
Chapel pier
Railing
Onion-shaped dome
Pitched roof
Shaped gable
Timber framing with ornamental woodwork
Nonesuch House
Crypt of Becket Chapel
Starling
Pier
Two-towered gate
Pointed Gothic stone arch
Oriel window
Timber framing

DONJON, COUCY-LE-CHATEAU, AISNE, FRANCE, 1225-1245

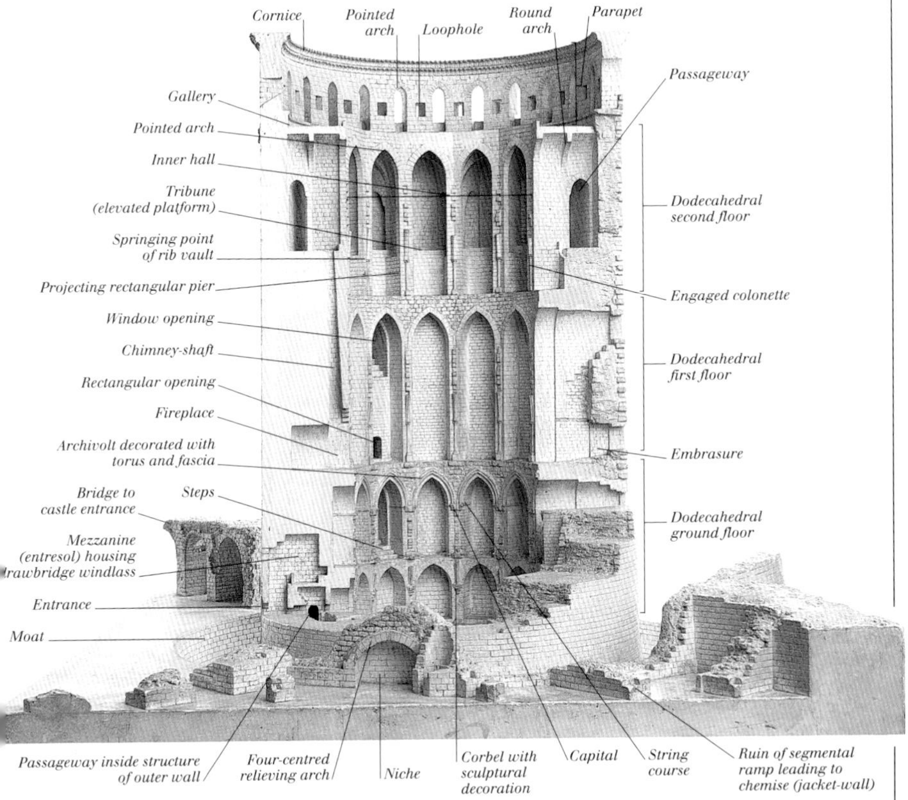

Cornice
Pointed arch
Loophole
Round arch
Parapet
Passageway
Gallery
Pointed arch
Inner hall
Tribune (elevated platform)
Springing point of rib vault
Projecting rectangular pier
Window opening
Chimney-shaft
Rectangular opening
Fireplace
Archivolt decorated with torus and fascia
Bridge to castle entrance
Steps
Mezzanine (entresol) housing rawbridge windlass
Entrance
Moat
Dodecahedral second floor
Engaged colonette
Dodecahedral first floor
Embrasure
Dodecahedral ground floor
Passageway inside structure of outer wall
Four-centred relieving arch
Niche
Corbel with sculptural decoration
Capital
String course
Ruin of segmental ramp leading to chemise (jacket-wall)

Medieval churches

DURING THE MIDDLE AGES, large numbers of churches were built in Europe. European churches of this period typically have high vaults supported by massive piers and columns. In the 10th century, the Romanesque style developed. Romanesque architects adopted many Roman or early Christian architectural ideas, such as cross-shaped ground-plans – like that of Angoulême Cathedral (opposite) – and the basilican system of a nave with a central vessel and side aisles. In the mid-12th century, flying buttresses and pointed vaults appeared. These features later became widely used in Gothic architecture (see pp. 470-471). Bagneux Church (opposite) has both styles: a Romanesque tower, and a Gothic nave and choir.

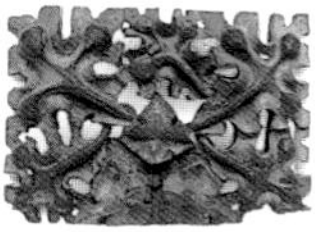

CHURCH-ROOF BOSS, BRITAIN

ROMANESQUE CAPITALS

"THE FLIGHT INTO EGYPT" CAPITAL, CATHEDRAL OF ST. LAZARE, AUTUN, FRANCE, 1120-1130

"CHRIST IN MAJESTY" CAPITAL, BASILICA OF ST. MADELEINE, VEZELAY, FRANCE, 1120-1140

ABBEY OF ST. FOI, CONQUES, FRANCE, c.1050-c.1130

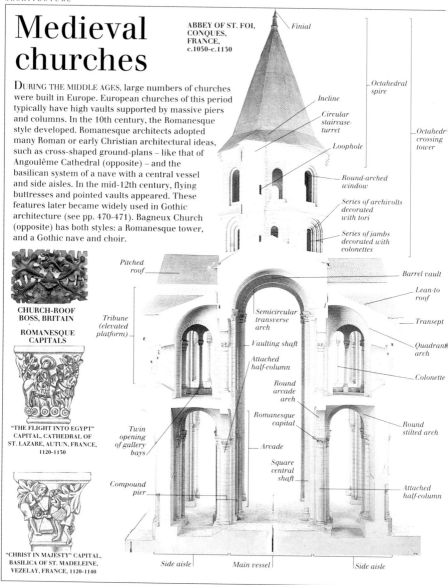

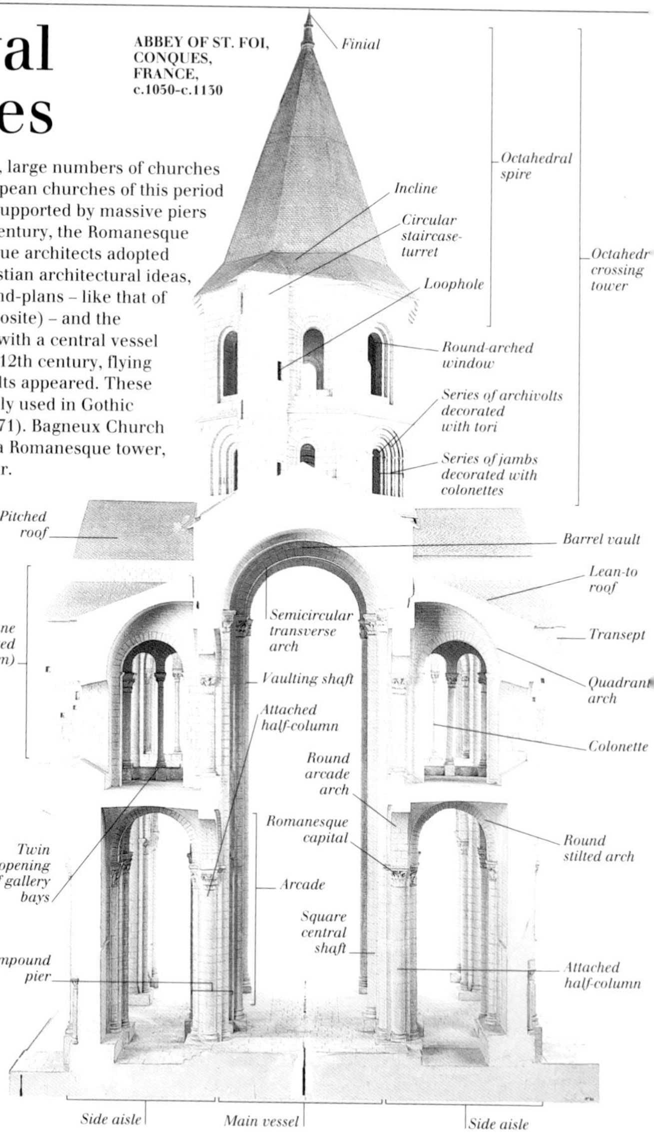

Finial
Octahedral spire
Incline
Circular staircase-turret
Octahedr crossing tower
Loophole
Round-arched window
Series of archivolts decorated with tori
Series of jambs decorated with colonettes
Pitched roof
Barrel vault
Lean-to roof
Tribune (elevated platform)
Semicircular transverse arch
Transept
Vaulting shaft
Quadrant arch
Attached half-column
Colonette
Round arcade arch
Romanesque capital
Round stilted arch
Twin opening of gallery bays
Arcade
Square central shaft
Compound pier
Attached half-column
Side aisle
Main vessel
Side aisle

GROUND-PLAN OF ANGOULEME CATHEDRAL, FRANCE, FROM c.1105

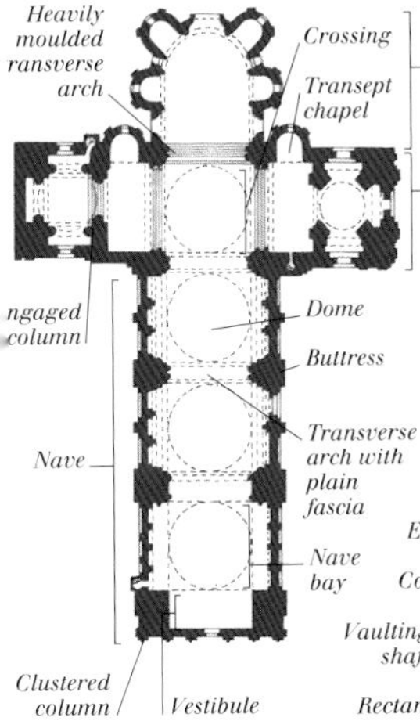
Heavily moulded transverse arch
Crossing
Chevet (choir with round apse and chapels)
Transept chapel
Transept
Engaged column
Dome
Buttress
Transverse arch with plain fascia
Nave
Nave bay
Clustered column
Vestibule

CHOIR, CHURCH OF ST. SERGE, ANGERS, FRANCE, c.1215-1220

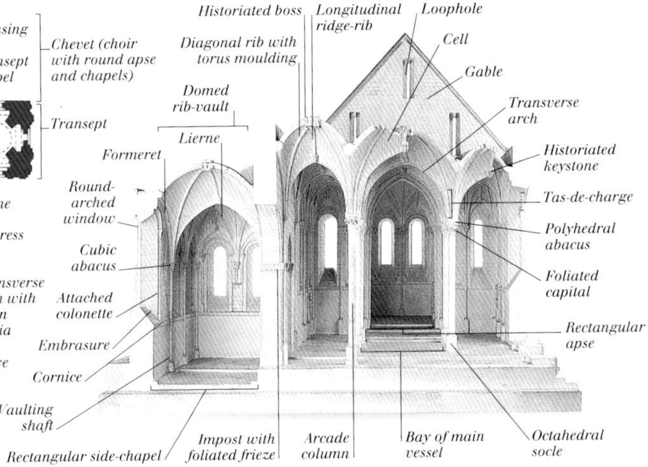
Historiated boss
Longitudinal ridge-rib
Loophole
Diagonal rib with torus moulding
Cell
Gable
Domed rib-vault
Transverse arch
Lierne
Formeret
Historiated keystone
Round-arched window
Tas-de-charge
Polyhedral abacus
Cubic abacus
Foliated capital
Attached colonette
Rectangular apse
Embrasure
Cornice
Vaulting shaft
Impost with foliated frieze
Arcade column
Bay of main vessel
Octahedral socle
Rectangular side-chapel

AGNEUX CHURCH, FRANCE, 1170-1190

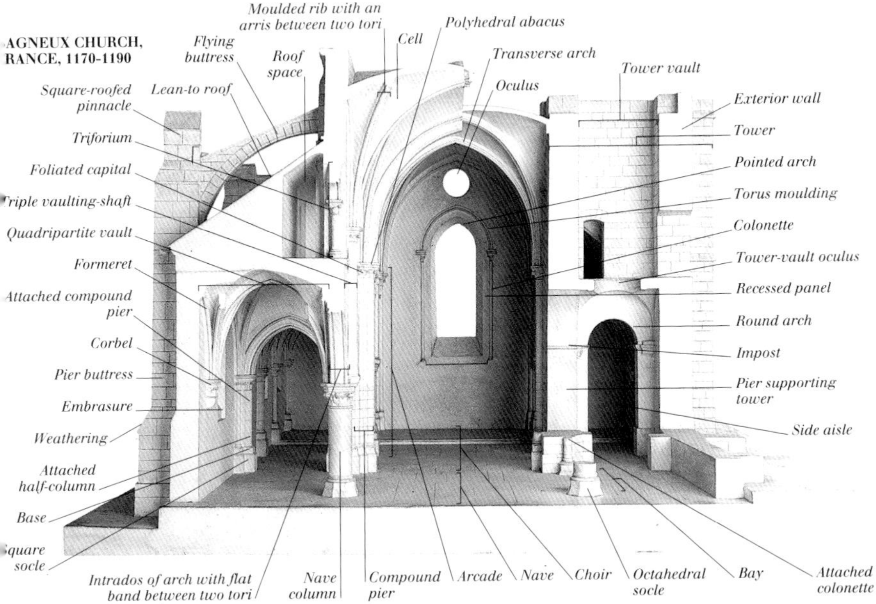
Moulded rib with an arris between two tori
Polyhedral abacus
Cell
Flying buttress
Roof space
Transverse arch
Tower vault
Oculus
Square-roofed pinnacle
Lean-to roof
Exterior wall
Tower
Triforium
Pointed arch
Foliated capital
Torus moulding
Triple vaulting-shaft
Colonette
Quadripartite vault
Tower-vault oculus
Formeret
Recessed panel
Attached compound pier
Round arch
Corbel
Impost
Pier buttress
Pier supporting tower
Embrasure
Side aisle
Weathering
Attached half-column
Base
Square socle
Intrados of arch with flat band between two tori
Nave column
Compound pier
Arcade
Nave
Choir
Octahedral socle
Bay
Attached colonette

Gothic 1

GOTHIC STAINED GLASS WITH FOLIATED SCROLL MOTIF, ON WOODEN FORM

GOTHIC BUILDINGS are characterized by rib vaults, pointed or lancet arches, flying buttresses, decorative tracery and gables, and stained-glass windows. Typical Gothic buildings include the Cathedrals of Salisbury and old St. Paul's in England, and Notre Dame de Paris in France (see pp. 472-473). The Gothic style developed out of Romanesque architecture in France (see pp. 468-469) in the mid-12th century, and then spread throughout Europe. The decorative elements of Gothic architecture became highly developed in buildings of the English Decorated style (late 13th-14th century) and the French Flamboyant style (15th-16th century). These styles are exemplified by the tower of Salisbury Cathedral and the staircase in the Church of St. Maclou (see pp. 472-473), respectively. In both of these styles, embellishments such as ballflowers and curvilinear (flowing) tracery were used liberally. The English Perpendicular style (late 14th-15th century), which followed the Decorated style, emphasized the vertical and horizontal elements of a building. A notable feature of this style is the hammer-beam roof.

GROUND-PLAN OF SALISBURY CATHEDRAL

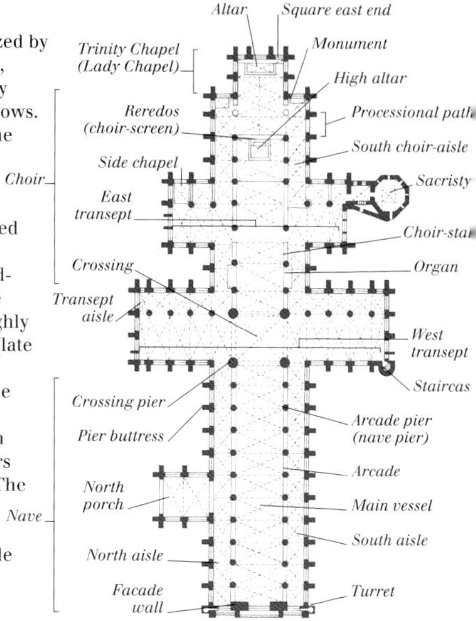
Altar
Square east end
Trinity Chapel (Lady Chapel)
Monument
High altar
Reredos (choir-screen)
Processional path
South choir-aisle
Side chapel
Choir
Sacristy
East transept
Choir-stal
Crossing
Organ
Transept aisle
West transept
Staircas
Crossing pier
Arcade pier (nave pier)
Pier buttress
Arcade
North porch
Main vessel
Nave
South aisle
North aisle
Facade wall
Turret

GOTHIC TORUS WITH BALLFLOWERS

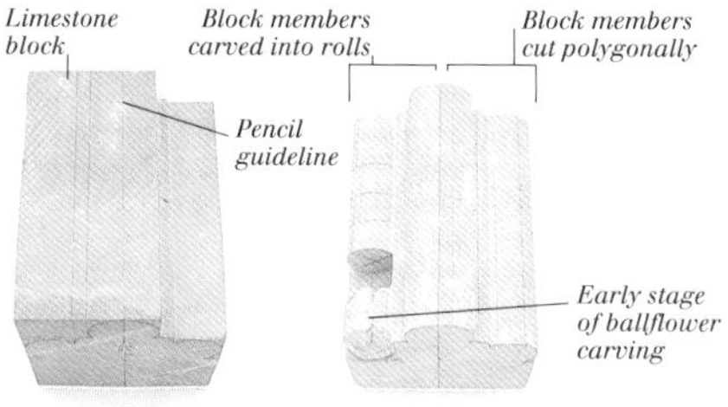
Limestone block
Block members carved into rolls
Block members cut polygonally
Pencil guideline
Early stage of ballflower carving
Torus
Ballflower
Fillet
Mason's mark

BLOCK AFTER INITIAL CUTTING

BLOCK WITH MEMBERS CUT INTO ROLLS

FINISHED BLOCK

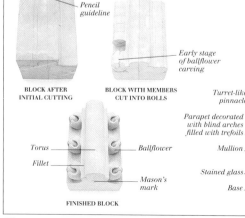

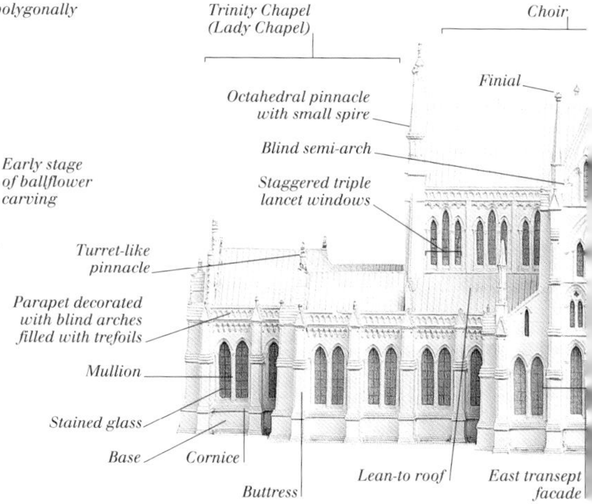
Trinity Chapel (Lady Chapel)
Choir
Finial
Octahedral pinnacle with small spire
Blind semi-arch
Staggered triple lancet windows
Turret-like pinnacle
Parapet decorated with blind arches filled with trefoils
Mullion
Stained glass
Base
Cornice
Buttress
Lean-to roof
East transept facade

NORTH SIDE, SALISBURY CATHEDRAL, BRITAIN, 1220-1280 (STEEPLE AND SPIRE ADDED DURING 14TH CENTURY)

WEST FACADE, SALISBURY CATHEDRAL

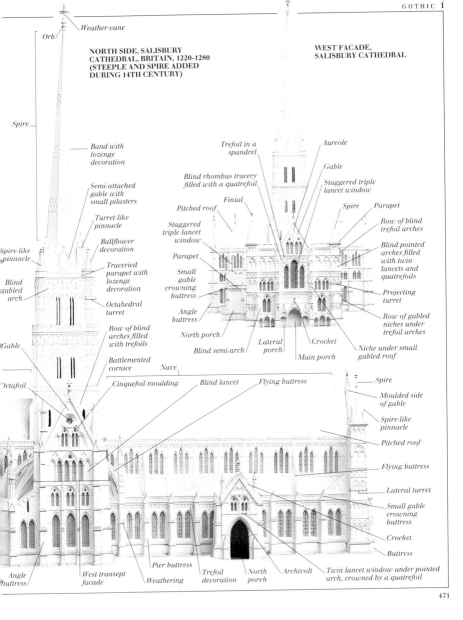

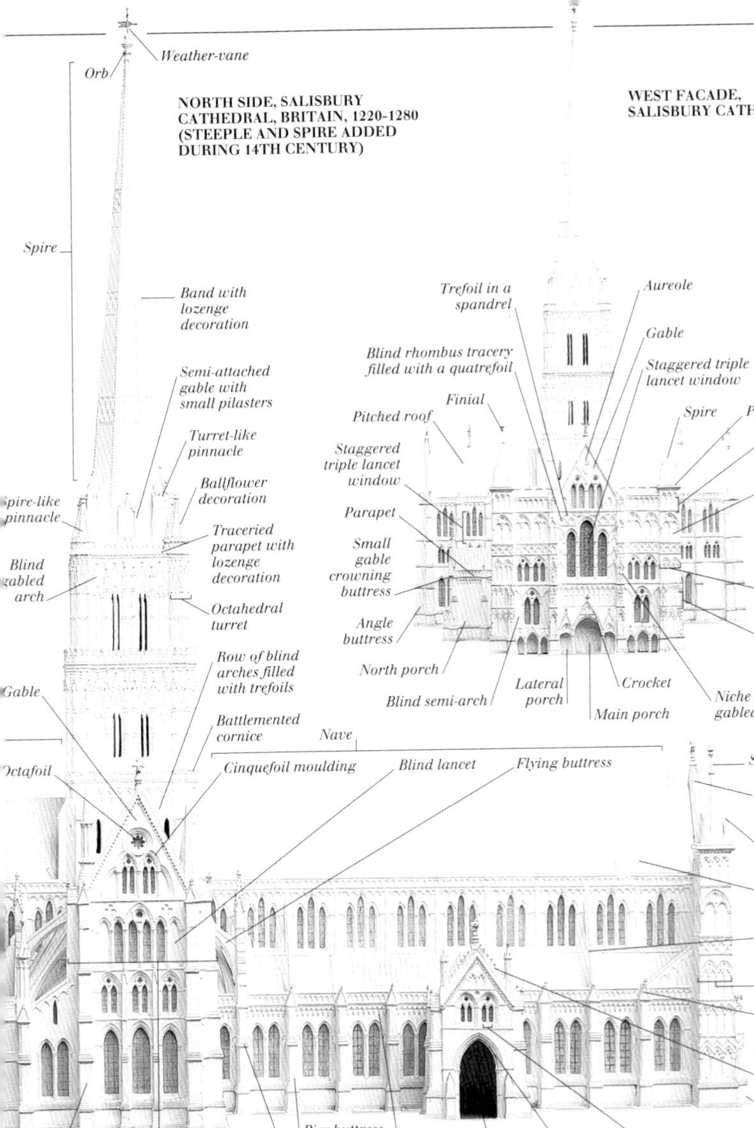
Weather-vane
Orb
Spire
Band with lozenge decoration
Semi-attached gable with small pilasters
Turret-like pinnacle
Ballflower decoration
pire-like pinnacle
Traceried parapet with lozenge decoration
Blind abled arch
Octahedral turret
Row of blind arches filled with trefoils
Gable
Battlemented cornice
Trefoil in a spandrel
Aureole
Gable
Blind rhombus tracery filled with a quatrefoil
Staggered triple lancet window
Finial
Pitched roof
Spire
Parapet
Staggered triple lancet window
Row of blind trefoil arches
Parapet
Blind pointed arches filled with twin lancets and quatrefoils
Small gable crowning buttress
Projecting turret
Angle buttress
Row of gabled niches under trefoil arches
North porch
Lateral porch
Crocket
Niche under small gabled roof
Blind semi-arch
Main porch
Nave
ctafoil
Cinquefoil moulding
Blind lancet
Flying buttress
Spire
Moulded side of gable
Spire-like pinnacle
Pitched roof
Flying buttress
Lateral turret
Small gable crowning buttress
Crocket
Buttress
Angle uttress
West transept facade
Pier buttress
Weathering
Trefoil decoration
North porch
Archivolt
Twin lancet window under pointed arch, crowned by a quatrefoil

Gothic 2

CURVILINEAR (FLOWING) TRACERY FROM A BALUSTRADE, 14TH OR 15TH CENTURY

Cyma reversa (reversed ogee curve)
Cavetto moulding
Plain fascia
Moulded cornice
Cavetto moulding with elongated lower part
Ogee curve
Mouchette (curved dagger)
Cusp
Drop shape
Cavetto moulding

SPIRAL STAIRCASE TO ORGAN, CHURCH ST. MACLOU, ROUEN, FRANCE, c.1519

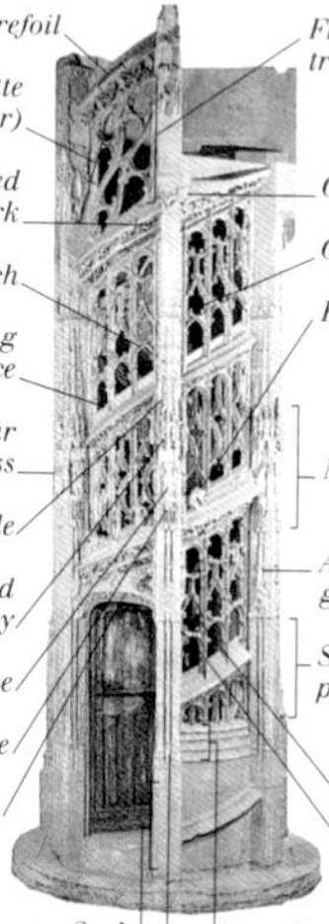
Trefoil
Flamboyant tracery
Mouchette (curved dagger)
Foliated scrollwork
Cherub
Crocket
Pointed arch
Figure
Winding cornice
Rectangular buttress
Niche
Attached gable
Attached gable
Gabled canopy
Square pillar
Statue
Base
Dagger
Basket arch
Round arch
Socle
Base decorated with ovolo mouldings
Cross motif

TOWER AND PART OF THE NAVE AND CHOIR, OLD ST. PAUL'S CATHEDRAL, LONDON, BRITAIN, 1087-1666

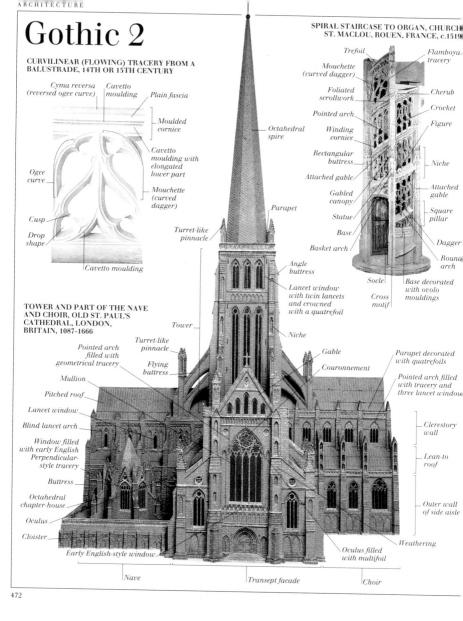

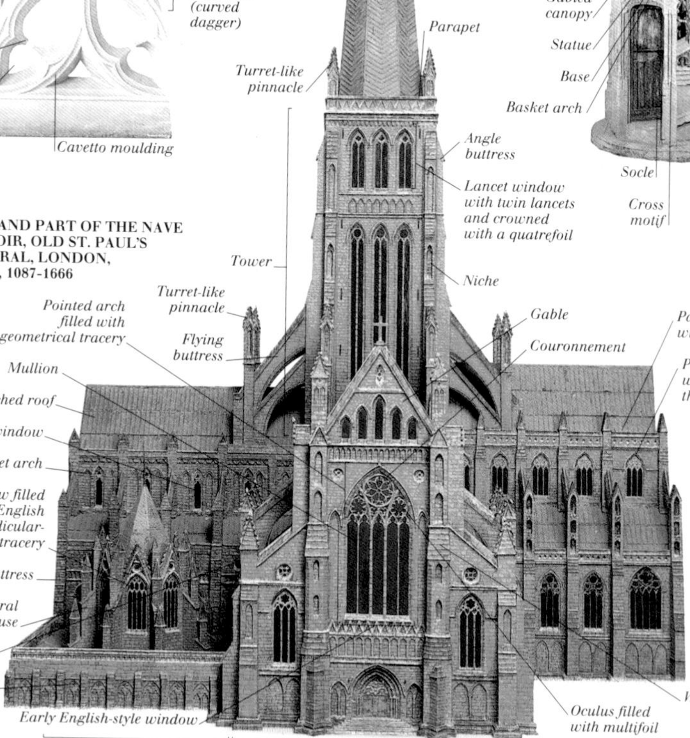
Octahedral spire
Parapet
Turret-like pinnacle
Angle buttress
Lancet window with twin lancets and crowned with a quatrefoil
Tower
Niche
Turret-like pinnacle
Pointed arch filled with geometrical tracery
Gable
Flying buttress
Couronnement
Parapet decorated with quatrefoils
Mullion
Pointed arch filled with tracery and three lancet windows
Pitched roof
Lancet window
Blind lancet arch
Clerestory wall
Window filled with early English Perpendicular-style tracery
Lean-to roof
Buttress
Octahedral chapter-house
Outer wall of side aisle
Oculus
Cloister
Weathering
Early English-style window
Oculus filled with multifoil
Nave
Transept facade
Choir

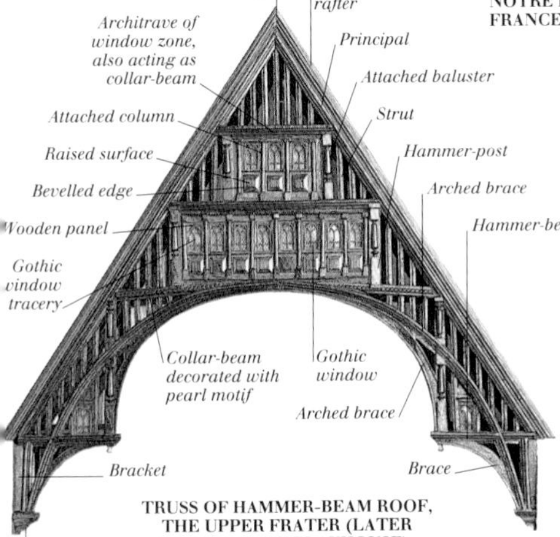
Ridge
Common rafter
Architrave of window zone, also acting as collar-beam
Principal
Attached baluster
Attached column
Strut
Raised surface
Hammer-post
Bevelled edge
Arched brace
Wooden panel
Hammer-beam
Gothic window tracery
Collar-beam decorated with pearl motif
Gothic window
Arched brace
Bracket
Brace
Impost

TRUSS OF HAMMER-BEAM ROOF, THE UPPER FRATER (LATER BLACKFRIARS' PLAYHOUSE), LONDON, BRITAIN, PROBABLY 14TH CENTURY

TYPICAL GOTHIC FEATURES

FLYING BUTTRESS OVER SIDE AISLES, MILAN CATHEDRAL, ITALY, C.1385-1485

GARGOYLE, HORSLEY CHURCH, DERBYSHIRE, BRITAIN, C.1450

HAMMER-BEAM ROOF, CHURCH OF ST. BOTOLPH, TRUNCH, NORFOLK, BRITAIN, 1360-1380

SPIRE AND TRANSEPT ROOF, CATHEDRAL OF NOTRE DAME DE PARIS, FRANCE, c.1163-1250

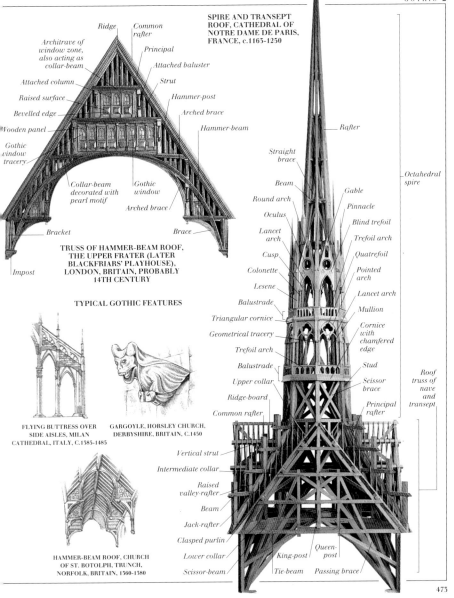

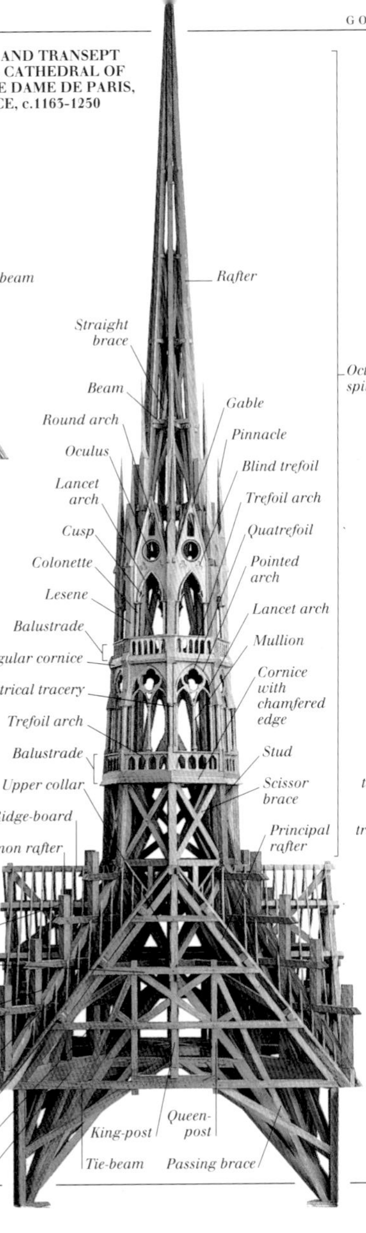
Rafter
Octahedral spire
Straight brace
Beam
Gable
Round arch
Pinnacle
Oculus
Blind trefoil
Lancet arch
Trefoil arch
Cusp
Quatrefoil
Colonette
Pointed arch
Lesene
Lancet arch
Balustrade
Mullion
Triangular cornice
Cornice with chamfered edge
Geometrical tracery
Trefoil arch
Stud
Balustrade
Scissor brace
Upper collar
Roof truss of nave and transept
Ridge-board
Principal rafter
Common rafter
Vertical strut
Intermediate collar
Raised valley-rafter
Beam
Jack-rafter
Clasped purlin
Queen-post
Lower collar
King-post
Scissor-beam
Tie-beam
Passing brace

Renaissance 1

THE RENAISSANCE was a European movement – lasting roughly from the 14th century to the mid-17th century – in which the arts and sciences underwent great changes. In architecture, these changes were marked by a return to the classical forms and proportions of ancient Roman buildings. The Renaissance originated in Italy, and the buildings most characteristic of its style can be found there, such as the Palazzo Strozzi shown here. Mannerism is a branch of the Renaissance style that distorts the classical forms; an example is the Laurentian Library staircase. As the Renaissance style spread to other European countries, many of its features were incorporated into the local architecture; for example, the Château de Montal in France (see pp. 476-477) incorporates aedicules (tabernacles).

FACADE ON TO PIAZZA, PALAZZO STROZZI

SIDE VIEW OF PALAZZO STROZZI, FLORENCE, ITALY, 1489 (BY G. DA SANGALLO, B. DA MAIANO, AND CRONACA)

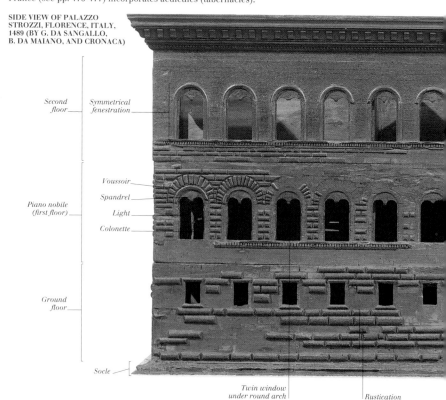

DETAILS FROM ITALIAN RENAISSANCE BUILDINGS

PANEL FROM DRUM OF DOME, FLORENCE CATHEDRAL, 1420-1436

COFFERING IN DOME, PAZZI CHAPEL, FLORENCE, 1429-1461

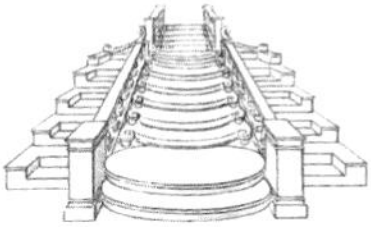

STAIRCASE, LAURENTIAN LIBRARY, FLORENCE, 1559

PORTICO, VILLA ROTUNDA, VICENZA, 1567-1569

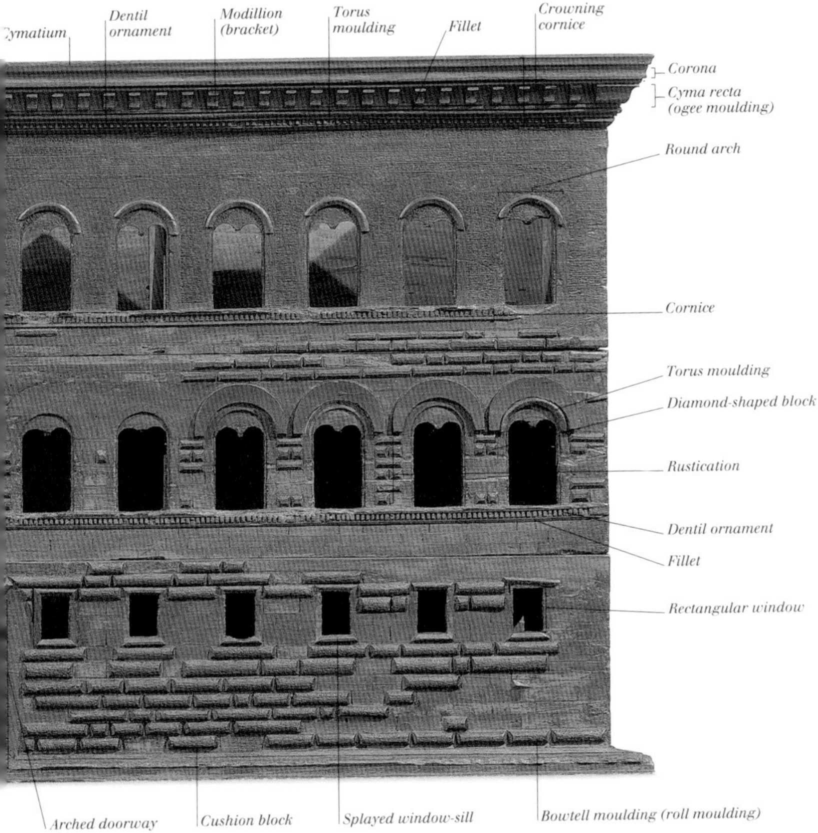
Cymatium
Dentil ornament
Modillion (bracket)
Torus moulding
Fillet
Crowning cornice
Corona
Cyma recta (ogee moulding)
Round arch
Cornice
Torus moulding
Diamond-shaped block
Rustication
Dentil ornament
Fillet
Rectangular window
Arched doorway
Cushion block
Splayed window-sill
Bowtell moulding (roll moulding)

Renaissance 2

DETAILS FROM EUROPEAN RENAISSANCE BUILDINGS

STONE WALL, QUOINS, AND SHELL DECORATION, CASA DE LAS CONCHAS, SALAMANCA, SPAIN, 1475-1483

SPIRAL-STAIRCASE TOWER, CHATEAU DE BLOIS, FRANCE, 1514-1530

CONICAL DOME, CHATEAU DE CHAMBORD, FRANCE, 1519-1547

PAIR OF CHIMNEY-STACKS, PALAIS DE FONTAINEBLEAU, FRANCE, FROM 1528

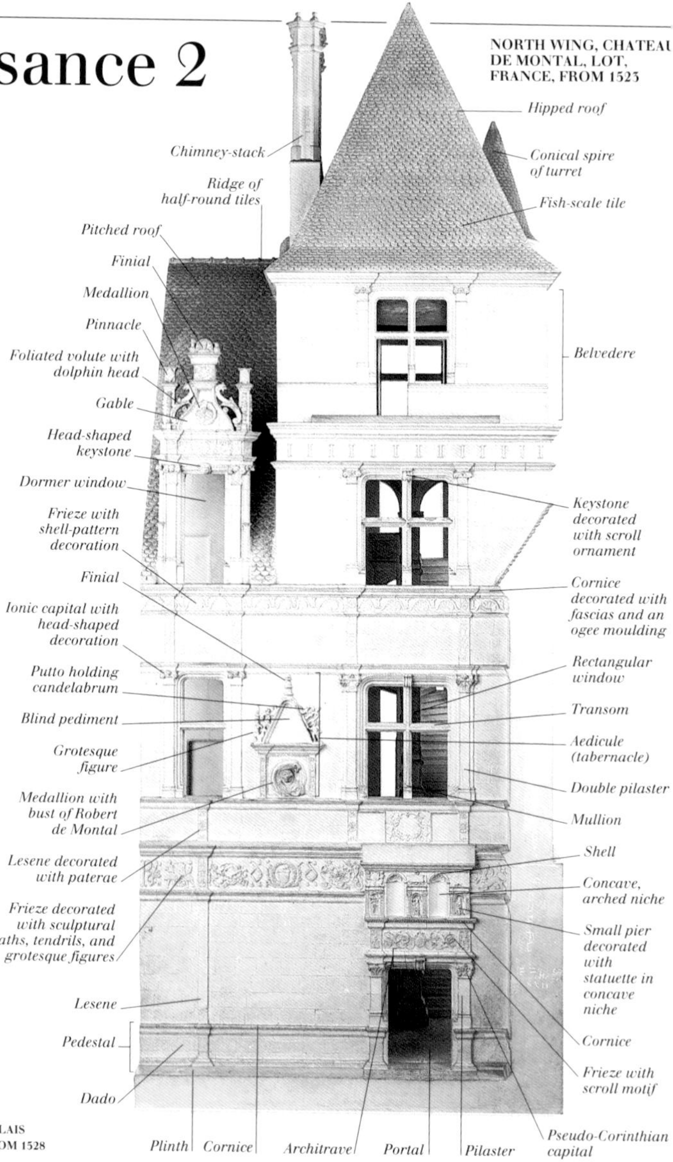
Chimney-stack
Ridge of half-round tiles
Pitched roof
Finial
Medallion
Pinnacle
Foliated volute with dolphin head
Gable
Head-shaped keystone
Dormer window
Frieze with shell-pattern decoration
Finial
Ionic capital with head-shaped decoration
Putto holding candelabrum
Blind pediment
Grotesque figure
Medallion with bust of Robert de Montal
Lesene decorated with paterae
Frieze decorated with sculptural wreaths, tendrils, and grotesque figures
Lesene
Pedestal
Dado
Plinth
Cornice
Architrave
Portal
Pilaster
Hipped roof
Conical spire of turret
Fish-scale tile
Belvedere
Keystone decorated with scroll ornament
Cornice decorated with fascias and an ogee moulding
Rectangular window
Transom
Aedicule (tabernacle)
Double pilaster
Mullion
Shell
Concave, arched niche
Small pier decorated with statuette in concave niche
Cornice
Frieze with scroll motif
Pseudo-Corinthian capital

NORTH WING, CHATEAU DE MONTAL, LOT, FRANCE, FROM 1523

NORTH-WING STAIRCASE, CHATEAU DE MONTAL

Hipped roof
Conical spire
Turret
Eaves with versailing fascias and fillets
Loophole
Cornice with fascias and ogee mouldings
Rib vault
Column
Conical corbel
Second-floor landing
First-floor landing
Flight of stairs
Lesene
Pier supporting flight of stairs
Handrail
Pier supporting first-floor landing
Riser
Tread

CAMPANILE, CHURCH OF ST. EUSTACHE, PARIS, FRANCE, 1532-1640

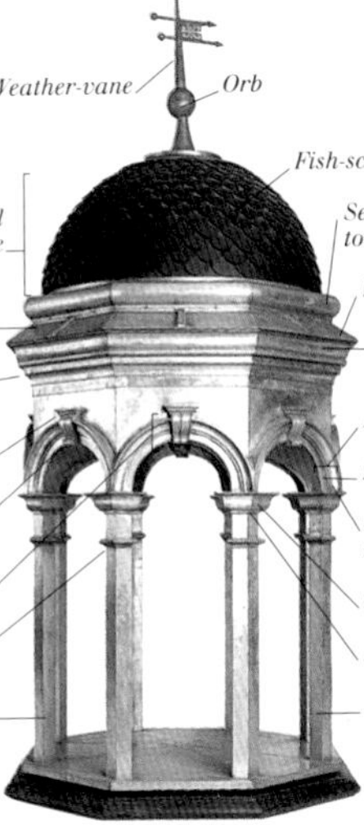
Weather-vane
Orb
Fish-scale tile
Hemispherical dome
Semicircular torus moulding
Weathering
Fillet
Ogee moulding
Plain fascia
Small architrave
Archivolt
Plain fascia
Volute
Cavetto moulding
Emphasized keystone
Capital
Cincture
Fillet
Zinc plating
Square pillar

GLOBE THEATRE, LONDON, ITAIN, 1599

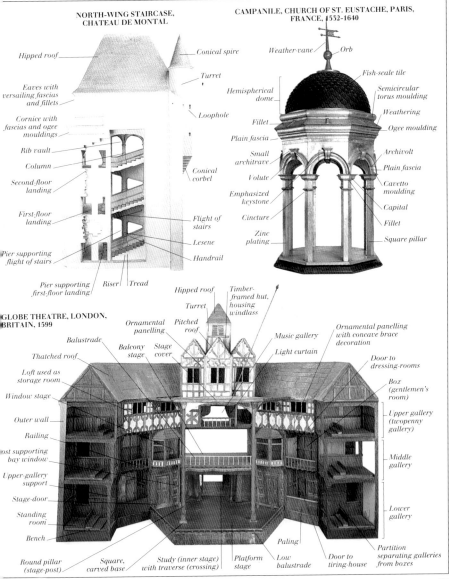

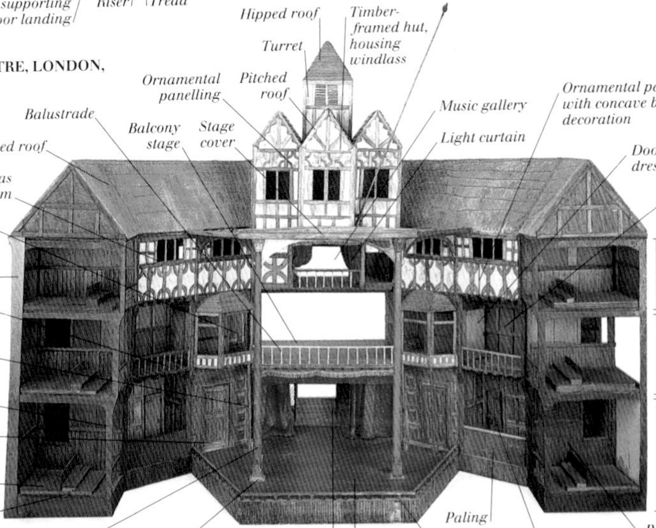
Hipped roof
Timber-framed hut, housing windlass
Turret
Ornamental panelling
Pitched roof
Balustrade
Music gallery
Ornamental panelling with concave brace decoration
Balcony stage
Stage cover
Light curtain
Thatched roof
Door to dressing-rooms
Loft used as storage room
Box (gentlemen's room)
Window stage
Upper gallery (twopenny gallery)
Outer wall
Railing
ost supporting bay window
Middle gallery
Upper-gallery support
Stage-door
Lower gallery
Standing room
Bench
Paling
Partition separating galleries from boxes
Round pillar (stage-post)
Square, carved base
Study (inner stage) with traverse (crossing)
Platform stage
Low balustrade
Door to tiring-house

Baroque and neoclassical 1

THE BAROQUE STYLE EVOLVED IN THE EARLY 17TH CENTURY in Rome. It is characterized by curved outlines and ostentatious decoration, as can be seen in the Italian church details (right). The baroque style was particularly widely favoured in Italy, Spain, and Germany. It was also adopted in Britain and France, but with adaptations. The British architects Sir Christopher Wren and Nicholas Hawksmoor, for example, used baroque features – such as the concave walls of St. Paul's Cathedral and the curved buttresses of the Church of St. George in the East (see pp. 480-481) – but they did so with restraint. Similarly, the curved buttresses and volutes of the Parisian Church of St. Paul-St. Louis are relatively plain. In the second half of the 17th century, a distinct classical style (known as neoclassicism) developed in northern Europe as a reaction to the excesses of baroque. Typical of this new style were churches such as the Madeleine (a proposed facade is shown below), as well as secular buildings such as the Cirque Napoleon (opposite) and the buildings of the British architect Sir John Soane (see pp. 482-483). In early 18th-century France, an extremely lavish form of baroque developed, known as rococo. The balcony from Nantes (see pp. 482-483) with its twisted ironwork and head-shaped corbels is typical of this style.

DETAILS FROM ITALIAN BAROQUE CHURCHES

SCROLLED BUTTRESS, CHURCH OF ST. MARIA DELLA SALUTE, VENICE, 1631-1682

STATUE OF THE ECSTASY OF ST. THERESA, CHURCH OF ST. MARIA DELLA VITTORIA, ROME, 1645-1652

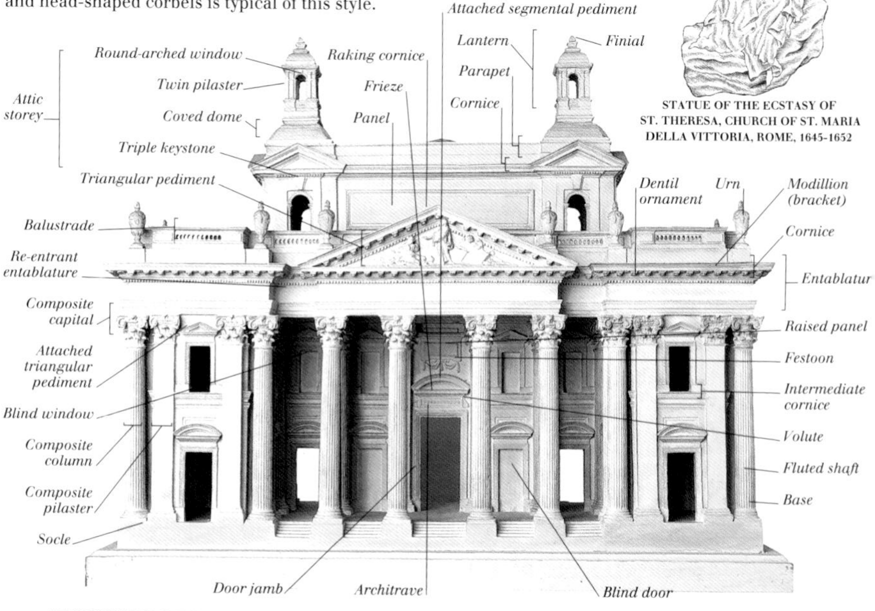
Attached segmental pediment
Round-arched window
Raking cornice
Lantern
Finial
Attic storey
Twin pilaster
Frieze
Parapet
Coved dome
Panel
Cornice
Triple keystone
Triangular pediment
Dentil ornament
Urn
Modillion (bracket)
Balustrade
Cornice
Re-entrant entablature
Entablatur
Composite capital
Raised panel
Attached triangular pediment
Festoon
Intermediate cornice
Blind window
Volute
Composite column
Fluted shaft
Composite pilaster
Base
Socle
Door jamb
Architrave
Blind door

PROPOSED FACADE, THE MADELEINE (NEOCLASSICAL), PARIS, FRANCE, 1764 (BY P. CONTANT D'IVRY)

CIRQUE NAPOLEON (NEOCLASSICAL), PARIS, FRANCE, 1852 (BY J.I. HITTORFF)

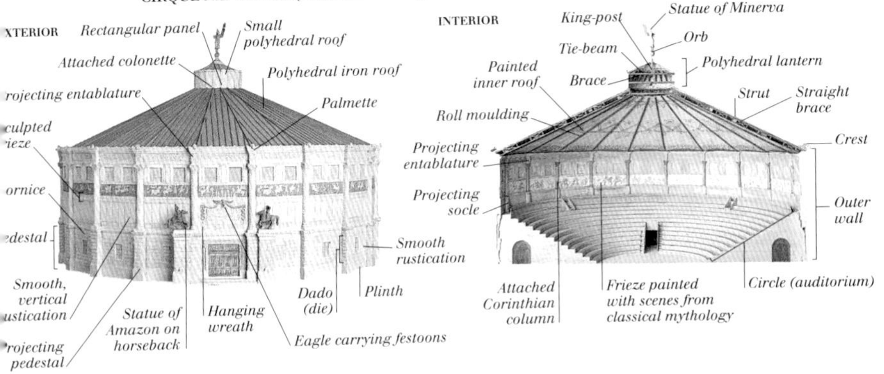
XTERIOR
Rectangular panel
Small polyhedral roof
Attached colonette
Polyhedral iron roof
rojecting entablature
Palmette
culpted rieze
ornice
edestal
Smooth rustication
Smooth, vertical ustication
Statue of Amazon on horseback
Hanging wreath
Dado (die)
Plinth
rojecting pedestal
Eagle carrying festoons
INTERIOR
King-post
Statue of Minerva
Orb
Tie-beam
Polyhedral lantern
Painted inner roof
Brace
Strut
Straight brace
Roll moulding
Crest
Projecting entablature
Projecting socle
Outer wall
Attached Corinthian column
Frieze painted with scenes from classical mythology
Circle (auditorium)

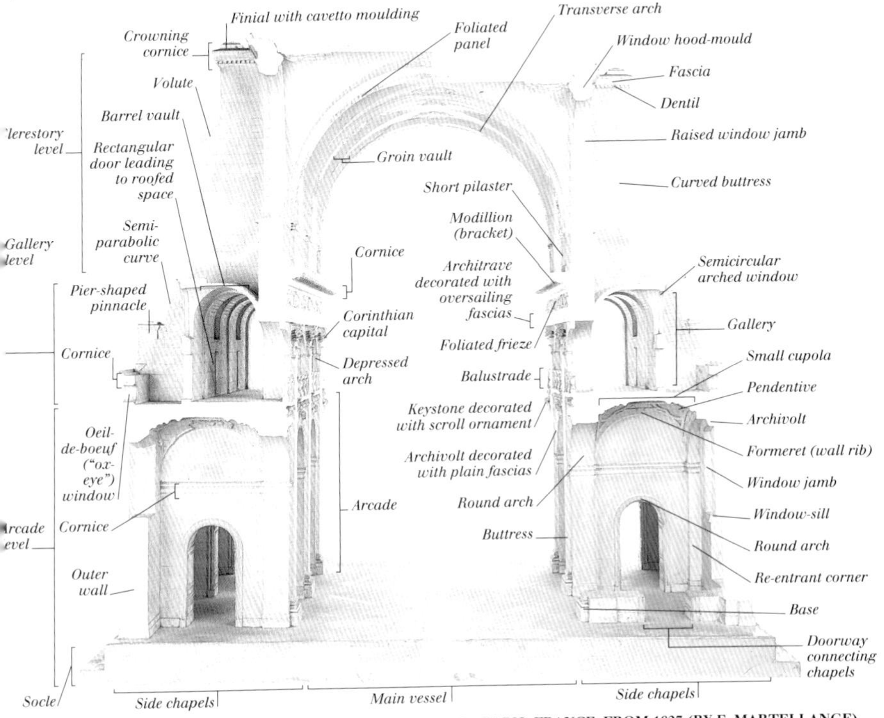
Finial with cavetto moulding
Crowning cornice
Foliated panel
Transverse arch
Window hood-mould
Fascia
Dentil
Volute
Barrel vault
lerestory level
Rectangular door leading to roofed space
Raised window jamb
Groin vault
Curved buttress
Short pilaster
Modillion (bracket)
Gallery level
Semi-parabolic curve
Cornice
Architrave decorated with oversailing fascias
Semicircular arched window
Pier-shaped pinnacle
Corinthian capital
Gallery
Foliated frieze
Cornice
Depressed arch
Small cupola
Balustrade
Pendentive
Keystone decorated with scroll ornament
Archivolt
Oeil-de-boeuf ("ox-eye") window
Formeret (wall rib)
Archivolt decorated with plain fascias
Window jamb
Arcade
Round arch
Window-sill
rcade evel
Cornice
Buttress
Round arch
Outer wall
Re-entrant corner
Base
Doorway connecting chapels
Socle
Side chapels
Main vessel
Side chapels

NAVE, CHURCH OF ST. PAUL-ST. LOUIS (FRENCH BAROQUE), PARIS, FRANCE, FROM 1627 (BY E. MARTELLANGE)

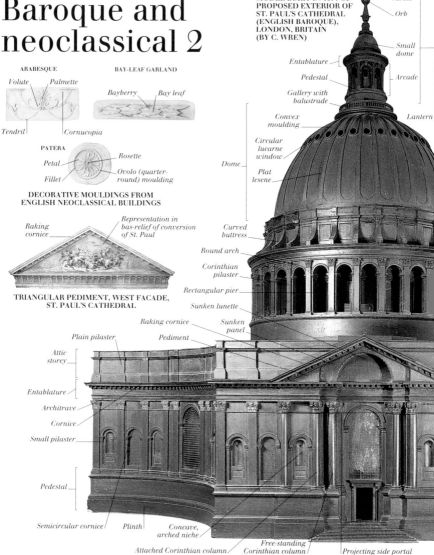

Baroque and neoclassical 2

ARABESQUE

Volute
Palmette
Tendril
Cornucopia

BAY-LEAF GARLAND

Bayberry
Bay leaf

PATERA

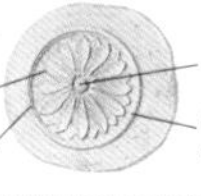
Petal
Fillet
Rosette
Ovolo (quarter-round) moulding

DECORATIVE MOULDINGS FROM ENGLISH NEOCLASSICAL BUILDINGS

Raking cornice
Representation in bas-relief of conversion of St. Paul

TRIANGULAR PEDIMENT, WEST FACADE, ST. PAUL'S CATHEDRAL

MODEL BUILT IN 1674 OF PROPOSED EXTERIOR OF ST. PAUL'S CATHEDRAL (ENGLISH BAROQUE), LONDON, BRITAIN (BY C. WREN)

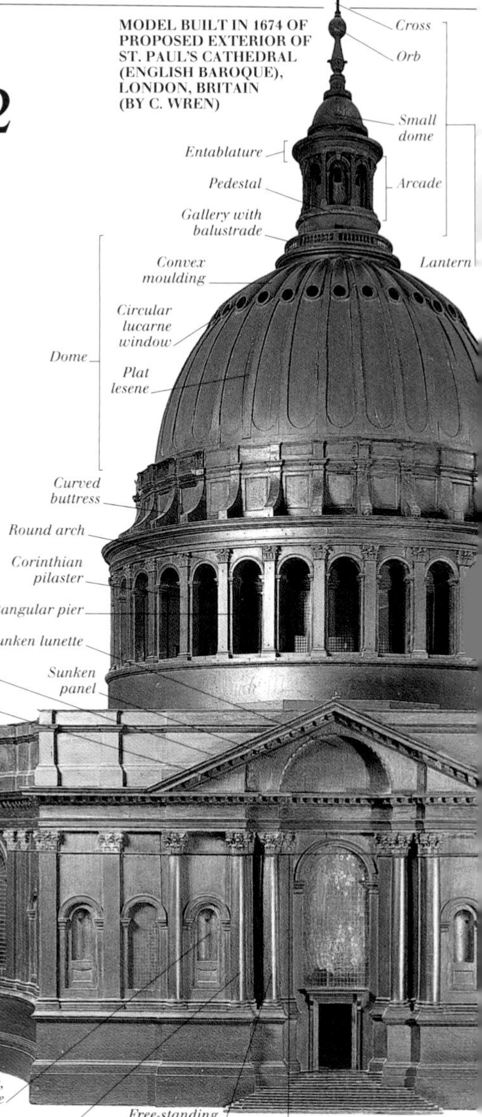
Cross
Orb
Small dome
Entablature
Arcade
Pedestal
Gallery with balustrade
Lantern
Convex moulding
Circular lucarne window
Dome
Plat lesene
Curved buttress
Round arch
Corinthian pilaster
Rectangular pier
Sunken lunette
Raking cornice
Sunken panel
Plain pilaster
Pediment
Attic storey
Entablature
Architrave
Cornice
Small pilaster
Pedestal
Semicircular cornice
Plinth
Concave, arched niche
Attached Corinthian column
Free-standing Corinthian column
Projecting side portal

CHURCH OF ST. GEORGE IN THE EAST (ENGLISH BAROQUE), LONDON, BRITAIN, 1714-1734 (BY N. HAWKSMOOR)

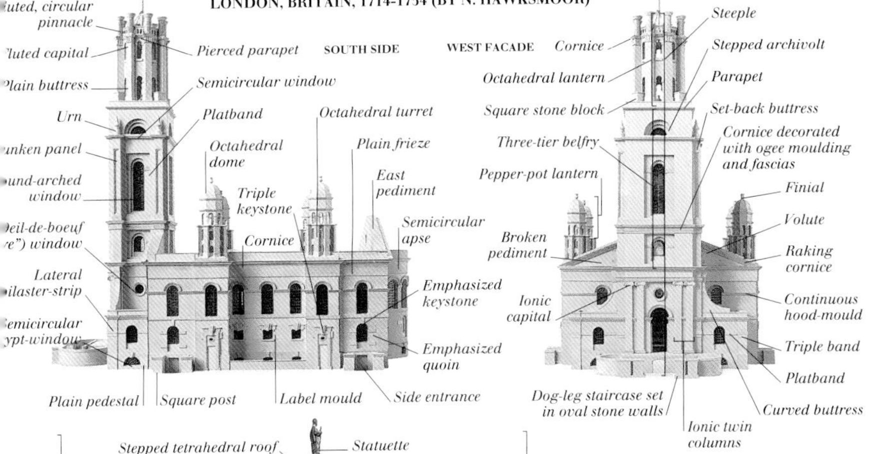
SOUTH SIDE
WEST FACADE
uted, circular pinnacle
luted capital
Plain buttress
Urn
unken panel
und-arched window
Deil-de-boeuf ("e") window
Lateral pilaster-strip
emicircular ypt-window
Pierced parapet
Semicircular window
Platband
Octahedral dome
Triple keystone
Cornice
Octahedral turret
Plain frieze
East pediment
Semicircular apse
Emphasized keystone
Emphasized quoin
Plain pedestal
Square post
Label mould
Side entrance
Cornice
Octahedral lantern
Square stone block
Three-tier belfry
Pepper-pot lantern
Broken pediment
Ionic capital
Dog-leg staircase set in oval stone walls
Ionic twin columns
Steeple
Stepped archivolt
Parapet
Set-back buttress
Cornice decorated with ogee moulding and fascias
Finial
Volute
Raking cornice
Continuous hood-mould
Triple band
Platband
Curved buttress

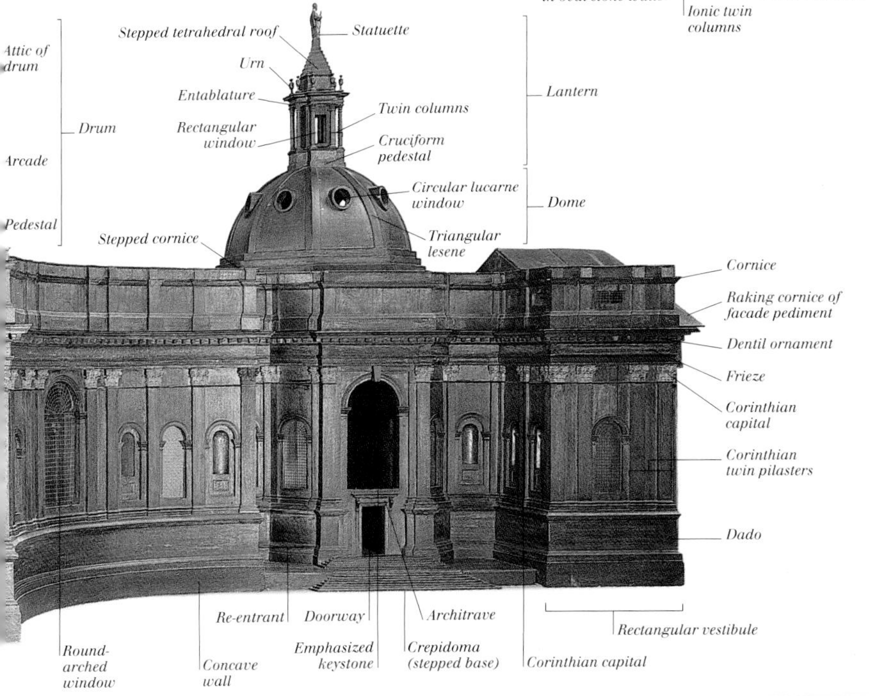
Attic of drum
Drum
Arcade
Pedestal
Stepped tetrahedral roof
Statuette
Urn
Entablature
Twin columns
Rectangular window
Cruciform pedestal
Circular lucarne window
Triangular lesene
Stepped cornice
Lantern
Dome
Cornice
Raking cornice of facade pediment
Dentil ornament
Frieze
Corinthian capital
Corinthian twin pilasters
Dado
Re-entrant
Doorway
Architrave
Rectangular vestibule
Round-arched window
Concave wall
Emphasized keystone
Crepidoma (stepped base)
Corinthian capital

Baroque and neoclassical 3

DETAILS FROM BAROQUE, NEOCLASSICAL, AND ROCOCO BUILDINGS

PORTICO, THE VYNE, HAMPSHIRE, BRITAIN, 1654 (NEOCLASSICAL)

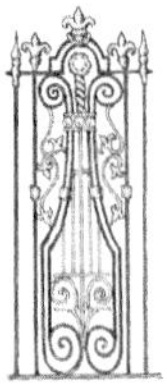

GILT IRONWORK FROM SCREEN, PALAIS DE VERSAILLES, FRANCE, 1669-1674 (FRENCH BAROQUE)

WINDOW, PALAZZO STANGA, CREMONA, ITALY, EARLY 18TH CENTURY (ROCOCO)

ATLAS (MALE CARYATID), UPPER BELVEDERE, VIENNA, AUSTRIA, 1721 (GERMAN-STYLE BAROQUE)

BALCONY, NANTES, FRANCE, 1730-1740 (ROCOCO)

MASONRY OF A NICHE IN THE ROTUNDA (NEOCLASSICAL), BANK OF ENGLAND, LONDON, BRITAIN, 1794 (BY J. SOANE)

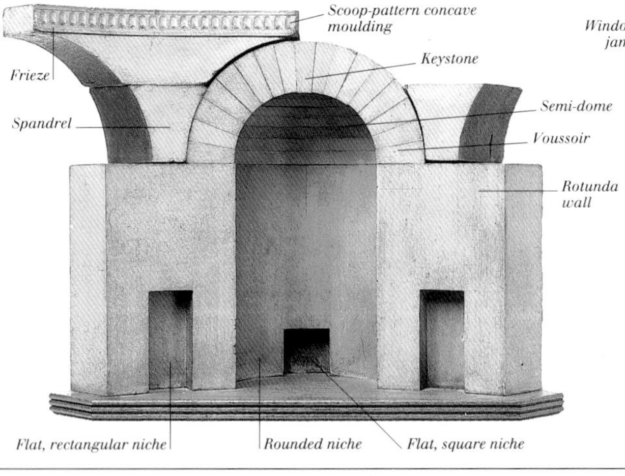
Scoop-pattern concave moulding
Frieze
Keystone
Spandrel
Semi-dome
Voussoir
Rotunda wall
Flat, rectangular niche
Rounded niche
Flat, square niche

CORNER OF THE NEW STATE PAPER OFFICE (NEOCLASSICAL), LONDON, BRITAIN, 1830-1831 (BY J. SOANE)

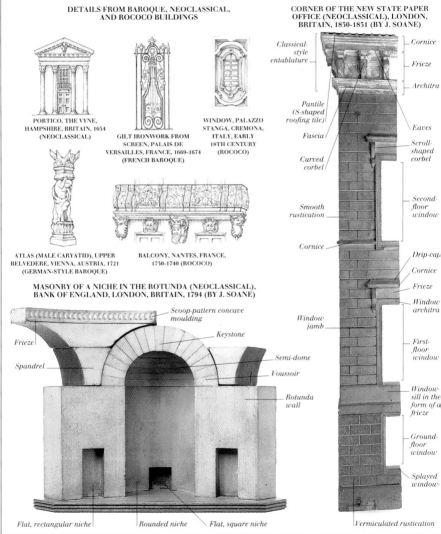

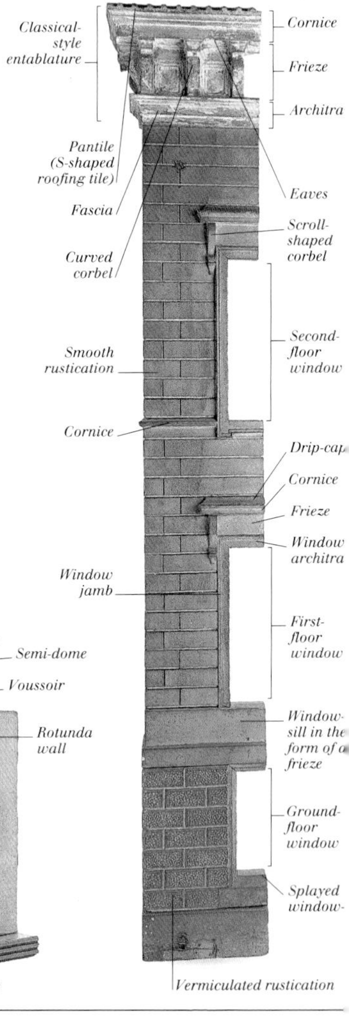
Classical-style entablature
Cornice
Frieze
Architra
Pantile (S-shaped roofing tile)
Eaves
Fascia
Scroll-shaped corbel
Curved corbel
Second-floor window
Smooth rustication
Cornice
Drip-cap
Cornice
Frieze
Window architra
Window jamb
First-floor window
Window-sill in the form of a frieze
Ground-floor window
Splayed window-
Vermiculated rustication

TYRINGHAM HOUSE (NEOCLASSICAL), BUCKINGHAMSHIRE, BRITAIN, 1793-1797 (BY J. SOANE)

ROOF LEVEL (ATTIC LEVEL)

- Space for illumination above unroofed central hall
- Chimney-stack
- Space above unroofed main staircase
- Flat roof
- Oculus illuminating secondary staircase
- Parapet rail
- Balustrade
- Baluster
- Cornice
- Attic storey of convex portico
- Cornice

FIRST-FLOOR LEVEL (CHAMBER FLOOR)

- Upper level of central hall, open to floor below
- Main staircase
- Secondary staircase
- Triangular pilaster
- Abacus
- Pilaster capital
- First-floor storey of convex portico
- Attached Tuscan twin pilasters
- Window-sill
- Bow front

GROUND-FLOOR LEVEL (PRINCIPAL FLOOR)

- Withdrawing-room
- Central hall
- Main staircase
- Library and breakfast-room
- Water-closet (toilet)
- Eating-room
- Secondary staircase
- Segmented lintel course
- Band incised with Greek-style fret ornament
- Window-sill
- Window jamb
- Window architrave
- Basement
- Base
- Plinth
- Ground-floor storey of convex portico
- Horizontal rustication
- Vestibule (entrance hall)

FACADE OF TYRINGHAM HOUSE

- Voussoir
- Chimney-stack
- Basement window
- Entrance door
- Circular entrance steps

PROSTYLE COLONNADE

- Rail
- Baluster
- Parapet
- Balustrade
- Cornice
- Entablature
- Capital
- Shaft
- Ionic column
- Base

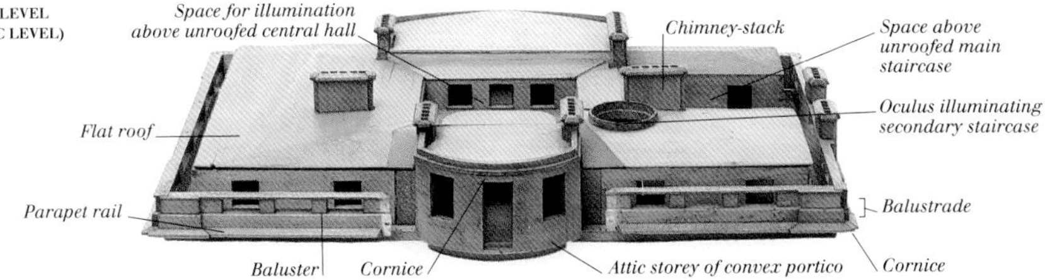

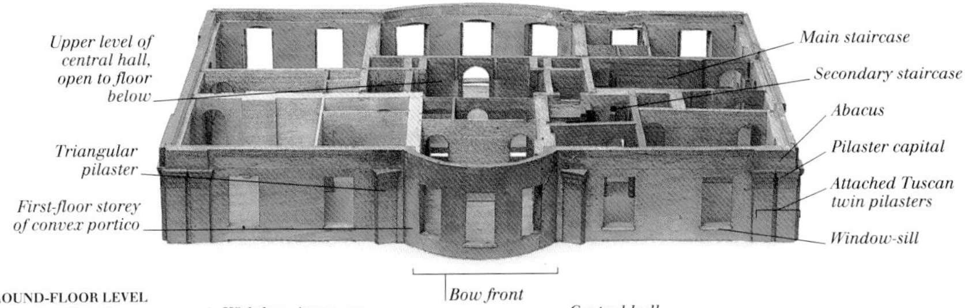

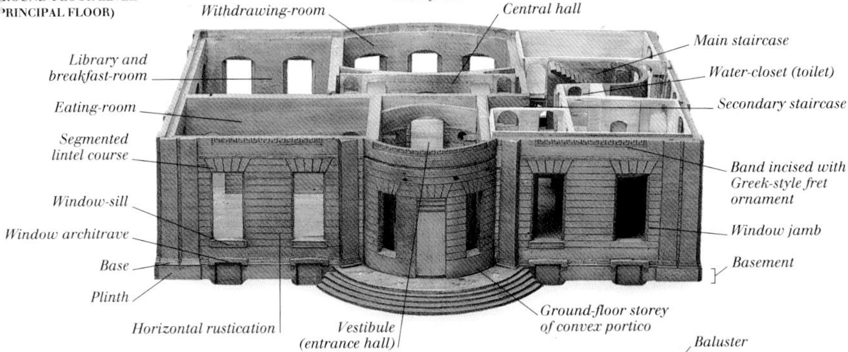

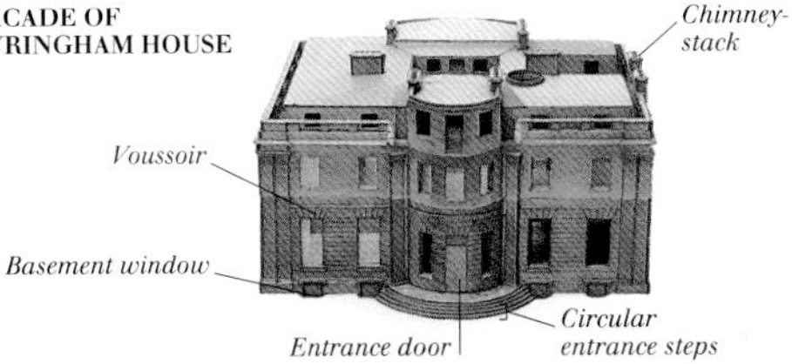

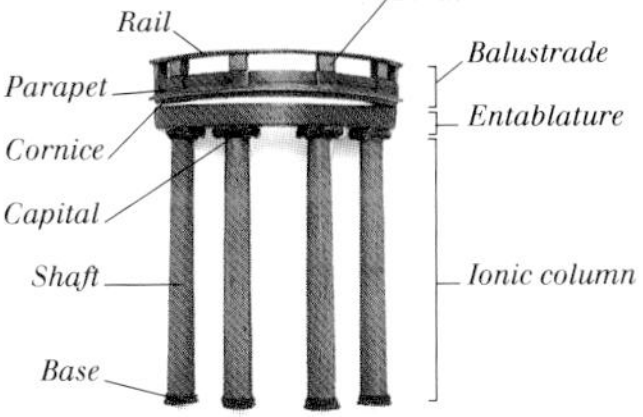

Arches and vaults

ARCHES ARE CURVED STRUCTURES used to bridge spans and to support the weight of upper parts of buildings, such as domes, as in St. Paul's Cathedral (below) and the antique temple (opposite). The voussoirs (wedge-shaped blocks) that form an arch (right) support each other and convert the downward force of the weight of the building into an outward force. This outward force is in turn transferred to buttresses, piers, or abutments. A vault is an arched roof or ceiling. There are four main types of vault (opposite). A barrel vault is a single vault, semicircular in cross-section; a groin vault consists of two barrel vaults intersecting at right-angles; a rib vault is a groin vault reinforced by ribs; and a fan vault is a rib vault in which the ribs radiate from the springing point (where the arch begins) like a fan.

PARTS OF AN ARCH

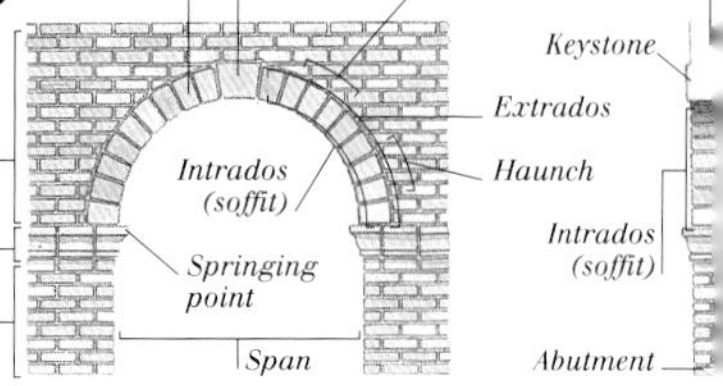
Voussoir
Keystone
Crown
Abutment
Keystone
Extrados
Abutment
Intrados (soffit)
Haunch
Impost
Intrados (soffit)
Springing point
Abutment
Span
Abutment
FRONT
SI

ARCHES AND BASE OF DOME, ST. PAUL'S CATHEDRAL, LONDON, BRITAIN, 1675-1710 (BY C. WREN)

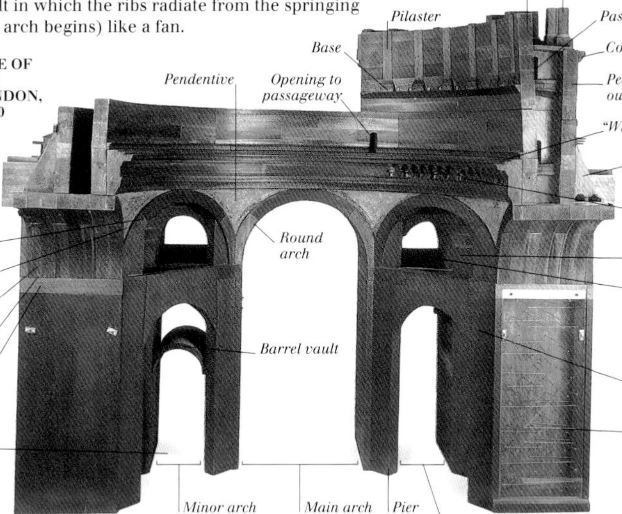
Inner dome
Colonnade
Pilaster
Passageway
Base
Cornice
Pendentive
Opening to passageway
Pedestal of outer dome
"Whispering Gallery
Triangular buttress
Upper arch (concealing difference in heights between main arch and minor arches)
Moulded bracket
Round arch
Extrados
Semi-dome
Intrados (soffit)
Upper barrel-vaulted passag opening on to side aisle
Springing point
Barrel vault
Impost
Abutment
Passage leading to side aisle
Strut built into masonry to strengthen pier (added in the 20th century)
Minor arch leading to side aisle
Main arch leading to nave
Pier
Minor arch

TYPES OF ARCH

HORSESHOE ARCH (MOORISH ARCH), GREAT MOSQUE, CORDOBA, SPAIN, 785

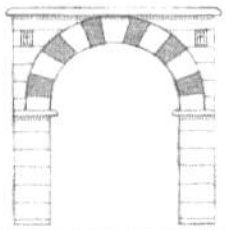
BASKET ARCH (SEMI-ELLIPTICAL ARCH), PALATINE CHAPEL, AIX-LA-CHAPELLE, FRANCE, 790-798

TUDOR ARCH, TOWER OF LONDON, BRITAIN, C.1086-1097

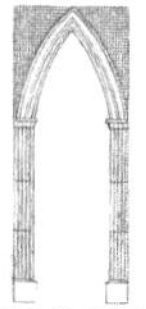
LANCET ARCH, WESTMINSTER ABBEY, LONDON, BRITAIN, 1503-1519

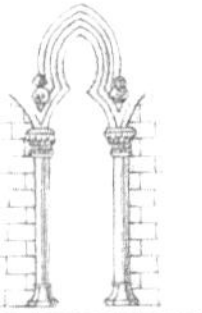
TREFOIL ARCH, BEVERL MINSTER, YORKSHIRE BRITAIN, C.1300

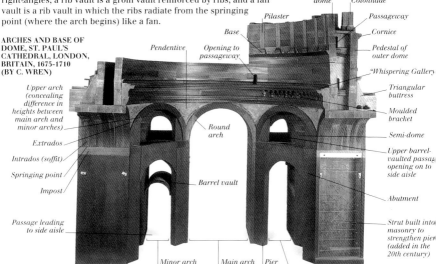

TYPES OF VAULT

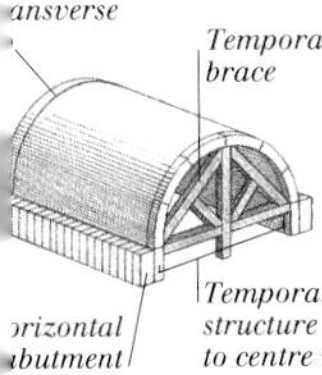

EL VAULT (TUNNEL VAULT; WAGON VAULT)

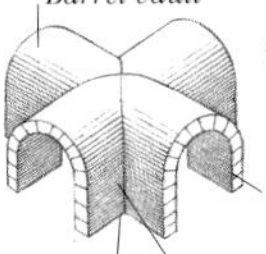
Barrel vault
Voussoir
Right-angled intersection
Groin

GROIN VAULT

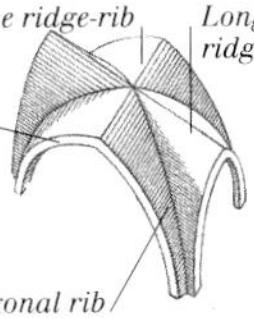
Transverse ridge-rib
Longitudinal ridge-rib
Transverse arch
Diagonal rib

RIB VAULT

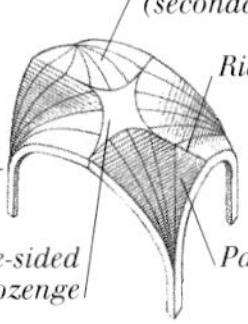
Tierceron (secondary rib)
Ridge-rib
Springing point
Concave-sided lozenge
Panel

FAN VAULT

ƆMPOSITE ODEL OF NTIQUE RENCH TEMPLE

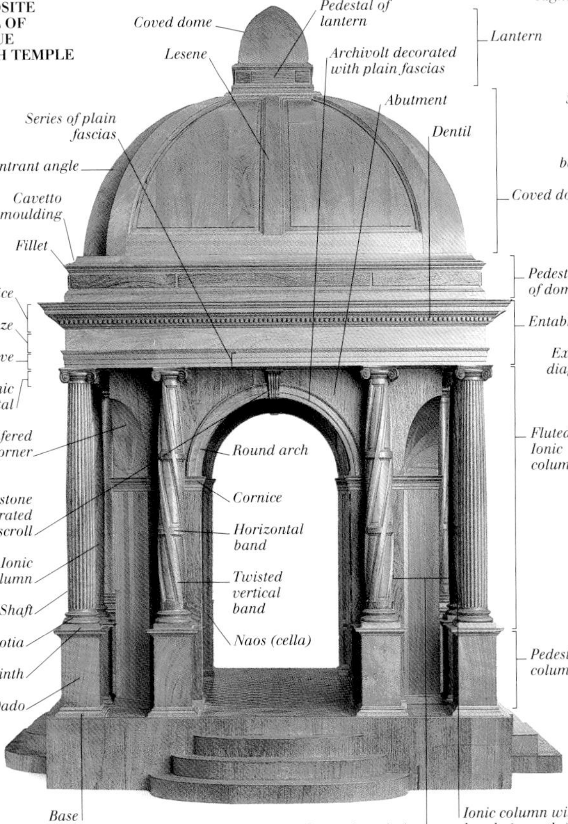
Coved dome
Pedestal of lantern
Lantern
Lesene
Archivolt decorated with plain fascias
Abutment
Series of plain fascias
Dentil
Re-entrant angle
Cavetto moulding
Coved dome
Fillet
Pedestal of dome
Cornice
ain frieze
Entablature
rchitrave
Ionic capital
Chamfered corner
Round arch
Fluted Ionic column
Cornice
Keystone decorated with scroll
Horizontal band
Plain Ionic column
Twisted vertical band
Shaft
Scotia
Naos (cella)
Plinth
Pedestal of column
Dado
Base
Intercolumniation
Ionic column with twisted vertical bands (wreaths) and horizontal bands

ENGLISH BOND BRICKWORK OF GROIN VAULT AND RIB VAULT

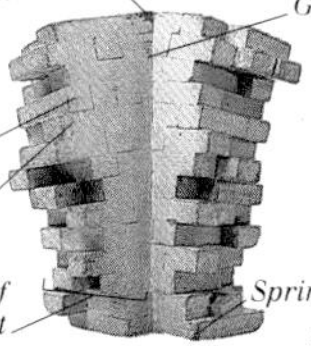
Right-angled intersection
Groin
Header
Stretcher
Cell of barrel vault
Springing point

EXTRADOS OF GROIN VAULT

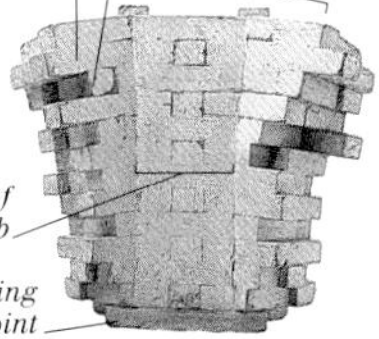
Stretcher
Header
Cell
Extrados of diagonal rib
Springing point

EXTRADOS OF RIB VAULT

INTERIOR DECORATION OF COFFERED VAULT

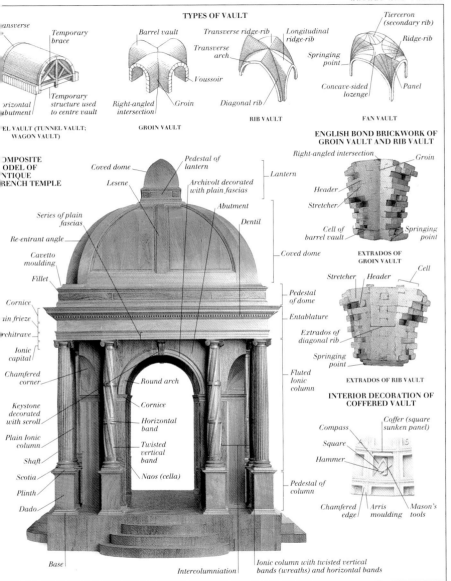

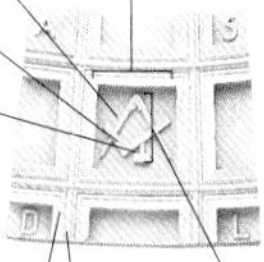
Compass
Coffer (square sunken panel)
Square
Hammer
Chamfered edge
Arris moulding
Mason's tools

Domes

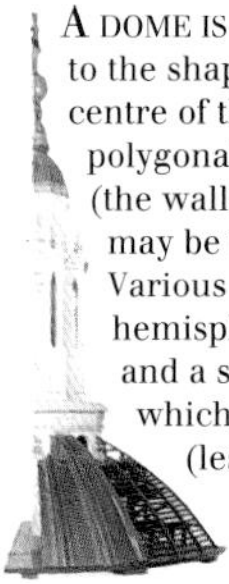

LANTERN AND UPPER DOME TIMBERING, ST. PAUL'S CATHEDRAL

A DOME IS A CONVEX ROOF. Domes are categorized according to the shapes of both the base and the section through the centre of the dome. The base may be circular, square, or polygonal (many-sided), depending on the plan of the drum (the walls on which the dome rests). The section of a dome may be the same shape as any arch (see pp. 484-485). Various types of dome are illustrated here: a hemispherical dome, which has a circular base and a semicircular section; a saucer dome, which has a circular base and a segmental (less than a semicircle) section; a polyhedral dome, which is a dome on a polygonal base whose sides meet at the top of the dome; and an onion dome, which has a circular or polygonal base and an ogee-shaped section. Many domes have a lantern (a turret with windows) to provide light inside.

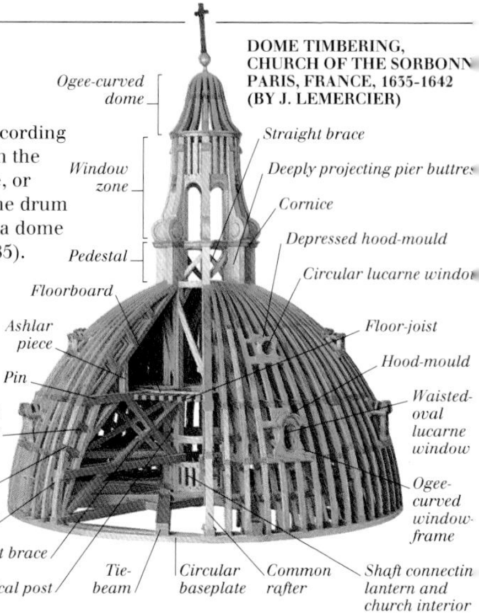

Ogee-curved dome
Window zone
Pedestal
Floorboard
Ashlar piece
Pin
Short strut
Mortise-and-tenon joint
Principal rafter
Straight brace
Vertical post
Tie-beam
Circular baseplate
Common rafter
Shaft connecting lantern and church interior
Straight brace
Deeply projecting pier buttress
Cornice
Depressed hood-mould
Circular lucarne window
Floor-joist
Hood-mould
Waisted-oval lucarne window
Ogee-curved window-frame

DOME TIMBERING, CHURCH OF THE SORBONNE, PARIS, FRANCE, 1635-1642 (BY J. LEMERCIER)

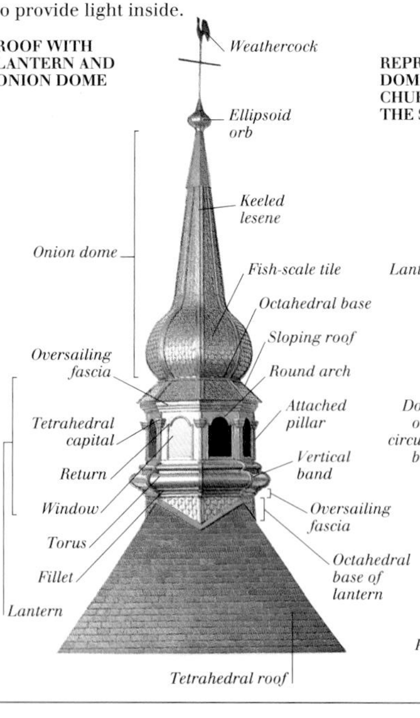

Weathercock
Ellipsoid orb
Keeled lesene
Onion dome
Fish-scale tile
Octahedral base
Sloping roof
Oversailing fascia
Round arch
Attached pillar
Tetrahedral capital
Vertical band
Return
Window
Oversailing fascia
Torus
Octahedral base of lantern
Fillet
Lantern
Tetrahedral roof

ROOF WITH LANTERN AND ONION DOME

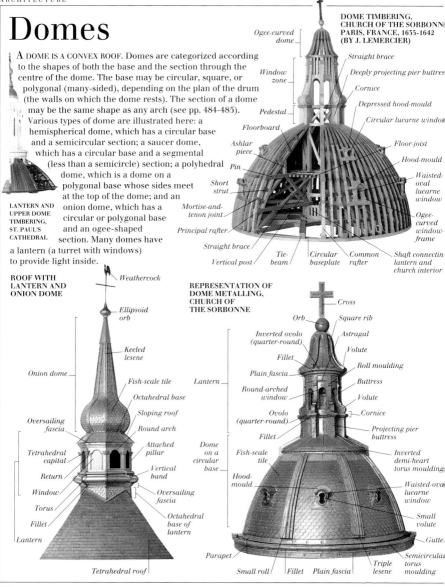

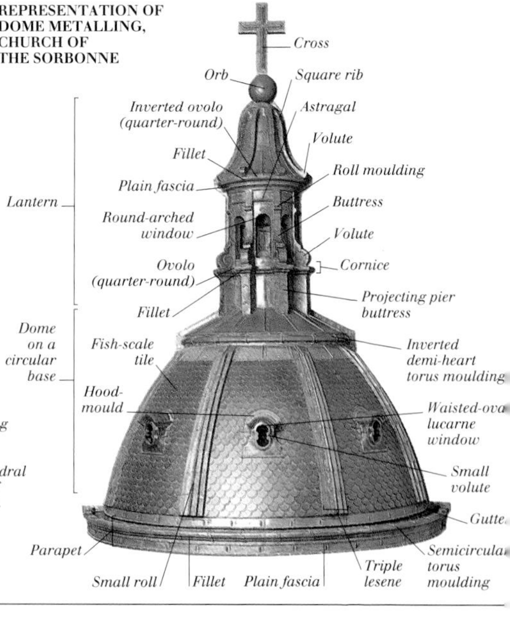

Cross
Orb
Square rib
Inverted ovolo (quarter-round)
Astragal
Volute
Fillet
Roll moulding
Plain fascia
Lantern
Buttress
Round-arched window
Volute
Ovolo (quarter-round)
Cornice
Projecting pier buttress
Fillet
Dome on a circular base
Fish-scale tile
Inverted demi-heart torus moulding
Hood-mould
Waisted-oval lucarne window
Small volute
Gutter
Parapet
Small roll
Fillet
Plain fascia
Triple lesene
Semicircular torus moulding

REPRESENTATION OF DOME METALLING, CHURCH OF THE SORBONNE

YPES OF DOME

DOME OF THE
OCK, JERUSALEM,
RAEL, FROM C.684
HEMISPHERICAL
DOME)

CHURCH OF SANTA SOPHIA,
ISTANBUL, TURKEY, 532-537
(SAUCER DOME)

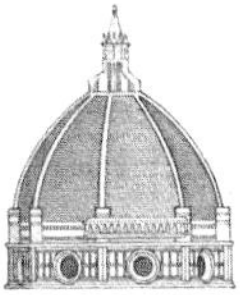

FLORENCE CATHEDRAL,
ITALY, 1420-1436
(POLYHEDRAL DOME)

ST. BASIL'S CATHEDRAL,
MOSCOW, RUSSIA,
1555-1561
(ONION DOME)

OME, ST. PAUL'S ATHEDRAL, LONDON, RITAIN, 1675-1710 3Y C. WREN)

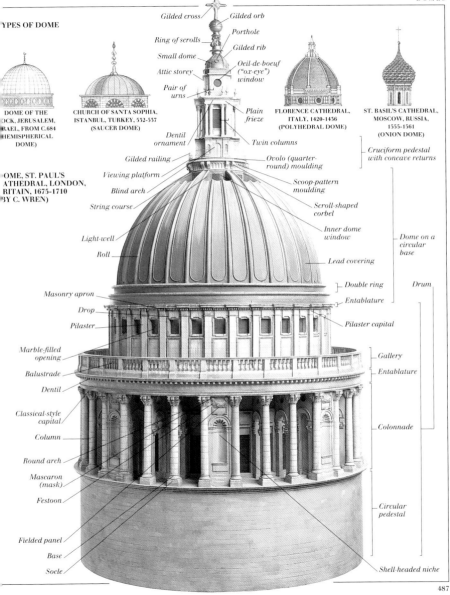

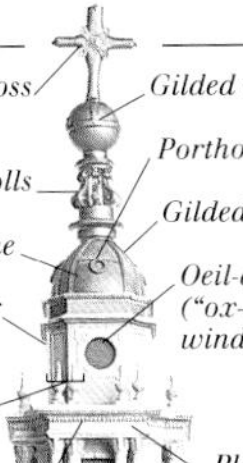
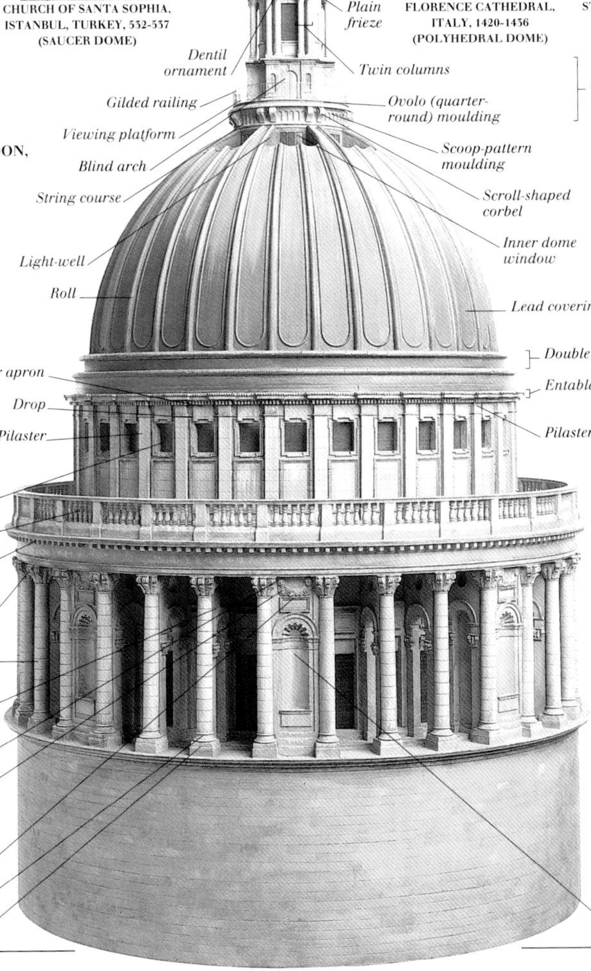
Gilded cross
Gilded orb
Porthole
Ring of scrolls
Gilded rib
Small dome
Oeil-de-boeuf ("ox-eye") window
Attic storey
Pair of urns
Plain frieze
Dentil ornament
Twin columns
Cruciform pedestal with concave returns
Gilded railing
Ovolo (quarter-round) moulding
Viewing platform
Scoop-pattern moulding
Blind arch
String course
Scroll-shaped corbel
Inner dome window
Light-well
Dome on a circular base
Roll
Lead covering
Double ring
Drum
Masonry apron
Entablature
Drop
Pilaster
Pilaster capital
Marble-filled opening
Gallery
Balustrade
Entablature
Dentil
Classical-style capital
Colonnade
Column
Round arch
Mascaron (mask)
Festoon
Circular pedestal
Fielded panel
Base
Socle
Shell-headed niche

Islamic buildings

OPUS SECTILE MOSAIC DESIGN

THE ISLAMIC RELIGION was founded by the prophet Mohammed, who was born in Mecca (in present-day Saudi Arabia) about 570 AD. In the following three centuries, Islam spread from Arabia to North Africa and Spain, as well as to India and much of the rest of Asia. The worldwide influence of Islam remains strong today. Common characteristics of Islamic buildings include ogee arches and roofs, onion domes, and walls decorated with carved stone, paintings, inlays, or mosaics. The most important type of Islamic building is the mosque – the place of worship – which generally has a minaret (tower) from which the muezzin (official crier) calls Muslims to prayer. Most mosques have a mihrab (decorative niche) that indicates the direction of Mecca. As figurative art is not allowed in Islam, buildings are ornamented with geometric and arabesque motifs, and inscriptions (frequently Koranic verses).

Bud-like onion dome
Depressed arch surrounding mihrab
Painted roof pavilion
Lotus-flower pendentive
Arabic inscripti
Turkish-crescent finial
Crest
Painted minaret with censer (incense burner)
Spandrel
Series of recessed arches
Semi-dome
Arched niche within a niche
Mural resembling tomb
Polyhedral niche
Recessed colonette

MIHRAB, JAMI MASJID (PRINCIPAL OR CONGREGATIONAI MOSQUE), BIJAPUR, INDIA, c.1636

Shield
Herring-bone pattern
Tablet flower
Spandrel with floral design
Ogee arch
Carved stone
Undulating band
Cusp
Volute
Impost
Capital with stylized floral design
Panel with fret pattern
Band with Arabic inscriptions praising Allah (God)
Attached colonette
Jali (latticed screen) with geometrical patterns

ARCH, THE ALHAMBRA, GRANADA, SPAIN, 1333-1354

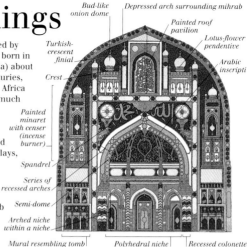

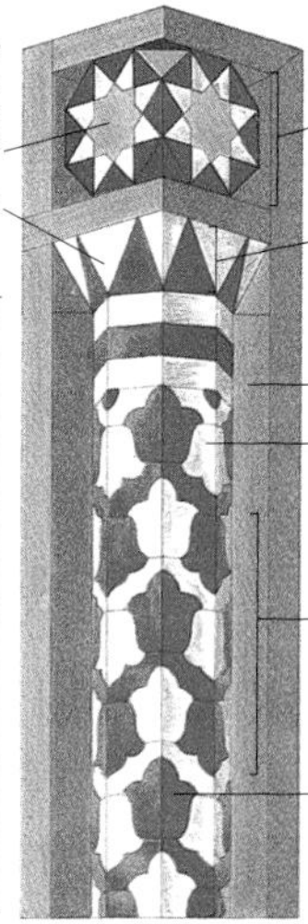

Enamelled turquoise earthenware tile
Cube with chamfered corners
Trigon
Polygonal capital
Niche
Enamelled white earthenware tile
Column shaft
Arabesques of stylized plants
Enamelled lapis blue earthenware tile

MIHRAB WITH COLUMN, EL-AINYI MOSQUE, CAIRO, EGYPT, 15TH CENTURY

EXAMPLES OF ISLAMIC MOSAICS, EGYPT AND SYRIA

Star-shaped motif
Greek cross of red marble
Triangle of yellow marble
Rhombus of black marble
Stone band

STAR AND GREEK-CROSS MOSAIC

Stone
Black marble
Mosaic tessellation
Turquoise glass
Tessera (small mosaic piece)

FRET-PATTERN MOSAIC

Greek cross of black and yellow marble
Star-shaped motif
Stone band
Rhombus of red marble

STAR AND GREEK-CROSS MOSAIC

Parallelogram of black marble
Symmetrical quadrilateral of stone
Triangle of yellow marble
Star-shaped motif
Rhombus of red marble

MOSAIC OF HEXAGONS, TRIANGLES, AND SYMMETRICAL QUADRILATERALS

Hexagonal design
Band of black marble
Band of stone

HEXAGON AND BAND MOSAIC

Triangle of turquoise glass
Parallelogram of mother-of-pearl

DANCETTE-PATTERN MOSAIC

Symmetrical quadrilateral of black marble
Hexagon of red marble
Triangle of stone

MOSAIC OF HEXAGONS, TRIANGLES, AND SYMMETRICAL QUADRILATERALS

MARBLE TOMB OF ITIMAD-UD-DAULA, AGRA, INDIA, c.1622-1628

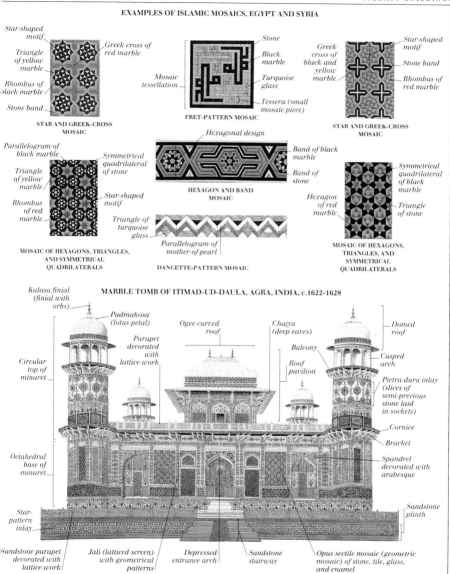

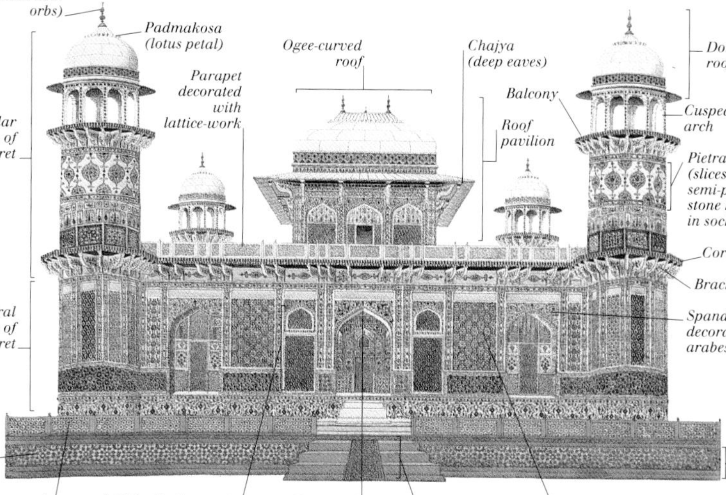

Kalasa finial (finial with orbs)
Padmakosa (lotus petal)
Ogee-curved roof
Chajya (deep eaves)
Domed roof
Parapet decorated with lattice-work
Balcony
Cusped arch
Circular top of minaret
Roof pavilion
Pietra dura inlay (slices of semi-precious stone laid in sockets)
Cornice
Bracket
Octahedral base of minaret
Spandrel decorated with arabesque
Star-pattern inlay
Sandstone plinth
Sandstone parapet decorated with lattice-work
Jali (latticed screen) with geometrical patterns
Depressed entrance arch
Sandstone stairway
Opus sectile mosaic (geometric mosaic) of stone, tile, glass, and enamel

South and east Asia

THE TRADITIONAL ARCHITECTURE of south and east Asia has been profoundly influenced by the spread from India of Buddhism and Hinduism. This influence is shown both by the abundance and by the architectural styles of temples and shrines in the region. Many early Hindu temples consist of rooms carved from solid rock-faces. However, free-standing structures began to be built in southern India from about the eighth century AD. Many were built in the Dravidian style, like the Temple of Virupaksha (opposite) with its characteristic antarala (terraced tower), perforated windows, and numerous arches, pilasters, and carvings. The earliest Buddhist religious monuments were Indian stupas, which consisted of a single hemispherical dome surmounted by a chattravali (shaft) and surrounded by railings with ornate gates. Later Indian stupas and those built elsewhere were sometimes modified; for example, in Sri Lanka, the dome became bell-shaped, and was called a dagoba. Buddhist pagodas, such as the Burmese example (right), are multistoreyed temples, each storey having a projecting roof. The form of these buildings probably derived from the yasti (pointed spire) of the stupa. Another feature of many traditional Asian buildings is their imaginative roof-forms, such as gambrel (mansard) roofs, and roofs with angle-rafters (below).

SEVEN-STOREYED PAGODA IN BURMESE STYLE, c.9TH-10TH CENTURY

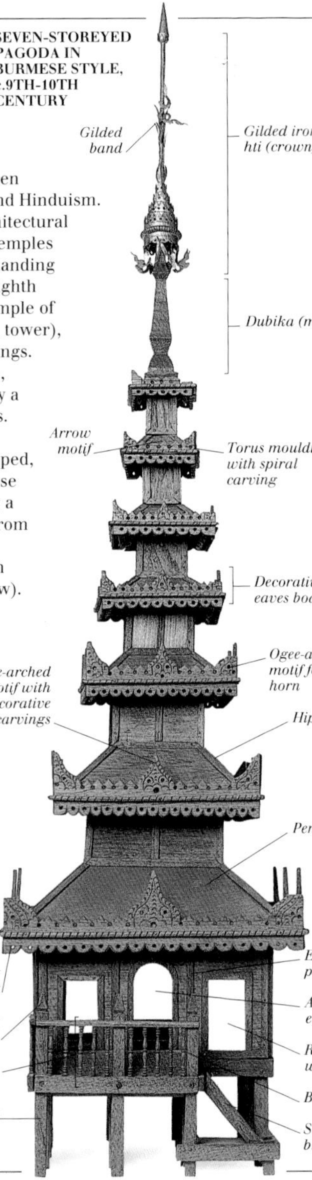

Gilded band
Gilded iron hti (crown)
Dubika (mast)
Arrow motif
Torus moulding with spiral carving
Decorative eaves board
Ogee-arched motif with decorative carvings
Ogee-arched motif forming horn
Hip-rafter
Pentroof
Engaged pillar
Undulating moulding
Arched entrance
Baluster finial
Rectangul window
Balustrade
Baluster
Pillar
Straight brace

DETAILS FROM EAST ASIAN BUILDINGS

KASUGA-STYLE ROOF WITH SUMIGI (ANGLE-RAFTERS), KASUGADO SHRINE OF ENJOJI, NARA, JAPAN, 12TH-14TH CENTURY

TERRACES, TEMPLE OF HEAVEN, BEIJING, CHINA, 15TH CENTURY

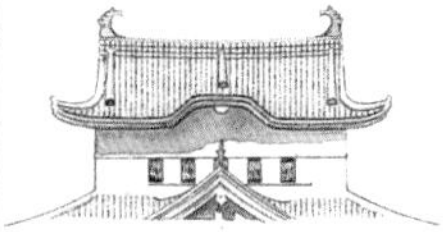

GAMBREL (MANSARD) ROOF WITH UPSWEPT EAVES AND UNDULATING GABLES, HIMEJI CASTLE, HIMEJI, JAPAN, 1608-1609

CORNER CAPITAL WITH ROOF BEAMS, POPCHU-SA TEMPLE, POPCHU-SA, SOUTH KOREA, 17TH CENTURY

ERFORATED STONE WINDOWS, TEMPLES OF VIRUPAKSHA ND MALLIKARJUNA, PATTADAKAL, INDIA, 8TH CENTURY

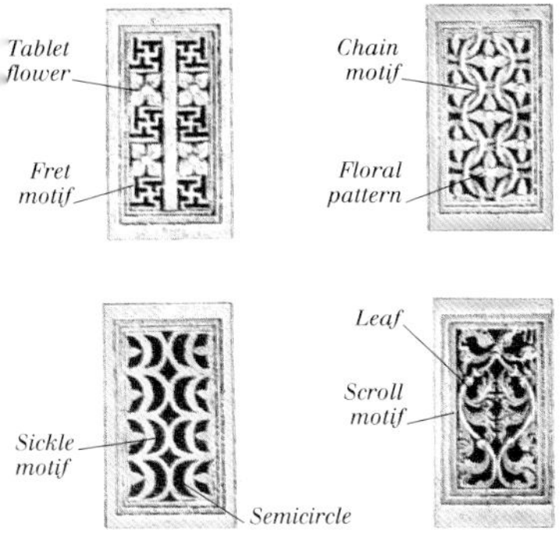
Tablet flower
Fret motif
Chain motif
Floral pattern
Leaf
Scroll motif
Sickle motif
Semicircle

DAGOBA STUPA, KANDY, SRI LANKA, c.2ND CENTURY BC-7TH CENTURY AD

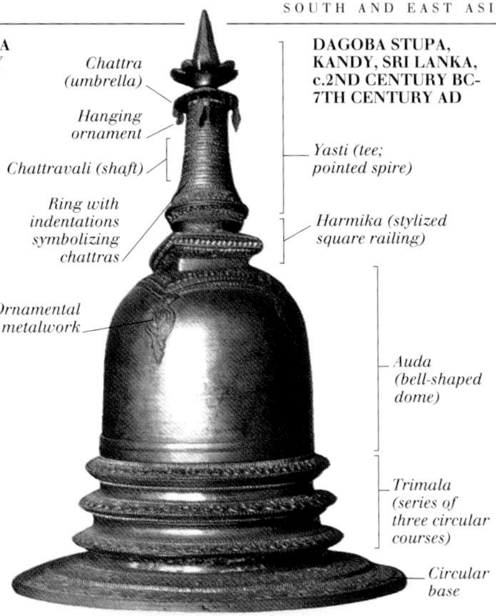
Chattra (umbrella)
Hanging ornament
Chattravali (shaft)
Ring with indentations symbolizing chattras
Ornamental metalwork
Yasti (tee; pointed spire)
Harmika (stylized square railing)
Auda (bell-shaped dome)
Trimala (series of three circular courses)
Circular base

IDE VIEW AND LAN VIEW, EMPLE OF IRUPAKSHA, ATTADAKAL, NDIA, c.746

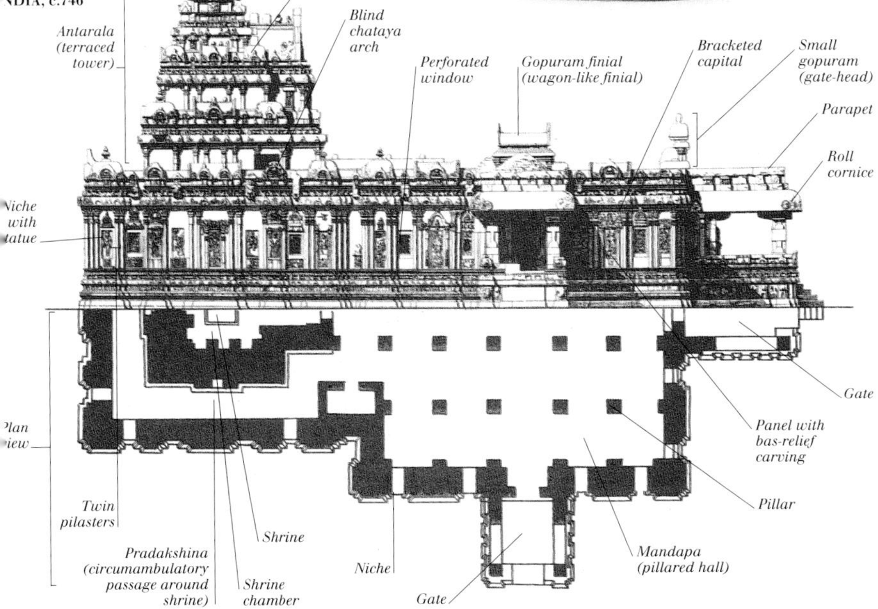
Stupica (small stupa) of the Dravidian order
Dravidian finial
Blind chataya arch
Antarala (terraced tower)
Perforated window
Gopuram finial (wagon-like finial)
Bracketed capital
Small gopuram (gate-head)
Parapet
Roll cornice
Niche with tatue
Gate
Panel with bas-relief carving
Pillar
lan iew
Twin pilasters
Shrine
Pradakshina (circumambulatory passage around shrine)
Shrine chamber
Niche
Gate
Mandapa (pillared hall)

The 19th century

BUILDINGS OF THE 19TH CENTURY are characterized by the use of new materials and by a great diversity of architectural styles. From the end of the 18th century, iron and steel became widely used as alternatives to wood for the framework of buildings, as in the flax-spinning mill shown here. Built in Britain in 1796, this mill exemplifies an architectural style that became common throughout the industrialized world for more than a century. The Industrial Revolution also brought mass-production of building parts – a development that enabled the British architect Sir Joseph Paxton to erect London's Crystal Palace (a building made entirely of iron and glass) in only nine months, ready for the Great Exhibition of 1851. The 19th century saw a widespread revival of older architectural styles. For example, in the USA and Germany, Neo-Greek architecture was fashionable; in Britain and France, Neo-Baroque, Neo-Byzantine, and Neo-Gothic styles (as seen in the Palace of Westminster and Tower Bridge) were dominant.

SECTION THROUGH A FLAX-SPINNING MILL

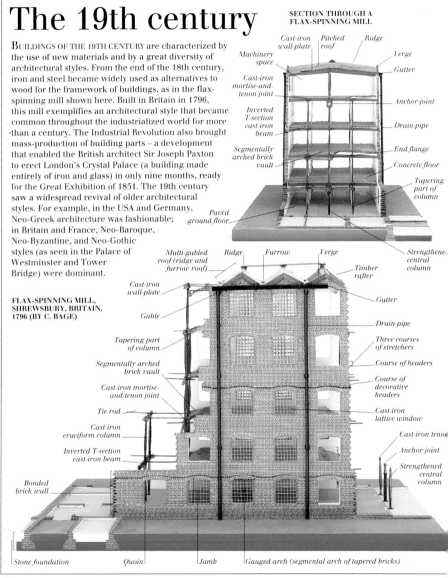

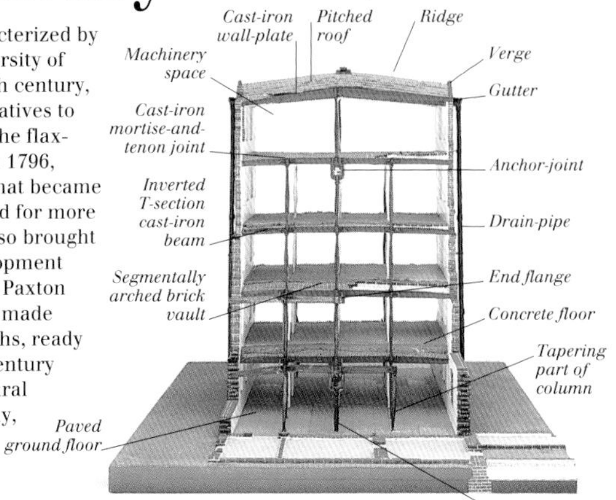
Cast-iron wall-plate
Pitched roof
Ridge
Machinery space
Verge
Gutter
Cast-iron mortise-and-tenon joint
Anchor-joint
Inverted T-section cast-iron beam
Drain-pipe
Segmentally arched brick vault
End flange
Concrete floor
Tapering part of column
Paved ground floor
Strengthene central column

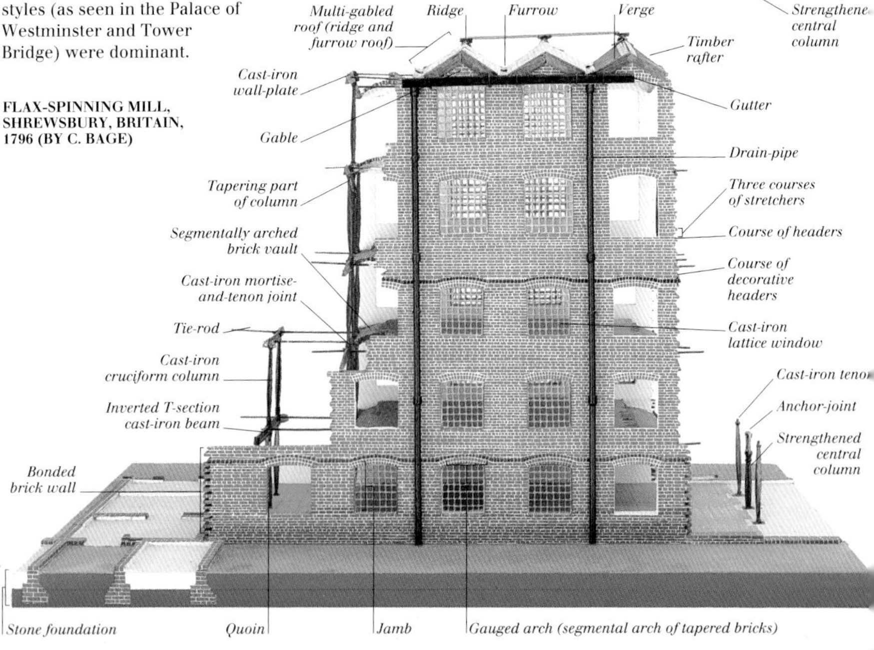
Multi-gabled roof (ridge and furrow roof)
Ridge
Furrow
Verge
Timber rafter
Cast-iron wall-plate
Gutter
Gable
Drain-pipe
Tapering part of column
Three courses of stretchers
Course of headers
Segmentally arched brick vault
Course of decorative headers
Cast-iron mortise-and-tenon joint
Tie-rod
Cast-iron lattice window
Cast-iron cruciform column
Cast-iron teno
Anchor-joint
Inverted T-section cast-iron beam
Strengthened central column
Bonded brick wall
Stone foundation
Quoin
Jamb
Gauged arch (segmental arch of tapered bricks)

FLAX-SPINNING MILL, SHREWSBURY, BRITAIN, 1796 (BY C. BAGE)

CLOCK TOWER ("BIG BEN"), PALACE OF WESTMINSTER, LONDON, BRITAIN, 1836-1868 (BY C. BARRY AND A.W.N. PUGIN)

Finial
Spire
Skylight
Iron tracery
Dormer window
Cornice
with
shields
Round arch filled with open tracery
Tetrahedral spire
Iron
Bell chamber
Balustrade
orb
Orb
Ogee tracery arch filled with trefoil
Flying buttress
Pinnacle
Spandrel
Octahedral shaft with billet decoration
Dial
Cornice
Moulded corbel
Star-shaped corner buttress
Panelled field filled with tracery
Slender diagonal buttress
Narrow window
String course
Carved panel

DETAILS FROM BUILDINGS IN REVIVALIST STYLES

CUPOLA, MERCHANTS' EXCHANGE, PHILADELPHIA, USA, 1832-1834 (NEO-GREEK)

SCULPTURE AND PEDIMENT, OPERA HOUSE, PARIS, FRANCE, 1861-1874 (NEO-BAROQUE)

DOMED TURRET, WESTMINSTER CATHEDRAL, LONDON, BRITAIN, 1894-1903 (NEO-BYZANTINE)

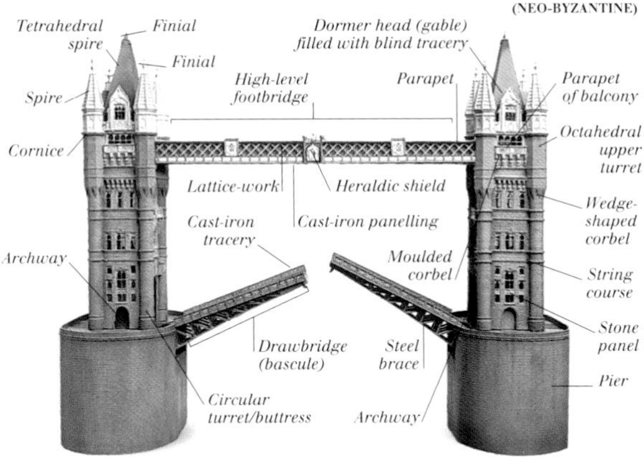
Tetrahedral spire
Finial
Finial
Spire
Cornice
High-level footbridge
Lattice-work
Heraldic shield
Cast-iron panelling
Cast-iron tracery
Archway
Drawbridge (bascule)
Circular turret/buttress
Dormer head (gable) filled with blind tracery
Parapet
Parapet of balcony
Octahedral upper turret
Wedge-shaped corbel
Moulded corbel
String course
Stone panel
Steel brace
Pier
Archway

TOWER BRIDGE, LONDON, BRITAIN, 1886-1894 (BY H. JONES)

CRYSTAL PALACE EXHIBITION HALL, LONDON, BRITAIN, 1851 (BY J. PAXTON)

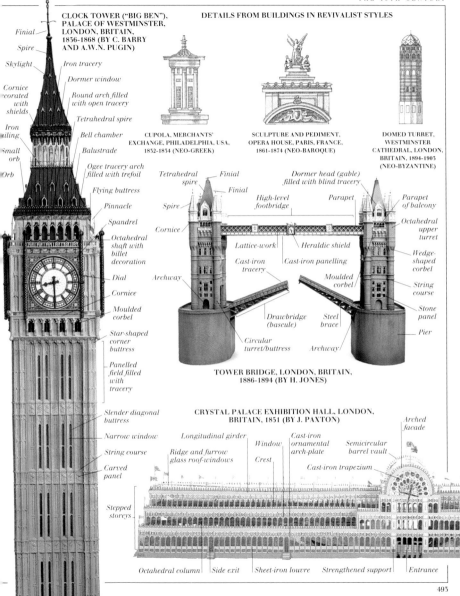

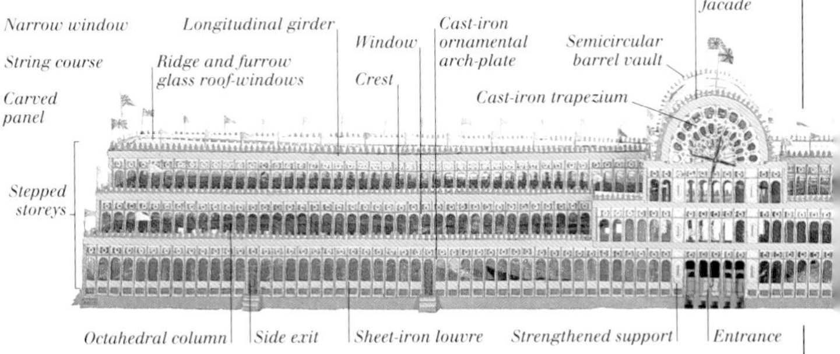
Longitudinal girder
Window
Cast-iron ornamental arch-plate
Semicircular barrel vault
Arched facade
Ridge and furrow glass roof-windows
Crest
Cast-iron trapezium
Stepped storeys
Octahedral column
Side exit
Sheet-iron louvre
Strengthened support
Entrance

The early 20th century

ARCHITECTURE OF THE EARLY 20TH CENTURY is notable for radical new types of steel-and-glass buildings – particularly skyscrapers – and the widespread use of steel-reinforced concrete. The steel-framed skyscraper was pioneered in Chicago in the 1880s, but did not become widespread until the first decades of the 20th century. As construction techniques were refined, skyscrapers became higher and higher; for example, the Empire State Building (right) of 1929-1931 has 102 storeys. Many buildings of this period were constructed from lightweight concrete slabs, which could be supported by cantilever beams or by pilotis (stilts), as in the Villa Savoye (below). The early 20th century also produced a great variety of architectural styles, some of which are illustrated opposite. Despite their diversity, the styles of this period generally had one thing in common: they were completely new, with few links to past architectural styles. This originality is in marked contrast to 19th-century architecture (see pp. 492-493), much of which was revivalist.

VILLA SAVOYE, POISSY, FRANCE, 1929-1931 (BY LE CORBUSIER)

TOP VIEW

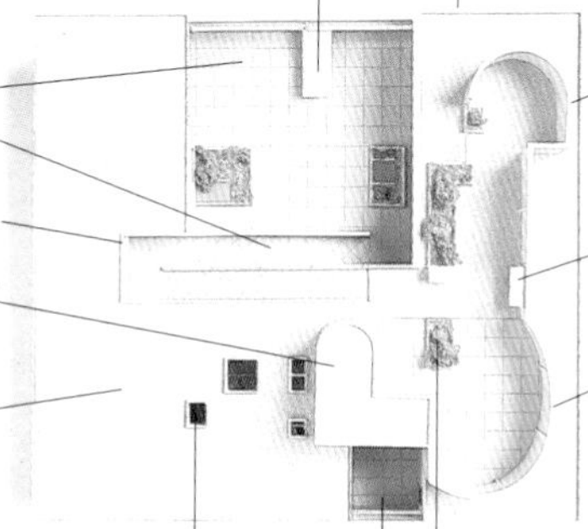
Fixed table
Parapet
Slab floor
Screen
Ramp
Handrail
Window-sill
Flat roof
Flat roof
Curved wall
Directional skylight
Terrace
Raised planting bed

SIDE VIEW

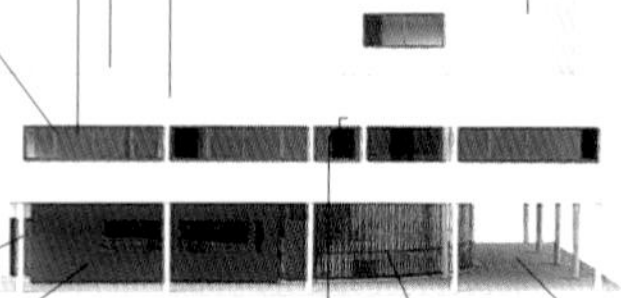
Terrace
Cement-rendered wall of lightweight slabs
Sliding pane of glass
Solarium
Mullion
Piano nobile (first floor)
Reinforced-concrete pilotis (stilt)
Rooms for staff
Ribbon window of long living-room
Curved glazing
Covered driveway

EMPIRE STATE BUILDING, NEW YORK, USA, 1929- (BY R. H. SHREVE T. LAMB, AND A. L. HARMON)

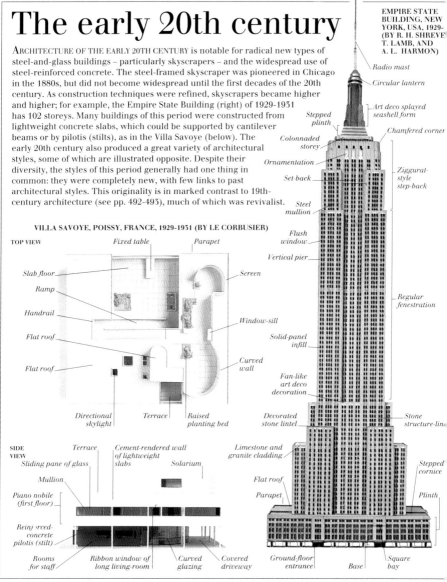

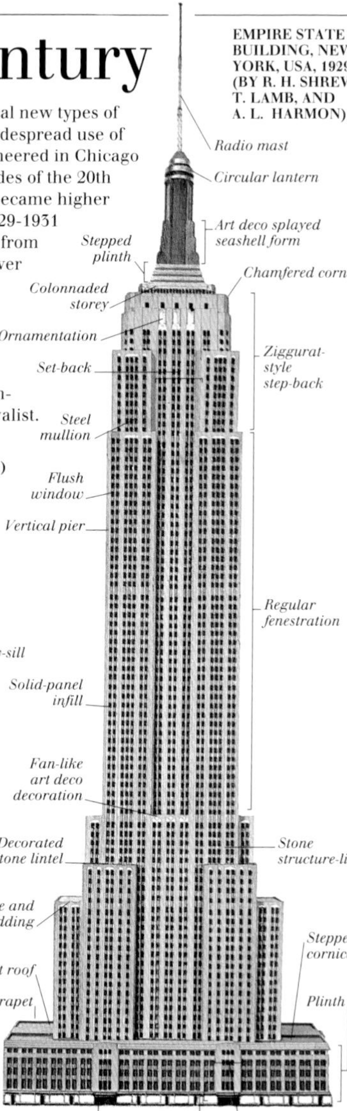
Radio mast
Circular lantern
Art deco splayed seashell form
Stepped plinth
Chamfered corner
Colonnaded storey
Ornamentation
Ziggurat-style step-back
Set-back
Steel mullion
Flush window
Vertical pier
Regular fenestration
Solid-panel infill
Fan-like art deco decoration
Decorated stone lintel
Stone structure-lin
Limestone and granite cladding
Stepped cornice
Flat roof
Parapet
Plinth
Ground-floor entrance
Base
Square bay

MIDWAY GARDENS, CHICAGO, USA, 1914 (BY F. L. WRIGHT)

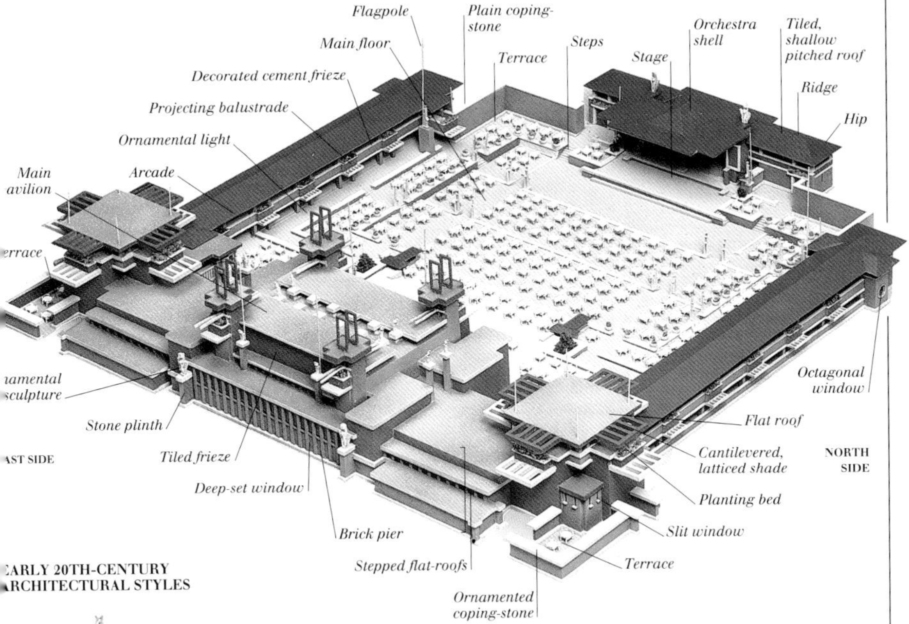
Flagpole
Plain coping-stone
Main floor
Steps
Orchestra shell
Tiled, shallow pitched roof
Terrace
Stage
Decorated cement frieze
Ridge
Projecting balustrade
Hip
Ornamental light
Main avilion
Arcade
errace
ıamental sculpture
Stone plinth
Octagonal window
Flat roof
AST SIDE
Tiled frieze
Cantilevered, latticed shade
NORTH SIDE
Deep-set window
Planting bed
Slit window
Brick pier
Terrace
Stepped flat-roofs
Ornamented coping-stone

ARLY 20TH-CENTURY RCHITECTURAL STYLES

DORMER WINDOW, STUDIO ELVIRA, MUNICH, GERMANY, 1902 (ART NOUVEAU)

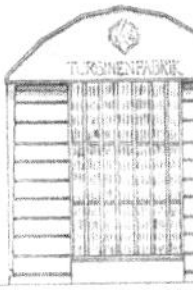

AEG TURBINE HALL, BERLIN, GERMANY, 1909 (DEUTSCHER WERKBUND)

ROBIE HOUSE, CHICAGO, USA, 1909-1910 (PRAIRIE STYLE)

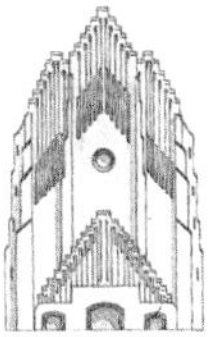

GRUNDTVIG CHURCH, OPENHAGEN, DENMARK, 1920 (EXPRESSIONIST)

VERTEX, CHRYSLER BUILDING, NEW YORK, USA, 1928-1930 (ART DECO)

TOWER, TOWN HALL, HILVERSUM, NETHERLANDS, 1930 (DUTCH CUBIST)

CASA DEL FASCIO, COMO, ITALY, 1932-1936 (GRUPPO SEVEN CUBIST)

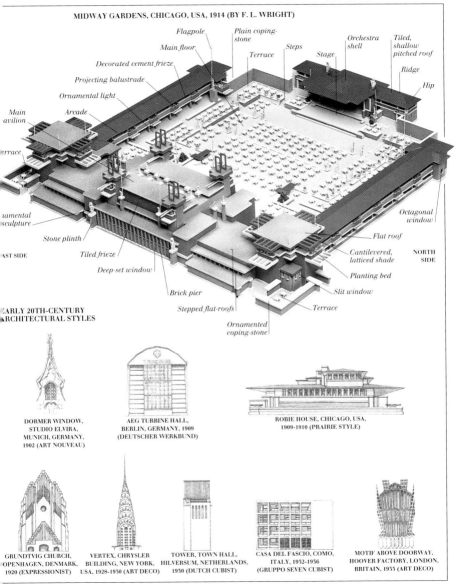

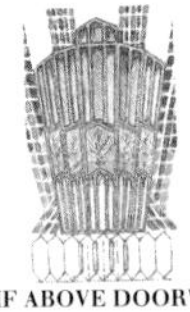

MOTIF ABOVE DOORWAY, HOOVER FACTORY, LONDON, BRITAIN, 1933 (ART DECO)

Modern buildings 1

ARCHITECTURE SINCE ABOUT THE 1950s is generally known as modern architecture. One of its main influences has been functionalism – a belief that a building's function should be apparent in its design. Both the Centre Georges Pompidou (below and opposite) and the Hong Kong and Shanghai Bank (see pp. 498-499) are functionalist buildings: on each, elements of engineering and the building's services are clearly visible on the outside. In the 1980s, some architects rejected functionalism in favour of post-modernism, in which historical styles – particularly neoclassicism – were revived, using modern building materials and techniques. In many modern buildings, walls are made of glass or concrete hung from a frame, as in the Kawana House (right); this type of wall construction is known as curtain walling. Other modern construction techniques include the intricate interlocking of concrete vaults – as in the Sydney Opera House (see pp. 498-499) – and the use of high-tension beams to create complex roof shapes, such as the paraboloid roof of the Church of St. Pierre de Libreville (see pp. 498-499).

KAWANA HOUSE, JAPAN, FROM 1987 (BY N. FOSTER)

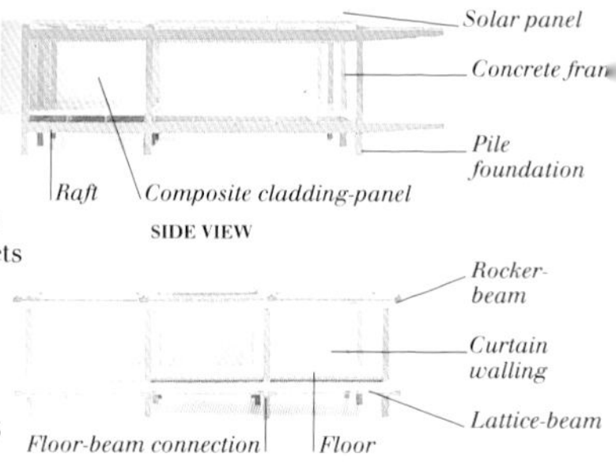
Solar panel
Concrete fram
Pile foundation
Raft
Composite cladding-panel
SIDE VIEW
Rocker-beam
Curtain walling
Lattice-beam
Floor-beam connection
Floor
FRONT VIEW

SERVICES FACADE, CENTRE GEORGES POMPIDOU, PARIS, FRANCE, 1977 (BY R. PIANO AND R. ROGERS)

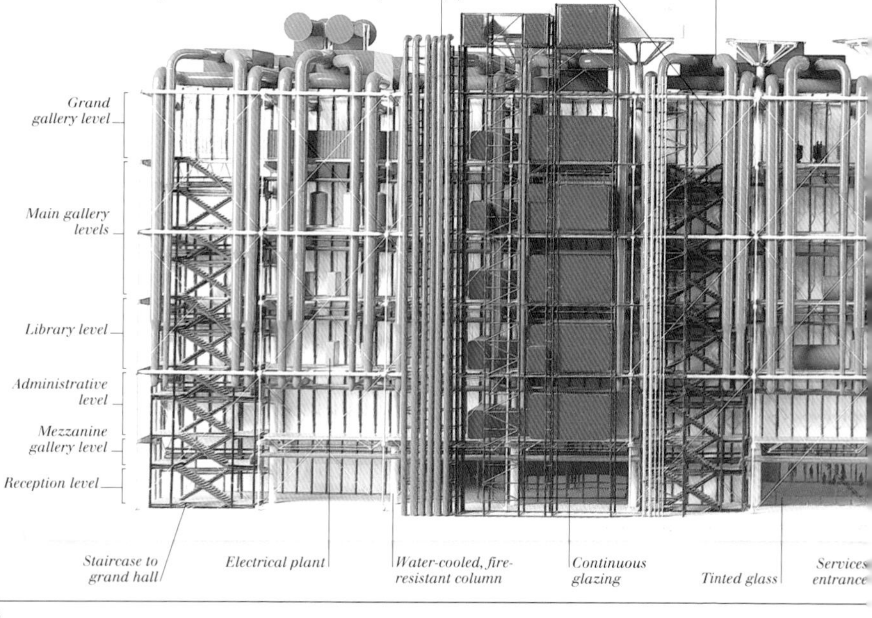
Metal-faced, fire-resistant panel
Air-conditioning duct
Cooling tower
Water-pipe
Grand gallery level
Main gallery levels
Library level
Administrative level
Mezzanine gallery level
Reception level
Staircase to grand hall
Electrical plant
Water-cooled, fire-resistant column
Continuous glazing
Tinted glass
Services entrance

PRINCIPAL FACADE, CENTRE GEORGES POMPIDOU

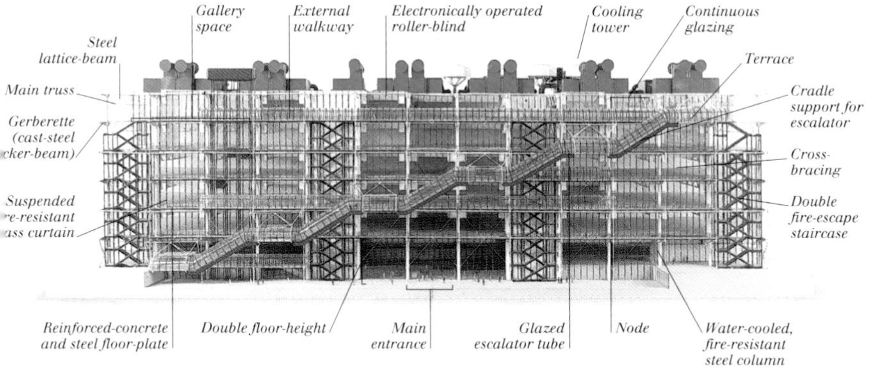
Gallery space
External walkway
Electronically operated roller-blind
Cooling tower
Continuous glazing
Steel lattice-beam
Terrace
Main truss
Cradle support for escalator
Gerberette (cast-steel cker-beam)
Cross-bracing
Suspended re-resistant ass curtain
Double fire-escape staircase
Reinforced-concrete and steel floor-plate
Double floor-height
Main entrance
Glazed escalator tube
Node
Water-cooled, fire-resistant steel column

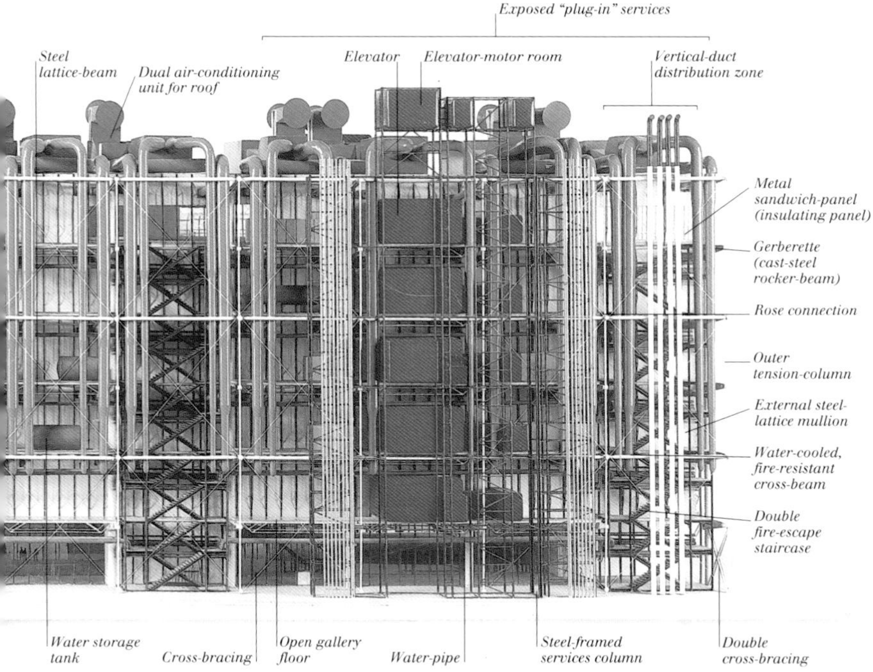
Exposed "plug-in" services
Steel lattice-beam
Dual air-conditioning unit for roof
Elevator
Elevator-motor room
Vertical-duct distribution zone
Metal sandwich-panel (insulating panel)
Gerberette (cast-steel rocker-beam)
Rose connection
Outer tension-column
External steel-lattice mullion
Water-cooled, fire-resistant cross-beam
Double fire-escape staircase
Water storage tank
Cross-bracing
Open gallery floor
Water-pipe
Steel-framed services column
Double cross-bracing

Modern buildings 2

HONG KONG AND SHANGHAI BANK, HONG KONG, 1981-1985 (BY N. FOSTER)

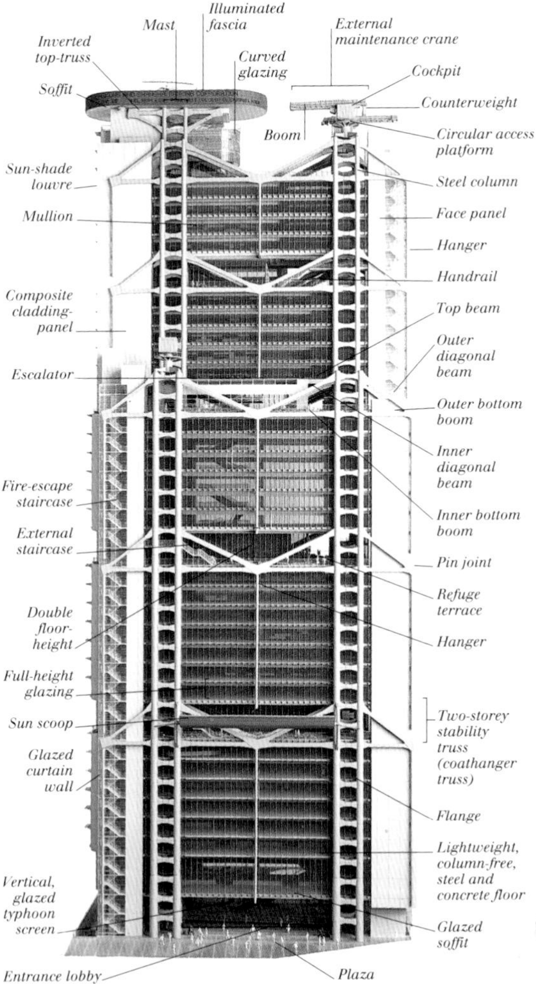
Mast
Illuminated fascia
Inverted top-truss
Curved glazing
External maintenance crane
Cockpit
Soffit
Counterweight
Boom
Circular access platform
Sun-shade louvre
Steel column
Mullion
Face panel
Hanger
Handrail
Composite cladding-panel
Top beam
Outer diagonal beam
Escalator
Outer bottom boom
Inner diagonal beam
Fire-escape staircase
Inner bottom boom
External staircase
Pin joint
Refuge terrace
Double floor-height
Hanger
Full-height glazing
Sun scoop
Two-storey stability truss (coathanger truss)
Glazed curtain wall
Flange
Lightweight, column-free, steel and concrete floor
Vertical, glazed typhoon screen
Glazed soffit
Entrance lobby
Plaza

SOUTH FACADE

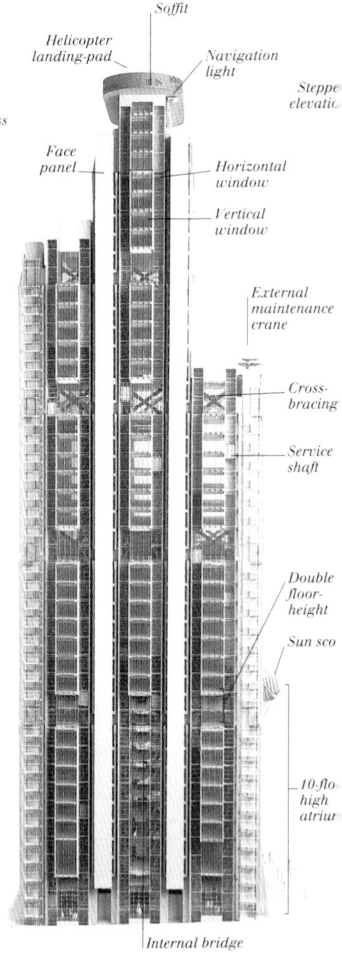
Soffit
Helicopter landing-pad
Navigation light
Face panel
Horizontal window
Vertical window
External maintenance crane
Cross-bracing
Service shaft
Double floor-height
Internal bridge

EAST SIDE

[C]HURCH OF ST. PIERRE, [L]IBREVILLE, GABON, 1990

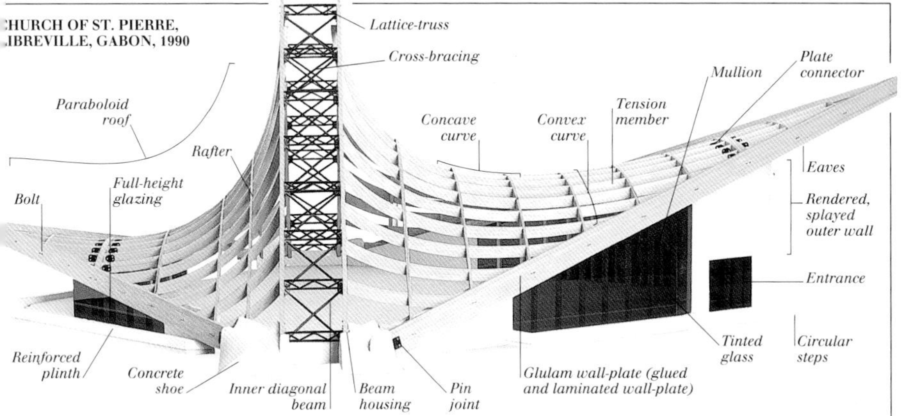

OPERA HOUSE, SYDNEY, AUSTRALIA, 1959-1973 (BY J. UTZON)

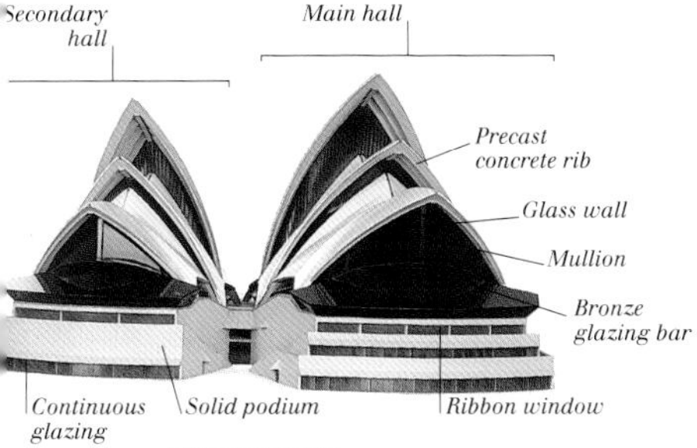

HARBOUR FACADE

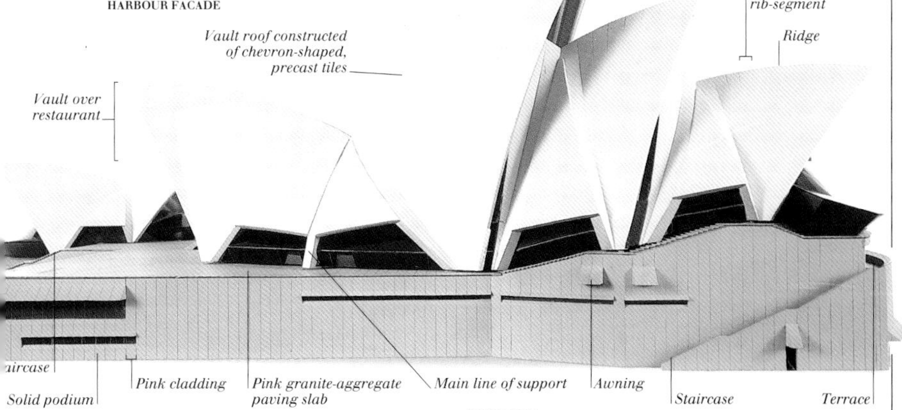

WEST SIDE

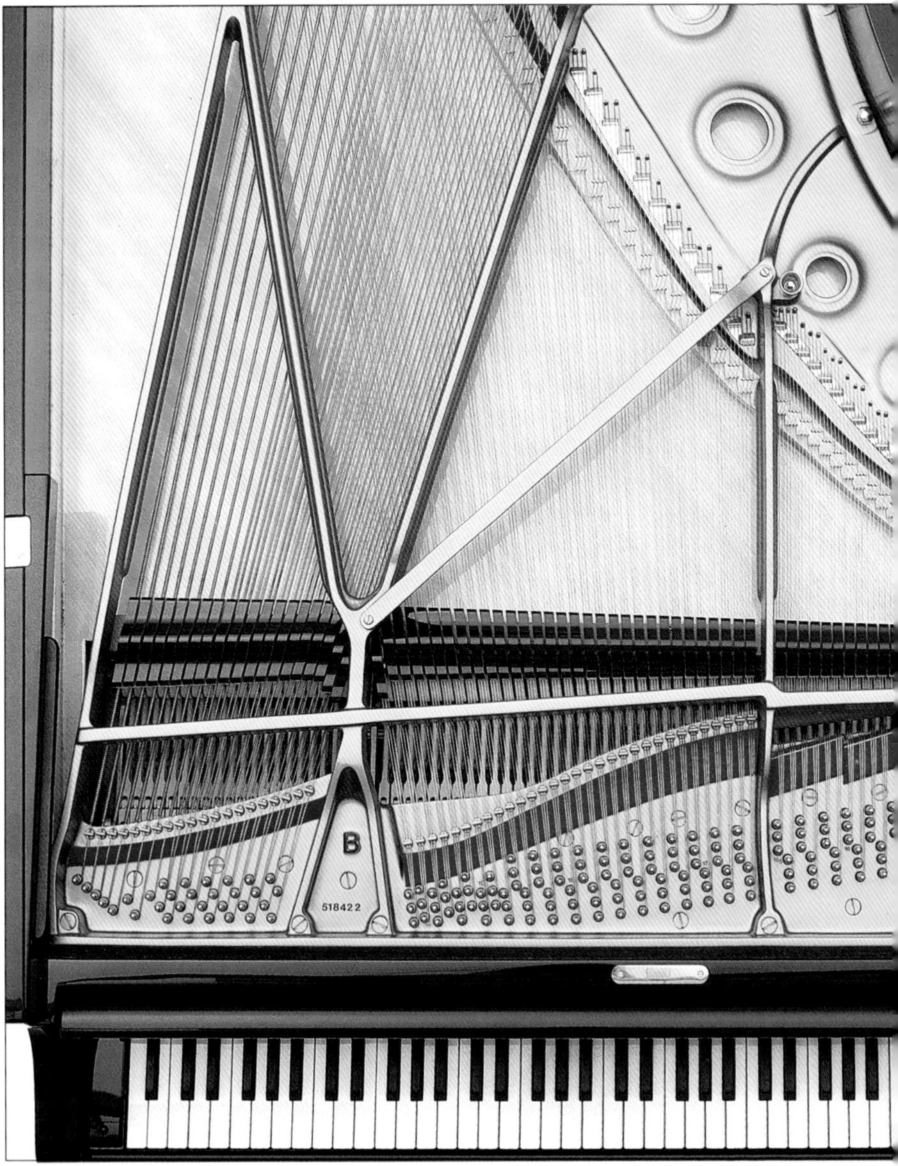
B
518422

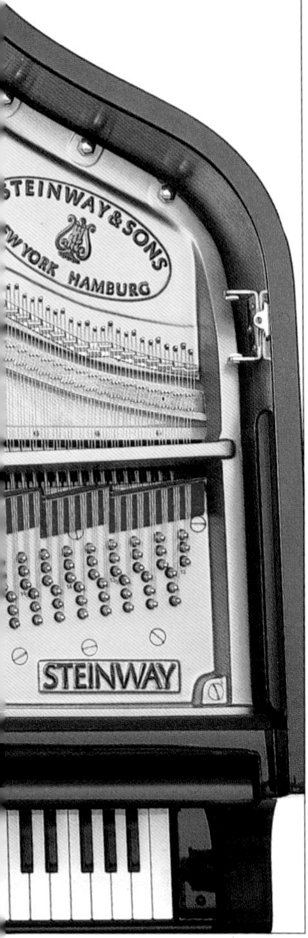
STEINWAY & SONS
NEW YORK HAMBURG
STEINWAY

Music

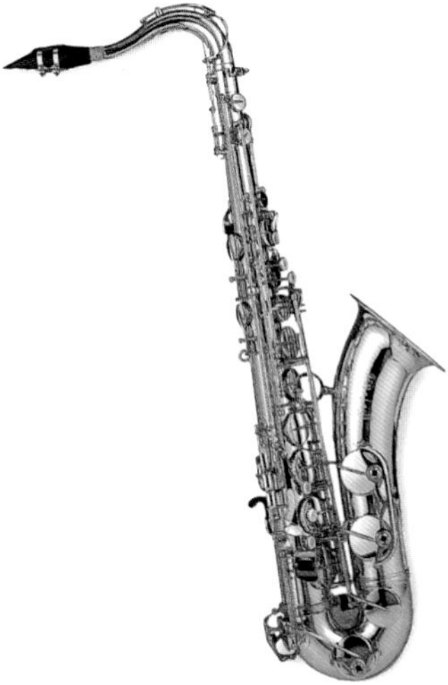

Musical notation

MUSICAL NOTATION IS ANY METHOD by which sounds are written down so that they can be read and performed by others. The present-day conventional system of notation uses a five-line stave (staff) – divided by vertical lines into sections known as bars – on which notes, rests, clefs, key signatures, time signatures, accidentals, and other symbols are written. A note indicates the duration of a sound and, according to its position on the stave, its pitch. Notes can be arranged on the stave in order of pitch to form a scale. A silence in the music is indicated by a rest. The clef, which is placed at the begininng of a stave, fixes the pitch. The key signature, which is placed after the clef, indicates the key. The time signature, placed after the key signature, shows the number of beats in a bar. Accidentals are used to indicate the raising or lowering of the pitch of a note.

ELEMENTS OF MUSICAL NOTATION

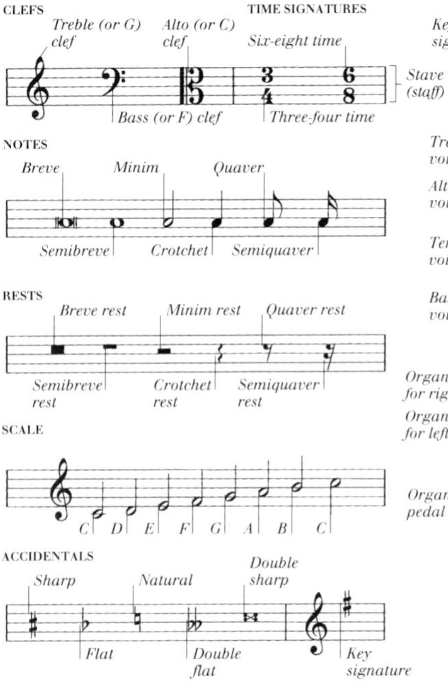
CLEFS
Treble (or G) clef
Alto (or C) clef
Bass (or F) clef
TIME SIGNATURES
Six-eight time
Three-four time
Stave (staff)
NOTES
Breve
Minim
Quaver
Semibreve
Crotchet
Semiquaver
RESTS
Breve rest
Minim rest
Quaver rest
Semibreve rest
Crotchet rest
Semiquaver rest
SCALE
C D E F G A B C
ACCIDENTALS
Sharp
Natural
Double sharp
Flat
Double flat
Key signature

EXAMPLE OF AN ORIGINAL MANUSCRIPT: THE PRODIGAL SON, ARTHUR SULLIVAN, 1869

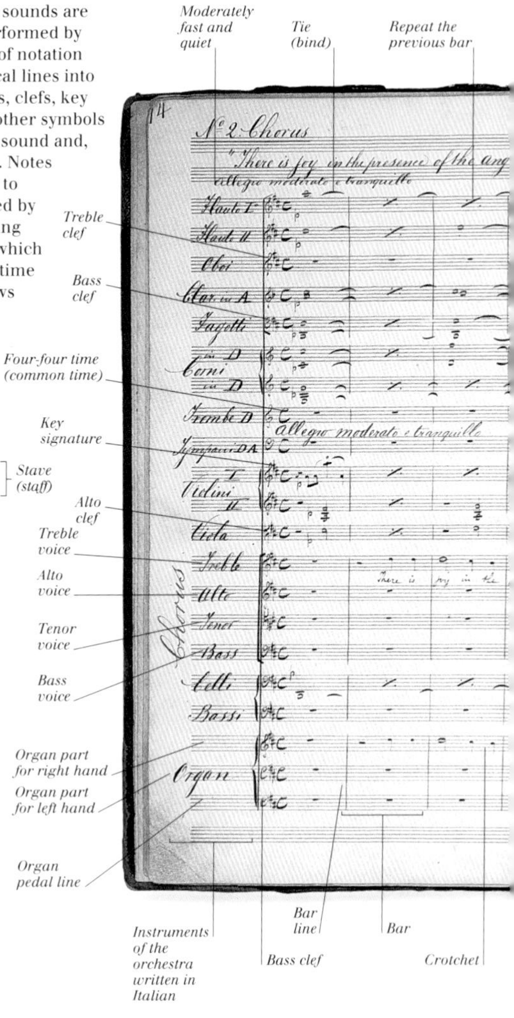
Moderately fast and quiet
Tie (bind)
Repeat the previous bar
Treble clef
Bass clef
Four-four time (common time)
Key signature
Alto clef
Treble voice
Alto voice
Tenor voice
Bass voice
Organ part for right hand
Organ part for left hand
Organ pedal line
Instruments of the orchestra written in Italian
Bass clef
Bar line
Bar
Crotchet

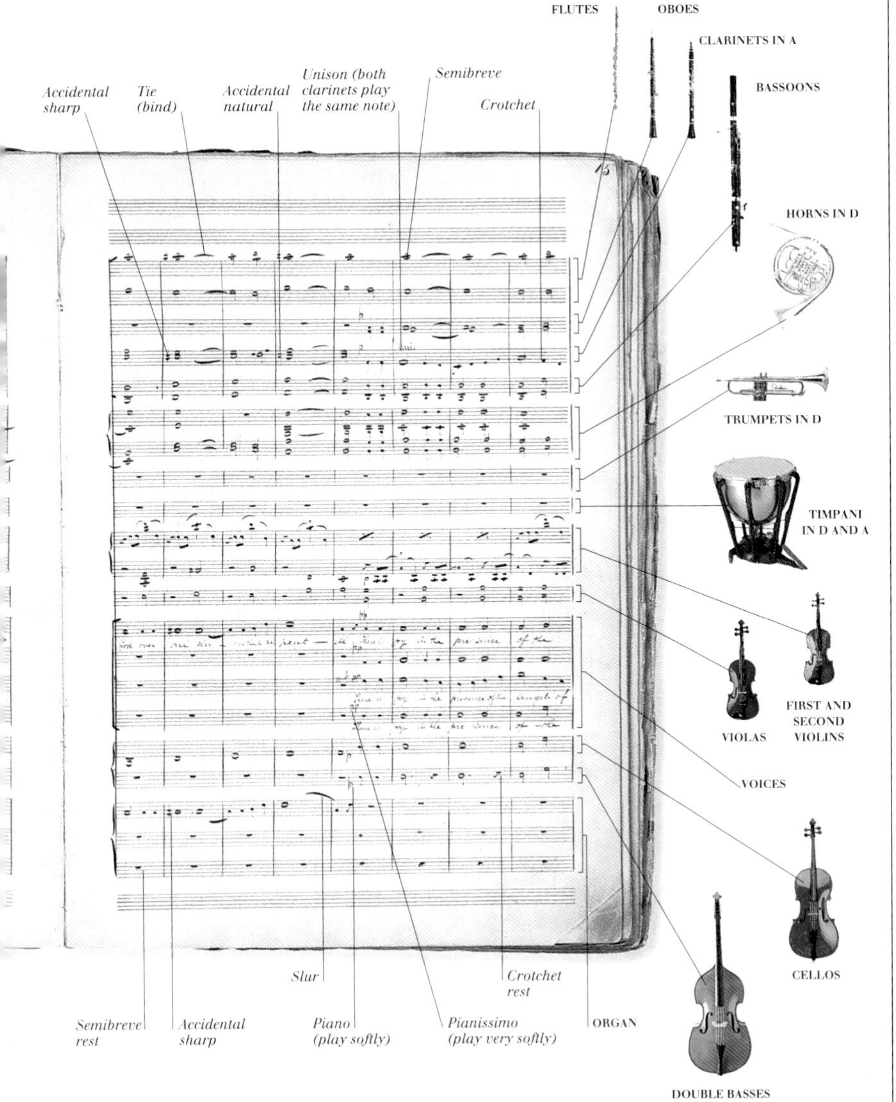
FLUTES
OBOES
CLARINETS IN A
BASSOONS
HORNS IN D
TRUMPETS IN D
TIMPANI IN D AND A
FIRST AND SECOND VIOLINS
VIOLAS
VOICES
CELLOS
DOUBLE BASSES
ORGAN
Accidental sharp
Tie (bind)
Accidental natural
Unison (both clarinets play the same note)
Semibreve
Crotchet
Slur
Crotchet rest
Semibreve rest
Accidental sharp
Piano (play softly)
Pianissimo (play very softly)

Orchestras

AN ORCHESTRA IS A GROUP of musicians that plays music written for a specific combination of instruments. The number and type of instruments included in the orchestra depends on the style of music being played. The modern orchestra (also known as a symphony orchestra) is made up of four sections of instruments – stringed, woodwind, brass, and percussion. The stringed section consists of violins, violas, cellos (violoncellos), double basses, and sometimes a harp (see pp. 510-511). The main instruments of the woodwind section are flutes, oboes, clarinets, and bassoons – the piccolo, cor anglais, bass clarinet, saxophone, and double bassoon (contrabassoon) can also be included if the music requires them (see pp. 508-509). The brass section usually consists of horns, trumpets, trombones, and the tuba (see pp. 506-507). The main instruments of the percussion section are the timpani (see pp. 518-519). The side drum, bass drum, cymbals, tambourine, triangle, tubular bells, xylophone, vibraphone, tam-tam (gong), castanets, and maracas can also be included in the percussion section (see pp. 516-517). The musicians are usually arranged in a semi-circle – strings spread along the front, woodwind and brass in the centre, and percussion at the back. A conductor stands in front of the musicians and controls the tempo (speed) of the music and the overall balance of the sound, ensuring that no instruments are too loud or too soft in relation to the others.

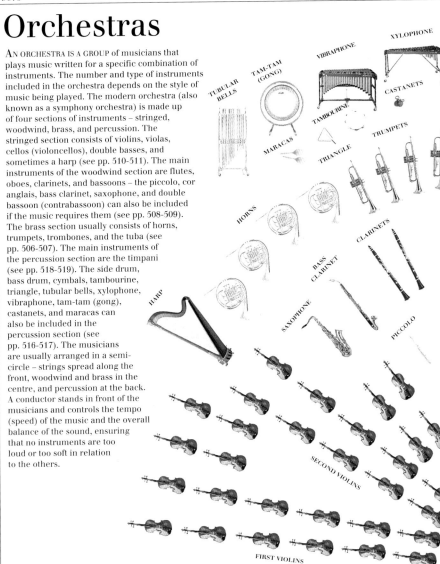

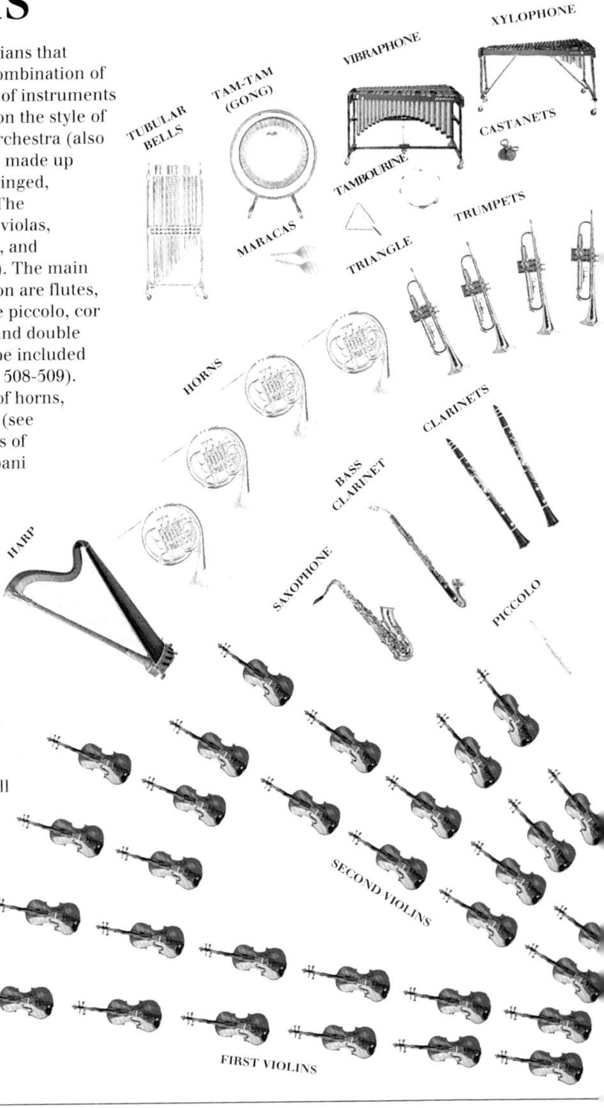
XYLOPHONE
VIBRAPHONE
TAM-TAM (GONG)
TUBULAR BELLS
CASTANETS
TAMBOURINE
MARACAS
TRIANGLE
TRUMPETS
HORNS
CLARINETS
BASS CLARINET
HARP
SAXOPHONE
PICCOLO
SECOND VIOLINS
FIRST VIOLINS

EXAMPLE OF A LAYOUT OF THE INSTRUMENTS FOR A MODERN (SYMPHONY) ORCHESTRA

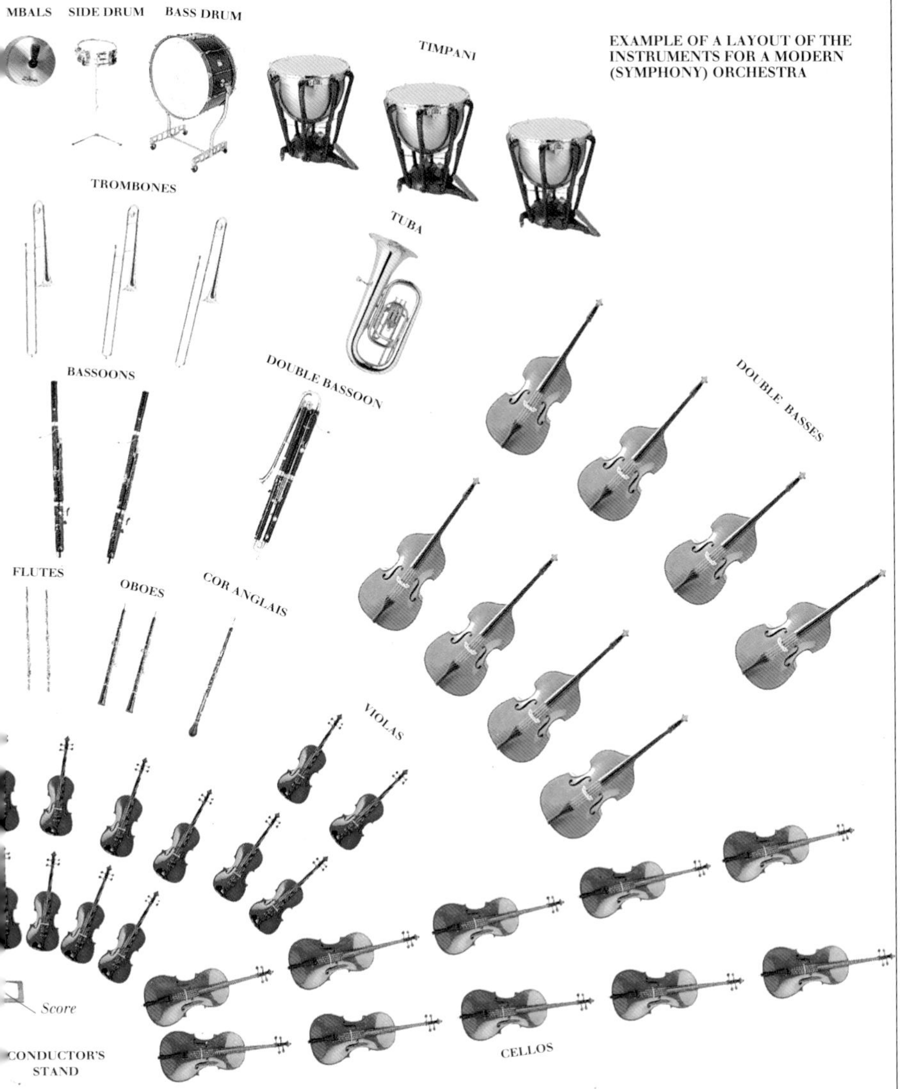
MBALS
SIDE DRUM
BASS DRUM
TIMPANI
TROMBONES
TUBA
BASSOONS
DOUBLE BASSOON
DOUBLE BASSES
FLUTES
OBOES
COR ANGLAIS
VIOLAS
Score
CONDUCTOR'S STAND
CELLOS

Brass instruments

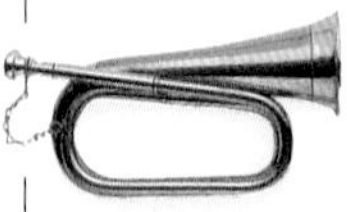

BUGLE

Brass instruments are wind instruments that are made of metal, usually brass. Although they appear in many different shapes and sizes, all brass instruments have a mouthpiece, a length of hollow tube, and a flared bell. The mouthpiece of a brass instrument may be cup-shaped, as in the cornet, or cone-shaped, as in the horn. The tube may be wide or narrow, mainly conical, as in the horn and tuba, or mainly cylindrical, as in the trumpet and trombone. The sound of a brass instrument is made by the player's lips vibrating against the mouthpiece, so that the air vibrates in the tube. By changing lip tension, the player can vary the vibrations and produce notes of different pitches. The range of notes produced by a brass instrument can be extended by means of a valve system. Most brass instruments, such as the trumpet, have piston valves that divert the air in the instrument along an extra piece of tubing (known as a valve slide) when pressed down. The total length of the tube is increased and the pitch of the note produced is lowered. Instead of valves, the trombone has a movable slide that can be pushed away from or drawn toward the player. The sound of a brass instrument can also be changed by inserting a mute into the bell of the instrument.

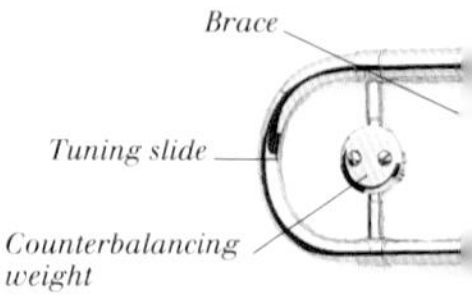
Brace
Tuning slide
Counterbalancing weight

SIMPLIFIED DIAGRAM SHOWING HOW A PISTON VALVE SYSTEM WORKS

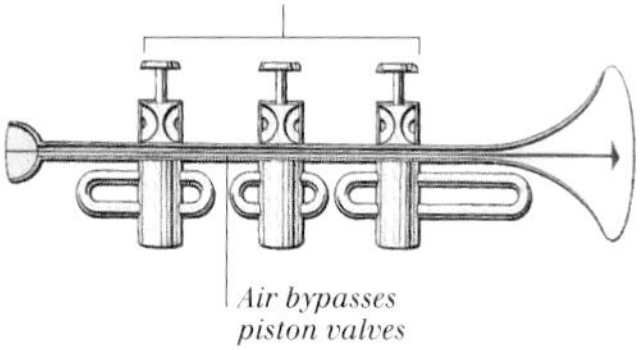
Piston valves at rest
Air bypasses piston valves

PISTON VALVES AT REST

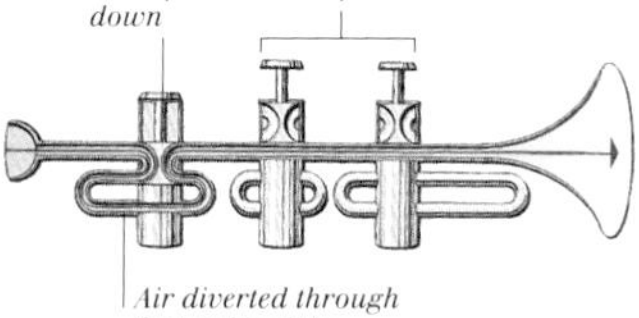
First piston valve pressed down
Second and third piston valves at rest
Air diverted through first valve slide

PISTON VALVE PRESSED DOWN

TRUMPET

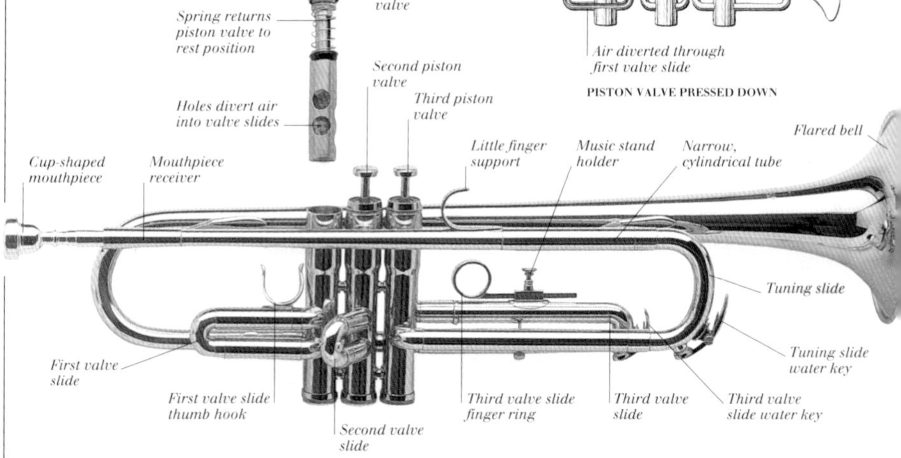
Finger button
First piston valve
Spring returns piston valve to rest position
Holes divert air into valve slides
Second piston valve
Third piston valve
Cup-shaped mouthpiece
Mouthpiece receiver
Little finger support
Music stand holder
Narrow, cylindrical tube
Flared bell
Tuning slide
Tuning slide water key
First valve slide
First valve slide thumb hook
Second valve slide
Third valve slide finger ring
Third valve slide
Third valve slide water key

SECTIONS OF A TROMBONE

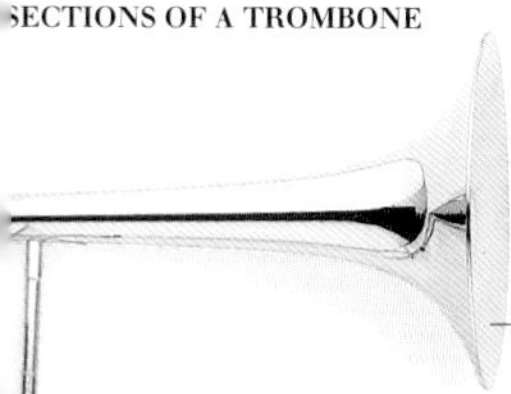
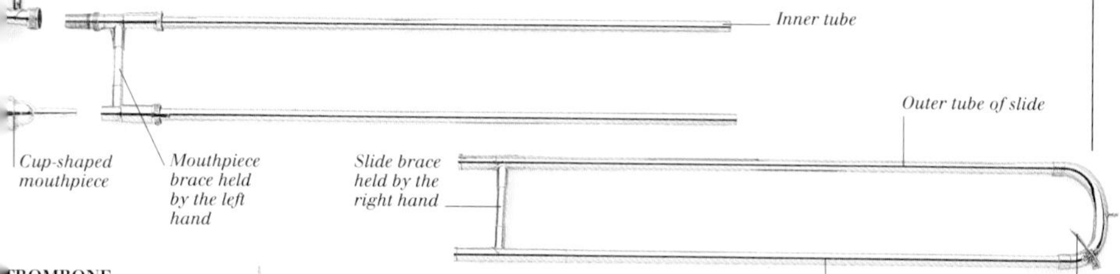
Flared bell
Inner tube
Outer tube of slide
Cup-shaped mouthpiece
Mouthpiece brace held by the left hand
Slide brace held by the right hand
Narrow, cylindrical tube
Water key

EXAMPLES OF MUTES

CUP MUTE
TENOR MUTE
ALTO MUTE

TROMBONE

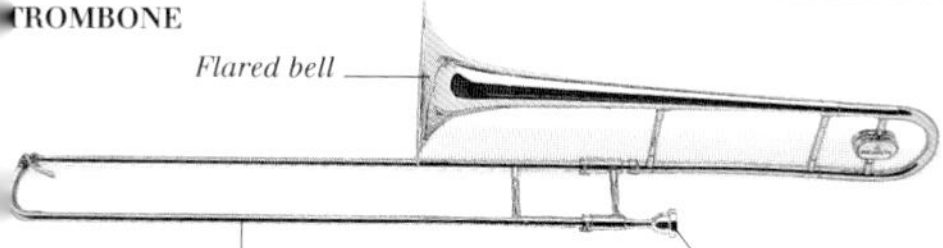
Flared bell
Outer tube of slide
Cup-shaped mouthpiece

FLUGELHORN

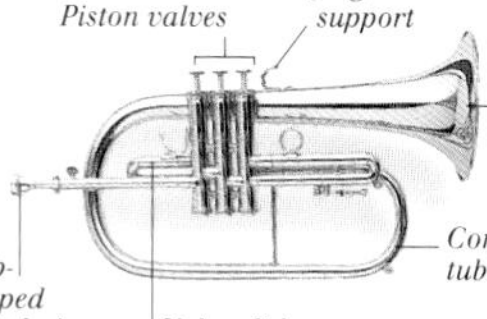
Little finger support
Piston valves
Flared bell
Conical tube
Cup-shaped mouthpiece
Valve slide

TUBA

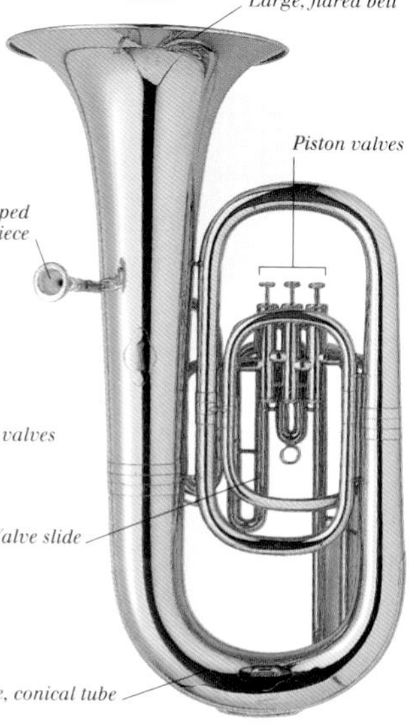
Large, flared bell
Piston valves
Cup-shaped mouthpiece
Valve slide
Wide, conical tube

HORN

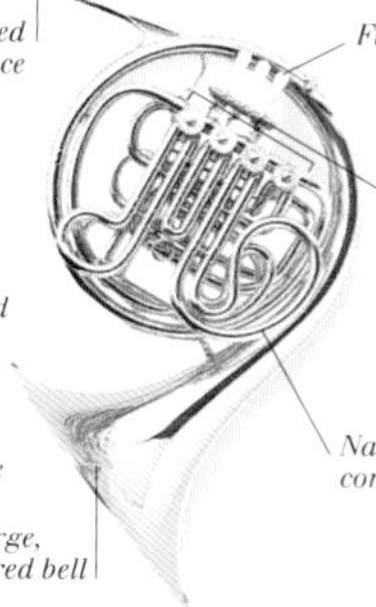
Cone-shaped mouthpiece
Finger key
Rotary valves
Narrow, conical bore
Large, flared bell

CORNET

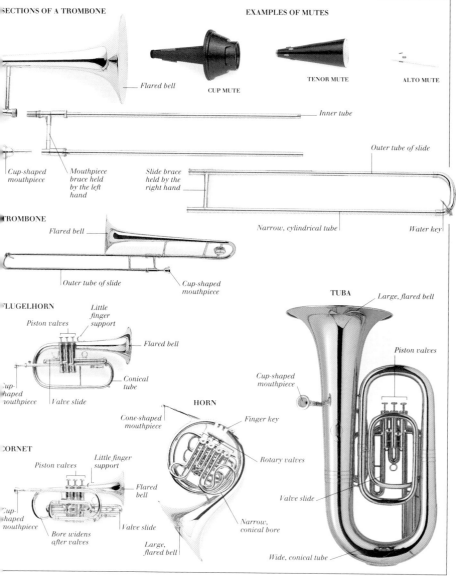

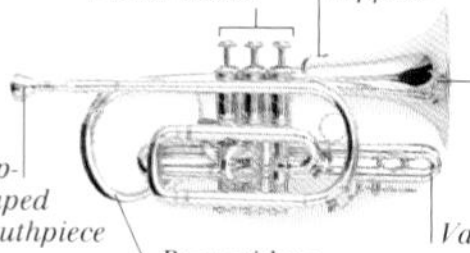
Piston valves
Little finger support
Flared bell
Cup-shaped mouthpiece
Valve slide
Bore widens after valves

Woodwind instruments

WOODWIND INSTRUMENTS ARE wind instruments that are generally made of wood, although some are made of metal or plastic. The sound of a woodwind instrument is produced by the vibration of air in a hollow tube. The air is made to vibrate by blowing across a blow hole – as in the flute and piccolo – or by blowing through a single reed – as in the clarinet and saxophone – or a double reed – as in the bassoon, cor anglais, and oboe. The pitch of a woodwind instrument can be changed by opening or closing holes cut into the tube of the instrument.

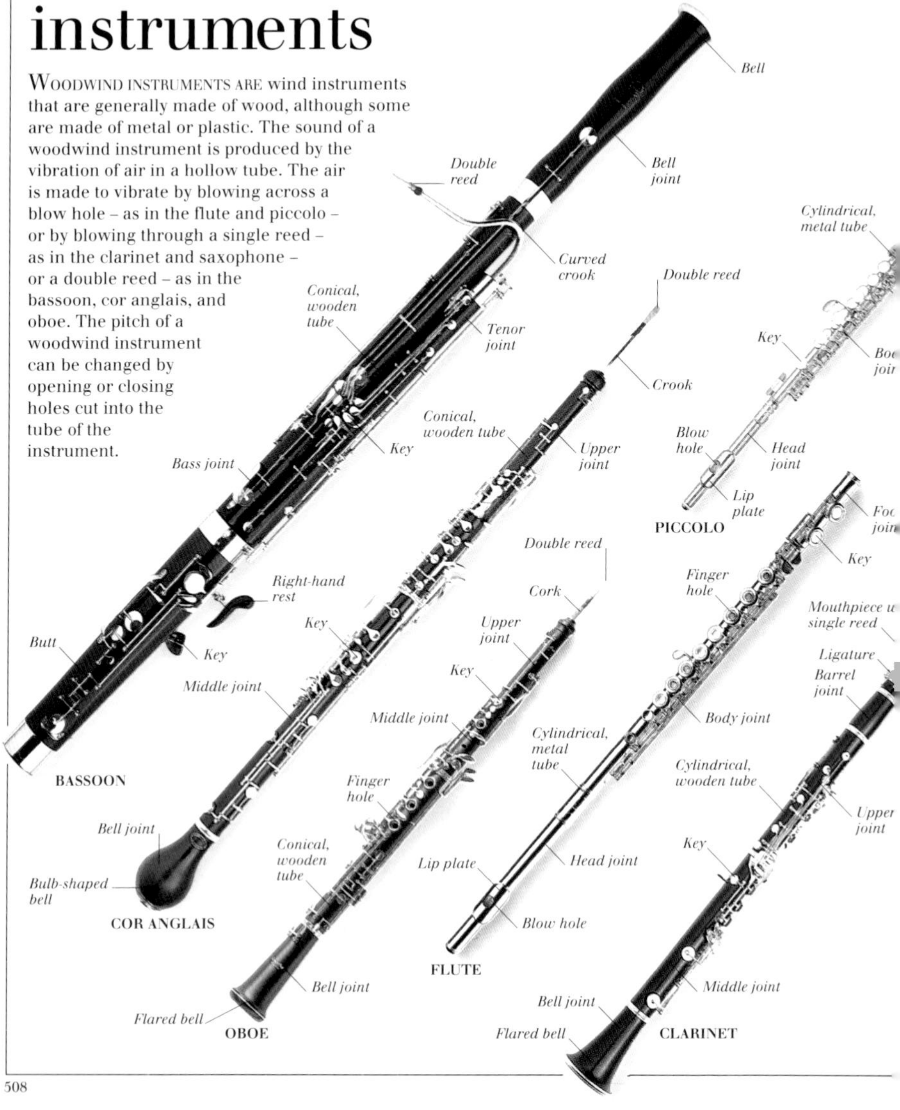
Bell
Double reed
Bell joint
Curved crook
Conical, wooden tube
Tenor joint
Key
Bass joint
Right-hand rest
Butt
Key
BASSOON
Double reed
Crook
Conical, wooden tube
Upper joint
Key
Middle joint
Bell joint
Bulb-shaped bell
COR ANGLAIS
Double reed
Cork
Upper joint
Key
Middle joint
Finger hole
Conical, wooden tube
Bell joint
Flared bell
OBOE
Cylindrical, metal tube
Key
Blow hole
Head joint
Lip plate
PICCOLO
Finger hole
Key
Body joint
Cylindrical, metal tube
Head joint
Lip plate
Blow hole
FLUTE
Ligature
Barrel joint
Cylindrical, wooden tube
Upper joint
Key
Middle joint
Bell joint
Flared bell
CLARINET

TENOR SAXOPHONE

Upturned, flared bell
Conical, metal tube

SECTIONS OF A TENOR SAXOPHONE

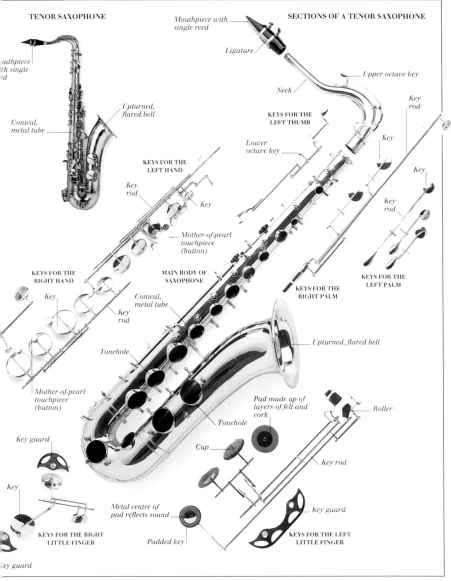

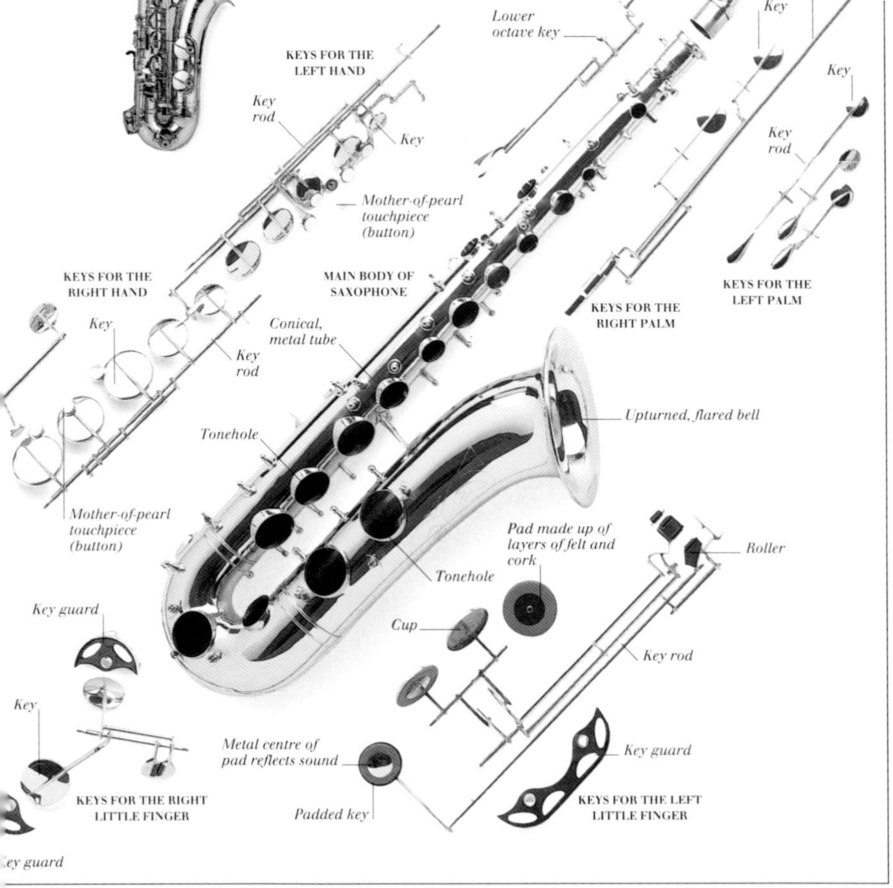
Mouthpiece with single reed
Ligature
Upper octave key
Neck
Key rod
KEYS FOR THE LEFT THUMB
Lower octave key
Key
KEYS FOR THE LEFT HAND
Key rod
Key
Key
Mother-of-pearl touchpiece (button)
Key rod
KEYS FOR THE RIGHT HAND
MAIN BODY OF SAXOPHONE
KEYS FOR THE LEFT PALM
KEYS FOR THE RIGHT PALM
Key
Conical, metal tube
Key rod
Upturned, flared bell
Tonehole
Mother-of-pearl touchpiece (button)
Pad made up of layers of felt and cork
Roller
Tonehole
Key guard
Cup
Key rod
Key
Metal centre of pad reflects sound
Key guard
KEYS FOR THE RIGHT LITTLE FINGER
Padded key
KEYS FOR THE LEFT LITTLE FINGER

Stringed instruments

STRINGED INSTRUMENTS PRODUCE SOUND by the vibration of stretched strings. This may be done by drawing a bow across the strings, as in the violin; or by plucking the strings, as in the harp and guitar (see pp. 512-513). The four modern members of the bowed string family are the violin, viola, cello (violoncello), and double bass. Each consists of a hollow, wooden body, a long neck, and four strings. The bow is a wooden stick with horsehair stretched across its length. The vibrations made by drawing the bow across the strings are transmitted to the hollow body, and this itself vibrates, amplifying and enriching the sound produced. The harp consists of a set of strings of different lengths stretched across a wooden frame. The strings are plucked by the player's thumbs and fingers – except the little finger of each hand – which produces vibrations that are amplified by the harp's soundboard. The pitch of the note produced by any stringed instrument depends on the length, weight, and tension of the string. A shorter, lighter, or tighter string gives a higher note.

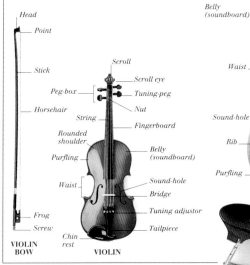

Head
Point
Stick
Horsehair
Frog
Screw

VIOLIN BOW

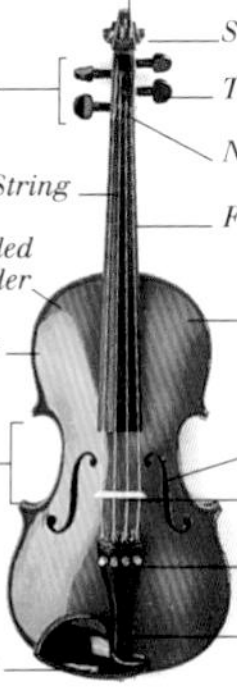
Scroll
Scroll eye
Peg-box
Tuning-peg
Nut
String
Fingerboard
Rounded shoulder
Belly (soundboard)
Purfling
Waist
Sound-hole
Bridge
Tuning adjustor
Tailpiece
Chin rest

VIOLIN

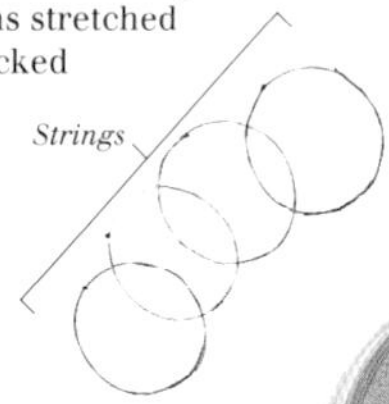
Strings

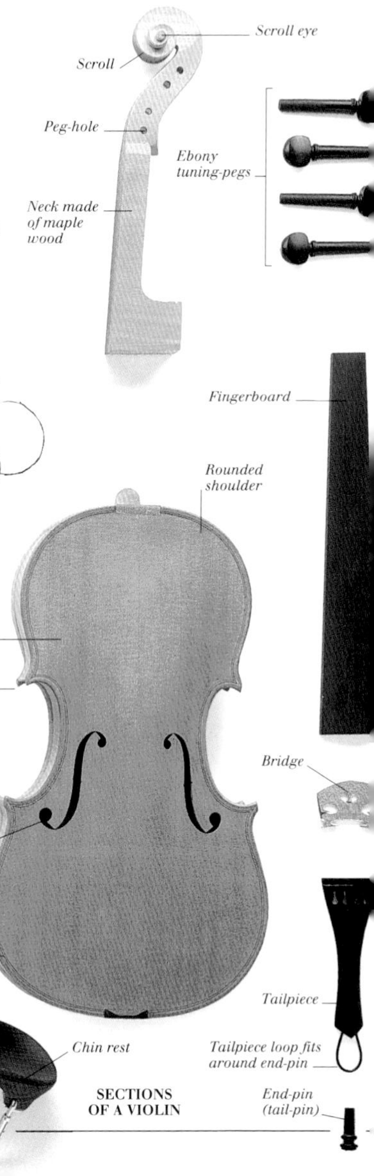
Scroll eye
Scroll
Peg-hole
Ebony tuning-pegs
Neck made of maple wood
Fingerboard
Rounded shoulder
Belly (soundboard)
Waist
Bridge
Sound-hole
Rib
Purfling
Tailpiece
Tailpiece loop fits around end-pin
End-pin (tail-pin)

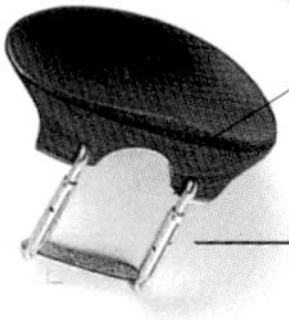
Chin rest

SECTIONS OF A VIOLIN

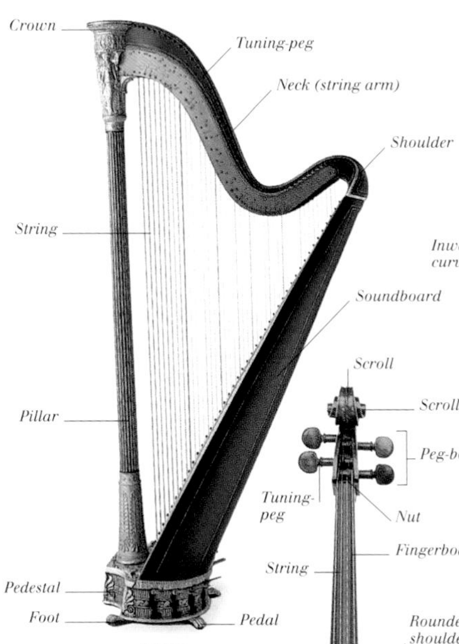
Crown
Tuning-peg
Neck (string arm)
Shoulder
String
Soundboard
Pillar
Pedestal
Foot
Pedal

HARP

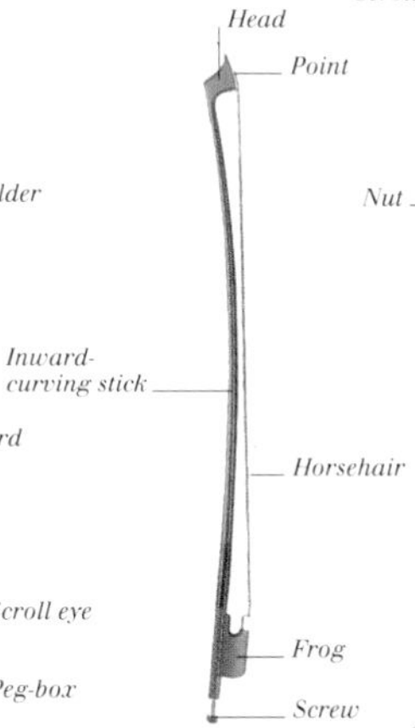
Head
Point
Inward-curving stick
Horsehair
Frog
Screw

DOUBLE BASS BOW

Scroll
Scroll eye
Tuning-pegs at back of peg-box
Nut
Fingerboard
String
Sloping shoulder
Belly (soundboard)
Purfling
Waist
Bridge
Rib
Sound-hole
Sound-hole
Tailpiece
Spike

DOUBLE BASS

Scroll
Scroll eye
Peg-box
Tuning-peg
Nut
Fingerboard
String
Rounded shoulder
Belly (soundboard)
Waist
Sound-hole
Bridge
Purfling
Tuning adjustor
Tailpiece
Spike

CELLO (VIOLONCELLO)

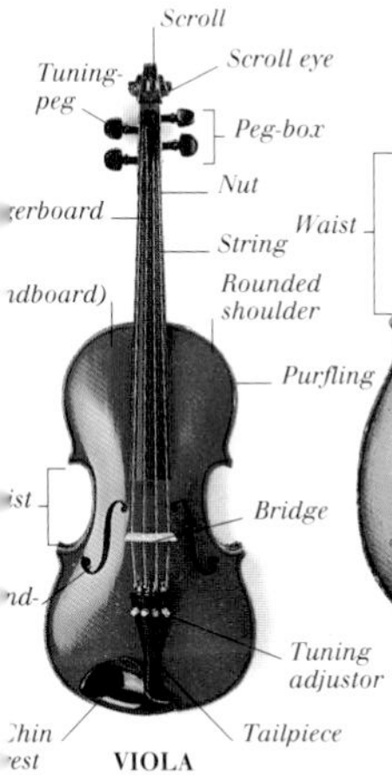
Scroll
Tuning-peg
Scroll eye
Peg-box
Nut
String
Rounded shoulder
Purfling
Bridge
Tuning adjustor
Tailpiece

VIOLA

Guitars

THE GUITAR IS A PLUCKED stringed instrument (see pp. 510-511). There are two types of guitar – acoustic and electric. Acoustic guitars have hollow bodies and six or twelve strings. Plucking the strings produces vibrations that are amplified by their hollow bodies. Electric guitars usually have solid bodies and six strings. Pick-ups placed under the strings convert their vibrations into electronic signals that are magnified by an amplifier, and sent to a loudspeaker where they are converted into sounds (see pp. 520-521). Electric bass guitars are very similar in structure to electric guitars, and produce sound in the same way, but have four strings and play bass notes.

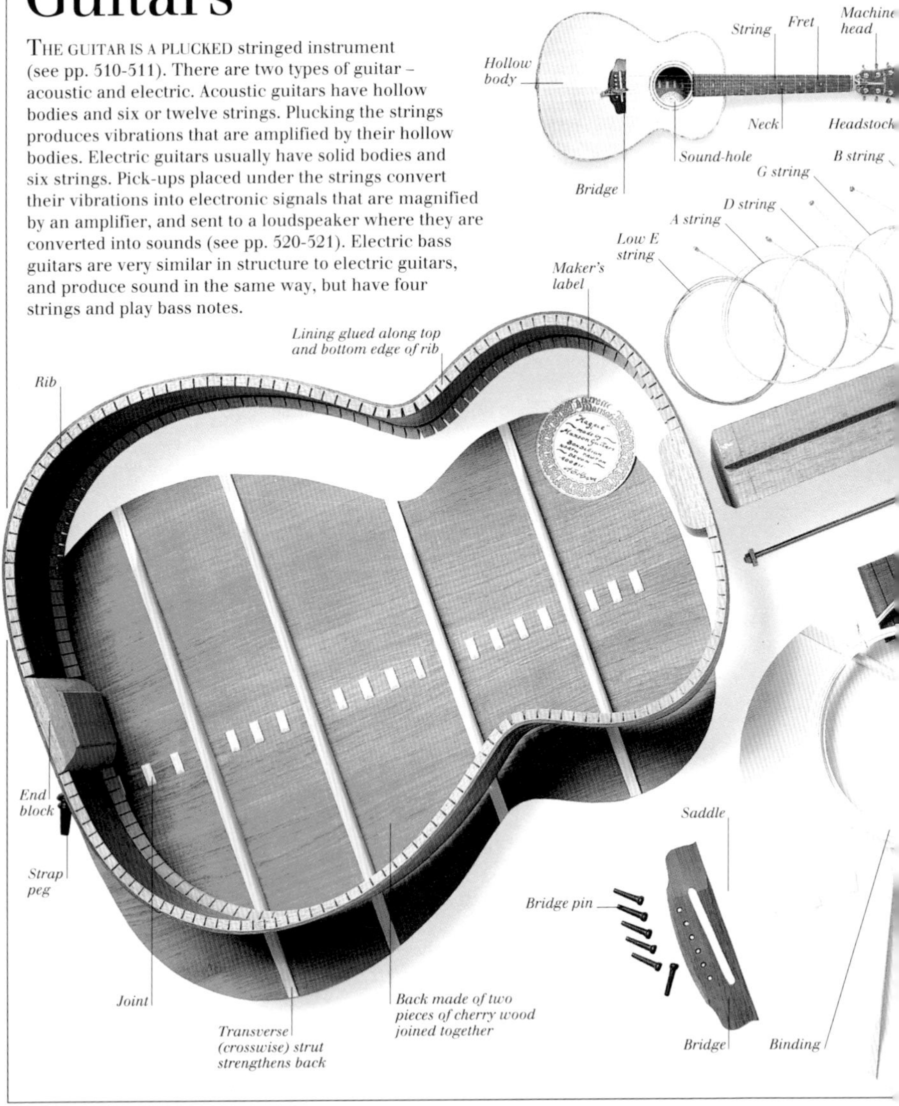
ACOUSTIC GUITAR
Hollow body
String
Fret
Machine head
Neck
Headstock
Sound-hole
Bridge
B string
G string
D string
A string
Low E string
Maker's label
Lining glued along top and bottom edge of rib
Rib
End block
Strap peg
Joint
Transverse (crosswise) strut strengthens back
Back made of two pieces of cherry wood joined together
Saddle
Bridge pin
Bridge
Binding

COMPONENTS OF AN ACOUSTIC GUITAR

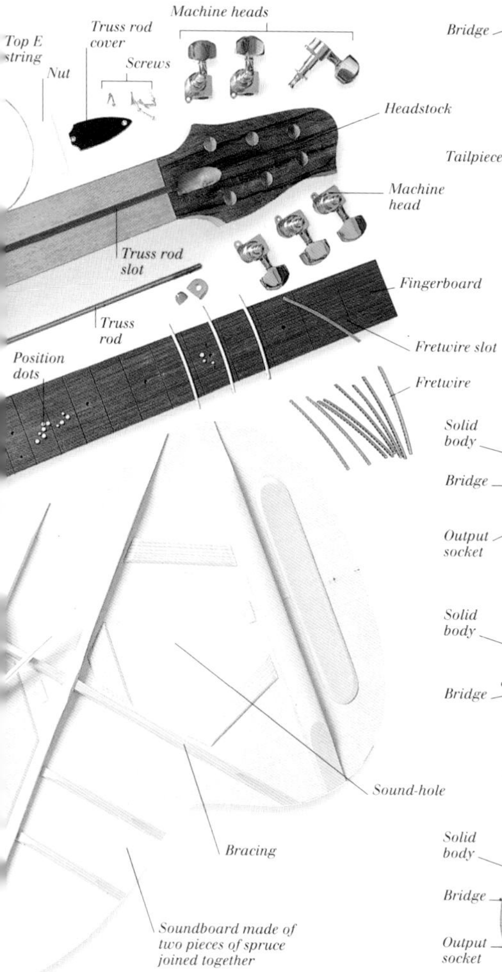
Machine heads
Truss rod cover
Top E string
Screws
Nut
Headstock
Machine head
Truss rod slot
Fingerboard
Truss rod
Fretwire slot
Position dots
Fretwire
Sound-hole
Bracing
Soundboard made of two pieces of spruce joined together

EXAMPLES OF ACOUSTIC GUITARS

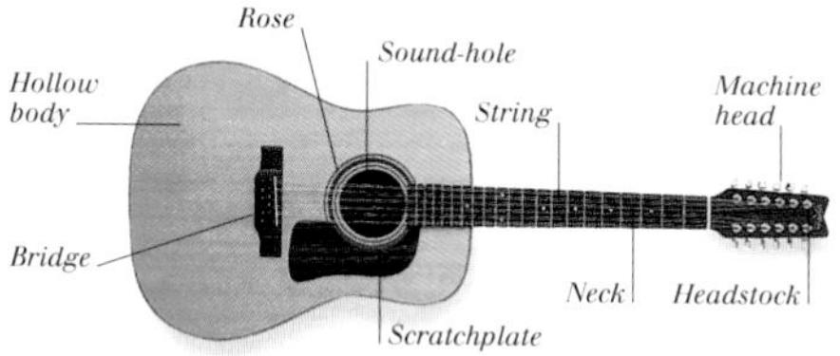
Rose
Sound-hole
Hollow body
String
Machine head
Bridge
Neck
Headstock
Scratchplate

WASHBURN TWELVE-STRING

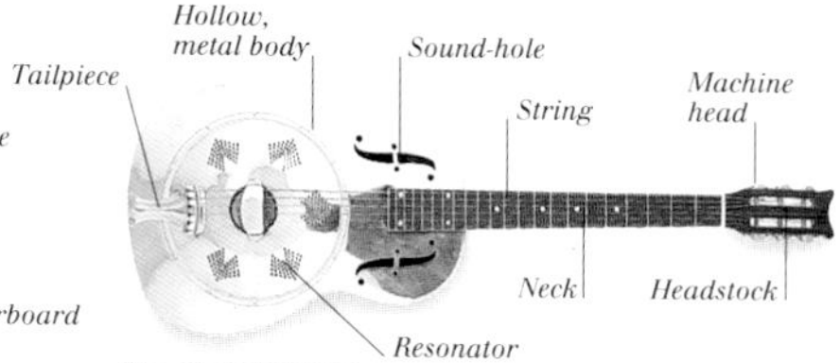
Hollow, metal body
Sound-hole
Tailpiece
String
Machine head
Neck
Headstock
Resonator

DOBRO RESONATOR

EXAMPLES OF ELECTRIC GUITARS

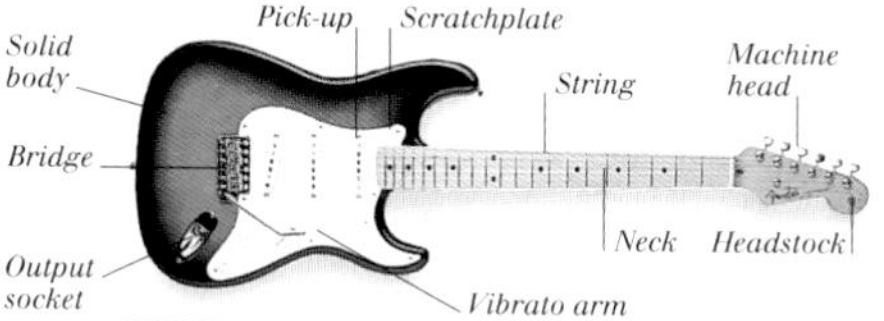
Pick-up
Scratchplate
Solid body
String
Machine head
Bridge
Neck
Headstock
Output socket
Vibrato arm

FENDER STRATOCASTER

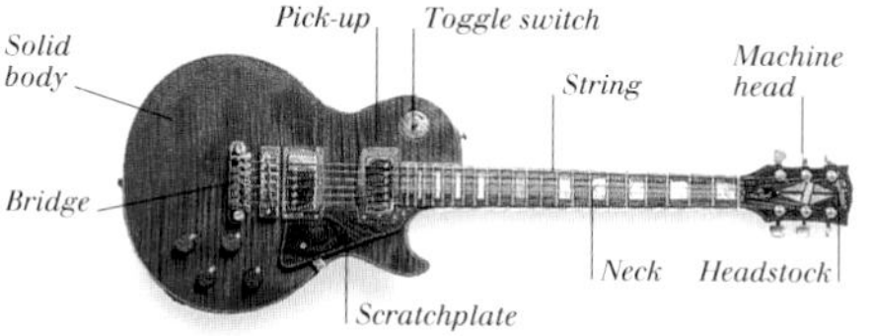
Pick-up
Toggle switch
Solid body
String
Machine head
Bridge
Neck
Headstock
Scratchplate

GIBSON LES PAUL

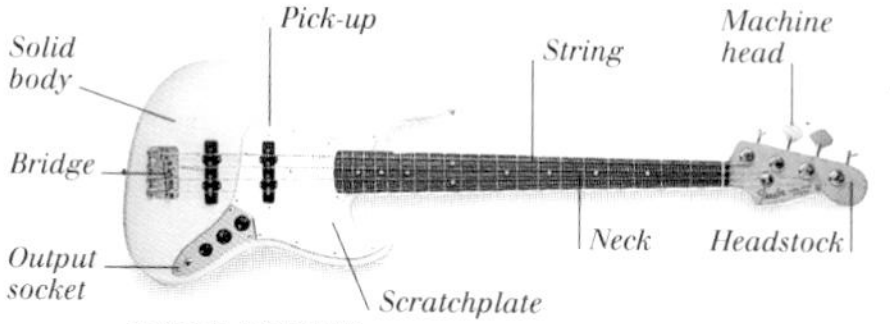
Pick-up
Solid body
String
Machine head
Bridge
Neck
Headstock
Output socket
Scratchplate

FENDER JAZZ BASS

Keyboard instruments

ORGAN PIPE

KEYBOARD INSTRUMENTS are instruments that are sounded by means of a keyboard. The organ and piano are two of the principal members of the keyboard family. The organ consists of pipes which are operated by one or more manuals (keyboards) and a pedal board. The pipes are lined up in rows (known as ranks or registers) on top of a wind chest. The sound of the organ is made when air is admitted into a pipe by pressing a key or pedal. The piano consists of wire strings stretched over a metal frame, and a keyboard and pedals that operate hammers and dampers. The piano frame is either vertical – as in the upright piano – or horizontal – as in the grand piano. When a key is at rest, a damper lies against the string to stop it vibrating. When a key is pressed down, the damper moves away from the string as the hammer strikes it, causing the string to vibrate and sound a note.

UPRIGHT PIANO

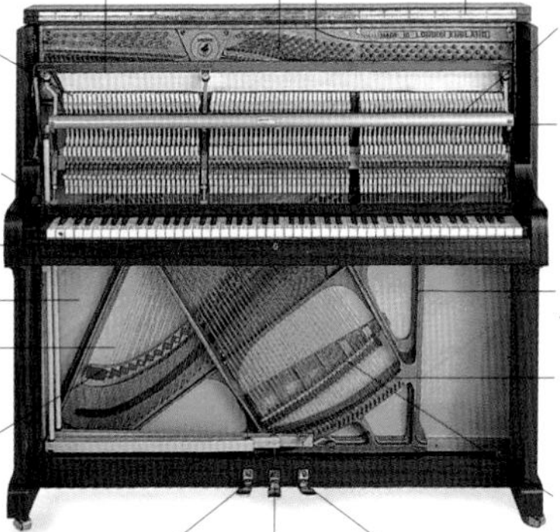

Muffler felt
Pressure bar
Tuning pin
Pin block
Hammer
88-note keyboard
Keybed
Soundboard
String
Treble bridge
Una corda (soft) pedal
Sostenuto pedal
Damper (sustaining) peda

ORGAN CONSOLE

Pipe
Pedal stop
Swell stop
Swell manual (keyboard)
Great manual (keyboard)
Choir manual (keyboard)
Toe piston
Pedal board
Foot pedal
Swell pedal
Music stand
Choir stop
Great stop
Thumb piston

UPRIGHT PIANO ACTION

KEY AT REST

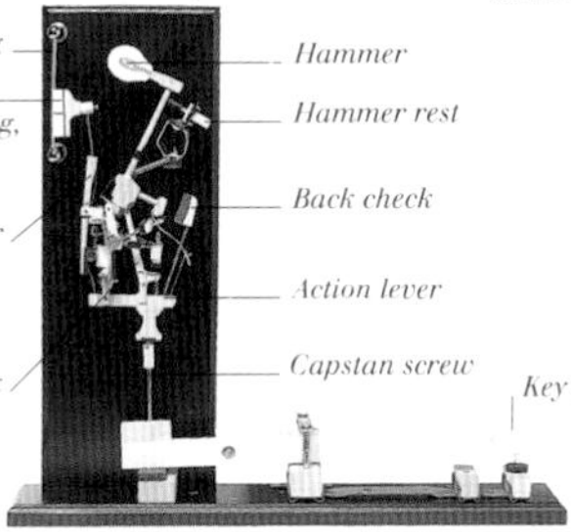

String
Damper lies against string, and stops it vibrating
Damper lever
Jack
Hammer
Hammer rest
Back check
Action lever
Capstan screw
Key released

KEY PRESSED DO

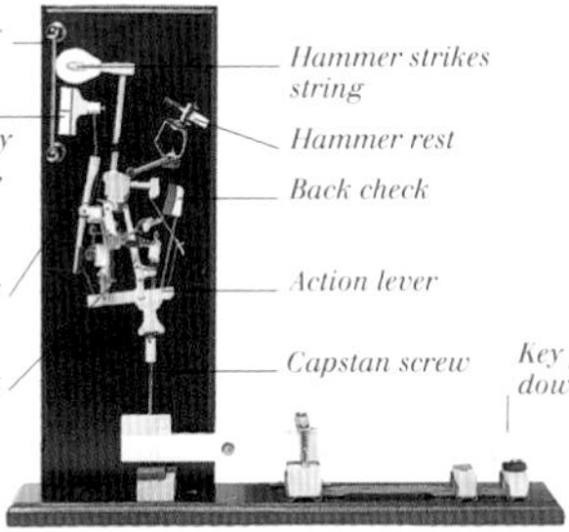

String
Damper moves away from string, allowing it to vibrate
Damper lever
Jack
Hammer strikes string
Hammer rest
Back check
Action lever
Capstan screw
Key pressed down

CONCERT GRAND PIANO (VIEWED FROM ABOVE)

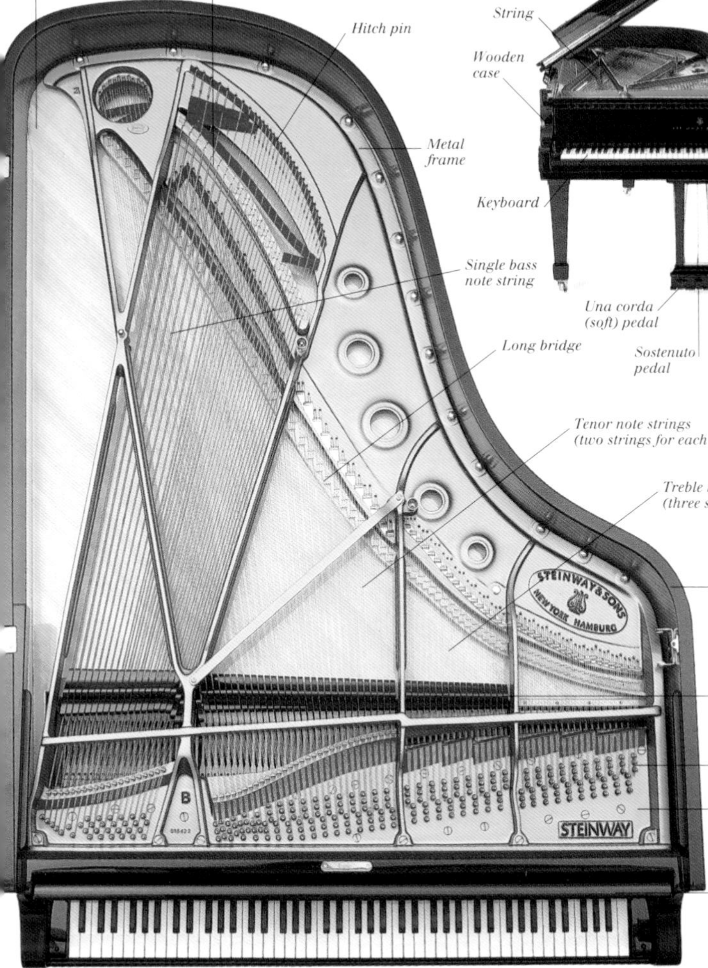
Soundboard
Bass bridge
Hitch pin
Metal frame
Single bass note string
Long bridge
Tenor note strings (two strings for each note)
Treble note strings (three strings for each note)
STEINWAY & SONS NEW YORK HAMBURG
Wooden case
Hammer
Tuning pin
Wrest plank
STEINWAY
Keyboard lid
88-note keyboard

CONCERT GRAND PIANO (FRONT VIEW)

Lid
String
Wooden case
Keyboard
Una corda (soft) pedal
Damper (sustaining) pedal
Sostenuto pedal

Percussion instruments

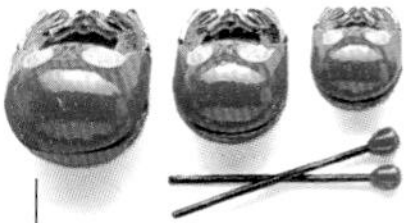

TEMPLE BLOCKS

PERCUSSION INSTRUMENTS are a large group of instruments that produce sound by being struck, shaken, scraped, or clashed together. Most percussion instruments – such as the tam-tam (gong), cymbals, and maracas – do not have a definite pitch and are used for rhythm and impact, and the distinctive timbre (colour) of their sound. Other percussion instruments – such as the xylophone, vibraphone, and tubular bells – are tuned to a definite pitch and can play melody, harmony, and rhythms. The xylophone and vibraphone each have two rows of bars that are arranged in a similar way to the black and white keys of a piano. Metal tubes are suspended below the bars to amplify the sound. The vibraphone has electrically operated fans that rotate in the tubes and produce a vibrato (wavering pitch) effect.

TUBULAR BELLS

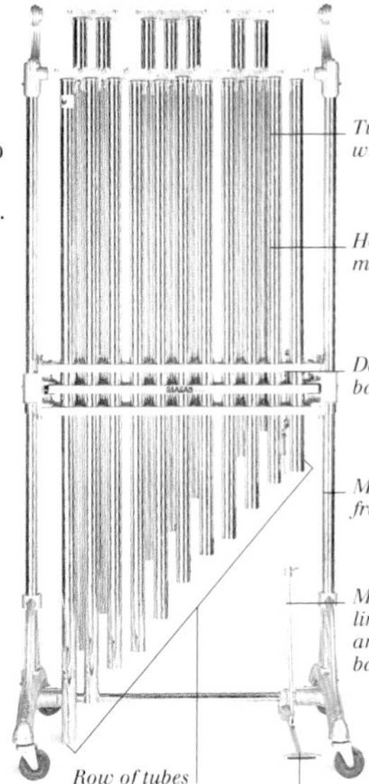
Tube struck with mallet
Hollow, metal tube
Damper bar
Metal frame
Mechanism linking pedal and damper bar
Row of tubes graduated in length and pitch
Damper pedal

EXAMPLES OF BEATERS

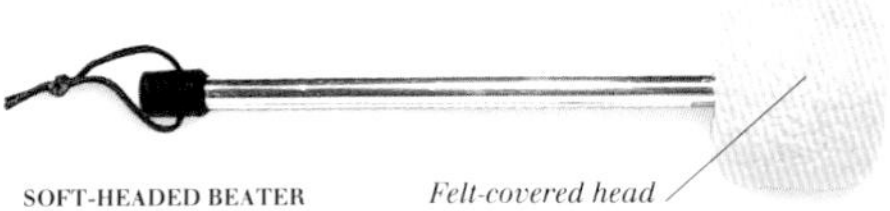
Felt-covered head

SOFT-HEADED BEATER

Rosewood head

HARD-HEADED BEATER

Leather-covered head

MALLET

XYLOPHONE

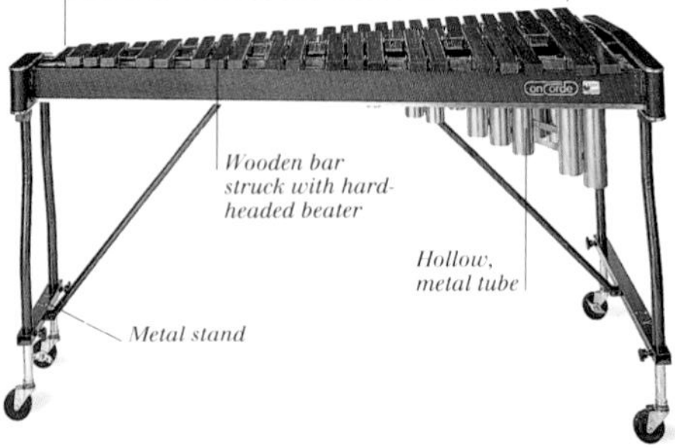
Row of bars graduated in length and pitch
Wooden bar struck with hard-headed beater
Hollow, metal tube
Metal stand

TAM-TAM (GONG)

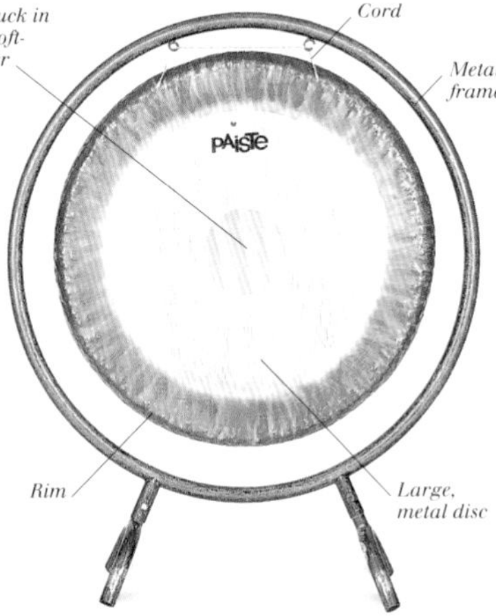
Tam-tam struck in centre with soft-headed beater
Cord
Metal frame
PAISTE
Rim
Large, metal disc

CYMBALS

Leather strap fits around player's hand
Pad protects hands from vibrations
Zildjian
Thin, convex disc of copper and tin alloy

SECTIONS OF A MARACA

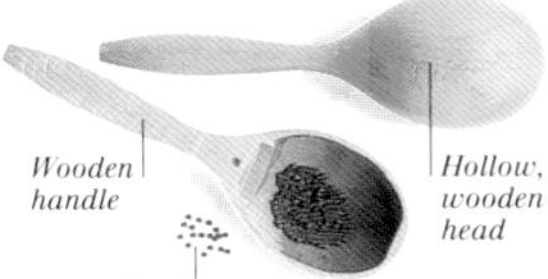
Wooden handle
Hollow, wooden head
Lead shot

TRIANGLE

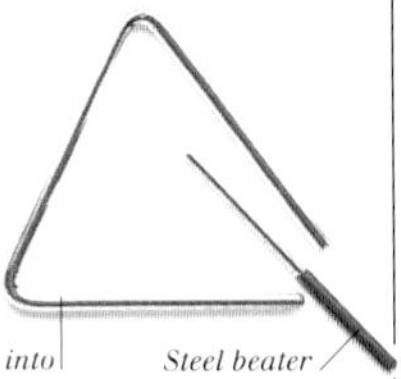
Steel rod bent into triangular shape
Steel beater

CLAVES

Hardwood sticks clashed together to give a sharp crack

CASTANETS

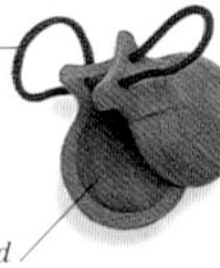
Cord
Hollowed wood

VIBRAPHONE

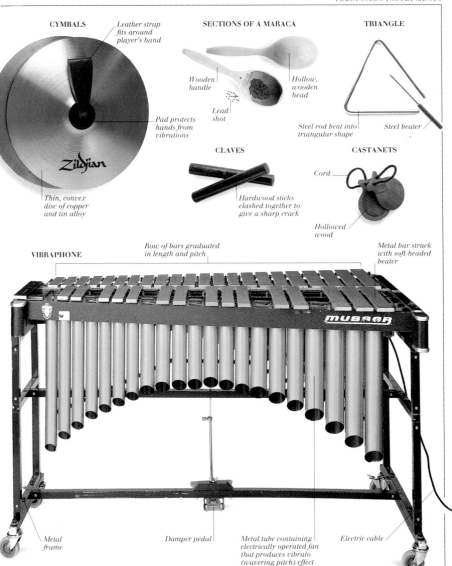

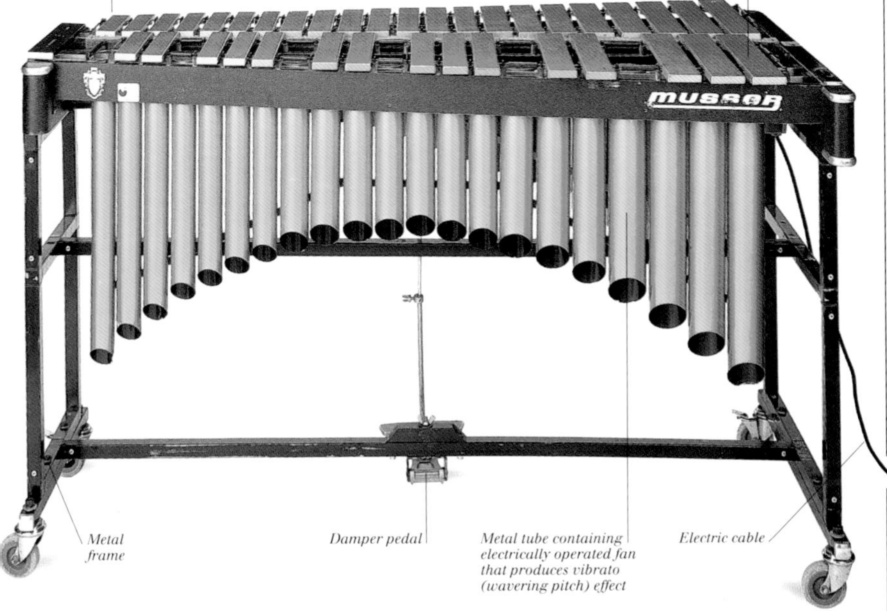
Row of bars graduated in length and pitch
Metal bar struck with soft-headed beater
Metal frame
Damper pedal
Metal tube containing electrically operated fan that produces vibrato (wavering pitch) effect
Electric cable

Drums

TAMBOURINE

A DRUM IS A percussion instrument that consists of a drumhead, made of skin or plastic, stretched over one or both ends of a hollow vessel (the body-shell). Drums are played in most parts of the world and are made in a number of different shapes and sizes. They can be divided into three groups according to the shape of the body-shell: frame drums (e.g., tambourines), bowl-shaped drums (e.g., timpani), and tubular drums (e.g., congas). Drums are usually sounded by striking the drumhead with the hands or with beaters, such as a hard-headed stick. The drumhead vibrates, and its vibrations are amplified by the hollow body-shell. The snare drum has wires – known as snares – stretched across the lower drumhead; the snares vibrate against the lower drumhead when the drum is played. Most drums, such as congas, do not have a definite pitch and can play only rhythms (see pp. 516-517). Other drums, such as timpani, have a definite pitch and can play melody, harmony, and rhythms. They can be tuned by adjusting the tension of the drumhead. Different types of drum can be combined together with other percussion instruments to form a drum kit. The basic components of the drum kit are bass drum, tom-toms, floor tom (tenor drum), snare drum, and cymbals.

DRUM KI

Crash cymbal
Tension key
Tension rod
Tom-tom
Lug
Hi-hat cymbal
Snare drum
Tripod stand
Chain
Tension screw
Felt-covered beater
Pedal
Pedal

SNARE DRUM (VIEWED FROM BELOW)

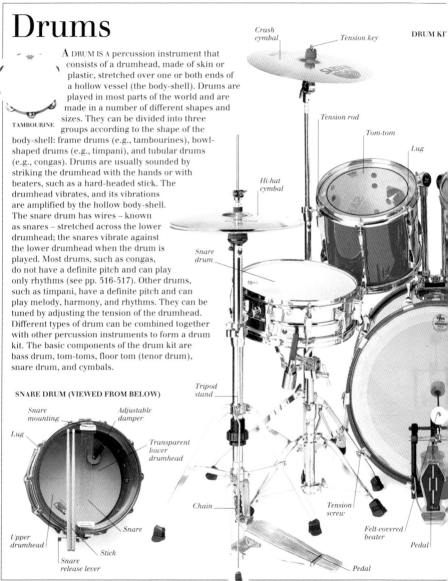

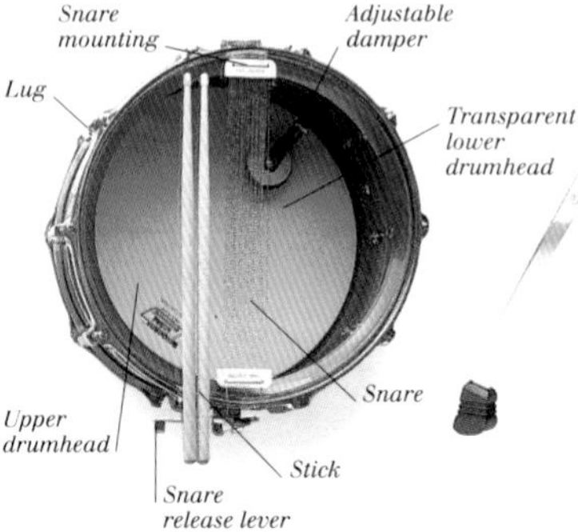
Snare mounting
Adjustable damper
Lug
Transparent lower drumhead
Snare
Upper drumhead
Stick
Snare release lever

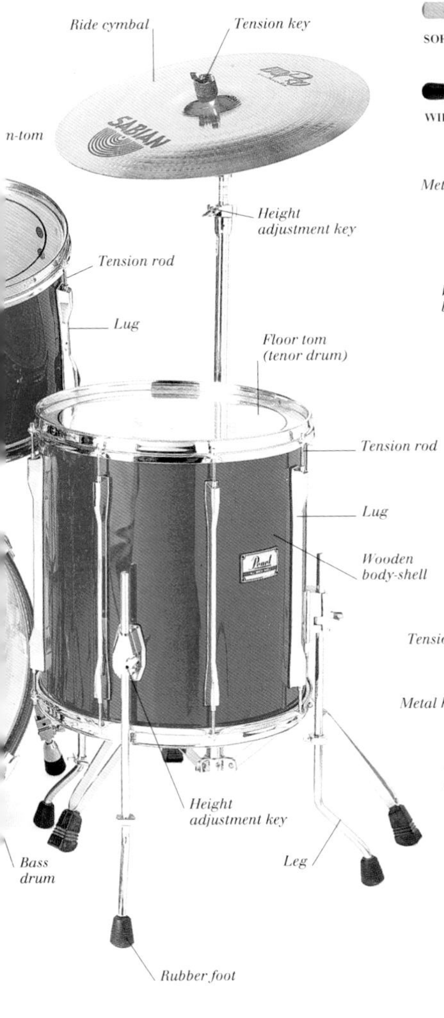
Ride cymbal
Tension key
n-tom
Height
adjustment key
Tension rod
Lug
Floor tom
(tenor drum)
Tension rod
Lug
Wooden
body-shell
Height
adjustment key
Bass
drum
Leg
Rubber foot

EXAMPLES OF BEATERS

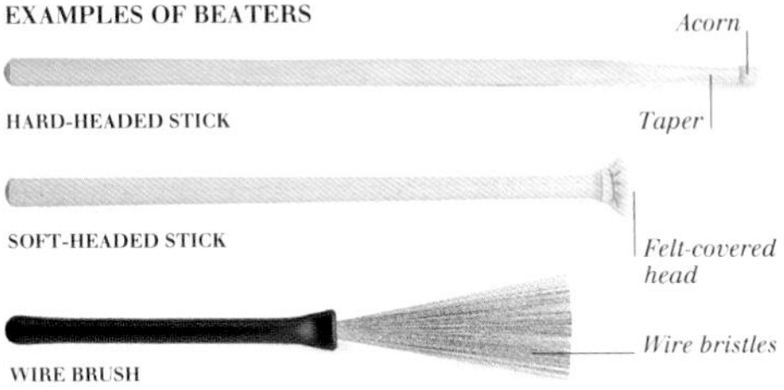
Acorn
HARD-HEADED STICK
Taper
SOFT-HEADED STICK
Felt-covered
head
WIRE BRUSH
Wire bristles

CONGAS

Drumhead
Metal hoop
Tension rod
Wooden
body-shell
Tripod
stand
Leg

TIMPANUM (KETTLE DRUM)

Drumhead
Tension rod
Metal hoop
Tuning
gauge
Copper
body-shell
Strut
Crown
Tension rod
Tuning pedal
Castor

Electronic instruments

ELECTRONIC INSTRUMENTS generate electronic signals that are magnified by an amplifier, and sent to a loudspeaker where they are converted into sounds. Synthesizers, and other electronic instruments, simulate the characteristic sounds of conventional instruments, and also create entirely new sounds. Most electronic instruments are keyboard instruments, but electronic wind and percussion instruments are also popular. A digital sampler records and stores sounds from musical instruments or other sources. When the sound is played back, the pitch of the original sound can be altered. A keyboard can be connected to the sampler so that a tune can be played using the sampled sounds. With a MIDI (Musical Instrument Digital Interface) system, a computer can be linked with other electronic instruments, such as keyboards and electronic drums, to make sounds together or in sequence. It is also possible, using music software, to compose and play music on a home computer.

ELECTRONIC DRUMS

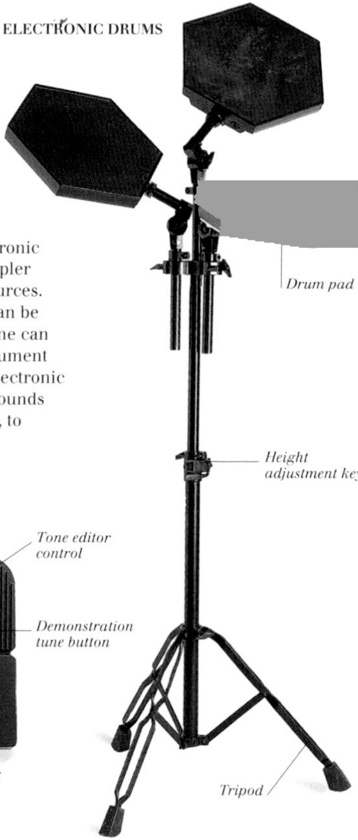
Drum pad
Height adjustment key
Tripod

HOME KEYBOARD

Power button
Volume control
Function display
Memory record button
Tone editor control
Demonstration tune button
Pitch modulator
Multi-accompaniment system control
Tone and rhythm pattern selector
Key
CASIO

SYNTHESIZER

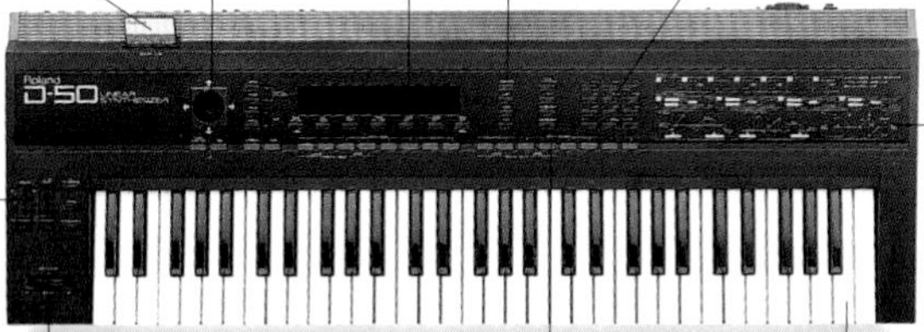
Memory card slot
Joystick
Function display
Edit control
Data entry key pad
Sound structure guide
Volume control
Pitch modulator
Sound selection control
Key
Roland
D-50

WIND SYNTHESIZER

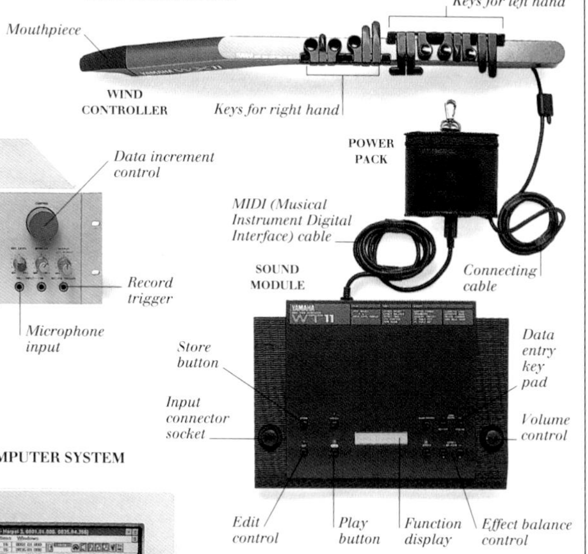
Keys for left hand
Mouthpiece
WIND CONTROLLER
Keys for right hand
POWER PACK
MIDI (Musical Instrument Digital Interface) cable
SOUND MODULE
Connecting cable
Data entry key pad
Store button
Input connector socket
Volume control
Edit control
Play button
Function display
Effect balance control

DIGITAL SAMPLER

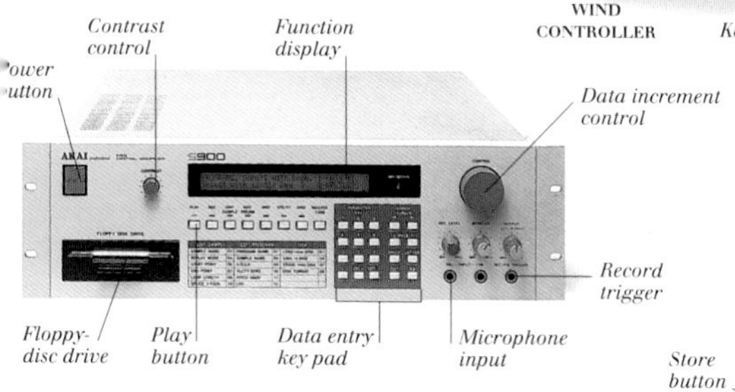
Contrast control
Function display
ower
utton
Data increment control
Record trigger
Floppy-disc drive
Play button
Data entry key pad
Microphone input

HOME COMPUTER SYSTEM

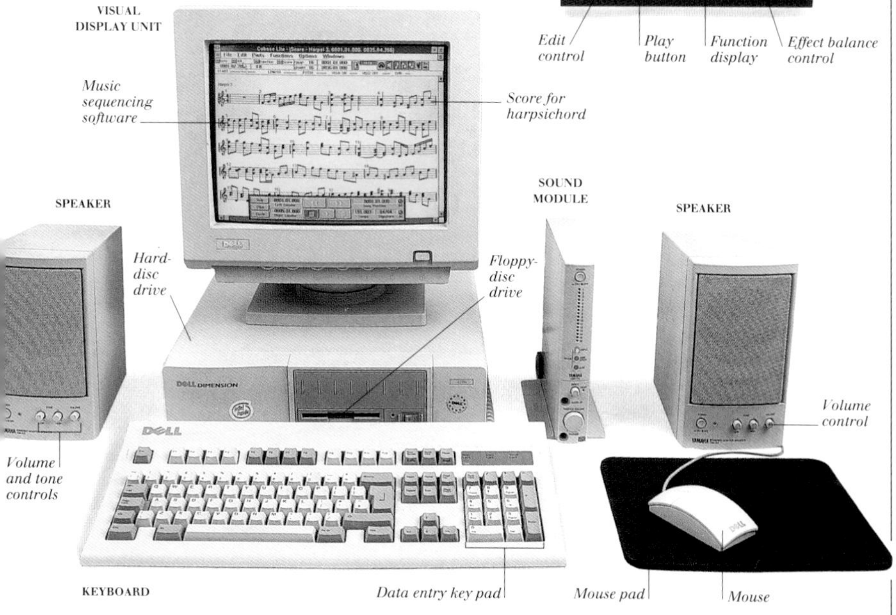
VISUAL DISPLAY UNIT
Music sequencing software
Score for harpsichord
SPEAKER
SOUND MODULE
SPEAKER
Hard-disc drive
Floppy-disc drive
Volume control
Volume and tone controls
KEYBOARD
Data entry key pad
Mouse pad
Mouse

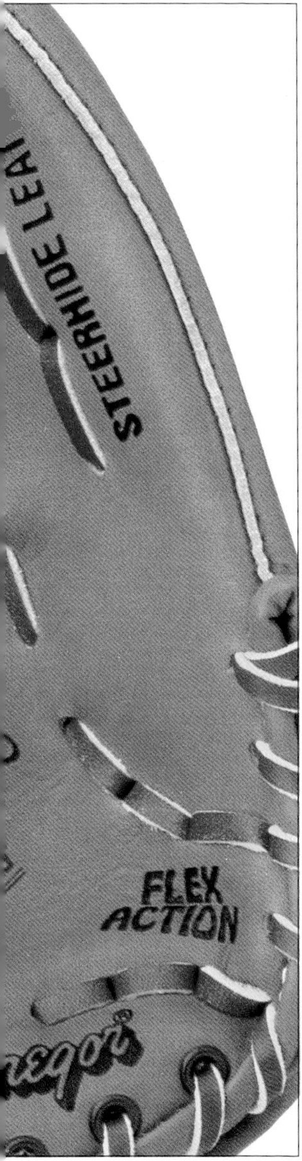

SPORTS

Soccer

GAMES INVOLVING KICKING A BALL have a long history and were recorded in China as early as 300 BC; in medieval Europe, street football was banned as a menace to the public; only in 1863 were the rules established, specifically banning carrying the ball for all players except the goalkeeper, and separating rugby from soccer. Soccer, officially termed association football, is a team sport in which players attempt to score goals by passing and dribbling the ball down the field past opposing defenders, and kicking or heading the ball into the goal net, outwitting the defending goalkeeper. Each team consists of ten outfield players (defenders, midfielders, and strikers) and a goalkeeper. Players from the opposing team may challenge the player in possession of the ball, but an illegal or foul tackle results in a penalty if a foul occurs inside the penalty area or a free kick if outside the penalty area. The round ball used in soccer is more easily controlled than the oval balls used in American, Canadian, and Australian rules football and in rugby. The result is a more "open" or flowing game which is played and watched by millions of people worldwide.

LINESMAN'S FLAG

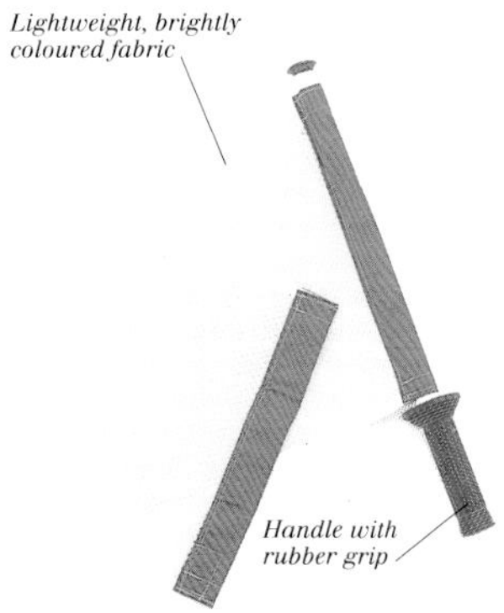

Lightweight, brightly coloured fabric
Handle with rubber grip

REFEREE'S EQUIPMENT

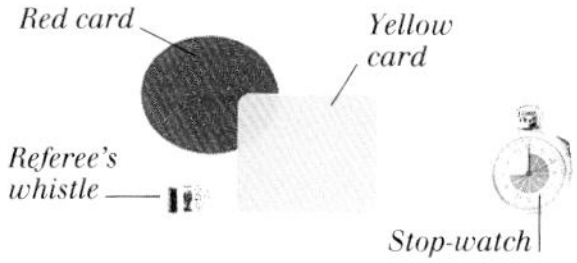

Red card
Yellow card
Referee's whistle
Stop-watch

SOCCER PITCH

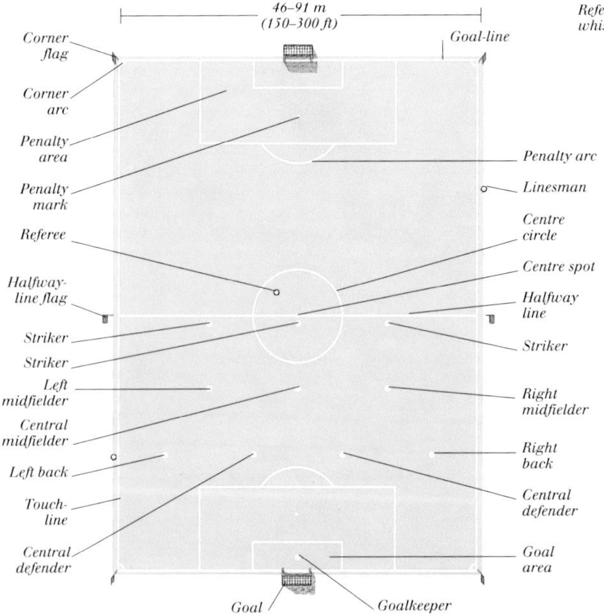

46–91 m (150–300 ft)
Corner flag
Goal-line
Corner arc
Penalty area
Penalty arc
Penalty mark
Linesman
Referee
Centre circle
Centre spot
Halfway-line flag
Halfway line
Striker
Striker
Striker
Left midfielder
Right midfielder
Central midfielder
Right back
Left back
Touch-line
Central defender
Central defender
Goal area
Goal
Goalkeeper

PITCH MARKINGS

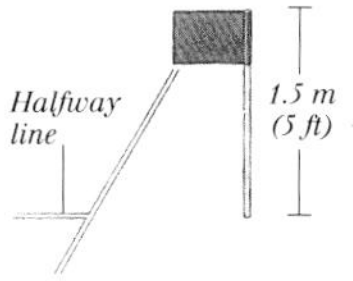

Halfway line
1.5 m (5 ft)

HALFWAY-LINE FLAG

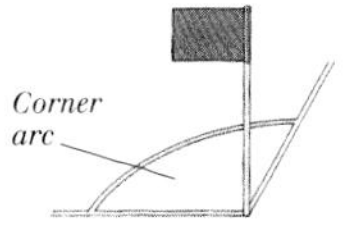

Corner arc

CORNER FLAG

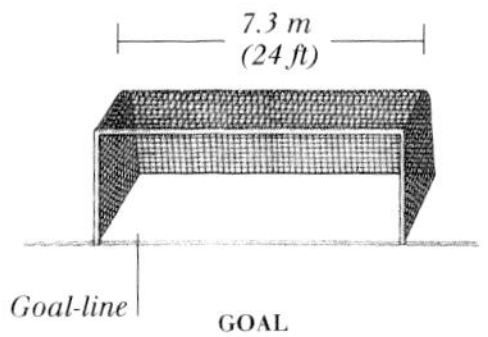

7.3 m (24 ft)
Goal-line

GOAL

GOALKEEPER

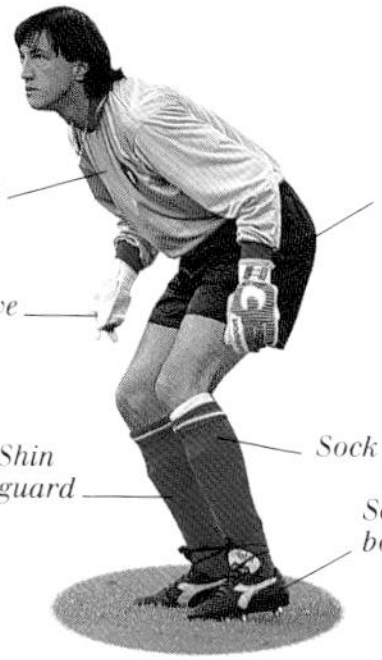
Goalkeeper's shirt
Shorts
Glove
Sock
Shin guard
Soccer boot

SOCCER STRIP

Open-neck collar
Lightweight, man-made fabric team shirt
Team logo
Manufacturer's logo
lotto
Motta
Ribbed welt
Sponsor's logo
Long cotton sock
Club crest
Team shorts

MAKING A SOCCER BALL

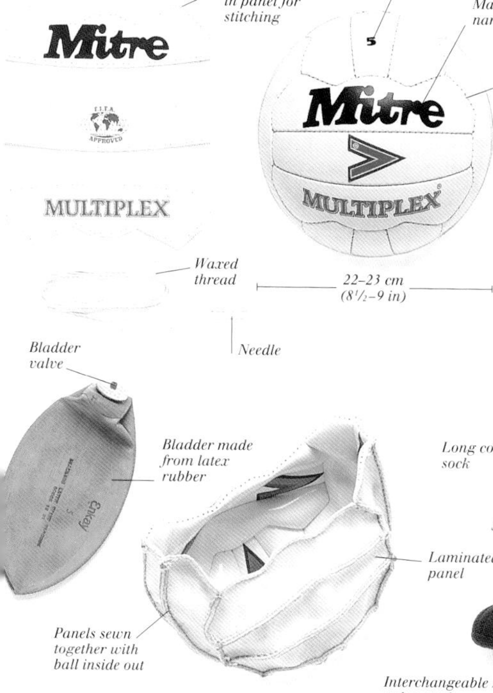
Hole punched in panel for stitching
Mitre
MULTIPLEX
Ball size number
5
Manufacturer's name
Edge cut to fit perfectly
Mitre
MULTIPLEX
Waxed thread
22–23 cm (8½–9 in)
Needle
Bladder valve
Bladder made from latex rubber
Enkay
Laminated panel
Panels sewn together with ball inside out

Synthetic bootlace
Reebok
Interchangeable nylon stud

SOCCER BOOT

American football

In American and Canadian football, the object of the game is to get the ball across the opponent's goal line, either by passing or carrying it across (a touch-down), or by kicking it between their goalposts (a field goal). An American football team has 11 players on the field at a time, although up to 40 players can appear for each side in a single game. The agile "offence" tries to score points, and the heavy hitting "defence" holds back the opposition. When in possession of the ball, a team has four chances ("downs"), to move it at least ten yards (nine metres) up the field to make a "first down". The opposition gains possession if they fail, or by tackling and intercepting the ball. Canadian football is played on a larger field, with 12 men on each side. A team has only three chances to achieve a first down. Otherwise, the game is very similar to American football. Helmets, face masks, and layers of body padding are worn by the players for protection.

AMERICAN FOOTBALL PLAYING FORMATION

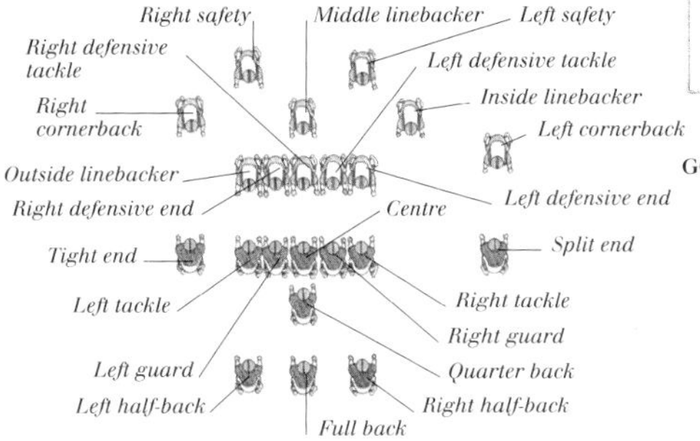

Right safety
Middle linebacker
Left safety
Right defensive tackle
Left defensive tackle
Right cornerback
Inside linebacker
Left cornerback
Outside linebacker
Left defensive end
Right defensive end
Centre
Tight end
Split end
Left tackle
Right tackle
Right guard
Left guard
Quarter back
Left half-back
Right half-back
Full back

CANADIAN FOOTBALL PLAYING FORMATION

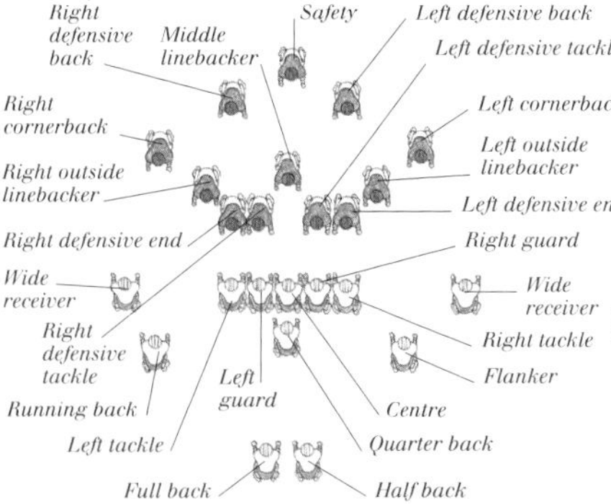

Right defensive back
Middle linebacker
Safety
Left defensive back
Left defensive tackle
Right cornerback
Left cornerback
Left outside linebacker
Right outside linebacker
Left defensive end
Right defensive end
Right guard
Wide receiver
Wide receiver
Right defensive tackle
Right tackle
Flanker
Left guard
Running back
Centre
Left tackle
Quarter back
Full back
Half back

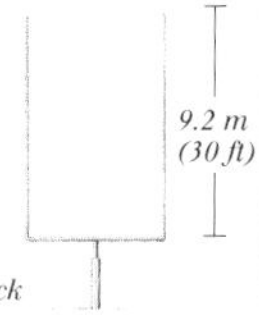

9.2 m
(30 ft)

GOALPOST

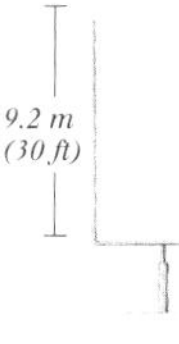

9.2 m
(30 ft)

GOALPOST

AMERICAN FOOTBALL FIELD

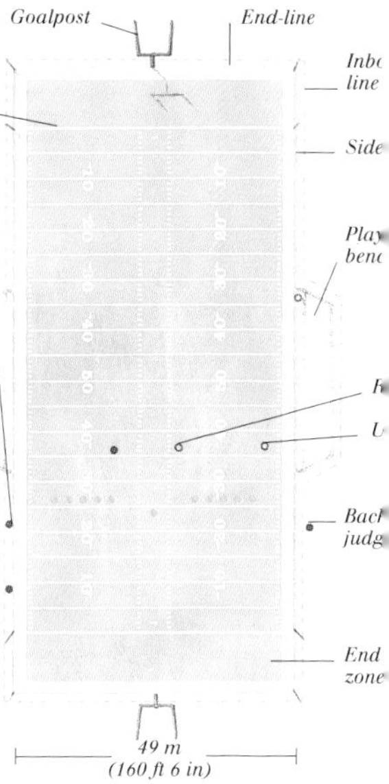

Goalpost
End-line
Goal-line
Line judge
End zone
49 m
(160 ft 6 in)

CANADIAN FOOTBALL FIELD

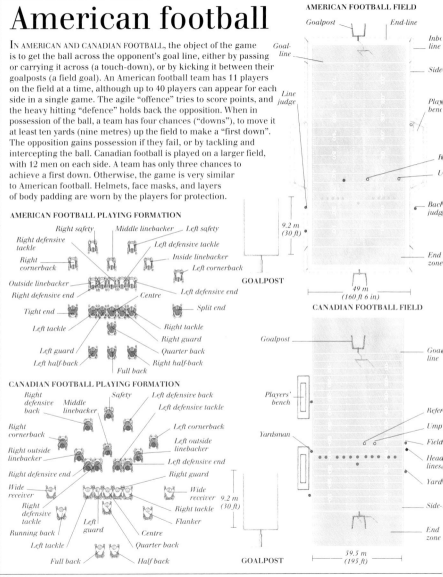

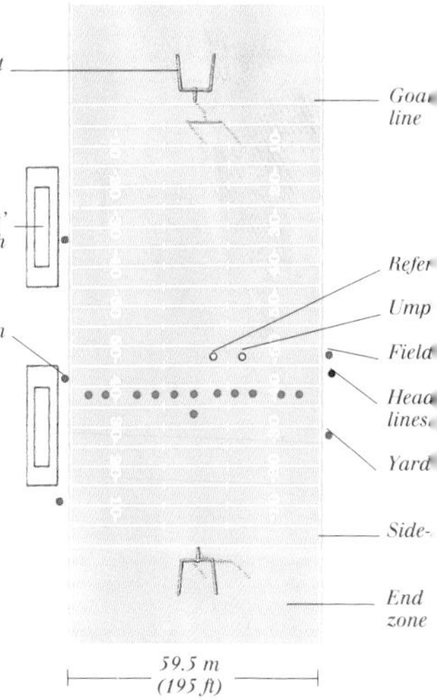

Goalpost
Players' bench
Yardsman
line
End zone
59.5 m
(195 ft)

PLAYER

Team logo

Helmet

Wrist pad

Player's number

igh *d*

Pants

Tie to shoulder pads

Studded shoe

PROTECTIVE EQUIPMENT

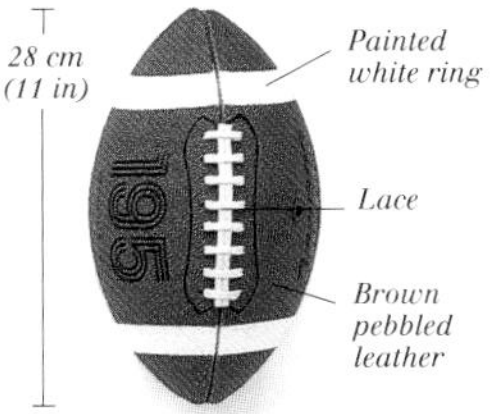

28 cm (11 in)

Painted white ring

Lace

Brown pebbled leather

FOOTBALL

HELMET

Non-breakable plastic

Rubber-coated plastic

Shock absorber

Riddell

SHOULDER PAD

BIKE

AIR·LITE

BLUE LASER 40-42

BIKE

Chest protector weight up to 2.5 kg (5 lb 8 oz)

UPPER ARM PAD

BIKE

BIKE

RIB PADS

Strap ties on to shoulder pad

Tail bone pad

Foam-sponge filling

ELBOW PAD

HIP PAD

BIKE AL82

BIKE

BIKE AL82

FINGERLESS GLOVE

Rigid plastic covering

Screw-in stud

PONY

BOOT

Fold-over leather tongue

PANTS

THIGH PAD

KNEE PAD

REFEREE'S SIGNALS

TIME OUT

TOUCH-DOWN OR FIELD GOAL

RSONAL *FOUL*

OFFSIDE OR ENCROACHMENT

OLDING

ILLEGAL MOTION

FIRST DOWN

PASS INTERFERENCE

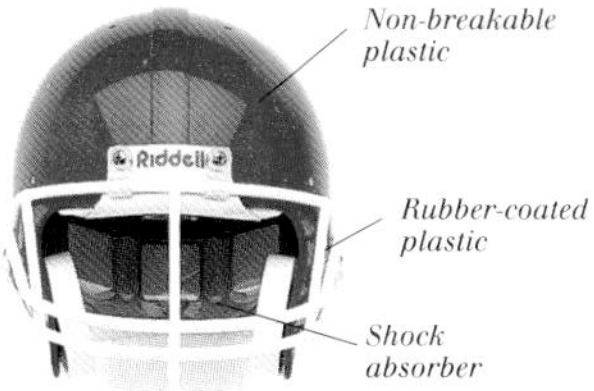

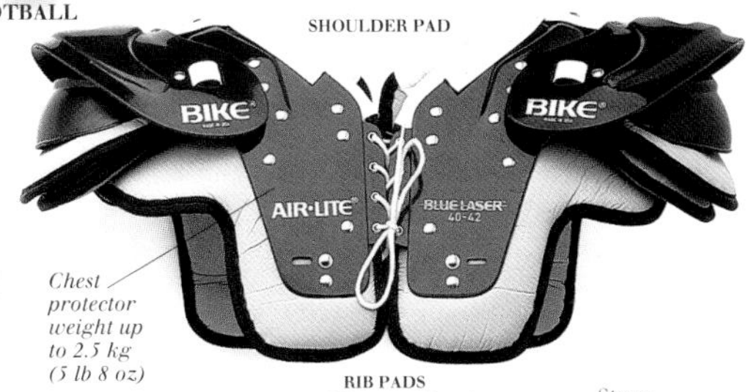

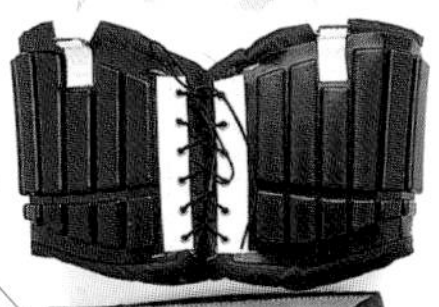

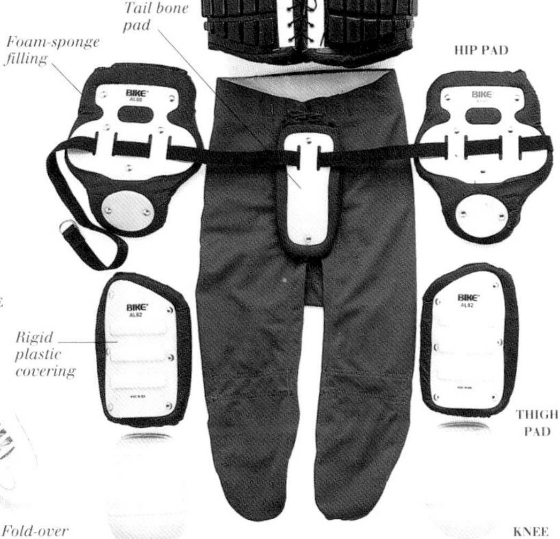

Australian rules and Gaelic football

VARIETIES OF FOOTBALL have developed all over the world and Australian rules football is considered to be one of the roughest versions, allowing full body tackles although participants wear no protective padding. The game is played on a large, oval pitch by two sides, each of 18 players. Players can kick or punch the ball, which is shaped like a rugby ball, but cannot throw it. Running with the ball is permitted, as long as the ball touches the ground at least once every ten metres. The full backs defend two sets of posts. Teams try to score "goals" (six points) between the inner posts or "behinds" (one point) inside the outer posts. Each game has four quarters of 25 minutes, and the team with the most points at the end of the allotted time is the winner. In Gaelic football, an Irish version of soccer (see pp. 524–525), a size 5 soccer ball is used. Each team can have 15 players on the field at a time. Players are allowed to catch, fist, and kick the ball, or dribble it using their hands or feet, but cannot throw it. Teams are awarded three points for getting the ball into the net, and one point for getting it through the posts above the crossbar. Gaelic football is rarely played outside of Ireland.

START OF PLAY

Field umpire

SCORING

GOAL (6 POINTS)
BEHIND (1 POINT)

AUSTRALIAN RULES FOOTBALL FIELD

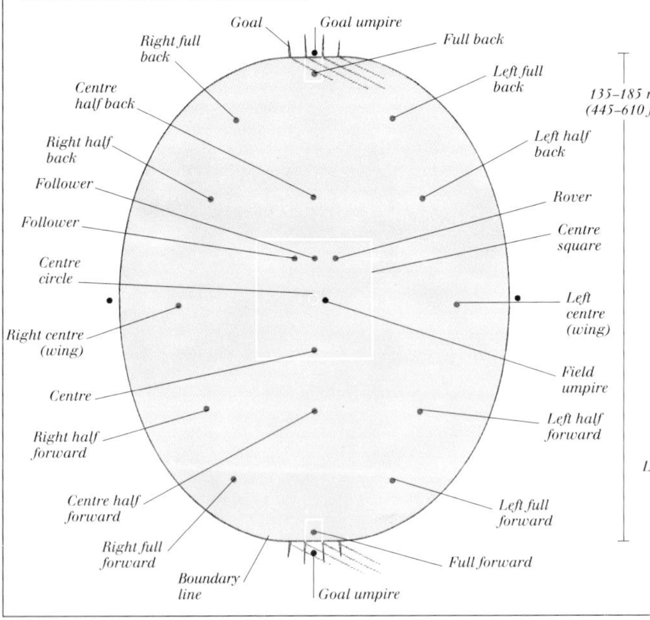
Goal
Goal umpire
Right full back
Full back
Left full back
Centre half back
135–185 m (445–610 ft)
Right half back
Left half back
Follower
Rover
Follower
Centre square
Centre circle
Left centre (wing)
Right centre (wing)
Field umpire
Centre
Left half forward
Right half forward
Centre half forward
Left full forward
Right full forward
Full forward
Boundary line
Goal umpire

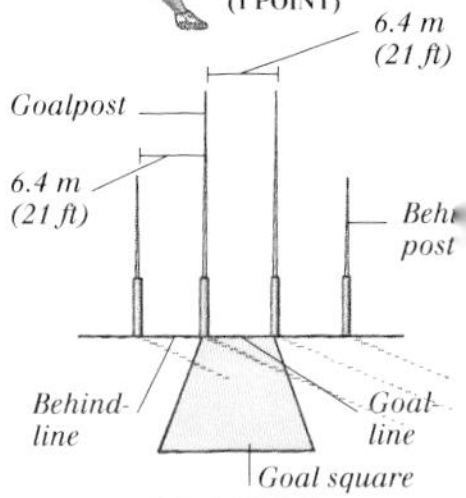
6.4 m (21 ft)
Goalpost
6.4 m (21 ft)
Behind-line
Goal square

GOALPOSTS

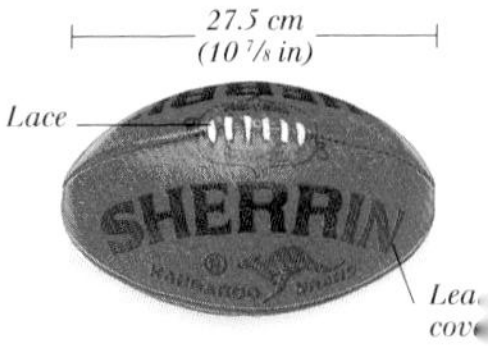
27.5 cm (10 7/8 in)
Lace
SHERRIN

AUSTRALIAN RULES FOOTBAL

STRALIAN RULES FOOTBALL SKILLS

NNING WITH THE BALL

KICKING

TACKLING

TAKING A MARK

PASSING THE BALL

AUSTRALIAN RULES FOOTBALL DRESS

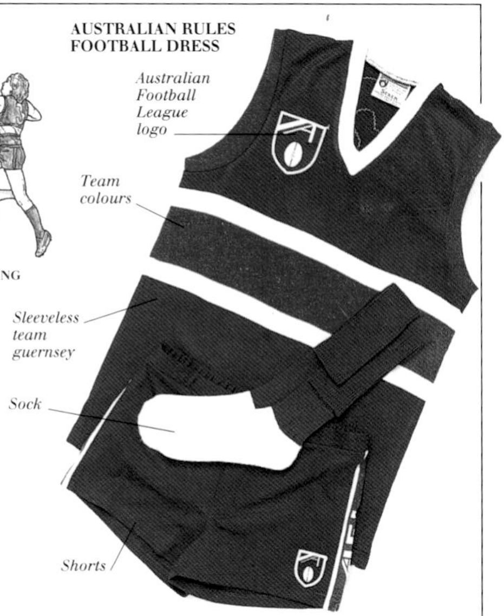
Australian Football League logo
Team colours
Sleeveless team guernsey
Sock
Shorts

AELIC FOOTBALL PITCH

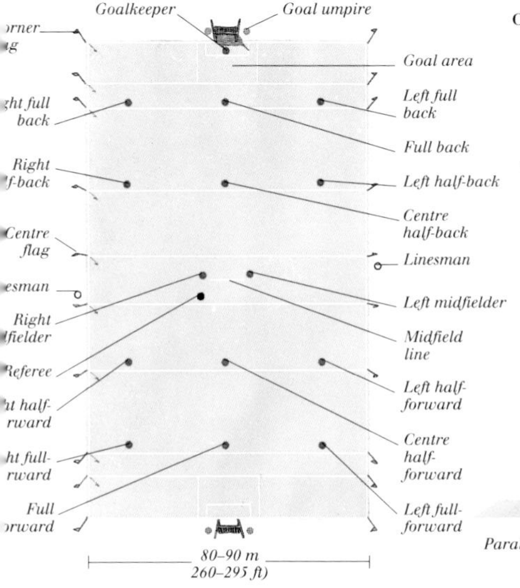
Goalkeeper
Goal umpire
rner
g
Goal area
ght full back
Left full back
Full back
Right
f-back
Left half-back
Centre half-back
Centre flag
Linesman
esman
Left midfielder
Right
fielder
Midfield line
Referee
ht half-
rward
Left half-forward
Centre half-forward
ht full-
rward
Full
rward
Left full-forward
80–90 m
260–295 ft)

CONTROLLING THE BALL

SCORING IN GAELIC FOOTBALL

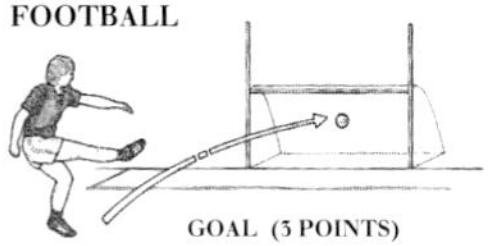

GOAL (3 POINTS)

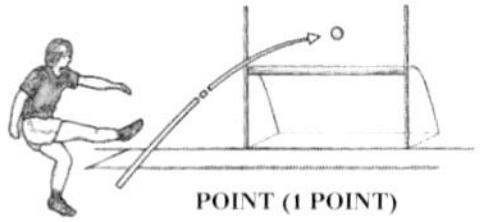

POINT (1 POINT)

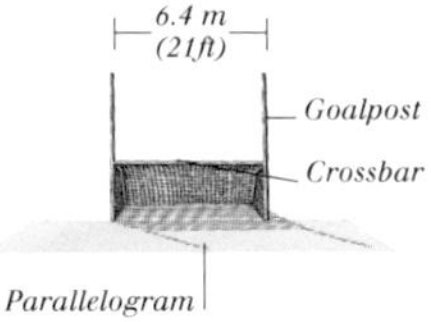
6.4 m
(21ft)
Goalpost
Crossbar
Parallelogram

GOAL

22–23 cm
(8 1/2–9 in)
O'neills
all-ireland

GAELIC FOOTBALL

Rugby

RUGBY IS PLAYED WITH AN OVAL BALL which may be carried, thrown, or kicked. There are two codes of rugby. Rugby Union is an amateur game played by two teams of 15 players. They can score points in two ways: by placing the ball by hand over the opponents' goal-line (a try, scoring four points) or by kicking it over the crossbar of the opponent's goal (a conversion of a try, scoring two points; a penalty kick, scoring three points; or a drop-kick, scoring three points). Rugby League developed from the Union game but is played by 13 players at amateur and professional levels. In League games, a try scores four points; a conversion of a try scores two points; a drop goal scores three points, and a penalty kick scores two points. Scrummages occur in both forms of the game when play stops following an infringement.

RUGBY UNION SCRUMMAGE

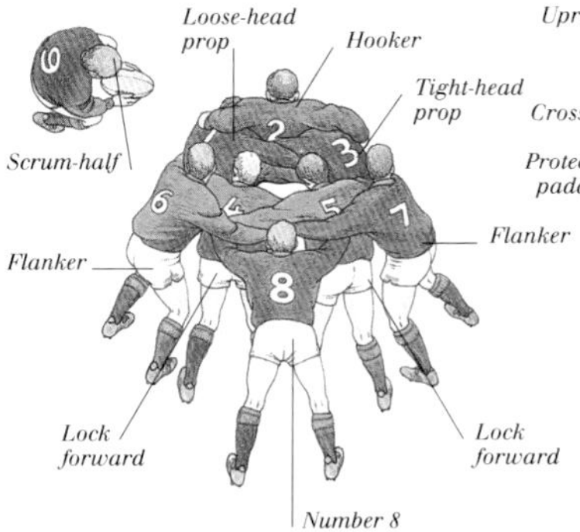

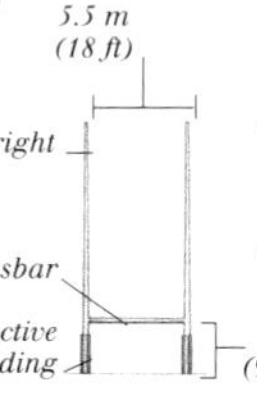

RUGBY UNION GOALPOST

RUGBY UNION PITCH

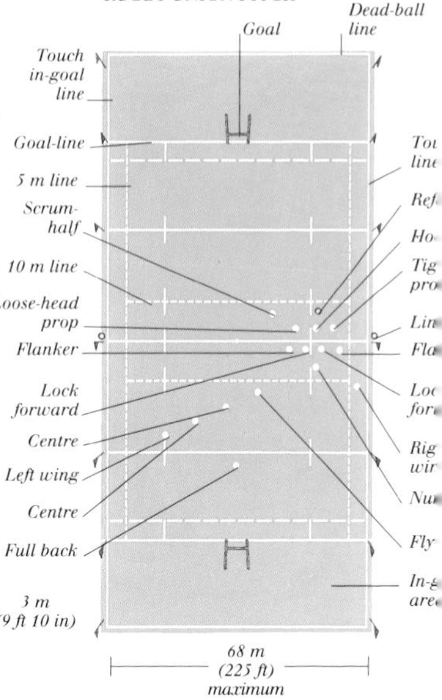

RUGBY LEAGUE SCRUMMAGE

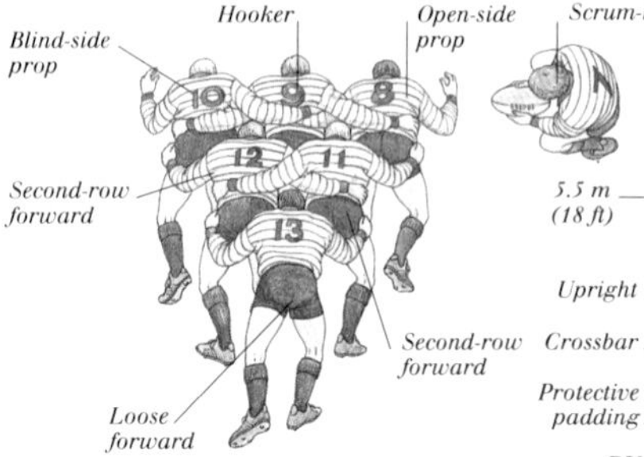

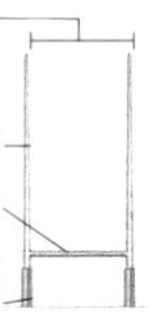

RUGBY LEAGUE GOALPOST

RUGBY LEAGUE PITCH

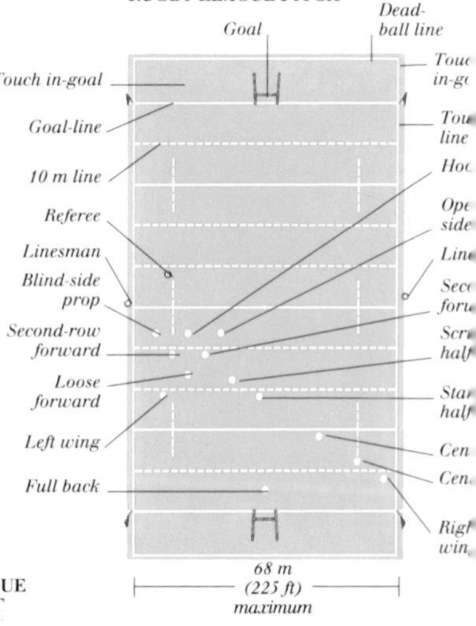

RUGBY SCORING AND SKILLS

GOAL

TRY

PASS

PLACE KICK

FLYING TACKLE

RUGBY UNION PLAYER

Shirt in team colour
Team shorts
Knee-high sock
Studded boot

RUGBY UNION BALL

Laminated leather panel covered with textured plastic
Mitre
MULTIPLEX
Four-panel construction
28–30 cm (11–12 in)

RUGBY LEAGUE BALL

Four-panel construction
Mitre
MULTIPLEX
Laminated leather panel covered with smooth plastic
28 cm (11 in)

Button-up collar
RUGBY LEAGUE SHIRT
Official logo of the British Rugby Football League
Three-quarter sleeve
UMBRO
Team crest
RUGBY UNION SHIRT
FFR
Team crest
Long sleeve
Team colour

RUGBY SHIRTS

RUGBY BOOT

Basketball

BASKETBALL IS A BALL GAME for two teams of five players, originally devised in 1890 by James Naismath for the Y.M.C.A. in Springfield, Massachusetts, U.S.A. The object of the game is to take possession of the ball and score points by throwing the ball into the opposing team's basket. A player moves the ball up and down the court by bouncing it along the ground or "dribbling"; the ball may be passed between players by throwing, bouncing, or rolling. Players may not run with or kick the ball, although pivoting on one foot is allowed. The game begins with the referee throwing the ball into the air and a player from each team jumping up to try and "tip" the ball to a team-mate. The length of the game and the number of periods played varies at different levels. There are amateur, professional, and international rules. No game ends in a draw. An extra period of five minutes is played, plus as many extra periods as are necessary to break the tie. In addition to the five players on court, each team has up to seven substitutes, but players may only leave the court with the permission of the referee. Basketball is a non-contact sport and fouls on other players are penalized by a throw-in awarded against the offending team; a free throw at the basket is awarded when a player is fouled in the act of shooting. Basketball is a fast-moving game, requiring both physical and mental coordination. Skilful tactical play matters more than simple physical strength and the agility of the players makes the game an excellent spectator sport.

INTERNATIONAL BASKETBALL COURT

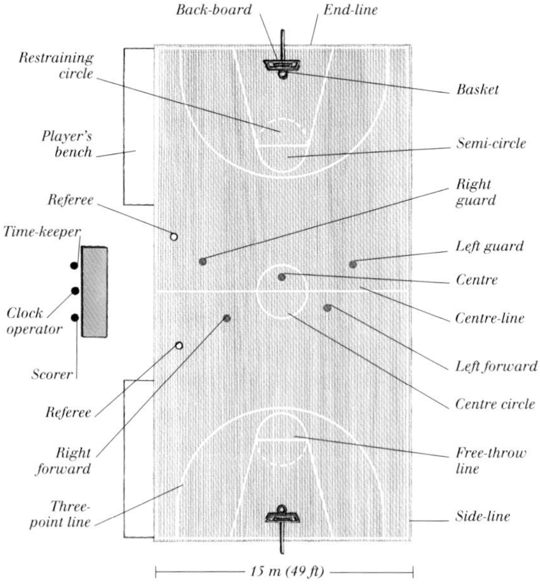
Back-board
End-line
Restraining circle
Basket
Player's bench
Semi-circle
Referee
Right guard
Time-keeper
Left guard
Centre
Clock operator
Centre-line
Left forward
Scorer
Referee
Centre circle
Right forward
Free-throw line
Three-point line
Side-line
15 m (49 ft)

BASKET AND BACK-BOARD

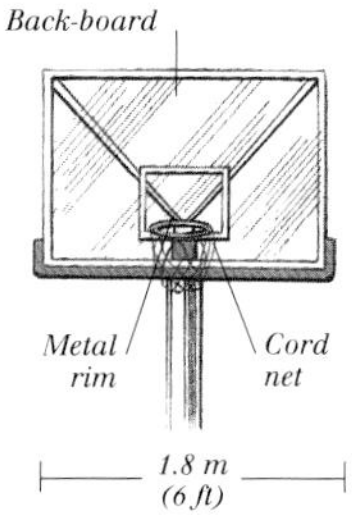
Back-board
Metal rim
Cord net
1.8 m (6 ft)

BASKET AND BACK-BOARD STRUCTURE

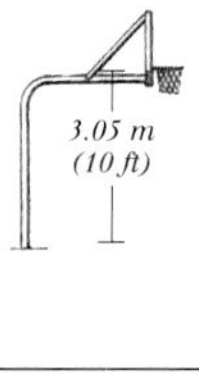
3.05 m (10 ft)

BASKETBALL SKIL

CHEST PASS
DRIBBLE
OVERHEAD PASS
LAY-UP SHOT
JUMP SHOT
LONG PASS

ZONE DEFENCES

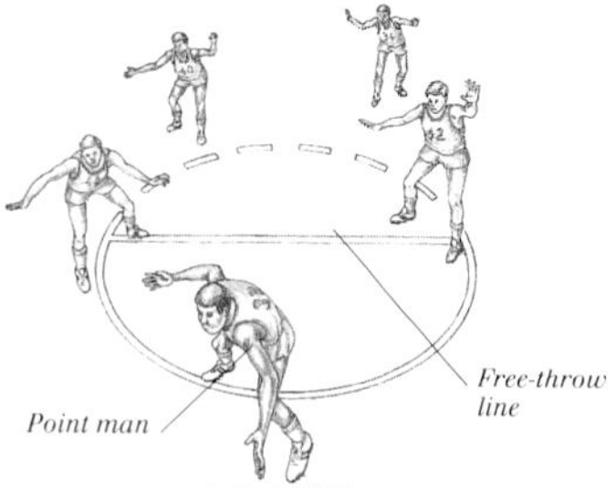
Point man
Free-throw line

1 – 2 – 2 ZONE

1 – 3 – 1 ZONE

2 – 3 ZONE

AMERICAN BASKETBALL VEST

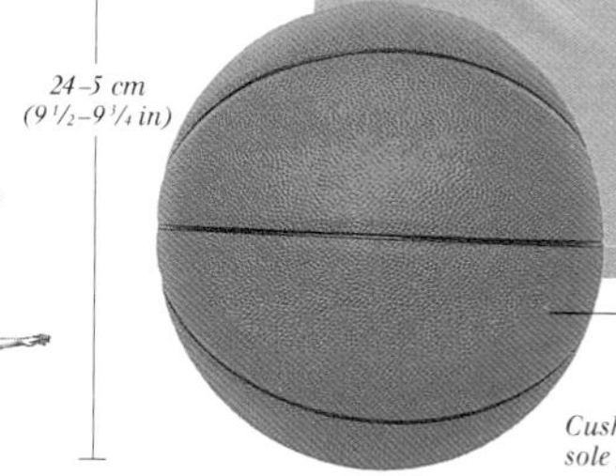
24–5 cm (9½–9¾ in)
Textured surface for good grip

BASKETBALL

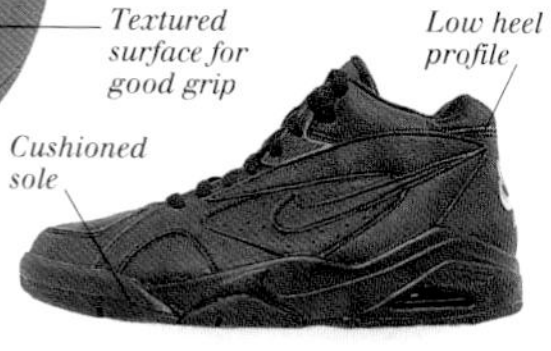
Low heel profile
Cushioned sole

BASKETBALL SHOE

INTERNATIONAL REFEREE'S SIGNALS

TECHNICAL FOUL
INTENTIONAL FOUL
JUMP BALL
STOP CLOCK FOR FOUL
SUBSTITUTION
RSONAL FOUL: FREE THROWS
TRAVELLING
ILLEGAL DRIBBLE
CHARGING WITH THE BALL
ONE FREE THROW
STOP CLOCK

Volleyball, netball, and handball

VOLLEYBALL, NETBALL, AND HANDBALL are fast-moving team sports played with balls on courts with a hard surface. In volleyball, the object of the game is to hit the ball over a net strung across the centre of the court so that it touches the ground on the opponent's side. The team of six players can take three hits to direct the ball over the net, although the same player cannot hit the ball twice in a row. Players can hit the ball with their arms, hands or any other part of their upper body. Teams score points only while serving. The first team to score 15 points, with a two-point margin over their opponent, wins the game. Netball is one of the few sports played exclusively by women. Similar to basketball (see pp.532–533), it is played on a slightly larger court with seven players instead of five. A team moves the ball towards the goal by throwing, passing, and catching it with the aim of throwing the ball through the opponents' goal net. Players are confined by their playing position to specific areas of the court. Team handball is one of the world's fastest games. Each side has seven players. A team moves the ball by dribbling, passing, or bouncing it as they run. Players may stop, catch, throw, bounce, or strike the ball with any part of the body above the knees. Each team tries to score goals by directing the ball past the opposition's goalkeeper into the net, which is similar to a soccer net.

VOLLEYBALL SHOTS

OVERHAND SERVE

SPIKE (SMASH)

UNDERHAND SERVE

FOREARM PASS (DIG)

VOLLEYBALL KIT

Team colours
Ribbed cuff
Cotton-knit jersey
Elasticated waist
Shorts

VOLLEYBALL COURT

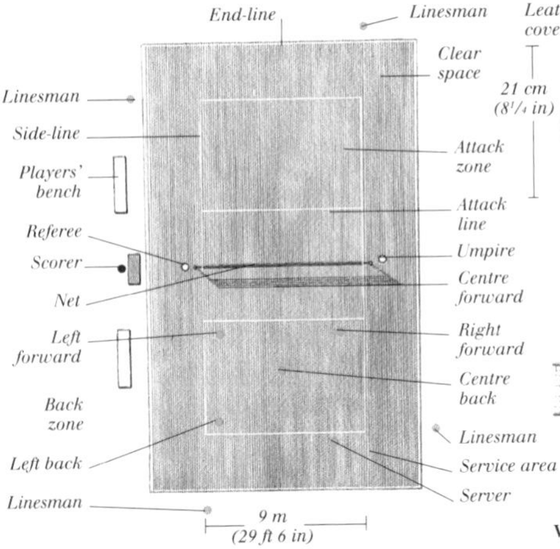
End-line
Linesman
Clear space
Linesman
Side-line
Players' bench
Attack zone
Attack line
Referee
Umpire
Scorer
Centre forward
Net
Left forward
Right forward
Centre back
Back zone
Linesman
Left back
Service area
Server
Linesman
9 m
(29 ft 6 in)

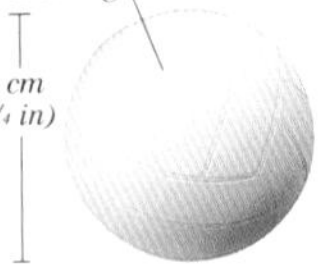
Leather covering
21 cm
(8¼ in)

VOLLEYBALL

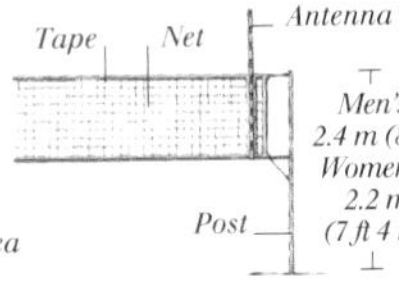
Antenna
Tape
Net
Men's:
2.4 m (8 ft)
Women's:
2.2 m
(7 ft 4 in)
Post

VOLLEYBALL NET

Elasticated knit fabric
Injecte
mould
paddi

KNEE PADS

ETBALL COURT

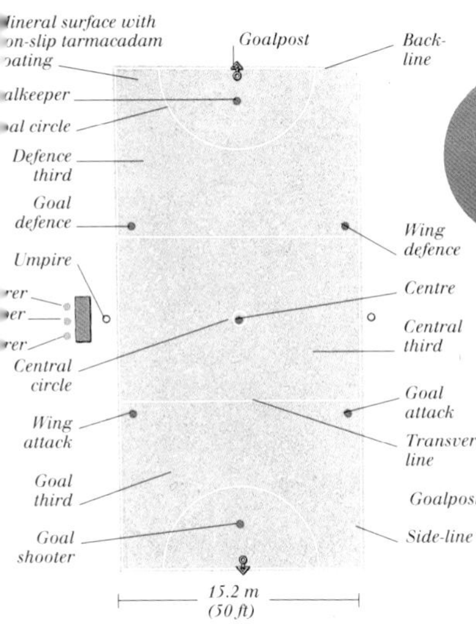

lineral surface with
on-slip tarmacadam
oating
Goalpost
Back-
line
alkeeper
al circle
Defence
third
Goal
defence
Wing
defence
Umpire
rer
er
rer
Centre
Central
third
Central
circle
Goal
attack
Wing
attack
Transverse
line
Goal
third
Goal
shooter
Side-line
15.2 m
(50 ft)

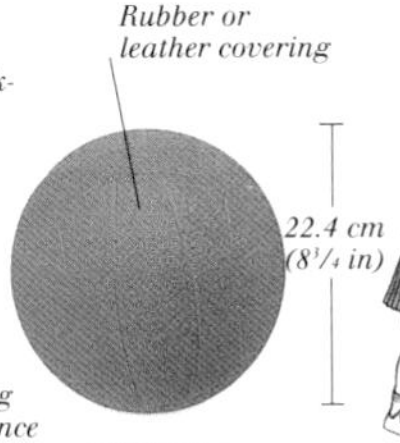

Rubber or
leather covering
22.4 cm
(8¾ in)

NETBALL

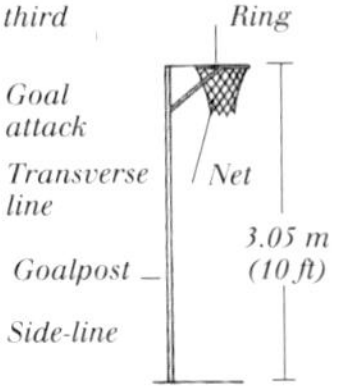

Ring
Net
Goalpost
3.05 m
(10 ft)

NETBALL GOALPOST AND NET

NETBALL PASSES

CHEST PASS

UNDERARM PASS

SHOULDER PASS

BOUNCE PASS

HANDBALL COURT

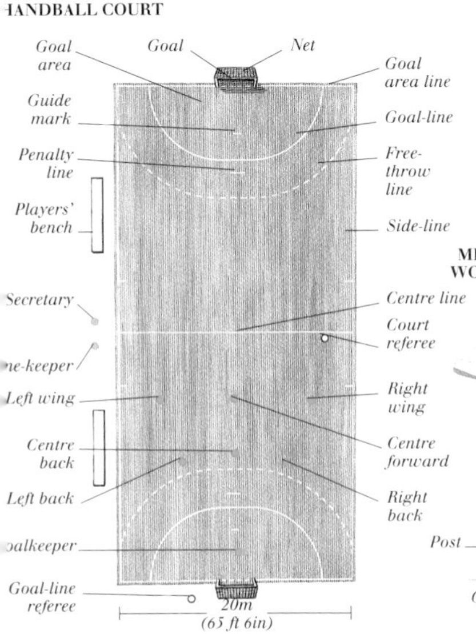

Goal
area
Goal
Net
Goal
area line
Guide
mark
Goal-line
Penalty
line
Free-
throw
line
Players'
bench
Side-line
Secretary
Centre line
Court
referee
ne-keeper
Left wing
Right
wing
Centre
back
Centre
forward
Left back
Right
back
oalkeeper
Goal-line
referee
20m
(65 ft 6in)

Leather
covering

HANDBALL
MEN'S: 18.8 CM (7½ IN)
WOMEN'S: 17.5 CM (7 IN)

HANDBALL SHOE

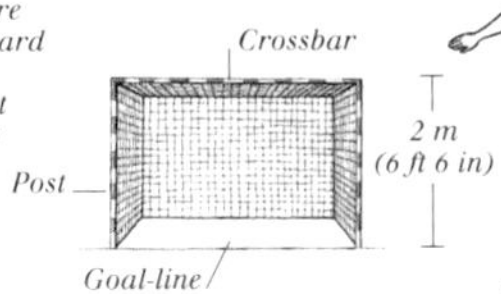

Crossbar
2 m
(6 ft 6 in)
Post
Goal-line

HANDBALL NET

HANDBALL SKILLS

OVERARM PASS

DRIBBLE

BOUNCE PASS

JUMP SHOT

Baseball

BASEBALL IS A BALL GAME for two teams of nine players. The batter hits the ball thrown by the opposing team's pitcher, into the area between the foul lines. He then runs round all four fixed bases in order to score a run, touching or "tagging" each base in turn. The pitcher must throw the ball at a height between the batter's armpits and knees, a height which is called the "strike zone". A ball pitched in this area that crosses over the "home plate" is called a "strike" and the batter has three strikes in which to try and hit the ball (otherwise he is "struck out"). The fielding team tries to get the batting team out by catching the ball before it bounces, tagging a player of the batting team with the ball who is running between bases, or by tagging a base before the player has reached it. Members of the batting team may stop safely at a base as long as it is not occupied by another member of their team. When the batter runs to first base, his team-mate at first base must run on to second – this is called "force play". A game consists of nine innings and each team will bat once during an inning. When three members of the batting team are out, the teams swap roles. The team with the greatest number of runs wins the game.

BATTER'S HELMET

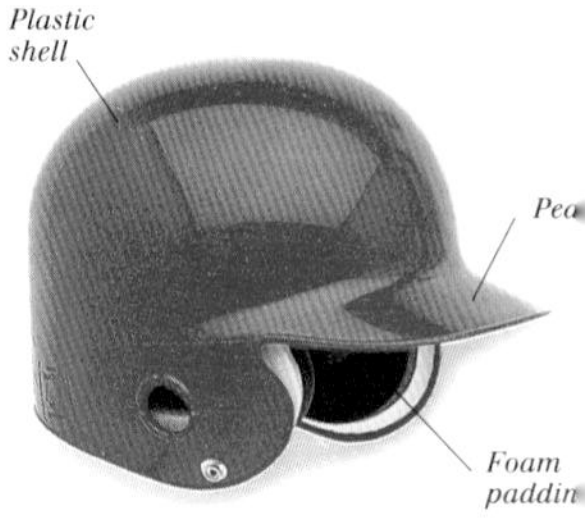
Plastic shell
Pea
Foam
paddin

Wire coated in strong nylon
Plastic-coated foam padding

CATCHER'S MASK

BASEBALL PITCH

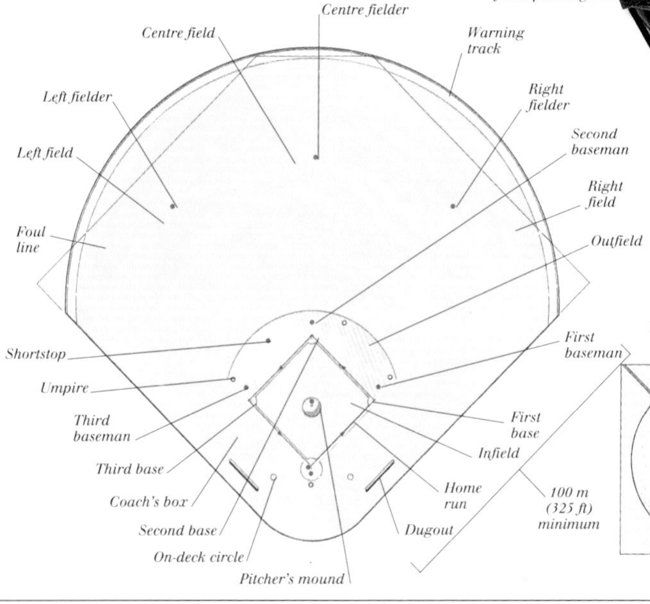
Centre fielder
Centre field
Warning track
Left fielder
Right fielder
Left field
Second baseman
Right field
Foul line
Outfield
Shortstop
First baseman
Umpire
Third baseman
First base
Infield
Third base
Home run
Coach's box
100 m (325 ft) minimum
Second base
Dugout
On-deck circle
Pitcher's mound

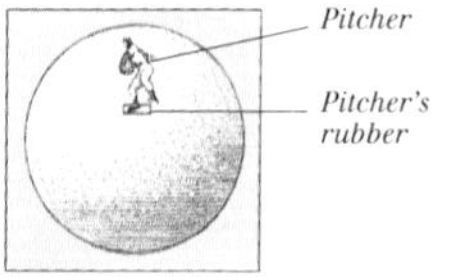
Pitcher
Pitcher's rubber

PITCHER'S MOUND

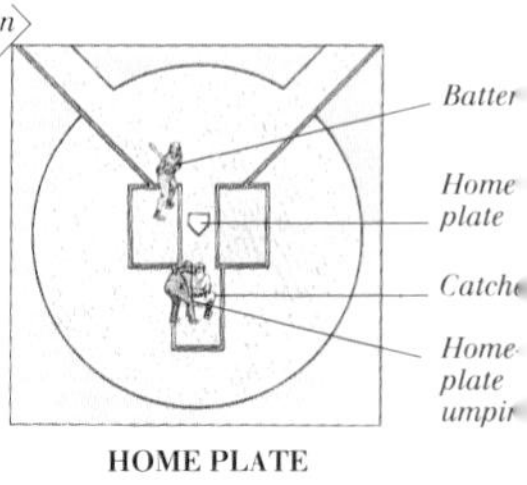
Batter
Home plate
Catche
Home-plate umpir

HOME PLATE

AKING A BASEBALL

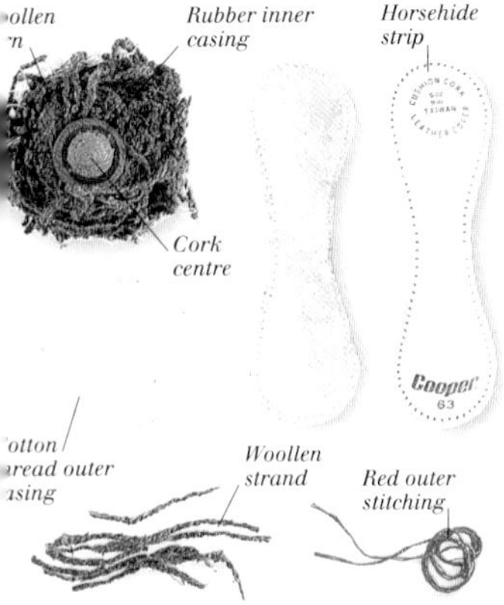

HE PITCHING SEQUENCE

HE WIND-UP 1 | THE WIND-UP 2 | THE WIND-UP 3

HE WIND-UP 4 | THE RELEASE | THE FOLLOW-THROUGH

MPIRING SIGNALS

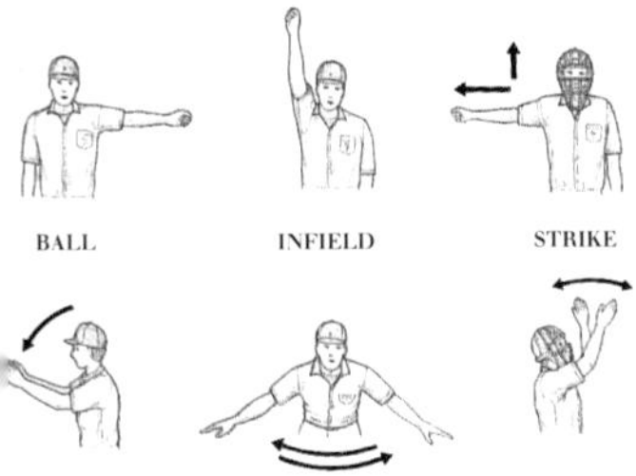

BALL | INFIELD | STRIKE

FAIR BALL | RUNNER IS SAFE | FOUL TIP

BASEBALL EQUIPMENT

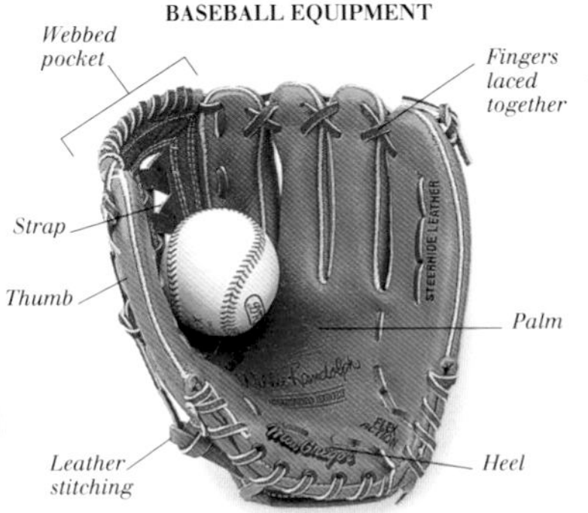
Webbed pocket
Fingers laced together
Strap
Thumb
Palm
STEERHIDE LEATHER
Leather stitching
Heel

FIELDER'S GLOVE AND BALL

PONY
Metal heel plate
Metal toe plate

AMERICAN BASEBALL BOOT

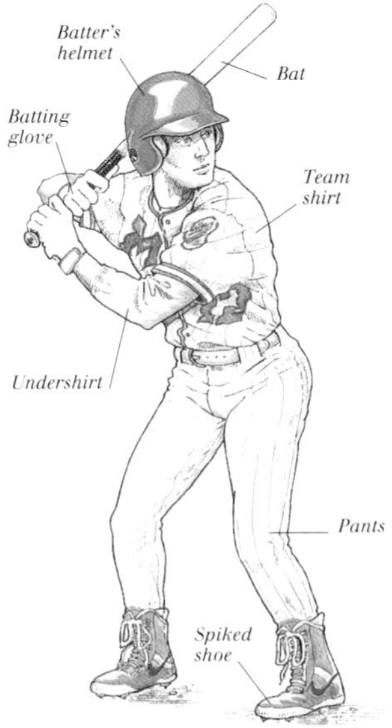
Batter's helmet
Bat
Batting glove
Team shirt
Undershirt
Pants
Spiked shoe

BATTER

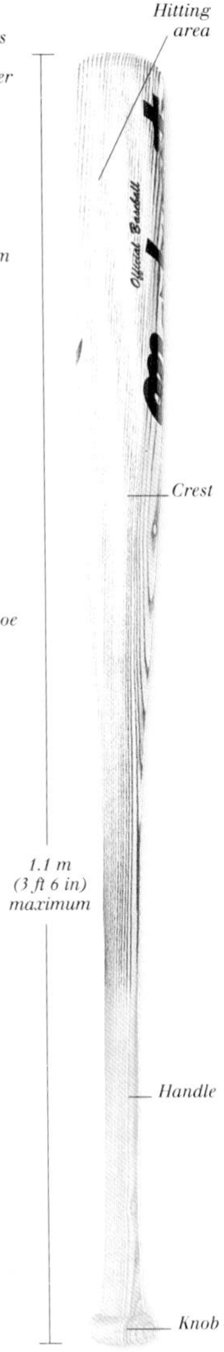
Hitting area
Official Baseball
Crest
1.1 m
(3 ft 6 in)
maximum
Handle
Knob

BAT

Cricket

CRICKET IS A BALL GAME PLAYED by two teams of eleven players on a pitch with two sets of three stumps (wickets). The bowler bowls the ball down the pitch to the batsman of the opposing team, who must defend the wicket in front of which he stands. The object of the game is to score as many runs as possible. Runs can be scored individually by running the length of the playing strip, or by hitting a ball which lands outside the boundary ("six"), or which lands inside the boundary but bounces or rolls outside ("four"); the opposing team will bowl and field, attempting to dismiss the batsmen. A batsman can be dismissed in one of several ways: by the bowler hitting the wicket with the ball ("bowled"); by a fielder catching the ball hit by the batsman before it touches the ground ("caught"); by the wicket-keeper or another fielder breaking the wicket while the batsman is attempting a run and is therefore out of his ground ("stumped" or "run out"); by the batsman breaking the wicket with his own bat or body ("hit wicket"); by a part of the batsman's body being hit by a ball that would otherwise have hit the wicket ("leg before wicket" ["lbw"]). A match consists of one or two innings and each innings ends when the tenth batsman of the batting team is out, when a certain number of overs (a series of six balls bowled) have been played, or when the captain of the batting team "declares" ending the innings voluntarily.

CRICKET STROKES

CRICKET PITCH

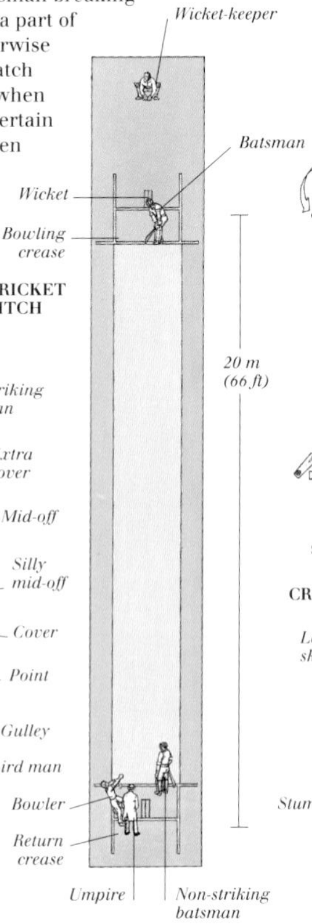
Wicket-keeper
Batsman
Wicket
Bowling crease
20 m (66 ft)
Bowler
Return crease
Umpire
Non-striking batsman

POSSIBLE FIELD POSITIONS FOR AN AWAY SWING BOWLER TO A RIGHT-HANDED BATSMAN (IN RED) AND OTHER FIELD POSITIONS

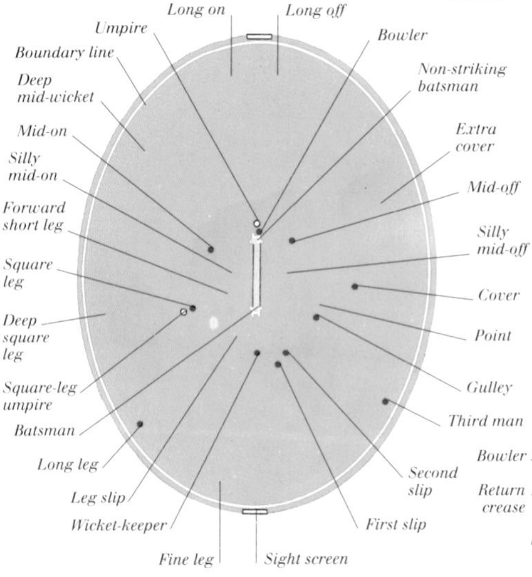
Long on
Long off
Umpire
Bowler
Boundary line
Non-striking batsman
Deep mid-wicket
Extra cover
Mid-on
Silly mid-on
Mid-off
Forward short leg
Silly mid-off
Square leg
Cover
Deep square leg
Point
Square-leg umpire
Gulley
Batsman
Third man
Long leg
Second slip
Leg slip
Wicket-keeper
First slip
Fine leg
Sight screen

CRICKET BALL AND WICK

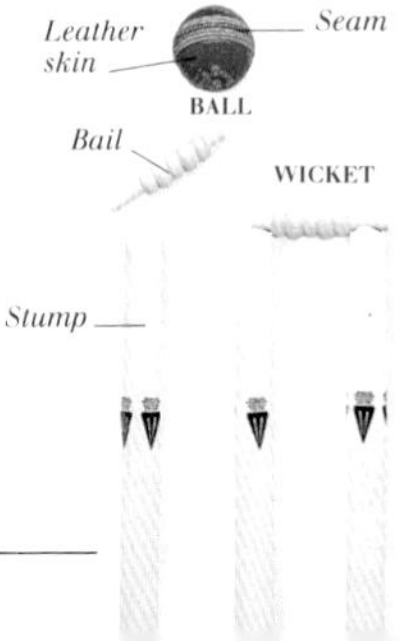
Leather skin
Seam
BALL
Bail
WICKET
Stump

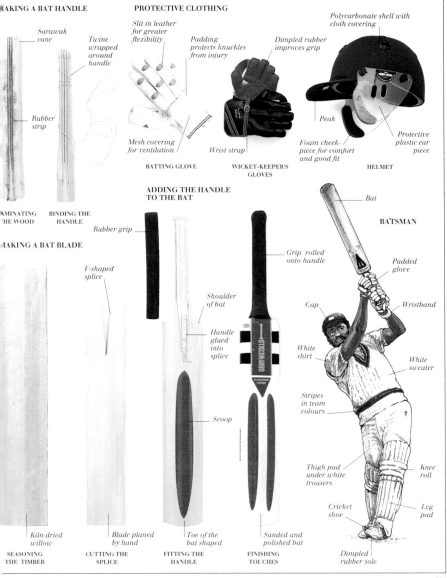

MAKING A BAT HANDLE

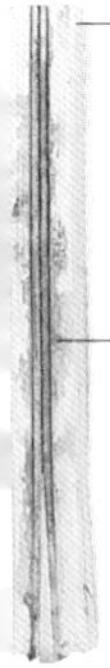
Sarawak cane
Rubber strip

LAMINATING THE WOOD

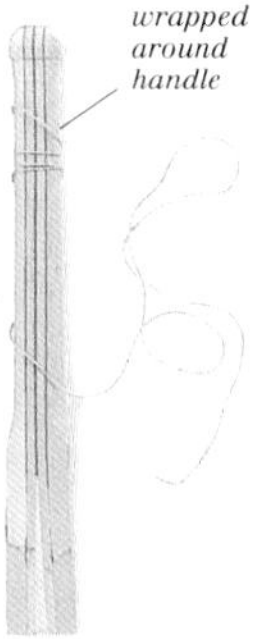
Twine wrapped around handle

BINDING THE HANDLE

PROTECTIVE CLOTHING

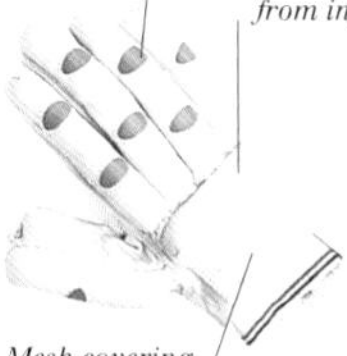
Slit in leather for greater flexibility
Padding protects knuckles from injury
Mesh covering for ventilation

BATTING GLOVE

Dimpled rubber improves grip
Wrist strap

WICKET-KEEPER'S GLOVES

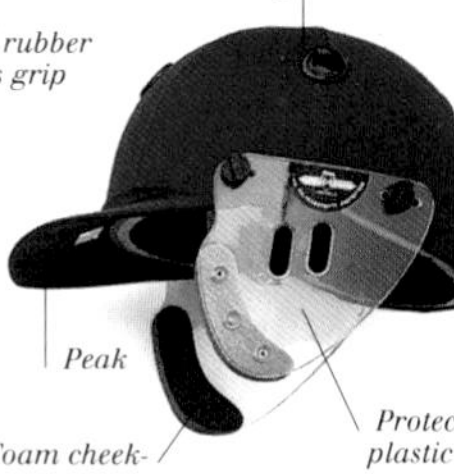
Polycarbonate shell with cloth covering
Peak
Foam cheek-piece for comfort and good fit
Protective plastic ear piece

HELMET

MAKING A BAT BLADE

Kiln-dried willow

SEASONING THE TIMBER

V-shaped splice
Blade planed by hand

CUTTING THE SPLICE

ADDING THE HANDLE TO THE BAT

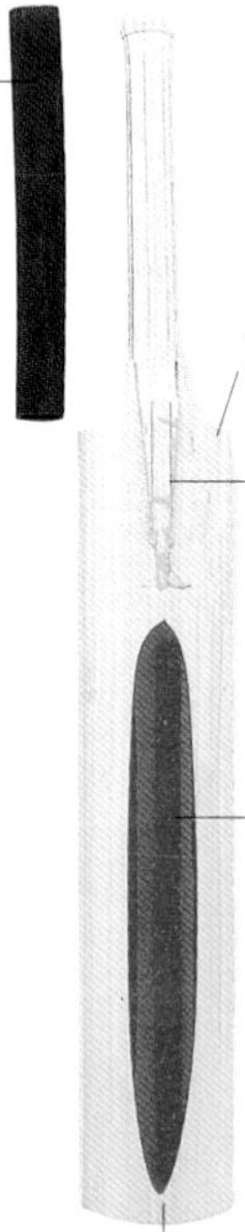
Rubber grip
Shoulder of bat
Handle glued into splice
Scoop
Toe of the bat shaped

FITTING THE HANDLE

Grip rolled onto handle
GRAY-NICOLLS
Sanded and polished bat

FINISHING TOUCHES

Bat
Padded glove
Wristband
Cap
White shirt
White sweater
Stripes in team colours
Thigh pad under white trousers
Knee roll
Leg pad
Cricket shoe
Dimpled rubber sole

BATSMAN

Hockey, lacrosse, and hurling

ALL OVER THE WORLD, TEAM GAMES have evolved which require that a ball be struck or carried, and tossed at the end of a stick. Early forms of these games include hurling, shinty, bandy, and pelota. Hockey is played by men and women: two teams of eleven players try to gain and keep possession of the ball and score goals by using the hockey stick to propel the ball into their opponents' goal net. Skills such as passing, pushing, or hitting the ball by slapping or lifting it in a flicking movement, and shooting at goal are crucial. Hockey is played indoors and outdoors on grass or synthetic pitches. Lacrosse is played internationally as a 12-a-side game for women and as 10-a-side game for men. The women's pitch has no absolute boundaries but the men's pitch has clearly defined side-lines and end-lines. The ball is kept in play by being carried, thrown or batted with the crosse, and rolled or kicked in any direction. In men's and women's lacrosse, play can continue behind the marked goal areas. Similar skills are required in hurling – a Gaelic field game played on the same pitch as Gaelic football (see pp. 528–529), using the same goalposts and net. In hurling, the ball may be struck with or carried on the hurley and, when off the ground, may be struck with the hand or kicked. Goals (three points) are scored when the ball passes between the posts and under the crossbar; one point is scored when it passes between the posts and over the crossbar.

HOCKEY STICK AND BALL

STICK

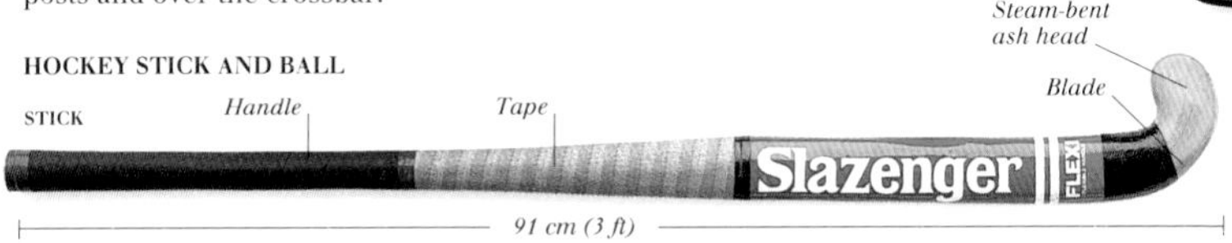
Handle
Tape
Steam-bent ash head
Blade
Slazenger
FLEX
91 cm (3 ft)

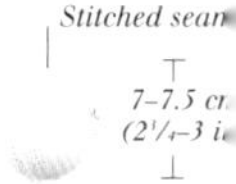
Stitched seam
7–7.5 cm
(2¾–3 in)
BALL

HOCKEY FIELD

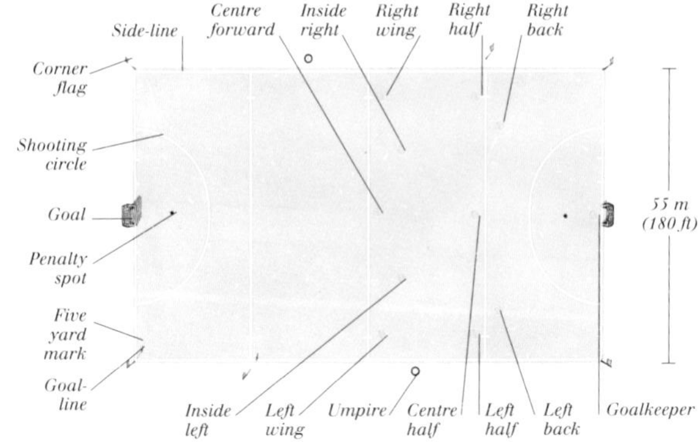
Side-line
Centre forward
Inside right
Right wing
Right half
Right back
Corner flag
Shooting circle
Goal
Penalty spot
Five yard mark
Goal-line
55 m (180 ft)
Inside left
Left wing
Umpire
Centre half
Left half
Left back
Goalkeeper

GOALKEEPER'S EQUIPMENT

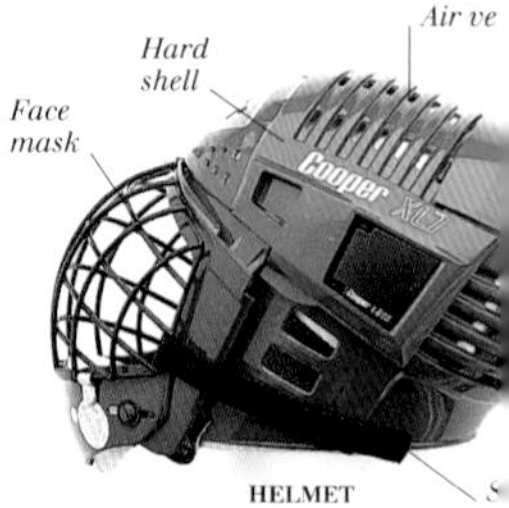

HELMET

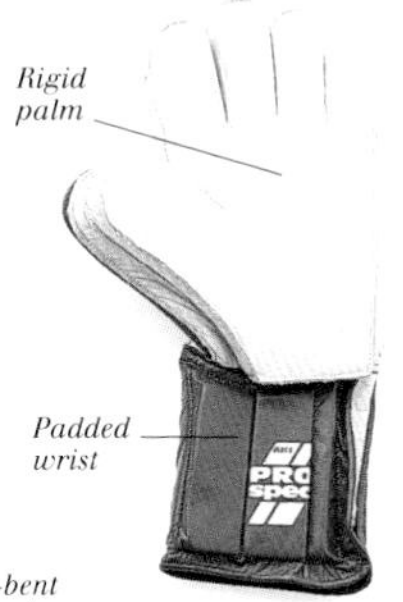

GAUNTLET

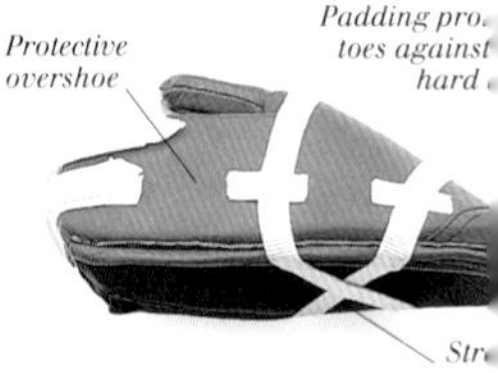

GOALKEEPER'S KICKER

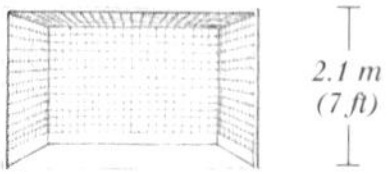
2.1 m
(7 ft)
HOCKEY GOAL

MEN'S LACROSSE FIELD

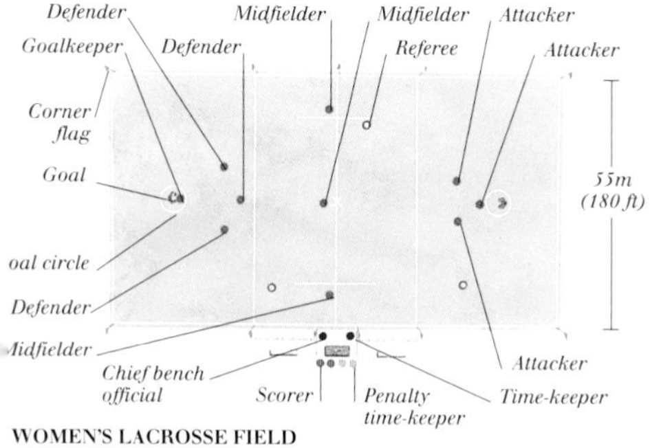
Defender
Goalkeeper
Defender
Midfielder
Midfielder
Attacker
Referee
Attacker
Corner flag
Goal
55m (180 ft)
oal circle
Defender
Iidfielder
Chief bench official
Scorer
Penalty time-keeper
Time-keeper
Attacker

LACROSSE SKILLS

CRADLING

THROWING

SIDE-SHOOTING

WOMEN'S LACROSSE FIELD

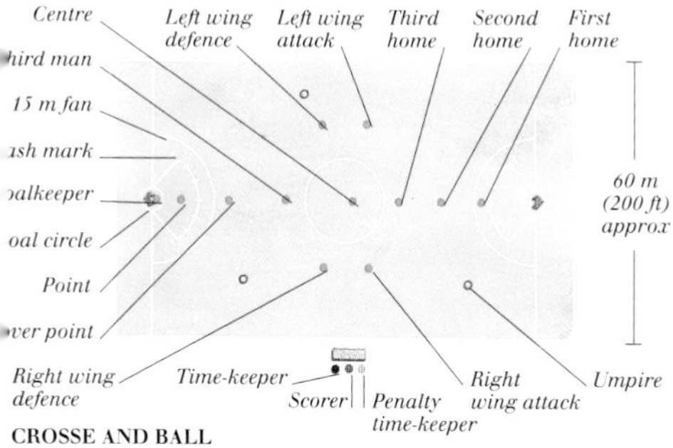
Centre
Left wing defence
Left wing attack
Third home
Second home
First home
hird man
15 m fan
ash mark
oalkeeper
oal circle
Point
ver point
60 m (200 ft) approx
Right wing defence
Time-keeper
Scorer
Penalty time-keeper
Right wing attack
Umpire

LACROSSE GOALKEEPER

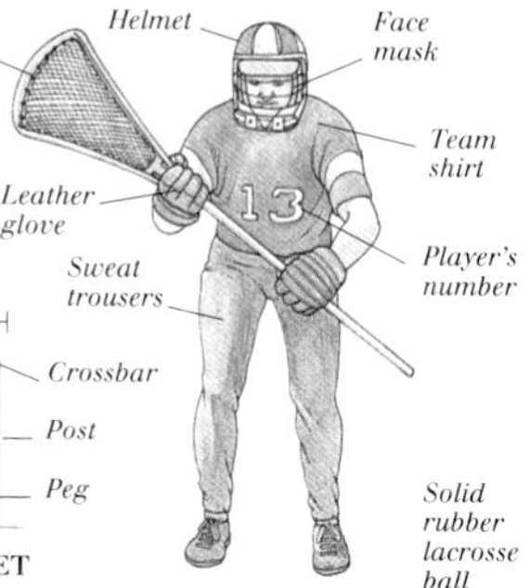
Helmet
Face mask
Goalkeeper's stick
Team shirt
Leather glove
Player's number
Sweat trousers

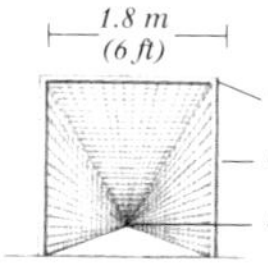
1.8 m (6 ft)
Crossbar
Post
Peg

LACROSSE NET

CROSSE AND BALL

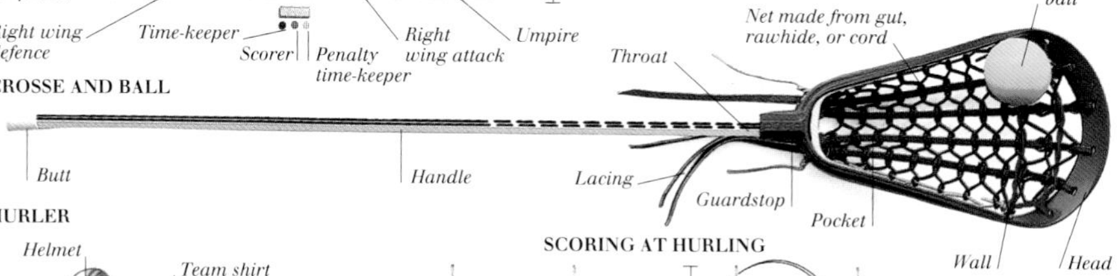
Solid rubber lacrosse ball
Net made from gut, rawhide, or cord
Throat
Butt
Handle
Lacing
Guardstop
Pocket
Wall
Head

HURLER

Helmet
Team shirt
Hurley
Shorts
Sock
Boot

SCORING AT HURLING

GOAL (3 POINTS)

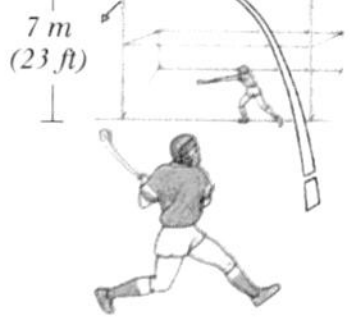
7 m (23 ft)

POINT (1 POINT)

Leather cover around a cork centre

HURLING BALL

HURLEY AND HURLING BALL

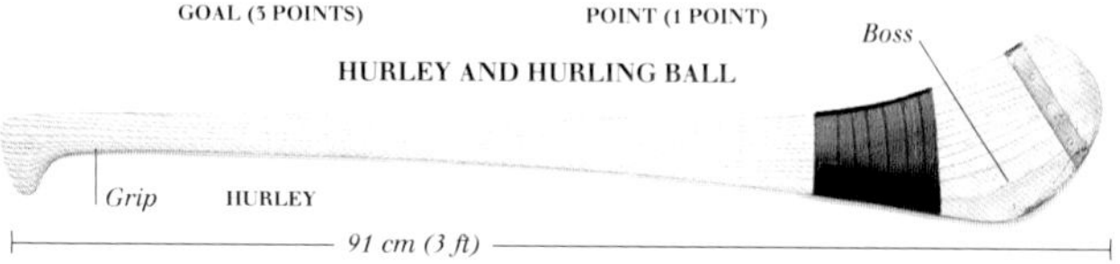
Boss
Grip
91 cm (3 ft)

HURLEY

Athletics

THE SPORTS that make up athletics are divided into two main groups: track events – which include sprinting, middle, and long distance running, relay running, hurdling, and walking – and field events which require jumping and throwing skills. Contests designed to test the speed, strength, agility, and stamina of athletes were held by the ancient Greeks over 4,000 years ago. However, the abolition of the Olympic Games in 393 AD meant that athletics were neglected until the revival of large-scale competitions in the mid-nineteenth century. Modern stadia offer areas reserved for the long jump, triple jump, and pole vault usually situated outside the running track. The javelin, shot, hammer, and discus are thrown within the track area. Most athletes specialize in one or two events but, in the heptathlon, women compete in seven events, held over two days: 200 m and 800 m races, 100 m hurdles, javelin, shot put, high jump, and long jump. In the decathlon, men compete in ten events over two days: 100 m, 400 m, and 1,500 m races, 110 m hurdles, javelin, discus, shot put, pole vault, high jump, and long jump.

FIELD EVENT EQUIPMENT

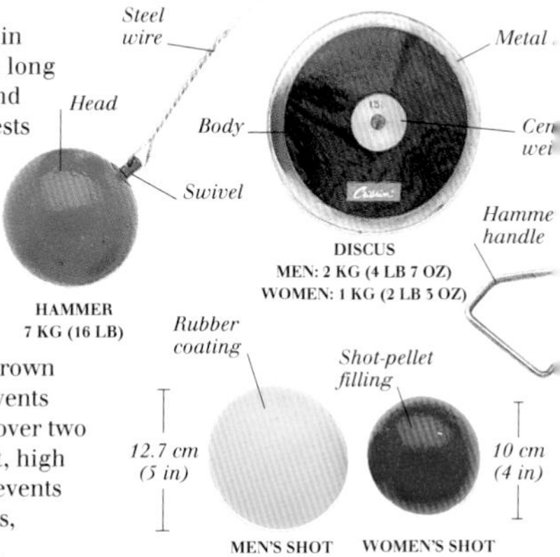
Steel wire
Head
Swivel
Body
Metal
Cen
wei
Hamme
handle
Rubber coating
Shot-pellet filling
12.7 cm (5 in)
10 cm (4 in)

HAMMER
7 KG (16 LB)

DISCUS
MEN: 2 KG (4 LB 7 OZ)
WOMEN: 1 KG (2 LB 3 OZ)

MEN'S SHOT
7 KG (16 LB)

WOMEN'S SHOT
4 KG (8 LB 12 OZ)

JAVELIN

Cord grip
Shaft
Tip
Men: 2.6 m (8 ft 6 in)
Women: 2.3 m (7 ft 6 in)

ATHLETICS TRACK AND FIELD

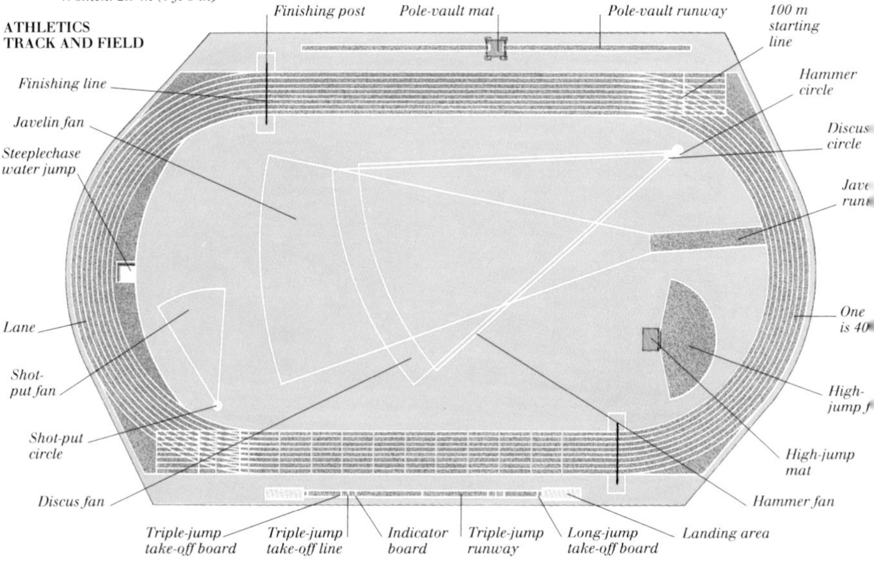
Finishing post
Pole-vault mat
Pole-vault runway
100 m starting line
Finishing line
Hammer circle
Javelin fan
Discus circle
Steeplechase water jump
Jave
runi
Lane
One
is 40
Shot-put fan
High-
jump f
Shot-put circle
High-jump mat
Discus fan
Hammer fan
Triple-jump take-off board
Triple-jump take-off line
Indicator board
Triple-jump runway
Long-jump take-off board
Landing area

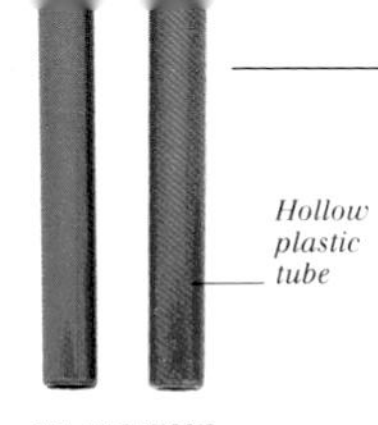
Hollow
plastic
tube

RELAY BATONS

TYPES OF SHOE

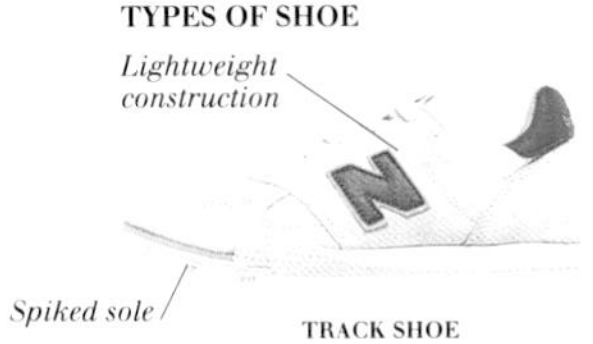
Lightweight
construction
Spiked sole

TRACK SHOE

Air "pumping" device
for comfort and fit
Reflective
side strip
Wedge
heel
Air-cushioned
sole

RUNNING SHOE

ISCUS THROW

Swing
Shift
Twist
Release

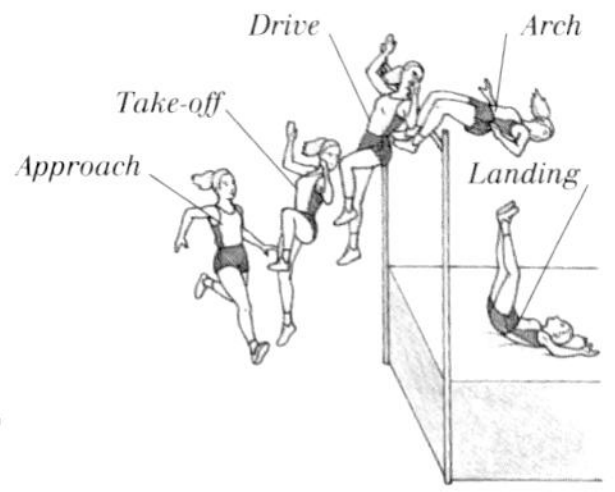
Drive
Arch
Take-off
Approach
Landing

HIGH JUMP

HOT PUT

Crouch
Shift
Thrust
Release

AMMER THROW

Swing
Entry
Lift
Release

AVELIN THROW

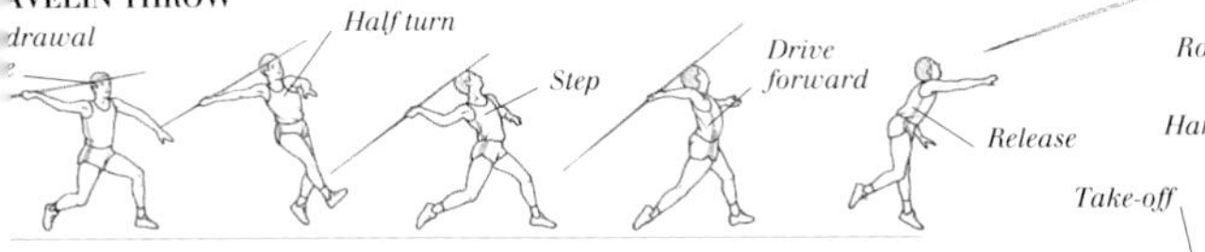
drawal
Half turn
Step
Drive
forward
Release

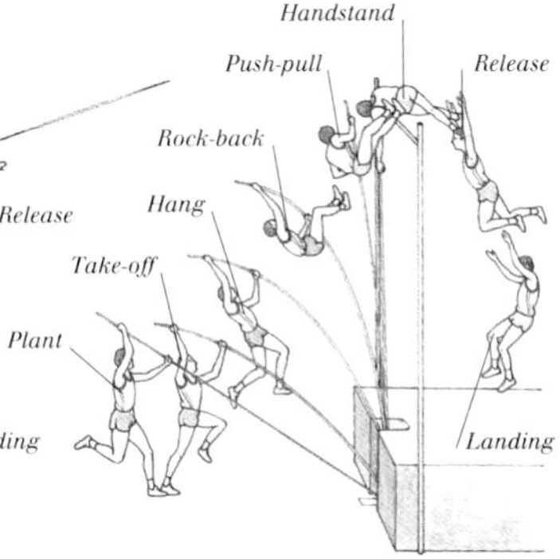
Handstand
Push-pull
Release
Rock-back
Hang
Take-off
Plant
Landing

POLE VAULT

ONG JUMP

Take-off
Flight
Hitch-kick
Stretch
Landing
Take-off
board

RIPLE JUMP

ake-off
Hop
Skip
Jump
Take-off
board
Land on foot
used for take-off
Land on
opposite foot

Racket sports

PROTECTIVE EYEWEAR

THE OBJECT OF ALL RACKET SPORTS is to make shots the opponent cannot return. Games are played by two players (singles) or four players (doubles). Racket shape and size is tailored to each sport, but all rackets are constructed of wood, plastic, aluminium, or high-performance materials such as fibreglass and carbon graphite. Racket strings are usually synthetic, although natural gut is still used. Tennis is played on a court divided by a low net. Opposing players serve alternate games. At least six games must be won to gain a set, and two or sometimes three sets are needed to win a match. Tennis courts may be concrete, grass, clay, or synthetic, each surface requiring a different style of play. Badminton is an indoor sport that is played with light, flexible rackets and a feather shuttlecock on a court with a high net. Players can score points only on their serve. The first to reach 15 points (11 points for women's singles) wins the game. Two games are needed to win a match. Squash and racketball are both played in enclosed courts. One player hits the ball against the front wall, and the other tries to return it before it bounces on the floor more than once. Squash rackets have smaller, rounder heads and stiffer frames than badminton rackets. In America, the game is played on a narrower court than an international court using a much harder ball. Squash games are played to nine points (international) or 15 points (American). In racketball, players use a ball that is larger and bouncier than a squash ball. The racket is thick and sturdy, with a large head, short handle, and a thong that loops around the wrist. Points can be won only when serving, and the first player to reach 21 points wins.

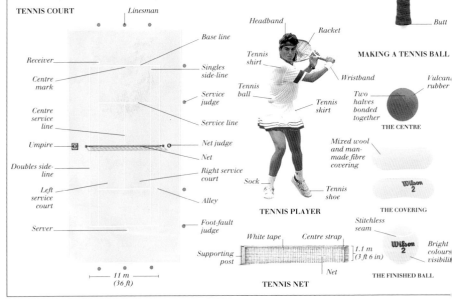

TENNIS RACKET

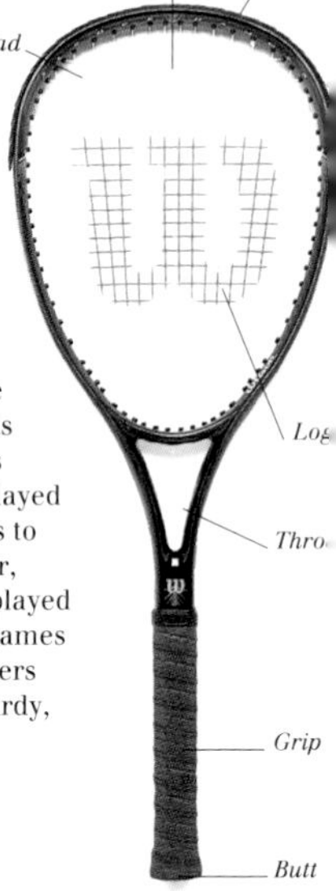
Synthetic string
Fram
Head
Log
Thro
Grip
Butt

TENNIS COURT

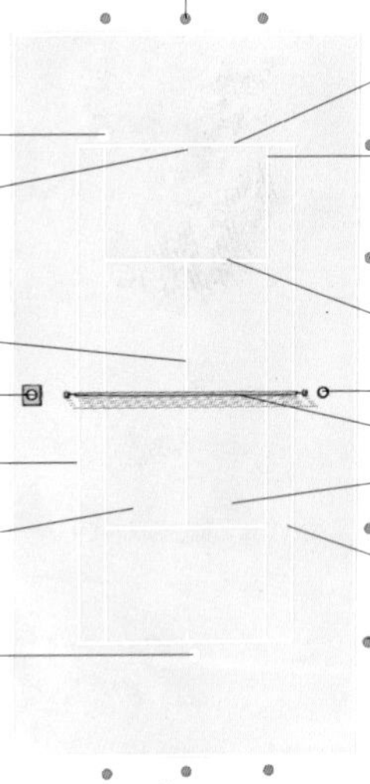
Linesman
Base line
Receiver
Singles side-line
Centre mark
Service judge
Centre service line
Service line
Umpire
Net judge
Net
Doubles side-line
Right service court
Left service court
Alley
Server
Foot-fault judge
11 m (36 ft)

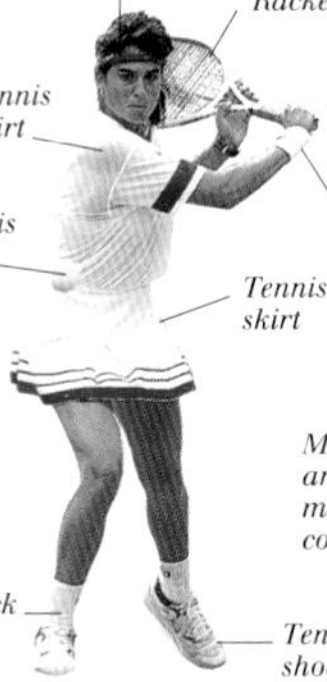
Headband
Racket
Tennis shirt
Wristband
Tennis ball
Tennis skirt
Sock
Tennis shoe

TENNIS PLAYER

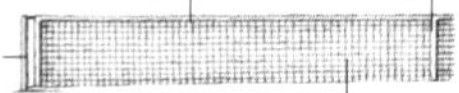
White tape
Centre strap
Supporting post
1.1 m (3 ft 6 in)
Net

TENNIS NET

MAKING A TENNIS BALL

Vulcan rubber
Two halves bonded together

THE CENTRE

Mixed wool and man-made fibre covering

Wilson
2

THE COVERING

Stitchless seam
Wilson
2
Bright colours visibili

THE FINISHED BALL

BADMINTON RACKET AND SHUTTLECOCK

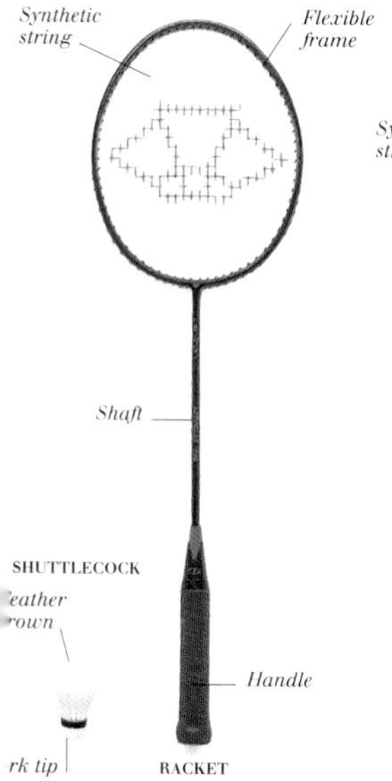

SQUASH RACKET AND SQUASH BALLS

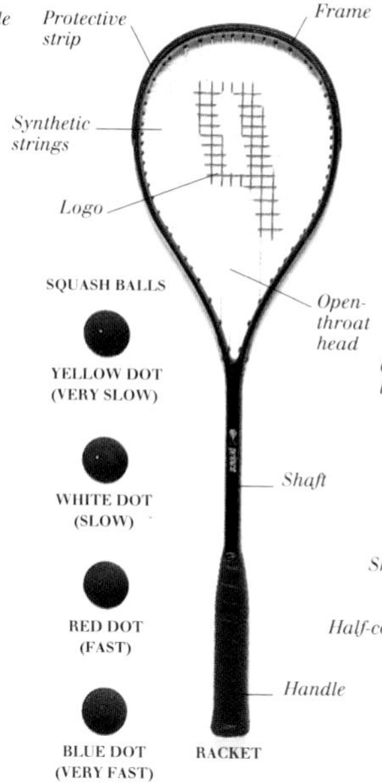
Protective strip
Frame
Synthetic strings
Logo
Open-throat head
Shaft
Handle
SQUASH BALLS
YELLOW DOT (VERY SLOW)
WHITE DOT (SLOW)
RED DOT (FAST)
BLUE DOT (VERY FAST)
RACKET

AMERICAN SQUASH COURT

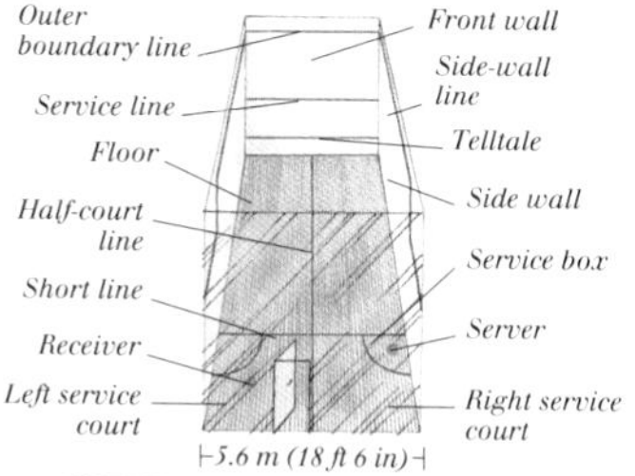
Outer boundary line
Front wall
Side-wall line
Service line
Telltale
Floor
Side wall
Half-court line
Service box
Short line
Server
Receiver
Left service court
Right service court
5.6 m (18 ft 6 in)

INTERNATIONAL SQUASH COURT

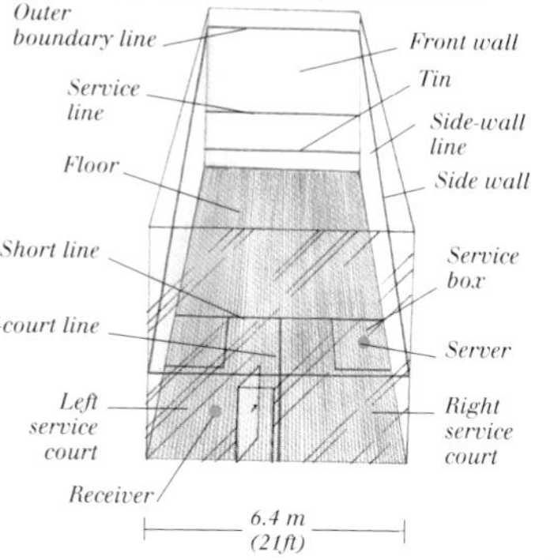
Outer boundary line
Front wall
Service line
Tin
Side-wall line
Floor
Side wall
Short line
Service box
Half-court line
Server
Left service court
Right service court
Receiver
6.4 m (21ft)

BADMINTON COURT

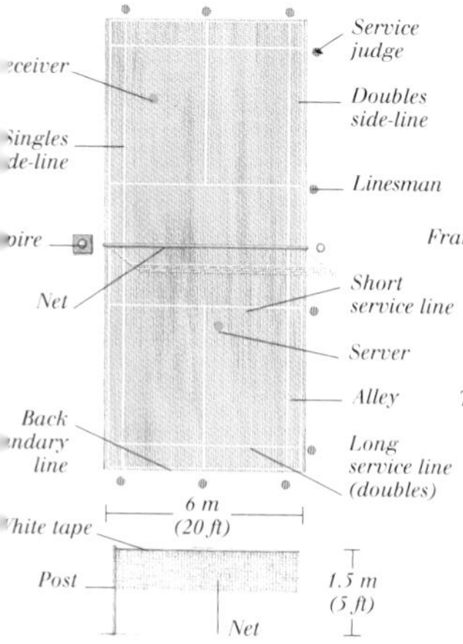
Service judge
eceiver
Doubles side-line
Singles de-line
Linesman
pire
Net
Short service line
Server
Alley
Back ndary line
Long service line (doubles)
6 m (20 ft)
hite tape
Post
1.5 m (5 ft)
Net

BADMINTON NET

RACKETBALL RACKET, BALL, AND GLOVE

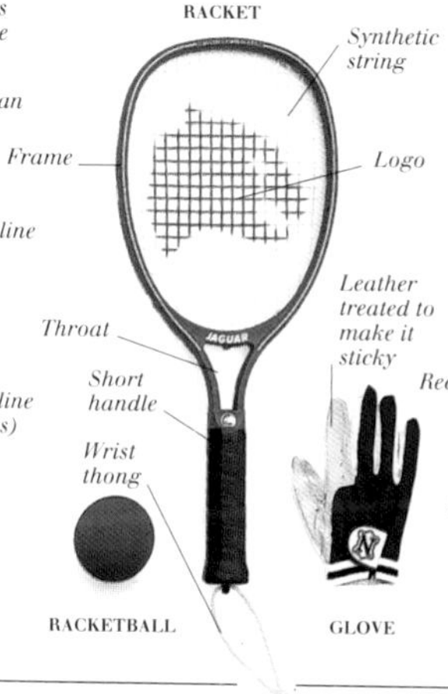
RACKET
Synthetic string
Frame
Logo
Throat
JAGUAR
Short handle
Leather treated to make it sticky
Wrist thong
RACKETBALL
GLOVE

RACKETBALL COURT

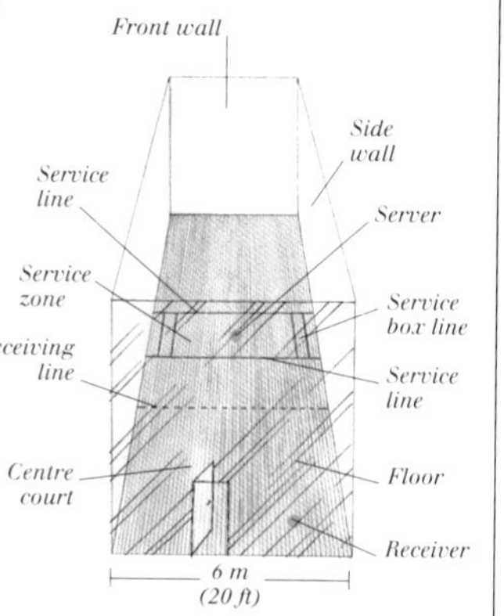
Front wall
Side wall
Service line
Server
Service zone
Service box line
Receiving line
Service line
Centre court
Floor
Receiver
6 m (20 ft)

Golf

GOLF BALL AND TEE

THE GAME OF GOLF was first played in Scotland some 400 years ago. Players are required to hit a ball, using a wooden or iron club, from a smooth level point or "teeing ground", down the "fairway", and on to a putting green where the target hole is located. The fairway is a strip of clear land along which there are natural hazards – such as ponds and streams, man-made hazards – such as bunkers (sand-pits), and rough (areas of uncut grass). Championship golf courses have 18 holes. The object of the game is to hit the ball into each hole in turn, and to complete the "round" using as few strokes as possible. Players compete individually or in teams, playing the course together in groups of two, three, or four. The two basic forms of competition are match play and stroke play. In match play, the side winning the majority of holes over a certain number of rounds wins the match. In stroke play, the winner is the player who finishes a certain number of rounds having made the fewest strokes.

GOLF BALL WITH BALATA SURFACE

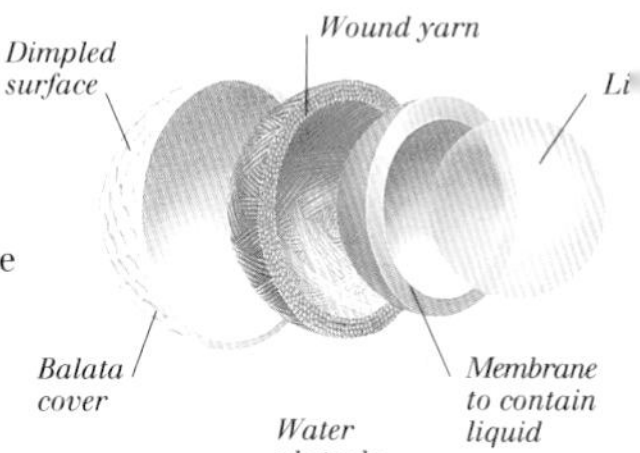

Dimpled surface
Wound yarn
Balata cover
Membrane to contain liquid

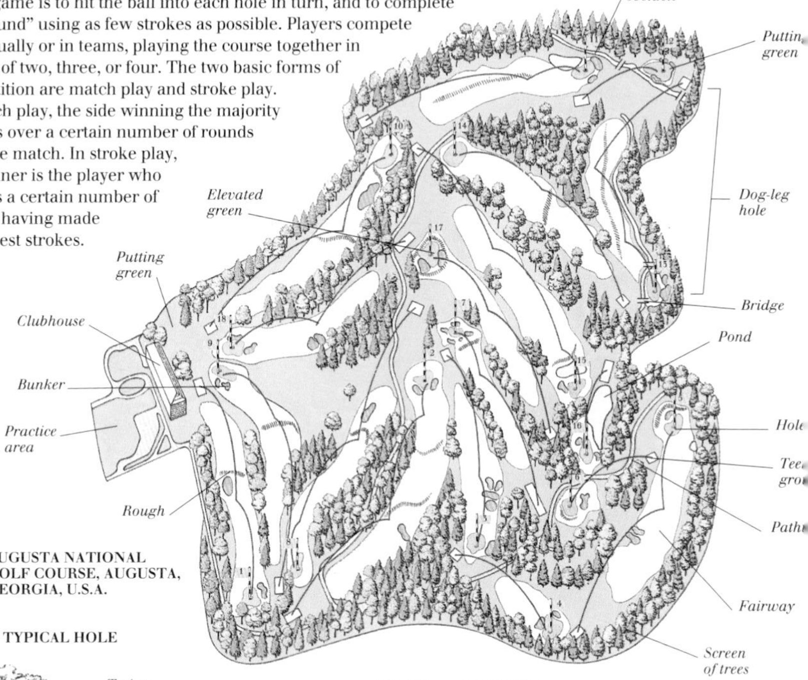

Water obstacle
Dog-leg hole
Elevated green
Putting green
Bridge
Pond
Clubhouse
Bunker
Practice area
Rough
Fairway
Screen of trees

AUGUSTA NATIONAL GOLF COURSE, AUGUSTA, GEORGIA, U.S.A.

A TYPICAL HOLE

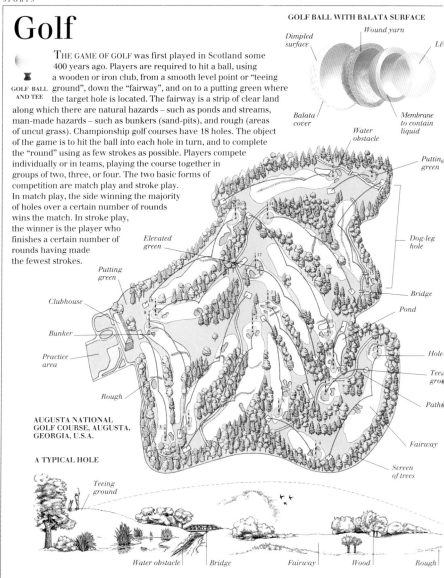

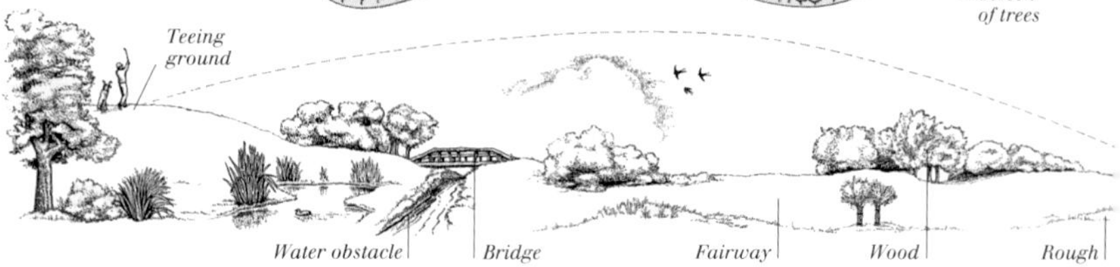

Teeing ground
Water obstacle
Bridge
Fairway
Wood
Rough

MAKING A WOODEN CLUB

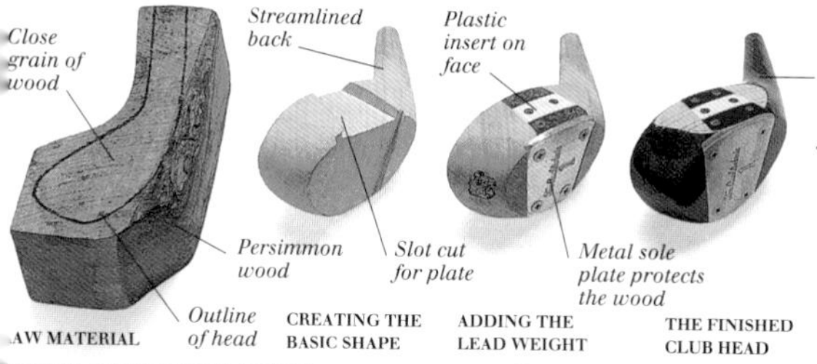
Close grain of wood
Persimmon wood
Outline of head
AW MATERIAL
Streamlined back
Slot cut for plate
CREATING THE BASIC SHAPE
Plastic insert on face
Metal sole plate protects the wood
ADDING THE LEAD WEIGHT
Sand, stain, and varnish finish
THE FINISHED CLUB HEAD

RANGE OF WOODEN CLUBS

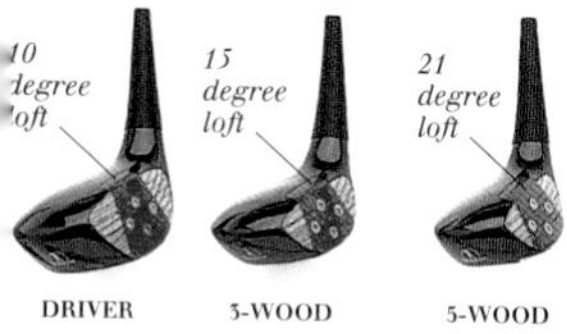
10 degree loft
DRIVER
15 degree loft
3-WOOD
21 degree loft
5-WOOD

RANGE OF IRON CLUBS

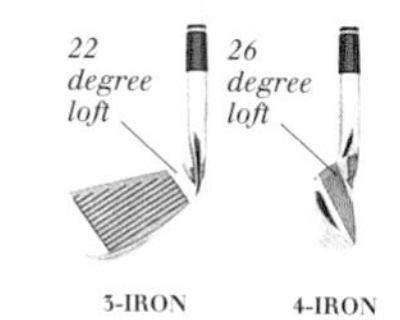
22 degree loft
3-IRON
26 degree loft
4-IRON

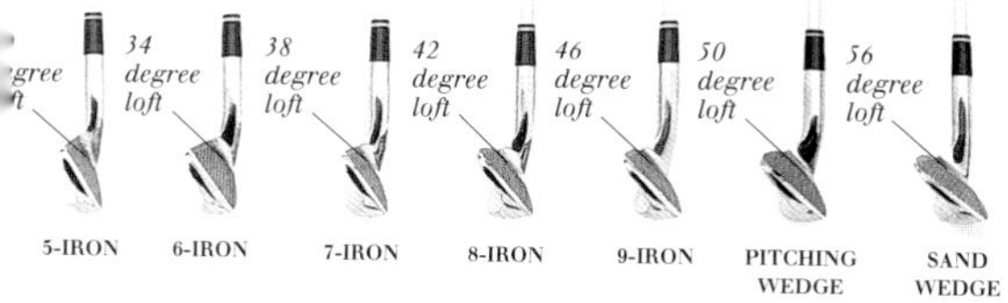
5-IRON
34 degree loft
6-IRON
38 degree loft
7-IRON
42 degree loft
8-IRON
46 degree loft
9-IRON
50 degree loft
PITCHING WEDGE
56 degree loft
SAND WEDGE

GOLF ACCESSORIES

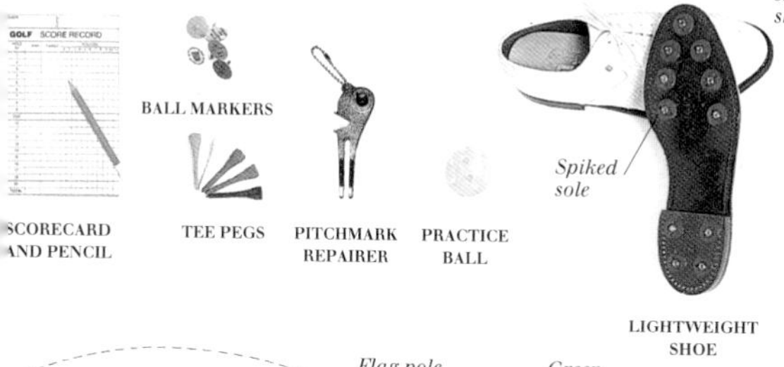
GOLF SCORE RECORD
SCORECARD AND PENCIL
BALL MARKERS
TEE PEGS
PITCHMARK REPAIRER
PRACTICE BALL
Spiked sole
LIGHTWEIGHT SHOE

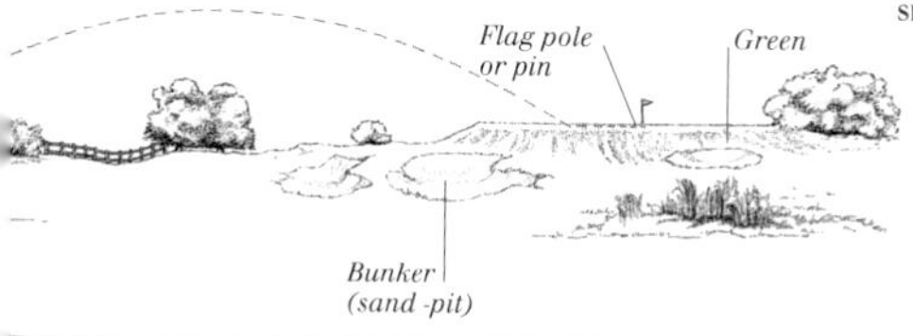
Flag pole or pin
Green
Bunker (sand -pit)

PUTTER, WOOD, AND IRON

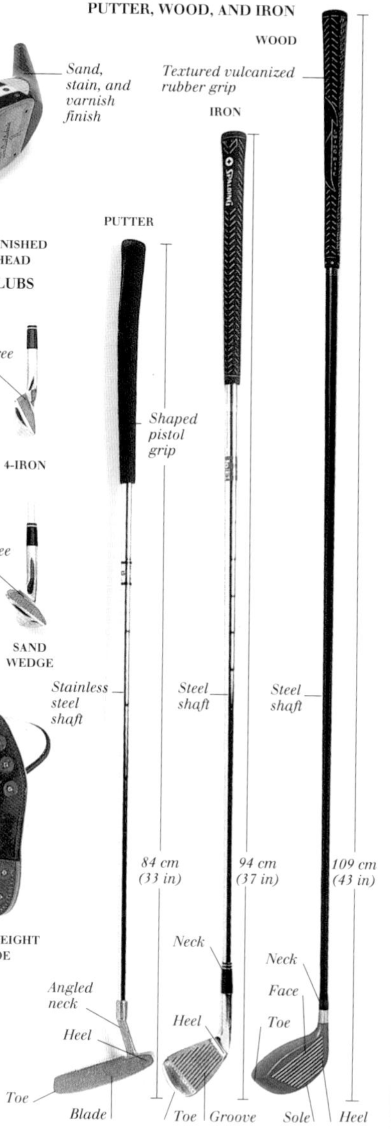
WOOD
Textured vulcanized rubber grip
IRON
PUTTER
Shaped pistol grip
Stainless steel shaft
Steel shaft
Steel shaft
84 cm (33 in)
94 cm (37 in)
109 cm (43 in)
Angled neck
Heel
Toe
Blade
Neck
Heel
Toe
Groove
Neck
Face
Toe
Sole
Heel

Archery and shooting

TARGET SHOOTING AND ARCHERY EVOLVED as practice for hunting and battle skills. Modern bows, although designed according to the principles of early hunting bows, use laminates, fibreglass, dacron, and carbon, and are equipped with sights and stabilizers. Competitors in target archery shoot over distances of 30 m (100 ft), 50 m (165 ft), 70 m (230 ft), and 90 m (300 ft) for men, and 30 m (100 ft), 50 m (165 ft), 60 m (200 ft), and 70 m (230 ft) for women. The closer the shot is to the centre of the target, the higher the score. The individual scores are added up, and the archer with the highest total wins the competition. Crossbows are used in match competitions over 10 m (33 ft), and 30 m (100 ft). Rifle shooting is divided into three categories: smallbore, bigbore, and air rifle. Contests take place over a variety of distances and further subdivisions are based on the type of shooting position used: prone, kneeling, or standing. The Olympic biathlon combines cross-country skiing and rifle shooting over a course of approximately 20 km ($12^1/_2$ miles). Additional magazines of ammunition are carried in the butt of the rifles. Bigbore rifles fitted with a telescopic sight can be used for hunting and running game target shooting. Pistol shooting events, using rapid-fire pistols, target pistols, and air pistols, take place over 10 m (33 ft), 25 m (82 ft), and 50 m (165 ft) distances. In rapid-fire pistol shooting, a total of 60 shots are fired from a distance of 25 m (83 ft).

CROSSBOW AND BOL

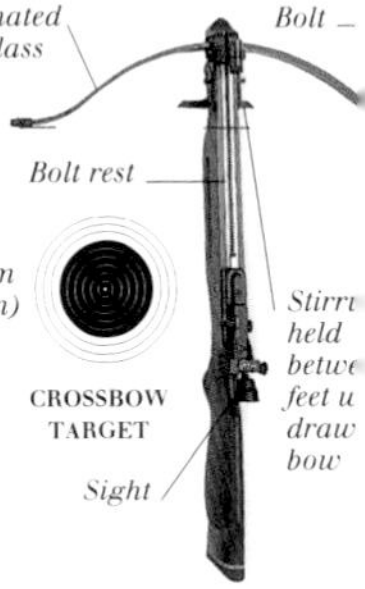
Laminated fibreglass bow
Bolt
Bolt rest
Stirr
held
betwe
feet u
draw
bow
Sight
45 mm ($1^3/_4$ in)

CROSSBOW TARGET

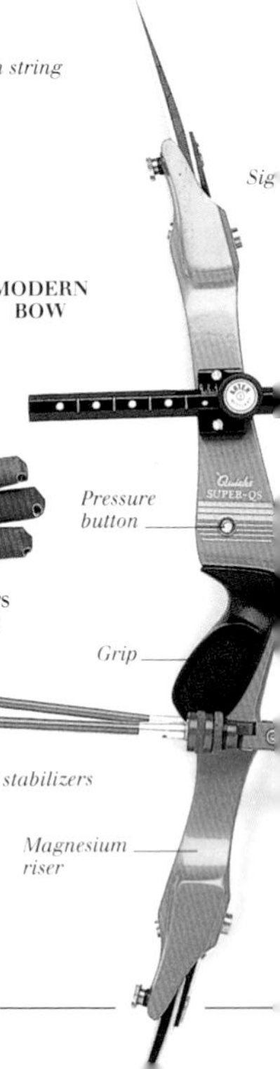
Hardwood laminate limb
Dacron string
Sig
Pressure button
Grip
V-bar stabilizers
Weight
Magnesium riser

MODERN BOW

Plastic fletch
Nock
Aluminium shaft
Waistband
Accessory pouch

QUIVER

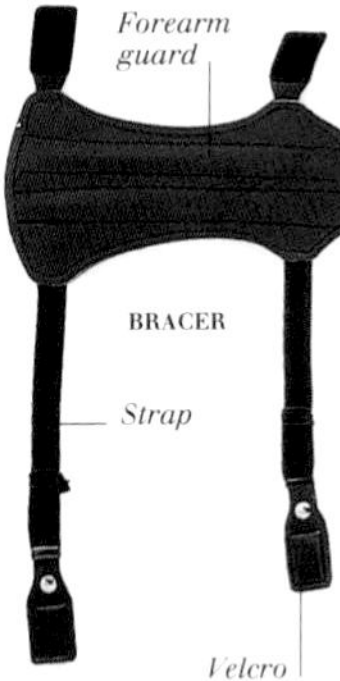
Forearm guard
Strap
Velcro fastening

BRACER

Finger hole

FINGER TAB

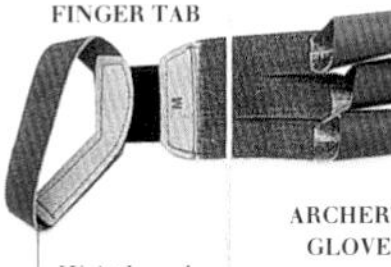
Wristband

ARCHER'S GLOVE

ARCHERY EQUIPMENT

SMALLBORE BIATHLON RIFLE

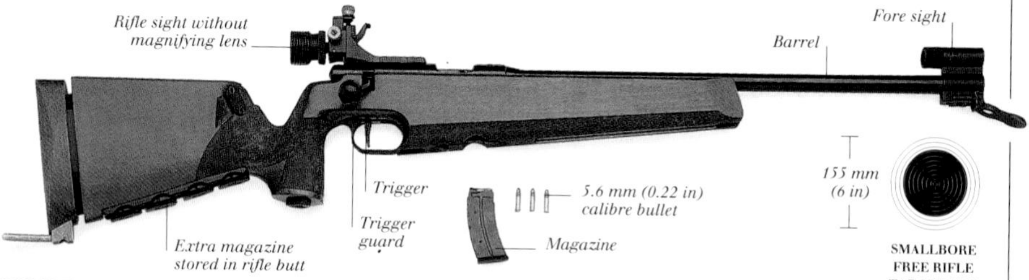
Rifle sight without magnifying lens
Fore sight
Barrel
Trigger
Trigger guard
5.6 mm (0.22 in) calibre bullet
Magazine
Extra magazine stored in rifle butt
155 mm (6 in)

SMALLBORE FREE RIFLE TARGET FOR 50 M (165 FT) RANGE

BIGBORE HUNTING RIFLE

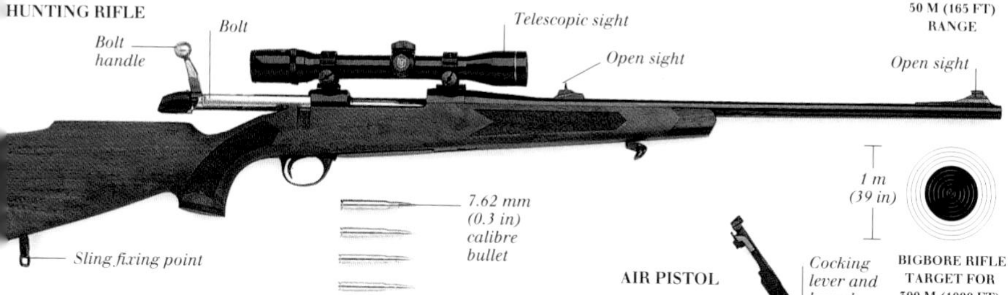
Bolt handle
Bolt
Telescopic sight
Open sight
Open sight
7.62 mm (0.3 in) calibre bullet
Sling fixing point
1 m (39 in)

BIGBORE RIFLE TARGET FOR 300 M (1000 FT) RANGE

AIR PISTOL

Cocking lever and barrel
Wooden grip shaped to fit the hand
Piston
Trigger
Air-pistol pellet

TARGET PISTOL

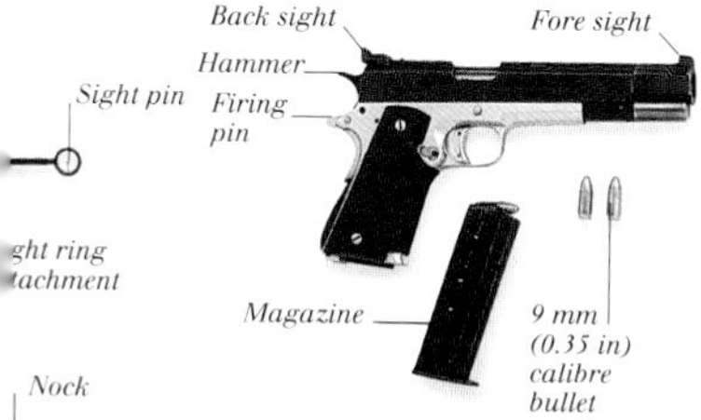
Back sight
Fore sight
Hammer
Firing pin
Sight pin
ght ring
tachment
Magazine
9 mm (0.35 in) calibre bullet

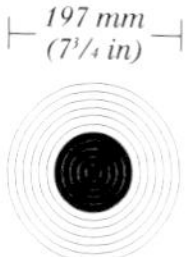

PISTOL TARGET FOR 18 M (60 FT) RANGE

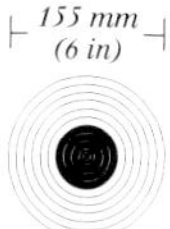
155 mm (6 in)

AIR-PISTOL TARGET FOR 10 M (33 FT) RANGE

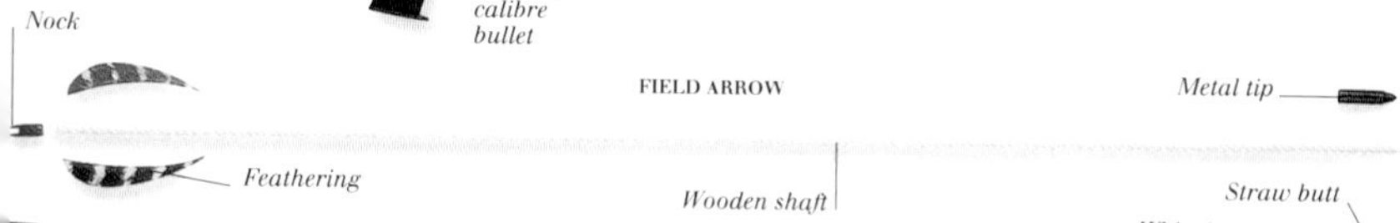
Nock
Metal tip
Feathering
Wooden shaft

FIELD ARROW

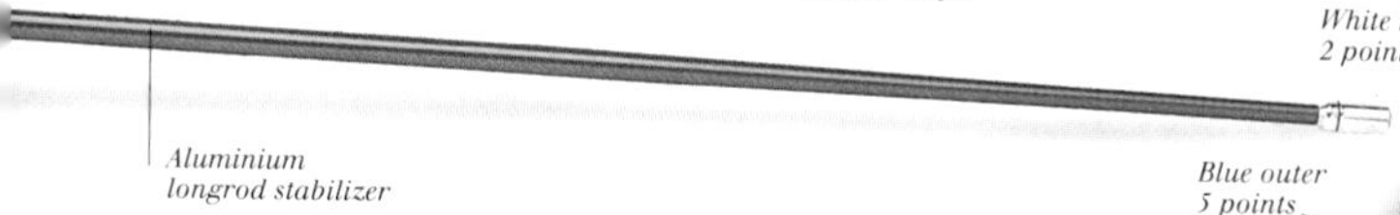
Aluminium longrod stabilizer

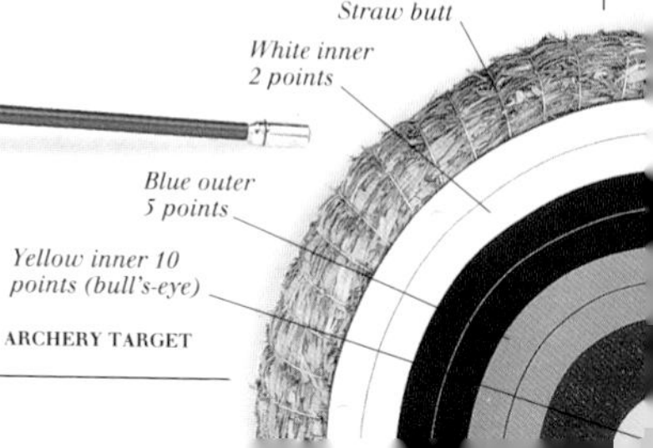
Straw butt
White inner 2 points
Blue outer 5 points
Yellow inner 10 points (bull's-eye)

ARCHERY TARGET

Ice hockey

ICE HOCKEY IS PLAYED by two teams of six players on an ice rink, with a goal net at each end. The object of this fast, and often dangerous, game is to hit a frozen rubber puck into the opposing team's net with a ice hockey stick. The game begins when the referee drops the puck between the sticks of two players from opposing teams, who "face off". The rink is divided into three areas: defending, neutral, and attacking zones. Players may move with the puck and pass the puck to one another along the ice, but may not pass it more than two zones across the rink markings. A goal is scored when the puck entirely crosses the goal-line between the posts and under the crossbar of the goal. A team may field up to 20 players although only six players are allowed on the ice at one time; substitutions occur frequently. Each game consists of three periods of 20 minutes, divided by breaks of 15 minutes.

GOALKEEPER

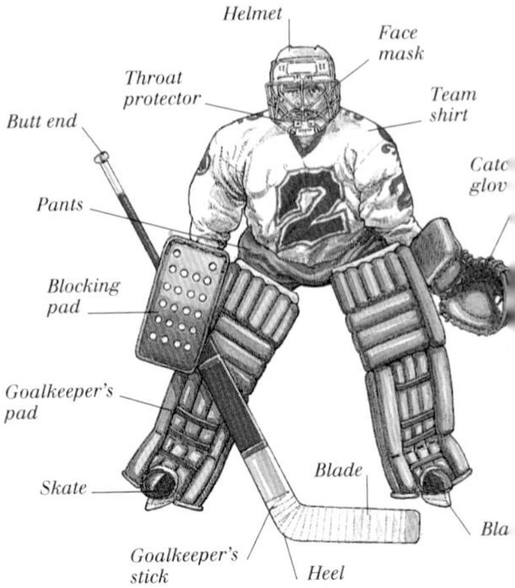
Helmet
Face mask
Throat protector
Team shirt
Butt end
Pants
Blocking pad
Goalkeeper's pad
Skate
Blade
Goalkeeper's stick
Heel

ICE HOCKEY RINK

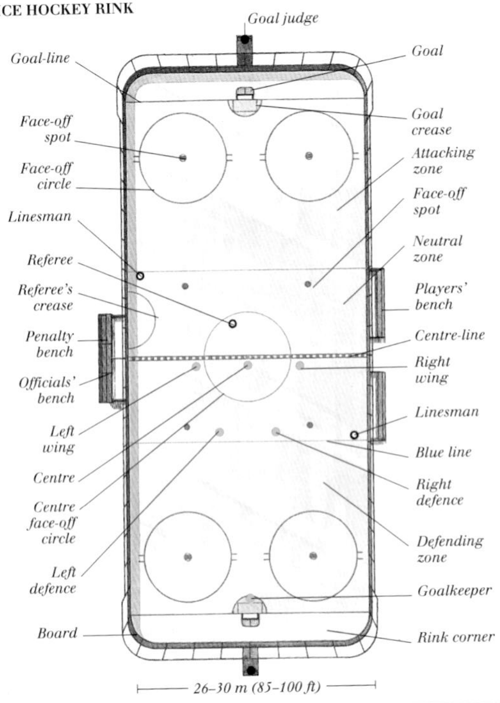
Goal judge
Goal-line
Goal
Goal crease
Face-off spot
Face-off circle
Attacking zone
Face-off spot
Linesman
Neutral zone
Referee
Players' bench
Referee's crease
Penalty bench
Centre-line
Officials' bench
Right wing
Left wing
Linesman
Blue line
Centre
Right defence
Centre face-off circle
Defending zone
Left defence
Goalkeeper
Board
Rink corner
26–30 m (85–100 ft)

THE FACE-OFF

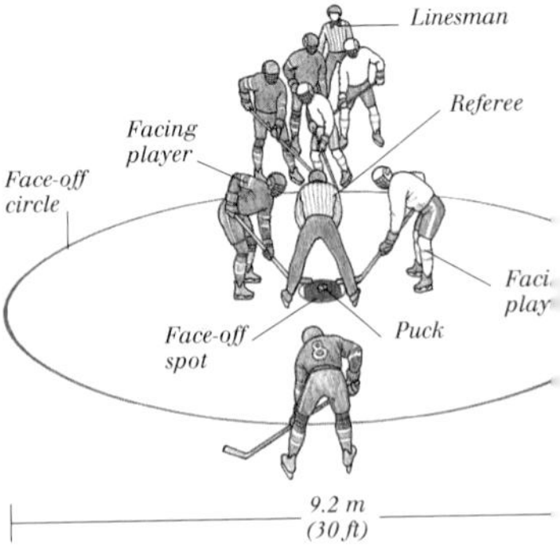
Linesman
Referee
Facing player
Face-off circle
Face-off spot
Puck
9.2 m (30 ft)

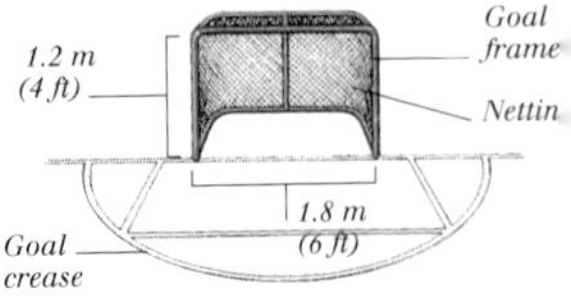
1.2 m (4 ft)
Goal frame
Nettin
1.8 m (6 ft)
Goal crease

ICE HOCKEY GOAL

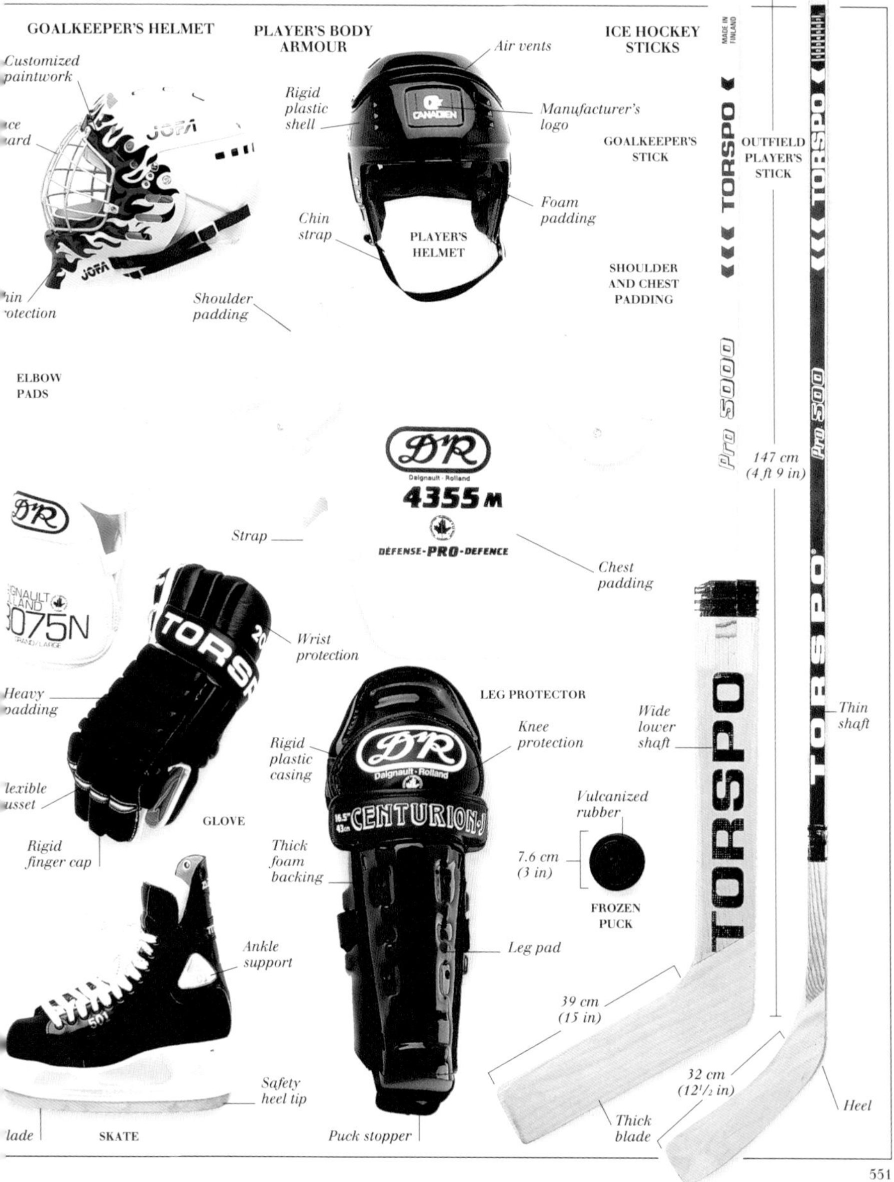
GOALKEEPER'S HELMET
Customized paintwork
ice
ard
hin
rotection
PLAYER'S BODY ARMOUR
Air vents
Rigid plastic shell
Manufacturer's logo
Foam padding
Chin strap
PLAYER'S HELMET
Shoulder padding
ELBOW PADS
SHOULDER AND CHEST PADDING
Strap
Chest padding
Wrist protection
Heavy
padding
lexible
usset
Rigid finger cap
GLOVE
LEG PROTECTOR
Rigid plastic casing
Knee protection
Thick foam backing
Leg pad
Puck stopper
Ankle support
Safety heel tip
lade
SKATE
Vulcanized rubber
7.6 cm (3 in)
FROZEN PUCK
ICE HOCKEY STICKS
GOALKEEPER'S STICK
OUTFIELD PLAYER'S STICK
147 cm (4 ft 9 in)
Wide lower shaft
Thin shaft
39 cm (15 in)
32 cm (12½ in)
Thick blade
Heel

Alpine skiing

Helmet
Ski goggles
One-piece lycra ski suit
Wrist strap
Ski pole
Basket
Ski boot
Safety binding
Tail
DOWNHILL SKIER

COMPETITIVE ALPINE SKIING is divided into four disciplines: downhill, slalom, giant slalom, and super-giant slalom (Super-G). Each one tests different skills. In downhill skiing, competitors race down a slope marked out by control flags, known as "gates", and are timed on a single run only. Competitors wear crash helmets, one-piece Lycra suits, and long skis with flattened tips to minimize air resistance. Slalom and giant slalom skiiers negotiate a twisting course requiring balance, agility, and quick reactions. Courses are defined by pairs of gates. Racers must pass through each pair of gates to complete the course successfully. Competitors are timed on two runs over different courses, and the skier who completes the courses in the shortest time wins. The equipment and protective guards used by slalom skiiers are shown opposite. In Super-G races, competitors ski a single run that combines the technical challenge of slalom with the speed of downhill. The course requires skiers to complete medium-to-long radius turns at high speed, and contain up to two jumps. Clothing is the same as for downhill, but slightly shorter skis are used.

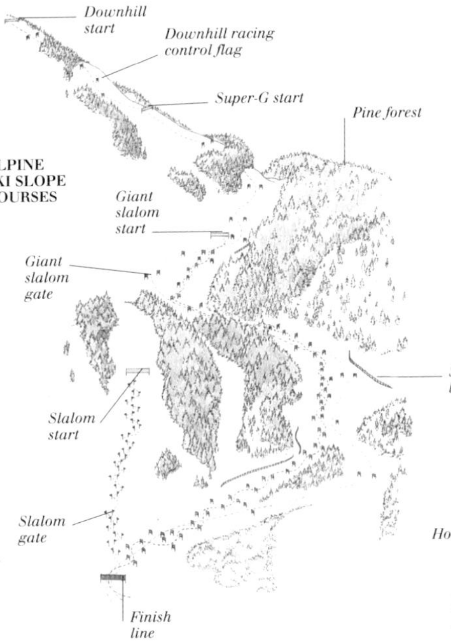
Downhill start
Downhill racing control flag
Super-G start
Pine forest
Giant slalom start
Giant slalom gate
Safety barrier
Slalom start
Slalom gate
Finish line
ALPINE SKI SLOPE COURSES

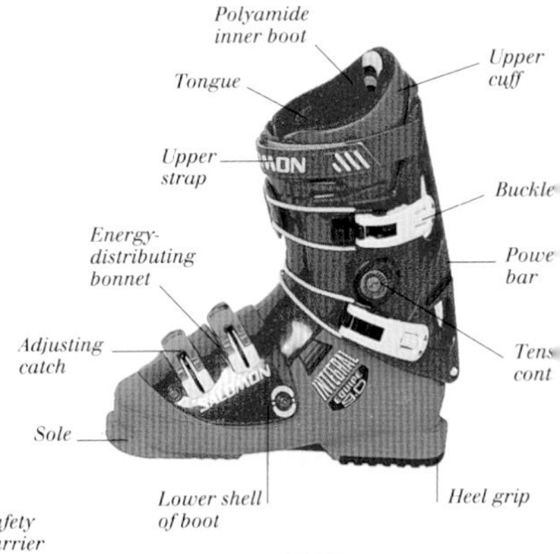
Polyamide inner boot
Tongue
Upper cuff
Upper strap
Buckle
Energy-distributing bonnet
Powe bar
Adjusting catch
Tens cont
Sole
Lower shell of boot
Heel grip
SKI BOOT

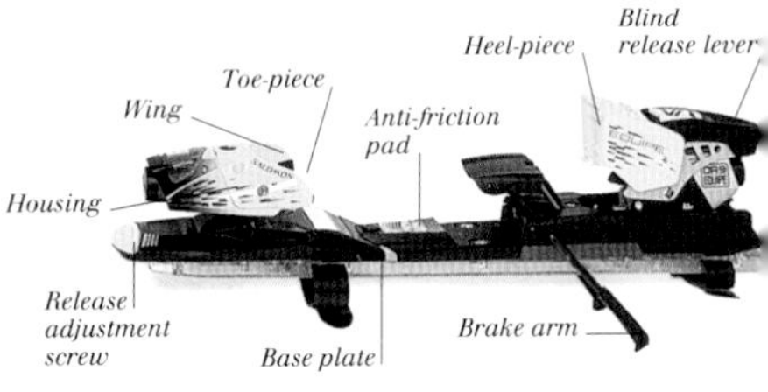
Blind release lever
Heel-piece
Toe-piece
Wing
Anti-friction pad
Housing
Release adjustment screw
Base plate
Brake arm
SAFETY BINDING

SLALOM CLOTHING AND EQUIPMENT

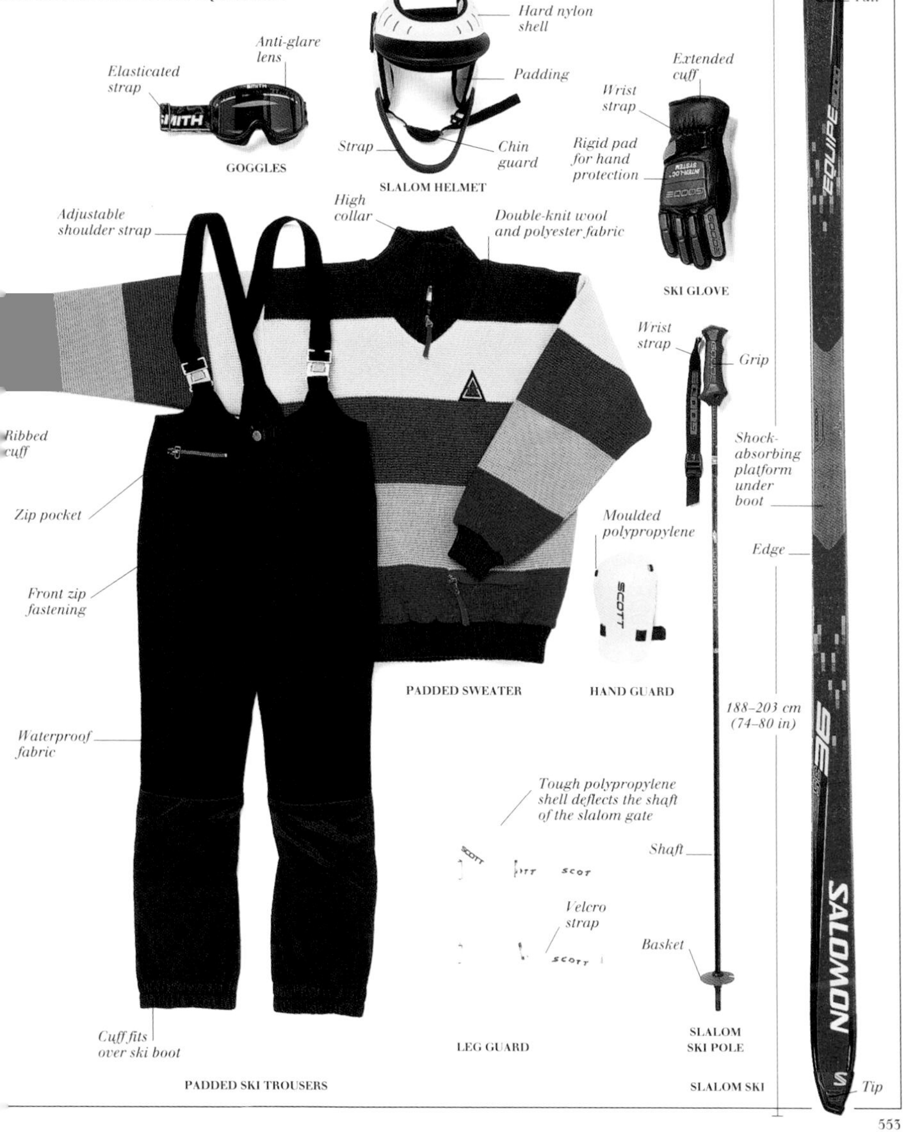

Elasticated strap
Anti-glare lens
GOGGLES
Hard nylon shell
Padding
Strap
Chin guard
SLALOM HELMET
Extended cuff
Wrist strap
Rigid pad for hand protection
SKI GLOVE
Adjustable shoulder strap
High collar
Double-knit wool and polyester fabric
Ribbed cuff
Zip pocket
Front zip fastening
Waterproof fabric
Cuff fits over ski boot
PADDED SKI TROUSERS
PADDED SWEATER
Moulded polypropylene
HAND GUARD
Tough polypropylene shell deflects the shaft of the slalom gate
Velcro strap
LEG GUARD
Wrist strap
Grip
Shaft
Basket
SLALOM SKI POLE
Tail
Shock-absorbing platform under boot
Edge
188–203 cm (74–80 in)
Tip
SLALOM SKI

Equestrian sports

EQUESTRIAN SPORTS HAVE TAKEN place throughout the world for centuries: events involving mounted horses were recorded in the Olympic Games of 642 BC. Showjumping, however, is a much more recent innovation, and the first competitions were held at the beginning of the 1900s. In this sport, horse and rider must negotiate a course of variable, unfixed obstacles, making as few mistakes as possible. Showjumping fences consist of wooden stands, known as standards or wings, that support planks or poles. Parts of the fence are designed to collapse on impact, preventing injury to the horse and rider. Judges penalise competitors for errors, such as knocking down obstacles, refusing jumps, or deviating from the course. Depending on the type of competition, the rider with the fewest faults, most points, or fastest time wins. There are two basic forms of horse racing – flat races and races with jumps, such as steeplechase or hurdle-races. Thoroughbred horses are used in this sport, as they have great strength and stamina and can achieve speeds of up to 65 kph (40 mph). Jockeys wear "silks" – caps and jackets designed in distinctive colours and patterns which help identify the horses. In harness racing, the horse is driven from a light, two-wheeled carriage called a sulky. Horses are trained to trot and to pace, and different races are held for each of these types of gait. In pacing races, the horses wear hobbles to prevent them from breaking into a trot or gallop. Breeds such as the Standardbred and the French Trotter have been developed especially for this sport.

SHOWJUMPING SADDLE

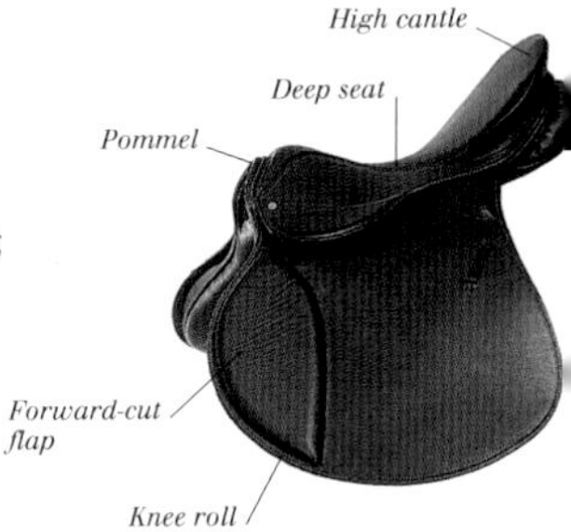
High cantle
Deep seat
Pommel
Forward-cut flap
Knee roll

SHOWJUMPING FENCES

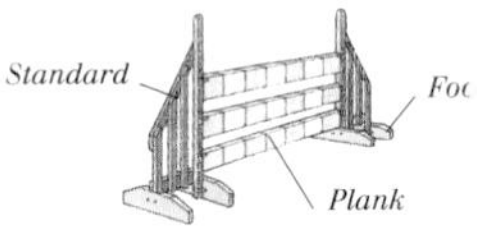
Standard
Plank

UPRIGHT PLANKS

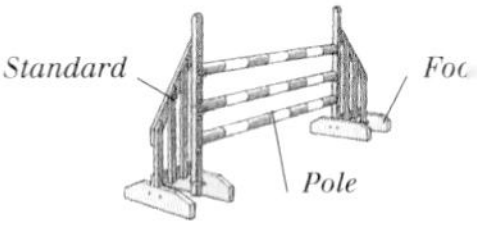
Standard
Pole

UPRIGHT POLES

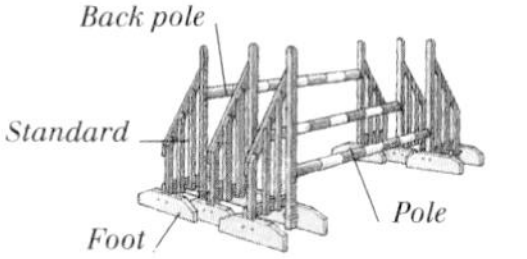
Back pole
Standard
Foot
Pole

TRIPLE BAR (STAIRCASE)

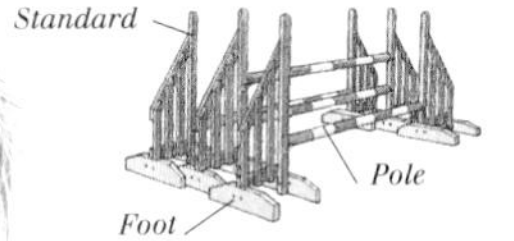
Standard
Pole
Foot

HOG'S-BACK

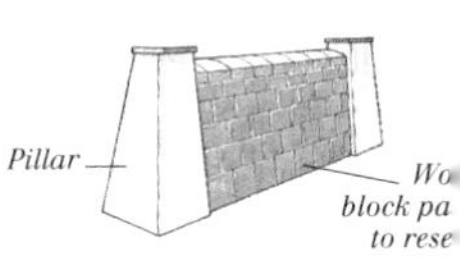
Pillar

WALL

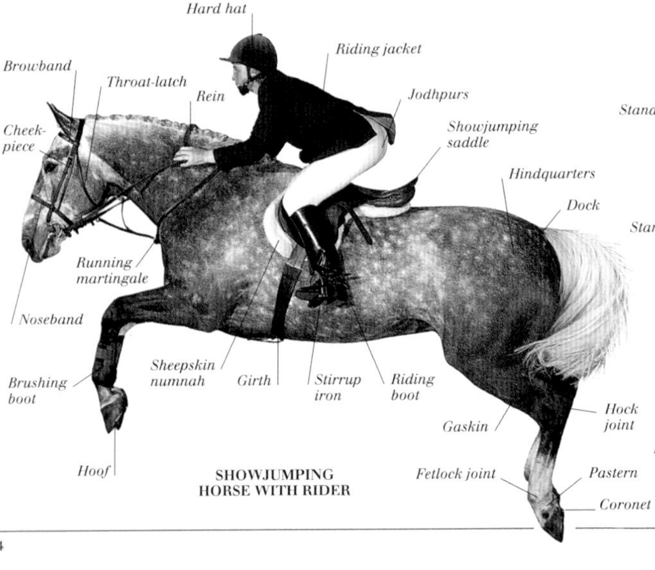
Hard hat
Riding jacket
Browband
Throat-latch
Rein
Jodhpurs
Cheek-piece
Showjumping saddle
Hindquarters
Dock
Running martingale
Noseband
Sheepskin numnah
Girth
Stirrup iron
Riding boot
Brushing boot
Gaskin
Hock joint
Hoof
Fetlock joint
Pastern
Coronet

SHOWJUMPING HORSE WITH RIDER

ACING SADDLE

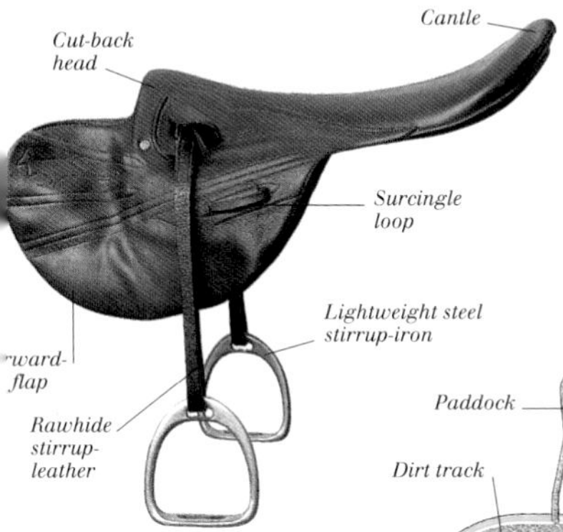
Cantle
Cut-back head
Surcingle loop
Lightweight steel stirrup-iron
ward- flap
Rawhide stirrup-leather

RACING SILKS

Plain cap
Spotted cap
Quartered cap
Plain sleeve
Plain sleeve
Striped jacket
Plain jacket
Spotted sleeve
Jacket with sash

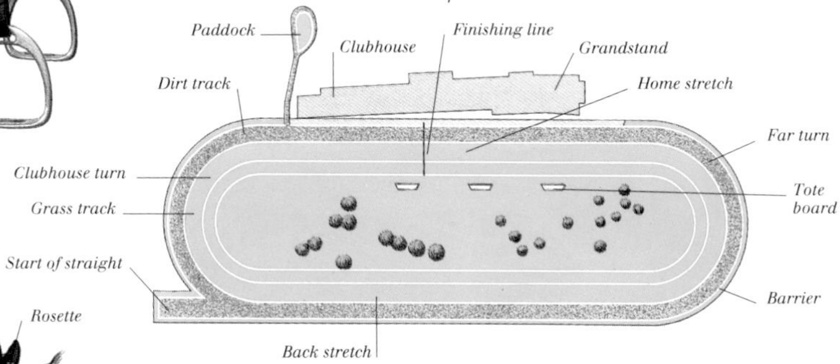
Paddock
Finishing line
Clubhouse
Grandstand
Dirt track
Home stretch
Far turn
Clubhouse turn
Tote board
Grass track
Start of straight
Barrier
Back stretch

SARATOGA RACE COURSE, SARATOGA, NEW YORK, U.S.A.

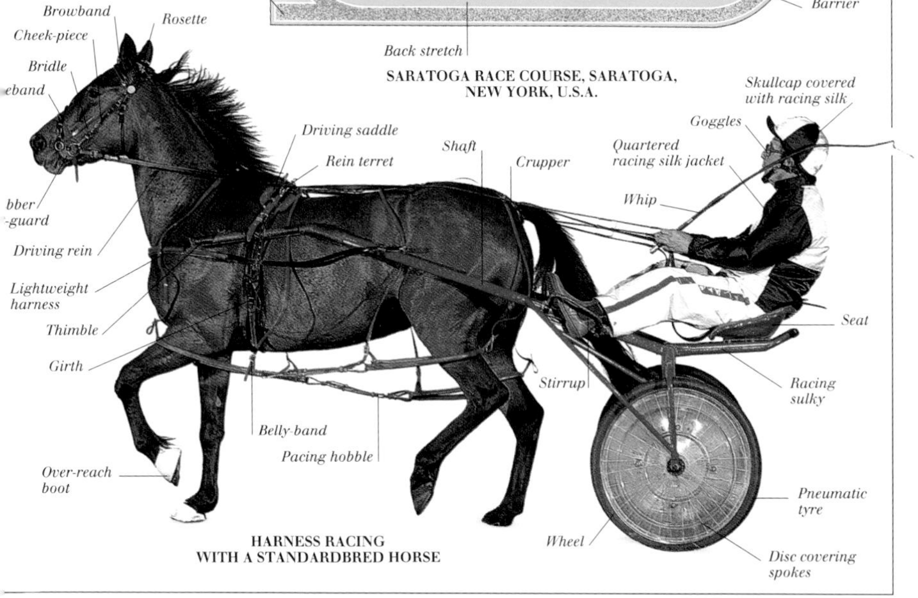
Browband
Rosette
Cheek-piece
Bridle
eband
Skullcap covered with racing silk
Goggles
Driving saddle
Shaft
Quartered racing silk jacket
Rein terret
Crupper
bber -guard
Whip
Driving rein
Lightweight harness
Thimble
Seat
Girth
Stirrup
Racing sulky
Belly-band
Pacing hobble
Over-reach boot
Pneumatic tyre
Wheel
Disc covering spokes

HARNESS RACING WITH A STANDARDBRED HORSE

Judo and fencing

COMBAT SPORTS ARE BASED ON THE SKILLS used in fighting. In these sports, the competitors may be unarmed – as in judo and boxing – or armed – as in fencing and kendo. Judo is a system of unarmed combat developed in the East. Translated from the Japanese the name means “the gentle way”. Students learn how to turn an opponent’s force to their own advantage. The usual costume is loose white trousers and a jacket, fastened with a cloth belt. The colour of belt indicates the student’s level of expertise, from white-belted novices to the expert “black belts”. Competitions take place on a mat or “shiaijo”, 9 or 10 m (30 or 33 ft) square in size, bounded by “danger” and “safety” areas to prevent injury. Competitors try to throw, pin, or master their opponent by applying pressure to the arm joints or neck. Judo bouts are strictly monitored, and competitors receive points for superior technique, not for injuring their opponent. Fencing is a combat sport using swords, which takes place on a narrow “piste” 14 m (46 ft) long. Competitors try to touch specific target areas on their opponent with their sword or “foil” while avoiding being touched themselves. The winner is the one who scores the greatest number of hits. Fencers wear clothing made from strong white material, which affords maximum protection while allowing freedom of movement, steel mesh masks with padded bibs to protect the fencer’s neck, and a long white glove on their sword hand. Fencing foils do not have sharpened blades, and their tips end in a blunt button to prevent injuries. Three types of swords are used – foils, épées, and sabres. Official foil and épée competitions always use an electric scoring system. The sword tips are connected to lights by a long wire that passes underneath each fencer’s jacket. A bulb flashes when a hit is made.

JUDO HOLDS AND THROWS

SIDE FOUR QUARTER HOLD

SINGLE WING

BODY DROP

ONE ARM SHOULDER THROW

SHOULDER WHEEL

SWEEPING LOW THROW

STOMACH THROW

KNEE WHEEL

JUDO MAT

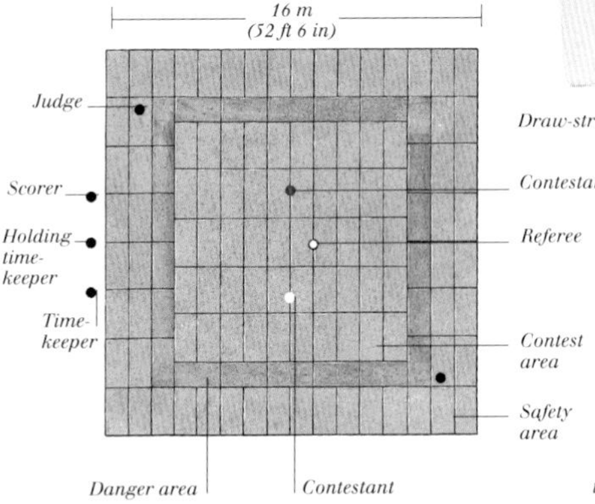
16 m
(52 ft 6 in)
Judge
Scorer
Holding time-keeper
Time-keeper
Danger area
Contestant
Contestant
Referee
Contest area
Safety area

JUDO KIT

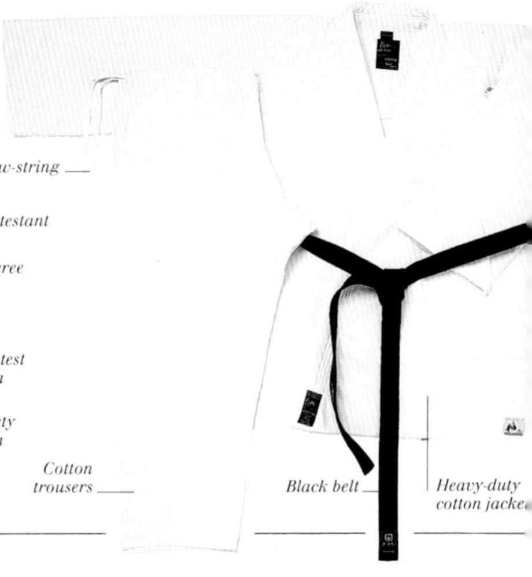
Draw-string
Cotton trousers
Black belt
Heavy-duty cotton jacke

ENCING PISTE

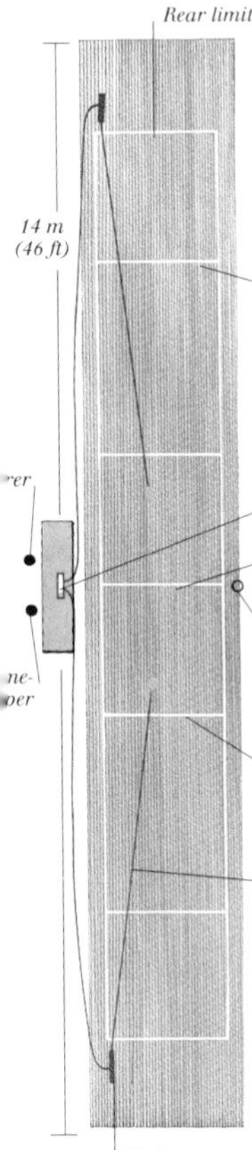
Rear limit line
14 m
(46 ft)
Sabre and épée warning line
rer
Electrical scoring apparatus
Centre line
President
ne-
per
On-guard line
Body wire
Reel

FENCING EQUIPMENT

Steel wire mesh
Padded bib

MESH MASK

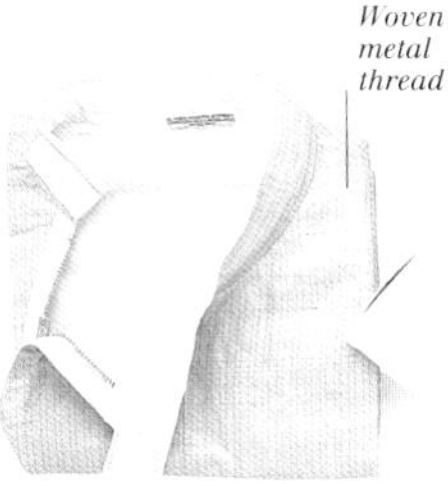
Woven metal thread

METAL JACKET

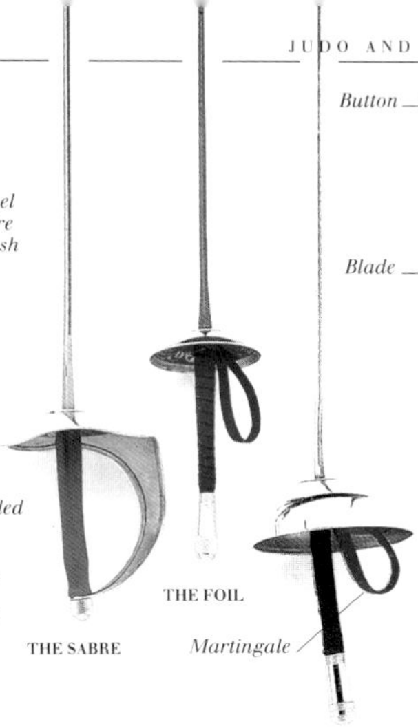
Martingale

THE SABRE

THE FOIL

THE EPEE

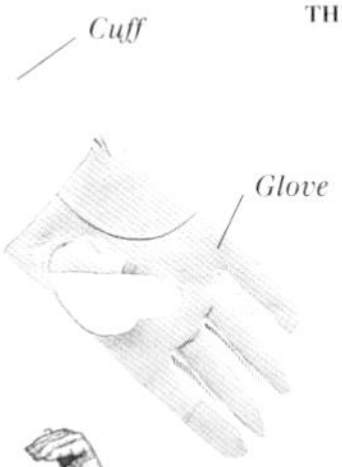
Cuff
Glove

GAUNTLET

PARTS OF THE SWORD

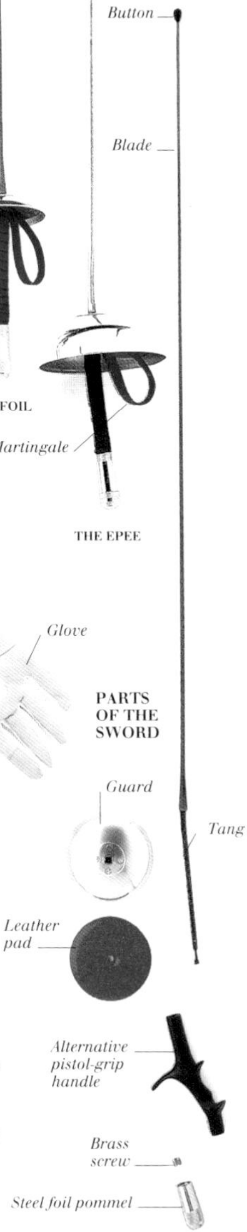
Button
Blade
Guard
Tang
Leather pad
Alternative pistol-grip handle
Brass screw
Steel foil pommel

TARGET AREAS ON THE UPPER BODY

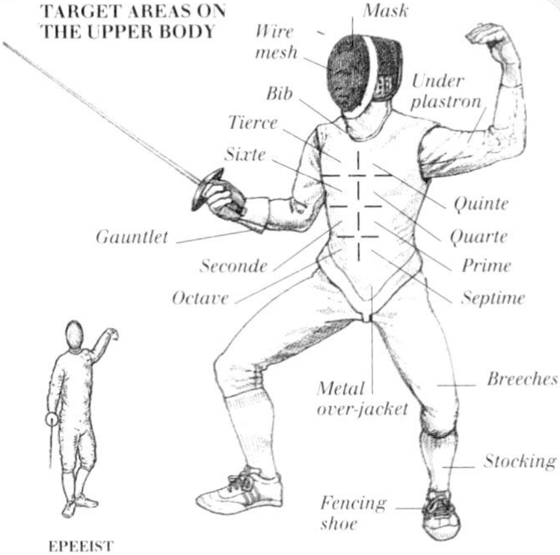
Mask
Wire mesh
Bib
Under plastron
Tierce
Sixte
Quinte
Quarte
Gauntlet
Prime
Seconde
Octave
Septime
Breeches
Metal over-jacket
Stocking
Fencing shoe

ENCING TARGET AREAS

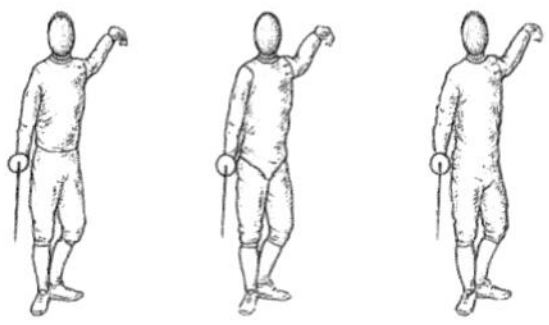

SABREUR

FOILIST

EPEEIST

Swimming and diving

SWIMMING GOGGLES

SWIMMING WAS INCLUDED in the first modern Olympic Games in 1896 and diving events were added in 1904. Swimming is both an individual and a team sport and races take place over a predetermined distance in one of the four major categories of stroke – freestyle (usually front crawl), butterfly, breaststroke, and backstroke. Competition pools are clearly marked for racing and anti-turbulence lane lines are used to separate the swimmers and help keep the water calm. The first team or individual to finish the race is the winner. Competitive diving is divided into men's and women's springboard and platform (highboard) events. There are six official groups of dives: forward dives, backward dives, armstand dives, twist dives, reverse dives, and inward dives. Competitors perform a set number of dives and after each one a panel of judges awards marks according to the quality of execution and the degree of difficulty.

STYLES OF DIVES

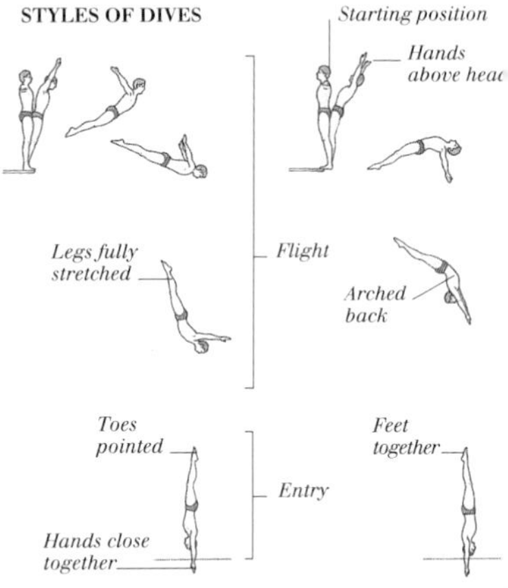
Starting position
Hands above heac
Legs fully stretched
Flight
Arched back
Toes pointed
Entry
Feet together
Hands close together
FORWARD DIVE
BACKWARD DIVE

SWIMMING POOL

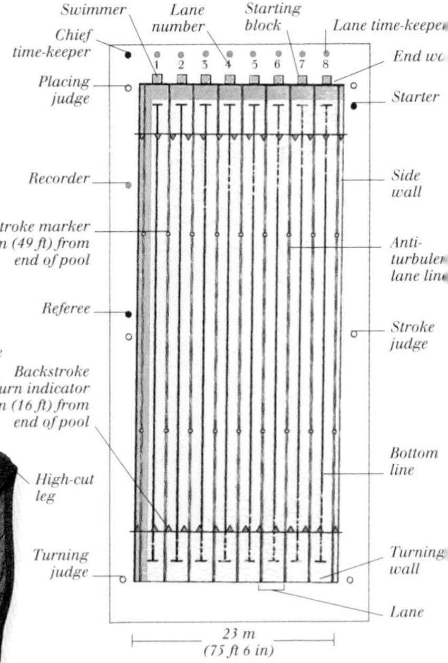
Swimmer
Lane number
Starting block
Lane time-keeper
Chief time-keeper
1 2 3 4 5 6 7 8
End wa
Placing judge
Starter
Recorder
Side wall
Backstroke marker 15 m (49 ft) from end of pool
Anti-turbuler lane lin
Referee
Stroke judge
Backstroke turn indicator 5 m (16 ft) from end of pool
Bottom line
Turning judge
Turning wall
Lane
23 m (75 ft 6 in)

SWIMWEAR

Latex rubber moulds to shape of head
SPEEDO
CAPS
Rubber-covered wire
NOSE CLIP
Moulded rubber
EARPLUG
High neckline
Man-made stretch fabric
Drawstring
High-cut leg
Strong seam
SWIMSUIT
TRUNKS

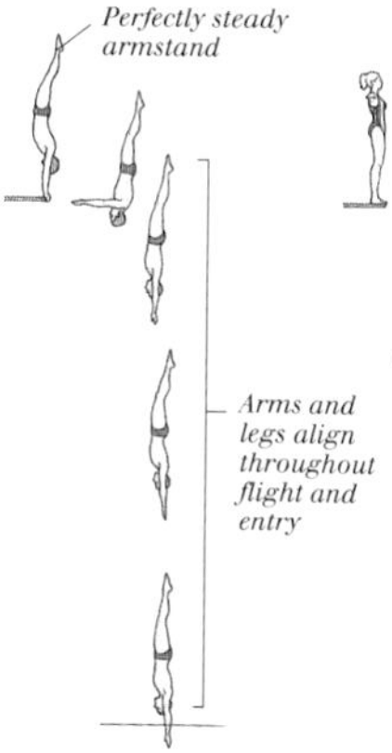
Perfectly steady armstand
Arms and legs align throughout flight and entry

ARMSTAND DIVE

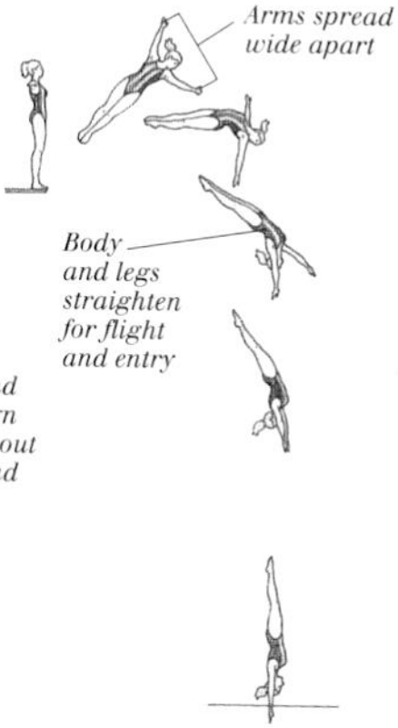
Arms spread wide apart
Body and legs straighten for flight and entry

TWIST DIVE

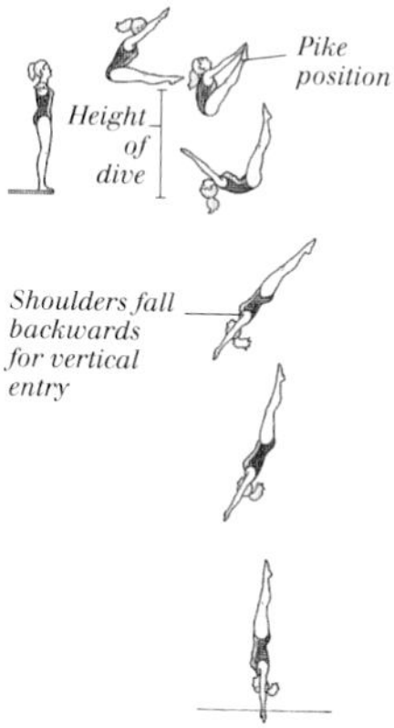
Pike position
Height of dive
Shoulders fall backwards for vertical entry

REVERSE DIVE PIKED

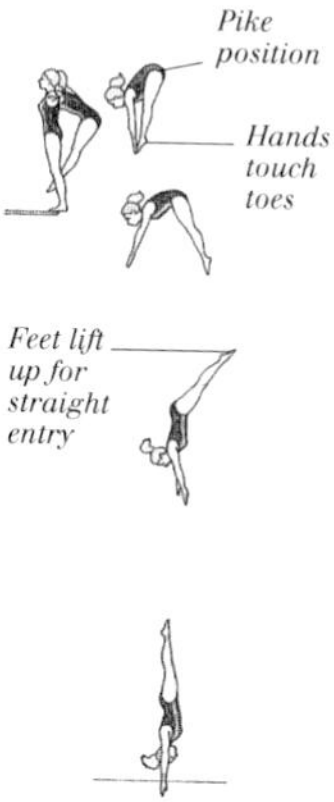
Pike position
Hands touch toes
Feet lift up for straight entry

INWARD DIVE PIKED

FRONT CRAWL

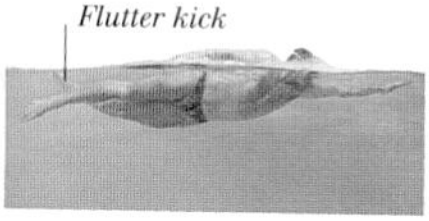
Flutter kick

FULL BODY STRETCH

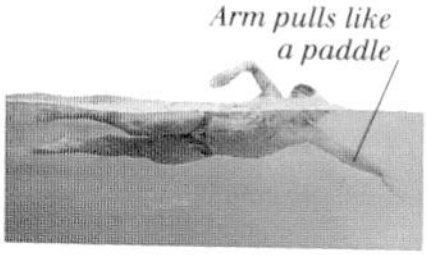
Arm pulls like a paddle

LOWER ARM PULL

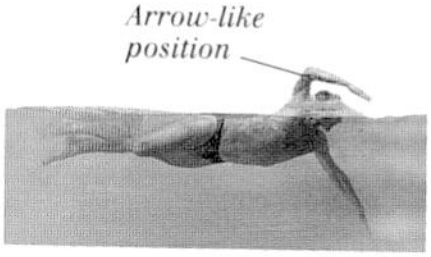
Arrow-like position

STREAMLINED ARM ENTRY

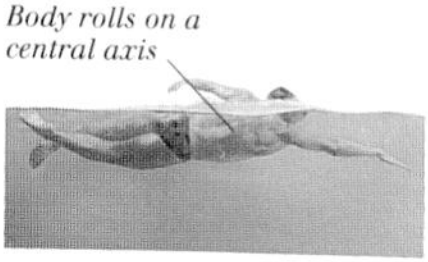
Body rolls on a central axis

SIDE-TO-SIDE BODY ROLL

BREASTSTROKE

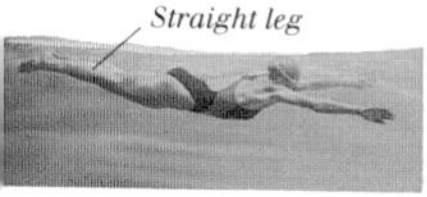
Straight leg

BODY GLIDE

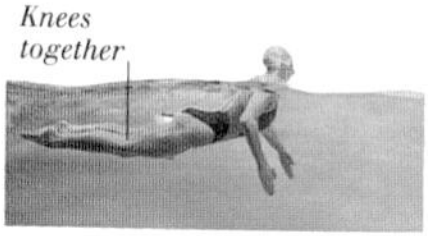
Knees together

DOUBLE ARM PULL

Elbows tucked in

SQUEEZING THE WATER

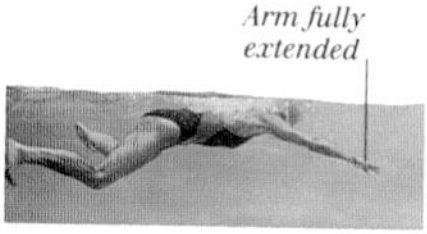
Arm fully extended

FROG KICK

BACKSTROKE

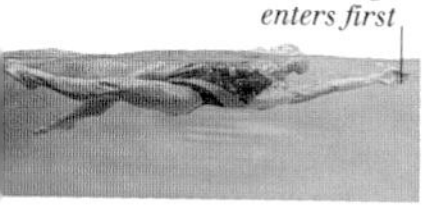
Little finger enters first

BODY ROLL

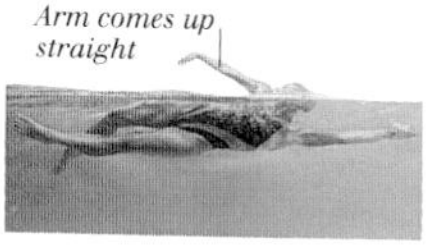
Arm comes up straight

PULLING THROUGH

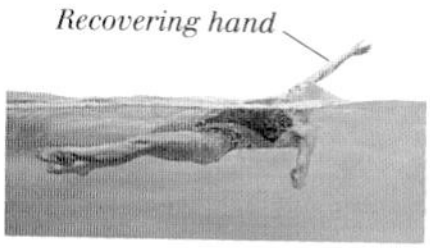
Recovering hand

STRAIGHTENING OUT

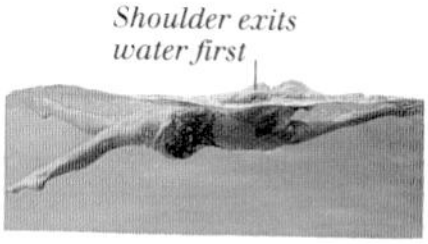
Shoulder exits water first

SHOULDER LIFT

BUTTERFLY

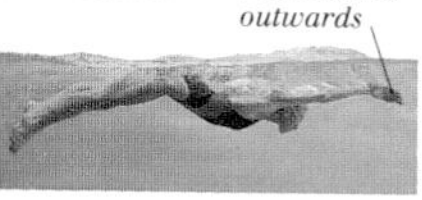
Palm turned outwards

CATCHING THE WATER

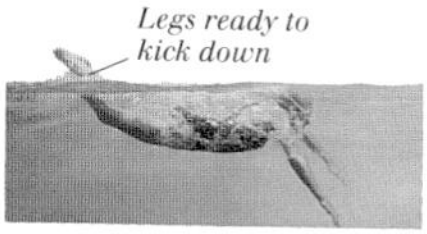
Legs ready to kick down

DOUBLE ARM PULL

Head clears the water

KICKING DOWN

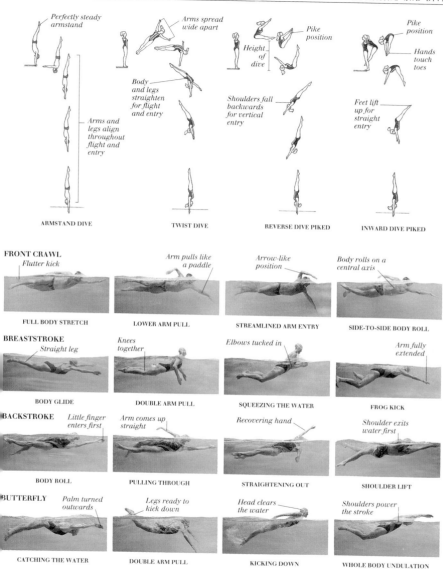

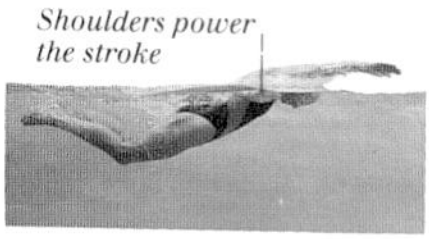
Shoulders power the stroke

WHOLE BODY UNDULATION

Canoeing, rowing, and sailing

WATERBORNE SPORTS are as varied as the crafts used. There are two disciplines in rowing; sweep rowing, in which each rower has one oar and sculling, in which rowers use two oars. There are a number of different Olympic and competitive rowing events for both men and women. The number of rowers and weight classes vary. Some rowing events use a coxswain; a steersman who does not row but directs the crew. Kayaks and canoes are used in straight sprint and slalom races. Slalom races take place over a course consisting of 20 to 25 gates, including at least six upstream gates. In yacht racing, competitors must complete prescribed courses, organized by the race committees, in the shortest possible time, using sail power only. Olympic events include classes for keel boats, dinghies, and catamarans.

SAILING GEAR

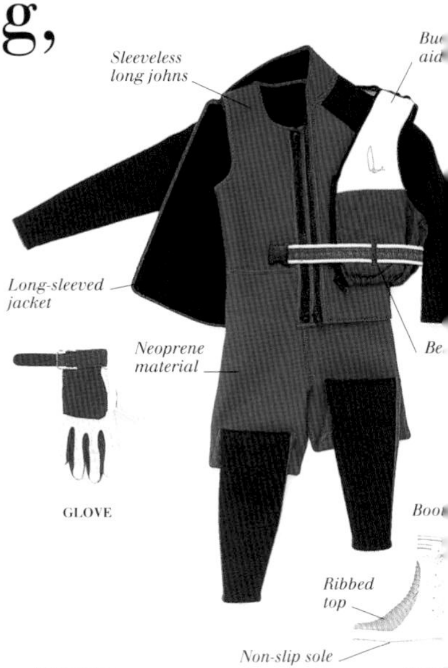
Sleeveless long johns
Long-sleeved jacket
Neoprene material
GLOVE
Ribbed top
Non-slip sole
BOOT

ONE-PERSON KAYAK AND PADDLE

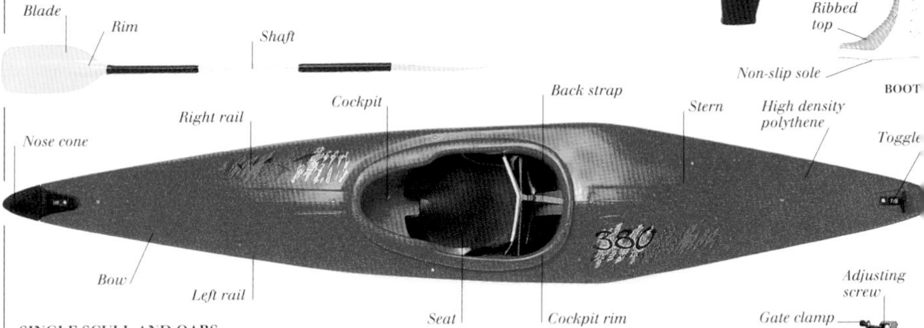
Blade
Rim
Shaft
Cockpit
Right rail
Back strap
Stern
High density polythene
Nose cone
Toggle
Bow
Left rail
Seat
Cockpit rim

SINGLE SCULL AND OARS (WITH CLOTH DECKING REMOVED)

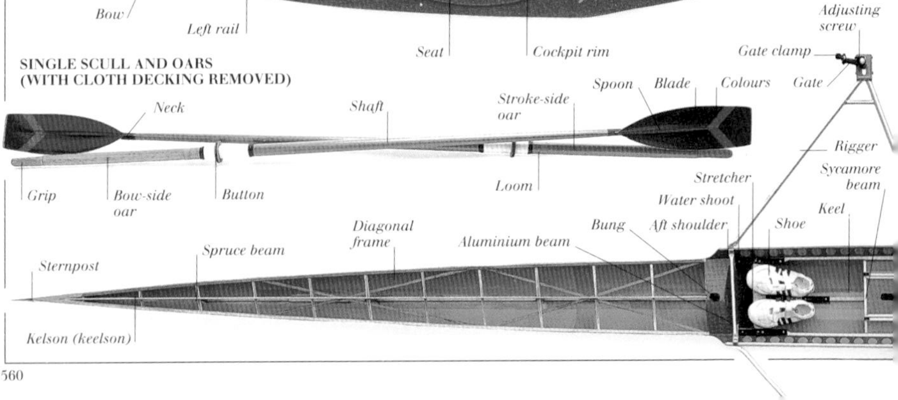
Adjusting screw
Gate clamp
Gate
Spoon
Blade
Colours
Neck
Shaft
Stroke-side oar
Rigger
Grip
Bow-side oar
Button
Loom
Stretcher
Sycamore beam
Water shoot
Keel
Diagonal frame
Bung
Aft shoulder
Shoe
Aluminium beam
Spruce beam
Sternpost
Kelson (keelson)

LIFEJACKET

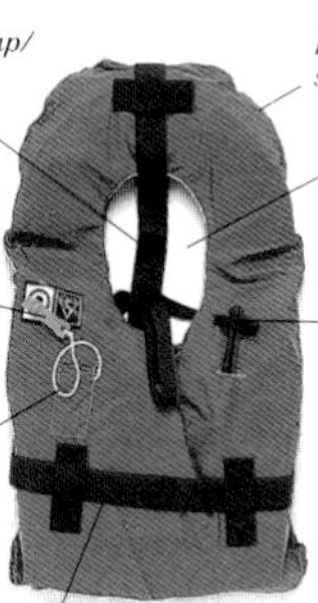

SAILING DINGHY

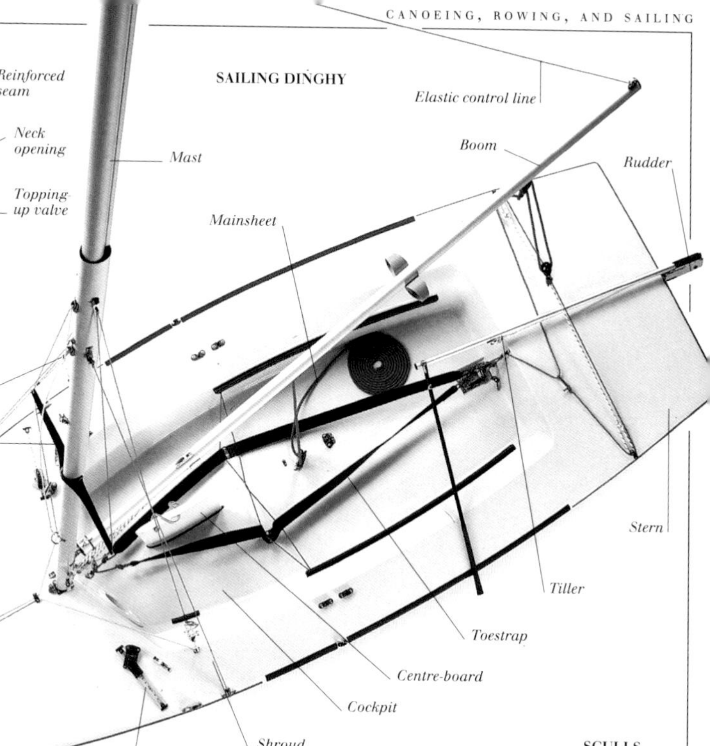

Elastic control line
Boom
Rudder
Mast
Mainsheet
Standing rigging
Spreader
Bow
Stern
Tiller
Toestrap
Centre-board
Cockpit
Shroud
Jib fairlead
Non-slip deck surface

SCULLS

DOUBLE SCULL

SINGLE SCULL

SWEEP-ROWING BOATS

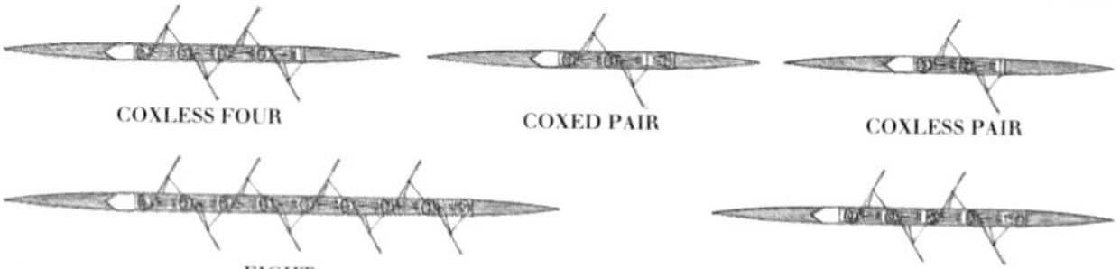

COXLESS FOUR

COXED PAIR

COXLESS PAIR

EIGHT

COXED FOUR

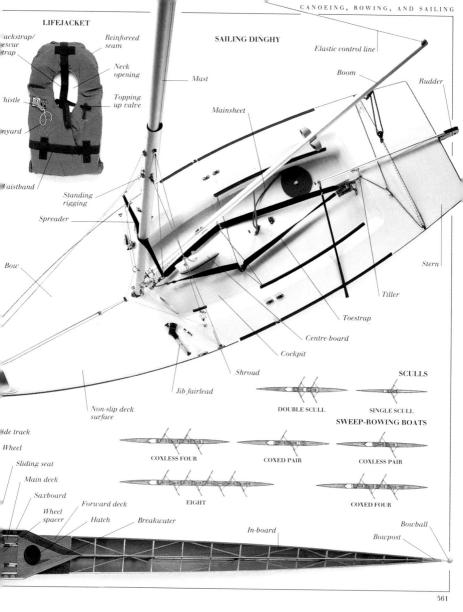

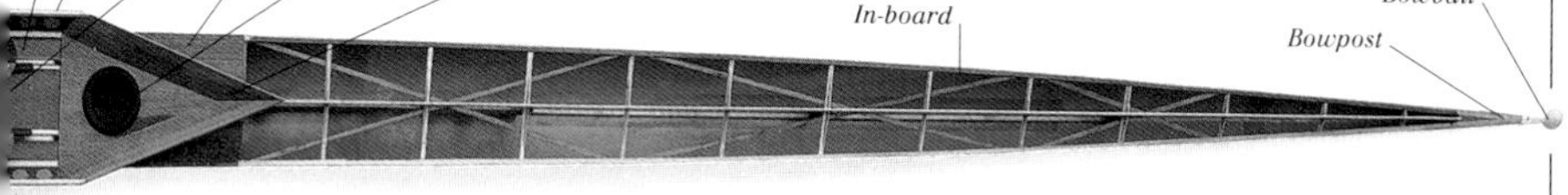

ide track
Wheel
Sliding seat
Main deck
Saxboard
Wheel spacer
Forward deck
Hatch
Breakwater
In-board
Bowball
Bowpost

Angling

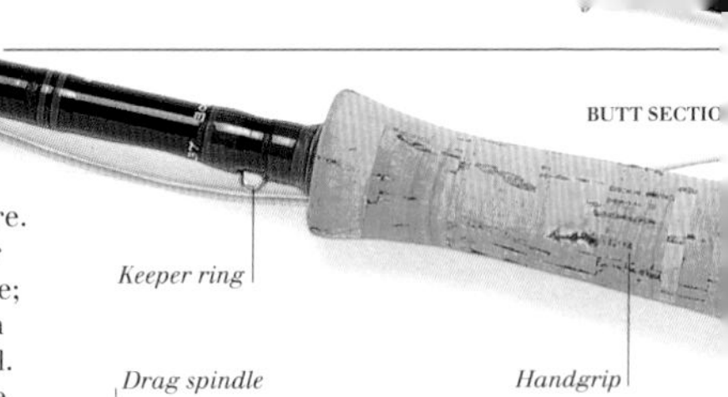

ANGLING MEANS FISHING WITH A ROD, reel, line, and lure. There are several different types of angling: freshwater coarse angling, for members of the carp family and pike; freshwater game angling, for salmon and trout; and sea angling, for sea fish such as flatfish, bass, and mackerel. Anglers use a variety of methods of catching fish. These include bait fishing, in which bait (food to allure the fish) is placed on a hook and cast into the water; fly fishing, in which a natural or artificial fly is used to lure the fish; and spinning, in which a lure that looks like a small fish revolves as it is pulled through the water. The angler uses the rod, reel, and line to cast the lure over the water. The reel controls the line as it spills off the spool and as it is wound back. Weights may be fixed to the line so that it will sink. Swivels are attached to prevent the line from twisting. When a fish bites, the hook must become embedded in its mouth and remain there while the catch is reeled in.

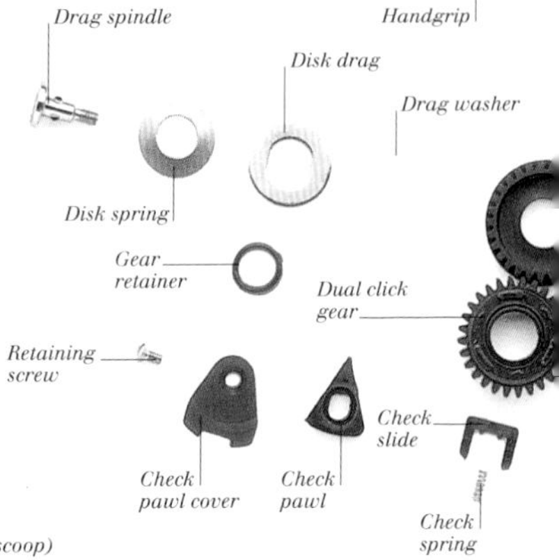
Drag spindle
Disk drag
Drag washer
Disk spring
Gear retainer
Dual click gear
Retaining screw
Check slide
Check pawl cover
Check pawl
Check spring

REELS

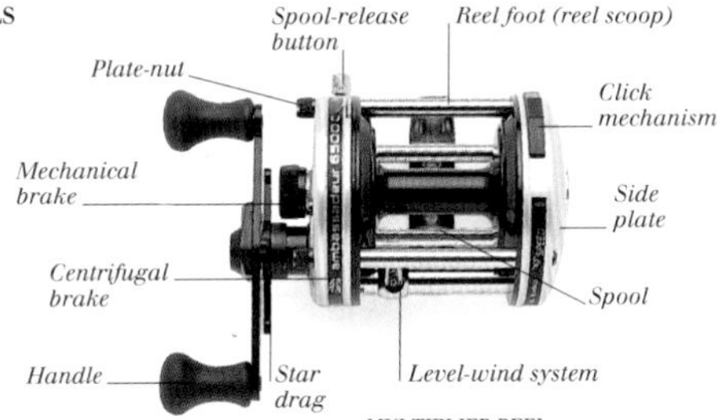
Spool-release button
Reel foot (reel scoop)
Plate-nut
Click mechanism
Mechanical brake
Side plate
Centrifugal brake
Spool
Handle
Star drag
Level-wind system

MULTIPLIER REEL

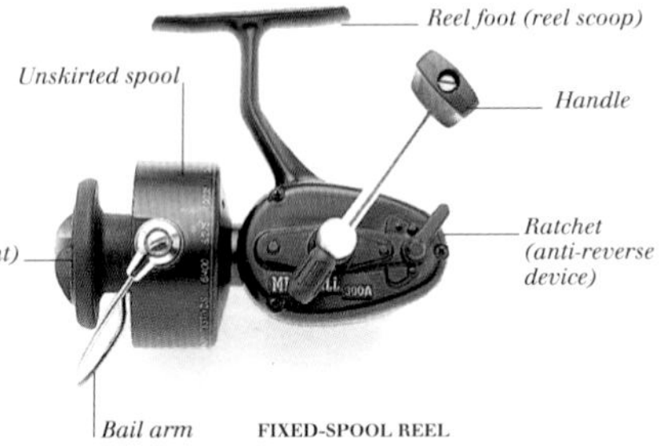
Reel foot (reel scoop)
Unskirted spool
Handle
Tension nut (drag adjustment)
Ratchet (anti-reverse device)
Bail arm

FIXED-SPOOL REEL

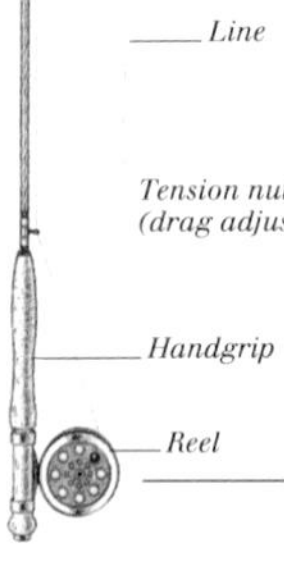
Line
Handgrip
Reel

HOOKS, SWIVELS, AND WEIGHTS

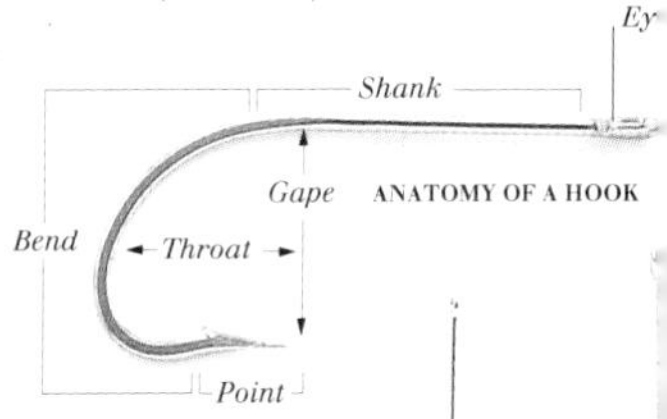
Ey
Shank
Gape
Bend
Throat
Point

ANATOMY OF A HOOK

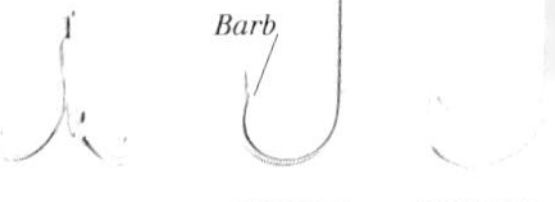
Barb

TREBLE HOOK

ABERDEEN HOOK

REVERSED BEND HOOK

EXAMPLES OF BARREL SWIVELS

HILLMAN ANTI-KINK WEIGHT

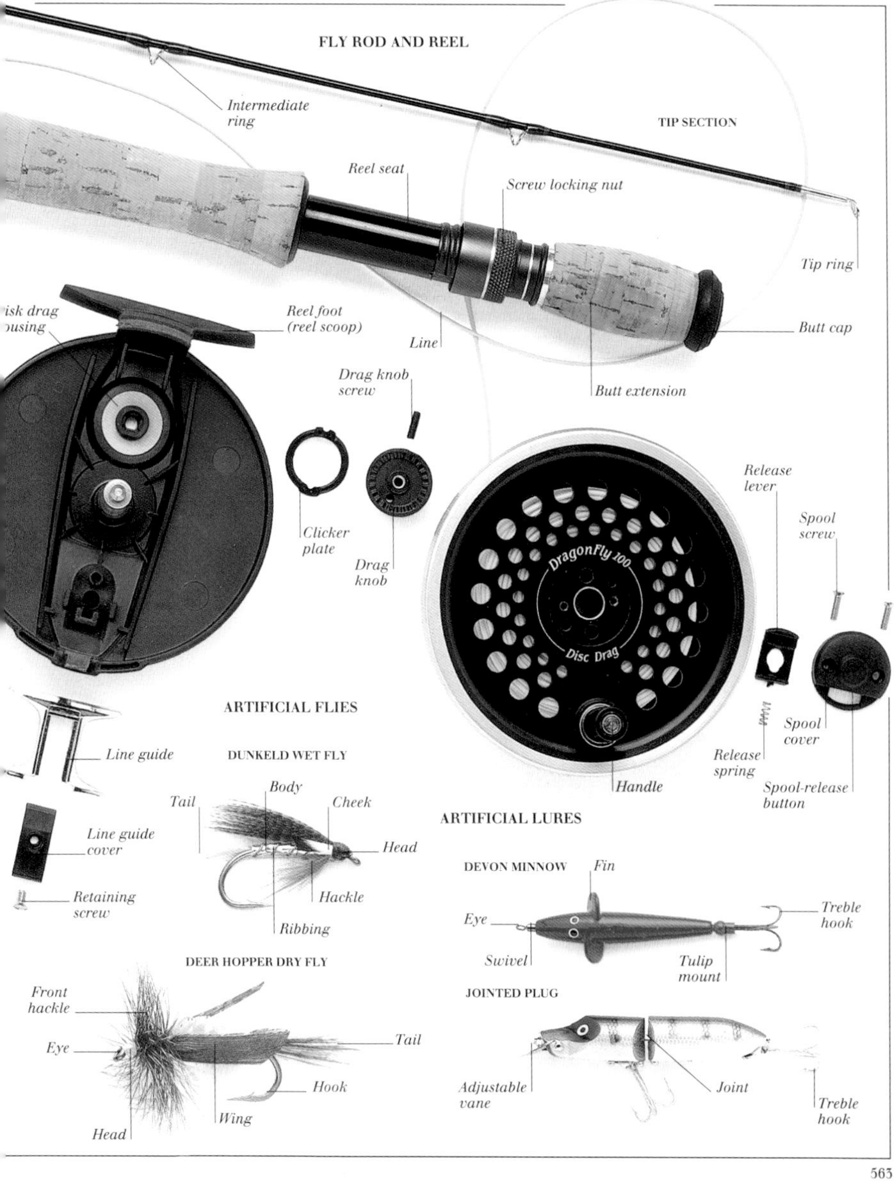
FLY ROD AND REEL
Intermediate ring
TIP SECTION
Reel seat
Screw locking nut
Tip ring
isk drag
ousing
Reel foot (reel scoop)
Line
Butt cap
Drag knob screw
Butt extension
Clicker plate
Drag knob
DragonFly 100
Disc Drag
Release lever
Spool screw
Spool cover
Release spring
Spool-release button
Handle
ARTIFICIAL FLIES
Line guide
DUNKELD WET FLY
Body
Tail
Cheek
Head
Line guide cover
Hackle
Retaining screw
Ribbing
ARTIFICIAL LURES
DEVON MINNOW
Fin
Eye
Treble hook
Swivel
Tulip mount
DEER HOPPER DRY FLY
Front hackle
Eye
Tail
Hook
Wing
Head
JOINTED PLUG
Adjustable vane
Joint
Treble hook

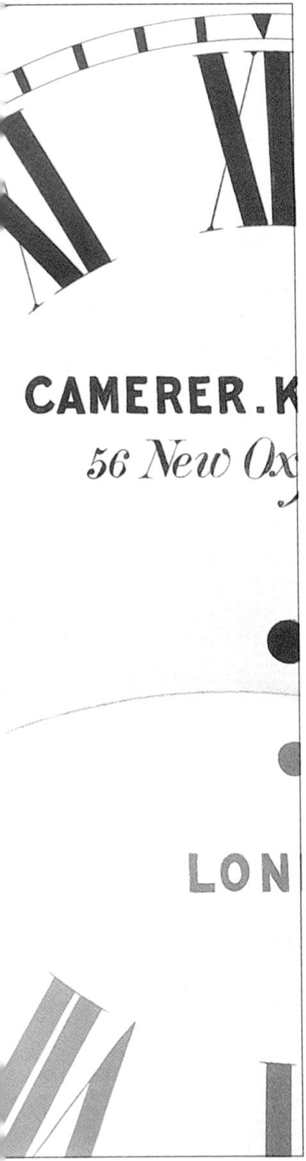

Everyday Things

Drills

THE ELECTRICALLY POWERED MOTOR OF A POWER DRILL, cooled by a fan, turns a shaft at high speed. The shaft connects, in turn, to a system of gears that rotates a chuck even faster. Clamped by the chuck, a sharp bit cuts out the hole, and at the same time the bit's screw-shaped grooves channel the waste out of the hole. For drilling hard materials, many power drills have a hammer mechanism: when this is operated a ratchet in the gearcase causes the chuck and bit to pound in and out as they drill. A hand drill, although slower and less forceful than a power drill, is easier to control. For cutting wide holes, carpenters often prefer a brace-and-bit. This acts like a lever: the bowed handle of the brace moves a larger distance than the bit, turning the bit with extra force.

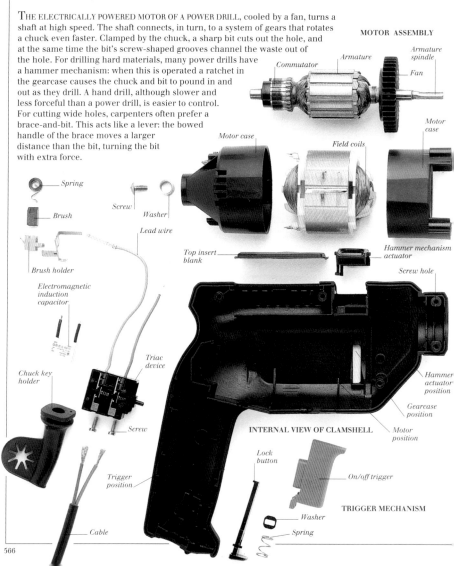

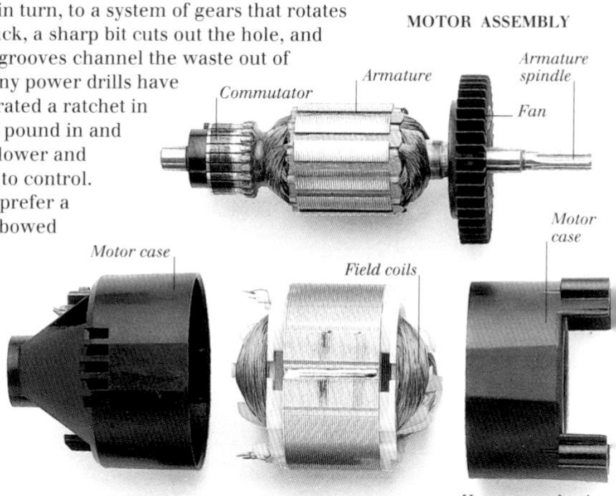
MOTOR ASSEMBLY
Armature spindle
Armature
Commutator
Fan
Motor case
Motor case
Field coils

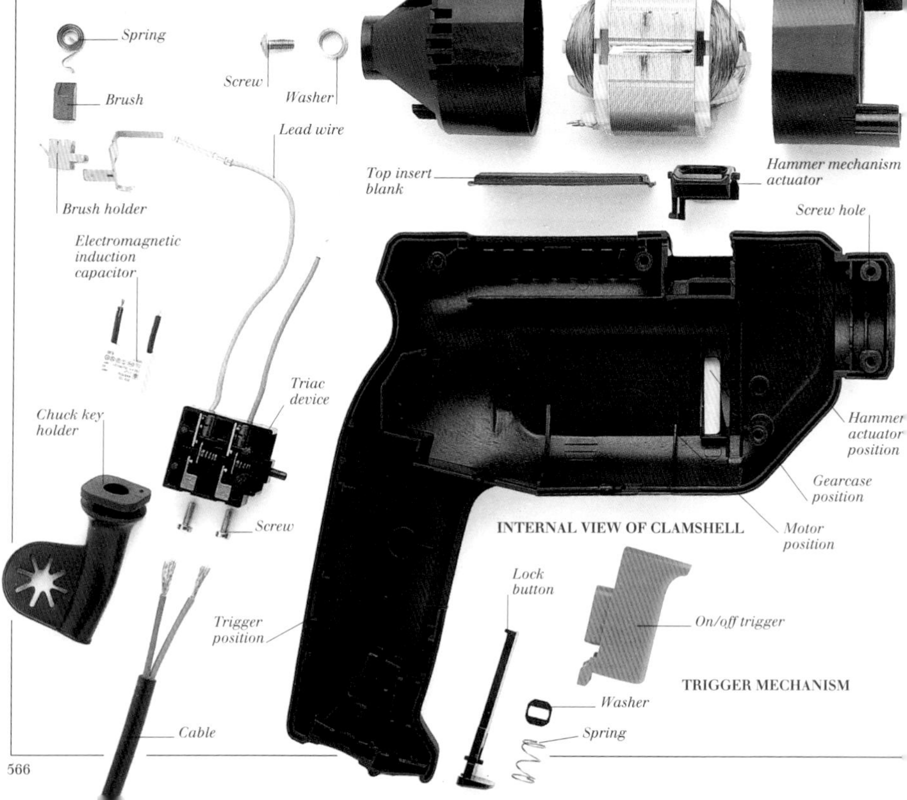
Spring
Screw
Washer
Brush
Lead wire
Brush holder
Top insert blank
Hammer mechanism actuator
Screw hole
Electromagnetic induction capacitor
Triac device
Chuck key holder
Hammer actuator position
Gearcase position
Screw
INTERNAL VIEW OF CLAMSHELL
Motor position
Lock button
Trigger position
On/off trigger
TRIGGER MECHANISM
Washer
Cable
Spring

GEAR MECHANISM

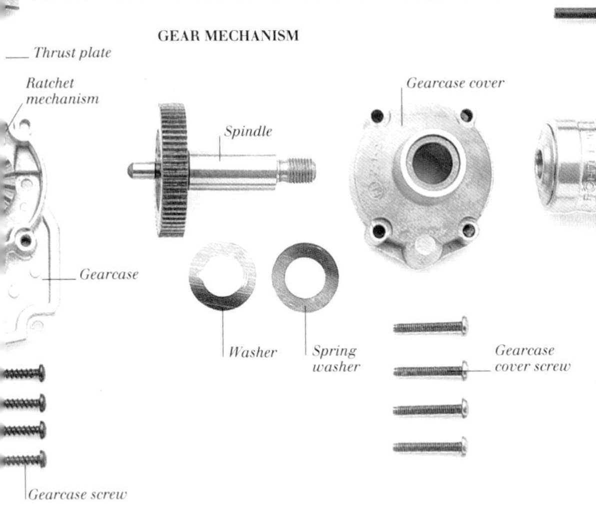

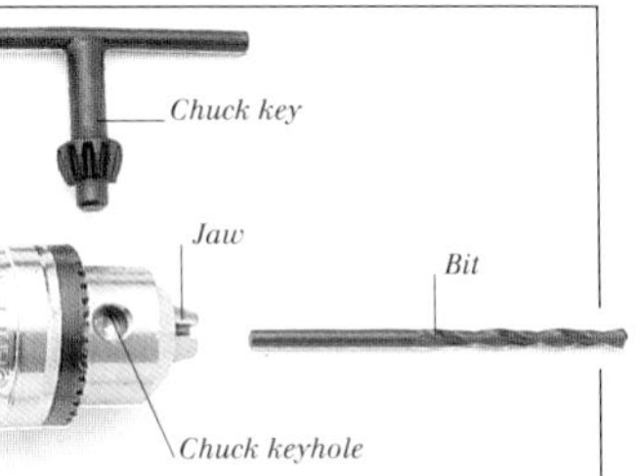

POWER DRILL

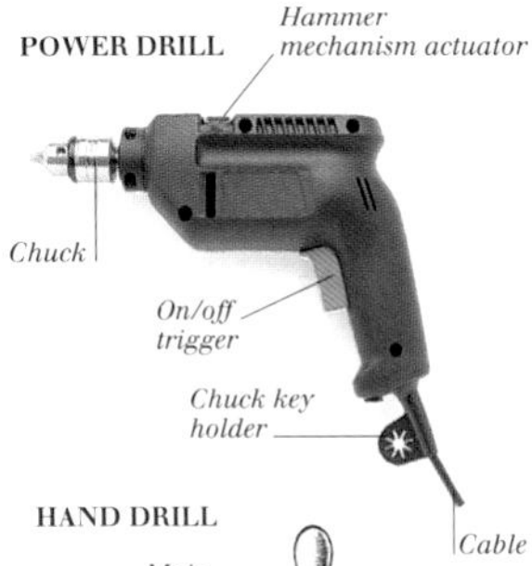

HAND DRILL

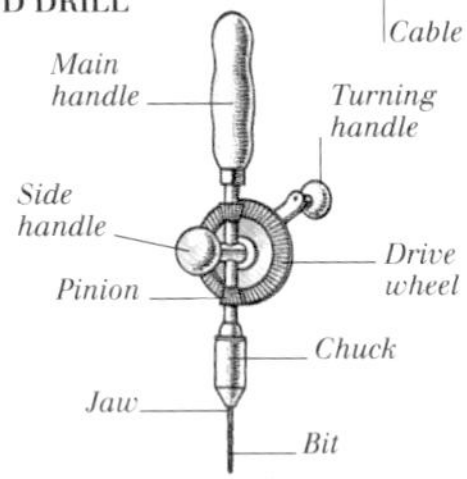

EXTERNAL VIEW OF CLAMSHELL

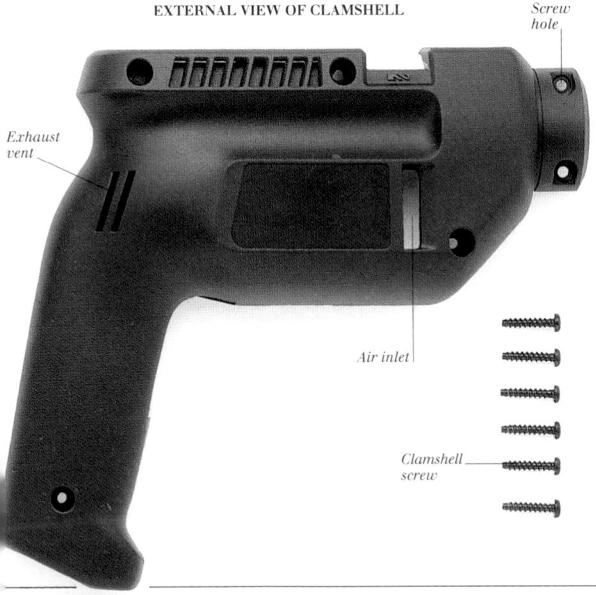

BRACE-AND-BIT

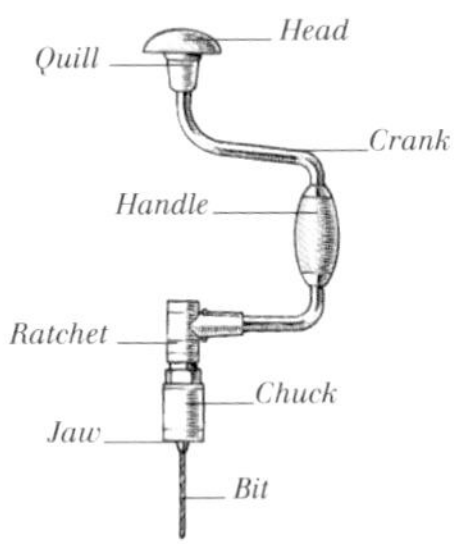

Shoes

WELL-MADE SHOES PROTECT THE FEET and are also comfortable and long-lasting. The best shoemakers use a wooden or plastic mould, called a last, which matches the shape of the customer's foot. The different parts of a shoe are stitched and glued together around the last; rivets and nails are used only in the heel, which is built up from layers of leather and rubber. The steel shank gives support to the arch of the foot and, with the seat lift, helps the wearer maintain posture. The layers of the sole give strength, while the soft insole cushions the foot. The leather welt sewn between the leather uppers and the sole ensures a strong join.

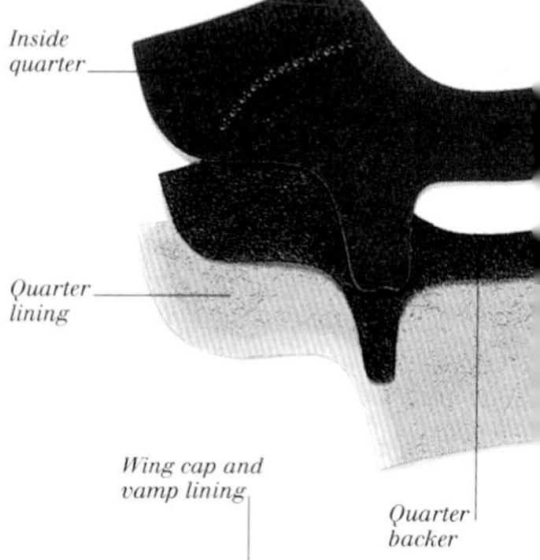
Inside quarter
Quarter lining
Quarter backer

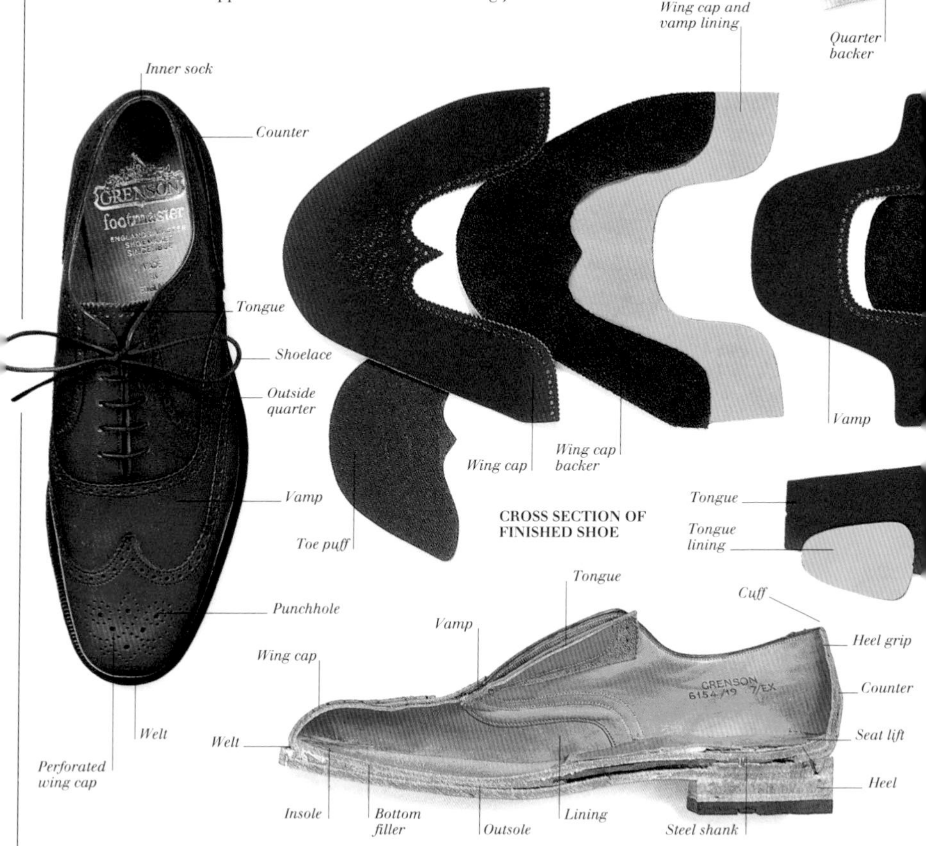
Wing cap and vamp lining
Inner sock
Counter
GRENSON
footmaster
Tongue
Shoelace
Outside quarter
Vamp
Punchhole
Welt
Perforated wing cap
Toe puff
Wing cap
Wing cap backer
Vamp
Tongue
Tongue lining
Tongue
Cuff
Vamp
Heel grip
Wing cap
GRENSON
6154/19 7/EX
Counter
Welt
Seat lift
Heel
Insole
Bottom filler
Outsole
Lining
Steel shank

CROSS SECTION OF FINISHED SHOE

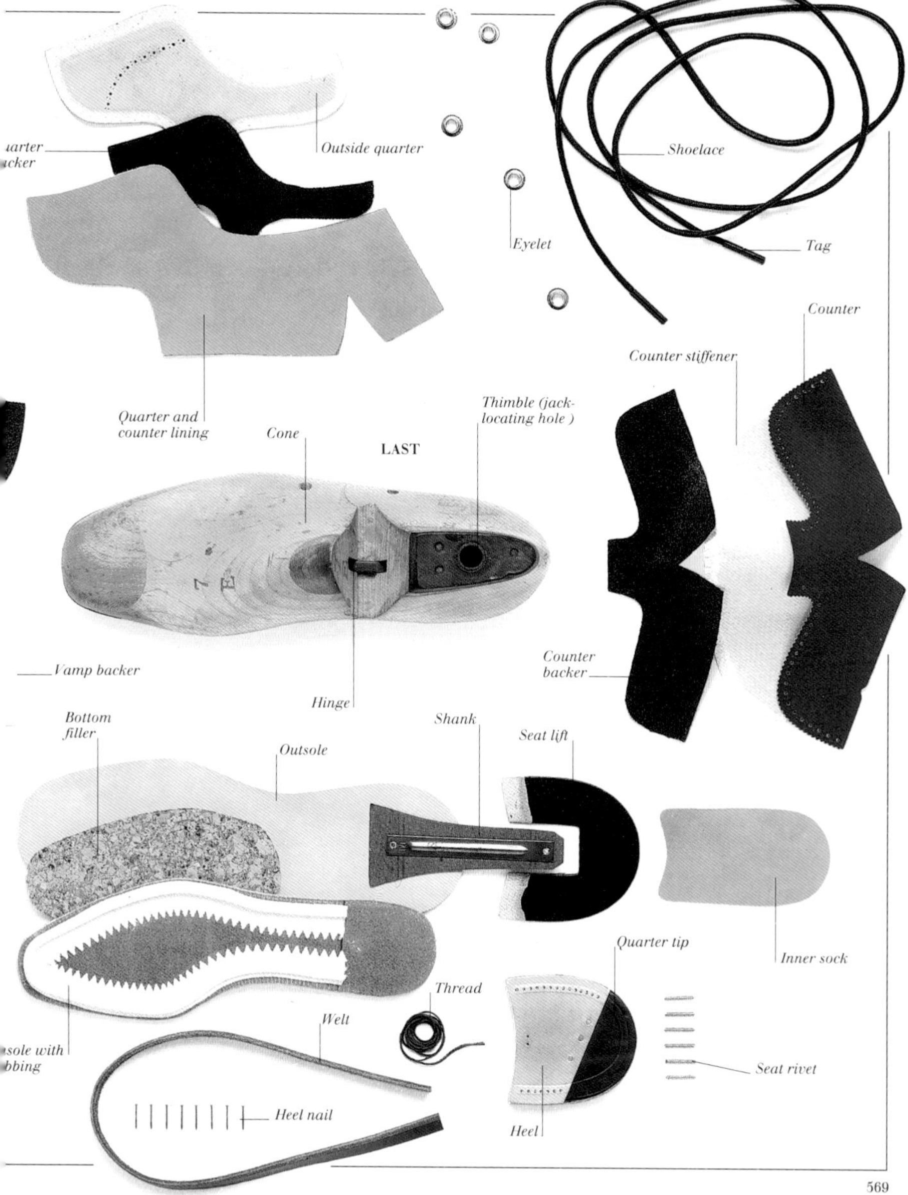

uarter
cker
Outside quarter
Shoelace
Eyelet
Tag
Counter
Counter stiffener
Quarter and
counter lining
Cone
LAST
Thimble (jack-
locating hole)
Vamp backer
Hinge
Counter
backer
Bottom
filler
Outsole
Shank
Seat lift
Inner sock
Quarter tip
Thread
Welt
sole with
bbing
Seat rivet
Heel nail
Heel

Clock

MECHANICAL CLOCKS HAVE TWO essential elements: a mainspring and a pendulum. When the clock is wound with the key, the mainspring is tightened. As the mainspring unwinds, it turns the gears, which move the minute and hour hands at different speeds around the face of the clock. The pendulum ensures that the hands move at a regular pace. At the top of the pendulum are two hooks called pallets. As the pendulum swings, the pallets allow the escape wheel to turn slowly and evenly.

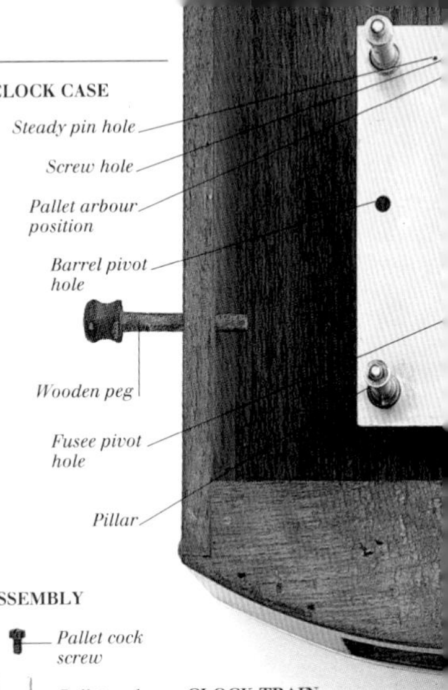
CLOCK CASE
Steady pin hole
Screw hole
Pallet arbour position
Barrel pivot hole
Wooden peg
Fusee pivot hole
Pillar

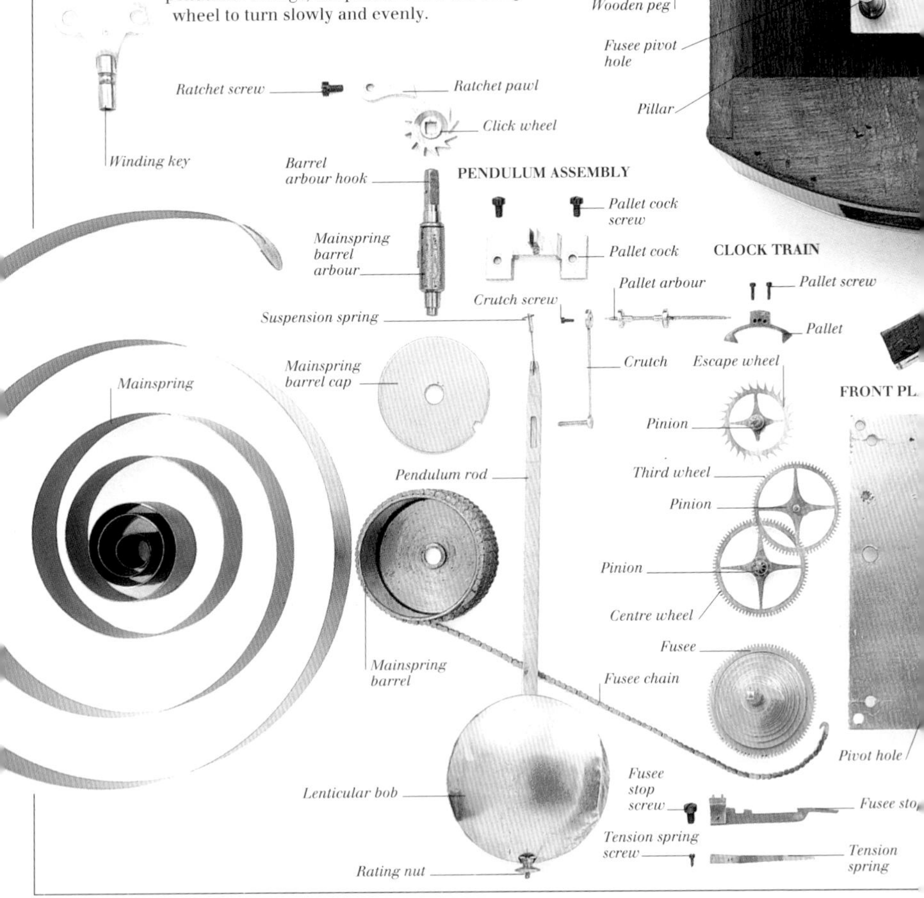
Ratchet screw
Ratchet pawl
Click wheel
Winding key
Barrel arbour hook
PENDULUM ASSEMBLY
Pallet cock screw
Mainspring barrel arbour
Pallet cock
CLOCK TRAIN
Pallet arbour
Pallet screw
Crutch screw
Suspension spring
Pallet
Crutch
Escape wheel
Mainspring barrel cap
Mainspring
FRONT PL.
Pinion
Pendulum rod
Third wheel
Pinion
Pinion
Centre wheel
Fusee
Mainspring barrel
Fusee chain
Pivot hole
Fusee stop screw
Lenticular bob
Fusee sto
Tension spring screw
Tension spring
Rating nut

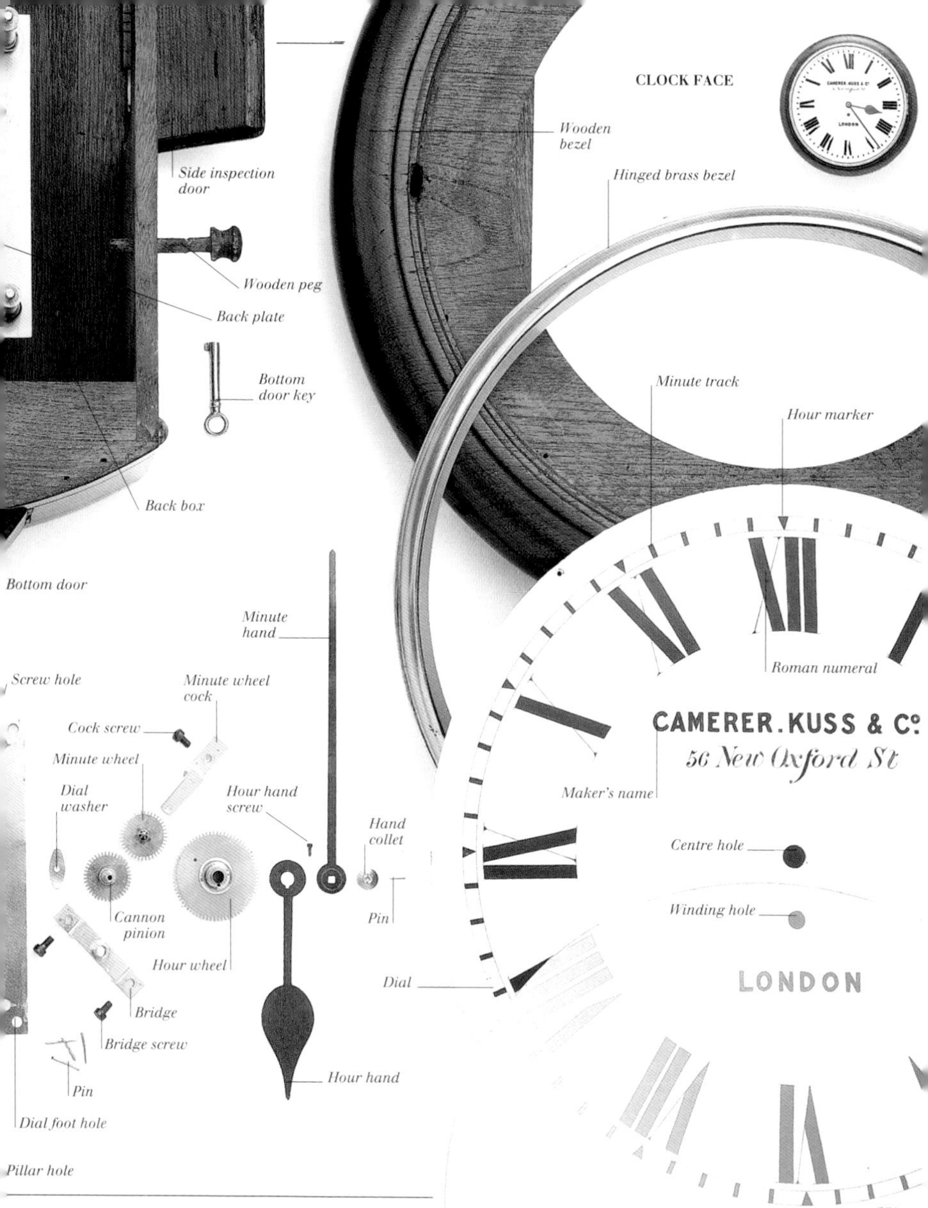
CLOCK FACE
Wooden bezel
Hinged brass bezel
Side inspection door
Wooden peg
Back plate
Bottom door key
Back box
Bottom door
Minute track
Hour marker
Roman numeral
CAMERER. KUSS & Co
56 New Oxford St
Maker's name
Centre hole
Winding hole
LONDON
Dial
Minute hand
Screw hole
Minute wheel cock
Cock screw
Minute wheel
Dial washer
Hour hand screw
Hand collet
Pin
Cannon pinion
Hour wheel
Bridge
Bridge screw
Pin
Hour hand
Dial foot hole
Pillar hole

Lamp

THE FIRST SPRING-TENSIONED, adjustable work lamp was designed in 1934 by George Carwardine. This type of lamp imitates the human arm in the way that it can be kept in a fixed position or moved easily and precisely. In the arm, such control is achieved by coordinating the opposing action of paired muscles (e.g., when the biceps contracts, the triceps relaxes and the arm bends). In the work lamp, one muscle of a pair is represented by the springs that pull on the rigid bars of the lamp; the other muscle is represented by the nuts, bolts, screws, and washers in the lamp's joints that resist the pull of the springs. By balancing the pull of the springs against the resistance in the joints, the lamp's height and angle can be adjusted with minimal pressure.

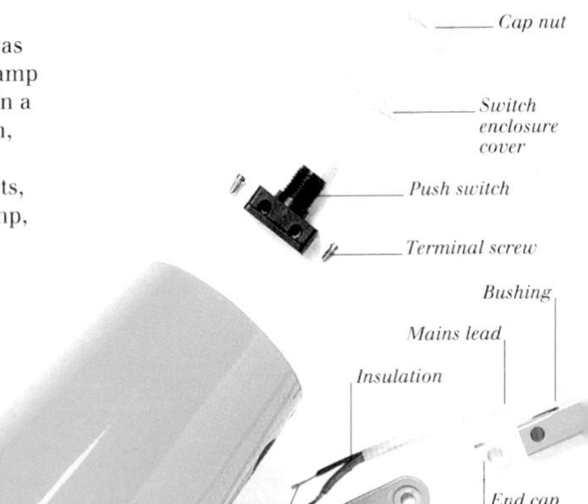
Cap nut
Switch enclosure cover
Push switch
Terminal screw
Bushing
Mains lead
Insulation
End cap

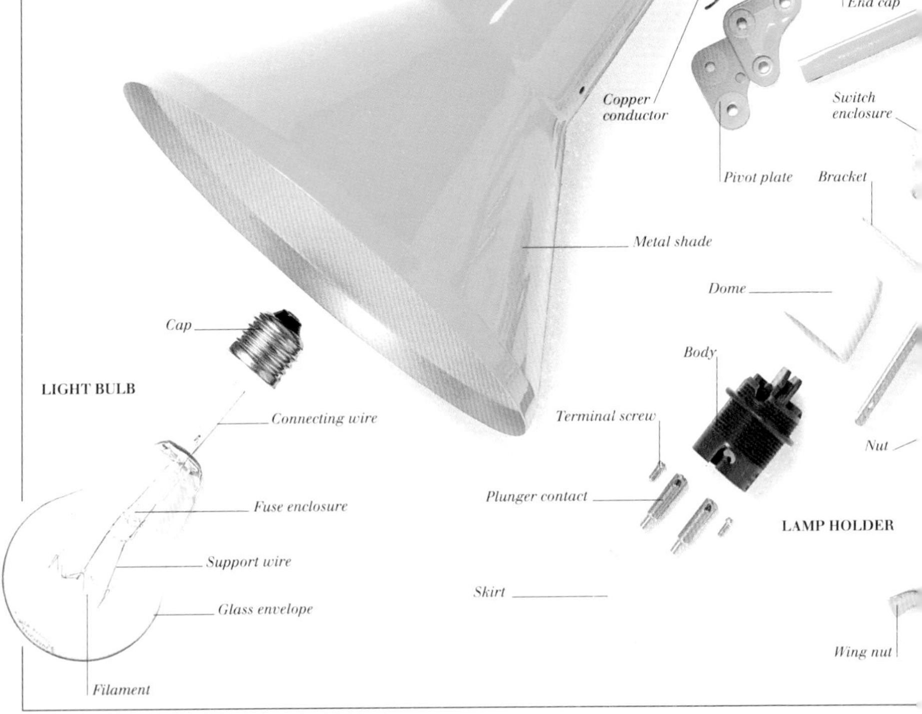
Copper conductor
Switch enclosure
Pivot plate
Bracket
Metal shade
Dome
Cap
LIGHT BULB
Connecting wire
Body
Terminal screw
Nut
Plunger contact
LAMP HOLDER
Fuse enclosure
Support wire
Skirt
Glass envelope
Wing nut
Filament

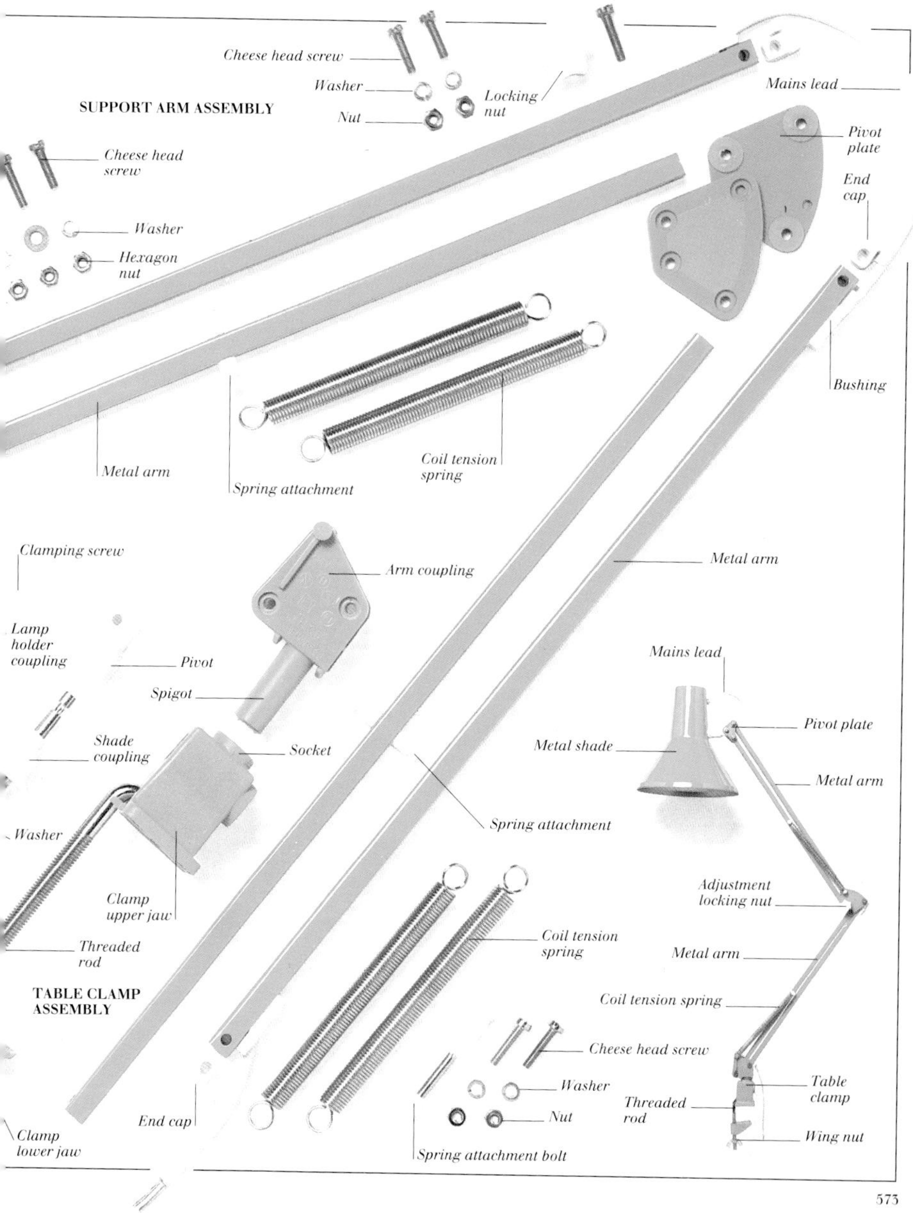
SUPPORT ARM ASSEMBLY
Cheese head screw
Washer
Nut
Locking nut
Mains lead
Pivot plate
End cap
Cheese head screw
Washer
Hexagon nut
Bushing
Metal arm
Spring attachment
Coil tension spring
Clamping screw
Arm coupling
Metal arm
Lamp holder coupling
Pivot
Spigot
Mains lead
Pivot plate
Socket
Metal shade
Shade coupling
Metal arm
Spring attachment
Washer
Clamp upper jaw
Adjustment locking nut
Coil tension spring
Threaded rod
Metal arm
TABLE CLAMP ASSEMBLY
Coil tension spring
Cheese head screw
Washer
Table clamp
Threaded rod
Nut
End cap
Wing nut
Clamp lower jaw
Spring attachment bolt

Mini-television

MINIATURIZED TELEVISION SETS are small enough to be held in the hand while being watched. A signal sent by a broadcast transmitter is picked up by the television aerial and passed to an electron gun at the back of the television set. In response to the signal this gun produces an electron beam that is passed through a deflection yoke. The yoke contains magnets and coils that cause the beam to scan across the screen in a series of lines. The screen is coated with phosphor, which glows when hit by the beam. As the beam scans the screen, its strength is varied so that the phosphor glows with different intensities in different parts of the screen. A continuous sequence of 25 black-and-white pictures per second appears on the screen so rapidly that the illusion of a moving picture is created.

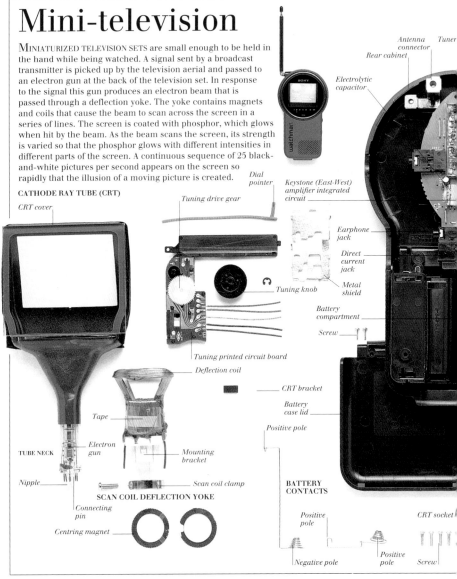

Antenna connector
Tuner
Rear cabinet
Electrolytic capacitor
Keystone (East-West) amplifier integrated circuit
Earphone jack
Direct current jack
Metal shield
Battery compartment
Screw
Battery case lid
CRT socket

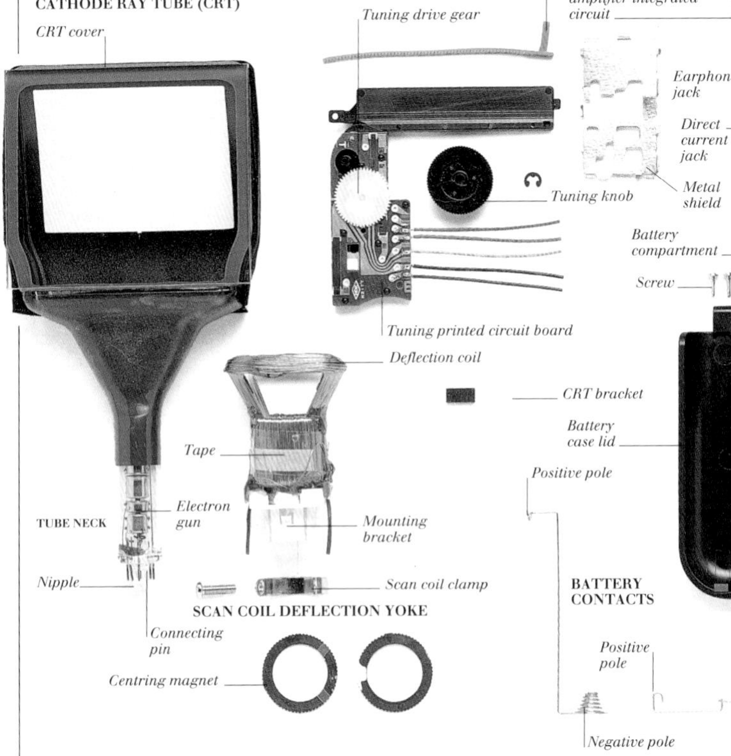
CATHODE RAY TUBE (CRT)
CRT cover
Dial pointer
Tuning drive gear
Tuning knob
Tuning printed circuit board
Deflection coil
CRT bracket
Tape
Electron gun
TUBE NECK
Mounting bracket
Nipple
Scan coil clamp
SCAN COIL DEFLECTION YOKE
Connecting pin
Centring magnet
Positive pole
BATTERY CONTACTS
Positive pole
Negative pole
Positive pole
Screw

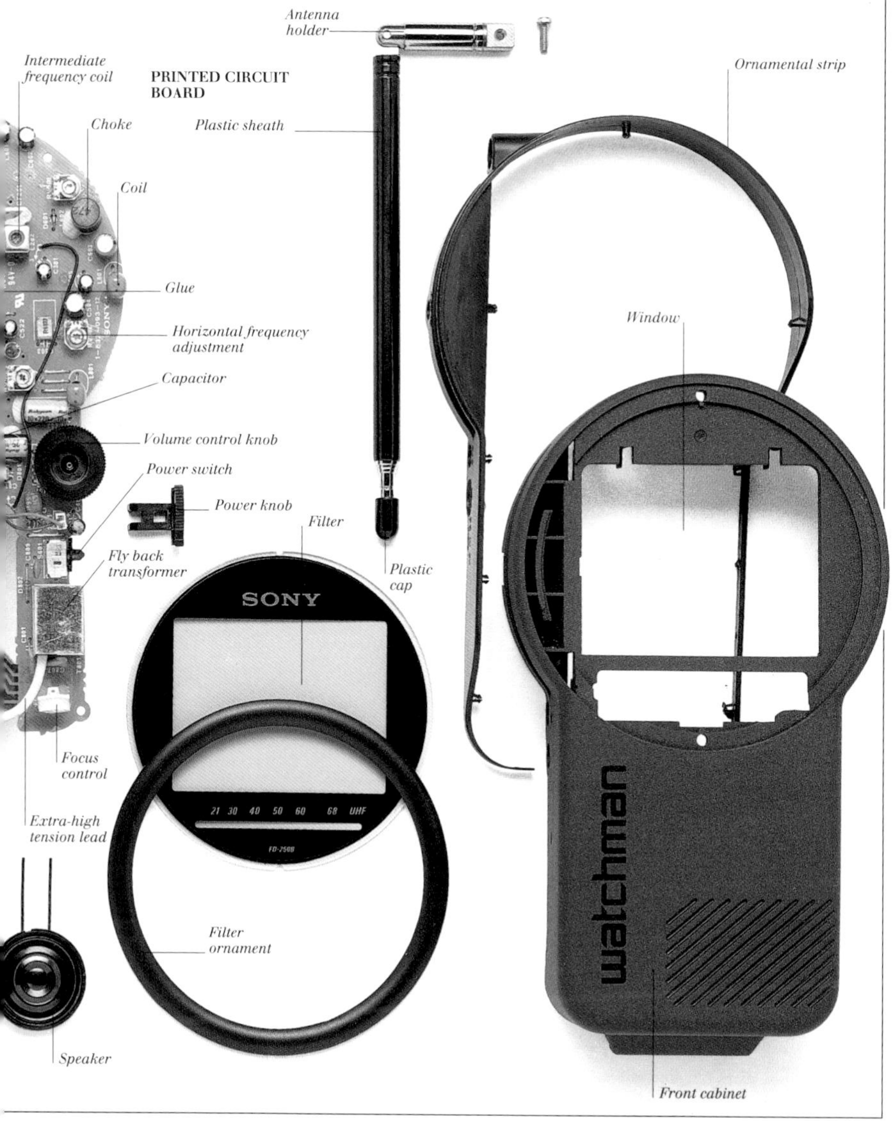
Antenna holder
Intermediate frequency coil
PRINTED CIRCUIT BOARD
Ornamental strip
Choke
Plastic sheath
Coil
Glue
Window
Horizontal frequency adjustment
Capacitor
Volume control knob
Power switch
Power knob
Filter
Fly back transformer
Plastic cap
SONY
21 30 40 50 60 68 UHF
FD-250B
Focus control
Extra-high tension lead
Filter ornament
watchman
Speaker
Front cabinet

Chair

A TRADITIONALLY MADE DINING CHAIR, such as the Regency-style carver shown here, is held together, not by nails or bolts, but by snugly fitting joints, screws, dowels, and glue. Its curved arms and top splats, as well as its tapering legs, are cut from seasoned – that is, dried – mahogany. Mortice slots in the back legs receive the tenon tongues of the top and bottom splats; angled grooves at the top of the back legs, called rebates, take the curved arm rail. Though the various joints are so tight-fitting that they could produce a solid frame on their own, screws and glue are used to give the joints added strength. The comfortable, upholstered seatpad shown here consists of a patterned cover, calico lining, and foam stuffing that has been treated for fire safety; it is supported by webbing stretched across a wooden frame.

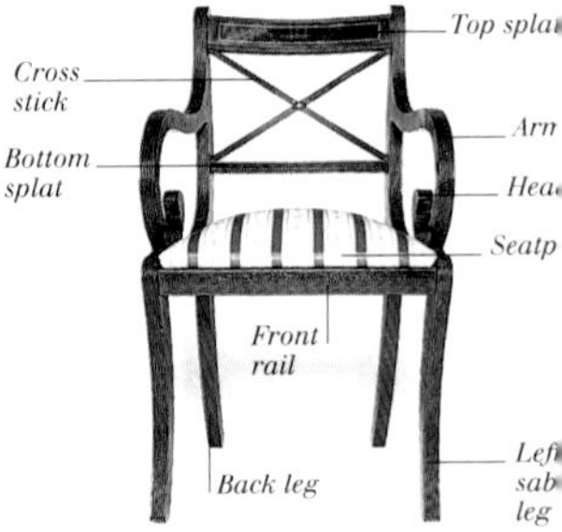
Cross stick
Bottom splat
Front rail
Back leg

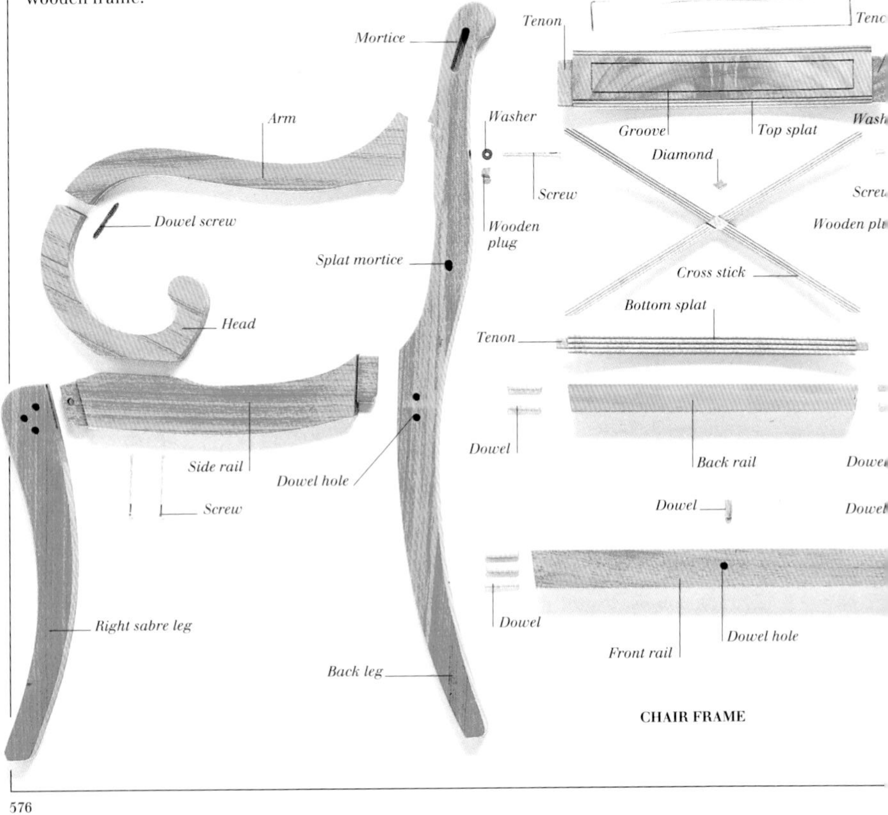
Square brass line
Tenon
Mortice
Arm
Washer
Groove
Top splat
Diamond
Screw
Dowel screw
Wooden plug
Splat mortice
Cross stick
Head
Bottom splat
Tenon
Side rail
Dowel
Back rail
Dowel hole
Screw
Dowel
Dowel
Dowel hole
Front rail
Right sabre leg
Back leg

CHAIR FRAME

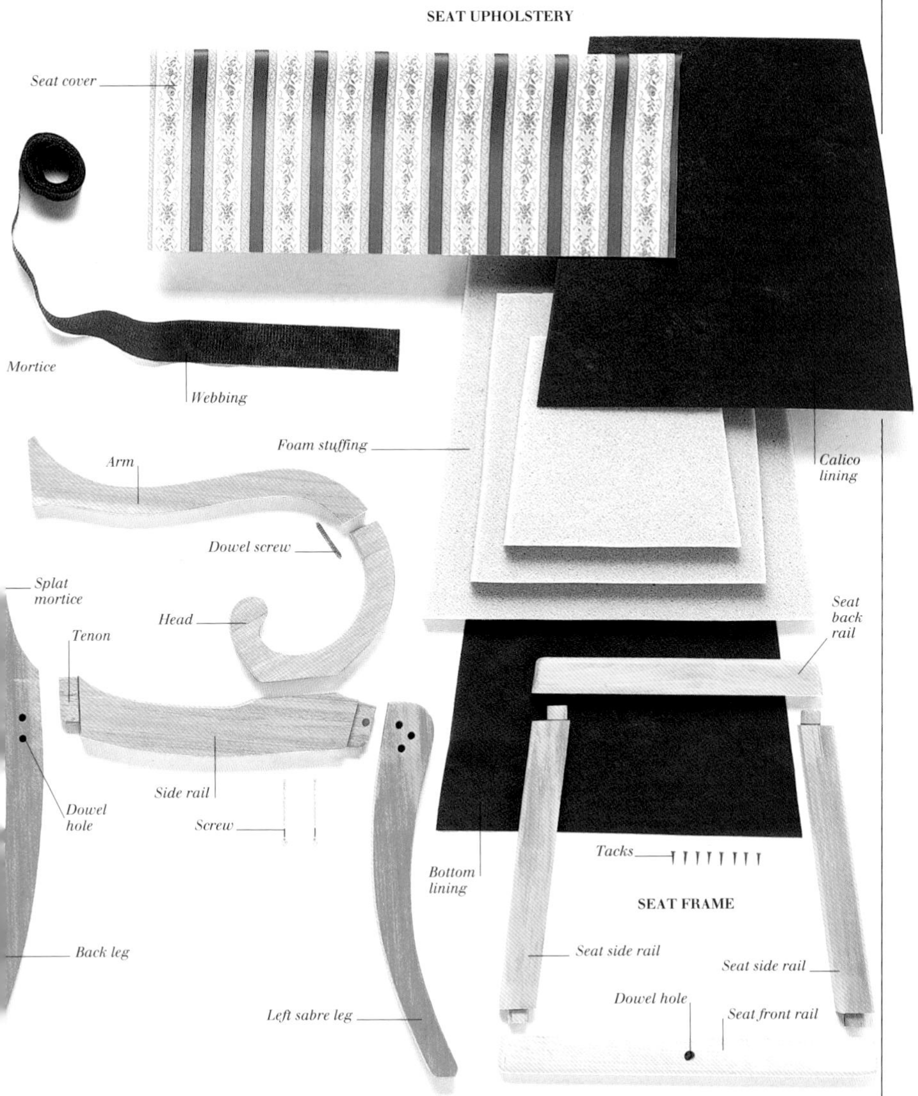
SEAT UPHOLSTERY
Seat cover
Mortice
Webbing
Foam stuffing
Calico lining
Arm
Dowel screw
Splat mortice
Head
Tenon
Seat back rail
Side rail
Dowel hole
Screw
Tacks
Bottom lining
SEAT FRAME
Back leg
Seat side rail
Seat side rail
Dowel hole
Seat front rail
Left sabre leg

Toaster

MOST ELECTRIC TOASTERS NOT ONLY GRILL slices of bread, they also pop them up when ready. While the slices rest on a spring-loaded rack, electric heating elements toast the bread. At the same time, a bimetallic strip heats and expands. One of the two metals in this strip expands more quickly than the other, causing the strip to curve. As it bends, it completes an electrical circuit and activates an electromagnet. The magnet attracts a catch, releasing the spring that holds the rack down in the toaster. The elements switch off, and the toasted slices pop up.

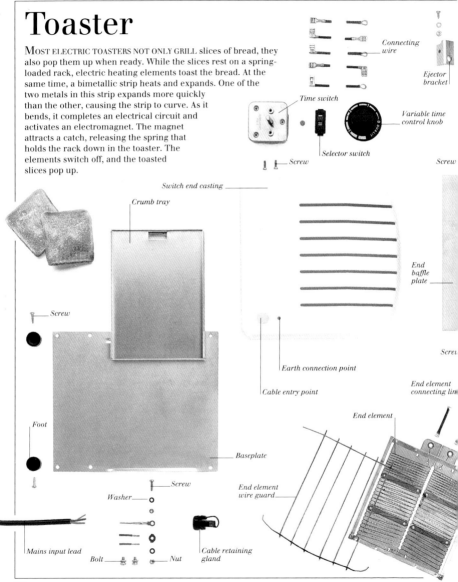

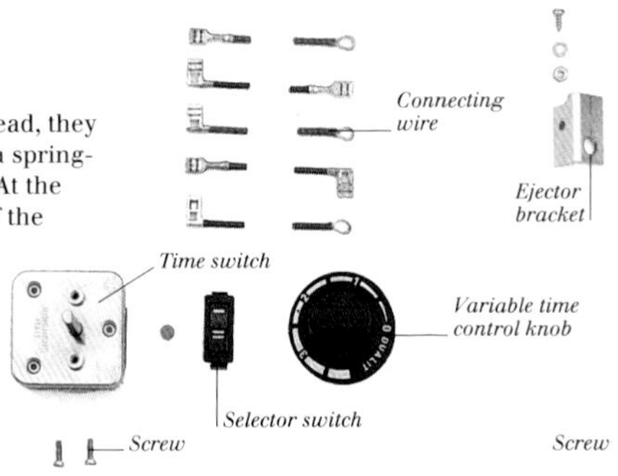

Connecting wire
Ejector bracket
Time switch
Variable time control knob
Selector switch
Screw
Screw

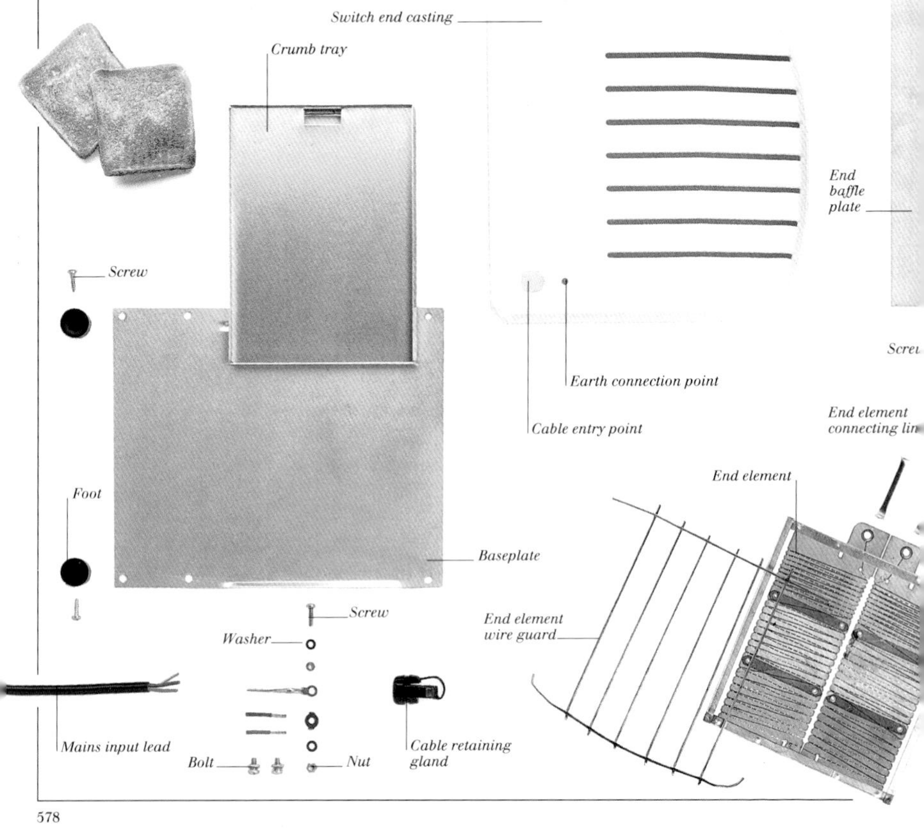

Switch end casting
Crumb tray
End baffle plate
Screw
Earth connection point
Cable entry point
End element
Foot
Baseplate
Screw
Washer
End element wire guard
Mains input lead
Bolt
Nut
Cable retaining gland

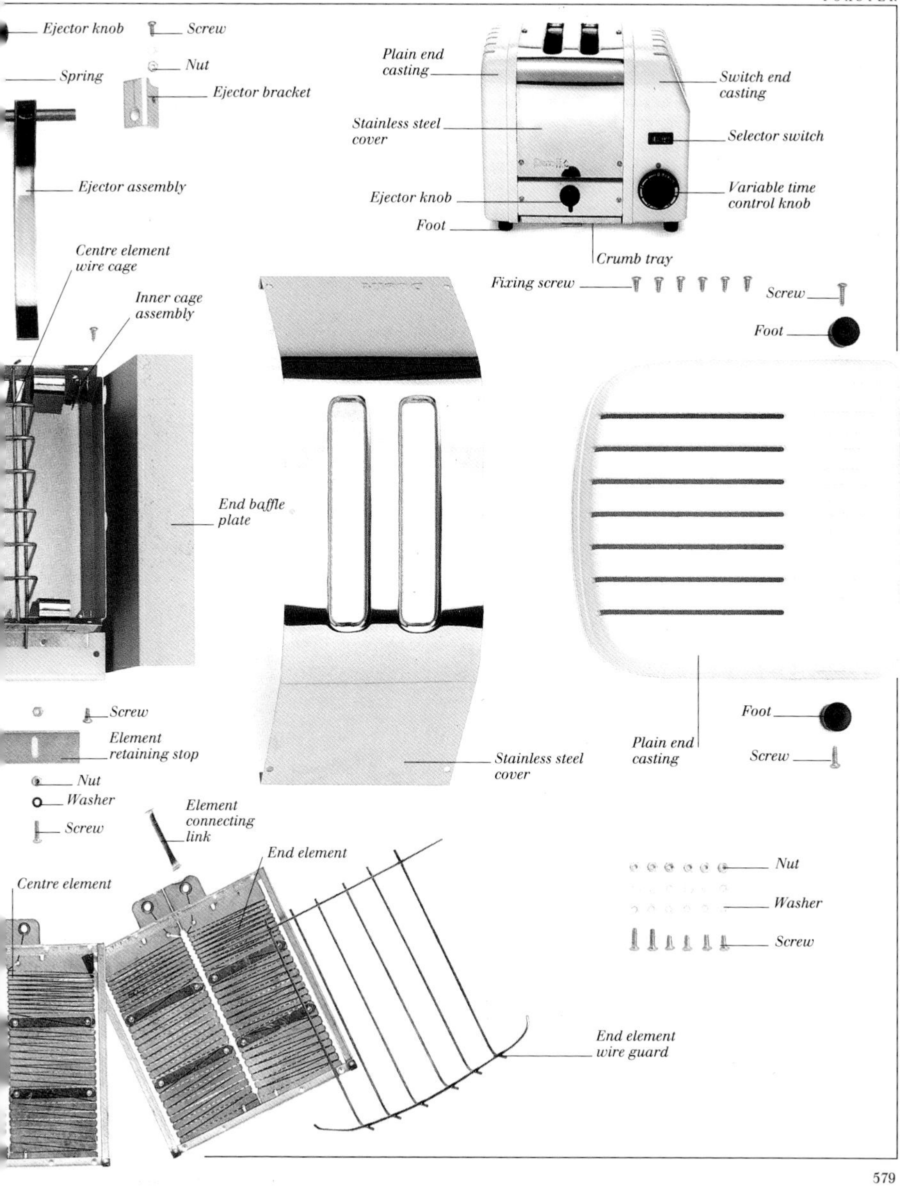
Ejector knob
Screw
Nut
Spring
Ejector bracket
Ejector assembly
Centre element
wire cage
Inner cage
assembly
End baffle
plate
Screw
Element
retaining stop
Nut
Washer
Screw
Element
connecting
link
End element
Centre element
Plain end
casting
Switch end
casting
Stainless steel
cover
Selector switch
Variable time
control knob
Ejector knob
Foot
Crumb tray
Fixing screw
Screw
Foot
Stainless steel
cover
Foot
Plain end
casting
Screw
Nut
Washer
Screw
End element
wire guard

Lawnmower

THE SHARP BLADES OF A LAWNMOWER – whether driven by electrical, petrol, or human power – shave grass close to the ground. The petrol-powered type shown here has a small engine that is electrically ignited by a battery and spark plug. This engine rotates a horizontal blade at the base of the lawnmower that slices the grass against a fixed blade. A grass bag at the back of the machine collects the cuttings. As the engine rotates the blades, it also turns the rear wheels, moving the lawnmower forwards. Gears ensure that the horizontal blade spins faster than the wheels so that all of the grass is cut neatly before the lawnmower moves on.

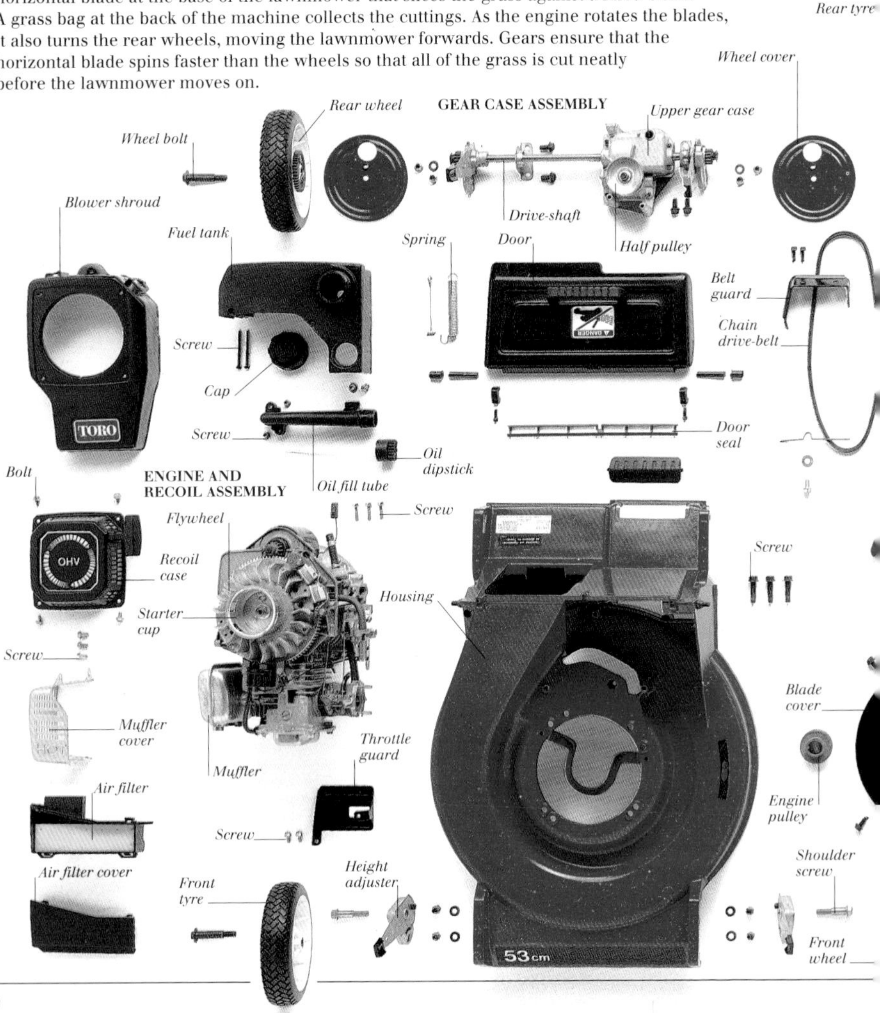
Rear tyre
Wheel cover
Rear wheel
GEAR CASE ASSEMBLY
Upper gear case
Wheel bolt
Blower shroud
Drive-shaft
Fuel tank
Spring
Door
Half pulley
Belt guard
Chain drive-belt
Screw
Cap
TORO
Screw
Door seal
Oil dipstick
Bolt
ENGINE AND RECOIL ASSEMBLY
Oil fill tube
Screw
Flywheel
OHV
Recoil case
Housing
Screw
Starter cup
Screw
Blade cover
Muffler cover
Throttle guard
Muffler
Air filter
Engine pulley
Screw
Shoulder screw
Air filter cover
Front tyre
Height adjuster
Front wheel
53cm

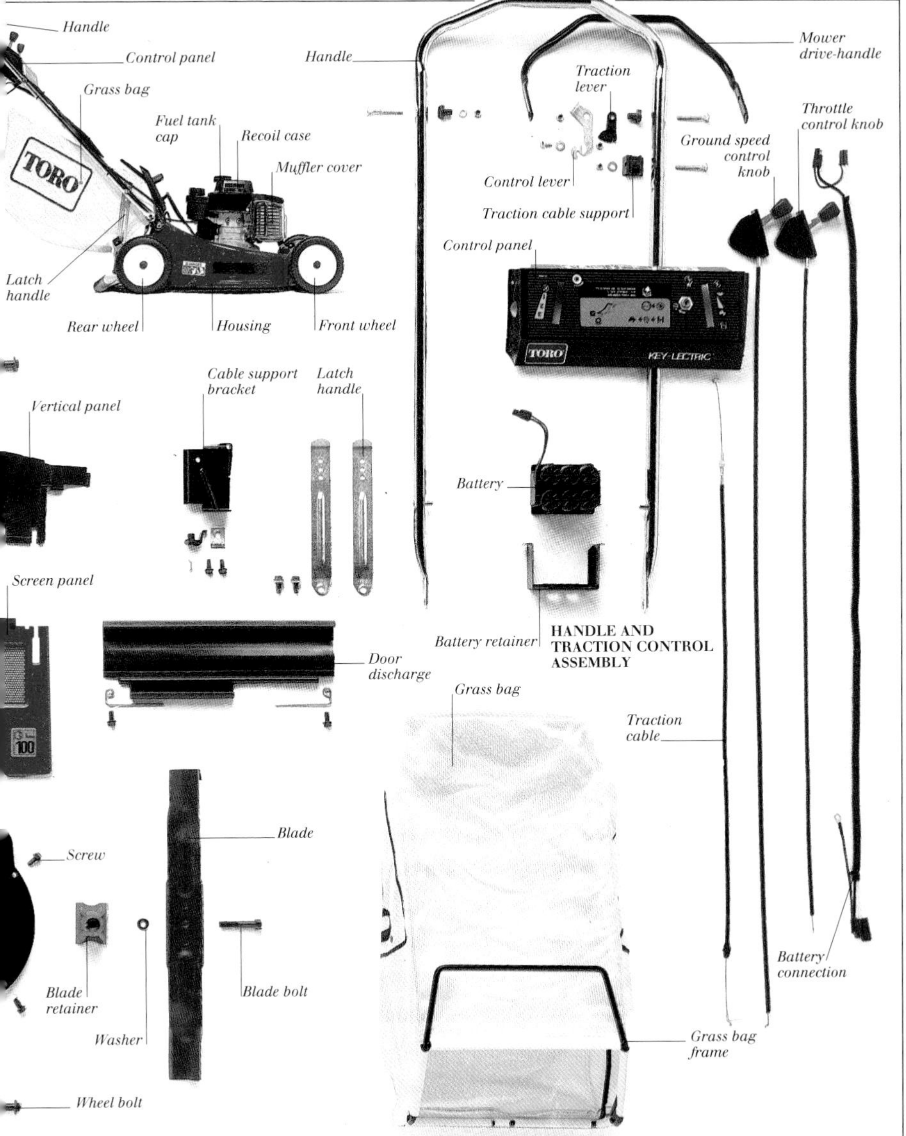
Handle
Control panel
Grass bag
Fuel tank cap
Recoil case
Muffler cover
TORO
Latch handle
Rear wheel
Housing
Front wheel
Handle
Mower drive-handle
Traction lever
Throttle control knob
Ground speed control knob
Control lever
Traction cable support
Control panel
TORO
KEY-LECTRIC
Cable support bracket
Latch handle
Vertical panel
Battery
Screen panel
100
Battery retainer
HANDLE AND TRACTION CONTROL ASSEMBLY
Door discharge
Grass bag
Traction cable
Blade
Screw
Blade bolt
Blade retainer
Washer
Battery connection
Grass bag frame
Wheel bolt

Saddle

THE FIRST HORSE RIDERS HAD NO SADDLES; they sat bareback, clinging to the animal's mane. Next came a simple cloth saddle. The leather saddle, which was invented about 2,000 years ago by the warriors of the Asian steppes, revolutionized horse riding. On this saddle, horsemen could gallop towards the enemy, fire arrows in all directions, and stay on their horses. Modern saddles are of two main types. The Western saddle is a heavy, working saddle used mainly by ranch hands in the United States. It has a metal horn at the front for securing a lasso and a high cantle at the back to keep the rider on the horse. The English saddle is a much lighter affair. Designed for sport, it allows the horse to gallop fast. Its drawback is that it provides less stability; to stay on the horse, the rider must grip the animal with the knees.

ENGLISH SADDLE

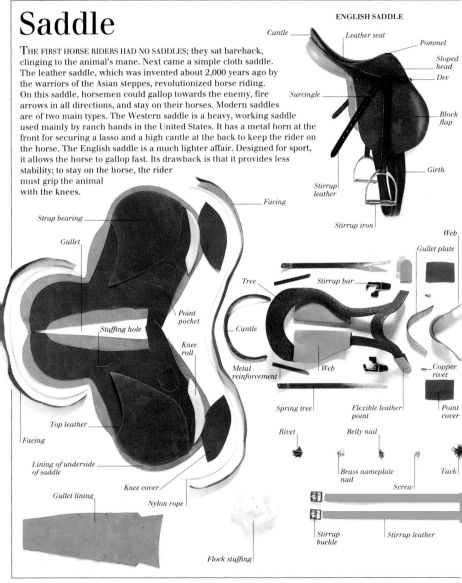

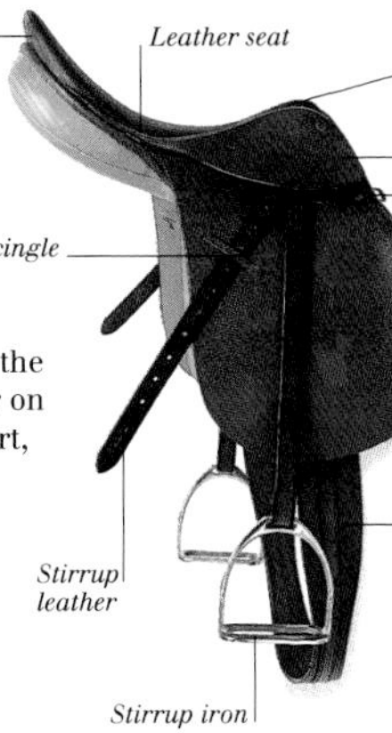
Cantle
Leather seat
Pommel
Sloped head
Dee
Surcingle
Block flap
Girth
Stirrup leather
Stirrup iron

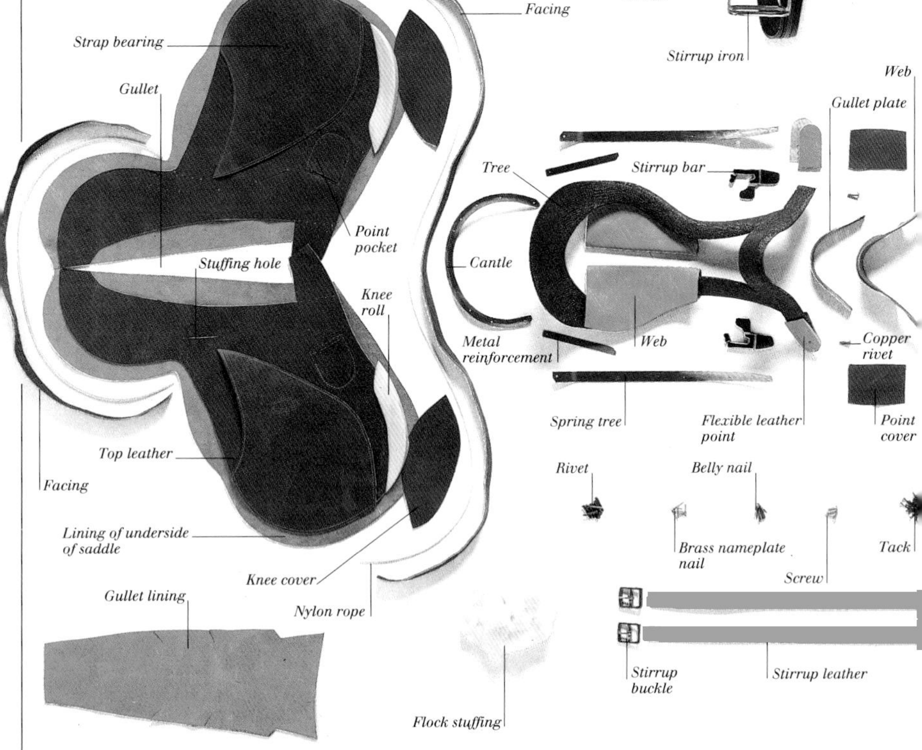
Facing
Strap bearing
Gullet
Point pocket
Stuffing hole
Knee roll
Top leather
Facing
Lining of underside of saddle
Knee cover
Nylon rope
Gullet lining
Flock stuffing
Web
Gullet plate
Tree
Stirrup bar
Cantle
Metal reinforcement
Web
Copper rivet
Spring tree
Flexible leather point
Point cover
Rivet
Belly nail
Brass nameplate nail
Screw
Tack
Stirrup buckle
Stirrup leather

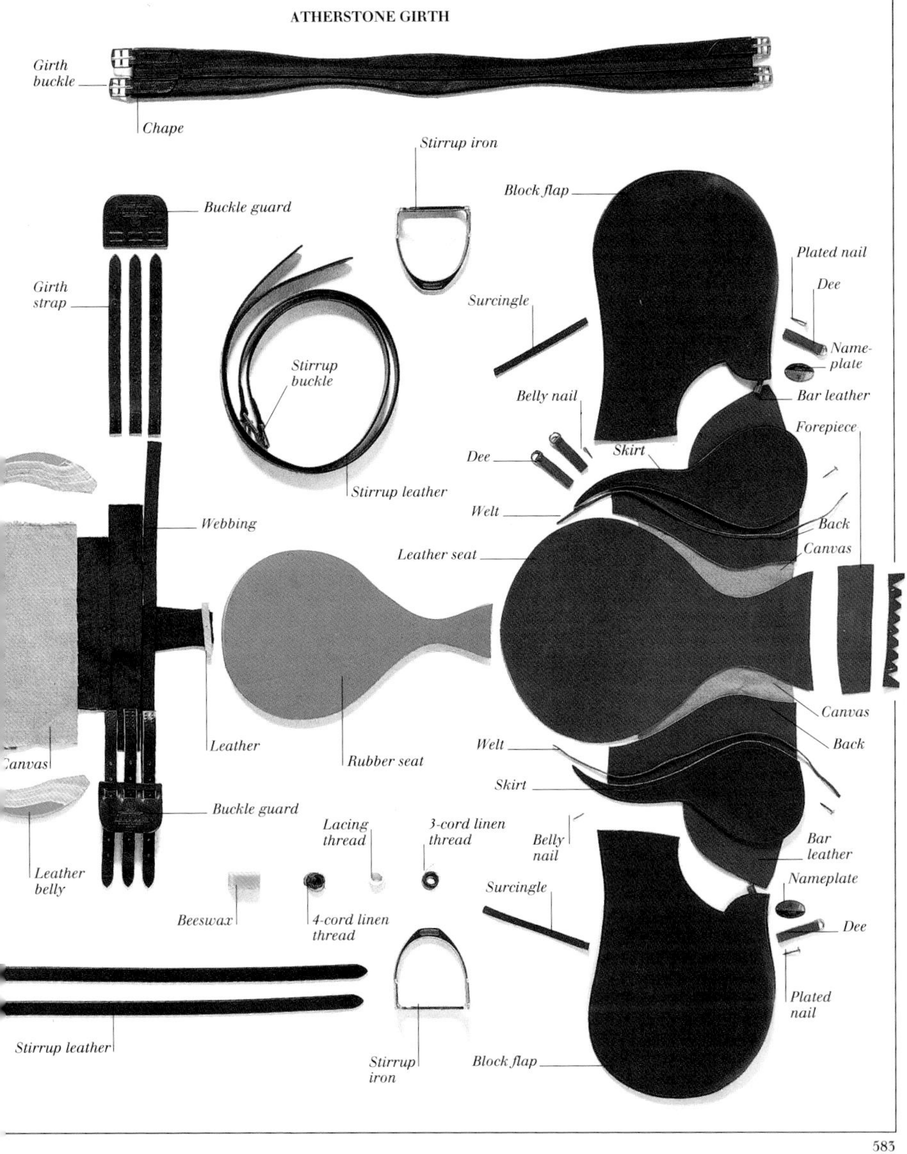
ATHERSTONE GIRTH
Girth buckle
Chape
Stirrup iron
Block flap
Buckle guard
Plated nail
Dee
Girth strap
Surcingle
Name-plate
Stirrup buckle
Bar leather
Belly nail
Forepiece
Dee
Skirt
Stirrup leather
Welt
Webbing
Back
Leather seat
Canvas
Canvas
Back
Leather
Welt
Canvas
Rubber seat
Skirt
Buckle guard
Lacing thread
3-cord linen thread
Belly nail
Bar leather
Leather belly
Nameplate
Surcingle
Beeswax
4-cord linen thread
Dee
Plated nail
Stirrup leather
Stirrup iron
Block flap

CD-ROM

A CD-ROM IS A TYPE OF COMPACT DISC (CD) that can be used to produce images on a computer screen. ROM stands for Read Only Memory, which means that the digitally recorded data registered in pits on the surface of the disc is fixed and cannot be altered or replaced. The CD is loaded into the CD-ROM player, where the data on the spinning disc is read by a laser. CD-ROMs are different from vinyl records in that they are not read along a spiral groove, from outer circumference to inner edge: instead each image or piece of information has a co-ordinate on the disc, which is located by the laser. Information picked up by the laser is relayed to the computer, where it is translated into the text and images that appear on screen. The information is relayed through a SCSI (Small Computer System Interface), which processes the electronic impulses between the disc drive and the computer system. The user can move around the program by clicking on different parts of the screen with a mouse (a hand-held tool with a clicking button whose movement on its pad is mimicked by an icon on the screen). The image in the viewing area (see opposite) can be changed by clicking on the active scrolling button: this moves a rectangular panel down the scrolling figure in the navigational panel. Clicking on active text will provide a new screen with more information, either in the form of text and diagrams, or as narrated animated sequences.

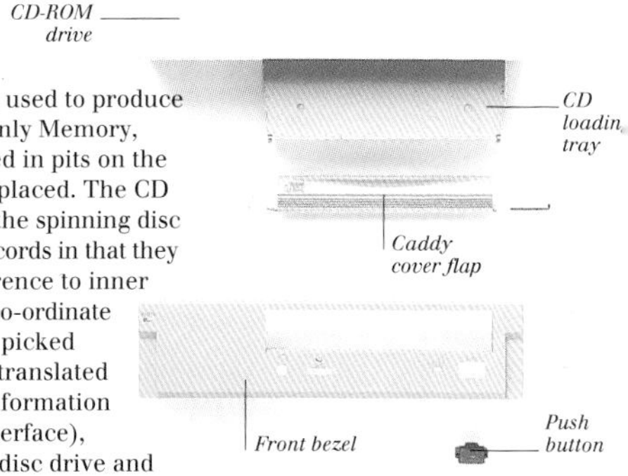
CD-ROM drive
CD loadin tray
Caddy cover flap
Front bezel
Push button

CD-ROM CASING

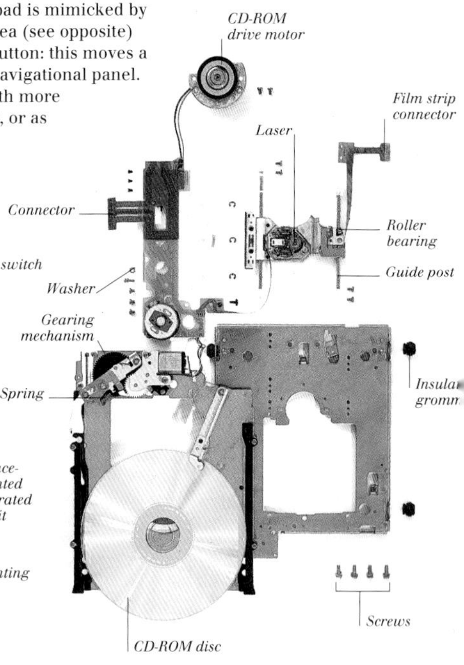
CD-ROM drive motor
Film strip connector
Laser
Connector
Roller bearing
Guide post
Washer
Gearing mechanism
Spring
Insula gromm
Screws
CD-ROM disc

CD-ROM LOADING MECHANISM

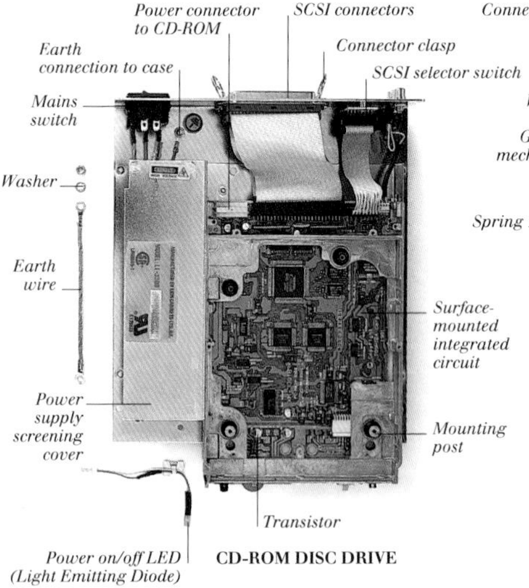
Power connector to CD-ROM
SCSI connectors
Connector clasp
SCSI selector switch
Earth connection to case
Mains switch
Washer
Earth wire
Surface-mounted integrated circuit
Power supply screening cover
Mounting post
Transistor
Power on/off LED (Light Emitting Diode)

CD-ROM DISC DRIVE

CONTENTS PAGE

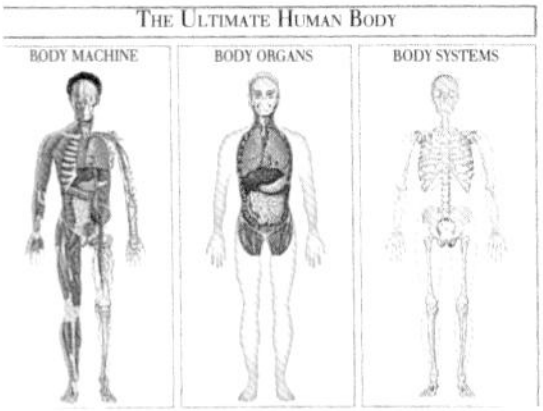
THE ULTIMATE HUMAN BODY
BODY MACHINE
BODY ORGANS
BODY SYSTEMS

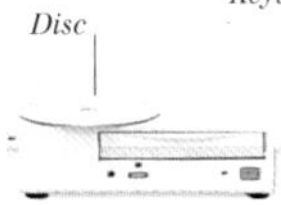
Disc

CD-ROM PLAYER

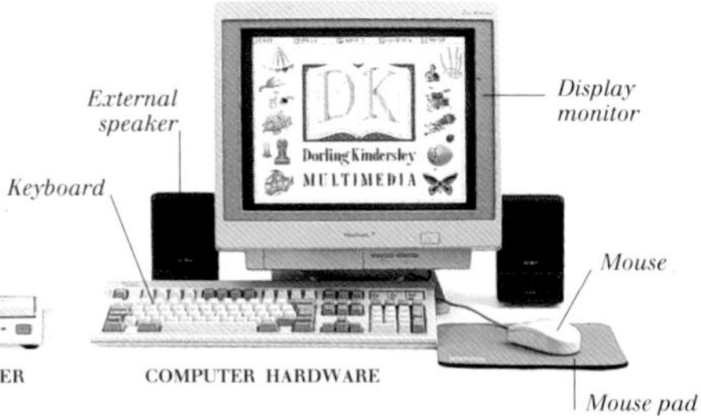

COMPUTER HARDWARE

SCREEN FROM A CD-ROM PROGRAM

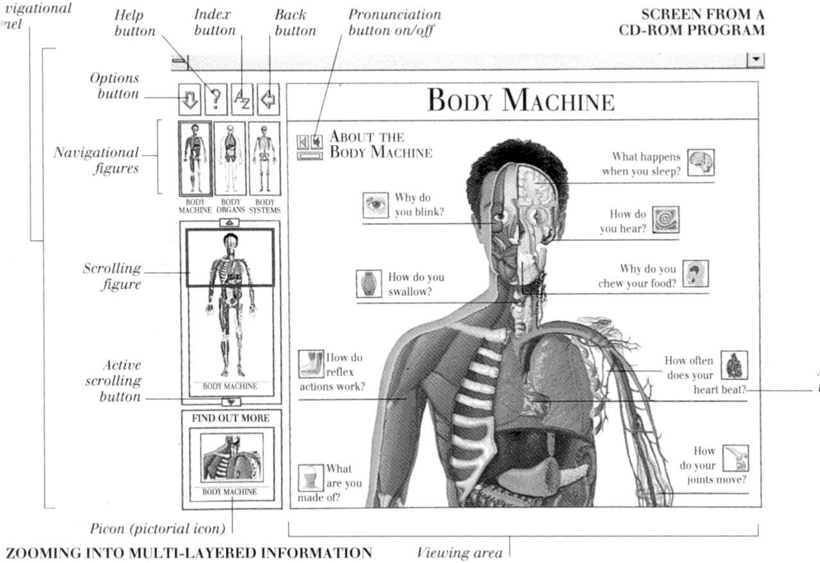
vigational
nel
Help button
Index button
Back button
Pronunciation button on/off
Options button
Navigational figures
Scrolling figure
Active scrolling button
Picon (pictorial icon)
Viewing area
Active text
BODY MACHINE
ABOUT THE BODY MACHINE
BODY MACHINE
BODY ORGANS
BODY SYSTEMS
FIND OUT MORE
What happens when you sleep?
Why do you blink?
How do you hear?
How do you swallow?
Why do you chew your food?
How do reflex actions work?
How often does your heart beat?
What are you made of?
How do your joints move?

ZOOMING INTO MULTI-LAYERED INFORMATION

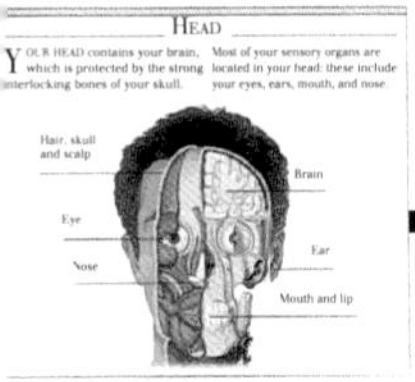
HEAD
YOUR HEAD contains your brain, which is protected by the strong interlocking bones of your skull.
Most of your sensory organs are located in your head: these include your eyes, ears, mouth, and nose.
Hair, skull and scalp
Brain
Eye
Ear
Nose
Mouth and lip

INITIAL SCREEN UNDER BODY ORGANS MENU

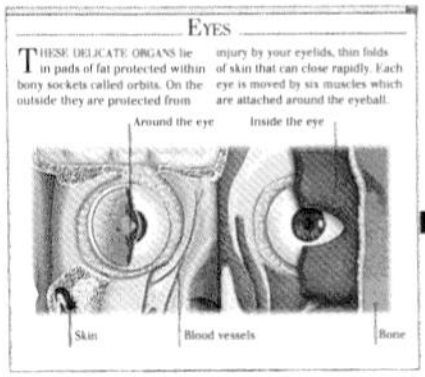
EYES
THESE DELICATE ORGANS lie in pads of fat protected within bony sockets called orbits. On the outside they are protected from injury by your eyelids, thin folds of skin that can close rapidly. Each eye is moved by six muscles which are attached around the eyeball.
Around the eye
Inside the eye
Skin
Blood vessels
Bone

CLICKING ON "EYES" LABEL PRODUCES MORE INFORMATION

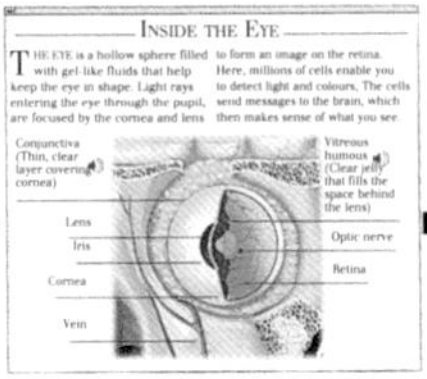
INSIDE THE EYE
THE EYE is a hollow sphere filled with gel-like fluids that help keep the eye in shape. Light rays entering the eye through the pupil, are focused by the cornea and lens to form an image on the retina. Here, millions of cells enable you to detect light and colours. The cells send messages to the brain, which then makes sense of what you see.
Conjunctiva (Thin, clear layer covering cornea)
Vitreous humous (Clear jelly that fills the space behind the lens)
Lens
Iris
Cornea
Vein
Optic nerve
Retina

EACH LABEL PRODUCES A FURTHER SCREEN

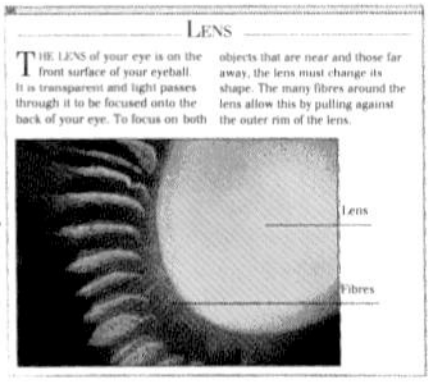
LENS
THE LENS of your eye is on the front surface of your eyeball. It is transparent and light passes through it to be focused onto the back of your eye. To focus on both objects that are near and those far away, the lens must change its shape. The many fibres around the lens allow this by pulling against the outer rim of the lens.
Lens
Fibres

THE FINAL IMAGE SHOWS MICROSCOPIC DETAIL

Books

THOUGH THE PROCESS OF BOOKBINDING today is usually mechanized, some books are still bound by hand. The pages of a book are printed on large sheets of paper called sections, or signatures. When folded, sections usually make 8, 16, or 32 pages. To assemble a hand-bound hardback book, the binder first places the folded sections in the correct order within the endpapers. Next, he or she sews the sections together along the spine edge using strong thread and then pastes them with glue for extra strength. After trimming the pages, the binder puts the book in a press and hammers the spine to round it. The binder then glues one or more linings to the spine. The cover, or case, comes last. To make this, the bookbinder sticks cover boards to the endpapers, front and back, and then covers them with cloth or leather.

HALF-BOUND BOOK

LEATHER-BOUND BO

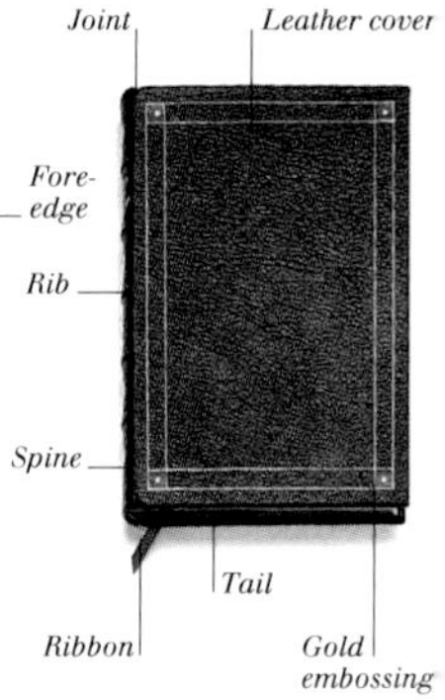

HALF-BOUND BOOK

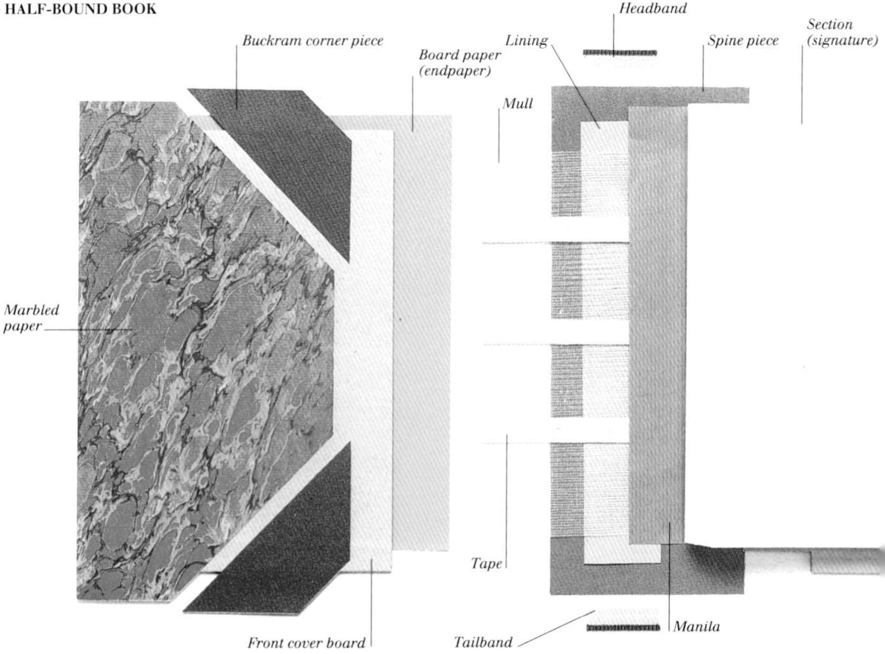

ATHER-BOUND BOOK

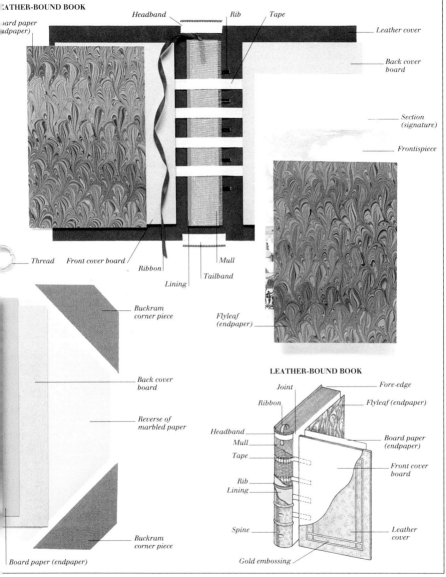

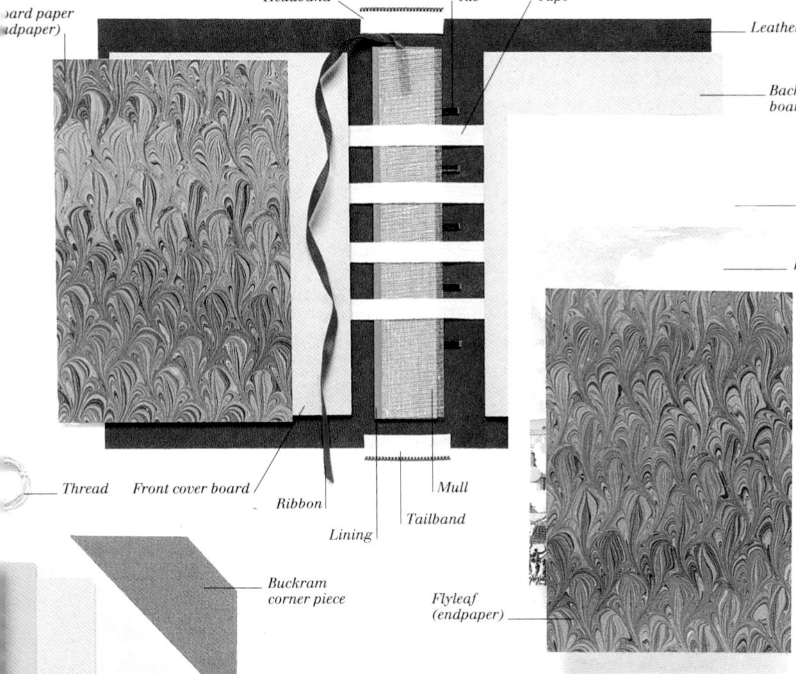
ard paper
dpaper)
Headband
Rib
Tape
Leather cover
Back cover board
Section (signature)
Frontispiece
Thread
Front cover board
Ribbon
Lining
Tailband
Mull
Flyleaf (endpaper)

Buckram corner piece
Back cover board
Reverse of marbled paper
Buckram corner piece
Board paper (endpaper)

LEATHER-BOUND BOOK

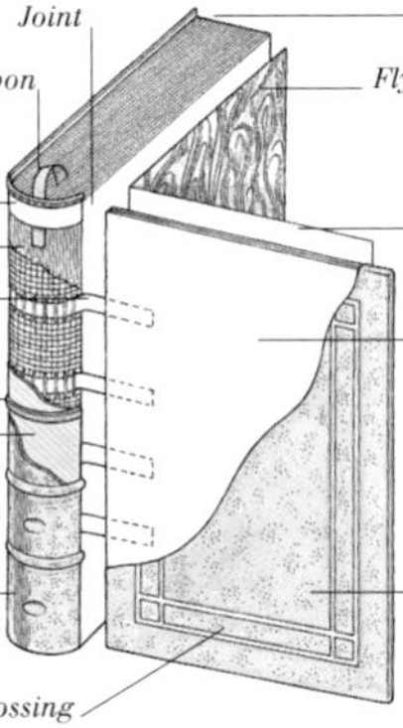
Joint
Fore-edge
Ribbon
Flyleaf (endpaper)
Headband
Mull
Board paper (endpaper)
Tape
Front cover board
Rib
Lining
Spine
Leather cover
Gold embossing

Camera

A CAMERA IS AN INSTRUMENT for recording images on photographic film. It consists of a light-tight box with a shutter, a lens containing a diaphragm, and a viewing system. When the shutter is released, the film is exposed to light from the subject that is being photographed. Adjusting the shutter speed alters the time for which the film is exposed to light. The diaphragm, by altering the aperture of the lens, controls the intensity of light entering the camera. The total amount of light entering the camera is called the exposure. The lens focuses the light on to the film. When there is insufficient light to produce an adequate image, a flashgun may be used to give extra light.

FRONT VIEW OF CAMERA

FRONT BOARD ASSEMBLY

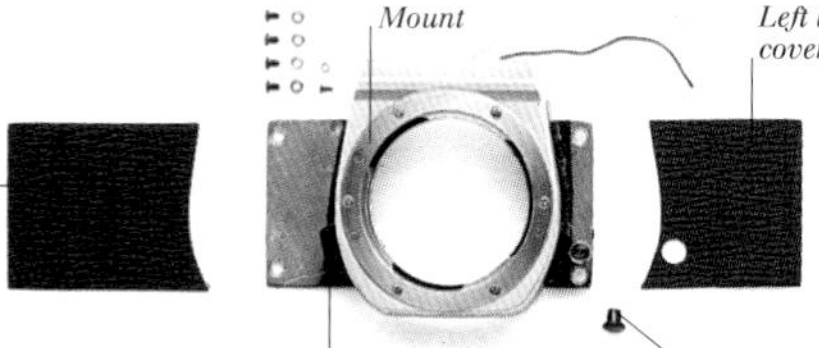
Mount
Left body
covering
Right body covering
Lens lock release lever
X-flash
sync cap

BOTTOM COVER ASSEMBLY

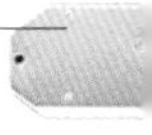
Tripod socket ho
Bottom
cover
Battery
Battery
chamber
cap

REAR VIEW OF CAMERA

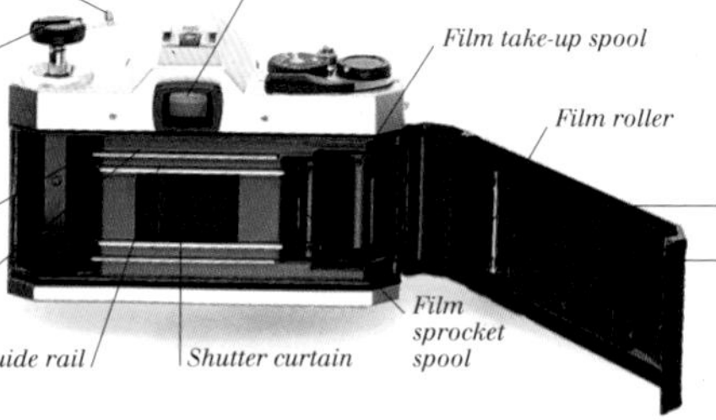
Film rewind
crank
Viewfinder
eyepiece
Film take-up spool
Film rewind/
back cover release
knob
Film roller
Back cover
Film chamber
Film pressure
plate
Film rail
Film
sprocket
spool
Film guide rail
Shutter curtain

LENS BARREL ASSEMBLY

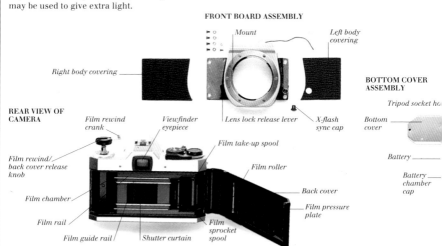

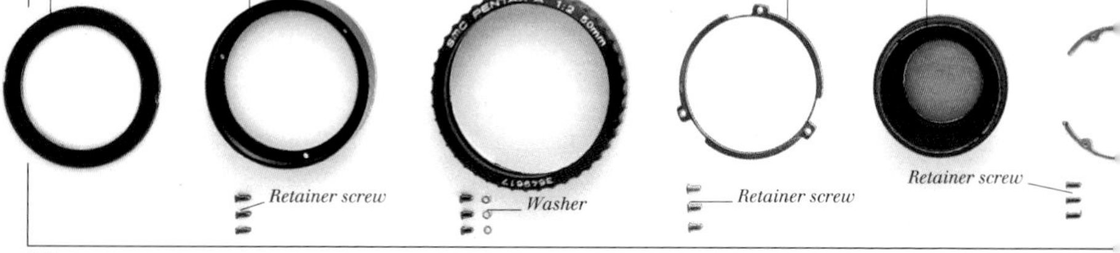
Ornament ring
Cover frame
Nameplate ring
Front lens frame
retainer plate
Front lens
group
Installing rir
retainer plat
smc PENTAX-A 1:2 50mm
Retainer screw
Washer
Retainer screw
Retainer screw

P COVER ASSEMBLY
Shutter dial knob spring
Film speed indicator
Shutter speed dial
Speed dial knob
Retainer screw
Film wind lever
Counter dial housing
Exposure counter dial
Wind lever install spring
Wind lever collar
Top cover
X-contact
Hot shoe
Rewind shaft
Film rewind/ back cover release knob
Retainer screw
Washer
Shutter release button
Shutter speed index
Rewind shaft collar
Film rewind crank
indow
Prism retainer plate
Prism retainer spring
IN BODY
Pentaprism
Cover frame
Retainer screw
Viewfinder eyepiece
ap lug
TOP VIEW OF CAMERA
Focusing ring
Distance scale (focal length scale)
Depth-of-field guide
Aperture/distance index
Lens alignment node
Aperture auto-lock button
Lens lock release lever
le for film vind button
Shutter release button
Cocked indicator
Exposure counter
Retainer screw
Film rewind crank
Film rewind/back cover release knob
Hot shoe
X-contact
Shutter speed index
Film speed indicator
Shutter speed dial
Film wind lever
upporter ring etainer plate
Supporter ring
Diaphragm blade
Installing ring
Main barrel assembly
Rear lens group
Opening and closing plate

Appendix: useful data

UNITS OF MEASUREMENT

Metric unit	Equivalent
Length	
1 centimetre (cm)	10 millimetres (mm)
1 metre (m)	100 centimetres
1 kilometre (km)	1,000 metres
Mass	
1 kilogram (kg)	1,000 grams (g)
1 tonne (t)	1,000 kilograms
Area	
1 square centimetre (cm^2)	100 square millimetres (mm^2)
1 square metre (m^2)	10,000 square centimetres
1 hectare	10,000 square metres
1 square kilometre (km^2)	1,000,000 square metres
Volume	
1 cubic centimetre (cc)	1 millilitre (ml)
1 litre (l)	1,000 millilitres
1 cubic metre (m^3)	1,000 litres
Capacity (liquid and dry measures)	
1 centilitre (cl)	10 millilitres (ml)
1 decilitre (dl)	10 centilitres
1 litre (l)	10 decilitres
1 decalitre (dal)	10 litres
1 hectolitre (hi)	10 decalitres
1 kilolitre (kl)	10 hectolitres

Imperial unit	Equivalent
Length	
1 foot (ft)	12 inches (in)
1 yard (yd)	3 feet
1 rod (rd)	5.5 yards
1 mile (mi)	1,760 yards
Mass	
1 dram (dr)	27.344 grains (gr)
1 ounce (oz)	16 drams
1 pound (lb)	16 ounces
1 hundredweight (cwt) (long)	112 pounds
1 hundredweight (cwt) (short)	100 pounds
1 ton (long)	2,240 pounds
1 ton (short)	2,000 pounds
Area	
1 square foot (ft^2)	144 square inches (in^2)
1 square yard (yd^2)	9 square feet
1 acre	4,840 square yards
1 square mile	640 acres
Volume	
1 cubic foot	1,728 cubic inches
1 cubic yard	27 cubic feet
Capacity (liquid and dry measures)	
1 fluidram (fl dr)	60 minims (min)
1 fluid ounce (fl oz)	8 fluidrams
1 gill (gi)	5 fluid ounces
1 pint (pt)	4 gills
1 quart (qt)	2 pints
1 gallon (gal)	4 quarts
1 peck (pk)	2 gallons
1 bushel (bu)	4 pecks

TEMPERATURE SCALES

To convert from Celsius (C) to Fahrenheit (F): $F = (C \times 9 \div 5) + 32$
To convert from Fahrenheit to Celsius: $C = (F - 32) \times 5 \div 9$
To convert from Celsius to Kelvin (K): $K = C + 273$
To convert from Kelvin to Celsius: $C = K - 273$

Celsius	-20	-10	0	10	20	30	40	50	60	70	80	90	100
Fahrenheit	-4	14	32	50	68	86	104	122	140	158	176	194	212
Kelvin	253	263	273	283	293	303	313	323	333	343	353	363	373

AREAS AND VOLUMES

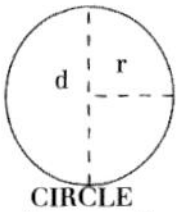

Radius r
Diameter
$d = 2 \times r$

CIRCLE
Circumference = $2 \times \pi \times r$
Area = $\pi \times r^2$
($\pi = 3.1416$)

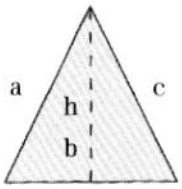

Height h
Sides a, b

TRIANGLE
Perimeter = $a + b + c$
Area = $\frac{1}{2} \times b \times h$

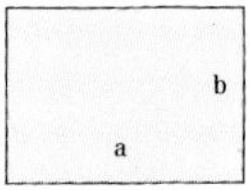

Sides a, b

RECTANGLE
Perimeter = $2 \times (a + b)$
Area = $a \times b$

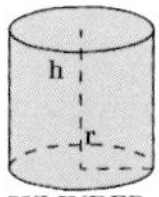

Height h
Radius r

CYLINDER
Surface area = $2 \times \pi \times r \times h$
(excluding ends)
Volume = $\pi \times r^2 \times h$

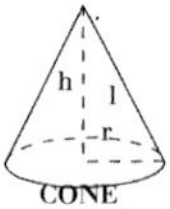

Height h
Radius r
Side l

CONE
Surface area = $\pi \times r \times l$ (excluding base)
Volume = $\frac{1}{3} \times \pi \times r^2 \times l$

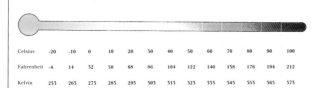

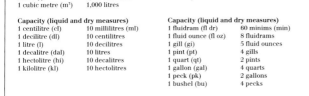

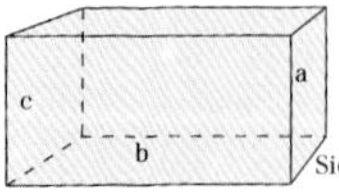

Sides a, b

RECTANGULAR BLOCK
Surface area = $2 \times (a \times b + b \times c + a \times c)$
Volume = $a \times b \times c$

METRIC - IMPERIAL CONVERSIONS

To convert	Into	Multiply by
Length		
Centimetres	inches	0.3937
Metres	feet	3.2810
Kilometres	miles	0.6214
Metres	yards	1.0940
Mass		
Grams	ounces	0.0352
Kilograms	pounds	2.2050
Tonnes	long tons	0.9843
Tonnes	short tons	1.1025
Area		
Square centimetres	square inches	0.1550
Square metres	square feet	10.7600
Hectares	acres	2.4710
Square kilometres	square miles	0.3861
Square metres	square yards	1.1960
Volume		
Cubic centimetres	cubic inches	0.0610
Cubic metres	cubic feet	35.3100
Capacity		
Litres	pints	1.7600
Litres	gallons	0.2200

IMPERIAL - METRIC CONVERSIONS

To convert	Into	Multiply by
Length		
Inches	centimetres	2.5400
Feet	metres	0.3048
Miles	kilometres	1.6090
Yards	metres	0.9144
Mass		
Ounces	grams	28.3500
Pounds	kilograms	0.4536
Long tons	tonnes	1.0160
Short tons	tonnes	0.9070
Area		
Square inches	square centimetres	6.4520
Square feet	square metres	0.0929
Acres	hectares	0.4047
Square miles	square kilometres	2.5900
Square yards	square metres	0.8361
Volume		
Cubic inches	cubic centimetres	16.3900
Cubic feet	cubic metres	0.0283
Capacity		
Pints	litres	0.5683
Gallons	litres	4.5460

NUMBER SYSTEMS

Roman	Arabic
I	1
II	2
III	3
IV	4
V	5
VI	6
VII	7
VIII	8
IX	9
X	10
XI	11
XII	12
XIII	13
XIV	14
XV	15
XX	20
XXI	21
XXX	30
XL	40
L	50
LX	60
LXX	70
LXXX	80
XC	90
C	100
CI	101
CC	200
CCC	300
CD	400
D	500
DC	600
DCC	700
DCCC	800
CM	900
M	1,000
MM	2,000

PHYSICS SYMBOLS

Symbol	Meaning
α	alpha particle
β	beta ray
γ	gamma ray; photon
ε	electromotive force
η	efficiency; viscosity
λ	wavelength
μ	micro-; permeability
ν	frequency; neutrino
ρ	density; resistivity
σ	conductivity
c	velocity of light
e	electronic charge

MATHEMATICS SYMBOLS

Symbol	Meaning
+	plus
−	minus
±	plus or minus
×	multiplied by
÷	divided by
=	equals
>	is greater than
<	is less than
≥	is greater than or equal to
≤	is less than or equal to
%	per cent
√	root
π	pi (3.1416)
°	degree
∞	infinity
≈	is approximately equal to
∠	angle
‖	parallel to

CHEMISTRY SYMBOLS

Symbol	Meaning
+	plus; together with
−	single bond
•	single bond; single unpaired electron; two separate parts or compounds regarded as loosely joined
=	double bond
≡	triple bond
R	group
X	halogen atom
Z	atomic number

BIOLOGY SYMBOLS

Symbol	Meaning
○	female individual (used in inheritance charts)
□	male individual (used in inheritance charts)
♀	female
♂	male
×	crossed with; hybrid
+	wild type
F_1	offspring of the first generation
F_2	offspring of the second generation

POWERS OF TEN USED WITH SCIENTIFIC UNITS

Factor	Name	Prefix	Symbol
10^{18}	quintillion	exa-	E
10^{15}	quadrillion	peta-	P
10^{12}	trillion	tera-	T
10^{9}	billion	giga-	G
10^{6}	million	mega-	M
10^{3}	thousand	kilo-	k
10^{2}	hundred	hecto-	h
10^{1}	ten	deca-	da
10^{-1}	one tenth	deci-	d
10^{-2}	one hundredth	centi-	c
10^{-3}	one thousandth	milli-	m
10^{-6}	one millionth	micro-	μ
10^{-9}	one billionth	nano-	n
10^{-12}	one trillionth	pico-	p
10^{-15}	one quadrillionth	femto-	f
10^{-18}	one quintillionth	atto-	a

NOTE: The American system of numeration for denominations above one million is used in this book. In this system, each of the denominations above one billion (1,000 millions) is 1,000 times the preceding one.

Index

E

G

H

I

J

K

L

M

O

Q

R

T

U

V

W

Acknowledgments

Dorling Kindersley would like to thank (in order of sections):

The Universe
(consultant editors – Sue Becklake, Gevorkyan Tatyana Alekseyevna):
John Becklake; the Memorial Museum of Cosmonautics, Moscow; The Cosmos Pavilion, Moscow; The United States Space and Rocket Centre, Alabama; Broadhurst, Clarkson and Fuller Ltd; Susannah Massey

Prehistoric Earth
(consultant editors – William Lindsay, Martyn Bramwell, Dr Ralph E. Molnar, David Lambert):
Dr Monty Reid, Andrew Neuman, and the staff of the Royal Tyrrell Museum of Palaeontology, Drumheller, Alberta; Dr Angela Milner and the staff of the Department of Palaeontology, the Natural History Museum, London; Professor W. Ziegler and the staff, in particular Michael Loderstaedt, of the Naturmuseum Senckenburg, Frankfurt; Dr Alexander Liebau, Axel Hunghrebüller, Reiner Schoch, and the staff of the Institut und Museum für Geologie und Paläontologie der Universität, Tübingen; Rupert Wild of the Institut für Paläontologie, Staatliches Museum für Naturkunde, Stuttgart; Dr Scheiber of the Stadtmuseum, Nördlingen; Professor Dr Dietrich Herm of Staatssammlung für Paläontologie und Historische Geologie, München; Dr Michael Keith-Lucas of the Department of Botany, University of Reading; Richard Walker; American Museum of Natural History, New York

Plants
(consultant editor – Richard Walker):
Diana Miller; Lawrie Springate; Karen Sidwell; Chris Thody; Michelle End; Susan Barnes and Chris Jones of the EMU Unit of the Natural History Museum, London; Jenny Evans of Kew Gardens, London; Kate Biggs of the Royal Horticultural Society Gardens, Wisley, Surrey; Spike Walker of Microworld Services; Neil Fletcher; John Bryant of Bedgebury Pinetum, Kent; Dean Franklin

Animals
(consultant editor – Richard Walker):
David Manning's Animal Ark; Intellectual Animals; Howletts Zoo, Canterbury; John Dunlop; Alexander O'Donnell; Sue Evans of the Royal Veterinary College, London; Dr Geoff Potts and Fred Frettsome of the Marine Biological Association of the United Kingdom, Plymouth; Jeremy Adams of the Booth Museum of Natural History, Brighton; Derek Telling of the Department of Anatomy, University of Bristol; the Natural History Museum, London; Andy Highfield of the Tortoise Trust; Brian Harris of the Aquarium, London Zoo; the Invertebrate Department, London Zoo; Dr Harold McClure of the Yerkes Regional Primate Research Center, Emory University, Atlanta, Georgia; Nielson Lausen of the Harvard Medical School, New England Regional Primates Research Centre, Southborough, Massachusetts; Dr Paul Hopwood of the Department of Veterinary Anatomy, University of Sydney; Dean Franklin

The Human Body
(consultant editors – Dr Frances Williams, Dr Fiona Payne, Richard Cummins FRCS):
Derek Edwards and Dr Martin Collins, British School of Osteopathy; Dr M.C.E. Hutchinson of the Department of Anatomy, United Medical and Dental Schools of Guy's and St Thomas' Hospitals, London. Models – Barry O'Rorke (Bodyline Agency) and Pauline Swaine (MOT Model Agency)

Geology, Geography, and Meteorology
(consultant editor – Martyn Bramwell):
Dr John Nudds of the Manchester Museum, Manchester; Dr Alan Wooley and Dr Andrew Clark of the Natural History Museum, London; Graham Bartlett of the National Meteorological Library and Archive, Bracknell; Tony Drake of BP Exploration, Uxbridge; Jane Davies of the Royal Society of Chemistry, Cambridge; Dr Tony Waltham of Nottingham Trent University, Nottingham; staff of the Smithsonian Institute, Washington; staff of the United States Geological Survey, Washington; staff of the National Geographic Society, Washington; staff of Edward Lawrence Associates (Export Ltd), Midhurst; John Farndon; David Lambert

Rail and Road
***Rail* (consultant editor – John Coiley)**
Michael Ashworth of the London Transport Museum

***Road* (consultant editors – David Burgess-Wise, Hugo Wilson)**
The National Motor Museum, Beaulieu; Alf Newell of Renault UK Ltd; David Suter of Cheltenham Cutaway Exhibits Ltd; Francesca Riccini of the Science Museum, London. Signore Amadelli of the Museo dell' Automobile Carlo Biscaretti di Ruffia; Paul Bolton of the Mazda MCL Group; Duncan Bradford of Reg Mills Wire Wheels; John and Leslie Brewster of Autocavan; David Burgess-Wise; Trevor Cass of Garrett Turbo Service; John Corbett of The Patrick Collection; Gary Crumpler of Williams Grand Prix Engineering Ltd; Mollie Easterbrooke and Duncan Gough of Overland Ltd; Arthur Fairley of the Vauxhall Motor Company; Paul Foulkes-Halbard of Filching Manor Motor Museum; Frank Gilbert of I. Wilkinson and Son Ltd; Paolo Gratton of Gratton Museum; Colvin Gunn of Gunn and Son; Judy Hogg of Ecurie Bertelli; Milton Holman of Dream Cars; Ian Matthews of IMAT Electronics; Eric Neal of Jaguar Cars Ltd; Paul Niblett, Keith Davidson, Mark Reumel, and David Woolf of Michelin Tyre plc; Doug Nye; Kevin O'Keefe of O'Keefe Cars; Seat UK; Roger Smith; Jim Stirling of Ironbridge Gorge Museum, Staffordshire; Jon Taylor; Doug Thompson; Martyn Watkins of Ford Motor Company Ltd; John Cattermole, Customer Services Manager at London Northern Buses; F. W. Evans Cycles Ltd; Trek UK Ltd (Bicycle); Sam Grimmer

Physics and Chemistry
(consultant editor – Jack Challoner)

Sea and Air
***Sea* (consultant editors – Geoff Hales and Harvey B. Loomis):**
David Spence, Gillian Hutchinson, David Topliss, Simon Stephens, Robert Baldwin, Jonathan Betts, all of the National Maritime Museum, London; Ian Friel; Simon Turnage of Captain O.M. Watts of London Ltd; Davey and Company Ltd, Great Dunmow; Avon Inflatables Ltd, Llanelli; Musto Ltd, Benfleet; Peter Martin of Spencer Rigging Ltd, Southampton; Peter Rowson of Ratseys Sailmakers, Southampton; Swiftech Ltd, Wallingford; Colin Scattergood of the Barrow Boat Company Ltd, Colchester; Professor J.S. Morrison of the Trireme Trust, Cambridge; The Cutty Sark Maritime Trust; Adrian Daniels of Kelvin Hughes Marine Instruments, London; Arthur Credland of Hull City Council Museums and Art Galleries; The Hull Maritime Society; Gerald Clark; Peter Fitzgerald of the Science Museum, London; Alec Michael of HMB Subwork Ltd, Great Yarmouth, and Ray Ward of the OSEL Group, Great Yarmouth; Richard Bird of UWI, Weybridge; Walker Marine Instruments, Birmingham; The International Sailing Craft Association; The Exeter Maritime Museum; Jane Wilson of the Trinity Lighthouse Company, London; The Imperial War Museum Collections; Thorn Security Ltd; Michael Bach

***Air* (consultant editor – Bill Gunston):**
Aeromega Helicopters, Stapleford; Aero Shopping, London; Avionics Mobile Services Ltd, Watford; Roy Barber and John Chapman of the RAF Museum, Hendon; Mitch Barnes Aviation, London; Mike Beach; British Caledonian Flight Training Ltd; Fred Coates of Helitech (Luton) Ltd; Michael Cuttell and CSE Aviation Ltd, Oxford; Dowty Aerospace Landing Gear, Gloucester; Guy Hartcup of the Airship Association; Anthony Hooley, Chris Walsh, and David Cord of British Aerospace Regional Aircraft Ltd; Ken Huntley of Mid-West Aero Engines Ltd; Imperial War Museum, Duxford; The London Gliding Club, Dunstable; Musée des Ballons, Calvados; Noel Penny Turbines Ltd; Andy Pavey of Aviation Scotland Ltd; Tony Pavey of Thermal Aircraft Developments, London; the Commanding Officer and personnel of RAF St Athan; the Commanding Officer and personnel of RAF Wittering; The Science Museum, London; Ross Sharp of the Science Museum, Wroughton; The Shuttleworth Collection; Skysport Engineering; Mike Smith; Solar Wings Ltd, Marlborough; Julian Temple of Brooklands Museum Trust Ltd; Kelvin Wilson of Flying Start

Architecture
(consultant editor – Alexandra Kennedy):
Stephen Cutler for advice and text; Gavin Morgan of the Museum of London, London; Chris Zeuner of the Weald and Downland Museum, Singleton, Sussex; Alan Hills and James Putnam of the British Museum, London; Dr Simon Penn and Michael Thomas of the Avoncroft Museum of Buildings, Bromsgrove,

Worcestershire; Christina Scull of Sir John Soane's Museum, London; Paul Kennedy and John Williamson of the London Door Company, London; Lou Davis of The Original Box Sash Window Company, Windsor; Goddard and Gibbs Studios Ltd, London, for access to stained glass windows; The Royal Courts of Justice, Strand, London; Charles Brooking and Peter Dalton for access to the doors and windows in the Charles Brooking Collection, University of Greenwich, Dartford, Kent; Clare O'Brien of the Shakespeare Globe Trust, Shakespeare's Globe Museum, Bear Gardens, Southwark, London; Ken Teague of the Horniman Museum, London; Canon Haliburton, Mike Payton, Ken Stones, and Anthony Webb of St Paul's Cathedral, London; Roy Spring of Salisbury Cathedral; Reverend Gillean Craig of the Church of St George in the East, London; the Science Museum, London; Dr Neil Bingham; Lin Kennedy of Historic Royal Palaces; Katy Harris of Sir Norman Foster and Partners; Production Design, Thames Television plc, London, for supplying models; Dominique Reynier of Le Centre Georges Pompidou, Paris; Denis Roche of Le Musée National des Monuments Français, Paris; Franck Gioria and students of Les Compagnons du Devoir, Paris, for access to construction models; Frank Folliot of Le Musée Carnavalet, Paris; Dr Martina Harms of Hessische Landesmuseums, Darmstadt; Jefferson Chapman of the University of Tennessee, Knoxville, for access to the model of the Hypostyle Hall, Temple of Amon-Re; staff of the Palazzo Strozzi, Florence; staff of the Sydney Opera House, Sydney; staff of the Empire State Building, New York; Nick Jackson; Ann Terrell

The Visual Arts
(consultant editor – Pip Seymour):
Rosemary Simmons; Michael Taylor of Paupers Press, London; Tessa Hunkin and Emma Biggs of Mosaic Workshop, London; John Tiranti, Jonathan Lyons of Alec Tiranti Ltd, London; Chris Hough; Dr Ashok Roy; Satwinder Sehmi of Alphabet Soup, London; Phillip Poole of Cornelissens, London; George Weil and Sons Ltd, London; The National Gallery, London; Chris Webster of the Tate Gallery, London; China Art Cultural Centre, London; London Graphic Centre, London; A.P. Fitzpatrick, London; Flowers Graphics, London; Intaglio Printmaker, London; Falkiner Papers, London; Edgar Udny and Co, London; John Green

Music
(consultant editor – Susan Sturrock):
Boosey and Hawkes Music Publishers Ltd, London, for permission to reproduce extract from The Prodigal Son by Arthur Sullivan; The Bass and Drum Cellar, London; Empire Drums and Percussion, London; Argents (part of World of Music), London; Bill Lewington Ltd, London; Frobenius organ at Kingston Parish Church, Surrey; Yamaha-Kemble Music (UK) Ltd, Tilbrook, Milton Keynes; Yamaha Atelier, London; Akai (UK) Ltd, Hounslow, Middlesex; Casio Electronics Co. Ltd, London; Roland (UK) Ltd, Fleet, Hampshire; Richard Schulman

Sports
The Sports Council Information Centre, London; The British Olympic Games Committee; Brian Crennell of Black's Leisure Group (First Sport); Lillywhites of Piccadilly, London; Mitre Sports International Ltd, Huddersfield; David Bloomfield of the Football Association; Denver Athletics Ltd, Norfolk; Greg Everest and Keith Birley of the British League of Australian Rules Football; Peter McNally of the Gaelic Athletic Association; Rex King of the Rugby Football Union, Twickenham; Neil Tunnicliffe of the Rugby Football League, Leeds; Wayne Patterson of the Basketball Hall of Fame, Springfield, Connecticut; Brian Coleman of the English Basketball Association; All American Imports, Northampton; George Bulman of the English Volleyball Association; Julie Longdon of Mizuno Mallory (UK) Ltd; Juliet Stanford of the All-England Netball Association; Jeff Rowland of the British Handball Association; Cally Melin of Adidas UK Ltd; Patrick Donnely of the Baseball Hall of Fame, Cooperstown, New York; Ian Lepage and Stephen Barlow of the Hockey Association, Milton Keynes; Alison Taylor and Anita Mason of the All England Women's Lacrosse Association, Birmingham; David Shuttleworth of the English Lacrosse Union; Les Barnett and Jock Bentley of the British Athletic Federation Ltd, Birmingham; Mike Gilks of the Badminton Association of England; Gurinder Purewall for advice on archery; Chris McCartney of the US Archery Association; Geoff Doe of the National Smallbore Rifle Association, Bisley, Surrey, for information and reference material on shooting; Fagan Sports Goods Distributors, Surrey; Konrad Bartelski for advice on skiing; The British Ski Federation, Edinburgh; Mike Barnett of Snow and Rock of London; Sally Spurway of Mast-Co. Ltd, Reading; Sarah Morgan for advice on equestrian sports; Steve Brown and the New York Racing Association Inc, New York; Danrho of London; Alan Skipp and James Chambers of the Amateur Fencing Association, London; Carla Richards of the US Fencing Association; Hamilton Bland and John Dryer of the Amateur Swimming Association, Loughborough; Cotswold Camping Ltd, London; Tim Spalton of Glyn Locke (Racing Shells) Ltd, Chalgrove; Terry Friel of the US Rowing Association; House of Hardy; Leeda Fishing Tackle

Everyday Things
City Clocks (Clocks); Christopher Cullen of Babber Electronics; Sony UK Ltd (Mini-television); Black and Decker Ltd (Drills); British Footwear Manufacturing Federation; Grenson Shoes Ltd (Shoes); The Folio Society; R S Bookbinders (Books); Pentax UK Ltd (Camera); F E Murdin of the Decorative Lighting Association; Habitat (Lamp); Chingford Reproductions Ltd (Chair); Dualit Ltd (Toaster); J B Dove; Toro Wheelhorse UK Ltd (Lawnmower); WandH Gidden Ltd (Saddle)

PHOTOGRAPHY:
M. Alexander; Peter Anderson; Charles Brooks; Jane Burton; Peter Chadwick; Simon Clay; John Coiley; Andy Crawford; Geoff Dann; Philip Dowell; John Downs; Mike Dunning; Torla Evans; David Exton; Robert and Anthony Fretwell of Fretwell Photography Ltd.; Philip Gatward; Anna Hodgson; Gary Kevin; J. Heseltine; Cyril Laubscher; John Lepine; Lynton Gardiner (American Museum of Natural History, New York); Steve Gorton; Michelangelo Gratton; Judith Harrington; Peter Hayman; Anna Hodgson; Colin Keates; Gary Kevin; Dave King; Bob Langrish; Brian D.Morgan; Nick Nicholls; Nick Parfitt; Tim Parmenter and Colin Keates (Natural History Museum, London); Tim Ridley; Dave Rudkin; Philippe Sebert; James Stevenson; Clive Streeter; Harry Taylor; Matthew Ward; Jerry Young

PHOTOGRAPHIC ASSISTANCE:
Kevin Zak; Gary Ombler

ILLUSTRATORS:
Julian Baum; Rick Blakeley; Kuo Kang Chen; Karen Cochrane; Simone End; Ian Fleming; Roy Flooks; Mark Franklin; David Gardner; Will Giles; Mick Gillah; David Hopkins; Selwyn Hutchinson; Mei Lim; Linden Artists; Nick Loates; Chris Lyon; Kathleen McDougall; Coral Mula; Sandra Pond; Dave Pugh; Colin Rose; Graham Rosewarne; John Temperton; John Woodcock; Chris Woolmer

MODEL ,AKERS:
Roby Braun; David Donkin; Morrison Frederick; Gordon Models; John Holmes; Graham High and Jeremy Hunt of Centaur Studios; Richard Kemp; Kelvin Thatcher; Paul Wilkinson

ADDITIONAL DESIGN ASSISTANCE:
Stefan Morris; Ulysses Santos; Suchada Smith

ADDITIONAL EDITORIAL ASSISTANCE:
Helen Castle; Colette Connolly; Camela Decaire; Nick Harris; Andrea Horth; Stewart McEwen; Damien Moore; Melanie Tham

INDEX: Kay Wright

Picture credits:

Action Plus 330tc; Anglo Australian Telescope Board 11cl, 11cra, 11cbl, 12tr, 12bc, 13tl, 13bl, 14tl, 16b, 17tc, 17bl, 22tl/D.Malin 16tl, 26tr, 27tl; Austin Brown and the Aviation Picture Library 426tl; Baptistery, Florence/Alison Harris 453r; Biophoto Associates 217ca, 217cra, 228cbc, 228cbc 230tr; Paul Brierley 311bra; British Aerospace/Anthony Hooley 412tl, 415tl; British Aerospace (Commercial Aircraft) Ltd 416tl; By prmission of the British Library 432tl, 445bl; British Museum 459tl, 459tr, 460tr, 460tc, 460tb, 489b; BP Exploration 299; Duncan Brown 25tl; Frank Lloyd Wright, American, 1867-1959, Model of Midway Gardens, 1914, executed by Richard Tickner, mixed media, 1987, 41.9 x 81.3 x 76.2, 1989.48. view 1. Photography courtesy of the Art Intitute of Chicago 495t; J.A. Coiley 331cr; Bruce Coleman Ltd/Andy Price 272tl; Courtesy of the Board of Trustees of the Victoria and Albert Museum, London 454-455b; European Passenger Services 329tl; ESA /PLV 11bl; French Railways 329c; Geoscience Features 311cla; Robert Harding Picture Library 62tl; Michael Holford /British Museum 372bl, Michael Holford 374tr; Hutchison Picture Library 60cl; The Image Bank/Edward Bower 306tr; Jet Propulsion Laboratory 11cbr; 30bc; 31bc; 31bcr; 38tl; 42crb; 44cb; 44cbr; 44bc; 44br; 46tl; 46cr; 46cb; 46bc; 46br; 50tl; 50cra; 50cl; 50c; 50cr; 50br; KeyMed Ltd 248bl, 249bl, 249bcl; Department of Prints and Drawings, Uffizi, Florence/Philip Gatward 431tc/Uffizi, Florence/Philip Gatward 433tl; Dr D.N. Landon (Institute of Neurology) 228bl,br; Life Science Images/Ron Boardman 244bl, 244br; The Lund Observatory 15bc; Brian Morrison 329tl, 329tr; © The Henry Moore Foundation 455tr; Musée d'Orsay, Paris/Philippe Sebert 437tc, 441tc; Musée du Louvre, Paris/Philippe Sebert 453tl, 453l, 453br; NASA/AUI 13tr; NASA/JPL 11 cbr, 11br, 30tl, 30bl, 30br, 30bc, 31bc, 31bcr, 31bl, 34cr, 38tl, 40tl, 40cr, 42cr, 44tl, 44cb, 44cbr, 44bc, 44br, 44cr, 46crb, 46tl, 46cr, 46cb, 46bc, 46br, 48tl, 48cra, 48bca, 48bc, 48br, 50tl, 50bc, 50bc, 50cbr, 50br, 50cr, 52cr; National Maritime Museum 373br, 392-393b; National Medical Slide Bank 217cr; Nature Photographers/Paul Sterry 286tl; Newage International 317bl; Oxford Scientific Films/Breck P. Kent 166tl; Planet Earth 274tr; Quadrant 326tr; Margaret Robinson 332tl; Giotto The Expulsion of the Merchants from the Temple Scala 435tc, 435bl, 435br; Science Photo Library 10bl, 13tr, 28tr, 214bcr, 214bl, 236tr/Michael Abbey 225tc/ Agema Infrared Systems 318tl/AGFA 220tl/ Biophoto Associates: 217crb/Dr Jeremy Burgess/Science Photo Library 132tr; Dr Jeremy Burgess 235bcl/CNRI 214tl, 214cl, 214c, 214cr, 214bl, 214clb, 214crb, 214blc, 214br, 217cb, 235bcr, 238tl, 249bcr, 253tr, 253cra, 256tl; Science Photo library /Earth Satellite Corporation 288cl, 293br/Dr Brian Eyden 228cbr/ Professor C. Ferlaud 245bl/Vaughan Fleming 311tl/Simon Fraser/U.S. Dept.of Energy 214bcl, 266tl/Eric Grave 217br/Hale Observatories 32br/Max Planck Institute for Radio Astronomy 15tl/Jan Hinsch 225tc/Jodrell Bank 11 tr, 13c / Manfred Kage 217c, 235br, 237br/Dr William C. Keel 13br/Keith Kent 316tl/Russ Lappa 310bra/ Astrid & Hans-Freider Michler 217tr/Dennis Milon 52bl/NASA 11cla, 12tl, 15tr, 30c, 31br, 32tl, 35tl, 36tl, 36cl, 36cr, 36bc, 42br, 42tr, 44tl 52tl, 291tr, 300tl/National Optical Astro Observatory 52tr/NIBSC 253crb/Novosti Press Agency 42bc/Omikron 244bc/David Parker 63bl, 304-305, 308br/Philippe Plailly 308tl, Roussel-UCLAF/CNRI 217tc/Rev Ronald Royer 32cr/Royal Observatory, Edinburgh/D Malin 11tl, 11cr,12c, 16cl, 16cr, 17br/David Scharf 235bl/Dr Kaus Schiller 248bcl, 248bcr, 248br/ Secchi-Lecaque/Roussel-UCLAF/CNRI 253br/ H. Sochurek 214cb/Stammers/Thompson 230tl/ Sheila Terry 234tl/US Department of Energy 310bc/U.S Geological Survey/Science Photo Library 8-9, 30bcr, 42tl, 42bl/Tom Van Sant/ Geosphere Project, Santa Monica/Science Photo Library 273tr, 281tr, 296tr, 297tl/ Dr Christopher B. Williams/(Saint Marks Hospital)249br; Oxford Scientific Films/ Animals Animals/Breck P. Kent 167tl; Pratt & Whitney Canada 418-419b, 419t; Science Museum 306bl,306bcl. 306 bcr, 324t, 326-327b, 330tr, 331ct, 331 cb; Sporting Pictures 524tl, 544cr; Tony Stone Worldwide 280tl; David Bomberg St Pauls and River 1945/Dinora Davies-Rees/Tate Gallery 431bc; David Hockney A Bigger Splash 1967/ © David Hockney/Tate Gallery 443tc; J.M.W. Turner The Burning of the Houses of Parliament Tate Gallery 439tc; Vision 26tr, 27c; Jerry Young 306tl; Dr Robert Youngson 241cr; Zefa 217bc/ Janicek 276tl/H. Sochurek 210tl, 250tl, 254tl,/ G. Steenmans 292tl

(t=top, b=bottom, a=above, l-left, r=right, c=centre)

Every effort has been made to trace the copyright holders. Dorling Kindersley apologises for any unintentional omissions and would be pleased, in any such cases, to add an acknowledgment in future editions.

Some pages in this book previously appeared in the *Visual Dictionary* series published by Dorling Kindersley. Contributors to this series include:

Project Art Editors:
Duncan Brown, Ross George, Nicola Liddiard, Andrew Nash, Clare Shedden, Bryn Walls

Designers:
Lesley Betts, Paul Calver, Simone End, Ellen Woodward

Additional design assistance:
Sandra Archer, Christina Betts, Alexandra Brown, Nick Jackson, Susan Knight

Project Editors:
Fiona Courtney-Thompson, Paul Docherty, Tim Fraser, Stephanie Jackson, Mary Lindsay

Editorial Assistant:
Emily Hill

Additional editorial assistance:
Susan Bosanko, Edward Bunting, Candace Burch, Deirdre Clark, Jeanette Cossar, Danièle Guitton, Jacqui Hand, David Harding, Nicholas Jackson, Edwina Johnson, David Lambert, Gail Lawther, David Learmount, Paul Jackson, Christine Murdock, Bob Ogden, Cathy Rubinstein, Louise Tucker, Dr Robert Youngson

Picture Researchers:
Vere Dodds, Danièle Guitton, Anna Lord, Catherine O'Rourke, Christine Rista, Sandra Schneider, Vanessa Smith, Clive Webster

Series Editor:
Martyn Page

Series Art Editor:
Paul Wilkinson

Managing Art Editors
Philip Gilderdale, Steve Knowlden

Art Director
Chez Picthall

Managing Editor
Ruth Midgley

Production:
Jayne Simpson